New Testament Life and Belief

A Study in History, Culture, and Meaning

Jerry Hullinger, Th.D.

Winston-Salem, North Carolina

ISBN-13: 978-1503038776

CONTENTS

PART III: MEANING

TO THE READER

The Aesop fable entitled *The Crow and the Pitcher* tells the story of a crow dying of thirst. The crow comes upon a pitcher which had once been full of water. His only hope of survival is to drink the water that remains. However, after repeated attempts, his beak is unable to reach the water at the bottom of the pitcher. With all hope but gone, the crow begins to drop pebble after pebble into the pitcher until the remaining water rises to the top. The crow drinks, and his life is saved. Though often attributed to Plato, the oft-quoted phrase that possibly originated with this fable is that "necessity is the mother of invention." In the case of this book, *limitation* is the mother of invention.

The task of adequately covering the entire New Testament in one undergraduate or graduate class is well-nigh impossible. This textbook was produced out of this limitation to serve as a rounded supplement when dealing with New Testament studies by bringing together three essential elements.

Part One provides a brief **historical** survey of international developments leading up to the time of the New Testament in an effort to ground the New Testament in its archival roots. Part Two presents a sampling of **cultural** details in an effort to illuminate the biblical text.

Finally, Part Three examines the **meaning** of the New Testament. This is achieved by combining four ingredients. The first is an overview of each New Testament book. The second, which grows out of the first, is a comprehensive purpose statement for each book. This statement is an attempt to merge the entire content of each book (answering the question "what?") and the reason for communicating that content (answering the question "why?") into a single sentence. One of the greatest safeguards of proper interpretation and application is to be aware of the "why" for the "what." Ingredient three is an interpretive, argumentative outline of each book. That is, instead of merely presenting a factual and structural outline of the material, the wording in this outline seeks to reflect the meaning of the text and how each part builds upon the preceding material to show the development of the writer's flow of thought, i.e., argument. The final ingredient of Part Three is the inclusion of over 350 interpretive notes interspersed throughout the outline. While books on New Testament survey intend to give a general overview of the major sections of each book, the intent of the interpretive notes is to provide a more substantive examination of some of the most important, most discussed, and most obscure passages in the New Testament. Though there will never be unanimity on all of these passages, disagreement as well as agreement spurs one on to further study.

It is hoped that the melding of history, culture, and meaning of the New Testament in one volume will contribute to a more well-rounded understanding of this part of God's word.

-Jerry Hullinger

PART I: HISTORY

CHAPTER 1
SETTING THE STAGE[1]

The theocracy[2] is grinding to a halt as the New Testament era approaches. Israel has repeatedly defied obedience to the Mosaic Law[3] leading to judgment, exile, and God's inactivity in working through the nation. This persistent disobedience leads to the Times of the Gentiles[4] officially formulated by Daniel in chapters 2 and 7 of his prophecy. In Daniel 2 Nebuchadnezzar[5] dreamed of a statue of a man which caused him to be afraid.[6] Daniel's interpretation indicated what course the Times of the Gentiles would take; namely, from the time of Nebuchadnezzar's final siege of Jerusalem in 586 B.C. until the destruction of the final Gentile power which will occur at Messiah's second coming.[7]

---

[1] On the importance of New Testament backgrounds, Barnett writes in the preface to his book on New Testament times: "If I may be permitted an expression of regret, it is that I did not venture forth upon this project years earlier. Having completed it I feel that after a lifetime of attempting to do so by other means, I am now at last beginning to grasp the message and meaning of the New Testament" (*Jesus & the Rise of Early Christianity* [Downers Grove, IL: InterVarsity Press, 1999], 11).

[2] The theocracy is God's rule on earth through a mediator. See Chapter 8, Section 1: The Theocracy for a detailed discussion.

[3] The Mosaic Law was the constitution of the nation of Israel. Though it had eleven discernible purposes (see J. Dwight Pentecost, "The Purpose of the Law, *Bibliotheca Sacra* 128:511 [Jul 1971], 227-233), the major intent of the Law was to provide the means by which Israel would receive the blessings described in the Abrahamic Covenant (expanded in the subsidiary Palestinian, Davidic, and New Covenants). This yielded the simple principle: obedience brings blessing (temporal) and disobedience brings cursing (temporal). See Chapter 8, Section 1: The Theocracy for further discussion.

[4] The Times of the Gentiles refers to the period of history when Jerusalem is under Gentile domination or legitimate threat by the Gentiles. Theoretically therefore, the Jews can control Jerusalem and still be in the Times of the Gentiles since their control is not stable. During Messiah's reign in the kingdom, Jerusalem will have absolutely no threats to her national security. See Chapter 8, Section 2 for more discussion on the Times of the Gentiles.

[5] Nebuchadnezzar was the greatest monarch in the Neo-Babylonian period. He is also considered to be one of the most competent rulers of the ancient Near East. He secured dominance for Babylon with his defeat of Pharaoh Neco (Egyptian) at Carchemish in 605 B.C. Nineveh (the capital of Assyria) was overthrown by the Medes and the Babylonians in 612 B.C. terminating the Assyrian empire and bringing Babylon to the fore.

[6] When Daniel is recounting the dream in 2:31 he refers to the appearance of the statue with the Hebrew word דְּחִיל. The term has been variously translated as "frightening," "terrible," or "awesome." The sense of "frightening" is to be preferred since the term comes from the root meaning "to fear." Even more specifically, the form of the verb used in 2:31 is a passive participle meaning "to make afraid."

[7] Though not germane at this juncture, the fact that Messiah's kingdom is instituted when the final Gentile power is crushed and replaced is extremely significant when it comes to the nature of Christ's reign. The amillennial position is that Christ's kingdom was inaugurated during the church age (e.g. G. K. Beale, "The Millennium in Revelation 20:1-10: An Amillennial Perspective," *Criswell Theological Review* 11:1 [Fall 2013], 29). In fact, Beale prefers the designation "inaugurated millennialism" rather than "amillennialism" (Ibid, 30). It should be pointed out, however, that in Daniel's vision, and as borne out by historical fulfillment, the successive empires in Daniel's vision actually superseded the preceding one. It is argued by dispensational premillennialists therefore, that consistent interpretation would demand Christ's kingdom judging the final Gentile power which is then replaced by his earthly reign. Consequently, the future part of the vision regarding the Times of Gentiles awaits future fulfillment to transpire at the Second Advent, followed by the age of the Kingdom. It should also be noted that contra historic/covenant premillennialists the concept of an earthly, mediatorial kingdom rests firmly on the Old Testament data and not Revelation

Cycle 1: Chapter 2	
Head of Gold	Babylon
Chest of Silver	Medo-Persia
Belly and Thighs of Bronze	Greece
Legs of Iron	Final Gentile Power
Smiting Stone	Smiting Stone

Cycle 2: Chapter 7	
Winged Lion	Babylon
Bear	Medo-Persia
Winged Leopard	Greece
Beast	Final Gentile Power

On the occasion of the three sieges of Jerusalem by Nebuchadnezzar, captives were taken back to Babylon.[8] One of the significant changes to come to the nation of Israel during the exile was the adoption of the Aramaic language.[9] Aramaic became the native tongue during the inter-testamental period, the common language in Israel in the first century, and was likely Jesus' native tongue.

The fortunes of Israel changed, however, when Babylon was defeated by Medo-Persia[10] on October 16, 539 B.C. When Babylon fell to Cyrus,[11] "Persia was raised to the position of a world empire, which encompassed the whole Near East."[12] The unique feature about Persian rule in contrast to Babylonian rule was their policy regarding conquered peoples. Whereas Babylon resettled their captives in order to disrupt national cohesion, the Persians allowed the exiles to return to their homeland to promote goodwill.

20:1-6.

[8] In 605 B.C. Daniel and his companions were taken to Babylon to be trained as administrators. The second siege took place in 597 B.C. in response to the rebellion of Jehoiachin. One of the notable exiles of approximately 10,000 at this time was the prophet Ezekiel. Nebuchadnezzar's third return to Jerusalem occurred in 588 B.C. which culminated in 586 B.C. after which the Jews who were not killed were deported to Babylon. Nebuchadnezzar died in 562 B.C. and was succeeded by his son Evil-Merodach, followed by Neriglissar (Nebuchadnezzar's son-in-law), and then Nabonidus.

[9] Aramaic was a Northwest Semitic language that became the *lingua franca* (a shared language used for communication among different peoples) of the ancient Near East from the time of Assyrian dominance to after Alexander's military victories. It is a cognate Semitic language with Hebrew. In fact, some portions of the Old Testament use Aramaic (two words in Genesis 31:47 [*Jegar-sahadutha*]; Ezra 4:8-6:18; 7:12-26; Daniel 2:4b-7:28; Jeremiah 10:11).

[10] In the Daniel 7 vision Medo-Persia is likened to a lop-sided bear. The fact that one side of the bear is higher than the other suggests that one of the empires in this alliance would be dominant. If true, the higher side of the bear would represent Persia which was the greater of the two empires. The three ribs in the bear's mouth would represent its three major conquests: Babylon, Lydia, and Egypt (525 B.C.).

[11] Xenophon (430-355; Greek historian, soldier, and possible student of Socrates) wrote a work entitled *Cyropedia* in which he discussed the upbringing of Cyrus: "He ruled over these nations, even though they did

During the first year of the reign of Cyrus (king of Persia), he allowed the Jews who had been taken captive by the Babylonians to return to Jerusalem to rebuild their temple and city.[13] His magnanimous nature was demonstrated even further by allowing the exiles to take their valuable temple treasures with them which had been stolen by the Babylonians. Moreover, the Jews who chose not to return were taxed by Cyrus to fund the trip of those who wanted to return. In addition, as a savvy politician, he publicly worshiped the gods of those nations he had conquered.[14]

---

not speak the same language as he, nor one nation the same as another; for all that, he was able to cover so vast a region with the fear which he inspired, that he struck all men with terror and no one tried to withstand him; and he was able to awaken in all so lively a desire to please him, that they always wished to be guided by his will. Moreover, the tribes that he brought into subjection to himself were so many that it is a difficult matter even to travel to them all, in whatever direction one begin one's journey from the palace, whether toward the east or the west, toward the north or the south" (Xen. *Cyrop*. 1.1.5).

There is debate as to whether the transference of power from Babylon to Medo-Persia fulfills the prophecy of Jeremiah 50-51. This has significant ramifications regarding the mention of Babylon in Revelation 17-18. If the prophecy was fulfilled, then Babylon will not be rebuilt. If the prophecy was not fulfilled, then Revelation 17-18 would indicate a rebuilt city of Babylon during the Tribulation period which would then be destroyed during that time, thus fulfilling the Jeremiah prophecy. For a fuller discussion of the issues see W. Glyn Evans, "Will Babylon Be Restored? Part 1," *Bibliotheca Sacra* 107:427 (Jul 1950), 335-342; Homer Heater, "Do The Prophets Teach That Babylonia Will Be Rebuilt In The *Eschaton*?" *Journal of the Evangelical Theological Society* 41:1 (March 1998), 23-43; Charles Dyer, "The Identity of Babylon in Revelation 17-18: Part 1," *Bibliotheca Sacra* 144:575 (Jul 1987), 305-316; Part 2 144:576 (Oct 1987), 433-449.

[12] E. Stern, "The Archeology of Persian Palestine," in *The Cambridge History of Judaism*. W.D. Davies and L. Finkelstein, eds. (Cambridge University Press, 1984), 1:70.

[13] The "Cyrus Cylinder," has inscribed on it (along with other exploits) words consistent with the edict allowing the exiles to return to Jerusalem and is dated 538 B.C. The Cylinder is made of baked clay and is currently in the possession of the British Museum in London. See Chapter 8, Section 3 for a translation of the Cylinder.

[14] Besides this being the Persian period of history, there are two other time-related terms relevant for Biblical studies (Mark Strauss, *Four Portraits, One Jesus* [Grand Rapids: Zondervan, 2007], 94). *The first* is the "Second Temple Period." The second temple is a reference to the temple completed under Zerubbabel's leadership in 516 B.C. which occurred during the Persian era (the first temple, of course, was Solomon's temple which was destroyed by the Babylonians in 587-86 B.C.). This second temple was destroyed by the Romans in A.D. 70. This entire period from 516 B.C. to A.D. 70 is known as the "Second Temple Period." Subsisting within this time frame is the "intertestamental period" marking the close of the ministry of Israel's last prophet Malachi to the birth of Jesus Christ. The intertestamental period is also known as the "400 silent years" since God gave no new revelation to his people Israel during this era. *The second* has to do with the abbreviations BC/AD and BCE/CE. BC refers to the time before Christ and is placed after the date or century it is describing while AD (*Anno Domini*) means "in the year of our Lord" and is placed before the date or century. Some opt to use BCE/CE instead of BC/AD when referring to dates. These abbreviations refer to "before the common era" and "common era."

Babylonian/Medo-Persian Timeline	
Nabopollasar	626 BC
Nineveh Overthrown	612 BC
Assyrians Seek Help	609 BC
Nebuchadnezzar to Jerusalem	605 BC
Nebuchadnezzar Returns to Jerusalem	597 BC
Nebuchadnezzar Returns to Jerusalem	588-586 BC
Nebuchadnezzar Dies	562 BC
Nabonidus Belshazzar	549 BC
Cyrus Captures Babylon	539 BC
Cyrus Allows Jews to Return	538 BC
Daniel's Last Vision	538 BC

Babylonian/Medo-Persian Sequence of Events			
586 BC: Jerusalem destroyed by Babylon →	539 BC: Babylon falls to Medo-Persia →	538 BC: Cyrus permits Jews to return →	
536 BC: First Return under Zerubbabel →	535 BC: Altar, sacrifice, foundation restored →	535-34 BC: Samaritan opposition →	
534 BC: Work Ceases	534-20 BC: Zurubbabel, Governor and Joshua, High Priest	520 BC: Zechariah and Haggai encourage to resume work	516 BC: Temple is finished

CHAPTER 2
THE GREEK PERIOD

Alexander the Great

As the Times of the Gentiles progressed in keeping with Daniel's prophecy, the Grecian empire (pictured by the belly and thigh of bronze and the winged leopard) overthrew the rule of the Medes and Persians.[15] While the leopard is known for its speed, the wings on Daniel's leopard would emphasize even more the rapidity with which this empire would rise to ascendancy. Alexander the Great[16] (356-323 B.C.) invaded Asia Minor in 334 B.C. and within some ten years had conquered the entire Medo-Persian empire to the borders of India.[17]

Hellenization

This period of Greek rule would span approximately 270 years from 332-63 B.C. and would have a profound effect on the Jewish nation. The most important effect was Hellenization[18] which influenced entertainment (the theater), athletics[19], dress, schools, government, and very importantly—language. Hellenistic Greek[20] became the common language of the day and the one in which the New Testament would be written. In the meantime, the Hellenized Jews began to lose touch with their native tongue and therefore could not understand the Hebrew Scriptures. This led to the translation of the Hebrew text into Greek yielding what is known as the Septuagint (LXX).[21] This version of the Scripture came to be the translation utilized in synagogue worship and is actually quoted more by the writers of the New Testament than is the original Hebrew text.[22]

---

[15] The last 100 years of Persian dominance was chaotic with the kings being characterized by excessive cruelty. The Satraps (provincial governors) often revolted and declared independence.

[16] Alexander the Great was a Macedonian king in ancient Greece who is considered to be one of the greatest military geniuses of all time. Three changes he made in field warfare have been noted by Burge, Cohick, and Green (*The New Testament in Antiquity*, Grand Rapids: Zondervan, 2009), 28 . 1) The Macedonian Phalanx. This was a 256 man square armed with an eighteen foot spear. The Phalanx was heavily armed and disciplined enough to move without a commander, 2) Heavy cavalry. These were horses with armor and men who could break through enemy lines, and 3) the siege train. These were wagons which could resupply what was needed for the army's continued fighting. Interestingly, one of the unique challenges faced by Alexander in India was the use of armored elephants with blades on their tusks. Their use, however, could prove dangerous for if they became afraid they could trample their own troops (Ibid.).

[17] Alexander died at the age of thirty-two from exhaustion, war wounds, excessive drinking and disease (D. Larry Gregg, "Alexander," in *Eerdmans Dictionary of the Bible* [Grand Rapids: Eerdmans], Logos 5. Upon his death, his kingdom was divided into four parts to his four generals: (1) Antipater, and later Cassander, gained control of Greece and Macedonia; (2) Lysimachus ruled Thrace and a large part of Asia Minor; (3) Seleucus I Nicator governed Syria, Babylon, and much of the Middle East (all of Asia except Asia Minor and Palestine); and (4) Ptolemy I Soter controlled Egypt and Palestine. This post-mortem division is predicted by Daniel 7:6 where the four heads of the leopard are referenced.

[18] Hellenization was the spread of Greek culture (i.e. Hellenism). This growth of a foreign culture proved to be dangerous for Israel as they were forced more and more to lose their identity as God's chosen people. One of the key literary works which deals with the struggles of the Jews during Hellenization was the Book

Diadochi[23]

Upon the death of Alexander the Great, since he had no heir,[24] the empire was divided into four parts by his generals who were called *didachoi.* The two most important divisions at this juncture for studying the New Testament are those belonging to Seleucus and Ptolemy.

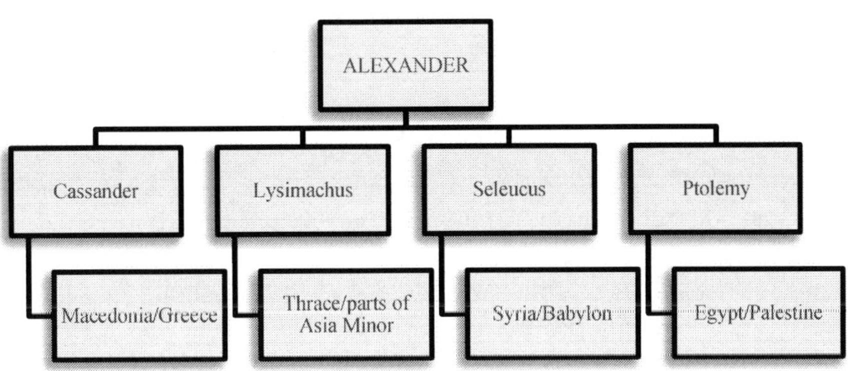

of Maccabees.

[19] Gymnasiums were built where athletes practiced in the nude. This led some Jewish young men to try to undo their circumcision (the sacred sign of the Abrahamic Covenant). The book of Maccabees declares: "So they built a gymnasium in Jerusalem, according to Gentile custom, and removed the marks of circumcision, and abandoned the holy covenant. They joined with the Gentiles and sold themselves to do evil" (1 Maccabees 1:14-15). This was due to the fact that circumcision was distasteful to the Greeks. Not only were the circumcised ridiculed, but their mothers were humiliated. Two passages from the Apocrypha will illustrate. "According to the decree, they put to death the women who had their children circumcised, and their families and those who circumcised them; and they hung the infants from their mothers' necks" (1 Maccabees 1:60-61). "For example, two women were brought in for having circumcised their children. These women they publicly paraded about the city, with their babies hung at their breasts, then hurled them down headlong from the wall" (2 Maccabees 6:10) (*The Apocrypha: Revised Standard Version of the Old Testament* [NY: Thomas Nelson, 1957]).

[20]Hellenistic Greek refers to the form of the Greek language from the time of Alexander to the writing of the New Testament. It also goes by the name of "Koine" (Greek for "common") because it did not have some of the nuances of Classical Greek and was distinguished from literary Greek.

[21] The Latin *Septuaginta* means "seventy" which is rounded down from the tradition that seventy-two scholars did the translation work (which legend says they did supposedly in an astounding seventy-two days!). Material for the origin of the LXX is usually traced back to the pseudepigraphal book *Letters of Aristeas.*

[22] De Silva offers this clarification regarding the term *Septuagint*, "Translations of the Torah began in the third-century B. C. E. and shortly after the Prophets and Writings were translated. They usually are lumped together under the title 'Septuagint.' This usage of the term *Septuagint* is somewhat misleading since it is anachronistic (our edited versions of the Septuagint are based primarily on four- and fifty-century C. E. codices) and since it tends to obscure the variations that have been found between Greek translations known to exist in the first century" (David de Silva, *An Introduction to the New Testament: Contexts, Methods & Ministry Formation* [Downers Grove: IVP Academic, 2004], 807).

[23] Greek for "Successors"

[24] Roxanne, a Bactrian princess, was pregnant at the time of his death. The child, Alexander IV, was murdered by Cassander in 310 B.C.

The Ptolemies

The Ptolemaic Empire (named after Ptolemy) was centered in Egypt with Alexandria as its capital. It controlled commerce, agriculture, and finance through a bureaucracy which levied heavy taxes. Many Jews flocked to Alexandria looking for employment and built Jewish communities there.

The following is a description of the significance of Alexandria:

> Located on the coast of the western Delta where a major branch of the Nile reaches the sea, the city had enormous economic potential. Two harbors served a fleet that exported grains, papyrus, and glass, among other things. Imports included metals and timber. The famous lighthouse of Pharos, one of the seven wonders of the ancient world, towered over the port. The early Ptolemies fostered the development of Hellenistic culture by supporting a large group of scholars at the Museum, an academy of learning, and building a library world renowned as the greatest repository of literary works in the ancient world.[25]

It is during this time that the translation of the Septuagint began due to the growing ignorance of Hebrew on the part of the diaspora.[26] Early tradition says this translation project started during the reign of Ptolemy Philadelphus.[27] Less is known about the Ptolemaic reign in Palestine than is known about its reign in Egypt. This is due to less evidence from archaeology, literature, and especially Josephus.[28] He writes a long account about the translation of the Septuagint (which many consider to be spurious) in his *Antiquities* but says little else about the period until he comes to the Maccabean era where he provides much detail. One thing that is known is that the Ptolemies treated Palestine as a temple-state which was a land dedicated to one of their gods. Significantly, the high priest in Jerusalem served as the *liaison* between the Jews there and the Ptolemaic government. He served as the civil and religious authority and was responsible to collect taxes.

---

[25] T. V. Brisco, "The Hellenistic Period," in *Holman Bible Atlas* (Nashville: Broadman & Holman Publishers, 1998), 179.

[26] The term "diaspora" will become a key one in studying the New Testament. It refers to the Jews not living in Palestine who had been dispersed among the Gentile nations. Its origination was the Assyrian and Babylonian deportations.

[27] Philadelphus succeeded Ptolemy I Soter as second ruler of the dynasty and reigned from 285-246 B.C.

[28] Flavius Josephus is a key source in studying the New Testament. He was a Jew appointed by the Roman emperor Vespasian (A.D. 69-79) to be the court historian who provides important historical background for the New Testament. Though his importance should not be underestimated, there is a general consensus that his numbers can be inflated at times and the description of some events should be read with historical balance. His key works are *The Jewish War* and *The Antiquities of the Jews* both of which are readily available online.

The Seleucids

The Seleucid Empire (named after Seleucus) would come to rule Syria, Babylon, and Asia Minor.[29] Some of the difficulties faced by the Seleucids were the defense and political administration of the empire due to the vastness of its geographical holdings and a varied ethnic population respectively. To address these problems, military colonies were established throughout the Empire and Hellenization was aggressively pursued.

The most important point to remember for the Seleucids is their clashes with the Ptolemies and the consequent unrest which this created in Palestine as they attempted to gain control over that region. A turning point in this tension occurred when the expansionist Antiochus III defeated Egypt in 198 B.C.

On the one hand, many of the Jews in Palestine were happy over this victory because of their weariness over oppressive Ptolemaic taxation. This loyalty was rewarded by lesser taxes, repair of the temple, and more local autonomy. This segment of the Jewish population was associated with the house of Tobias. On the other hand, some Jews supported Egypt and were associated with the house of Onias. Antiochus III's expansionistic policies finally got the better of him when he was eventually defeated by the Romans at Magnesia who then demanded financial reparations and the return of land in Asia Minor. He died in 187 B.C.

Antiochus III was succeeded by his son Seleucus IV who was then murdered. This led to the accession of the nefarious Antiochus IV in 175 B.C. who claimed the title of "Epiphanes," likening himself to a manifestation of God on earth. Antiochus IV set in motion a movement that would change the political and religious landscapes in Jerusalem for decades to come by virtue of his efforts to impose Hellenism on the Jews.

The Jewish high priest at the beginning of Antiochus IV's rule was Onias III who was of the conservative party which opposed Antiochus IV. Consequently, he accepted a bribe from Jason the brother of Onias III, who then became high priest. Jason was a Hellenist who attempted to transform Jerusalem into a Greek city. This effort was opposed by a Jewish group called the "Hasidim" (the devout).[30]

Before embarking on a military invasion in Egypt, Antiochus IV replaced Jason with another high priest who was also a Hellenist named Menelaus. His appointment was based on his promise to collect higher taxes from the people of Palestine. The high priesthood of God's chosen nation had now become a corrupt, political office under the guise of a Greek-city state. As Epiphanes was on the cusp of victory in Egypt, Rome intervened under the leadership of the Roman general Popillius Laenas and demanded that he withdraw from the region.[31] Rather than risk war with Rome, he acquiesced to their order. When news of these

[29] Key cities in the empire included Syrian Antioch (as opposed to Pisidian Antioch in Asia Minor) on the Orontes River and Seleucia on the Tigris River.

[30] The Hasidim or Hasideans were pious Jews who were strict observers of the Mosaic Law. They came to the fore in Jerusalem during the Hellenistic period in opposition to Greek proselytization.

[31] It is said that Laenas drew a circle in the sand around Antiochus with his cane from which he was not to

affairs reached Palestine (even rumors that Antiochus IV had been killed), Jason seized the opportunity to return to Jerusalem and wrested control of the city from Menelaus.

Antiochus IV was embittered by his recent defeat and viewed events in Jerusalem as a sign of rebellion against his rule. He had lost Egypt but he was not willing to lose Jerusalem. This prompted him to send troops to punish those in rebellion and reinstate Menelaus to the high priesthood. In the process, these soldiers looted the temple and slaughtered many Israelites.[32] Sometime later he sent a general named Apollonius to Jerusalem to enforce Hellenization on the Jews. The following atrocities are some of what took place: taxation; Judaism became illegal; Jerusalem plundered and burned; circumcision, celebration of Jewish festivals and observance of the Sabbath were forbidden; pagan sacrifices were mandatory; prostitution was practiced in the temple; and in the winter of 167 B.C. the temple became a place of worship for Zeus as a pagan altar was built on which pigs were sacrificed.

The Maccabean Revolt

In the tiny village of Modein (Modin) located some twenty miles northwest of Jerusalem, soldiers of Antiochus IV demanded that the people offer a pagan sacrifice to Zeus thus showing their loyalty to the empire. When one of the Jews was ready to comply with these demands, an elderly priest named Mattathias[33] drew his sword, killed the man and the royal envoy, destroyed the altar, and took flight to the mountains together with his five sons. This event was the catalyst for the Maccabean revolt.[34]

---

leave until he had given his answer to the demand for withdrawal. According to the Roman historian Livy (59 B.C-A.D. 17): "After receiving the submission of the inhabitants of Memphis and of the rest of the Egyptian people, some submitting voluntarily, others under threats, [Antiochus] marched by easy stages towards Alexandria. After crossing the river at Eleusis, about four miles from Alexandria, he was met by the Roman commissioners, to whom he gave a friendly greeting and held out his hand to Popilius. Popilius, however, placed in his hand the tablets on which was written the decree of the senate and told him first of all to read that. After reading it through he said he would call his friends into council and consider what he ought to do. Popilius, stern and imperious as ever, drew a circle round the king with the stick he was carrying and said, "Before you step out of that circle give me a reply to lay before the senate." For a few moments he hesitated, astounded at such a peremptory order, and at last replied, "I will do what the senate thinks right." Not till then did Popilius extend his hand to the king as to a friend and ally. Antiochus evacuated Egypt at the appointed date, and the commissioners exerted their authority to establish a lasting concord between the brothers, as they had as yet hardly made peace with each other" (Titus Livius, *The History of Rome,* Canon Roberts trans., London: J.M. Dent & Sons, London, 1905 [6:45.12]).

[32] For a description of the desecration of the temple by Antiochus, see Chapter 8, Section 4: Antiochus desecrates the Temple.

[33] Mattathias was a priest who killed a compromising Jewish worshiper and envoy of Antiochus IV thus sparking the Maccabean revolt. Mattathias' family was known as the Hasmoneans named after Hasmon, the great-grandfather of Mattathias. They were also known as the Maccabees. Maccabeus, which means "hammer," was a cognomen given to Judas. Thus the title "Maccabean Revolt" is often the tag used for this uprising.

[34] The Maccabean revolt was the response of pious Jews to the efforts of Antiochus Epiphanes to Hellenize them.

Following the death of Mattathias in 166 B.C., his son Judas assumed leadership over the movement.[35] Judas led the Jewish rebels in successful guerrilla warfare winning a series of strategic battles ultimately leading to the recapture of Jerusalem and rededication of the temple. The highlight of the revolt occurred in 164 B.C. when Judas and his brothers arrived at the temple. 1 Maccabees 4:38-40 describes the pathos of what they saw: "They saw the sanctuary desolate, the altar profaned, and the gates burned. In the courts they saw bushes sprung up as in a thicket. They saw also the chambers of the priests in ruins. Then they rent their clothes, and mourned with great lamentation, and sprinkled themselves with ashes. They fell face down on the ground, and sounded the signal on the trumpets, and cried out to Heaven." Judas then ordered that the temple be rededicated and proper worship resumed. This began the feast which is known as Hanukkah (dedication).[36] Jesus Christ would attend this festival two

---

[35] Mattathias' family was known as the Hasmoneans named after Hasmon, the great-grandfather of Mattathias. They were also known as the Maccabees. Maccabeus, which means "hammer," was a cognomen given to Judas. Thus the title "Maccabean Revolt" is often the tag used for this uprising.

[36] What follows is an account of the restoration of temple worship from 1 Maccabees 4:41-59: "Then Judas detailed men to fight against those in the citadel until he had cleansed the sanctuary. He chose blameless priests devoted to the law, and they cleansed the sanctuary and removed the defiled stones to an unclean place. They deliberated what to do about the altar of burnt offering, which had been profaned. And they thought it best to tear it down, lest it bring reproach upon them, for the Gentiles had defiled it. So they tore down the altar, and stored the stones in a convenient place on the temple hill until there should come a prophet to tell what to do with them. Then they took unhewn stones, as the law directs, and built a new altar like the former one. They also rebuilt the sanctuary and the interior of the temple, and consecrated the courts. They made new holy vessels, and brought the lampstand, the altar of incense, and the table into the temple. Then they burned incense on the altar and lighted the lamps on the lampstand, and these gave light in the temple. They placed the bread on the table and hung up the curtains. Thus they finished all the work they had undertaken. Early in the morning on the twenty-fifth day of the ninth month, which is the month of Chislev, in the one hundred and forty-eighth year, they rose and offered sacrifice, as the law directs, on the new altar of burnt offering which they had built. At the very season and on the very day that the Gentiles had profaned it, it was dedicated with songs and harps and lutes and cymbals. All the people fell on their faces and worshiped and blessed Heaven, who had prospered them. So they celebrated the dedication of the altar for eight days, and offered burnt offerings with gladness; they offered a sacrifice of deliverance and praise. They decorated the front of the temple with golden crowns and small shields; they restored the gates and the chambers for the priests, and furnished them with doors. There was very great gladness among the people, and the reproach of the Gentiles was removed. Then Judas and his brothers and all the assembly of Israel determined that every year at that season the days of dedication of the altar should be observed with gladness and joy for eight days, beginning with the twenty-fifth day of the month of Chislev."
2 Maccabees 10:1-9 offers a further description: **1** Now Maccabeus and his followers, the Lord leading them on, recovered the temple and the city; **2** they tore down the altars that had been built in the public square by the foreigners, and also destroyed the sacred precincts. **3** They purified the sanctuary, and made another altar of sacrifice; then, striking fire out of flint, they offered sacrifices, after a lapse of two years, and they offered incense and lighted lamps and set out the bread of the Presence. **4** When they had done this, they fell prostrate and implored the Lord that they might never again fall into such misfortunes, but that, if they should ever sin, they might be disciplined by him with forbearance and not be handed over to blasphemous and barbarous nations. **5** It happened that on the same day on which the sanctuary had been profaned by the foreigners, the purification of the sanctuary took place, that is, on the twenty-fifth day of the same month, which was Chislev. **6** They celebrated it for eight days with rejoicing, in the manner of the festival of booths, remembering how not long before, during the festival of booths, they had been wandering in the mountains and caves like wild animals. **7** Therefore, carrying ivy-wreathed wands and beautiful branches and also fronds of palm, they offered hymns of thanksgiving to him who had given success to the purifying of his own holy place. **8** They decreed by public edict, ratified by vote, that the whole nation of the Jews should observe these days every year. **9** Such then was the end of Antiochus, who was called Epiphanes."

times during his earthly ministry. Meanwhile, Antiochus IV died while campaigning in the east in 163 B.C.

The Hasmonean Dynasty[37]

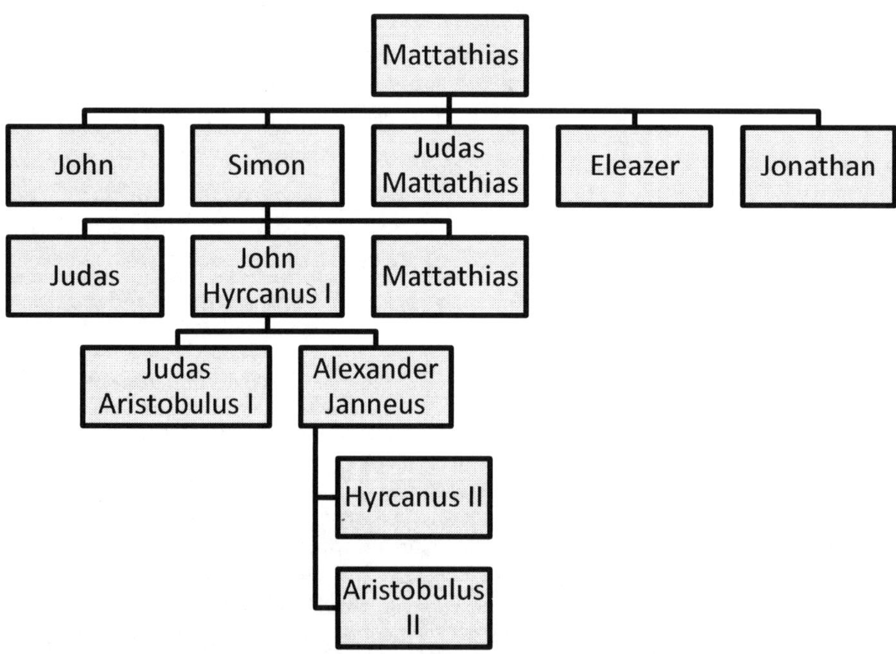

The descendants of Mattathias formed the first Jewish dynasty which had been known for hundreds of years. Lysias, a Seleucid nobleman, seized power through Antiochus' son, Antiochus V. Lysias attacked Judas at the behest of some Jews who pled for intervention against the conservatives in Jerusalem. Lysias won this battle but was forced to make concessions to the Jews which gave them religious freedom. This overturned the previously oppressive policies of Antiochus IV and satisfied most of the conservative Jews. From this point forward, however, the issue was not so much over religious issues but whether orthodox or hellenists would control leadership.

The history of the Hasmonean Dynasty would degenerate into an ambitious struggle for power. Importantly, there emerged three discernible factions within Judaism:

Hellenized Jews	Hasmoneans	Hasidim
• Embraced Greek Culture • "Sadducees"	• Power Brokers • Autocratic	• Religious Purity • "Pharisees"

[37] The Hasmonean Dynasty refers to the dynasty of Jewish priests and kings who ruled Judea from the Maccabean revolt until the time of Roman conquest in 63 B.C.

CHAPTER 3
THE ROMAN PERIOD

Pompey and Julius Caesar

Rome began in the mid-8th century B.C. traditionally dated in 753 B.C.[38] This unimpressive, melting pot of people would become the most powerful empire in the ancient world and would provide the background for the entire New Testament. Key military victories by Pompey[39] and Julius Caesar[40] would extend the territory of Rome.

Among the military goals of Pompey was the desire to provide a geographical buffer between the Roman Empire to the west and the Parthian threat to the east. The conquest of Palestine was important to him for this purpose. Taking advantage of a struggle for the Jewish throne in Jerusalem between Aristobulus and Hyrcanus (sons of Alexander Janneus in the Hasmonean Dynasty), Pompey tried to enter Jerusalem but was barred by the people. A three month siege ensued and Rome broke into Jerusalem in the autumn of 63 B.C. killing some 12,000 Jews. Pompey entered the Holy of Holies in the temple without plundering it and allowed the religious system to continue. However, he appointed a high priest whom he chose, set Roman rulers over the province, freed the cities of the Decapolis,[41] and organized troops to deal with any resistance. Thus there ended eighty years of Jewish independence under the Hasmonean Dynasty.[42]

Roman Emperors, 31 BC – AD 96

Augustus or Octavian	• 31 BC-AD14 • "Augustus" (reverend) was a title given to Octavian by the Roman senate • Reigned and ordered census at Jesus' birth • declared a god at his death
Tiberius	• AD 14-37 • ruled during Jesus' public ministry and death • He is referred to in Luke 3:1 • He is the referent whenever "Caesar" is mentioned in the Gospels

[38] D. R. W. Wood and I. Howard Marshall. *New Bible Dictionary* (Leicester, England; Downers Grove, IL: InterVarsity Press, 1996). Logos 5.

[39] Pompey, also called Pompey the Great, was a Roman statesman and celebrated general. He was an associate and later an opponent of Julius Caesar. Pompey's victories in Judea and Jerusalem would prove crucial in the political background of the region during the period of the New Testament.

[40] Julius Caesar was a Roman statesman and general who conquered Gaul and emerged from the Roman republic as a virtual dictator. He was famously assassinated by a group of senators led by Marcus Brutus. "Caesar" would later be used as a title for the emperor.

[41] The cities of the Decapolis were a league of ten Hellenistic cities under Jewish control located south and east of the Sea of Galilee. It is mentioned three times in the New Testament (Matt. 4:25; Mark 5:20; 7:31).

[42] For a fuller description of these events, see Chapter 8, section 5: Pompey; where sections are cited from Alfred Edersheim and Josephus.

Gaius (Caligula)	• AD 37-41 • cruel, immoral despot • not mentioned in NT • ordered his image to be put in the temple, though never was • assassinated
Claudius	• AD 41-54 • expelled Jews from Rome in AD 49 • Two expelled at this time were Aquila and Priscilla who then went to Corinth (Acts 11:28; 18:2) • The famine predicted by the prophet Agabus occurred during Claudius' reign
Nero	• AD 54-68 • Paul appeals to him in Acts 25:10; 28:19) • Peter and Paul martyred during his reign • Began first major persecution against Christians by blaming them for a fire in Rome (see Ch. VIII, Section 6, Tacitus on Nero's Persecution)
Vespasian	• AD 69-79 • Nero gave him command of the war against the Jews in 66 • Proclaimed emperor in 69
Titus	• AD 79-81 • Son of Vespasian • Took over the war against the Jews and led the defeat of Jerusalem in AD 70 • Coliseum completed during his rule
Domitian	• AD 81-96 • Son of Vespasian, brother of Titus • Second emperor to persecute Christians • Emperor during writing of Revelation

Roman Government

The Emperors

The highest ruler of the Roman Empire was given the title Emperor (*Imperator*-Lat.). He was the political, military, judicial, and religious leader.[43] The chart below lists the emperors most relevant for New Testament studies.[44]

The Administration

The Roman Empire was divided in to two types of provinces—senatorial and imperial. The senatorial provinces were the older, richer, peaceful areas which were governed by a proconsul who was appointed to a one-year term by the Roman Senate. Proconsuls mentioned in the New Testament include Sergius Paulus (Acts 13:7-8) and Gallio (Acts 18:12).[45]

---

[43] Since the emperor was a virtual dictator with no way to constitutionally remove him from office, assassination was the best method to end his reign.

[44] After the death of Domitian there was great relief in the Empire due to the terror during his reign (e.g., rivals executed, philosophers banished from Rome, Christian persecution). This led to a peaceful era through the reigns of the next five emperors: Nerva, Trajan, Hadrian, Antonius Pius, and Marcus Aurelius from AD 96-180. Aurelius' son Commodus was incompetent and was strangled to death in AD 192. Generally speaking, the subsequent years experienced Rome's decline.

[45] The reference to Gallio is one of the most crucial pieces of data when it comes to the chronology of

The imperial provinces were new, unruly frontier areas governed by a legate who was appointed by the Emperor.[46] The proconsuls and legates were from the Senate representing the aristocracy. However, another ranking of governors known as "prefects" and later "procurators" ruled over smaller or problematic imperial provinces for the emperor. Primarily, the function of all of these rulers was to keep the peace and collect taxes.[47] One of the key prefects for New Testament studies was Pontius Pilate. He was the fifth Roman governor of Judea and was the one who ordered Jesus' crucifixion.[48] He had a tenuous relationship with the Jewish leadership; and, it is no wonder. On one occasion at night, Pilate brought images of the emperor into Jerusalem which greatly offended the Jews.

Josephus recounts the incident:

> He introduced Caesar's effigies, which were upon the ensigns, and brought them into the city; whereas our law forbids us the very making of images; on which account the former procurators were wont to make their entry into the city with such ensigns as had not those ornaments. Pilate was the first who brought these images to Jerusalem, and set them up there; which was without the knowledge of the people, because it was done in the night-time; but as soon as they knew it, they…interceded with Pilate many days, that he would remove the images; and when he would not grant their requests...and when the Jews petitioned him again, he gave a signal to the soldiers to encompass them round, and threatened that their punishment should be no less than immediate death.[49]

Paul's ministry. Luke indicates that Gallio was proconsul while Paul was in Corinth. Proconsuls served a 1-2 year term beginning in the early summer (John Polhill, *Acts* [Nashville: Broadman Press, 1992], 387). Gallio, also known as Lucius Junius Gallio, was the brother of Lucius Annaeus Seneca who was a philosopher and tutor to Nero (de Silva, *An Introduction to the New Testament,* 378). Archaeologists have found an inscription in Central Greece at Delphi which dates a proclamation of the Roman Emperor Claudius in early 52 AD. The inscription mentions that Gallio was proconsul at this time. However, because of an illness he was forced to leave Corinth early. Therefore, the incident in Acts 18 would be dated around AD 51-52 (Darrell Bock, *Acts* [Grand Rapids: Baker, 2007], 580). For a discussion and translation of the Delphi inscription, see Adolf Deissmann, "Appendix I: The Proconsulate of L. Junius Gallio: An Epigraphical Study towards the Absolute Chronology of St. Paul's Life," in *St. Paul: A Study in Social and Religious History* (NY: Hodder and Stoughton, 1912), 233-260.

[46] A "legate" was essentially a military governor.

[47] There were two types of taxes: *tributum soli* was a fixed rate property tax and *tributum capitis* was a poll tax. Other taxes could also be introduced. The Jews also paid a temple tax to help maintain the temple and the priesthood. In order to collect taxes, the right to collect taxes would be bid for and the highest bidder would send out "publicans" to actually collect the money. Publicans were also known as "tax farmers" since they raised money like a farmer raised crops. Related to the collection of taxes was the "census." This was basically a headcount in each family in order to determine the taxes for that family. For the issues related to the census in terms of Quirinius and the translation of πρώτη see Chapter IX, Luke, Notes 4 and 5.

[48] The first four were Coponius, M. Ambivius, Annius Rufus, and Valerius Gratus. Later prefects to be named in the New Testament besides Pilate were Felix (Acts 23, 24) and Festus (Acts 24:27).

[49] *Antiquities of the Jews,* 18.3.1.

There were four types of cities in the Empire. The Roman colonies were founded by citizens of Rome who had been sent out from Italy. They were compensated for this by being exempt from tribute and most taxation as well as other benefits. One biblical example of a colony is Philippi. The municipalities were cities which were granted full rights of Roman citizenship. These cities were self-governing as long as they promised to support Rome. The third type of city was the temple city. In these cities one would find a fusion of politics and religion dedicated to the worship of a deity. And finally, there were Greek cities which continued as they had been in the old Grecian Empire.

Jewish Rulers

Herod the Great

The Romans allowed natives of Palestine to rule under their authority. One of the most significant of these Jewish rulers was Herod the Great.[50] He was required to gain control of Palestine by force. With the help of Romans troops, he was able to accomplish this in three months.[51] Though he was disliked by many Jews because he was of Idumean ancestry,[52] Herod ruled for thirty-three years and was a classic politician trying to keep both Rome and his Jewish subjects satisfied. Scott describes Herod the Great as a man of "powerful body and by nature wild, passionate, harsh, arrogant, calculating, and ruthless."[53] Some quick facts about Herod's reign are included below:

- Tried to gain Jewish favor by refraining from pork. This led to the comment by Augustus that it would be better to be Herod's pig than his son since he killed three of his sons (the comment by Augustus is possibly legend though the other facts are correct).
- Tried to gain Jewish favor by divorcing his Idumean wife Doris and marrying a Hasmonean woman
- Mentioned in the birth narratives (Matt. 2:2 and Lk. 1:5)
- Built a harbor at Caesarea Maritima beneath the shadow of a temple dedicated to Augustus
- Beautified the temple in Jerusalem with much gold, limestone, jewels, and marble which took over eighty years to complete[54]

---

[50] Herod the Great (or Herod I) was the King of Judea from 37-4 B.C. Through the motion of Antony and Octavian, Herod was declared king of the Jews by the Roman senate. Several descriptions of Herod the Great gleaned from Schurer include: a skillful rider, huntsman, marksman, wild, passionate, harsh, unbending, ruled with an iron hand, cunning, unpitying (even toward those he loved), energetic, insatiable ambition (Emil Schurer, *A History of the Jewish People in the Time of Jesus*, Nahum Glatzer ed. [NY: Shocken Books, 1967], 128-129).

[51] F. F. Bruce, *New Testament History* (NY: Doubleday, 1980), 14.

[52] An Idumean was a descendant of Esau.

[53] J. Julius Scott, *Jewish Backgrounds of the New Testament* (Grand Rapids: Baker, 2000), 95.

[54] For a description of the temple by Josephus, see Chapter 8, section 7: The Temple. To provide a base for the temple, Herod's engineers constructed a marble platform measuring 912 feet (south) by 1,536 feet (east),

- At the northwest corner of the temple he rebuilt a Maccabean fortress now known as the Fortress of Antonia (after Mark Antony who appointed him). This fortress will figure prominently in the Gospels and the book of Acts.[55]
- He rebuilt the walls of Jerusalem and added a water system and theaters.[56]
- He financed his building projects by heavy taxation contributing to his hatred by the Jews.
- "He was the incarnation of brute lust, which in turn became the burden of the lives of his children. History tells of few more immoral families than the house of Herod, which by intermarriage of its members so entangled the genealogical tree as to make it a veritable puzzle. As these marriages were nearly all within the line of forbidden consanguinity, under the Jewish law, they still further embittered the people of Israel against the Herodian family."[57]
- When Herod knew his death was close, he moved to Jericho where he had built palaces and pools. He ordered Jewish families to come to Jericho where they were then rounded up into the hippodrome (horserace track). He ordered his soldiers to kill them at the moment of his death so that there would be mourning when he died; otherwise, because of Jewish hatred for him he wanted to ensure there would at least be some type of mourning. While lying on his death bed he had his son Antipater killed. However, the soldiers at the hippodrome released the Jewish prisoners.[58]

---

by 1,035 (north), by 1,590 (west) which is the equivalent of about fifteen football fields. The platform was supported by walls of chiseled masonry with some stones being forty feet in length (measurements taken from Barnett, *Jesus & the Rise of Early Christianity*, 76).

[55] "It stood 115 feet high and was partly surrounded by a deep ravine 165 feet wide. It functioned as headquarters for the Roman soldiers, a palace and a barracks. Herod constructed a secret passage from the fortress to the Temple. While overlooking Jerusalem, the Antonia Fortress was garrisoned with 600 Roman soldiers, who watched over the Temple courts in order to preserve order" (http://www.bible-history.com/jerusalem/firstcenturyjerusalem antonia-_fortress.html, accessed 6/21/14).

[56] Scott offers this summary of some of Herod's building exploits: "They included whole cities such as Samaria...and Caesarea Maritima with its magnificent artificial harbor. Many cities were beautified and received pagan temples, sports facilities, and other important buildings. He virtually rebuilt Jerusalem with all the features expected in a Hellenistic city. His own palace was magnificent and well fortified. The Antonia, the military citadel he built at the northwest corner of the temple mount, is mentioned in connection with Paul's arrest (Acts 21:31-40), and was possibly the location of part of the trial and torture of Jesus. A series of fortress palaces provided places of luxurious refuge for Herod and his family" (Scott, *Jewish Backgrounds of the New Testament*, 96).

[57] Henry Dosker, "Herod," in *International Standard Bible Encyclopedia*, James Orr, ed. (Grand Rapids: Eerdmans, 1980), 3:1381.

[58] See Chapter 8, section 8: Herod's last days from Edersheim and Josephus.

Archelaus

When Herod died in the spring of 4 B.C. his kingdom was divided among his sons (see chart below).[59] *Archelaus* assumed the rule of Judea. His rule was so cruel that it inspired fear in the people (see Matthew 2:22 for the explanation of why Mary and Joseph avoided this area when leaving Egypt with Jesus). Edersheim describes his cruelty thusly: "He began his rule by crushing all resistance by the wholesale slaughter of his opponents…But he far surpassed him [his father] in cruelty, oppression, luxury, the grossest egotism, and the lowest sensuality, and that, without possessing the talent or the energy of Herod."[60] The rule of Archelaus proved so inept that he was removed from the throne by Augustus in A.D. 6 and banished to Gaul.

The Herodian Dynasty

Herod the Great [61]
King of Judea
37-4 BC, *Matthew 2:1*

Herod Phillip I
Mark 6:17, Luke 3:1

Herod Antipas,
Tetrarch of Galilee
4 BC – AD 39

Aristobulus

Archelaus,
Ethnarch of Judea/Samaria
4 BC - AD 6,
Matthew 2:22

Herod Phillip II
4 BC – AD 34

Herod Agrippa I,
King of Judea
AD 37-44, *Acts 12:1*

Herodias
Mark 6:17

Bernice
Acts 25:13

Herod Agrippa II,
Tetrarch and King of Chalcis
AD 48-70,
Acts25:13

Drusilla
Acts 24:24

Salome
Matthew 14:6

[59] "By the final testament of Herod, as ratified by Rome, the kingdom was divided as follows: Archelaus received one-half of the kingdom, with the title of king, really 'ethnarch,' governing Judea, Samaria and Idumaea; Antipas was appointed 'tetrarch' of Galilee and Peraea; Philip, 'tetrarch' of Trachonitis, Gaulonitis and Paneas. To Salome, his intriguing sister, he bequeathed Jamnia, Ashdod and Phasaelus, together with 500,000 drachmas of coined silver" (Henry Dosker, "Herod," in *The International Standard Bible Encyclopedia* [Grand Rapids: Eerdmans, 1980], 3:1381). See the chart on the "Herodian Dynasty" below.

[60] Alfred Edersheim, *The Life and Times of Jesus the Messiah* (Grand Rapids: Eerdmans, 1980), 1:220. For Josephus' account of the slaughter of those in the temple, see Chapter 8, Section 9: Archelaus' Slaughter. For the hatred of Archelaus by the Jews, see Josephus, *Antiquities,* 17.11.1-4.

[61] This chart is not exhaustive but is intended to highlight individuals named in the New Testament. A "tetrarch" was the governor of one-fourth of a province. An "ethnarch" was the ruler of an ethnic group. Herod Philip I in the chart was the son of Herod the Great's wife Miriamne II while Herod Philip II in the chart was the son of Herod the Great's wife Cleopatra.

Herod Antipas[62]

Herod Antipas ruled over Galilee and Perea until he was dethroned and exiled by the Roman emperor Caligula in A.D. 39. Some of the most notable facts about him include the following: 1) he reigned during Jesus' earthly ministry; 2) he had John the Baptist executed because of his objection to Antipas' consanguineous marriage to Herodias; 3) he was paranoid that John the Baptist had risen from the dead; 4) Jesus called him "that fox"[63]; 5) Jesus stood before Antipas during one of his six trials before crucifixion; 6) he built a capital for himself on the Sea of Galilee and named it Tiberius after the current Roman emperor. This is why the Sea of Galilee is sometimes called the Sea of Tiberius.

Philip II

The third of Herod's sons who received a portion of his empire was Philip II. He is mentioned only one time in the New Testament in Luke 3:1 where he and the territories over which he reigned are named. Other than his reign in the northern part of the region, he is best known for two building projects. The more important of the two was the building of Caesarea Philippi which was named after him. It was here that Jesus asked the disciples "Who do men say that I am?" This drew out Peter's classic response, "You are the Christ, the son of the living God." The other project was the enlargement of the city of Bethsaida renamed Bethsaida Julias in honor of Augustus' daughter.[64] This city was the hometown of Peter, Andrew, and Philip (John 1:44). In addition, many of Jesus' miracles took place here including the feeding of the 5,000 and the healing of a blind man using spittle.

Herod Agrippa I/Herod Agrippa II

There are only two other rulers from the Herodian dynasty to be mentioned in the New Testament: Herod Agrippa I and Herod Agrippa II. Herod Agrippa I was the grandson of Herod the Great and the son of Herod Antipas. Agrippa I enjoyed a privileged upbringing in Rome:

> When six years of age he was sent to Rome for his education, and there enjoyed the companionship of the gifted Drusus Cæsar, son of Tiberius. The extravagance of court life accustomed him to splendor and luxury, and his prospects, which were brilliant, were the means of furnishing him with a never-failing supply of money, of which he availed himself in the style of a spendthrift. But his circumstances were changed in the year 23, when his friend and patron, Drusus, died suddenly. From that hour the emperor declined to receive the high-spirited young

[62] "Antipas" is an abbreviation of the Greek term ἀντιπατρός which means "instead of his father."

[63] For a complete word study on the sense of "fox," see Harold Hoehner, *Herod Antipas*, (Cambridge: At the University Press, 1972), 343-347. Hoehner's conclusion on the term is that "fox" refers to a person who is "insignificant or base." He "lacks real power and dignity, using cunning deceit to achieve his aims" (347).

[64] He would die here in AD 34.

> man, and very soon his boon companions also forsook Agrippa. Destitute of all resources, he meditated suicide…[65]

After an unhappy stint as ruler over Tiberius (due to tensions with his brother-in-law), Agrippa returned to Rome where he came to be on good terms with Caligula. Agrippa carelessly remarked on one occasion that he wished the aged Tiberius would die so that Caligula would assume the throne. When these remarks reached Tiberius, he promptly fettered Agrippa in chains and cast him into prison. Eventually Caligula did become the emperor of Rome at which time he freed Agrippa from incarceration and gave to him the tetrarchy enjoyed by his uncle Philip. In addition, he was given the title "king" and then the title "praetor"[66] by the Roman senate.[67] Upon the death of Caligula, his boyhood friend Claudius made him king over all Judea and gave him authority over the temple and the high priesthood.

Agrippa I is well known from the New Testament for his order to execute James the Apostle.[68] When Agrippa saw that this pleased his Jewish subjects, he proceeded to arrest Peter presumably to have him put to death the next day. Though God in his sovereignty ordained James' death, he chose to spare Peter leading to one of the three jailbreak miracles in Acts.[69] What is of further interest from the Acts 12 text is the description of Agrippa's death by Luke in conjunction with the description provided by Josephus. Luke writes:

---

[65] "Agrippa-I," *Jewish Encyclopedia,* accessed August 23, 2013; http://www.jewish-encyclopedia.com/articles/912-agrippa-i.

[66] A "praetor" was a senior magistrate.

[67] Jewish Encyclopedia, "Agrippa-i."

[68] This is the only actual execution of an apostle mentioned in the New Testament.

[69] One of the clear themes of Scripture is the "Godhood of God;" part of which involves God doing all of his pleasure. More narrowly one of the emphases of Acts is to present the Gospel as a juggernaut which moved its way through the known world directed by the hand of God. Worthy of note is the reaction of the young church in Acts 4 after Peter's first appearance before the Sanhedrin. As they offer their prayer, they address God as "Lord" (4:24). One might expect the Greek word to be κύριος however in this instance δέσποτα is used. The word denotes one who has "legal control and authority over persons" (Walter Bauer, William Arndt, and F. Wilbur Gingrich, *A Greek-English Lexicon of the New Testament and Other Early Christian Literature,* 2nd ed., rev F. Wilbur Gingrich and W. Danker [Chicago: University of Chicago Press, 1979], 176). Schnabel comments: "the omnipotent ruler whose authority extends over all. He is sovereign because he is the Creator of all visible and invisible realities" (Eckhard Schnabel, *Zondervan Exegetical Commentary on the New Testament: Acts* [Grand Rapids: Zondervan, 2012], 254). God's rule as "despot" is described in the same verse with the verb "made" (ποιήσας). Schnabel continues by noting the correspondence of this verse to the LXX version of Psalm 146:6: "This individual psalm praises Yahweh as Creator of the world, before whom foreign rulers are powerless in the long run and who providentially cares for his people, particularly those who suffer afflictions. As Peter and John have been threatened by the rulers of the Jewish people, the psalm puts their plight in perspective, assuring them of God's sovereign control over these rulers and over future events that they attempt to control" (Ibid.).

> Now Herod had been very angry with the people of Tyre and Sidon; but they came to him with one accord, and having made Blastus the king's personal aide their friend, they asked for peace, because their country was supplied with food by the king's country. So on a set day Herod, arrayed in royal apparel, sat on his throne and gave an oration to them. And the people kept shouting, "The voice of a god and not of a man!" Then immediately an angel of the Lord struck him, because he did not give glory to God. And he was eaten by worms and died.

Josephus[70] corroborates Luke's version with some added details:

> Now when Agrippa had reigned three years over all Judea he came to the city Caesarea, which was formerly called Strato's Tower; and there he exhibited spectacles in honor of Caesar, for whose well-being he'd been informed that a certain festival was being celebrated. At this festival a great number were gathered together of the principal persons of dignity of his province. On the second day of the spectacles he put on a garment made wholly of silver, of a truly wonderful texture, and came into the theater early in the morning. There the silver of his garment, being illuminated by the fresh reflection of the sun's rays, shone out in a wonderful manner, and was so resplendent as to spread awe over those that looked intently upon him. Presently his flatterers cried out, one from one place, and another from another, (though not for his good) that he was a god; and they added, "Be thou merciful to us; for although we have hitherto reverenced thee only as a man, yet shall we henceforth own thee as superior to mortal nature." Upon this the king neither rebuked them nor rejected their impious flattery. But he shortly afterward looked up and saw an owl sitting on a certain rope over his head, and immediately understood that this bird was the messenger of ill tidings, just as it had once been the messenger of good tidings to him; and fell into the deepest sorrow. A severe pain arose in his belly, striking with a most violent intensity. He therefore looked upon his friends, and said, "I, whom you call a god, am commanded presently to depart this life; while Providence thus reproves the lying words you just now said to me; and I, who was by you called immortal, am immediately to be hurried away by death. But I am bound to accept what Providence allots, as it pleases God; for we have by no means lived ill, but in a splendid and happy manner." When he had said this, his pain became violent. Accordingly he was carried into the palace, and the rumor went abroad everywhere that he would certainly die soon. The

[70] For an overview of the life and writings of Josephus see J. Julius Scott, *Jewish Backgrounds of the New Testament* (Grand Rapids: Baker, 2000), 35-38.

> multitude sat in sackcloth, men, women and children, after the law of their country, and besought God for the king's recovery. All places were also full of mourning and lamentation. Now the king rested in a high chamber, and as he saw them below lying prostrate on the ground he could not keep himself from weeping. And when he had been quite worn out by the pain in his belly for five days, he departed this life, being in the fifty-fourth year of his age and in the seventh year of his reign.[71]

The final ruler from the Herodian dynasty mentioned in the New Testament, as well as the last of this House to hold a kingdom, was Herod Agrippa II. When his father died unexpectedly, as described above, Agrippa II was seventeen years of age and pursuing an education in Rome. Though too young to rule at this point, he was gradually given territories to rule by various Roman rulers. When he was given a large part of Galilee by Nero, he renamed Caesarea Philippi "Neronius." Paul made his defense here before Agrippa II in Acts 26. Upon hearing Paul's appeal, Agrippa wryly commented "you almost persuade me to become a Christian" (Acts 26:28) and then recommended to Festus that Paul be released. Agrippa would later die in Rome in the early 90s and with him the race of Herods.

[71] Flavius Josephus, *Antiquities of the Jews* in *The Works of Flavius Josephus,* William Whiston, trans. (Grand Rapids: Baker, 1980), 19.8.2 [106-108]. The arresting confirmation of Luke by Josephus is impressive to Eusebius (Eusebius, *Eusebius: The Church History,* Translation and Commentary by Paul Maier [Grand Rapids: Kregel, 2007], 60-61).

PART II: CULTURE

CHAPTER 4
CULTURAL BACKGROUND

"Culture" simply refers to customary beliefs, social norms, or a way of life of a particular people at a particular time. Several relevant aspects of culture from the world of the New Testament are outlined below.

Language

There were four languages relevant for the land of Palestine. *Latin* was the official language of the Roman Empire but was used mainly in the West. *Greek* was the common language in the East and was widely understood in Palestine.[72] *Aramaic* was a Semitic language related to Hebrew and was used by the majority of Jews in the first century.[73] They began to use Aramaic instead of Hebrew during their time of exile since this was the *lingua franca* of the ancient Near East. *Hebrew* was primarily used by the rabbis and scribes since they were the guardians of the Hebrew Scriptures.[74] Jesus would have utilized Aramaic as he taught the people; Hebrew when he interacted with the religious leaders; and Greek when he spoke to non-Jews.

Social classes

Society at this time was broken down into four social classes. The small *upper class* in Rome was composed of wealthy businessmen, military generals, tax collectors, and administrators.[75] The upper class in Palestine consisted of the Roman hierarchy, landowners, and the leading priests and rabbis. The Romans of this class together with those Jews who cooperated with them were disdained by the masses.

---

[72] Of course the New Testament (as well as the LXX, and Apostolic Fathers) was written in Greek. However, it is important to understand that the Greek language has been through multiple stages beginning in the third millennium BC and going to Modern Greek in the present. The Greek of the New Testament is referred to as κοινή. "Koine" is an adjective which means "common" referring to the Greek typically spoken in the Mediterranean world. The stage of Koine Greek can be dated 330 BC to AD 330. The reason this is important is to prevent the misinterpretation of words in the New Testament. As any language goes through historic development, the significance, nuance, and use of words change. Since Koine Greek was the common language, it lost the subtleties often found in earlier Greek. Moreover, later forms of Greek were different in this regard from Koine. Therefore, the interpreter must be careful in reading earlier meanings forward to the New Testament and later meanings backward to the New Testament. These errors are typically referred to as the "semantic obsolescence fallacy" and the "anachronistic fallacy" respectively.

[73] There was a northern and southern dialectical form of Aramaic in Palestine during the first century (Matt. 26:73).

[74] During the services in the synagogue the Hebrew Scriptures would be read. However, a "targum" would also be read. A Targum is a dynamic translation of the Hebrew text by the rabbis.

[75] The upper class was also known as "equestrians."

The second class during this time was the *common people* who had been freeborn.[76] In Rome this strata would be populated by farmers, merchants, educators, and lower government officials for example. In Palestine this class was made up of poor people who farmed or who ran small businesses. These individuals made up the vast majority of society.[77] *Freedmen* were a social class of former slaves. Roman slaves could be released by becoming the property of a god or released by their masters. Once slaves were freed they could become socially mobile and occupy positions held by the common people or upper class. The Jewish master was required to set free slaves every seventh year. The fourth social class was *slaves*. Slaves were the property of their masters with no rights whatsoever. Slaves outnumbered free people in the Roman Empire and many times were more educated and skillful than their masters in areas such as medicine and education.

Homes

Palestinian homes were normally made of sun-baked bricks composed of mud and straw. They were low with flat roofs and sometimes had a guest room on the roof. The roofs were plastered with mud and in addition to a possible guest room were used for sleeping in hot weather, curing food, relaxing, and praying.[78] The floor of the main room was made of hardened earth, and in the poorer homes a mat was laid for sleeping. Poorer Palestinians lived in a ground level apartment building. Furniture in a typical lower class home would have included a bed, stove, table, chairs, and containers for storage.[79]

Houses in the western part of the Empire were made of brick or concrete in the cities. Most homes did not have windows facing the street because of crime at night. Gundry describes other features of the home:

> Roofs were tile or thatch. In the kitchen an open hearth, or an earthen or stone oven, served for cooking. Oil lamps provided lighting. Plumbing and heating were well developed. A central furnace heated some houses, pipes conveying the warm air to different rooms. Many Roman lavatories had Running water, and Pompeian houses had at least one toilet convenience, sometimes two...In larger cities lower- and middle-class people often rented flats in multi-storied apartments. The upper classes might enjoy expensive villas in the countryside as well as luxurious dwellings in the city.[80]

---

[76] This class is also known as the "plebians." The term is an adjective from the Latin term "plebes" the common people. There really was no "middle" class in the ancient world; rather, the great majority of people simply eked out a living in their profession.

[77] The middle class in Palestine was known as the *'am ha-ares* (people of the land). The Pharisees tended to look down on them while Jesus freely communed with them as "sheep without a shepherd." Estimates go as high as 90% for the percentage of the population belonging to this class.

[78] Robert Gundry, *A Survey of the New Testament* (Grand Rapids: Zondervan, 2003), 30-31.

[79] J. Julius Scott, *Jewish Backgrounds of the New Testament*, 247.

[80] Robert Gundry, *A Survey of the New Testament*, 30. For more exhaustive details on homes in Palestine

Work

Royalty, wealthy merchants, and politicians came from the upper class in Roman Society. Since the upper class was small, most people worked as farmers,[81] merchants, fishermen, and craftsman.

The poorest of the poor were hired as day workers who lived on what they made each day. The typical industry at this time was the craftsman who produced goods and sold them directly to the public and worked from sunrise to sunset with an afternoon break. One of the best discussions of the various craftsmen in Jerusalem has been provided by Jeremias.[82] After discussing the esteem for crafts in Judaism (manual labor was looked down on by upper class Greeks), he offers the following organizational description:[83]

Industries which Served the General Public

Goods for Domestic Use	• Weaving • Tailor • Smith	• Fuller • Leather industry • Potter
Food Trades	• Oil • Butchers	• Bakers • Water Sellers (see Mark 14:13)
Luxury Goods	• Ointments and spices	• Scrivener (a person who would write out documents)
Building Workers	• Ordinary building from stone	• Skilled Craftsmanship • Road Sweepers
Other Trades	• Doctors • Money Changers	• Barbers

such as gates, roofs, floors, doors, furniture, lighting, and decoration, see H.G. Stigers, "House," in *Zondervan Pictorial Encyclopedia of the Bible,* Merrill Tenney, ed. (Grand Rapids: Zondervan, 1975), 3:217-220.

[81] Small farms could be managed by a handful of slaves or laborers. Larger farms could be leased to tenant famers or extra day workers could be hired. The two most important crops were olives and grapes. Olives had a variety of uses including cooking, seasoning, fuel, and soap. Grapes were grown primarily for making wine (Mark Strauss, *Four Portraits, One Jesus* [Grand Rapids: Zondervan, 2007], 158-159). Related to the farmer was the work of the shepherd. It is often asserted that the Jews despised shepherds because they were unclean. This has provided fodder for dramatic Christmas sermons as to how the message of the incarnation went initially to the "despised" shepherd. However, this Jewish attitude is uncertain and could come from later Judaism. The Greeks and Romans apparently did look down on shepherds. Aristotle wrote that shepherds are lazy and idle. "The laziest are shepherds, who lead an idle life, and get their subsistence without trouble from tame animals; their flocks having to wander from place to place in search of pasture, they are compelled to follow them, cultivating a sort of living farm. Others support themselves by hunting, which is of different kinds. Some, for example, are brigands, others, who dwell near lakes or marshes or rivers or a sea in which there are fish, are fishermen, and others live by the pursuit of birds or wild beasts. The greater number obtains a living from the cultivated fruits of the soil" (*Politics*, 1.8).

[82] Joachim Jeremias, *Jerusalem in the Time of Jesus* (Philadelphia: Fortress Press, 1989), 5-30.

[83] I have taken the liberty of putting Jeremias' material in chart form.

Those in the same trade were often organized into "guilds" (somewhat similar to modern trade unions) which helped set standards for their profession as well protecting their economic interests. The guilds could pose two potential problems for converts to Christianity both of which were linked to the patron Roman deity of that guild. One problem related to the manufacture of those things identified with idol worship. For example, we are introduced to the guild in Ephesus composed of silversmiths and craftsmen who made images of the Roman god Artemis (Acts 18:24-25). To refuse this kind of work would put one's livelihood into jeopardy. Witherington notes the pagan reaction to their work being threatened by the missionaries:

> The social situation of artisans was tenuous. They might make a good deal of money, but money was the only basis for their status claims. Their lack of education or a proper family background meant they were looked down upon by the elite of society...Anything that threatened their income also threatened the status and standard of living they had worked so hard to obtain in a highly stratified society.[84]

The second problem related to the participation in the feasts associated with the deity of a particular guild. Ramsay observes the difficulty faced by Christians in Thyatira (Revelation 2:18-29):

> The clubs bound their members closely together in virtue of the common sacrificial meal, a scene of enjoyment following on a religious ceremony. They represented in its strongest form the pagan spirit in society...To hold aloof from the clubs was to set oneself down as a mean-spirited, grudging, ill-conditioned person, hostile to existing society, devoid of generous impulse and kindly neighbourly feeling an enemy of mankind...Such revels were not merely condoned by pagan opinion, but were regarded as a duty, in which graver natures ought occasionally to relax their seriousness, and yield to the impulses of nature, in order to return again with fresh zest to the real work of life...Thus, this controversy was of the utmost importance in the early Church. It affected and determined more than any other, the relation of the new religion to the existing forms and character of Graeco-Roman city society.[85]

---

[84] Ben Witherington III, *The Acts of the Apostles: A Socio-Rhetorical Commentary* (Grand Rapids: Eerdmans, 1998), 593.

[85] William Ramsay, *The Letters to the Seven Churches* (Grand Rapids: Baker, 1985), 348-350. For a discussion of Christianity as a "club," see Robert Wilken, *The Christians as the Romans Saw Them* (New Haven: Yale Press, 1984), 31-47.

Of special interest for those who study the New Testament are the references to Jesus as a "carpenter" and the son of a "carpenter" (Matthew 13:55; Mark 6:3) as well as Paul as a "tentmaker" (Acts 18:3). The word used in the New Testament for "carpenter" is τέκτων. The term referred to one who was a builder using various materials such as wood, stone, and metal. Perhaps a better translation would simply be "builder." J.I. Packer suggests "that though 'carpenter' is the common rendering here, *tekton* could equally mean 'mason' or 'smith' (as indeed some of the Fathers took it); or it could mean that Joseph and Jesus were builders, so that both carpenter and masonry would have been among their skills."[86] Some have posited that Joseph worked at Sepphoris which was an hour's walk from Nazareth. It was being rebuilt by order of Herod Antipas and would have required a number of skilled workers.[87]

Campbell expands on the "building" concept noted above by making a compelling case that Jesus was in the construction business.[88] He surveys the relevant terms in Greek literature and the words/illustrations used by Jesus in his teaching ministry including knowledge of finance, types of building projects, architecture, and management. All of this points to the fact that building was the family occupation of Jesus.

In a land of omnipresent stone and few trees, a craftsman worked primarily in stone, and much less in wood or metal. Such a craftsman is called "a builder," and he worked on all the structures mentioned by Jesus in his parables, as described above, as well as wine-presses, millstones, olive press stones, tomb stones, cisterns, farm terraces, vineyards, watch towers, house extensions, etc. An examination of the material culture of Nazareth confirms this review of the terminology of Jesus' occupation.[89]

Regarding the term "tentmaker," the term used is σκηνοποιός. Most commentators lean to the sense of general leather-working or a cloth of woven goat's hair for this word.[90] If Paul's situation was typical, he would have gone through an apprenticeship as a teenager at the conclusion of which he would have been given his own tools. These tools could have been transported by him wherever he traveled. BAGD discusses the intriguing suggestion that Paul built props for the theater.[91]

---

[86] J.I. Packer, "Carpenter, Builder, Workman, Craftsman, Trade," in *The New International Dictionary of New Testament Theology,* Colin Brown, ed. (Grand Rapids: Zondervan, 1981), 1:279.

[87] Barnett, *Jesus & the Rise of Early Christianity*, 90-91; Hoehner, *Herod Antipas*, 85. For a fairly recent discussion of Sepphoris, see Mark Chancey and Eric Meyers, "How Jewish was Sepphoris in Jesus' Time?" *Israel: An Archaeological Journey* (Washington, D.C.: Biblical Archaeology Society, 2009), 26-43.

[88] Ken Campbell, "What was Jesus' Occupation?" *Journal of the Evangelical Theological Society* 48:3 (Sep 2005), 502-519.

[89] Ibid, 519.

[90] Darrell Bock, *Acts* Baker Exegetical Commentary on the New Testament (Grand Rapids: Baker, 2007), 578; F.F. Bruce, *The Book of Acts* The New International Commentary on the New Testament (Grand Rapids: Eerdmans, 1980), 367; Richard Longenecker, *The Acts of the Apostles*, in The Expositor's Bible Commentary (Grand Rapids: Zondervan, 1981), 9:480; John Polhill, *Acts* The New American Commentary (Nashville: Broadman Press, 1992), 383.

[91] *A Greek-English Lexicon of the New Testament and Other Early Christian Literature,* Walter Bauer,

A key industry in Palestine as mentioned in the Gospels was fishing. The types of nets are described by Jeffers:

> The cast net, or circular throwing net, was about fifteen feet in diameter, made of fine mesh and weighted with leaden sinkers (Mk 1:16). It was used in shallow water. The dragnet was a large net used with two boats. Once they came to the fishing area, the net was loaded half into one boat and half into the other. The boats then separated, letting out the net as they went. As they both sailed toward the shore, they pulled in the net on both sides and eventually dragged the net and its contents onto the shore (Mt 13:47-48). At times they just dragged the fish into the boats (Lk 5:6-9). Peter protested Jesus' instruction to fish at night (Lk 5:5), probably because he knew the fish at that time would be in deep water and his cast net would be useless. Fishermen had to keep their nets mended (Mk 1:19). They also had to salt down and sell their fish.[92]

The money earned in these various occupations could be spent or saved. If an individual wanted to protect his money, he could deposit it in the temple (hoping the gods would protect it), bury it, or put it in the hands of professional bankers.[93]

Travel

There were two major modes of travel in the first century. Most significant from the Roman Empire was its system of roads. They were crafted as straight as possible with multiple layers of stone beneath the thick pavement and wide enough for two chariots to pass side by side.[94] Roads throughout Palestine were inferior to the famous Roman roads and both systems were traveled by foot, various animals, carriage, or chariot.

William Arndt, F. Wilbur Gingrich, and Frederick Danker (Chicago: University of Chicago Press, 1979), 755.

[92] James Jeffers, *The Greco-Roman World of the New Testament Era: Exploring the Background of Early Christianity* (Downers Grove: InterVarsity, 1999), 22.

[93] These bankers also provided loans and money-changing services which was particularly necessary in the Temple. This is due to the fact that only Jewish coins could be used in the temple since Roman coins often had the image of a deified emperor considered to be idolatrous. If a loan was not repaid, the creditor could enslave the debtor (Jeffers, *The Greco-Roman World of the New Testament Era*, 24).

[94] One of the most famous roads was the *Via Egntia.* Walker describes this road as follows: "The Romans had paved this in the second century BC—450 miles in length and, in places, up to 20 feet in width—to establish the main communication corridor from Rome to its eastern provinces. It could be incredibly busy. Cicero had once delayed departing Thessalonica, waiting for when there was less traffic (*Letters* 69); his letters also indicate that it could be dangerous, due to occasional attacks by barbarians. At various points along the road there were places to exchange animals and places to stay" (Peter Walker, *In the Steps of Paul: An Illustrated Guide to The Apostle's Life and Journeys* [Grand Rapids: Zondervan, 2008], 105-106). As a caveat to the safety issue is the fact that due to the *Pax Romana*, one would not be traveling through areas with regional skirmishes.

Camel caravans, often of impressive length, brought goods from a distance to Jerusalem.[95] The next major mode of travel was by sea. This was the fastest method but could also be dangerous as testified by the three shipwrecks experienced by Paul.[96] It has been estimated that Paul traveled nearly 10,000 miles (recorded in Acts alone) during his ministry as an apostle.[97]

Weights, Distance, and Money

UNIT	EQUIVALENT	NT EXAMPLE
Measure (μετρητής κορός σατόν χοῖνιξ βατός)	Various units of capacity	Matt. 13:33: 12 quarts; Luke 16:7: 11-17 bushels; John 2:6: 18-27 gallons per jar; Rev. 6:6: one quart
Talent (weight) (τάλαντον)	58-80 pounds	Rev. 16:21
Talent (money)	Value differed according to metal	Matt. 18:24; 25:15ff.
Sabbath day's journey	Little over ½ mile	Acts 1:12
Mile (Roman) (μίλιον)	4,854 feet/1,000 paces	Matt. 5:41
Furlong (στάδιος)	Around 600 feet	Luke 24:13
Cubit (πῆχυς)	18 inches/length of forearm	Matt. 6:27
Fathom (ὀργυιά)	6 feet	Acts 27:28
Measuring rod (κάλαμος)	10 feet	Rev. 11:1
Stadion (στάδιος)	Around 600 feet	1 Cor. 9:24; Rev. 21:16
Drachma (Greek) (δραχμή)	A day's wage	Luke 15:8
Denarius (δηνάριον) (Roman)	A day's wage	Luke 10:35; Rev. 6:6
Farthing/Penny (ἀσσάριον)	1/16 of drachma/denarius	Matt. 10:29
Mite (λεπτός)	1/28 of drachma/denarius	Mark 12:42

---

[95] Jeremias, *Jerusalem in the Time of Jesus,* 31.

[96] The most vital trade route by sea was from Rome to Alexandria, Egypt. "There were thousands of ships involved in this trade [grain] and they would often travel in large convoys. Since the prevailing winds were north-westerly, the southbound journey could take less than fifteen days; the return journey from Alexandria, however, often required an extensive detour along the shores of the eastern Mediterranean and was marked by a continuous process of 'taking' back the wind…Sailing on the open seas could be dangerous, not so much because of storms, but because cloudy weather made it impossible to fix one's location with any accuracy. So far over 600 wrecks of Roman ships have been found off the shores of Europe" (Ibid. 176).

[97] Ronald Hock, *The Social Context of Paul's Ministry: Tentmaking and Apostleship* (Philadelphia: Fortress, 1980), 27.

Mina (μνᾶ)	100 drachmas	Luke 19:13
Shekel (στατήρ)	4 drachmas	Matt. 17:27

Hospitality

Generous hospitality was a core value of the Middle East and was a point of honor going back to the hospitality shown by Abraham in Genesis 18. In Greco-Roman culture this practice was traceable back to Zeus. Dio Chrysostom in speaking to the Roman emperor Trajan said the following:

> It was my purpose, after finishing the description of the good king, to discuss next that supreme king and ruler whom mortals and those who administer the affairs of mortals must always imitate in discharging their responsibilities, directing and conforming their ways as far as possible to his pattern. Indeed, this is Homer's reason for calling true kings "Zeus-nurtured" and "like Zeus in counsel"; and Minos, who had the greatest name for righteousness, he declared was a companion of Zeus. In fact, it stands to reason that practically all the kings among Greeks or barbarians who have proved themselves not unworthy of this title have been disciples and emulators of this god. For Zeus alone of the gods has the epithets of "Father" and "King," "Protector of Cities," "Lord of Friends and Comrades," "Guardian of the Race," and also "Protector of Suppliants," "God of Refuge," and "God of Hospitality," these and his countless other titles signifying goodness and the fount of goodness. He is addressed as "King" because of his dominion and power; as "Father," I ween, on account of his solicitude and gentleness; as "Protector of Cities" in that he upholds the law and the commonweal; as "Guardian of the Race" on account of the tie of kinship which unites gods and men; as "Lord of Friends and Comrades" because he brings all men together and wills that they be friendly to one another and never enemy or foe; as "Protector of Suppliants" since he inclines his ear and is gracious to men when they pray; as "God of Refuge" because he gives refuge from evil; as "God of Hospitality" because it is the very beginning of friendship not to be unmindful of strangers or to regard any human being as an alien; and as "God of Wealth and Increase" since he causes all fruitage and is the giver of wealth and substance, not of poverty and want. For all these functions must at the outset be inherent in the royal function and title.[98]

A further and practical reason for showing hospitality was the ill-repute of inns in the ancient world. Williams offers his assessment of inns at this time:

[98] Dio Chrysostom, *The First Discourse on Kingship,* 1.37-41 (http://penelope.uchicago.edu/Thayer/E/Roman/Texts/Dio_Chrysostom/Discourses/1, accessed 6/16/2014).

> The traveler who survived the human terrors of the road and the often rugged terrain still had to endure the "hospitality" of such wayside accommodation as he might happen to find. The archaeological and literary evidence indicates that the establishments catering to travelers were generally cramped and undecorated. They were frequented by carters, drunkards, prostitutes, and the riffraff of society. The beds they offered seemed to harbor every known insect, and the proprietor, as likely as not, was a rogue.[99]

Surprisingly, the matter of hospitality is addressed several times in the New Testament epistles. For instance, Paul asserts in 1 Timothy 3:2 that the one aspiring to the office of bishop must be given to hospitality.[100] John rebukes a man named Diotrephes for not showing hospitality in 3 John 10. However, he balances this out in 2 John 10 by telling the church not to show hospitality to false teachers (in the sense of giving them room and board which would be tantamount to supporting their work).[101]

Honor and Shame

There was a great concern in the first century for being well-thought of by others. Conversely, losing that esteem was a serious matter. Consequently, Jewish culture was rife with competition as individuals sought honor for their pious acts or position at a feast. The same was true in Greco-Roman culture as illustrated by the mess in the Corinthian church. The major problem in that church was that the congregants had brought the competitive nature of Greek culture of getting ahead and being recognized into the church. Interestingly, Jesus turned this concept on its head by teaching his disciples that the way to honor and exaltation in his kingdom was not through self-assertion but through humility and service. Both Jesus (Matthew 5:5; 10:32-33; 18:4) and the Apostles (2 Timothy 2:12; 1 John 2:28; Revelation 2:26; 3:21) taught that the believer will experience honor/exaltation or shame during Messiah's earthly reign.[102] Richards summarizes well the concept of honor/shame in the ancient world:

---

[99]David Williams, *Paul's Metaphors: Their Context and Character* (Peabody, MA: Hendrickson Publishers, 2004), 199-200.

[100] This essentially has the idea of taking in travelers as guests.

[101] "In the ancient world, inns were notoriously bad. In one of Aristophanes's plays Heracles asks his companion where they will lodge for the night; and the answer is: 'Where the fleas are fewest.' Plato speaks of the inn-keeper being like a pirate who holds his guests to ransom. Inns tended to be dirty and expensive and, above all, immoral…In the Christian Church there were wandering teachers and preachers who needed hospitality…It was of the greatest blessing that Christians should have Christian homes ever open to them in which they could meet people like-minded to themselves" (William Barclay, *The Letters to Timothy, Titus, and Philemon* [Philadelphia: Westminster Press, 1975], 82).

[102] In a striking text addressed to believers, the possibility exists for some to be put to shame at the coming of Christ. In 1 John 2:28 the apostle is clearly addressing Christians since he calls them "little children" and is encouraging them to abide in fellowship with God. The purpose of this abiding is so that they would not be ashamed at his coming. The passive voice of the verb could indicate not merely that they will be ashamed, but that they will be put to shame.

Recent sociological studies have provided meaningful insights into the NT, particularly for my purposes here in the elucidation of the honor/shame dynamic of the first-century Mediterranean world. This culture has been labeled "agonistic" (from ἀγών, "contest"). Honor was a limited good in the ancient world. Two types of honor were available: ascribed and acquired (or achieved). Ascribed honor came from one's birth (family lines, village, etc.) or as a gift (adoption) from a more honorable person. Honor could also be acquired (or achieved). A life of consistent virtue brought honor (as Jewish Wisdom literature often asser-ted). Singular acts could also bring honor, such as exceptional bravery, loyalty, or Torah-obedience in the case of the Jews.[103]

Communication

Since there were no sophisticated media in the ancient world, news was communicated through posted notices, word of mouth, papyrus, tablets, and pieces of pottery. Important documents were made of leather or parchment.[104] Though not as often considered, street announcing and graffiti were also common forms of communication. Town criers would either be involved in the official capacity of announcing news and events, or of the more hawkish variety to gain attention from the crowds. Regarding graffiti, Muir notes that there were two types.[105] The first included handbills and announcements painted on public public walls as well as advertisements and arena events. The second type was informal in nature and consisting of sketches and subversive sayings quickly scribbled on walls. Muir remarks:

> The exterior walls of an elite home were public space, and homeowners would have to send slaves out in the morning to scrub off the writings which had sprung up overnight. Like graffiti today, street wall space involved an on-going battle between the graffiti artist and the property owner.[106]

Public Services

Most important cities had paved streets, underground sewage systems, and libraries. Antioch of Syria had two and one-half miles of streets "colonnaded and paved with marble and a complete system of night lighting."[107] Moreover, entertainment was enjoyed at the amphitheater, sporting events,[108] plays, concerts and other venues. One of the most significant contributions to citizens was the *thermae* or public baths. The term actually refers to a "complex of rooms designed for public bathing, relaxation, and social activity."[109]

---

[103] E. Randolph Richards, "An Honor/Shame Argument for Two Temple Clearings," *Trinity Journal* 29:1 (Spring 2008), 30-31.

[104] Gundry, *A Survey of the New Testament*, 29

[105] Steven Muir, "Vivid Imagery in Galatians 3:1—Roman Rhetoric, Street Announcing, Graffiti, and Crucifixions," *Biblical Theology Bulletin* 44:2 (2014), 82.

[106] Ibid.

[107] Ibid, 29.

[108] For example, there were chariot races. "The Circus Maximus had a seating capacity of at least 25,000

The following chart lists some quick facts about the Roman baths taken from Jerome Carcopino's lengthy discussion.[110]

The Roman Baths
The baths put hygiene on the daily agenda of the Romans and focused on exercise and care of the body.
The baths were lavishly decorated to make this an enjoyable experience.
The baths were accessible to the rich and the poor. In the early days of the Empire, the men's and women's baths were separate.
Nero, under whose reign Paul was executed, built a bath on the Campus Martius.[111]
Hot, cold, hot-air, swimming, and tubs were provided.
Adjacent to the baths were crowded shops, gardens, promenades, massage rooms, gymnasiums, libraries, and even museums. The *thermae* was basically a small picture of the best the Empire had to offer.

---

people. As it grew in capacity over the years, so did the number and variety of events. By the time of Claudius the Roman calendar included 159 days expressly set aside as holidays, of which ninety-three were devoted to events in the circus at the public expense. The number of races held on any one day increased until, again by the time of Claudius, twenty-four had become the norm. Other events were added for the sake of variety, and the chariot races themselves were diversified by the number of horses in each team: sometimes two, sometimes three, sometimes even six or eight or ten. Most commonly, however, the chariots were *quadrigae*, drawn by four horses. A race started at the sound of a trumpet, which the presiding magistrate signaled. As he stood, the chariots were drawn up for the start below him. While the horses pawed the ground, branches on their heads, tail held in air by a tight knot, mane starred with pearls, breastplate studded with plaques and amulets, neck bearing a flexible collar and a ribbon died with the colours of their party,' all eyes were on the charioteer. 'He stood upright in his chariot, helmet on head; whip in hand, leggings swathed round calf and thigh, clad in a tunic the colour of his *factio*, his reins bound round his body, and by his side the dagger that would sever them in case of accident.

The moment of greatest danger occurred when the chariot was turning at the *metae*, which were always on the left (the races ran counterclockwise). The success of this maneuver depended on the strength and agility of the two outside horses. If the chariot hugged the turning post too closely, it ran the risk of crashing into it; if it swung too widely, it either lost position or was in danger of being overrun and wrecked by the other competitors.

Philippians 3:13-14 describes the charioteer, intent on the race, his eyes fixed on the front, not daring to look behind lest the slightest pressure on the reins (wrapped around his body) produce a false move and cause him to lose the race and possibly his life. Thus, 'forgetting what lies behind, and **straining forward** to what lies ahead, **I drive on toward the finishing line**.' He is explaining to his readers, by means of metaphor, that those who long to be like Christ faced danger in looking back. Past achievements (breeding complacency) and past failures (promoting despondency) are best forgotten in the interest of pressing on toward the objective" (Williams, *Paul's Metaphors*, 261-62).

[109] "Thermae," Encyclopedia Britannica, accessed August 29, 2013, http://www.britan-nica.com/thermae.

[110] Jerome Carcopino, *Daily Life in Ancient Rome* (NY: Bantam, 1971), 290-99.

[111] "In ancient Rome, a floodplain of the Tiber River, the site of the altar of Mars and the temple of Apollo in the 5th century bc. Originally used primarily as a military exercise ground, it was later drained and, by the 1st century bc, became covered with large public buildings—baths, amphitheatre, theatres, gymnasium, crematorium, and many more temples. The Pantheon is the most notable structure extant. The historian Livy (1st century bc) called the area *campus ignifer* because of the volcanic smoke often seen there" (Campus Martius, Encyclopedia Britannica, accessed August 29, 2013, http://www. britannica.com/Campus-Martius.

At the center of the *thermae* were the baths themselves. One would enter the dressing rooms, then a warm, vaulted hall. To the north of this hall was the *frigidarium*[112] and to the south of the hall was the *caldarium.*[113]
To the south of the *caldarium* was the *sudatoria* which was like a steam room.
The baths were surrounded by the *palaestrae* where naked bathers exercised.
During the reign of Domitian, under whose reign John was exiled to Patmos, there was no prohibition of mixed bathing though private bathing was also available.

The Foulness of the City

The plumbing and sewage conveniences of the larger cities did not reach many of the other cities. This led to conditions of squalor including human waste in the streets and no running water.[114] Williams provides a descriptive summary of the situation:

> Sewage disposal – the system only collected the outfall of a few private houses and of public lavatories that dotted its routes. Most people had either to use the lavatories (at a small fee) or to dispose of their sewage as best they could. They might clatter down the stairs to empty their pot in the vat provided by the landlord or find the nearest dung pit outside (travelers could reputedly smell Rome before reaching it). But there were always some who found the stairs too steep or the hour too late and, to save themselves further trouble, would empty their pots from a window into the street. So much the worse for the passerby who happened upon the wrong place at the wrong time! The evidence suggests this occurred with some regularity.[115]

[112] The *frigidarium* contained the pool into which bathers jumped.

[113] The *caldarium* "was a rotunda lit by the sun at noon and in the afternoon, and heated by vapour circulating between the *suspensurae* laid beneath its pavement. It was surrounded by little bathing boxes where people could bathe in private; and a giant bronze basin of water in the centre was kept at the required temperature by the furnace immediately below" (Carcopino, *Daily Life in Ancient Rome*, 292).

[114] For a picture of illness during this time frame, see Chapter 8, Section 10: Illness.

[115] Williams, *Paul's Metaphors*, 10-11.

The Family

General characteristics. The following chart lists some normal features in the typical household.

Greco-Roman	Jewish
Patriarchal[116]	Patriarchal[117]
Extended families were the norm[118]	Extended families were the norm
Low birth rate	High birth rate
Boys were favored[119]	Boys were favored, birth of a girl was disappointing
Inherent superiority of men over women	Boys were circumcised the eighth day No surnames[120]
Did not allow polygamy	Allowed polygamy but did not encourage it

Ancestory

Pure ancestory was of great importance to the Jew. In order to hold office, one had to produce his genealogy. Even the average layman would know his immediate ancestors and to which tribe he belonged. Jeremias suggests that each Jew would have at least known the last few generations of his ancestory.[121] A pure ancestory gave a "true Israelite" various rights including: a woman's right to marry into a priestly family, being able to hold an office of public trust, having a vicarious share in Abraham's righteousness, and assurance in a share of Messianic salvation.[122] The significance of this biblically is that the Messianic hope rested on one of a particular pedigree. Toussaint explains the importance of this for Christ's messianic claims:

---

[116] At one time the husband was the absolute master of all of its members. This was referred to by the term "paterfamilias." By the time of Paul, those days of the father's absolute power of life and death had waned, but Roman society still remained patriarchal.

[117] Certainly Scripture and even the moral law which God has put within each person would indicate that we are to be kind, respectful and nurturing of all people including our parents. However, most readers of texts like Ephesians 6:2 at the time and culture in which it was given would have seen instruction on caring for their aging parents. This would fit well with the last half of the verse "...that your days may be long in the earth." The idea being that as I care for my elderly parents and lay that example, it is going to be more likely that my children would do that for me and so it would go. For further statements of importance in Judaism, see the apocryphal *The Wisdom of Sirach* 3:6-8, 12-15.

[118] Living under the same roof or in close vicinity would be the husband/wife, unmarried children, married sons, daughters-in-law, grandchildren, and slaves.

[119] Baby girls were commonly left to die, many of whom were raised as prostitutes. For a sketch of abortion in the ancient world, see Chapter 8, Section 11: Abortion in the ancient world.

[120] People were identified by attaching to their given name: the name of their father (Simon son of Zebedee), their political association (Simon the Zealot), place of residence (Simon of Cyrene), or occupation (Simon the tanner). The same is true for Jesus. Since this was a common name, his name is usually qualified in the New Testament (e.g., Jesus of Nazareth, Jesus the Christ).

[121] Jeremias, *Jerusalem in the Time of Jesus,* 276.

[122] Gentile converts to Judaism who had been circumcised, baptized, and offered sacrifice were still considered legally as Gentiles.

> One of the primary questions a Jew would ask concerning a claimant to the title of Messiah would be, "Is he a son of Abraham and of the house of David?...Because this question concerning the King of Israel is so important, and because it forms a logical starting point for a document which sets about to prove the Messiahship of Christ, Matthew presents the first genealogy of Jesus (1:1-1:17).[123]

Importantly, there is no record in the New Testament that the opponents of Jesus ever questioned his physical qualifications to assume David's throne. This would have been an easy way to debunk his Messianic claims so it is highly likely this area would have been explored by Jesus' enemies.[124]

Marriage, Divorce, and Remarriage in Greco-Roman Culture[125]

Men usually married in their mid to late twenties while girls were normally in their middle to late teens. Most Roman weddings[126] occurred in April or the second half of June at which time the bride (the legal minimum age was twelve) sacrificed her childhood toys and clothes to the gods. On the morning of the wedding, a pig would be sacrificed and she would be dressed in a white tunic and bright orange veil with her face exposed.[127] Divorce was common, but the major importance of it for New Testament studies relates to the *kind* of divorce which was practiced. No-fault divorce (unilateral) could be initiated by either spouse by simply telling the other to leave without naming any grounds or choosing to move out.[128] This method of divorce had infiltrated the Corinthian church and it is against this backdrop that Paul gives the fullest apostolic teaching on the subject in 1 Corinthians 7. His point in this regard is that the believer should never be the initiator of a no-fault divorce; however, if the other partner insisted on it and reconciliation proved impossible, the innocent party was free to remarry.[129]

---

[123] Stanley Toussaint, *Behold the King: A Study of Matthew* (Portland: Multnomah Press, 1981), 35.

[124] Not only does Matthew's genealogy of Jesus confirm his kingly descent, but the configuration of it does as well. The Matthew 1 genealogy falls into three sections of fourteen names each. Matthew uses a "gematria" in his account. Gematria assigns a numerical value to letters. The Hebrew letters (consonants) DVD have a value of 14 (D=4, D=6, D=4).

[125] It is important to distinguish between marriage customs in Greco-Roman and Jewish cultures. Confusion between the two will result in reading one culture into another and thus misinterpretation of the key texts. For example, Jesus' teaching on divorce and remarriage in Matthew 19 is addressing the rabbinic interpretation of Deuteronomy 24:1 while Paul in 1 Corinthians 7 is dealing with the infiltration of unilateral divorce into the Corinthian church.

[126] Only marriages between Roman citizens were considered legal which meant only they would receive legal protection. Children born to mixed marriages, in terms of citizenship, were considered illegitimate. See the intimation of Timothy's illegitimacy in 1 Timothy 1:2 where Paul speaks of him as legitimate spiritually speaking. Jesus was accused of being illegitimate by the Pharisees in John 8:41.

[127] Edwin Yamauchi "Cultural Aspects of Marriage in the Ancient World," *Bibliotheca Sacra* 135 (1978) 247. For a fuller treatment of this aspect of the wedding, see Chapter 8, Section 12: Roman Marriage.

[128] David Instone-Brewer, *Divorce and Remarriage in the Bible: The Social and Literary Context* (Grand Rapids: Eerdmans, 2002), 190.

[129] Under Roman law, either the man or woman could initiate a divorce.

Marriage, Divorce, and Remarriage in Jewish Culture

Jewish marriages underwent four major phases. The first phase was the betrothal.[130] Females were normally betrothed before puberty[131] and males were encouraged to marry as minors to lessen the likelihood of immorality. The fathers of the bride and groom arranged the marriage which culminated in the betrothal which was contractually binding so much so that the couple was considered husband and wife.[132] The betrothal could only be dissolved due to death or divorce. Marriages were arranged affairs probably due to the fact that the couple was not merely beginning a new family but becoming a part of one already in place.[133]

Since the betrothal was a matter of business, there would be negotiations in drawing up the contract often with the aid of one who had been hired as a sort of marriage broker. He would be aware of the bride-price (*mohar*) willing to be paid.[134] The bride-price would compensate for the loss of a daughter since she would have offered significant help in the household and fields. It would also show that the groom had resources to be a good provider for his wife. This payment could be in the form of cash, a gift, or some kind of service. Another part of the transaction was the "dowry."[135] The dowry was paid by the groom's father to the bride and could consist of gifts or coins which would help to contribute to the marriage or help the woman in case of divorce.[136]

The second phase of the Jewish marriage was the "betrothal period." Once the legal arrangements of the betrothal were finalized, the "married" couple embarked on the betrothal period which normally lasted one year. The purpose of this time span was to test the faithfulness of each partner to the other.[137] If immorality did occur during this time on the part of the woman, this would be considered as adultery since the betrothal contract made the couple husband and wife. The husband could pursue a private divorce which did not require a trial; a public divorce which did require a trial; or, he could have her executed by stoning.[138] The Talmud instructs:

---

[130] The "betrothal" was an event which preceded the actual marriage and was therefore different. It was essentially an agreement of marriage which was considered to be binding.

[131] Roughly 12 ½ years of age or when the first signs of puberty appeared.

[132] Note Matthew 1:18-19 where the couple is said to be betrothed (ESV, NAU, NJB, NKJ, and YLT) and Joseph is referred to as Mary's "husband."

[133] Love typically came after betrothal. See Genesis 24:67 which indicates that when Isaac and Rebekah were married they had never even seen each other.

[134] The *mohar* was the price paid by the groom to the bride's father. This payment sealed the betrothal (see Genesis 24:53; Exodus 22:16-17).

[135] Some have mistakenly equated the "bride-price" with the "dowry" when in fact they are two separate things. This is partially due to the mistranslation of *mohar* with "dowry" on three occasions by the KJV (Genesis 34:12; Exodus 22:17; 1 Samuel 18:25). See also Edwin Yamauchi "Cultural Aspects of Marriage in the Ancient World," 244.

[136] This is presumably what led to the frenetic search of the woman in Luke 15:8 for a coin which was possibly a part of her dowry. Jesus' point is to illustrate the passion with which God seeks lost individuals.

[137] This is why Joseph was aghast when Mary became pregnant—this occurred during the betrothal period. It took no less than an angelic visitor to convince him that she was faithful to him—"that which is conceived in her is of the Holy Spirit" (Matthew 1:20).

[138] Typically in Jewish culture, only the man could initiate a divorce (Bruce, *New Testament History*, 28).

> If witnesses appeared against her in the house of her father-in-law that she had played the harlot in her father's house she is stoned at the door of her father's house, as if to say, "See the plant that you have reared": If witnesses came against her in her father's house that she played the harlot in his house she is stoned at the entrance of the gate of the city.[139]

During the betrothal period, the husband would busy himself preparing a place in his father's house to which he would bring his bride after the wedding ceremony. In addition, the bridegroom would send out a messenger informing his friends of the betrothal along with an invitation to the wedding and subsequent wedding banquet. Since the betrothal period lasted one year, they would have plenty of time to make arrangements. There would then be a second invitation issued to the same guests announcing the exact time of the wedding (see Matthew 22:1-14).[140]

The third phase of the Jewish marriage was the actual day of the wedding ceremony. While the bride was at her home in the evening, the friends of the bridegroom would accompany him in a torchlight procession as he left his father's house to pick up his bride as he was dressed in holiday attire. The bride would be decked in jewels and marvelous dress completely veiled. The bridegroom and his closest friends would enter the bride's house where the bride's father would hand his daughter over to the groom and they would enjoy a festive banquet. After the banquet, the procession would make its way back to the bridegroom's house. It is here that the most important event transpired—entry into the bridegroom's house and a pronouncement of blessing by the groom's father followed by his placement of the bride's hand into that of his son's. This "presentation" completed the marriage ceremony as the father handed over the bride he had purchased with the *mohar* to give to his son. She would now remove her veil and look clearly into her husband's face. The marriage was then consummated in the "bridal chamber."

The final phase of the Jewish wedding was the "wedding feast." The feast would last seven days[141] or more and would be marked by eating extravagant food, drinking wine, dancing, and singing. The feast was normally arranged by the father of the bridegroom and to run out of anything, especially wine, was considered to be a serious social *faux pas*.[142] Interestingly (particularly from a theological perspective), though the bride was splendidly adorned, the focus of attention would be on the bridegroom.

On the shame of public trails, see the Mishnah, Tractate Sotah 5.1, 5.5. For the process of getting a divorce see the Mishnah, Tractate Gittin 2.5; 9.3-4, 8.

[139] *Babylonian Talmud*: Kethuboth 44b; 45a; Yebamoth 29a. See also Sanhedrin 7.4.

[140] To reject this kind of an invitation would be an insult. See the apocryphal *Sirach* 13:9-10 for an example.

[141] For a statement of seven day celebration, see *Tobit* 11:18.

[142] A.C. Bouquet, *Everyday Life in New Testament Times* (New York: Charles Scribner, 1955), 148.Carson observes that "to run out of supplies would be a dreadful embarrassment in a 'shame' culture; there is some evidence it could also lay the groom open to a lawsuit from aggrieved relatives of the bride" (D.A. Carson, *The Gospel According to John* [Grand Rapids: Eerdmans, 1998], 169). Without getting into a lengthy discussion on whether Jesus created alcoholic wine in John 2, the idea that this was merely grape juice is

Unlike Graeco-Roman marriages, a Jewish marriage was expected to last a lifetime. However, the Old Testament and Rabbinic Law did provide grounds for divorce and remarriage. These grounds did not make a divorce mandatory, but allowed it in extreme cases. The culture of Jesus' day generally followed one of the two rabbinic schools on this matter. The major issue of debate among the rabbis was the interpretation of the Hebrew phrase עֶרְוַת דָּבָר (*'erwat dabar*) in Deuteronomy 24:1. This phrase has been variously translated in our English versions as "something indecent," "some uncleanness," "some impropriety," "something objectionable," and "not finding grace." The conservative school of Shammai interpreted the phrase to refer to some kind of immorality on the part of the wife. The more liberal school of Hillel[143] understood the phrase very loosely to refer to anything in the wife which displeased the husband. This could include a variety of things such as immorality, ruining a meal, or simply if he found another woman who was more attractive.[144] It is thus seen that despite the expectations of a Jewish marriage, it was relatively easy to obtain a divorce. When the religious leaders questioned Jesus on these matters in Matthew 19:3-12, they were essentially asking him with which rabbinic school he agreed.[145]

Food

The Romans ate four meals a day consisting of such items as bread,[146] cheese, vegetables, soup, porridge, olives, fruit, bacon, sausage, fish,[147] and diluted wine with dinner being the main meal of the day. The Jews ate two meals a day—the first at noon and the second in the evening. Their diet included bread, vegetables, fruit, fish, and milk. Other meats were usually reserved for special occasions. Since sugar was not known during this time, raisins, figs, and honey were used for sweetening. At formal banquets guests would recline on their left arms and eat with their right hand around a low table. These meals demonstrated social status with the more favored guests sitting at the right and left of the host. When the banquet began, the host would close the door and no one else was allowed admittance (Matt. 25:10).

"intrinsically silly" (Ibid., 169). Since the women's quarters at the feast were near the storage area for the wine, Mary became aware that the wine supply was running low and let Jesus know to avoid the embarrassment which could last for years (Craig Keener, *The IVP Bible Background Commentary: New Testament* [Grand Rapids: Eerdmans, 1993], 268).

[143] Gamaliel (Acts 5:34) was the son or grandson of Hillel. Gamaliel's protégé was a young man named Saul. The pupil disregarded his mentor's advice for caution (Acts 5:35-39) by wreaking havoc among the early Christians (Acts 8:3).

[144] Shammai: "A man should divorce his wife only because he has grounds for it in unchastity." Hillel: "Even if she spoiled his dish." Aqiba: "Even if he found someone else prettier than she" (Mishnah, Gittin 9.10).

[145] What the Bible teaches on the entire matter of divorce and remarriage (including concomitant issues such as the role of the divorced in the church) has long been a bone of contention among Christians. The literature is extensive and the exegesis of certain passages such as Deuteronomy 24:1 and Matthew 19:9 is technical. I have included one of the better discussions on the matter in Chapter 8, Section 13: Divorce and Remarriage by David Instone-Brewer.

[146] Bread was made from wheat flour or barley flour. Bread made from wheat was superior and therefore more expensive than that made from barley. During the Tribulation period, inflation will be so great that one

Clothing/Style

Jewish men wore a tunic made of linen or wool,[148] a belt around the waist, leather (usually) sandals and a hat or scarf. In cold weather they donned a heavy outer coat and their garments were usually white. Rabbis of the day had their heads covered, and so more than likely Jesus also wore some kind of turban on his head. Jewish women wore a shorter tunic as an undergarment over which was worn a brightly colored outer garment which extended to the feet.[149] Greco-Roman women usually wore a tunic to the ankles over which was worn a belted gown. Unmarried women were unveiled while a veil was worn over the head by married women with the face remaining uncovered.[150] Strauss helpfully comments that "a woman's covering symbolized modesty and respect for her husband, preventing sexual attention from other males. Uncovered hair was a sign of promiscuity or even prostitution…In general, the farther east you went in the Mediterranean world, the more women were expected to cover up. Persian women in the East were completely veiled in public, while Roman and Greek women more often had their heads and arms uncovered."[151]

Jewish men wore beards with longer hair, but not shoulder-length as is often portrayed in Christian art. Jewish women wore their hair long while prostitutes sometimes wore their hair shorter. Unique to the Roman male was the donning of a toga, under which was worn a knee-length tunic. [152] Roman men wore their hair short and were clean-shaven (during the New Testament era) while Greek men wore their hair long. Wealthy Greco-Roman women wore make-up, jewelry, and elaborate hairstyles. While the Bible does not condemn such things per se, it does prohibit fashion excesses in the church meeting (1 Timothy 2:9-10). Hurley observes:

---

measure of wheat will cost a denarius and three measures of barley will cost a denarius (Revelation 6:6). Osborne explains the terms: "Wheat was a better grain and a major staple, and barley was less expensive but also less nutritious. The poor ate barley, while the wealthy ate wheat for the most part. A 'denarius' was the average days' wage for a laborer. A quart of wheat was enough food for one person for a day, and three quarts of barley enough for a small family (there were few small families except among the wealthy in the ancient world). Therefore a man's entire earnings were barely enough to feed himself, let alone his family, and all the other costs like home or incidentals could not be met" (Grant Osborne, *Revelation*, Baker Exegetical Commentary on the New Testament [Grand Rapids: Baker, 2006], 280).

[147] Romans especially favored fish. The lower classes ate fish preserved in brine while the rich enjoyed turbot, sturgeon, and mullet. Other meats could include pork, venison, ass (wild), flamingo, stork, crane, and peacock (J. Balsdon, *Romans and Aliens* (London: Duckworth, 1979), 224.

[148] A tunic was like a shirt that went down to the knees.

[149] Gundry, *A Survey of the New Testament*, 32.

[150] Of interest are Paul's words in 1 Corinthians 11:4 where he says that it is a shame for a man to pray with a covered head. This could be a reference to the Roman practice of men making idol sacrifice where he would lift the back of the toga over his head. See the illustration in Ben Witherington III, *New Testament History: A Narrative Account* (Grand Rapids: Baker, 2001), 307.

[151] Mark Strauss, *Four Portraits, One Jesus* (Grand Rapids: Zondervan, 2007), 154.

[152] A ceremonial garment characteristic of male Roman citizens in Rome was the "toga." The toga was a large piece of woolen fabric which was carefully folded and draped over the body. Because of its size and covering over one arm, there were certain togas worn for various occasions ("Toga," A Dictionary of Greek and Roman Antiquities, accessed August 23, 2013, http://www.penelope.uchicago.edu /Thayer/E/Roman/Texts).

> The sculpture and literature of the period make it clear that women often wore their hair in enormously elaborate arrangements with braids and curls interwoven or piled high like towers and decorated with gems and/or gold and/or pearls. The courtesans wore their hair in numerous small pendant braids with gold droplets or pearls or gems every inch or so, making a shimmering screen of their locks.[153]

Morality

There were certainly many decent people in the world of the first century. However, just like other eras of history, immorality was flagrant in the Roman world. Male and female prostitution was practiced in pagan worship ceremonies, divorce was acceptable, and homosexuality (most commonly pederasty) was accepted by this society.[154] Interestingly though, homosexual relationships were proper if they conformed to social values related to status.[155] In addition to these sins, murder was common as was abortion and the euthanasia of female babies through drowning or exposure. In a letter dated 1 BC, a Roman man wrote to his pregnant wife back home: "I am still in Alexandria...I ask and beg you to take good care of our baby son, and as soon as I receive payment I shall send it up to you. If you are delivered (before I come home), if it is a boy, keep it, if a girl, discard it."[156]

Name	Color	Meaning
Toga virilis	White	Everyday use for male Roman citizen
Toga praetexta	White with purple border	Senator—stripe width indicated position
Toga pulla	Gray or brown	During a period of mourning
Toga candida	Bright white	Political candidate symbolizing honesty
Toga picta	Purple with gold embroidery	Victorious general

[153] James Hurley, *Man and Woman in Biblical Perspective* (Grand Rapids: Zondervan, 1981), 199. The problem created by excessive attire in the church meeting (which is just as true for men as women) is threefold: 1) attention is drawn to people rather than focusing on God (going to church is not intended to be a fashion show, even at Christmas and Easter!), 2) it would accentuate the socio-economic differences within the body of Christ thus weakening its unity, and 3) this type of dress can reflect a power-play in an effort to obviate role distinctions.

[154] Barclay notes that "this sin had swept like a cancer through Greek life and from Greece, invaded Rome. We can scarcely realize how riddled the ancient world was with it....Fourteen of the first fifteen Roman Emperors practised this unnatural vice. At this very time Nero was emperor. He had taken a boy called Sporus and had him castrated. He then married him with a full marriage ceremony and took him home in procession to his palace and lived with him as wife...When Nero was eliminated and Otho came to the throne one of the first things he did was to take possession of Sporus" (William Barclay, *The Letters to the Corinthians* [Philadelphia: Westminster Press, 1975], 53-54). Durant observes that "even our generation has not yet rivaled the popularity of homosexualism in ancient Greece or Rome" (Will Durant, *The Lessons of History* [NY: Simon and Schuster, 1968], 40).

[155] See Chapter 8, Section 14: Socially Acceptable Homosexuality in the Roman World.

[156] This is a statement found in the Oxyrhynchus Papyrus 744. The Oxyrhynchus Papyri are a collection of

If the child was rescued, it quite likely was for the purpose of being reared as a prostitute. Against the backdrop of the evil and violence in the cities is the Pauline metaphor of darkness.

> The night especially was a time to be afraid. As dusk fell, the city shut down and anyone who ventured out after "closing" was at risk. Juvenal laments that to go out to supper in Rome without having first made your will was to be guilty of an act of gross negligence. The pages of the *Digest* show how real and pervasive was the danger that Romans faced from murderers and housebreakers and muggers. At night the city's narrow streets were plunged into impenetrable darkness. Little or no attempt was made at lighting them. Night fell over the city—any city—like the shadow of a great danger, and most people fled to their homes, shut themselves in, and barricaded their doors. But some welcomed the night as a cloak for their deeds. Paul enlists their actions—orgies and drunkenness, sexual indulgence and debauchery—as a metaphor of immoral conduct in general, "the works of darkness," he calls them, **"darkness"** characterizing "the children of this age." Doors were commonly barred against thieves and the like, but Paul spoke of doors that we sometimes, surprisingly, opened.[157]

The Athletic games

The Pauline corpus is laden with doctrinal truth and exhortations to Christian living based on this illustration. One of Paul's favorite methods for applying and illustrating Christian responsibility is through the use of athletic metaphors. For example, he uses words for "running" and the "race" on numerous occasions (Acts 13:25; 20:24; Rom. 9:16; 1 Cor. 9:24; Gal. 2:2; 5:7; Phil. 2:16; 2 Thess. 3:1; 2 Tim. 4:7). In addition, he refers to other sports such as boxing (1 Cor. 9:26) and wrestling (Eph. 6:12). Besides references to specific sports, Paul also uses words which would have conjured up images of the games in his readers' minds. These include such words as "prize" (1 Cor. 9:24), "crown" (1 Cor. 9:25), "goal" (Phil. 3:14), being disqualified (1 Cor. 9:27), "strive lawfully" (2 Tim. 2:5), and the giving of the crown by the righteous judge (2 Tim. 4:8).[158]

It is clear from the above examples that a large part of Paul's admonitions are bound closely with athletic imagery from the first century during which time he and his readers lived. Therefore, it is evident that if the full impact of the Apostle's words is to be felt, there must be some understanding of this part of his historical milieu.[159]

---

manuscripts found near Oxyrhynchus, Egypt in the late 19th and early 20th centuries. They contain, among other things, Greek writings dating back to the first century AD.

[157] David Williams, *Paul's Metaphors: Their Context and Character*, 8.

[158] John also refers to these concepts in Revelation 2-3 when he urges the members of the seven churches to be "overcomers."

[159] For a fuller discussion, see Chapter 8, Section 15: Paul's Athletic Allusions.

Gladiatorial combat

One of the most macabre yet alluring spectacles of the ancient world was gladiatorial combat (basically an event of debauched voyeurism!). Spectators sat encircled on multi-levels around the floor of the amphitheater as they waited for the *venatio* to begin.[160] Criminals of the lower status-whether males, females, or children-were mauled to death or eaten by animals as a means of execution. Additionally, an unbelievable number of animals were slaughtered.

Of the number of animals killed, occasional references give us some indication. As early as 169 BCE, 63 African animals (probably lions or leopards), 40 bears, and several elephants had been killed in a single show (Livy, *Hist.* 44.18). New species were gradually introduced to Roman spectators—tigers, crocodiles, giraffes, lynxes, rhinoceroses, ostriches, hippopotamuses—and killed for their pleasure (Pliny, *Nat.* 8.65ff.). Pliny tells of single shows that featured 100, 400, and 600 lions respectively, plus other animals (*Nat.* 8.53; cf. Dio Cassius, *Rom. Hist.* 39.38). Augustus is said to have given twenty-six wild beast shows in Rome during his principate, in which 3,500 animals were killed (see K. Hopkins, *Death and Renewal* [Cambridge: Cambridge University Press, 1983], 9). In one day of the *munera* with which Titus inaugurated the Colosseum in 80 CE, 5000 beasts were killed (Suetonius, *Tit. 7).* In 108-109 CE Trajan celebrated his conquest of Dacia with games, lasting 123 days, in which 'some eleven thousand animals wild and tame were killed and ten thousand gladiators fought' (Dio Cassius, *Rom. Hist.* 68.15). Caelius Rufus's badgering of Cicero, at that time the governor of Cilicia, to send him 100 panthers for the games to be held under his aedileship seems, by comparison, a modest request (see Cicero, *Fam.* 8.9)! The emperor Commodus himself killed five hippopotamuses, two elephants, a rhinoceros, and a giraffe in a show that lasted two days (Dio Cassius, *Rom. Hist.* 72.19). On another occasion, he killed 100 animals (lions or bears) in a single morning (Herodian, *Hist. 1.15*). It is not surprising that the lion, the tiger, the hippopotamus, and the elephant became extinct in large areas—within and beyond the borders of the empire—in which once they had freely roamed.[161]

However, the *venatio* was not the most breathtaking of the events. There remained the *munus gladiatorum* and the *naumachia*.[162] Unwilling gladiators consisted of prisoners of war, criminals, and slaves. However, some voluntarily chose to participate in the hopes of becoming famous. Though some survived, this was not expected and most died in the arena.

The night before the event, the gladiators would be fed an elegant, final meal known as the *cena libera.* There has been discussion on why the host of the games would be so lavish for those who most likely would die the next day. Tertullian[163] argued in his *De Spectaculis* ("the shows") that the blood of the gladiators was sacrificial in nature:

---

[160] Latin for the "chase" or "hunt."

[161] Williams, *Paul's Metaphors*, 281.

[162] Latin for "offerings of gladiatorial shows" and "naval battle" respectively.

[163] Tertullian was born in AD 160, the son of a Roman centurion. He was a major Western apologist and

> The ancients thought that in this solemnity they rendered offices to the dead; at a later period, with a cruelty more refined, they somewhat modified its character. For formerly, in the belief that the souls of the departed were appeased by human blood, they were in the habit of buying captives or slaves of wicked disposition, and immolating them in their funeral obsequies. Afterwards they thought good to throw the veil of pleasure over their iniquity. Those, therefore, whom they had provided for the combat, and then trained in arms as best they could, only that they might learn to die, they, on the funeral day, killed at the places of sepulture. They alleviated death by murders. Such is the origin of the "Munus." But by degrees their refinement came up to their cruelty; for these human wild beasts could not find pleasure exquisite enough, save in the spectacle of men torn to pieces by wild beasts. Offerings to propitiate the dead then were regarded as belonging to the class of funeral sacrifices.[164]

Brettler and Poliakoff agree with Tertullian by citing sources which aver that the "vile blood of the prisoner or slave was ritually unsuited for the funeral offerings" and so the meal "functioned as a ritual for turning an undesirable man into a free and noble victim." And, the last meal made a "worthy sacrificial victim: his blood becomes then, in the rabbis' words, 'sweet.'"[165]

The combat was made compelling (for one example) by pitting a slow, heavily armed individual with a lightly armed man who was quicker. Other combinations were added using blacks, dwarfs, and women. The combatant taken to his back would raise his left arm to appeal for his life. The host of the event would decide the fighter's fate. At times, the host would consult the crowd. In such cases, the gladiator did not want to hear the cry "*jugular*" (cut his throat). Unbelievably, for the *naumachia* the arena would be flooded and stocked with warships.

Burial

Death came relatively early by modern Western standards in the Roman world. Jeffers observes that around 80 percent of the burial inscriptions found in the Roman city of Ostia were for people under the age of thirty.[166]

---

theologian. Wright describes him as follows: "sophistic brilliance and literary versatility, ruthless vigor as disputant and polemicist, fecundity in uttering memorable dicta, and fervent religious immediacy make him a captivating writer as well as a priceless mirror of early African Christianity" (David Wright, "Tertullian," in *The New International Dictionary of the Christian Church,* J.D. Douglas, editor [Grand Rapids: Zondervan, 1981], 961).

[164] *Ante-Nicene Fathers 3: Latin Christianity: Its Founder, Tertullian*, "De Spectaculis" (Buffalo: The Christian Literature Company, 1885), Chapter 12.

[165] Marc Avi Brettler and Michael Poliakoff, "Rabbi Simeon ben Lakish at the Gladiator's Banquet: Rabbinic Observations on the Roman Arena," *The Harvard Theological Review* 83:1 (1990) 94, 97.

[166] Jeffers, *The Greco-Roman World of the New Testament*, 44.

During the time of the New Testament most Romans practiced cremation as opposed to burial, though this changed in time.[167] Several fascinating details (general and selected) emerge from the Roman practice.[168] When the individual was about to die, the nearest relative attempted to catch his last breath in his mouth. A coin was placed in the mouth to pay the ferryman to hades and the corpse was prepared for burial and lay in state in the house for as long as a week dressed in the best robe owned with feet facing the door.

A nighttime procession followed and the body was burned on a pyre (pile of wood). Depending on the wealth of the deceased, the process could be quite elaborate including mourning, actors who imitated his words and actions, and the wearing of wax masks depicting the individual's ancestors. The ashes were put in an urn which was placed in one of the niches in the family tomb. Nock writes that "the poor, above all the slaves and freedmen of great households and foreign groups, associated in gilds and built communal repositories for the ash-urns of their dead, each occupying its niche or columbarium."[169] Tombs were often ornate with one of the most common ornaments being a horse's head which signified departure. The attendees then returned home and went through purification rituals including sprinkling with water, stepping over a fire, and sweeping out the house with a special broom. The Romans would return to the tomb at various times to present gifts and sacrifices.

Paul instructs the Thessalonians in 1 Thessalonians 4:13 that they should sorrow at the death of a loved one, but not as those "who have no hope." Paul certainly was alluding to the pagan sense of hopelessness at the death event. For example, Theocritus has Corydon say: "Cheer up, brave lad! Tomorrow may ease thee of thy pain: <u>Aye for the living are there hopes, past' hoping are the slain</u>: And now Zeus sends us sunshine, and now he sends us rain."[170] Hogg and Vine cite Moschus speaking of the plants which die in his garden and Catullus respectively: "Alas! Alas!...these live and spring again in another year; but we…when we die, deaf to all sound in the hollow earth, sleep a long, long, endless sleep that knows no waking," "Suns may set and rise again but we, when once our brief light goes down, must sleep an endless night."[171]

Deissmann quotes a letter from the second century written to a bereaved friend:

---

[167] Arthur Nock, "Cremation and Burial in the Roman Empire," *The Harvard Theological Review* 25:4 (1932): 322.

[168] Much of the material is taken from John Heller, "Burial Customs of the Romans," *The Classical Weekly* XXV:24 (1932) 193-197; "Funus," in *A Dictionary of Greek and Roman Antiquities by Various Authors,* William Smith, ed., (London: John Murray, 1875), 558-562. Though this work is extremely dated, and therefore should not be used indiscriminately, it still contains much valuable material of interest.

[169] Nock, "Cremation and Burial in the Roman Empire," 322.

[170] Theocritus, *Idyll IV. The Herdsman.*

[171] C.F. Hogg and W.E. Vine, *The Epistles of Paul the Apostle to the Thessalonians* (Shreveport, LA: Lambert Book House, 1977), 133.

> Irene to Taonnophris and Philo, good comfort. I am as sorry and weep over the departed one as I wept for Didymas. And all things, whatsoever were fitting, I have done, and all mine, Epaphroditus and Thermuthion and Philion and Apollonius and Plantas. But, nevertheless, against such things one can do nothing. Therefore, comfort ye one another.[172]

In contrast to the Romans of this period, the Jews practiced burial rather than cremation. The deceased was buried on the day of his death which was preceded by the preparation of the body with various spices and then wrapped in linen. Personal and hired musicians publicly demonstrated the grief of the survivors in the procession to the burial site. According to the Mishnah, even poor families were required to hire a minimum of two flute players and one mourning woman: "Even the poorest man in Israel should not have less than two mourning pipes, and one mourning woman."[173] Jones observes that it was normal to visit a grave within three days to make sure the person was dead, since mistakes could be made in light of the rapidity with which the dead were buried![174] Once the body had decomposed about a year later, the wealthy would place the bones into a specially prepared box known as an ossuary. Christians also often buried their dead in underground tunnels and rooms called catacombs.

Crucifixion

Christians were held in disdain because they worshiped *hominem noxium et crucem eius* (a criminal and his cross) or worse, they worshiped "an ass in the temple."[175] For Jews who had not embraced Christ as Messiah, his death on the cross was a sign of God's displeasure[176] while for the Greeks and Romans his claim to divinity was proved sheer folly since their gods were immortal.

---

[172] A. Deissmann, *Light from the Ancient East* (Grand Rapids: Baker, 1978), 176.

[173] Mishnah, *Ketubot* 4.4. http://www.sefaria.org/Mishnah_Ketubot.4. Accessed 5/11/2014.

[174] J. Julius Scott, *Jewish Backgrounds of the New Testament*, 251. Later rabbinic belief indicated that the soul of the deceased would hover over the body for the first three days of death with the intent of re-entering it. However, when decomposition began to set in, it would depart with the belief that death was irreversible. Some doubt that this belief held true during Jesus' ministry; however, some commentators feel this is implied in such texts as John 11:17 (D. A. Carson, *The Gospel According to John* [Grand Rapids: Eerdmans, 1991], 411).

[175] This was a common anti-Jewish sentiment (Martin Hengel, *Crucifixion* [Philadelphia: Fortress Press, 1982], 19). See also Everett Ferguson, *Backgrounds of Early Christianity* (Grand Rapids: Eerdmans, 1993), 559-61.

[176] In order for the Messiah to return to earth and establish his kingdom, this sentiment will have to be reversed by the Jewish remnant. Two Old Testament texts are on point here. The first is Isaiah 53:4-5 where the prophet shows how the thinking of the nation will change. Notice how the New Living Translation catches the idea: "Yet it was our weaknesses he carried; it was our sorrows that weighed him down. And we thought his troubles were a punishment from God for his own sins! But he was wounded and crushed for our sins. He was beaten that we might have peace. He was whipped, and we were healed!" The second text is Zechariah 12:10 where before the second coming of the Messiah, Israel will "look for the one whom <u>they</u> pierced" (New Jerusalem Bible).

While the death of Christ is the most famous of Roman crucifixions,[177] the practice actually goes back to the Assyrians, Phoenicians, Persians, Greeks, and Seleucids. In fact, even though the preferred method of capital punishment in Judaism was stoning, crucifixion was at times used. Josephus writes of Alexander Jannaeus (a Maccabean king) who crucified 800 Jews in one day.

> Now as Alexander fled to the mountains, six thousand of the Jews hereupon came together [from Demetrius] to him out of pity at the change of his fortune; upon which Demetrius was afraid, and retired out of the country; after which the Jews fought against Alexander, and being beaten, were slain in great numbers in the several battles which they had; and when he had shut up the most powerful of them in the city Bethome, he besieged them therein; and when he had taken the city, and gotten the men into his power, he brought them to Jerusalem, and did one of the most barbarous actions in the world to them; for as he was feasting with his concubines, in the sight of all the city, he ordered about eight hundred of them to be crucified; and while they were living, he ordered the throats of their children and wives to be cut before their eyes.[178]

In the century prior to the coming of Christ, the Romans used crucifixion as an instrument of torture and humiliation (not execution) for non-Romans, but this eventually evolved into a method of capital punishment. Crucifixion of individuals during a time of war was done without much concern for method as thousands could be put to death in a short period of time. This is seen, for example, when the revolt of Spartacus was quelled with 6,000 being crucified on the road from Capua to Rome:

> On account of this vote Crassus tried in every way to come to an engagement with Spartacus so that Pompey might not reap the glory of the war. Spartacus himself, thinking to anticipate Pompey, invited Crassus to come to terms with him. When his proposals were rejected with scorn he resolved to risk a battle, and as his cavalry had arrived he made a dash with his whole army through the lines of the besieging force and pushed on to Brundusium with Crassus in pursuit. When Spartacus learned that Lucullus had just arrived in Brundusium from his victory over Mithridates he despaired of everything and brought his forces, which were even then very numerous, to close quarters with Crassus. The battle was long and bloody, as might have been expected with so many thousands of desperate men. Spartacus was wounded in the thigh with a spear and sank upon his

[177] Though originally a pre-Christian symbol, early believers remembered the cross by means of the "staurogram." This ⳩ symbol combines the Greek capital letters *tau* (T) and *rho* (R) which when superimposed on each other: pictures a figure on a cross.

[178] *Antiquities*, 13.14.2.

> knee, holding his shield in front of him and contending in this way against his assailants until he and the great mass of those with him were surrounded and slain. The Roman loss was about 1000. The body of Spartacus was not found. A large number of his men fled from the battle-field to the mountains and Crassus followed them thither. They divided themselves in four parts, and continued to fight until they all perished except 6000, who were captured and crucified along the whole road from Capua to Rome.[179]

However, during times of peace, this method of execution was carried out in a specified manner.[180] Once sentence had been passed, the process was supervised by the *carnifex serarum.* The victim would be stripped and tied to a column at which time he would be beaten with a rod or *flagellum* (a short handle to which was attached leather strips with pieces of bone or metal at the ends). There was no set amount of lashes to be delivered under Roman law, and though some died during this flogging, it was not the intent to kill the victim at this point. Blinzler gives a more detailed description:

> The Roman scourging was carried out in a barbarous manner. The delinquent was stripped, bound to a post or a pillar, or sometimes simply thrown on the ground, and beaten by a number of torturers until the latter grew tired and the flesh of the delinquent hung in bleeding shreds. In the provinces of the empire this was the task of soldiers. Three different kinds of implements were customary. Rods were used on freemen; military punishments were inflicted with sticks, but for slaves scourges or whips

---

[179] *The Histories of Appian: The Civil Wars*, Loeb Classical Library, E.H. Warmington, ed. (Cambridge: Harvard University Press, 1912), I.120. Hengel cites Quintilian as to the deterrent which public crucifixion created: "Whenever we crucify the guilty, the most crowded roads are chosen, where the most people can see and be moved by this fear. For penalties relate not so much to retribution as to their exemplary effect" (Hengel, *Crucifixion*, 50).

[180] One of the most important finds in crucifixion studies was the accidental discovery of Yehohanan "the crucified man." Archaeologist Vassilios Tzaferis was allowed to investigate construction areas in Jerusalem following the Six Day War in 1968. While investigating a tomb, he discovered an ossuary (essentially a box containing the bones of a dead person) on which was inscribed "Yehohanan son of HGQWL [untranslatable]." His findings were published in "Crucifixion—The Archaeological Evidence," *Biblical Archaeology Review* 11:01 (1985). Tzaferis did not know the individual had been crucified until he found the heel bones of a young man still attached with a single iron spike. Astonishingly, he claimed, this was the only victim of crucifixion ever to have been found. Evidently, the spike had not been removed because the nail had hit a knot in the wood and curled. From the evidence of all the remains, the specifics were reconstructed that this was a 5 foot 6 inch man in his mid to late twenties who engaged in moderate muscular activity with no marks of disease or nutritional deficiency. In addition, it was surmised that he had a cleft right palate, an asymmetrical facial appearance, and came from a comfortable situation financially speaking. The main significance of the discovery was the posture in which Yehohanan had been crucified. Namely, the man's ankles had been placed sideways on top of each other. It was then argued that the victim's legs were in a semi-flexed position on the cross. However, this reconstruction was challenged by Joseph Zias and Eliezer Sekeles who reexamined the remains. Their analysis was published in "The Crucified Man from Giv'at ha-Mivtar: A Reappraisal," *Israel Exploration Journal* 35:1 (1985) 22-27. It is probably best to say that the crucifixion posture was with the feet facing forward on either side of the vertical beam.

> were used, the leather thongs of these being often fitted with a spike or with several pieces of bone or lead joined to form a chain. The scourging of Jesus was carried out with these last-named instruments. Unlike Jewish law, Roman law prescribed no maximum number of strokes.[181]

The condemned then had the *patibulum* (horizontal piece of the cross weighing somewhere between 75-125 lbs.) placed on the neck and balanced on his shoulders which he carried to the site of his execution. The outstretched arms were typically tied to the crossbeam. At the head of the procession would be a soldier who carried the *titulus* which was a piece of wood on which was inscribed the person's name and crime of which he was accused. On other occasions the *titulus* would be hung around the neck of the condemned.[182]

Once the procession arrived at the place of death, as the victim lay down, his arms were either tied or nailed to the *patibulum* which was then affixed to the vertical beam, though generally nails were used for the hands and feet.[183] The *titulus* was then attached to the top of the cross. The cross was then raised by means of ropes which dropped with a thud into a hole which had already been prepared.[184] Within a short amount of time breathing would become difficult and the victim would attempt to raise himself by his arms in order to breathe. This would become more and more difficult and the crucified would die of asphyxiation in a matter of hours. As death was progressing, insects would burrow into the wounds, nose, and eyes while birds of prey would pick at the wounds.

In order to prevent death to occur so quickly, the Romans devised two additional features which were attached to the cross. The first was the *sedile*. This was a small wooden seat attached midway down the vertical beam of the cross which would lure the victim to "sit" between attempts to breathe. To enhance the cruelty of this device, it was sometimes pointed so as to inflict pain when it was utilized. The second was the *suppedaneum* which was a foot support which would also aid in breathing. These two features could prolong the victim's life from hours to days.

While the Romans allowed the person to die slowly, the Jews required that a person be buried on the same day they were crucified. Thus, the victim's legs were broken so that the breathing process was suspended and the person could be buried before nightfall.[185]

---

[181] Josef Blinzler, *The Trial of Jesus* (Westminster, MD: The Newman Press, 1959), 222.

[182] According to the Mishnah (*Sanhedrin,* 43a), the women of Jerusalem could offer a narcotic drink to the criminal to numb the pain. The pertinent passage reads as follows: "When one is led out to execution, he is given a goblet of wine containing a grain of frankincense, in order to benumb his senses, for it is written, Give strong drink unto him that is ready to perish, and wine unto the bitter in soul. And it has also been taught; the noble women in Jerusalem used to donate and bring it."

[183] Hengel, *Crucifixion*, 31.

[184] Though crosses were of differing heights, the feet of the crucified were normally not far from the ground—probably a matter of feet, if not inches.

[185] For ancient statements on crucifixion, see Chapter 8, Section 16: Selected Miscellaneous Statements on Crucifixion in Antiquity. For some medical aspects of crucifixion, see Chapter 8, Section 17: Medical

Education

Schools were instituted in the Hellenistic period and continued relatively unchanged during Roman times. There were no professional schools except for schools of medicine and rhetoric. Those trained in rhetoric, through a five-year program, were prepared for careers in law, politics, and public administration. Otherwise, there were three levels of education which included primary schools—where students learned reading, writing, music, and athletics; middle schools—where students learned to read classical poets;[186] and prep school—where students would be trained in athletics or for the military.

While education does not come to mind when one hears the word "gymnasium," part of the function of the gymnasium in Greek cities was education for the young and old, and male and female. Scott explains:

> There were various levels of training in the gymnasium, both formal for the young and informal for adult male citizens. Most crucial was the training of the *ephebus* (an eighteen year old male who had just become a citizen). Some instruction was given to girls as well. The list of subjects included "reading, writing, recitation, arithmetic, painting, playing on and singing to the lyre, comedy, tragedy, verse and song writing, and general know-ledge, besides running, wrestling, boxing, and in some cases military exercises such as archery."[187]

Aspects of Crucifixion. This section on "crucifixion" is simply presented for historical and cultural interest which is the purpose of this chapter. The fact of crucifixion in the ancient world is irrelevant biblically in the sense that it was a common event. The New Testament does not so much attach importance to the act per se, but to the theological import of Jesus' death. Significantly, the horrors of crucifixion were not the issue of significance for Jesus. When he staggered in the garden at the thought of his death, it was not the thought of physical suffering which frightened him, but the prospect of separation from his Father, an experience he never had before in his infinite existence. When he was on the cross, Christ never is recorded to have said anything about the physical pain (once he says he is thirsty, but this is not a complaint but a request so that his final cry could be heard), but the cry of lament which occurred when the Father turned his back on his Son. This produced the excruciating cry "my God, my God, why have you forsaken me?" Jesus died spiritually at that moment. When we moderns cringe at the barbarism of crucifixion more than the spiritual ramifications, it shows that we understand very little of the cross event.

[186] Slaves became "pedagogues" for some students and were responsible for their daily supervision until they reached puberty. Paul likens the Mosaic Law to a pedagogue (schoolmaster) in Galatians 3:24 "to bring us unto Christ." In this verse, Paul is not speaking of the revelatory function of the Law in exposing man's sin, but rather indicating to the Galatians that while the Law functioned as a pedagogue during the time of Israel's immaturity, since Christ had died, the nation was no longer under its jurisdiction. Or stated differently, just as the pedagogue had a temporary function over a child, so the Mosaic Law had a temporary function over Israel. Thus, Israel should not return to their infancy by putting themselves back under the Law. Smith correctly writes that "From Paul's argument in the book [Galatians] two main concepts are evident: the temporary nature of the Law and the matter of guardianship. Although the concept of the pedagogue includes other ideas, these two aspects seem to be the focus of what Paul had in mind as he used this analogy" (Michael Smith, "The Role of the Pedagogue in Galatians, " *Bibliotheca Sacra* 650:163 [2006], 207).

[187] J. Julius Scott, *Jewish Backgrounds of the New Testament* (Grand Rapids: Baker, 2000), 114. The quote marks in Scott's quotation is his citation of A. H. M. Jones, *The Greek City from Alexander to Justinian* (Oxford: Clarendon, 1940), 222-223.

Jewish children were taught reading, writing, history, religion, and practical skills by their parents. Jewish boys attended the local synagogue beginning at five years of age where they learned the Jewish Scriptures and Jewish tradition.[188] Undoubtedly, Jesus (a very common name at this time) experienced the normal track of education during his boyhood.[189]

Roman Citizenship

Citizenship in the Roman Empire was a prized commodity.[190] Roman citizenship could be purchased, received by heredity, through naturalization, retirement from the army, emancipation from slavery by a Roman master, and granted by the emperor for service to the Empire. Citizens asserted their status through the Latin phrase "*civis Romanus sum*" ("I am a Roman citizen"). Privileges of citizenship included freedom from degrading forms of punishment, any kind of punishment meant to elicit information, forced labor, imprisonment without a formal trial, and freedom from crucifixion unless ordered by the Emperor. In addition, the citizen had the right to appeal to Caesar, the right to vote and own property, and essentially any right which would be enjoyed by one who lived in Rome. To falsely claim Roman citizenship could mean execution.[191] Adams explains why this threat was in place:

---

[188] The Mishnah gives ages which are appropriate for each area of life (*Avoth* 5.21):

1. At five years of age the study of Scripture;
2. At ten the study of Mishnah;
3. At thirteen subject to the commandments;
4. At fifteen the study of Talmud;
5. At eighteen the bridal canopy;
6. At twenty for pursuit [of livelihood];
7. At thirty the peak of strength;
8. At forty wisdom;
9. At fifty able to give counsel;
10. At sixty old age;
11. At seventy fullness of years;
12. At eighty the age of "strength";
13. At ninety a bent body;
14. At one hundred, as good as dead and gone completely out of the world.

[189] For more on the synagogue, see the Chapter V on "Religious Background." For more details on the education of Jewish children, such as what Jesus would have received, see J.W. Shepard, *The Christ of the Gospels* (Grand Rapids: Eerdmans, 1946), 49-50.

[190] Jeffers estimates that only about five million of the over fifty million people in the Empire at the time of Christ were free and full citizens (*The Greco-Roman World of the New Testament*, 197).

[191] On the other hand, to violate the rights of a Roman citizen was also a serious matter. Livy writes in his *History of Rome* 10.9.3-5 "[3] In the same year Marcus Valerius, consul, procured a law to be passed concerning appeals; more carefully enforced by additional sanctions. This was the third time, since the expulsion of the kings, of this law being introduced, and always by the same family. [4] The reason for renewing it so often was, I believe, no other, than that the influence of a few was apt to prove too powerful for the liberty of the commons. [5] However, the Porcian law seems intended, solely, for the security of the persons of the citizens; as it visited with a severe penalty any one for beating with stripes or putting to death a Roman citizen (Livy. *History of Rome by Titus Livius, Books Nine to Twenty-Six*. Edited by Spillan, D. The History of Rome by Titius Livius [Spillan-Evans-McDevitte] Medford, MA: Henry G. Bohn, 1849).

> In the ancient world the declaration that a person was a Roman citizen called for an immediate cessation of punishment until the claim of citizenship could be supported or proven false. As a result of this, there were a number of incidents of people falsely claiming Roman citizenship to escape punishment or be given respite. This was highly distasteful to the Romans, and so to deter this sort of action a steep punishment was assigned, sometimes resulting in the execution of the person. As a result of these severe punishments there was a strong deterrent to wrongly claim citizenship to attempt to escape a punishment.[192]

Witherington suggests that "Paul, an inveterate traveler, quite possibly carried with him a certificate of citizenship, or at least a *libellus*, which vouched for citizenship and stated that the original was on file in a municipal register in one's hometown."[193]

Geography of Rome

Rome was organized into provinces and ruled from their capital cities. Consult the map and map key below for the provinces, key cities with capital city in bold type, and biblical reference. The province list moves in a generally eastward direction. During the reign of Augustus, the Empire consisted of twenty-eight provinces.[194] The major ones will be listed below.

Map of Selected Roman Provinces

---

[192] Sean Adams, "Paul the Roman Citizen: Roman Citizenship in the Ancient World and its Importance for Understanding Acts 22:22-29," http://www.academia.edu/-3793625/Paul_the_Roman_Citizen_Roman_Citizenship_in_the_Ancient_World_and_its_Importance_for_Understanding_Acts_22_22-29, accessed 6/16/2014.

[193] Ben Witherington III, *New Testament History: A Narrative Account* (Grand Rapids: Baker, 2001), 305.

[194] Paul Achtemeir, "Provinces," in *Harper's Bible Dictionary* (San Francisco: Harper & Row, 1985), 832.

PROVINCE	KEY CITIES	SELECTED NEW TESTAMENT REFERENCES
Italia (Italy)	**Rome**, Puteoli	Acts 18:2; 27:1, 6; 28:13-14; Heb. 13:24
Sicilia (Sicily)	**Syracuse**	Acts 28:12
Macedonia	Amphipolis, Apollonia, Berea, Neapolis, Philippi, **Thessalonica**	Acts 16:11-12; 17:1, 10; 2 Cor. 8:1; 9:2-4; 11:9-10; Phil. 4:14-17
Achaia	**Corinth**, Athens, Cenchrea	Acts 17:17, 24; 18:12, 18; 19:21; Rom. 15:26; 16:1-2; 2 Cor. 1:1; 9:2-4; 11:9-10; 1 Thess. 1:7-8
Pamphylia	**Perga**, Myra, Pamphylia, Patara	Acts 2:10; 13:13; 14:24; 15:38; 21:1-2; 27:5-6; Gal. 4:13
Galatia	**Ancyra**, Pisidian Antioch, Lystra, Derbe, Iconium, Lycaonia	Acts 13-14; 20:4; 16:1-5; 18:23; 2 Tim. 3:11
Asia	**Ephesus**, Colosse, Laodicea, Pergamum, Philadelphia, Sardis, Smyrna, Troas, Thyatira, Patmos	Acts 16:6-8; 18:19; 19:1, 10, 31; 20:9-12; 21:1; Col. 1:2; 2:1; 4:12; 1 Peter 1:1; Rev. 1:4, 9; 2-3
Bithynia et Pontus	**Nicomedia** (Bithynia)	Acts 2:9; 16:7; 18:2; 1 Peter 1:1
Cappadocia	Caesarea	Acts 2:9; 1 Peter 1:1
Crete	Claudia, Lasea	Acts 27:8, 16; Titus 1:5
Cyprus	Salamis, **Paphos**	Acts 11:19-20; 13:5, 6
Cilicia	**Tarsus**	Acts 21:39; 22:3; 23:34; 27:5
Aegyptus (Egypt)	**Alexandria**	Matt. 2:13-14; Acts 2:10; 27:6; 28:11
Syria	Antioch of Syria, Caesarea Philippi, **Damascus**, Decapolis, Seleucia, Tyre	Matt. 16:13-20; Mark 5:20; 7:31; Acts 9:2, 10; 11:19-20; 13:1-4; 15:35-36; 18:22-23; Gal. 2:11-13
Iudea (Judea)	Caesarea Sebaste, **Jerusalem**, Jamnia, Joppa, Ptolemais	Matt. 21:9, 10; 23:37; John 4:45; Acts 6:5; 10:1-2, 24; 11:11-12; 21:8-9, 37; 22:24; 23:10, 16, 32

Geography of Palestine

Speaking of the land promise made to the patriarchs in Israel's covenants, Walt Kaiser commented that "In fact, אֶרֶץ, 'land,' is the fourth most frequent substantive in the Hebrew Bible. Were it not for the larger and more comprehensive theme of the total promise…the theme of Israel and her land could well serve as the central idea or the organizing rubric of the entire canon."[195]

[195] Walt Kaiser, "The Promised Land: A Biblical-Historical View," *Bibliotheca Sacra* 138:552 (1981), 303.

Clearly, the most important facet of "land" in the Bible is not so much topographical as it is theological.[196] However, secondarily, the layout and geography of Palestine is vital in understanding the Biblical text. This land can be divided into five longitudinal zones.[197]

A Topographical Overview of Israel				
Zone 1: Coastal Plains	**Zone 2: Coastal Hills**	**Zone 3: Central Mountains**	**Zone 4: Jordan Valley**	**Zone 5: Eastern Plateau**
• Mt. Carmel to south of Gaza • Fishing villages • Home of Cornelius • Paul's Caesarean imprisonment	• East of Caesarea Philippi in the north to Beersheba in the south • Fertile	• Samaria in the north to south of Hebron • Limestone for building • Valleys with rich soil • Hebron, Jerusalem, Sechem • Small villages like Bethlehem	• Land descends for some ten miles, dropping almost 3,500 feet • The valley is 70 miles long • The Jordan River runs 200 miles from Mt. Hermon to the Dead Sea • Many Old Testament events and Jesus' baptism occurred here	• The plateau rises on the east side of the Jordan • Also known as Perea • Herod Antipas ruled here • Cereal crops grown here

[196] The point here is that a specific piece of real estate was unconditionally promised to Abraham's descendants. Much of Old Testament prophecy is taken up with their return, restoration, and prosperity in that land. This will be realized at Messiah's Second Advent. That the land is to be taken as literal is supported by a number of considerations (these are adapted from John Walvoord, "Part 1: Does the Church Fulfill Israel's Program?" *Bibliotheca Sacra* 137:545 [Jan 80], 25-30): 1) Abraham left his home in Mesopotamia for a new land. If the land promised by God was not literal, he could have stayed where he was, 2) when he arrived in the land, God said he would give that land to Abraham and his descendants, 3) in the dispute with Lot over the land, God told Abraham to look around in every direction and that land would be his, 4) in Genesis 15:13-14 God said that Abraham's seed would be strangers in a land not theirs. This was literally fulfilled in the Egyptian exile. If that was literal, then it follows that the promise to be returned to their land was literal, 5) after Moses died, Joshua was promised the same land promised to Abraham, 6) God had warned the nation in Deuteronomy 28-30 that if they were disobedient in the land, they would be removed. This occurred during the exiles, 7) almost every prophet (pre and post exilic) promise a return and possession of the land, and 8) there is no text in Scripture which ever changes the identity of this land. Therefore, since Abraham and his descendants all proceeded on the basis that the land was literal; and since history shows the land promises were never fulfilled as envisioned by the prophets; we anticipate a day of future, literal fulfillment.

[197] One of the most helpful ways of dividing the land of Israel has been provided by Burge, Cohick, and Green in their volume *The New Testament in Antiquity* (Grand Rapids: Zondervan, 2009), 54-62. Their categories are followed above.

CHAPTER 5

JEWISH RELIGIOUS BACKGROUND

The Temple[198]

Israel's temple has passed through multiple phases, with two phases still in the future. Foreshadowed by the Tabernacle, the First Temple began construction under Solomon's leadership in 966 BC and was completed in 959 BC. This temple was destroyed by the Babylonians in 586 BC. When the Medo-Persians overtook Babylon, the Persian king Cyrus allowed the exiles of the Babylonian captivity to return to Jerusalem in order to rebuild their temple. This became the Second Temple and was completed in 515 BC through the encouragement of Haggai and Zechariah. A significant part of the history of the Second Temple was the massive renovations during the reign of King Herod which started in 20-19 BC and continued until AD 62. The Second Temple was destroyed by the Romans in AD 70. Daniel, Jesus, and Paul indicate that in the future a temple will be desolated by idolatry; therefore, assuming a future fulfillment of these prophecies, it is necessary to posit a Third Temple. The Fourth Temple will be built during Jesus' future earthly reign. This temple is most notably described in Ezekiel 40-48.[199]

The Second Temple is most relevant for this study since it was in place for most of the New Testament era.[200] The temple (not the platform) "measured 360,000 square feet (equivalent to nine football fields). Fifty-ton stones were lifted into place—a process that still today defies explanation...Twenty-four priestly families—numbering over 7,000 priests—worked alongside 9,600 Levities in the day-to-day tasks."[201] The temple was a place of worship, sacrifice,[202] prayers, and tithes. In addition, it was a center for judicial and community life.[203]

---

[198] The term "temple" (Heb. הֵיכָל Gr. *ναός*) refers to the dwelling place of a deity. This was first experienced by Israel in the Tabernacle and later in the Temple. Depending on one's perspective, the building was meant to protect the people from God's glory and protect God's glory from the uncleanness of the people.

[199] For a defense of the idea that Ezekiel's temple awaits realization, see Chapter 8, Section 18: The Realization of Ezekiel's Temple.

[200] Assuming a late date for the Epistles of John and Revelation, they would have been written after the destruction of the Second Temple while the other New Testament books would have been written before its destruction.

[201] Burge, Cohick, Green, *The New Testament in Antiquity*, 68. For a full description of the Temple see Chapter 8, Section 7: The Temple.

[202] For an explanation of the various sacrifices and their origin in Leviticus, see Chapter 8, Section 19: The Five Major Offerings.

[203] The temple was the only place where the Romans allowed the Jews to be armed. In Acts 4:1 Luke refers to the "captain of the temple." He was second in charge in the temple behind the high priest. He essentially was a chief of police employed to keep order in the temple. Josephus refers to this individual frequently in his

Besides the captain of the temple, officiants in the temple included the high priest, the priests, the Levites, and the Sanhedrin. The *high priest* occupied the highest religious position in Judaism.[204] This office was hereditary in the family of Aaron and was conferred for life (Num. 25:10-13).[205] He oversaw temple worship, collected taxes, and acted as a general administrator.[206] Perhaps his most solemn responsibility was to perform the blood manipulation ritual on the Day of Atonement which included his sole entrance into the Holy of Holies. The high priest was so revered it was believed that his death had atonement powers. For example, when a high priest died, all who had committed homicide and fled to cities of refuge could return home. "The death of the high priest had, by virtue of his office, expiated the guilt incurred by accidental homicide."[207]

The most significant high priestly family for New Testament background was that of Annas. Annas was installed in the office of high priest by Quirinius in AD 6 and served until AD 13.[208] One of the most famous members of the family was Caiaphas who oversaw the trial of Jesus (Jn 11:49); however, it was Annas who was most involved in the questioning of Jesus indicating that he still maintained a level of importance even though he had been succeeded. One of the other well-known members of the family for biblical purposes who served as high priest was Ananias before whom Paul stood when he was questioned by the Sanhedrin (Acts 23:2; 24:1).

The *priests* were Levites who were also descendants of Aaron. The active priesthood was divided into twenty-four groups with each group being in charge of the temple service for a week at a time (see 1 Chron. 24:3-4 for the origin of the courses). Daily duties were assigned by lot and included at least fifteen responsibilities: burning incense, cleaning the lamps, putting out the bread on the Table of Showbread each Sabbath, keeping the fire burning on the altar of burnt offering, clearing ashes, offering the morning and evening sacrifices, sprinkling blood, putting various animal parts on the altar, blowing silver trumpets at festivals, inspecting unclean persons, administering oaths, instructing in the Law, collecting tithes, maintaining the grounds, and pronouncing blessings.

The *Levites* were descendants of Levi who generally assisted the Aaronic priests in the temple.[209] They constituted the temple police force,[210] and according to the Mishnah supplied music in temple worship both instrumental but particularly vocal.[211] Levites are mentioned only three times in the New Testament (Luke 10:32; John 1:19; Acts 4:36).

---

writings (e.g., *War of the Jews,* 2.17.2; 6.5.3; *The Antiquities of the Jews,* 20.6.2).

[204] His power, however, was under the supervision of Rome.

[205] In all, there were eighty-three high priests: Aaron in 1657 BC to Phannias in AD 70.

[206] For the dress of the high priest, see Chapter 8: Section 20: The Dress of the High Priest.

[207] Jeremias, *Jerusalem in the Time of Jesus,* 149.

[208] Powell, Mark Allan, ed. "Annas." The HarperCollins Bible Dictionary, 2011. Logos 5.

[209] Within the tribe of Levi, descendants of Aaron were to be priests; but those within the tribe of Levi not descended from Aaron were to be their assistants.

[210] Alfred Edersheim, *The Temple: Its Ministry and Services as they were at the Time of Christ* (Grand Rapids: Eerdmans, 1972), 89.

[211] *Sukkah* 5.4; *Kelim* 15.6; *Tamid* 7:3,.4, et al.

The final major player in temple life was the *Sanhedrin.*[212] The Sanhedrin was the highest judicial and religious court in Jerusalem. It included seventy-one members composed of Sadducees (which predominated), Pharisees, elders, scribes and the high priest who presided over the council. However, it was only necessary for 23 members to be present to have a quorum (the number required to transact official business). Jesus, Peter, John, Stephen, and Paul all appeared before this body. The Sanhedrin met in the temple precincts.[213]

Temple Hierarchy

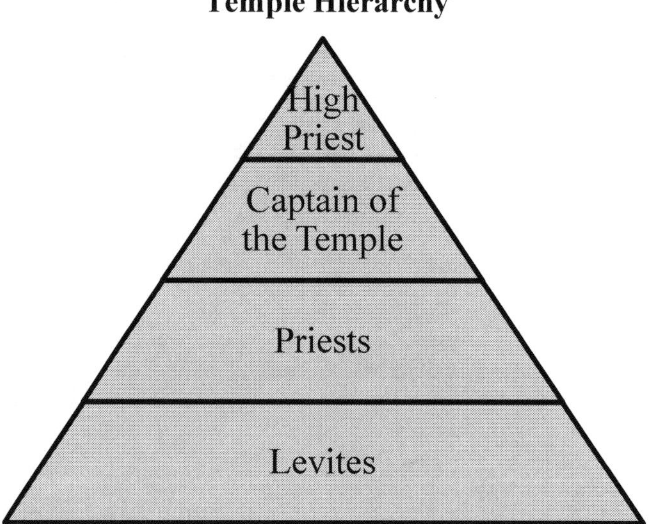

The Synagogue

The term "synagogue" (συναγωγή) refers to "a gathering place" or "a place of assembly."[214] Numerous synagogues emerged in various places in Palestine, including Jerusalem, and around the Roman world as buildings where the Jews could gather to worship, study the Torah, pray, discuss civic issues of importance, and informally fellowship with friends. Thus the synagogues became the "unrivalled hub of the social and religious life of each community."[215] The synagogues did not replace the temple but supplemented its ministry. The earliest synagogues apparently appeared in Babylon following the exile.[216] On numerous

[212] In the New Testament, the Sanhedrin goes by a variety of names including: the "council," "body of elders," and the "senate."

[213] For some idea of how the Sanhedrin operated, see Chapter 8, Section 21: Excerpts from the Mishnah Tractate *Sanhedrin.* Keep in mind that the Mishnah was not completed until around AD 200, so caution must be used in reading procedure back into the first century. Regarding the authority of the Sanhedrin to execute Jesus, it is probably best to conclude that though they could pass sentence they could not carry out an execution on their own.

[214] BAGD, *A Greek-English Lexicon*, 782-83.

[215] Uri Kaploun, *The Synagogue* (Philadelphia: Jewish Publication Society of America, 1973), 3.

[216] Negev, Avraham. *The Archaeological Encyclopedia of the Holy Land.* New York: Prentice Hall Press, 1990. Logos 5.

occasions, Jesus entered the synagogue to teach and help those who attended (Matt. 4:23; 9:35; 12:9; 13:54; Mark 1:21, 23, 39; 3:1; 6:2 Luke 4:15, 16, 44; 6:6; 13:10; John 6:59; 18:20). Jesus also castigated the Pharisees for their hypocrisy when attending the synagogues (Matt. 6:2, 5; 23:6).[217]

Regarding the time and nature of the synagogue service, Scott writes:

> Services were held on the Sabbath (often more than one), and possibly on Mondays and Thursdays as well. There were also special assemblies on feast days and other important occasions of the religious and civil calendars. The liturgy was simple but services could be several hours in length. The principal parts of the service included recitation of the *Shema*, the daily prayer...and reading of the Law and the Prophets. The reading was accompanied by a translation-interpretation (a targum), and frequently a sermon-homily. All elements of the service were preceded and usually concluded with blessings. At the close of each prayer the congregation joined in saying Amen."[218]

While any male could take part in the synagogue service, the organization centered around three individuals. The first was the head of the synagogue who presided over its activities and maintained order. The second was the *Hazzan* (minister or attendant). LaSor and Eskenazi observe that his duties included signaling the approach of the Sabbath by the blowing of trumpets from the roof, he took the sacred scroll from the ark to give to the reader and then returned it to the ark, indicated when the benediction was to be pronounced, sometimes led in prayer as well as other duties.[219] The third key individuals consisted of the elders. They were the "mainstays of the synagogue" "from whom the head of the synagogue was chosen."[220]

The Sects

The overwhelming majority of Jews in the first century lived outside of the land of Palestine. This majority collectively was known as the "diaspora" which comes from a Greek word meaning "to scatter." These Jews had either been exiled or immigrated to other lands and therefore faced the challenge of maintaining their religious identity. For those Jews who stayed in Palestine, some 90 per cent of them were unattached to any of the Jewish sects. However, it is imperative to be aware of the various sects in order to have a full picture of what was going on in the New Testament. The six major sects of Judaism are

[217] One of the most serious penalties in Jewish culture was receiving the "ban," that is, being put out of the synagogue. This was the fear of the parents of the healed blind man in John 9:18-23 when questioned by the religious leaders. See the following sections from the Mishnah, Ta'anit 3.8; Nedarim 1.1; 'Eduyyot 5.6; Middot 2.2.

[218] J. Julius Scott, *Jewish Backgrounds of the New Testament* (Grand Rapids: Baker, 2000), 141.

[219] LaSor, W. S., and T. C. Eskenazi. "Synagogue." Edited by Geoffrey W. Bromiley. *The International Standard Bible Encyclopedia, Revised.* Wm. B. Eerdmans, 1979–1988. Logos 5.

[220] Ibid.

summarized below.

PHARISEES[221]	SADDUCEES
"The Pharisees are friendly to one another, and are for the exercise of concord and regard for the public."[222]	"But the behavior of the Sadducees one towards another is in some degree wild; and their conversation with those that are of their own party is as barbarous as if they were strangers to them."[223]
Originated from the Hasidim of the Maccabean period	Originated from priestly/aristocratic families of Maccabean period
Middle class (mostly laity)[224]	Upper class
Strong influence among common people[225]	Strong influence on a political level
Tried not to be involved in politics	Willingly cooperated with Rome so they would have more control
Supernaturalists	Anti-supernatural
Affirmed God's sovereignty	Rejected God's sovereignty
Believed in hierarchy of angels/demons	Denied existence of angels
Believed in immortality and resurrection	Denied immortality and a bodily resurrection[226]
Believed in a final judgment with reward and punishment	Denied a final judgment

[221] Closely related to the Pharisees were the Scribes. Thousands of years before the coming of Christ, spoken language was encoded in written form. This necessitated the work of a scribe. "The complexities that cuneiform presented its students made long and rigorous training of scribes a necessity throughout the ancient Near East. For use in schools and chancelleries were developed sign lists, word lists, grammars, bilingual texts, and similar studies. Archives and libraries were built to house important documents. Cuneiform texts encompass every genre: legal documents (contracts, accounts, and receipts), letters, mathematical problems and statistical tables, astronomical and medical observations, omens, rayers, dedications and votive offerings, royal statements, and a variety of literature in prose and poetry" (Allen Meyers, "Writing," in *Eerdmans Bible Dictionary* [Grand Rapids: Eerdmans, 1987], 1071). The work of the scribe naturally led to his expertise in the knowledge contained in these documents. Consequently for the Jews, scribes became esteemed teachers of the Mosaic Law. In the New Testament era, the scribes are almost always presented as opponents of Jesus and could belong to any of the sects though most of them appear to have been Pharisees. The major difference between a scribe and a Pharisee is that the former would describe a profession, whereas the latter would describe a theological position (D.A. Carson, "Matthew" in *The Expositor's Bible Commentary* [Grand Rapids: Zondervan, 1984], 471).

[222] Josephus, *The Wars of the Jews*, Translated by William Whitson (Grand Rapids: Baker, 1980), 2.8.14.

[223] Ibid.

[224] There were strict rules of admissions to this sect including a time of probation to see if the ritual laws of purity could be followed (Jeremias, *Jerusalem in the Time of Jesus,* 251).

[225] There is an interesting question to be considered when pondering the popularity of the Pharisees with the average person: if they were so hypocritical, as claimed by Jesus in Matthew 23, then how does one explain their popularity among the people? This question is most recently examined by Roland Deines in his article "The Pharisees—Good Guys with Bad Press," *Biblical Archaeology Review* (July/August 2013). He asks, "How is it, then, that the Pharisees are described as the people's party in the New Testament as well as in Josephus? Why would the people follow their example if they were nothing but hypocrites, eager to burden others with heavy halakhic [legal] bundles" (22)? Deines' solution is that one must not mistake "the polemical stance of the New Testament against the Pharisees as an objective description of the Pharisees…" (22). He proposes that the Pharisees were actually the "good guys" in that day for they attempted to make purity and holiness more practical and easier for the average person to attain (57, 58).

[226] For statements, see Josephus, *Antiquities* 18.1.4; *Jewish War* 2.8.14.

Authority of Scripture and Tradition	Affirmed the Hebrew Scriptures (only the Pentateuch) but denied Pharisaic tradition
Focused on dietary laws, ritual purity and Sabbath observance[227]	Denied a coming Messiah
Zealous adherence to the Law	Sophisticated and educated
Jealous of Jesus' influence with the people	Opposed Jesus
Offended by Jesus' divine claims	Condemned for pride and taking advantage of people
Jesus condemned their self-righteousness and hypocrisy	Took responsibility for Jesus' arrest and trial
Continued after AD 70	Disappeared after AD 70

ESSENES	ZEALOTS
Concerned with the corruption of the priesthood in Jerusalem	Jewish nationalists
Isolationists	Minimal influence until the Jewish War which began in AD 66
Believed they were the "righteous remnant"	Wanted open war with Rome which they believed would cause God to intervene for them
Little influence since they withdrew from society	Similar beliefs as Pharisees but with a violent element added
Largest settlement was Qumran near the Dead Sea	
Majored on apocalyptic ideas	
Ascetic	
Lived in communes	

[227] J. Neusner, *The Rabbinic Traditions about the Pharisees before 70*, (Leiden: Brill, 1974), 3:304.

SICARII[228]	HERODIANS
Name is Greek for "dagger-men" because they carried concealed daggers[229]	Originated during Herodian dynasty
Extremist wing of the zealots/terrorists	Wealthy/powerful Jews who supported the Herods
Violently opposed Rome	Accepted foreign occupation
Fanatic patriots	Amenable to Hellenization and cooperating with foreigners

The Festivals[230]

The constitution of the nation of Israel was the Mosaic Law. Since the nation was a theocracy, there were a number of festivals and holy days to be celebrated throughout the year as stipulated in the Law. The origin and most exhaustive biblical text for the religious calendar are found in Leviticus 23—these days continued to be celebrated during the New Testament era.

---

[228] Some have assumed that Paul was mistaken as a member of the Sicarii because of the reference to "assassins" in Acts 21:38 (J. Julius Scott, *Jewish Backgrounds of the New Testament*, 101). However, it is more likely that the Egyptian's men were distinct from the sicarii (Darrell Bock, *Acts* [Grand Rapids: Baker, 2007], 657-658). For a description of the background of the Egyptian's insurrection, see Eckhard Schnabel, *Acts* (Grand Rapids: Zondervan, 2012), 897.

[229] The Sicarii would mingle with the crowds on festival days and stab Roman sympathizers. Josephus writes: "When the country was purged of these, there sprang up another sort of robbers in Jerusalem, which were called Sicarii, who slew men in the day time, and in the midst of the city; this they did chiefly at the festivals, when they mingled themselves among the multitude, and concealed daggers under their garments, with which they stabbed those that were their enemies; and when any fell down dead, the murderers became a part of those that had indignation against them; by which means they appeared persons of such reputation, that they could by no means be discovered. The first man who was slain by them was Jonathan the high priest, after whose death many were slain every day, while the fear men were in of being so served was more afflicting than the calamity itself; and while everybody expected death every hour, as men do in war, so men were obliged to look before them, and to take notice of their enemies at a great distance; nor, if their friends were coming to them, durst they trust them any longer; but, in the midst of their suspicions and guarding of themselves, they were slain. Such was the celerity of the plotters against them, and so cunning was their contrivance" (*Jewish War* 2.13.3). And again, "Upon Festus's coming into Judea, it happened that Judea was afflicted by the robbers, while all the villages were set on fire, and plundered by them. And then it was that the sicarii, as they were called, who were robbers, grew numerous. They made use of small swords, not much different in length from the Persian acinacae, but somewhat crooked, and like the Roman sicae, [or sickles,] as they were called; and from these weapons these robbers got their denomination; and with these weapons they slew a great many; for they mingled themselves among the multitude at their festivals, when they were come up in crowds from all parts to the city to worship God, as we said before, and easily slew those that they had a mind to slay. They also came frequently upon the villages belonging to their enemies, with their weapons, and plundered them, and set them on fire. So Festus sent forces, both horsemen and footmen, to fall upon those that had been seduced by a certain impostor, who promised them deliverance and freedom from the miseries they were under, if they would but follow him as far as the wilderness. Accordingly, those forces that were sent destroyed both him that had deluded them and those that were his followers also" (*Antiquities*, 20.8.10).

[230] There are three major Old Testament texts which describe the various feasts. The three lists probably are emphasizing different aspects as follows: Deuteronomy 16—the pilgrimage; Numbers 28-29—the offerings; Leviticus 23—the feats themselves (Timothy Hui, "The Purpose of Israel's Annual Feasts," *Bibliotheca Sacra* 147:586 [Apr 1990], 144).

The Sabbath[231]

The word "Sabbath" comes from the Hebrew term שׁבּת (*Shabbat*) which simply means "to cease, desist, rest."[232] The Sabbath was the sign of the Mosaic Covenant and Jewish families (not the priesthood) were to stay home and cease from normal, daily labor (see Leviticus 23:3 "it is a Sabbath unto Jehovah in all your dwellings)."[233]

Very importantly, in Jesus' day the Jews reckoned their days from dusk to dusk (nightfall to nightfall) rather than from midnight to midnight as we do. Therefore, the Sabbath began at sundown on Friday evening and continued until sundown on Saturday evening. While there were Sabbath prohibitions set down by God in the Law,[234] their function was to help mankind. Thus, Jesus taught that the "Sabbath was made for man." The Rabbis, however, had turned that around and believed that man was created to observe the Sabbath. Thus, their view was that "man was made for the Sabbath." This led to endless controversy between Jesus and the religious leaders of Israel. It should not be missed, however, that Jesus did abide by the Sabbath rules according to the Mosaic Law; the friction came in abiding by that which had been added to the Law and a misunderstanding of the spirit of the Law.[235] In fact, the rabbis had passed around 1,500 additional Sabbath regulations by which the people were to abide.[236] What was to be a day of rest had become a day of burden. What follows is the Table of Contents from the Babylonian Talmud, *Tract Sabbath*, Volumes I and II. This will give the reader an idea of the various categories which head the numerous Sabbath regulations.[237]

Volume I

Chapter I: Regulations Regarding Transfer on Sabbath
Chapter II: Regulations Concerning The Sabbath And 'Hanukah Light'
Chapter III: Regulations Concerning Stoves, Hearths, and Ovens

[231] The Sabbath was the sign of the Mosaic Covenant, and therefore, along with the Law, the Sabbath has been abrogated with all of its regulations during the Church age. For a full discussion see Arnold Fruchtenbaum, *Israelology: The Missing Link in Systematic Theology* (Tustin, CA: Ariel Ministries, 2001), 652-673.

[232] Brown, Driver, and Briggs, *A Hebrew and English Lexicon of the Old Testament: with an Appendix Containing the Biblical Aramaic* (Oxford: Clarendon Press, n.d.), 991.

[233] For an excellent and thorough treatment of the Sabbath see D.A. Carson, ed., *From Sabbath to Lord's Day: A Biblical, Historical, and Theological Investigation* (Grand Rapids: Zondervan, 1982); Arnold Fruchtenbaum, *Israelology: The Missing Link in Systematic Theology* (Tustin: CA, Ariel Ministries, 2001).

[234] The key Sabbath texts in Moses are: Exodus 16:23-30; 20:8-11; 23:12; 31:12-17; 34:21; 35:1-3; Leviticus 16:31; 19:3, 30; 23:3, 11, 15-16, 32, 38; 24:5-9; 26:2; Numbers 15:32-36; 28:9-10; Deuteronomy 5:12-15.

[235] The gospel writers record five Sabbath controversy pericopes (plucking grain, healing a deformed man, healing a woman with a back condition, healing a man with edema, and healing a crippled man in Jerusalem).

[236] Arnold Fruchtenbaum, *The Sabbath* (Ariel Ministries Digital Press), 60.

[237] The reader should keep in mind that the Talmud was not in written form until well after the time of Christ. For an explanation, see the later section "Literary Background."

Chapter IV: Regulations Concerning Victuals, Where They May or May Not Be Deposited to Retain Their Heat for the Sabbath

Chapter V: Regulations Concerning What May and May Not Be Worn by Animals on the Sabbath

Chapter VI: Regulations Concerning What Garments Women May Go Out With On the Sabbath

Chapter VII: The General Rule Concerning the Principal Acts of Labor on Sabbath

Chapter VIII: Regulations Concerning the Prescribed Quantities of Victuals and Beverages Which Must Not Be Carried About on the Sabbath

Chapter IX: Rabbi Aqiba's Regulations On Different Subjects

Chapter X: Further Regulations Concerning The Prescribed Quantity of Things To Be Stored

Volume II

Chapter XI: Regulations Concerning Throwing From One Ground Into Another.

Chapter XII: Regulations Concerning Building, Ploughing, etc., On the Sabbath

Chapter XIII: Regulations Concerning Weaving, Tearing, Hunting, etc., on the Sabbath

Chapter XIV: Regulations Concerning the Catching of Reptiles, Animals and Birds

Chapter XV: Regulations Concerning the Tying and Untying of Knots on the Sabbath

Chapter XVI: Regulations Concerning Articles Which May be Saved From a Conflagration on Sabbath

Chapter XVII: Regulations Concerning Handling of Utensils and Furniture on the Sabbath

Chapter XVIII: Regulations Regarding the Clearing Off of Required Space, the Assistance To Be Given Cattle When Giving Birth To Their Young and To Women About To Be Confined

Chapter XIX: Regulations Ordained by R. Eliezer Concerning Circumcision on the Sabbath

Chapter XX: Regulations Concerning Certain Acts of Labor Which Must Be Performed Differently on a Sabbath and on a Festival

Chapter XXI: Regulations Concerning the Pouring Out of Wine From Vessels Covered With a Stone (Which Must Not Be Lifted), and the Clearing Off of Crumbs, etc., From the Table

Chapter XXII: Regulations Concerning Preparation of Food and Beverages

Chapter XXIII: Borrowing, Casting Lots, Waiting for the Close of the Sabbath, and Attending to a Corpse

Chapter XXVI: Regulations Concerning a Man Who is Overtaken by Dusk on the Eve of Sabbath While Travelling, and Concerning Feeding of Cattle.

The Passover

Having mentioned the weekly Sabbath, Moses now moves on to describe the seven annual feasts. The original, historical incident of the Passover is found in Exodus 12 in which Abraham's seed is delivered from Egyptian bondage. The Hebrew term translated "Passover" in the English translations is פֶּסַח (*pesah*). The sense could be that God would "pass over" the homes which had followed his directions with the idea that he would "protect" them.[238] This would make excellent sense in light of Exodus 12:23: "for the Lord will pass through to smite the Egyptians; and when he sees the blood upon the lintel, and on the two side posts, the Lord will pass over the door, and will not permit the destroyer to come into your houses to smite you." Wells correctly states: "In this regard, it is evident that the verb *psh* has its meaning of 'protect' (as seen clearly in Isaiah 31:5) rather than 'pass over.'"[239]

The Jewish culture was an agrarian one and therefore the annual feasts were not only times to remember what Yahweh had done, but also a time to celebrate the agricultural seasons. The Passover began on the first month of the spring (Nisan) on the 15th day at the beginning of the barley harvest. Next to wheat, barley was the most important cereal crop in the land. It was used to make bread and beer. Burge gives a general description of the Passover event:

> A man and perhaps his sons would carry their Passover animal to the temple, and there a priestly assistant (a Levite) would inspect it and manage its slaughtering. Blood from the lamb was caught in a silver or gold bowl, passed to other Levites, and then was cast at the base of the sacrificial altar. All the while, the Levites were chanting Psalms 113-118, the Hallel (or "praise") Psalms. The carcass was then hung on meat hooks on the temple walls and pillars, and its kidneys and liver removed and burned (Lev. 3:3-4); then the body was returned to the waiting family for roasting. Even here the law specifies how it should be roasted—on a wooden skewer (not a metal one or a grill)—and it was often basted with fruit juice…Then on the night of the Passover, they fulfilled the law by eating the Passover meal inside the city itself. Families would join together until there were enough people to consume the roasted young lamb or goat that had been sacrificed that afternoon. This was the ideal scenario…In Jesus' day, we believe it was organized around four cups of

---

[238] There have been several suggestions as to the sense of this term. 1) "pass over" in the sense that God's destructive power would not visit that dwelling—he would bypass it; 2) "to limp" so that the Passover describes a religious dance; 3) "to appease" a deity; 4) "to defend, or protect"; and 5) a "strike" or "blow" so that the Passover is the last blow. The sense of "to defend, or protect" is favored by the writer. For a fuller discussion of these options see R. Laird Harris, Gleason Archer, and Bruce Waltke, *Theological Wordbook of the Old Testament: Volume II Nun-Taw* נ-ת (Chicago: Moody Press, 1980) 728-29.

[239] Bruce Wells, "Exodus" in *Zondervan Illustrated Bible Backgrounds Commentary: Volume 1 Genesis, Exodus, Leviticus, Numbers, Deuteronomy*, John Walton, ed. (Grand Rapids: Zondervan, 2009), 205.

> (red) wine, the singing of the Hallel Psalms (Psalms 113-118), and the eating of bitter herbs, unleavened bread (yeast-free bread), and a dish called *haroset* (a mixture of apples, nuts, and wine). In the first century, the telling of the Passover story (Heb. *Haggadah*) became common so that the meal was also an instructional evening particularly for children. After the fourth cup of wine, the gathering dispersed into the night.[240]

The following is the timeline as it would have occurred on the final Passover week (and slightly beyond) of Jesus' life.[241]

Chronology and Synopsis of the Passion Week

Galilean (Sunrise to Sunrise)	**Judean** (Sunset to Sunset)	**Modern** (Gregorian Dating [C.E.])	**Event**	**Reference(s)**
			To Judea	Matt 19:1-2 Mark 10:1
			On Divorce and Kingdom Eunuchs	Matt 19:3-12 Mark 10:2-12
			Jesus Blesses the Children	Matt 19:13-15 Mark 10:13-16 Luke 18:15-17

---

[240] Gary Burge, *Jesus and the Jewish Festivals* (Grand Rapids: Zondervan, 2012), 55-57. The bitter herbs were a reminder of the tears shed in Egypt, the *haroset* was a reminder of the mortar used in brick work, and the unleavened bread was a reminder of the hasty departure from Egypt.

The issues of the Passover related to Jesus are extremely complicated and present one of the greatest challenges in New Testament studies in two regards: when did he eat his last meal? Did he eat the Passover meal or not? Bock explains more fully the issues involved: "Bound up in this discussion is one of the most complex chronological issues in the NT. Two questions surround the problem. (1) What kind of meal did Jesus and the disciples have: a Passover meal, another type of special meal, or a regular evening meal? (2) How is the date of the meal to be reckoned? The clear impression from the Synoptics is that Jesus eats a Passover meal as the date moves from Nisan 14 to Nisan 15. On the other hand, John appears to have Jesus eat the meal the day before Passover, since Passover preparation begins while Jesus is on the cross. Many pit Luke 22:7=Matt. 26:17=Mark 14:12 against John 18:28, where Jewish guards hesitate to enter Pilate's pretorium for fear of defiling themselves for the Passover meal. How can this be if the meal was already eaten? Related to this is the possibility that different calendars—one popular, the other official—were in use. If so, what is the evidence for them, which one was used, and where" (Darrell Bock, *Luke: Volume 2: 9:51-24:53* Baker Exegetical Commentary on the New Testament [Grand Rapids: Baker Books, 1998], 1951). After an erudite discussion, Bock concludes that Jesus ate a Passover meal on Thursday night, Nisan 15 (1960). For the same conclusion see D. A. Carson's discussion ("Matthew," in *The Expositor's Bible Commentary* [Grand Rapids: Zondervan, 1984], 528-532).

[241] https://bible.org/article/chronology-synopsis-passion-week, accessed 4/24/2014. The chronology in this chart was created by Peter Smith. See also Andreas Kostenberger and Justin Taylor, *The Final Days of Jesus* (Wheaton: Crossway Books, 2014). For the same general layout, but with some minor differences, see Harold Hoehner, *Chronological Aspects of the Life of Christ* (Grand Rapids: Zondervan, 1977). For a full chronology of Christ's entire life, see Chapter 8, Section 22: Chronological Table of Christ's Life.

On a related note, given the adopted timeline, Jesus would have been in his late 30s when he died. This is based on a birth date of 5/4 BC and a death date of AD 33 as well as calculations regarding the beginning of John the Baptist's ministry, beginning of Christ's ministry, and length of Christ's ministry. For a lengthy treatment validating these dates, see Hoehner, *Chronological Aspects of the Life of Christ*, 11-114. In addition (though excluding data on the birth date), see the summary from Kostenberger/Taylor , Chapter 8, Section 23: Key Dates in the Life of Jesus.

			The Rich Young Man	Matt 19:16-22 Mark 10:17-22 Luke 18:18-23
			Commenting on the Rich Man Incident	Matt 19:23-30 Mark 10:23-31 Luke 18:24-30
			The Parable of the Laborers in the Vineyard	Matt 20:1-16
Kislew 25?	Kislew 25?		Jesus at the Feast of Dedication/Hanukkah	John 10:22-39
			Jesus Withdraws	John 10:40-42
			Jesus Recieves News of Lazarus's Death	John 11:1-16
			The Raising of Lazarus	John 11:17-44
			Conspiracy Council	John 11:45-53
			Jesus Retires to Ephraim	John 11:54-57
			Another Prediction of the Passion	Matt 20:17-19 Mark 10:32-34 Luke 18:31-34
			The Request by the Sons of Zebedee	Matt 20:20-28 Mark 10:35-45 Luke 22:24-27
			Healing of the Blind (Jericho)	Matt 20:29-34 Mark 10:46-52 Luke 18:35-43
			Zacchaeus (Jericho)	Luke 19:1-11
			The Parable of the Pounds	(Matt 25:14-30) (Mark 13:34) Luke 19:11-28
Nisan 9	Nisan 8	Saturday, 28 March 33	The Anointing at Bethany by Mary	Matt 26:6-13 Mark 14:3-9 (Luke 7:36-50)? John 12:1-8
Nisan 9	Nisan 8	Saturday, 28 March 33	The Plot to Kill Lazarus	John 12:9-11
Nisan 10	Nisan 9	Sunday, 29 March 33	Approaching Jerusalem On Colt (Hosanna!)	Matt 21:1-9 Mark 11:1-10 Luke 19:28-40 John 12:12-19
Nisan 10	Nisan 9	Sunday, 29 March 33	Jesus Weeps for Jerusalem	Luke 19:41-44
Nisan 10	Nisan 9	Sunday, 29 March 33	Jesus at the Temple	Matt 21:10-17 Mark 11:11
Nisan 10	Nisan 9	Sunday, 29 March 33	Return to Bethany	Matt 21:17 Mark 11:11 (Luke 21:37)
Nisan 11	Nisan 10	Monday, 30 March 33	The Cursing of the Fig Tree	Matt 21:18-19 Mark 11:12-14
Nisan 11	Nisan 10	Monday, 30 March 33	The Cleansing of the Temple	Matt 21:12-13 Mark 11:15-17 Luke 19:45-46

			Crowd's Reaction and Conspiracy Efforts	Mark 11:18-19 Luke 19:47-48
Nisan 11	Nisan 10	Monday, March 30, 35	Left Jerusalem	Mark 11:19 (Luke 21:37)
Nisan 12	Nisan 11	Tuesday, 31 March 33	The Fig Tree is Withered (Morning)	Matt 21:20-22 Mark 11:20-26
Nisan 12	Nisan 11	Tuesday, 31 March 33	The Question about Authority	Matt 21:23-27 Mark 11:27-33 Luke 20:1-8
Nisan 12	Nisan 11	Tuesday, 31 March 33	The Parable of the Two Sons	Matt 21:28-32
Nisan 12	Nisan 11	Tuesday, 31 March 33	The Parable of the Wicked Husbandmen	Matt 21:33-46 Mark 12:1-12 Luke 20:9-19
Nisan 12	Nisan 11	Tuesday, 31 March 33	The Parable of the Great Supper	Matt 22:1-14 (Luke 14:15-24)
Nisan 12	Nisan 11	Tuesday, 31 March 33	On Paying Tribute to Ceasar	Matt 22:15-22 Mark 12:13-17 Luke 20:20-26
Nisan 12	Nisan 11	Tuesday, 31 March 33	Resurrection Debate with the Sadducees	Matt 22:23-33 Mark 12:18-27 Luke 20:27-40
Nisan 12	Nisan 11	Tuesday, 31 March 33	The Great Commandment	Matt 22:34-40 Mark 12:28-34 (Luke 10:25-28)
Nisan 12	Nisan 11	Tuesday, 31 March 33	The Question about David's Son	Matt 22:41-46 Mark 12:35-37a Luke 20:41-44
Nisan 12	Nisan 11	Tuesday, 31 March 33	Woe to the Scribes and Pharisees	Matt 23:1-36 Mark 12:37-40 Luke 20:45-47
Nisan 12	Nisan 11	Tuesday, 31 March 33	Jesus' Lament over Jerusalem	Matt 23:37-39 (Luke 13:34-35)
Nisan 12	Nisan 11	Tuesday, 31 March 33	The Widow's Mite	Mark 12:41-44 Luke 21:1-4
Nisan 12	Nisan 11	Tuesday, 31 March 33	The Greeks Seek Jesus	John 12:20-36
Nisan 12	Nisan 11	Tuesday, 31 March 33	The Unbelief of the People	John 12:37-43
Nisan 12	Nisan 11	Tuesday, 31 March 33	Judgment by the Word	John 12:44-50
Nisan 12	Nisan 11	Tuesday, 31 March 33	The Olivet Discourse (Leaving Temple)	
Nisan 12	Nisan 11	Tuesday, 31 March 33	(OD) Prediction of the Temple's Destruction	Matt 24:1-2 Mark 13:1-2 Luke 21:5-6
Nisan 12	Nisan 11	Tuesday, 31 March 33	Signs before the End (Mount of Olives)	Matt 24:3-8 Mark 13:3-8 Luke 21:7-11

Nisan 12	Nisan 11	Tuesday, 31 March 33	Persecutions Foretold	Matt 24:9-14 (Matt 10:17-22; 24:24) Mark 13:9-13 Luke 21:12-19 (John 16:2; 15:21;14:26)
Nisan 12	Nisan 11	Tuesday, 31 March 33	The Desolation	Matt 24:15-22 Mark 13:14-20 Luke 21:20-24 (Luke 19:43-44; 17:31)
Nisan 12	Nisan 11	Tuesday, 31 March 33	False Christs and False Prophets	Matt 24:23-28 (Matt 24:4-5, 11) Mark 13:21-23 (Mark 13:5-6) (Luke 17:23-24; 17:37; 21:8;17:20-21)
Nisan 12	Nisan 11	Tuesday, 31 March 33	The Coming of the Son of Man	Matt 24:29-31 Mark 13:24-27 Luke 21:25-28
Nisan 12	Nisan 11	Tuesday, 31 March 33	The Time of the Coming: Fig Tree Parable	Matt 24:32-36 Mark 13:28-32 Luke 21:29-33
Nisan 12	Nisan 11	Tuesday, 31 March 33	Conclusion: Take Heed and Watch	(Matt 25:13-15; 24:42) Mark 13:33-37 Luke 21:34-36 (Luke 19:13-13; 12:40; 12:38)
Nisan 12	Nisan 11	Tuesday, 31 March 33	Conclusion: The Parable of the Flood	Matt 24:37-44 (Luke 17:26-36; 12:39-40)
Nisan 12	Nisan 11	Tuesday, 31 March 33	Conclusion: The Parable of the Servants	Matt 24:45-51 (Mark 12:41-46)
Nisan 12	Nisan 11	Tuesday, 31 March 33	Conclusion: The Parable of the Ten Virgins	Matt 25:1-13
Nisan 12	Nisan 11	Tuesday, 31 March 33	Conclusion: The Parable of the Talents	Matt 25:14-30 (Mark 13:34) (Luke 19:11-27)
Nisan 12	Nisan 11	Tuesday, 31 March 33	Conclusion: Sheep and Goats/Last Judgment	Matt 25:31-46
Nisan 12	Nisan 12	Tuesday, 31 March 33	Lodged on Mt. Olives	Luke 21:37-39
Nisan 13	Nisan 12	Wednesday, 1 April 33	The Plot to Kill Jesus	Matt 26:1-5 Mark 14:1-2 Luke 22:1-2 (John 11:47-53)

Nisan 13	Nisan 12	Wednesday, 1 April 33	Judas's Betrayal Agreement	Matt 26:14-16 Mark 14:10-11 Luke 22:3-6 (John 13:2;13:27; 6:70-71)
Nisan 14	Nisan 13	Thursday, 2 April 33	Passover Preparations (3-5PM Slaying of Lamb)	Matt 26:17-20 Mark 14:12-17 Luke 22:7-14
Nisan 14	Nisan 14	Thursday, 2 April 33	Washing the Disciples' Feet (SUNSET/During Supper)	[Luke 22:24-30] John 13:1-20
Nisan 14	Nisan 14	Thursday, 2 April 33	Jesus Foretells his Betrayal	Matt 26:21-22 Mark 14:18-19 Luke 22:21-23 John 13:21-22
Nisan 14	Nisan 14	Thursday, 2 April 33	The Inquiry of Peter about Betrayer's Identity	John 13:23-25
Nisan 14	Nisan 14	Thursday, 2 April 33	Jesus Identifies Betrayer	Matt 26:23 Mark 14:20 Luke 22:21 John 13:26
Nisan 14	Nisan 14	Thursday, 2 April 33	Jesus' Woe to the Btrayer	Matt 26:24 Mark 14:21 Luke 22:22
Nisan 14	Nisan 14	Thursday, 2 April 33	Judas Iscariot's Response	Matt 26:25 Luke 22:23
Nisan 14	Nisan 14	Thursday, 2 April 33	The Last Supper (SUNSET)	Matt 26:26-29 Mark 14:22-25 Luke 22:15-20 1 Cor 11:23-25
Nisan 14	Nisan 14	Thursday, 2 April 33	The Exit of Judas	John 13:26-30
Nisan 14	Nisan 14	Thursday, 2 April 33	The New Commandment of Love	[Luke 22:24-30] John 13:31-35
Nisan 14	Nisan 14	Thursday, 2 April 33	The Denial of Peter Predicted	Matt 26:30-35 Mark 14:26-31 Luke 22:31-34 John 13:36-38
Nisan 14	Nisan 14	Thursday, 2 April 33	The Two Swords	Luke 22:35-38
Nisan 14	Nisan 14	Thursday, 2 April 33	The Farwell/Upper Room Discourse	
Nisan 14	Nisan 14	Thursday, 2 April 33	Let Not Your Hearts Be Troubled	John 14:1-14
Nisan 14	Nisan 14	Thursday, 2 April 33	The Promise of the Helper	John 14:15-26
Nisan 14	Nisan 14	Thursday, 2 April 33	The Gift of Peace	John 14:27-31
Nisan 14	Nisan 14	Thursday, 2 April 33	Jesus the True Vine (On the Way to the Garden)	John 15:1-8

Nisan 14	Nisan 14	Thursday, 2 April 33	Remaining in My Love	John 15:9-17
Nisan 14	Nisan 14	Thursday, 2 April 33	The World's Hatred	John 15:18-25
Nisan 14	Nisan 14	Thursday, 2 April 33	The Witness of the Helper	John 15:26-27
Nisan 14	Nisan 14	Thursday, 2 April 33	On Persecutions	John 16:1-4
Nisan 14	Nisan 14	Thursday, 2 April 33	The Work of the Helper	John 16:5-15
Nisan 14	Nisan 14	Thursday, 2 April 33	Sorrow Turned to Joy	John 16:16-22
Nisan 14	Nisan 14	Thursday, 2 April 33	Prayer in the Name of Jesus	John 16:23-28
Nisan 14	Nisan 14	Thursday, 2 April 33	Prediction of the Disciples's Flight	John 16:29-33
Nisan 14	Nisan 14	Thursday, 2 April 33	Jesus' Intercessory Prayer	John 17:1-26
Nisan 14	Nisan 14	Thursday, 2 April 33	Jesus' Prayer For Himself (Gethsemane)	Matt 26:36-46 Mark 14:32-42 Luke 22:39-46 John 18:1
Nisan 14	Nisan 14	Thursday, 2 April 33	Jesus' Betrayal and Arrest	Matt 26:47-50 Mark 14:43-46 Luke 22:47-48 John 18:2-9
Nisan 14	Nisan 14	Thursday, 2 April 33	Peter Cuts Off Malchus's Ear	Matt 26:51-55 Mark 14:47-49 Luke 22:49-53 John 18:10-12
Nisan 14	Nisan 14	Thursday, 2 April 33	The Flight of the Disciples	Matt 26:56-56 Mark 14:50-52
Nisan 14	Nisan 14	Friday, 3 April 33	Preliminary Hearing Before Annas	John 18:13-14, John 18:19-24
Nisan 14	Nisan 14	Friday, 3 April 33	Peter's First Denial	Matt 26:69-70 Mark 14:54, 66-68 Luke 22:54-57 John 18:15-18
Nisan 14	Nisan 14	Friday, 3 April 33	Trial Before Caiaphas	Matt 26:57-68 Mark 14:53-65 Luke 22:54, 63-65 John 18:24
Nisan 14	Nisan 14	Friday, 3 April 33	Peter's Second Denial	Matt 26:71-72 Mark 14:69-70a Luke 22:58 John 18:25

Nisan 15	Nisan 14	Friday, 3 April 33	Trial Before Sanhedrin	Matt 27:1 Mark 15:1 Luke 22:66-71
Nisan 15	Nisan 14	Friday, 3 April 33	Peter's Third Denial and Rooster's Crow	Matt 26:73-75 Mark 14:70-72 Luke 22:59-62 John 18:26-27
Nisan 15	Nisan 14	Friday, 3 April 33	Trial Before Pilate	Matt 27:1-2 Mark 15:1 Luke 23:1 John 18:28-38
Nisan 15	Nisan 14	Friday, 3 April 33	Judas Iscariot's Suicide	Matt 27:3-10
Nisan 15	Nisan 14	Friday, 3 April 33	Trial Before Pilate	Matt 27:11-14 Mark 15:2-5 Luke 23:2-5 John 18:28-38
Nisan 15	Nisan 14	Friday, 3 April 33	Trial Before Herod	Luke 23:6-12
Nisan 15	Nisan 14	Friday, 3 April 33	Pilate Declares Jesus Innocent	Luke 23:13-16
Nisan 15	Nisan 14	Friday, 3 April 33	Jesus or Barabbas?	Matt 27:15-23 Mark 15:6-14 Luke 23:17-23 John 18:39-40
Nisan 15	Nisan 14	Friday, 3 April 33	The Message From Pilate's Wife	Matt 27:19
Nisan 15	Nisan 14	Friday, 3 April 33	The Choice to Release Barabbas	Matt 27:24-26
Nisan 15	Nisan 14	Friday, 3 April 33	Jesus Condemned	Matt 27:24
Nisan 15	Nisan 14	Friday, 3 April 33	"Behold the Man!"	Matt 27:28-31a Mark 15:17-20a John 19:1-15
Nisan 15	Nisan 14	Friday, 3 April 33	Pilate Delivers Jesus to be Crucified	Matt 27:24-26 Mark 15:15 Luke 23:24-25 John 19:16
Nisan 15	Nisan 14	Friday, 3 April 33	Jesus Mocked by the Soldiers	Matt 27:27-31a Mark 15:16-20a John 19:2-3
Nisan 15	Nisan 14	Friday, 3 April 33	The Road to Golgatha	Matt 27:31-32 Mark 15:20-21 Luke 23:26-32 John 19:17a
Nisan 15	Nisan 14	Friday, 3 April 33	Simon of Cyrene Carries the Cross	Matt 27:32 Mark 15:21 Luke 23:26
Nisan 15	Nisan 14	Friday, 3 April 33	The Followers to Golgatha	Luke 23:27-32

Nisan 15	Nisan 14	Friday, 3 April 33	Arrival at Golgatha	Matt 27:33 Mark 15:22 Luke 23:33a John 19:17b
Nisan 15	Nisan 14	Friday, 3 April 33	Jesus Rejects Wine and Myrrh	Matt 27:34 Mark 15:23
Nisan 15	Nisan 14	Friday, 3 April 33	Jesus' Crucifixion (9AM)	Matt 27:35a Mark 15:24-25 Luke 23:33b John 19:18a
Nisan 15	Nisan 14	Friday, 3 April 33	The Criminals Crucified on Left & Right	Matt 27:38 Mark 15:27 Luke 23:33b John 19:18b
Nisan 15	Nisan 14	Friday, 3 April 33	(1)"Father Forgive Them..."	Luke 23:34a
Nisan 15	Nisan 14	Friday, 3 April 33	Jesus Clothes Divided	Matt 27:35b Mark 15:24b Luke 23:34b John 19:23-24
Nisan 15	Nisan 14	Friday, 3 April 33	The Guard Sitting	Matt 27:36
Nisan 15	Nisan 14	Friday, 3 April 33	Posted Charges	Matt 27:37 Mark 15:26 Luke 23:38 John 19:19-20
Nisan 15	Nisan 14	Friday, 3 April 33	The Reaction to the Charges	John 19:21-22
Nisan 15	Nisan 14	Friday, 3 April 33	Mocking of Jesus on Cross by Passerbys	Matt 27:39-40 Mark 15:29-30 Luke 23:35
Nisan 15	Nisan 14	Friday, 3 April 33	Mocking of Jesus on Cross by Jewish Leadership	Matt 27:41-43 Mark 15:31-32a Luke 23:35
Nisan 15	Nisan 14	Friday, 3 April 33	Mocking of Jesus on Cross by Soldiers	Luke 23:36-37
Nisan 15	Nisan 14	Friday, 3 April 33	Jesus Offered Wine and Vinegar	Luke 23:36
Nisan 15	Nisan 14	Friday, 3 April 33	Mocking of Jesus on Cross by Criminals	Matt 27:44 Mark 15:32b Luke 23:39
Nisan 15	Nisan 14	Friday, 3 April 33	The Repentant Criminal	Luke 23:40-42
Nisan 15	Nisan 14	Friday, 3 April 33	(2)Jesus Responds to the Repenant Criminal	Luke 23:43
Nisan 15	Nisan 14	Friday, 3 April 33	(3)Jesus Designates His Mother's Provision	John 19:25-27
Nisan 15	Nisan 14	Friday, 3 April 33	Darkness (12-3PM)	Matt 27:45 Mark 15:33 Luke 23:44-45a

Nisan 15	Nisan 14	Friday, 3 April 33	(4)"My God My God…" (3PM)	Matt 27:46 Mark 15:34
Nisan 15	Nisan 14	Friday, 3 April 33	(4)"I am Thirsty" (3PM)	John 19:28
Nisan 15	Nisan 14	Friday, 3 April 33	Crowd's Reaction to Utterance	Matt 27:47 Mark 34:35
Nisan 15	Nisan 14	Friday, 3 April 33	Jesus Offered Wine and Vinegar	Matt 27:48 Mark 15:36a John 19:29
Nisan 15	Nisan 14	Friday, 3 April 33	"Let's See if Elijah Saves Him"	Matt 27:49 Mark 15:36b
Nisan 15	Nisan 14	Friday, 3 April 33	Jesus Receives the Wine and Vinegar	John 19:30a
Nisan 15	Nisan 14	Friday, 3 April 33	Jesus' Loud Cry	Matt 27:50a Mark 15:37a Luke 23:46a
Nisan 15	Nisan 14	Friday, 3 April 33	(5)"Father, into your hands I commit my Spirit"	Luke 23:46b
Nisan 15	Nisan 14	Friday, 3 April 33	(5)"It is finished"	John 19:30b
Nisan 15	Nisan 14	Friday, 3 April 33	Jesus' Death	Matt 27:50b Mark 15:37b Luke 23:46c John 19:30c
Nisan 15	Nisan 14	Friday, 3 April 33	The Temple Curtain is Torn	Matt 27:51a Mark 15:38 Luke 23:45b
Nisan 15	Nisan 14	Friday, 3 April 33	Earthquake	Matt 27:51b
Nisan 15	Nisan 14	Friday, 3 April 33	Resurrection of Dead	Matt 27:52-53
Nisan 15	Nisan 14	Friday, 3 April 33	Centurion's Reaction	Matt 27:54 Mark 15:39 Luke 23:47
Nisan 15	Nisan 14	Friday, 3 April 33	The Beating of the Breast	Luke 23:48
Nisan 15	Nisan 14	Friday, 3 April 33	Jews Request to Pilate	John 19:31
Nisan 15	Nisan 14	Friday, 3 April 33	The Soldiers Break Legs of Criminals	John 19:32
Nisan 15	Nisan 14	Friday, 3 April 33	Soldier Pirces Side of Jesus with Spear	John 19:33-34
Nisan 15	Nisan 14	Friday, 3 April 33	The Witnesses of the Death	Matt 27:55-56 Mark 15:40-41 Luke 23:49 John 19:35-37
Nisan 15	Nisan 14	Friday, 3 April 33	Joseph of Arimathea Requests Body of Jesus	Matt 27:57-58a Mark 15:42-43 Luke 23:50-52 John 19:38a

Nisan 15	Nisan 14	Friday, 3 April 33	Pilate's Surprise at Jesus' Quick Death	Mark 15:44a
Nisan 15	Nisan 14	Friday, 3 April 33	Pilate's Confirmation Hearing of Jesus' Death	Mark 15:44-45a
Nisan 15	Nisan 14	Friday, 3 April 33	Pilate Gives Permission to Joseph of Arimathea	Matt 27:58b Mark 15:45b John 19:38b
Nisan 15	Nisan 14	Friday, 3 April 33	Joseph Buys Linen Cloth	Mark 15:46a
Nisan 15	Nisan 14	Friday, 3 April 33	Nicodemus Brings 75lbs. of Myrrh and Aloes	John 19:39
Nisan 15	Nisan 14	Friday, 3 April 33	Joseph Removes Jesus' Body from the Cross	Mark 15:46b Luke 23:53a
Nisan 15	Nisan 14	Friday, 3 April 33	Jesus' Body is Wraped in Linen Cloth and Spices	Matt 27:59 Mark 15:46c Luke 23:53b John 19:40
Nisan 15	Nisan 14	Friday, 3 April 33	Nicodemus and Joseph Place Jesus in Tomb	Matt 27:60a Mark 15:46d Luke 23:53c John 19:41-42
Nisan 15	Nisan 14	Friday, 3 April 33	Female Witnesses Saw Jesus Laid in Tomb	Matt 27:61 Mark 15:47 Luke 23:55
Nisan 15	Nisan 14	Friday, 3 April 33	Stone Rolled in Front of Tomb Enterance	Matt 27:60b Mark 15:46e
Nisan 15	Nisan 14	Friday, 3 April 33	Joseph of Arimathea Leaves	Matt 27:60c
Nisan 15	Nisan 14	Friday, 3 April 33	Women Leave and Prepare Spices	Luke 23:56a
Nisan 16	Nisan 15	Saturday 4 April 33	Women Rested on Sabbath	Luke 23:56b
Nisan 16	Nisan 15	Saturday 4 April 33	Jewish Leaders Requests Guard from Pilate	Matt 27:62-64
Nisan 16	Nisan 15	Saturday 4 April 33	Pilate Orders Tomb Security	Matt 27:65
Nisan 16	Nisan 15	Saturday 4 April 33	Tomb is Sealed	Matt 27:66a
Nisan 16	Nisan 15	Saturday 4 April 33	Tomb Guard is Posted	Matt 27:66b
Nisan 17	Nisan 16	Sunday, 5 April 33	The Women at the Tomb	Matt 28:1-8 Mark 16:1-8 Luke 24:1-12 John 20:1-13
Nisan 17	Nisan 16	Sunday, 5 April 33	Jesus Appears to the Women	Matt 28:9-10 (Luke 24:10-11) John 20:14-18
Nisan 17	Nisan 16	Sunday, 5 April 33	The Report of the Guard	Matt 28:11-15

Nisan 17	Nisan 16	Sunday, 5 April 33	Jesus Appears to Simon Peter	1 Cor 15:5 Luke 24:34
Nisan 17	Nisan 16	Sunday, 5 April 33	Jesus Appears on Emmaus Road	Luke 24:13-35
Nisan 17	Nisan 17	Sunday, 5 April 33	Jesus Appears to his Disciples -Thomas Absent	Luke 24:36-43 John 20:19-23
Nisan 24	Nisan 23	Sunday, 12 April 33	Jesus Appears to his Disciples -Thomas Present	1 Cor 15:5 John 20:24-29
			Jesus Appears to Eleven on Galilean Mountain	Matt 28:16-20
			Jesus Appears to More Than 500	1 Cor 15:6
			Jesus Appears to James	1 Cor 15:7
		Thursday, 14 May 33	Jesus' Last Words and Ascension	Luke 24:44-53 Acts 1:1-11
		?	Judas's Replacement is Chosen	Acts 1:12-26
	Siwan 7	Sunday, 24 May 33	Pentecost: Helper Arrives	Acts 2
			Jesus Appears to Saul on Damascus Road	Acts 9:1-25 1 Cor 15:8

The Feast of Unleavened Bread

This feast was a seven-day agricultural festival which began the day after Passover to celebrate the incoming harvest (though treated separately here, it came to be a part of the Passover).[242] In addition, it commemorated the hasty departure from Egypt and a break from the sustenance of Egypt. The combination of the Passover and Feast of Unleavened bread also reminded the Israelites of the necessity of living a pure life since redemption by the lamb had been experienced.

The Feast of First Fruits

The Feast of First Fruits was a presentation of the first part of the barley harvest. The Jews regarded this as a pledge that God would bless them with more harvest during the coming year.

The Feast of Weeks (Pentecost)

This was a one day feast which fell on the 50th day after Passover during which the people thanked God for the completion of the first harvest.[243] In later Judaism, it was also a commemoration of the giving of the Mosaic Law.

---

[242] See Josephus, *Antiquities* 17.9.3.

[243] Significantly, the Holy Spirit was poured out on the day of this festival in Acts 2. One is tempted to see the completion of the first harvest of salvation of the Church Age.

The Feast of Trumpets (Rosh Hashanah)

This feast fell on the first day of the 7th month and was marked by the blasts of trumpets to gather the people of God to the sanctuary. This day was the first day of the civil year much like our New Year's Day. Moreover, it alerted the people to the upcoming Day of Atonement.

The Day of Atonement

This marked the holiest day in Israel's calendar. It was the time when the high priest went into the holy of holies by himself in order to cleanse the sanctuary from the sins and uncleanness of the people.[244]

The Feast of Tabernacles (Booths)

The harvest season had come to an end as grapes, olives, figs and other produce was gathered in. Since this marked the end of the harvest, the people celebrated with various samples of their harvests. On the 15th day of Tishri the pilgrims to Jerusalem gathered and lived in outdoor, temporary shelters made from tree branches outside the city walls.[245] Residents of the city most likely built them on their rooftops. In addition to a time of thanksgiving and worship to God for his provision, this was an opportunity to remember how God had provided for Israel's needs as they wandered in the wilderness. This feast also had eschatological overtones and looked forward to dwelling in God's presence during the kingdom age.[246]

It is important to point out in conjunction with the Feast of Tabernacles that two ceremonies took place during Jesus' time. The first was a *water ceremony.* This feast took place in the late fall which was a time of relative drought in Israel. The water ceremony during this Feast presented a double entendre in which the people desired of God both physical and spiritual refreshment. Each day of the feast a procession of priests would make their way to the Gihon Spring where a priest filled a golden pitcher with water.[247] The filled pitcher was then taken back to the temple where the priest poured the water into two silver bowls with spouts on the bottoms. As he did so, the water drained onto the altar. On the final day of the feast, this ceremony was done seven times.

The second was the *light ceremony.* In the Court of Women in the temple were large bowls filled with oil. They were located on top of gigantic pillars which could only be accessed via ladders. During the feast, the priests would light the lamps and (according to the rabbis) this would illumine all of Jerusalem. The people would bring in smaller torches and sing and dance all through the night in one of the most joyous occasions of the year.[248]

---

[244] See Chapter 8, Section 24: The Day of Atonement for a full description of this ritual.

[245] For the tradition of waving palm branches and quoting the Hallel Psalms see Mishnah, *Sukkah* 3.1, 8-9, 11-12; 4.5, 8.

[246] See Chapter 8, Section 25: The Eschatological Significance of the Feast of Booths.

[247] As this was done, Isaiah 12:3 was chanted: "With joy you will draw water from the wells of salvation" (ESV). For some details from the Mishnah on this ceremony, see *Sukkah* 4.9.

[248] Mishnah, Sukkah 5.1-4.

In light of this festival background, Jesus' attendance at this feast is remarkable.

> *In the last day, that great day of the feast, Jesus stood and cried out saying, If any man thirst, let him come unto me, and drink. He that believeth on me, as the scripture hath said, out of his heart shall flow rivers of living water* (John 7:37-38).

> *Then spoke Jesus again unto them saying, I am the light of the world; he that follows md shall not walk in darkness, but shall have the light of life* (John 8:12).

Summary of Festivals[249]

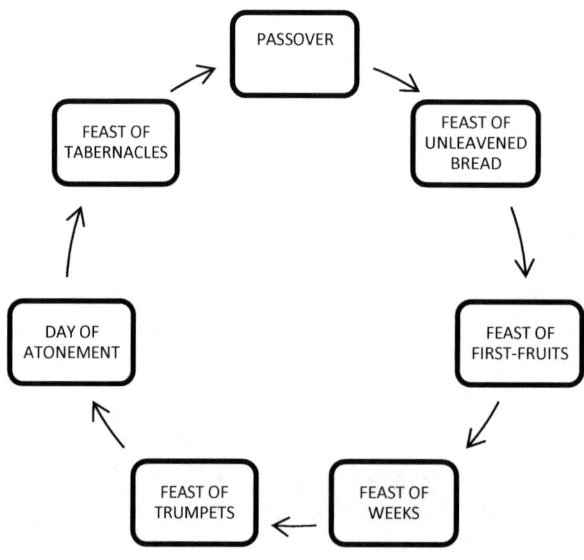

Jewish Festivals

Festival	**Passover**	**Unleavened Bread**	**First-Fruits**
Sacred Month	1 (Nisan)	1 (Nisan)	1 (Nisan)
Civil Month	7	7	7
Modern	March/	March/	March/

[249] There are two other more minor Jewish festivals not mentioned in Leviticus since they were added later. The first is the Feast of Purim which remembered the deliverance of the Jews during the time of Esther in the Persian Empire, and the second is the Feast of Dedication (Hanukkah) which remembered the rededication of the Temple and the victory of the Maccabees.

Month	April	April	April
Day/s of the Month	15	15-21	Day after Sabbath following Passover
Male Attendance Required	No	Yes	No
Season	Spring	Spring	Spring
Relation to Agriculture	Beginning of cereal harvest	1	10
Purpose	Remember deliverance from Egypt	Celebrate initial provision of God	Celebrate God's full provision & commemorate the giving of the Law

Festival	**Weeks (Pentecost)**	**Trumpets**	**Day of Atonement**	**Tabernacles (Booths)**
Sacred Month	3 (Sivan)	7 (Tishri)	7 (Tishri)	7 (Tishri)
Civil Month	9	1	1	1
Modern Month	May/ June	September/ October	September/ October	September/ October
Day/s of the Month	4	1	10	15-21
Male Attendance Required	Yes	No	No	Yes
Season	Fall	Fall	Fall	Fall
Relation to Agriculture	Completion of the cereal harvest			End of the harvest year
Purpose	Celebrate God's full provision & commemorat e the giving of the Law	Prepare for Day of Atonement	Day of national repentance & cleansing of Sanctuary	Remember God's provision in wilderness & look for-ward to the Kingdom

CHAPTER 6
GRECO-ROMAN RELIGIOUS BACKGROUND

As the message of Christianity spread throughout the Roman world, a variety of religious views were confronted. In Athens, for example, "It was said that there were more statues of the gods in Athens than in all the rest of Greece put together, and that in Athens it was easier to meet a god than a man."[250] Schnabel describes the drama Paul would have encountered as he surveyed Athens: "Looking south across the agora, Paul would have seen a large number of temples with their cult images and altars dedicated to the worship of Zeus, Athena, Aphrodite, Apollo, Ares, Hephaistos, the Mother of the gods, Nike, the twelve gods, mystery religions, and the emperor Augustus"[251] and the "unknown god." Deissmann explains the rationale of having an altar to an unknown god:

> The Greek inscription which St. Paul read on an altar at Athens, 'To an unknown god,' and which he viewed and interpreted with the eyes of a monotheistic missionary, has often been illustrated by literary evidence culled from Pausanias, Philostratus, and Diogenes Laertes. We must conclude from this that in Greek antiquity cases were not altogether rare in which 'anonymous' altars 'To unknown gods' or 'To the god whom it may concern' were erected, when people were convinced, *e.g.*, after experiencing some deliverance, that a deity had been gracious to them, but were not certain of the deity's name. Altars to 'unknown gods' on the way from Phalerum to Athens, at Athens, and at Olympia are specially mentioned by Pausanias (second century a.d.) and Philostratus (third century a.d.).[252]

Major Roman/Greek Gods and Goddesses		
Roman	**Greek**	**Description**
Jupiter	Zeus	Ruled sky/supreme/threw lightning bolts
Neptune	Poseidon	Ruled sea/brother of Zeus/carried trident
Pluto	Hades	Ruled underworld/brother of Zeus/helmet made invisible
Juno	Hera	Protector of marriage/sister-wife of Zeus/punished women Zeus loved
Mars	Ares	God of war/liked vultures and dogs

---

[250] William Barclay, *The Acts of the Apostles* (Philadelphia: Westminster Press, 1976), 130.

[251] Eckhard Schnabel, *Acts* (Grand Rapids: Zondervan, 2012), 723. As Paul approached the city of Corinth, he would have seen the Acrocorinth rising up some 1800 feet above the plain on which sat the temple of Aphrodite.

[252] Adolf Deissmann, "Appendix II: On the Altar of an Unknown God," in *St. Paul: A Study in Social and Religious History* (NY: Hodder and Stoughton, 1912), 261.

Minerva	Athena	Daughter of Zeus/came from his head full grown/protected civilized life and agriculture
Venus	Aphrodite	Daughter of Zeus/goddess of love and beauty
Mercury	Hermes	Son of Zeus/wings on shoes and hat/swift/messenger
Apollo	Apollo	Son of Zeus/musician/sun god
Diana	Artemis	Daughter of Zeus/Apollo's twin sister/huntsman to the gods
Vulcan	Hephaestus	God of fire/only ugly and deformed god/makes weapons and armor under volcano
Bacchus	Dionysus	Goddess of wine and debauchery
Ceres	Demeter	Goddess of fertility/grain
Asclepius	Aesculapius	God of medicine
Saturn	Cronus	Ruler of the Titans
Cupid	Eros	God of love
Victoria	Nike	Goddess of victory

Religious Thought

Mythology

There were several major strands of religious thought which accosted the early church. The first was *mythology.* The quest of the pagan was to achieve health, prosperity, and protection. The gods could help him fulfill these quests with some hope for immortality.[253] At the head of the chain of gods was Zeus with all of the gods accessing earth from Mount Olympus in Greece.[254]

The Emperor Cult

The *Emperor Cult* began as a post-mortem ascription after the death of Augustus Caesar.[255] Subsequently, the Roman Senate began to deify emperors

---

[253] One example would be in reference to the town of Iconium which Paul visited on his first missionary journey. The mythology stated that Prometheus and Athena had re-created mankind after a flood by making images of people out of mud and breathing life into them. The town name "Iconium" is from the Greek word for "icon" (εικών) (Richard Longenecker, *The Acts of the Apostles* [Grand Rapids: Zondervan, 1981], 431-432).

[254] J. E. Zimmerman lists over 2,000 entries from Abas to Zodiac in *Dictionary of Classical Mythology* (NY: Bantam Books, 1971). Culpably, "we are all Athenians in a sense…" (vii).

[255] The dedicatory inscription on Augustus' temple reads: "Caesar Augustus, son of a god, pontifex maximus…father of the fatherland" (Peter Walker, *In the Steps of Paul* [Grand Rapids: Zondervan, 2008], 86).

after they died. Participation in this worship system was a way to bring solidarity in and loyalty to Rome as a cohesive of this vast empire. This, of course, was a threat to Christianity for it was an assault on the Lordship of Christ. The early Christians understood that Christ can only be worshiped truly if he is worshiped solely. Refusal to conform would be a sign of disloyalty to Rome.[256] Eusebius noted in his description of persecution from Diocletian to Galerius that "prisons prepared for murderers and grave robbers were now filled with bishops, presbyters and deacons…so that there was no room for criminals."[257] It does not appear that Christians were persecuted for their theological beliefs per se, but that they did not fit into Rome's religious theory. During the reign of Domitian,

> When on trial, if they [Christians] worshiped the pagan gods, that is, the emperor and the imperial cult, they would be freed. If not, they would suffer all manner of punishments and death. All the suspected Christian had to do was sprinkle a few sacrificial grains of incense into the eternal flame burning in front of the statue of the emperor. Since the punishments were so horrible and the means of escape so easy, many Christians gave in. Many did not and were burned alive, killed by lions in the arena, or crucified.[258]

Mystery Religions and Cults

The third strand of religious thought was represented by the *mystery religions* and *cults*. The mystery religions were popular for those who wanted to feel a personal connection with a deity. Some of these religions were native to Greece while others had been imported from the East. These cults often were centered on myths and were marked by various rites, direct revelation from the deity, and the promise of immortality. Some of the chief mystery cults included the Eleusinian (a Greek fertility cult in honor of the goddess Demeter), the Mithraic (Mithra-Persian, only open to men), the Isiac (an Egyptian cult in honor of Osiris and

---

[256] Other "legal" grounds on which Christians were harassed included charges of cannibalism, atheism, and incest (C.G. Thorne, "Persecution." in *The New International Dictionary of the Christian Church* [Grand Rapids: Zondervan, 1981], 766). It should be noted, however, that Rome was generally very tolerant of various religions as long as they did not disrupt the Empire. In fact, the Jewish religion was under the protection of the State to the extent that emperor worship was not demanded (except during the time of Caligula). Rome was satisfied as long as sacrifice was made in the temple twice each day for Caesar and the Roman people (Emil Schurer, *The History of the Jewish People in the Age of Jesus Christ* [London: Bloomsbury T & T Clark, 2014], 1:379.

[257] Eusebius, *The Church History,* Translation and Commentary by Paul Maier [Grand Rapids: Kregel, 2007], 8.6.

[258] Donna R. Ridge and E. Ray Clendenen. "Emperor Worship." in *Holman Illustrated Bible Dictionary* (Nashville, TN: Holman Bible Publishers, 2003), 486. For a survey of persecution in this regard under Nero, Domitian, and Marcus Aurelius, see Justo Gonzalez, *The Story of Christianity: The Early Church to the Present Day* (Peabody, MA: Prince Press, 2010), 33-48; for persecution from AD 100 to the Edict of Milan in AD 313 (the decree from Constantine giving freedom to all religions) see Earle Cairns, *Christianity through the Centuries* (Grand Rapids: Zondervan, 1981), 91-93. Whether the Edict of Milan was actually an edict; whether it was actually issued from Milan; and, whether it was issued solely by Constantine is beside the point here. To read the full edict, see Chapter 8, Section: 26 The Edict of Milan.

Isis—mother of all things), the Dionysiac (in honor of the Greek god of wine and animals Dionysus), and the Cybelan cult (in honor of the fertility goddess Cybele of Asia Minor).

Superstition and Astrology

A fourth strand of religious thought was *superstition* and *astrology.* This was extremely prevalent in the ancient world and was often encountered by Paul on his missionary journeys. Just as Peter had to confront a sorcerer named Simon in Samaria (Acts 8:9-24), so Paul met a sorcerer named Bar-Jesus on the island of Cyprus (Paphos-Acts 13:8). Roman officials were notoriously superstitious so it was not unusual in this instance for Sergius Paulus, a proconsul, to have a magician with him.[259] Perhaps one of the most well-known instances of superstition is in Acts 19 and the salvation of many of the Ephesian magicians. To show the genuineness of their experience, they voluntary burned their books publicly. These books undoubtedly contained spells and magical formulas,[260] and according to Luke, were valued at 50,000 days' wage for a day laborer.[261]

Gnosticism

A final, major aspect of Greco-Roman religious thought was *Gnosticism.* From the Greek word for "knowledge" (γνῶσις), Gnosticism was in an incipient form toward the end of the first century and reached its full development in the second century.[262] Thus, disorganized gnostic ideas will be battled by John (1-3 John) and Paul (Colossians). Some of the outstanding gnostic ideas included: 1) eclecticism (syncretism), 2) stress on the subjective, 3) God's immanence, 4) a dualistic universe in which spirit was good and matter was evil. This led to Christological heresies such as Docetism and Cerinthianism plus a warped view of the created order, 5) asceticism or licentiousness, and 6) a reliance on immediate, higher knowledge for salvation.[263]

---

[259]William Neil, *The Acts of the Apostles* (Grand Rapids: Eerdmans, 1981), 155.

[260] These spells and formulas would be an attempt to manipulate a deity into acting in the interest of an individual.

[261] Witherington, *The Acts of the Apostles: A Socio-Rhetorical Commentary*, 582-583.

[262] "Full development" is not meant to imply that gnostic thought reached a particular, monolithic form since there was not a uniform set of beliefs held by all Gnostics. Rather, these various ideas had become more entrenched by the second century. In the text above six characteristics are mentioned. Geisler lists twelve of them in his article on Gnosticism (Norman Geisler, "Gnosticism," in *Baker Encyclopedia of Christian Apologetics* [Grand Rapids: Baker, 1999], 274).

[263] Of illustrative interest is Paul's statement on contentment when he says to the Philippians that he had been "instructed" both to be hungry and to be full, both to abound and to suffer need (KJV). The term translated "instructed" in the Authorized Version is the Greek term from the lemma μυέω. It is defined by BAGD as being initiated into the mystery religions (529). Part of the knowledge imparted through this thought system was gained when one was initiated into Gnosticism. It is possible that Paul was sarcastically using the term in this instance. See for example H.C.G. Moule's brief discussion in *The Epistle to the Philippians* (Grand Rapids: Baker, 1981), 85-86, and Moises Silva's caution on this in *Philippians* (Grand Rapids: Baker, 2008), 204.

Philosophical Thought

Just as there were many strands of religious thought in the Greco-Roman world, so there were many strands of philosophical thought. These included: Platonism, Epicureanism, Stoicism, Cynicism, and Aristotelianism. Philosophy deals with five distinct subjects including logic, esthetics, ethics, politics, and metaphysics.[264]

Platonism

Plato (429-380 BC) lived some four centuries before Christ and taught that the physical world is not true reality but a shadow or copy of the spiritual world.[265] Other platonic ideas included the dialectical method of testing and questioning truth claims (for which he was indebted to Socrates), and the teaching that the soul is a divine spark trapped in the body.

Epicureanism

Epicurus (341-271 BC) believed in chance, no divine involvement, the survival of the fittest, and no future judgment. Bock likens them to "agnostic secularists."[266] The well-known statement of Diogenes is cited by Witherington:[267] "Nothing to fear in God; Nothing to feel in death; Good can be attained; Evil can be endured." Probably that for which the Epicureans are best known is their belief that the highest good of man is the pursuit of pleasure. While this is true, we must not define pleasure in the modern sense; rather, it pictured pleasure as a freedom from fear and a state of tranquility.

Stoicism

Zeno the Cypriot (340-265 BC) was the founder of *Stoicism.* The roofed colonnade where Zeno taught in the agora[268] was called the "stoa" (στοά) hence his followers were called *Stoics.* The Stoics were pantheists, self-sufficient, strong believers in virtue and reason, and had a reputation for being arrogant.

Cynicism

Antisthenes (contemporary of Socrates) was a devoted follower of Socrates and Diogenes of Sinope (412-323 BC) and was the most famous pupil of this school known as cynics.[269] They were sarcastic, non-comformists who lived very simple lives.

---

[264] Will Durant, *The Story of Philosophy* (NY: Simon and Schuster, 1961), 3.
[265] Colin Brown, *Philosophy & the Christian Faith* (Downers Grove, IL: InterVarsity Press, 1968), 15.
[266] Darrell Bock, *Acts* (Grand Rapids: Baker, 2007), 561.
[267] Witherington, *The Acts of the Apostles: A Socio-Rhetorical Commentary*, 514.
[268] A public, open place in ancient Greece used for assemblies and markets.
[269] Josiah Renick Smith, *Xenophon: Memorabilia (*Medford, MA: Ginn and Company, 1903), 1.6.10.

Aristotelianism

Aristotle (384-322) attended the Academy of Plato in Athens for twenty years. He was known for teaching while strolling with his students. This came to be called "Peripatetic Philosophy" ("peripatetic" is from the Greek verb περιπατέω which means "to go about" or "to walk around). Aristotle believed that there was a First Cause and that ideas existed only as they were expressed in individual objects (*contra* Plato).[270] He was deeply interested in sound logic and reasoning as the standard for measuring truth.

Interestingly, as Paul interacted with the Stoics and Epicureans in Acts 17, they called him a "babbler." The Greek term σπερμολόγος (*spermologos*) refers to a scavenger such as a bird which would randomly pick up seeds here and there. They derogatorily pictured Paul as an unsophisticated philosopher who picked up scraps of information and tried to pass them off as profound truth. This assessment was particularly expressed when Paul began to speak of the resurrection since the Epicureans did not believe in the afterlife and the Stoics believed that only the soul continued to exist.

[270] Colin Brown, *Philosophy and the Christian Faith*, 16.

CHAPTER 7
LITERARY BACKGROUND

Jewish Sources

Several written, Jewish and Greco-Roman sources become invaluable when studying the New Testament. The major ones are organized in the charts below.

NAME	DATE[271]	DESCRIPTION	CONTENTS
The Scriptures	ca. 1446 -432 BC[272]	Sacred writings given directly by God	The Law, Prophets, and Writings[273]
Septuagint (LXX)	ca. 200 BC	Greek translation of the Hebrew Scriptures	The 39 OT books plus the apocryphal books of Judith, Tobit, Baruch, Sirach (or Ecclesiasticus), the Wisdom of Solomon, 1st and 2nd Maccabees, 1st and 2nd Books of Esdras, additions to the Book of Esther, additions to Daniel, and the Prayer of Manasseh
Philo	20 BC-AD 50	Jewish philosopher who lived in Alexandria, Egypt	49 treatises have survived. His works include commentaries on the Bible, philosophy, apologetics. His commentaries are

[271] Many dates are approximate.

[272] Assuming Mosaic authorship of the Pentateuch and a 1446 BC date for the Exodus, the Pentateuch would be written sometime between 1446 and 1406 (Moses' death). Generally speaking, Malachi should be dated well after 516 BC based on the fact that the completion of the temple is presupposed along with many religious and social abuses. More specifically, an approximate date could be posited from the following facts: 1) the Persian name for governor Pechah puts the date during the Persian empire in Israel (539-333 BC), 2) sacrifices were being offered which points to after 516, and 3) the moral decline is best represented by the time of Nehemiah after his second return. Thus a date of around 432 (the date of Nehemiah's return to Babylon) or after is plausible.

[273] The Law (Torah) includes the five books of Moses; the Prophets appear in the following order: former prophets—Joshua, Judges, Samuel, Kings; latter prophets—Isaiah, Jeremiah, Ezekiel, and the twelve minor prophets; the Writings include Psalms, Proverbs, Job, Song of Solomon, Ruth, Lamentations, Ecclesiastes, Esther, Daniel, Ezra/Nehemiah, Chronicles.

			marked by heavy allegorization.[274]
Josephus[275]	37-100 AD	First century Jew appointed by Roman Emperor Vespasian to be court historian	Most famous works are: *The Antiquities of the Jewish People* and *The History of the Jewish War Against the Romans.* The former is a 20-volume work which traces the history of the Jews to Josephus' day. The latter is a 7-volume account of the Jewish revolution against the Romans
Dead Sea Scrolls	1947 (discovered)	Nearly 800 scrolls discovered in caves just off the northwest shore of the Dead Sea	Copies of OT books (most famous is the Isaiah scroll), Apoc. and Pseud. texts, commentaries on OT books (largest is on Habakkuk), collections of OT passages on themes, sectarian writings of the Qumran community
Apocrypha	Intertestamental and NT era (250 BC-AD 100)	Jewish writings included in the LXX (except II Esdras). Protestants reject these and Roman Catholics accept	1,2 Esdras, Tobit, Judith, Additions to Esther, Wisdom of Solomon, Ecclesiasticus, Baruch, Letter of

[274] For Philo, the immature reader would only see the literal meaning or the milk of a passage, whereas the mature reader would see the allegorical reading or the meat, for texts are not saying what they appear to say, but something different. Here are some quick examples of this from Philo's commentaries on the Pentateuch: Cain represents a person who can speak fluently but is insufficient in content, while Abel represents a person who is solid in content but not fluent in speech. A fluent person can kill a person who is not fluent. The Passover symbolized the passing of the soul out of its body. The 7-branched menorah represented 7 planets. Abraham and Sarah represented the mind and virtue. See *The Works of Philo,* Complete and Unabridged, Translated by C. D. Yonge (Peabody, MA: Hendriksen, 1995). For more examples of Philo's allegorical method, see virtually any of the sections in his works such as: "On the Creation," "On the Cherubim," "Allegorical Interpretation, I," "Allegorical Interpretation, II," etc.

[275] Bock and Herrick offer a balanced critique of Josephus: "These texts are crucial because they give us insight into how a major figure living in Jesus' day viewed Israel's history and key political events…Josephus is usually fairly reliable as a source, but his perspective needs critical assessment" (Darrell Bock and Gregory Herrick, eds. *Jesus in Context: Background Readings for Gospel Study* [Grand Rapids: Baker, 2005], 19-20).

		them as fully authoritative[276]	Jeremiah, Prayer of Azariah and the Song of the Three Young Men, Susanna, Bel and the Dragon, Prayer of Manasseh, 1,2 Maccabees
Pseude-pigrapha	Intertestamental and NT era	Jewish writings, some of which claim to have been written by a dead OT figure, not included in the OT or Apocrypha	1,2 Enoch, 2,3 Baruch, Sibylline Oracles, Testaments of the Twelve Patriarchs, Testament of Job, Lives of the Prophets, Assumption of Moses, Martyrdom of Isaiah, Paralipomena of Jeremiah, Jubilees, Life of Adam and Eve, Psalms of Solomon, Letter of Aristeas, 3, 4 Maccabees
Babylonian Talmud	Late 5th century	Mishnah plus the Babylonian Gemarah. Considered to be the authoritative edition. Longer than the PT (35 volumes in the BT)	The complete body of Jewish oral law
PalestinianTalmud[277]	Late 4th/early 5th century	Mishnah plus the Palestinian Gamarah	The complete body of Jewish oral law
Mishnah	Compiled early 3rd century AD	The body of oral tradition put into written form	Rabbinic rulings on various issues and application of Torah

[276] The original 1611 KJV included the Apocrypha.

[277] Scott offers this helpful summary and caution regarding the rabbinic Jewish writings. "Most of the religious and related traditions of Intertestamental Judaism were circulated orally. Only after the A.D. 70 destruction of Herod's temple was a concerted effort made by the rabbis to collect and reduce this material to writing...Material was collected selectively, abridged, expanded, adapted, and partly created to meet the needs of the post-70 situations. The result was collections such as the Mishnah (codified by the Tannaim, A.D. 90-200), Gemara (codified by the Amoraim, A.D. 200-500...the Tosephta, targums, and midrashim. The rabbinic writings may, at places, reflect the intertestamental Jewish period. However, this first-century information stands side by side and is often intertwined with records that reflect situations and practices that arose after that era. Accordingly, those using rabbinic writings as a source for the intertestamental period must do so with caution and critical skill" (J. Julius Scott, *Jewish Backgrounds of the New Testament* [Grand Rapids: Baker, 2000], 33).

			to daily life. Two types of material: *halakah* (legal rulings and interpretations) and *haggadah* (non-legal portions)
Gemara(h)	3rd-5th centuries	Commentary on the Mishnah by the rabbis	Includes expositions, descriptions of customs, proverbs, and folklore
Tosefta	Same as Gemarah	Additions to the Mishnah, thus dealing with issues in a more complete form	Collection of more elucidated and complete maxims
Targums	------	Aramaic and Hebrew commentary on the Scriptures (interpretive paraphrases)	
Midrashim	------	Collections of comments on the Scriptures	

Greco-Roman Sources

Name	Date	Description
Polybius	203-120 BC	Greek historian who wrote 40-volume history of Rome
Diodorus of Sicily	Died ca. 21 BC	Greek contemporary of Julius Caesar who wrote a treatise on Antiochus Epiphanes
Strabo	63 BC-AD 21	Greek historian and geographer. 17 of his 47 volumes describe the geography of Palestine
Plutarch	AD 50-ca. 120	Greek who wrote sketches of Roman statesman
Dio Cassius	AD 155-ca. 230	Greek Proconsul of Africa. 18 of his 80 volume Roman history is extant
Cicero	106-43 BC	Roman historian who wrote a history of Syria
Livy	59 BC-AD 17	Roman historian who wrote a complete Roman history. All 35 volumes are extant
Tacitus	AD 55-ca. 120	Considered the most reliable Roman historian
Pliny the Younger	AD 62-113	Roman historian who wrote a letter to Roman Emperor Trajan seeking advice on how to handle Christians. Earliest reference by a Roman author to Christ
Suetonius	AD 69-ca. 121	Roman historian who wrote *The Lives of the Twelve Emperors* (Caesar to Domitian). Refers to history, customs, and chronology

Besides having a basic grasp of the literary world of the New Testament, it is helpful to have an understanding of how the Scriptures particularly were interpreted.

Ancient Jewish Hermeneutics

Most scholars begin discussion of the history of hermeneutics with the time of Ezra.[278] When the nation of Israel returned to Jerusalem following the Babylonian Captivity, the Bible says in Nehemiah 8:8 that Ezra and the Levites *...read distinctly from the book, in the Law of God; and they gave the sense, and helped them to understand the reading*. There is every indication that their explanation and interpretation of the text followed the normal laws of understanding language.

However, the teachers of the nation eventually began interpreting Scripture using methods not always consistent with how language is normally interpreted. By the time of Christ, Jewish hermeneutics could be divided into four categories:

The Plain

The first category could be called the plain meaning. That is, the text was understood in its normal, obvious, literal, historical sense. This was referred to as *peshat.*

Midrash

The second category could be called *Midrash.* This word comes from a Hebrew verb which means "to search." This was a Jewish method of exegesis which sought to discover deeper meanings in the text beyond the literal one.[279]

Pesher

This method was particularly practiced by the Qumran community.[280] In Judaism there was a monastic sect known as the Essenes and one of their communities was located at Qumran on the Northwest shore of the Dead Sea. They believed that what the ancient prophets had written was to be imminently fulfilled through their community. They were living in the last days which would culminate in the Messianic Kingdom. *Pesher* interpretation has plagued and continues to plague the Christian community as people constantly see in the news headlines the fulfillment of prophecy and make statements like "the Lord is

---

[278] See for example, Henry Virkler, *Hermeneutics: Principles and Processes of Biblical Interpretation* (Grand Rapids: Baker Academic, 2007), 44-45.

[279] Midrash included *halakah* dealing with the practice of religious laws and *haggadah* including stories, legends, etc. Paul actually condemns this method of interpretation in 1Timothy 1:4 where he speaks of fables and endless genealogies. For validation of this point, see George Knight, *The Pastoral Epistles* The New International Greek Testament Commentary (Grand Rapids: Eerdmans, 2000) 73-74.

[280] Qumran is the name of a wadi (the bed or valley of a stream) near the Northwest shore of the Dead Sea and even more broadly a reference to the caves in the surrounding cliffs (Wood, D. R. W., & Marshall, I. H. (1996). *New Bible Dictionary* (3rd ed). Leicester, England; Downers Grove, IL: InterVarsity Press. Logos 5. The Essenes were a major Jewish sect believed to be the inhabitants of Qumran.

coming soon" or "we are the terminal generation."

Allegorical

Allegorical interpretation believed that beneath the literal, plain meaning of the text lay the true, spiritual meaning called the *hyponoia*. Allegorization can be traced back to the Greeks who were dealing with the fact that in some of their mythology, the gods were behaving immorally. To explain this, the stories were interpreted allegorically so that the real truth of the story lay at a deeper level beneath the surface of the literal story. The characters, objects, and events were all symbols of other things. Or stated differently, the text has a meaning other than its apparent meaning.

One of the most famous names associated with this method was Philo. Philo was an Alexandrian Jew who followed the Greek method of hermeneutics in interpreting the Mosaic writings. The immature reader would only see the literal meaning or the milk, whereas the mature reader would see the allegorical reading or the meat, for texts are not saying what they appear to say, but something different. Here are some quick examples of this from Philo's commentaries on the Pentateuch: Cain represents a person who can speak fluently but is insufficient in content, while Abel represents a person who is solid in content but not fluent in speech. A fluent person can kill a person who is not fluent. The Passover symbolized the passing of the soul out of its body. The 7-branched menorah represented 7 planets. Abraham and Sarah represented the mind and virtue.[281]

New Testament Hermeneutics

The New Testament writers cite and allude to the Old Testament hundreds of times. There is much scholarly discussion in the field of hermeneutics in this area—in fact, there are entire books written just on this one issue. While not intending to get into that fray here; it can be observed that the New Testament writers used neither the *pesher* method of the Essenes nor the Hellenistic approach of allegorization.[282]

[281] See *The Works of Philo,* Complete and Unabridged, Translated by C. D. Yonge (Peabody, MA: Hendriksen, 1995).

[282] There is a significant amount of literature on the issue of how the New Testament writers used the Old Testament. For a sampling, see Kenneth Berding and Jonathan Lunde eds. *Three Views on the New Testament Use of the Old Testament* (Grand Rapids: Zondervan, 2008); Walter Kaiser, *Uses of the Old Testament in the New* (Eugene, OR: Wipf & Stock Publishers, 2001); G. K. Beale, *The Right Doctrine from the Wrong Texts? Essays on the Use of the Old Testament in the New* (Grand Rapids: Baker Academic, 1994). A separate but related issue is how the New Testament writers use the term "fulfill." See Charles Dyer, "Biblical Meaning of 'Fulfillment,'" in *Issues in Dispensationalism* (Chicago: Moody Press, 1994) 51-72. For a fuller discussion see Chapter IX, 1 Peter, Note #3. For a brief survey of how the interpretation of Scripture developed to the present day, see Chapter 8, Section 27: Biblical Interpretation—Patristic to the Present.

CHAPTER 8

FOR FURTHER STUDY

Section 1: The Theocracy[283]

The Meaning of the Term "Kingdom"

The core idea behind the term "kingdom" is simply the divine rule—or God's rule.

The Aspects of the Kingdom

In the Bible, there are two expressions of the kingdom. The first is the "eternal aspect." The eternal aspect of the kingdom is characterized by four features. The first feature is that it is timeless. That is, God has always possessed absolute sovereignty; He has always ruled as King; and He always will. The second feature is universality. Because God is omnipresent, there is nothing in creation which has ever been outside of God's rule. The third feature of the eternal kingdom is that it represents God's immediate rule. That is, generally speaking God will exercise this rule directly through his providence or miracles, for example. The fourth feature is that it always exists efficaciously regardless of the attitude of its subjects.

The second expression of the kingdom is the theocratic kingdom or the theocracy. It is this aspect of the kingdom which is most critical when it comes to biblical interpretation. As with the eternal kingdom, so there are four features of the theocratic kingdom. The first feature is that, whereas the eternal kingdom is timeless, the theocratic kingdom is temporal. That is, there are periods of time when the theocratic kingdom is not. Again, the eternal kingdom is always present, it is always functioning, and it experiences no hiatus to it. By contrast, however, the theocratic kingdom is temporal. It occurs in time and it may come and go. The second feature of the theocratic kingdom is that it is local. Again, in contrast to the eternal kingdom which is universal covering Jupiter, Mars, Saturn, Tokyo, London, Paris, Chicago, heaven and hell in its reign, the theocratic kingdom is localized to a place on earth. The third feature is that it is mediated. While generally speaking, in the eternal kingdom God will act directly, in the theocratic kingdom, God will work through a mediator. He will work through a representative He has chosen. The fourth feature is that its success is dependent upon the obedience of the subjects. That is, as the subjects and mediator are obedient to God, that will determine the blessing which they experience in the

[283] The material in this section is greatly in debt to the work of J. Dwight Pentecost, *Thy Kingdom Come: Tracing God's Program and Covenant Promises Throughout History* (Wheaton: Victor Books, 1990) and Alva McClain, *The Greatness of the Kingdom: An Inductive Study of the Kingdom of God* (Winona Lake, IN: BMH Books, 1983).

theocracy.

The Development of the Theocracy

The development in Eden. God decided to create the heavens and the earth which he did *ex nihilo, per verbum.* This creation would be the new sphere which would experience the divine rule. The last thing God created in this sphere, and therefore the climactic thing, was man. Man was not only in the *imago dei* that is, made in the image of God but he also was the *imago dei* on earth. Being the "image of God," indicated that man would stand as God's representative on earth. He would be God's vizier, God's regent.

This validated in Genesis 1:26, 28 where the Bible says that Adam and Eve were given the image and likeness so that they could have dominion over all living things and subdue them. Eden, therefore, becomes the first form of the theocratic kingdom. God had always ruled in his eternal kingdom, but now he had localized his rule in the garden, at a particular time, through a mediator, the man and the woman.

However, another aspect of the theocracy is that its success is dependent on the obedience of its subjects and mediator. When the first couple disobeyed God, the theocracy was shattered. Physical death came, spiritual death came, and the creation was cursed. To put it in the words of Romans 5:12 sin burst onto the scene and brought death with it. Paradise had been lost, will paradise ever be regained? The theocracy was lost; will the theocracy ever be restored? This will begin the plot line of the entire Bible until the culmination of history when the Messiah returns to earth and restores paradise lost.

The development through Abraham. The rebellion of Adam did not thwart God's theocratic plan. Thus, the next major phase of the theocracy or the mediatorial kingdom comes in Genesis where God calls Abraham, whom Joshua 24:2 describes as a pagan idolater. By the gracious call of God, Abraham will become the next figure through whom God will mediate His kingdom. After God called Abraham, God made a covenant with him known as the Abrahamic Covenant. There were three essential features to this covenant. The first was a seed promise where God told Abraham he would have numerous descendants. The second was a land promise where it was said that these descendants would possess a specific piece of land as an everlasting possession. The land aspect is essential because if there is going to be dominion (going back to Genesis) and a rule, there must be a locus in which this is carried out. And the third was a universal promise where it was indicated that all of the families of the earth would be blessed through this people. "Through" indicates that they, the seed from Abraham, would have a mediatorial function in the world. These promises are reiterated and expanded throughout the entire Pentateuch, the rest of the Old Testament, and the New Testament.

The development through Moses. After these promises are made to Abraham, his seed begins to grow as God had promised, and they find themselves in bondage in the land of Egypt. In order to rule and bless the world, however, these people had to be gathered into a nation and put under an organized government. Moses will become the next key player in the theocratic kingdom as he will lead the people out and accomplish this. In the last two verses of Exodus 2 before God appears to Moses at the burning bush, the text says: "God heard their groaning [that is, the groaning of Abraham's seed] and God remembered his covenant with Abraham, with Isaac, and with Jacob." When the people are brought out of Egypt they assemble at the foot of Mt. Sinai and receive the Law which forms them into a nation.

The development in Exodus. The rule of life in this Code was given by God to Israel, never to the Church and never to the Gentiles. This raises the important question, why was the Law given? And how did it contribute to the theocracy? One key reason the Law was given to Israel was that it revealed the means by which the nation would enjoy the blessings of the Abrahamic Covenant.

The enjoyment and realization of the blessings would only come about as the nation lived in obedience to God. Obedience to the Law was the means of blessing in the theocracy. Just as with Adam, obedience was necessary for his blessing in the garden, so obedience to the Law was necessary for Israel to be blessed. It was the means by which the nation would see the progressive outworking of the promises made to Abraham.

The development in Deuteronomy. In the book of Deuteronomy, Moses gives a series of sermons based on the terms of the Mosaic Law to the nation of Israel as they ae poised to go into the Promised Land. In five sermons Moses makes three critical points regarding the theocracy. The first is an expansion of the land promised made to Abraham recorded back in the book of Genesis. This expansion is known as the Palestinian Covenant and is recorded in Deuteronomy 30:1-10. Moses states that even though Israel will be dispersed from the land because of disobedience, they will be brought back to the land which they will enjoy forever.

The second critical point made by Moses in Deuteronomy related to the theocracy has to do with the simple principle: obedience brings blessing and disobedience brings cursing. Stated in an expanded fashion: if the nation obeyed the stipulations of the Mosaic Law they would experience the blessings promised to Abraham, but if they disobeyed the Mosaic Law they would experience the curses enumerated in Deuteronomy. Moses lists the blessings which involve material blessings, peace, and prosperity for Israel as a nation. But then he lists the curses for disobedience including panic, disease, drought, physical and mental disease, oppression, exile, economic ruin, siege, and permanent exile.

The third critical point made by Moses is the means of restoration. Moses makes it clear to the nation that if they are disobedient and were experiencing cursing from God, the remedy to be restored was repentance. Involved in this repentance was humility, prayer, the seeking of God's face, and the forsaking of sin. If those means were met, then God would resume working out the Abrahamic promises on behalf of the nation.

The development through David. God raised up David to be the next representative of his dynasty on earth. Very importantly, God made a covenant with David and his house. This is known as the Davidic Covenant and expands the seed promise made to Abraham. The provisions of this covenant included three crucial features: 1) an eternal seed—every generation would have a descendant with right to the throne, 2) an eternal kingdom—this referred to a realm of rule, and 3) an eternal throne—this referred to the right to royal dominion. Thus the three key words of the promises are "house," "kingdom," and "throne."

The implications in the development of the Covenant are that Israel must remain in God's program and David's Son must reign over a literal kingdom. This continued to be Israel's expectation as they waited for the one who would ultimately bring all of these promises to fulfillment. This is why Jesus is linked to the covenant as the Son of David in Matthew 1:1, and Luke 1:31-33 (where Gabriel's birth announcement centers around the key terms "throne," "house," and "kingdom"), and then proceeds to offer the kingdom. After the intercalation of the church age, Christ is again seen in His fulfillment of the covenant as the "lion of the tribe of Judah, the root of David" (Rev. 5:5). Finally, Christ returns as the King of Kings (Rev. 19:16) and reigns forever as the "root and offspring of David" (Rev. 22:16). All of this is anticipated in the Davidic Covenant.

The development through the prophets. By the time of the prophets, the nation had departed from obedience to the Mosaic Law. Because of this, the disciplines went into effect about which Moses had warned the nation in Deuteronomy. And so God raised up the prophets and their message was threefold: 1) they pointed out how the nation had departed from the Mosaic Law, 2) they called the nation to repent (also in keeping with Moses' instructions in Deuteronomy), and 3) they pictured an ultimate Messiah/King who would come and bring the fulfillment of all of the kingdom promises to earth as they give glorious depictions of what that kingdom will be like.

God continued to send prophet after prophet to the nation and they continued to live in disobedience, even after the discipline of the Babylonian exile was over. Finally, God had sent his last prophet, the nation was left in her sin, and the covenant promises made to Israel remained unfulfilled.

The development through the New Testament. The period of darkness ended, however, when God sent another prophet named John the Baptist. His message was "Repent, for the kingdom of heaven is at hand." The concept of repentance goes back to Moses and the prophets as the means for Israel to be restored to

God's covenant program. The kingdom continues to be what it was in the Old Testament—the earthly, mediated kingdom.

Once more, however, the nation rejected this message. There certainly were many individuals, who repented and put their faith in their Messiah, but the bulk of the nation including the leadership rejected what was being offered to them and had their Messiah killed. Because of this rejection, Jesus pronounced judgment on the nation. This judgment was experienced in AD 70 when the Romans destroyed Jerusalem. The kingdom program, the covenant program remained in a state of unfulfillment. However, Jesus is clear in the Gospels that this program will be realized at some point in the future. Of crucial importance is to note that in Matthew 23 when Jesus pronounced judgment on the nation, he said: *You shall not seem henceforth, until you shall say, blessed is he who comes in the name of the Lord.* The theocratic program is still in view, even at Israel's darkest hour. This concept is still on the apostles' radar when they inquire of Jesus in Acts 1:5, "will you at this time restore again the kingdom to Israel?" Jesus replies, not by correcting their notion of the kingdom, but by instructing them as to their mission until the time when the Father sees fit to bring the kingdom.

As this day is being anticipated, God begins to work through a new entity known as the Church which begins on the day of Pentecost. As the Gospel is preached through this entity, the message is taken to the ends of the earth that the forgiveness of sins is available through the work of the Messiah and those who place their faith in him will be a part of his kingdom when he returns. At an unspecified time, this church age will come to a close. God will then resume his work with the nation of Israel during the Tribulation period or Daniel's 70th week. One of the main purposes of this period is to bring Israel to a point of repentance at which time they will look to the one whom they pierced for deliverance and say "blessed is he who comes in the name of the Lord." The Messiah will then return to earth and fulfill all of the promises made to Abraham and developed by the prophets in the Old Testament. This will have brought the kingdom program full circle: paradise was lost through the first Adam, but it is restored through the second Adam.

Section 2: The Times of the Gentiles[284]

The times of the Gentiles can be defined as: that long period of time from the Babylonian Empire to the Second Coming of the Messiah during which time Gentiles have dominance over the city of Jerusalem. This does not rule out temporary Jewish control of the city, but all such Jewish control will be temporary until the Second Coming. If Jewish control takes place, it is to be viewed as temporary and does not mean that the Times of the Gentiles have ended. This period can only end when the Gentiles cannot overtake Jerusalem. There are four

[284] The material in this section consists of the author's summary and/or citation of the discussion found in: Arnold Fruchtenbaum, *The Footsteps of the Messiah* (Tustin, CA: Ariel Ministries, 2002), 21-44.

key passages which detail the Times of the Gentiles.

Daniel 2:31-45

There are four metals on this image. The head of gold is Nebuchadnezzar and the Babylonian Empire. The two arms of silver are the two nations of the Medes and Persians. The belly and two thighs of brass represent the Greek or Hellenic Empire. The rest of the image represents the fourth Gentile Empire. This empire goes through several stages, three of which are presented in this passage. First, there is the united stage (v. 40). This united stage gives way to the two-division stage (v. 41). Eventually, however, this fourth Gentile Empire gives way to a ten-division stage as is seen in the ten toes (vv. 42-43). The fifth empire which will follow will not be Gentile but Jewish (vv. 44-45). The "stone" is a reference to the Messiah and the fact "that is cut out without hands" speaks of divine origin. "Mountain" in prophetic scripture speaks of a king/kingdom which will emerge when Gentile domination (seen by the image) will be smashed.

Daniel 7:1-28

The first vision (1-6) begins with the Great Sea (Mediterranean) which represents the Gentile world. Four beasts arise from this sea, the first of which is eagle-winged and lion-like representing the Babylonian Empire. The second is bear-like representing the Medo-Persian Empire. The bear is lopsided, being raised up on one side; for although the Medes and Persians were confederate, the Persians were by far the dominant power and it was a lopsided alliance. Further, the bear is found to have three ribs in its mouth, having devoured the flesh. Historically, these three ribs represent the three kingdoms conquered by the Medo-Perisan forces giving them their empire status: Lydia, Babylonia, and Egypt. The third is leopard-like representing the Hellenistic Empire. The leopard is less majestic than the lion or bear but it is swifter than both. With leopard-like speed Alexander the Great conquered the Medo-Persian Empire. At his death, the empire split into four kingdoms. The four wings represent the four kingdoms rising out of Alexander's empire, and the four heads represent the four generals who took control of the four kingdoms: Ptolemy over Egypt, Israel and Arabia Petrea; Seleucus over Syria, Babylonia, and as far east as India; Cassander over Macedonia and Greece; and Lysimachus over Thrace and Bithynia.

The second vision (7-8) describes a fourth beast. This fourth beast is described as being diverse. It completely subdues and breaks in pieces all that precedes it. It appears as far more ferocious than the previous three. The fourth beast has ten horns, but while it begins with ten horns, an eleventh horn arises, the little horn, which uproots three of the ten others. Having uprooted the other three, it begins to speak great things. With the uprooting of the three horns, seven of the original remain, and the little horn is now an eighth rather than an eleventh. The fourth beast represents a fourth Gentile Empire.

The third vision takes place in heaven (9-12). There is a throne of God the Father who is referred to as the Ancient of Days. He is viewed as a judge, and the book of judgment is opened. He is surrounded by myriads of angels who will be responsible to carry out these judgments; the object of which is the fourth Gentile Empire (11-12). In verse 11, it is the fourth beast, particularly the little horn, which is judged and destroyed.

The fourth vision in the passage (13-14) describes the setting up of the Kingdom of God following the destruction of the fourth Gentile Empire.

The interpretation of these four visions is given in 15-27. The summary interpretation is in 17-18 and includes the following details: coming out of the sea emphasizes their Gentile identity; arising out of the earth emphasizes their humanity--these are human, not divine, kingdoms; the little horn causes three of the ten horns to fall; he speaks great things; he wars against the saints and is allowed to prevail. Finally, he is personally defeated by the Ancient of Days. Once the judgment is passed on the little horn, he will be done away with and the kingdom will pass over to the saints.

Daniel 7:23-26 gives the interpretation of the fourth beast. In 23a, the fourth empire is seen in its United Stage, and it is in this first stage that its diverseness from the previous three empires is seen. This is followed by the second stage, that of a one-world government, for in verse 23b it states that the fourth empire will devour the whole earth. This stage will be followed by the ten kingdom stage (24a) which, in turn, will be followed by the little horn, or the antichrist stage (24b-26). These verses state that he arises after the ten division stage (24b). While the fourth empire is diverse from the previous three, the little horn is diverse from the other ten (24c). He eventually puts down three of these kings (24d) and verse 25 again points out his speaking great things against God and the saints. He seeks to change the times and the seasons, and he will be allowed to rule for only a time, times, and half a time, which from other passages means 3 ½ years (Dan. 9:27; 12:7; Rev. 11:2, 3; 12:6, 14; 13:5). Finally, his dominion is destroyed (v. 26).

With the destruction of the little horn, the Messianic kingdom is set up for the saints (27). The saints in Daniel refer to righteous Israel, or the remnant of Israel, and not the church. The following is a summary of these two important chapters.

Daniel 2	**Daniel 7**
1. The Babylonian empire	1. The Babylonian empire
2. The Medo-Persian empire	2. The Medo-Persian Empire
3. The Hellenistic empire	3. The Hellenistic empire
a. the united stage	
b. the four division stage	
4. The Fourth empire	4. The Fourth Empire
a. the united stage	a. the united stage
b. the two division stage	b. the one world government stage
c. the ten division stage	c. the ten division stage
d. the antichrist stage	

5. The Messianic kingdom 5. The Messianic kingdom

Elaboration of the Fourth Empire

The fourth empire of Daniel's vision goes through five different stages, with Rome being merely the first of these five stages, for Rome cannot be viewed as the entire fourth empire. Both Daniel passages make it clear that the fourth Gentile Empire begins with the end of the third and continues until Messiah comes to set up his kingdom. The long continuous existence of the empire is to go through five successive stages.

The United Stage—Rome

The first stage was the united stage, which was the Roman Empire. It has become customary to think in terms of a revival of the old Roman Empire in the future, but no such concept is really warranted. It is more consistent to simply follow through the five stages with the Roman Empire being the first stage or the untied stage, which lasted from 63 BC to AD 364. Neither of the Daniel passages allows for gaps or for a revival of the old Roman Empire.

The Two Division Stage

The second stage of the empire was the two division stage. This stage was foreseen by Daniel 2, but not by Daniel 7. It is a stage that began in 364 AD when Emperor Valentinian divided the Roman Empire into an east and west division. From that point on, the empire was divided into an east-west balance of power (there was an earlier division in AD 285 but this was short-lived when Constantine reunited the empire in AD 312-313. The division in AD 364 was permanent).

The eastern division of power remained in Constantinople until 1453 when it collapsed in the Turkish invasion. When Constantinople fell, the political rulers, scribes, and scholars fled northward into Russia and infiltrated the government there, setting up a Roman type of government. The rulers called themselves Czars, which is Russian for "Caesar." After a while, Russia gave herself the official title of the Third Roman Empire. Eventually, the eastern balance of power was centered in the Soviet Union and included the Communist block of nations. With the collapse of European communism, the eastern balance shifted to Russia the Commonwealth of Independent States.

The western division of power remained in Rome from 364 to 476, when Rome fell. From there it shifted to France, especially with the power gained by Charlemagne in AD 800. He called his domain the Holy Roman Empire of the Frankish Nation. In 962, Otto I of Germany defeated the Franks and set up the Holy Roman Empire of the German Nation. The leaders called themselves Kaisers, which is German for "Caesar." Since then, especially after World War I, the western balance of power has been centered in the democratic nations of the west. So, the two division stage began in 364 and continues to the present day.

The One World Government Stage

The next three stages of the empire are all future. At some point the east-west balance of power will break down, leading to a one world government. This stage is seen in Daniel 7. Daniel 7:23 states that at some point the fourth empire devours the whole earth. This is something that Rome never did. Some attempt to make this expression mean the "then-known world," but it cannot be said that Rome even conquered the then-known world. The third stage will happen at some point when the two division stage collapses.

The Ten Division Stage

This stage was seen both in Daniel 2 and 7 in the ten toes and ten horns respectively. The ten division stage is stated to come out of the one world government stage. For some reason not given in the text, the one world government will divide into ten kingdoms that will cover the whole world—not merely Europe. It has been common today to refer to the ten kingdoms as being in Europe only, especially in the former Common Market, now the European Union. But the text does not allow for this kind of interpretation. At the very best, the European Union might become one of the ten, but it could hardly become all of the ten. A careful reading of the Daniel passage states that once the fourth empire rules the whole world, then this one world government will split into ten kingdoms. This requires the ten kingdoms to cover the entire world, not just the territory known as Europe.

The Antichrist Stage

It is during the ten kingdom stage that the antichrist will begin his rise to power. Eventually, he will be strong enough to uproot three of the ten kings, and the other seven will simply submit to his authority. Once the other seven submit their authority to the antichrist, this will begin the fifth and final stage of the fourth Gentile Empire, the antichrist stage, which is the stage of absolute imperialism.

Revelation 13:1-10

The sea in Revelation 13 is the same as the one in Daniel 7 which represents the Gentile world. However, Revelation 13 is completely focused on the fourth empire, emphasizing a particular stage of the fourth empire, namely, the fifth stage, and the antichrist stage. The Beast John saw is the same beast that Daniel saw in chapter 7. The ten horns are found in Daniel 7, and they represent the ten kingdoms, which is the fourth stage of the empire. A new element is introduced by Revelation 13:1; the beast has seven heads (this will be explained in the Rev. 17 passage).

Revelation 17:7-14

The text says that the seven heads are seven mountains. The word "mountain" is used symbolically for a king, kingdom, or throne in prophetic literature. In verse 10, these seven mountains represent seven kings. If this refers to Rome the city, then five hills should no longer be in existence, only one should be there now, with another to rise in the future. Contextually, this is an impossible interpretation. The ten horns are kings that are contemporary with each other. They all rise and reign at the same time. The seven heads though are chronological. At the time of the writing of Revelation, five had already gone into history and were no more. The sixth head was present and in control, and there was one more to go (the antichrist stage). The five could be types of government or five fallen heads representing five previous empires: Egypt, Assyria, Babylon, Medo-Persia, and Greece. The sixth is Rome, with the seventh being the antichrist at the first half of the Tribulation, and eighth being the antichrist at the second half of the Tribulation [Or, alternatively, the "seven" refers to heads while the "eight" refers to the horns in which case the antichrist is the eighth in that he is an eighty contemporary king reigning with the seven who have submitted to his authority].

Section 3: Translation of the Cyrus Cylinder[285]

1. [When ... Mar]duk, king of the whole of heaven and earth, the .... who, in his ..., lays waste his ....
2. [...]broad ? in intelligence, ... who inspects} (?) the wor]ld quarters (regions)
3. [..] his [first]born (=Belshazzar), a low person was put in charge of his country,
4. but [..] he set [a (…) counter]feit over them.
5. He ma[de] a counterfeit of Esagil, [and ....]... for Ur and the rest of the cult-cities.
6. Rites inappropriate to them, [impure] fo[od- offerings ……………………………………………] disrespectful […] were daily gabbled, and, as an insult,
7. he brought the daily offerings to a halt; he inter[fered with the rites and] instituted [.......] within the sanctuaries. In his mind, reverential fear of Marduk, king of the gods, came to an end.
8. He did yet more evil to his city every day; … his [people ....], he brought ruin on them all by a yoke without relief.
9. Enlil-of-the-gods became extremely angry at their complaints, and […] their territory. The gods who lived within them left their shrines,

[285] "Cyrus Cylinder," British Museum-Cyrus Cylinder, accessed July 8, 2012, http://www.Britishmuseum.org/explore/highlights/articles/c/cyrus_cylinder__translation.aspx.

10. angry that he had made (them) enter into Shuanna (Babylon). Ex[alted Marduk, Enlil-of-the-Go]ds, relented. He changed his mind about all the settlements whose sanctuaries were in ruins,
11. and the population of the land of Sumer and Akkad who had become like corpses, and took pity on them. He inspected and checked all the countries,
12. seeking for the upright king of his choice. He took the hand of Cyrus, king of the city of Anshan, and called him by his name, proclaiming him aloud for the kingship over all of everything.
13. He made the land of Guti and all the Median troops prostrate themselves at his feet, while he shepherded in justice and righteousness the black-headed people
14. whom he had put under his care. Marduk, the great lord, who nurtures his people, saw with pleasure his fine deeds and true heart,
15. and ordered that he should go to Babylon He had him take the road to Tintir (Babylon), and, like a friend and companion, he walked at his side.
16. His vast troops whose number, like the water in a river, could not be counted, were marching fully-armed at his side.
17. He had him enter without fighting or battle right into Shuanna; he saved his city Babylon from hardship. He handed over to him Nabonidus, the king who did not fear him.
18. All the people of Tintir, of all Sumer and Akkad, nobles and governors, bowed down before him and kissed his feet, rejoicing over his kingship and their faces shone.
19. The lord through whose help all were rescued from death and who saved them all from distress and hardship, they blessed him sweetly and praised his name.

----

20. I am Cyrus, king of the universe, the great king, the powerful king, king of Babylon, king of Sumer and Akkad, king of the four quarters of the world,
21. son of Cambyses, the great king, king of the city of Anshan, grandson of Cyrus, the great king, ki[ng of the ci]ty of Anshan, descendant of Teispes, the great king, king of the city of Anshan,
22. the perpetual seed of kingship, whose reign Bel (Marduk)and Nabu love, and with whose kingship, to their joy, they concern themselves. When I went as harbinger of peace i[nt]o Babylon
23. I founded my sovereign residence within the palace amid celebration and rejoicing. Marduk, the great lord, bestowed on me as my destiny the great magnanimity of one who loves Babylon, and I every day sought him out in awe.
24. My vast troops were marching peaceably in Babylon, and the whole of [Sumer] and Akkad had nothing to fear.

25. I sought the safety of the city of Babylon and all its sanctuaries. As for the population of Babylon […, w]ho as if without div[ine intention] had endured a yoke not decreed for them,
26. I soothed their weariness; I freed them from their bonds(?). Marduk, the great lord, rejoiced at [my good] deeds,
27. and he pronounced a sweet blessing over me, Cyrus, the king who fears him, and over Cambyses, the son [my] issue, [and over] my all my troops,
28. that we might live happily in his presence, in well-being. At his exalted command, all kings who sit on thrones,
29. from every quarter, from the Upper Sea to the Lower Sea, those who inhabit [remote distric]ts (and) the kings of the land of Amurru who live in tents, all of them,
30. brought their weighty tribute into Shuanna, and kissed my feet. From [Shuanna] I sent back to their places to the city of Ashur and Susa,
31. Akkad, the land of Eshnunna, the city of Zamban, the city of Meturnu, Der, as far as the border of the land of Guti - the sanctuaries across the river Tigris - whose shrines had earlier become dilapidated,
32. the gods who lived therein, and made permanent sanctuaries for them. I collected together all of their people and returned them to their settlements,
33. and the gods of the land of Sumer and Akkad which Nabonidus – to the fury of the lord of the gods – had brought into Shuanna, at the command of Marduk, the great lord,
34. I returned them unharmed to their cells, in the sanctuaries that make them happy. May all the gods that I returned to their sanctuaries,
35. every day before Bel and Nabu, ask for a long life for me, and mention my good deeds, and say to Marduk, my lord, this: "Cyrus, the king who fears you, and Cambyses his son,
36. may they be the provisioners of our shrines until distant (?) days, and the population of Babylon call blessings on my kingship. I have enabled all the lands to live in peace.
37. Every day I increased by [… ge]ese, two ducks and ten pigeons the [former offerings] of geese, ducks and pigeons.
38. I strove to strengthen the defences of the wall Imgur-Enlil, the great wall of Babylon,
39. and [I completed] the quay of baked brick on the bank of the moat which an earlier king had bu[ilt but not com]pleted its work.
40. [I …… which did not surround the city] outside, which no earlier king had built, his workforce, the levee [from his land, in/int]o Shuanna.
41. [… ....with bitum]en and baked brick I built anew, and [completed] its [work].
42. [………………………………………………] great [doors of cedarwood] with bronze cladding,

43. [and I installed] all their doors, threshold slabs and door fittings with copper parts. [.........................] I saw within it an inscription of Ashurbanipal, a king who preceded me;
44. [...] his ... Marduk, the great lord, creator (?) of [...]
45. [...] my [... I presented] as a gift.....................] your pleasure forever.

"Now in the first year of Cyrus king of Persia, that the word of the LORD by the mouth of Jeremiah might be fulfilled, the LORD stirred up the spirit of Cyrus king of Persia, so that he made a proclamation throughout all his kingdom, and also put it in writing, saying, Thus says Cyrus king of Persia: All the kingdoms of the earth the LORD God of heaven has given me. And He has commanded me to build Him a house at Jerusalem which is in Judah. Who is among you of all His people? May the LORD his God be with him, and let him go up!" - 2 Chronicles 36:22-23

"Who says of Cyrus, 'He is My shepherd, And he shall perform all My pleasure, Saying to Jerusalem, "You shall be built," And to the temple, "Your foundation shall be laid." ' - Isaiah 44:28

"King Cyrus also brought out the articles of the house of the LORD, which Nebuchadnezzar had taken from Jerusalem and put in the temple of his gods; and Cyrus king of Persia brought them out by the hand of Mithredath the treasurer, and counted them out to Sheshbazzar the prince of Judah. This is the number of them: thirty gold platters, one thousand silver platters, twenty-nine knives, thirty gold basins, four hundred and ten silver basins of a similar kind, and one thousand other articles. All the articles of gold and silver were five thousand four hundred. All these Sheshbazzar took with the captives who were brought from Babylon to Jerusalem." - Ezra 1:7-11

Section 4: Antiochus Desecrates the Temple

"Now the fifteenth day of the month Casleu, in the hundred forty and fifth year, they set up the abomination of desolation upon the altar, and builded idol altars throughout the cities of Judah on every side and burnt incense at the doors of their houses, and in the streets." -1 Maccabees 1:54-55

"And when they saw the sanctuary desolate, and the altar profaned, and the gates burned up, and shrubs growing in the courts as in a forest, or in one of the mountains, yea, and the priests' chambers pulled down" -1 Maccabees 4:38

Section 5: Pompey

But already another power had appeared on the scene. Pompey was on his victorious march through Asia when both parties appealed to him for help. Scaurus, whom Pompey detached to Syria, was, indeed, bought by Aristobulus, and Aretas was ordered to raise the siege of Jerusalem. But Pompey quickly discovered that Hyrcanus might, under the tutelage of the cunning Idumæan, Antipater, prove an instrument more likely to serve his ulterior purposes than Aristobulus. Three deputations appeared before Pompey at Damascus—those of the two brothers, and one independent of both, which craved the abolition of the Asmonæan rule and the restoration of the former mode of government, as we understand it, by the 'Chebher' or Eldership under the presidency of the High-Priest. It need scarcely be said that such a demand would find no response. The consideration of the rival claims of the Asmonæans Pompey postponed. The conduct of Aristobulus not only confirmed the unfavourable impression which the insolent bearing of his deputies had made on Pompey, but sealed his own fate and that of the Jewish people. Pompey laid siege to Jerusalem. The adherents of Hyrcanus surrendered the City, but those of Aristobulus retired into the Temple. At last the sacred precincts were taken by storm amidst fearful carnage. The priests, who were engaged in their sacred functions, and who continued them during this terrible scene, were cut down at the altar. No fewer than 12,000 Jews are said to have perished.

With the taking of Jerusalem by Pompey (63 b.c.) the history of the Maccabees as a reigning family, and, indeed, that of the real independence of Palestine, came to an end. So truly did Jewish tradition realise this, that it has left us not a single notice either of this capture of Jerusalem or of all the subsequent sad events to the time of Herod. It is as if their silence meant that for them Judæa, in its then state, had no further history. Still, the Roman conqueror had as yet dealt gently with his prostrate victim. Pompey had, indeed, penetrated into the Most Holy Place in contemptuous outrage of the most sacred feelings of Israel; but he left the treasures of the Temple untouched, and even made provision for the continuance of its services. Those who had caused the resistance of Jerusalem were executed, and the country made tributary to Rome. But Judæa not only became subject to the Roman Governor of Syria, its boundaries were also narrowed. All the Grecian cities had their independence restored; Samaria was freed from Jewish supremacy; and the districts comprised within the so-called Decapolis (or 'ten cities') again obtained self-government. It was a sadly curtailed land over which Hyrcanus 2, as High-Priest, was left Governor, without being allowed to wear the diadem (Ant. 20. 10). Aristobulus 2 had to adorn as captive the triumphal entry of the conqueror into Rome.[286]

Now when Pompey had pitched his camp at Jericho, [where the palm tree grows, and that balsam which is an ointment of all the most precious, which upon

[286] Alfred Edersheim, *The Life and Times of Jesus the Messiah* (Grand Rapids: Eerdmans, 1980), 2:679-680.

any incision made in the wood with a sharp stone, distills out thence like a juice,] he marched in the morning to Jerusalem. Hereupon Aristobulus repented of what he was doing, and came to Pompey, had [promised to] give him money, and received him into Jerusalem, and desired that he would leave off the war, and do what he pleased peaceably. So Pompey, upon his entreaty, forgave him, and sent Gabinius, and soldiers with him, to receive the money and the city: yet was no part of this performed; but Gabinius came back, being both excluded out of the city, and receiving none of the money promised, because Aristobulus's soldiers would not permit the agreements to be executed. At this Pompey was very angry, and put Aristobulus into prison, and came himself to the city, which was strong on every side, excepting the north, which was not so well fortified, for there was a broad and deep ditch that encompassed the city and included within it the temple, which was itself encompassed about with a very strong stone wall.

Now there was a sedition of the men that were within the city, who did not agree what was to be done in their present circumstances, while some thought it best to deliver up the city to Pompey; but Aristobulus's party exhorted them to shut the gates, because he was kept in prison. Now these prevented the others, and seized upon the temple, and cut off the bridge which reached from it to the city, and prepared themselves to abide a siege; but the others admitted Pompey's army in, and delivered up both the city and the king's palace to him. So Pompey sent his lieutenant Piso with an army, and placed garrisons both in the city and in the palace, to secure them, and fortified the houses that joined to the temple, and all those which were more distant and without it. And in the first place, he offered terms of accommodation to those within; but when they would not comply with what was desired, he encompassed all the places thereabout with a wall, wherein Hyrcanus did gladly assist him on all occasions; but Pompey pitched his camp within [the wall], on the north part of the temple, where it was most practicable; but even on that side there were great towers, and a ditch had been dug, and a deep valley begirt it round about, for on the parts towards the city were precipices, and the bridge on which Pompey had gotten in was broken down. However, a bank was raised, day by day, with a great deal of labor, while the Romans cut down materials for it from the places round about. And when this bank was sufficiently raised, and the ditch filled up, though but poorly, by reason of its immense depth, he brought his mechanical engines and battering-rams from Tyre, and placing them on the bank, he battered the temple with the stones that were thrown against it. And had it not been our practice, from the days of our forefathers, to rest on the seventh day, this bank could never have been perfected, by reason of the opposition the Jews would have made; for though our law gives us leave then to defend ourselves against those that begin to fight with us and assault us, yet does it not permit us to meddle with our enemies while they do anything else.

Which thing when the Romans understood, on those days which we call Sabbaths they threw nothing at the Jews, nor came to any pitched battle with them; but raised up their earthen banks, and brought their engines into such forwardness, that they might do execution the next day. And any one may hence learn how very great piety we exercise towards God, and the observance of his laws, since the priests were not at all hindered from their sacred ministrations by their fear during this siege, but did still twice a-day, in the morning and about the ninth hour, offer their sacrifices on the altar; nor did they omit those sacrifices, if any melancholy accident happened by the stones that were thrown among them; for although the city was taken on the third month, on the day of the fast, upon the hundred and seventy-ninth olympiad, when Caius Antonius and Marcus Tullius Cicero were consuls, and the enemy then fell upon them, and cut the throats of those that were in the temple; yet could not those that offered the sacrifices be compelled to run away, neither by the fear they were in of their own lives, nor by the number that were already slain, as thinking it better to suffer whatever came upon them, at their very altars, than to omit anything that their laws required of them. And that this is not a mere brag, or an encomium to manifest a degree of our piety that was false, but is the real truth, I appeal to those that have written of the acts of Pompey; and, among them, to Strabo and Nicolaus [of Damascus]; and besides these two, Titus Livius, the writer of the Roman History, who will bear witness to this thing.

But when the battering-engine was brought near, the greatest of the towers was shaken by it, and fell down, and broke down a part of the fortifications, so the enemy poured in apace; and Cornelius Faustus, the son of Sylla, with his soldiers, first of all ascended the wall, and next to him Furius the centurion, with those that followed on the other part, while Fabius, who was also a centurion, ascended it in the middle, with a great body of men after him. But now all was full of slaughter; some of the Jews being slain by the Romans, and some by one another; nay, some there were who threw themselves down the precipices, or put fire to their houses, and burnt them, as not able to bear the miseries they were under. Of the Jews there fell twelve thousand, but of the Romans very few. Absalom, who was at once both uncle and father-in-law to Aristobulus, was taken captive; and no small enormities were committed about the temple itself, which, in former ages, had been inaccessible, and seen by none; for Pompey went into it, and not a few of those that were with him also, and saw all that which it was unlawful for any other men to see but only for the high priests. There were in that temple the golden table, the holy candlestick, and the pouring vessels, and a great quantity of spices; and besides these there were among the treasures two thousand talents of sacred money: yet did Pompey touch nothing of all this, on account of his regard to religion; and in this point also he acted in a manner that was worthy of his virtue. The next day he gave order to those that had the charge of the temple to cleanse it, and to bring what offerings the law required to God; and restored the high priesthood to Hyrcanus, both because he had been useful to him in other respects, and because he hindered the Jews in the country from giving Aristobulus any assistance in his war against him. He also cut off those that had been the authors of that war; and bestowed proper rewards on Faustus, and those others that mounted the wall with such alacrity; and he made Jerusalem tributary to the

Romans, and took away those cities of Celesyria which the inhabitants of Judea had subdued, and put them under the government of the Roman president, and confined the whole nation, which had elevated itself so high before, within its own bounds. Moreover, he rebuilt Gadara, which had been demolished a little before, to gratify Demetrius of Gadara, who was his freedman, and restored the rest of the cities, Hippos, and Scythopolis, and Pella, and Dios, and Samaria, as also Marissa, and Ashdod, and Jamnia, and Arethusa, to their own inhabitants: these were in the inland parts. Besides those that had been demolished, and also of the maritime cities, Gaza, and Joppa, and Dora, and Strato's Tower; which last Herod rebuilt after a glorious manner, and adorned with havens and temples, and changed its name to Caesarea. All these Pompey left in a state of freedom, and joined them to the province of Syria.

Now the occasions of this misery which came upon Jerusalem were Hyrcanus and Aristobulus, by raising a sedition one against the other; for now we lost our liberty, and became subject to the Romans, and were deprived of that country which we had gained by our arms from the Syrians, and were compelled to restore it to the Syrians. Moreover, the Romans exacted of us, in a little time, above ten thousand talents; and the royal authority, which was a dignity formerly bestowed on those that were high priests, by the right of their family, became the property of private men. But of these matters we shall treat in their proper places. Now Pompey committed Celesyria, as far as the river Euphrates and Egypt, to Scaurus, with two Roman legions, and then went away to Cilicia, and made haste to Rome. He also carried bound along with him Aristobulus and his children; for he had two daughters, and as many sons; the one of which ran away, but the younger, Antigonus, was carried to Rome, together with his sisters.[287]

At this treatment Pompey was very angry, and took Aristobulus into custody. And when he was come to the city, he looked about where he might make his attack; for he saw the walls were so firm, that it would be hard to overcome them; and that the valley before the walls was terrible; and that the temple, which was within that valley, was itself encompassed with a very strong wall, insomuch that if the city were taken, that temple would be a second place of refuge for the enemy to retire to.

Now as he was long in deliberating about this matter, a sedition arose among the people within the city; Aristobulus's party being willing to fight, and to set their king at liberty, while the party of Hyrcanus were for opening the gates to Pompey; and the dread people were in occasioned these last to be a very numerous party, when they looked upon the excellent order the Roman soldiers were in. So Aristobulus's party was worsted, and retired into the temple, and cut off the communication between the temple and the city, by breaking down the bridge that joined them together, and prepared to make an opposition to the

[287] Flavius Josephus, *Antiquities of the Jews* in *The Works of Flavius Josephus*, William Whiston, trans. (Grand Rapids: Baker, 1980) 14.4.1-5 [285-289].

utmost; but as the others had received the Romans into the city, and had delivered up the palace to him, Pompey sent Piso, one of his great officers, into that palace with an army, who distributed a garrison about the city, because he could not persuade any one of those that had fled to the temple to come to terms of accommodation; he then disposed all things that were round about them so as might favor their attacks, as having Hyrcanus' party very ready to afford them both counsel and assistance.

But Pompey himself filled up the ditch that was oil the north side of the temple, and the entire valley also, the army itself being obliged to carry the materials for that purpose. And indeed it was a hard thing to fill up that valley, by reason of its immense depth, especially as the Jews used all the means possible to repel them from their superior situation; nor had the Romans succeeded in their endeavors, had not Pompey taken notice of the seventh days, on which the Jews abstain from all sorts of work on a religious account, and raised his bank, but restrained his soldiers from fighting on those days; for the Jews only acted defensively on sabbath days. But as soon as Pompey had filled up the valley, he erected high towers upon the bank, and brought those engines which they had fetched from Tyre near to the wall, and tried to batter it down; and the slingers of stones beat off those that stood above them, and drove them away; but the towers on this side of the city made very great resistance, and were indeed extraordinary both for largeness and magnificence.

Now here it was that, upon the many hardships which the Romans underwent, Pompey could not but admire not only at the other instances of the Jews' fortitude, but especially that they did not at all intermit their religious services, even when they were encompassed with darts on all sides; for, as if the city were in full peace, their daily sacrifices and purifications, and every branch of their religious worship, was still performed to God with the utmost exactness. Nor indeed when the temple was actually taken, and they were every day slain about the altar, did they leave off the instances of their Divine worship that were appointed by their law; for it was in the third month of the siege before the Romans could even with great difficulty overthrow one of the towers, and get into the temple. Now he that first of all ventured to get over the wall, was Faustus Cornelius the son of Sylla; and next after him were two centurions, Furius and Fabius; and every one of these was followed by a cohort of his own, who encompassed the Jews on all sides, and slew them, some of them as they were running for shelter to the temple, and others as they, for a while, fought in their own defense.

And now did many of the priests, even when they saw their enemies assailing them with swords in their hands, without any disturbance, go on with their Divine worship, and were slain while they were offering their drink-offerings, and burning their incense, as preferring the duties about their worship to God before their own preservation. The greatest part of them were slain by their own countrymen, of the adverse faction, and an innumerable multitude threw themselves down precipices; nay, some there were who were so distracted among the insuperable difficulties they were under, that they set fire to the buildings that were near to the wall, and were burnt together with them. Now of the Jews were slain twelve thousand; but of the Romans very few were slain, but a greater number was wounded.

But there was nothing that affected the nation so much, in the calamities they were then under, as that their holy place, which had been hitherto seen by none, should be laid open to strangers; for Pompey, and those that were about him, went into the temple itself whither it was not lawful for any to enter but the high priest, and saw what was reposited therein, the candlestick with its lamps, and the table, and the pouring vessels, and the censers, all made entirely of gold, as also a great quantity of spices heaped together, with two thousand talents of sacred money. Yet did not he touch that money, nor anything else that was there reposited; but he commanded the ministers about the temple, the very next day after he had taken it, to cleanse it, and to perform their accustomed sacrifices. Moreover, he made Hyrcanus high priest, as one that not only in other respects had showed great alacrity, on his side, during the siege, but as he had been the means of hindering the multitude that was in the country from fighting for Aristobulus, which they were otherwise very ready to have done; by which means he acted the part of a good general, and reconciled the people to him more by benevolence than by terror. Now, among the Captives, Aristobulus's father-in-law was taken, who was also his uncle: so those that were the most guilty he punished with decollation; but rewarded Faustus, and those with him that had fought so bravely, with glorious presents, and laid a tribute upon the country, and upon Jerusalem itself.[288]

Section 6: Tacitus on Nero's Persecution

Cornelius Tacitus (AD 56-120) was a Roman historian who believed Christianity was a superstition, but nonetheless thought the arson charge leveled against Christians was wrong. In his *Annals* (which incidentally contains the earliest non-Christian reference to the crucifixion of Christ) he described Nero's persecution of the Christians following the great fire:

> The next thing was to seek means of propitiating the gods, and recourse was had to the Sibylline books, by the direction of which prayers were offered to Vulcanus, Ceres, and Proserpina Juno, too, was entreated by the matrons, first, in the Capitol, then on the nearest part of the coast, whence water was procured to sprinkle the fane and image of the goddess. And there were sacred banquets and nightly vigils celebrated by married women. But all human efforts, all the lavish gifts of the emperor, and the propitiations of the gods, did not banish the sinister belief that the conflagration was the result of an order. Consequently, to get rid of the report, Nero fastened the guilt and

[288] Flavius Josephus, *The Wars of the Jews* in *The Works of Flavius Josephus*, William Whiston, trans. (Grand Rapids: Baker, 1980), 1.7.1-6 [28-31].

> inflicted the most exquisite tortures on a class hated for their abominations, called Christians by the populace. Christus, from whom the name had its origin, suffered the extreme penalty during the reign of Tiberius at the hands of one of our procurators, Pontius Pilatus, and a most mischievous superstition, thus checked for the moment, again broke out not only in Judaea, the first source of the evil, but even in Rome, where all things hideous and shameful from every part of the world find their centre and become popular. Accordingly, an arrest was first made of all who pleaded guilty; then, upon their information, an immense multitude was convicted, not so much of the crime of firing the city, as of hatred against mankind. Mockery of every sort was added to their deaths. Covered with the skins of beasts, they were torn by dogs and perished, or were nailed to crosses, or were doomed to the flames and burnt, to serve as a nightly illumination, when daylight had expired. Nero offered his gardens for the spectacle, and was exhibiting a show in the circus, while he mingled with the people in the dress of a charioteer or stood aloft on a car. Hence, even for criminals who deserved extreme and exemplary punishment, there arose a feeling of compassion; for it was not, as it seemed, for the public good, but to glut one man's cruelty, that they were being destroyed.[289]

Section 7: The Temple

Now this temple, as I have already said, was built upon a strong hill. At first the plain at the top was hardly sufficient for the holy house and the altar, for the ground about it was very uneven, and like a precipice; but when king Solomon, who was the person that built the temple, had built a wall to it on its east side, there was then added one cloister founded on a bank cast up for it, and on the other parts the holy house stood naked. But in future ages the people added new banks, 12 and the hill became a larger plain. They then broke down the wall on the north side, and took in as much as sufficed afterward for the compass of the entire temple. And when they had built walls on three sides of the temple round about, from the bottom of the hill, and had performed a work that was greater than could be hoped for, [in which work long ages were spent by them, as well as all their sacred treasures were exhausted, which were still replenished by those tributes which were sent to God from the whole habitable earth,] they then encompassed their upper courts with cloisters, as well as they [afterward] did the lowest [court of the] temple. The lowest part of this was erected to the height of three hundred cubits, and in some places more; yet did not the entire depth of the foundations appear, for they brought earth, and filled up the valleys, as being desirous to make them on a level with the narrow streets of the city; wherein they made use of stones of forty cubits in magnitude; for the great plenty of money they then had, and the liberality of the people, made this attempt of theirs to succeed to an incredible degree; and what could not be so much as hoped for as

[289] Tacitus, *Annals* 15:44.

ever to be accomplished, was, by perseverance and length of time, brought to perfection.

Now for the works that were above these foundations, these were not unworthy of such foundations; for all the cloisters were double, and the pillars to them belonging were twenty-five cubits in height, and supported the cloisters. These pillars were of one entire stone each of them, and that stone was white marble; and the roofs were adorned with cedar, curiously graven. The natural magnificence, and excellent polish, and the harmony of the joints in these cloisters, afforded a prospect that was very remarkable; nor was it on the outside adorned with any work of the painter or engraver. The cloisters [of the outmost court] were in breadth thirty cubits, while the entire compass of it was by measure six furlongs, including the tower of Antonia; those entire courts that were exposed to the air were laid with stones of all sorts. When you go through these [first] cloisters, unto the second [court of the] temple, there was a partition made of stone all round, whose height was three cubits: its construction was very elegant; upon it stood pillars, at equal distances from one another, declaring the law of purity, some in Greek, and some in Roman letters, that "no foreigner should go within that sanctuary" for that second [court of the] temple was called "the Sanctuary," and was ascended to by fourteen steps from the first court. This court was four-square, and had a wall about it peculiar to itself; the height of its buildings, although it were on the outside forty cubits, 13 was hidden by the steps, and on the inside that height was but twenty-five cubits; for it being built over against a higher part of the hill with steps, it was no further to be entirely discerned within, being covered by the hill itself. Beyond these thirteen steps there was the distance of ten cubits; this was all plain; whence there were other steps, each of five cubits a-piece, that led to the gates, which gates on the north and south sides were eight, on each of those sides four, and of necessity two on the east. For since there was a partition built for the women on that side, as the proper place wherein they were to worship, there was a necessity for a second gate for them: this gate was cut out of its wall, over against the first gate. There was also on the other sides one southern and one northern gate, through which was a passage into the court of the women; for as to the other gates, the women were not allowed to pass through them; nor when they went through their own gate could they go beyond their own wall. This place was allotted to the women of our own country, and of other countries, provided they were of the same nation, and that equally. The western part of this court had no gate at all, but the wall was built entire on that side. But then the cloisters which were betwixt the gates extended from the wall inward, before the chambers; for they were supported by very fine and large pillars. These cloisters were single, and, excepting their magnitude, were no way inferior to those of the lower court.

Now nine of these gates were on every side covered over with gold and silver, as were the jambs of their doors and their lintels; but there was one gate that was without the [inward court of the] holy house, which was of Corinthian brass, and greatly excelled those that were only covered over with silver and gold.

Each gate had two doors, whose height was severally thirty cubits, and their breadth fifteen. However, they had large spaces within of thirty cubits, and had on each side rooms, and those, both in breadth and in length, built like towers, and their height was above forty cubits. Two pillars did also support these rooms, and were in circumference twelve cubits. Now the magnitudes of the other gates were equal one to another; but that over the Corinthian gate, which opened on the east over against the gate of the holy house itself, was much larger; for its height was fifty cubits; and its doors were forty cubits; and it was adorned after a most costly manner, as having much richer and thicker plates of silver and gold upon them than the other. These nine gates had that silver and gold poured upon them by Alexander, the father of Tiberius. Now there were fifteen steps, which led away from the wall of the court of the women to this greater gate; whereas those that led thither from the other gates were five steps shorter.

As to the holy house itself, which was placed in the midst [of the inmost court], that most sacred part of the temple, it was ascended to by twelve steps; and in front its height and its breadth were equal, and each a hundred cubits, though it was behind forty cubits narrower; for on its front it had what may be styled shoulders on each side, that passed twenty cubits further. Its first gate was seventy cubits high, and twenty-five cubits broad; but this gate had no doors; for it represented the universal visibility of heaven, and that it cannot be excluded from any place. Its front was covered with gold all over, and through it the first part of the house, that was more inward, did all of it appear; which, as it was very large, so did all the parts about the more inward gate appear to shine to those that saw them; but then, as the entire house was divided into two parts within, it was only the first part of it that was open to our view. Its height extended all along to ninety cubits in height, and its length was fifty cubits, and its breadth twenty. But that gate which was at this end of the first part of the house was, as we have already observed, all over covered with gold, as was its whole wall about it; it had also golden vines above it, from which clusters of grapes hung as tall as a man's height. But then this house, as it was divided into two parts, the inner part was lower than the appearance of the outer, and had golden doors of fifty-five cubits altitude, and sixteen in breadth; but before these doors there was a veil of equal largeness with the doors. It was a Babylonian curtain, embroidered with blue, and fine linen, and scarlet, and purple, and of a contexture that was truly wonderful. Nor was this mixture of colors without its mystical interpretation, but was a kind of image of the universe; for by the scarlet there seemed to be enigmatically signified fire, by the fine flax the earth, by the blue the air, and by the purple the sea; two of them having their colors the foundation of this resemblance; but the fine flax and the purple have their own origin for that foundation, the earth producing the one, and the sea the other. This curtain had also embroidered upon it all that was mystical in the heavens, excepting that of the [twelve] signs, representing living creatures.

When any persons entered into the temple, its floor received them. This part of the temple therefore was in height sixty cubits, and its length the same;

whereas its breadth was but twenty cubits: but still that sixty cubits in length was divided again, and the first part of it was cut off at forty cubits, and had in it three things that were very wonderful and famous among all mankind, the candlestick, the table [of shew-bread], and the altar of incense. Now the seven lamps signified the seven planets; for so many there were springing out of the candlestick. Now the twelve loaves that were upon the table signified the circle of the zodiac and the year; but the altar of incense, by its thirteen kinds of sweet-smelling spices with which the sea replenished it, signified that God is the possessor of all things that are both in the uninhabitable and habitable parts of the earth, and that they are all to be dedicated to his use. But the inmost part of the temple of all was of twenty cubits. This was also separated from the outer part by a veil. In this there was nothing at all. It was inaccessible and inviolable, and not to be seen by any; and was called the Holy of Holies. Now, about the sides of the lower part of the temple, there were little houses, with passages out of one into another; there were a great many of them, and they were of three stories high; there were also entrances on each side into them from the gate of the temple. But the superior part of the temple had no such little houses any further, because the temple was there narrower, and forty cubits higher, and of a smaller body than the lower parts of it. Thus we collect that the whole height, including the sixty cubits from the floor, amounted to a hundred cubits.

Now the outward face of the temple in its front wanted nothing that was likely to surprise either men's minds or their eyes; for it was covered all over with plates of gold of great weight, and, at the first rising of the sun, reflected back a very fiery splendor, and made those who forced themselves to look upon it to turn their eyes away, just as they would have done at the sun's own rays. But this temple appeared to strangers, when they were coming to it at a distance, like a mountain covered with snow; for as to those parts of it that were not gilt, they were exceeding white. On its top it had spikes with sharp points, to prevent any pollution of it by birds sitting upon it. Of its stones, some of them were forty-five cubits in length, five in height, and six in breadth. Before this temple stood the altar, fifteen cubits high, and equal both in length and breadth; each of which dimensions was fifty cubits. The figure it was built in was a square, and it had corners like horns; and the passage up to it was by an insensible acclivity. It was formed without any iron tool, nor did any such iron tool so much as touch it at any time. There was also a wall of partition, about a cubit in height, made of fine stones, and so as to be grateful to the sight; this encompassed the holy house and the altar, and kept the people that were on the outside off from the priests. Moreover, those that had the gonorrhea and the leprosy were excluded out of the city entirely; women also, when their courses were upon them, were shut out of the temple; nor when they were free from that impurity, were they allowed to go beyond the limit before-mentioned; men also, that were not thoroughly pure, were prohibited to come into the inner [court of the] temple; nay, the priests themselves that were not pure were prohibited to come into it also.

Now all those of the stock of the priests that could not minister by reason of some defect in their bodies, came within the partition, together with those that had no such imperfection, and had their share with them by reason of their stock, but still made use of none except their own private garments; for nobody but he that officiated had on his sacred garments; but then those priests that were without any blemish upon them went up to the altar clothed in fine linen. They abstained chiefly from wine, out of this fear, lest otherwise they should transgress some rules of their ministration. The high priest did also go up with them; not always indeed, but on the seventh days and new moons, and if any festivals belonging to our nation, which we celebrate every year, happened. When he officiated, he had on a pair of breeches that reached beneath his privy parts to his thighs, and had on an inner garment of linen, together with a blue garment, round, without seam, with fringe work, and reaching to the feet. There were also golden bells that hung upon the fringes, and pomegranates intermixed among them. The bells signified thunder, and the pomegranates lightning. But that girdle that tied the garment to the breast was embroidered with five rows of various colors, of gold, and purple, and scarlet, as also of fine linen and blue, with which colors we told you before the veils of the temple were embroidered also. The like embroidery was upon the ephod; but the quantity of gold therein was greater. Its figure was that of a stomacher for the breast. There were upon it two golden buttons like small shields, which buttoned the ephod to the garment; in these buttons were enclosed two very large and very excellent sardonyxes, having the names of the tribes of that nation engraved upon them: on the other part there hung twelve stones, three in a row one way, and four in the other; a sardius, a topaz, and an emerald; a carbuncle, a jasper, and a sapphire; an agate, an amethyst, and a ligure; an onyx, a beryl, and a chrysolite; upon every one of which was again engraved one of the forementioned names of the tribes. A mitre also of fine linen encompassed his head, which was tied by a blue ribbon, about which there was another golden crown, in which was engraven the sacred name [of God]: it consists of four vowels. However, the high priest did not wear these garments at other times, but a more plain habit; he only did it when he went into the most sacred part of the temple, which he did but once in a year, on that day when our custom is for all of us to keep a fast to God. And thus much concerning the city and the temple; but for the customs and laws hereto relating, we shall speak more accurately another time; for there remain a great many things thereto relating which have not been here touched upon.

Now as to the tower of Antonia, it was situated at the corner of two cloisters of the court of the temple; of that on the west, and that on the north; it was erected upon a rock of fifty cubits in height, and was on a great precipice; it was the work of king Herod, wherein he demonstrated his natural magnanimity. In the first place, the rock itself was covered over with smooth pieces of stone, from its foundation, both for ornament, and that any one who would either try to get up or to go down it might not be able to hold his feet upon it. Next to this, and before you come to the edifice of the tower itself, there was a wall three cubits high; but within that wall all the space of the tower of Antonia itself was built upon, to the height of forty cubits. The inward parts had the largeness and form of a palace, it being parted into all kinds of rooms and other conveniences, such as courts, and places for bathing, and broad spaces for camps; insomuch that, by having all conveniences that cities wanted, it might seem to be composed of several cities, but by its magnificence it seemed a palace. And as the entire structure resembled that of a tower, it contained also four other distinct towers at its four corners; whereof the others were but fifty cubits high; whereas that which lay upon the southeast corner was seventy cubits high, that from thence the whole temple might be viewed; but on the corner where it joined to the two cloisters of the temple, it had passages down to them both, through which the guard [for there always lay in this tower a Roman legion] went several ways among the cloisters, with their arms, on the Jewish festivals, in order to watch the people, that they might not there attempt to make any innovations; for the temple was a fortress that guarded the city, as was the tower of Antonia a guard to the temple; and in that tower were the guards of those three 14. There was also a peculiar fortress belonging to the upper city, which was Herod's palace; but for the hill Bezetha, it was divided from the tower Antonia, as we have already told you; and as that hill on which the tower of Antonia stood was the highest of these three, so did it adjoin to the new city, and was the only place that hindered the sight of the temple on the north. And this shall suffice at present to have spoken about the city and the walls about it, because I have proposed to myself to make a more accurate description of it elsewhere.[290]

Section 8: Herod's Last Days

After that the end came rapidly. On his return from Callirhoe, feeling his death approaching, the King had summoned the noblest of Israel throughout the land to Jericho, and shut them up in the Hippodrome, with orders to his sister to have them slain immediately upon his death, in the grim hope that the joy of the people at his decease would thus be changed into mourning. Five days before his death one ray of passing joy lighted his couch. Terrible to say, it was caused by a letter from Augustus allowing Herod to execute his son Antipater—the false accuser and real murderer of his half-brothers Alexander and Aristobulus. The death of the wretched prince was hastened by his attempt to bribe the jailer, as the noise in the palace, caused by an attempted suicide of Herod, led him to suppose his father was actually dead. And now the terrible drama was hastening to a close. The fresh access of rage shortened the life which was already running out. Five days more, and the terror of Judæa lay dead. He had reigned thirty-seven years—thirty-four since his conquest of Jerusalem. Soon the rule for which he had so long plotted, striven, and stained himself with untold crimes, passed from his descendants...It need scarcely be said, that Salome (Herod's sister) and her husband were too wise to execute Herod's direction in regard to the noble Jews

[290] Flavius Josephus, *The Jewish Wars*, in *The Works of Flavius Josephus*, William Whiston, trans. (Grand Rapids: Baker, 1980), 5.5.1-8 [372-379].

shut up in the Hippodrome. Their liberation, and the death of Herod, were marked by the leaders of the people as joyous events.[291]

But now Herod's distemper greatly increased upon him after a severe manner, and this by God's judgment upon him for his sins; for a fire glowed in him slowly, which did not so much appear to the touch outwardly, as it augmented his pains inwardly; for it brought upon him a vehement appetite to eating, which he could not avoid to supply with one sort of food or other. His entrails were also ex-ulcerated, and the chief violence of his pain lay on his colon; an aqueous and transparent liquor also had settled itself about his feet, and a like matter afflicted him at the bottom of his belly. Nay, further, his privy-member was putrefied, and produced worms; and when he sat upright, he had a difficulty of breathing, which was very loathsome, on account of the stench of his breath, and the quickness of its returns; he had also convulsions in all parts of his body, which increased his strength to an insufferable degree. It was said by those who pretended to divine, and who were endued with wisdom to foretell such things, that God inflicted this punishment on the king on account of his great impiety; yet was he still in hopes of recovering, though his afflictions seemed greater than anyone could bear.[292]

Section 9: Archelaus' Slaughter

Now, upon the approach of that feast of unleavened bread which the law of their fathers had appointed for the Jews at this time, which feast is called the Passover, and is a memorial of their deliverance out of Egypt (when they offer sacrifices with great alacrity; and when they are required to slay more sacrifices in number than at any other festival; (214) and when an innumerable multitude came thither out of the country, nay, from beyond its limits also, in order to worship God), the seditious lamented Judas and Matthias, those teachers of the laws, and kept together in the temple, and had plenty of food, because these seditious persons were not ashamed to get it. (215) And as Archelaus was afraid lest some terrible thing should spring up by means of these men's madness, he sent a regiment of armed men, and with them a captain of a thousand, to suppress the violent efforts of the seditious, before the whole multitude should be infected with the like madness; and gave them this charge, that if they found any much more openly seditious than others, and more busy in tumultuous practices, they should bring them to him. (216) But those that were seditious on account of those teachers of the law, irritated the people by the noise and clamors they used to encourage the people in their designs; so they made an assault upon the soldiers, and came up to them, and stoned the greatest part of them, although some of them ran away wounded, and their captain among them; and when they had thus done, they returned to the sacrifices which were already in their hands. (217) Now Archelaus thought there was no way to preserve the entire government, but by

---

[291] Alfred Edersheim, *The Life and Times of Jesus the Messiah* (Grand Rapids: Eerdmans, 1980), 1:218-219.

[292] Flavius Josephus, *Antiquities of the Jews*, *The Works of Flavius Josephus*, William Whiston, trans. (Grand Rapids: Baker, 1980), 17.6.5 (495).

cutting off those who made this attempt upon it; so he sent out the whole army upon them, and sent the horsemen to prevent those that had their tents without the temple, from assisting those that were within the temple, and to kill such as ran away from the footmen when they thought themselves out of danger; (218) which horsemen slew three thousand men, while the rest went to the neighboring mountains.[293]

Section 10: Illness[294]

Comparative evidence for preindustrial societies suggests that the average life expectancy at birth in the Roman world was twenty to thirty years. Infant mortality was high, with a quarter or more of those born not surviving their first year and perhaps only a half living beyond the age of ten. Those who did survive childhood diseases and the rigors of their upbringing faced a somewhat less hazardous future and could expect to live to the age of fifty or longer, their chance of longevity improving the farther they lived from the city, any city, for in the cities disease of every kind was endemic. But no one was ever safe from the threat of disease or sickness or accident. And those affected by such disasters found little help. There were medical schools and some skilled doctors, but such doctors were not accessible to most people. Many, in desperation, resorted to practitioners who were doctors in name only, "charlatans with a…smattering of superstitious medical knowledge," like the cobbler in Phaedrus's tale, who was so incompetent with his needle that no one entrusted him with their shoes, but so persuasive with his tongue that people let him do what he would with their bodies. But for most people (for better or for worse) there were no doctors at all. "There are thousands," writes Pliny, "who live without doctors, but do not live without medicine." They used remedies that had been passed down from father to son and were largely herbal in nature, derived from leaves, roots, and the like, and from bread (a common ingredient in these ancient potions)—medicines that sometimes proved to be fatal to a patient who might otherwise have survived and recovered!

At birth, the Roman child was regarded as barely human and as something that needed yet to be formed: such formation was especially important in the case of a boy. For the first few months the baby was imprisoned in its cradle, wrapped in swaddling bands tied particularly tight around its elbows, wrists, knees, hips, and ankles. Its hands were kept open and splints were used to keep its legs straight. Its arms were strapped straight against its body. After two months of this regime, the bands were loosed a little, and the right hand was freed to ensure that the child grew up right-handed. It was bathed only in cold water, and at bath time, its various parts were manipulated in an attempt to give them the desired shape,

[293] Flavius Josephus, *Antiquities of the Jews*, *The Works of Flavius Josephus*, William Whiston, trans. (Grand Rapids: Baker, 1980), 17.9.3 (502-503).

[294] This section consists of excerpts from David Williams, *Paul's Metaphors: Their Context and Character* (Peabody, MA: Hendrickson Publishers, 1999), 86-87.

including kneading the head and stretching the foreskin. Bath time was never popular with Roman children!

But no one was ever safe from the threat of disease or sickness or accident. It is difficult to ascertain the diseases to which the ancient world was prone. The Romans seem to have been mainly subject to eye infections (which they treated with ointments), stomachaches, skin diseases, and summer and autumn fevers. Insomnia was also a problem.

They used remedies that had been passed down from father to son and were largely herbal in nature." Traditionally, in both Greek and Roman circles, the *paterfamilias* prepared the medicines for the entire household, including women, children, and slaves. In the *Il.* 2.728-733, Homer mentions the two sons of Asclepius (the renowned healer) among those assembled for the attack on Troy and notes that they were "both good healers themselves," for Asclepius, like any father, had bequeathed to them his medical knowledge. Similarly, Cato was the latest custodian of a medical tradition passed on from father to son. Deeply suspicious of professional doctors, all of whom were Greeks in his time, he believed that they were out to poison the people. He looked after his own household with advice culled from a huge book—which had long been in his family—about medical treatments (see Pliny, *Nat.* 29.4-16). He treated sciatica, for example, with juniper wood wine (Cato, *Agr.* 123) and always kept a pomegranate extract at the ready to combat colic and worms. But best of all was cabbage. It aided digestion, facilitated urination, made a powerful diuretic, and emetic, and a cure for colic. As a poultice it could heal ulcers, open sores generally, and dispel any tumor. It was good for infected wounds. Eating it could soothe most aches and pains. Fried in hot fat and taken on an empty stomach, it helped to induce sleep. Dried, it could be taken as snuff. Its juice, dropped into the ears, was a sure cure for deafness. Incantations generally accompanied the treatment and might even be used on their own (see Horace, *Ep.* 1.1.36-37). Cato had an astonishing procedure for healing dislocations and fractures.

Paul had some medical advice to give as a "father" to his "son." "Stop drinking water," he said, and take "a little wine for the sake of your stomach" (1 Tim 5:23). He was speaking to Timothy, who (it seems from Paul's evidence) was frequently ill. Paul appears to have attributed Timothy's condition to the water supply, which in Ephesus was as likely a cause as any. In 2 Cor 12:7 he speaks of a "thorn in [his] flesh." In Eph 5:27, he speaks of Christ as presenting his bride (the church) to himself "free from spot." A "spot" could refer to a minor blemish, or it could apply to the symptoms of certain conditions (for example, venereal diseases) that were regarded as the result of divine retribution. "Wrinkle" could also refer to such diseases or to leprosy or to the aftermath of major surgery. Neither term, as used in Eph 5:27, merely describes the outcome of old age. Longevity is not the issue, but the defilement of sin and its purification.

Ephesus was an ancient and decaying city. Its harbor was silting up, and a sewage system is often the first casualty in such an event. This, in turn, can lead to pollutants infiltrating the groundwater in wells (although Greek and Roman cities took as much of their water as possible from natural springs). So disease spreads. Moreover, we know that in Rome lead piping was used for reticulation and that this was the cause of poisoning. This, too, could have been a source of Timothy's problems. See E.M. Blaiklock, *The World of the New Testament* (London: Ark, 1981), 25.

Section 11: Abortion in the Ancient World[295]

Abortion was not uncommon. Because the fetus was not considered to be a person until it was born (it was regarded as a part of the maternal viscera), abortion was not illegal in Roman law (in Greek law it was). That is not to say that everyone approved of the practice. In fact, a number of attempts were made to restrain it. But it appears to have flourished at all levels of society. Contraception was practiced by both chemical and mechanical means, the simplest being the "pagan custom" of washing after sexual intercourse. A vase decorated with reliefs found in Lyons shows a man carrying a pitcher of water to a couple busily occupied in bed. If contraception failed, many of the same potions recommended in that connection, together with other expedients, were applied in the attempt to procure an abortion.

The physician Soranus, writing in the early second century CE, prescribed exercise: walking, riding jumping, and carrying loads. Failing this (or as an alternative), various concoctions could be taken to bring on menstruation. "Laxatives are helpful," he suggested, "as well as pungent clysters [enemas]." He recommended bathing in a decoction of herbs and then applying a herbal poultice. If the pregnancy persisted, more drastic treatments, such as bleeding" and the use of suppositories, were employed. Another physician, Dioscorides, writing a little earlier than Soranus, has many of the same prescriptions. And they seem to have worked, so that abortions were very much a fact of life (or of death) in the ancient world, but at what cost in the lives and the health of women we cannot tell.

Paul has a metaphor of abortion in 1 Cor 15:8. He was speaking of Jesus' postresurrection appearances, of which the appearance to him was the last. "He appeared," he says, "to James, then to all of the apostles, and last of all, to me, as to *an abortion*." To be precise, he speaks of himself here as "*the* abortion" (*to ektromati*), as though he were the only one to whom such a name could properly be applied. In the light of verse 9, he may have been using the word as an expression of his disgust at what he had once been, a persecutor of the church. Or he may have been echoing an epithet coined for him by others—his Jewish or even his Jewish Christian opponents—as a term of abuse, the article indication something that was commonly said: that "abortion of a man," as they call me. Or he may have been thinking of his lack (compared with the others named in 1 Cor 15) of a proper "period of gestation" in becoming what he now was, a leader in

[295] This section consists of excerpts from David Williams, *Paul's Metaphors: Their Context and Character* (Peabody, MA: Hendrickson Publishers, 1999), 57-58.

the church, an apostle. But Paul had received none of these advantages. His glimpse of the risen Christ had torn him, so to speak, like an aborted fetus, unformed, unprepared, from what he had been to what he became.

Section 12: Roman Marriage

> On the day fixed for the wedding the bride, whose hair had been imprisoned the night before in a crimson net, put on the costume which custom dictated: a tunic woven in the ancient way (tunica recta), secured round the waist by a knotted girdle of wool (*cingulum herculeum*). Over this she wore a cloak or *palla* of saffron colour; on her feet sandals of the same shade; round her neck a metal collar. Her coiffure was protected by six pads of artificial hair (*seni crines*) separated by narrow bands, such as the Vestals wore during the whole period of their service; and over it she wore a veil of flaming orange—hence called the *flammeum*—which modestly covered the upper part of her face. On top of the veil was placed a wreath, woven simply of verbena and sweet marjoram in the time of Caesar and Augustus, and later of myrtle and orange blossom. After she was duly dressed she stood amid her own people and welcomed her groom, his family, and friends. Everyone then adjourned either to a neighbouring sanctuary, or into the atrium of the house to offer a sacrifice to the gods. After the animal sacrifice had been consummated—sometimes a ewe, rarely an ox, most often a pig—the auspex and the witnesses played their part. The witnesses, probably ten in number, selected from the circles of the two contracting parties, played a silent role and simply affixed their seal to the marriage contract. The drawing up of a contract was not obligatory, however. The auspex, on the other hand, was indispensable. His untranslatable title indicated that he fulfilled the function of a personal, family augur without sacerdotal investiture and without official appointment. After examining the entrails, he gave his guarantee that the auspices were favourable. Without this, the marriage would have been disapproved by the gods and invalid. As soon as he had solemnly made his pronouncement amid respectful silence, the couple exchanged their mutual vows in his presence…This concluded the marriage rite and the guests burst into congratulations and good wishes.[296]

[296] Jerome Carcopino, *Daily Life in Ancient Rome* (NY: Bantam, 1971), 91-92.

Section 13: Divorce and Remarriage[297]

Introduction

My [Brewer] overall conclusions on all the biblical material are:

- Both Jesus and Paul condemned divorce without valid grounds and discouraged divorce even for valid grounds
- Both Jesus and Paul affirmed the OT grounds for divorce
- The OT allowed divorce for adultery and for neglect or abuse
- Both Jesus and Paul condemned remarriage after an invalid divorce, but not after a valid divorce

The Ancient Near East

Marriage in the ANE was contractual, involving payments, agreed stipulations, and penalties. If either partner broke the stipulations of the contract, the innocent partner could opt for a divorce and keep the dowry. Exact parallels to these practices are found in the Pentateuch.

The Pentateuch

The Law of Moses was different from the rest of the ANE with regard to the rights of women in marriage and divorce. They had greater rights within marriage, and a greater opportunity to remarry after divorce. The divorce certificate, which gave women the right to remarry, was unknown elsewhere in the ANE.

The Later Prophets

Malachi's criticism of divorce is directed at those who cause the divorce by breaking their vows

Intertestamental Period

There was an increase in both the rights of women and the security of marriages within Judaism. Polygamy and divorce were starting to be criticized. Outside Judaism, divorce became easier to initiate by both men and women.

---

[297] The literature on this subject is immense. In working through the material both biblical and extra-biblical, the writer is in the most substantial agreement with David Instone-Brewer (*Divorce and Remarriage in the Bible: The Social and Literary Context* [Grand Rapids: Eerdmans, 2002]). Brewer's summary statements from his work are included in this section. The writer has either cited Brewer directly or attempted to replicate his points as accurately as possible. The reader is encouraged to work through the various volumes, key biblical texts, and religious/cultural backgrounds to come to a conclusion. In addition to the plethora of articles on the subject, other works include: William Heth and Gordon Wenham, *Jesus and Divorce* (London: Hodder and Stoughton), 1984; J. Carl Laney, *The Divorce Myth* (Minneapolis: Bethany House), 1981; Guy Duty, *Divorce & Remarriage* (Minneapolis: Bethany House), 1983; John Murray, *Divorce* (Phillipsburg, NJ: Presbyterian and Reformed), 1961; *Divorce and Remarriage: Four Christian Views*, Wayne House, ed (Downers Grove: InterVarsity), 1990; Craig Keener, *...And Marries Another* (Peabody, MA: Hendrickson), 1991.

Rabbinic Teaching

The rabbis agreed that the grounds for divorce were childlessness, material neglect, emotional neglect, and unfaithfulness. Divorce was generally regarded as undesirable but sometimes necessary. Remarriage was generally accepted, but if it followed an invalid divorce, it was treated as adultery.

Divorce in the rabbinic world of the first century could be based on the grounds of infertility, sexual unfaithfulness, or material and emotional neglect. Women were able to ask a court to persuade their husbands to divorce them if they suffered neglect. The Hillelites also allowed groundless divorces by interpreting Deut. 24:1 as "any matter," but the Shammaites (and Jesus) said that "any matter" divorces were invalid. There was little stigma attached to divorce, and remarriage after a divorce was expected, though remarriage after an invalid divorce was considered to be adultery in a literal sense.

Jesus' Teaching

The Pharisees came to Jesus to test him and asked "is it lawful for a man to divorce his wife [for any matter—Deut. 24:1] according to the Hillelite interpretation? He answered that from the beginning of creation the two were made one flesh and should not be separated. They responded: why then did Moses command to give a certificate of divorce? He answered: what did Moses command you? They said that Moses commanded a man to write a certificate of divorce and to put her away. But Jesus said: for the hardness of your heart he wrote you this command. Moses allowed you to divorce but from the beginning it was not to be. In the house, the disciples asked him again about this matter. He said: whoever divorces his wife [except for the matter of indecency—Deut. 24:1] and marries another commits adultery against her; and if she divorces her husband [except for indecency] and marries another, she commits adultery.

And Pharisees came up and in order to test him asked: Is it lawful for a man to divorce his wife on the grounds of "any matte" as the Hillelites say? Jesus answered: have you not read that in the beginning of creation men could marry only one woman? These verses (Gen. 1:27; 2:24) show that God made them, so it is God who joins them and makes them one flesh. Therefore if God has joined them together, neither of them should divorce the other. The Pharisees replied: but if they should not divorce, then why did Moses command a husband to give a certificate of divorce to an adulteress and to put her away? He answered them: Moses did not command this, but he allowed it. He allowed it in the situation of stubborn hardness of heart. But this is not what God wanted from the beginning. Later in private, the disciples asked him again about this matter. And Jesus said to them, if a man divorces his wife for any matter and not for a matter of indecency (the correct interpretation of Deut. 24:1), he does not have a valid divorce. If he then marries another woman, he is committing adultery, because he is still married to his first wife. Similarly, if a woman forces her husband to divorce her for any matter and not for a matter of indecency, and she marries another, she is also committing adultery.

Jesus was teaching six specific things:

1. **Monogamy**: an individual can be married to only one person at a time.
2. **Marriage should be lifelong**: it is against God's will to break up a marriage. Many Rabbis were already teaching that marriage should be lifelong, but they also allowed divorce for any matter.
3. **Divorce is not compulsory**: even in cases of adultery.
4. **Divorce is allowable**: if there is a stubborn refusal to stop committing adultery.
5. **Marriage is not compulsory**: so infertility is not a ground for divorce.
6. **Divorce for "any matter" is invalid**: and so remarriage after this divorce is adulterous.

Paul's Teaching

Paul was aware of Jesus' teaching on divorce and agreed with it, though he was addressing a different problem. The Corinthians lived under Roman law where men and women could divorce their partners by separating from them. Paul told the Corinthians that Christians should not divorce in this way, and that they should never cause a divorce. However, if they were divorced by a non-Christian who refused to be reconciled, they were free to remarry, though they must marry a Christian. He also pointed out that their circumstances made it an inopportune time for them to marry, for practical reasons.

In the Greco-Roman world divorce by separation was practiced. Paul forbade this kind of separation and reminded them of their marital obligations. Paul had to face the problem of those who had been divorced against their will by separation. He decided to apply a pragmatic solution and declare that such divorces are valid, so that the believer is free to remarry. A widow can also remarry without worrying about levirate marriage (she can marry whomsoever she wills). However, Paul advised all who were unmarried to remain single during the "present crisis" (probably a famine), presumably because it would be difficult to support a family.

Spouses whose partners deserted them against their will had a right to divorce because of the neglect of the marital obligations. However, it is clear that Paul would have counseled caution in the use of these grounds for divorce, as contemporary Jews did. In the end, however, when believers tried reconciliation and failed, Paul said that they were free to accept that the marriage had ended, and (by implication) they were free to remarry. A believer should never cause a divorce, but if the marriage ends despite his best efforts, he or she is entitled to divorce and is free to remarry.

Section 14: Socially Acceptable Homosexuality in the Ancient World[298]

Pederasty was the most common male homosexual act in the ancient world. That is because sexual propriety was judged according to social values: "The

---

[298] Excerpts taken from: David Garland, *1 Corinthians* Baker Exegetical Commentary on the New Testament (Grand Rapids: Baker, 2003), 217-218.

ancients did not classify kinds of sexual desire or behavior according to the sameness or difference of the sexes of the persons who engaged in a sexual act; rather, they evaluated sexual acts according to the degree to which such acts either violated or conformed to the norms of conduct deemed appropriate to individual sexual actors by reason of their gender, age, and social status." A person's rank and status determined what was considered acceptable or unacceptable. On one side were free males; on the other side were women and slaves. A free male was free to choose women, men, or boys as sexual objects without the majority taking offense as long as he did not demean his status as a free male. A free male could not "indulge in passive acts of love like a woman or a slave" without incurring a stigma. But he could use boys, slaves, or persons of no account with impunity as long as he remained "on top." "Phallic insertion functioned as a marker of male precedence; it also expressed social domination and seniority...Any sexual relation that involved the penetration of a social inferior (whether inferior in age, gender, or status) qualified as sexually normal for a male, irrespective of the penetrated person's anatomical sex, whereas to *be* sexually penetrated was always potentially shaming, especially for a free male of citizen status [e.g., Tacitus, *Annales* 11.36]." Homosexual acts between free males were regarded with contempt because one partner would have to take on the passive role (insertivity) suited only to women and slaves. We see this cultural attitude manifested in Petronius's novel, *Satyricon* (91-100). Two close friends, Encolpius and Ascyltus, fight over sexual favors of their slave boy, Giton; but they never engage in any homosexual act between themselves.

It should be noted also that "neither sexual desire nor sexual pleasure represented an acceptable motive for a boy's compliance with the sexual demands of his lover." The younger partner was not to be motivated by, or express, passionate sexual desire for his senior lover, lest he compromise his own future status as a man. As a result, sexually receptive or effeminate males were ridiculed. Society would have considered same-sex sexual acts between two men of equal standing to be shameful. What some in modern society find acceptable—male same-sex eroticism between equals in a committed relationship—would have been condemned in ancient society. Penetration was not regarded as an expression of love but "as an aggressive act demonstrating the superiority of the active to the passive partner."

Section 15: Paul's Athletic Allusions[299]

The Pauline corpus is laden with doctrinal truth and exhortations to Christian living based on that truth. One of Paul's favorite methods for applying and illustrating Christian responsibility is through the use of athletic metaphors. For example, he uses words for "running" and the race" on numerous occasions (Acts 13:25; 20:24; Rom. 9:16; 1 Cor. 9:24; Gal. 2:2; 5:7; Phil. 2:16; 2 Thess. 3:1; 2

[299] Jerry Hullinger, "The Historical Background of Paul's Athletic Allusions," *Bibliotheca Sacra* 161:643 (2004) 343-359. Portions used by permission.

Tim. 4:7). In addition, he refers to other sports such as boxing (1 Cor. 9:26) and wrestling (Eph. 6:12). Besides references to specific sports, Paul also uses words which would have conjured up images of the games in his readers' minds. These include such words as "prize" (1 Cor. 9:24), "crown" (1 Cor. 9:25), "goal" (Phil. 3:14), being disqualified (1 Cor. 9:27), "strive lawfully" (2 Tim. 2:5), and the giving of the crown by the righteous judge (2 Tim. 4:8).

It is clear from the above examples that a large part of Paul's admonitions are bound closely with athletic imagery from the first century during which time he and his readers lived. Therefore, it is evident that if the full impact of the Apostle's words are to be felt, there must be some understanding of this part of his historical milieu.[300]

The Olympic Games[301]

The king of athletic contests was the Olympic Games. Founded in 776 B.C., these games were held every four years. In 472 B.C. the Olympics were extended to a length of five days. The first day was occupied with sacrifices to the gods, general activity, and the taking of the oaths by the judges and competitors. The second morning began with the naming of the competitors by the herald, and was followed by chariot races, horse races, and the pentathlon for men. Contests for boys were held on the third day. On the fourth day the men's games in foot racing, jumping, wrestling, boxing, and the pankration were held. The final day of the games was spent in sacrifices and an evening banquet where the victors were entertained.

The Other Crown Games

In addition to the Olympic Games, many other athletic contests were spawned. Papalas noted that "the Isthmian, Pythian, Nemean, Panathenaean and many lesser athletic festivals were established. Greeks who had not been able to afford trips to Olympia could now see first rate athletics in the vicinity of their own polis."[302]

The Isthmian Games

For the purpose of this study, an understanding of the Isthmian Games is the most crucial. This is due to the fact that they were held in Corinth, and form the backdrop for the central passage 1 Corinthians 9:24-27. Concerning the

---

[300] Though not exhaustive, the key New Testament passages are 1 Corinthians 9:24-27; 2 Timothy 2:5; 4:7-8. A word of caution is also apropos at the beginning of this study. One must resist the temptation when dealing with any theme of foisting that theme on passages where it does not belong. This is true of the theme in this article; however, the number of athletic allusions in Paul are so numerous, that this data must at least be considered in interpretation.

[301] This material regarding the Olympics is taken from Frederick Wright, "Olympic Games," in *The Oxford Classical Dictionary* (Oxford: Clarendon, 1949), 621.

[302] A. Papalas, "The Development of Greek Boxing," *The Ancient World* 9 (1984), 74. For a summary of the four major crown games, see Waldo Sweet, *Sport and Recreation in Ancient Greece*, (NY: Oxford, 1987), 573.

mythology behind the origin of these games, Pausanias wrote: "The story about the Molourian Rock is that Ino threw herself into the sea from it, holding the younger of her sons, named Melikertes; her husband had killed her older son Learchus. They say that they the body of Melikertes was carried to the Isthmus of Corinth by a dolphin. Among the other honors which were given to Melikertes, whose name was changed to Palaimon, was the establishment of the Isthmian Games in his honor."[303]

The games themselves were one of the great festivals of the ancient world and ranked only below the Olympic Games in magnitude. Broneer offered this description of their splendor:

> Corinth played host to the athletes and visitors at the Isthmian Games celebrated every other year. Next to the Olympic Games, which were held every four years, the celebrations at the Isthmia were the most splendid and best attended of all the national festivals of Greece. Preparation for these events occupied the attention of the citizens several months in advance, and when the throngs arrived to view the contests in the Isthmian stadium, the vendors and entertainers from Corinth were on hand to reap profit from the occasion.[304]

Thus it can be seen that this festival drew thousands of people, both as competitors and spectators, from all over the empire. Further, the greater athletes were honored in Isthmia itself by monuments, statues, and inscriptions.[305] The glory of this spectacle is further illustrated by the sanctuary dedicated to Poseidon at Isthmia. Pausanias, in his guidebook to Greece, noted that the Isthmus belongs to Poseidon. In addition, he wrote: "Worth seeing here are a theatre and a white marble stadium. "Within the sanctuary of the god stand on the one side portrait statues of athletes who have won victories at the Isthmian games, on the other side pine trees growing in a row, the greater number of them arising up straight."[306]

Concerning the games themselves, they consisted of foot races, horse races, chariot contests, jumping wrestling, boxing, and throwing of the discus and

[303] Pausanias, *Description of Greece*, (Cambridge, MA: Harvard, 1978), 1.44.11. Likewise, Broneer wrote that "The Isthmian Games were dedicated to Poseidon, the pagan god of the sea, and to the boy-god Palaimon" (Oscar Broneer, "The Apostle Paul and the Isthmian Games," *The Biblical Archaeologist* 25 (1962), 2; see also Sweet, *Sport and Recreation in Ancient Greece,* 7-8; *The Oxford Classical Dictionary*, "Isthmia," by Frederick Wright, 461. While this was the legend adopted by the Corinthians, Wright also described the myth held to by the Athenians.

[304] Oscar Broneer, "Corinth: Center of Paul's Missionary Work in Greece," *The Biblical Archaeologist* 14 (1951), 95.

[305] Gordon Fee, *The First Epistle to the Corinthians*, (Grand Rapids, MI: Eerdmans, 1987), 433, note 58; see also Jerome Murphy-O'Connor, *St. Paul's Corinth*, (Wilmington, DE: Michael Glazier, 1983), 14.

[306] Pausanias, 1.7; Pausanias also observed that when Corinth was decimated by Mummius, the Games were not even interrupted but were entrusted to the Sicyonians until they were restored back to Corinth (2.2).

javelin.[307] Dio Chrysostom of Prusa, who was almost a contemporary of Paul, described a visit to the Isthmian Games: "When the time came for the Isthmian Games...all were at the Isthmus...And at that time it was that you could hear in the arena around the Temple of Poseidon any number of luckless sophists shouting and abusing each other, and their notorious students wrangling among themselves, and many authors reciting their silly compositions, poets declaiming their verses to the applause of their colleagues, magicians showing off their marvels, soothsayers interpreting omens, tens of thousands of lawyers twisting lawsuits, and no small number of hucksters peddling whatever goods each one happened to have for sale."[308]

In light of the popularity and splendor of these games, it is no wonder that Paul uses an abundance of athletic metaphors in his writings. They no doubt had a tremendous impact on his readers.[309] In fact, it is very likely that Paul was in Corinth when the games of 49 or 51 AD were held. As Murphy-O'Connor suggests, "it can hardly be coincidence that Paul's first sustained development of this theme (athletics) occurs in a letter to the Corinthians."[310] A further reason which lends weight to the idea that Paul attended these games was his profession as a tentmaker.[311] Livy suggested that the popularity of the games at Corinth had to do with the geographical setting of the city. Because the Isthmus had the resources of two seas, it was a natural meeting place for many people.[312] This being the case, a ripe opportunity was in place for Paul. Every two years the city would host a multitude of people including athletes, delegates, visitors, and merchants for the games. This would be a means of communicating for Paul, since he could meet with the Jews in the synagogue on the Sabbath, and come in contact with foreigners through his business as a tent-maker. Broneer explained: "At such occasions large numbers of tents would be needed to provide shelter for the crowds of visitors...In April, or early May, when the Isthmian Games were held, the air is chilly enough to require shelter; and frequent showers and violent gusts of wind that buffet the Isthmian region make such shelter imperative. Paul and his companions would find plenty of customers."[313]

Because of these facts, it was Broneer's conclusion that this was the decisive reason Paul chose Corinth as the chief base of his missionary work in Greece.[314]

---

[307] Arthur Ross, "Games," in *The Zondervan Pictorial Bible Dictionary*, ed. Merrill Tenney (Grand Rapids: Zondervan, 1976), 298.

[308] Dio Chrysostom, *Concerning Virtue* (London: William Heinemann, 1961), 6. 9. 14. 15.

[309] Smith observed that "the early christians, therefore, whether Jewish or Gentile origin, were able to understand, and the latter at any rate to appreciate, references either to the games in general, or to details of their celebration" (William Smith, "Games," in *The International Standard Bible Encyclopedia*, ed. James Orr [Grand Rapids: Eerdmans, 1980], 2:1171).

[310] Murphy-O'Connor, *St. Paul's Corinth,* 16.

[311] Even if Paul were not technically speaking a "tent-maker" but rather a leather-worker, this would not have precluded his making or repairing of tents or shelters.

[312] Livy, *Book XXIII: From the Founding to the City* (Cambridge, MA: Harvard, 1966), 23.32.

[313] Oscar Broneer, "The Apostle Paul and the Isthmian Games," *The Biblical Archaeologist* 25 (1962), 4, 5, 20; see also Murphy-O'Connor, *St. Paul's Corinth,* 17.

[314] Oscar Broneer, "Paul and the Pagan Cults at Isthmia," *Harvard Theological Review* 64 (1971),169.

This yields the conclusion that Paul would have been intimately familiar with the ancient games being an eyewitness to many of the events.[315]

The Specific Athletic Allusions Made by Paul

The Foot Race

Of all of the athletic events in the games, Paul referred to the foot race the most (1 Cor. 9:24; Gal. 2:2; Phil. 2:16; 2 Tim. 4:7). The word used by Paul in this regard is τρέχω. In Classical Greek it meant to move quickly, to run, especially at a contest in the stadium.[316] In the LXX it meant to run in a literal sense (Gen. 18:7; 1 Kings 18:46), and in a figurative sense referred to the living of one's life in the commandments of God (Ps. 119:32), or running into lies (Ps. 61:5), and in the expression of "running in the way of immorality" (4 Macc. 14:5). Likewise in the New Testament it was used in a literal sense when the disciples ran to the empty tomb (Matt. 27:48), and in the figurative sense where Paul expressed how the Christian life is to be directed toward a goal.

Concerning the races themselves, the contests took place in an enclosure of about 600 feet in length called a stadium.[317] Within these stadia there were at least three types of races which were held: "In the stade-race the competitors had to run a single length of the stadium, a distance of 192.28 meters. In the *diaulo*, which was the middle distance event at the ancient Olympics, they ran twice the length of the stadium, once in each direction, which means that they covered 384.56 meters. In the long-distance event, i.e., the *dolichos*, they had to run twenty-four lengths of the stadium, a total distance of 4614.72 meters."[318]

---

[315] Poliakoff noted that "The Greek, and later the Greco-Roman, world was packed with athletic festivals, ranging from small contests that admitted only local citizens to the great national festivals, to which the whole ancient world thronged" (Michael Poliakoff, *Combat Sports in the Ancient World*, [New Haven, CT: Yale, 1987], 18). This knowledge of sport was also known in Jerusalem. Josephus wrote: "In the first place he [Herod] appointed solemn games to be celebrated every fifth year, in honor of Caesar, and built a theatre in Jerusalem...He celebrated these games every five years, in the most solemn and splendid manner...Those that strove for the prizes in such games, were invited out of every land, both by the hopes of the rewards to be bestowed, and by the glory of victory to be there gained" (*Antiquities of the Jews*, trans. William Whiston [Grand Rapids, MI: Baker, 1979], Book IV, Ch. 8, Sec. l; see also *The Wars of the Jews*, [Grand Rapids, MI: Baker, 1979], Book I, Ch. 21, sec. 8. In addition, Romano wrote that "the great number of preserved stadia attests to the importance of athletics and competition in ancient Greece...Classical stadia have been excavated at Isthmia, Olympia, and Haliesis" (David Romano, "The Ancient Stadium: Athletes and Arete," *The Ancient World* 7 (1983), 9, 11. Ross, *The Zondervan Pictorial Bible Dictionary*, 298; Smith, *International Standard Bible Encyclopedia*, 2:1171).

[316] G. Ebel, "πορεύομαι," in *New International Dictionary of New Testament Theology*, ed. Colin Brown, (Grand Rapids: Zondervan, 1981), 3:946.

[317] Smith, "Games," in *International Standard Bible Encyclopedia*, 2:1172; Moulton and Milligan explained that stadios was a measurement of 600 Greek feet, and as a stade was the length of the Olympic course, the word came to be used of a race course (*Vocabulary of the Greek Testament*, 586).

[318] Ludwig Drees, *Olympia* (NY: Frederick Praeger, 1968), 78-79; Pausanias referred to these three races in these words: "Polites also you will consider a great marvel. This Polites was from Ceramus in Caria, and showed at Olympia every excellence in running. For from the longest race, demanding the greatest stamina, he changed, after the shortest interval, to the shortest and quickest, and after winning a victory in the long race and immediately afterwards in the short race, he added on the same day a third victory in the double course" (Pausanias, *Description of Greece* [Cambridge, MA: Harvard, 1978], 6.13.3).

Considering the stamina required by the long-distance event, it is probable that this is the running event to which Paul makes reference in his epistles. This is due to the fact that the Christian life is likened to a race which encompasses the entire earthly life. Therefore, what would be needed the most would be the spiritual stamina and endurance needed to complete it. This is evident especially in Hebrews 12:1 where it says that the believer is to "run with patience the race that is set before us" (KJV). Thus as Ebel noted, "what matters is applying all one's strength and holding out to the end."[319]

It is also interesting to observe that the writer to the Hebrews bid his readers to "fix their eyes on Jesus" as they run their race (Heb. 12:1). And Paul told the Philippians to "press toward the goal" (Phil. 3:14). The Greek word "σκοπός" means the goal or mark.[320] This is most likely a reference to the square pillars which were located at each end of the track on which the runner could fix his eyes so that he would be able to run straight as well as have something to keep in his sight so as to encourage him. Gardiner explained that "it is obvious that in a straight two hundred yards race the runner must have some point to fix his eye on if he is to run straight, and a post with a distinguishing mark would have been of great value as a guide."[321] The question has been raised as to how all of the runners would be able to turn around one post at the end of the track and run back without all of them crowding around the one post. In addition, this could have been an invitation to bumping, colliding, and foul play.[322] A possible solution to this problem has been suggested by Gardiner: "In the crowding at the turn a runner might easily lose three or four yards, a matter of vital importance for this distance, but of less importance in a three-mile race where the runners spread out rapidly...We may probably conclude then, that in the '*diaulos*' each runner raced to and turned round his own post."[323]

The Serious Nature of Athletics

It is appropriate at this point to discuss the passion with which athletics were approached in the ancient world. This will serve to illumine the reason Paul applied this imagery to the Christian life.

It is demonstrable that when it came to sporting events, the Greeks were not moderate. The goal was not merely to take part, but to win. To lose, in many cases, was a disgrace.[324] Pindar noted that "the athlete delights in the toil and the

[319] Ebel, in *New International Dictionary of New Testament Theology,* 3:947.

[320] Walter Bauer, William F. Arndt, and F. Wilbur Gingrich, *A Greek-English Lexicon of the New Testament and Other Early Christian Literature*, 2nd ed., rev. Frederick W. Danker (Chicago: University of Chicago Press, 1979), 756.

[321] E. Norman Gardiner, *Athletics of the Ancient World* (Chicago, IL: Ares, 1930), 135. It becomes evident that the races were not around a curved track as today, but rather up and down a straight track, 128 (see also H.A. Harris, *Sport in Greece and Rome* [Ithaca, NY: Cornell, 1972], 27); Gardiner further suggested that possibly each post was distinguished by some special sign or color (E. Norman Gardiner, *Greek Athletic Sports and Festivals* (London: Macmillan, 1910), 279).

[322] Harris, *Sport in Greece and Rome*, 31.

[323] Gardiner, *Athletics of the Ancient World*, 137.

[324] Sweet, *Sport and Recreation in Ancient Greece*, 118.

cost."[325] And Philo wrote of his experience: "I know wrestlers and *pankratiasts* often persevere out of love for honor and zeal for victory to the point of death, when their bodies are giving up and they keep drawing breath and struggling on spirit alone, a spirit which they have accustomed to reject fear scornfully...Among these competitors, death for the sake of an olive or celery crown is glorious."[326]

Epictetus noted the same common belief: "In the Olympic Games you cannot just be beaten and then depart, but first of all, you will be disgraced not only before the people of Athens or Sparta or Nikopolis but before the whole world. In the second place, if you withdraw without sufficient reason you will be whipped. And this whipping comes after your training which involves thirst and broiling heat and swallowing handfuls of sand."[327]

The word used by Paul to depict this spirit is αγωνίζομαι (1 Cor. 9:25). It can be used in reference to an athletic contest in which it could be translated "engaging in a contest," or it could be used generically of any struggle.[328] In classical Greek the word originally referred to a gathering, or a gathering place of the gods on Mt. Olympus, or of ships in a harbor, and then to a fight itself.[329] The word occurred primarily in the Apocrypha in this last sense.[330] Paul's use of the word with athletic overtones could refer to an "expression of the contestants' manly discipline."[331] Stauffer provided this excellent description of the force of the word:

> First is the thought of the goal which can be reached only with the full expenditure of all our energies...a passionate struggle, a constantly renewed concentration of forces on the attainment of the goal...The struggle for the reward does not demand not only full exertion but also rigid denial. The final assault is so exacting that all forces must be reserved, assembled, and deployed in it. The final goal is so high and glorious that all provisional ends must fade before it...If a man is not ready to set aside his egotistic needs and desires and claims and reservations, he is not fit for the arena.[332]

---

[325] Pindar, *The Olympian Odes* (Cambridge, MA: Harvard, 1961), I.V.10.

[326] Philo, *Every Good Man is Free* (Cambridge, MA: Harvard, 1929), 110.113.

[327] Epictetus, *Discourses* (London: William Heinemann, 1969), 3.22.52. See also Raubitschek who notes that "the 'agnostic' attitude was from the very beginning not confined to athletic exercises but it constituted a code of conduct, the striving for excellence and for its recognition in the form of honor" (Antony Raubitschek, "The Agonistic Spirit in Greek Culture," *The Ancient World* 7 [1983]:7).

[328] Bauer, Arndt, Gingrich, *A Greek-English Lexicon of the New Testament and Other Early Christian Literature*, 15.

[329] A. Ringwald, "αγών," in *The New International Dictionary of New Testament Theology*, ed. Colin Brown, vol. 1 (Grand Rapids: Zondervan, 1981), 644; see also Epictetus, *Discourses*, 3.25.3; Herodotus, *Book VIII*, 102; 9.60.1.

[330] See for example Wisdom 4:2; 2 Maccabees 8:16.

[331] Ringwald, in *The New International Dictionary of New Testament Theology*, 1:647.

[332] Ethelbert Stauffer, "αγών" in *Theological Dictionary of the New Testament*, ed. Gerhard Kittle, vol. 1 (Grand Rapids: Eerdmans, 1971), 137. Pfitzner argued well that though the idea of maximum exertion is present in Paul's use of the word αγών, his usage in 1 Corinthians 9 emphasizes more the idea of the self-

The Crown

Paul stated in 1 Corinthians 9:25 that the reason he exerts himself in his ministry is that he may obtain an incorruptible crown (cf. 1 Tim. 2:5; 2 Tim. 4:8). The word used by Paul for this crown is στέφανος. In Classical usage the word originally referred to anything which encircled such as a besieging army or the wall around a city. The usual meaning in secular Greek was a crown or wreath won at the various athletic contests.[333] In the LXX the word was used of a royal crown (2 Sam. 12:30) and of a festal ornament (Prov. 1:9; 4:9; Song of Songs 3:11; Isa. 28:1). In the New Testament the word occurs eighteen times (eight of which are in Revelation) and often refers to the prize of the athletic victor as a metaphor for the eternal reward of the faithful (1 Cor. 9:25; 2 Tim. 2:5; James 1:12; 1 Peter 5:4; Rev. 3:11; 4:4, 10).

Because of this type of usage which stresses the crown of victory, some have distinguished between στέφανος and διάδημα. Trench, for instance, commented that "We must not confuse these words because our English word 'crown' stands for them both. I greatly doubt whether anywhere in Classical literature...στέφανος is used of the kingly or imperial crown...In the New Testament it is plain that the...στέφανος whereof Paul speaks is always the conqueror's and not the king's."[334]

While the words of Trench seem justified, Moulton and Milligan warned that though στέφανος came to denote a crown of victory, "it should be noted that the distinction between στέφανος, crown of victory, and διάδημα, crown of royalty, must not be pressed too far as by Trench, for στέφανος is not infrequently used in the latter sense."[335]

It could be noted in passing that related to the crown of victory mentioned by Paul is the prize (βραβεῖον used in 1 Cor. 9:24; Phil. 3:14). Ringwald noted that the word is such a technical term for sporting events that it is rare in secular Greek. The prizes included the crowns, money, oil, barley, and certain rights throughout the victor's home city.[336] The emphasis on the prize as given by Paul seems to be related to the prize of the conflict which one can only win if he throws himself and his resources entirely into the struggle.[337]

The mythology of the crown

In light of the fact that pine was the most common of trees in the Isthmus region, the victors of the games were crowned with wreaths made from the

---

restriction which the athlete must endure. This idea would fit well with the ideas Paul develops in chapters 8 and 9 (Victor Pfitzner, *Paul and the Agon Motif* [Leiden: E.J. Brill, 1967], 87).

333 C.J. Hemer, "στέφανος," in *New International Dictionary of New Testament Theology,* ed. Colin Brown, vol. 1 (Grand Rapids: Zondervan, 1981), 405.

334 R.C. Trench, *Synonyms of the New Testament* (Grand Rapids, MI: Eerdmans, 1985), 79.

335 Moulton and Milligan, *Vocabulary of the Greek Testament*, 589.

336 A. Ringwald, "βραβεῖον," in *New International Dictionary of New Testament Theology*, ed. Colin Brown, vol. 1 (Grand Rapids: Zondervan, 1981), 648-649.

337 Ethelbert Stauffer, "βραβεύω," in *Theological Dictionary of the New Testament*, ed. Gerhard Kittel, vol. 1 (Grand Rapids: Eerdmans, 1971), 638; Smith, *International Standard Bible Encyclopedia*, 2:1173.

branches of these trees. However, this material was also associated with an ancient myth. The story was that a famous monster named Sinis made travel unsafe. This monster received the nickname "*Pityokamptos*" from his habit of inviting travelers to a pine-bending contest. After the two had forced a tree to the ground, Sinis told the traveler to hold it down, but when the monster let go of it, the tree would spring up and toss the traveler to his death.[338]

Another possible myth behind the fact of the pine crown was told by Plutarch: "The pine, and why it was used for the crown at the Isthmian games, was the subject of a discussion at a dinner given us in Corinth itself during the games by Lucanius, the chief priest. Praxiteles, the official guide, appealed to mythology, citing the legend that the body of Melicertes was found cast up by the sea at the foot of a pine."[339]

The value of the crown

Because of the hardship that the athlete endured in order to win a crown which would wither away in a short length of time, the question naturally arises as to whether a leafy crown was worth the effort employed to win it. Further, since the crown withered away quickly after winning it, does this not weaken Paul's analogy of the crown in relation to the Christian life? Why refer to this as a reward for the believer, if it is short-lived?

The answer to these questions lies in the fact that it was not the crown in and of itself which was desired, but rather what the crown represented, for the "*stephanos* to be won at Olympia had only ideal worth."[340] This ideal worth can be seen in the works of the Classical writers.

For example, Herodotus recorded the response to the question of a Persian as to what prize was offered at the various events of the games: "They told him of the crown of olive that was given to the victor. Then Tigranes son of Artabanus uttered a most noble saying...when he heard that the prize was not money but a crown, he could not hold his peace, but cried 'Zounds Mardonius,' what manner of men are these that you have brought us to fight withal? 'Tis not for money they contend but for glory of achievement!"[341] Dio Chrysostom also wrote of the worth and honor of the crowns:

---

[338] Oscar Broneer, "Paul and the Pagan Cults at Isthmia," *Harvard Theological Review* 64 (1971):185-186; Broneer also suggested that the competition in the pine-bending contest is an allusion to the striving for mastery in the games (186).

[339] Plutarch, *Plutarch's Lives: Marcellus* (London: William Heinemann, 1917), 5.3.1. There were also periods when the crowns were made of celery or even olive leaves, but at the foundation of the games the wreaths were made of pine which was reintroduced alongside the celery during Roman times. For a fuller discussion of this issue, see: Broneer, "Paul and the Pagan Cults at Isthmia," 186; Broneer, "Corinth: Paul's Center of Missionary Work in Greece, *The Biblical Archaeologist* 14 (1951):96; Broneer, "The Isthmian Victory Crown," *American Journal of Archaeology* 66 (1962):261; Oppian, *Cynegetica* (London: William Heinemann, 1933), 4.197; Plutarch, Plutarch's Lives, 5.3.3; Marcellus Poliakoff, *Combat Sports in the Ancient World*, 18.

[340] Otto Bauernfeind, "τρέχω," in *Theological Dictionary of the New Testament*, ed. Gerhard Kittel, vol. 8 (Grand Rapids: Eerdmans, 1971), 227.

[341] Herodotus, *Book VIII*, 8.26.3.

> For the pillar, the inscription, and being set up in bronze are regarded as a high honor by noble men, and they deem it a reward worthy of their virtue not to have their name destroyed along with their body and to be brought level with those who have never lived at all, but rather to leave an imprint and a token, so to speak, of their manly prowess.

You see what hardships these athletic competitors endure while training, spending money, and finally often even choosing to die in the very midst of the games. Why is it? If we were to abolish the crown for the sake of which they strive, and the inscription which will commemorate their victory at the…games, do you think that they would endure for even one day the heat of the sun?[342]

In addition to the glory represented by the crown, there is some indication to suggest that the victor acquired divine status. At the Olympic Games, the olive leaves were cut with a golden sickle from the most sacred olive trees before they were handed to the victor. Drees explained the significance: "The victors were placed on the same level as the gods and entered into communion with them. This bond was clearly demonstrated in the temple of Zeus in Olympia, for Phildias represented Zeus wearing a crown of wild olive. When the victors were honored they wore the same mark of distinction as the god; a wreath woven from the evergreen branches of the wild olive tree."[343]

The ceremony of the crown

On the last day of the games the victors were crowned in an elaborate ceremony. In the morning, the victors, judges, and members of the various groups proceeded in a solemn parade to the temple of Zeus which was observed by all of the spectators which were present at the games. It was at this temple where the victors were crowned. The judge, who wore a purple robe, placed the crown upon the victor's head. The wreath was made from a single branch which was supposed to imply magical associations, for this wreath linked the victor with the god at the moment it was placed on his head. Drees described the electricity of this moment: "[This] was one of the great moments of his life—he felt not only the pride and joy of victory but also the sense of pious awe induced by a divine sacrament. Certainly this was the case for as long as the sacred games retained their religious character."[344]

It can clearly be seen that what was at stake for the athlete was much more than a crown made from a dead plant. Rather, the possession of this crown meant extreme spiritual, emotional, financial, and social benefits. The apostle Paul explained to his readers that as grand as this earthly attainment was, it paled in

[342] Dio Chrysostom, *The Thirty-First Discourse: To the People of Rhodes* (London: William Heinemann, 1961), 31.20-21.

[343] Ludwig Drees, *Olympia*, 36; for other remunerations represented by the crown, see also Waldo Sweet, *Sport and Recreation in Ancient Greece*, 119-120; David Young, "Professionalism in Archaic and Classical Greek Athletics," *The Ancient World* 7 (1983):46-48.

[344] Drees, *Olympia,* 86.

significance when compared to the heavenly reward for the faithful believer (1 Cor. 9:25).

Boxing

Paul referred to the sport of boxing when he wrote: "so fight I, not as one that beats the air" (1 Cor. 9:26, KJV). The phrase "not as one that beats the air" could refer to a boxer who is unable to make contact with his blows, or rather than referring to an actual boxing match, could speak of the practice of shadow boxing, which was a favorite method of training in antiquity.[345] Because of Paul's reference in 9:26a to not running uncertainly (that is, with a goal in mind), it is more likely that Paul was referring to shadow boxing since his goal was to win the match. Therefore, his point was that unlike the one who is shadow boxing, he is involved in the actual boxing match and thus bears the marks of that contest in his body. Poliakoff wrote: "Paul insists that in his religious struggles he is a genuine fighter and does not act like a shadow boxer who punches the air: 'I bruise my body and bring it into subjugation.' In other words, he bears the scars of contest on his frame."[346]

This idea is in keeping with the historical data for boxing was considered to be the most injurious of all sports. Indeed, Paul had witnessed the boxers engaged in this violent (and sometimes deadly) sport as they strapped their knuckles with leather strips in order to make the blows more punishing. Such allusions to this sport would bring these thoughts readily to the Corinthians' minds.[347] Drees noted the violence of the sport when he observed that "many of the contestants left the stadium with broken teeth, swollen ears and squashed noses; many sustained serious injuries to their eyes, ears and even their skulls."[348] Part of the reason for this is that there were no rounds in Greek boxing. The opponents fought until they were both too exhausted to continue, and by mutual consent stopped for a breather. But if this did not happen, "usually the fight went on until one of the two was incapable of fighting any more, or acknowledged defeat by holding up his hand."[349]

Lucillius related the following account of the disfigurement that could take place in a boxing match: "O Augustus, this man Olympikos, as he now appears,

[345] Harris, *Sport in Greece and Rome,* 24.

[346] Poliakoff, *Combat Sports in the Ancient World,* 86.

[347] Broneer, "Corinth: Center of Paul's Missionary Work in Greece," 96.

[348] Drees, *Olympia,* 82; Papalas also noted that "certain Greek boxing practices from the modern point of view seem unsportsmanlike. It was perfectly acceptable to hit a man while he was down. This is where the hammer punch, a chopping blow to the back of the head, was useful…Furthermore, kicking was permitted, though we do not know under what circumstances. The most puzzling tactic however was striking with the open hand" (A. Papalas, "The Development of Greek Boxing," *The Ancient World* 9 (1984):73.

[349] Gardiner, *Athletics of the Ancient World,* 415; Paul also alluded to temperance in 9:25 and discipline in 9:27. It is also possible that temperance could enter into the realm of boxing as well as in the realm of running. Gardiner wrote concerning this that in boxing "forcing tactics do not pay, the boxer who makes the pace too fast exhausts himself to no purpose; in the descriptions of fights which we possess it is usually the clumsy, untrained boxer who forces the pace and tries to rush his opponent, with disastrous effects to himself. Caution was therefore the rule of the Greek boxer; and the fighting was therefore usually slow" (416).

used to have nose, chin, forehead, ears, and eyelids. But then he enrolled in the guild of boxers, with the result that he did not receive his share of his inheritance in a will. For in the lawsuit about the will his brother shows the judge a portrait of Olympikos, who was judged to be an imposter, bearing no resemblance to his own picture."[350]

Though it is impossible to be dogmatic, it is probable that in Paul's reference to boxing, he is showing his earnestness in his apostolic ministry by this allusion. He says that his ministry is characterized by self-discipline (1 Cor. 9:27), and striving (1 Cor. 9:25), and marks of being involved in the actual battle (1 Cor. (9:26) rather than just standing on the sidelines.

The Herald

Another possible reference to the games by Paul (though debated more than the others) is his mention of "preaching to others" (1 Cor. 9:27). The Greek word is κῆρυξ meaning a herald whose duty it is to make public proclamations.[351] The term was used of a subordinate official who made announcements at the games of Oxyrhynchus.[352] Be this as it may, some view this allusion in the New Testament as questionable.[353] However, given the athletic imagery which is strongly in the context, it is not improbable that Paul would also have this setting in mind when speaking of "preaching to others." If this is the case, then it would be observed that one of the assignments of the herald was to go out and announce the games before their commencement.[354]

In doing this he would proclaim a truce to all of the Greek cities who wished to take part in the games. This truce would then be engraved on a bronze disc. During the truce nobody was allowed to take up arms and the personal safety of all who attended the games was guaranteed. When the time of the games drew near, the herald would be sent out to announce the precise date of the upcoming games.[355]

At the time of the games the herald proclaimed the laws, conditions, and qualifications of the games as well as the names and countries of each competitor.[356] He then started the actual events by calling "go,"[357] and then pronouncing the judge's verdict of the winner.

When the games were over, the herald announced the name, country, and

---

[350] Lucillius, *Greek Anthology*, 11.75; Poliakoff also mentioned vase paintings which show blood pouring from boxers' noses, as well as cuts to the face, and eyes struck out. Furthermore, it was considered a bad omen to dream of boxing, for this could mean possible misfortune (Poliakoff, *Combat Sports in the Ancient World,* 86-87; see also Pausanias, *Description of Greece,* 6.15.5).

[351] Bauer, Arndt, Gingrich, *A Greek-English Lexicon of the New Testament and Other Early Christian Literature,* 431.

[352] Moulton and Milligan, *The Vocabulary of the Greek Testament*, 343.

[353] C.K. Barrett, *Commentary on First Corinthians* (NY: Harper & Row, 1968), 218; Moulton and Milligan, *Vocabulary of the Greek Testament*, 343.

[354] Stephen Miller, "Excavations at Nemea," *Hesperia* 48 (1979):79.

[355] Nicos Papahatizis, *Ancient Corinth*, 37; Drees, *Olympia*, 36-37, 54.

[356] Pfitzner, *Paul and the Agon Motif,* 94.

[357] Drees, *Olympia*, 69.

father of each victor and handed over the wreath of victory to the judge.[358] Thus Paul was not saying that in his apostolic ministry he is performing each job as did the herald at the games. Rather, as both a competitor and preacher related to the Christian life, if he were to be disqualified this would be an extreme tragedy. Plummer puts it well: "He was not only the herald to summon competitors and teach them the conditions of the contest; he was a competitor himself. How tragic, therefore, if one who had instructed others as to the rules to be observed for winning the prize, should himself be rejected for having transgressed them."[359]

Disqualification

In dealing with disqualification from the prize in the games, two passages are relevant—2 Timothy 2:5 and 1 Corinthians 9:27. These will be examined in logical order.

2 Timothy 2:5. Paul stated in this text that one "is not crowned except he strive lawfully." The word he uses for "lawfully" is νομός. Bauer defined the word as "in accordance with the rules or law of athletes, compete according to the rules."[360] Νόμος is well attested in Classical Greek with this sense (as will be documented in the following paragraph). The word is found as an adjective in the LXX only once which speaks of "lawful ways of living" (2 Macc. 4:11).[361] In the New Testament it is found only as an adverb (1 Tim. 1:8; 2 Tim. 2:5).

There were basically two areas in which an athlete had to "strive lawfully." The first was in the realm of training and the second was in the contest itself before which the athlete would take an oath. The first was illustrated by Epictetus who writes: "Give me proof, whether you have striven lawfully, eaten what is prescribed, taken exercise, heeded your trainer."[362] The same writer described this training process at length:

> You say 'I want to win at Olympia.' Hold on a minute. Look at what is involved both before and after, and only then, if it is to your advantage, begin the task. If you do, you will have to obey instructions, eat according to the regulations, keep away from desserts, exercise on a fixed schedule at definite hours, in both heat and cold; you must not drink cold water nor can you have a drink of wine whenever you want. You must hand yourself

[358] Walter Grundmann, "στέφανος," in *Theological Dictionary of the New Testament*, ed. Gerhard Kittel, vol. 7 (Grand Rapids: Eerdmans, 1971), 620; Arthur Ross, "Games," in *Zondervan Pictorial Dictionary of the Bible*, ed. Merrill Tenney (Grand Rapids: Zondervan, 1976), 299; Smith, *International Standard Bible Encyclopedia*, 2:1172.

[359] Alfred Plummer, *A Critical and Exegetical Commentary on the First Epistle of St. Paul to the Corinthians* (Edinburgh: T. & T. Clark, 1983), 197.

[360] Bauer, Arndt, Gingrich, *A Greek-English Lexicon of the New Testament and Other Early Christian Literature*, 541.

[361] W. Gutbrod, "νόμος," in *Theological Dictionary of the New Testament*, ed. Gerhard Kittel, vol. 4 (Grand Rapids: Eerdmans, 1971), 1088.

[362] Epictetus, Discourses, 3.10.8.

over to your coach exactly as you would to a doctor.[363]

The second area of striving lawfully related to an oath which would be taken by the athletes before the games began. In this oath the contestant would affirm that he had trained in the prescribed manner and would observe the rules of his event. At Olympia, for example, Philostratus related how the athletes, along with their fathers, brothers and trainers would swear that they would commit no foul play and that they had trained faithfully. Their instructions were: "If you have labored so hard as to be entitled to go to Olympia and have banished all sloth and cowardice from your lives, then march boldly on; but as for those who have not so trained themselves, let them depart withersoever they like."[364]

Conybeare added concerning the oath that they had to swear they had been in training for ten months and that then they would practice in the gymnasium before the games under the directions of the judges or umpires.[365] A good description of the oath-taking ceremony was supplied by Drees: "The oath taking ceremony was then performed…in front of the statue of Zeus. This statue, which was called 'Zeus God of Oaths,' was most awe-inspiring. It seems that the athletes, their fathers and brothers and also their trainers were required to swear over the entrails of a boar that he would not cheat at the Olympic Games. The athletes were then called upon to give a further oath to the effect that they had carefully prepared for the games over a period of ten months."[366]

1 Corinthians 9:27. The question arises as to the consequences of not "striving lawfully" or "according to the rules." What were the results if an athlete either broke training or broke the rules during the games? According to 2 Timothy 2:5, this person would not receive a crown. Or, to put it another way, he would be disqualified from winning the prize (1 Cor. 9:27). The word Paul used for being disqualified is αδόκιμος. The antonym (δόκιμος) refers to what is "valid, recognized, approved or accepted" (Rom. 14:18; 16:10; 1 Cor. 11:19; 2 Cor.

[363] Ibid., 15.2-5; see also *Encheiridion* (London: William Heinemann, 1969), 29.b; Pausanias related the story of a long distance runner who won once at Olympia, twice at Delphi, three times at the Isthmus and five times at Nemea. He was thought to be the first man ever to have eaten meat while preparing for the games "for athletes in training before him used to eat only a particular kind of cheese" (Pausanias, *Description of Greece*, 6.7.10). As was noted in the citation by Epictetus in the text, the athlete had to submit to their trainer as to their doctor. Lee tells of pictures of trainers on vases where they are carrying a staff about the height of a man which is sometimes forked. At times athletes would be struck for breaking the rules (Hugh Lee, "Athletic Arete in Pindar," *The Ancient World* 7 [1983]:32). The place where the athletes trained was in the γυμνασία (gymnasium) and was an important feature of every Greek city. The word is found in 1 Maccabees 1:14 and 2 Maccabees 4:9 where the allusion is to places of Greek amusement at Jerusalem. A form of the word is also found in 1Timothy 4:8 (W.J. Conybeare, *The Life and Epistles of St. Paul* [Grand Rapids, MI: Eerdmans, 1966], 539, note 2; Moulton and Milligan, *Vocabulary of the Greek Testament*, 133).

[364] Philostratus, *The Life of Apollonius of Tyana* (London: William Heinemann, 1926), Book V, Ch. 43; see also Gardiner, *Athletics of the Ancient World,* 278-279; Poliakoff, *Combat Sports in the Ancient World,* 20.

[365] The judges and umpires had to have been instructed in the details of the games for ten months (Conybeare, *The Life and Epistles of St. Paul,* 539, note 2; see also J.N.D. Kelly, *A Commentary on the Pastoral Epistles* (Grand Rapids, MI: Baker, 1983), 175-176; Pausanias, *Description of Greece,* 5.25.9-10.

[366] Drees, *Olympia,* 68; see also Sweet, *Sport and Recreation in Ancient Greece,* 240.

10:18). Conversely, αδόκιμος would refer to what is worthless, rejected or proved to be a sham.[367]

The idea of disqualification is seen in three incidents recounted by Pausanias. In the first he described a case with an Egyptian boxer from Alexandria who arrived late for the Olympiad in 107 A.D. He said that the reason for his lateness was adverse winds that had delayed his ship. But Heraclides, another Alexandrian boxer, was able to disprove this story by proving that Appollonius had really gone to the Ionian games to win prize money. Because of this, Apollonius was disqualified and Heraclides was pronounced the winner.[368] He also told of a case where an athlete was disqualified, and his crown was awarded to his competitor even though the competitor was dead.[369] And finally, one Cleomedes, was disqualified by the judges, went mad and returned to Asypalaea and attacked a school of about sixty children by pulling down a pillar which held up the roof.[370]

The interesting point in relation to Paul's argument in 1 Corinthians (and elsewhere) is that Paul considered it a real possibility that he could someday be refused a crown from the heavenly judge. Just as the athlete could be refused a reward in the athletic contests by not abiding by the rules, so the Christian someday will be refused reward if he does not run the race of life according to God's rules.[371] Thus it is imperative that the believer in the Lord Jesus strive as earnestly in the Christian life as the ancient athlete did in the games.

Section 16: Selected Miscellaneous Statements on Crucifixion in Antiquity

Plutarch

"And as every malefactor about to pay the penalty of his crime in his person <u>bears his cross</u> [Some translations have "carry his own cross on his back." This is a reference to the *patibulum*], so vice fabricates for itself each of its own torments, being the terrible author of its own misery in life, wherein in addition to shame it has frequent fears and fierce passions and endless remorse and anxiety."[372]

Tacitus

---

[367] Bauer, Arndt, Gingrich, *A Greek-English Lexicon of the New Testament and Other Early Christian Literature*, 18; H. Haarbeck, "δόκιμος," in *New International Dictionary of New Testament Theology,* ed. Colin Brown, vol. 3 (Grand Rapids: Zondervan, 1981), 808.

[368] Pausanias, *Description of Greece,* V.21.12-14.

[369] Ibid., VIII.40.1-2.

[370] Ibid., 6.9.6; Broneer saw a reference to the oath in 2 Timothy 4:7-8. He translated it: "I have competed in the good olympic games; I have finished the foot race, I have kept the pledge (i.e. to compete honestly, with reference to the athletic oath). What remains to me is to receive the crown of righteousness, which has been put aside for me; it will be awarded to me by the Lord, the just umpire, on that day" (Oscar Broneer, "The Apostle Paul and the Isthmian Games," *The Biblical Archaeologist* 25 [1962], 31).

[371] In the writer's opinion, this point has not been brought out strongly enough when it comes to the debate on whether the "overcomer" in Revelation 2-3 is a reference to all believers or only faithful believers. It would seem that the latter view is more probable given the cultural milieu, and that this is how the "overcomer" terminology would have been understood by the readers.

[372] Plutarch. *Moralis*, "On Those who are Punished by the Deity Late," 9.554 A.

"Nero fastened the guilt and inflicted the most exquisite tortures on a class hated for their abominations, called Christians by the populace. Christus, from whom the name had its origin, suffered the extreme penalty during the reign of Tiberius at the hands of one of our procurators, Pontius Pilatus, and a most mischievous superstition, thus checked for the moment, again broke out not only in Judaea, the first source of the evil, but even in Rome, where all things hideous and shameful from every part of the world find their centre and become popular. Accordingly, an arrest was first made of all who pleaded guilty; then, upon their information, an immense multitude was convicted, not so much of the crime of firing the city, as of hatred against mankind. Mockery of every sort was added to their deaths. Covered with the skins of beasts, they were torn by dogs and perished, or were nailed to crosses, or were doomed to the flames and burnt, to serve as a nightly illumination, when daylight had expired."[373]

"You confess that he did cry out that he was a Roman citizen; but that the name of citizenship did not avail with you even as much as to cause the least hesitation in your mind, or even any brief respite from a most cruel and ignominious punishment."

"A spot commanding a view of Italy was picked out by that man, for the express purpose that the wretched man who was dying in agony and torture might see that the rights of liberty and of slavery were only separated by a very narrow strait, and that Italy might behold her son murdered by the most miserable and most painful punishment appropriate to slaves alone."

Cicero

"Even if death is set before us, we may die in freedom. But the executioner, the veiling of heads, and the very word 'cross,' let them all be far removed from not only the bodies of Roman citizens but even from their thoughts, their eyes, and their ears."[374]

Origen

Nor do we at all say, as Celsus scoffingly alleges, "Believe that he whom I introduce to thee is the Son of God, although he was shamefully bound, and disgracefully punished, and very recently was most contumeliously treated before the eyes of all men…"[375]

Josephus

"And when I was sent by Titus Caesar with Cerealins, and a thousand horsemen, to a certain village called Thecoa, in order to know whether it were a place fit for a camp, as I came back, I saw many captives crucified, and

[373] Tacitus. *Annals,* 15.44.

[374] Cicero. *Against Verres,* 2.5.165; 2.5.169; *Speech before Roman Citizens on Behalf of Gaius Rabirius, Defendant against the Charge of Treason,* 16.

[375] Origen. *Contra Celsum,* 6.10.

remembered three of them as my former acquaintance. I was very sorry at this in my mind, and went with tears in my eyes to Titus, and told him of them; so he immediately commanded them to be taken down, and to have the greatest care taken of them, in order to their recovery; yet two of them died under the physician's hands while the third recovered."

"But the best men, and those of the noblest souls, did not regard him, but did pay a greater respect to the customs of their country than concern as to the punishment which he threatened to the disobedient; on which account they every day underwent great miseries and bitter torments; for they were whipped with rods, and their bodies were torn to pieces, and were crucified, while they were still alive, and breathed. They also strangled those women and their sons whom they had circumcised, as the king had appointed, hanging their sons about their necks as they were upon the crosses."

"Upon this, Varus sent a part of his army into the country, to seek out those that had been the authors of the revolt; and when they were discovered, he punished some of them that were most guilty, and some he dismissed: now the number of those that were crucified on this account were two thousand."

"Now there was about this time Jesus, a wise man, if it be lawful to call him a man; for he was a doer of wonderful works, a teacher of such men as receive the truth with pleasure. He drew over to him both many of the Jews and many of the Gentiles. He was [the] Christ. And when Pilate, at the suggestion of the principal men amongst us, had condemned him to the cross, those that loved him at the first did not forsake him; for he appeared to them alive again the third day; as the divine prophets had foretold these and ten thousand other wonderful things concerning him. And the tribe of Christians, so named from him, are not extinct at this day."

"And besides this, the sons of Judas of Galilee were now slain; I mean of that Judas who caused the people to revolt, when Cyrenius came to take an account of the estates of the Jews, as we have showed in a foregoing book. The names of those sons were James and Simon, whom Alexander commanded to be crucified." "Nay, they proceeded to that degree of impiety, as to cast away their dead bodies without burial, although the Jews used to take so much care of the burial of men, that they took down those that were condemned and crucified, and buried them before the going down of the sun."

"Now it happened at this fight that a certain Jew was taken alive, who, by Titus's order, was crucified before the wall, to see whether the rest of them would be affrighted, and abate of their obstinacy."

"This miserable procedure made Titus greatly to pity them, while they caught every day five hundred Jews; nay, some days they caught more: yet it did not appear to be safe for him to let those that were taken by force go their way, and to set a guard over so many he saw would be to make such as great deal them useless to him. The main reason why he did not forbid that cruelty was this, that he hoped the Jews might perhaps yield at that sight, out of fear lest they might themselves afterwards be liable to the same cruel treatment. So the soldiers, out of the wrath and hatred they bore the Jews, nailed those they caught, one after one way, and another after another, to the crosses, by way of jest, when their multitude was so great, that room was wanting for the crosses, and crosses wanting for the bodies."[376]

Section 17: Medical Aspects of Crucifixion[377]

Medical aspects of scourging

"As the Roman soldiers repeatedly struck the victim's back with full force, the iron balls would cause deep contusions, and the leather thongs and sheep bones would cut into the skin and subcutaneous tissues. Then, as the flogging continued, the lacerations would tear into the underlying skeletal muscles and produce quivering ribbons of bleeding flesh. Pain and blood loss generally set the stage for circulatory shock. The extent of blood loss may well have determined how long the victim would survive on the cross...when the soldiers tore the robe from Jesus' back, they probably reopened the scourging wounds."

Medical aspects of crucifixion

"Furthermore, with each respiration, the painful scourging wounds would be scraped against the rough wood of the stipes [a post or tree trunk]. As a result, blood loss from the back probably would continue throughout the crucifixion ordeal. With arms outstretched but not taut, the wrists were nailed to the *patibulum*. It has been shown that the ligaments and bones of the wrist can support the weight of a body hanging from them, but the palms cannot. Although a nail in either location in the wrist might pass between the bony elements and thereby produce no fractures, the likelihood of painful periosteal injury would seem great. Furthermore, the driven nail would crush or sever the rather large sensorimotor median never. The stimulated nerve would produce excruciating bolts of fiery pain in both arms."

"Most commonly, the feet were fixed to the front of the stipes by means of an iron spike. It is likely that the deep peroneal nerve and branches of the medial and lateral plantar nerves would have been injured by the nails. Although scourging may have resulted in considerable blood loss, crucifixion per se was a relatively bloodless procedure. The major pathophysiologic effect of crucifixion was a marked interference with normal respiration, particularly exhalation. The weight of the body, pulling down on the outstretched arms and shoulders would tend to fix the intercostals muscles in an inhalation sate and thereby hinder passive exhalation. Accordingly, exhalation was primarily diaphragmatic, and

---

[376] Josephus. *The Life of Flavius Josephus,* 75; *Antiquities,* 12.5.4, 17.10.10, 18.3.3, 20.5.2; *Jewish Wars,* 4.5.2, 5.6.5, 5.11.1.

[377] The following statements are taken from William Edwards, Wesley Gabel, and Floyd Hosmer, "Crucifixion (and related incidents) on the Physical Death of Jesus Christ," *Journal of the American Medical Association* 255:11 (1986).

breathing was shallow. Adequate exhalation required lifting the body by pushing up on the feet and by flexing the elbows and adducting the shoulders. However, this maneuver would place the entire weight of the body on the tarsals and would produce searing pain. Furthermore, flexion of the elbows would cause rotation of the wrists about the iron nails and cause fiery pain along the damaged median nerves. Lifting of the body would also painfully scrape the scourged back against the rough wooden stipes. As a result, each respiratory effort would become agonizing and tiring and lead eventually to asphyxia. The two most prominent causes of death probably were hypovolemic shock and exhaustion asphyxia. Other possible contributing factors included dehydration, stress-induced arrhythmias, and congestive heart failure with the rapid accumulation of pericardial and perhaps pleural effusions. Curcifracture (breaking the legs below the knees), if performed, led to an asphyxic death within minutes. Death by crucifixion was, in every sense of the word, excruciating (Latin, *excruciates*, or 'out of the cross')."

Section 18: The Realization of Ezekiel's Temple[378]

The Time of Realization of the Temple

The Ideal View

There have been several proposals as to when the temple of Ezekiel is to be, or was, realized. Some have taken the temple vision of Ezekiel as an apocalyptic dream or ideal in which God gave to Ezekiel an ethereal vision of what God would do for His people. Craigie wrote:

> Only in the vision did this marvelous temple exist; it was a sign to him that God would not always be absent from His people… but the prophet is not prophesying a physical and geographical transformation; rather, in the symbolism of the vision, he is anticipating the extraordinary transformation that would overcome the people of Israel, when once again the temple in their midst was the residence of God.[379]

The Historical View

The historical view of Ezekiel's temple attempts to find a historical

[378] For a fuller discussion of the issues see Jerry Hullinger, "The Realization of Ezekiel's' Temple," in *Dispensationalism Tomorrow & Beyond: A Theological Collection in Honor of Charles C. Ryrie* (Fort Worth, TX: Tyndale Seminary Press, 2008), 375-396. Portions are used by permission.

[379] Peter Craigie, *Ezekiel* (Philadelphia: Westminster, 1983), 281, 313. Another part of this view which creates problems is the characteristic statement by Craigie that "the writing is apocalyptic in style expressing in a profoundly symbolic manner the nature of the restored Israel that God would establish in the future" (275). There seems to be no textual basis to corroborate his statement of the "profoundly symbolic manner" of the passage. The text seems to militate against this understanding. Further, granting the fact of a "restored Israel that God would establish in the future" is the issue of what form this would take. Assuming for sake of argument that a futuristic view of 40-48 is correct, how much clearer could this have been set forth by God through the prophet?

fulfillment for chapters 40-48. The historical referents for this realization are said to be either the Solomonic temple or Zerubbabel's post-exilic temple. In this view, Ezekiel was looking at a literal return which would result in a literal temple in Jerusalem in the sixth century. The underlying rationale for this position was stated by Terry. "All Jewish-carnal theories of a literal restoration of Jerusalem and the Jewish state…The notion…that at Christ's second coming Jerusalem and the temple will be rebuilt and become the throne center of the kingdom of the Messiah is inconsistent with a rational interpretation of the prophets and the spiritual nature of the kingdom."[380]

The Church/Christ View

Others have seen the Ezekiel passage fulfilled either in Christ or the Christian Church. This was the position of many of the Reformers and was stated by Fairbairn: "The whole representation was not intended to find in either Jewish or Christian times an express and formal realization, but was a grand complicated symbol of the good God had in reserve for his Church, especially under the coming dispensation of the Gospel."[381]

Those who link the prophecy with Christ rely heavily on: a) the symbolism of the river in Ezekiel and its connection with John 7, and b) the temple and its connection with the person of Christ. Grigsby is representative of this understanding when he stated that "the resurrected Christ fulfills the role of the new temple in Ezekiel 47:1-12 and dispenses living water to a barren world with John 7:37-39."[382] Klein noted on John 7:37-39:

> The stream of Ezekiel 47 may even provide a new level of meaning to an incident at the crucifixion of Jesus, when a soldier pierced his side with a spear and at once there came out blood and water (John 19:24). If God's presence in his temple means new life for his people, John's symbolism would suggest that the body of Jesus is now that temple, and that God was never more "with" his people than when Jesus hung on a cross.[383]

---

[380] Milton Terry, *Biblical Hermeneutics*, 131-32. Terry's comment also implies the common false dichotomy between a "spiritual" kingdom and a "literal, earthly" kingdom. The Scripture does not present one in opposition with the other. Rather, the mediatorial kingdom always had and will always have a spiritual base. This was seen in the Edenic theocracy where God made requirements of the first couple; it is seen in Israel's theocracy in the Mosaic commandments; and, it will be seen during the future kingdom age in which the kingdom is characterized by "holiness unto the Lord" (Zech. 14:20).

[381] Patrick Fairbairn, *An Exposition of Ezekiel*, reprint ed., (Grand Rapids: Zondervan, 1960), 434-35. Luther wrote that "this building of Ezekiel is not to be understood to mean a physical building, but like the chariot at the beginning so this building at the end (40-48) is nothing else than the kingdom of Christ, the holy church or Christendom here on earth until the last day" (Martin Luther, *Luther's Works,* E. Theodore Bachmann, ed., [Philadelphia: Muhlenberg Press, 1960], 35:293). However, Luther also relates the Ezekiel vision to the heavenly Jerusalem (*Works,* 35:283).

[382] Bruce Grigsby, "Gematria and John 21:11—Another Look at Ezekiel 47:10," *The Expository Times* 95 (1984): 177.

[383] Klein, *Ezekiel: The Prophet and His Message*, 182. See also for Jesus as the temple, David Holwerda, *Jesus & Israel: One Covenant or Two?* (Grand Rapids: Eerdmans, 1995), 74-75.

The Eternal State View

The next view identifies the vision of 40-48 with the eternal state. Keil represents this view and suggested that the vision "is partly to be regarded as the Old Testament outline of the New Testament picture of the heavenly Jerusalem in Revelation 21 and 22."[384] Likewise, Hoekema wrote:

> The details about the temple and sacrifices are to be understood not literally but figuratively. The closing chapters of the book of Revelation, in fact, echo Ezekiel's vision. In Revelation 22, we read about the counterpart of the river which Ezekiel saw...What we have in Ezekiel 40-48, therefore, is not a description of the millennium, but a picture of the final estate on the earth, in terms of the religious symbolism with which Ezekiel and his readers were familiar...All that was foreshadowed in such visions John sees fulfilled.[385]

The Kingdom View

A final view holds that Ezekiel 40-48 will be realized during the future kingdom period. This position holds that the descriptions given by Ezekiel in 40-48 will be literally implemented on earth during the visible reign of Christ in His millennial kingdom. This includes the building of the glorious temple, the restoration of animal sacrifices, the presence of God with His people, and the various topographical phenomena which are mentioned. This subsection will present arguments in favor of this interpretation and will attempt to deal with the two major objections.

Arguments in Favor of the Kingdom View

The first strength of the kingdom view is that it is able to deal with the supernatural elements of the passage. As noted previously, there are elements in the prophecy that did not occur historically and must therefore have a future fulfillment. Allen specifically pointed out regarding the Dead Sea, circumstances that have never taken place. "The healing effect of the river upon the Dead Sea is described in 8-10. It was to become a freshwater lake, able to sustain an enormous abundance of fish. The upper half of the west shore of the Dead Sea is portrayed as a fisherman's paradise. In its backwaters, however, would be left salt water to provide salt for cultic and human needs."[386]

Another statement of this point is provided by Davidson:

> The fact that the subject of the passage is the final blessedness of the people accounts for the supernatural elements in the picture. But both the

---

[384] F. Keil, *Ezekiel*, 417.

[385] Anthony Hoekema, *The Bible and the Future* (Grand Rapids: Eerdmans, 1979), 205-6.

[386] Leslie Allen, *Ezekiel 20-48*, 279. It is interesting to point out that in the Ancient Near East the home or temple of a god was often situated on a river or a stream. El's home, for example, in the Ugaritic texts is located by two rivers (Klein, *Ezekiel: The Prophet and His Message*, 181; Coogan, *Studies from Ancient Canaan* [Philadelphia: Westminster Press, 1978], 95; Richard Clifford, *The Cosmic Mountain in Canaan and the Old Testament* [Cambridge: Harvard University Press, 1972], 158).

natural and the supernatural features of the peoples' condition are to be understood literally. The temple, the services, and the like are meant in a real sense, and no less literally meant is the supernatural presence of Jehovah in His house, the transfiguration of nature, the turning of the desert into a garden, and the sweetening of the waters of the Dead Sea.[387]

The other views of the passage do not account well for these supernatural elements. If a historical view is taken, then these supernatural issues are stripped of any reality. If a Christian Church view is adopted, then the language of the text is reduced to the whim of the interpreter. And finally, if the passage is placed into the eternal state, then the contradictions between Ezekiel and John must be reconciled, as well as the inconsistent methodology.

It can also be pointed out that the returnees to Jerusalem did not compare their rebuilt temple with Ezekiel but rather with the temple of Solomon (Haggai 2:3). And concerning the altar, Stalker has observed that there is no evidence that it was modeled on the description given by Ezekiel.[388]

A second support for this view is the seemingly clear meaning of the text.[389]

---

[387] A. B. Davidson, *Ezekiel,* xvi.

[388] D. M. G. Stalker, *Ezekiel* (London: SCM Press Ltd., 1971), 291; Roland de Vaux, *Ancient Israel* (New York: McGraw-Hill, 1961), 412.

[389]One could object to this statement in that, if the text is so clear, why does so much disagreement exist? This leads to the important hermeneutical debate between premillennialists and amillennialists (i.e., "literal" versus "symbolic" tendencies in interpreting prophecies). Of course, the question is really not an issue of a strictly literal versus a strictly symbolic approach, because even the most extreme literalist takes some things as symbolic. Conversely, even the most stringent symbolist interprets some things as literal. Frequently, dispensational literalism is made to look inconsistent by producing a passage which clearly has to be interpreted symbolically. While a number of responses could be made, one important point is that literal interpretation is more than deciding whether a text should be taken figuratively or literally, for this is a question with which all interpreters wrestle. Rather, literal is a framework brought to the text from which the literal vs. figurative is decided (Mike Stallard, "Literal Interpretation: The Key to Understanding the Bible," *The Journal of Ministry and Theology* 4 [2000]: 27). Therefore, it is a red herring to point to an isolated passage which could be taken figuratively as arguing against dispensational literalism. For a discussion of this issue and clarification of the meaning of "literal" in today's discussion, see the following: Thomas Ice, "Dispensational Hermeneutics," in *Issues in Dispensationalism* (Chicago: Moody Press, 1994), 29-49; Elliott Johnson, "Premillennialism Introduced: Hermeneutics," in *The Coming Millennial Kingdom* (Grand Rapids: Kregel, 1997), 15-34; "A Traditional Dispensational Hermeneutic," in *Three Central Issues in Contemporary Dispensationalism* (Grand Rapids: Kregel, 1999), 65, 67, 76; "What I Mean by Historical-Grammatical Interpretation and How That Differs from Spiritual Interpretation," *Grace Theological Journal* 11 [1990]: 157-158; "Literal Interpretation: A Plea for Consensus," *When the Trumpet Sounds,* (Eugene, OR: Harvest House, 1995), 213, 216, 217; Robert L. Thomas, "A Critique of Progressive Dispensational Hermeneutics," in *When the Trumpet Sounds* (Eugene, OR: Harvest House, 1995), 413-425); Bernard Ramm, *Protestant Biblical Interpretation* (Boston: W. A. Wilde, 1950), 64; Geisler, *Systematic Theology*, 415-21, 423-26, 441-48; Mike Stallard, "The Rediscovery of the Jewish Perspective of the Bible," in *The Gathering Storm* (Springfield, MO: 21st Century Press, 2005): 57-71. There are basically three definitions of "literal": 1) a letterism which excludes figures of speech, 2) a normal reading of the text that allows for figures, historical, contextual, and progressiveness, and 3) a normal approach which takes most prophetic material as symbolic and figurative, most of which is applied to the Church (Alexander, "Ezekiel," 905-6). But as evinced by Hoekema's comments in the text, there is a trend among some amillennialists to move slightly away from this (and possibly a trend among progressive dispensationalists to move toward it, at least methodologically). This article falls into the camp described as #2 above, with the well-known caveat of Lange: "The literalist is not one who denies figurative language, that symbols are used in prophecy, nor does he deny that spiritual truths are set forth therein; his position is,

Beasley-Murray cogently explained that "to tackle the vision verse by verse and try to take symbolically 'thirteen cubits,' 'hooks a handbreath long,' 'the sixth part of an ephah,' place names like Berothat and Hauran, is out of the question, to contradict all reason."[390] If God or Ezekiel did not intend the language to be taken in their normal, sense, then they were being blatantly deceptive.[391]

A third argument in favor of the kingdom view is the emphasis in the passage

---

simply, that the prophecies are to be normally interpreted (i.e. according to revealed laws of language) as any other utterances are interpreted—that is manifestly figurative being so regarded" (J. P. Lange, "The Revelation of St. John," in *Lange's Commentary on the Holy Scriptures*, ed. Philip Schaff, vol. 12, reprint ed., [Grand Rapids: Zondervan, 1980, 98]. Ramm continues to provide six defenses for this approach: 1) it is the normal approach in all language, 2) secondary meanings parables, types, etc., depend on a literal meaning of terms, 3) most of the Bible makes sense this way, 4) it does not rule out symbols and figures, 5) it is the only safe check on interpretation, and 6) it is consistent with plenary inspiration (Ibid., 54ff.). Having examined the interpretive approaches to the realization of Ezekiel's temple, it is seen why this issue is important and how the other views do not treat the text in this manner. As Terry observed: "Its (allegorism's) habit is to disregard the common signification of words and give wing to all manner of fanciful speculation. It does not draw out the legitimate meaning of an author's language, but foists onto it whatever whim or fancy of an interpreter may desire" (Milton Terry, *Biblical Hermeneutics*, 224). Again, Ramm noted that "spiritualizing is an open door to almost uncontrolled speculation and imagination. For this reason we have insisted that the control in interpretation is the literal method" (Ramm, *Protestant Biblical Interpretation*, 65). Even Allis agreed that if the allegorical or symbolic method is "used to empty words of their plain and obvious meaning, to read out of them what is clearly intended by them, then allegorizing or spiritualizing is a term of reproach which is well merited" (Allis, *Prophecy and the Church*, 18). There are visions in Ezekiel that merit a symbolic interpretation due to their presentation, such as wheels within wheels, dry bones coming to life, etc. However, to spiritualize 40-48, which does not employ such symbolism, seems to belie the prejudice of the interpreter. The text speaks of historical places, solid buildings, exact measurements, and precise cultic sacrificial language as found in the legislative portions of the Pentateuch, and therefore seems to demand a normal and literal interpretation. For interpreting prophetic portions of Scripture see, C. C. Ryrie, *The Basis of the Premillennial Faith*, 40-46; J. Randolph Jaeggli, "The Interpretation of Old Testament Prophecy," *Detroit Baptist Seminary Journal* 2 (1997): 3-17. One final noteworthy observation has been made by John Walton, "Inspired Subjectivity and Hermeneutical Objectivity," *The Master's Seminary Journal* 13 (2002). He points out that there are two distinct methods of interpretation. "One is defined by hermeneutical guidelines and is objective in nature. The other is subjective in nature but finds its authority not in the science that drives it, but in its source—inspiration from God. If you have inspiration, you do not need historical-grammatical hermeneutics. If you do not have inspiration, you must proceed by the acknowledged guidelines of hermeneutics. The credibility of any interpretation is based on the verifiability of either one's inspiration or one's hermeneutics" (70). "We must push on in our question to preserve the objectivity of our hermeneutics, for it provides the foundation for our commitment to biblical authority....For an interpretation of the text to claim credibly that it represents the authoritative teaching of the text, it must depend on either hermeneutical objectivity or inspired subjectivity" (77). Since we are not writing Scripture today, we cannot rely on the subjective (as perhaps the apostles did), but we need to lean as heavily as possible on what is objective. In the writer's view, this is best done by taking Ezekiel at face value.

[390] Beasley-Murray, *Ezekiel*, 663; Cameron MacKay, "Why Study Ezekiel 40-48," *Evangelical Quarterly* 37 (1965), 155.

[391] For a good description of the temple as Ezekiel described it, see T. Chary, "Le Temple d'Ezechiel," 34-38. In this article, Chary conducts a tour through the temple beginning from the exterior through the main gate into the court and its various annexes. This is followed by the temple proper (interior). He describes the details with great precision. Interestingly, Ezekiel had a profound influence on the Qumran community (E. Cothenet, "Influence d'Ezechiel sur la spiritualite de Qumran," *Revue de Qumran* 13 [1988], 431-39). For example, in the Qumran text "Description of the New Jerusalem," the author says that he had a vision in which he was shown buildings and streets with their measurements. In this vision, he was shown a city which had the last chapters of Ezekiel as its model. Particularly notable are the enormous streets and massive city (Jacob Licht, "An Ideal Town Plan from Qumran—The Description of the New Jerusalem," *Israel Exploration Journal* 29 [1979], 45-59).

on the distribution of the land[392] which is reminiscent of the promises made to the Patriarchs. It is clear that Israel has never dwelt in the land with the divisions presented by Ezekiel. Therefore, if 40-48 is to be taken seriously, a fulfillment of this aspect of Ezekiel's vision must be proleptic.[393]

Allen observed:

> This passage functions as an introduction to 48:1-29 where the allocation of the land is described. Verse 14 lays down a theological premise, the revival of the theme of the land promised to the Patriarchs, which runs through the Pentateuchal sources.... There is a tradition deeply embedded in Israel's faith that inextricably linked together are the fortunes of the temple and the land. To worship in the temple carried with it the privileges of dwelling in the land and enjoying God's blessings there.[394]

Another indication which supports the kingdom interpretation is the emphasis in 40-48 on the glory of Yahweh. The passage stresses the fact that the new sanctuary will again be His dwelling place. Thus Ezekiel records the divine

---

[392]The importance of the land cannot be overstated. Consider the following statement: "In the Old Testament few issues are as important as that of the promise of the land to the patriarchs and the nation Israel. In fact, ארץ 'land' is the fourth most frequent substantive in the Hebrew Bible. Were it not for the larger and more comprehensive theme of the total promise with all its multifaceted provisions, the theme of Israel and her land could well serve as the central idea or the organizing rubric for the entire canon...The land of Israel cannot be reduced to a sort of mystical land defined as a new spiritual reality...the Bible is most insistent on the fact that the land was promised to the patriarchs as a gift where their descendants would reside and rule as a nation" (Walter Kaiser, "The Promised Land: A Biblical-Historical View," *Bibliotheca Sacra* 138 [1981], 302). Later postexilic prophets continue to pledge to Israel their restoration to the land. As Kaiser notes, "the sheer multiplicity of texts...is staggering" (309); see also Jeffrey Townsend, "Fulfillment of the Land Promise in the Old Testament," *Bibliotheca Sacra* 142 [1985], 321-332). Moreover, in Ezekiel's discussion of the New Covenant, he not only describes spiritual blessings which will occur, but physical blessings also. He states that towns and ruins will be rebuilt (36:33, 35) and desolate land will be cultivated (36:34). The fact that the New Covenant presents spiritual *and* physical blessings provides support that the temple Ezekiel envisions is consistent with his physical concerns.

[393] Some have argued that the fulfillment of the land promise was fulfilled historically either during the time of Joshua or during the reign of David and Solomon. Yet premillennialists have maintained that the promise will find its ultimate fulfillment during the kingdom period. Amillennialists have contended that the promise is spiritualized in the church (older), was conditional, and therefore forfeited during the Conquest, or will be realized during the eternal state (some newer). The problem faced by premillennialists is that the text states that the promise was fulfilled (Josh. 21:43-45; 23:14-15; Neh. 9:8). With this in mind, there are several points to remember. First, the historical allocations of land were never made according to Ezekiel's plan, nor accompanied with the concomitants he presents. Second, the Abrahamic Covenant and its land extension in the Palestinian Covenant are unconditional. Third, the covenant was made with the physical seed of Abraham. Fourth, Israel never completely removed the Canaanites from the whole land so as to possess all of it (Josh. 11:16-17; 12:7; 13:2-6; Judges 3:3). Fifth, the Lord was faithful to give Israel the land (Josh. 21:43), but Israel was still responsible to obey the directives of the Mosaic Covenant in order to maintain possession. Thus the land was given to the nation by Yahweh and was theirs to take, but they forfeited the full blessings of the land through disobedience. This demonstrated the truth of Leviticus 26 and Deuteronomy 28-30 that the enjoyment of the blessings of the unconditional Abrahamic Covenant was obedience. So, while historically Israel enjoyed a partial taste of this fulfillment, it will not be until the enactment of the New Covenant (Ezekiel 36), by a gracious God, that they will permanently enjoy the full blessings of the Covenant during the kingdom age as they are restored to the land.

[394] Allen, *Ezekiel 20-48*, 280, 285.

initiative in Ezekiel 37:26b, "I will put my sanctuary among them." In fact, the glory of God is one of the unifying themes of the entire book. Ezekiel sees a vision of the glory of God in chapter 1, sees the departure of the glory of God in 8-11, and then sees the return of God's glory in 40-48. Clearly, this return of God's glory has never been experienced by the nation as evinced from their present condition. Alexander commented that “the return of God's glory…is the climax of the book. The context implies that this could only occur after Israel has been restored to her promised land and cleansed...When God's glory returns, it will remain in Israel's midst forever. The development of this unifying factor in Ezekiel would argue strongly for a future fulfillment of 40-48.”[395]

A fifth consideration in favor of the kingdom view revolves around the fact that the features presented by Ezekiel are different than those of the programs of Moses, Solomon, or Zerubbabel. Surely if Ezekiel were looking at these as models, there would have been a great deal of similarity, but in fact there are a great number of dissimilarities. This strongly suggests that he is looking into the future. In addition, economically speaking, the returnees to the land were bankrupt and in no condition even to attempt what Ezekiel was suggesting. This leads to the conclusion suggested by Eichrodt: “It becomes evident that the prophet is especially interested in something far wider than the familiar features of the old future hope, for he names new miracles by the covenant of God through which the fulfillment takes on a tone all of its own (e.g., Spirit is imparted, rebuilding, obedience, united kingdom, etc.)."[396]

The provenance of Ezekiel 40-48 presents another support for this view. It is quite possible that 40-48 is continuing the message of 34-39, and belongs to them as an extended oracle of salvation. In particular, it would be a direct outworking of the New Covenant in chapter 37. Thus, "the four motifs of new temple, covenant, king and land find here a practical grounding and a detailed development."[397] Therefore, since Israel has never experienced the full blessings of the New Covenant, their future fulfillment would be placed into the eschaton along with the realization of Ezekiel's temple.

A final strength of the position adopted here is the parallel that exists between

---

[395] Alexander, *Ezekiel*, 944. Another argument related to the glory of God is to note Ezekiel's strong concern for God's name in his book. This is seen by the recurrent phrase “they will know that I am Yahweh.” Zimmerli has observed that of the 947 verbal occurrences of the stem “to know” “not less than 99 are found in Ezekiel, with virtually all of them making significant theological statements” (Walther Zimmerli, *I Am Yahweh* [Atlanta: John Knox Press, 1982], 29-30). He further defined this knowledge as a “form of self-revelation of a person in his name” (Walther Zimmerli, *Ezekiel: A Commentary on the Book of the Prophet Ezekiel*, vol. 2 [Philadelphia: Fortress Press, 1979], 38). The result of this concern for the divine name is an indirect assurance of salvation to Israel. This is absolutely necessary if God's name is to be vindicated because of Israel's sin. Ezekiel 40-48 convincingly argues for a restored Jewish temple and land with the resultant phrase “the house of Israel will never again defile my holy name” (43:7). If the events of 40-48 are not fulfilled as laid out by the prophet, then God's plans and covenants with the nation have been frustrated, and His preeminence as God will not be established.

[396] Eichrodt, *Ezekiel: A Commentary*, 37.

[397] Allen, *Ezekiel 20-48*, 213. Regarding the New Covenant context of Jeremiah 31, it is striking that one of the provisions of the New Covenant regards the very city that Jeremiah was before long to see destroyed by the Chaldeans. In the future, the city will be rebuilt and incapable of devastation.

Ezekiel's ideas and those of other prophets. Some commentators dismiss the idea of a literal, future fulfillment of Ezekiel 40-48 by simply referring to it as an apocalyptic dream or spiritualizing it into oblivion. However, it needs to be observed that several other prophets foresaw the same future for Israel when sacrifices in a temple would again be instituted (e.g., Isaiah 56:7; 66:20-23; Jer. 33:18; Zech. 14:16-21; Mal. 3:3-4). Isaiah saw a temple in the holy land (Isa. 2:2-3; 56:3; 60:13) where animal sacrifices would be offered on its altar by the Egyptians (19:21) and the Arabians (60:7). Of these sacrifices, Yahweh says, "even these I will bring to my holy mountain and make them joyful in my house of prayer. Their burnt offerings and their sacrifices will be acceptable on my altar" (56:6-7; cf. 66:19-20). Hosea also speaks of sacrifices to be resumed in the last days (3:4-5). Jeremiah says the same thing (33:17-22), as does Amos (9:11), and Zechariah (14:21). And even more significant is the fact that Jeremiah spoke of these sacrifices after noting the demise of the Old Covenant and its replacement by the New Covenant.[398]

Arguments against the view

There are, of course, objections to the kingdom position. The two primary objections involve envisioned topography and the renewal of animal sacrifices.[399] Concerning the first, Taylor remarked: "There are elements which are so impracticable that a completely literal interpretation of the vision must be ruled out (e.g. the setting of the temple on a very high mountain, 40:2; the impossible source and course of the river of life, 47:1-13; the unreality of the boundaries of the tribes which could never be worked out geographically in hilly Israel)."[400] Martyn Lloyd-Jones added the same complaint:

> Let us turn for instance, to the prophecy of Ezekiel from chapters 40 to the end...Read those chapters and try to interpret them literally. If you work out all those measurements about the restored Temple, you will find that you have measurements which cannot be fitted into a literal Palestine. If

---

[398] See also for the kingdom view: Alexander, "Ezekiel," 945; Lamar Cooper, Sr., *The New American Commentary, Ezekiel* (Nashville: Broadman & Holman, 1994), 353, 381; Dyer, "Ezekiel," 1302-04; Paul Enns, "Ezekiel" (Grand Rapids: Zondervan, 1986), 180; Charles Feinberg, The Prophecy of Ezekiel (Chicago: Moody, 1969): 233-39; Hobart Freeman, *An Introduction to the Old Testament Prophets* (Chicago: Moody, 1968), 312.

[399] A third objection sometimes made by those opposed to the dispensational premillennial scheme is that this reduces the kingdom into a carnal hope. However, two points should be kept in mind. First, the so-called "carnal" (physical) aspects of the kingdom were instituted in creation and have merely been marred by sin. It is only fitting that God should undo these effects. Curiously, those who are not dispensational have produced some of the best work arguing for the goodness of creation (see for example, Michael Horton's excellent and enjoyable volumes, *Where in the World is the Church* [Chicago: Moody, 1995]; *Putting Amazing Back into Grace* [Grand Rapids: Baker, 1995], 38-40, 42, 199-200). Second, as mentioned previously, the kingdom always has a spiritual base as is seen by the glory of God, cleansing, the work of the Spirit, the regenerate nature of those who enter, etc. The "carnal" objection attempts to force one into an either/or decision which does not exist. For further rebuttal to this objection, see John Walvoord, "Spiritual Life in the Millennium," *Bibliotheca Sacra* 115 (1958): 97-108.

[400] Taylor, *Ezekiel*, 252.

> you work out what you are told there about the river, you will find that river will have to rise and flow up over mountains—impossible if you take it literally! But if you understand Ezekiel's words pictorially and spiritually there is no difficulty. A literal interpretation of these chapters involves us in believing that a day is coming when the Jews will again occupy the whole of the land of Palestine with a literal Temple again built in Jerusalem. Not only that, but burnt offerings and sacrifices for sins will again be offered.[401]

Three responses are in order here. First, it has always been maintained by premillennialists that the kingdom will be one in which changes in topography and in the course of nature will occur. This will be accomplished by the power of God and is anticipated in all of the prophets (e.g. Isa. 11:6-9; Joel 3:18-21; Amos 9:13-15; Obad. 19-21; Zech. 14).[402] It should be no more difficult to accept this than it should be to accept the changes regarding the eternal state.

The second response deals with the issue of miracles. Geisler defines a miracle as "a divine intervention into, or an interruption of, the regular course of the world that produces a purposeful but unusual event that would not (or could not) have occurred otherwise. The natural world is the world of regular, observable, and predictable events. Hence, a miracle by definition cannot be predicted by natural means."[403] Unless one denies all of the miraculous throughout the biblical history, this is a bogus objection. Why would this be any different?

A third response deals with dispensationalism's philosophy of history. Showers correctly notes that several consequences resulted from Adam's rebellion.[404] These included the theocracy being lost from planet earth, Satan usurping the "rule" of the world, and nature being subjected to the curse. In response to these consequences, the "ultimate purpose of history is the

---

[401] Martyn Lloyd-Jones, *The Church and the Last Things* (Wheaton, IL: Crossway, 1998), 108-09. Likewise, Keil stated: "It is upset by the fact that not only are its supporters unable to make anything of the description of the spring which issues from the threshold of the temple, flows through the land, and makes the waters of the Dead Sea sound, but they are also unable to explain the separation of the temple from the city of Jerusalem; as it would never have occurred to any Jewish patriot" (Keil, *Ezekiel,* 385). Also, O. Palmer Robertson, *The Christ of the Prophets,* (Phillipsburg, NJ: Presbyterian & Reformed, 2004), 298-99. And what can rival Luther's way of putting it: "The blind Jews do not see the absurdity. This cannot be any physical building; still less can it be at the place where Jerusalem was situated, as they falsely hope. There shall also be a great flow of water out of the temple into the Dead Sea (Ezek. 47:1-12) (which the papists—fools that they are!—take to be their holy water); but this in no way squares with the topography of Israel" (*Works,* 35:292).

[402] Alva McClain, *The Greatness of the Kingdom* (Winona Lake, IN: BMH Books), 230.

[403] Norman Geisler, *Miracles and Modern Thought* (Grand Rapids: Zondervan, 1982), 13.

[404] Renald Showers, *What on Earth is God Doing?* (Neptune, NJ: Loizeaux Brothers, 1973), 14-16. These consequences relate mostly to dispensationalism's goal of history. For a development of the anthropological consequences see Augustine's seven-fold list cited by Philip Schaff, *History of the Christian Church* (Grand Rapids: Eerdmans, 1981), 3:825-829.

demonstration of God's sovereignty."[405] To accomplish this purpose, God must undo all of the above consequences. This means that God must restore the theocracy, crush Satan, and remove the curse from nature. All of these will occur during the Kingdom age. This is the goal toward which history is moving, and if paradise lost is not paradise regained then God has lost the war.[406] Eugene Merrill writes in his *magum opus*:

> The creation account is thus the beginning of the sacred narrative, and it is there that the central theological theme is introduced. The fall and its tragic consequences become the sotto voce of everything that subsequently follows in the narrative; but the notes of divine redemption, growing ever more audible and clear, eventually drown out the despair of the human dilemma and point to the triumphant day of full restoration of God's eternal and glorious designs.[407]

The second argument against the kingdom view is the anticipation of the renewal of animal sacrifices. The logic also includes the claim of literal interpretation and goes as follows: one of the major *sine qua non* of dispensationalism is the insistence on a normal, literal interpretation of the prophets. If the literal interpretation of the prophets is abandoned when it comes to Ezekiel 40-48, then dispensationalism is undercut for the logic of the entire system is weakened. If, however, literal interpretation is maintained, then the dispensationalist is left with a renewal of animal sacrifices which appears to demean the cross of Christ and is contradicted by the Book of Hebrews. Adherents of other eschatological schemes are quick to note this apparent discrepancy. Snowden remarked:

> It is a cardinal principle of premillennarianism that the prophecies of the Messianic kingdom in the Old Testament apply, not to the first, but to the second coming of Christ and to the millennial kingdom he will inaugurate...It is a further principle of this system that these prophecies must be interpreted in a literal sense...Premillennialism is therefore required by its own logic to take the prophecy of Ezekiel 40-48 literally...If any premillenarians pause at this or say that they do not hold it, we must repeat that we are not dealing with individuals but with the

[405] Showers, *What on Earth is God Doing?* 18. For an expanded definition see Renald Showers, *There Really is a Difference! A Comparison of Covenant and Dispensational Theology* (Bellmawr, NJ: The Friends of Israel, 1990), 1-6.

[406] Geisler, *Systematic Theology,* 565.

[407] Eugene Merrill, *Everlasting Dominion: A Theology of the Old Testament* (Nashville: Broadman & Holman, 2006), 647. Ross adds: "It is important to note that contrary to popular opinion the ultimate destiny of God's people is an earthly destiny. The Bible places the redeemed on the new earth and not only in a heavenly realm; they will reign with Christ on earth (Rev. 5:10)" (Allen Ross, *Recalling the Hope of Glory* [Grand Rapids: Kregel, 2006], 495).

logic and literature of the system.[408]

Concerning the same matter and the return to animal sacrifices, Hamilton concurred, "If the literal method of interpretation of all Old Testament prophecies is to be followed, this is exactly what will be necessary…This is a picture upon which premillennialists do not like to dwell."[409] And more recently, Hoekema has said: "These words [that sacrifices are not literal] convey a far-reaching concession on the part of the dispensationalists. If the sacrifices are not to be taken literally, why should we take the temple literally? It would seem that the dispensational principle of literal interpretation of Old Testament prophecy is here abandoned, and that a crucial foundation stone for the entire dispensational system has here been set aside."[410]

These objections are valid in that they insist on hermeneutical consistency. If one is committed to the truth of dispensational theology, he must interpret Ezekiel literally with whatever apparent difficulties that may entail. However, one additional observation is appropriate. The impression from the above quotations is that these authors feel that they have dispensationalists in a no-win situation. Yet, it is equally clear, that the postmillennialist and amillennialist have no basis on which to allegorize Ezekiel 40-48. While it is granted that there could be "problems" associated with these sacrifices, these problems are not diminished by unwarranted license with the text. There are as many problems if one accepts a non-literal view of the passage as when one accepts a literal view of it. As suggested by Alexander, "The figurative or 'spiritualizing' interpretive approach does not seem to solve any of the problems of Ezekiel 40-48; it tends to create new ones."[411] There is no reasonable explanation concerning the numerous details of the temple service, worship, and re-allotment of the land which can be given by advocates of a symbolic view. The spiritualization of this prophecy in applying it to the church or the eternal state is unsound hermeneutically and results in confusion when the immense number of details is examined. The allegorists' interpretations of these chapters border on exegetical license and subjective theories.[412]

---

[408] James Snowden, *The Coming of the Lord*, 207-9, 217.

[409] Floyd Hamilton, *The Basis of the Millennial Faith*, 41.

[410]Hoekema, *The Bible and the Future*, 204. Similar statements are made by LaSor: "This would appear contrary to the prophetic emphasis on the spiritual nature of the cult and of Yahweh as the God who does not delight in blood offerings. It is certainly contrary to the New Testament view" (William LaSor, *Old Testament Survey* [Grand Rapids: Eerdmans, 1982], 477; see also Keil, *Ezekiel*, 388; Stalker, *Ezekiel*, 42).

[411] Ralph Alexander, "Ezekiel," 4:943. Or Feinberg: "The non-literal approach has no system of its own; it dwells on negation and offers no positive exposition of the revelatory material" (Charles Feinberg, "The Rebuilding of the Temple," in *Prophecy in the Making,* Carl F. H. Henry, ed. [Carol Stream, IL: Creation House, 1971], 109).

[412] Hobart Freeman, *An Introduction to the Old Testament Prophets,* 310-11. Sauer likewise commented that "Ezekiel pictures a future temple with so very many particulars and measurements that it will be simply impossible to declare that all this is only figurative and must therefore be spiritualized...how can this be spiritualized" (Erich Sauer, *The Triumph of the Crucified* [Grand Rapids: Eerdmans, 1952], 179-80)? For a discussion of the tension of interpretation between millennial systems, see David Turner, "The Continuity of Scripture and Eschatology: Key Hermeneutical Issues," *Grace Theological Journal* 6 (1985): 275-87.

Section 19: The Five Major Offerings[413]

The Burnt Offering (עֹלָה)

Leviticus 1:1-17. The first offering mentioned in Leviticus is the burnt offering.[414] The word used refers to "that which goes up."[415] This could be a reference either to the fact that the offering goes up to the altar or that the smoke of the sacrifice being totally consumed goes up to God (except for the hide which goes to the priest as his prebend-Lev. 7:8).[416] The majority of scholars favor the latter understanding since the peculiarity of this sacrifice is that it was completely incinerated on the altar.[417]

There appear to be at least two demonstrable purposes for the burnt offering. The first is that the offering symbolized the complete and utter devotion of the offerer to God. This is based on the fact that the complete animal was consumed and that the animal was very costly (Lev. 1:3).[418] When the proper animal was brought in an unblemished state, it[419] was said to be "acceptable to the Lord" (Lev. 1:3).[420]

Ironically, some of those opposed to interpreting Ezekiel 40-48 literally provide a series of maps of the various details in the vision.

[413] Jerry Hullinger, "The Function of the Sacrifices in Ezekiel's Temple, Part 1" *Bibliotheca Sacra* 167:665 (2010) 40-57; "The Function of the Sacrifices in Ezekiel's Temple, Part 2" *Bibliotheca Sacra* 167:666 (2010) 166-179. Portions used are by permission.

[414] The performance of this sacrifice can be enumerated as follows: The worshiper may choose to bring (v. 3) a bull (vv. 3-5), sheep or goat (v. 10), or a bird (v. 14). He then lays (press) his hand on its head (v. 4). He slaughters it on the north side of the altar (vv. 4-5)

The priest throws (splashes) the blood around the altar after it is collected by his fellow priests (v. 5). The worshiper flays and cuts the animal into pieces (v. 6). The priest puts fire and wood on the altar (v. 7). The priest lays the pieces on the fire (v. 8). The priest washes its legs and entrails in water (v. 9). The priest burns the whole on the altar (v. 9).

[415] Brown, Driver, and Briggs, *A Hebrew and English Lexicon of the Old Testament*, 750.

[416] In keeping with one of the suggested purposes of this offering (total dedication), it is fitting that the whole carcass is consumed (for the exception of larger hides and "feathers" see Lev. 1:16; 7:8). This would then make the offering useless, and therefore an irrevocable gift.

[417] Roland de Vaux, *Studies in Old Testament Sacrifice* (Cardiff: University of Wales Press, 1964), 27; George Buchanan Gray, *Sacrifice in the Old_Testament: Its Theory and Practice*, 7; W. O. E. Oesterley, *Sacrifices in Ancient Israel* (London: Hodder and Stoughton, 1937) 85; N. H. Snaith, *Leviticus and Numbers*, 15; S. C. Gayford, *Sacrifice and Priesthood: Jewish and Christian*, 42.

[418] Derek Kidner, "Sacrifice—Metaphors and Meaning," *Tyndale Bulletin* 33 (1982), 131; A. Noordtzij, *Leviticus*, 30; Gayford, *Sacrifice and Priesthood*, 43; H. Ringgren, *Sacrifice in the Bible*, 15; Joseph Dan, "Sacrifice," in *Encyclopedia Judaica*, 14:602.

[419] The pronoun can be properly translated either "it" or "he." The translation "it" is being followed because the first part of the verse (1:3a) puts the emphasis on the state of the animal. The following verse (1:4) deals with the atonement on behalf of the worshiper, and therefore his acceptance. Hartley adds that "the next verse [v. 4] says it will be accepted for him…suggesting that the offering is the antecedent in this verse" (John Hartley, *Leviticus* [Dallas: Word, 1992], 13).

[420] "To be accepted by the Lord" carries the idea of being accepted for worship since "not to be accepted" means rejection (Ps. 77:7) and restriction from enjoying the temple festivals (Ps. 51:8, 13-19). Acceptability would depend on the adherence to the regulations (e.g. Lev. 22:21) and the spiritual condition (e.g. Jer. 6:20). Rooker similarly argues that the noun form of רָצוֹן ("acceptable") is cognate to the verb form meaning "to be pleased with." The sacrificial offering was thus to elicit favor from God (Rooker, *Leviticus,* 88).

A second purpose of the burnt offering involves atonement. The text states concerning the burnt offering in Leviticus 1:4b, "that it may be accepted on his behalf to make atonement for him." This is probably included here because it would have been unthinkable to approach God without some form of atonement.[421] Therefore, it probably functioned to secure a positive response from God and to protect the person from His wrath so that worship could be continued. The "atonement" therefore, had the ultimate effect of propitiation.[422] Levine states this view in these words:

> "The *'olah* was a signal to God that His worshippers desired to bring their needs to His attention; its purpose was to secure an initial response from Him...Proximity to God was inherently dangerous for both the worshiper and the priest, even if there had been no particular offense to anger Him. The favorable acceptance of the *'olah* signaled God's willingness to be approached and served as a kind of ransom, or redemption, from divine wrath."[423]

The Grain Offering (מִנְחָה)

[421] There are other Old Testament texts which assign an atoning function to the burnt offering (Lev. 9:7 [with the purgation offering]; 14:20; 16:24; Job 1:5; Ezek. 45:15, 17 [with the other sacrifices]); and, passages in which the burnt offering was used as a part of the tabernacle-purging process (Richard Averbeck, "עֹלָה" in *New International Dictionary of Old Testament Theology and Exegesis*, Willem A. VanGemeren, gen. ed. [Grand Rapids: Zondervan, 1997], 3:409). Milgrom has suggested that the purification and reparation offerings were the primary expiatory offerings to be offered for very specific reasons (Milgrom, *Leviticus 1-16* [NY: Doubleday, 1991], 176). This would indicate that any atoning function assigned to the burnt offering was more general in nature necessary because the worshiper was approaching God (Wenham, *Leviticus,* 57). This implies that the burnt offering's atoning significance was to secure a positive response from God. See also Milgrom, *Leviticus 1-16,* 488. For diachronic explanations of the atoning significance of the burnt offering, see Averbeck, *New International Dictionary of Old Testament Theology and Exegesis,* 3:409-10. Regarding the textual order of the offerings, Rainey holds that the ritual order of sacrifice was expiation, consecration, fellowship (A. F. Rainey, "The Order of Sacrifices in Old Testament Ritual Texts," *Biblica* 51 [1970], 498). Therefore, the burnt offering could be offered before the peace offering, but never before the primary expiatory offerings (purification and reparation). However, others argue that the order in the text is not the order of being carried out but simply to aid the memory of the priest (Rooker, *Leviticus*, 81 note 4). Or, as suggested by Ross, the burnt offering is listed first because it was one of the most frequent, not normally the first offering (Ross, *Holiness to the LORD,* 85). This is probably the best option in light of the evidence.

[422] The wording here is in light of the later discussion regarding the main sense of "atonement." It will be argued that "atonement" deals with the wiping and purification of uncleanness. However, this still finally results in God being satisfied. Hence "atonement" properly reflects the maintenance of relationship with God.

[423] Levine, *Leviticus*, 7. For the idea of attraction, Levine uses the illustration of the Elijah narrative in 1 Kings 18 where Elijah prepares a burnt offering and the priests of Baal prepare their offerings. Their common objective was to secure a response from their deity. As 1 Kings 18:24 says, "The god who responds with fire, that one is God" (6). For this same view see G. J. Wenham, *The Book of Leviticus*, 57-63; H. H. Rowley, *Worship in Ancient Israel: Its Forms and Meaning*, 120-21; de Vaux, *Studies in Old Testament Sacrifice,* 36. The quote by Levine in the text, "even if there had been no particular offense" is an important one. Other sacrifices atoned for more specific transgressions and shortcomings while the burnt offering seems to be more general in its approach form any sin so that he can proceed with other forms of worship. Though not in the priestly literature, it is interesting that Job offered burnt offerings for his sons when he was thinking "perhaps my children have sinned and cursed God in their hearts" (Job 1:5).

Leviticus 2:1-14. The burnt offering and the grain offering are often mentioned together in the Old Testament (Josh. 22:23, 29; Judges 13:19; 23; 1 Kings 8:64; 2 kings 16:13, 15). In usage[424] outside tabernacle or temple worship the מִנְחָה could refer to offerings in general (Gen. 4:3-5) and frequently was used to speak of tribute (Judg. 3:15, 17-18; 2 Sam. 8:6; 10:25; 2 Kings 17:3). Closely connected to this was when a gift would be sent by an inferior to a superior (1 Kings 10:25; 2 Kings 8:8). The word could also denote devotion and commitment (Gen. 43:11-34; Judges 3:14; 1 Chron. 18:2, 6; 1 Kings 4:21). The term in Leviticus, however, always refers to a grain offering.[425] In addition to being offered with the burnt offering, it was brought at times of joy including the cleansing of a leper (Lev. 14:10, 20, 21, 31), the successful consummation of a Nazirite vow (Num. 6:15, 19), and the presentation of a peace offering (Num. 15:3ff).[426]

The procedure for making the מִנְחָה was to use semolina, mix olive oil into the dough, and apply frankincense to it. The מִנְחָה could be cooked on a griddle or in an oven, and a fistful of the dough was burned on the altar while the rest was eaten by the priests in the sanctuary. Interestingly, it is emphasized that salt was by no means to be left out of the offering as a symbol of the covenant (Lev. 2:13).[427] Because the usage of the word מִנְחָה emphasizes the gift aspect of an inferior to a superior, and because of the emphasis on the salt of the covenant, the purpose of this offering was probably to attribute homage to God and to express fidelity to the covenant.[428] Eichrodt suggests:

> The category is the conception of sacrifice as a gift to deity. Just as an inferior being brings a present to a superior, or a client to his patron, or a vassal to his lord, as the normal expression of his subjection…so the pious worshiper makes an offering to his God. Naturally only something valuable…is suitable for such an offering. Hence food—and that only at its best—accords admirably with the idea of gift, because it is essential to

[424] Brown, Driver, and Briggs, *A Hebrew and English Lexicon of the Old Testament*, 585

[425] Wenham, *The Book of Leviticus,* 69.

[426] The general ritual for the cereal offering included the following:
He shall bring a cereal offering (Lev. 2:1, 8, 14).
He shall pour oil on it (Lev. 2:1, 15).
He shall put frankincense on it (Lev. 2:1, 15).
He shall bring it to Aaron's sons (Lev. 2:2, 8).
The priest shall bring it to the altar (Lev. 2:8).
The priest shall take from it a handful (Lev. 2:2, 9).
The priest shall burn a memorial part.

[427] For other references to salt showing commitment to a covenant see Numbers 18:19; 2 Chronicles 8:5; 2 Samuel 23:5-7; and Isaiah 55:3. For other references which show this offering as being a time of joy see 2 Chronicles 31:5; 32:28; Psalm 4:7; Isaiah 16:10; 22:13; 24:7; 25:6; 27:2; Jeremiah 31:12; 48:33; Hosea 14:7; and Zechariah 10:7.

[428] Though not as prominent, there are cases where a propitiatory element is present (Gen. 32:14, 19, 21: 33:10; Lev. 5:11-13; 1 Sam. 26:19).

life.[429]

The same is stated well by Rooker: "The grain offering was a gift to the Lord that honored him as the source of life and of the fertility of the land. It represented the dedication to God of the fruit of one's labor. In the grain offering the worshiper offered the best of the kernels of wheat to indicate that he was offering the best to God, which signified the dedication of one's life and work to God."[430]

The Peace Offering (שֶׁלֶם)

Leviticus 3:1-17. The next offering listed in Leviticus is the "peace offering." This word indicates not only an absence of war, but a state of completeness, soundness, and welfare.[431] Critical to understand is that this offering was not one which *made* peace with God, but rather one which expressed that the worshiper was *already* at peace with God.[432] Thus peace exists when this offering is brought. Gayford notes that if "the name was used in this sense [to make peace] the Peace Offering would be beyond all others the atoning sacrifice."[433] The preceding fact is confirmed by the instances in which this offering was specified.[434] It was to be made during the celebration of the Feast of Weeks (Lev. 23:19-20) and in the ritual for the completion of the Nazirite vow (Num. 6:17-20). The peace offering was made as well after successful military campaigns (1 Sam. 11:15), cessation of famine or pestilence (2 Sam. 24:25), a time of spiritual renewal (2 Chron. 29:31-36), family reunions (1 Sam. 20:6), and at the harvesting of the first-fruits (1 Sam. 9:11-13, 22-24; 16:4-5).[435] Thus in many cases the peace

[429] Eichrodt, Theology of the Old Testament, 144. See also Wenham, The Book of Leviticus, 69, 71.

[430] Rooker, Leviticus, 99. This observation illuminates the reason Cain's offering was rejected in Genesis 4. In the Genesis narrative, the offerings are designated by the term מִנְחָה. The issue therefore was not blood but the state of Cain's heart. Abel went out of his way to please God, while Cain simply discharged his duty.

[431] Francis Brown, S. R. Driver, and Charles Briggs, A Hebrew and English Lexicon of the Old Testament, (Oxford: Clarendon Press, 1951), 1022-23.

[432] There is difference of opinion concerning the most appropriate way to translate the word. Some have suggested the idea of "shared offering" or "fellowship offering" based on the ritual at the end of the sacrifice (N. H. Snaith, Leviticus and Numbers, [London: Thomas Nelson, 1967] 37; NEB, TEV). Another possibility is that this could be a "covenant sacrifice." However, in one sense all sacrifices were covenant related (see Davies' article, "An Interpretation of Sacrifice in Leviticus," Zeitschrift fur die alttestamentliche Wissenschaft 89 [1977]: 387-99). Still another view is that connection should be made with the Akkadian shulmanu meaning "a gift." But again, in a sense all sacrifices were gifts. It seems more probable that the word is to be connected with the Ugaritic *shlmm* carrying the idea of "peace" (KJV, ESV, NAS, RSV).

[433] S. C. Gayford, Sacrifice and Priesthood: Jewish and Christian [London: Methuen & Co., 1953], 35. See also Derek Kidner, "Sacrifice—Metaphors and Meaning," Tyndale Bulletin 33 (1982): 133; H. H. Rowley, Worship in Ancient Israel (London: SPCK, 1967) 123; H. Ringgren, Sacrifice in the Bible (NY: Association Press, 1962) 23.

[434] Regarding Exodus 29:28, 33 where the peace offering is said to make atonement, it should be remembered that varying sacrifices could have overlapping functions. While its blood could make atonement, usage shows that this was not its chief intent.

[435] At these times the kidneys and intestines of the animal were burned. In the Old Testament, these were the seat of the emotions (Job 19:27; Ps. 16:7; Jer. 4:14; 12:2). This probably demonstrated the deepest and best emotions of peace being expressed in this offering to God (G. J. Wenham, *Leviticus* [Grand Rapids: Eerdmans, 1985], 80-81).

offering expressed thanksgiving to God for His blessings which were a sign of a peaceful relationship. As Eichrodt wrote, this offering "springs spontaneously from man's need to give public and material expression to his gratitude from some deliverance or marvelous benefit."[436]

The unique part of this offering was that it was the only one in which part of the sacrifice was eaten by the worshiper (3:17).[437] Every peace offering culminated in a communal meal. Except for the portions burned on the altar or given to the priest, the rest was given to the offerer as food for his family and the Levites in his community (Deut. 12:12, 18-19). The communal meal in social life cemented an alliance of friendship and was an expression of joy and communion. Noordtzij observed that this meal "brought an expression of joy and thanksgiving produced by this newly awakened communion with God."[438] On other occasions people are said to have eaten and drunk "before the Lord" (Exod. 18:12; Deut. 12:7, 18; 14:23, 26; 15:20) signifying intimate fellowship at which God was perceived to be the honored guest. Further, the expression "before the Lord" really denotes God's face as a symbol of His presence (cf., Exod. 33:14).[439]

The Purgation Offering (חַטָּאת)

Leviticus 4:1-5:13. The final two offerings of Leviticus 1-7 differ from the first three primarily in that they were the major propitiatory offerings which effected atonement.[440] The central passage for the חַטָּאת is Leviticus 4:1-5:13.[441]

---

[436] Walther Eichrodt, *Theology of the Old Testament* (Philadelphia: Westminster, 1961), 147.

[437] See Averbeck's helpful comments on the prohibition in Leviticus 17 about eating blood which deals solely with the peace offering (Richard Averbeck, שׁלם," in *New International Dictionary of Old Testament Theology and Exegesis*, Willem A. VanGemeren, gen. ed. [Grand Rapids: Zondervan, 1997], 4:138).

[438] A. Noordtzij, *Leviticus* (Grand Rapids: Zondervan, 1982) 51; Eduard Konig, *Geschichte der Alttestamentlichen Relgion* (Gutersloh: C. Bertelsmann, 1924), 537ff.

[439] Ringgren, *Sacrifice in the Bible,* 25-26; Baruch Levine, *Leviticus: The Traditional Hebrew Text with the New JPS Translation,* (Philadelphia: The Jewish Publication Society, 1989) 14; Gayford, *Sacrifice and Priesthood,* 38; A. Noordtzij, *Leviticus* (Grand Rapids: Zondervan, 1982), 4.

[440] For the purification offering see Exodus 29:10-14, 36; Leviticus 4:1-35; 6:10, 17-23, 7:7, 37; 8:2, 14-15; 9:2-3, 7-15, 22; 10:16-20; 12:6-8; 14:13, 22, 31; 15:15 30: 16:3, 5, 6, 9, 11, 14-15, 18-19, 25, 27-28; 23:19; Numbers 6:11, 14, 16; 7:16, 22, 28, 34, 40, 46, 52, 58, 64, 70, 76, 82, 87; 8:7, 8, 12; 15:24, 25, 27, 18:9; 19:9, 17; 28:15, 22; 29:5, 11, 16, 19, 22, 25, 28, 31, 34, 38.

[441] On the material regarding this offering, Wenham suggests the following outline (87) which will be followed in the above discussion.

4:1-35—for inadvertent sin
2—general introduction
3-21—blood sprinkled in the holy place
3-12—for the high priest
13-21—for the whole congregation
22-35—blood smeared on the main altar
22-26—for the tribal leader
27-31—for an ordinary person offering a goat
32-35—for an ordinary person offering a lamb
5:1-13—for sins of omission
1-6—offering—lamb or goat
7-10—offering—birds

The term for this offering comes from חָטָא which is rendered "to miss, to go wrong, sin."[442] Because of this, the חַטָּאת has been traditionally rendered as "sin offering." However, when the occasion and purposes of this offering are examined, it will be seen that a better translation would be "purification or purgation offering." Though this will be pointed out in the subsequent discussion, it can at least be stated here that the term occurs in contexts where it is unlikely that sin is present (e.g., Lev. 12:6-7; 15:14-15, 29-30; 14:19, 22, 31; Num. 6:10-11, 14).[443]

Leviticus 4:3-13. Instructions are given here if the priest sins. Of note are four things: 1) the priest's sin brings guilt on all of the people (4:3),[444] 2) he sprinkles blood seven times[445] in front of the veil (4:6), 3) he daubs the blood on the horns of the inner altar[446] of incense (4:7), and 4) the animal (a bull), except for its suet, is burned outside the camp in a place ceremonially clean (4:12).

Leviticus 4:13-21. These verses give the ritual in the event that the whole Israelite community sins unintentionally. The important points to be noticed in this case are: 1) the blood (of a bull) is again sprinkled in front of the veil, and 2) again daubed on the horns of the altar.

Leviticus 4:22-26. In this scenario, a leader is pictured as sinning unintentionally. In this case, the blood (this time of a male goat) is put on the horns of the altar of burnt offering with the rest being poured out at the base of the altar.

Leviticus 4:27-35. This last form of ritual is when a member of the community sins unintentionally. The blood manipulation is performed in the same manner as the preceding except a female goat is used. In this discussion of ritual there are two key points to be noted. First, in the first two cases the blood is sprinkled in closer proximity to the Most Holy Place than the last two. Second, the animals decrease in value in each instance.[447]

11-13—offering—flour

[442] Brown, Driver, and Briggs, *A Hebrew and English Lexicon of the Old Testament*, 306.

[443] This fact is acknowledged by many including N. Kiuchi, *The Purification Offering in the Priestly Literature: Its Meaning and Function* (Sheffield: Sheffield Academic Press, 1987), 16, 162; Colin Brown, "θύω," in *New International Dictionary of New Testament Theology*, edited by Colin Brown (Grand Rapids: Zondervan, 1975), 3:419. Milgrom states dogmatically that the rendering as "sin offering" is "incorrect on all grounds: contextually, morphologically, and etymologically…The very range of the חַטָּאת gainsays the notion of sin…Purification offering is certainly the more accurate translation" (Jacob Milgrom, "Two Kinds of Hatta't," *Vetus Testamentum* 26 [1976], 237).

[444] This is due to the fact that sins and impurities had a contagious effect which could spread throughout the entire community.

[445] The blood was sprinkled seven times because to the Semitic mind this was the number of completeness or totality (Noordtzij, *Leviticus*, 57-58).

[446] The need to purify the altar is seen by the fact that it was a symbol of God's presence. In the earliest periods it commemorated a theophany (Gen. 12:7; 26:24-25). In addition, it is at times referred to as the table of Yahweh (Ezek. 44:16; Mal. 1:7, 12). The horns on the altar could also be emblems of God (H. Obbink, "The Horns of the Altar in the Semitic World, Especially in Yahwism," *Journal of Biblical Literature* 56 [1937], 43-49; Roland de Vaux, *Studies in Old Testament Sacrifice* [Cardiff: University of Wales Press, 1964], 413).

[447] The laying-on-of-hands ritual is significant in the process of sacrifice. Different views as to what this signified include: the transfer and/or substitution theory; the identification theory; the consecration/dedication

The Occasion of the חַטָּאת

The general occasion for the חַטָּאת is when anyone "sins unintentionally and does what is forbidden in any of the Lord's commands" (Lev. 4:2). This type of sin is one which is done in error or inadvertence.[448] The nominal form שְׁגָגָה occurs some nineteen times in the Old Testament and is used mainly in relation to the חַטָּאת (Lev. 4:2, 22, 27; Num. 15:24-29), and in the law of asylum (Num. 35:11; Josh 20:3, 9). It is used as parallel to expressions such as "without knowledge" (Josh. 20:3), and "he does not know" (Lev. 5:17). The opposite of this word seems to be that of sins committed with a high hand. So it seems best to retain the translation of "inadvertent" or "unintentional"[449] (NASB, ESV, NKJV, NIV). Davidson concurs:

> [It] comprehended all sins done not in a spirit of rebellion against the law

---

theory; the appropriation and/or designation theory; the Manumissio theory. For an adequate discussion of these see Angel Rodriguez, *Substitution in_the Hebrew Cultus* (Berrien Springs, MI: Andrews University Press, 1979) 201-32. It is commonly thought that by the laying on of hands, the sacrificial animal received that which induced the person to present it as an offering. Thus the animal became the successor to the person who offered it with the resultant punishment that was due him—hence transference and substitution. Levine states this view: "The sacrificial victim substitutes for the person, or persons, who offended God or who are impure. Impurity is transferred from them to the sacrificial victim, thus freeing the offenders from God's punishment. God accepts the sacrifice in lieu of the life of the offenders, whom He then pardons" (Levine, *Leviticus*, 21-22). For other adherents of this view see Geerhardus Vos, *Biblical Theology* (Grand Rapids: Eerdmans, 1977) 162; Derek Kidner, "Sacrifice—Metaphors and Meaning," *Tyndale Bulletin* 33 (1982): 131 (Kidner comes to the same conclusion using Num. 8:10ff as a starting point); Noordtzij, *Leviticus*, 33; Alfred Edersheim, *The Temple and its Ministry* (Grand Rapids: Eerdmans, 1972) 113; probably also S. C. Gayford, *Sacrifice and Priesthood: Jewish and Christian*, 63; H. Ringgren, *Sacrifice in the Bible*, 30; N. H. Snaith, *Leviticus and_Numbers* (London: Thomas Nelson Printers, 1967) 42. It could be objected that a transference of sin to an animal makes it unfit for sacrifice since it would then be polluted. This dilemma is what Feldman has called the "pattern of paradox" in the defilement and sanctity tension (Emanuel Feldman, *Biblical and Post-Biblical Defilement and Mourning: Law as Theology* [NY: KTAV, 1977] 63, 70). Rodriguez suggests the following solution, "What this tension proclaims is the superiority of holiness over against impurity. When sin/impurity is, through repentance and confession, given to Yahweh, He controls it. In the sanctuary the power of sin is overcome. We can therefore conclude that nether flesh of the animal, nor the priest, nor the blood, lose their holiness by bearing the sin of the offerer. They are the means by which sin is brought before the Lord" (Angel Rodriguez, *Substitution in the Hebrew Cultus* [Berrien Springs, MI: Andrews University Press, 1979] 218-19). This view, however, seems to contradict the inherent purpose of the sacrificial system. The purpose of the system is to purify and remove impurities as much as possible from the sanctuary. If sin or uncleanness were transferred to the animal, just the opposite would be occurring if impure blood were taken into the tabernacle. (It should be pointed out that in Lev. 16:21 the sins of the Israelites are expressly said to be put on the goat's head. However, in this sole instance the goat is led *away* from the tabernacle.) This point is substantiated by the fact that they blood of the purgation offering contaminated that which it touched after it had done its purifying work (Lev. 6:20, 21; 16:27-28; Num. 19:7, 8, 10). Because of this problem it is probably better to see the rite as one of ownership or declaration where the animal is set part as that which is designated to be offered to God.

[448] Brown, Driver, and Briggs, *A Hebrew and English Lexicon of the Old Testament*, 993.

[449] The translation "inadvertent" or "unintentional" has been used for convenience by many interpreters and is accurate as far as it goes. However, there are times when this offering was required for sins which were by nature known and intentional (Lev. 5:1). Yet, as Davidson points out, an intentional sin can be intentional and not necessarily premeditated in distinction to those intentional sins committed in a spirit of rebellion. This does not negate the fact that some of these "sins" which required this sacrifice were also committed "inadvertently" or "unintentionally" (as the examples in the text will illustrate) and therefore this translation is retained.

> or ordinance of YHWH—sins committed through human imperfection, or human ignorance or human passion; sins done when the mind was directed to some end connected with human weakness or selfishness, but not formally opposed to the authority of the Lawgiver. The distinction was thus primarily a distinction in regard to the state of mind of the transgressor.[450]

The first specific occasion for the חַטָּאת is when the priest commits some inadvertent sin (Lev. 4:3-12). Interestingly, his "sin" brings guilt on the entire nation. This is due to the fact that as the representative of the people before God (Exod. 28:12, 29, 38) the priest was to manifest at all times the holiness that God expects of His people. Thus as the representative of the entire congregation, his sin carried the greatest weight and brings guilt on the entire congregation. This would seem to imply that the mistake that he made was in some ritual matter in the tabernacle since there he was performing a ceremony which would affect the whole group.[451] However, Leviticus 10:6 would seem to extend this even beyond his cultic duties where Moses warns Aaron, Eleazar, and Ithamar, "Do not let your hair become unkempt, and do not tear your clothes, or you will die and the Lord will be angry *with the whole community.*"

The second specific occasion for the offering is found in Leviticus 4:13-21. In this case, the offering was presented when the whole community of Israel had committed some intentional sin.

The third occasion was when a leader sinned unintentionally (Lev. 4:22-26). It should be observed again that in this instance there was no blood rite performed near the veil or on the horns of the altar.

The fourth prescribed occasion for the offering is found in Leviticus 4:27-35. In this instance, an individual in the community had sinned.

Leviticus 5:1-4 presents four more instances in which the purgation offering is to be made. These include withholding evidence,[452] touching something

---

[450] A. B. Davidson, *The Theology of the Old Testament* (Edinburgh: T. & T. Clark, 1904), 315. See also Numbers 15:29, 20 which has unintentional vs. defiant; Leviticus 4:22, 23 with not aware vs. in ignorance; Numbers 35:11, 15 with manslaughter vs. murder. The unintentional nature of these sins is underscored by the fact that in three cases it is said that the offender may be "unaware of the matter" (Lev. 4:13, 23, 28). For a further discussion of various classes of sin in the Old Testament including inadvertent sin, advertent sin, and demonstrative sin, see Megory Anderson and Philip Culbertson, "The Inadequacy of the Christian Doctrine of Atonement," *Anglican Theological Review* 7 (1977), 308-9.

[451] Snaith, *Leviticus and Numbers,* 41; Levine, *Leviticus,* 20.

[452] By way of explanation, Leviticus 5:1 would be concerned not with the perpetrator of the various offences, but with one who knows about them and fails to divulge this information to the authorities. Thus for whatever reason, he has chosen to cover this up. Even though no one would know that this person knew something but himself, this sin could bring disaster on the entire community. This is illustrated (though not the same sin but the same principle) by Achan's sin. He was the only one who knew about it, yet the whole congregation suffered defeat at Ai. It was therefore imperative that this person be brought forth. Phillips explains the rationale: "The priestly legislators were...confronted with the problem of deliberate but undetectable offences which contaminated the cult....Such persons would be self-defeating for then there would be no incentive for the offender to admit his guilt and so enable his sin to be removed from the

ceremonially unclean such as an animal, touching any human uncleanness, or carelessly taking an oath.

Outside of Leviticus 4:1-5:13, there were other occasions when a purgation offering was required. These included childbirth (Lev. 12:1-18), a man with an unclean discharge (Lev. 15:13-15), a woman with an unclean discharge (Lev. 15:25-30), a leper (Lev. 14:1-32), and the Nazirite who defiled himself (Num. 6:11). Kiuchi made the following comment concerning these five occasions:

> These five cases...have one important thing in common: the contamination is unintentional, or at least the person was not in a position in which he/she could have avoided the defilement. Three of these cases describe a defilement produced by a disease. The first three are directly related to blood defilement, while the fifth is a defilement produced by a dead body.[453]

Along the same lines, Kurtz observed:

> These conditions...were involuntary and to a certain extent inevitable...Yet by requiring a sin-offering for the removal of the higher forms of uncleanness, it indicates a primary connection between them and sin, so far, that is to say, as the processes occurring in the body are dependent upon the influences and effects of the universal sinfulness...which required sacrificial expiation by means of a sin-offering, in the same manner as sinful acts unconsciously performed.[454]

The purgation offering was also given at religious feast times. These included the beginning of the month (Num. 28:11-15); the first day of unleavened bread (Num. 28:16-25); the feast of weeks (Lev. 23:15-21); the feast of the seventh month (Num. 29:1-38); the feast of the blowing of trumpets (Num. 29:1-6); and the feast of expiation (Num. 29:7-11). Again it is to be noted that no specific sin is given as the reason for offering. These festivals were joyous occasions and the purgation offering was probably made as recognition of impurity that needed to be cleansed simply by virtue of the fact that they would be approaching Yahweh.

A final class of occasions for the purgation offering included special times such as: 1) the anticipation of the consecration of the tabernacle and altar (Exod. 29:35-37); 2) the consecration of Aaron, his sons, and the altar (Lev. 8:14-17); 3) the installation of Aaron and his sons (Lev. 9:1-11, 15-17); 4) the Day of Atonement to cleanse the sanctuary (Lev. 16); 5) the fulfillment of a Nazirite vow

---

community" (Anthony Phillips, "The Undetectable Offender and the Priestly Legislators," *Journal of Theological Studies* 36 [1985]: 150).

[453] N. Kiuchi, *The Purification Offering in the Priestly Literature: Its Meaning and Function* (Sheffield: Sheffield Academic Press, 1987) 103.

[454] J. H. Kurtz, *Sacrificial Worship of the Old Testament* (Edinburgh: T. & T. Clark, 1863), 416.

(Num. 6:13-16); and 6) the dedication of the altar (Num. 7). It needs to be stressed again, according to the argument of this paper, that atonement/purification is being made on behalf of persons or to objects that could not possibly have sinned.[455] In other instances (e.g., the Day of Atonement), purgation was needed because sin or uncleanness had defiled an object.

The Purpose/Function of the חַטָּאת

From the above occasions observed, it can be seen that the purpose of the purgation offering was purification or cleansing of sancta which had been defiled either from unintentional mistakes or the unavoidable contracture of uncleanness. It is also evident that the blood of the offering was required to purify even when no specific sin is mentioned as needing atonement.[456] This being the case, the blood of the sacrifices was not an offering to God, but rather a means of purification.

Milgrom has argued that the חַטָּאת only functioned to purify sancta and not people. He states that the חַטָּאת is "confined to the sanctuary but it is never applied to a person...the priest purges the most sacred objects and areas of the sanctuary on behalf of the person who caused their contamination."[457] If purification by blood[458] did not follow, disastrous consequences would result.

[455] For example, Kiuchi states that "nowhere in Leviticus 8 is there a hint that the purification of the altar was necessitated by particular sins of Aaron and his sons. Since the occasion is the consecration of the altar and priests, could it be that the purification concerns uncleanness which is assumed to be present before the common becomes holy" (Kiuchi, *The Purification Offering in the Priestly Literature,* 42).

[456] Milgrom asserts that not only was the purgation offering "unrelated to sin in Rabbinic thought, most authorities deny emphatically that the impurity itself was caused by sin. And even the minority who see a causal connection between sin and affliction...concur with the majority that the primary purpose of the *hatta't* is for ritual purification" (Jacob Milgrom, "Sin Offering or Purgation Offering?" *Vetus Testamentum* 21 [1971]: 238).

[457] The blood of the purgation offering is often said to purify, purge, and decontaminate (Exod. 29:36; Lev. 8:15; 12:7, 8; 14:19, 20, 31, 52; 16:19; 2 Chon. 29:24; Ezek. 43:20, 22, 23; 45:18; Jacob Milgrom, "Israel's Sanctuary: The Priestly Picture of Dorian Gray," *Revue biblique* 83 [1976], 391). See also, Jacob Milgrom, *Cult and Conscience: The Asham and the Priestly Doctrine of Repentance* (Leiden: E. J. Brill, 1976), 72, 76, 77; Allen Ross, *Holiness to the LORD* (Grand Rapids: Baker, 2002) 124-25. Likewise, Gayford: "The offenses for which it was appointed, had the effect of making the offender unclean....The sin offering purified him and reconsecrated him. He was restored to membership of the people made holy to the Lord" (Gayford, *Sacrifice and Priesthood,* 49). (See also Feldman for his idea that "impurity is a metaphor for estrangement and desacralization" [Feldman, *Biblical and Post-Biblical Defilement and Mourning: Law as Theology,* 34]). Gammie also wrote that "a restoration of purity and separation from uncleanness is what the sacrificial system—and in particular the so-called sin offerings—sought to restore" (John Gammie, *Holiness in Israel* [Minneapolis: Fortress, 1989], 43-44).

[458] The atoning power of blood is linked to its nature as the essence of animation (Noam Zohar, "Repentance and Purification: The Significance and Semantics of חטאת in the Pentateuch," *Journal of Biblical Literature* 107 [1988]: 611). This is in keeping with the ancient idea that the life-force had its specific seat in the blood which belongs to God (Martin Noth, *Leviticus: A Commentary* [Philadelphia: Westminster, 1977], 132). This has been agreed on by many, for example Levine writes: "sacrificial blood being especially instrumental because it was the symbol of life...God accepts the blood of the sacrifices in lieu of human blood" (Levine, *Leviticus,* 115). Likewise, de Vaux noted that "according to the Hebrew conception, the blood contains the life, it is life itself" (Roland de Vaux, *Studies in Old Testament Sacrifice*, 93. See also Ringgren, *Sacrifice in the Bible,* 37; Ralph Elliott, "Atonement in the Old Testament," *Review and Expositor* 59 [1962], 23).

This section, then, concludes with Rodriguez's comments on the function of this offering.

> Its function is purificatory...The function of the *hatta't* then would be to remove that impurity...Thus, man's relationship with God is re-established. From this discussion we may conclude that sin or impurity, if not expiated, would result in the sinner's permanent separation from God and the cultic community. To be severed from God and his sanctuary is to be disjointed form the source of life and blessings. The final result of that experience is death. It is within this conceptual framework that the *hatta't* operates.[459]

The Reparation Offering (אָשָׁם)

אָשָׁם As Reparation Offering

Leviticus 5:14-6:7. The fifth offering listed is the guilt offering.[460] Contextually, it will be seen that this offering would be better rendered as "reparation offering" rather than as "guilt-offering." While the root word means "guilty,"[461] the ritual of this offering suggests the meaning "guilty" in the sense of "liable to pay." This so-called guilt offering was due in all cases where damage had been done and loss had been suffered.[462] BDB agree that "this offering seems to have been confined to offences against God or man that could be estimated and so covered by compensation."[463] This is further supported by the fact that this offering is unique in its use of "return, restore" in Numbers 5:7; 18:9. Finally, a legal situation in the offering is presented: damage is done and restitution is

---

Some have argued that the blood represented death rather than life (Leon Morris, "The Biblical use of the Term Blood," *Journal of Theological Studies* 3 [1952], 216-27; R. K. Harrison, *Leviticus: An Introduction and Commentary* [Downers Grove, IL: InterVarsity Press, 1980], 182). For a rebuttal to this idea that blood represents death rather than life, McCarthy has noted that blood was associated with death in the ancient world in nations other than Israel, so that in seeing spilled blood as a life-force Israel was unique in viewing blood as representing life and not death in contrast to her neighbors (Dennis McCarthy, "Further Notes on the Symbolism of Blood and Sacrifice," *Journal of Biblical Literature* 92 [1973]: 210; see also his "The Symbolism of Blood and Sacrifice," *Journal of Biblical Literature* 88 [1969]: 166-76). For specific rebuttal to Morris's view see Lindsay Dewar, "The Biblical use of the Term Blood," *Journal of Theological Studies* 4 (1953), 204-8.

[459] Rodriguez, Substitution in the Hebrew Cultus, 144, 149. So, Alex Luc, "חַטָּאת" in *New International Dictionary of Old Testament Theology and Exegesis*, 2:97.

[460] Some have seen no noticeable difference between the חַטָּאת and the אָשָׁם (e.g., George Buchanan Gray, *Sacrifice in the Old Testament* [NY: KTAV Publishing House, 1971], 65; de Vaux, *Studies in Old Testament Sacrifice*, 102). Besides the differences which will be noted in the textual part of this section, see Norman Snaith, "The Sin-Offering and the Guilt-Offering," *Vetus Testamentum* 15 (1965), 73-80; Angel Rodriguez, *Substitution in the Hebrew Cultus*, 190.

[461] Brown, Driver, and Briggs, *A Hebrew and Eng. Lexicon of the Old Testament*, 79.

[462] N. H. Snaith, *Leviticus and Numbers*, 17.

[463] Brown, Driver, and Briggs, *A Hebrew and English Lexicon of the Old Testament*, 79. See also Kellerman who discusses the issue of reparation applicable in such cases as leprosy and sexual impurity (D. Kellermann, "אָשָׁם" in *Theological Dictionary of the Old Testament* [Grand Rapids: Eerdmans, 1974], 1:433-34) and the differences between the reparation offering and the purification offering (1:434).

ordered. It is the only offering in the roster of sacrifices that is commutable to currency (Lev. 5:15, 18, 25; 1 Sam. 6:3).[464] In sum, this offering did bring cleansing to the sanctuary as did the חַטָּאת since God's honor had been violated. However, the unique feature of this offering is that it also squared matters with the one offended.[465]

The Occasion of the **אָשָׁם**

The term מָעַל refers to the act of unfaithfulness or treachery which was redressed by the reparation offering.[466] מָעַל is used in the Old Testament to refer to a number of serious sins committed against God and man including adultery (Num. 5:12, 27); worshiping pagan deities (Num. 31:16; Ezek. 20:27), marrying foreigners (Ezra 10:2, 10), Achan's sin (Josh. 7:1), and Uzziah's violation (2 Chron. 26:16, 18).

Violation of Sancta. The first category of sins which required this offering was a violation or misappropriation of the Lord's holy things (Lev. 5:15) or that property which belonged to the Lord, the sanctuary, and the priests.[467] Milgrom has pointed out the cases of this violation (מָעַל) on temple sancta in Chronicles.[468] Uzziah is charged with this offense for offering incense inside the temple (2 Chron. 26:16-18). Ahaz is charged for tampering with the temple sancta (2 Chron. 28:19, 22-25) and suspending their use (2 Chron. 29:19). In addition, Chronicles pinpoints violation of temple sancta (מָעַל) as the reason for the downfall of Judah because "they contaminated the house of the Lord which He had sanctified in Jerusalem" (2 Chron. 36:14). This idea of trespass against sacred property is seen elsewhere in the dangers of contact with sancta by apodictic law ("the stranger who encroaches shall be put to death"—Num. 1:51; 3:10, 38; 18:7); the rebellion of Korah (Num. 16—18); Achan's violation (מָעַל) against the booty at Jericho (Josh. 7), and the Nadab and Abihu incident (Lev. 10).[469]

---

[464] Jacob Milgrom, *Cult and Conscience: The Asham and the Priestly Doctrine of Repentance*, 13-14. Gayford noted that "it presupposed a legal compensation...consisting of entire restitution of the loss inflicted, plus a fine of an additional fifth of the loss (Lev. 6:5; Num. 5:7)" (Gayford, Sacrifice and Priesthood, 45). For further support of this rendering, see Wenham, *The Book of Leviticus*, 104; Snaith, *Leviticus and Numbers*, 50; Noordtizj, *Leviticus*, 69; Leviticus 5:6, 19; Numbers 5:7, 8; 1 Samuel 6:4; Proverbs 14:9.

[465] Leon Morris suggested in his article (" 'Asham,' " *Evangelical Quarterly* 30 [1958], 196-209) that exegetes have "tended to concentrate too much on the money aspect and to overlook those substitutionary and expiratory aspects which may well be more fundamental. Our contention is that it is in these aspects that the essential meaning of this offering is to be found" (207). As noted above, the majority of the offerings had substitutionary and expiatory aspects. The question becomes: What is the unique contribution of a particular offering? Concerning the אָשָׁם;, the answer is that its unique contribution lies in its aspect of reparation. That is why this aspect is concentrated upon (though not meant to exclude the atoning aspect).

[466] Brown, Driver, and Briggs, A Hebrew and English Lexicon of the Old Testament, 591.

[467] Martin Noth, Leviticus: A Commentary, 46.

[468] Milgrom, Cult and Conscience, 1.

[469] This sin against sancta was one of the most dreaded in antiquity. See for example, "Prayer to Every God" (391) and "The Curse of Agade" (647-51) in James Pritchard, Ancient Near Eastern Texts (NJ:

Violation Against the Lord's Commands. This offering was also presented in cases where one suspected that he transgressed one of the Lord's commands for which he later felt guilty (Lev. 5:17-19). Wenham suggests that the offerer only suspected he had committed a transgression, though he could not be certain.[470]

Violation Against a Fellow Israelite. The third instance in which the אָשָׁם was offered was when one member of the nation defrauded his fellow Israelite. The sins listed in this regard seem to include types of embezzlement, theft, extortion, etc. (Lev. 6:2-3). In these cases, the reparation offering required that the offender bring a ram before the Lord to make expiation for his sin. In addition to this, however, he was required to make full restitution to the offended party as well as adding a fifth of its value (Lev. 6:4-7). Both of these acts resulted in his forgiveness. Eichrodt observes:

> A breach of trust between human beings involved the payment of compensation. The same obligation toward God was expressed in the guilt offering or sacrifice of reparation. Moreover, the proper legal compensation had to be made either directly to the injured fellow citizen or to the sanctuary at the time of sacrifice.[471]

One violation that may need slight explanation is the reference to "swearing falsely" (Lev. 6:3). At times, there was no other means of settling a dispute than to take an oath before Yahweh (Exod. 22:9) that had to be accepted by the claimant with no further action contemplated. Evidently this is due to the belief that divine judgment would follow if the oath were false (Num. 5:11ff.).[472] If

---

Princeton University Press, 1969). The Bible does not define the scope of the sancta, but it is reasonable to conclude that it had a wide meaning including the furniture, sacrifices, and ritual from the time of dedication until, if it were food, eaten or incinerated (Milgrom, Cult and Conscience, 44; F. Duane Lindsey, "Leviticus," in The Bible Knowledge Commentary: Old Testament, edited by John Walvoord and Roy Zuck [Wheaton: Victor, 1985], 183; Harrison, Leviticus, 71). It could be pointed out additionally that sancta trespass was in violation of the stipulations of the covenant (Lev. 19:30; 21:23; 26:2). Moreover, sancta trespass can bring God's wrath on people in the nation besides the one who committed the act (Josh. 22:18, 31; 2 Chron. 28: 19). This shows the horizontal as well as vertical ramifications of "sin" in the theocratic context.

[470] Wenham, The Book of Leviticus, 107-8. See also Lindsey, "Leviticus," in The Bible Knowledge Commentary, 183.

[471] Eichrodt, *Theology of the Old Testament,* 161. See also W. A. Van Gemeren, "Offerings and Sacrifices in Bible Times," in *The Evangelical Dictionary of Theology* (Grand Rapids: Baker, 1984), 790, for a discussion.

[472] Numbers 5:5-10 deals further with the law of recompense. When a person had wronged another person, he was to confess the sin and provide full restitution plus twenty percent. This corresponds with Leviticus 6, but goes on to describe a case not covered in Leviticus 6 (if the defrauded man was dead). In this case, a ram was required as a reparation offering to be given to the priest as well as the returned goods. In emphasizing the restitution idea that is unique to this offering, Milgrom remarks concerning Numbers 5:7, "The 'asham' is the only sacrifice that regularly uses the verb *heshiv* (Num. 5:7, 8) meaning 'restore' and implying monetary compensation" (Jacob Milgrom, *Numbers* [NY: The Jewish Publication Society, 1990], 35). Allen describes the full ritual for restitution in these verses. "The steps in the ritual...include 1) a condition of guilt—that person is guilty (v. 6), which excludes that person from active participation in the community as surely as a serious skin disease or contact with a dead body; 2) a public confession of that sin (v. 7a), presumably in the precincts of the sacred shrine, before witnesses and priests; 3) full restitution plus one-fifth to the one

Yahweh did not choose to bring quick judgment, the offender had in a sense "gotten away" with his false oath until God took whatever action He deemed necessary. This stipulation in the אָשָׁם is evidently to persuade the person to come forward.[473]

Summary: Functions for the Five Major Offerings	
Offering	**Function**
עֹלָה	Express devotion and make acceptable for worship by making atonement
מִנְחָה	A tribute or gift to a superior being
שְׁלָם	Express thanksgiving and celebrate the communion of fellowship
חַטָּאת	Cleanse or purge sancta on behalf of persons from inadvertent sins and contamination from impurity
אָשָׁם	Atonement for the sanctuary and reparation for misappropriation of sancta, suspected transgression, defrauding of fellow man

Section 20: The Dress of the High Priest

The High Priest in his robes

1. Linen drawers. These reached from the waist to the thigh (Exodus 28:42). Someone has said that these were to be worn as an evidence that the divine worship sanctioned no such sexual impurities as were associated with idolatrous

---

wronged (see Lev. 22:14; 27:11-13, 31); 4) a sacrifice to the Lord of a ram offering for atonement" (Ronald Allen, "Numbers," in *The Expositor's Bible Commentary* [Grand Rapids: Zondervan, 1990], 2:741).

[473] Phillips, "The Undetectable Offender and the Priestly Legislators," *Journal of Theological Studies*, 147. Ezekiel pronounces exile on the nation because its king violated a solemn oath (Ezek. 17:19-2). A similar oracle reveals that the gods sent a plague on the Hittites because of violation of the sancta and violation of their treaty oath (*Ancient Near Eastern Texts*, 395; see also A. Malamat, "Doctrines of Causality in Historiography," *Vetus Testamentum* 5 [1955], 1-12). It is a bit confusing as to why a purified leper would have to bring a reparation offering since his leprosy is not traceable to sancta trespass or any other cause (Lev. 14:12-17). Milgrom suggests that the answer is to be found in Leviticus 5:17-19 where it intimates that he may have desecrated sancta. He writes, "My hypothesis would rank as sheer conjecture were it not for the corroboration offered from an unexpected source. The Chronicler relates that Uzziah was stricken with leprosy precisely at the moment when, and because, he encroached upon sancta. It is no accident that Uzziah's sin is twice labeled *ma'al*" (Milgrom, *Cult and Conscience*, 80-81).

The question could arise as to why Leviticus 6-7 repeats much of what is in 1-5. Hoffmann suggests that 6-7 were written immediately after Exodus 29, and then 1-5 were written sometime later to clarify for the layman how to bring sacrifice (D. Hoffmann, *Das Buch Leviticus* [Berlin: Poppelauer, 1905-06], 1:70ff). However, it seems best to not make such a hard division between the two sections, but to regard 1-5 as concerning primarily the worshiper, and 6-7 as concerning primarily the priest. For further discussion of the occasions for the reparation offering, see, D. Kellermann "אָשָׁם," in *Theological Dictionary of the Old Testament*, 1:429-37.

worship, and that this is also the reason for the command in Exodus 20:26—"And do not go up to my altar on steps, lest your nakedness be exposed on it."

2. Tunic or shirt. It was made of white linen, all one piece, had sleeves, and is believed to have reached to the ankles, and to have been of a checker pattern. (Exodus 28:39, 40; 29:5)

3. Sash or girdle. This was wound around the tunic between the waist and the shoulders. Josephus says it was four fingers broad, and "so loosely woven that you would think it were the skin of a serpent." It was embroidered in colors. (Exodus 28:39)

4. Turban or miter. It was made of linen.

Garments that were peculiar to the high priest:

1. Robe. This was woven of blue cloth, in one piece, with an opening by which it might be put on over the head. It was worn over the tunic, but whether it reached to the knees or to the ankles is uncertain. It was beautifully ornamented at the bottom with pomegranates in purple and scarlet. Little gold bells hung between these, and made a tinkling sound whenever the wearer moved. (Exodus 39:22–26).

2. Epod. The ordinary priest wore an epod (see 1 Samuel 22:18), but it was different in material and style from that of the high priest. This was made of made "of gold, and of blue, purple and scarlet yarn, and of finely twisted linen" (Exodus 39:2). After that they "hammered out thin sheets of gold and cut strands to be worked into the blue, purple and scarlet yarn and fine linen—the work of a skilled craftsman" (Exodus 39:3), who must have learned his skill while he was a slave in Egypt, for the art of weaving was well known to the ancient Egyptians. The epod was in two pieces, one for the back and one for the breast. The two pieces were joined by "shoulder pieces," which were a continuation of the front part of the epod (Exodus 28:7; 39:4). On the shoulder pieces were two precious stones, each having the names of six of the tribes of Israel. There stones were placed in gold settings, which some think made clasps for fastening the shoulder pieces together. (Exodus 28:9–12) The two parts of the epod were fastened around the body by means of a waistband (girdle, KJV), which was really a portion of the front part of the epod (Exodus 28:8). The epod had no sleeves.

3. Breastplate. This was made of the same material as the epod. It was half a cubit wide (9") and a cubit long (18"), but when doubled it became a half cubit square (9"), and formed a pouch or pocket. On the front of this were four rows of precious stones, three in each row, and on them were engraved the names of the twelve tribes. These stones were set in gold. The breastplate was fastened to the epod by golden chains. (Exodus 28:15–29) Connected with this breastplate were the Urim and Thummim—Lights and Perfections—but precisely what these were no one knows. They were used as means of consulting the LORD in case of doubt

(Numbers 27:21; 1 Samuel 28:6). How they were used is not known. Some think that the twelve stones were the Urim and Thummim, the stones themselves being the Urim, or Lights, and the names of the tribes engraved on them being the Thummim, or Perfections, because they represented the tribes in their tribal integrity. From the fact that the Urim and Thummim are said to be in the breastplate, others think that they were separate from the twelve stones and were put into the pocket behind them. Some believe them to have been three precious stones that were placed in this pouch of the breastplate to be used for casting lots to decided questions of doubts; and that on one of the stones was engraved Yes, on another No, the third being without inscription. The stone drawn out by the high priest would indicate the answer: affirmative, negative, or no answer to be given. This may be so, but there is no proof of it. Someone further suggested that the Urim and Thummim was a diamond, kept in the pocket of the breastplate, and having the ineffable name of the Deity inscribed on it. This one believed that this is the "white stone" referred to in Revelation 2:17. Again, there is no proof of this, and all such things are only speculations best left until the LORD clarifies it all in the ages to come.

4. Diadem. This was a plate of pure gold fastened around the miter or turban by a blue cord (lace, KJV), and having engraved on it the words: "HOLINESS TO THE LORD." The NIV verses read: "Make a plate of pure gold and engrave on it as on a seal: HOLY TO THE LORD. Fasten a blue cord to it to attach it to the turban; it is to be on the front of the turban" (Exodus 28:36–37).[474]

Section 21: Excerpts from the Mishnah Tractate *Sanhedrin*

Physical Arrangement

4.3 The Sanhedrin sat in the form of a semi-circle so that they might all see each other; and two judges' clerks stood in front, one on the right and one on the left, taking down the evidence for the prosecution and the defence. R. Jehuda holds that there were three: one taking down evidence for the prosecution, the second for the defence, and the third taking down both. Before them sat three rows of disciples, each knowing his own place. If it became necessary to appoint another judge, he was appointed from the front row, while one from the second row took his place, and one from the third row that of the second. And for the third row one of the assembled audience was chosen. He did not sit in the place just vacated, but in a place for which he was suited.

Verdicts in Capital Trials to be Reached in Daytime

4.1 In noncapital cases they hold trial during the daytime and the verdict may be reached during the night; in capital cases they hold the trial during the daytime

[474] James M. Freeman and Harold J. Chadwick. *Manners & Customs of the Bible*. North Brunswick, NJ: Bridge-Logos Publishers, 1998, Logos 5.

and the verdict must also be reached during the daytime. In noncapital cases the verdict, whether of acquittal or of conviction, may be reached the same day; in capital cases a verdict of acquittal may be reached on the same day, but a verdict of conviction not until the following day.

Criteria for Conviction

5.1 They used to prove witnesses with seven inquiries: In what week of years? In what year? In what month? On what day? In what hour? In what place? (R. Jose says: [They aked only,] On what day? In what hour? In what place?) [They also asked:] Do you recognize him? Did you warn him? If a man committed idolatry [they asked the witnesses], What did he worship? and, How did he worship it?

5.2. The more a judge tests the evidence the more he is deserving of praise: Ben Zakkai once tested the evidence even to inquiring about the stalks of figs. Wherein do the inquiries differ from the cross-examination? If to the inquiries one [of the two witnesses] answered, "I do not know," their evidence becomes invalid; but if to the cross-examination one answered, "We do not know," their evidence remains valid. Yet if they contradict one another, whether during the inquiries or the cross-examination, their evidence becomes invalid.

5.3. If one said, "On the second of the month," and the other said, "On the third," their evidence remains valid since one may have known the month was intercalated and the other did not know the month was intercalated; but if one said, "On the third," and the other said, "On the fifth," their evidence becomes invalid. If one said, "At the second hour," and the other said, "At the third," their evidence remains valid; but if one said, "At the third hour," and the other said, "At the fifth," their evidence becomes invalid. R. Judah says: It remains valid; but if one said, "At the fifth hour," and the other said, "At the seventh," their evidence becomes invalid since at the fifth hour the sun in in the east and at the seventh it is in the west.

5.4. They afterward brought in the second witness and proved him. If their words were found to agree together they begin [to examine the evidence] in favor of acquittal. If one witness said, "I have somewhat to argue in favor of his acquittal," or if one of the disciples said, "I have somewhat to argue in favor of his acquittal," they bring him up and set him among them and he does not come down from thence the whole day. If there is any substance in his words they listen to him. Even if the accused said, "I have somewhat to argue in favor of my acquittal," they listen to him, provided there is any substance to his words.

Postponement of Final Sentence Until the Day After Trial

5.5 If they found him innocent they set him free; otherwise they leave his sentence over until the morrow. [In the meantime] they went together in pairs, they ate a little (but they used to drink no wine the whole day), and they discussed the matter all night, and early on the morrow they came to the court. He that favored acquittal says: "I declared him innocent and I still declare him innocent"; and he that favored conviction says, "I declared him guilty and I still declare him guilty." He that favored conviction may now acquit, but he that had favored acquittal [the day before] may not retract and favor conviction."

Stoning

6.1. When sentence has been passed, they take him forth to stone him. The place of stoning was outside the court, as it is written, Bring forth him that hath cursed without the camp. One stands at the door of the court with a towel in his hand, and another, mounted on a horse, far away from him [but where he is able] to see him. If one [in court] said, "I have somewhat to argue in favor of his acquittal," that man waves the towel and the horse runs and stops him [the stoner]. Even if he himself said, "I have somewhat to argue in favor of my acquittal," they must bring him back, be it four times or five, provided that there is any substance in his words. If they found him innocent, they set him free; otherwise he goes forth to be stoned. A herald goes out before him [announcing], "Such-a-one, the son of such-a-one, is going forth to be stoned for that he committed such or such an offense. Such-a-one and such-a-one are witnesses against him. If any man knoweth anything in favor of his acquittal, come let him plead it."

6.2. When he was about ten cubits from the place of stoning they used to say to him, "Make your confession," for such is the way of them that have been condemned to death to make confession, for every one that makes his confession has a share in the world to come. For so we have found it with Achan. Joshua said to him, My son, give, I pray thee, glory to the Lord, the God of Israel, and make confession unto him, and tell me now what you have done; hide it not from me. And Achan answered Joshua and said, Of a truth I have sinned against the Lord, the God of Israel, and thus and thus have I done. Whence do we learn that his confession made atonement for him? It is written, And Joshua said, Why have you troubled us? The Lord shall trouble thee this day—this day you shall be troubled, but in the world to come you shall not be troubled. If he knows not how to make his confession they say to him, "Say, May my death be an atonement for all my sins." R. Judah says: If he knew that he was condemned because of false testimony he should say, "Let my death be an atonement for all my sins excepting this sin." They said to him: If so, every one would speak after this fashion to show his innocence."

6.3. When he was four cubits from the place of stoning, they stripped off his clothes. A man is kept covered in front and a woman both in front and behind. So R. Judah. But the Sages say: a man is stoned naked but a woman is not stoned naked.

6.4. The place of stoning was twice the height of a man. One of the witnesses knocked him down on his loins; if he turned over on his heart the witness turned him over again on his loins. If he straightaway died that sufficed; but if not, the second took the the stone and dropped it on his heart. If he straightaway died, that sufficed; but if not, he was stoned by all Israel, for it is written, The hand of the witnesses shall be first upon him to put him to death and afterward all the hand of all the people. All that have been stoned must be hanged. So R. Eliezer. But the Sages say: None is hanged save the blasphemer and the idolater. A man is hanged with his face to the people and a woman with her face to the gallows. So R. Eliezer. But the Sages say: A man is hanged but a woman is not hanged. R. Eliezer said to them: Did not Simeon ben Shetah hang women in Ashkelon? They answered: He hanged eighty women, whereas two ought not to be judged in one day. How did they hang a man? They put a beam into the ground and a piece of wood juttted from it. The two hand were brought together and it was hanged. R. Jose days: The beam was made to lean against a wall and one hanged the corpse thereon as butchers do. And they let it down at once: if it remained there overnight a negative command is thereby transgressed, for it is is written, His body shall not remain all night upon the tree, but thou shall surely bury him the same day; for he that is hanged is a curse against God; as if to say, Why was this one hanged? Because he blessed the Name, and the Name of Heaven was found profaned.

[*Other forms of capital punishment under Jewish law included burning, decapitation, and strangulation, each of which has its own set of crimes meriting such punishment.*]

Crimes Meriting Stoning

7.4 These are they that are to be stoned: he that has connexion with his mother, his father's wife, his daughter-in-law, a male, or a beast, and the woman that suffers connexion with a beast, and the blasphemer and the idolator, and he that offers any of his seed to Molech, and he that has a familiar spirit and a soothsayer, and he that profanes the Sabbath, and he tht curses his father or his mother, and he that has a connexion with a girl that is betrothed, and he that beguiles [others to commit idolatry], and he that leads [a whole town] astray, and the sorcerer and a stubborn and rebellious son.

Section 22: Chronological Table of Christ's Life[475]

EVENT	DATE
Christ's birth	Winter 5/4 BC
Herod the Great's death	March/April 4 BC
Prefects began to rule over Judea and Samaria	AD 6
Christ at the temple when twelve	Passover, April 29, AD 9
Caiaphas became high priest	AD 18
Pilate arrived in Judea	AD 26
Commencement of John the Baptist's	AD 29

[475] While there is debate on many chronological issues found in the gospels, the dates above are a good, general guide taken from Harold Hoehner, *Chronological Aspects of the Life of Christ* (Grand Rapids: Zondervan, 1977), 143.

ministry	
Commencement of Christ's ministry	Summer/autumn AD 29
Christ's first Passover	April 7, 30
John the Baptist imprisoned	AD 30/31
Christ's second Passover	April 25, 31
John the Baptist's death	AD 31/32
Christ at the Feast of Tabernacles (John 5:1)	October 22-28, 31AD
Christ's third Passover	April 13/14, 32
Christ at the Feast of Tabernacles (John 7:2, 10)	September 10-17, 32 AD
Christ at the Feast of Dedication	December 18, 32
Christ's final week	March 28-April 5, 33 AD
Arrived at Bethany	Saturday, March 28
Crowds at Bethany	Sunday, March 29
Triumphal entry	Monday, March 30
Cursed the fig tree and cleansed Temple	Tuesday, March 31
Temple controversy and Olivet Discourse	Wednesday, April 1
Christ ate Passover, betrayed, arrested and tried	Thursday, April 2
Christ tried and crucified	Friday, April 3
Christ laid in the tomb	Saturday, April 4
Christ resurrected	Sunday, April 5
Christ's ascension	Thursday, May 14
Day of Pentecost	Sunday, May 24

Section 23: Key Dates in the Life of Jesus[476]

The Year John the Baptist's Ministry Began

Luke implies that John the Baptist began his public ministry shortly before Jesus did, and he gives us a historical reference point for when the Baptist's ministry began: "In *the fifteenth year of the reign of Tiberius Caesar…*" (Luke 3:1).

We know from Roman historians that Tiberius succeeded Augustus as emperor and was confirmed by the Roman Senate on August 19, AD 14. He ruled until AD 37. "The fifteenth year of the reign of Tiberius Caesar" sounds like a straightforward date, but there are some ambiguities, beginning with when one starts the calculation. Most likely, Tiberius's reign was counted either from the day he took office in AD 14 or from January 1 of the following year, AD 15. The earliest possible date at which Tiberius's "fifteenth year" began is August 19, AD 28, and the latest possible date at which his "fifteenth year" ended is December 31, AD 29. So *John the Baptist's ministry began anywhere from mid-AD 28 until sometime in AD 29.*

[476] Material in this section is taken verbatim from the work of Kostenberger/Taylor: http://www.firstthings.com/web-exclusives/2014/04/april-3-ad-33, accessed 4/22/2014.

The Year Jesus's Ministry Began

If Jesus, as the Gospels seem to indicate, began his ministry not long after John, then based on the calculations above, the earliest date for Jesus's baptism would be in late AD 28 at the very earliest. However, it is more probable to place it sometime in the first half of the year AD 29, because a few months probably elapsed between the beginning of John's ministry and that of Jesus (and the year AD 30 is the latest possible date). So *Jesus's ministry must have begun between the end of AD 28 at the earliest and AD 30 at the latest.*

This coheres with Luke's mention that "Jesus, when he began his ministry, was *about thirty years of age*" (Luke 3:23). If he was born in 6 or 5 BC, as is most likely, Jesus would have been *approximately thirty-two to thirty-four years old* in late AD 28 until AD 30, which falls well within the range of him being "about thirty years of age."

The Length of Jesus's Ministry

Now we need to know how long Jesus's public ministry lasted, because if it went on for two or more years, this would seem to rule out spring of AD 30 as a possible date for the crucifixion.

John's Gospel mentions that Jesus attended at least three Passovers (possibly four), which took place once a year in the spring:

- There was a Passover in Jerusalem at the start of his public ministry (John 2:13, 23).
- There was a Passover in Galilee midway through his public ministry (John 6:4).
- There was a final Passover in Jerusalem at the end of his public ministry, that is, the time of his crucifixion (John 11:55; 12:1).
- And Jesus may have attended one more Passover not recorded in John but perhaps in one or several of the Synoptic Gospels (i.e., Matthew, Mark, and Luke).

Even if there were only three Passovers, this would still make a date of AD 30 all but impossible for the date of the crucifixion. As noted above, the earliest likely date for the beginning of Jesus's ministry from Luke 3:1 is late AD 28. So the first of these Passovers (at the beginning of Jesus' ministry; John 2:13) would fall on Nisan 14 in AD 29 (because Nisan is in March/April, near the beginning of a year). The second would fall in AD 30 at the earliest, and the third would fall in 31 at the earliest. This means that if Jesus's ministry coincided with at least three Passovers, and if the first Passover was in AD 29, he could not have been crucified in AD 30.

But if John the Baptist began his ministry in AD 29, then Jesus probably began his ministry in late AD 29 or early AD 30. Then the Passovers in John would occur on the following dates:

Nisan 14	AD 30	John 2:13

Nisan 14	AD 31	Either the unnamed feast in John 5:1 or else a Passover that John does not mention (but that may be implied in the Synoptics)
Nisan 14	AD 32	John 6:4
Nisan 14	AD 33	John 11:55, the Passover at which Jesus was crucified

Jesus Was Crucified on the Day of Preparation for the Passover

John also mentions that Jesus was crucified on "the day of Preparation" (John 19:31), that is, the Friday before the Sabbath of Passover week (Mark 15:42). The night before, on Thursday evening, Jesus ate a Passover meal with the Twelve (Mark 14:12), his "Last Supper."

In the Pharisaic-rabbinic calendar commonly used in Jesus's day, Passover always falls on the fourteenth day of Nisan (Exodus 12:6), which begins Thursday after sundown and ends Friday at sundown. In the year AD 33, the most likely year of Jesus's crucifixion, Nisan 14 fell on April 3, yielding April 3, AD 33, as the most likely date for the crucifixion. In *The Final Days of Jesus*, we therefore constructed the following chart to show the dates for Jesus's final week in AD 33:

April 2	Nissan 14	Thursday (Wednesday nightfall to Thursday nightfall)	Day of Passover preparation	Last Supper
April 3	Nissan 15	Friday (Thursday nightfall to Friday nightfall)	Passover; Feast of Unleavened Bread, begins	Crucifixion
April 4	Nissan 16	Saturday (Friday nightfall to Saturday nightfall)	Sabbath	
April 5	Nissan 17	Sunday (Saturday nightfall to Sunday nightfall)	First day of the week	Resurrection

Conclusion

The above calculations may appear complicated, but in a nutshell the argument runs like this:

Beginning of Tiberius's reign	AD 14
Fifteenth year of Tiberius's reign: Beginning of John the Baptist's ministry	AD 28
A few months later: Beginning of Jesus's ministry	AD 29
Minimum three-year duration of Jesus' ministry: Most likely date of Jesus's crucifixion	AD 33 (April 3)

Section 24: The Day of Atonement

The pinnacle of the Mosaic sacrificial system was the Day of Atonement. It has been correctly termed the "Good Friday" of the Old Testament, and the rabbis simply called it "the day."[477] Herr agrees that this was the "most important day of the liturgical year."[478] However, this facet of God's revelation is not complete until it is correlated with Hebrews 9-10, for these two chapters are the New Testament commentary on the Old Testament Day. The Day of Atonement was instituted in light of the deaths of Nadab and Abihu (Lev. 10). This institution was to protect the high priest from experiencing a similar fate. Moreover, in light of the context in Leviticus 11-15, the wide-ranging nature of the uncleanness rules threatened to pollute the presence of God in the sanctuary.

The Purpose of the Day of Atonement

There are two demonstrable purposes for the Day. First and foremost, this was the day when the sanctuary was cleansed from the various pollutions that had infiltrated it due to the sin and uncleanness of the congregation and priests (Lev. 16:16, 19).[479] This would then permit the holy presence of God to continue dwelling among the people.

Second, the Day of Atonement was the culminating day of sacrifice in the Mosaic system. Gayford has commented that the offerings of this day were "the highest in importance of all the atoning sacrifices; they summed up all the atoning power of the others."[480] Likewise Kurtz states that "it was the highest, most perfect, and most comprehensive of all the acts of expiation."[481] And finally Ringgren writes, "This comprises a large number of expiatory practices to atone for sins of the high priest and the people during the preceding year."[482] The sacrifice on this occasion was the most potent blood manipulation possible.[483]

The Ritual of the Day of Atonement

The central passage for examining the Day of Atonement is Leviticus 16.[484] Leviticus 16:1-10 provides a general description of the ritual. The description is introduced with a warning: Aaron was not to come into the Holy of Holies whenever he chose.[485] This was due to God's presence above the mercy seat

[477]C. F. Keil and F. Delitzsch, *The Pentateuch* (repr., Commentary on the Old Testament; Grand Rapids: Eerdmans, 1980), 395-96.

[478] Moshe David Herr, "Day of Atonement," *Encyclopedia Judaica*, 5:1376.

[479] G. J. Wenham, *The Book of Leviticus*, New International Commentary on the Old Testament (Grand Rapids: Eerdmans, 1985), 228. Margolis agrees that "by these rites the most holy place was rendered free from all impurities attaching to it through the intentional and unintentional entrance of the unclean persons into the sanctuary" (Max Margolis, "Atonement, Day of," *The Jewish Encyclopedia*), 2:284.

[480] S. C. Gayford, *Sacrifice and Priesthood: Jewish and Christian* (London: Methuen & Co., 1953), 85.

[481] J. H. Kurtz, *Sacrificial Worship of the Old Testament* (repr., Minneapolis: Klock & Klock, 1980), 386.

[482] H. Ringgren, *Sacrifice in the Bible* (NY: Association Press, 1962), 38. See also Allen Ross, *Holiness to the Lord: A Guide to the Exposition of the Book of Leviticus* (Grand Rapids: Baker, 2002), 313-14; Alfred Edersheim, *The Temple: Its Ministry and Services* (repr., Grand Rapids: Eerdmans, 1972), 303; Barclay, *The Letter to the Hebrews*, (DSB; Philadelphia: Westminster, 1958), 98.

[483] N. Kiuchi, *The Purification Offering in the Priestly Literature: Its Meaning and Function* (Sheffield: Sheffield Academic Press, 1987), 159.

[484] Other Old Testament references to the Day of Atonement include Exodus 30:10; Leviticus 23:26-32; Leviticus 25:9; Numbers 18; and Numbers 29:7-11.

[485] "That he is not to come" is not an apodictic prohibition but merely a warning (J. Bright, "The Apodictic Prohibition: Some Observations," *Journal of Biblical Literature* 92 [1973], 195-204). It is interesting that

which would result in Aaron's death if he entered without proper preparation. Therefore, the rest of the chapter explains how he was to make his entrance.

A detailing of the ritual is found in Leviticus 16:11-28. The first part of the ritual was the offering of the bullock (16:11-14) by Aaron to make atonement for his own sins. He took the blood of the bull along with a censer full of hot coals into the Holy of Holies. While Keil suggests that the incense was to prevent God from seeing the sinner, it seems better with Hertz and Hoffmann to understand this act as an attempt to protect the high priest from gazing on the divine presence and thereby averting his death.[486] This appears to be the idea of verse 13 which says that the smoke covers the mercy seat rather than the high priest.[487] Consequently, the result was that "the high priest was unable to see the Lord, and this fact saved his life."[488] When he had entered the inner sanctuary, the high priest sprinkled some of the blood of the bull on the mercy seat and some in front of the mercy seat.

The second part of the ritual dealt with the offering of the first goat (16:15-19) on behalf of the nation. Interestingly, no mention is made of the ceremony of the casting of lots regarding the two goats (cf., Lev. 16:8-9). Perhaps this casting of lots was done during the preparation phase of the ceremony. The lots were drawn and one was placed on the head of each goat.[489]

At this point, the high priest killed the goat which was designated for the Lord in order to offer it for the people. He then took its blood into the Holy of Holies and sprinkled it in the same manner as he had the blood of the bull (16:15). In addition, the sanctuary of the Holy Place needed to be cleansed (16:16). The text states that the holy place was defiled by the sin of the people. Morris explains: "The point of this is that the circumstances of everyday life made it easy for people to contract forms of ceremonial defilement…All this meant that they had defiled the place where they came to worship and this part of the day's ceremonies was directed to removing uncleanness."[490]

The third part of the Day of Atonement ritual was the sending away of the second, live goat into the wilderness (16:20-22). This part of the ceremony had two phases. In the first, the high priest laid both of his hands on the goat's head while confessing the sins of the people (16:21a). This symbolized the transference

---

nothing is said about a fixed time for Aaron to enter the adytum. Milgrom suggests that the purgation rite was initially an emergency measure, and therefore Aaron could enter the adytum whenever he chose, but his successors could do so only on the annual Day of Atonement (Jacob Milgrom, *Leviticus 1—16* [NY: Doubleday, 1991], 1012-13).

486 Keil & Delitzsch, *The Pentateuch*, 399; J. H. Hertz, *Leviticus* (London: Oxford, 1932), 156; D. Hoffmann, *Das Buch Leviticus I-II*, (Berlin: Poppelauer, 1905-06), 1:447.

487 Wenham, *The Book of Leviticus*, 231; Leon Morris, *The Atonement: Its Meaning and Significance* (Downers Grove: InterVarsity, 1983), 70.

488 R. K. Harrison, *Leviticus: An Introduction and Commentary*, Tyndale Old Testament Commentary (Downers Grove: InterVarsity, 1980), 172.

489 For the details on this phase from Mishnaic sources, see Milgrom, *Leviticus 1-16*, 1019-20.

490 Leon Morris, *The Apostolic Preaching of the Cross* (Grand Rapids: Eerdmans, 1965), 71.

of the guilt of the people to the goat (16:21b; cf. Isa. 53:4).[491] The second aspect of this part of the ritual involved the actual sending of the goat into the wilderness by a man appointed specifically for this job (16:21c-22).[492] While there has been considerable debate regarding the term "Azazel" (scapegoat) and the sending of the goat into the desert, what is being portrayed is clear.[493] The dismissal of this goat signified to the people that the consequences of their sins were removed from the presence of the Lord (cf., Ps. 103:12). W. Moeller summarizes the meaning of the dismissal of this goat:

> In order to make this transfer all the more impressive, both the hands are here brought into action, while in Leviticus 1:4 only one hand is used. The fact that the goat is accompanied by somebody and that it is to be taken to

---

[491] Kiuchi has also noted: "the guilt that Aaron has borne in purifying the defiled sancta is devolved upon the Azazel goat. Thus the relationship of the two rites is a continuous one" (Kiuchi, *The Purification Offering in the Priestly Literature*, 156).

[492] Geikie observes that in New Testament times, in order to prevent the goat returning to Jerusalem, it was led to a high mountain where it was pushed off and certainly killed (Cunningham Geikie, *The Holy Land and the Bible* [NY: James Pott & Co., 1888], 1:224-25).

[493] The etymology of the word "Azazel" is uncertain. Some derive "to drive away, something driven away" (Keil, *The Pentateuch*, 398; Hertz, *Leviticus*, 154; *Brown, Driver, Briggs*, 736b). Others follow the Septuagint and Vulgate and translate it as "scapegoat" (N. H. Snaith, *Leviticus and Numbers* [London: Thomas Nelson, 1967], 113; R. de Vaux, *Ancient Israel* [NY: McGraw-Hill, 1961], 508ff.), while others suggest an Arabic etymology meaning "rough ground" or "precipice" (G. R. Driver, "Three Technical Terms in the Pentateuch," *Journal of Semitic Studies* 2 [1956], 98). Besides this, there have been four options proposed for understanding the phrase "for Azazel" (for a further discussion of all these options see Kurtz, *Sacrificial Worship of the Old Testament,* 396; Wenham, *The Book of Leviticus,* 234-35; Harrison, *Leviticus,* 170-71; Charles Feinberg, "The Scapegoat of Leviticus Sixteen " *Bibliotheca Sacra* 115 [1958], 320-33): 1) the description of a place, 2) the description of the goat, 3) an evil demon to whom the goat is sent (possibly Satan) , and 4) an abstract noun signifying complete removal. The majority of commentators opt for the third view (e.g., Keil and Delitzsch, *The Pentateuch,* 1:404; George Bush, *Leviticus* [repr., Minneapolis: James Family Christian Publishers, 1979], 149; Morris, *The Apostolic Preaching of the Cross,* 98). This view is supported by the parallelism of "for the Lord" and "for Azazel," later Jewish literature which cites Azazel as the name of a demon (Enoch 8:1; 9:6), and the biblical citations looking at the wilderness as the haunt of demons (Lev. 17:17; Isa. 13:21; 34:14; Matt. 12:43; Mark 1:13). But as Hertz points out, "The offering of sacrifices to satyrs is spoken of as a heinous crime in the very next chapter (17:7); homage to a demon of the wilderness cannot, therefore be associated with the holiest of the Temple rites into the chapter immediately preceding" (Hertz, *Leviticus,* 156). This view is further weakened by the fact that both goats are said to constitute one sin offering to the Lord. In the writer's opinion, the best view is the fourth. First, this option fits the dual aspect of the one sacrifice. Second, this is a legitimate etymology of the word (*Brown, Driver, Briggs*, 736). Third it avoids the pitfall of offering an appeasement to a demon. Fourth, it is supported by the translation of the Septuagint (Wilhelm Moeller, "Azazel," *International Standard Bible Encyclopedia,* 1:344. Fifth, the function of the live goat is expressly said to bear the sins away into the wilderness (Lev. 16:21c-22). Thus the word visually symbolizes the removal of sin from the people (Feinberg, "The Scapegoat of Leviticus 16," 333; Harrison, *Leviticus,* 171; Hoffmann, *Das Buch Leviticus I-II,* 1:444; Hertz, *Leviticus,* 154).

Whichever view is adopted, however, Hoffmann's words are apropos. "Whether Azazel means, the mountain where the goat is destroyed, the sin which is given to destruction, or the evil angel who is given a bribe so that he does not become an accuser, it all comes back to the same basic idea: that sin is exterminated from Israel" (Hoffmann, 1:444; so, Ross, *Holiness to the Lord,* 319). The New Testament does not mention the scapegoat as typical of Christ directly, but since the Epistle of Barnabas (written c.a. AD 200), Christians have seen it as a type of Christ. As it was led out to die in the wilderness bearing the sins of the people, Christ was crucified outside the city of Jerusalem for the sins of the people (N. Micklem, "The Book of Leviticus," *Interpreter's Bible*, 2:79ff.).

> an uninhabited place is to indicate the absolute impossibility of its return, i.e., the guilt has been absolutely forgiven and erased, a deep thought made objectively evident in a transparent manner and independently of the explanation of Azazel.[494]

It is probably best to see the two goats of this part of the ceremony as forming one offering. It is clearly stated in 16:5 that the two goats constituted a sin offering.[495] Crawford suggests consequently that the two goats embodied two aspects of one sacrifice; the first exhibited the means, and the other the results of the atonement.[496] Erdman corroborates this thought. "The first goat signified the means of reconciliation to God, namely, by the death and sprinkled blood of a vicarious offering, so the dismissal of the second goat typified the effect of the expiation in the removal of the sin from the presence of a holy God."[497]

Following the ritual of the two goats, the next stage of the procedure was the washing of the participants (16:23-28) so that new contamination to areas just cleansed would be prevented. Therefore, all who were involved in the activities were required to wash their clothes and flesh. The high priest at this point removed his white garments and put on his normal priestly garb (16:23-24). The fat of the sin offering was then burned on the altar while the bull and first goat were burned outside the camp.

The final part of the ritual involved duties which were incumbent on the people. First, they were to observe this day once each year on the given date. Second, they were to "afflict themselves." This probably carried the idea of self-examination, prayer, and fasting.[498] Third, they were to do no work on this day.

Section 25: The Eschatological Significance of the Feast of Booths

When Jesus predicted that some standing with Him would "see the Son of Man coming in his kingdom," He had reference to the transfiguration to occur about a week later, which in turn was an eschatological picture of the future.[499] Hence, the prediction had a double referent. Lane stated well "The immediate sequel to Jesus' solemn promise is the account of the transfiguration. This indicates that Mark understood Jesus' statement to refer to this moment of transcendent glory conceived as an enthronement and an anticipation of the glory

---

[494] Moeller, "Azazel," 1:344.

[495] Thus the living goat was the "alter ego" of the first as *hircus redivivus* (Kurtz, *Sacrificial Worship of the Old Testament,* 396; Edersheim, *The Temple: Its Ministry and Services,* 312). The first died as a sin offering, while the second visibly and strikingly conveyed the idea of the complete dismissal of sin.

[496] T. J. Crawford, *Doctrine of Holy Scripture Respecting Atonement* (NY: William Blackwood, 1888), 225.

[497] Charles Erdman, *The Book of Leviticus* (NY: Fleming Revell, 1951), 75. See also George Smeaton, *The Apostles' Doctrine of the Atonement* (repr., Grand Rapids: Zondervan, 1957), 25; Edersheim, *The Temple: Its Ministry and Services,* 319.

[498] Wenham, *The Book of Leviticus,* 236.

[499] The sense of the verse, therefore, stated interpretively, is that Jesus was introducing the "transfiguration of chapter 17, which anticipated, in vision, the glory of the Son of man coming in His kingdom" (John Walvoord, *Matthew: Thy Kingdom Come* [Chicago, IL: Moody, 1974], 126; see also A. C. Gaebelein, *The Gospel of Matthew* [Neptune, NJ: Loizeaux Brothers, 1961], 358).

which was to come."[500] Smalley also observed: The natural point of reference…is the Transfiguration itself. A short while after this announcement, the disciples "see" a further irruption of the power and sovereignty of God, and this, in typically dynamic fashion is proleptic…Immediate events in this way contain the eschatological future, and only the present is invested with chronological definition. As a result, this particular saying would cause no difficulty if its ultimate fulfillment were delayed since its immediate fulfillment, itself proleptic…soon came to pass.[501]

There are a number of supports which can be given to demonstrate the pre-transfiguration prediction to be fulfilled in the Transfiguration itself.[502] First, all of the Synoptics placed the transfiguration immediately after the prediction, thus making a link between the two. Bruce noted that "the three evangelists who relate the event so carefully note the time of its occurrence with reference to that announcement and the conversation which accompanied it."[503] Green concurred: "In all three gospels it [the transfiguration] follows immediately on the promise of Jesus that some of His hearers would not taste death until the kingdom came with power."[504]

A second support concerns Jesus' statement that "some" would not taste of death until they saw this event. The fact that only three of the apostles saw the glory of Christ on the mount fits much better with the transfiguration view than with any of the others since the multitudes witnessed them. Thus Plummer counseled that "no interpretation can be correct that does not explain εισίν τινές

[500] William Lane, *The Gospel of Mark* (Grand Rapids, MI: Eerdmans, 1979], 313-314.

[501] Stephen Smalley, "The Delay of the Parousia," *Journal of Biblical Literature* 83 (1964), 46; for further support of the prediction being fulfilled in the transfiguration, see J.F. Walvoord, *Matthew: Thy Kingdom Come*, 126; D. Edmond Hiebert, *Mark: A Portrait of the Servant* (Chicago, IL: Moody, 1974), 211; A.C. Gaebelein, *The Gospel of Matthew*, 358; F.C. Synge, "The Transfiguration Story," *The Expository Times* 82 (1970), 83; Walter Wessell, "Mark," in *The Expositor's Bible Commentary* (Grand Rapids, MI: Zondervan, 1984), 8:698 (Wessell holds to the parousia view but understands the transfiguration as an anticipation and guarantee of the parousia). See also Darrell Bock who suggested: "the remarks anticipate the transfiguration, with its glimpse of the future glory of Jesus. This kind of 'patterned' event, where a short-term event patterns one coming later, is common in Jesus' teaching" (*Jesus According to Scripture* [Grand Rapids, MI: Baker, 2002], 234). Bock also combined with this view, though, an "already form of the inaugurated kingdom" based on Jesus' words that the disciples would "see" the kingdom (*Luke 1:1-9:50* [Grand Rapids, MI: Baker, 1999], 859).

[502] S. Lewis Johnson, Jr., "The Transfiguration of Christ," *Bibliotheca Sacra* 124 (1967), 140-141.

[503] A.B. Bruce, *The Training of the Twelve* (Grand Rapids, MI: Kregel, 1971), 191.

[504] Michael Green, *The Second Epistle of Peter and the Epistle of Jude* (Grand Rapids, MI: Eerdmans, 1973), 82. It is not germane at this point whether those cited agree with the writer's view of the kingdom and the eschatological ramifications of the transfiguration account. At this point a link is simply being demonstrated between the prediction and the event. See also W.L. Liefeld, "μεταμορφόω," *The New International Dictionary of New Testament Theology* 3 (1971), 862; Stanely Toussaint, *Behold the King: A Study of Matthew* (Portland, OR: Multnomah, 1981), 210. Concerning the phrase "after six days," McCurley suggested that this was a common literary device in Semitic literature which "points to a climactic action on the seventh day after a preparatory period of six days" (Foster McCurley, "And After Six Days: A Semitic Literary Device," *Journal of Biblical Literature* 93 [1974], 81). For a discussion of this temporal phrase, as well as Luke's about eight days" and Old Testament parallels see McCurley and Charles Carlston, "Transfiguration and Resurrection," *Journal of Biblical Literature* 80 (1961), 238; B.D. Chilton, "The Transfiguration: Dominical Assurance and Apostolic Vision," *New Testament Studies* 27 (1980), 120-121.

which implies the exceptional privilege of some, as distinct from the common experience of all."[505]

A third possible factor which favors this view is that the verb "to see" used by Christ is in harmony with the transfiguration event as witnessed by the disciples.[506]

Fourth, Peter interpreted the significance of the event in this matter in 2 Peter 1:16-18. Peter's words will be examined below.

A fifth reason is that this was the predominant view of the early church.[507] Probably the earliest evidence of this interpretation is found in the Apocalypse of Peter. In this text the story opens on the Mount of Olives where the disciples ask Jesus the same question which they ask preceding the Olivet Discourse, namely, "what are the signs of the parousia and of the end of the world?" Jesus' answer consists of descriptions of the parousia and a lengthy description of the punishment of the wicked and the blessings of the righteous. Following this, Jesus takes the disciples to another mountain where two glorious men appear and Jesus is transfigured. Peter then asks where the other patriarchs are, in response to which Jesus shows him paradise and tells him the same glory awaits them all. Also included in the story are the request of Peter, the heavenly voice, the cloud, and the ascent of Jesus into heaven. Thus, it was not uncommon for the early church to see the pre-transfiguration prediction fulfilled in the transfiguration and in the transfiguration a picture of the Second Coming.

Sixth, as will be shown, the transfiguration is packed with eschatological terminology pointing to the kingdom age rather than to Christ's resurrection, the church age, or the destruction of Jerusalem.[508]

---

[505] Alfred Plummer, *An Exegetical Commentary on the Gospel According to Saint Matthew* (Grand Rapids, MI: Baker, 1982), 249; Cranfield, *The Gospel According to St. Mark*, 288.

[506] Johnson, "The Transfiguration of Christ," 140-141; Cranfield, *The Gospel According to St. Mark*, 288; Hiebert, *Mark: A Portrait of the Servant*, 211-212.

[507] Boobyer, "St. Mark and the Transfiguration," 119; Trench, *Studies in the Gospels*, 120; Hiebert, *Mark: A Portrait of the Servant*, 211; Jerome Neyrey, "The Apologetic Use of the Transfiguration," *The Catholic Biblical Quarterly* 42 (1980), 510, 513. For general comments on the value and cautions of appealing to the early church views, see Bill Heth and Gordon Wenham, *Jesus and Divorce* (London: Hodder and Stoughton, 1984), 19-22; Paul Enns, *The Moody Handbook of Theology* (Chicago, IL: Moody, 1989), 403; Millard Erickson, *Christian Theology* (Grand Rapids, MI: Baker, 1983-1985), 26-27.

[508] One view that is not as widespread as the ones discussed is held by Brower who appears to relate the prediction to the crucifixion. He wrote: "Mark 9:1 can best be understood as a combination threat/promise that the kingdom of God would come in power in the lifetime of at least some of the hearers. These shall see the kingdom in power, albeit power in weakness, and it may not be perceived as power. Nevertheless, in the cross of Jesus, God's rule has been decisively established, shown by the darkness at noon and the rending of the veil, and witnessed to by the Roman centurion" (Brower, "Mark 9:1: Seeing the Kingdom in Power," 41). This position has recently been argued for by Michael Bird, "The Crucifixion of Jesus as the Fulfillment of Mark 9:1," *Trinity Journal* 24 (2003):23-36. This interpretation must redefine what the kingdom has been throughout Scripture until this point. Furthermore, even after the transfiguration, the kingdom is still being defined as an earthly entity (Matt. 19:28; 25:34; 26:29; Mark 10:40; Acts 1:6). Another view was the one held by Dodd (and others) from their perspective of realized eschatology. He argued that the kingdom had already arrived when Jesus was speaking but that the disciples would come to recognize this later at Pentecost (C.H. Dodd, *The Parables of the Kingdom* [London: Nisbet, 1936], 28). For a full listing of all of the views see Darrell Bock, Luke 1:1-9:50, 858-860; Hiebert, *Mark: A Portrait of the Servant*, 211-212;

Thus far it has been argued generally that the pre-transfiguration prediction made by Christ was fulfilled in the transfiguration. It has also been suggested that this event served as a preview of the coming earthly kingdom. If this is correct, then the transfiguration account provides another piece of support that the kingdom terminology in the Gospels be understood primarily in its literal, earthly sense. It will now be necessary to see if the details of the transfiguration support this understanding.

The Transfiguration Proper

The Future of the Kingdom

One of the prime purposes[509] of the transfiguration was to confirm to the disciples a future kingdom as prophesied in the Old Testament.[510] Thus, regardless of the fact that this kingdom had been rejected by Israel, this event served as a pledge that it would still be a reality someday. It therefore becomes a miniature picture of what lies in the future. In the words of McClain: "Christ gives to the three of His disciples a prevision, in miniature, of His coming in the Kingdom."[511] And Ramsey observed that "all the imagery can be, and the imagery of light and shining garments is most readily, associated with an eschatological picture...Peter and his companions on the mountain are spectators in advance of the glory that is going to be declared."[512] The aspects in the text which deal with

---

Plummer, *A Critical and Exegetical Commentary on the Gospel According to S. Luke*, 249; Lange, "The Gospel According to Matthew," 8:304; Liefeld, *New Dimensions in New Testament Study*, 162-165.

[509] There certainly were several purposes for the transfiguration of Christ. Involved in the broad context, as far as theological chronology is concerned, the King and kingdom had been rejected by Israel. In the narrow context (Matt. 16:13-28; Mark 8:27-38; Luke 9:18-26), Peter's confession, the passion prediction, and the prediction of the coming of the Son of Man all must be taken into account (see comments by E. F. Harrison, "The Transfiguration," *Bibliotheca Sacra* 93 [1936]:316-317; Alfred Edersheim, *The Life and Times of Jesus the Messiah* [Grand Rapids, MI: Eerdmans, 1980], 2:91; Walter Liefeld, "Luke," 166. The fact that the covenanted kingdom was now in abeyance, combined with Jesus prediction of His death, called for some stunning event which would verify that God's theocratic program for the nation was not forever gone (L.S. Chafer, *Systematic Theology* (Dallas, TX: Dallas Seminary Press, 1978], 5:89; G.N.H. Peters, *The Theocratic Kingdom*, 5:558; Alva McClain, *The Greatness of the Kingdom* [Winona Lake, IN: BMH Books, 1983], 337; Harrison, "The Transfiguration," 317). Thus, at least three things were confirmed by this event: 1) the faith of the disciples as expressed in Peter's confession, 2) the person of Christ in light of his coming death, and 3) the future of the kingdom. In fact, Johnson sees the following purposes: the authentication of the Son by the Father's voice, the anticipation of the kingdom as a prelude and pledge, an illustration of the inhabitants of the kingdom, an illustration of personal resurrection, confirmation of Old Testament prophecy, a proclamation of the costliness of His sacrifice for sin, and an evaluation of the strength of His passion for souls (Johnson, "The Transfiguration of Christ," 139-143). Baltensweiler listed the following purposes: Christological, Heilsgeschichtlich-a new covenant is begun; proof of Messianic claim; pedagogical regarding the resurrection body; eschatological (Heinrich Baltensweiler, *Die Verklarung Jesu: Abhandlungen zur Theologie des Alten und Neuen Testaments* [Zurich: Zwingli-Verlag, 1959], 9-10).

[510] Chafer pointed out correctly that "unless the transfiguration is approached with the background of all that the Old Testament revelation concerning the earthly Davidic Kingdom presents, there can be no understanding of this major event in the life of Christ. The premillenarian alone is able to give this peculiar portrait its full and worthy signification and explanation" (L. S. Chafer, *Systematic Theology*, 5:85)

[511] Alva McClain, The Greatness of the Kingdom, 336.

[512] Arthur Ramsey, The Transfiguration and the Glory of Christ (London: Longmans, Green and Co., 1949), 118. It is noteworthy that many non-dispensationalists see far eschatology portrayed in the

this fact will now be examined.

Jesus' Transformation

Jesus invited Peter, James, and John onto a high mountain to witness His glory. The high mountain is probably reminiscent of the theophanies seen by Moses and Elijah on Sinai and Horeb respectively (Exod. 24; 1 Kings 19).[513] While they were on the mountain, Jesus was "transfigured" (μεταμορφόω) or "changed in form"[514] before them. The idea of transformation from one appearance or form into another was common in Classical literature. For example, Ovid presented a series of takes in which supernatural beings and humans experienced various transformations.[515] Apuleius described in autobiographical style of being transformed into an ass, and then later being restored back into a human by the power of the goddess Isis.[516] There are no significant linguistic data in the Old Testament related to the word, however, some background to the idea could be seen in Exodus 34:29-35 when the face of Moses shone after his conversation with God on Mt. Sinai.[517] The best way of understanding the transformation of Christ is to see His divine glory as shining through His flesh under which it was concealed (as opposed to His body temporarily changing into a heavenly, spiritual body). Bernardin explained this view: "The background of the idea is briefly this: The Messiah was a supernatural, heavenly, pre-existent figure dwelling in the presence of God...As such He was clothed with glory...When the Messiah came down to earth...His glory was concealed for the time being beneath the human flesh which He assumed. But here on the mount the glory was permitted to shine through."[518]

This view appears to fit better with the orthodox understanding of the incarnation. This was stated well by Harrison: "This metamorphosis of Christ should be considered in the light of Philippians 2. There the word is *morphe* translated "form," the same root word that is found in metamorphosis, occurs twice. Christ being originally in the form of God emptied himself taking the form

---

transfiguration proper. Because of this they are usually forced to deny that the transfiguration is the fulfillment of the pre-transfiguration prediction speaking of the kingdom, else, they would be forced to see that the transfiguration lends support to the fact that the kingdom consists of more than God's invisible rule in the world or in the heart of the believer. For example, D.A. Carson is representative when he comments on Matthew 16:28 that the prediction is a manifestation of Christ's kingly reign which is exhibited by the rapid multiplication of disciples. But then in expounding Matthew 17 he speaks of the parousia, Jesus' coming exaltation, the eschatological overtones of the Feast of Tabernacles, and the eschatological associations of the "cloud" terminology ("Matthew," 382, 384-386).

[513] Lane, The Gospel of Mark, 318; Boobyer noted that the mountain has prominence both in the New Testament and in other Christian and Jewish literature as an appropriate place for eschatological revelations—Matthew 24:3; Mark 13:3; Revelation 21:10 (G. H. Boobyer, "St. Mark and the Transfiguration," The Journal of Theological Studies 41 [1940], 127). While mountains can have other associations, in this context, the point is valid.

[514] Walter Bauer, William F. Arndt, and F. Wilbur Gingrich, A Greek-English Lexicon of the New Testament and Other Early Christian Literature, 2nd ed., rev. Frederick W. Danker (University of Chicago Press, 1979), 511.

[515] Ovid, Metamorphoses, Vol. III, The Loeb Classical Library.

[516] Apuleius, The Golden Ass, The Loeb Classical Library.

[517] The word is used four times in the New Testament (Matt. 17:2; Mark 9:2; Rom. 12:2; 2 Cor. 3:18).

[518] Joseph Bernardin, "The Transfiguration," *Journal of Biblical Literature* 52 (1933), 183-184.

of a servant...But here on the mount He stands forth with the veil parted, the glory of His deity shining through."[519]

For the purposes of this study, it is also important to note that this glory in the transfiguration is to be viewed in an eschatological sense, namely, the glory of the coming kingdom. Betteridge explained that "it [glory] is also used to describe the idea Messianic kingdom of the future. It is applied to Christ to describe His royal majesty when He comes to set up His kingdom. So James and John as to sit, one on His right hand and one on His left in His glory."[520] Boobyer concurred: "both in Judaism and in the New Testament, then, transformation into a glistening body of δόξα has outstanding reference to the events of the last days. It was a current apocalyptic hope, which in the New Testament focuses strongly upon the fashion of Jesus at His Second Coming."[521] This is especially seen in Mark's account when the references to δόξα are examined. He uses the term only three times and in each instance it refers to the coming of the kingdom (8:38; 10:37; 13:26).[522]

The Son of Man

A further point that supports the fact that the transfiguration relates to a literal kingdom is the fact that Christ (in the pre-transfiguration prediction) referred to Himself as the "Son of Man." The key to this title is Daniel 7:13-14 where the Son comes in the clouds of heaven to establish His kingdom. Peters observed:

> To Jewish hearers who invariably linked the coming of the Son of Man in glory with the prediction of Daniel 7:13-14...our Savior proceeds now to give His disciples...an assurance that He will give some of them a specimen of this coming in glory...The scene enacted in the transfiguration is a representation of the very appearance that the Son of man will assume when He comes in glory at His Second Coming in His kingdom.[523]

The Question of Peter

When Christ was transfigured before the disciples, Peter asks the Lord if they

[519] E.F. Harrison, "The Transfiguration," 318-319; see also D. Edmond Hiebert, *Mark: A Portrait of the Servant*, 213. Thus what happened to Christ was "a revelation of the glory which [He] possessed continually but not openly" (S. Aalen, "δόξα," *New International Dictionary of New Testament Theology* 2 [1981], 48. Not only was this glory preincarnate but also the same glory revealed of deity in the Old Testament when there was a manifestation (J. D. Pentecost, *The Words and Works of Jesus Christ* [Grand Rapids, MI: Zondervan, 1981], 256; Bernard Ramm, *Them He Glorified* [Grand Rapids, MI: Eerdmans, 1963], 40; John 12:41).

[520] Walter Betteridge, "Glory," in *International Standard Bible Encyclopedia* (Grand Rapids, MI: Eerdmans, 1980), 2:1239.

[521] Boobyer, "St. Mark and the Transfiguration," 130. Likewise, Kee explains that "the only thing that can be inferred from the radiance is that Jesus was seen as entering proleptically in the eschatological glorification that Jewish apocalyptic expected the righteous to share in" (Howard Kee, "The Transfiguration in Mark: Epiphany or Apocalyptic Vision," in *Understanding the Sacred Text* [Valley Forge, PA: Judson Press, 1972], 144). This point was even conceded by Thrall who does not take this view (Thrall, "Elijah and Moses in Mark's Account of the Transfiguration," 309).

[522] Boobyer, "St. Mark and the Transfiguration," 129; Wessell, "Mark," 8:698.

[523] G.N.H. Peters, *The Theocratic Kingdom*, 2:554-555.

should build three booths. Quite often Peter is chided for this question by commentators. For example, Caird stated that "Peter's offer was a very foolish one, which he would never have made if he had not been bewildered; he simply blurted out the first thing that came to his head."[524] Or, Lenski suggested that Peter was foolish because he thought that those in an exalted state needed shelter like ordinary mortals.[525] Those who feel that Peter's question was foolish usually take one of two approaches. The first is that Peter was trying to dissuade Christ from going to the cross. Johnson advocated this understanding in these words: "The counsel that comes from Peter at this point is not only not infallible, it is senseless and sinful...In effect, they would turn Him from His destined earthly goal, the cross. Our Lord thinks so little of the suggestion that He does not answer it."[526]

A second approach (and related to the preceding) is that Peter was simply trying to prolong the situation on the mount. Hiebert felt that "it may mean that the experience was good and one which he wished to prolong."[527] Plummer agreed that Peter "wishes to make present glory and rapture permanent."[528] While there is no doubt that Peter wished to perpetuate the situation, there is probably a better explanation.

The word Peter used for "booths" was σκῆνος. The term was particularly used in the Old Testament to refer to the Tabernacle. However, it was also used to refer to the booths made out of leafy branches by the Israelites during the Feast of Tabernacles (Lev. 23:42ff; Neh. 8:14-17). The Feast of Tabernacles was the last in the cycle of Israel's annual feasts, and was a memorial of their deliverance out of Egypt and their wilderness wanderings where they celebrated God's sovereignty and provision.[529]

Besides the historical implications to this celebration, there was also an eschatological implication as well, namely the time during the kingdom age when all nations would celebrate this feast together as God Himself dwelled among His people (Ezek. 37:27; 43:7, 9; Joel 3:21; Zech. 2:10; 8:3, 8; 14:16-19). Boobyer stated this point well:

> Frequently in Judaism, the day of salvation was depicted as a day when

---

[524] G.B. Caird, "The Transfiguration," *The Expository Times* 67 (1956), 292.

[525] Lenski, *The Interpretation of St. Matthew's Gospel* (Minneapolis, MN: Augsburg, 1961), 657. Close to this idea is that Peter erred in putting Jesus on par with Moses and Elijah since he advocated building a booth for all of them. Thus Trench commented: "Putting those other two at all on the same level with Him, he plainly declared that he did not yet perceive how far that Master transcended all other, even the princes of the elder dispensation" (R.C. Trench, *Studies in the Gospels*, 217); see also Walter Liefeld, "Luke," in *The Expositor's Bible Commentary*, 8:927.

[526] Johnson, "The Transfiguration of Christ, 138; J.P. Lange, "The Gospel According to Matthew," 307.

[527] Hiebert, *Mark: A Portrait of the Servant*, 214.

[528] Plummer, *A Critical and Exegetical Commentary on the Gospel According to S. Luke*, 252; see also Liefeld, "Luke," 927; Geldenhuys, *The Gospel of Luke*, 282; F.L. Godet, *Luke*, 1:429; I. Howard Marshall, *Commentary on Luke*, 380.

[529] Marshall, Commentary on Luke, 386; Pentecost, The Words and Works of Jesus Christ, 257; Mitch Glaser, The Fall Feasts of Israel, 157.

> Yahweh would once more pitch His *skene* with His people, as He had done in forty years of wilderness wandering...The Feast of Tabernacles itself had in fact...acquired eschatological significance. Not only did it look back to the deliverance from Egypt and God's preservation...It also looked forward to the New Age when Yahweh would again tabernacle with His people; and one of the special features of that great day would be the muster of members of all nations in Jerusalem to celebrate the Feast of Tabernacles and worship God as King.[530]

During Peter's day the nation was being oppressed by Rome and was anticipating deliverance (possibly even to a fault which caused them to downplay the spiritual basis of the kingdom). Naturally, therefore, when he sees the glory of the Son of Man, his mind goes to the Feast of Tabernacles. Thus Peter's suggestion "about building three tabernacles is not, of course, a *gauche* remark, as it used so often to be said to be: it is a natural part of the eschatological symbolism of the story. The Jews had come to look forward to the tabernacling presence of the Messiah with his righteous elect ones."[531] If Peter's request were legitimate, then why was he rebuked? The answer is that while Peter was correct in his eschatology, he was incorrect as to the timing of that eschatology (cf. Acts 1:6-7). The fulfillment of what was anticipated in the Feast of Tabernacles was conditioned on the repentance of Israel. Liefeld corroborated this understanding: "There can be no doubt that the Feast of Tabernacles had eschatological significance. One might, therefore, surmise that this proposal was not wrong in itself, but simply wrong in its timing. That is, Jesus the Messiah was to usher in the time of eschatological rest, but the anticipated festival of Tabernacles could not yet be celebrated. The response to his suggestion then, should be understood as, 'yes, but not yet.'"[532]

---

[530] Boobyer, "St. Mark and the Transfiguration," 134. The eschatological aspect to this feast is well attested: Ernst Lohmeyer, "Die Verklarung Jesus nach dem Markus-Evangelium," *Zeitschrift fur die neutestamentliche Wissenschaft* 21 (1922), 191ff; Norman Hillyer, "1 Peter and the Feast of Tabernacles," Tyndale Bulletin 21 (1970), 63, 67; Kee, "The Transfiguration in Mark: Epiphany or Apocalyptic Vision," 147; Lane, *The Gospel of Mark*, 317.

[531] Richardson, *An Introduction to the Theology of the New Testament* (London: SCM Press, 1958), 183; Carlston, "Transfiguration and Resurrection," 239; Wessell, "Mark," 699; Lane, *The Gospel of Mark*, 319; Carson, "Matthew," 383-386; Pentecost, *The Words and Works of Jesus Christ* 257; Boobyer, "St. Mark and the Transfiguration," 134. Roehers made the interesting point that the transfiguration and the Feast of Tabernacles should be seen in the perspective of God's eternal plan to dwell among His people, and that the glory of God was tabernacled in Israel provisionally by way of anticipation (Walter Roehers, "God Tabernacles Among Men," *Concordia Theological Monthly* 35 [1964], 18, 20-21).

[532] Walter Liefeld, "Theological Motifs in the Transfiguration Narrative," 175. Otto has argued strenuously against this position. He cited Davies and Allison who wrote that no one has yet put forward a convincing theological or literary explanation for Peter's remarks about the booths. Otto then rejects the notion that the feast of booths or the eschatological dwelling of God is in view. Rather, building on a strict Sinaitic background to the narrative, he suggests that Peter's request for booths is made out of fear death. Essentially, the booths are desired for protection (Randall Otto, "The Fear Motivation in Peter's Offer to Build Τρεις Σκηνας," *Westminster Theological Journal* 59 [1997], 102-112). It is certainly true that this was one of the functions of the Tabernacle and that God is biblically viewed as a *numen tremendum,* but the view presented above finds its justification in the kingdom context and expectation of the entire narrative. Penner

Moses and Elijah

The disciples not only saw the glorification of the Lord, but they also witnessed the appearance of Moses and Elijah. One of the more common explanations concerning their presence is they represented the Law and the Prophets.[533] However, as pointed out by McCurley: "the argument that these two heroes of antiquity represent the Law and the Prophets respectively leaves something to be desired for neither in the Old Testament or in later Jewish literature are they designated in such a way."[534]

It seems better to explain their appearance in light of the eschatological overtones of the passage. Moses had predicted that God would raise up a prophet to whom the people would listen (Deut. 18:15, 18). This fact is probably echoed in the words of the Father "hear ye him." Since this passage was given Messianic implications, Moses became the prototype of the Messiah. He was the model of the eschatological Prophet. Manek explained the significance of this. "For Luke it is very important to construct a positive relation between Moses and Jesus. Moses is the leader of the Exodus—Jesus is the leader of the Exodus....Moses was chosen by God to lead the Exodus from Egypt to the Promised Land. Christ was chosen by God to lead the new and final exodus, and so He introduced into history the eschatological era."[535]

If Moses was the model of the eschatological Prophet, then Elijah was the forerunner of that Prophet. When Jesus and Elijah are mentioned together in the New Testament, the eschaton or the preparation for it is in view. It is clear in Jewish expectation that Elijah played this role of being an eschatological figure of

---

also denies that Peter was thinking of the Feast of Tabernacles who wrote that "though possible, this seems unlikely." One of the reasons given is that "eschatological characteristics also appear to be downplayed in Matthew's account, with an emphasis on Mosaic allusions instead" (James A. Penner, "Revelation and Discipleship in Matthew's Transfiguration Account," *Bibliotheca Sacra* 152 [1995]:205). While it may be true that there are Mosaic motifs in the account, this does not argue against the eschatology of the passage, but instead argues for it since Moses was the model of the eschatological Prophet. Moreover, if any gospel writer were to downplay prophetic allusion, it certainly would not be Matthew since that and kingdom themes are two of his major concerns.

[533] Johnson, "The Transfiguration of Christ," 137; Calvin, *Commentary on the Harmony of the Evangelists,* 1:311; Geldenhuys, *The Gospel of Luke,* 281; Plummer, *St. Luke,* 251; Hiebert, *Mark: A Portrait of the Servant,* 213-214; Lenski, *The Interpretation of St. Matthew's Gospel,* 654; Swete, *Commentary on Mark,* 189; A.C. Gaebelein, *The Gospel of Matthew*, 363. For still other views see Bock, *Luke 1:1-9:50,* 868-869.

[534] McCurley, "And After Six Days: A Semitic Literary Device," 80; see also Liefeld, "Theological Motifs in the Transfiguration Narrative," 171.

[535] Jindrich Manek, "The New Exodus in the Books of Luke," *Novum Testamentum* 2 (1957), 20-21; see also Caird, "The Transfiguration," 292. This point is also brought out by the fact that in Luke's account it is said that they discussed Jesus' "decease" (or better "exodus"). This shed light on how Jesus viewed His death, and is reminiscent of the exodus out of Israel from the bondage of Egypt. Significantly, Luke speaks of the birth of Christ as his "incoming" (Acts 13:24). When the imagery is taken as a whole, the bondage to which Christ was subject was His incarnate state (Phil. 2), and His "exodus" would refer not only to His death, but to His resurrection and ascension as well—back into His state of glory and liberty. On this discussion and further validation see Harrison, "The Transfiguration," 320; Manek, "The New Exodus in the Books of Luke," 13, 19; Edersheim, *The Life and Times of Jesus the Messiah* 2:97; Plummer, *A Critical and Exegetical Commentary on the Gospel According to S. Luke* 251; Godet, *A Commentary on the Gospel of St. Luke* 1:427-428; Marshall, *Commentary on Luke* 380, 384; Lenski, *The Interpretation of St. Matthew's Gospel* 656; Pentecost, *The Words and Works of Jesus Christ* 257.

announcing the End. Kee stated the case thusly:

> The evidence [Apocalypse of Elijah; Ecclesiasticus; Assumption of Moses; Malachi] thus points to the conclusion that Elijah was considered in first century Judaism as an almost exclusively eschatological figure. There is no hint of his being numbered among the prophets, but his roles in relation to the establishment of God's rule are manifold, and all of them crucial. It is in this history-of-religions backgrounds that we must look for light on the meaning of Elijah as one of the companions.[536]

2 Peter 1:16-18

Also important to the thesis of this study is the recollection of Peter to the transfiguration event in his Second Epistle. One of the prime purposes of the writing of 2 Peter was to buttress the hope of the Second Coming of Christ in His kingdom and glory (1:11; 3:3, 4, 9, 10, 12, 13). This fact was being scoffed at by false teachers (3:3-4). Neyrey commented on this occasion. "The real occasion is the advent of heretics scoffing at the parousia-traditions. The opponents charge that the parousia prophecy is but a humanly concocted myth…The transfiguration is functioning in the apologetic argument as a prophecy of the Parousia…The transfiguration is the premier prophecy of the parousia."[537] This being the case, it is most significant that Peter uses the transfiguration as an authentication of the Old Testament prophecies. Peter does not relate the transfiguration to the resurrection, the destruction of Jerusalem, or the Church Age.[538] Rather, he

---

[536] Kee, "The Transfiguration in Mark: Epiphany or Apocalyptic Vision," 146; Wessell, "Mark," 679; Carson, "Matthew," 385; Hiebert, *Mark: A Portrait of the Servant* 213. One could also conclude from the eschatological significances to Elijah that since John the Baptist did not accomplish his work because of the rejection by the nation, it would follow that the Kingdom is also postponed until the future. Thus, this fits with the contention of this article that the transfiguration is a proleptic preview of the Millennium. In his superb article, Boobyer also pointed out that there were many prominent figures in Hebrew history who were associated with Hebrew eschatology—Enoch, Elijah, Moses, Ezra, Baruch, Jeremiah, and perhaps even Job (130; see also Hermann Strack and Paul Billerbeck, *Kommentar zum neuen Testament* vol. 1: *Das Evangelium nach Matthaus erlautert aus Talmud und Midrash* [Munich: C.H. Beck'sche Verlagsbuchhandlung, 1961], 1:753-758; Lohmeyer, "Die Verklarung Jesu nach dem Markus-Evangelium," 191). Moreover, Matthew 8:11 speaks of those who will come from the east and west to sit down with Abraham, Isaac, and Jacob in the kingdom. However, Luke adds in 13:28ff that they shall see "Abraham, Isaac, and Jacob, *and the prophets* in the kingdom." Surely, then, Moses and Elijah are included and therefore are related to the consummation of the kingdom and not to some point in religious history. This interpretation is also strengthened by the question asked by the disciples after the transfiguration regarding the coming of Elijah and Jesus' response concerning the restoration of all things (John A. McClean, "Did Jesus Correct the Disciples' View of the Kingdom?" *Bibliotheca Sacra* 151 [1994], 219-220; John Walvoord, "Interpreting Prophecy: Part 4—The Kingdom of God in the New Testament," *Bibliotheca Sacra* 139 [1982], 305). See also the discussion by Walter C. Kaiser, "The Promise of the Arrival of Elijah in Malachi and the Gospels," *Grace Theological Journal* 3 (1982), 233.

[537] Jerome Neyrey, "The Apologetic Use of the Transfiguration," *The Catholic Biblical Quarterly* 42 (1980), 519. Kelly also noted that "the rest of the letter shows that the future coming was what was raising doubts in the readers' minds" (J.N.D. Kelly, *A Commentary on the Epistles of Peter and Jude* [Grand Rapids, MI: Baker, 1987], 317-318).

[538] It should again be observed that there are non-dispensationalists who see the transfiguration as a reference to the parousia. However, as has been pointed out previously, the pre-transfiguration prediction relating to the kingdom was fulfilled in the transfiguration. This being the case, it is best to invest the term

related it to the future coming of Christ in His kingdom. As Ramsey stated: "it bore witness to the prophetic word. It confirmed the truth of the whole body of prophetic teaching which spoke of the Messianic Age. This for Peter is the supreme importance of the transfiguration...It shows that the prophets are not annulled. Vindicated and confirmed by the Transfiguration, their word endures."[539] Or, in the words of Johnson, "the transfiguration, then, is a foretaste and a foreshadowing of the Messianic Kingdom to come and, thus a convincing pledge of its consummation according to its Old Testament terms of description."[540]

Section 26: The Edict of Milan[541]

When I, Constantine Augustus, as well as I, Licinius Augustus, fortunately met near Mediolanurn (Milan), and were considering everything that pertained to the public welfare and security, we thought, among other things which we saw would be for the good of many, those regulations pertaining to the reverence of the Divinity ought certainly to be made first, so that we might grant to the Christians and others full authority to observe that religion which each preferred; whence any Divinity whatsoever in the seat of the heavens may be propitious and kindly disposed to us and all who are placed under our rule. And thus by this wholesome counsel and most upright provision we thought to arrange that no one whatsoever should be denied the opportunity to give his heart to the observance of the Christian religion, of that religion which he should think best for himself, so that the Supreme Deity, to whose worship we freely yield our hearts) may show in all things His usual favor and benevolence. Therefore, your Worship should know that it has pleased us to remove all conditions whatsoever, which were in the rescripts formerly given to you officially, concerning the Christians and now any one of these who wishes to observe Christian religion may do so freely and

"kingdom" with the qualities found in the transfiguration which are most consistent with the Old Testament description of it. Thus when writers are cited who are not dispensational but who hold the parousia view, this is strictly for their contribution of placing the transfiguration in the realm of far eschatology and not necessarily to their understanding of what the kingdom is in the present age.

539 Ramsey, *The Glory of God and the Transfiguration of Jesus Christ,* 126.

540 Johnson, "The Transfiguration of Christ," 141; Gaebelein, *The Gospel of Matthew* 361; Caird, "The Transfiguration," 292, Blum, "2 Peter," 273; Kelly, *A Commentary on the Epistles of Peter and Jude* 317; McClain, *The Greatness of the Kingdom* 336. There are a few other miscellaneous indications in the transfiguration narrative which could lend support to the far eschatological argument: 1) the color white was used of heavenly dwellers (Mark 16:5; Acts 1:10; Rev. 3:4-5; 7:9-13) and because of this had possible eschatological ramifications (Strack and Billerbeck, *Kommentary zum neuen Testament* 1:752; T.D. Angel, "λευκός," *New International Dictionary of New Testament Theology*, 1 [1981], 204-205), 2) so perhaps also is the reference of Matthew to "light," 3) clouds are often associated with the future coming of the Son of Man (Isa. 4:5; Dan. 7:13; 2 Baruch 53:1-12; 4 Ezra 13:3; Mark 14:62; Luke 21:27 and with the two prophets in Rev. 11:12). It could rightly be argued that clouds have other significances in the Bible, namely the divine presence, but the divine presence, of course, will be dwelling on earth during the kingdom age and would go along nicely with the "kingdom" overtones of the passage, and 4) the fact that the disciples are later instructed to tell no man of this event fits nicely with the dispensational understanding of the rejection of the kingdom.

541 Ray Petry, ed., A History of Christianity: Readings in the History of the Church, Volume 1 The Early and Medieval Church (Grand Rapids: Baker, 1981), 57-58.

openly, without molestation. We thought it fit to commend these things most fully to your care that you may know that we have given to those Christians free and unrestricted opportunity of religious worship. When you see that this has been granted to them by us, your Worship will know that we have also conceded to other religions the right of open and free observance of their worship for the sake of the peace of our times, that each one may have the free opportunity to worship as he pleases; this regulation is made we that we may not seem to detract from any dignity or any religion.

Moreover, in the case of the Christians especially we esteemed it best to order that if it happens anyone heretofore has bought from our treasury from anyone whatsoever, those places where they were previously accustomed to assemble, concerning which a certain decree had been made and a letter sent to you officially, the same shall be restored to the Christians without payment or any claim of recompense and without any kind of fraud or deception, Those, moreover, who have obtained the same by gift, are likewise to return them at once to the Christians. Besides, both those who have purchased and those who have secured them by gift, are to appeal to the vicar if they seek any recompense from our bounty, that they may be cared for through our clemency. All this property ought to be delivered at once to the community of the Christians through your intercession, and without delay. And since these Christians are known to have possessed not only those places in which they were accustomed to assemble, but also other property, namely the churches, belonging to them as a corporation and not as individuals, all these things which we have included under the above law, you will order to be restored, without any hesitation or controversy at all, to these Christians, that is to say to the corporations and their conventicles: providing, of course, that the above arrangements be followed so that those who return the same without payment, as we have said, may hope for an indemnity from our bounty. In all these circumstances you ought to tender your most efficacious intervention to the community of the Christians, that our command may be carried into effect as quickly as possible, whereby, moreover, through our clemency, public order may be secured. Let this be done so that, as we have said above, Divine favor towards us, which, under the most important circumstances we have already experienced, may, for all time, preserve and prosper our successes together with the good of the state. Moreover, in order that the statement of this decree of our good will may come to the notice of all, this rescript, published by your decree, shall be announced everywhere and brought to the knowledge of all, so that the decree of this, our benevolence, cannot be concealed.

Section 27: Biblical Interpretation—Patristic to the Present

Patristic Hermeneutics

Patristics refers to the study of the early Christian writers also known as the Church Fathers. This period would take us from approximately the time of the apostles to the Council of Chalcedon or from roughly A.D. 100 to A.D. 450. This period featured three major schools of interpretation.

The first was the Alexandrian school. The Alexandrian school focused on allegorical interpretation insisting that the text had a deeper, spiritual, symbolic meaning as illustrated from Philo above. Probably the two most famous individuals associated with this method were Clement of Alexandria (ca. 150-215) and Origen (185-254). To add to the illustrations of this method given from Philo, Clement said that the two fish in the feeding of the five thousand were the merging of Greek philosophy with Christian theology. For Origen, the tree planted beside rivers of water in Psalm 1 represented the cross and baptism; Rahab's scarlet cord and the two spies were prophetic of the Trinity and the work of Christ; the 318 servants of Abraham were predictive of Christ's death based on corresponding letters in Greek; Rebekah drawing water from the well meant that we must meet Christ daily in the Scriptures; Noah's ark was the church; Noah was Christ; in Jesus' triumphal entry, the donkey represented the Old Testament while its colt was the New Testament and on it went. This was the Alexandrian school. [542]

The second was the Antiochian school. The Antiochian school reacted to the Alexandrian by stressing literal, historical, grammatical interpretation. They taught that every passage of Scripture had one meaning. Though they normally practiced this commendable type of hermeneutics, they did occasionally slip into extreme typology but generally the normal reading was the philosophy. Three famous names associated with this method were Chrysostom (ca. 344-407), Theodore of Mopsuestia (ca. 350-428), and Theodoret (ca. 386-458) who has left us a brilliant exegesis of the epistles of Paul. Unfortunately, this school would begin to lose its influence.

The third school was the Western school. The third school was more of an eclectic method which embraced features of the Alexandrian and Antiochian schools. Two key individuals taking this view were Jerome (ca. 345-419) and Augustine (ca. 354-430). Jerome was influenced by Origen and consequently his first commentary which was on the book of Obadiah was allegorical. He then came to be influenced by the Antiochian school and his last commentary, on Jeremiah, was literal in its approach.

Augustine was the greatest thinker of his era and according to some the greatest thinker in Christian history. Augustine tended to a more literal interpretation but drifted into excessive allegorization.[543] One of the most

---

[542]Origen taught that Scripture should be interpreted figuratively according to its spiritual method (Origen. *De Principiis* F. Crombie, Trans. In A. Roberts, J. Donaldson & A. C. Coxe Eds, *The Ante-Nicene Fathers, Volume IV: Fathers of the Third Century: Tertullian, Part Fourth; Minucius Felix; Commodian; Origen, Parts First and Second* (Buffalo, NY: Christian Literature Company), 252.

[543] He writes in his *On Christian Doctrine*: "For what more liberal and more fruitful provision could God have made in regard to the Sacred Scriptures than that the same words might be understood in several senses, all of which are sanctioned by the concurring testimony of other passages equally divine? (Augustine of Hippo. "On Christian Doctrine". translated by Shaw, J. F. In *A Select Library of the Nicene and Post-Nicene Fathers of the Christian Church, First Series, Volume II: St. Augustin's City of God and Christian Doctrine*. Buffalo, NY: Christian Literature Company, 1887), 3.27. Though Augustine includes the safety net of the analogy of faith in this statement, his biblical exegesis still robs the author of an intended meaning. The

shocking is from his homilies in Genesis where he writes that the drunkenness of Noah is a "figure of the death and passion of Christ."[544]

Medieval Hermeneutics

The next period in the history of interpretation was medieval hermeneutics. Generally speaking little progress was made in the area of hermeneutics from the fifth century A.D. to the time of the Protestant Reformation. Interpretation was bound by tradition and the prominent method of hermeneutics was the allegorical one articulated by Augustine.

Reformation Hermeneutics

It would be accurate to say that the Protestant Reformation of the 16th century did not only consist of a reformation in doctrine but also a reformation in hermeneutics. There were two issues at stake during the Reformation. The first is what is known as the "material principle." This dealt with the doctrine of justification. The second issue is known as the "formal principle" concerning the final locus of authority. For the Reformers, the final seat of authority was not the bishops or tradition but Scripture alone which we know by the slogan *sola scriptura*. This, along with the Hebrew contributions of Johannes Reuchlin and the Greek contribution by Desiderius Erasmus, logically led to an emphasis on the literal exegesis of Scripture and a moving away from allegorization. The authority of Scripture rested in its literal sense. Martin Luther wrote on one occasion: "When I was a monk, I was an expert in allegories. I allegorized everything. But after lecturing on the Epistle to the Romans...I saw that Christ was no allegory." When taking Erasmus to task for his view of free will, Luther asserted that our sentiment should be "...that the simple, pure, and natural meaning of the words is to be adhered to, which is according to the rules of grammar, and to that common use of speech which God has given to men."[545] Throughout his works he blasts allegorization as "mere jugglery," "a merry chase," "monkey tricks," and "looney talk." Thus, Luther followed (though not always consistently!) the *sensus unum* (single meaning) and the *sensus literalis* (literal sense).

The method advocated by Luther was followed by Melanchthon, Calvin,

---

analogy of faith principle is only valid when corroborated with properly exegeted passages, not truth in general. See also Augustine's exposition of the "7 Rules of Tichonius" which "penetrate the secrets of the sacred writings" (Augustine of Hippo. "On Christian Doctrine". translated by Shaw, J. F. In *A Select Library of the Nicene and Post-Nicene Fathers of the Christian Church, First Series, Volume II: St. Augustin's City of God and Christian Doctrine*. Buffalo, NY: Christian Literature Company, 1887), 3.30.42ff.

[544]Augustine, *Reply to Faustus the Manichæan.* R. Stothert, Trans. In P. Schaff, Ed, *A Select Library of the Nicene and Post-Nicene Fathers of the Christian Church, First Series, Volume IV: St. Augustine: The Writings against the Manichaeans and against the Donatists,* (Buffalo, NY: Christian Literature Company), 190.

[545] Martin Luther, *The Bondage of the Will,* Henry Cole trans. (Grand Rapids: Baker, 1983), 205. "When some ascribe to the Scriptures the flexibility of a waxen nose, and say that it is like bending a reed, this is due to the work of those who misuse the Holy Word of God for their incompetent and unstable opinions and glosses. They reach the

point where the Word of God, which is fitting for everything, fits nothing" (Martin Luther, *Works of Luther, Volume 14: Selected Psalms III* (St. Louis: Concordia Publishing House, 1955), 338.

Zwingli, and before him Tyndale. John Calvin, the greatest exegete of the period, who surpassed Luther in matching up hermeneutic theory with exegesis, wrote correctly when explaining the purpose of one who expounds Scripture, "...it is almost his only work to lay open the mind of the writer whom he undertakes to explain, the degree in which he leads away his readers from it, in that degree he goes astray from his purpose, and in a manner wanders from his own boundaries."[546] He writes further: "It is therefore an audacity, closely allied to a sacrilege, rashly to turn Scripture in any way we please, and to indulge our fancies as in sport; which has been done by many in former times."[547]

Post-Reformation hermeneutics

During the post-reformation era, there were two major influences in the history of hermeneutics. The first was pietism which emphasized the application of Scripture to one's own personal life. While this is good, many later pietists began to depend on subjective impressions and pious reflections on the text which had nothing to do with the Scriptural author's intended meaning.[548]

The second major influence during this time was rationalism which said that human reason determined what was true and false. Therefore, if something in the Bible appears unreasonable, then it may be rejected. This led, of course, eventually to liberal Christianity and extreme biblical criticism. It is important to insert here one caveat lest it be thought that we come mindlessly to the Bible when we interpret it. Luther distinguished between the magisterial and the ministerial use of reason. The ministerial use of reason meant that we use human reason to help us understand the Bible. The magisterial use of reason meant that we use human reason to stand in judgment over the Bible. When we speak of rationalism and decry it, of course we are speaking of the magisterial use of reason.[549]

---

[546] John Calvin, "The Epistle Dedicatory to Simon Grynaeus: A Man Worthy of All Honour," in *Commentaries on the Epistle of Paul the Apostle to the Romans.* Henry Beveridge ed. (Grand Rapids: Baker, 1979), xxiii.

[547] Ibid. xxvii.

[548] Norman Geisler and William Nix, *A General Introduction to the Bible* (Chicago: Moody Press, 1977), 109. A personal concern within Christianity has to do with the elevation of one's devotional life as the most important part of the Christian life. Of course, each individual Christian should have a close walk with God which includes private Bible study and prayer--this goes without saying. This has degenerated, however, into a contemplative, subjective time with God where we are waiting for the Holy Spirit zap the mind with various "insights" as to what the Bible means. Many times these insights have nothing to do with the meaning of the text ultimately leading to a man-made version of the Christian life and doctrine. Certainly the Holy Spirit will use the Word in our lives, but he will not give us interpretations which cannot be sustained through proper hermeneutical method. Private bible study should not be an exercise in which we wait for God to speak, but one in which we pour ourselves into discerning the meaning of the text. The Holy Spirit will then do his work through his word.

[549] It is important to balance these two aspects of reason in Luther's thought. On the one hand, he made some very stinging comments against the use of reason. For example: "But the Devil's bride, reason, the lovely whore comes in and wants to be wise, and what she says, she thinks, is the Holy Spirit" ("Sermons 1," *Luther's Works*, Vol. 51 [Philadelphia: Fortress Press, 1959], 374). On the other hand, he could praise reason as "the most important and highest in rank among all things, and, in comparison with other things of this life, the best and something divine" ("Career of the Reformer IV," *Luther's Works*, Vol. 34 [Philadelphia: Fortress

Modern Hermeneutics

The modern era is dated around 1800 to the present day. There are at least three movements of note in modern hermeneutics.

Liberalism

The philosophical rationalism of post-reformation hermeneutics led to liberalism in theology. It was now being posited that there were degrees of inspiration of the biblical text, or that we were free to reject whatever did not fit into our sophisticated way of viewing things. Put differently, the Bible is a human book, not a divine one.

Neoorthodoxy

The highly influential Swiss theologian Karl Barth reacted to liberalism in his famous commentary on Romans in 1919.[550] He argued that the Bible was not a human document. However, he went on to posit that the Bible is a record of revelation, not revelation itself. And that the Bible becomes the Word of God as we have a divine/human encounter with it.[551]

Reader-Response.

The primary aim of hermeneutics is to determine what the author of the text intended when he wrote the text. By contrast, "reader-response" hermeneutics puts the reader at the center of the process so that the reader derives meaning through his study of the text--and so what the text means to one reader is not what it means to another reader. At the end of the day, this approach leads to a sort of hermeneutical nihilism where the text cannot sustain any objective meaning. This can also be linked with another hermeneutical approach known as "deconstructionism" where the reader is invited to enjoy interpretive creativity.[552]

Press, 1960], 137). The Reformer is not contradicting himself, but showing the role of reason in the different spheres of life. In the realm of man, human reason is of great value; however, in the realm of spiritual things, reason must be subservient to divine revelation. It is not that reason is useless in the realm of Scripture (indeed we must use reason to interpret Scripture), but when truths emerge such as salvation through faith alone, the Trinity, the hypostatic union, etc. which may not make sense to one's reason, then it must bow to the knowledge of a more intelligent being and acknowledge its own limitations. If this is not the case, then it is futile to even think in terms of a God.

[550] Karl Barth, *The Epistle to the Romans* (London: Oxford, 1933).

[551] See similarly Emil Brunner, *Theology of Crisis* (NY: Scribner, 1929).

[552] For a further development of these themes see Henry Virkler and Karelynne Gerber Ayayo, *Hermeneutics: Principles and Processes of Biblical Interpretation* 2nd ed (Grand Rapids: Baker, 2007), 43-78.

PART III: MEANING

CHAPTER 9

ARGUMENTATIVE ANALYSIS OF EACH NEW TESTAMENT BOOK WITH INTERPRETIVE NOTES[553]

MATTHEW

Authorship

A. The external evidence for the authorship of Matthew:

1. The *Didache*[554] (ca. AD 110) quotes Matthew more than any other Gospel.

2. The letters of Ignatius and Polycarp (ca. AD 110) show knowledge of the book.

3. The Christians in Rome were acquainted with the book by AD 120.

4. The *Epistle of Barnabas* (ca. AD 130) uses the expression, "It is written" in quoting Matthew 20:16 and 22:14.

5. Many of the church fathers attributed the book to Matthew. For example, Irenaeus wrote that "Matthew published also a book of the Gospel among the Hebrews in their own dialect" (*Against Heresies*. 3.1.1). Origen wrote that, "Among the four gospels… I have learned by tradition that the first was written Matthew" (Eusebius, *Ecclesiastical. History*, 6.25.4). Papias noted that, "Matthew composed the *logia* in the Hebrew tongue" (cited by Eusebius, 3.39.16). Though the meaning of *logia* is disputed in the statement by Papias, it is reasonable to conclude that it is a reference to the Gospel for the following reasons: 1) it agrees with the earliest title (see below under internal evidence), 2) it agrees with Papias' own usage of *logia* (Donald Guthrie, *New Testament Introduction* [Downers Grove: InterVarsity, 1970] 34-35), and 3) in the New Testament and the Fathers *logia* is synonymous with the Scriptures (Everett Harrison, *Introduction to the New Testament* [Grand Rapids: Eerdmans, 1964], 159).

B. The internal evidence for the authorship of Matthew:

1. The Gospel's superscription is the oldest known testimony to its authorship: KATA MAΘΘAION. This is indisputably attested by the close of the second century and found in uncials Aleph, B, and D. Furthermore, this superscription is found on all known manuscripts of the Gospel (see D. Edmond Hiebert, *An Introduction to the New Testament* [Chicago: Moody Press, 1975], 1:47-49).

2. Matthew calls himself a "publican" in the lists of disciples while the others call him "Matthew."

3. Matthew was knowledgeable of Jewish, Greek, and Roman culture and would be able to speak Aramaic and Greek as are evinced in the book.

4. The attention in Matthew to the details of coinage would be characteristic of a tax

[553] Interpretive notes will be interspersed throughout the text in *italics*.

[554] The *Didache* is a manual of church practice and morals dating from the early second century AD.

collector. Matthew includes three *hapax legomenon* for money which may reflect his background. Matthew also includes the only account of the payment of the temple tax.

Date

The question concerning the date of Matthew involves whether or not one accepts the possibility of predictive prophecy. Those who disavow the possibility of predictive prophecy, namely in such passages as Matthew 24:1-28, date the book as late as AD 80-100 (see Guthrie's discussion *New Testament Introduction,* 45-46). Even some conservatives date it as late as AD 70-80 (Harrison, *Introduction to the New Testament,* 166), while others date it as early as AD 50-60.

The writer accepts a date at least before AD 70 because of the Lord's prediction of the destruction of Jerusalem in Matthew 24. In addition, since Luke's Gospel is earlier than Acts, and Matthew is earlier than Luke, it is felt that Matthew must have prepared his Gospel around AD 50. And finally, the phrase "unto this day" (Matt. 27:8) and "until this day" (Matt. 28:15) imply a date some time after the resurrection and ascension, which if Matthean priority is held could be as early as AD 50. If Marcan priority is held, then a date of around AD 60 would be held.

Original Language

One of the most debated subjects in the introduction to Matthew is whether the original was written in Aramaic or Greek. Those who opt for the former point to the statement by Papias quoted by Eusebius (see above A5) which states that Matthew wrote in Hebrew and then interpreted it (see for this view Hiebert, *An Introduction to the New Testament,* 1:54-56). Others, however, hold that the original was originally written in Greek. This is due to the facts that the Greek text explains certain Aramaic words, the author explains certain Palestinian customs, and there is very little evidence that the extant Greek manuscripts are translations (Guthrie, *New Testament Introduction,* 46-47).

Origin

There have been several suggestions regarding the origin of Matthew. These include: 1) Palestine, based on the comment of Irenaeus that Matthew "produced his gospel among the Hebrews," 2) Antioch, based on the fact that Ignatius' writings of the early second century indicate a knowledge of Matthew (Harrison, *Introduction to the New Testament,*164), and 3) Syria, based on the fact that there were a large number of Jewish Christians living in that area (Acts 11:19, 27; Hiebert, *An Introduction to the New Testament,* 63).

Destination

The strong Jewish flavoring of the Gospel indicates that it was written to early Jewish converts though this does not argue for a specific locale.

Characteristics

The following are some of the outstanding characteristics of Matthew:

A. Events found only in Matthew

1. The announcement of Mary's pregnancy to Joseph.

2. The journey of the Magi.

3. The flight into Egypt to flee from Herod.
4. The suicidal death of Judas.
5. The dream of Pilate's wife about Jesus' innocence.
6. The resurrection of bodies at/after (?) Christ's resurrection.
7. The bribery of the Roman guard to spread the rumor about the stolen body.

B. Parables found only in Matthew
1. The wheat and the tares.
2. The treasure hidden in the earth.
3. The net and the fish.
4. The unmerciful servant.
5. The ten virgins.
6. The sheep and the goats.

C. The word "church" occurs only in this **Gospel** (2 times in 16 and 1 time in 18).

D. The book is structured around five great discourses (The Sermon on the Mount in 5-7, the Mission Discourse in 10, the Kingdom Parables in 13, the Discipleship Discourse in 18, and the Olivet Discourse in 24-25).

E. The Jewish character of the book.
1. The term "kingdom of heaven."
2. The term "son of man."
3. The reference to Old Testament prophecies.
4. The reference to the Sabbath.
5. The reference to defilements.
6. Some 129 Old Testament references.
7. Prophecy in the Kingdom parables and the Olivet Discourse.
8. The emphasis on the Law in the Sermon on the Mount.
9. The emphasis on the Kingdom.
10. The content forms a logical bridge from the prophets of the Old Testament to the New Testament.
11. There is a concern for the Gentiles seen which would be remi-niscent of the promise of the Abrahamic Covenant (8:11-12; 15:24; 21:43; 28:19).

Purposes

Oftentimes it is thought that the Gospels are simply recording historical facts so that the reader will know more about that period in history. While the Gospels are certainly historical, the writers concentrate on only small and selective facts in order to emphasize a given purpose or purposes. Guthrie has written well that "it is customary to think of the Gospels as accounts of the life of Christ…Their dominant purpose is not solely a record of facts…Their purpose was something more than historical" (Guthrie, *New Testament Introduction,* 13). With this in mind, several purposes of Matthew's Gospel can be pointed out.

A. Matthew wanted to demonstrate that Christ is the rightful heir to the Abrahamic and

Davidic covenants. This is shown by the genealogy and the many allusions to Old Testament fulfillment. In combination with this, Matthew also proves and presents Christ as the King of Israel. This is done by the many prophecies fulfilled, the repetition of the word "kingdom," the repetition of the title "Son of David," and the expectation brought from the Old Testament.

B. Matthew wanted to explain to Jewish believers why the Kingdom had not been established if Christ was indeed the rightful heir to the covenants.

C. In light of the postponement of the Kingdom for Israel, Matthew wanted to give some details concerning the Kingdom program (Matt. 13 and Matt. 24-25) and how his Jewish readers were to live in light of its rejection (the Sermon on the Mount).

D. A further purpose (intimated in #C) was instruction. This is seen by the structure around the five great discourse sections and the catch-phrase "when Jesus finished these sayings" (7:28; 11:1; 13:53; 19:1; 26:1).

In light of these purposes, a general purpose statement could be put thusly:

> Matthew records selected events in the life of Christ in order to demonstrate that He is the covenanted Messiah and to shed light on the Kingdom program in light of the rejection of the King so that persecuted Jewish Christians would be encouraged and receive instruction on how they should live in the present age.[555]

Summary of Argument

I. MATTHEW RECORDS THE GENEALOGY, CHILDHOOD, AND PREPARATION OF CHRIST IN ORDER TO AUTHENTICATE THAT HE IS THE RIGHTFUL HEIR TO THE Davidic THRONE, AND THAT HIS PROTECTION BY GOD AND FULFILLMENT OF OLD TESTAMENT PROPHECY IS FURTHER PROOF THAT HE IS THE PROPHESIED KING WHO WILL REIGN—1:1-4:11

A. Matthew records the genealogy of Christ from Abraham through David in order to show that He was a son of Abraham and from the house of David since promises were made to them which were to be fulfilled by the Messiah—1:1-17

Note #1: Messiah

The Hebrew term for "messiah" is simply a passive adjective for any individual who had been anointed king. It came to be a title for the one who would fulfill God's covenants made with Israel. According to Old Testament prophecies, this would be a

---

[555] The purpose statements in this chapter are composed of three elements: 1) the *content* of the book, 2) the *purpose* for recording this content, and 3) the *goal* for the readers. Thus, "Matthew records selected events in the life of Christ (1) *in order to* demonstrate that He is the covenanted Messiah and to shed light on the Kingdom program in light of the rejection of the King (2) *so that* persecuted Jewish Christians would be encouraged and receive instruction on how they should live in the present age (3)." For some statements, #s 2 and 3 will be combined for sake of clarity.

divine-man of the proper Davidic lineage who would bring God's kingdom to earth. One of the obvious themes of Matthew is that Christ is the fulfillment of this expectation.

1. Matthew records a summary statement that Jesus was of the royal line of David in order to establish the motif that Jesus is the son of David—1:1
2. Matthew records the genealogy from Abraham to David during which time the kingdom was being waited for and during which time the Abrahamic covenant was made to show that Christ would fulfill it—1:2-6a
3. Matthew records the genealogy from David to the Babylonian Captivity during which time the Davidic Covenant was made in order to show that Christ would fulfill that—1:6b-11
4. Matthew records the genealogy from the Babylonian Captivity to the time of Christ during which time the New Covenant was made in order to show that Christ would fulfill that—1:12-16
5. Matthew summarizes the genealogy by noting that in each of the three lists there are fourteen generations (note: he is not saying that there are only fourteen) which is the numerical value of DVD in order to further emphasize the fact of Christ's Davidic descent—1:17

B. Matthew records the events in the childhood of Christ which show God's intervention in His conception and protection in order to emphasize to the readers that He is the Messiah sent from God who will someday reign and to show the beginnings of Jewish rejection and Gentile acceptance of the King—1:18-2:23

1. Matthew records the virgin conception of Christ showing that it was of supernatural origination and in fulfillment of Old Testament prophecy (Isa. 7:14) in order to demonstrate that Christ was the promised Messiah—1:18-25

Note #2: Relationship between Isaiah 7 and Matthew 1

The historical background of Isaiah 7 revolves around four players in 734 BC: Assyria with king Tiglathpileser III, Syria with king Rezin, Ephraim with king Pekah, and Judah with king Ahaz. Syria and Ephraim had formed an alliance against Judah causing Ahaz to panic. In response, he turned to Assyria for help. God sent Isaiah to the king to inform him that trusting in Assyria was foolish since it would turn on Judah despite the alliance. To show Ahaz he could trust God instead, Isaiah told Ahaz to ask any sign he wished as an indication that God would protect Judah from the Syria/Ephraim alliance. Ahaz, who was a wicked unbeliever, piously refused the offer, but Isaiah gave a sign anyway revolving around a child to be born of a virgin (7:14). When the child reached a certain age of being able to tell right from wrong, the threatening alliance would dissolve. Amazingly, the prophecy was fulfilled when TP III defeated Damascus and Samaria, the capital of Ephraim.

If this were the end of the matter, this passage would be relatively simple. However, centuries later, Matthew would cite 7:14 and apply it to the birth of Christ (1:23). This has led to three major interpretations regarding the child of Isaiah 7:14: 1) the historical view which sees the prophecy as a reference to a child born by natural means in the 8th century only, 2) the messianic view which sees a direct prediction to Christ only, and 3) the combination view which sees a double reference—a child born in the 8th century plus *a prediction of Christ. The first view is typically held by those who do not believe in predictive prophecy and therefore adopt an entirely naturalistic interpretation. The second view has four supports. First, after Ahaz rejects the offer of a sign, Isaiah begins to speak about the entire house of David in 7:13. This would indicate the prophecy has taken on a new scope. Second, the word "virgin" refers to a woman who has never had sexual relations* <u>*and*</u> *therefore she is carrying a child while still a virgin. Third, if the reference is to a natural birth in the 8th century, then how can this be said to be a miraculous sign? And fourth, the fact that Matthew applies this passage to Jesus shows that it was intended to be a strict prophecy.*

I believe that the third view is the most compelling with my reasons and explanation of the texts listed below.

1. There are strong reasons in Isaiah 7-8 that a child born at that time would fulfill the prophecy, a) the prophecy would have had no meaning as a sign to Ahaz in his current crisis if it were entirely future, b) the coalition which frightened Ahaz was to be destroyed when the boy reached a particular age. The fact that a child specifically is said to reach a certain age when the alliance was broken in 732 BC with the destruction of Damascus (the capital of Syria) argues for a historical fulfillment, c) the word "Immanuel" is used twice in Isaiah 8 (8, 10) forging the historical birth of Mahershalalhasbaz with the chapter 7 prophecy, d) the child's name contains imperatives carrying the idea of "one who hurries to plunder" which would be apropos to the defeat of Damascus, e) in 8:1-2 God told Isaiah to write on a large surface Mahershalalhashbaz to announce the attack on Syria and the birth of his son. Moreover, two men were selected to witness the writing on the document to note its official character to show that Isaiah had predicted these events (8:3), and f) Isaiah had relations with his wife who bore a son whom she named Immanuel and he named Mahershalalhashbaz. Based on these considerations, Wolf is correct when he writes that "the context of chapter 7 demands some sort of contemporary fulfillment as a sign to King Ahaz" (Herbert Wolf, "A Solution to the Immanuel Prophecy in Isaiah 7:14-8:22," Journal of Biblical Literature 91 [December 1972], 449). The "virgin," therefore, is Isaiah's fiancée and the promised child is their son. This is validated by the above points as well as the fact that Isaiah's sons are referred to as "signs" in 8:18.

2. The Messianic view has apparently assumed that the word "sign" always refers to the miraculous. While the word "sign" often refers to a miraculous event (however most of these uses refer to the same event, namely, the exodus), this is not always the case. The Hebrew word translated "sign" (אוֹת) in 7:14 is used 79 times in the Old Testament and many times does not refer to something which would be classified as "miraculous." For example, the following are called "signs" using the same Hebrew word: circumcision (Gen. 17:11), blood on the doorposts (Exod. 12:13), the Sabbath (Exod. 31:17), eating (2 Kings 19:29), Isaiah's naturally born children (Isa. 8:18), Isaiah walking naked and barefoot (Isa. 20:3), and Isaiah's diet (Isa. 37:30). This is why the lexicons will use a variety of terms in translating the word such as sign, pledge, token, symbol, miracle, memorial, and standard (Brown, Driver, Briggs, Hebrew and English Lexicon of the Old Testament [Oxford: Clarendon, n.d.], 16).

Chisholm nicely sums up these first two points. "A child would soon be born and named 'Immanuel' (meaning 'God is with us') because he would serve as living proof of God's ability to deliver Judah from her enemies. Before the child reached the age when he could discern good from evil, the Lord would eliminate the Aramean-Israelite threat. At that time people would be able to point to the child Immanuel as a reminder that the

Lord was sovereign over the nation's destiny and had announced in advance the demise of the enemy...The immediate fulfillment of the Immanuel prophecy is recorded in chapter 8. Isaiah made careful preparations for the birth of a sign-child, and the 'prophetess' gave birth to a child named Maher-Shalal-Hash-Baz (meaning 'quick to the plunder, swift to the spoil'). Like Immanuel, this child's growth pattern, when viewed in conjunction with developments on the international scene, would be a reminder of God's providential control over his people's destiny" (Robert Chisholm, "A Theology of Isaiah," in A Biblical Theology of the Old Testament [Chicago: Moody Press, 1991], 315).

3. How to translate the term "virgin" (אלמה) in Isaiah 7:14 has been the subject of considerable discussion. Though the term at times refers to a virgin, it does not inherently carry that sense. "The word is simply the feminine form of the corresponding masculine noun... 'young man.' The Aramaic and Ugaritic cognate terms are both used of women who are not virgins. The word seems to pertain to age, not sexual experience, and would normally be translated 'young woman'" (New English Translation [Biblical Studies Press, 2001], 1238, footnote 13tn). The other issue at point here is whether the phrase "a virgin shall conceive" means that the young woman will be a virgin in the technical sense while she is pregnant or is this a simple future tense verb indicating that the young woman who at that time was a virgin would in the future become pregnant. Albert Barnes is correct when he writes: "It does not, however, imply that the person spoken of should be a virgin 'when the child' should be born; or that she should ever after be a virgin. It means simply that one who was 'then' a virgin, but who was of marriageable age, should conceive, and bear a son. Whether she was 'to be' a virgin 'at the time' when the child was born, or was to remain such afterward, are inquiries which cannot be determined by a philological examination of the word" (Albert Barnes, Notes on the Old Testament: Isaiah [Grand Rapids: Baker, 1950], 255).

4. Matthew quotes the Immanuel prophecy of Isaiah 7:14 and applies it to Mary and Jesus (1:23). This is illustrative of a common phenomenon in prophetic literature in which a New Testament writer will be guided by the Holy Spirit to assign a fuller meaning to an Old Testament text. It is therefore seen that the Isaiah 7:14 prophecy had significance for both a child born in the 8th century BC and the Lord Jesus born in 5-4 BC. Though the gospel narratives make it abundantly clear that Mary was a virgin, the sinlessness of Christ does not hinge on this fact. Rather, it is because of the Spirit's conception and protection that Christ was both sinless by nature and act.

5. Matthew records events in the childhood of Christ in Bethlehem, Egypt, and Nazareth in order to show that He is under the sovereign protection of God and to foreshadow the rejection of the nation of the kingdom—2:1-23.

Note #3: How did the magi become three kings of the orient?

Matthew writes, "Now after Jesus was born in Bethlehem of Judea in the days of Herod the king, behold, wise men from the East came to Jerusalem" (2:1 NKJV). The word translated "wise men" in the ESV, KJV, NKJV, NLT, NRSV and "magi" in the NASB and NIV is the Greek word μάγος. The term refers to one who was an "expert in astrology, interpretation of dreams and various other secret arts" (Bauer, Arndt, Gingrich, Danker, A Greek-English Lexicon of the New Testament and other Early Christian Literature [Chicago: University of Chicago Press, 1979), 484). Or as stated by Turner, "the magi were not kings but...priestly professionals who studied the stars and discerned the signs of the times" (David Turner, Matthew [Grand Rapids: Baker Academic, 2008], 79).

In his stimulating study on the Magi, Yamauchi traces various legends concerning them back to the Apocryphal Gospels and early Christian art where "the number of Magi varied from two to four but was eventually stabilized at three. The three Magi, dressed in Persian garb, were usually depicted bearing gifts to the infant Jesus, resting on the lap of his mother, as in the epitaph of Severa" (Edwin Yamauchi, "The Episode of the Magi," in Chronos, Kairos, Christos: Nativity and Chronological Studies Presented to Jack Finegan [Eisenbrauns, 1989], 16). Yamauchi goes on to suggest that the magi originally were from one of the tribes of the Medes and functioned as priests, diviners, astrologers, and later practiced magic and sorcery (23-27).

Later in this text Matthew indicates that the magi had seen the star in the "east" (2:9). Brown has outlined the three major suggestions as to what Matthew meant by "the east" (Raymond Brown, The Birth of the Messiah: A Commentary on the Infancy Narratives in Matthew and Luke [Garden City, NY: Image Books, 1979], 168-170) to include Parthia/Persia (favored by the history of the term magi), Babylon (favored by astrological implications), or Arabia (favored by the gifts brought). After a thorough discussion the third view might be the strongest. "Evidence in favor of an Arabian origin of the Magi includes the testimony of church fathers, the designation of the land of the Magi as east of the Jordan River, and the friendly relationships between the Jews and their Arabian kin that made the messianic hope common among them. In addition, the gifts offered by the Magi pledging loyalty to Christ were well-known products of ancient Arabia, which Messiah was predicted at the dawn of His kingdom (Isa. 60:5-6)" (Tony Maalouf, "Were the Magi from Persia or Arabia?" Bibliotheca Sacra 156:624 [Oct 1999], 441).

C. Matthew presents the preparation of the Christ including His forerunner, baptism, and temptation in order to show the readers that Christ was properly prepared to be introduced to the nation as their King—3:1-4:11

1. Matthew is interested in showing that Christ, as the King of the Jews, should properly be introduced to the nation as their King and therefore presents the ministry of John the Baptist (himself a fulfillment of Isa. 40:3) in order to attest His Kingship —3:1-4

Note #4: "Repent for the kingdom of heaven is at hand"

The term "repent" has the idea of a turnaround of mind which leads to action. Its background is in the Old Testament where the people had strayed from the covenant and were urged by the prophets to return to God and be blessed (Deut. 22, 30; Mal. 5:7-12). This was the condition for blessing (2 Chron. 7:14).

However, caution must be exercised when interpreting "repentance texts." The interpreter must take into account the various Hebrew and Greek words translated by the English word "repent;" realize that there is not a monolithic understanding of what repentance entails; and take into account whether the audience told to repent is an unbeliever or believer. For example, when Israel is called on to repent under the covenant system, they are being called upon to adjust their lives to the Mosaic Law so as to experience the temporal blessings promised in the covenants. However, when individuals are called upon to repent in the salvation context, they are being asked to change their mind about spiritual realities which leads to the action of placing faith in Christ.

There are at least eight views of the identity of the kingdom. McClain lists the following (Alva McClain, The Greatness of the Kingdom [Winona Lake, IN: BMH Books, 1983], 7-15).

The National Kingdom - *This associates the kingdom as Israel's earthly kingdom*

The Millennial Kingdom - *The kingdom to be established by Christ at the Second Coming. McClain correctly observes that this was the prevailing view in the Church until the time of Augustine*

The Celestial Kingdom - *The reign of God in heaven*

The Ecclesiastical Kingdom - *The kingdom identified with the Church*

The Spiritual Kingdom - *God ruling over the hearts of men*

The Moral Kingdom - *The reign of the moral law over the lives of men*

The Liberal Social Kingdom - *Social organization to improve the world*

The Modern Eschatological Kingdom - *Either Christ's deluded desire for the kingdom or a kingdom which exists outside of time*

The best option for understanding the kingdom is view #1: the literal one presented in the Old Testament for at least the following reasons: there was no formal definition given by Christ; the spiritual rule of God had always existed; Jewish expectation; and the fact that it was drawing near showed that it was not on the scene. The term "kingdom" is used fifty-one times in Matthew, and each time it occurs it refers to the same thing: the earthly reign of the Messiah which fulfills the covenants God made with Israel in the Old Testament. For an excellent study of the term in Matthew see Stanley Toussaint, "The Kingdom and Matthew's Gospel," in Essays in Honor of J. Dwight Pentecost (Chicago: Moody Press, 1986), 19-34.

The phrase "to be at hand" suggested contingency based on repentance—a concept clearly taught in God's arrangement with Israel. Six key passages in this regard include Deuteronomy 28-30 where Moses indicates that only repentance will bring covenant fulfillment; Leviticus 26:40; Jeremiah 3:11-18; Hosea 5:15; Zechariah 12-14; and Matthew 23:39 where Jesus tells the nation that they would not see him again <u>*until*</u> *they said "blessed is he who comes in the name of the Lord."*

2. Matthew records the baptism of Christ by John to show that Christ fulfilled all righteousness and was authenticated in His Messiahship by the Father—3:1-17.

3. Matthew records the temptation of Christ by Satan in order to show that Christ was morally worthy to reign —4:1-11 (note: the word τότε which Matthew uses around ninety times—"then"—ties the temptation into the baptism. The baptism provided the divine approval of His sonship. Satan now tests this declaration that was made at the baptism. The word πειράζω means to test, or try, or prove. Christ was not tempted to see if He could sin, rather He was tempted to demonstrate that He could not sin. This is supported by the nature of the will in that choices are made consistent with one's nature. Thus Christ was impeccable, not peccable.)

Note #5: Christ's temptation as an attack on the Trinity

Scripture presents the Trinity from ontological and economic perspectives. Ontologically, each member of the Trinity is identical in essence or "godness." Economically, however, there is a functional difference as certain members of the godhead agree to submit to the other in the outworking of matters pertaining to salvation (one of the mistakes of Arius [see "John," note #5] was the failure to make this distinction. Hence, when he saw economic statements about Christ, he interpreted those ontologically). It is my suggestion that each Satanic temptation of Christ was ultimately an attack on the economic Trinity. The temptation to turn stones to bread would have disrupted the Trinity since at that time it was the Father's will that the Son be hungry. The loyalty of the Son in the first temptation is then twisted in the second temptation to jump from the pinnacle of the temple (possibly the 450 feet distance from the southeast corner of the temple to the ground below). The sense of the temptation could be something like, "you have shown your loyalty to the Father by remaining hungry, let's see if he is loyal to you by catching you when you jump." The third temptation was to gain the inheritance of the world (Daniel 7:14) through a means not ordained by the Father. Thus the heart of the temptations was to drive a wedge through the economic Trinity.

II. MATTHEW PRESENTS THE INTRODUCTORY MINISTRY OF CHRIST IN ORDER TO GIVE A BRIEF EXAMPLE OF HIS WORK AS KING AND THE ETHICS OF THE KING IN ORDER TO SHOW THE KIND OF BEHAVIOR HE EXPECTED OF ALL THOSE WHO BECAME HIS SUBJECTS—4:12-7:29

A. Matthew records the beginning ministry of Christ in order to provide the nation with a brief résumé of His work and the kind of kingdom He would provide for them—4:12-25

1. Jesus withdraws into Capernaum because of the opposition brought against John the Baptist and in fulfillment of Isaiah 9:1-2—4:12-16

2. Jesus' message is repent for the kingdom of heaven is at hand—4:17

3. Jesus calls four disciples in order to demonstrate His authority—4:18-22

4. Jesus conducts his ministry which included teaching in the synagogues, preaching the gospel of the kingdom, and healing in order to give a preview of the kingdom—4:23-25

B. Matthew records Jesus' Sermon on the Mount in which He develops the theme of true righteousness in order to show the kind of behavior which was characteristic of His kingdom and expected of His subjects—5:1-7:29

Note #6: The Sermon on the Mount

The Sermon on the Mount is considered to be Jesus' greatest recorded discourse and consequently the subject of much discussion. One area of discussion has to do with the interpretation of the Sermon. There is a general misconception among non-dispensational scholars that there is but one dispensational approach, namely, the Kingdom approach to the Sermon on the Mount. Moreover, this lone option is often misrepresented as well. Since dispensationalists believe the following:

1. Jesus offered the Davidic Kingdom to Israel at his first coming
2. Jesus gave the Sermon on the Mount during the time of this offer

And

3. Israel rejected the kingdom offer by rejecting the Messiah

    Then

4. The Sermon on the Mount has no application today

Observe the three following citations:

> *At the other extreme [the first extreme being Tolstoi and the Christian Marxist] is the earlier American Dispensationalism which relegated the Sermon to the millennial Kingdom, leaving a historical dichotomy between the present and the future..."*[556]

> *Some teach a dispensational view of the Sermon on the Mount, saying that it has nothing whatsoever to do with modern Christians...It says, in effect, that the Sermon on the Mount has nothing to do with us...According to this view I need not read the Sermon on the Mount; I need not be concerned about its precepts; I need not feel condemned because I am not doing certain things; it has no relevance for me...We must likewise ignore the gracious promises in this sermon. We must not say that we must let our light shine before men.*[557]

> *As a result of this theological structure (dispensationalism), the Sermon on the Mount has no immediate relevance or application to the Christian...This theological construction is so all-embracing that it is extremely difficult for a member of this school of thought to accept a different interpretation of any particular passage without endangering the entire system...In dispensationalism, the interpretation of Matthew's Gospel is one of the crucial support pillars of the theological structure. Remove it (or any one of a dozen other pillars), and the structure collapses.*[558]

There are some who have held to the position stated above; however, these can best be classified as ultra-dispensationalists and are the rare exception.[559] *The above statements reveal two points of misunderstanding. First, the Kingdom View is misrepresented. It has been observed by dispensationalists Ryrie and Campbell (both of whom hold the Kingdom View and represent an earlier form of Dispensationalism) that while they relate the Sermon primarily to the millennial age, it still has application to the present.*[560] *The same is true for other earlier dispensationalists including Scofield and Chafer.*[561] *Second, Dispensationalism is misrepresented. It is assumed either that all dispensationalists hold or must hold to the Kingdom approach which is why it is called*

---

556 Robert Guelich, *The Sermon on the Mount: A Foundation for Understanding* (Waco: Word Books, 1982), 18.

557 D. M. Lloyd-Jones, *Studies in the Sermon on the Mount* (Grand Rapids: Baker, 1986), 1:14-15.

558 D. A. Carson, *The Sermon on the Mount: An Evangelical Exposition* (Grand Rapids: Baker, 1984), 155-156.

559 See for example E. W. Bullinger, "Matthew," in *The Companion Bible* (London: Oxford University Press, n.d.), 1:1316.

560 C. C. Ryrie, *Dispensationalism Today* (Chicago: Moody Press, 2007), 114; Donald K. Campbell, "Interpretation and Exposition of the Sermon on the Mount" (ThD diss., Dallas Theological Seminary, 1953), 49.

561 *The Scofield Reference Bible*, 999-1000; *The New Scofield Reference Bible*, 997; Lewis S. Chafer, *Systematic Theology* (Dallas: Dallas Seminary Press, 1947-1948), 5:97.

the "dispensational interpretation." [562] *Yet, this view is not an essential of dispensational theology and is not held by many dispensationalists.* [563] *There is not a uniform dispensational approach to the Sermon any more than there is a uniform amillennial approach to it. See Appendix 1 at the end of Matthew for a further discussion of dispensational options.*

The view adopted by the writer is that the Sermon on the Mount presents the follower of Christ with a timeless, present ethic grounded in an eschatological hope. That the Sermon presents an applicable ethic to the present day is demonstrated in Note 20. That it is grounded in an eschatological hope is demonstrated by the following table (Harvey McArthur, Understanding the Sermon on the Mount [New York: Harper, 1960], 90-91).

The Eschatology of the Sermon on the Mount

Explicit Eschatology	Possible Eschatology	No Eschatology
5:3-12 Beatitudes		
		5:13-16 Salt, Light
5:17-20 The Old Law		
5:21-26 Murder		
5:27-30 Adultery		
		5:31-32 Divorce
		5:33-37 Swearing
		5:38-42 Retaliation
		5:43-48 Love of enemies
	6:1-4 Almsgiving	
	6:5-8 Prayer	
6:9-15 Lord's Prayer		
	6:16-18 Fasting	
	6:19-21 Treasures	
		6:22 The sound eye
		6:24 Two masters
		6:25-32, 34 Anxiety
6:33 Seek the Kingdom		
	7:1-2 Judging	
		7:3-5 Beam and mote

[562] In addition to the quotes from Guelich, Lloyd-Jones, and Carson, see also Carl F. Henry, *Christian Personal Ethics* (Grand Rapids: Eerdmans, 1957), 292; T. A. Hegre, *The Cross and Sanctification* (Minneapolis: Bethany, 1960), 6; C. Norman Kraus, *Dispensationalism in America* (Richmond: John Knox Press, 1958), 13; G. T. Burke, "Sermon on the Mount," in *Evangelical Dictionary of Theology* (Grand Rapids: Baker, 1984), 1006; Robert Govett, *The Sermon on the Mount* (Miami Springs, FL: Conley & Schoettle, 1984), iii; George Ladd, *Crucial Questions about the Kingdom of God* (Grand Rapids: Eerdmans, 1952), 104; *A Theology of the New Testament* (Grand Rapids: Eerdmans, 1983), 123; Harvey McArthur, *Understanding the Sermon on the Mount* (NY: Harper & Row, 1960), 69.

[563] One example is Dwight Pentecost who taught during the "golden age" of normative dispensationalism. Though not taking the Kingdom View, he wrote that "while we recognize that the Sermon on the Mount in its historical setting was Christ's instruction to the generation to which he was offering Himself as Saviour and Sovereign, we realize that it has a present-day application...it becomes a guide as to demands that God's holiness makes upon believers today" (*The Sermon on the Mount: Contemporary Insights for a Christian Lifestyle* [Portland: Multnomah Press, 1980], 16-17).

		7:6 Profaning the holy
		7:7-11 Asking
		7:12 Golden rule
7:13-14 The narrow gate		
7:15-20 False prophets		
7:21-23 Lord...Lord		
7:24-27 The two houses		

1. Matthew presents the setting of the Sermon on a mountain to which Jesus goes after seeing the multitudes and assumes a rabbinic teaching position by sitting down—5:1-2
2. Matthew presents the beatitudes in order to show the character of those who follow the king and that those who display such characteristics will be rewarded during the kingdom—5:3-12
3. Matthew presents the calling and position in the world of a true disciple as salt and light in order to show them what the impact of their character will be—5:13-16
4. Matthew presents Jesus' teaching about the nature of true righteousness in order to challenge true disciples to live in this manner—5:17-7:12
5. Matthew presents three of Jesus' parables having to do with warning and invitation to encourage his disciples to live righteously—7:13-27
6. Matthew presents the response of the people to be amazement because of His authority and content—7:28-29

III. MATTHEW PRESENTS SEVERAL MIRACLES OF JESUS IN ORDER TO DEMONSTRATE HIS SUPERNATURAL POWER AND WHAT CONDITIONS WOULD BE LIKE IN THE KINGDOM SO THAT THE PEOPLE WOULD SEE THAT HE IS THEIR MESSIAH—8:1-11:1

A. Matthew records several incidents of Jesus' miracles and His calls to discipleship in order to show that He was the Messiah and had the authority to have disciples based on his works— 8:1-9:34

Note #7: Why did Jesus perform miracles?

There are several legitimate answers to this question, but one stands out in relation to the fact that Jesus comes as Israel's king offering the kingdom. In the Old Testament numerous prophecies are made depicting the rejuvenation of nature in the kingdom. One of the purposes of miracles was to give a foretaste of kingdom conditions. This connection is made by the writer of Hebrews as he states that the Jews who witnessed the miraculous had "tasted the powers of the age to come" (6:5; see also 2:4-5 where the miraculous is linked to "the world to come of which we are speaking"). When the Old Testament prophecies regarding millennial conditions are categorized, it is observed that Jesus performed at least one miracle for every category. Showers suggests eight categories to illustrate, which I have organized below (Renald Showers, What on earth is God doing? Satan's Conflict with God *[Neptune, NJ: Loizeaux Brothers, 1974], 55).*

Christ's Miracles and the Kingdom

Category	Old Testament Reference	New Testament Miracle
Natural elements	Isaiah 30:23-36; Ezekiel 47:1-12; Joel 2:21, 26; 3:18; Zechariah 14:8	Walking on water; calming two storms
Growth and fruit of trees	Isaiah 41:19-20; Ezekiel 36:8, 29-30; 47:6-7, 12; Joel 2:21-22	Cursing of the fig tree so that it withered showing control over its growth
Productivity of animals including fish	Ezekiel 36:11; 47:8-10	Two miraculous catches of fish
Abundant food supply	Psalm 72:16; Isaiah 30:23-24; Ezekiel 34:25-30; 36:29-30; Joel 2:21-26; Zechariah 8:11-12	Feeding of the five thousand from five loaves and two fish; feeding of the four thousand
Abundance of wine	Isaiah 25:6; Joel 2:21-26; Amos 9:13	Water into wine at Cana
Nature of animals	Isaiah 11:6-9; 65:25; Hosea 2:18	Triumphal entry riding on a colt never broken; a fish is caused to come to Peter with a coin in its mouth
Healing of disease and deformity	Isaiah 29:18; 33:24; 35:5-6	Healing of the lame, deaf, a withered hand, an issue of blood, dropsy, replacement of severed ear
Longevity of life	Isaiah 65:20-22	Raising of Lazarus, Jairus' daughter, and widow's son from the dead showing a lengthening of their life spans

Not surprisingly, when Jesus was asked to state plainly if he was the Messiah, he replied, "I told you, and you believed not; the works I do in my Father's name, they bear witness of me" (John 10:24-25).

1. Matthew records three miracles of healing in order to show that Jesus was the Messiah and to show the characteristics of the kingdom He was offering—8:1-17

Note #8: Is there physical healing in the atonement?

According to Matthew 8:16 Christ healed a variety of physical illnesses. Matthew then says in 8:17 that this fulfilled the prophecy of Isaiah 53:4-5. Many argue on the basis of this text and 1 Peter 2:24 that the believer has the right to physical healing in the present just as he has a right to spiritual healing. Several comments are in order:

1. The terms "griefs" and "sorrows" in Isaiah 53 contextually refer to spiritual issues.

2. There are nine uses (three different Hebrew words) of terms related to sin in Isaiah 53 which shows the intent of the passage is to deal with sin not sickness.
3. Isaiah uses the term "heal" (רפא) six times in his book. All of the uses outside of 53:5 refer to spiritual healing. Given the context of the book as a whole and the context of this chapter, the same use is most probable in this instance.
4. When Matthew quotes Isaiah 53:4, instead of using the Greek term φέρω ("to bear") as found in the LXX version of Isaiah, he uses λαμβάνω ("took") and βαστάζω ("carry"). Mayhue explains the reason for the change: "Matthew is saying that Christ 'took away'...their sicknesses. Christ did not 'bear'...in a substitutionary sense the sickness of Peter's mother-in-law...Later, he would 'bear' sin on Calvary, but at this point in Matthew 8 he had only 'taken away' their sicknesses (Richard Mayhue, "For What Did Christ Atone in Isa 53:4-5?" Masters Seminary Journal 6:2 [Fall 95], 133). Thus, while Isaiah 53 speaks of the atonement in its relation to spiritual redemption, Matthew applies the passage to physical illness as an illustration of the spiritual truth.
5. The words of J. I. Packer summarize the theological issue well: "We must carefully observe that perfect physical health is promised, not for this life, but for heaven, as part of the resurrection glory that awaits us in the day when Christ 'will change our lowly body to be like His glorious body, by the power which enables Him even to subject all things to Himself.' Full bodily wellbeing is set forth as a future blessing of salvation rather than a present one. What God has promised, and when He will give it, are separate questions" (J. I. Packer, "Poor Health May be the Best Remedy," Christianity Today 21 [1982], 15).

2. Matthew records Jesus' call to discipleship in order to show His authority to have disciples and the radical nature of discipleship—8:18-22

Note #9: The "Son of Man" title

Jesus used this designation of himself more than any other title. The title goes back to Genesis 1 where man was told to subdue the earth and dominate it. This was forfeited in its completion due to sin. Christ is seen to do what man failed to do (Psalm 8 and Hebrews 2) which will be culminated in the Millennium.

The title also has roots in Daniel 7:13 where the Son of Man is given possession of the Kingdom by the Ancient of Days. Thus it has strong Messianic connotations.

3. Matthew records a second group of miracles in order to demonstrate the power of Christ—8:23-9:8

4. Matthew records the new type of behavior which should characterize his disciples 9:9-17 (Apparently, Jesus and his disciples did not fast [9:14]. This is due to the fact that the bridegroom was present).

5. Matthew records three miracles of restoration in order to show that Jesus was the Messiah who would restore all things in the kingdom despite the opposition He was facing—9:18-34

B. Matthew records the concern of Christ over the nation, and in light of His miracles, His right to commission His disciples to go to the nation in order to show that He was truly offering the kingdom to them—9:35-11:1

1. Matthew notes the compassion of Jesus on the nation which leads Him to heal many of them and exhort His disciples of the greatness of the work to be done—9:35-38

2. Matthew records the instructions to the twelve in sending them out to offer the kingdom in order to show His offering of the kingdom and concern for the nation—10:1-11:1

Note #10: The mission discourse

Beginning in chapter 10 Matthew records the second major discourse in his gospel in which Jesus sends out the Twelve to preach the Gospel of the Kingdom. One of the difficulties in this section revolves around Jesus' words in 10:23 "When they persecute you in this city, flee to another. For assuredly, I say to you, you will not have gone through the cities of Israel before the Son of Man comes." The question is: in what sense could Jesus be said to have returned before the disciples finished their mission? The major suggestions as to what this return is include, a simple reference to Jesus meeting up with the disciples again, the resurrection, the destruction of Jerusalem, or the coming of the Spirit at Pentecost.

The key to understand this statement is to take into account the "theocratic chronology" at this point in time (the reader is referred to Chapter VIII, Section 1: The Theocracy for an explanation of the full theocratic program). Jesus' commission of the apostles occurs at a time when the theocratic kingdom is being offered to Israel and is contingent on their response (see Note #3 in this section). Moreover, God's revelation up until this point in time depicted a succession of four major Messianic events.

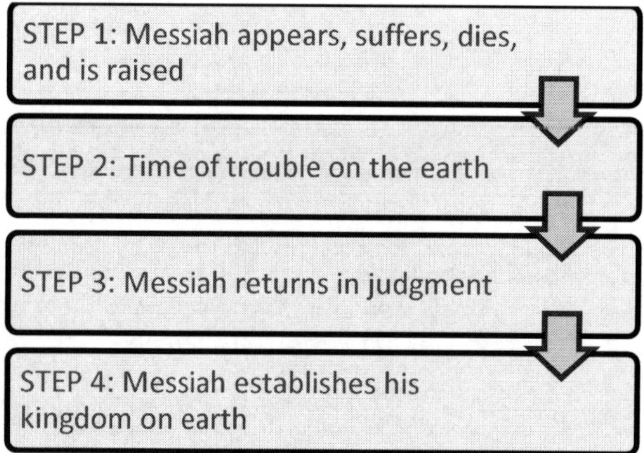

Had Israel repented and accepted the Kingdom message, this program would have played out with Christ dying at the hands of the Romans. Since the message was not accepted there is a gap of time between steps 1 and 2. This is why Jesus told the nation in Matthew 23:39 that they would not see him again <u>*until*</u> *they say "blessed is he who comes in the name of the Lord." It is noteworthy that in the Olivet Discourse the same series of steps is laid out with one difference: the Messiah has been officially rejected by the nation at that point; however, the same program will be enacted, just at a later time.*

A key term to understand in this regard is "apotelesmatic." Though lengthy, the following citation expands on this critical concept:

Apotelesmatic interpretation recognizes that some Old Testament texts present the messianic program as a single event, but they actually intend a near and far historical fulfillment, separated by an indeterminate period of time. Dispensational writers have referred to this as an "intercalation" or a "gap." However, prophetic postponement better expresses this concept. Prophetic, because we understand a purposeful, preordained act in the divine program, and postponement, because it retains the original idea of an interruption in fulfillment, while supplementing it with the notion that such a delay is only temporary. Old Testament texts hinted at this postponement when referring to Israel's hardening (Isaiah 6:9-13; Zechariah 7:11-12) and judicial exile (Deuteronomy 4:27-30; 28:36-37, 49-50, 64-68), but the postponement was not fully revealed until the New Testament (John 12:37-40; Acts 28:25-28; Romans 11:25-26). Accordingly, this postponement in the fulfillment of Israelite history is not so much an interruption of redemption as an extension of a predicted hardening (Romans 11:7-10). The exile, which was a punishment for national disobedience, has therefore been prolonged during the church age until the appointed time for Israel's national restoration (Acts 1:7; 3:21; Romans 11:25-27). So that none can question the infallibility of the divine promise to Israel (Romans 9:6; 11:29), individual Israelite redemption is presently being fulfilled within the church (Romans 11:1-5). This salvation of the remnant during the present age (Romans 9:8; 11:24, 27) testifies to the ultimate salvation of all Israel in the age to come (Romans 11:26). This previously unrevealed aspect of the messianic plan (Romans 16:25-26; Ephesians 3:3-6) declares that Christ will redeem Israel (Romans 11:23) as surely as He is saving individual Jews and Gentiles now (Romans 11:12, 15, 23, 31)...An objection to this concept of postponement has been that in such cases the units of time or space must be understood to run continuously and successively. Prophetic postponement does not affect the fulfillment of measured events. The same chronological events are fulfilled in the same temporal order as if no interruption occurred. From the human perspective the clock has stopped, and the fulfillment may seem to have failed. From the divine viewpoint, however, nothing has changed, and all is proceeding according to schedule (because "the times of the Gentile" was always an intended part of the fulfillment...Jesus also recognized the principle of prophetic postponement in His use of Isaiah 61:1-2 (Luke 4:16-21). He differentiates the time of fulfillment for two messianic events that follow one another immediately in the text. In Luke 4, Jesus went against Jewish tradition in public reading, abruptly ending His selected passage in mid-sentence. The rest of the sentence reads, "...and the day of vengeance of our God; to comfort all who mourn." Jesus knew that the day of Gentile judgment was to be postponed, and so He read only that portion of the verse that pertained to the present fulfillment" (Randall Price, "Prophetic Postponement," in The Popular Encyclopedia of Bible Prophecy *[Eugene, OR: Harvest House, 2004], 300, 301, 302).*

IV. MATTHEW RECORDS THE EVIDENCE OF THE REJECTION OF JESUS AND JESUS' RESPONSE TO THAT REJECTION BY RECORDING HIS KINGDOM PARABLES IN ORDER TO SHOW THOUGH THE KINGDOM WILL NOT COME

IMMEDIATELY BECAUSE OF REJECTION BY THE NATION IT HAS NOT BEEN DONE AWAY FOR GOOD—11:2-13:53

A. Matthew presents the opposition to the ministry of John the Baptist and Himself in order to illustrate the hostility of the nation and the reason that the Kingdom was not established—11:2-30

1. Matthew records the opposition to John the Baptist who was the forerunner of Christ in order to show the opposition to Him—11:2-19

Note #11: The relation of John the Baptist to Malachi's prophecy

The writer feels that the Malachi prophecies (3:1 and 4:6) were not calling for a reincarnated Elijah but one coming in the "spirit and power" of Elijah (Luke 1:17). It seems that John would have fulfilled the prophecies if the nation had repented. When John denied that he was Elijah (John 1:21), he was not denying that he could fulfill the prophecy, but that he was not Elijah reincarnated. Further, the individual in the tribulation will not be Elijah or John the Baptist but one in the spirit and power of Elijah (Rev. 11:3-6).

2. Matthew records the indifference of the people to the message of Jesus in order to further illustrate the rejection—11:20-24

3. Matthew records an invitation by Christ to the nation who are under the burden of the religiosity of the Pharisees in order to further point out the rejection motif since there is a call to separate from the rebellious segment—11:25-30

B. Matthew presents the tension and opposition that revolved around Jesus' ministry in order to show its increase and to show finally that the nation, through its leaders, had rejected Jesus as their Messiah—12:1-50

1. Matthew records the contention concerning the Sabbath to demonstrate the opposition and rejection of Christ by the nation—12:1-21

2. Matthew records the contention concerning the source of Jesus' power—12:22-37

3. Matthew records the contention regarding the signs presented by Christ—12:38-45

4. Matthew records the contention about one's relationship to Christ in which Jesus notes that a true relationship to Him is based on the new birth and not on physical descent in order to show His rejection by the nation—12:46-50

Note #12: The unpardonable sin

Matthew 12:22-32 contains the account of the ominous "unpardonable," "unforgivable" sin. After Jesus performed a miracle of healing, the people asked in amazement "is not this the Son of David?" They were asking if he was the Messiah who would sit on David's throne and rule over Israel in the kingdom. The reason this question would be asked is because Jesus had performed a miracle which resonated with the conditions to be experienced when the Kingdom was instituted. The religious leaders could not deny a miracle had occurred, and so they came up with an explanation which said that the source of Jesus' power was Beelzeboul, the head of the demonic household, rather than the Holy Spirit. This blasphemous statement was a rejection of the final witness which testified to the person of Christ. Because all witnesses pointing to the Messiahship of Jesus had been refused, the nation was now in an unpardonable state. This is illustrated later in the chapter by the parable of the swept house and Jesus' statement at the end of verse 45 "even so shall it be also unto this wicked generation." It should be carefully noted that this was a national sin, not a personal sin. That is, individuals could still be saved, but the nation as a nation was now put under judgment. This judgment would be experienced in AD 70. In this light, the sin envisioned in this chapter cannot be committed today. Notice the connection between the events in this chapter and the following chapter as stated in point "C" below.

C. Matthew presents a series of parables which reveal new truths concerning the Kingdom as to its preparation and establishment in light of the preceding rejection of the Kingdom in order to demonstrate to the readers that the Kingdom had not been done away and would still be inaugurated in the future—13:1-52

Note #13: The Kingdom parables

There is a difference of opinion among dispensationalists as to whether these parables are introducing a "mystery form" of the kingdom or whether they are only presenting new truths about the kingdom. This is a fine, but important point of distinction. If the former is correct, this can lead to a redefining of the kingdom into a form it was never envisioned as in the Old Testament. When this view is adopted by normative dispensationalists, the logic is similar to progressive dispensationalists and the "already not yet" understanding of the kingdom in historic/covenant premillennialism. See Note 21 for two statements taking this view to task.

1. Jesus presents the parables of the soils as an introductory parable to explain the responses which had been given to the Kingdom message—13:1-23
2. Jesus presents the parable of the wheat and the weeds to show that not until the separation at the end of the age would one be able to distinguish the good from the bad—13:24-30
3. Jesus presents the parable of the mustard seed to show the rapid growth of the Kingdom (cf. Dan. 4)—13:31-32
4. Jesus presents the parable of the leaven in order to show the pervasive influence of the Kingdom—13:33
5. Matthew notes that Jesus' parables were in fulfillment of Psalm 78:2—13:34-35
6. Jesus presents the explanation of the first parable to the disciples—13:36-43
7. Jesus presents the parable of the hidden treasure in which the treasure is the kingdom program of Israel; the hidden period of the kingdom is before Christ came; its discovery is at His coming when He offered the Kingdom; its hiding is the removal of the Kingdom offer; the man is Christ who then condescends to the cross in order to show the cost to Christ of the Kingdom program—13:44
8. Jesus presents the parable of the pearl of great price to show the value of the kingdom—13:45-46
9. Jesus presents the parable of the dragnet to show the judgment that would occur before the establishment of the Kingdom—13:47-50
10. Jesus concludes this section with a non-Kingdom parable directed to the disciples to show their responsibility to dispense this Kingdom truth—13:51-53

Summary of the Kingdom Parables	
Sower/Soils	-Different responses to the Kingdom message -Shows the message was poorly received because of the state of men's hearts
Weeds	-Explains the conflict of the sons and enemies of the kingdom -Separation will occur at Messiah's second coming to establish the kingdom
Mustard seed	-Though the kingdom has a small beginning (the 11), it will grow to worldwide proportions
Leaven	-The kingdom program has an inherent dynamic for growth
Hidden treasure	-The kingdom program was hidden in that the theocracy had not been operative since the Babylonian exile -Jews in Jesus' day who were not looking for the kingdom were willing to make sacrifice for it when they became aware of its offer by the king
Pearl	-Jews in Jesus' day who were looking for the kingdom were willing to make any sacrifice for it
Dragnet	-Unbelievers will not be allowed entrance into the kingdom
Homeowner	-The disciples are to teach old truth about the kingdom (that which had been revealed) and new truth about the kingdom (that which Christ was revealing to them)

V. MATTHEW RECORDS THE WITHDRAWAL OF CHRIST FROM THE NATION IN ORDER TO SHOW HIS REACTION TO THEIR REJECTION AND THE INSTRUCTION OF THE DISCIPLES IN ORDER TO PREPARE THEM FOR THE COMING PASSION—13:54-19:2

A. Matthew presents the continued opposition to Christ and His reaction to that opposition to be one of withdrawal in order to show the consequences of their actions—13:54-16:12

1. Matthew notes the scorn shown to Jesus in His hometown of Nazareth in order to set the stage for His withdrawal—13:54-58

2. Matthew notes the opposition of Herod and the reaction of Christ of withdrawal—14:1-36

3. Matthew notes the opposition of the Scribes and Pharisees to Christ and His consequent withdrawal—15:1-39

4. Matthew presents opposition from the Pharisees and Sadducees in which they seek for a sign and are rebuked by Christ for their blindness and because of this He abandons them—16:1-16:12

B. Matthew records the instruction of the disciples by Christ in order to prepare them for His passion and the Kingdom program—16:13-19:2

1. Jesus reveals to His disciples truth about His person in order to stress to them His Messiahship and deity—16:13-17

2. Jesus reveals to His disciples truth about the program and work that would now be instituted in light of the Jewish rejection—16:18-17:13

Note #14: Is the Church built on Peter? Yes!

The debate is well known as to what Jesus meant when he said to Peter, "And I tell you, you are Peter and upon this rock I will build my church" (16:18). What follows are some summary observations about this text.

1) In 16:18, the first "you" is a dative, singular noun; while the second "you" is a nominative singular noun. The "you" in 16:15 is a nominative plural noun. Thus, while all of the disciples are asked the question by Jesus, now Peter is being addressed alone.

2) The proper name "Peter" (Πέτρος, *petros*) *means "stone" (Bauer, Arndt, Gingrich, Danker,* A Greek-English Lexicon of the New Testament and Other Early Christian Literature, *654) and occurs 156 times in the New Testament. With the exception of John 1:42, it is only used for the Apostle.*

3) The noun "rock" (πέτρα , *petra) can be used of bedrock, rock formations, a piece of rock, rocky soil, etc. The term can also be used figuratively to speak of a hardened mind, or a strong character (Bauer, Arndt, Gingrich, Danker, 654).*

4) Matthew 16:18 is the only place in the New Testament where πέτρος and πέτρα are used in the same verse.

5) *The "rock" upon which the church is to be built has been variously interpreted as God, Jesus' teachings, Jesus, Peter's confession, and Peter.*

6) It is my opinion that the reason the "Peter" interpretation has been rejected by Protestants is because this is the view taken by most Roman Catholic interpreters. However, one's exegesis must not be guided by reaction , but the meaning of the text. Moreover, as will be pointed out below, to take the "Peter" view does not necessitate the implications drawn from that by Rome.

7) Regarding the gender difference between "Peter" and "rock," observe the following citation: The most likely explanation for the change from "Peter" (Πέτρος) to πέτρα is that petra was the normal word for "rock." Because the feminine ending of this noun made it unsuitable as a man's name, however, Simon was not called petras but Petros...There is no good reason to think that Jesus switched from petros to petra to show that he was not speaking of the man Peter but of his confession as the foundation of the church. The words "on this rock" indeed refer to Peter. Because of the revelation that he had received and the confession that it motivated in him, Peter was appointed by Jesus to lay the foundation of the future church (H. N. Ridderbos, Matthew *[Grand Rapids: Eerdmans, 1987], 303). Jesus probably uses the term "rock" for the effect of the wordplay with Peter's name. This fact would argue that he is referring to Peter since*

Jesus could have used the more common word for stone, λίθος (the noun is used 79 times in the New Testament as opposed to the term petra which is used 15 times). If Jesus had meant that the church was to be built on Peter's confession, for example, he certainly could have said so.

8) Any linguistic distinction between petros and petra were probably not observed during this time (D. A. Carson, "Matthew," in The Expositor's Bible *Commentary [Grand Rapids: Zondervan, 1984], 8:368).*

9) The "and" which occurs between "Peter" and "upon" in verse 18 shows Peter to be in view. Otherwise, a contrastive particle would have been used.

10) The view argued for in this note does not support the doctrine of succession or the doctrine of the papacy as taught by Rome. In fact, Jesus' statement to Peter is not even an exclusive one. Paul will later add in Ephesians 2:20 that the church is built on the foundation of all of the apostles. Thus, the Church *__is__* *built on Peter...and John...and Paul, etc. with Christ being the chief cornerstone. If there is any perpetuity to be found, it is in the apostolic teaching, not the apostolic office.*

3. Jesus reveals to His disciples some of His principles in order to guide them while He is absent—17:14-18:35

Note #15: The discipleship discourse

When studying the discourses in the gospels, it is important to interpret each one as a unit of material in order to make sure the various sayings are interpreted correctly as they are connected to the whole. The Matthew 18 discourse is a case in point. The flow of the discourse can be seen through a number of summaries.

__18:1-2__. The disciples are arguing as to who will be greatest in the kingdom. Notice that they are still viewing the kingdom as something that is a future entity, not something that was inaugurated by Christ at his coming or merely spiritual in nature. This discussion is to be seen in light of the Transfiguration of chapter 17, which validates our suggested purpose for that event as a mini foreshadowing of the kingdom (see Chapter VIII, Section 25: The Eschatological Significance of the Feast of Booths).

__18:3-4__. Jesus responds to the disciples' dispute by setting a child in their midst and telling them they must be converted. The word translated "converted" (στρέφω) has led some to believe that salvation is in view. However, the term simply means "to turn," or "to change," and is thus rendered in the ESV and NIV. Contextually, the disciples are to change their attitude of pride and contention to that of childlike humility. Just as they had expressed that attitude in the past, so it was to be continued.

__18:5-9__. The "little ones" in view in this section is not a reference to children but to the humble disciple. If an unbeliever in the world causes the disciple to stumble thus impeding his mission, he will be judged by God. The sense of "receiving" in 18:5 should be interpreted in light of the disciples' mission as seen in chapter 10.

__18:10-14__. Whereas the previous section addressed the problem of the world impeding the progress of the disciple, now Jesus turns his attention to disciples impeding other disciples. In this context, that would involve the competitive problem of pride. Jesus illustrates the posture of humility through the parable of a lost sheep. The point of the parable is not the lost sheep, but the joy when the sheep is found. If the joy is so great when the sheep is found, it must be terribly serious to be the one who caused the sheep to go astray in the first place. The parable is summarized in verse 14 where it is stated that *it is not the will of God that any of the humble disciples "perish" or be "lost." Again, the discourse is not talking about salvation, and so the reference here is to the wasted life of a disciple who is caused to go astray.*

18:15-20. The question now is: what is their responsibility toward a fellow disciple who causes one to go astray. These verses lay out the process to be followed in this instance. For the interpretation of 19-20 see note #16 below.

18:21. This prompts Peter to ask the question: "Lord, how often shall my brother sin against me and I forgive him?" Having just heard Jesus talk about the responsibility toward the offender, Peter logically is asking how many times should this process be followed?

18:22-35. Jesus responds with the parable of the unforgiving servant to show that they should be ready to forgive to the same degree they had been forgiven.

Note #16: Matthew 18:19-20: where two or three are gathered together—is this even talking about prayer?

This is undoubtedly one of the most abused texts in the Gospels. If nothing else, it is absurd to think that God is giving a carte blanche *for prayer as long as at least two believers agree on that which is asked. Several textual considerations lead to a different conclusion: 1) the term πρᾶγμα (anything) can refer to a lawsuit or a dispute, or even "a matter" (Walter Bauer, William Arndt, and F. Wilbur Gingrich,* A Greek-English Lexicon of the New Testament and Other Early Christian Literature, *2nd ed., rev. F. Wilbur Gingrich and Frederick W. Danker (Chicago: University of Chicago Press, 1979) 697. The lawsuit or dispute sense would fit nicely in this context and is attested elsewhere in the New Testament in 1 Corinthians 6:1, 2) the preceding context deals with the restoration of an erring brother, 3) the "two" who agree are the two individuals in the dispute—the offender and the one offended, 4) the verb αἰτέω (ask) can refer to the pursuit of a claim (D. A. Carson, "Matthew," in* The Expositor's Bible Commentary, *403), but if not would refer to their request to the one presiding over the case, 5) as these guidelines are followed, they have God's endorsement, and 6) the following context supports this interpretation, for Peter then asks "Lord, how often shall my brother sin against me, and I forgive him?" The sense of the question is: how often shall I go through the process just described? Is there a limit? Therefore, this text is probably not speaking of prayer but reconciliation.*

4. Jesus continues His journey to Jerusalem—19:1-2

VI. MATTHEW RECORDS 1) THE OFFICIAL PRESENTATION AND REJECTION OF CHRIST BY THE NATION IN WHICH HE CONTINUES TO RECORD JESUS' INSTRUCTIONS TO THE DISCIPLES, 2) CHRIST'S OFFICIAL PRESENTATION TO THE NATION, 3) THEIR REJECTION OF HIM AND HIS REJECTION OF THEM, AND 4) HIS PREDICTIONS ABOUT THE NATION'S FUTURE IN LIGHT OF THIS REJECTION—19:3-25:46

A. Matthew presents Jesus' continued instruction to the disciples to prepare them for their ministry after His departure—19:3-20:34

1. Jesus instructs the disciples concerning divorce and remarriage—19:3-12

2. Jesus instructs the disciples concerning childlikeness in order to show them that the character of those who enter the kingdom is childlike—19:13-15

3. Jesus instructs the disciples concerning wealth using the incident of the rich young ruler. He asks Christ what he must do to gain eternal life to which Jesus responds he should sell his possessions. Because of his refusal to do this, Jesus notes that salvation is the work of God—19:16-26

4. Jesus instructs the disciples concerning rewards in the kingdom— 19:27-20:16

5. Jesus instructs the disciples concerning His passion in which He, for the first time, notes the means of His death—20:17-19

6. Jesus instructs the disciples concerning positions in the Kingdom on the occasion of the request of James and John in which it is seen that positions are reserved for those for whom they are prepared, but before this came they would have to face suffering . The greatest in the Kingdom was linked with humility and service—20:20-28

7. Jesus heals two blind men in order to show that though He has been rejected, he continues to offer His person to those who want to enter the Kingdom—20:29-34

B. Matthew presents the official presentation of Christ including His triumphal entry and cleansing of the temple in order to set in concrete the rejection of the nation and the response of Christ to this—21:1-17

1. Matthew notes the preparations made by Christ for the entry into Jerusalem and the fulfillment of prophecy—21:1-7

2. Matthew notes the official presentation of Christ by His entrance into Jerusalem—21:8-11

3. Matthew notes the entrance by Christ into the temple—21:12-17

C. Matthew records the rejection of Christ by the nation which consists of His cursing of the fig tree and proved by the conflict He has with the religious leaders—21:18-22:46

1. Jesus curses the fig tree which did not have fruit in order to picture the judgment on the nation for not producing the fruit they should have been and in order to give the disciples a lesson on faith—21:18-22

2. Matthew presents the conflict between Christ and the Chief Priests and Elders involving the question of authority and three parables in order to show the conflict and rejection of Christ—21:23-22:14

3. Matthew presents the conflict between Jesus, the Pharisees, and Herodians regarding tribute in order to show the bitter opposition against Jesus since the Pharisees and Herodians were enemies and yet here were acting in concert, and to instruct the disciples that in His absence they were to abide by earthly law—22:15-22

4. Matthew presents the conflict with the Sadducees regarding the resurrection in order to show more opposition—22:23-33

5. Matthew presents the conflict with the Pharisees regarding the greatest commandment and Christ's person—22:34-46

D. Matthew records the rebuke of Christ to the religious leaders and His lament over Jerusalem to show that Christ had rejected the nation— 23:1-39

1. Christ warns the multitudes of the Pharisees—23:1-12
2. Christ condemns the Pharisees with a series of "woes" in order to reveal their hypocrisy and show His condemnation of them—23:13-36
3. Christ laments over Jerusalem in order to show His sorrow over their rejection, the certainty of judgment because of that, and Jesus' rejection of them in regard to the Kingdom program; and yet, by the word "until" intimates that He would yet return and establish the Kingdom—23:37-39

Note #17: The interpretation of the Olivet Discourse

There are three major views on how to interpret the Olivet Discourse. The first is the preterist view which sees the events of the discourse fulfilled in the destruction of Jerusalem in AD 70[564] *and can be diagrammed as follows.*

Preterist View
1. Jesus Delivers Olivet Discourse Matt. 24-25; Mark 13; Luke 21
2. Death of Christ
3. Destruction of Jerusalem in AD 70 (Olivet Discourse Fulfilled)
4. The Present Age
5. Second Coming of Christ
6. Eternal State

---

[564] For an assessment of this view see Stanley Toussaint, "A Critique of the Preterist View of the Olivet Discourse," *Bibliotheca Sacra* 161:644 (October, 2004), 469-490. For a preterist/futurist debate see Thomas Ice and Kenneth Gentry, *The Great Tribulation Past or Future? Two Evangelicals Debate the Question* (Grand Rapids: Kregel, 1999). In his historical study on the early church and preterism, H. Wayne House concludes: "An examination of the patristic literature from the late first century of the Christian era through the eighth century reveals that this sampling [*Epistle of Barnabas,* Clement of Alexandria, Tertullian, Irenaeus, Hippolytus, Origen, Athanasius, Cyril of Jerusalem, Basil, Jerome, Chrysostom, Augustine, John of Damascus] of the words of the Fathers demonstrates that what is known as Preterism held virtually no sway in the eschatological perspectives taught by the Church Fathers. Though not all were pre-millennialists, nor futurists in the contemporary sense, nonetheless the overwhelming consensus was that the Second Coming of Christ was future from each of the writer's time frame and that it included the revelation of the Antichrist before the coming of Christ, an apostasy, a tribulation of the saints, and for some a millennial kingdom following the coming. Though the perspectives on the place of the Jews in the future kingdom of God, the millennial reign of David's Son, and other important doctrines were not consistent among the Fathers, largely I believe dependent on the influence of the apostles in Asia and neo-Platonic thought in Egypt, nevertheless the Church looked for a future coming of Christ in judgment on a rejecting sinful world but a Blessed Hope of the coming of Christ for His Church" (H. Wayne House, "The Understanding of the Church Fathers Regarding the Olivet Discourse and the Fall of Jerusalem" Paper presented at the Pre-Trib Conference, 2009).

There are three stripes of modern preterism. Thomas Ice provides a summary: "Mild preterism holds that the Tribulation was fulfilled within the first three hundred years of Christianity...Moderate preterism [this is the form being interacted with in this lecture]...sees the Tribulation and the bulk of prophecy as fulfilled in events surrounding the destruction of Jerusalem and the temple in A.D. 70, but they still hold to a Second Coming, a physical resurrection of the dead, an end to temporary history and the establishing of the consummate new heaven and new earth. Extreme...preterism believes that the Second Coming, and thus the resurrection of believers, is all past. For all practical purposes all Bible prophecy has been fulfilled and we are beyond the millennium and even now in the new heaven and the new earth" (Thomas Ice and Kenneth Gentry, *The Great Tribulation Past or Future? Two Evangelicals Debate the Question*, 7).

The second major view is the "historic (present)" view which believes that the Discourse has been in the process of fulfillment throughout church history. It is diagrammed below.

Historic (Present) View
1. Jesus Delivers Olivet Discourse Matt. 24-25; Mark 13; Luke 21
2. Death of Christ
3. The Olivet Discourse is being fulfilled throughout history
4. Emphasis on present events which will precede the Parousia
5. Second Coming of Christ

The final view is the futuristic one and it is the one adopted by the writer. It takes Jesus' words in this discourse as describing God's future work with Israel during the Tribulation period up to the Second Coming of Christ to earth to establish his kingdom. One of the most frequent objections to the futuristic understanding is the phrase "this generation" in 24:34. See Note 22 for a discussion of this phrase.

Futurist View
1. Jesus Delivers Olivet Discourse Matt. 24-25; Mark 13; Luke 21
2. Death of Christ
3. Destruction of Jerusalem in AD 70 gives near fulfillment of Jesus' prediction about the destruction of the Temple
4. The Church Age
5. Rapture of the Church
6. Tribulation Period; Olivet Discourse Fulfilled
7. Second Coming of Christ
8. The Kingdom Age

E. Matthew records the Olivet Discourse as given by Christ in which He makes a series of predictions regarding Israel's future together with a series of parables illustrating them in order to show that though Israel has been set aside for the present, the Kingdom program would be resumed at a future time—24:1-25:46

1. The setting of the discourse includes the previous lament as well as Jesus' statement to the disciples that the buildings of the temple would one day be torn down—24:1-2

2. The disciples ask when these things would occur—24:3

Note #18: How many questions did the disciples ask?

That the disciples are asking two questions has been noted by many. Blomberg writes: "By not repeating the definite article ('the') before 'end of the age,' Matthew's rendering of Jesus' words is most likely linking the coming of Christ and the end of the age together as one event" (Craig Blomberg, Matthew [Nashville: Broadman Press, 1992], 353. Toussaint concurs: "While many see three questions here, the disciples are really asking two. The words 'coming' (παρουσιάς) and 'end' (συντελείας) are joined by one article and the conjunction 'and' (και,); therefore, these two words actually are two parts of one question"(Stanley Toussaint, Behold the King: A Study of Matthew

[Portland: Multnomah Press, 1981], 268-269). See also David Turner, Matthew *[Grand Rapids: Baker Academic, 2008], 569, f.n. 3).*

Though Jesus indicated that there would be judgment on Jerusalem which turned out to take place in AD 70, the disciples had correctly understood the correlation between the destruction of the city and Messiah's return as occurring at the same time. This was based on their understanding of Zechariah 14 which links together three events: the destruction of the city; the return of the Messiah in judgment; and, the establishment of the kingdom. To understand the fulfillment of Jerusalem's destruction based on Jesus' words about "one stone shall not be left on another" in AD 70, does not cancel out the Zechariah prophecy. Rather, it is an illustration of a common phenomenon in prophecy known as near/far fulfillment.

3. Christ outlines the events of the Tribulation and Second Coming in order to give the disciples insight as to Israel's future program— 24:4-31

Note #19: Matthew 24/Revelation 6 parallels

Matthew 24		*Revelation 6*
5	*False Messiahs*[565]	*2*
6-7	*War*[566]	*2-4*
7	*Famine*[567]	*5-6*
7	*Death*	*7-8*
9	*Persecution*[568]	*9-11*
7	*Earthquakes*[569]	*12*

4. Christ instructs the disciples through a series of parables in order to illustrate and lend significance to the things He has just said— 24:32-25:30

5. Christ closes the Olivet Discourse with a description of the judgment on the nations immediately before His Kingdom is established on earth—25:31-46

[565] It is sometimes wrongly assumed that the Tribulation begins with the rapture of the Church. According to Daniel 9:27 the period begins with the covenantal arrangement between Antichrist and Israel. There is an unspecified amount of time between the rapture and this event. This is why it is fitting that Jesus would begin his description of the Tribulation with the presence of false messiahs. Evidently many will make messianic claims at this time; however, only one will be persuasive enough to convince Israel to enter into a political agreement with him. Evidence from Josephus has been presented to show that while there were prophetic claims before the destruction of Jerusalem, there is no record of any messianic claims. This would be one piece of evidence militating against a preterist understanding of the Discourse (Robert Gundry, *Matthew* [Grand Rapids: Eerdmans, 1994], 477); Heinrich Meyer, *Critical and Exegetical Handbook to the Gospel of Matthew* [Edinburgh: T. & T. Clark, 1879], 2:128).

[566] The reminder needs to constantly be given that warfare in the present day is not to be found in this passage. The events listed will occur during the future Tribulation.

[567] The famine in the world is probably the direct result of the warfare just mentioned.

[568] The Tribulation will be a time of unprecedented evangelism through the preaching of the gospel of the kingdom. This preaching will be done by the 144,000 mentioned in Revelation 7, the two witnesses mentioned in Revelation 11, and those who have fled Jerusalem upon hearing of the Abomination of Desolation. Many of those who accept the message will experience martyrdom.

[569] Only six seal judgments are mentioned in this chart since the seventh seal contains the trumpet judgments recorded in Revelation 8-9.

VII. MATTHEW RECORDS THE PASSION AND RESURRECTION OF CHRIST IN ORDER TO SHOW THAT HE IS THE SON OF GOD AND TO SHOW THAT CHRIST HAS PROVIDED THE MEANS WHEREBY MEN CAN ENTER THE KINGDOM ABOUT WHICH HE HAS BEEN SPEAKING—26:1-28:20

A. Matthew presents the crucifixion events including the pre-paration, arrest, trials, cross, and burial—26:1-27:66

1. Matthew notes all of the preparations before Christ's arrest by the Jewish leaders in order to portray His preparation as the sacrificial lamb—26:1-46

2. Matthew notes the betrayal and arrest of Christ in order to show that Christ was in complete command of what was happening and that all of this was in fulfillment of prophecy which demonstrated that He was the covenanted Messiah—26:47-56

3. Matthew notes the trials of Christ which were illegal in order to emphasize Christ's righteousness and the guilt of the nation—26:57-27:26

4. Matthew records the crucifixion of Christ—27:27-56

5. Matthew records a) the burial of Christ in the tomb of Joseph of Arimathea to show this was in fulfillment of Isaiah 53:9, and b) the sealing of the large stone in front of the tomb—27:57-66

B. Matthew presents the resurrection of Christ and commissioning of the disciples in order to show that He is the triumphant King of Israel with the authority to commission disciples—28:1-20

1. Matthew observes the empty tomb which he validates by the witnesses of the angels, soldiers, women, and the religious leaders in order to show the triumph of the King—28:1-10

2. Matthew notes the false report spread about the resurrection in order to show the hardness of the leaders as well as the origination of this false theory—28:11-15

3. Matthew records the commission of the disciples by Christ in which he stresses the all-inclusive authority given to Christ which would include all Kingdom-authority so that He can delegate a mission to the disciples of making disciples—28:16-20

Note #20: Interpreting the Sermon on the Mount[570]

The Millennial View (aka the Kingdom View)

Statement of the view

This view applies the Sermon primarily to the future earthly Kingdom which the Lord announced as being at hand, and has been held by numerous dispensationalists during the mid-twentieth century approximately.[571] *As stated above, since the Sermon was delivered during the time when the Kingdom was being offered, its prime referent point is the time of the Kingdom. Since the Kingdom was rejected, its application today becomes secondary.*

---

[570] I am indebted to Dr. John Martin for the categories and concepts in this section (class taken at Dallas Theological Seminary, Bible 329 "The Sermon on the Mount," Spring 1986).

[571] Some representatives include Chafer, Gaebelein, Kelly, Pettingill, Ryrie, Scofield, and Campbell.

Support of the view

The chief support for this view is the Sermon's setting during the Kingdom offer. Since the kingdom was rejected and consequently postponed, so also is the kingdom's constitution and rule of life, namely, the Sermon on the Mount. So, because the Sermon appears in the first half of Matthew's Gospel, some millennial interpreters have dismissed it as only applicable to the Jews in Jesus' day.

A second support is Matthew's law/grace distinction. This position assumes that Jesus was speaking under the old dispensation of law, which has been superseded by the dispensation of grace. Therefore, the Discourse was merely an Old Testament ethic not applicable today.

Closely akin to the preceding, a third argument for this view is the impossibility of keeping the demands of the Sermon. This argues for its place under the dispensation of law. These legal demands were done away when God began to deal with people in a new way in the dispensation of the church.

A fourth premise of this view is the interpretation of "law" in the Sermon. It is assumed that this is a technical term referring to the Mosaic legal code from which the believer has been delivered.

One final pillar upon which the millennial view rests is the "fact" that neither Christ nor the early Church actually sought to follow it. This is based on a comparison of Matthew 5:39 and John 18:23.

Weaknesses of the view

The first problem with the millennial view is the many references throughout the Sermon which are incongruous with the millennial kingdom. Disciples will be reviled and persecuted (5:11-12); wickedness must be prevalent since the disciples are to be salt (5:13-16); and Pharisees, thieves, and false prophets will be present (5:17-10; 6:19; 7:15).

If Satan will be bound during the millennium, why pray in 6:13, "Deliver us from the evil one?" This is a strange kingdom indeed where Christ is said to "rule with a rod of iron." It should be pointed out in fairness, however, that the adherents of the view are aware of this problem. Their explanation is that these things belong to the tribulation period before the actual millennium. In positing this large block of material to the tribulation period, the "millennialists" really destroy their own position. For by doing this, they are applying a great deal of the Discourse to a period other than the millennium.

A second difficulty with this view is that the Sermon is made a ground for admission into the kingdom. This immediately gives rise to at least three problems; (1) the kingdom would be sparsely populated, (2) to make the Sermon's ethics an entrance requirement implies a period of testing which would obviously be before the kingdom. This then, applies the Sermon to a time other than the millennium, and (3) it makes entrance into the kingdom a matter of merit rather than of grace.

A third weakness relates both to the time of composition and the original readers of Matthew. The point therefore, is that if Matthew lived in the church age, and wrote to a people in the church age, it is doubtful that his material would be relegated to a time before then. It could be argued that Matthew's recording of the Sermon was simply historical and therefore not necessarily meant for the Church. However, the ethical demands are confirmed throughout Scripture and cannot be confined to one time period.

Further, if this logic were followed through, the Sermon would not have validity even in the millennium, since it was simply part of an historical record.

The next difficulty lies in the anticipatory nature of the Sermon in relation to the kingdom. There is not the slightest intimation that the ethics here are only for the kingdom. Rather, it looks forward to people entering the kingdom (5:21); receiving rewards in the kingdom (5:12, 19, 46; 6:1, 2, 4); praying for the coming of the kingdom (6:10); and prior to that, persecution and false prophets (5:11-12; 7:15-18).

A fifth problem is the insistence that the life-style portrayed in the Sermon is impossible to live out in the church age. This is a weak point for two reasons: (1) neither Testament ever excuses anyone from a command because of its difficulty. There are many New Testament commands impossible to fulfill completely (e.g., 1 Pet. 1:15; I John 2:1; Col. 3:3). Godly standards, though unattainable completely in this life, are nevertheless to be the goal of every believer through dependence on the Holy Spirit and (2) this argument is used selectively in the Sermon, The main place it is used is Jesus' retaliation in John 1:23, thus contradicting Matthew 5:39. It is then concluded that the demands are impossible and will only be fulfilled in the millennium. Yet, no such suggestion is made for the sections dealing with murder/hatred and adultery/lust. But these ethical instructions are all found in the same section of the Sermon.

Another difficulty exists with the purpose of the law. This misrepresents the function of the Law. The Law was given for the sanctification of a redeemed people. It was not intended to blast people out, but to guide them in the path of holiness.

A seventh difficulty also surrounds the Law. Those espousing the millennial view assume the mention of the Law to be a reference to the Mosaic Law. Yet, when the two references in the Sermon are examined (5:17; 7:13), it is evident that more is being referred to than simply the Mosaic Law.

An eighth problem with this view is the presence of the Sermon in Luke's Gospel not related to a kingdom motif. It is admitted by "millennialists" that if Luke and Matthew are recording the same Sermon, doubt would be cast on their interpretation. Yet, it is widely accepted by Roman Catholic and Protestant scholars alike, that the two are the same. This is important, for Matthew and Luke do not follow the same theological chronology in their Gospel. Luke apparently expected his readers to follow these things. Thus, if the two accounts are of the same sermon, the "millennialists" chief support (the Sermon's placement by Matthew within the kingdom-offer setting) would be shattered.

A ninth objection to the millennial view concerns the charge that the early church did not seek to implement its teachings. If this were true, one would not expect to find many references to the Sermon in the writings of the early church. The opposite is true however. The Didache (dated from the end of the first to the middle of the second century) emphasizes love of enemies, turning the other cheek, and the Lord's Prayer.

The Penitential View

Statement of the view

The penitential view (also called the Lutheran view) was popularized in theological circles by the famous German Gerhard Kittel. It was also held by such scholars as Machen, Tholuck, and Gore. Those who subscribe to this position view the Sermon as a body of law which makes the individual cognizant of his sin, and drives him to God. It shows the need of depending on Jesus alone for salvation. A variation of this view also is related to the Mosaic Law, and is thus presented here. It sees the Sermon as presenting the righteousness needed to enter the kingdom which is being offered by Christ. As the

Law was an exposition of the holiness of God, and what that demanded, so the Sermon on the Mount reveals the demands of a holy God.

Support of the view

One support for this view is an emphasis on 5:17-20 where Jesus talks about fulfilling the law and the prophets. Speaking in a legal setting, the effect of the Sermon would be the same as the effect of the law—no one can be justified by it and must find another means of justification (cf., Gal. 3:24).

A second foundation of this view is the fact that Jesus told His hearers that their righteousness had to surpass that of the Pharisees (5:20, 43).

A third reason this approach is taken is the belief that the primary audience is the unbelieving multitude. It is pointed out by the supporters of this view that the text states the multitudes were present as Jesus began and closed the Sermon (5:1; 7:28). In addition, Luke notes that "a great throng of people from all Judea and Jerusalem and the coastal region of Tyre and Sidon" were present (Luke 6:17).

Finally, the invitation of Matthew 7:13, the warning of judgment in Matthew 7:21-23, and the parable of the two foundations in Matthew 7:24-27 must be directed to unbelievers.

Weaknesses of the view

The first problem with this position is that Matthew does not picture the Pharisees as the most righteous people of their day. Rather, he pictures them as hypocritical (Matt. 6, 23). It is doubtful that only Jesus noticed their pretentious lives. This is seen by the objurgation of them by John the Baptist (Matt. 3:7-12).

Another obstacle in this view is that Jesus did not identify his coming simply with the Mosaic Law, but with the whole Old Testament (Matt. 5:17). Thus his demands in the Sermon fulfilled those of the Old Testament. He was asking for obedience to the revealed will of God just as the prophets had done.

A third weakness has to do with the audience referent. While unbelievers were certainly present, and perhaps addressed at times by Christ, the internal evidence of his words shows them to be primarily applicable to believers (e.g., Matt. 5:13, 14, 16; 6:9, 32). Also, both Matthew and Luke identify them as the primary audience (Matt. 5:1; Luke 6:20).

A fourth problem has to do with the law/grace distinction as discussed under the millennial view. The reader is referred to that section.

Interim Ethic View

Statement of the view

This approach views the Sermon as an ethic for the time preliminary to the establishment of the kingdom. This idea, called Intermsethik, *was proposed by Albert Schweitzer. He viewed the kingdom as entirely eschatological which would be brought about by a catastrophic irruption of God into the world. Since Jesus' preaching occurred before this event, the Discourse was to be in force until that time.*

A parallel to this idea can be seen in the special laws that go into effect during a time of war. The disciples were soldiers awaiting the kingdom. They were to conduct themselves by these stringent measures until the kingdom came, and the interim period was over. The kingdom did not come, however, and apparently Jesus died in despair and disillusionment. Such to Schweitzer was "the historical Jesus"—a deluded first-century apocalyptist. Consequently, the Sermon has little relevance to the contemporary Christian. While obviously dispensationalists who hold this view (e.g., Toussaint)[572] *would reject Schweitzer's conclusion, the concept of an ethic for an interim period remains attractive.*

Support of the view

Part of the appeal in this view is the avoidance of the problems associated with the millennial view (e.g., incongruities between the Sermon and kingdom, the Sermon as a ground for admission into the kingdom, the identity of the Law, the anticipatory nature of the Sermon, etc.). Another support is the utilization of the grammatico-historical method of interpretation. It connects the Sermon with the offer of the kingdom.

Second, the message of the kingdom is anticipatory, noting a time lapse before the establishment of the kingdom. It looks forward to people entering the kingdom (5:20; 7:21); and it speaks of future rewards (5:12; 6:1, 2, 4, 5).

A third strength is that it identifies the audience as disciples. They are called salt (Matt. 5:13), admonished in righteousness (Matt. 5:19-7:12), and God is called their Father (Matt. 5:16, 19, 46; 6:1, 2, 5).

Weaknesses of the view

Despite the strengths of this view, there remain some serious problems. The first has to do with the termination of the interim period. If it ends when Jesus is rejected by the religious leaders in Matthew 12, then one is forced to conclude that the Sermon has no bearing on the Church today. Thus, the ethic was only in force for a few years, and the interpreter ends up with the same conclusion as the "millennialist." If, on the other hand, the interim period ends when Christ does set up the kingdom, then the Sermon is in force today. There is a great deal of ambiguity when it comes to answering this question. Does the interim period end with the rejection of Christ in Matthew 12, or when Christ inaugurates the kingdom?

A second problem arises with the question—why would Jesus change the Law? Were not the moral principles God revealed in the Old Testament appropriate for all times?

A final objection to this approach is that the material in the Sermon cannot be shown to be different from the ethics of the Old Testament. In fact, just the opposite is true. Friedlander, in his classic work, The Jewish Sources of the Sermon on the Mount, *suggests that all the material in the Sermon has its roots in early Jewish literature. In addition, parallels are also presented for the rest of the Sermon. While the dispensationalist would not reach the Friedlander's ultimate conclusion, namely, that since Jesus' teaching is not unique it can be ignored, nevertheless, it does show that much of what Jesus taught is grounded in the Old Testament.*

Hence, it becomes clear the words of the entire Sermon were not a new and special ethic for an interim period. Rather, they were the same moral principles which God has desired from His people for a long, long time.

The Discipleship Ethic View

Statement of the view

[572] "Those who come to the Sermon on the Mount with the interim interpretation see in it an ethic for the time preliminary to the establishment of the kingdom" (Stanley Toussaint, *Behold the King: A Study of Matthew* [Portland: Multnomah Press, 1981], 91).

It has been seen thus far, that the millennial approach teaches that the primary application of the Sermon on the Mount is the future kingdom age, and thus today enjoys only a secondary application. Likewise, the interim ethic view would also consider the Sermon to have a secondary application to the present. The believer's (discipleship) ethic view, however, affirms the Discourse to be categorically for today, as well as for any dispensation.

Support of the view

In enumerating the various supports for this position, there naturally will be a small amount of overlap from some of the other sections. In such cases, no elaboration will be given. The following points are offered in support of the discipleship ethic view.

First, the Gospel of Matthew is interested primarily in the teaching aspects of Jesus' ministry. This is evident from the material Matthew includes. It has been observed already that this bulk of material has been arranged in five great discourse sections. This is very significant in light of Jesus' words in 28:20 where He commands the disciples "to teach them all things whatsoever I have commanded you." For the original readers of the gospel, the "all things" would have included these five great discourses.

Second, nowhere in the Gospel does Jesus abolish the words of the Sermon from being binding in the lives of His disciples.

Third, the Sermon's applicability in Luke 6 (generally considered to be a condensation of the same message) is not tied to the kingdom-offer setting.

Fourth, the Sermon on the Mount had great influence on later New Testament thought. There is a plethora of references to this in the writings of Paul (e.g., Rom. 6:13; 12:14; Gal. 5:19, 22; 1 Cor. 7:10, 11). James (e.g., 1:2, 12, 26; 2:8, 12, 13; 5:12), and Peter (e.g., 1 Pet. 2:12).

Fifth, it would appear that if the precepts of the sermon do not bind us, then we are not a part of the kingdom of which it speaks. For, if the characterizations of it do not apply to us, then neither would the penalties or rewards.

Sixth, as was previously observed, the Beatitudes, as the rest of the Sermon on the Mount contain nothing that was either entirely new or unknown, but based on passages of the Old Testament. Thus, even though the words were spoken when the kingdom was being offered, they maintain their validity.

Seventh, the eschatological and non-eschatological sections of the sermon argue that the ethic is for the present, while the blessings will be realized in the future (5:5, 10; 6:10; 7:21).

Eighth, it is true that Jesus spoke these words while the people were still under the time frame of the Law. Nevertheless, Matthew recorded them during the age of the church as a teaching tool for church people.

Ninth, true disciples were the primary audience for Jesus' teaching.

Tenth, this view sees the historical context as being in a time which anticipates the prophesied kingdom. While the present day context is not exactly the same, it is true that believers today anticipate the same kingdom, and should behave in the same manner. In fact, it could be successfully argued that the invitation at the end of the sermon regarding the narrow road is not an invitation to salvation as it is often presented, but rather, an invitation to Jesus' disciples to embrace the ethic he has expounded. This makes much more sense in light of the fact that the bulk of the sermon is on righteous living and not on the Gospel message.

Note #21: A "mystery form" of the Kingdom?

It is often alleged that the Lord predicted a form of the kingdom for the church age in His parables, particularly those in Matthew 13. For many years dispensationalists have referred to these parables as teaching a mystery form or a new form of the kingdom...However, nowhere in Matthew 13 or anywhere else does the Lord Jesus use the term "mystery form." Rather, He refers to the "mysteries of the kingdom of heaven" (v. 11); that is, the Lord in these parables is giving to His disciples new truths about the kingdom that were hitherto unknown. It is strange that so many dispensationalists claim that a new form of the kingdom is introduced in Matthew 13. Dispensationalists argue strenuously for a literal, earthly kingdom that is the fulfillment of the Old Testament when John, Jesus, and His disciples announce its nearness. Then suddenly these dispensationalists change the meaning in Matthew 13. How much better to say that the same kingdom is being discussed but now the Lord Jesus is providing further revelation about that kingdom.[573]

The fiction of a present "kingdom of heaven" established on earth in the Church, has been lent some support by an incautious terminology sometimes used in defining the "mysteries of the kingdom of heaven" (Matt. 13:11). The parables of this chapter...describe the kingdom of heaven as now existing in "mystery form" during the Church age. Now it is true that these parables present certain conditions related to the Kingdom which are contemporaneous with the present age. But nowhere in Matthew 13 is the establishment of the Kingdom placed within this age. On the contrary, in two of these parables the setting up of the Kingdom is definitely placed at the end of the "age" (vss. 39 and 49 ASV, with 41-43). And it is to be noted that in each of these references, our Lord is speaking as the infallible interpreter of His own parable.

What is certain in the teaching of these difficult parables is that the present age, viewed from the standpoint of the Kingdom, is a time of preparation. During this period the Son of man is sowing seed (vs. 37), gathering and developing a spiritual nucleus for the future Kingdom, a group called "sons of the kingdom" (vs. 38, ASV). At the same time He is permitting a parallel development of evil in the world under the leadership of Satan (vss. 38-39). It is the purpose of God to bring both to a "harvest," when the good and bad will be separated, and then to establish the Kingdom in power and righteousness (vss. 41-43, 49).[574]

Note #22: The problem of "this generation."

Perhaps the most discussed passage in the Olivet Discourse occurs in Matthew 24:34 where Jesus says to his disciples "Truly, I say to you, this generation will not pass away until all these things take place" (ESV). The key question has to do with what Jesus meant when he referred to "this generation" (γενεὰ αὕτη). The importance of the issue lies in the fact that one's interpretation of this phrase will impact the time the discourse is fulfilled. There have been at least seven interpretations which will be briefly mentioned here.

---

[573] Stanley Toussaint, "Israel and the Church of a Traditional Dispensationalist," in *Three Central Issues in Contemporary Dispensationalism: A Comparison of Traditional and Progressive Views* (Grand Rapids: Kregel, 1999), 237.

[574] Alva McClain, *The Greatness of the Kingdom* (Winona Lake, IN: BMH Books, 1983), 440-441.

1. Some imply that the "generation" was Jesus' disciples. Since all of the events did not occur during their lifetime, Jesus made a mistake due to his humanness.[575]

2. This second view also sees the generation as Jesus' disciples, but since the events did not occur literally during their lifetime, Jesus was speaking metaphorically and find their fulfillment in AD 70. This is the common approach of preterism.

3. Others interpret "generation" as a race of people. Thus Jesus meant that the Jewish race would not come to an end before events of the Discourse had been fulfilled.

4. Another suggested possibility centers around the verb "take place" which can have the sense of "to begin." This would take the verb as an ingressive aorist focusing on the beginning of the events. Therefore the events of the Discourse would begin in the days of the present disciples but would not be completed until the Lord returned.

5. A fifth possibility is to see the Discourse as an instance of a prophecy which has multiple fulfillments. There is then a fulfillment in AD 70 and another fulfillment in the future Tribulation and Second Coming.

6. Another option is to take "this generation" as a technical phrase referring to an evil class of people which opposes Jesus' disciples and God's program.

7. A final suggestion is that the phrase "this generation" should be governed by the phrase "all these things." So, this generation refers to the generation which witnesses "the things" mentioned in the discourse. In other words, the generation which is alive at the time will see the beginning and ending of these events.

It should be noted that views 3-7 are all compatible (though not all equally valid) with the futuristic understanding of the discourse. I am most inclined to view #6. For a full defense of this position see Neil Nelson, "'This Generation' in Matthew 24:34: A Literary Critical Perspective," Journal of the Evangelical Theological Society 38:3 (September, 1996). See also the discussion in Susan Rieske, "What is the Meaning of 'This Generation' in Matthew 23:36," (24:36) [sic] Bibliotheca Sacra 165:658 (April-June 2008), 209-226.

[575] McNeile writes that "it is impossible to escape the conclusion that Jesus, as Man, expected the End within the lifetime of His contemporaries" (Alan McNeile, *The Gospel According to St. Matthew* [Grand Rapids: Baker, 1980], 355). A variation of this theological concept related to the humanity of Christ is often used to explain Matthew 24:36 "But of that day and hour no one knows, not even the angels of heaven, but My Father only" (NKJV). It is then suggested that Jesus was speaking from the limitations of his humanity and really did not know when he was to return. Though this explanation is common, this schizophrenic understanding of the theanthropic person of Christ has seemed rather odd. This is particularly the case since Jesus had just given extensive details on the future in the previous part of the discourse. Perhaps a better explanation is to see Jesus' statement in light of the economic trinity in the sense that it was not his place to make this announcement (see the use of "know" in Matthew 25:12 which also does not refer to ignorance). I am indebted for this observation to https://bible.org/byverse/matthew24:36, accessed 10/12/2013.

MARK

Authorship

The traditional view identifies John Mark, an associate of Peter, as the author of this Gospel. This position is supported by both external and internal evidence.

A. External Evidence

The earliest statement of external evidence comes from Papias (ca. A.D. 135-140) as cited by Eusebius in *Ecclesiastical History* 3.39.15-16. This early evidence is confirmed also by testimony from the other church fathers (Guthrie, *New Testament Introduction,* 69-71; Hiebert, *An Introduction to the New Testament,* 1:84-86).

B. Internal Evidence (the internal evidence is not demonstrative but compatible)

1. There are several items in the book which suggest the author's connection with Peter (1:16-20; 5:21-24; 9:14-15; 11:4-6) as well as the inclusion of the phrase "and Peter" in 16:7.
2. The author is also familiar with Palestine (5:1; 6:53; 8:10), its Aramaic language (5:41; 7:11, 34; 14:36), and Jewish customs (1:21; 2:14; 7:2-4).
3. Mark's association with Peter is also seen in 1 Peter 5:13. For further support that John Mark is the author see Hiebert, *An Introduction to the New Testament,* 1:87-90; Harrison, *Introduction to the New Testament,* 174-175; Guthrie, *New Testament Introduction,* 69-72; William Lane, *The Gospel of Mark* (Grand Rapids: Eerdmans, 1979), 21-33.

Date

Part of the debate concerning the date revolves around the statement of Irenaeus that Mark wrote after the "departure" of Peter and Paul (after 67 or 68) by which he probably meant death (cf. Luke 9:31 and 2 Peter 1:15). On the other hand, Clement of Alexandria and Origen say that the Gospel was written during Peter's lifetime. Because of this conflict, the book is usually dated either between AD 67-69 (written after the deaths of Peter and Paul) or prior to AD 64-68 (when Peter was martyred thus during his lifetime).) On the other hand, some take the "departure" to be a reference to the departure of Peter from the place where Mark was and thus date the book as early as the late 40s or 50s (Robert Gundry, *A Survey of the New Testament* [Grand Rapids: Zondervan, 2003] 128). Grassmick dates the book between AD 57-59 based on Mark antedating Acts which ends with Paul is in prison prior to his first release (ca. AD 62) and the probability that Mark could have been in Rome in the late 50s during Nero's reign ("Mark" in *The Bible Knowledge Commentary* [Wheaton: Victor, 1983], 99). This matter is hard to settle, but it is felt that it can at least be said that the date is before AD 70 based on Mark 13:14-23. Thus the writer accepts the traditional view that the book was written sometime during Peter's lifetime (AD 64-68).

Origin and Destination

The traditional view is that Mark was written in Rome primarily for Gentile Christians in Rome. This is supported by almost universal testimony of the Church

Fathers, the internal evidence of Jewish customs being explained (7:3-4; 14:12), and Latin loanwords (5:9; 6:27; 12:15; 15:16).

Occasion

If Mark were written in Rome in the mid-late 60s, then it is quite possible that the church was facing persecution under the reign of Nero.

The Synoptic Problem

The synoptic problem deals with the differences in the same accounts presented by Matthew, Mark, and Luke and the questions this raises concerning the sources they used and their relationship to each other. While most conservatives will grant that the gospel writers used sources, the liberal critic sees the sources as the resource which an editor used to put the gospel together. The methods suggested for this include: the fragment theory, the urevangelium theory (an original gospel from which all three drew their information), the two-document theory, the four-document theory, and *Formgeschichte*. Probably the best solution is to conclude that there was not dependence among the gospels but a universal dependence on the same events (for this view see Charlie Dyer, "Do the Synoptics Depend on Each Other?" *Bibliotheca Sacra* 138:551 [Jul 1981], 230-244).While it is not necessary to deny there were various sources, it can be said that these also included eyewitness accounts, conversations with eyewitnesses, written sources in circulation, etc. Further, it should be noted that: 1) each gospel writer had a different emphasis in writing, and thus included and omitted certain things in order to serve his purpose in writing, and 2) Christ promised that through the Holy Spirit, He would guide the apostles to an accurate recording the facts.

Characteristics

- **A.** It is a book of action. The word *ethus* (immediately)[576] is used 41 times in Mark compared to 10 times in Matthew, Luke, John, and Acts combined. The Roman mind would be more interested in what Christ did.
- **B.** Over 90% of the content is found elsewhere.
- **C.** Mark does contain some unique material: the parable of the seed growing secretly (4:26-29), the healing of the blind man at Bethsaida (8), the flight of the young man (14), and that Jesus was too busy to eat (3:20).
- **D.** It is the shortest Gospel with no genealogy or birth and only two discourses.
- **E.** It has a simple and rough style.
- **F.** It is very realistic speaking of the dullness of the disciples, their criticism of Jesus, and the recording of Jesus' human emotions (sighs, hunger, sorrow, anger, etc.).
- **G.** There is an emphasis on Christology in 1:1 and the testimony of the Father, demons, and the centurion.
- **H.** There is a Gentile interest. This is seen in that the book does not presuppose a knowledge of the Old Testament (Mark quotes only one OT passage), no prohibition in the sending of the twelve, he translates Aramaic expressions, he explains some Palestinian geography (e.g., the Jordan was a river and the Mt. of

[576] I am assuming the common translation "immediately" here; however, with the understanding that this is overly simplistic. For a discussion of the semantic range and syntax of the term in Mark see Rodney Decker, "The Use of εὐθύς ('immediately') in Mark," *Journal of Ministry and Theology* 1:1 (Spring 1997), 90-121.

Olives overlooks the temple area).

Discipleship

One of the major themes for Mark is discipleship. This is also a major area of debate within current scholarship. One view holds that discipleship is a part of the Gospel. John MacArthur writes that "the gospel Jesus proclaimed was a call to discipleship, a call to follow Him in submissive obedience" (*The Gospel According to Jesus* [Grand Rapids: Zondervan, 1988], 21). Similarly, "we maintain that being a believer and a disciple are the same. A believer/disciple has salvation" (Robert Lescelius, *Lordship Salvation: Some Crucial Questions and Answers* [Ashville, NC: Revival Literature, 1992], 65). J. I. Packer concurs: "In our presentation of Christ's Gospel, therefore, we need to lay a similar stress on the cost of following Christ, and making sinners face soberly before we urge them to respond to the message of free forgiveness. In common honesty, we must not conceal the fact that free forgiveness in one sense will cost us everything" (*Evangelism and the Sovereignty of God* [Downers Grove: InterVarsity, 1961], 73). The other view stresses that the Gospel and discipleship are separate.

All of the major lexicons simply define a disciple as: a pupil, follower, learner, apprentice, etc. Of note in this regard is the fact that in the 267 New Testament uses of "disciple" (μαθητής) there are no occurrences in the epistles. While this is an argument from silence, it is odd that if discipleship is a part of the gospel that Paul never mentions it in his justification texts in Galatians and Romans. In his excellent articles on the subject (Charles Bing, "Why Lordship Faith Misses the Mark for Salvation" *Journal of the Grace Evangelical Society* 12:1 [Spring 1999]; "Why Lordship Faith Misses the Mark for Discipleship," *Journal of the Grace Evangelical Society* 12:2 [Autumn 1999]), Bing notes the distinctions between salvation and discipleship.

Salvation	Discipleship
Justification	Sanctification
By grace • Through faith • Free • Christ's love for me • Christ's commitment to me • Christ's cross for me • Eternal life	By works • Through faithfulness • Costly • My love for Christ • My commitment to Christ • My cross for Christ • Eternal rewards
An unbeliever's response	A believer's response
Instantaneous	Progressive
One condition	Many conditions
Inclusive	Exclusive

Purpose

While Matthew stresses the deity of Christ in the role of a King, Mark stresses the deity of Christ in the role of a servant. His deity is seen in the beginning statement (1:1) and in the climax of the confession of the Roman centurion (15:39). His servanthood is seen in his activity as God's busy servant. There is also an emphasis on suffering and discipleship for Christ's followers. With these facts in mind, the statement of purpose of Mark could be put thusly: <u>Mark presents the deity of Christ in the role of a servant of</u>

God in order to give the suffering Roman church a pattern of discipleship in the midst of adversity so that they would be encouraged to stand as strong disciples during difficult times.

Summary of Argument

I. MARK ASSERTS THE DEITY OF CHRIST AND PRESENTS THE INTRODUCTION OF HIM AS THE SERVANT OF GOD THROUGH THE EVENTS OF HIS FORERUNNER, BAPTISM, AND TEMPTATION—1:1-13.

A. Mark asserts the deity of Christ by calling Him the Son of God by which he sets the tone for the rest of the book to be seen in this light—1:1

B. Mark presents the introduction of the Servant by His forerunner John the Baptist as he records John's baptism and message of One who is coming after him—1:2-8

C. Mark presents the baptism of Jesus in order to show His submission to this ordinance and His divine approval from the Father—1:9-11

D. Mark presents the temptation of Christ by Satan noting that the Spirit drove Him to this to again emphasize His submission to the will of God —1:12-13

II. MARK PRESENTS THE MINISTRY OF THE SERVANT GEOGRAPHICALLY IN ORDER TO DEMONSTRATE HIS CONSTANT ACTIVITY ON BEHALF OF THE FATHER AND THE DISCIPLESHIP WHICH HE DEMANDS OF HIS FOLLOWERS—1:14-13:37

A. Mark presents the early ministry of Christ in Galilee which consists of many rapidly recorded events in order to stress the servanthood of Christ—1:14-4:34

1. Mark gives a summary of Jesus' preaching content which is said to be the Gospel of the Kingdom, namely, repent for the Kingdom of Heaven is at hand—1:14-15
2. Mark records the calling of the first four disciples in order to emphasize the quick obedience on their part as what is required of those who would follow Christ—1:16-20

3. Mark records the ministry of Christ in Capernaum—1:21-34
4. Mark records the ministry of Christ in His tour of Galilee—1:35-45

Note #23: The cleansing of a leper

Lepers were considered to be unclean and so any contact with them would spread this uncleanness. In light of this fact, the contrast between the teaching of the rabbis and Jesus is marked. "Their burdens were needlessly increased. True, as wrapped in mourner's garb the leper passed by, his cry 'Unclean!' was to incite others to pray for him—but also to avoid him. No one was even to salute him; his bed was to be low, inclining towards the ground. If he even put his head into a place, it became unclean. No less a distance than four cubits (six feet) must be kept from a leper; or, if the wind came from that direction, a hundred were scarcely sufficient. Rabbi Meir would not eat an egg purchased in a street where there was a leper. Another Rabbi boasted, that he always threw stones at them to keep them far off, while others hid themselves or ran away. To such extent did Rabbinism carry its inhuman logic in considering the leper as a mourner, that it even forbade him to wash his face" (Alfred Edersheim, The Life and Times of Jesus the Messiah *[Grand Rapids: Eerdmans, 1980], 1:495). By contrast, lepers would run to Jesus asking for mercy and in this instance he actually touch the man (1:41). The Law required a leper to go through an elaborate ritual of cleansing before he could be accepted back into society (Lev. 14). Therefore, after Jesus healed the man, he sent him to the priest for this reason and for a testimony to the proof of His Messiahship. However, Jesus told the man not to tell anyone but the priest about the healing. Though often referred to as the "messianic secret," probably Jesus did not want news of this healing to spread so as to avoid premature opposition from the leaders.*

5. Mark presents the conflicts between Jesus and the religious leaders in order to show that service to God often brings harsh conflicts— 2:1-3:6

Note #24: Sickness

According to the religious leaders, sickness was a sign of God's displeasure, therefore only God could remove sin. Thus in this section, Christ is claiming the prerogatives of God in forgiving sin and healing the sick.

6. Mark notes the large crowds which were following Jesus and His ministry among them—3:7-12
7. Mark records the appointment of the twelve apostles—3:13-19
8. Mark records further opposition to Christ in order to show the suffering of the true disciple which, in this case, climaxes in the unpardonable sin—3:20-35
9. Mark records Christ's parabolic teaching to the multitudes in order to hide truth from those who had been opposing Him and to reveal truth to those who had accepted His person—4:1-34

B. Mark presents the withdrawals of Christ from Galilee in order to show His response to the opposition, and many miracles in order to authenticate His person and give encouragement to his readers in the midst of their opposition—4:35-9:50

1. Mark presents the first withdrawal and return of Christ and the disciples—4:35-6:29

2. Mark presents the second withdrawal and return of Christ and the disciples—6:30-7:23

3. Mark presents the third withdrawal and return of Christ and the disciples—7:24-8:13

4. Mark presents the fourth withdrawal and return of Christ and the disciples—8:14-9:50

C. Mark presents the journey of Christ to Jerusalem—10:1-52

1. Mark records Jesus' departure from Galilee and entrance into Judea—10:1
2. Mark records Jesus' teaching on divorce—10:2-12
3. Mark records Jesus' teaching on divorce—10:2-12Mark records Jesus' blessing of the little children in order to show that it takes childlike character to enter the Kingdom—10:13-16

4. Mark records Jesus' teaching on wealth and eternal life to the rich young ruler and how salvation is impossible apart from the work of God—10:17-27
5. Mark records Peter's question about reward and Jesus' response that all who follow Him would be amply rewarded—10:28-31
6. Jesus gives the third announcement of His passion—10:32-34
7. Mark records the desire for prominent positions among the disciples in the Kingdom—10:35-45

Note #25: A contradiction?

There is an apparent contradiction between Mark 10:35-37 and Matthew 20:20-21. Matthew says that all three disciples came to Jesus and that their mother made the requests, while Mark says that James and John asked. It could have been a joint effort where James and John seconded their mother's request and Matthew was shielding James and John. For Mark, he could have stressed their role, for they in a sense, were speaking through Salome.

8. Jesus heals blind Bartimaeus at Jericho—10:46-52

D. Mark presents the ministry of Christ in Jerusalem—11:1-13:37

1. Mark records several preparatory events surrounding Jerusalem leading up to His public teaching—11:1-25

Note #26: How many cleansings of the temple?

The Gospels appear to present two different cleansings of the temple. John presents a temple cleansing at the beginning of Jesus' ministry (John 2), while the Synoptics place a temple cleansing during the Passover week. A vast number of scholars argue for one cleansing which John relocates in his gospel at the beginning of Christ's ministry. There are several differences between the two which reasonably show them to be distinct: 1) in the first (John 2), Jesus was immediately confronted while he was not at the second, 2) at the first he responded with a reference to His death while in the second he denunciated the abuse, and 3) in the first he replied to the religious leaders while in the second he responded to all present. For more discussion see D. A. Carson, The Gospel according to John *(Grand Rapids: Eerdmans, 1991), 176-178; Andreas Kostenberger,* John *(Grand Rapids: Baker, 2004), 109, "additional note;" Leon Morris,* The Gospel according to John *(Grand Rapids: Eerdmans, 1979), 196-198; E. Randolph Richards, "An Honor/Shame Argument for Two Temple Clearings,"* Trinity Journal *29:1 [Spring 2008], 20-43).*

2. Mark records the public teaching of Christ in Jerusalem—11:27-12:44
3. Mark presents the teaching of the Olivet Discourse to His disciples in order to show the future of Israel in light of the rejection of Christ by the nation—13:1-37

III. MARK PRESENTS THE SUFFERING OF THE SERVANT IN ORDER TO SHOW THAT DISCIPLESHIP LEADS TO SUFF-ERING AND PRESENTS A TRIUMPHANT EXAMPLE OF SUFFERING FOR RIGHTEOUSNESS SO AS TO ENCOURAGE THE READERS—14:1-15:47

A. Mark records the pre-Passover events in order to show a contrast between the friends and enemies of Christ—14:1-11

1. Mark notes the plotting of the chief priests and scribes as to how they could take Him and put him to death—14:1-2
2. Mark notes the anointing of Christ by Mary of Bethany in order to show a contrast with the leaders and to present an anointing of Christ for His burial—14:3-9
3. Mark notes the agreement between Judas and the leaders as to how he would betray Christ—14:10-11

B. Mark records the events of the Passover observance—14:12-25

1. Mark records the sending of the two disciples by Jesus in order to make the proper arrangements for the Passover—14:12-16
2. Mark records the announcement by Christ that one of the disciples would betray Him—14:17-21
3. Mark records the institution of the Lord's Supper and the relation of His blood to the ratification of the New Covenant—14:22-25

C. Mark records the events in the Garden of Gethsemane—14:26-52

1. Jesus makes three revelations as they are en route to the garden—14:26-31
2. Mark notes the agony of Christ in the garden—14:32-42
3. Mark notes the betrayal and arrest of Christ as well as the forsaking of Him by the disciples—14:43-52

D. Mark records the events surrounding the trials of Jesus together with the denials by Peter, and the mockery of the soldiers—14:53-15:20

1. Mark notes the trial of Christ before the Sanhedrin in which Christ affirms His sonship for which He is struck for blasphemy—14:53-65

Note #27: The trials of Jesus

The Six Trials of Christ		
Type of Trial	**Charge**	**Details**
Religious Trials	Blasphemy	**Annas:** John 18—He was the father-in-law of Caiaphas the high priest who questioned Him about His disciples and doctrine to determine what course the leaders would follow. He sent Christ to Caiaphas.
		Caiaphas: Matt. 26; Mark 14; Luke 22; John 18—He asked Christ to say if He was the Son of God. When Jesus answered in the affirmative, He ripped his garments because of blasphemy.

		Sanhedrin: Matt. 27; Mark 15; Luke 22—Here Christ told them that He was the Christ for which they sentenced Him to death.
Civil Trials	Treason	**Pilate:** Matt. 27; Mark 15; Luke 23; John 18—Christ said that He was the King of the Jews but this was no threat to Pilate so he sought to release Him. Pilate saw that the crowds did not want Him released and was afraid of their threat to tell Caesar.
		Herod: Luke 23—When Pilate had heard that Herod was in town from Galilee, he saw this as a chance to get out of his predicament so he sent him to Herod who was in Jerusalem and declared him innocent.
		Pilate: Matt. 27; Mark 15; Luke 23; John 18-19—Herod sent Christ back to Pilate who found Him innocent again but gave Him over to the crowd anyway.

2. Mark records the three denials of Peter and his subsequent remorse—14:66-72
3. Mark records the trial before Pilate—15:1-15
4. Mark records the mockery by the soldiers—15:16-20

E. Mark presents the account of the crucifixion—15:21-41

1. Mark notes the procession to Golgotha including the carrying of the cross by Simon and the offering of the drink to Jesus—15:21-23
2. Mark notes His agony on the cross which climaxes in the confession of the Roman centurion that this was the Son of God—15:24-39
3. Mark notes that there were many faithful women standing within view—15:40-41

F. Mark presents the account of His burial—15:42-47

IV. MARK PRESENTS THE RESURRECTION OF THE SERVANT IN ORDER TO VALIDATE HIS DEITY AND SHOW THAT THE LIFE OF DISCIPLESHIP AND SERVICE WILL BE REWARDED IN THE END—16:1-8

A. Mark records the arrival at the tomb of the women who discover that He has risen from the dead—16:1-8

Note #28: The disputed ending of Mark

There is serious manuscript debate as to whether Mark 16:9-20 should be included in the text. This could be the major textual problem in the New Testament.

Some evidence for the long ending:

1. *The scribe of B left a blank column after verse 8 suggesting he knew of an ending.*
2. *Mark would have been expected to include a resurrection appearance.*
3. *The versions and late MSS include it.*
4. *Ireneaus, Tatian, and Justin Martyr accepted it.*
5. *The majority of MSS include including A, C, D, K, X, etc., as well as the lectionaries.*

Some evidence against the long ending

1. *The Sinaiticus and Vaticanus (a and B the two oldest Greek uncials) omit 9-20.*
2. *Jerome, Eusebius, Origen, and Clement do not take it.*
3. *About 1/3 of the significant words are non-Marcan.*
4. *The Greek is not vivid.*
5. *Matthew and Luke parallel Mark until verse 8 and then diverge.*
6. *There is a description of Mary in verse 9 after a description in verse 1.*
7. *There is a different word for "week" in verses 2 and 9.*
8. *It is absent in most Armenian and Ethiopic versions.*

It is the opinion of the writer that the evidence favors the fact that the long ending was not part of the original. If this is the case, there still remains the difficulty as to whether Mark intended to end his Gospel at verse 8, or if he finished it and that part was lost. It is the writer's view that Mark purposely finished his gospel at verse 8. Verses 9-20 were written by an anonymous writer and added. Though not written by Mark, they are still historically and doctrinally accurate. This fact would explain why there was no attempt to match the vocabulary, etc. Be that as it may, given the difficulty of the question, the passage should be included in modern translations as long as it is noted that it may not be authentic. "The prevailing view in contemporary scholarship is that Mark intended to end his Gospel with v. 8. The problem then becomes to explain why he did so" (James Brooks, Mark, *New American Commentary [Nashville: Broadman & Holman Publishers, 1991], 274). Wessell concurs by stating "both the external and internal evidence are clearly against the authenticity of this ending [the long ending]" (Walter Wessell, "Mark" in* The Expositor's Bible Commentary *[Grand Rapids: Zondervan, 1984], 8:791). For further discussion, see any scholarly commentary on Mark, Bruce Metzger,* A Textual Commentary on the Greek New Testament *(NY: United Bible Societies, 1971), 122-126; James White,* The King James Only Controversy: Can You Trust the Modern Translations? *(Minneapolis: Bethany House, 1995), 255-257.*

B. *Christ appears to Mary Magdalene but the disciples refuse to believe—16:9-11*
C. *Christ appears to two followers but the rest do not believe until Christ later appears to them and rebukes them for their unbelief—16:12-14*
D. *Christ commissions His disciples—16:15-18*
E. *Christ's ascension—16:19-20*

LUKE

Author

Neither Luke nor Acts directly states who the author was. The only places in the New Testament where Luke is mentioned is Colossians 4:14, 2 Timothy 4:11, Philemon 24, and the "we" sections of Acts. Despite this fact, there are a number of reasons which support Lucan authorship of Luke.

A. External Evidence - Lucan authorship is attested in the early church by the Muratorian Canon, the Anti-Marcinonite Prologue (ca. AD 160-200), Irenaeus (*Against Heresies*), Tertullian of Carthage (*Against Marcion*), Clement of Alexandria, Origen, Eusebius, and Jerome (see Hiebert, *An Introduction of the New Testament,* 114-117).

B. Internal Evidence - As in many cases, the internal evidence does not prove a particular author but it does add solid support for external tradition.

1. A unity of authorship between Luke and Acts is evident for several reasons: both are dedicated to Theophilus, the reference in Acts 1:1 to the "first account" is most naturally understood as the gospel of Luke, there is a strong similarity in language and style, and both have common interests.

2. The "we" sections of Acts suggest that the author was an eye-witness and traveling companion of Paul. Only Titus and Luke are mentioned in Acts as close companions of Paul.

Date

While a number of dates have been suggested for the time of writing, a date before AD 60 (ca. 58-60) is the most likely for several reasons: 1) Acts does not mention the fall of Jerusalem (AD 70), Paul's death (AD 65-66), Nero's persecution (AD 64), or the death of James (AD 62). Luke must have written prior to these dates since it was written before Acts, and 2) Luke used primary sources.

Origin and Destination

The suggestions for the origin of the book are pure conjecture. Regarding the destination, it is stated in the prologue that the book is written to the individual Theophilus.

Characteristics

1. Luke wrote primarily for Gentiles. This is seen from the facts that he explains Jewish locales (4:31; 8:26; 21:37; 23:51; 24:13), he traces the genealogy of Christ back to Adam rather than to Abraham as does Matthew, he refers to Roman emperors in the birth accounts, he uses words which would be more familiar to Gentiles, he quotes from the LXX (2:23-24; 3:4-6; 4:4, 8; 7:27; 10:27; 18:20; 20:17; 22:37), there is very little said about the fulfillment of prophecy, he substitutes Greek for Aramaic terms, and he omits the Hosanna cry in the triumphal entry.

2. Luke speaks about the universality of the Gospel. This is implied in the preceding point, but is also seen by his references to sinners, the poor and the outcast, Samaritans, women, and children.

3. Luke has the most distinctive material from the other Synoptics (over 50%).

4. Luke emphasizes forgiveness (3:3; 5:18-26; 6:37; 7:36-50; 11:4; 12:10). This is probably in keeping with his stress on the Gentiles and the universality of the Gospel.

5. Luke emphasizes prayer (3:21; 5:16; 6:12; 9:18, etc.).

6. Luke says a lot about money.

7. Luke contains 17 (18 counting the rich man and Lazarus) unique parables.

Purposes

From the content of the book, it appears that there are at least two demonstrable purposes. The first is to confirm the faith of Theophilus (1:1-4). It is important to note that he is not writing to inform Theophilus, but rather to convince him and edify him that the faith rests on a sure foundation. The second purpose is seen by the presentation of Christ as the Son of Man to the Gentiles. Because Christ had been rejected by Israel, He is now being presented to the Gentiles for their acceptance. Thus there appears to be both a historical purpose (relating to Theophilus) and a theological purpose (relating to the Gentile world). A synthetic purpose statement could be stated in these words: Luke records selected events from the life of Christ in order to confirm Theophilus in the faith and to present Christ as the Son of Man to the Gentile world so that they would know that they are included in the Kingdom program and offered salvation.

Summary of Argument

I. LUKE PRESENTS THE PROLOGUE TO HIS GOSPEL IN WHICH HE STATES THAT AS OTHERS HAD WRITTEN CONCERNING THE GOSPEL SO HE WAS DOING THE SAME THAT THEOPHILUS WOULD BE CONFIRMED IN THE FAITH BY THE PRESENTATION OF THE GOSPEL IN A RELIABLE FASHION—1:1-4

Note #29: Luke's sources

The sources used by Luke have been of interest. It appears that there are several sources from which he could have drawn. These include the apostles who were spreading the gospel message, personal contact with Paul (who had contact with Peter, James, and John), Philip and Agabus whom he met in Jerusalem (Acts 21), written records, oral traditions, and eyewitnesses, etc. Whichever sources Luke used, it is certain that his information was accurate and penned under the supervision of the Spirit. For a full and critical discussion of how Luke's sources affect the Synoptic problem related to interdependence, the Augustinian hypothesis, Griesbach hypothesis, and the four-source theory, see Darrell Bock, Luke 1:1-9:50 *(Grand Rapids: Baker, 1999), 7-12. For the historical reliability of the gospels and the New Testament as a whole, see J. Ed Komoszewski, M. James Sawyer, and Daniel B. Wallace,* Reinventing Jesus: What the DaVinci Code and other Novel Speculations don't Tell You *(Grand Rapids: Kregel, 2006).*

Note #30: "In order" (KJV)

When Luke says that he wrote "in order," this does not necessarily mean that he was attempting to present a strict chronological order. Rather, he meant that he was presenting a narrative which would be a connected whole. Thus, he was giving an account which formed a logical package so that it would be worthy of belief.

II. LUKE PRESENTS THE BIRTH AND CHILDHOOD NARRATIVES OF JOHN THE BAPTIST AND JESUS IN ORDER TO STRESS THEIR HISTORICITY AND SUPERNATURAL CHARACTER TO SHOW THE GENTILES THAT CHRIST WAS IDENTIFIED WITH ALL MEN TO PROVIDE FOR THEIR SALVATION THROUGH HIS IDENTITY WITH THE OLD TESTAMENT COVENANTS—1:5-2:52

A. Luke records the events surrounding the announcement of the birth of John the Baptist—1:5-25

1. Luke introduces the parents of John the Baptist, Zacharias and Elizabeth, in order to show their righteous character—1:5-7

Note #31: Zacharias

Zacharias was of the priestly division of Abijah. Since the time of David (for about 1000 years) the priests were divided into 24 groups who performed their duties two separate weeks each year. The course of Abijah was eighth in the list in 1 Chronicles 24:10. After the Babylonian exile, only a few orders existed, but the surviving priests were again divided into 24 orders with their original names. One of the prized duties of a priest was the offering of incense in the temple. According to Geikie, this was done only once in the lifetime of a priest and was determined by lot (Cunningham Geikie, The Life and Words of Christ *[NY: Appleton, 1893], 86-87). On this occasion the lot had fallen on Zacharias. Bock adds these details: "Zechariah is performing the greatest ministry of his priestly career. At this special moment, God makes an announcement for the pious priest and for the nation of God's people. By the casting of lots Zechariah received the honor of giving the sacrifice. The custom of casting lots—required because of the large number of priests—occurred twice a day to determine which priest would offer the incense with the whole burnt offering. Only once in his life would a priest receive the special honor of offering incense in the Holy Place as part of the preparation for the sacrificial offering (Bock,* Luke 1:1-9:50, *79). The drama of the event is portrayed by Shepard, "Zacharias entered the Holy Place, lit by the sheen of the seven-branched candle-stick on the right, bearing in his hand the golden censer. On his left was the table of shew-bread. In front of him beyond the altar was the thick curtain which separated the Holy of Holies. The people outside were prostrate in silent worship. Zacharias alone in the Holy Place awaited the kindling of the incense on the altar, when he too would bow in worship and then withdraw in reverence" (J. W. Shepard,* The Christ of the Gospels *[Grand Rapids: Eerdmans, 1946], 20-21).*

2. Luke presents the angelic announcement to Zacharias—1:8-23
3. Luke presents the pregnancy of Elizabeth—1:24-25

B. Luke records the events surrounding the announcement of the birth of Jesus—1:26-56

1. Luke introduces the parents of Jesus by noting that they were in the betrothal period and that Mary was a virgin—1:26-27
2. Luke presents the angelic announcement to Mary—1:28-38
   a. Luke notes that Mary was "highly favored" by which he did not mean that she was immaculate, but rather that she was being blessed with a special honor and privilege, namely that of bearing the Messiah—1:28-31
   b. Gabriel predicts several characteristics of the Messiah—1:32-33
   c. Mary was confused how this would happen since she was a virgin to which the angel explains that this would be the work of the Holy Spirit—1:34-38
3. Luke records the visit of Mary to Elizabeth's house—1:39-56
   a. Luke notes the joyous meeting between Mary and Elizabeth concerning the news they had been given—1:39-45
   b. Mary responds with a song of praise to God in order to demonstrate the Messiahship of Christ—1:46-55

C. Luke records the births and childhoods of John and Jesus—1:57-2:52
1. Luke presents the birth and childhood of John—1:57-80
   a. Luke notes the events surrounding the birth of John the Baptist including his naming, the obedience to the Law by his parents concerning his circumcision, and the awareness of the people that he was an unusual child—1:57-66
   b. Luke records the prophecy and psalm of Zechariah in order to show that the Messiah had come to fulfill the covenants of the Old Testament—1:67-79
   c. Luke records that John grew in the privacy of the desert until the day he started his ministry to Israel—1:80
2. Luke presents the birth and childhood of Jesus in order to show His link with humanity as the Son of Man and as divine so as to be the Savior of man—2:1-52
   a. Luke records the birth of Jesus—2:1-7

Note #32: When was Jesus born?

Christ was born during the reign of Caesar Augustus who reigned from 44 BC to AD 14. Within this limit, the earliest point for Christ's birth was the census of Quirinius and the latest point is the death of Herod the Great. According to Matthew 2:1 and Luke 1:5, Christ's birth came before Herod's death which was in 4 BC. Thus, Christ could not have been born later than 4 BC. According to Luke 2, a census was taken just before Christ's birth, so He could not have been born before the census. Luke states that the census took place before Quirinius was governor of Syria (AD 6-7 and possibly 3-2 BC). The exact year of the census was probably between 6-4 BC since Matthew and Luke indicate that the census and Christ's birth were shortly before Herod's death. Thus Christ was probably born in 5-4 BC.

Oddly therefore, Christ was born "before Christ." The reason for this is traceable back to a sixth century individual named Dionysius Exiguus. He estimated Christ's birth to be 755 years after Rome's foundation. Though this date was off by several years and later rejected, it has become the basis of the Anno Domini *calendar (L. Feehan, "Dionysius Exiguus," in* The New International Dictionary of the Christian Church *[Grand Rapids: Zondervan, 1981], 300).*

Another chronological problem revolves around Luke's statement that Quirinius was governor of Syria (AD 6-7) which was too late for Jesus' birth. Therefore, does the word "first" in 2:2 refer to an earlier census? This would mean that one would have to posit an earlier governorship for Quirinius around 4 BC. Another possible solution is to take "first" to mean "former" or "prior." The verse would then read "this was the census that took place before Quirinius was governor of Syria" (i.e., before AD 6).

Note #33: Lactantius on the Roman census

Lactantius (c.240-c.320) was a Roman convert to Christianity who became a foremost apologist in the Christian church. Schaff includes him in a list consisting of the most important Latin defenders of the faith (Philip Schaff, History of the Christian Church: Volume II Ante-Nicene Christianity A.D. 100-*325 [Grand Rapids: Eerdmans, 1980], 105) while his style earned him the title "the Christian Cicero" (C. Peter Williams, "Lactantius," in* The New International Dictionary of the Christian Church *[Grand Rapids: Zondervan, 1981], 575). In his work entitled* De mortibus persectuorum, *Chapter XXIII, Lactantius describes a Roman census.*

"But that which gave rise to public and universal calamity, was the tax imposed at once on each province and city. Surveyors having been spread abroad, and occupied in a general and severe scrutiny, horrible scenes were exhibited, like the outrages of victorious enemies, and the wretched state of captives. Each spot of ground was measured, vines and fruit-trees numbered, lists taken of animals of every kind, and a capitation-roll made up. In cities, the common people, whether residing within or without the walls, were assembled, the market-places filled with crowds of families, all attended with their children and slaves, the noise of torture and scourges resounded, sons were hung on the rack to force discovery of the effects of their fathers, the most trusty slaves compelled by pain to bear witness against their masters, and wives to bear witness against their husbands, In default of all other evidence, men were tortured to speak against themselves; and no sooner did agony oblige them to acknowledge what they had not, but those imaginary effects were noted down in the lists. Neither youth, nor old age, nor sickness, afforded any exemption. The diseased and the infirm were carried in; the age of each was estimated; and, that the capitation-tax might be enlarged, years were added to the young and struck off from the old. General lamentation and sorrow prevailed. Whatever, by the laws of war, conquerors had done to the conquered, the like did this man presume to perpetrate against Romans and the subjects of Rome, because his forefathers had been made liable to a like tax imposed by the victorious Trajan, as a penalty on the Dacians for their frequent rebellions. After this, money was levied for each head, as if a price had been paid for liberty to exist; yet full trust was not reposed on the same set of surveyors, but others and others still were sent round to make further discoveries; and thus the tributes were redoubled, not because the new surveyors made any fresh discoveries, but because they added at pleasure to the former rates, lest they should seem to have been employed to no purpose. Meanwhile the number of animals decreased, and men died; nevertheless taxes were paid even for the dead, so that no one could either live or cease to live without being subject to impositions. There remained mendicants alone, from whom nothing could be exacted, and whom their misery and

wretchedness secured from ill-treatment. But this pious man had compassion on them, and determining that they should remain no longer in indigence, he caused them all to be assembled, put on board vessels, and sunk in the sea. So merciful was he in making provision that under his administration no man should want! And thus, while he took effectual measures that none, under the reigned pretext of poverty, should elude the tax, he put to death a multitude of real wretches, in violation of every law of humanity" (Roberts, Alexander, James Donaldson, and A. Cleveland Coxe, eds. Fathers of the Third and Fourth Centuries: Lactantius, Venantius, Asterius, Victorinus, Dionysius, Apostolic Teaching and Constitutions, Homily, and Liturgies. *Vol. 7. The Ante-Nicene Fathers. Buffalo, NY: Christian Literature Company, 1886). Logos 5.*

Note #34: A second look at the first Christmas

Is it possible that the birth of Christ has too often been viewed through Western eyes rather than Middle Eastern eyes? Is it conceivable that this bias has trumped the culture behind and the meaning of the Matthean/Lukan birth narratives? While the birth of a baby is a joyous occasion in all civilized cultures, is it likely that the people of Bethlehem were so heartless that they would not help a woman give birth; leading Joseph and Mary to find the lonely quarters of an animal stable to have their child? Consider the following observations:

1. Luke indicates in 2:6 that after Joseph and Mary arrive in Bethlehem, "the days were accomplished that she should be delivered." Thus, there was a space of time (some suggest as long as a month) after their arrival before Jesus was born. The idea that they arrive at night scurrying around to find a place for the birth is not found in the passage. The fact they would have been in Bethlehem for a period of time before Christ was born argues for the thesis in this note that Christ was born in a house.

2. There is strong evidence to submit the idea that Christ was born in a private home and not a stable based on the following facts:

a) Family members were culturally bound to help those to whom they were related. This is not dissimilar to our Western culture.

b) The word translated "inn" (ESV, KJV, NKJV, NASB, NIV, NLT, NRSV) is κατάλυμα and would best be translated as "guest room." Bailey lists six reasons why the translation of "inn" is not adequate (Kenneth Bailey, "The Manger and the Inn: The Cultural Background of Luke 2:7," Bible and Spade *20:4 [Fall 2007], 104).*

1) *The word for a commercial inn (πανδοχεῖον—Luke 10:34) also translated as "inn" is not the word used in the Luke 2 text.*
2) *The only other uses of the Luke 2 term (κατάλυμα) in the Bible are Luke 22:11 and Mark 14:14 where it does not refer to an "inn," but to a "guest room." Interestingly, all of the versions translate it as such,*
3) *A man returning to his home village would have insulted his family by going to an "inn."*
4) *There is no evidence there were any inns in Bethlehem. Bailey notes that "We are not aware of any evidence for a commercial inn near or in the village after the exile. Inns, then as now, were found on major roads. No major Roman road passed through Bethlehem, and small villages on minor roads had no inns" (104).*

5) *It was not culturally acceptable to have a child in an inn. Yet, the text does not say that the κατάλυμα was inappropriate for the birth, but that it was full.*
6) *For 1,900 years Syriac and Arabic versions have never translated the term as "inn."*

c) It was not unusual for peasant homes to consist of a main floor where animals were kept at night, a raised terrace where the family slept and lived, and at times an adjacent guest room. When Mary and Joseph arrived, the guest room was occupied. Regarding the terrace, Bailey writes, "The raised terrace on which the family ate, slept and lived was unsoiled by the animals, and taken out each day and during which time the lower level was cleaned. Their presence was in no way offensive" (105), since animals were kept on the main floor of the house, feeding troughs were built into the floor (see also R. T. France, The Evidence for Jesus [Downers Grove, IL: InterVarsity Press, 1986], 159. For an alternative view that Christ was born in a stable adjacent to the house see Verlyn Verbrugge, A Not-So-Silent Night (Grand Rapids: Kregel, 2009), 57.

3. The magi, who were not kings (see "Matthew" note #3), arrive well after Jesus was born and visit him in a house (Matt. 2:11). This not only shows that they were not present when Jesus was a baby, but also lends support to the idea that Jesus was born in a house.

4. There was probably no star or meteor guiding the magi to Bethlehem (which was only a few miles from Jerusalem). The word translated "star" (ἀστήρ) simply refers to a "luminous body visible in the sky." This could refer to an angel which is a common use of the term in Revelation. In addition, angels are prominently involved in previous aspects of the birth narrative (Matthew 1 and Luke 2). The way the "star" moves in guiding them to the house and resting over it seems an unlikely description of a meteor, etc. However, for an alternate explanation as to how Jupiter could have remained almost stationary for three hours, see "The Star of the Magi and Babylonian Astronomy," in Chronos, Kairos, Christos: Nativity and Chronological Studies Presented to Jack Finegan *(Eisenbrauns, 1989), 49; and, for other options including a supernova, comet, or planetary conjunction, see Raymond Brown, The Birth of the Messiah, 171-173.*

5. Despite the words of "Away in a Manger" ("no crying he makes"), though without sin, Christ came to earth as a human baby doing all of the things babies do.

b. Luke records the announcement to the shepherds of Jesus' birth and their subsequent worship of Him in order to show that the salvation of the Messiah extended to the most lowly—2:8-20

Note #35: Peace on earth, good will toward men (?)

Only the King James Version translates Luke 2:14 as "Glory to God in the highest and on earth peace, good will toward men." All other versions have something like "peace with whom he is pleased," or "peace on whom his favor rests." The KJV follows the inferior textual tradition of the Textus Receptus *which has the nominative form of "good will" (εὐδοκία), thus making it the subject of the clause (interestingly, Theodore Beza who followed Erasmus' TR reading of this text, included a note disputing it). However, the other versions follow the oldest manuscripts which have the genitive form of the term (εὐδοκίας). Generally speaking, other than King James Only advocates, the latter reading is accepted by scholars. Besides the textual arguments, Bock summarizes the essence of the phrase," God's peace extends to...men of his good pleasure, which is almost a technical phrase in first-century Judaism for God's elect, those on whom God has poured out his favor...Thus, to argue that the term should be seen as broad, almost universal, in light of 2:10 fails to note its technical force. It also fails to note the difference between those whom Jesus comes for (all people 2:10) and those who benefit from his coming (men of his good pleasure; 2:14)" (Bock,* Luke 1:1-9:50, *220).*

c. Luke records the circumcision of Jesus in order to show that Jesus was placed in the sphere of the Abrahamic Covenant who was thus eligible to fulfill its promises—2:21

d. Luke records the presentation of Jesus in the temple and the obedience to the Law by His parents in order to show that Jesus was the perfect man thus prepared to complete His mission—2:22-38

e. Luke records the growth of Jesus in Nazareth in order to stress His humanity and also the fact that the Spirit of God was with Him—2:39-40

f. Luke records the visit of Jesus and his parents to the temple to observe the Passover in order to stress that Jesus was aware of His mission as Messiah and to show that as the perfect man, He was obedient and submissive to parental authority—2:41-50

g. Luke notes His continued growth again emphasizing His obedience and development—2:51-52

III. LUKE PRESENTS THE MINISTRY OF JOHN THE BAPTIST, THE BAPTISM, GENEALOGY, AND TEMPTATION OF JESUS IN ORDER TO SHOW THE PERFECT PREPARATION OF CHRIST IN ANTICIPATION OF HIS MINISTRY—3:1-4:13

A. Luke records the events in the ministry of John the Baptist in order to show how he performed the introductory preparation for the ministry of Christ—3:1-20

1. Luke presents an introduction to the ministry of John the Baptist—3:1-6

a. Luke briefly describes the political scene at the time of John and that while he was in the wilderness the word of the Lord came to him—3:1-2

b. Luke notes that John preached repentance and the forgiveness of sin—3:3

c. Luke associates John's ministry with Isaiah 40:3-5 (which speaks of God smoothing the way for the return of the exiles from Babylon to Judah) in order to show that as His messenger, John was clearing the path for the Messiah—3:4-6

2. Luke presents the message John preached to the multitudes—3:7-14

a. John challenges the people to bring forth fruit which demonstrated true repentance and that merely being related to God ethnically did not bring salvation—3:7-9

b. John gives three evidences the people could show to demonstrate true repentance: generosity, honesty, and contentment—3:10-14

3. Luke presents the role of John in relation to Christ in order to show that he was not the Christ—3:15-17

a. Luke notes that the people were musing whether John was the Messiah or not—3:15
b. Luke notes that their ministry was different by pointing out the differences between their baptisms—3:16-17

Note #36: Baptism by fire

The baptism by fire could refer either to the purifying aspect of the spirit baptism at Pentecost or to the purifying work of judgment that the Messiah would accomplish (Mal. 3:2-3). Due to the context in 3:9 and 3:17, the latter is probably in view.

4. Luke records that John was imprisoned by Herod—3:18-20

B. Luke records the baptism of Christ in order to show the beginning of His ministry, His anointing with the Spirit for that ministry, and His approval by the Father who refers to Psalm 2:7 and Isaiah 42:1—3:21-22

C. Luke records the genealogy of Jesus back to Adam in order to stress the universality of the Gospel which Jesus came to present and His identification with the whole human race—3:23-28

D. Luke records the temptation of Christ in order to show that Christ was the perfect Son of Man who overcame temptation and submitted to the will of God and was thus fit to offer salvation to the whole world— 4:1-13

1. Luke notes that Jesus was led by the Spirit into the wilderness—4:1-2
2. Luke notes that Jesus resists the temptation in the realm of physical need—4:3-4
3. Luke notes that Jesus resists the temptation in the realm of glory and dominion—4:5-8
4. Luke notes that Jesus resists the temptation in the realm of gaining the acceptance of the people without going to the cross—4:9-13

IV. LUKE PRESENTS THE MINISTRY OF JESUS IN GALILEE IN ORDER TO AUTHENTICATE THE MINISTRY OF CHRIST BY HIS MIRACLES, TO SHOW HIS AUTHORITY IN CALLING DISCIPLES, AND TO SHOW THE EXTENSION OF HIS MESSAGE TO THE GENTILES IN LIGHT OF JEWISH OPPOSITION—4:14-9:50

A. Luke presents a trend in the ministry of Jesus which included His declaration of His Messiahship, His rejection by the Jews, and His inclusion of the Gentiles in salvation in order to show the universality of His message—4:14-30

1. Luke notes that the initial response to Jesus' Spirit-filled ministry was one of reception—4:14-15
2. Jesus proclaims His Messiahship by reading Isaiah 61:1-2 in His hometown of Nazareth which is rejected by the people —4:16-24
3. Because of their rejection, Jesus gives two examples (Elijah and the widow of Zarephath) of grace which was shown to Gentiles during a period of Jewish unbelief at which the people became furious—4:25-30

B. Luke presents a series of miracles and calls to discipleship in order to validate His person and authority in the light of Jewish rejection—4:31-6:16

1. Luke validates Christ's authority by presenting three miracles of healing, a statement about Christ's ministry, and Christ's calling of His first disciples—4:31-5:11
    - **a.** Jesus heals a man with an unclean spirit—4:31-37
    - **b.** Jesus heals Peter's mother-in-law—4:38-39
    - **c.** Jesus heals scores of people with demons and sicknesses—4:40-41
    - **d.** Jesus told the people that He had to move on to other areas for His ministry needed to extend to all people—4:42-44
    - **e.** Luke records the calling of disciples—5:1-11
2. Luke validates Christ's authority by presenting two miracles of healing and the call of Matthew to discipleship—5:12-39
    - **a.** Luke describes the healing of a leper—5:12-16
    - **b.** Luke describes the healing and forgiveness of a paralytic—5:17-26
    - **c.** Luke describes the call of Matthew and the subsequent banquet to show that Jesus came to call all of the unrighteous to repentance and salvation and that His way did not mix with that of the religious leaders—5:27-39
3. Luke records a Sabbath controversy consisting of the disciples picking of grain and the healing of a man in order to show that Jesus had authority over the Sabbath and the incident of the calling of the twelve in order to further show His authority—6:1-16
    - **a.** Luke records the controversy over the harvesting of the grain on the Sabbath in order to show that Jesus had authority over the Sabbath—6:1-5
    - **b.** Luke records the healing of a man by Christ on the Sabbath—6:6-11
    - **c.** Luke records the calling of the twelve—6:12-16

C. Luke records a portion of the Sermon on the Mount in order to show how the disciples He has called, and all others who would follow him, should conduct their lives—6:17-49

Note #37: The Sermon on the Plain

It is probably best to understand the "Sermon on the Plain" as a condensed version of the same sermon recorded by Matthew (5-7). Both of the sermons contain the same beatitudes, have the same parables at the end, and have the same general content. The reason this statement is problematic is the location of its presentation as recorded by Matthew (on a mountainside) and by Luke (on a level place). This then raises the problem of sources, etc. A suggested solution has been presented in the following sequence of events (Norval Geldenhuys, The Gospel of Luke *[Grand Rapids: Eerdmans, 1979], 209): Jesus went up in the hills to pray (6:12). He then called the twelve apostles. He then went down on a level place to talk and heal diseases (6:17-19). After this, He went up higher to get away from the crowds and teach the disciples (Matt. 5:1). The multitudes climbed the mountain and heard the sermon (Matt. 7:28; Luke 7:1). It is significant to note that Luke, writing to Gentiles, omits certain Jewish parts of the sermon such as the interpretation of the Law.*

1. Luke presents the setting of the sermon to be on a plain where Jesus is pressed by the crowds for healing—6:17-19
2. Jesus presents a series of contrasted blessings and woes in order to show His disciples what kind of character they should have and under what conditions they would be blessed—6:20-26
   a. Jesus presents a series of blessings—6:20-23
      1) Blessed are the ones who are poor—6:20
      2) Blessed are the ones who hunger now—6:21a
      3) Blessed are the ones who weep now—6:21b
      4) Blessed are the ones who are persecuted—6:22-23
   b. Jesus presents a series of woes—6:24-26
      1) Woe to those who are rich—6:24
      2) Woe to those who are well fed now—6:25a
      3) Woe to those who laugh now—6:25b
      4) Woe to those who are well-liked now—6:26
3. Jesus presents an exposition of what true righteousness is—6:27-45
   a. He notes that true righteousness is characterized by love and mercy—6:27-38
      1) Love is unconditional and is not based on anything that will be received in return—6:27-35
         a) He said to love your enemies—6:27a
         b) He said to do good to those who hate you—6:27b
         c) He said to bless those who curse you—6:28a
         d) He said to pray for those who mistreat you—6:28b
         e) He said to not retaliate—6:29a
         f) He said to freely give—6:29b-30
         g) He said to treat people the way you want to be treated—6:31-35
      2) Mercy should be shown to others and is reciprocal—6:36-38
         a) Mercy leads to mercy—6:36
         b) Judgment leads to judgment—6:37a
         c) Condemnation leads to condemnation—6:37b
         d) Pardon leads to pardon—6:37c
         e) Giving leads to giving—6:38
   b. He notes that true righteousness would be revealed by actions—6:39-45
4. Jesus states that a true follower would act on the words He had spoken—6:46-49
   a. Obedience is more important than mere words—6:46
   b. Jesus notes that the one who acts on His words is secure but the one who does not would be destroyed—6:47-49

D. Luke records some further incidents in Jesus' ministry in Capernaum and surrounding cities including miracles and teaching in order to authenticate that He was the Messiah and had the authority to teach the people—7:1-8:56
1. Luke records the miracles of the healing of a centurion's servant and the raising of a widow's son in order to show that Jesus was the Messiah and to provide a basis for His teaching authority—7:1-17
   a. Jesus heals the servant of a centurion in order to show the necessity of having faith in His Person and that His ministry extended to the

Gentiles—7:1-10

b. Jesus raises a widow's son from the dead in order to provide the basis for His subsequent teaching—7:11-17

2. Luke records the teaching of Jesus in which He states that His miracles authenticate who He is—7:18-35

a. Luke notes that John the Baptist was confused as to whether Christ was the Messiah because the Kingdom had not been established—7:18-20

b. Luke notes that Jesus sends John's messengers back to him to tell him of the miracles that had been occurring (Isaiah 61:1-2) in order to demonstrate to him that He was the Messiah because He was performing Messianic works—7:21-23

c. Jesus commends John's ministry to the people by stating that He was not just another religious prophet but was the forerunner of the Messiah—7:24-29

d. Jesus condemns the Pharisees for their rejection of John's and His ministry—7:30-35

3. Jesus had just said (7:35) that the ones who were following Jesus and John were proof of the correctness of their teaching and now He provides a contrast to prove this point—7:36-50

a. He speaks of a Pharisee who had Him over to dinner but did not arrange to have His feet washed—7:36

b. A "sinful" woman proceeded to wash and anoint His feet—7:37-38

c. The Pharisee became skeptical that Jesus was a prophet otherwise He would not have let a sinner touch Him—7:39

d. In response to the thought of the Pharisee, Jesus told the parable of the two debtors in which He taught that one who has been forgiven more loves more—7:40-43

e. Jesus noted that the woman showed love to Him because of her realization of her forgiveness, but on the other hand, Simon did not treat Jesus in a special manner thus showing his feeling of righteousness—7:44-50

4. Jesus continues to build on the preceding points by noting the different responses to His ministry—8:1-21

a. Luke notes a band of women who had responded positively to Jesus' ministry—8:1-3

Note #38: How to interpret a parable

Luke includes more of Jesus' parables in his gospel than any of the other gospel writers. The Greek word for "parable" (παραβολή) occurs forty-eight times in the Synoptics. The word is derived from the verb παραβάλλω which means "to throw alongside" or "to compare." The idea is that something is thrown alongside a truth in order to illustrate that truth. Most commonly the word parable refers to a true-to-life story, but the term also is used to refer to similitudes, proverbs, or even riddles. The key term to remember for a parable is comparison. *This comparison will come through a story. Here are some good, more technical definitions:*

> *A parable is a composed story that describes a particular situation analogous to some theological truth* (E. Linnemann, *Jesus of the Parables: Introduction and*

Exposition [NY: Harper & Row, 1966], 3-8).

The typical parable uses a common event of natural life to emphasize or clarify an important spiritual truth (Henry Virkler, *Hermeneutics: Principles and Processes of Biblical Interpretation* [Grand Rapids: Baker Academic, 2007], 152).

A parable is ultimately a literary, rhetorical form of argument. Its purposes include instructing believers, hiding truth from those who reject the message, and shocking the listener through its imagery into reconsidering how one sees the world and God (Darrell Bock, *Luke 1:1-9:50* [Grand Rapids: Baker, 1999], 947).

When interpreting a parable, four questions should be asked.

Question 1: *Why was the parable given?*

Question 2: *What are the cultural details of the parable?*

Question 3: *What is the main point of the parable?*

Question 4: *What is the desired response?*

Question 1: *When Jesus told a parable it was in response to a discussion or event which had just occurred. When we take note, therefore, of the verses just preceding the parable, or maybe an entire unit before the parable, this will often give us tremendous insight as to the parable's meaning. For example, the kingdom parables of Matthew 13 are given in response to the committing of the unpardonable sin by the leaders of Israel in chapter 12. In Luke 10:29 the question is asked: who is my neighbor? This is followed by the parable of the Good Samaritan. In Matthew 18:21 Peter asks Jesus how many times he should forgive his brother. Jesus responds with the parable of the unmerciful servant. The parable of the rich man and Lazarus was given because the Pharisees loved money.*

Question 2: *Since parables are drawn from everyday life—be it commercial, farming, domestic, or social referents—to make the most sense of the parable we need to understand those areas of life in first century, Palestinian culture.*

Question 3: *Throughout church history, there have been individuals who have come to the parables and allegorized every detail of the story with the result that the parable's meaning had little or no resemblance to why it was originally given. One of the most famous examples of this is Augustine's treatment of the parable of the Good Samaritan. And I would remind you that Augustine is considered to be one of the if not the greatest thinker in Christian history even having been elevated to one of the doctors of the church in the Roman Catholicism. Fee and Stuart summarize Augustine's interpretation (How to Read the Bible for All It's Worth [Grand Rapids: Zondervan, 2003], 150).*

the man going down to Jericho = Adam
Jerusalem = heavenly city from which Adam fell
Jericho = the moon (signifying Adam's mortality)
Robbers = the devil and his angels

stripping him = taking away his immortality
beating him = persuading him to sin
leaving him half-dead = as a man lives, but is dead spiritually, therefore he is half-dead
priest and Levite = priesthood and ministry of the Old Testament
the Samaritan = Christ
binding of the wounds = binding the restraint of sin
wine = exhortation to work with fervent spirit
beast = flesh of Christ's incarnation
the inn = the church
two denarii = promise of this life and life to come
innkeeper = the apostle Paul

*In opposition to this method of finding some kind of significance in every detail, many have argued that each parable makes one major point. Obviously, this approach is much better than the preceding. However, there is a third approach to be preferred. This approach has been championed by Craig Blomberg (*Introduction to Biblical Interpretation *[Nashville: Thomas Nelson, 2004], 413-414; Interpreting the Parables [Downers Grove and Leicester: InterVarsity], 1990) and the essential idea is that though there may be one fundamental point, there are subsidiary points which Jesus' audience would have understood. One can see this illustrated through the parable of the lost son in Luke 15. While the main thrust of the parable is to show God's attitude toward sinners, an unavoidable point is also being made about the Pharisees. The younger brother is being compared to the sinner; the older brother is being compared to the religious leaders.*

Question 4: *Often the desired response of a parable is discovered by noting how the parable ends.*

b. Luke cites Jesus' parable of the sower and the soils in order to illustrate the various responses to the Word—8:4-15
  1) Luke notes that a large crowd had gathered—8:4
  2) Jesus states that when the farmer sows the seed it could land on either the pathway, on rock, on soil with thorns, or on good soil which brought forth a crop—8:5-8
  3) Jesus explains to His disciples that He used the parabolic form of teaching in order to hide truth and reveal it—8:9-10
  4) Jesus explains that the four soils represent those who hear and do not believe, those who listen at first and then fall away, those who listen but are distracted, and those who listen and produce, respectively—8:11-15

c. Jesus gives the parable of the lamp in order to show that those who receive the Word should make it known in which case they would receive more insight—8:16-18

d. Luke notes the response of Jesus' family in order to show that all who responded to the Word were His family including Jew and Gentile—8:19-21

5. Jesus authenticates His teaching through a series of miracles—8:22-56

a. Jesus demonstrates His power over the natural realm by stilling the storm—8:22-25
b. Jesus demonstrates His power over the demonic realm by casting out demons—8:26-39
c. Jesus demonstrates His power over the physical realm by raising Jairus' daughter and by healing the woman with the issue of blood—8:40-56

E. Luke presents a series of lessons which Christ taught the disciples in order to prepare them for ministry—9:1-50
   1. Jesus commissions the twelve to the ministry—9:1-6
      a. Jesus gives them the authority to perform the miracles He was performing—9:1
      b. Jesus sent them to preach the Kingdom and to heal the sick—9:2
      c. Jesus instructed them not to take supplies because of the brevity of their mission and because their treatment would be an evidence of the people's faith—9:3-6
   2. Luke records Herod's inquiry about Jesus' ministry in order to show that their ministry was having an impact—9:7-9
   3. Luke records the feeding of the 5,000 in order to teach the disciples and the people that He was sufficient for meeting the needs of the nation—9:10-17
   4. Jesus asks the disciples who people thought He was to which Peter gives His great confession—9:18-21
   5. Jesus teaches the disciples that His ultimate mission was to die—9:22
   6. Jesus taught the disciples that they too should be ready to follow Him to death in order to show the disciples that their ministry was not wasted for they would be rewarded for their efforts—9:23-26
   7. Jesus is transfigured before the disciples in order to show them that even though they might go to death there would still be a Kingdom—9:27-36
      a. Luke records Jesus' pre-transfiguration prediction—9:27

Note #39: The pre-transfiguration prediction

There has been a great deal of debate over this pre-transfiguration prediction. Views on the matter include the resurrection view, the destruction of Jerusalem view, the advance of the Gospel view, and the transfiguration view. This latter view is probably best and states that the kingdom was seen in miniature during the transfiguration. There are a number of supports to this view: 1) all the synoptists place the transfiguration immediately before the event, 2) Jesus stated that "some" would not taste death. The fact that only three of the apostles saw this event fits much better with this view than the other ones, 3) Peter interpreted the significance of this event in 2 Peter 1:16-18 which He referred to as this experience, 4) this was the predominant view of the early church, and 5) the event is packed with eschatological terminology.

      b. Jesus is transfigured (*metamorphoo*)—9:28-29
      c. Moses and Elijah appear and talk with Christ about His exodus from the earth—9:30-31
      d. Peter asks about building three booths which he thought would be appropriate in view of the eschatological nature of the setting, but was

rebuked, not because he was wrong in fact, but in timing— 9:32-33

  - **e.** Luke notes that the Father voiced His divine approval of the Son—9:34-36

8. Jesus heals an epileptic boy in order to show the disciples that their power depended on Him—9:37-43

9. Jesus again teaches the disciples that He must die—9:44-45

10. Jesus teaches the disciples that the one who would be greatest in the Kingdom is the one who is characterized by service—9:46-48

11. Jesus rebukes a spirit of sectarianism among His disciples— 9:49-50

V. LUKE RECORDS THE EVENTS SURROUNDING THE JOURNEY OF JESUS TOWARD JERUSALEM IN ORDER TO SHOW HOW JESUS WAS NOT ACCEPTED BY MOST OF THE NATION AND THUS TO INSTRUCT THE DISCIPLES ON HOW THEY SHOULD LIVE IN THE LIGHT OF OPPOSITION—9:51-19:27

A. Luke presents how Jesus was rejected by most of the people climaxing in their accusation of Him having demonic power—9:51-11:54

1. Luke notes the rejection of the Samaritans of the ministry of the disciples and their desire to destroy their city with fire—9:51-56

2. Luke notes the meeting of Christ with three men in order to show that those who would be His disciples must make strong commitments—9:57-62

  - **a.** Jesus told the first man who wanted to follow Him that he must be willing to give up the comforts of life—9:57-58
  - **b.** A second man was willing to follow Jesus after he had buried his father but Jesus responded that the dead (spiritually) can bury the dead (physically) and that it was more important for him to follow—9:59-60
  - **c.** A third man wanted to say good-bye to those at home first, but Jesus told him that the ministry was so important that the one who follows Him must not go back but continue to move straight ahead—9:61-62

3. Luke notes the sending of messengers by Jesus so that they could spread His message—10:1-24

  - **a.** Luke records the choosing of the 72 (or 70) and Jesus' commissioning of them in which He told them that there would be opposition, they should depend on hospitality for their needs, and that whoever rejected them would be severely judged—10:1-12
  - **b.** Jesus pronounces woes on Chorazin and Bethsaida (representative of other nations) if they rejected the message of the 72 and that they would be more severely judged because of the light they had received—10:13-16
  - **c.** Luke records the return of the 72 to Jesus who were exuberant over the success of their ministry and Jesus reminds them that their real cause of rejoicing should be that their names are written in heaven—10:17-20
  - **d.** Jesus rejoices over the report of the 72 and tells them that they are blessed to be seeing the things they were seeing—10:21-24

4. Luke records the parable of the Good Samaritan which shows that one should meet a need he is able to meet in order to give a tangible expression of the kind of righteousness necessary to enter the Kingdom and perhaps to show, in light of Jesus' rejection, that He was like the Samaritan (an outcast) who was reaching out to help those who were in need—10:25-37

  a. Luke provides the setting for the parable—10:25-29

  b. Luke records the parable of the Good Samaritan in order to give the man a concrete example of what it means to love one's neighbor—10:30-37

5. Luke presents the story of Mary and Martha in order to rebuke Martha, not because of her choice, but because of her attitude toward Mary's choice—10:38-42

6. Luke presents Jesus' teaching about prayer in order to instruct the disciples in this area—11:1-13

  a. The disciples request that Jesus teach them how to pray probably because they saw a contrast between the hypocritical praying of the Pharisees and the genuine praying of Christ—11:1

  b. Jesus presents a model prayer consisting of five requests—11:2-4

    1) The first was that God's name be hallowed—11:2a

    2) The second request was for the coming of the Kingdom—11:2b

    3) The third request was for the necessities of life—11:3

    4) The fourth request was for the forgiveness of sin—11:4a

    5) The fifth request was that they be delivered from situations which would cause them to sin—11:4b

  c. Jesus presents two parables about prayer in order to teach them lessons about it—11:5-13

Note #40: The gift of the Spirit

One of the good gifts promised in the Old Testament was the giving of the Holy Spirit (Ezek. 36:27; Joel 2), and thus would be prayed for as a part of the praying for the coming of the Kingdom. This coming of the Spirit would occur on the Day of Pentecost thus fulfilling part of Joel 2, the rest of which would have been fulfilled if the nation had repented (thus contingency; compare also Acts 1:5-6). Because of the rejection of the nation, these prophecies will be fulfilled during the Millennium.

7. Luke records the increased rejection of Jesus in order to set the stage for the message going to the Gentiles and Jesus' instruction of the twelve in light of opposition—11:14-54

  a. Luke presents the incident where Jesus is accused of doing miracles by demonic power—11:14-26

  b. Jesus emphasizes that spiritual relationship is more important than physical relationship in order to show the nation that their physical descent from Abraham was not sufficient—11:27-28

  c. Jesus refuses to give the nation any more signs other than the one of Jonah. He indicates that Nineveh and the Queen of Sheba (Gentiles) believed and would be a witness against the Jews in judgment because Christ was a greater witness than either Jonah or Solomon—11:29-32

Note #41: Why did the ancient Ninevites repent?

In Luke 11:29 Jesus refers to the "sign of Jonah." The genitive "Jonah" would best be taken as appositional to "sign" thus yielding the sense "the sign, that is, Jonah." In other words, Jonah was the sign to the Ninevites. This is confirmed by the repetition of the idea in 11:30 which this time says "for as Jonah became a sign to the Ninevites." This is intriguing wording for it implies that Jonah, not necessarily his preaching, was the motivating factor leading to the repentance of the Ninevites (I do not think this was salvific repentance; however, that is beside the point being made here). The question becomes: how was Jonah a sign? Nineveh, one of the oldest Assyrian cities in history (which incidentally means "fishtown"), was steeped in a myth that much of Assyrian culture was brought by a half-fish, half-man god which emerged from the Persian Gulf, known in Greek as Oannes. Maspero explains the myth: "But, in the first year, appeared a monster endowed with human reason named Oannes, who rose from out of the Erythraean sea, at the point where it borders Babylonia. He had the whole body of a fish, but above his fish's head he had another head which was that of a man, and human feet emerged from beneath his fish's tail; he had a human voice, and his image is preserved to this day. He passed the day in the midst of men without taking any food; he taught them the use of letters, sciences and arts of all kinds, the rules for the founding of cities, and the construction of temples, the principles of law and of surveying; he showed them how to sow and reap; he gave them all that contributes to the comforts of life. Since that time nothing excellent has been invented. At sunset this monster Oannes plunged back into the sea, and remained all night beneath the waves, for he was amphibious. He wrote a book on the origin of things and of civilization, which he gave to men" (Gaston Maspero, The Dawn of Civilization: Egypt and Chaldaea *[London: Society for Promoting Christian Knowledge, 1910], 546). It is very likely that Jonah's entrapment in the fish would have left physical marks, and it is reasonable that someone had witnessed his being vomited on the shore. Given the history of Nineveh, this would have made Jonah a powerful sign (Eugene Merrill, "The Sign of Jonah,"* Journal of the Evangelical Theological Society *23:1 [Mar 1980], 29-30).*

The indictment Jesus is making of Israel through this reference is stinging. A pagan, Gentile city repented at the sign of Jonah, but Israel would not repent even though a greater than Jonah was in their midst.

d. Jesus presents the parable of the lighted lamp in order to show that if the nation was in darkness it was the fault of the receiver and not the revealer for the good eye admits light whereas the bad eye does not admit light and thus lives in darkness—11:33-36

e. Jesus condemns the Pharisees and the lawyers—11:37-54

B. Luke records the teaching of Christ to His disciples and the multitudes in order to instruct them in the light of the rejection of the leaders—12:1-19:27

1. Jesus instructs the people to side with Him and His cause and to not be afraid of the consequences—12:1-12

a. He warns them to beware of the hypocrisy of the Pharisees because eventually everything would be made know anyway—12:1-3

b. He warns them that they can side with Him because they should not be afraid of men but of God who has the power over their destiny—12:4-7

c. He exhorts them to confess Him before men—12:8-10

Note #42: How does confession relate to salvation?

Concerning the relation of confession to salvation, it is important to underscore the fact that "confession" simply refers to the acknowledgment of a given fact. Related to this context, Pentecost has observed that the people were in a state of indecision. "They were weighing the threats that the Pharisees might carry out against them if they left Pharisaism and identified with Christ. They were also considering the truth of Christ's words as authenticated by his works. Christ impressed on them the fact that their destiny depended on their decision and again exhorted them to put faith in Himself" (J. Dwight Pentecost, The Words and Works of Jesus Christ *[Grand Rapids: Zondervan, 1981], 313).*

- **d.** He tells his disciples that in the hour of persecution they would be granted the aid of the Holy Spirit—12:11-12

2. Jesus teaches about wealth in order to show the people that it is more important to be rich toward God than rich in the world—12:13-34

- **a.** Luke presents the occasion for this teaching when a person asks Christ to be an arbitrator in an inheritance dispute to which Christ replied to beware of covetousness for one's life consists of more than what one possesses—12:13-15

Note #43: Christ as arbiter

A man from the crowd asked Jesus to settle an inheritance dispute. This was not a particularly odd request since people would often ask rabbis to settle legal disputes (Craig Keener, The IVP Bible Background Commentary: New Testament *[Downers Grove, IL: InterVarsity Press, 1993], 223). Jesus uses this opportunity to forcefully teach concerning greed. This incident is also interesting from another perspective. One of the roles of the Messiah in His Kingdom will be that of an arbiter or judge (Isa. 2:4; Ps. 72:2; Micah 5:2). This is brought out clearly in the Isaiah 2:4 text which indicates that Christ will "decide disputes" (ESV), "settle disputes" (NIV), "arbitrate" (NRSV). The progression of the Isaiah 2:1-4 passage (also known as the "little apocalypse") is fascinating.*

1. "In the last days" refers to the future period of Messiah's earthly kingdom. This could not refer to the time after Christ's first coming since the events of this passage have not occurred.

2. "The mountain of the house of the Lord" refers to the mountain home of the Lord. That it will be established as the highest mountain at the least indicates the exaltation of God over all during this time frame. It may additionally carry the idea of a literal mountain which is the tallest on earth. This is based on Ezekiel's description of the same time frame where he envisions a massive 50 mile-square plateau on the top of which will rest the millennial temple, the millennial Jerusalem, and a section for the tribe of Levi (Ezek. 40:1-4; 45:1-8; 48:8-20; see also Isa. 27:13; 56:6-8).

3. The nations will stream to the mountain of the Lord. The fact that they will stream "up" the mountain (streams always flow downward) indicates that they will have a hunger for revealed truth as the law will emanate from Zion. Smith observes on the phrase "that he may teach us" in 2:3: "The result clause 'so that he may teach us' has a hiphil *imperfect verb...that expresses a subjunctive idea of possible action....The phrase indicates that the people know why they are going to Zion. They have the clear purpose of learning what God says" (Gary Smith,* Isaiah 1-39 *[Nashville: B&H Publishing, 2007], 130).*

4. Another reason nations will come to the mountain of the Lord is to hear the Messiah's ruling on national and international disputes. Since the Messiah will act as arbiter, warfare will be nonexistent. The nations will neither learn of war anymore (i.e., be trained in warfare) nor have weapons of war which will be replaced by agricultural implements.

Since Jesus clearly presented himself as the Messiah, is it possible that the man was turning to him to fulfill one of the aspects of his office? Though the man wanted Him to fulfill this role, it was not time for Christ to impose His decision on the nation since he had been rejected. In this light, Jesus gives his stern rebuke of covetousness.

b. Jesus gives the parable of the rich fool in order to illustrate His point that life is more important than material possessions—12:16-21

Note #44: Covetousness

The Pharisees were covetous and probably based this on Deuteronomy 28 feeling that the rich were the ones who were being blessed by God. Thus the richer one was, the more this showed God's favor. In this parable, Christ presents a rich farmer who kept adding to his riches, and was unwilling to share with others thus showing his inner character. Christ calls this man a fool because he was investing solely in this life. Therefore, Christ is noting why greed and covetousness should be avoided.

c. Jesus teaches about anxiety in the realm of physical needs in order to balance what He had just said about not making wealth the goal of one's life—12:22-34

1) Jesus notes that anxiety is foolish since life consists of more than the material and that God cared for them more than mere birds—12:22-24

2) Jesus notes that anxiety is foolish since it will not change any situation—12:25-28

3) Jesus notes that anxiety is foolish because it is the attitude of pagans whereas they should seek the Kingdom first—12:29-31

4) Jesus tells them not to fear for they have been given the Kingdom and they could lay up incorruptible treasure—12:32-34

3. Jesus tells two parables about readiness in order to stress the attitude which should characterize those waiting for the Kingdom—12:35-48

a. Jesus gives the parable of servants waiting for their Master to return from a wedding banquet who, if they were watching and ready, would serve Him regardless of when He returned—12:35-40

b. Peter asks Christ whether the preceding parable applied to the disciples or everyone—12:41

c. Jesus tells the parable of the wise stewards in which he emphasized the responsibility of the servants to guard what had been entrusted to their care to show Peter that this applied to all who had received revelation—12:42-48

4. Jesus tells His disciples that in their ministry there would be division in order to prepare them for rejection and persecution—12:49-53

5. Jesus tells the people that though they can discern the signs of the weather, they are unable to discern spiritual signs concerning His person so that they would see He was the Messiah and respond to His offer—12:54-56
6. Jesus notes that it is wise to be reconciled with an opponent, even if it is on the way to court, so that he would not be penalized in order to show that much more they should be reconciled to God if He is their enemy—12:57-59
7. Luke presents two contemporary examples of destruction followed by a parable to show that not all calamities came as a result of divine judgment and that just because one escaped calamity does not mean he is right with God—13:1-9
   a. Luke presents the Galilean and tower of Siloam tragedies and Christ's call to repentance in order to show that being killed or not being killed is not a sign of righteousness and all needed to repent—13:1-5
   b. Christ presents the parable of the fig tree in order to show why those who did not repent would be judged, namely because they did not produce the fruit of the chosen nation which was in covenant with Yahweh—13:6-9
8. Luke presents the healing of a crippled woman (picturesque of the nation) in order to show that there was still hope for individuals in the nation to receive grace and mercy—13:10-17
9. Luke presents two parables of Christ in light of the nation's rejection in order to encourage His disciples concerning the Kingdom program—13:18-21
   a. Christ presents the parable of the mustard seed in order to show that though the opponents of the Kingdom outnumbered its followers, the Kingdom would still be populous in the future—13:18-19
   b. Christ presents the parable of the leaven in order to show that the Kingdom program would work effectively and irreversibly—13:20-21
10. Luke records a series of teachings by Christ in order to show the identity of those who would enter the Kingdom—13:22-17:10
    a. Jesus taught that much of Israel would be excluded from the Kingdom while many Gentiles would be included so that the disciples would not be surprised at the seeming lack of success of Jesus' preaching—13:22-35
       1) Luke notes that on the way to Jerusalem one asked Jesus if many would be saved—13:22-23
       2) Jesus answers this question by giving a parable of people locked out of a feast in order to show the Jews that many Gentiles would be let in the Kingdom while they would be denied admittance—13:24-30
       3) Luke records the warning by the Pharisees for Christ not to go to Jerusalem to which He responded that He would complete His mission and go there anyway—13:31-33
       4) Christ laments over Jerusalem and rejects it because of their rejection of Him but notes that He will ultimately come again as their ruler—13:34-35
    b. Jesus teaches that many Jewish outcasts and Gentiles would populate the Kingdom—14:1-24
       1) Jesus was eating at the home of a Pharisee where He healed a man of the dropsy in order to demonstrate mercy to one who

was considered ceremonially unclean—14:1-6

2) Jesus observed how many of the guests were picking places of honor near the host at the banquet—14:7
3) Jesus tells the parable about sitting in places of humility in order to show the measure of greatness in the Kingdom—14:8-11
4) Jesus tells the host that when he has a supper he should not only invite his friends but the outcasts of society in order to set the stage for the next parable—14:12-14
5) Jesus tells the parable of the great supper to illustrate who would be invited to attend the banquet of the Kingdom—14:15-24

Note #45: The millennial banquet

In 14:1-14 a Pharisee had extended hospitality to his friends which led Jesus to make the point that true righteousness is expressed when one extends hospitality to those who cannot offer any repayment. This will lead to lasting reward given by God. One of the guests who heard Jesus responded by saying "blessed is everyone who will eat bread in the kingdom of God." The picture of a banquet frequently speaks of the bountiful provision to be enjoyed in the Messiah's kingdom (Isa. 25:6; Amos 9:13-14; Luke 14:15; 22:16; Rev. 19:9). Since the topic had turned to the future messianic banquet, Jesus gave a parable to show that only those who responded to him would participate in that feast.

According to social customs of the day, a banquet would be planned requiring extensive preparation. At this stage invitations would be sent to the guests who would then respond as to whether they would be in attendance. When the banquet was ready, a servant would announce that the time for celebration had come. The invitation to the banquet of the kingdom had been to Israel through a long line of the prophets. Finally, John the Baptist had Jesus announced that the "kingdom was at hand." However, the invitation had repeatedly been scorned by the nation. Jesus continues the parable by noting that the master of the feast (God) was sending his servant (Jesus) to those considered unworthy to attend. Therefore, the invitation would be taken to the "streets" where all manner of people could be found, and to the "lanes" of the city. The Greek term "lanes" (ῥύμη) refers to the back alleys of the city where the dregs of society would feel more comfortable. Liefeld notes that these side paths would be "likely to harbor the loitering outcasts of society" (Walter Liefeld, Luke *The Expositor's Bible Commentary [Grand Rapids: Zondervan, 1984], 8:978). These were the same kinds of people Jesus had urged the host of the banquet he was attending to invite (14:13). Thus this parable indicates that the millennial banquet will be filled with those outside of the nation of Israel who responded the message.*

c. Luke notes that crowds began to follow Jesus and He took that opportunity to teach them about true discipleship so that they would see the seriousness of the matter—14:25-35

1) Jesus told them that the disciple had to have proper priorities even when it involved their families—14:25-26
2) Jesus told them that the disciple had to be willing to follow Christ even if it meant death—14:27

3) Jesus illustrates the teaching on discipleship with two illustrations—14:28-33

a) Jesus notes that before one undertakes a building project he should be able to pay the full cost of it, so the disciple needs to be sure that he is willing to pay the full cost of following Christ—14:28-30

b) Jesus notes that before a king goes to battle he would be willing to sacrifice victory if he knows he cannot win so the disciple must be willing to sacrifice for Christ—14:31-33

4) Jesus notes that the disciple must have these qualities or else he is worthless as a disciple—14:34-35

d. Jesus presents three parables in order to show what God's attitude was toward outcasts and sinners in order to show that these types would be in the Kingdom—15:1-32

1) The occasion for these parables is when Jesus is seen fellowshipping with tax collectors and sinners and the Pharisees and scribes showed disdain at this—15:1-2

Note #46: Tax collectors

Tax collectors were despised because they sold themselves to Rome, and sinners were the outcasts of society and yet Jesus fellowshipped with them. In the Gospels tax collectors are comfortably grouped with sinners through the recurrent phrase "tax collectors and sinners." Even in Jewish literature "Tax collectors were grouped with murderers and robbers. To avoid loss, one could deceive a tax collector. The word of a tax gatherer could not be trusted, nor could his oath be believed. As a consequence, he could not testify in a court of law or hold a communal office. Money in the pocket of a tax collector was considered stolen property" (Frank Stern, A Rabbi Looks at Jesus' Parables [Lanham, MD: Rowman & Littlefield, 2006], 141). The religious leaders believed that God hated the sinner. The issue in these parables then is what God's attitude is toward sinners. Also, the emphasis in each parable is on the person looking and not necessarily what is lost. This brings out the theological issue of the disposition of God's heart toward the sinner.

2) The parable of the searching shepherd shows a man searching for something that is valuable to him and rejoicing when he found it thus showing God's attitude toward the lost—15:3-7

3) The parable of the searching woman emphasizes the diligence of God as He searches—15:8-10

Note #47: The woman's search

This diligence shown by this woman could (though there is not certainty as to the age of this custom) be related to the fact that the coins would have been the bride's dowry which were mounted on a headband. To lose one of the coins could be indicative of unfaithfulness (J. Dwight Pentecost, The Parables of Jesus *[Grand Rapids: Zondervan, 1982], 101. Pentecost elaborates on the difficulty of the search (illustrating God's diligence). "Palestinian homes had either a dirt floor or a stone floor. In order to keep down the dust, or to overcome the cold and dampness, the floors would be covered with straw. In order to find a coin that had fallen to the floor, it would be necessary to remove the straw, sift through it, and then sweep the floor. Such a search involved considerable labor, but the coin was of sufficient value that the labor was considered worthwhile" (101).*

4) The parable of the searching father showed the attitude of the father toward his rebellious son—15:11-32

Note #48: The father's search

The father evidently watched from a distance in order to see his son "a great way off." Several interesting cultural details help to make this parable unforgettable (several of these insights are taken from Craig Keener, The IVP Bible Background Commentary: New Testament *[Downers Grove, IL: InterVarsity Press, 1993], 232-234). The son says to his father that he wants his inheritance--and the sense is: "I want it now!" This is tantamount to saying to his father: I wish you were dead. According to the Mosaic Law under which the Jews were living, this could have been grounds for a serious beating or even death. The father was under no obligation of any kind to divide his inheritance. Moreover, in Jewish law, the father could divide the inheritance, but it would merely be telling his sons which fields they received, but they would not receive them until the father's death. In this instance the eldest son would have received 2/3 of the inheritance and the youngest son 1/3. Inexplicably, the father gives the son his portion. The son then squanders his money and is reduced to feeding unclean animals and eating what they eat. The son has managed to fritter away 1/3 of his father's life's earnings. The religious leaders would have liked the parable to end here. He got what he deserved, and indeed he did. But Jesus continues the story. Having come to an end of himself, the son ventures home on the tiny possibility that his father might take him back as a servant. In 15:20 the text says that while the son was a great way off, his father saw him. This could suggest that he routinely watched for his son's return. The father's next action is shocking. He runs to meet his son. In this culture, it was undignified for an older man to run--but the father does not care about social convention. He then kisses his son and literally falls on his son's neck. No Middle Eastern father would have reacted this way to a rebellious son. Refusing to listen to his son's prepared speech, he gives him the best robe in the house--probably his own which would have been long and flowing and suggestive of formal attire, the family signet ring showing he had been received back into the family, and sandals. Slaves usually did not wear sandals but carried their master's. A calf is then killed which would have been able to feed the whole village. Meanwhile, the elder brother did not rejoice over the son's return and did not attend the feast though he was invited. He was thus criticizing the father's treatment of the son. Likewise, the Pharisees were criticizing Christ's treatment of sinners. The father noted that the privileges for the younger son had always been there for the elder if he would have taken advantage of them. So, the fault lay with the elder brother. The parable ends with no record of the elder brother's response. The religious leaders were left to finish the story with the option of adopting the father's heart toward sinners or the elder brothers.*

e. Jesus teaches about wealth in order to correct false notions about it and the Kingdom—16:1-31

1) Jesus tells His disciples the parable of the unjust manager in order to show a good lesson from a bad example, namely, that they should plan ahead and use their wealth for the Kingdom—16:1-8a
2) Jesus makes three applications from this parable to His disciples—16:8b-13
   a) The disciples should use wealth wisely to reach others for the Kingdom—16:8b-9
   b) The disciples would be rewarded with Kingdom riches if they are faithful with wealth on earth—16:10-12
   c) The disciples cannot serve two masters—16:13
3) The Pharisees sneer at Jesus' teaching because they love money and assumed that a person's wealth was given in return for righteous conduct—16:14-17

Note #49: Pressing into the kingdom

Jesus speaks in 16:16 about "pressing into" the Kingdom. The interpretation centers around two issues: whether the verb "press, forces"(βιάζομαι) should be taken in a middle or passive sense, and whether this verb has the positive sense of enter, or a negative sense of some kind of violence. This yields four possible interpretations: 1) take the verb as middle with a positive sense—people are trying to enter the kingdom, 2) take the verb as middle with a negative sense—people act violently against the message of the kingdom, 3) take the verb as passive with a positive sense—people are being urged to enter the kingdom, or 4) take the verb as passive with a negative sense—people are being strongly urged not to enter the kingdom bespeaking the resistance of the message by the religious leaders. Given the context of rejection on the part of the Jewish leaders, option number 4 is probably the best. Therefore, the point Jesus is making is that the religious leaders are hindering the people to enter the kingdom because of their rejection of the Messiah.

4) Jesus illustrates their sin and breaking of the law by the example of obtaining another woman by divorcing their own wife and thus thinking they had not committed adultery—16:18
5) Jesus tells the parable of the rich man and Lazarus in order to show the Pharisees that wealth did not guarantee eternal life—16:19-31

f. Jesus teaches various obligations His disciples should have toward men and God—17:1-10
   1) Jesus taught that His disciples should not cause others to stumble and should be ready to forgive—17:1-4
   2) Jesus taught that His disciples should have faith in God and should humbly serve Him—17:5-10

11. Luke presents a series of events in the life of Christ in order to teach the disciples what attitudes should characterize their lives in view of the coming Kingdom—17:11-19:27
   a. Luke records the cleansing of the ten lepers and the return to thank Christ by the Samaritan in order to show the lack of gratitude of the nation and to show that thanksgiving is a recognition of

indebtedness—17:11-19

b. Luke records some answers of Christ concerning the Kingdom to the question of the Pharisees as to when the Kingdom would come—17:20-37

1) The Pharisees ask when the Kingdom would come—17:20a

2) Jesus told them that they would not be able to tell the coming of the Kingdom by their observation—17:20a

3) Jesus told them that the Kingdom was in their midst—17:21

Note #50: Is the kingdom in my heart?

Christ could not have meant that the Kingdom was "within you" for He was talking to the Pharisees. "Within you" could be translated "in your midst" or "among." Jesus was thus affirming that because the King was present the Kingdom was possible.

4) Jesus told the disciples that there would be a day when they would long to see Him but would not, that when the Kingdom came everyone would know it, and that He must suffer before the Kingdom came—17:22-25

5) Jesus gives the illustrations of the days of Noah and Lot's wife in order to show the lack of preparedness of people at the time of the coming of the Kingdom and the consequent judgment that would come on these people—17:26-37

c. Jesus presents two parables on prayer—18:1-14

d. Jesus used the example of children in order to illustrate the preceding parable to show that those who enter the Kingdom need to be humble and dependent on God—18:15-17

e. Luke records the incident concerning the rich young ruler in order to show what kind of righteousness was necessary to enter the Kingdom—18:18-30

1) The man asks Christ what he needed to do to have eternal life—18:18

2) Jesus notes that he should fulfill the Law's teaching toward his fellow man showing that he possessed true righteousness—18:19-20

3) The man replied that he had kept all these things—18:21

4) Jesus told him that the one thing he lacked was to give all of his wealth to the poor thus keeping the tenth commandment and follow Him—18:22

5) The man refused to do this and went away—18:23

6) Jesus notes that riches are often a hindrance to gaining eternal life but even still God can do the impossible and save them and that His disciples' sacrifice would be rewarded as well—18:24-30

Note #51: The eye of a needle

Luke uses the term for a sewing needle when he speaks of a camel going through the eye of a needle. There was not a gate in Jerusalem called "the needle's eye" that camels had to crouch down and remove their burdens to squeeze through. The earliest known reference to this is found in the 11th century in a commentary by a Greek commentator named Theophylact. The point of the passage is that it takes a miracle of God to save a rich man which is why the next phrase is: "all things are possible with God."

f. Jesus tells the disciples of His coming death at the hands of the Gentiles in order to again warn them and to show that though the Gentiles were receiving mercy they were still sinners—18:31-34

g. Luke records two examples of Christ's meeting with two men in order to show that outcasts in Jewish eyes were ones who could receive mercy thus also showing the nation what they could have—18:35-19:10

1) Jesus heals a blind beggar for his faith thus showing how the leaders should have the same kind of dependence on Him for help—18:35-43

2) Jesus meets and saves Zacchaeus the tax collector in order to illustrate His words in 18:27, to show that the wealthy Jews still need salvation, and to show that the outcast has a part with the Messiah—19:1-10

h. Jesus presents the parable of the ten minas in order to show what Christ expected of those who had made a commitment to Him during the time of the postponement of the Kingdom—19:11-27

Note #52: Archelaus

It is interesting to note the historical event that probably lies behind this parable. Archelaus, the son of Herod the Great, went to Rome to secure permission to reign (because of his father's death) over a territory in Samaria and Judea which was actually subject to Rome. This petition was opposed by some of Archelaus' own subjects, while his brother Antipas was trying to do the same thing. In spite of this, Archelaus was appointed ruler by the emperor. This would be in view in 19:12, 14. Similarly, Jesus claim to be king and his kingdom had been rejected.

It should also be observed that Matthew's version of this parable refers to Israel during the Tribulation period while Luke's version includes the period since the postponement of the Kingdom. Thus Luke is applying the truth of the parable to the whole period from the Messiah's rejection until his coming, while Matthew is applying the truth of the parable to the Jews alive during the 7 years prior to the coming of the Kingdom.

VI. LUKE PRESENTS THE MINISTRY OF CHRIST IN JERUSALEM, INCLUDING HIS ENTRANCE AND TEACHING, IN ORDER TO SHOW THAT HE HAD PRESENTED HIMSELF AS THE MESSIAH WHO COULD HAVE BROUGHT IN THE KLNGDOM--19:28-21:38

A. Luke records the entry of Christ into Jerusalem to show that He was publicly displaying Himself as the Messiah—19:28-44

1. Luke records the preparations for the entry of Christ into the city—19:28-34

2. Luke records the entrance of Christ into the city and the cries of the people in order to show that He was accepting their ascriptions of Him as the Messiah—19:35-40

3. Jesus laments over the city because, though He had presented Himself as the

Messiah, the Kingdom would still not be established until a future date and that the city would be judged—19:41-44

B. Luke records the events surrounding Christ in the temple in order to confirm the opposition of the religious leaders and to show the disciples the future of the nation in the light of that opposition—19:45-21:38

1. Luke presents the cleansing of the temple in order to show that Christ was utilizing His prerogatives as the Messiah and to validate the corruption of the nation—19:45-46

2. Luke presents the teaching of Christ in the temple—19:47-21:38

a. Luke introduces this teaching by noting that the crowds were delighted at His teaching while the leaders wanted to kill Him—19:47-48

b. The religious leaders question Jesus' authority to do what He is doing to which He responds by asking them a question concerning the authority of John thus implying that they were both operating under God's authority—20:1-8

c. Jesus tells the parable of the vineyard owner in order to show what would happen to the nation as a result of their rejection of the authority of Christ, namely judgment on Israel and the allowance of outcasts and Gentiles into the Kingdom before the Jews (18a views repentance and 18b judgment)—20:9-19

d. Jesus answers the Herodians that one should render to Caesar what is his and to God what is His—20:20-26

e. Jesus answers the Sadducees concerning the resurrection—20:27-38

f. Jesus answers the scribes concerning the nature of the Messiah—20:39-44

g. Jesus warns the people to beware of the hypocrisy of the religious leaders—20:45-47

h. Jesus notes the example of the widow, in contrast to the Pharisees, in order to show that the little she gave was worth more—21:1-4

i. Luke records the Olivet Discourse in order to show the future of the nation before Christ returns and to show the disciples how they should live in light of this—21:5-38

1) Luke records the fact that the disciples were impressed with the temple structure and Jesus noted that it would one day be destroyed and the disciples inquire as to what things would take place before the temple fell—21:5-7

2) Jesus notes several things that would occur before the destruction of the temple—21:8-19

a) Many would claim to be the Messiah—21:8

b) Wars would occur—21:9-10

c) Earthquakes and famine would occur—21:11

d) Persecution would occur—21:12-19

3) Jesus answers the disciples original question by noting that Jerusalem would be destroyed by Gentile armies and that this domination would occur as well in the Tribulation until the return of the Messiah—21:20-24

4) Jesus notes the signs that will precede His return in order to show that Gentile domination would one day be broken—21:25-28

5) Jesus presents the parable of the fig tree to show that one can tell what is coming by the signs preceding it—21:29-33
6) Jesus warns His disciples to be watchful—21:34-36
7) Luke concludes this section by noting that the crowds were intrigued by His teaching and wanted to hear more—21:37-38

Note #53: Luke's AD 70 parenthesis

It is important to observe that both Matthew and Luke's versions of the Olivet Discourse deal with the future time before Messiah returns to establish his kingdom. However, in Luke's version, he contains a segment dealing with the AD 70 destruction of the temple. For how these two fit together, see Note 54 for more details.

VII. LUKE RECORDS THE DEATH, BURIAL, AND RESURRECTION OF CHRIST IN ORDER TO BRING OUT THE HIGH POINT OF THE LEADERS' REJECTION AND TO ALSO SHOW THAT CHRIST WAS INNOCENT AND THAT HE WAS THE TRUE MESSIAH BY HIS VICTORY OVER DEATH—22:1-24:53

A. Luke presents the events surrounding the death, burial, and resurrection of Christ—22:1-23:56

1. Luke records the agreement by Judas to betray Jesus—22:1-6

2. Luke records the Passover and garden events as preparatory for the death of Christ—22:7-46

a. Luke records the events of the Passover meal including the preparation, the teaching of the New Covenant, the announcement of the betrayal, the argument over who would be the greatest in the Kingdom, the announcement of Peter's denial, and the new instructions for the disciples to provide for themselves as they went out to serve—22:7-38

b. Luke records Christ's agony in the garden in order to show His deep association with humanity and fear of eternal separation from the Father—22:39-46

3. Luke records the betrayal of Jesus by Judas—22:47-53

4. Luke presents the trials before Caiaphas, the Sanhedrin, Pilate, Herod, and Pilate—22:54-23:25

5. Luke records the death of Christ in order to show that He was the dying Son of Man who had come to provide forgiveness for all—23:26-49

6. Luke records the burial of Christ to show that He had actually died—23:50-56

B. Luke records the resurrection and appearances of Christ in order to confirm the bodily resurrection of Christ and to confirm the person of Christ to His disciples by His exposition of His suffering and glory—24:1-53

1. Luke records the discovery of the empty tomb by the women and Peter—24:1-12

2. Luke records the appearances to His followers in order to confirm His resurrection and His person as prophesied in the Old Testament—24:13-49

a. Jesus appears to two disciples on the road to Emmaus and teaches them concerning His person—24:13-35

1) Luke records that two disciples were walking and discussing the events that had taken place in Jerusalem and that they were joined by Jesus but did not recognize Him—24:13-16
2) Jesus asked them what they were discussing and they related that they were talking about the death of Jesus who they thought was going to bring in the Kingdom—24:17-24
3) Jesus expounded the prophecies concerning the Messiah from Moses and all the prophets in order to show them that they should have understood what had happened—24:25-27
4) Jesus broke bread with them and opened their eyes to see who He was at which they ran back to Jerusalem to confirm His resurrection to the others—24:28-35

3. Luke records the appearance to the eleven which included events to prepare them for their ministry as recorded in Acts—24:36-49

Note #54: Luke's AD 70 parenthesis expanded

In his superb work on the kingdom, Alva McClain has observed that in Luke's account of the Olivet Discourse, Jesus' answer to the disciples' first question about the destruction of the temple is recorded. This answer actually is parenthetical to the part of the discourse related to the Tribulation period. This important observation reveals two things: 1) the discourse is meant to have a futuristic interpretation since the AD 70 destruction of the temple is a parenthesis in Luke's account, and 2) it shows that the Roman destruction did not exhaust that part of the prophecy due to the events of Zechariah 14 and the other considerations in this chapter which indicate a future fulfillment. As Lowery observes regarding the AD 70 destruction: "But several factors suggest that an event of greater magnitude is being described here."[577] *Lowery posits three reasons for his statement. These include an over-exaggeration of the events if they only refer to 70, the citation of the Daniel "abomination" text which is associated with the end of time, and the resurrection of the righteous together with the separation of humanity at the second coming.*[578] *I have included below Luke's version of the Olivet Discourse from the American Standard Version (which was the one used by Dr. McClain) and put in bold type the parenthetical section. This is followed by McClain's comments.*

> [5] *And as some spake of the temple, how it was adorned with goodly stones and offerings, he said,* [6] *As for these things which ye behold, the days will come, in which there shall not be left here one stone upon another, that shall not be thrown down.* [7] *And they asked him, saying, Teacher, when therefore shall these things be? and what [shall be] the sign when these things are about to come to pass?* [8] *And he said, Take heed that ye be not led astray: for many shall come in my name, saying, I am [he]; and, The time is at hand: go ye not after them.* [9] *And when ye shall hear of wars and tumults, be not terrified: for these things must needs come to pass first; but the end is not immediately.* [10] *Then said he unto them, Nation shall rise against*

[577] David Lowery, "A Theology of Matthew," in *A Biblical Theology of the New Testament*, Roy Zuck editor, (Chicago: Moody Press, 1994), 60.

[578] Ibid, 60-61.

nation, and kingdom against kingdom; 11 *and there shall be great earthquakes, and in divers places famines and pestilences; and there shall be terrors and great signs from heaven.* 12 ***But before all these things, they shall lay their hands on you, and shall persecute you, delivering you up to the synagogues and prisons, bringing you before kings and governors for my name's sake.*** 13 ***It shall turn out unto you for a testimony.*** 14 ***Settle it therefore in your hearts, not to meditate beforehand how to answer:*** 15 ***for I will give you a mouth and wisdom, which all your adversaries shall not be able to withstand or to gainsay.*** 16 ***But ye shall be delivered up even by parents, and brethren, and kinsfolk, and friends; and [some] of you shall they cause to be put to death.*** 17 ***And ye shall be hated of all men for my name's sake.*** 18 ***And not a hair of your head shall perish.*** 19 ***In your patience ye shall win your souls.*** 20 ***But when ye see Jerusalem compassed with armies, then know that her desolation is at hand.*** 21 ***Then let them that are in Judaea flee unto the mountains; and let them that are in the midst of her depart out; and let not them that are in the country enter therein.*** 22 ***For these are days of vengeance, that all things which are written may be fulfilled.*** 23 ***Woe unto them that are with child and to them that give suck in those days! for there shall be great distress upon the land, and wrath unto this people.*** 24 ***And they shall fall by the edge of the sword, and shall be led captive into all the nations: and Jerusalem shall be trodden down of the Gentiles, until the times of the Gentiles be fulfilled.*** 25 *And there shall be signs in sun and moon and stars; and upon the earth distress of nations, in perplexity for the roaring of the sea and the billows;* 26 *men fainting for fear, and for expectation of the things which are coming on the world: for the powers of the heavens shall be shaken.* 27 *And then shall they see the Son of man coming in a cloud with power and great glory.* 28 *But when these things begin to come to pass, look up, and lift up your heads; because your redemption draweth nigh.* 29 *And he spake to them a parable: Behold the fig tree, and all the trees:* 30 *when they now shoot forth, ye see it and know of your own selves that the summer is now nigh.* 31 *Even so ye also, when ye see these things coming to pass, know ye that the kingdom of God is nigh.* 32 *Verily I say unto you, This generation shall not pass away, till all things be accomplished.* 33 *Heaven and earth shall pass away: but my words shall not pass away.* 34 *But take heed to yourselves, lest haply your hearts be overcharged with surfeiting, and drunkenness, and cares of this life, and that day come on you suddenly as a snare:* 35 *for [so] shall it come upon all them that dwell on the face of all the earth. 36 But watch ye at every season, making supplication, that ye may prevail to escape all these things that shall come to pass, and to stand before the Son of man.*

"The main events under consideration in these questions can be reduced to two: first, the judgment upon Jerusalem...second, the return of Christ to consummate the age. The problem of the interpreter now is to identify those portions of the entire discourse which deal with these two grand events respectively....Matthew and Luke point out that these things [wars, famines, earthquakes, etc.] are only the 'beginning of sorrows.' They are the first pangs of a world which must be born anew by the establishment of Messiah's Kingdom...and therefore are true signs of the end, not merely of the destruction of Jerusalem and its temple. It is precisely at this point in our Lord's discourse, however, that Luke records a section which has no exact parallel in the other two Gospels. It is, in fact, a literary parenthesis inserted in Luke's account of coming events. This parenthetical section begins with the words 'But before all these things' (21:12, ASV),

i.e., the things already referred to which will mark the beginning of the 'end.' The section ends with the words, 'And Jerusalem shall be trodden down of the Gentiles, until the times of the Gentiles be fulfilled' (21:24). It should be obvious that in this section of Luke's account we have the answer of Christ to the disciples' question about the judgment of Jerusalem and the temple...As for that vast interval of time between A.D. 70 and the arrival of the 'end,' Christ has no comment except that Jerusalem will continue under the Gentile heel until the end of Gentile world supremacy. And just as Gentile world supremacy began with the end of the Old Testament Theocratic Kingdom, even so, according to the prophets, Gentile supremacy can only end with the restoration of the Kingdom to Israel at the glorious advent of her Messianic King....If the student will now read the Lukan account, omitting the parenthesis in 21:12-24, it will become clear that verses 11 and 25 join perfectly in subject matter...In summary, it may be said that all three Synoptics record the teaching of Christ about His second coming and the end of the age, but only Luke clearly identifies and records separately what Christ said specifically regarding the judgment about to fall upon Jerusalem in A.D. 70."[579]

[579] McClain, *The Greatness of the Kingdom*, 363-365.

JOHN

Authorship

Though this Gospel does not name its author, the traditional view which was commonly accepted before the advent of biblical criticism was that John, the son of Zebedee, was the author (Raymond Brown, *The Gospel according to John I-XII* The Anchor Bible [Garden City, NY: Doubleday, 1966], xxiv). This position has both external and internal support in its favor.

External Evidence

There is unanimity among the church fathers that this Gospel was written by John (Irenaeus, Clement of Alexandria, Tertullian, Origen, Papias, Hippolytus, Eusebius, etc.).

Internal Evidence

The information in the book itself supports this universal opinion concerning authorship.

1. The author was a Jew. He quoted from the Old Testament (12:40; 13:18; 19:37); he knew and understood the Jewish religious feasts (2:23; 5:1; 6:4; 7:2; 10:22); he understood Jewish customs such as wedding feasts (2:1-10), ceremonial purification (11:55), and the manner of burial (11:38; 19:40); and he knew of the religious differences between Jews and Samaritans (4:9, 20).
2. He was a Jew of Palestine. For examples see 5:2; 11:18, 54; 18:1; 19:13.
3. He was an eyewitness. He beheld Christ's glory (1:14) and was at the crucifixion (19:33-35). See also 2:6; 1.2:5; 21:8, 11.
4. The author was an apostle. See 2:11, 17, 22; 4:27, 33; 6:19; 9:2, etc.
5. He refers to himself as the disciple whom Jesus loved (19:23).

Date

The date for this Gospel was probably sometime between AD 85 and 95 though some date the book as early as before AD 70 and others as late as AD 170. The date of 85-95 date is acceptable to most scholars.

Origin and Destination

Tradition has placed the composition of John at Ephesus where John spent his later years (Irenaeus, Polycrates). Furthermore, it is probable that the primary audience was Ephesian Gentiles due to the fact that various feasts and geographical locations are described for the readers.

Distinctive Features

1. Jesus' seven signs.
    a. Water into wine—2:1-11
    b. Healing of the nobleman's son—4:46-54
    c. Healing of the invalid at the Pool—5:1-18
    d. Feeding of the 5,000—6:5-14
    e. Walking on water—6:16-21
    f. Healing a blind man—9:1-7

   g. Raising Lazarus—11:1-45
2. Jesus' seven "I AMs."
   a. I am the bread of life—6:35
   b. I am the light of the world—8:12
   c. I am the gate for the sheep—10:7
   d. I am the good shepherd—10:11, 14
   e. I am the resurrection and the life—11:25
   f. I am the way the truth and the life—14:6
   g. I am the true vine—15:1
3. John's writing is simple in style but profound in nature.
4. John includes great topical discourses unique to Christ.
   a. The new birth—3:1-13
   b. The water of life—4:6-29
   c. The defense of His deity—5:19-47
   d. The bread of life—6:22-71
   e. The light of the world—8:12-59
   f. The good shepherd—10:1-30
   g. The upper room discourse—13:1-16:33
5. John presents a strong emphasis on the deity of Christ.
6. Over 90% of his content is unique.
7. John uses key words such as "believe," "signs," "life," etc.
8. John centers on Christ's visits to Jerusalem for the various feasts.

Purpose

Suggested purposes for the book include a supplement to the Synoptics, a polemic against unbelieving Jews, an apologetic against zealots for John the Baptist, and the combating of Gnosticism. While these could be subsidiary purposes, there is really no good reason to look beyond the clear statement of purpose by John in 20:31. Even with this purpose, however, one needs to be clear on the Johannine concept of "life" in order to grasp the significance of this statement.

For John, "life" and "eternal life" are both quantitative and qualitative ideas. That is, the life possessed by the believer is durative quantitatively, but it is also a life which can grow and deepen which therefore brings a qualitative idea into the picture. So, in John's thought, life (defined by Jesus in 17:3 as knowing the Father) is entered into at the moment of salvation. However, this life then needs to be cultivated into a fuller experience. In a sense, it could be said that the concept for John incudes both justification and sanctification. The first aspect will be stressed in the early chapters of the book while the latter will be emphasized as the ministry narrows more and more to the apostles.

For John, this life is entered into and continues to be deepened by belief. Interestingly, the Greek noun for "belief" is never found in this Gospel. Rather, John uses exclusively the verbal form nearly 100 times in various constructions in order to emphasize the act of believing.

Thus, the purpose of John's Gospel is: <u>John records selected signs and discourses from the ministry of Jesus in order to demonstrate that He is the Son of God who reveals the Father so that his readers would put their faith in Him and gain a dynamic and growing eternal life.</u>

I. JOHN PRESENTS THE PROLOGUE TO HIS GOSPEL IN ORDER TO INTRODUCE CHRIST AS THE DIVINE REVEALER OF THE FATHER IN PREPARATION FOR HIS INTRO-DUCTION TO THE NATION AS THE SON OF GOD—1:1-18

A. John introduces Christ in His preincarnate state and relation to the Father in order to show that He was qualified to reveal the Father to the world—1:1-2

Note #55: The prologue

The Prologue, or introduction, to John's Gospel in 1:1-18 is one of the most profound sections in the New Testament. It has been said that "Johannine theology is, in essence, Christology" (Hall Harris, "A Theology of John's Writings," in A Biblical Theology of the New *Testament [Chicago: Moody Press, 1994], 167). Setting the stage for this Christology is the first two verses written in chiastic form (to stress the distinct person and deity of Christ). McCoy defines chiasm as follows: "the use of inverted parallelism of form and/or content which moves toward and away from a strategic central component" (Brad McCoy, "Chiasmus: An Important Structural Device Commonly Found in Biblical Literature,"* Chafer Theological Seminary Journal *9:2 (Fall, 2003), 18. For the importance of observing chiasm in the New Testament see Ronald Man, "The Value of Chiasm for New Testament Interpretation,"* Bibliotheca *Sacra 141:562 (April-June 1984), 146-157, and Mark Wilson, "Revelation," in* Zondervan Illustrated Bible Backgrounds Commentary *(Grand Rapids: Zondervan, 2002), 317.*

Greek		English	
A	ἐν ἀρχῇ	A	in the beginning
B	ἦν	B	was
C	ὁ λόγος	C	the word
D	καὶ ὁ λόγος	D	and the word
E	ἦν	E	was
F	**πρὸς τὸν θεόν**	**F**	**with God**
F'	**καὶ θεός**	**F'**	**and God**
E'	ἦν	E'	was
D'	ὁ λόγος	D'	the word
C'	οὗτος	C'	he
B'	ἦν	B'	was
A'	ἐν ἀρχῇ πρὸς τὸν θεόν	A'	in the beginning with God

1. John notes the fact that Christ was preexistent before His advent into the world—1:1a

Note #56: The logos

Λόγος should not be understood philosophically, or as the principle governing the universe but in the Old Testament sense. Thus, the λόγος is not an impersonal term for "reason" or the "mind" but a reference to the second member of the trinity who has

become the incarnate speech of God.

Note #57: In the beginning

In 1 John 1:1, John uses the phrase ἀπ ἀρχῆς (from the beginning) referring to what took place from the starting point of the incarnation. Here John uses the phrase ‡Eν ἀρχῆ (in the beginning) dealing with the original beginning. It is also significant to note the verb ἦν ("was"). The imperfect tense implies continuous existence in the past. Thus, before the beginning of the world, the Word was already there. The Word predates creations and existed as far back as one can think. The Word is not merely pre-existent (Jehovah's Witnesses) but eternally existent.

2. John notes the fact that Christ was distinct from the Father before His incarnation—1:1b

Note #58: "With" God

The statement "the Word was with God" is an assertion of the Word's distinctiveness. The preposition πρὸς indicates both equality and distinction bespeaking the fellowship between the Logos and God. This argues against the ancient heresy of Sabellianism and its modern counterpart of Modalism (the one God revealing himself as Father, Son, and Spirit).

3. John notes the fact that Christ was deity before His incarnation—1:1c

Note #59: And the word was God—the anarthrous construction

*This is a clear statement of deity especially in light of the fact that the noun θεός is anarthrous (lacks the article) thus emphasizing character. To have included the article (*contra *Jehovah's Witnesses) would have been heretical in that this would have said that the Father and the Logos were the same person. The Jehovah's Witnesses* New World Translation *of the Bible renders 1:1c as "the word was a god" as opposed to "the Word was God." Their grammatical reasoning is that because the word "god" lacks the article in the Greek text, it should be translated indefinitely. Not only does this show a misunderstanding of Greek grammar, but the NWT is inconsistent in its use of this grammatical "rule." In fact, the Greek word for God θεός occurs over 1300 times in the New Testament. Of these over 1300 uses, 282 times the word "God" appears without the article as it does in the second use of God in John 1:1. Their premise, again, is that if God occurs without the article it should be rendered as "a god" referring to Christ as not having the same essence as the Father. And yet out of 282 instances, the New World Translation renders God with a small "g" only 16 times. They are therefore consistent with their own premise only 6% of the time and inconsistent with their own premise 94% of the time (Statistics are taken from Robert Countess, "The Translation of θεός in the New World Translation,"* Bulletin of the Evangelical Theological Society *10:3 [1967], 160).*

A historic watershed regarding the deity of Christ occurred in June of 325 B.C. when somewhere between 250 and 300 bishops convened at the request of the Emperor

Constantine. They gathered in a small town in northwestern Turkey by the name of Nicea. One of the items on the agenda was to discuss Arianism which was threatening the unity of the Church. The debate essentially centered around one Greek word "ousios" which means "essence." The issue at hand was what kind of essence does Jesus have compared to the kind of essence the Father has. The word used to describe the position of Arius was "heteroousios." He said that the essence of Christ is different than the essence of the Father. Then there was another position argued for by Eusebius. The word used to describe his position was "homoiousios" which meant that the Christ has a similar essence to that of the Father. And then, also present at the council was the mighty theologian Athanasius. Athanasius pressed for the term "homoousios" which meant that Christ was the same essence as the Father.

3 Views of Christ's Deity	
Arius	• Heteroousios • Different essence
Eusebius	• Homoiousios • Similar essence
Athanasius	• Homoousios • Same essence

In the providence of God, Athanasius won the day and the council condemned Arius as a heretic and exiled him to the Roman province of Illyricum. They hammered out what is known as the Nicean Creed, part of which reads:

> *I believe in one God, the Father Almighty, Maker of heaven and earth, and of all things visible and invisible. And in one Lord Jesus Christ, the only-begotten Son of God, begotten of the Father before all worlds; God of God, Light of Light, very God of very God; begotten, not made, being of one substance with the Father, by whom all things were made.*

4. John restates the truth about the Word in order to emphasize his point—1:2

B. John introduces Christ in His relation to creation by showing that He was the Creator in order to show His first revelatory act of the Father—1:3

Note #60: John's use of verb tenses

It will be noticed that in 1:1-2 John uses the same verb (εἰμί) four times. "In the beginning <u>was</u> the Word and the Word <u>was</u> with God and the Word <u>was</u> God. The same <u>was</u> in the beginning with God." In each of these instances John uses the imperfect tense of the verb to indicate that the Word was always existing. By contrast, in 1:3 he uses the verb "made" (γίνομαι) three times. In the first two uses the aorist form of the verb is used to draw a distinction between the eternal nature of the Son and the temporal nature of matter. In John's third use, he switches to the perfect tense of the verb. Thus in 1:3 we have a snapshot reference to the act of creation (the two aorist uses) and then a reference *to the continued state of creation (the perfect use). On the one hand Christ created matter, and on the other he sustains matter. This could refer to Christ upholding all things, or may even be a statement of "continuous creation." Edwards asked "To what purpose can it be to talk of God's preserving things in being, when there is no need of his preserving them? Or to talk of their being dependent on God for continued existence, when they would of themselves continue to exist without his help; nay, though he should wholly withdraw his sustaining power and influence? It will follow from what has been observed, that God's upholding created substance, or causing its existence in each successive moment, is altogether equivalent to an immediate production out of nothing, at each moment" (Jonathan Edwards, "The Great Christian Doctrine of Original Sin Defended," in* The Works of Jonathan Edwards *[Carlisle, PA: The Banner of Truth Trust, 1992], 1:224).*

- **C.** John introduces Christ in His relation to men in order to show that He came to reveal the Father to them so that they would come into the knowledge of the Father he had experienced—1:4-5
  - **1.** John notes that in Christ was life (the knowledge of the Father) which He was able to give because of His relationship to the Father—1:4a
  - **2.** John notes that Christ brought light (the knowledge of the Father) which could not be overcome by the powers of darkness—1:4b-5

Note #61: The most pathetic verses in the New Testament?

John 1:4-5 could well be the most pathetic verses in the entire New Testament. John has been presenting Christ as the ultimate revealer of the Father. He is qualified to be this revelation because he has lived in eternal intimacy with the Father. This is why John can say that in Christ was "life" because in the Johannine sense "life" refers to an intimate knowledge of and relationship with the Father. The word used by John translated "life" (ζωή) occurs 135 times in the New Testament with a whopping 66 found in the Johannine writings. Raymond Brown has correctly noted regarding this term, and its fuller description "eternal life," that it has to do with "the life by which God Himself lives, and which the Son of God possesses from the Father...There can be no doubt then, that for John 'eternal life' is qualitatively different from natural life" (Raymond Brown, The Gospel according to John I-XII *The Anchor Bible [Garden City, NY: Doubleday, 1966], 507). Thus Christ, the epitome of one who possesses the life of God in the sense of intimate fellowship, comes to offer this same kind of life to the world. What will be the response to such an offer?*

Note how the various translations record the response as found in 1:5 observing that the issue is how the verb (καταλαμβάνω) is to be translated.

ESV John 1:5 The light shines in the darkness, and the darkness has not ***overcome*** *it.*

KJV John 1:5 And the light shineth in darkness; and the darkness ***comprehended*** *it not.*

NAU John 1:5 The Light shines in the darkness, and the darkness did not ***comprehend*** *it.*

NIV John 1:5 The light shines in the darkness, but the darkness has not ***understood*** *it.*

NJB John 1:5 and light shines in darkness, and darkness could not ***overpower*** *it.*

NKJ John 1:5 And the light shines in the darkness, and the darkness did not ***comprehend*** *it.*

NLT John 1:5 The light shines through the darkness, and the darkness can never ***extinguish*** *it.*

NRS John 1:5 The light shines in the darkness, and the darkness did not ***overcome*** *it.*

YLT John 1:5 and the light in the darkness did shine, and the darkness did not ***perceive*** *it.*

Three views have been proposed as to how this response is to be interpreted: 1) the darkness was trying to understand the light but could not, 2) the darkness wanted to seize the light for its own, and 3) the darkness wanted to overtake the light with hostile intent. In the Gospel of John "darkness" is not merely the absence of light, but a moral category which is antagonistic to God. In addition, one of the thematic aspects of the book is the growing hostility of the darkness to the light. One of the best thematic studies of John is by Tenney who labels the major sections of the book as the period of consideration, controversy, conflict, and crisis. Once the crisis point has been reached, Christ withdraws and instructs the disciples privately. Following this conference, Christ re-emerges and is killed (Merrill Tenney, John: The Gospel of Belief *[Grand Rapids: Eerdmans, 1979], 13-15). In light of this development, one could well ask the question, "who then can be saved?" This is why John places such a strong emphasis on God's effectual calling and regeneration culminating in the recurring phrase "those whom you have given me" in Jesus' high priestly prayer in chapter 17. For more on this theme see Robert Yarbrough, "Divine Election in the Gospel of John," in* The Grace of God: The Bondage of the Will *(Grand Rapids: Baker, 1995), 47-62. In this light, view number 3 is to be preferred with the best expression being found in the NLT.*

The reason people hated the light was because it exposed their sinfulness and made them feel uncomfortable. To put it as bluntly as possible, people have always fought against God because they do not like who he is. One of the most delightful treatments of this subject is by Puritan Thomas Boston who breaks down the attributes of God and confronts the sinner with them. When we ask the question: "what is it that people don't like about God," the answer becomes "nearly everything" (Thomas Boston, Human Nature in its Fourfold State *[Carlisle, PA: The Banner of Truth Trust, 1989], 59-202. Jonathan Edwards concurred when he made the same point in light of the fact that God's attributes are immutable. "They are enemies in the natural relish of their souls. They have an inbred distaste and disrelish of God's perfections. God is not such a being as they would have. Though they are ignorant of God; yet from what they hear of him, and from what is manifest by the light of nature, they do not like him. By his being endowed with such attributes as he is, they have an aversion to him. They hear God is an infinitely holy, pure, and righteous Being, and they do not like him upon this account; they have no relish of such qualifications: they take no delight in contemplating them. It would be a mere task, a bondage to a natural man, to be obliged to set himself to contemplate those attributes of God. They see no manner of beauty or loveliness, nor taste any sweetness, in them. And on account of their distaste of these perfections, they dislike all his other attributes. They have greater aversion to him because he is omniscient and knows all things; and because his omniscience is a holy omniscience. They are not pleased that he is omnipotent, and can do whatever he pleases; because it is a holy omnipotence. They are enemies even to his mercy, because it is a holy mercy. They do not like his immutability, because by this he never will be otherwise than he is, an infinitely holy God" (Jonathan Edwards, "Men are Naturally God's Enemies," in* The Works of Jonathan Edwards *[Carlisle, PA: The Banner of Truth Trust, 1974], 2:131).*

D. John introduces the ministry of John the Baptist in order to stress that John the Baptist was only a witness of Christ the Light and not himself the Light—1:6-8

E. John presents the coming of the Light into time to show the purpose of His incarnation of revealing of the Father and the responses possible to this revelation—1:9-13

1. John states the Light comes into the world and affects men—1:9
2. John states that the light was not recognized by sinful man—1:10
3. John states that Christ was rejected in the world—1:11
4. John states that this rejection was not universal and that those who receive Him would become God's children due to the supernatural nature of regeneration—1:12-13

F. John describes the incarnate manifestation of the revelation of the Father by the Son in order to show that this revelation was dependent on incarnation—1:14-18

1. John declares that the logos became man and tabernacled among men to reveal the glory of the Father—1:14
2. John notes that the Baptist's testimony is in accord with this—1:15
3. John notes that in Christ was resident the full expression of grace and truth—1:16-17
4. John notes that Christ is the only one who truly knows and is able to make the Father known—1:18

II. JOHN PRESENTS THE MANIFESTATION OF CHRIST AS THE REVEALER OF THE FATHER TO THE NATION THROUGH A SERIES OF SIGNS AND DISCOURSES FOR CONSIDERATION OF WHO THE PROLOGUE SAYS HE IS AND TO SHOW THAT THIS REVELATION HAS ONLY TWO POSSIBLE RESPONSES: BELIEF OR UNBELIEF—1:19-12:50

A. John records the beginning ministry of Christ in order to show the early ministry of Christ the Revealer—1:19-4:54

1. John presents the witness of John the Baptist in order to show his confirmation of Christ as seen in the prologue—1:19-34
   - **a.** John's first witness is to a committee from the Jews in which he states that he is simply one who is preparing the way for the Messiah—1:19:28
   - **b.** John's second witness was to the disciples to whom he identified Christ as the Son of God who would take away the sin of the world and the one for whom he was preparing the way—1:29-34

2. John presents the witness of the first disciples of Jesus in order to show their confirmation of who Jesus was—1:35-51
   a. The first group of disciples follows Christ and acknowledge Him as the Messiah—1:35-42
   b. The second group of disciples follow Christ and acknowledge Him as the Son of God and King of Israel—1:43-51
3. John records the first sign of changing water into wine in order to reveal His glory and to show the glorious and joyful character of the Kingdom He was offering—2:1-11
   a. John notes that Jesus, Mary, and His disciples were invited to a wedding—2:1-2
   b. John notes that wine ran out at the banquet and the instructions of Jesus on how to deal with the problem—2:3-8
   c. John notes that the people were impressed with the quality of the wine—2:9-10
   d. John notes that this miracle manifested His glory and caused His disciples to move to a deeper level of faith—2:11

Note #62: The Wedding at Cana

The miracle performed at this wedding by Jesus is one of his most famous. This has led to a number of suggestions as to what the purpose of the miracle was. These proposals include 1) the "joke" view in which Jesus said to use water instead of wine. The headmaster of the feast entered into the spirit of the gag by saying sarcastically that this was the best "wine" of all, 2) this account was a heathen legend John adapted and used in his gospel, 3) Jesus' presence at the feast shows his approval of marriage, 4) the account shows the legitimacy of enjoying life, 5) the changing of water into wine shows Christ to be the creator. There are other questions related to this miracle such as, why did Jesus address his mother as he did? Did Jesus make alcoholic wine? and, what is the hour? The following summary statements can be made concerning this incident.

1. This was actually the final phase of the Jewish wedding known as the wedding feast. This feast could last up to a week or more and was marked by joyous celebration including, eating, drinking, and dancing. In a shame-oriented culture, running out of wine would be a serious matter with the ramifications lasting possibly throughout the family's lifetime.

2. Given the attendance at this event by Jesus, Mary, and the disciples, this could well have been the wedding of a family member or close friend. When Mary becomes aware that the wine had run out, she rushes to Jesus. In light of Mary's understanding of who Jesus was (see the "magnificat" in Luke 1) and Jesus' response, it is likely that she wants him to assert his Messiahship.

3. When Jesus responds to her request by calling her "woman," this indicated, not disrespectfully, that their relationship had changed. As Jesus was embarking on his public ministry, he was now on the timetable of his Father rather than that of his mother.

4. The phrase "what have I to do with you" has the idea of "what do you and I have in common in this situation?" This phrase was originally a Semitic idiom as illustrated by such passages as 2 Kings 3:13 and Hosea 14:8. Jesus expands on this by saying that "his hour" had not yet come. This is a reference to the process of his glorification as Messiah through his death, resurrection, exaltation, and return to reign.

Once more, Jesus is on the Father's schedule at this time. Mary grants this point and humbly submits to his will.

5. At the entrance to the feast are jars of water for purification. This would provide the guests with a means of being ritually clean as they ate at the feast. The amount of water in these jars could have been well over 100 gallons.

6. When Jesus transforms the water into wine, the headwaiter judges the wine to be better than that which was served at the beginning of the feast. Whereas normally the inferior wine was served when palates were dulled, he comments that the best had been saved for last. That this wine was fermented goes without question.

7. Regarding the purpose of this sign miracle, it is to be observed that the wedding feast and abundance of wine is consistently a picture of the joy and abundance of Messiah's kingdom in Scripture (Gen. 49:11, 13; Isa. 25:6-9; Hosea 2:22; Joel 2:24; 3:18; Amos 9:14; Zech. 9:15, 17; 10:7; Matt. 26:29; Luke 22:30; Rev. 19:9). Thus, this miracle is portraying the joy of the kingdom over which the Messiah will some day reign.

4. John presents an interlude in Capernaum—2:12

5. John presents Christ's first cleansing of the temple in order to show His unique relationship to the Father in that Christ is jealous for the holiness of the temple—2:13-22

6. John notes that Jesus went to Jerusalem where He performed many miracles and many believed, however Jesus would not commit Himself to them for He knew human nature—2:23-25

7. John presents Jesus' interview with Nicodemus in order to show that eternal life is gained through faith and to show that Christ as the Revealer knows what is in the heart of man—3:1-21

- **a.** A Pharisee named Nicodemus comes to Jesus and acknowledges Him as
  a teacher from God because of His miracles—3:1-2
- **b.** Jesus tells him that one cannot enter the Kingdom unless he is born from above—3:3
- **c.** Nicodemus thinks Jesus is talking about a physical birth showing he did not grasp the nature of regeneration—3:4
- **d.** Jesus tells him that one is born from above by the Spirit—3:5-8

Note #63: Born of "water and spirit"

Many interpretations have been posited for being born of "water and the Spirit" 1) water refers to natural birth and Spirit to supernatural birth. This has the strength of v. 4, but is a strange designation for natural birth. Moreover, 3:5 is not building on the misunderstanding of Nicodemus, but rather clarifying what it means to be born from above, 2) water refers to the Word of God, 3) water refers to baptism as a part of salvation, but this is contradicted by the rest of the Bible, 4) water refers to the Spirit as a symbol taking kai, as appositional, 5) water refers to the baptism of repentance under John, or 6) more likely, water and wind are both metaphors for the Holy Spirit, all of which originate from above, as does the new birth. For a full discussion of view 6 (the "water wind" view), see Zane Hodges, "Problem Passages in the Gospel of John Part 3: Water and Spirit—John 3:5," Bibliotheca Sacra *135:539 (Jul 1978), 206-220.*

e. In response to his lack of understanding Jesus noted that He had been the only one to permanently reside in heaven and come to earth and was therefore able to speak of these things—3:9-13

f. Jesus told him that He would be crucified and that the one who believed on Him would have eternal life—3:14-15

g. John offers several comments on the words of Jesus—3:16-21

   1) He notes the manner by which the Father showed his love was the gift of his Son for the purpose of giving eternal life to each one who believes—3:16

Note #64: Is God love-sick for the world?

"For God so loved" the world is often understood to mean God is love-sick for the world almost to the point of vulnerability. In fact, he is so in love with the world that he gave his only Son. While it is true that God loves all people, it is untrue that this goes to such an extent that God loses his independence and satisfaction within the Trinity. Additionally, it is doubtful that the construction of John 3:16 even refers to the intensity of God's love. After an exhaustive survey of the construction "so...that" (οὕτωςὥστε) ("For God ***so*** *loved the world* ***that****...") in extra-biblical Greek literature and the Gospel of John, Gundry and Howell contend that the construction communicates "in this way" or "this manner" and that the construction is supplementing something previously stated (Robert Gundry and Russell Howell, "The Sense and Syntax of John 3:14-17 with Special Reference to the use of "ΟΥΤΩΣ ΩΣΤΕ in John 3:16,"* Novum Testamentum *41 [Jan 1999], 25). Thus, 3:16 is not showing the intensity of God's love, but the manner in which he showed it to the world.*

   2) Christ was sent to save the world—3:17
   3) The instrumental means for salvation is belief—3:18
   4) Men are condemned because they love darkness rather than light and therefore shun the light—3:19-20
   5) Those who love the truth are drawn to the light—3:21

8. John records the final testimony of John the Baptist—3:22-30
9. John records an expansion on the theme of the Baptist about the supremacy of Christ—3:31-36
10. John presents the Samaritan ministry of Christ in order to show the acceptance of Christ as the Revealer of the Father as validated by his words and insight into men—4:1-42
    a. Jesus left Judea and was compelled to go through Samaria—4:1-4
    b. Jesus came into a city called Sychar and rested by Jacob's well—4:5-6
    c. Jesus talks to the woman at the well about living water—4:7-26

Note #65: Jews do not use dishes Samaritans have used

The animosity between Jews and Samaritans is well documented; however, there is an interesting exchange between Jesus and the woman regarding drawing water from the well. According to Leviticus, there were various ways in which one could contract uncleanness. This would lead to separation from the worshiping community lest the uncleanness spread and ultimately defile God's holiness. A list of uncleannesses is given in Leviticus 11-15—one of which was the loss of life fluids. Typically, an unclean person was quarantined and after cleansing was allowed to rejoin the community. The rabbis taught that Samaritan women were "menstruants from the cradle" (Mishnah, Naddah, *4.1. http://www.sefaria. org/Mishnah Niddah.4 , accessed 6/4/14) and thus perpetually unclean. This belief is apparently hinted at by the woman when she says that "Jews have no dealings with Samaritans" (4:9). The New International Version translates the phrase as "Jews do not associate with Samaritans," but has a footnote suggesting the translation "do not use dishes Samaritans have used." This sense fits well with 4:11 where the woman tells Jesus that he has nothing to draw with, i.e., some kind of utensil. Therefore the woman is somewhat surprised, not only that a Jewish male is talking to her, but that he would ask to share something she had used to drink which would render him unclean.*

Note #66: Worship in spirit and truth

This phrase is often interpreted to mean that true worship comes from the depths of the heart and is consistent with the revelation of Scripture. However, consider another option of what is meant here based on the following points:

1. To say that God is spirit means that he is invisible and does not have bodily parts.

2. The contrast in this passage is that God is immaterial while human beings are material.

3. While the term "spirit" can be a reference to the spirit of man, it could also be a reference to the Holy Spirit. The two interviews in this section of John (Nicodemus and the Samaritan woman have both been taken up with the work of the Holy Spirit whether in regeneration or living water).

4. The only way the incorporeal God can be known is if he chooses to reveal himself.

5. The major theme of John, going back to his prologue in 1:1-18, is that Christ is the revealer of the Father. He is the one in whom the Father may be known.

6. Christ is personified as the truth in 1:14 and 1:18. Very significantly the 1:18 text says that truth came by Jesus Christ, which is immediately followed by the phrase "no man has seen God."

7. Jesus declares plainly in 14:6 "I am the truth."

8. My conclusion: God is invisible and cannot be known or worshipped by man. Through the Spirit, a location has been given where God has revealed himself and that is in the Truth incarnate. The woman says in 4:25 that when Messiah comes he will show us all things—to which Jesus responds "I who speak to you am he." In other words, in keeping with the theme of the Gospel of John, Jesus is the locus of the full revelation of God and therefore to be worshiped.

d. The return of the disciples—4:27-38

1) The disciples return and are amazed that Jesus was talking with the woman—4:27

2) The woman reports of Jesus to the city and they come out to meet Him—4:28-30

3) Jesus told the disciples that His food was to do the will of God—4:31-34

4) Jesus told the disciples that unlike the agricultural year, the spiritual harvest is always ready—4:35-38
e. John records the faith of the Samaritans—4:39-42
11. John records the healing of the nobleman's son in order to authenticate the person of Christ and to explain that true faith is believing in the Word of God—4:43-54
a. Jesus went into Galilee and was accepted only on the basis of what they saw hinting at His upcoming rejection—4:43-45
b. A nobleman asked Jesus in Cana to heal his son who was in Capernaum—4:46-47
c. Jesus noted that faith that need signs was an immature faith—4:48
d. The nobleman again asks Jesus to come with him to heal his son—4:49
e. Jesus told him that his son was well and the man believed His word and left—4:50
f. The man learned on the way home that Jesus' word was true and He believed as well as His house—4:51-54

B. John presents Jesus' continued manifestation of Himself to the nation in Jerusalem in order to validate that He is the Son of God who reveals the Father and to show the beginnings of conflict and rejection of His person—5:1-47
1. Jesus heals a paralytic man at the pool of Bethesda—5:1-15
2. John writes that they sought to kill Jesus because He had done this on the Sabbath—5:16
3. John writes that they sought to kill Jesus because He made Himself equal with God—5:17-18
4. John presents Jesus' discourse concerning His relationship with the Father in order to show that He had authority because of this relationship—5:19-47
a. Jesus speaks of His relationship to the Father—5:19-29
1) Jesus said that He was subordinate to the Father—5:19
2) Jesus said that He is loved by the Father and knows Him—5:20
3) Jesus said He possesses the power of life like the Father—5:21
4) Jesus said He has been entrusted with judgment by the Father—5:22-23
5) Jesus said He is the one who is the means of salvation—5:24
6) Jesus said He would some day exercise His authority because of His inherent life and delegation of authority when He judges mankind—5:25-29
b. Jesus notes that there are other witnesses to His authority besides His own testimony—5:30-32
c. Jesus presents the witnesses to His testimony—5:33-47
1) The witness of John the Baptist—5:33-35
2) The witness of His works—5:36
3) The witness of the Father—5:37-38
4) The witness of the Scriptures—5:39-47

C. John presents Jesus' continued manifestation of Himself to the nation in Galilee in order to validate that He is the Son of God who reveals the Father and to show the continuation of conflict and rejection of His person—6:1-7:9

1. John records the feeding of the 5,000 in order to manifest His deity and to show the disciples that He was the one who could meet all needs on whom they needed to depend in their future ministries—6:1-14
2. John records the walking on water by Jesus to show the disciples that in difficult times ahead they would need to trust Him to protect them—6:15-21
3. John records the Bread of Life discourse in order to emphasize the kind of life that Christ came to give was eternal life and not the physical life provided by food—6:22-71
   a. John notes the mixed attitude of the crowd in Jerusalem toward Jesus in order to foreshadow the coming conflict—7:10-13
   b. John records Jesus' revelations concerning Himself during the feast to the responses of the people concerning His person—7:14-36
   c. Christ affirms that His learning came from the Father who sent Him—7:14-18
      1) Christ accused them of not keeping the Law because they wanted to kill Him and that they were hypocrites because they permitted circumcision on the Sabbath but not healing—7:19-24
      2) Christ affirms that He came from the Father because of the confusion of the people over His origination—7:25-29
      3) John notes that some believed on Him and the leaders tried to kill Him—7:30-32
      4) Christ affirms that after a while He would return to the Father—7:33-36
   d. John records Jesus' teaching on the last day of the feast—7:37-52
      1) On the last day of the feast Jesus proclaimed to the crowds that those who believed would be satisfied with the coming of the Holy Spirit—7:37-39
      2) The crowd was divided in their opinion of Jesus—7:40-44
      3) The leaders were against Christ but Nicodemus pointed out that he should get a fair hearing to which they dismissed him as ignorant as the Galileans—7:45-52
   e. John records Jesus' light of the world discourse in order to show that He was the Messiah who gave revelation and knowledge of the Father—8:12-8:59

Note #67: The woman caught in adultery

The majority of textual critics agree that 7:53-8:11 was not part of the original text of John. There are several reasons for this: 1) it is absent from most of the earliest MSS, 2) it is absent from the works of the earliest commentators, 3) when it does appear, it is found in different places, 4) it contains stylistic differences, and 5) it interrupts the flow of the context. It is possible that this was still historically true and would then be a rare instance of an extrabiblical tradition about Jesus. The point of the story seems to be that only a holy God has the ability to pass judgment and not unholy men. The Pharisees were using the woman to try to push Jesus into a corner. Theologically, this shows Jesus authority to forgive sin as well as His merciful character. In conclusion, "this entire section, 7:53-8:11, traditionally known as the pericope adulterae, *is not contained in the earliest and best MSS and was almost certainly not an original part of the Gospel of*

*John. Among modern commentators and textual critics, it is a foregone conclusion that the section is not original but represents a later addition to the text of the Gospel" (*New English Translation: First Beta Edition *[Biblical Studies Press, 2001], 1962). For a fuller discussion of the view that the* pericope *is not canonical but actually took place, see D. A. Carson,* The Gospel According to John *(Grand Rapids: Eerdmans, 1991), 333-337. For the view that the passage is authentic, see Zane Hodges, "Problem Passages in the Gospel of John Part 8: The Woman Taken in Adultery (John 7:53-8:11): The Text,"* Bibliotheca Sacra *136:544 [Oct 1979], 318-332.*

1) Jesus proclaims Himself to be the light of the world whose witness is testified to by the Father—8:12-20

2) Jesus proclaims that the consequence of unbelief in Him as the light of the world is eternal death—8:21-30

3) Jesus proclaims various truths in response to the antagonism of unbelief—8:31-59

(a) Jesus instructs those who believed on Him that if they continued in committed discipleship they would experience progressive freedom—8:31-32

(b) Some object to this idea of freedom for they operate on the false assumption that physical descent from Abraham was equivalent to spiritual char-acter—8:33

(c) Jesus tells them that only He could grant freedom and that their hate toward Him was unlike Abraham and showed rather their spiritual kinship with Satan—8:34-40

(d) They accuse Him of being illegitimate—8:41

(e) Jesus states that they showed they did not belong to God because they did not believe in Him—8:42-47

(f) They accuse Him of being demon-possessed—8:48

(g) Jesus states that His claims are not those of one who is possessed for he sought to honor the Father and that whoever kept His words would not see death—8:49-51

(h) They again say He has a demon for Abraham and the prophets had died and He could not be greater than they— 8:52-53

(i) Jesus states that He is honored by the Father and that Abraham rejoiced to see His day—8:54-56

(j) They said that He was not even fifty years old so He could not have known Abraham—8:57

(k) Jesus states that He existed before Abraham to which they sought to stone Him for blasphemy but He escaped—8:58-59

2. John records the healing of the blind man in order to confirm the Messiahship of Christ and to validate that as the light of the world He could give sight to the blind—9:1-41

a. Jesus heals the blind man and notes that His blindness was so that the works of God would be manifested in him—9:1-7

b. People initially asked the man how he was made to see and he told them that a man named Jesus did it—9:8-12

c. John presents the antagonism of the leaders to this sign—9:13-34

1) The first examination by the leaders is held and they said that He was not of God because He did not keep the Sabbath but the man says He is a prophet—9:13-17

2) The leaders question the parents of the man but they are afraid to answer for fear of being excommunicated from the temple and refer them back to their son—9:18-23

3) The leaders reexamine the man and get into a debate with him and the man confirms Jesus is from God—9:24-32

d. Jesus seeks out the man and leads him to a full belief in His deity while Jesus condemns the leaders for their blindness—9:33-41

3. John presents the Good Shepherd Discourse in order to contrast the ministry of the True Shepherd with that of the false shepherds of Israel in order to show that He was the Messiah of Israel—10:1-21

a. Jesus points out that He is the true shepherd—10:1-6

This first section is the picture of a sheepfold with sheep inside. Anyone who entered the sheepfold over the walls would do so for wrong reasons. By contrast, the true shepherd would enter the proper way. The sheep follow the voice of the true shepherd. The porter is John the Baptist and the fold is the nation. The point is to show that Christ is the "true" shepherd, that is, he fulfilled the prophecies of Himself; hence, he did not sneak into the fold. His words were meant to separate true believers from Pharisaism.

b. Jesus points out that He is the door—10:7-10

After the true sheep had been separated they were taken to pasture where there was an enclosure for the sheep. He becomes the door to that enclosure that protects and provides unlike the Pharisees.

c. Jesus points out that He is the good shepherd—10:11-18

This section shows that He is the caring shepherd who would lay down His life for the sheep. It also shows that there is a remnant of Israel which is distinguished from the Gentile remnant.

d. John notes that there was again a division among the people over these sayings—10:19-21

4. John records a final confrontation with the hostile in Jerusalem—10:22-42

a. He notes that at the feast of dedication in Solomon's Colonnade Christ is asked to tell plainly if He is the Christ—10:22-24

Note #68: Feast of Dedication

The Feast of Dedication (Hanukkah or Lights) commemorated the rededication of the temple by Judas Maccabeus on December 25, 165 B.C. This came after it was defiled three years earlier by Antiochus Epiphanes who offered a pig on the altar. His attempt to Hellenize Judea resulted in the Maccabean revolt.

b. Christ answers that His works testify of His person and that those who do not believe are not His sheep whereas the ones who do believe are His sheep who shall never perish because He is one with the Father—10:25-30

c. The Jews take up stones to stone Him because of blasphemy—10:31

d. He asked them for which works they wanted to stone Him and they responded that it was because of His claim to be God—10:32-33

e. He noted that in the Psalms humans were called gods (judges) so He could not be accused of blasphemy since He was God's Son on a mission from the Father—10:34-39

f. Jesus withdraws from Jerusalem—10:40-42

D. John records the raising of Lazarus from the dead in order to provide a climactic sign to the claims of Christ—11:1-57

1. John presents the setting for the sign by introducing Lazarus, Mary, and Martha and the news that Lazarus was sick and then Jesus declaration that he had died—11:1-16
2. John presents Jesus' conversation with Martha and Mary and His statement that He is the resurrection and the life and the one who believes this would have life—11:17-37
3. John presents the raising of Lazarus after being dead for four days in order to demonstrate irrefutably that He is the Messiah who reveals the Father—11:38-44
4. John notes that this revelation of the person of Christ brought two responses—11:45-57
   - **a.** Many of the people who saw the miracle believed—11:45
   - **b.** The others went and told the Pharisees who counseled together how they could put Jesus to death—11:46-57

E. John records the conclusion of Jesus' public ministry and the manifestations of belief and unbelief—12:1-50

1. John presents the anointing of Jesus by Mary and the opposition of this act by Judas in order to show the two responses to His person—12:1-8
2. John presents two more responses to the Lazarus miracle as many Jews came to see Jesus and Lazarus whereas the leaders plotted how to kill Lazarus because of his influence on many to believe—12:9-11
3. John presents the triumphal entry into Jerusalem in order to show Christ's public claim to be the Messiah and the negative response of the Pharisees toward His public acclaim—12:12-19
4. John presents the last public ministry of Christ in Jerusalem—12:20-36
   - **a.** Many God-fearing Greeks came to Philip (who had a Greek name) wanting to see Jesus—12:20-22
   - **b.** Jesus responds to this request by the Greeks—12:23-36
     - **1)** Jesus said that this confirmed that His glorification in death was near—12:23
     - **2)** Jesus gives the analogy of the grain of wheat in order to show that His death was necessary to gain a harvest of people— 12:24
     - **3)** Jesus points out that for those who would follow Him the principle is similar in that they must be willing to give up their lives for His sake—12:25-26

4) Jesus is troubled at the thought of death and prays that the Father would be glorified through it in response to which He endorses Christ's work—12:27-29
5) Jesus foretells His death but warns the crowds to believe on Him while they have opportunity—12:30-36

c. John presents Jesus' response to the unbelief of the nation—12:37-50
1) He notes that their unbelief was foreseen in Isaiah 53 and that they have been judicially blinded—12:37-43
2) He presents a call to the nation in which He reiterates that He came to reveal the light of the Father and that whoever believed would have life—12:44-50

III. JOHN PRESENTS THE PRIVATE MINISTRY OF CHRIST TO THE DISCIPLES IN ORDER TO PREPARE THEM FOR HIS DEATH AND TEACH THEM ABOUT THEIR MINISTRIES WHEN HE IS GONE—13:1-17:26

A. John records the events surrounding the Last Supper—13:1-30

1. John notes the incident of the washing of the disciples' feet in order to teach them that love for one another produces service and that in order to have fellowship with Christ they must be cleansed—13:1-17
2. John notes that at the supper Jesus predicts that the one He gave the sop to would betray Him at which time Judas immediately leaves—13:18-30

Note #69: The last supper

The bread was a flat cake which was filled with lamb, sprinkled with herbs, rolled up, dipped in a bitter sauce, and handed to a guest. The lamb was a reminder of God and salvation. In receiving the bread, each one acknowledged his sin and faith in a coming Messiah. The first piece went to the most honored guest, which in this arrangement was Judas (J. Dwight Pentecost, The Words and Works of Jesus Christ *[Grand Rapids: Zondervan, 1981], 431).*

There has been debate as to whether the Last Supper was a Passover meal. It is probably best to see it as such. For 14 reasons supporting this assertion, see Harold Hoehner, "Jesus' Last Supper," in Essays in Honor of J. Dwight Pentecost *(Chicago: Moody Press, 1986), 63-64. The following is a general overview of the events of the meal as outlined by Hoehner (65-74) which I have put into chart form:*

PREPARATION FOR PASSOVER

Morning	Afternoon	Late Afternoon
1.Work ceased 2. Leavened bread removed	1. Unleavened bread, wine, bitter herbs, fruit puree sauce set out 2. Couches or carpets for reclining were arranged 3. Lamps were prepared	1. Sacrifice of unblemished lamb 2. Lamb was taken to the temple 3. Lamb was slaughtered by the worshiper between 3-5 p.m. 4. The priests caught the blood in a golden bowl and the blood was tossed on the altar 5. Psalms 113-18 were sung 6. The lambs were put on hooks and flayed for sacrifice. 7. The pieces were placed on the altar of burnt offering

CELEBRATION OF PASSOVER

Before the Meal	Preliminary Course	Main Course	Conclusion
1. Lamb roasted 2. No bones were to be broken 3. To be eaten after sunset 4. Jesus and his disciples would have reclined around a U-shaped table	1. First cup of wine with benediction as a reminder of the promise to the enslaved Israelites 2. *Hors d'oeuvres* consisting of lettuce, bitter herbs, and fruit puree as a reminder of the bitter experience of Egyptian slavery	1. Serving of meal and second cup of wine though not consumed in order to arouse curiosity of the Passover liturgy 2. The father reviews the first Passover in Egypt 3. Part of the Hallel was sung from Psalms 113-118 4. Second cup of wine drunk 5. Grace said over unleavened bread 6. Passover meal eaten 7. Third cup of wine drunk and thanks	1. Second part of the Hallel sung 2. Fourth cup of wine drunk and blessing 3. Jesus did not drink the fourth cup but announced he would drink it with his people during the future kingdom age when they are restored

B. John records the final discourse of Jesus—13:31-16:33

1. Jesus notes that He would glorify the Father in His death and tells His disciples that they are to love one another as He had loved them which would be their identification as disciples—13:31-35
2. Peter asks Jesus where He is going and why he could not follow Him now—13:36-38
3. Christ answered that He was going to prepare the way for them and that He would return for them later—14:1-4
4. Thomas asks Jesus how they could know the way to where He was going—14:5

5. Christ answered that He was the way to the Father and that because they know Him they know the Father—14:6-7
6. Philip asks Christ to show them the Father—14:8
7. Christ answered that He and the Father were one as seen by His character, words, and works—14:9-11
8. Christ instructs the disciples concerning their future ministry—14:12-14
   a. He said that they would act as His agents in revealing the Father—14:12
   b. He said that as they went about this task they would be able to ask the help of the Father in His name—14:13-14

Note #70: Do I have to say "in Jesus' name" when I end a prayer?

While there is nothing wrong with ending a prayer in this manner, it is not necessary. Many Christians subconsciously think their prayers will not be effective without adding this formula; however, this was not the meaning of Jesus' words. To pray in Jesus' name is to recognize we are coming to God on his authority. In addition, his "name" represents all that he is. Therefore, prayer is to be consistent with his character and his holy will as laid out in Scripture.

9. Christ instructs the disciples concerning the Holy Spirit—14:15-26
   a. Christ tells them that obedience is a test of love—14:15
   b. Christ tells them that He would send another Comforter who would aid them in their ministry—14:16
   c. Christ says that the Spirit would be a communicator of truth—14:17
   d. Christ comforts them by telling them they would see Him shortly and repeats that they would demonstrate their love for Him by keeping His commandments—14:18-21
   e. Judas (not Iscariot) asks Jesus how He would manifest Himself to them and not to the world—14:22
   f. Jesus tells him that He is not manifested to those who are disobedient to His teaching but that they would be taught all things and have things brought to remembrance by the Comforter—14:23-26

Note #71: The apostles or all Christians?

The question arises as to whether the "bringing to remembrance all truth" applies to all believers or only the disciples. It is probably the latter for several reasons: 1) Jesus says that they would be helped to understand what they had not understood and reminded of things they had forgotten. The disciples were the only ones in a position for this, 2) they were the ones being commissioned by Christ, and 3) they were the ones who wrote Scripture and thus needed this.

10. Christ bequests His peace on the disciples which would give them a sense of calmness and adequacy for their task ahead—14:27-31
11. Christ instructs the disciples regarding relationships—15:1-16:4
    a. He instructs them on their relationship with Him—15:1-11
       1) Jesus tells them that they need to draw on His strength in order to bear fruit—15:1-8

Note #72: The branches that are burned

John 15:1-6 is a famous text in the debate among Calvinists (perseverance), Arminians (loss of salvation), and Free Grace (Christian discipline) especially when it comes to the burning of the branches in verse 6. One of the most helpful discussions of this passage which rightly takes into account viticultural practices of the day is found in Gary Derickson and Earl Radmacher, The Disciplemaker: What Matters Most to Jesus *(Salem, OR: Charis Press, 2001), 149-184; 326-329. Their discussion is largely followed here.*

1) Jesus is not focusing on true believers vs. false believers. He is focusing on those who are abiding and not abiding. The issue is communion with Christ, not union with Christ. Judas has left the room at this point and Jesus is instructing his true followers about their obedience to him.

2) A "vinedresser" is not merely a farmer but one who cares for each vine.

3) There are two kinds of branches present, those who bear fruit and those who do not.

4) The branches which do not bear fruit are "lifted up" to encourage fruit-bearing. The branches which are bearing fruit are pruned to encourage more growth. The point here (15:2) is that the vinedresser is doing all he can to encourage fruit from his vines. These words were spoken by Jesus in the Spring and is thus referring to spring training and trimming practices.

5) In 15:3 Jesus tells his disciples that they had been cleansed indicating that their season of fruitfulness is upon them.

6) Though they are ready to bear fruit, fruit-bearing is not automatic (15:4-5). The disciples must be obedient to Christ's command of abiding in him.

7) According to verse 6 (the "if...then" construction), the disciple may choose not to abide.

8) The work of the vinedresser in verse 2 is different than his work in verse 6. The former refers to the Spring pruning while the latter refers to the Fall pruning. Therefore, verse 6 is not a warning of judgment but simply a description of what happens to pruned materials. They are useless and therefore they are burned. This was true of all of the branches, even those that had borne fruit. The point of the illustration is that these branches are now useless. Therefore, if one does not choose to bear fruit, then he is useless just like the branches that are burned at the time of fall pruning.

9) The bottom line is that this whole illustration is not dealing with the perseverance of the saints, eternal security, or Christian discipline. Rather, it is meant for regenerate disciples of Christ to encourage them to a life of obedience so that they will live fruitful lives for the cause of Christ rather than a useless one.

- **2)** Jesus tells them that they would demonstrate their love for Him by keeping His commandments—15:9-11
- **b.** He instructs them on their relationship to one another that they should love one another—15:12-17
- **c.** He instructs them on their relationship to the world—15:18-16:4
  - **1)** He says that the world would hate them (first class condition) for several reasons—15:18-25
    - **a)** They had been chosen out of the world—15:18-19
    - **b)** They were friends with Christ whom the world hated—15:20

- **c)** The world does not know the Father—15:21
- **d)** The revelation of Christ offended the world—15:22-25

2) He tells them that they were still responsible to testify to the world because they had been with Christ—15:26-27

3) He shows them ways in which the world would show antagonism—16:1-2

- **a)** They would be put out of the synagogues—16:1-2a
- **b)** They would be murdered—16:2b

4) He tells them these things would be because He had warned them—16:3-4

12. Christ instructs the disciples concerning the Spirit's work—16:5-15

- **a.** Jesus notes that He would send the Spirit when He departed—16:5
- **b.** Jesus told them that the Spirit's work in the world would consist of convicting the world of sin, righteousness, and judgment—16:6-11
- **c.** Jesus tells them that the Spirit will testify of Christ not of Himself, guide them into all truth, and show them things to come—6:12-13
- **d.** Jesus tells them that the Spirit will glorify Christ—16:14-15

13. Jesus instructs the disciples on what the immediate future would hold for them—16:16-33

- **a.** Christ tells them that they would not see Him for a little while (His death and burial) and again in a little while they would see Him (His 40-day post-resurrection ministry)—16:16
- **b.** The disciples are confused over these time intervals—16:17-18
- **c.** Jesus told them that they would be sorrowful and the world would be happy (over His death) but that their sorrow would be turned to joy (after the resurrection), as when a woman gives birth, that no one would be able to take away—16:19-22
- **d.** Jesus notes that after His ascension there would be a change in that they would have to ask things of the Father—16:23-24
- **e.** Jesus tells them that later (after His resurrection) He would speak more plainly of the Father which would give them a greater intimacy with Him in prayer—16:25-28
- **f.** The disciples respond to Jesus by saying that they understand now—16:29-30
- **g.** Jesus tells them that their faith is not as strong as they think for they would abandon Him—16:31-32
- **h.** Jesus assures them that they have His peace and that He has overcome the world—16:33

C. John records Jesus' intercessory prayer on behalf of all the disciples—17:1-26

1. Christ prays for Himself that the Father would glorify Him (cross, resurrection, ascension, etc.) which in turn would glorify the Father for it would vindicate all He said about Him—17:1-5

2. Christ prays for His disciples—17:6-19

- **a.** He reviews their past by stating that they had the Father revealed to them which they received and obeyed—17:6-8
- **b.** He prays for them as the possession of the Father and Son—17:9-10
- **c.** He prays for their protection in an evil world and from the Evil One—

17:11-15

   d. He prays for their sanctification—17:16-19

3. Christ prays for future believers that they would be unified, i.e., enjoy a deep, genuine fellowship that flows out of the new birth—17:20-23

4. Christ prays for all that the Father has given Him to behold His glory—17:24

5. Christ pledges His continuing work of revealing the Father in order that the disciples may experience the love of the Godhead—17:25-26

IV. JOHN PRESENTS THE PASSION AND RESURRECTION OF CHRIST IN ORDER TO SHOW THE CULMINATION OF UNBELIEF AND THE ULTIMATE REVELATION OF THE FATHER AS HE PROVIDES A WAY OF FORGIVENESS THROUGH THE CROSS AND TRIUMPHS OVER THE GRAVE—18:1-20:31

A. John records the betrayal and arrest of Christ in the garden—18:1-11

B. John records an interchange of material of Jesus' trial before the Jewish court and Peter's denials in order to emphasize the steadfastness of Christ—18:12-27

1. Jesus appears before Annas—18:12-14
2. Peter denies Christ the first time—18:15-18
3. Jesus is questioned by Annas—18:19-24
4. Peter denies Christ the second and third times—18:25-27

C. John records Jesus' trial before Pilate at the Praetorium recording the events that took place outside and inside the palace—18:28-19:16

1. Outside the Jews demand the execution of Jesus—18:28-32
2. Inside Jesus affirms His kingship to Pilate—18:33-38a

Note #73: Whence the kingdom?

In 18:36a, Jesus was not commenting to Pilate about the location of His kingdom, but rather its source and origin. It would not be established as the other kingdoms with which Pilate was familiar, so he need not fear an insurrection among the people.

3. Outside Pilate's attempt at a bargain for Jesus is rejected—18:38b-40
4. Inside Jesus is scourged and mocked by the soldiers—19:1-3
5. Outside Pilate declares Jesus' innocence to the crowd—19:4-7
6. Inside Pilate declares his authority to have Jesus put to death—19:8-11
7. Outside Pilate hands Him over to be crucified—19:12-16

D. John records the crucifixion and death of Jesus reminiscent of the fact that the Word was made flesh—19:17-37

1. Jesus is crucified with the superscription put over Him—19:17-22
2. John notes that as He was hanging on the cross the soldiers cast lost for His garments and several women stood by the cross—19:23-27
3. Jesus gives up His spirit and dies—19:28-30
4. Jesus legs are not broken and His side thrust through with a spear—19:31-37

E. Nicodemus and Joseph of Arimathea bury the body of Jesus—19:38-42

Note #74: Burial

Burial took place shortly after death, and if no one intervened (19:38), the body of the executed was thrown into a common pit. "Bodies of Jewish criminals seem to have been buried with ignominy, in the valley of Hinnom; know, from this reason, as the Valley of Corpses" (Cunningham Geikie, The Life and Words of Christ *[NY: Appleton, 1893], 2:575). However, due to the bold action of Joseph of Arimathea, a wealthy member of the Sanhedrin, permission was secured from Pilate for him to take Jesus' body. His body and strips of cloth were covered with expensive spices to counteract the smell of putrefying flesh and then wrapped. In a garden belonging to Joseph, a new tomb had been cut for Joseph out of solid rock. Archaeology has revealed that inside the tomb would have been a room with three benches around a pit. Those who prepared the body would be able to prepare the body standing in the pit while the corpse lay on one of the benches. The body would then be placed into one of several niches which had been carved out of the inside rock walls. The opening to the tomb was sealed by a round stone which gently rolled down an incline to close the entrance. After about one year, the bones from the body would be placed into what was essentially a box called an "ossuary." Remarkably, when the disciples went to the tomb on the third day, the stone had been rolled up the incline and secured with a stopping stone. The disciples needed to stoop over in order to enter the tomb and when they did the body was gone except for the linen wrappings. For an excellent diagram of the tomb see Mark Strauss,* Four Portraits, One Jesus *(Grand Rapids: Zondervan, 2007), 576-577.*

F. John records the resurrection of Christ in order to vindicate His revelation concerning the Father—20:1-29

- **1.** The empty tomb is discovered first by Mary of Magdala and later Peter and John who see the orderliness of the tomb scene in order to stress that Jesus had been truly resurrected—20:1-10
- **2.** John records several appearances of the resurrected Christ in order to show the growth of faith based on this sign—20:11-29
  - **a.** Jesus reveals Himself to Mary at the tomb—20:11-18

Note #75: "Don't Touch Me"

When Jesus told Mary "do not touch me," the idea was more "do not cling to or restrain me." There would still be time to see him before his ascension to the Father. There is nothing mysterious in view here such as a secret ascension or defiling the resurrection body of Christ.

- **b.** Jesus reveals Himself to the disciples in the locked room in order to dissuade their fears and prepare them for ministry—20:19-23

Note #76: The breathing of the Spirit

John 20:22 refers to an initial enabling of the Spirit which fullness would be recognized at the Day of Pentecost. This was not the baptism of the Spirit, but a unique Old Testament receiving or empowering of the Spirit. It is evident they needed this because of their cowardice.

Note #77: Did the apostles have the power to absolve sins?

The Roman Catholic Church teaches that the apostles were given the power to forgive sins which has now passed on to the priesthood. Within the Sacraments of Mercy, Penance involves the process of confession, contrition, penance, and absolution. Only a priest or bishop can give absolution. Two examples from the Catechism of the Catholic Church *illustrate this belief: "The forgiveness of sins is associated with the Holy Spirit, the Church, and the Communion of Saints. Jesus said, 'Receive the Holy Spirit. If you forgive the sins of any, they are forgiven, if you retain the sins of any, they are retained'" (976). "The bishops (as successors of the apostles) and priests (as collaborators of the bishop), by the sacrament of Holy Orders, have the power to forgive all sins, 'in the name of the Father, and of the Son, and of the Holy Spirit'" (1461). There are at least two problems with this interpretation of John 20:23: 1) this view assumes the doctrine of apostolic succession. There are at least nine reasons to argue against succession (see Norm Geisler and Joshua Betancourt,* Is Rome the True Church? A Consideration of the Roman Catholic Claim *[Wheaton: Crossway, 2008], 162-164). If apostolic succession cannot be proved, then the Roman Catholic claim has no basis, and 2) there is no New Testament instance of a confession to an apostle or priest. It is one thing to proclaim forgiveness but quite another to confer it. What then, was Jesus teaching? Julius Mantey has argued convincingly that there is no instance in the New Testament where forgiveness was gained by proxy; that no one in church history claimed to forgive sins until the third century; and that the two perfect tense verbs in 20:23 ("forgiven" and "retained") should not be translated as presents or futures (Julius R. Mantey, "Evidence That the Perfect Tense in John 20:23 and Matthew 16:19 Is Mistranslated,"* Journal of the Evangelical Theological Society *16:3 [Summer 1973], 130-138). Therefore, the sense would be that the apostles proclaim the assurance of forgiveness in light of the fact that the individual has already received forgiveness from God.*

c. Jesus reveals Himself to Thomas and a second time to the disciples—20:24-29

Note: #78: Jesus' post-resurrection appearances

This is an approximate sequence of events that begin with the crucifixion and ends with the vision of John:

GOOD FRIDAY
Golgotha or Calvary - *Jesus is taken from the cross and placed in the garden tomb (Mt 27:57; Mk 15:42; Lk 23:50; Jn 19:31)* *There is no complete agreement by the various commentators on precisely how many different appearances Jesus made to his disciples*
EASTER SUNDAY IN AND AROUND JERUSALEM
The Garden Tomb - *Jesus appears to Mary Magdalene outside the tomb (Mk 16:9; Jn 20:11)* ***The Garden Tomb*** - *To Mary Magdalene and the other Mary (the mother of James the Younger and Joses - Mk 16:1) as they hurry from the tomb (Mt 28:8)*

The Garden Tomb *- To Peter (Lk 24:34; "Cephas" in 1Co 15:5)*
The Road to Emmaus *- To two disciples on the Emmaus road later in the day (Mk 16:12; Lk 24:13)*
The Upper Room *- To the apostles in a house in Jerusalem (Luke 24:36; Jn 20:19). Possibly the Upper Room where the Last Supper was held; Thomas was absent according to John 20:24.*

A WEEK LATER

The Upper Room *- To the eleven apostles, including Thomas in a house; probably the same house as [6] (Jn 20:26; possibly Mk 16:14)*

OVER THE NEXT WEEKS IN GALILEE

The apostles go to Galilee (Mt 28:16a); there Jesus appears ***to seven of them fishing*** *on the Sea of Galilee (Jn 21:1)*
Jesus appears ***to the apostles*** *on a mountain and gives his great commission to preach the Gospel to the world (Mt 28:16b)*
More than 500 disciples *in Galilee (1Co 15:6)*
To James*, his brother (1Co 15:7)*

ASCENSION DAY NEAR JERUSALEM

To the apostles *on the Mount of Olives (Olivet), near Bethany, as he ascends to Heaven (Lk 24:50, Acts 1:12)*

AFTER HIS ASCENSION

To Stephen *as he is stoned to death in Jerusalem (Ac 7:55)*
To Paul *on the road to Damascus (Ac 9:3; 26:13; 1Co 15:8)*
To John *in a vision on the island of Patmos (Rev 1:10)*

G. John notes that Jesus performed many signs which he had not written down, but that the ones he did record were designed to demonstrate Christ's deity and bring people to a full faith—20:30-31

V. JOHN PRESENTS THE EPILOGUE TO HIS GOSPEL IN ORDER TO CONFIRM AGAIN TO THE DISCIPLES CHRIST'S RESURRECTION, TO SHOW THE REINSTATEMENT OF PETER IN LIGHT OF HIS APOSTOLIC MINISTRY, AND TO CORRECT ANY FALSE NOTIONS ABOUT CHRIST'S RETURN—21:1-25

A. Christ provides the disciples with a miraculous catch of fish and eats a meal with them—21:1-14
B. Christ reinstates Peter to ministry and emphasizes to him that he must care for the sheep and follow Him and that He would be martyred—21:15-19
C. Christ tells Peter that the kind of death John would die was not his business but that did not mean that He would necessarily be alive when Christ returned—21:20-25

ACTS

The Importance of the Book

There are several reasons which can be given for the importance of the book of Acts: 1) it is the only historical sequel to the Gospels, 2) it is the only extant historical account of the first century church from a Christian perspective, 3) Acts forms a background for most of Paul's writings, and 4) Acts marks the transition from God dealing with the nation of Israel to the spread of the Gospel through the Church to the whole world.

The Bible contains 7,947 verses. Luke/Acts (which is one literary work probably separated into two parts because of the scroll size) comprises 27.1% or 2,157 of them. Compare this with the 2,032 verses in the Pauline writings and 1,407 in the Johannine writings (Kurt and Barbara Aland, *The Text of the New Testament* [Grand Rapids: Eerdmans, 1987], 29).

Author

It has already been pointed out in the discussion of the argument of Luke, that Luke was the author of both Luke and Acts. However, it can also be noted here that: 1) the external evidence uniformly supports this view (e.g., the Anti-Marcionite Prologue, the Muratorian Canon, Irenaeus in *Against Heresies*, and Clement of Alexandria), 2) the prologue of Acts 1:1 refers to a first account written by the same author, to the same recipient Theophilus and, 3) several features in the book indicate that the author accompanied Paul on several of his journeys (16:10-17; 20:5-21; 27:1-28), and Luke's association With Paul is attested in Colossians 4:14 and Philemon 24.

Date and Origin

It is safest to hold a date of around AD 60-62.This is due to the fact that Luke does not mention the destruction of Jerusalem (AD 70), the death of Paul (AD 66-68), or the Neronian persecutions (after the great fire in AD 64). While it is difficult to fully substantiate the place of origin, it is quite likely that Luke was in Rome at the time of Paul's release.

Structure

There are two internal items within Acts which contribute to its outline. The first is in 1:8 where Jesus instructs the apostles to be witnesses in Jerusalem, Judea/Samaria (one article in the Greek text covers both of these ethnocentric areas), and the uttermost parts of the earth. This yields a macrostructure of the book of 1:1-6:7—the progression of the gospel in Jerusalem; 6:8-9:31—the progression of the gospel in Judea/Samaria; 9:32-28:31—the progression of the gospel to the uttermost parts of the earth. Thus, in accord with the discussion on purpose below, Luke has given to Theophilus an orderly account of the gospel beginning with John the Baptist and ending with Paul in Rome. The second internal factor which contributes to the book's outline is the "progress reports." These reports show the progression of the gospel under the sovereign hand of God. Though some see more, there are at least seven progress reports which serve as structural markers in the book: 2:47; 6:7; 9:31; 12:24; 16:5; 19:20; 28:31.

The Purpose

Suggested purposes for Acts include: 1) an apologetic purpose, 2) a historical purpose, 3) to show the universality of the Gospel, 4) a conciliatory purpose, or 5) a catechetical purpose. While all of these views could be seen as subsidiary purposes with merit, they do not take into account all of the material in Acts. Furthermore, they fail to make a direct link with Luke's Gospel. This point is of prime importance, for as Longenecker notes: "The Acts of the Apostles was originally written as the second part of a two-volume work, and its inseparable relation to Luke's Gospel must be kept in mind if we are to understand the work" ("Acts," in *Expositor's Bible Commentary* [Grand Rapids: Zondervan, 1981], 9:231-232). Thus, coupling together Luke and Acts, it could be said that Luke wrote of the events that stretched from John the Baptist to the entrance of the Gospel in Rome. It will be remembered in the discussion of Luke's argument that Luke was recording events in the life of Christ in order to show how the Kingdom program had gone from the Jew to embrace the Gentile. Acts continues this movement from Jew to Gentile as the Gospel marches from Jerusalem to Rome. So Luke answers the question, "If Christianity has its roots in the Old Testament and in Judaism, how did it become a worldwide religion" (Stan Toussaint, "Acts," in *The Bible Knowledge Commentary* [Wheaton: Victor Books, 1983], 351)? It can also be shown that the Kingdom concept is replete in Acts. For example, the book begins with a question about the Kingdom (1:6) and ends with it (28:31). Toussaint has pointed out that the term "kingdom of God" occurs thirty-two times in Luke and six times in Acts, in addition to numerous references and inferences to eschatology (1:11; 2:19-21, 34-35; 3:19-25; 6:14; 10:42; 13:23-26, 32-33; 15:15-18; 17:3, 7, 31; 20:24-25, 32; 21:28; 23:6; 24:15-17, 21, 25; 26:6-8, 18; 28:20). With these things in mind, a purpose statement for Acts could be: Luke records the events surrounding the sovereign progression of the Gospel message from Jews in Jerusalem to Gentiles in Rome in order to show that the kingdom will be populated with believers from every race. The phrase "sovereign progress" is meant to emphasize that the story of the church in Acts will meet with numerous obstacles, none of which are able to thwart what God is doing. One way Luke will make this point is by his vocabulary: "plan," "foreknown," "foretold," "predestined," "promised," "ordained," things worked out by God's "choice" and "it is necessary."

Summary of Argument

I. LUKE RECORDS THE EVENTS SURROUNDING THE PROGRESSION OF THE GOSPEL IN JERUSALEM IN ORDER TO SHOW THE SOVEREIGN WORK OF GOD SPREADING FROM THE TWELVE APOSTLES THROUGH THE ESTABLISHMENT OF THE CHURCH—1:1-6:7

A. Luke presents the expectation of the coming of the Holy Spirit by the Apostles and their preparations for that event—1:1-26

1. Luke gives his prologue to the book in order to inform Theophilus concerning the actions of the Apostles—1:1-5

a. Luke reviews for Theophilus that in the former book he had written (the Gospel of Luke) about all that Jesus had begun to do until the time of His ascension—1:1-2a

b. Luke notes that before this ascension He had given instructions to the Apostles—1:2b

c. Luke notes that after His passion, He showed Himself to them and gave them convincing proof that He was alive—1:3a

d. Luke notes that during Christ's 40-day post-resurrection ministry He spoke to them about the Kingdom—1:3b

e. Luke notes that during this period, Jesus told the Apostles to remain in Jerusalem and wait for the gift of the Father—1:4-5

Note #79: The gift of the Father

The "gift" or "promise" of the Father was the gift of the Holy Spirit. Jesus had made this promise on behalf of the Father on a number of occasions (e.g. Luke 24:49; John 7:37-39; the Upper Room Discourse).

2. Luke presents the last meeting of the Apostles and Christ and their activities before the giving of the Spirit—1:6-26

a. The Apostles ask Christ if He is at this time going to restore the Kingdom to Israel—1:6

Note #80: The Kingdom

It should be observed that the question concerning the Kingdom in v. 6 is related to v. 5 by μὲν οὖν ("therefore," "so when"). According to Isaiah 32:15-20, Ezekiel 36, 39, Joel 2, and Zechariah 12:8-10, the giving of the Spirit was associated with the fulfillment of the New Covenant and the last days. Thus, the apostles associated the coming of the Spirit with the coming of the Kingdom and the fulfillment of the promises. There are strong indications in this text that the Kingdom was considered to be literal by the apostles. For example, their understanding of the kingdom was not corrected by Christ. In his response he deals with the timing of the kingdom, not the nature of it. In addition, the word for "restore" (ἀποκαθιστάνεις, the verbal form is used here and the nominative form is used in 3:21) has the idea of restoration or regeneration of an earthly kingdom. This theocracy ended when the Times of the Gentiles began under Nebuchadnezzar. Therefore, the Kingdom will not be inaugurated until the time of the Messiah's return. "Thus regarding the kingdom, it is best to say ***'no, not yet'*** *rather than; 'already, not yet' (Stanley Toussaint, Jay Quine, "No, Not Yet: The Contingency of God's Promised Kingdom,"* Bibliotheca Sacra *164:654 [Apr 2007], 131). For a fuller discussion of the view argued for in this note, see John McLean, "Did Jesus Correct the Disciples' View of the Kingdom?"* Bibliotheca Sacra *151:602 (Apr 1994), 215-227.*

b. Christ gives them two answers to this question—1:7-8

1) The first answer is that the time of the Kingdom is something under the control of the Father—1:7

2) The second answer is that their concern now is to witness on behalf of Christ to the uttermost parts of the earth—1:8

c. Christ is taken up to heaven out of the sight of the Apostles and the angel notes that this is the same way He would someday return—1:9-11

Note #81: The ascension

The ascension is important for several reasons: 1) it officially marked the end of Christ's earthly ministry, 2) it exalted Him to the right hand of the Father to begin His priestly work there, 3) it was necessary for the sending of the Holy Spirit, and 4) it was the official marking of the beginning of the ministry of the Apostles.

d. Luke notes that the Apostles went back into the city of Jerusalem into a room where they were staying and there joined together in prayer—1:12-14

Note #82: Prayer in the upper room

While some commentators state that the group was simply observing an appointed time of prayer, it is more likely that they were specifically praying for the coming of the Spirit. This is for several reasons: 1) the context has been talking about the giving of the Spirit, 2) Luke 11:13 speaks about praying for the Spirit, 3) chapter two would record an answer to this prayer, 4) there is the definite functioning article before the word "prayer," and 5) Luke notes in Luke 3:21 that the Spirit descended on Christ while He was praying.

e. Luke records the selection of the 12th Apostle to replace Judas—1:15-26

1) Peter reviews the account of Judas' betrayal and death and that it was in fulfillment of prophecy which now meant that they needed another to take his place—1:15-20

Note #83: Imprecatory psalms

Peter refers to Palms 69 and 109 both of which are royal imprecatory psalms which anticipate the King of Israel. While these psalms did not mention Judas by name, the psalms anticipated the enemies of the Messiah, which in this case, happened to be Judas. The imprecatory nature of both psalms applies to the destruction of Judas as an enemy of the Messiah. Because these royal psalms anticipated the Messiah, what happened to David was understood prophetically as applicable to Jesus.

It is also possible that choosing a replacement apostle was the first order of business because they were anticipating the Kingdom. Jesus had said in Matthew 19:28 that there would be twelve thrones in the Kingdom.

2) Peter notes that the qualifications for this replacement were that he had to have been with them during Jesus' earthly ministry and a witness of His resurrection—1:21-22

3) Matthias is made the next Apostle over Barsabbas after the Lord reveals this through the casting of lots—1:23-26

Note #84: The office and preparation of the apostles

The Office of Apostle

When the word "apostle" is examined throughout the history of the Greek language, it is discovered that the term could be used in a very general way to refer to someone/something who was sent away to do something. There are even occasions in the New Testament where the word is used to speak of a person who was sent forth as a messenger. And so the word did have a general sense to refer to someone or something that was sent forth. However, the dominant use of the term in the New Testament is a technical one referring to the office of apostle. Thus the apostles were those who were chosen and sent forth by Christ bearing the full authority of the One who had sent them. Those who were apostles in the technical sense shared certain characteristics/qualifications. First, an apostle had to receive a direct call and commission from the Lord Jesus. This is something that held true of the twelve who were appointed by Christ in the Gospels. This same fact was true of the Apostle Paul who was directly called and commissioned by Christ on the Road to Damascus. The only possible exception to this qualification would be the appointment of Matthias to replace Judas in Acts chapter 1. However, when the details of that story are examined, it is discovered that the eleven remaining apostles chose two candidates for the open position and then they prayed to the Lord and said "You Lord know which of these two you have chosen." And so the decision was not left up to the Church or up to the Apostles, but the decision rested with the Lord.

A second characteristic is that the person had to be a direct witness of the ministry of Jesus. The reason for this was so that he would be able to personally testify to what he had seen and heard. This was true of the original twelve, and it was also true of Matthias for Acts 1:22 says that the new apostle had to have been in the company of the Apostles from the baptism of John up until the ascension.

Regarding Paul, his conversion in Acts 9 would qualify him for being a witness of the resurrection. This is actually his own defense of his apostleship in 1 Corinthians 9:1 where he asks the question: "Am I not an apostle?" And the answer he gives which is also in the form of a question is: "Have I not seen Jesus Christ our Lord?" As far as being personally with the Lord and being taught by Him, Paul indicates in Galatians 1:16 and follow that after his conversion, he was taught directly by the Lord and receiving further revelation.

A third mark of an apostle is that he was the recipient of divine revelation. This means that when he spoke or wrote as an apostle he was indeed the voice of God. Paul refers to this phenomenon in Ephesians 3:3 when talking about the mystery of the Church. He indicates that what he was about to write "was given me by revelation."

The fourth characteristic of an apostle is infallibility. Since the apostles were communicating information directly from God, what they said or wrote in that capacity was infallible. And then finally, an apostle was able to perform miracles. When Christ commissioned the original apostles in Matthew 10:1-2, Jesus indicated that the miraculous would be worked through them including raising the dead, healing the sick, and casting out demons. This is also seen in Hebrews 2:3 where the writer says that salvation was "confirmed unto us by them that heard him [the apostles] God bearing them witness both with signs and wonders and with diverse miracles of the Holy Spirit." And in 2 Corinthians 12:12, where Paul is defending his apostleship, he says that the "signs of an apostle were wrought among you."

The fact that no one today has even one of these characteristics indicates that the apostolic office is no longer functioning and was therefore a transitional office as God began to work through the newly formed Church.

The Preparation of the Apostles

In the prologue to Acts, Luke outlines four stages in Jesus' preparation of these men to get them ready to carry on the ministry with which he would leave them. The first stage of preparation was that Jesus instructed the apostles. This is seen in 1:2 where the text says "he, through the Holy Spirit, had given commandments [instructions] unto the apostles whom he had chosen." There were basically two commandments given both of which are found at the end of the Gospel of Luke. The first commandment is in Luke 24:47 where Jesus instructs them to go into the world and be His witnesses. The second commandment is in Luke 24:49 where Jesus then tells them: "tarry in the city of Jerusalem, until you are endued with power from on high."

The second stage of preparation was that Jesus showed Himself to be alive to the apostles. Acts 1:3 says that Jesus demonstrated this through many "infallible proofs." The phrase translated "infallible proofs" is one word in the Greek text (τεκμήριον τεκμεριον) which is only found here in the New Testament. It refers to a proof that is convincing and decisive. There of course are many proofs which could be mentioned in the historical, legal, logical, and biblical categories of convincing proofs, but if confined to Luke's writings, there are two key passages. In Luke 24:13-32 Jesus carried on a conversation with the disciples on the Road to Emmaus and then ate with them. In 24:39-43 he ate with the eleven disciples and then showed them the nail scars in his hands and invited them to touch his body to show that it was made of flesh and bone. The sense of the text in Acts where it says that "he showed himself alive...being seen by them forty days," is that at various intervals during these forty days he would appear to them.

Stage three is that they were taught by Christ. According to 1:3 Jesus taught them for forty days truths about the Kingdom. And then the fourth stage of their preparation was that they were told by Christ to remain in Jerusalem and wait for the gift of the Father (1:4). The promise or gift of the Father was the Holy Spirit. There were three key passages where Jesus spoke about this to the disciples. The first passage was in Luke 24:49 where he talked to them about being "endued with power from on high." The second is recorded in John 7:37-39 where Jesus spoke of "rivers of living water" which John went on to identify as the reception of the Holy Spirit which would be given when Christ had ascended. And then the third key passage is the Upper Room Discourse where in John 14-16 Jesus once more spoke of the coming and reception of the Holy Spirit after His personal ascension. This was something which Jesus had clearly taught them and that is why at the end of verse 4 Jesus says that they had heard this from him.

For a discussion on the important issue of "apostolic succession," see Norman Geisler and Joshua Betancourt, Is Rome the True Church? A Consideration of the Roman Catholic Claim *(Wheaton: Crossway Books, 2008); Henry Hudson, Papal Power (Unicoi, TN: The Trinity Foundation, 2008); Robert Reymond,* The Reformation's Conflict with Rome: Why it Must Continue *(Great Britain: Christian Focus Publications, 2001), 21-66.*

B. Luke presents the coming of the Holy Spirit and the beginning of the Church in order to show in order to show the inception of the work of God in populating the Kingdom from Jerusalem—2:1-47

1. Luke records the descent of the Spirit on the Day of Pentecost in order to show the inauguration of this part of God's program—2:1-13

Note #85: Pentecost

"Pentecost" is from the Greek term meaning "50" because it fell on the 50th day after Passover and marked the completion of the wheat harvest. Passover anticipated Christ's death, while Pentecost anticipated His completed earthly ministry and thus the anticipation of the Spirit.

Note #86: The inauguration of the church age at Pentecost

The importance of when the church began helps determine whether there is a distinction between Israel and the Church. If the Church is a continuation of Israel, then it will have its origins in the Old Testament. This will affect how prophecies made to Israel during that era will be fulfilled in the Church. However, if the Church is a distinct entity, it will have a separate starting point and will not fulfill Israel's promises. Therefore, the issue is as large as how to read the entire Old Testament and its understanding in the New. Views regarding the origin of the Church include Adam, Abraham, Christ, John the Baptist, the ultra-dispensational view which sees a Jewish church at Pentecost and a later, Gentile church during the ministry of Paul, and the beginning of the Church at Pentecost. To begin with, the word "church" (ἐκκλησία) occurs 114 times in the New Testament and nearly 100 times in the LXX with 77 of those being in the canonical books. The word itself simply refers to an "assembly" (BAGD, 240) and the contexts vary as to the kind of assembly in view. The word is used of Israel in the Septuagint to refer to an assembly of the nation (e.g. Deut 18:16; Neh. 13:1); of an assembly of citizens in Ephesus (Acts 19:39); of a riotous mob (Acts 19:32, 41); and, of the body of Christ throughout the New Testament. It is seen that just because the word "assembly" is used in a text, this does not necessarily mean that it is being used in a technical sense. There are a number of reasons which support the beginning of the Church, as the body of Christ in its technical sense, at the day of Pentecost: 1) in Ephesians 3 Paul refers to the church as a "mystery." In the context of that chapter, the mystery is a reference to the Jew and Gentile in one body. Paul says that this was referred to the apostles, thus as a mystery, it was not revealed before that time, 2) in Matthew 16:18, Jesus uses a future tense verb when he speaks of building his church, 3) a body cannot function without a head. Jesus did not become head of his body until after his ascension (Eph. 1:22), 4) a body cannot function without gifts which were not given until after the ascension (Eph. 4:8), 5) the formation of the body of Christ is linked to Spirit baptism (1 Cor. 12:13) which Jesus said in Acts 1:5 was still future, naturally taking place at Pentecost, and 6) the word "church" is used only 3 times in 89 chapters of gospel material. Two of the three refer to the assembly of the apostles (Matt. 18:17) and the other is proleptic (Matt. 16:18). Compare this to 111 uses after the Day of Pentecost.

- **a.** Luke notes that the occasion was the Day of Pentecost when they were all gathered in one place—2:1
- **b.** Luke notes that there was the sound like a rushing wind and that tongues as of fire rested on each person—2:2-3

Note #87: The significance of "wind" vocabulary

In Luke's description of the events of Pentecost, it is significant that he uses the term "wind." The actual Greek word that is used here is the noun πνοη, which means a "blowing wind." What is of special importance however is to note that this word is part of a family of words all coming from the same root πνέω dealing with "spirit," "breath," "blow," etc. This strong connection between all of these terms is demonstrated by the fact that in Hebrew, Greek and even Latin the same word for "spirit" would also be used for "wind" or "breath." Thus when Luke uses the term "wind" those who thought in these languages would not have missed the connection or the symbolism of what was taking place.

In the Genesis 1 creation account, the Bible says that the Spirit of God was hovering over the waters. The implication of that in English is that the Spirit is lighting or skimming over the waters. But the correct idea is that the Holy Spirit, portrayed as God's breath, is moving and creating and being dynamic. While each member of the Godhead had a role to play in creation, the flow of the Genesis text would indicate that it was the Spirit who actually fashioned matter so that it was habitable for man. Thus the Spirit is the subject of the narrative from 1:3 onward. In Genesis 2 we are told of the creation of Adam where the Spirit breathes into him the breath of life and he becomes a living being.

In the New Testament Jesus said to Nicodemus in John 3 that he needed to be born again or literally born from above. Jesus then spoke of being born of water and the spirit. Just as God breathed into Adam the breath of life so that he became a living being, so Nicodemus would only become spiritually alive through the breath or wind of the Holy Spirit.

When this background is brought to Acts 2:2, and it says a wind came from heaven; this is very analogous to the story of the Spirit of God hovering over the waters at creation. Just as in Genesis 1 where the Holy Spirit is hovering over the waters at creation—protecting and watching and anticipating and participating in the creation—so now in Acts 2 at the Day of Pentecost here comes the wind of the Spirit of God again symbolizing the coming of the creative power of God to create and inaugurate a new era in which men and women will be given spiritual life and the Church would be created for its mission.

- **c.** Luke notes that each believer was filled with the Holy Spirit and began to speak in other tongues—2:4
- **d.** Luke notes the bewilderment of the people because they heard them speak in a variety of languages the wonderful works of God—2:5-12
- **e.** Luke notes that others made fun of them and said they were drunk—2:13

Note #88: Tongues

*Views on the identity of tongues include: 1) expository preaching, 2) a miracle of hearing, not speaking, 3) ecstatic speech, 4) languages in Acts and ecstatic speech in 1 Corinthians. However, the evidence points to the conclusion that tongues in the book of Acts and elsewhere refers to known languages. This is based on several factors from the text of Acts. First, the initial occurrence of speaking in tongues is found in Acts 2:4 where Luke writes that they "spoke with other tongues." Luke uses a plural form of the Greek noun γλῶσσα (*glossa*). In Classic Greek literature this term referred to the physical organ of the tongue, a language including obsolete terms of that language which might need to be explained, or something that was tongue-shaped. One will find the same three uses of* glossa *in the Septuagint and in Koine Greek which was the common Greek spoken in the first century AD. The word is used 50 times in the New Testament and it continues to have the sense of the physical organ, something that is tongue-shaped, or an actual language. The third use is by far the dominant one. There is no indication that* glossa *ever has the sense of an ecstatic utterance or unintelligible speech. Therefore, in the first historical instance of tongues speaking in the New Testament the reference is to a known language.*

The second reason concerns the synonym of glossa *in Acts 2. In 2:4 Luke says they spoke with other tongues—*glossa. *In verse 6 where Luke is expanding on this phenomenon he writes "And when this sound occurred, the multitude came together, and were confused, because everyone heard them speak in his own language." The word translated "language" is the Greek word διάλεκτος (*dialektos*). Notice that Luke himself, in this text, gives the definition of tongues,* glossa *as dialects. Third, in verse 8 he uses the word "dialect" for a second time and then in verses 9-11 gives a list of various dialects. The following chart is taken from Clinton Arnold, "Acts," in* Zondervan Illustrated Bible Backgrounds Commentary *(Grand Rapids: Zondervan, 2002), 233.*

Country	**Local Dialects**	**What Is Known About Judaism There**
1. Parthia 2. Media 3. Elam 4. Mesopotamia	Aramaic, Parthian, Iranian	It was to these countries in the East...that the tribes of Israel were exiled over seven hundred years earlier...Although they were given permission to return to Israel during the Persian empire...many chose to stay. By the time of the first century, the number of Jews in this region may have numbered in the hundreds of thousands.
5. Judea	Aramaic, Hebrew	This was the Roman province to which Jerusalem belonged. Jews from all of the surround villages streamed to Jerusalem for the festivals.
6. Cappadocia 7. Pontus 8. Asia 9. Phrygia 10. Pamphylia	Numerous local dialects include Phrygian, Pisidian, Lydian, Carian, Lycian, Celtic, Lycaonian, and others	These five countries were all ethnic territories within the Roman province of Asia Minor....There are numerous literary texts and archaeological evidences illustrating the extensive Jewish presence in Asia Minor from the second century B.C.
11. Egypt	Coptic	This was the largest Jewish community in the world at that time. The largest community was in the city of Alexandria, where there may have been as many as a

		hundred thousand Jews.
12. Libya (Cyrene)	Latin, Numidian	There is considerable evidence for Jewish presence in North Africa, especially in the city of Cyrene
13. Rome	Latin	Jews established a colony in Rome during the second century B.C. The Roman general Pompey brought a great number of Jews to the city from Palestine in 62 B.C. The Jewish population in Rome swelled to as high as twenty thousand by the first century A.D.
14. Crete	Greek	This large island had a sizeable Jewish population dwelling primarily in the area of Gorytna.
15. Arabia	Nabatean (a branch of Aramaic), Aramaic, Arabic	This would refer to the Nabatean Arabs who lived to the east of the Jordan River and to the south of Palestine. Their capital was Petra....There is ample evidence of Jewish presence in the key cities...and in the territory.

Since Acts 2 is the first historical instance of tongues speaking in the New Testament and the only passage which defines it, if speaking in tongues is different than what is found in Acts 2, then lexical and contextual evidence will have to be produced. After an exhaustive study of modern tongues, Samarin offers this assessment: "Over a period of five years I have taken part in meetings in Italy, Holland, Jamaica, Canada and the United States. I have observed old-fashioned Pentecostal and Neo-Pentecostals. I have been in small meetings in private homes as well as in mammoth public meetings. I have seen such different cultural settings as are found among Puerto Ricans of the Bronx, the snake handlers of the Appalachians and the Russian Molakans of Los Angeles...I have interviewed tongues speakers, and tape recorded and analyzed countless samples of tongues. In every case, glossolalia *[speaking with tongues] turns out to be linguistic nonsense. In spite of superficial similarities,* glossolalia *is fundamentally not language" (William Samarin,* Tongues of Men and Angels *(NY: Macmillan Co., 1972), 10-1. See also Samarin's study entitled "The Linguisticality of Glossolalia" in which he shows ways in which glossolalia is not language (http://philosophy-religion.info/handouts/-pdfs/Samarin-Pages 48-75, accessed 1/21/2014). For the identity of tongues in 1 Corinthians and their purpose, see notes 14 and 15 in that section.*

Note #89: The Significance of Pentecost

The event described in these verses is the inauguration of a new age which marked the coming of the Holy Spirit in a new way. The wind, fire, and tongues constituted the "fanfare" for this event. The coming of the Holy Spirit at this new dispensation effected the baptism, filling, formation of the Church, and other works of the Holy Spirit. There are several reasons to be noted as to why the events of Pentecost are unrepeatable: 1) a new era in God's dealings can only begin once, 2) the Holy Spirit can only be sent once, 3) all of the events associated with Pentecost have never recurred, and 4) many miraculous events have never recurred because they were not intended to (e.g., parting of the Red Sea, being taken to heaven in a fiery chariot, etc.).

2. Luke records Peter's sermon on the Day of Pentecost in which he proves that Christ is the covenanted Messiah—2:14-41
   a. Peter states that what was taking place was in fulfillment of Joel's prophecy—2:14-21

Note #90: Joel 2

In Acts 2:17-21 Peter quotes Joel 2:28-32. How Peter is using this quotation is one of the most difficult questions in the New Testament. Broadly, there are three approaches as to Peter's intent, 1) all of Joel's prophecy was fulfilled on the Day of Pentecost, 2) Joel was partially fulfilled, and 3) nothing from Joel was fulfilled, with the events of Pentecost serving as an illustration of what will happen when the Joel prophecy is fulfilled in the future. In my opinion, view 1 is the least likely since this would remove the prophecy from its original intent of referring to the restoration of Israel. Those who argue for view 2 suggest that Acts 2:17-18 was fulfilled on the Day of Pentecost while 2:19-21 awaits a future fulfillment. Toussaint explains "this clause does not mean, 'This is like that'; it means Pentecost fulfilled what Joel had described. However, the prophecies of Joel quoted in Acts 2:19-20 were not fulfilled. The implication is that the remainder would be fulfilled if Israel would repent" (Stan Toussaint, "Acts," in The Bible Knowledge Commentary *[Wheaton: Victor, 1983], 358). Fruchtenbaum is representative of those taking view 3 and suggests that Peter's use of Joel is an example of the "literal plus application" of the Old Testament use in the New: "Virtually nothing that happened in Acts 2 is predicted in Joel 2...However, there was one point of similarity, an outpouring of the Holy Spirit, resulting in unusual manifestations. Acts two does not change or reinterpret Joel two, nor does it deny that Joel two will have a literal fulfillment when the Holy Spirit will be poured out on the whole nation of Israel. It is simply applying it to a New Testament event because of one point of similarity" (Arnold Fruchtenbaum,* Israelology: The Missing Link in Systematic Theology *[Tustin, CA: Ariel Ministries, 2001], 844-845). Though it is difficult to be dogmatic on this issue, I tend ever so slightly to view 2 in that Peter is presenting an ongoing duty of the nation to repent in order to experience the promises. It is evident from Acts that there was not a national repentance, but growing antagonism toward the Messiah. Therefore, the fulfillment of the kingdom promises awaits a future, national repentance.*

   b. Peter states that Jesus is the Messiah—2:22-36
      1) Jesus' miracles authenticated His claim to be the Messiah—2:22
      2) Jesus' death was divinely ordained by God and coupled with His resurrection/ascension showed Him to be the Messiah which is further demonstrated by four proofs—2:23-35
         a) The presence of David's tomb shows that Psalm 16 had prophetic ramifications for the Messiah—2:25-31

b) There were witnesses of the resurrection—2:32
c) The supernatural events at Pentecost were sent by Christ—2:33
d) The Lord ascended into heaven—2:34-35

3) Peter concludes that the one they crucified is Lord and Christ—2:36

c. Peter applies the sermon—2:37-41

1) The people were convicted by this message and asked Peter what they should do—2:37

2) Peter tells them to repent and be baptized so that they would be forgiven and receive the Holy Spirit—2:38-41

Note #91: Is Baptism Necessary for Salvation?

Peter preaches in Acts 2:38 "Repent, and let every one of you be baptized in the name of Jesus Christ for the remission of sins; and you shall receive the gift of the Holy Spirit." Several religious traditions teach from this verse that water baptism is an essential ingredient to salvation. It is not the intent here to deal with the larger question of faith alone versus faith plus works/rites for salvation; rather, it is to deal with legitimate interpretations of 2:38; 1) take the preposition "for" to have a causal sense. Thus, be baptized for (because) of the forgiveness of sins. However, this presses an unusual use of the preposition, 2) baptism refers to Spirit baptism. Yet, Spirit baptism is not something people are ever told to do. Moreover, the following verses indicate people were baptized with water, 3) take the baptism clause as parenthetical. Since "repent" and "sins" are plural in number, and the command to be "baptized" is singular, it has been posited that the baptism clause is a parenthesis. So, "repent in reference to your sins, and be baptized." This is possible, but the singularity of the baptism clause could emphasize the responsibility of each one being addressed, 4) take baptism in its first century sense. By this I mean that baptism was associated with the forgiveness of sins in the sense that this was the natural, subsequent event, and 5) take the baptism to be in connection with verse 40 "save yourselves from this crooked generation." Just as John's baptism of repentance led people to separate from the religious order and identify with John's message, so Peter is urging his Jewish hearers to disassociate themselves from the generation that killed the Messiah, since that generation had been placed under judgment by Christ.

3. Luke describes some of the activities of the first church at Jerusalem—2:42-47

a. He notes that the people were steadfastly devoted to the Apostle's teaching and fellowship (which consisted of the breaking of bread and prayer)—2:42

b. He notes that the people were in awe at the miracles of the Apostles—2:43

c. He notes that the people voluntarily sold their possessions when there was a need in the church—2:44-45

d. He notes that they continued to meet daily and that many people were added to the church (progress report #1)—2:46-47

C. Luke presents the expansion of the Church at Jerusalem in order to show the sovereign spread of the Gospel message in that region—3:1-6:7

1. Luke records the ministry of Peter in Jerusalem and the opposition from without to show that the sovereign spread of the Gospel cannot be thwarted by men—3:1-4:31

a. Luke notes a miracle by Peter and his consequent sermon in order to give the occasion for opposition to the message—3:1-26

1) Peter heals a man, through the power of Christ, who had been crippled for forty years—3:1-10

2) Peter preaches his second sermon as recorded in Acts in which he shows that Christ was the covenanted Messiah whom they killed, but despite this they could still repent and enjoy covenant blessings—3:11-24

a) Peter notes the excitement over the miracle and asks the people why they were so surprised at this as though they had the power to perform this miracle—3:11-12

b) Peter offers an explanation for the miracle as attributable to Jesus and then notes three contradictions in their conduct toward Him when He was on earth in order to show their culpability—3:13-16

1) They demanded His death when Pilate wanted to release Him—3:13

2) They demanded His death while releasing a murderer—3:14

3) They killed the Author of Life who was raised from the dead—3:15-16

c) Peter exhorts the people that though they are guilty they can still repent and enjoy the covenant blessings—3:17-26

1) Peter notes that, though guilty, they had acted in ignorance because they did not comprehend fully who Jesus was—3:17-18

2) Peter exhorts the people to repent and that this would bring the Kingdom to earth—3:19-21

Note #92: Did Peter re-offer the kingdom?

This section is difficult in determining whether Peter was really offering to the nation the establishment of the Kingdom if they repented. There are two answers to this question. On the one hand, some say that the Kingdom was not really being offered but that Peter was stressing the responsibility of the nation to repent, which was always required of the nation. Christ then, would set up His Kingdom at the end of the world. On the other hand, some feel that the Kingdom would have been established if they had repented. This is the favored view for several reasons: 1) the word "restore" is related to the similar word in ch. 1 which refers to the restoration of the nation in their prophesied form, 2) the purpose clauses in vv. 20 and 21 are seen to be the purpose for the repentance in v. 19, 3) The sending of Christ meant the coming of the Kingdom, and 4) the repentance of Israel is the only prerequisite for the Kingdom. This view can be reconciled with Matthew 12-13 in that though Israel had been confirmed in her unbelief, Peter was still presenting a true fact. The same phenomenon was seen in the Old Testament where prophets like Isaiah delivered the message of the kingdom to Israel despite the fact he was told in advance by God that it would fall on deaf ears. The ultimate purpose of the offer, therefore, is to continue to validate the guilt of the nation regarding their rejection.

3) Peter notes that Christ would be the new Moses who would judge as Moses did—3:22-23
4) Peter notes that the prophets from Samuel on had written about this Messianic age—3:24-25
5) Peter notes that the divine pattern was that salvation be offered to the Jew first—3:26

b. Luke notes the opposition to the ministry of the Apostles in order to show that the ministry thrived in spite of it—4:1-31

1) Luke shows that the leaders were upset at the preaching concerning the resurrection so they incarcerated Peter and John and yet many believed the message still—4:1-4
2) Luke records Peter's address before the Jewish leaders in order to show that they had rejected the only means of salvation—4:5-12
   a) Luke presents the setting where the leaders are gathered and they ask them by what power they performed the miracle —4:5-7
   b) Peter is astonished that they are being tried for doing a good deed, and states that they performed this miracle by the power of the one they had crucified—4:8-10
   c) Peter quotes Psalm 118 in stating that Christ was the rejected stone—4:11

Note #93: The stone

While in Psalm 118 the stone probably referred to Israel as spurned by the other rations (other suggestions include David or an actual stone), Christ was the capstone of the Messianic program which was rejected by the nation.

   d) Peter notes that salvation (personal and national as anticipated in Psalm 118) was found in Christ—4:12
3) Luke notes that the leaders were astonished because of the boldness Peter had even though he was unschooled—4:13-14
4) Luke says that the leaders met privately and agreed they could not deny the miracle but at the same time had to get the apostles to stop spreading their teaching—4:15-17
5) Luke notes that they threatened them to stop teaching but could do no more because of the people—4:18-22
6) Luke presents the prayer of the early church when they learned that Peter and John had been released—4:23-31
   a) They praised God for His sovereignty—4:23-24
   b) They acknowledged that God's plan included persecution—4:25-28
   c) They ask for boldness to preach despite the opposition—4:29-31

2. Luke records the ministry of the church in Jerusalem and the opposition from within in order to show that the sovereign spread of the Gospel cannot be hindered by men—4:32-5:11

a. Luke shows the unity of the Church and their generosity toward one another in order to present a contrast with the opposition to that unity by Ananias and Sapphira—4:32-37

b. Luke shows the sin of Ananias and Sapphira as lying to the Holy Spirit in order to show that they were sinning against the unity of the body and to show that God was operating in this group in contrast to the nation as a whole—5:1-11

1) They sold property and gave only a part to the Apostles—5:1-2

2) Peter notes that their sin consisted of lying to the Holy Spirit—5:3-4

3) Luke notes that both were slain by the Lord and that great fear seized the church as a result—5:5-11

Note #94: Why did God kill Ananias and Sapphira for lying?

This couple sold a piece of property and gave the proceeds to the apostles. They lied by stating that they had given the full amount. As Peter is exposing the sin in 5:4 Ananias falls down and dies. The verb "heard" in 5:5 is a present participle indicating simultaneous action so that as Peter is speaking, Ananias dies. Sapphira is later given an opportunity to tell the truth, but continues the charade and she dies as well. The interpretation of the account is straightforward; however, it is rather puzzling as to why such a harsh penalty was imposed by God. By the standards of morality, even in the first century church, this sin was not a gross one. The question remains: why did God kill Ananias and Sapphira for lying? I would propose a solution through a number of observations.

1. This incident as recorded in 5:1-11 is part of a larger unit which begins in 4:32. In 4:32-37 a positive example of generosity and unity in the church, followed by the negative example in 5:1-11. This juxtaposition helps to establish the unity of the body of Christ as the main theme in the section.

2. Peter says in 5:3 that Satan had "filled" the heart of Ananias. Christians can not only be influenced by the Holy Spirit, but they can also be influenced by Satan. A major scriptural concept undergirds this point. Paul argues in Romans 6, for example, that the Christian is no longer the person he used to be spiritually by virtue of the fact that the old man was killed by God and he has been placed in Christ by Spirit baptism. While this is positionally true, the second half of chapter 6 calls on the believer to put this into practice. The same idea is found in Ephesians 4:22 where the believer is told to "put off the old man." Romans has already taught that the old man is dead, but now the Christian must live consistently with that. The same idea is present in 1 John 2:9-11 where a believer can be said to walk in darkness if he hates his brother. Darkness is the realm of sin and Satan from which the believer has been delivered, but he may still choose to live in that realm. Evidently, this was characteristic of Ananias and Sapphira leading to the influence of Satan in their lives.

3. The two key terms which inform the purpose of Ephesians is "love" and "unity" (see the introductory Ephesians notes) with all of the material revolving around that purpose. In 4:22-33 Paul lists a series of positives and negatives to be heeded by the believer in order to promote unity in the Church. Interestingly he notes in 4:30 that the sins listed "grieve the Holy Spirit." It would certainly be true that these sins would also grieve the Father and the Son. The reason the third member of the Trinity is singled out is because it is his work which creates the unity of the body. The Christian who commits sin against the body is especially grieving the Spirit since he is the member of the Godhead who forms the body of Christ.

4. When this idea is applied to Acts, in light of the fact that the Ananias and Sapphira incident occurs in a context dealing with Church unity and just recently at the Day of Pentecost the Spirit formed the body of Christ, it is not surprising that sin against the Church is being shown at an early date to be a serious matter. This does not indicate that every time a person sins against the unity of the body of Christ they will die, but again, a divine statement is being made at the beginning of the church age as to how seriously God regards the church.

3. Luke records the further authentication of the Apostles and the continued rejection by the nation of Israel of the Messiah in order to show their guilt and why the message was being spread to the ends of the earth—5:12-42
- **a.** Luke presents a series of miracles done by the Apostles in order to authenticate their message and to show that God was introducing a new era in God's dealings with Israel—5:12-16
- **b.** Luke notes that because of these miracles the Apostles were again arrested and put in jail but an angel released them—5:17-20
- **c.** Luke records the discovery of this fact by the leaders and that they were again preaching in the temple courts—5:21-25
- **d.** Luke records the re-arrest of the Apostles and their defense before the Sanhedrin—5:26-32
  - **1)** They arrested them and presented them before the High Priest who charged them with continuing to teach when they had been told not to—5:26-28
  - **2)** Peter told them that they had to obey God rather than men and that they were witnesses of the death and resurrection of Christ and the Holy Spirit which could bring salvation to the nation—5:29-32
- **e.** Luke records the response of the Sanhedrin to this defense and the release of the Apostles—5:33-42
  - **1)** The leaders were furious and wanted to put them to death—5:33
  - **2)** Gamaliel observed that false Messiah movements would fail whereas the true one would not and that they should leave them alone—5:34-39

Note #95: Gamaliel

The apostles probably would have been executed at this point if not for the intervention of Gamaliel. He was the leader of the Hillel branch within Pharisaism. He was called "rabban" ("our teacher") by the people which was a more respected title than "rabbi" ("my teacher"). He speech persuaded the Sanhedrin not to act rashly toward the apostles. This restraint, however, would be short-lived with the execution of Stephen in Acts 7.

  - **3)** The leaders agree and have the apostles flogged and release them—5:40

Note #96: Flogging

Flogging was a barbaric punishment which sometimes caused the victim to die. The tractate Makkoth *3.12-14 in the Mishnah describes the process.*

"How do we lash him? His two hands are bound on each side of the pillar and the administer of the gathering seizes his clothing. If they [the clothing] are torn, they are torn [i.e. so be it] and if they become unstitched, they are unstitched [i.e. so be it], until his heart is uncovered. And the stone is placed behind him, and the administrator of the gathering stands on it. And a strap from a calf is in his hand, doubled over once into two [straps] and a second time into four [straps] and there are two [other] straps go up and down with it [during the lashing]. The [strap's] handle is a handbreadth [wide] and it [the strap] is a handbreadth wide and its tip reaches to the mouth of his stomach. And he is lashed a third [of the lashes] in his front and two thirds from his back. And he is not lashed, neither standing nor sitting rather leaning over, as the verse says (Deuteronomy 25:2) "and the judge shall cause him to lie". And the one who hits, hits with one hand with all his strength. The reader would read, "If you do not keep the commandments... God will increase your beatings and the beatings of your children..."(Deuteronomy 28:58-59) and (if he finished) he would go back to the beginning of the reading. "And you shall keep the words of this covenant" (Deuteronomy 29:9) and he concludes "The all-merciful one who forgives sin...(Psalms 78:38) and if he finishes he goes back to the beginning. If he (the one being lashed) died during his whipping, the whipper is not responsible for his death. If the whipper added an extra strap to the whip and the sinner died the whipper is sent into exile. If the sinner either soiled or wet himself he is exempt from further lashes. Rabbi Yehuda says a man is only exempt if he soils himself, but a woman is exempt if she wets herself" ("Makkoth," http://www.sefaria.org/Mishnah_Makkot.3, accessed 6/15/2014).

4) The Apostles rejoiced over this and continued to preach the message about Christ—5:41-42

4. Luke records the administrative action in the Church to show the working together of Jews and Hellenistic Jews in the ministry and to prepare for the expansion of the Church outside Jerusalem—6:1-7

- **a.** The Hellenistic Jews (ones who could not speak Aramaic which was the native tongue of the Jews in Israel) were complaining to the Aramaic speaking ones that their widows were being overlooked in the daily distribution—6:1
- **b.** The Apostles suggested that they delegate this problem to men who were full of the Spirit and wisdom so that they could devote their time to the Word and prayer—6:2-4
- **c.** The church agrees to this and ordains some Hellenists in order to bridge the gap between the two groups—6:5-6
- **d.** Luke notes that the Word continued to spread and that many were added to the faith (progress report #2)—6:7

Note #97: Deacons

Many have felt that this Acts 6 passage contains the origin for the church office of deacon. This is unlikely for the following reasons 1) the different terms in the "deacon" word group occur around 100 times in the New Testament and usually refer to varying types of service unrelated to church office. Thus, terms used in this passage related to that word group prove nothing, 2) the verb "to serve" (from the "deacon" word group) in 6:2 is inconclusive since the term "ministry" (also from the "deacon" word group) in 6:4 is used of the apostles, 3) the demonstrative pronoun "this" in the phrase "this business" in 6:3 would suggest that the appointment of men in this chapter was to meet a particular need, 4) deacons are never mentioned in the book of Acts. If this were the institution of the office, one would expect this, 5) all of the men appointed have Greek names. This is a wise decision since the ones feeling neglected were Hellenists. However, this was an unwise decision if this were a permanent office since the native Jews would have no representation. Therefore, this event merely appoints men to deal with a temporary problem which arose in the early church.

II. LUKE RECORDS THE EVENTS SURROUNDING THE PROGRESSION OF THE GOSPEL IN JUDEA AND SAMARIA IN ORDER TO SHOW THE SOVEREIGN WORK OF GOD IN THE SPREADING OF THE MESSAGE AND TO SHOW THE INCLUSION OF PARTICIPANTS IN THE KINGDOM TO EXTEND BEYOND JERUSALEM—6:8-9:31

A. Luke presents the events surrounding the martyrdom of Stephen in order to vindicate Christianity in the face of opposition thus providing a basis for the spread of the message into Judea and Samaria—6:8-8:1

1. Stephen was performing miracles and teaching which could not be successfully debated by those who opposed him—6:8-10

2. These opposers persuaded some men to say that they had heard Stephen blaspheme Moses and God—6:11

3. They arrested Stephen and charged him with speaking against Moses, God, and the temple (in the Olivet Discourse Jesus had said the temple would be destroyed from which they inferred a change in the Mosaic system)—6:12-7:1

4. Luke presents the address of Stephen in which he reviews Israel's history in order to show that there is progress and change in God's program, that the blessings of God are not limited to the land of Israel and the temple area, and that Israel has always opposed God's working in order to vindicate Christianity—7:2-53

Note #98: Stephen's address

Stephen's address in Acts 7 is the hinge of the book of Acts and quite possibly in the entire New Testament as far as a transition in God's program is concerned. He asserts to the leaders of Israel that God is changing his work after Pentecost to working through the Church rather than through Israel. Stephen's sermon could be summarized as follows (The three major ideas of Stephen's discourse in the box below are taken from Stanley Toussaint, "Acts" in The Bible Knowledge Commentary *[Wheaton: Victor Books, 1983], 369-370).*

Stephen presents Israel's past history in order to vindicate the transition to Christianity		
There is progress and change in God's program	God's blessings are not limited to the land or temple	Israel has shown a pattern of opposition to God's program

a. *Stephen reviews the patriarchal period from Abraham to the Egypt experience—7:2-16*
b. *Stephen reviews the period of Moses and the Law—7:17-43*
c. *Stephen reviews the period of the Tabernacle and Temple—7:44-50*
d. *Stephen climaxes his discourse by chiding the leaders for being just like their fathers in always resisting God's plans and messengers—7:51-53*

Richard Rackham states:

> *"[Stephen] perceived, and evidently was the first to perceive clearly, the incidental and temporary character of the Mosaic Law with the temple and all its worship. This was the first germ of doctrine which S. Paul was afterward to carry out to its full logical and far-reaching consequences, viz. the perfect equality of Jew and Gentile in the church of God...S. Stephen then is the connecting link between S. Peter and S. Paul—a link indispensable to the chain. Stephen, and not Gamaliel, was the real master of S. Paul...For "the work" of Stephen lasts on till chapter xii...and then it is taken up by his greater pupil and successor—Paul." (Richard Rackham, The Acts of the Apostles [Grand Rapids: Baker. 1978, 88).*

Note #99: The problem of 400 years

There is a chronological problem in 7:6 where Stephen states that Israel would be enslaved and mistreated for 400 years while Paul in Galatians 3:17 implies that the period from the Abrahamic promise in Genesis 15 to Mt. Sinai was 430 years. The difference of 400 and 430 could be explained either by saying that Stephen was using round numbers or that 400 years could be the actual time of bondage and the 430 years was the time period from the confirmation of the Covenant to the Exodus. If the 430 years in Galatians refers to the period from the promise (Gen. 15) to the Exodus, then the bondage would be 215 years. But this presents a problem because Acts 7:6 says the bondage was 400 years. This can be reconciled by saying that Paul was looking at periods of time. The Covenant was reaffirmed in Genesis 46 to Jacob. So, the point of the end of the promises to the Patriarchs to the Exodus was 400 years.

5. Luke notes that the leaders responded to Stephen's message with fury and

proceeded to stone him to death and that this was approved of by one named Saul—7:54-8:1a

Note #100: Stoning

As in the case of flogging, the Mishnah also describes the procedure for stoning. The following is taken from Sanhedrin 6:1-4 ("Sanhedrin," http://www.sefaria.org/Mishnah_Sanhedrin.6, accessed 6/15/2014).

Once the verdict is reached, they bring him [the accused] out to stone him. The stoning area was outside the courthouse, as it is written (Leviticus 24) "bring out the cursor." One person would stand before the entrance to the courthouse and the cloths would be in his hand and another person would ride on a horse before them at a distance so that he would see him. If someone says 'I have a way to argue your innocence,' then he waves the cloths and the horse comes and supports him. And even if the accused says 'I have a way to argue my own innocence,' then he is returned, and this may happen even four or five times, so long as there is substance to his words. If he is found innocent, then he is exempt, and if not he is brought out to be stoned. And an announce comes out before him and announces, 'So-and-so, son of so-and-so is being brought out to be stoned for having committed such-and-such transgression, and so-and-so and so-and-so are his witnesses. Anyone who has any knowledge as to his innocence should come and argue for him.

Once he [the accused] is ten cubit from the stoning area they say to him, 'confess,' for such is the way of those sentenced to death to confess, for al who confess have a share in the world to come. This is what we have found by Achan, to whom Joshuah said (Joshuah 7) "Son, give honor, please, to Gd, the Lord of Israel and give him a confession...and Achan answered Joshuah and said, 'I have sinned to Gd the Lord of Israel..." And from where do we know that his confession atoned for him? As it is written (there), "And Joshuah said 'Once he is four cubits from the stoning area his clothes are removed. If it is a man, his front is covered. If it is a woman, her front and her back are covered, this is the opinion of Rabbi Yehudah. And the Sages say, both men and women are stoned naked. The stoning area was two stories high. One of the witnesses pushes him on his waist. If he rolls on his chest, they roll him to his back. If he dies from this, it is fulfilled. If not, the second (witness) picks up the rock and puts it on his chest. If he dies from this, it is fulfilled. If not, his stoning is by all of Israel as it says (Deuteronomy 17), "The hand of the witnesses will be against him first to kill him and the hand of the rest of the nation following."

As indicated in the above citation from Sanhedrin 3-4, the victim was to be stripped, pushed over a cliff some and a stone rolled off the cliff onto the victim. In the case of Stephen, however, it is difficult to assess how closely this procedure was followed since the picture which emerges is something like a "legal mob" act in which Stephen is pelted with stones. The members of the Sanhedrin are so incensed that they cover their ears and gnash their teeth. Moreover, in 7:58-59 the term "stoned" is used twice. The verb in each instance is the imperfect form of λιθοβολέω. The verb means "to throw stones," and the imperfect tense would indicate that this went on for some time.

B. Luke records the ministry of Philip in Samaria and to the Ethiopian eunuch in order to show the extension of the Gospel message from Jerusalem and the Jews—8:1b-40

1. Luke presents the work of Philip in Samaria—8:1b-25
   a. Luke notes that the persecution of the Church intensified as the Apostles were scattered throughout Judea and Samaria—8:1-3
   b. Luke notes that Philip preached Christ in Samaria as well as performing miracles in order to confirm the message—8:4-8
   c. Luke notes that there were many professions of faith in Samaria including Simon the sorcerer in order to show that the message was extending beyond the Jews—8:9-13
   d. Luke notes that the work was approved by the Jerusalem church which sent Peter and John to Samaria to confer the Spirit on them in order to validate Philip's work and to prevent schism in the body by having John and Peter welcome the Samaritans into the church—8:14-17
   e. Luke notes that Simon attempted to buy the ability from the Apostles of conferring the Spirit which brought the rebuke from Peter in order to show the superiority of the Christian movement over the occult—8:18-24
   f. Luke notes that Peter and John continued to preach the Gospel in many Samaritan villages—8:25

Note #101: The Samaritans' delay in receiving the Spirit

It is clear from this passage that the Samaritans receive the Holy Spirit some time after they believe the Gospel. This has led some to posit what is known as the doctrine of subsequence. The general idea is that while there is a reception of the Spirit at conversion, there is a later experience of Spirit baptism which must be sought and when received will result in greater spiritual power. It is sometimes taught that this experience will be validated by speaking in tongues. A number of comments are in order: 1) caution must be taken when building a normative practice on literature that is historic narrative. This does not mean that doctrine or binding practices are not found in narrative literature; but, when the primary text for such is narrative, then the support is very weak. If this method is adopted, one could find all kinds of "binding" practices from narrative throughout the Bible, 2) the book of Acts itself does not support subsequence. Reception of the Spirit is mentioned four times in Acts (2, 8, 10, 19) and this is the only instance of a delay. What is supposed to be normative in the doctrine of subsequence, therefore, is not even normative in the book. One would have to explain why the minority example is to be normative, 3) in none of the reception texts did anyone ever seek the Holy Spirit, 4) other Scripture indicates that at the moment of salvation everything a believer needs to live a full, godly life has been provided (e.g., 2 Peter 1:1-11), and 5) there is a better explanation for the delay. One of the purposes of Acts is to show that the Gospel is for all peoples which will bring them together into one spiritual body. There was a well-known rift between Jews and Samaritans. If the Jews had a "Jewish Pentecost" in Acts 2 and the Samaritans had a "Samaritan Pentecost" in Acts 8, there would have been two separate churches along ethnic lines. The reason there was a delay in the Samaritan's reception of the Spirit was to show the Jews that the Samaritans had the same experience they had; and to show the Samaritans they were linked to the authority of the Jewish apostles who mediated the Spirit to them. This event served to maintain the unity of the newly formed church. This idea would be continued as the Jewish apostle Peter will be called to go to a full-fledged Gentile Cornelius in Acts 10.

2. Luke presents the work of Philip to the Ethiopian eunuch, a Gentile worshipper of Yahweh, who was not a full-fledged proselyte (eunuchs were not allowed in the Lord's assembly—Deut. 23:1), in order to show the further widening of the Kingdom program—8:26-40
   a. Philip is ordered by an angel from the Lord to go onto a desert road—8:26
   b. Philip leaves and is told to go near the chariot of an Ethiopian official—8:27-29
   c. Philip speaks with the man about the prophet Isaiah and the man is converted— 8:30-35
   d. Philip baptizes the man and is then caught away—8:36-40

C. Luke records the conversion of Saul in order to show the victory of the Gospel over its most notorious enemy and to prepare the way for the spreading of the message to the Gentiles—9:1-31

Note #102: Did Paul undergo a name change?

There is really no evidence that Saul's name was changed to Paul after his conversion especially in light of the fact that he is not referred to as Paul until Acts 13:9. The reason the apostle would be known as both Saul and Paul is to be explained by the different names a Roman citizen would possess. It was characteristic of Roman citizens to have three names: a praenomen (like our first name), a nomen (a family name like our surname), and a cognomen (personal name). In addition, being Jewish, Paul had the Jewish name "Saul." As he embarked on his mission to the Gentiles, he appropriately used his Latin cognomen "Paul" (Paullus) rather than his Jewish name "Saul."

1. Luke records the supernatural conversion of Saul in order to validate his taking the message to the Gentiles—9:1-19a
2. Luke records the opposition against Saul in order to show the continued Jewish opposition to provide a basis for the gospel being spread to the Gentiles—9:19b-31 (progress report #3)

III. LUKE RECORDS THE EVENTS SURROUNDING THE PROGRESSION OF THE GOSPEL TO THE UTTERMOST PARTS OF THE EARTH IN ORDER TO SHOW THE UNIVERSAL NATURE OF THE MESSAGE BY ITS INCLUSION OF THE GENTILES—9:32-28:31

A. Luke presents a variety of events in order to show the gradual spread of the Gospel from Jerusalem to Antioch—9:32-12:24
   1. Luke records the events in the ministry of Peter which prepare him for this universal message—9:32-10:48
      a. Peter was ministering in areas which were populated by both Jews and Gentiles in order to prepare him for his ministry to Cornelius, a full-fledged Gentile—9:32-43
         1) Peter heals the cripple Aeneas (a Greek name) in order to confirm his

ministry and prepare him for Cornelius—9:32-35

2) Peter raises Dorcas from the dead in Joppa and resided with Simon the tanner (which was considered unclean—Lev. 11:40)—9:36-43

b. Peter carries the Gospel to the Gentile Cornelius in order to show that the Gospel was now going to full Gentiles and non-proselytes—10:1-48

1) Cornelius has a vision in which an angel tells him to send for Peter—10:1-8

2) Peter has the vision of the great sheet in order to show Peter that in this new economy nothing was unclean including the Gentiles—10:9-16

3) The messengers from Cornelius deliver the message to Peter and he invites them in—10:17-23a

4) The next day the group went to Caesarea where Peter explained to Cornelius and his house the message of the Gospel—10:24b-43

5) As a result of the acceptance of the message the believers received the Spirit, spoke in tongues, and were baptized in order to show the vindication of Peter's message to the Gentiles by validating this to the Jews—10:44-48

Note #103: Was Cornelius saved before he heard the gospel?

On the surface, there are several passages in the Cornelius account which seem to imply that Cornelius was saved before Peter brought the gospel to him. If this is true, there are many ramifications for both theology and missions. These indications include Cornelius was devout, prayed, gave alms, and feared God (10:2); an angel told Cornelius that his prayers had been heard (10:31); and that the one who works righteousness and fears God is accepted (10:35).

There are, however, a number of considerations which would argue that Cornelius was not saved before the gospel was brought to him. These considerations are listed below together with several propositions which put the issue in perspective.

1. *In Acts 2:5 Luke calls the people gathered in Jerusalem for Pentecost "devout" (2:5) but Peter tells them later that they must repent to receive the remission of sins (2:38). In 13:16 Paul calls on the Jews to listen to him whom he describes as those who "fear God." At the end of his sermon he tells them they must believe in order to be justified (13:39). To be devout, to fear God, or to do acts of piety are never viewed in the Bible as the means to receive the forgiveness of sins.*
2. *Peter asserts in his sermon to Cornelius that faith in Christ brings the forgiveness of sins (10:35).*
3. *When the angel appears to Cornelius and tells him to send for Peter, the angel indicates that he will hear from Peter the "words by which he will be saved" (11:14).*
4. *When Peter is recounting the story of Cornelius to the Jews in Jerusalem, they respond by saying that God had granted the Gentiles "repentance that leads to life" (11:18).*
5. *The large context of this story must be taken into account in order to interpret it accurately. One of the major issues addressed in the book of Acts is the transition from God working through Israel to God working through the Church. At*

Pentecost in chapter 2 the church is born. The rest of the book shows how this newly formed entity will be composed of Jew and Gentile on equal standing—a concept initially resisted since the Gentiles were considered to be ceremonially unclean. Acts 10:1-11:18 tells the story of how God initiated, through two visions, Gentile evangelism.

6. *Peter is prepared for this mission by the sheet vision in which he learns that "no man is common or unclean" (10:28). That is, there is no one who should not hear the gospel due to race, culture, ethnicity, etc.*
7. *Acts 10:35 teaches that "in every nation" there are those acceptable to God. The key is to note the difference between 10:28 and 10:35. While the former indicates that the gospel is to go to all, the latter teaches that "in" each group there are those (some) "acceptable" to God.*
8. *The "some" that are acceptable to God are those in whom God has been working to prepare them for reception of the gospel.*
9. *This conclusion would be consistent with what is being discussed at the Jerusalem Council where the Jew/Gentile salvation issue is being rehearsed. "Simon has declared how God first did visit the nations to take out of them a people for his name." This declaration is asserting the above points. The gospel goes to all, but out of them God is taking out a people for himself.*

2. Luke records the discussion among Peter and the Jewish believers concerning Peter's actions in order to validate for them this spread of the Gospel and prepare them for a similar mission—11:1-18
  - **a.** Luke notes that some of the Jewish believers criticized Peter for eating with Gentiles (a mark of fellowship)—11:1-3
  - **b.** Peter offers a defense of his actions—11:4-17
    - **1)** Peter recounts his vision—11:4-10
    - **2)** Peter recounts how at that precise moment the delegation from Cornelius arrived—11:11-14
    - **3)** Peter recounts how the Gentiles received the Holy Spirit just as they had at Pentecost—11:15-17
  - **c.** The group agrees that God had granted repentance to the Gentiles—11:18

3. Luke records the events in the church at Antioch in order to show its preparation for the universal spread of the Gospel—11:19-30
  - **a.** Luke notes the spread of the message into Gentile areas in order to show that for the first time the church was actively reaching out to Gentiles—11:19-21
  - **b.** Luke presents the support and generosity of the Jerusalem church toward the church at Antioch to show the unity between Jew and Gentile regarding this new dimension of God's program—11:22-30

4. Luke presents the persecution of the church at Jerusalem in order to validate the Jewish rejection of the Messiah and the validation for its spread to the Gentiles—12:1-24
  - **a.** Luke notes the martyrdom of James by Herod Agrippa I—12:1-2
  - **b.** Luke notes that Peter was imprisoned by Herod but that the church was praying—12:3-5
  - **c.** Luke notes that an angel released Peter from prison who went back to

John Mark's home which was followed by the execution of the guards—12:6-19

d. Luke notes that Herod was struck dead by God for his pride—12:20-23

e. Luke notes that the Word continued to increase and spread (progress report #4)—12:24

B. Luke presents a variety of events in the outreach of the early church in order to show its spread into Asia Minor—12:25-16:5

1. Luke records the call and ordination of Barnabas and Saul for their first missionary journey—12:25-13:3

2. Luke records the first missionary journey of Saul and Barnabas in order to document the spread of Christianity into Asia Minor—13:4-14:28

a. They first were directed to go down to Seleucia a seaport which was 16 miles from Antioch—13:4a

b. They then sailed to Cyprus (the homeland of Barnabas)—13:4b-12

1) They stopped first in the city of Salamis which was the largest city in the eastern half of Cyprus and proclaimed the Word in the Jewish synagogues with John Mark as their helper—13:4b-5

2) They then ministered in Paphos which was 100 miles southwest of Salamis where they met opposition from Bar-Jesus in order to show: the victory of
Christ over the demonic, the Gentile slant of the ministry which was seen in Paul's leadership in dealing with Bar-Jesus (Elymas), and the interest by Sergius Paulus in the message of Paul—13:6-12

c. John Mark defected at Perga and returned to Jeru-salem—13:13

d. They then sailed to Pisidian Antioch where Paul preached his first major sermon to the Jews concerning the Messiah—13:14-52

1) Luke notes that they went to the synagogue and were given the opportunity to speak—13:14-15

2) Paul preaches his first sermon in which he shows how Christ was the Messiah and that they needed to repent or suffer judgment—13:16-41

a) Paul surveys the history of Israel from the Egyptian bondage to the ministry of John the Baptist in order to show the preparation for the coming of the Messiah— 13:16-25 (for the chronological problem in 13:20 see Eugene Merrill, "Paul's Use of 'About 450 Years' in Acts 13:20," *Bibliotheca Sacra* 138:551 [Jul 1981], 246-254).

b) Paul reviews the crucifixion and resurrection of Christ in order to show the guilt of the Jewish nation—13:26-37

c) Paul warns the people to believe in the Messiah or suffer judgment—13:38-41

3) After the service, Paul and Barnabas were invited to return on the next Sabbath and speak—13:42-43

4) On the next Sabbath the Jews were filled with jealousy and opposed Paul—13:44-45

5) Paul and Barnabas responded by stating their obligation to preach to the Jews first but since they were rejecting the message they would turn to the Gentiles at which the Gentiles rejoiced and believed—

13:46-48

6) The Word continued to spread but so did the opposition of the Jews—13:49-52

e. They then went to Iconium where their ministry prospered among Jews and Gentiles in order to confirm their ministries—14:1-6

1) They enjoyed success in the synagogue—14:1
2) The Jews who did not believe stirred up opposition—14:2
3) They continued to preach boldly and performed miracles to confirm their message—14:3
4) There was a division among the people and a plot to stone the Apostles so that they fled—14:4-6

f. They fled to Lystra where Paul healed a crippled man and the people attempted to worship Paul and Barnabas but he told them to turn to the one God at which they stoned them—14:7-20a

Note #104: Why did the people think Paul and Barnabas were Hermes and Zeus?

Hermes was the son of Zeus, and among his many duties was to be a messenger for the gods (J. E. Zimmerman, Dictionary of Classical Mythology *(NY: Bantam, 1971], 124-125). Of interest from the biblical perspective is Acts 14:6-20 where Paul and Barnabas travel to Derbe and Lystra. The people refer to Barnabas as Zeus and Paul as Hermes since Paul did most of the speaking. Lystran legend taught that Zeus and Hermes had once visited an elderly couple there named Philemon and Baucis. The story is found in Ovid's* Metamorphoses *entitled "The Story of Baucis and Philemon." One key passage reads: "Here Jove with Hermes came; but in disguise of mortal men conceal'd their deities; one laid aside his thunder, one his rod; and many toilsome steps together trod: For harbour at a thousand doors they knocked, Not one of all the thousand was locked; at last an hospitable house they found; a homely shed; the roof not far from ground, was thatch'd with reeds, and straw together bound. There Baucis and Philemon liv'd, and there had liv'ed long marry'd and a happy pair..." (Ovid,* Metamorphoses *8.626ff).*

g. They went from there to Derbe where the word enjoyed success—14:20b-21a

h. They retraced their steps going through Lystra, Iconium, and Antioch to confirm the churches there, and then went through Pisidia, Pamphylia, Perga, Attalia, and back to Antioch where they reported that God had opened the door of faith to the Gentiles—14:21b-28

3. Luke presents the events of the Jerusalem Council in order to show the early church's acceptation of the Gentiles into God's program by faith alone which showed their equal footing with the Jews in the current age—15:1-35

Note #105: The Jerusalem Council

The Jerusalem Council recorded in Acts 15 is one of the most critical features of early church history. The tension which was fomenting dealt with the relationship between Jew and Gentile in the Church. Stated differently, the debate was over the nature of the Church. Was the Church distinct from Judaism, or a branch of Judaism? Did Gentile converts need to become Jewish or were they acceptable to God as Gentiles?

This debate began in Syrian Antioch and became so heated that it was brought to the Jerusalem Church for a decision. After hearing the various sides of the argument, James, the leader of the Church, announced that the Gentiles were not subject to the laws of Judaism and were accepted by God through faith alone. However, during this sensitive time as Jew and Gentile were coming together in the new body called the Church, the Gentiles were to abstain from things associated with idolatry so as not to offend their Jewish brethren. That the areas of abstinence dealt with idolatry, see the word studies by Charles Savelle, "A Reexamination of the Prohibitions in Acts 15," Bibliotheca Sacra *161:644 (Oct 2004), 452-457.*

a. Luke notes the dissension revolved around some Jews who insisted that circumcision was essential in order to be justified at which Paul and Barnabas were appointed to go to Jerusalem to deal with this matter—15:1-2

b. Luke notes that during the trip to Jerusalem they related how the Gentiles had been converted at which the believers were glad—15:3-4

c. Luke records the discussion concerning circumcision—15:5-12

- **1)** Some believing Pharisees suggest that the Gentiles need to be circumcised and obey the Mosaic Law—15:5
- **2)** The Apostles and elders meet to consider the question—15:6-7a
- **3)** Peter relates their conclusions—15:7b-11
  - **a)** Peter notes that God had chosen for the Gentiles to hear of salvation from his lips—15:7b
  - **b)** Peter notes that God accepted them which was shown by His giving of the Spirit to them and purifying their hearts by faith—15:8-9
  - **c)** Peter notes that imposing the Law would be to test God and to put an unbearable yoke on the neck of the disciples—15:10
  - **d)** Peter concludes that both groups are saved by grace and not any outward act—15:11
- **4)** Paul and Barnabas tell the group of the miracles they had performed and the Gentile belief as a result in order to confirm what Peter had just said—15:12

d. Luke records the official statement given by James regarding the matter—15:13-29

- **1)** James notes that the conclusions of the council were confirmed by the experience of Peter in taking the Gospel to Cornelius—15:13-14
- **2)** James notes that the conclusions of the council are confirmed by Scripture where he notes that Amos in particular foresaw Gentile salvation—15:15-18

Note #106: The tabernacle of David

There are at least three views of how to take the Amos prophecy: The first view of this passage in Acts is characteristic of amillennialists (though a form of it is also held by those who are not amillennial). The words "in that day" are said to refer to the kingdom in the Church at Pentecost. It logically follows from this that the "tabernacle of David" refers to the Church. A further inference from this view is that Christ is now seated on the Davidic throne (Lenski, Morgan, Ladd, Bruce). The strengths of this view grow out of the strengths of amillennial theology. Textually, it has seeming validity because it appears that James is intimating that the prophecy is being fulfilled. There are however many difficulties with this position: 1) James did not say that Amos was fulfilled, but simply that the salvation of the Gentiles was in agreement with the Old Testament. This is further corroborated by the fact that "prophets" is plural, thus expressing a general idea, 2) the verb "return" refers to an actual return (cf., Acts 5:22). 3) there is not one reference connecting Christ's present session with the Davidic throne, 4) the church was not revealed in the Old Testament (Rom 16:25; Eph. 3:5-6), thus it could not have been referred to in Amos, and 5) the Davidic covenant was unconditional in nature, and should be interpreted literally.

A second view, held by many premillenarians, sees four chronological movements in the passage. These include the Church Age, the return of Christ, the establishment of the Davidic kingdom, and the turning of the Gentiles to God (Ryrie, Walvoord). This view has merit in that it sees a logical progression of thought in the text. It also avoids the weaknesses of the preceding view. However, it has some problems. First, the view relies heavily on the words "after this." Yet, these words are neither in the LXX or MT. And second, if the words "after this" are conceded as valid, this position would be reading the Church into the prophecy of Amos.

A third possibility suggests that James was simply asserting that Gentiles will be saved in the Millennium when Christ returns. This view is favored by the writer for several reasons. First, it fits the purpose of the council. James' concern was to validate the inclusion of the Gentiles, not to give a panorama of prophecy. Second, it observes that James says that this inclusion of the Gentiles is in agreement with, not in fulfillment of Amos. Third, it preserves the literal, unconditional nature of the Davidic covenant. Fourth, it maintains a distinction between Israel and the Church. Fifth, it provides the usual interpretation of "House of David" as referring to the nation of Israel. Sixth, it properly interprets Amos' use of "in that day" as referring to the time after the Tribulation period. Seventh, many Old Testament prophets predicted the same thing (e.g., Isa. 42:6; 60:3; Mal. 1:11). Longenecker states this view well: "God's people will consist of two concentric groups who will share in the messianic blessings the result being that the Conversion of the Gentiles in the last days should be seen in an eschatological context" ("Acts," in The Expositor's Bible Commentary, *9:446).*

3) James sets forth a practical decision in which he states that they should not annoy the Gentiles but suggest that they abide by an ethic that would not offend those Jews—15:19-21

4) The church then determined to send some men with Paul and Barnabas to take this report to Antioch—15:22

5) They took with them a letter emphasizing the conclusions reached by the council—15:23-29

e. Luke records the joyful acceptance of the news by the church at Antioch—15:30-35

4. Luke records the confirmation of the churches in Asia Minor—15:36-16:5

a. Paul proposes to Barnabas that they return to the churches and see how

they are doing—15:36
b. They had a disagreement over whether to take John Mark with them with the result that Barnabas took Mark and Paul took Silas—15:37-41
c. Luke records the beginning of the second missionary journey as Paul comes to Derbe and Lystra and is joined by Timothy whom Paul had circumcised—16:1-4
d. Luke notes that the churches were strengthened and continued to grow (progress report #5)—16:5

C. Luke presents a variety of events in the outreach of the early church in order to show its spread into the Aegean area—16:6-19:20
1. Paul receives a vision to go and preach the Gospel in Macedonia in order to show that this extension of the Gospel to new places was in the plan of God—16:6-10
2. Luke records the victories and opposition to the Gospel in Macedonia in order to validate the message of Christianity—16:11-17:15
a. Luke presents the ministry of Paul and Silas in Philippi—16:11-40
1) Luke records the conversion of Lydia in order to show that Old Testament believers had to enter into full New Testament salvation and to show the sovereignty of God in salvation—16:11-15
2) Luke records the deliverance of the demon-possessed slave girl in order to show the power of God over the demonic and to show the occasion for the following persecution—16:16-18
3) Luke records the flogging and jailing of Paul and Silas and the subsequent events in order to show the opposition to the Gospel and the victory of the Gospel in this circumstance—16:19-40
a) The Apostles are dragged in front of the court by the owners of the slave girl—16:19-21
b) The Apostles were beaten and jailed—16:22-24
c) The Apostles were loosened by an earthquake from God the result of which the jailer asked how to be saved—16:25-30
d) The Apostles told the jailer he only had to believe; he and his household were saved and baptized—16:31-34
e) Paul and Silas were released by the magistrates—16:35-40
b. Luke presents the ministry of Paul and Silas in Thessalonica—17:1-9
1) Luke notes that Paul ministered in the synagogue concerning Christ's death and resurrection to which many Jews and Greeks believed—17:1-4
2) Luke notes that some Jews started stirring up trouble against them in order to emphasize the continuing Jewish rejection—17:5-9
c. Luke presents the ministry of Paul and Silas in Berea—17:10-15
1) They ministered in the synagogue and many believed because of their eagerness to search the Scriptures—17:10-12
2) The Jews in Thessalonica came down to Berea and continued to cause trouble so Paul was forced to flee—17:13-15
3. Luke records the work of Paul and Silas in Achaia in order to show the continued spread of the Word among the Gentiles—17:16-18:18
a. Luke presents the ministry of Paul in Athens—17:16-34

1) Paul is distressed over the number of idols in the city—17:16
2) Luke notes that he ministered in the synagogues to the Jews and God-fearing Greeks and in the marketplace to the philosophers—17:17
3) He was opposed by Epicurean and Stoic philosophers who called him a seed-picker and one who advocated foreign gods—17:18

Note #107: Stoics and Epicureans

Zeno the Cypriot (340-265 BC) was the founder of Stoicism. The roofed colonnade where Zeno taught in the agora was called the "stoa" (στοά) hence his followers were called Stoics. The Stoics were pantheists, self-sufficient, strong believers in virtue and reason, and had a reputation for being arrogant.

Epicurus (341-271 BC) believed in chance, no divine involvement, the survival of the fittest, and no future judgment. Bock likens them to "agnostic secularists" (Darrell Bock, Acts [Grand Rapids: Baker, 2007], 561). The well-known statement of Diogenes is cited by Witherington: "Nothing to fear in God; Nothing to feel in death; Good can be attained; Evil can be endured" (Ben Witherington, The Acts of the Apostles: A Socio-Rhetorical Commentary *[Grand Rapids: Eerdmans, 1998], 514). Probably that for which the Epicureans are best known is their belief that the highest good of man is the pursuit of pleasure. While this is true, we must not define pleasure in the modern sense; rather, it pictured pleasure as a freedom from fear and a state of tranquility.*

4) Luke notes that Paul was taken to the Areopagus where they wanted to hear what new ideas he had—17:19-21
5) Luke records another of Paul's sermons in which he stresses that the Creator has revealed Himself in creation and He commands all men to repent because they would give an account to Christ whom He raised from the dead—17:22-31
   a) Paul introduces his sermon by acknowledging the religiosity of the Athenians even noticing their altar to an unknown god—17:22-23
   b) Paul speaks of the true God who created everything and who was both sovereign and yet near to man—17:24-29
   c) Paul says that this God commands all men to repent and that they will be judged by the one who was raised from the dead—17:30-31
6) Luke notes that some scoffed at Paul's message while others believed—17:32-34

b. Luke presents the ministry of Paul in Corinth—18:1
   1) Luke states that Paul came to Corinth—18:1
   2) Paul meets Aquila and Priscilla who had been ordered to leave Rome because of an edict by Claudius (AD 49-50) and that they practiced their tent-making trades together—18:2-3
   3) Paul ministered to Jews and Greeks in the synagogue—18:4
   4) Luke notes that Paul was joined by Silas and Timothy and when he was opposed by the Jews, he declared that he was turning to the Gentiles—18:5-6
   5) Luke notes that when Paul ministered outside the synagogue he

experienced some success—18:7-8

6) Paul receives a vision from God in which He states that he should continue boldly in the city because there were some of God's elect there and he would be protected by God—18:9-11
7) The unbelieving Jews brought Paul to court before Gallio (a Roman proconsul) who was not interested in this "Jewish" problem which was important because any judgment handed down by Gallio would have set a legal precedent—18:12-17
8) Paul left Corinth and headed for Syria with Aquila and Priscilla—18:18

4. Luke records the conclusion to the second missionary journey in which he states that Paul traveled to Ephesus, to Caesarea, and then up to Jerusalem—18:19-22
5. Luke presents the record of the third missionary journey which began with the taking of the Gospel into Ephesus—18:23-19:20
   a. Luke initially states that Paul spent some time in Antioch, Galatia, and Phrygia strengthening the disciples—18:23
   b. Luke notes that a Jew named Apollos was preaching the Old Testament and the baptism of John, but he was led into full New Testament understanding by Priscilla and Aquila in order to show that Christianity was in a transitional period though grounded in the Old Testament scriptures—18:24-28
   c. Luke notes the ministry of the Gospel to various groups in Ephesus in order to note the transition in this period of church history—19:1-20
      1) Paul explains the way of Christ to about twelve men who are subsequently baptized, receive the Holy Spirit, speak with tongues, and prophesy in order to be a sign to the Jews present of this change in God's program—19:1-7
      2) Paul taught concerning the Kingdom in the synagogue but met with opposition and left—19:8-9a
      3) Paul preached in the lecture hall of Tyrannus as well as performing miracles to confirm his message—19:9b-12
      4) Paul ministered in opposition to the demon-possessed thus showing again God's power over the occult (progress report #6)—19:13-20

D. Luke presents the spread of the Gospel message into Rome and the events surrounding it in order to show the sovereign purpose of God in spreading the message to include both Jew and Gentile who would thus someday enjoy Kingdom blessings—19:21-28:31
   1. Luke records the completion of the third missionary journey—19:21-21:16
      a. Luke presents the riot at Ephesus in order to show part of the incentive for Paul to leave—19:21-41
         1) Luke notes that Paul had a desire to go to Jerusalem and then to Rome in order to show the ultimate goal of the message—19:21-22
         2) Luke notes that an uproar broke out in Ephesus because certain silversmiths were afraid of losing money because of people converting to Christianity—19:23-34
         3) Luke notes that the chief officer in the city quieted the crowd and it dismissed after the man appealed to the fact that Rome would not

appreciate this riot—19:35-41

b. Luke presents Paul's travels through Macedonia and Greece—20:1-6

c. Luke presents Paul's ministry in Troas—20:7-12

1) Paul met with the believers there on the first day of the week and spoke until midnight—20:7

2) Luke notes that a man named Eutychus fell out of a third story window while Paul was speaking and died—20:8-10

3) Paul revived the young man and they broke bread together—20:11-12

d. Luke records Paul's farewell to the Ephesian elders in Miletus in order to show his great love for these men and to charge them concerning their ministries—20:13-38

1) Paul summons the elders from Ephesus to come to Miletus—20:13-17

2) Paul reviews his past ministry in Ephesus in order to affirm to them his faithfulness and good motives—20:18-21

3) Paul describes his present situation as being burdened to go to Jerusalem despite any sufferings that may happen there but that in going he is innocent of the blood of all men because of his faithful preaching—20:22-27

4) Paul charges the elders regarding their future ministry when he leaves—20:28-31

a) They are to guard themselves and the flock—20:28a

b) They are to shepherd the flock—20:28b

c) They are to be on guard against heretics from within and without the church—20:29-31

5) Paul justifies his ministry with them in which he states that he did not covet but provided for his own needs—20:32-35

6) Luke notes that they wept and prayed and accompanied Paul to the ship—20:36-38

e. Luke records the events surrounding Paul's trip to Jerusalem—21:1-16

1) Luke notes that they sailed from Cos to Rhodes to Patara—21:1

2) Paul boarded a ship which went to Phoenicia with no stops—21:2

3) The ship landed at Tyre where Paul set out to find believers who warned him not to go to Jerusalem because they knew through the Spirit that he would suffer but he went anyway—21:3-6

4) The ship proceeded to Ptolemais for a one-day stop where they stayed with some brothers—21:7

5) They went to Caesarea where they stayed with Philip where Agabus prophesied that Paul would be bound in Jerusalem but despite their pleas for him not to go he did anyway—21:8-16

2. Luke records the captivity of Paul in Jerusalem in order to show the antagonism of unbelieving Jews toward Paul's ministry—21:17-23:32

- **a.** Luke presents the arrival of Paul in Jerusalem in which he emphasizes Paul's work among the Gentiles in order to contrast it with the coming persecution at the hands of the Jews and to show Paul's concern for unity by helping with the Nazirite vow—21:17-26
  - **1)** Paul arrives in Jerusalem and is greeted warmly by the brothers—21:17
  - **2)** Paul and his companions went to see James and the elders the next day and told them what God had been doing among the Gentiles—21:17-19
  - **3)** The men told Paul of a false rumor that was circulating that Paul was teaching Jews to disregard Jewish customs—21:20-22
  - **4)** They suggest that Paul join in purification rites of four men who had taken a vow and that afterward he help pay for the sacrifices which were required (Num. 6:13-17) in order to show his sympathy for the Law—21:23-24
  - **5)** They reiterate the decision of the ethical demands of the Jerusalem Council regarding Gentile believers—21:25-26
- **b.** Luke presents the violence of the unbelieving Jews who opposed Paul's ministry—21:27-36
  - **1)** Some Jews stirred up the crowd against Paul by stating that he taught against the Law and had defiled the temple by letting Greeks into it—21:27-29
  - **2)** They started beating Paul but intervention by Roman troops stopped the beating—21:30-32
  - **3)** The troops bound and arrested Paul while the mob was yelling that he be executed—21:33-36
- **c.** Luke presents the defense of Paul in order to justify the spreading of the Gospel to include both Jew and Gentile—21:37-23:10
  - **1)** Luke records Paul's defense before the mob—21:37-22:29
    - **a)** Paul asks the commander of the soldiers for permission to speak who thinks that he was an Egyptian insurrectionist but Paul assures him that he was a Jew and a citizen of Tarsus who could speak Greek but addressed the crowd in Aramaic—21:37-40
    - **b)** Paul reviews his conduct before his conversion—22:1-5
      - (1) Paul notes that he was a Jew of Tarsus who was trained in the Law under Gamaliel and zealous for it—22:1-3
      - (2) Paul notes that he persecuted the Christians and at one point was on his way to Damascus with letters from the high priest to take them to Jerusalem to have them punished—22:4-5
    - **c)** Paul reviews his conversion in which he explains the Damascus road experience, his blindness, and the ministry of Ananias—22:6-16
    - **d)** Paul reviews his commission to ministry—22:17-21
      - (1) He relates a trance he had in Jerusalem where God told him

to leave Jerusalem because the people would not accept his message—22:17-18

(2) Paul told the Lord that he thought the Jews would listen to him—22:19-20

(3) The Lord answered that it was His purpose for Paul to go minister among the Gentiles—22:21

e) Luke notes that the crowd was enraged at this statement and called for his death in order to reiterate the Jewish rejection of the Gospel—22:22

f) The commander ordered that Paul be flogged to which Paul pointed out that he was a born Roman citizen and therefore could not be flogged unless he had been proven guilty—22:23-29

2) Luke records Paul's defense before the Sanhedrin—22:30-23:10

a) The Roman commander had Paul brought before the Sanhedrin in order to find out why he was being accused by the Jews—22:30

b) Paul states that he had fulfilled his ministry in all good conscience at which Ananias the high priest had him struck on the mouth—23:1-2

c) Paul retorts that the high priest is a hypocrite for he was to uphold the Law but transgressed it by having Paul struck before he was proven guilty—23:3-5

d) Paul knew that justice was impossible in this setting and so said that he was a Pharisee and caused division among the Pharisees and Sadducees by mentioning the resurrection—23:6-9

e) Paul was taken back to the barracks because of the violence of the situation—23:10

d. Luke presents the plot among the Jews to kill Paul in keeping with his theme on Jewish opposition and the sovereignty of God over that opposition—23:11-32

1) Paul has a vision in which the Lord tells him to be encouraged because he would see to it that he got to Rome—23:11

2) Luke notes that about 40 Jews had vowed not to eat or drink until they had killed Paul—23:12-13

3) Luke notes that the Sanhedrin was in on this to call Paul before them again on the pretext of getting more information, so that while Paul was en route they would kill him—23:14-15

4) Paul's nephew heard of this plot and told Paul and then the commander of the troops—23:16-22

5) The commander made arrangements to have Paul transferred to Caesarea—23:23-33

a) Paul was provided with military protection and moved during the nighttime—23:23-24

b) A letter was sent with him to Governor Felix who reviewed the essentials of the case—23:25-30

c) Paul and the letter are handed over to Felix—23:31-32

3. Luke records the captivity of Paul in Caesarea and his defenses before

Felix, Festus, and Agrippa II—23:33-26:32

a. Paul is handed over to Felix and he decides to hear the case but until that time keeps Paul under guard in Herod's palace—23:33-35

b. Luke records the trial before Felix—24:1-27

- **1)** The high priest and a lawyer come down from Jerusalem to present their case before Felix—24:1
- **2)** The lawyer introduces his case by patronizing Felix for his political accomplishments—24:2-4
- **3)** The lawyer makes three accusations against Paul: he is a trouble-maker, he is a leader of the Nazarene sect, and he attempted to desecrate the temple—24:5-9
- **4)** Luke records Paul's defense—24:10-21
  - **a)** Paul states confidence in Felix's ability to judge the case—24:10
  - **b)** Paul states that he went up to Jerusalem to worship not cause a riot—24:11
  - **c)** Paul states that his accusers cannot prove he ever started a riot—24:12-13
  - **d)** Paul states that he worshiped God and believed in the Law and the Prophets—24:14-16
  - **e)** Paul states that after an absence, he returned to Jerusalem to bring an offering to the church—24:17
  - **f)** Paul states that his genuine accusers were not present and that the Sanhedrin had found him innocent—24:18-21
- **5)** Felix postponed the trial and granted him protection and some limited freedom—24:22-23
- **6)** Luke notes that Felix often listened to Paul but left him in prison in order to gain favor with the Jews—24:24-27

c. Luke records the trial before Festus in order to show that in Paul's appeal to Caesar he eventually ended up in Rome—25:1-12

- **1)** Luke notes that Festus went to Jerusalem where the religious leaders presented their charges against Paul and asked him to have Paul transferred there so that they could ambush him along the way and kill him, but Festus said he was going to try him in Caesarea—25:1-5
- **2)** Luke notes that the trial began as the Jews brought many serious but unprovable charges against Paul—25:6-7
- **3)** Paul states that he had done nothing wrong against the Law, the temple, or Caesar—25:8
- **4)** Festus asked Paul if he would be willing to be tried in Jerusalem in order to placate the Jews—25:9
- **5)** Paul refused this and appeals to Caesar—25:10-11
- **6)** Festus declares that he would send him to Caesar—25:12

d. Luke records the events surrounding Paul's defense before King Agrippa II—25:13-26:32

- **1)** King Agrippa came to Caesarea to pay his respects to Festus and Festus took this opportunity to review Paul's case with him and

Agrippa said that he would like to hear what Paul had to say—25:13-22

2) Paul is brought before Agrippa by Festus where he states that he found nothing worthy of death but before he could send him to Caesar he had to have some clear charges against him—25:23-27
3) Paul is granted permission to speak by Agrippa and proceeds to present his case—26:1-32
   a) Paul states his pleasure at being before Agrippa because he understood Jewish customs—2 6; 1-3
   b) Paul states that the Jews know that he was a Pharisee and lived in light of the promise made to the Patriarchs that they would be resurrected to enjoy the blessings of the Messianic age—26:4-8
   c) Paul states that he had been a zealous opponent to Christianity in his past—26:9-11
   d) Paul reviews his conversion on the Damascus road for Agrippa and the fact that he was commissioned by God to preach to the Gentiles—26:12-18
   e) Paul notes that in his ministry he was faithful to this commission and preached to Jews and Gentiles the truth about the Messiah including His resurrection—26:19-23
   f) Festus interrupted Paul and said he was insane because of his views on resurrection which to the Greek mind was impossible—26:24
   g) Paul addresses Agrippa as knowing that the things concerning Christ had taken place because Agrippa was acquainted with Christianity and affirmed to him that he knew he believed the Prophets—26:25-27
   h) Agrippa jokingly responds that Paul in a short time could persuade him to become a Christian—26:28
   i) Paul seriously responds that whether it took a long or short time he would be willing to spend it—26:29
   j) Agrippa declares Paul's innocence and states he could have been set free if he had not appealed to Caesar—26:30-32

4. Luke records the captivity of Paul in Rome in order to show that God had sovereignly directed events so as to .move the Gospel message out from Jerusalem to Rome in order to include both Jews and Gentiles in His program—27:1-28:31
   a. Luke records the various stops of the ship on the way to Rome as well as the difficulties in sailing on the Mediterranean Sea at this time of the year (late September-early October)—27:1-12
   b. Luke notes that the ship was caught by a sudden storm which they battled for many days and eventually gave up hope of surviving—27:13-20
   c. Paul addresses the crew by saying that they would survive because God had appeared to him in a vision saying that he would appear in Rome and that not one of them would be lost—27:21-26
   d. Luke records the shipwreck in order to emphasize the leadership of Paul (thus validating his ministry) and the sovereign protection of God in

order to have the message taken to the Gentile center of Rome—27:27-44

e. Luke records the stay at Malta where Paul performed two miracles of healing—28:1-10

f. Luke records the events surrounding Paul's time in Rome—28:11-31

   1) Luke notes the arrival in Rome and that Paul was allowed to live by himself with a soldier to guard him—28:11-16

   2) Paul addresses some Jewish leaders—28:17-20

      a) He tells them that he was innocent of damaging their customs—28:17

      b) He tells them that the Roman authorities thought he was innocent—28:18

      c) He appealed to Caesar because the Jews would not treat him fairly—28:19

      d) He states that the major reason he wanted to talk with them was the hope of Israel (i.e., the fulfillment of Old Testament prophecies)—28:20

   3) The Jewish leaders said they had not heard of him but wanted to hear his views—28:21-22

   4) They had a later meeting in which Paul taught about the Kingdom and the Messiah and some were starting to be convinced though not fully (imperfect tense) and others refused to believe—28:23-24

   5) Paul was upset at their unbelief and applied the words of Isaiah to them concerning their blindness—28:25-27

   6) Luke records the climax of the book in which he states that Paul was turning to the Gentiles who would listen—28:28

   7) Luke notes that for the next two years Paul rented a house and preached the Kingdom of God to all who would listen (progress report #7)—28:30-31

ROMANS

Importance

MISCELLANEOUS STATEMENTS REGARDING THE IMPORTANCE OF ROMANS
This Epistle is really the chief part of the New Testament and the very purest Gospel, and is worthy not only that every Christian should know it word for word, by heart, but occupy himself with it every day, as the daily bread of the soul (Martin Luther, *Commentary on Romans* [Grand Rapids: Kregel, 1977], xiii).
I think that the Epistle to the Romans is the most profound work in existence (Samuel Coleridge, *Table Talk* [Oxford: Oxford University Press, n.d.], 232).
Forasmuch as this epistle is the principal and most excellent part of the new Testament and most pure evangelion, that is to say glad tidings, and that we call gospel, and also is a light and a way unto the whole scripture; I think it meet that every christian man not only know it, by rote and without the book, but also exercise himself therein evermore continually, as with the daily bread of the soul. No man verily can read it too oft, or study it too well; for the more it is studied, the easier it is; the more it is chewed, the pleasanter it is; and the more groundly it is searched, the preciouser things are found in it, so great treasure of spiritual things lieth hid therein. ("Tyndale's Preface to Romans" http://www.luminarium.org/renlit/tyndalebib.htm, accessed 2/11/2014).
[I]t is unquestionably the most important theological work ever written (John Knox, "Romans: Introduction," in *The Interpreter's Bible*, 12 vols.; ed. George Arthur Buttrick [New York: Abingdon, 1954], 9:355).
It is the fullest, plainest and grandest statement of the gospel in the New Testament (John Stott, *The Message of Romans* [Leicester: InterVarsity, 1994], 19.
When any one gains knowledge of this Epistle, he has an entrance opened to him to all the most hidden treasures of Scripture (John Calvin, *Epistle to the Romans*, in *Calvin's Commentaries* 22 vols. [Grand Rapids: Baker, 1979], xxix).

Authorship

Almost no one denies that Paul was the author of Romans. Because of the almost universal acceptance of this fact, the point will not be belabored here, and Paul will be considered the author. However, the one who actually penned the letter was Tertius (16:22).

Date and Origin

Corinth is probably the place from which Romans was written since Phoebe, of nearby Cenchrea, was entrusted with carrying the letter (Rom. 16:1, 2). This is further confirmed by the fact that Gaius was Paul's host (Rom. 16:23) who was one of the converts during Paul's ministry in Corinth (1 Cor. 1:14). The letter was most likely written at the close of Paul's third missionary journey during his three months while he was in Greece (Acts 20:3) just before his return to Jerusalem with the offering. This indicates that the letter was written around AD 57.

Recipients

Paul addresses the letter to "all who are in Rome" (1:7). It is evident that a church did exist in Rome (16:5), but it is likely that there were several churches there and so he addressed it to all of the saints there rather than to one particular church. The question also arises as to the composition of these churches, whether Jew or Gentile. It is probably best to conclude that the church was mixed ethnically, but with Gentiles being the predominant element. That there were Jews is evident from the names Aquila, Andronicus, Junias and Herodion (16:7, 11). But Rome was a Gentile city (though there a Jewish colony there—Acts 28:17-28), and the church was most likely composed of mainly Gentiles. Further, Paul was considered the Apostle to the Gentiles. This mixture of people is also seen in that Paul directly addresses the Jew (2:17; 4:1, 12) and the Gentile (11:13).

Occasion/Purpose

The immediate occasion for Paul's writing of Romans was the projected trip of Phoebe to Rome (Rom. 16:2). There are several sub-purposes which could be given for motivating Paul to write this letter. First, he wanted to announce his plans to visit Rome (Rom. 15:24, 28-29). Second, he requested prayer for his safety. And third, he wanted to be a source of edification to them (Rom. 1:11). These are demonstrable purposes from the text, but they are called "sub-purposes" here because they do not take into account the body of the letter from 1:18-15:13.When the body of the letter is considered, it is the writer's opinion that there are four strands which make up the purpose of the book. First, the righteousness of God (subjective genitive). Thus, this refers to an activity of God in that He does what is right and just in His relationship to others. There are a number of observations which support the subjective use of "God": l) this is clearly the usage in 3:5, 25, 26, 2) the parallelism of structure between v. 17a and v. 18, and 3) this would fit well into the content of the book especially 9-11 as will be developed in the argument. This does not, however, rule out the fact that in God's dealing justly with people he justifies them in imparting Christ's righteousness to their account (genitive of source/origin). So in a sense, both are present, but the first seems to be the main thrust of the book.

Second, the doctrine of justification must be kept in mind. The major way in which Paul displays the righteousness of God is through his explanation of justification throughout the course of the letter.

Third, the Jewish/Gentile tension present in the first century must be remembered. The first question which would arise in this regard is how God could accept the "despicable" Gentile. In the course of Paul's argument, he shows how God can be right and just in His dealings with them. The second question is how God could be just and fair in His dealings with Israel as His covenant people and still set them aside (9-11). This question is also dealt with by the Apostle.

This tension must be put into historical perspective with God's change in economies. That is, it had been God's purpose through the Old Testament to be the God of Israel, who in turn would be a light and source of blessing to the Gentiles. This was the message brought to the nation by John the Baptist and Jesus as they offered the Kingdom to Israel. It is obvious throughout the Gospels that Christ came with a ministry to the Jew first. Because of Jewish rejection, however, Christ (and the Apostles) turned the message to include the Gentile as well. This is the great theme of Luke and Acts. In light of the rejection of the Messiah by the Jewish nation, a new dispensation was ushered in during which this chronological nature of the message was set aside, for God was no longer dealing with Israel as a nation. Thus, Paul's contribution to the explanation of this new program in Romans is to show that Jew and Gentile alike are sinners, and both are justified through faith (this does not mean to imply that justification ever came any other way than by faith, but that both Jew and Gentile are put on the same opportunistic plane in this present age). Because of this change in program, Paul deals with how God can be just in accepting the Gentiles, and presents his great section vindicating God's righteousness related to the Jew in 9-11. The above facts are buttressed when one goes through Acts with this in mind. The Apostles were constantly opposed by the Jews and used this as an occasion to turn to the Gentiles. So, there was the need in the first century, in light of this transition in dispensations, to present a thorough and comprehensive statement of God's righteous character in his dealings with mankind as it is revealed in justification.

Fourth, according to 15:20-24, Paul eventually wanted to take the Gospel message to Spain and needed the church's help in doing so. Therefore, he was presenting in the book of Roman the message he would be taking there so as to garner the support for the mission from the Christians in Rome.

Thus, a purpose statement for Romans could be put as follows: Paul presents a comprehensive statement of justification by faith which is available to both Jew and Gentile in order to show that God is just in His dealings with both groups in order to unify them thereby gaining support for his Spanish mission.

Summary of Argument

I. PAUL PRESENTS HIS INTRODUCTION TO THE EPISTLE BY GREETING THE ROMANS, NOTING HIS INTEREST IN THEM, AND STATING THE PROPOSITION OF HIS EPISTLE IN ORDER TO LAY THE GROUNDWORK FOR THE REST OF THE LETTER—1:1-17

A. Paul opens the letter with a salutation in which he identifies himself, states the subject of the letter, and names the recipients of the letter—1:1-7

1. Paul identifies himself and states that he is a servant of Christ who was called to be an Apostle and separated unto the Gospel of God in order to show his authority for what he is about to write—1:1

2. Paul identifies the subject of the letter as the Gospel of Jesus Christ—1:2-6

a. Paul notes that the Gospel message has its historical roots in the Old Testament in order to show that the message was not novel with him—

1:2

b. Paul notes that the Gospel message has as its content the person of Christ—1:3-6
   1) Paul says that in Christ's birth he was the Son of David in order to emphasize His humanity and Messiahship—1:3

   2) Paul says that Christ was appointed and vested with the privileges of being the Son of God (Psalm 110) declared in time at the resurrection—1:4a
   3) Paul says that His name is Jesus Christ—1:4b

Note #108: Romans 1:3-4

Romans 1:3-4 is one of the most difficult passages in the New Testament to interpret. The following is my summary of these two verses.

The Son is described through two participial clauses with a kata phrase in common

v. 3	v. 4
who has come	who was appointed
from the seed of David	Son of God in power
according to the flesh	*according* to the spirit of holiness from the resurrection

The Son was eternally Son. He entered human existence by birth which was followed by a further appointment.

These two verses are then parallel to Philippians 2 contrasting the two phases of Christ's work: incarnation and reigning at his future exaltation

"seed of David according to the flesh"	Incarnation with a kingly future
"appointed"	To install and invest with privilege
"according to the spirit of holiness"	Just as "according to the flesh" characterizes Christ physically; so, "according to the spirit of holiness" characterizes Christ spiritually. That is, a holy consecration to God marked his ministry

   4) Paul says that through Him he received gracious apostleship (hendiadys) to call for obedience from among the Gentiles—1:5-6

c. Paul notes that the recipients of the letter are the saints in Rome—1:7

B. Paul expresses his interest in the Romans in order to show his concern for them and desire to see them—1:8-15

1. Paul gives several proofs of his interest in the Romans—1:8-10
   a. He thanks God for their well-known faith—1:8
   b. He constantly prays for them—1:9

c. He prays that he would be able to come and visit them—1:10

2. Paul gives several reasons for why he wants to visit them—1:11-15

a. He wanted to impart to them a spiritually-oriented gift, namely, that theywould be encouraged—1:11-12

b. He wanted to have a spiritual harvest among them—1:13

c. He wanted to fulfill his obligation as a debtor of the Gospel—1:14-15

C. Paul states the proposition of the epistle in order to show the theme he will be developing in the letter—1:16-17

1. He states that the gospel is the power of God unto salvation to everyone who believes—1:16

Note #109: Salvation

"Salvation" in Romans has a plenary sense of all that salvation does and entails. S. Lewis Johnson correctly observed that "it may come as something of a surprise to learn that Paul more often than not in Romans uses the concept of salvation in its third sense that of future salvation (cf. 5:9; 11:11; 13:11; 11:26). This fact, coupled with the contextual evidence of the book as a whole, namely, that in the book he expounds in detail the three phases of salvation, leads to the conclusion that this completed sense is the force required in 1:16. Thus, the apostle's meaning is simply this: The gospel is the power of God that leads to complete salvation, salvation from the penalty, power, and ultimately the presence of sin ("The Gospel that Paul Preached" Bibliotheca Sacra 128:512 [October 1971], 332).

Note #110: From faith to faith

Major discussion has turned on the phrase from "faith to faith" (for a list of options see C.E.B. Cranfield, Romans Volume I *I-VIII [Edinburgh: T. & T. Clark, 1985], 99-100). It is the writer's opinion that the phrase is to be taken as a pleonasm where Paul is using emphasis by repetition. Thus justification comes altogether through faith.*

2. He states that the gospel is a revelation of God's righteousness received through faith alone—1:17

II. PAUL DEMONSTRATES THE SINFULNESS OF ALL MEN IN ORDER TO SHOW THAT GOD IS JUST AND RIGHTEOUS IN CONDEMNING ALL MANKIND AND TO SHOW THEIR NEED OF HIS DEALING WITH THEM THROUGH JUSTIFICATION—1:18-3:20

A. Paul discusses the condemnation of the unrighteous in order to show that the Gentile is under God's wrath because of their rejection of Him—1:18-32
   1. Paul states that God's wrath (an expression of His personal righteousness) is being revealed (present tense) against.
      human sinfulness because of their suppression of the truth—1:18
   2. Paul states that the revelation of the knowledge of God is seen in natural revelation in order to show that men are without excuse in suppressing the truth—1:19-20
   3. Paul states how men are rejecting the knowledge of God in order to illustrate their suppression of the truth—1:21-23
      a. They did not give glory to God—1:21a
      b. They did not give thanks go God—1:21b
      c. Their thinking became futile and darkened—l:21c-22
      d. They became idolatrous—1:23
   4. Paul states that God reacted to this suppression of the truth with a judicial handing over of man to sin in order to reveal His righteousness and utter condemnation of sinful man—1:24-32

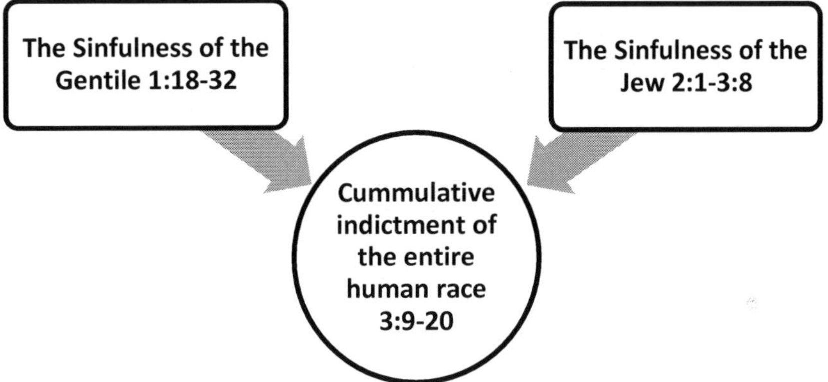

Note #111: God "gave them up"

The word for "give them up" (παραδίδωμι, 1:24, 26, 28) does not have the sense of a passive letting go of mankind. Rather, it denotes an active abandonment of God as a judicial act. This abandonment of the human race took place after the Fall.

      a. God abandoned man to impurity—1:24-25
      b. God abandoned man to perversion—1:26-27
      c. God abandoned man to reprobate thinking—1:28-32
         1) God abandoned man to a depraved mind and all of its expressions because they did not think God worthy of their thoughts—1:28-31
         2) Paul shows man's animosity toward God in that even though they know God disproves of sinful behavior they continue in it and approve of others who do the same—1:32

B. Paul discusses the condemnation of the Jew in order to show that though he may have not reached visible degrees of degradation as just described he is just as culpable in the sight of God—2:1-16
   1. Paul shows God's condemnation of the Jew in order to show that His

judgment is based on principles of divine standards—2:1-16

a. Paul states that God's judgment is based on truthfulness—2:1-5
   1) The Jews' judgment of others leads to his own judgment since he has violated his own standard of judgment—2:1
   2) God's judgment is based on reality not on the Jews' perception of it—2:2
   3) The fact that God does not judge in the present does not mean that He will not judge in the future but gives opportunity, for repentance—2:3-5

b. Paul states that God's judgment is based on man's works and is impartial in order to show that man will receive the appropriate punishment —2:6-11

Note #112: Does Paul indicate salvation by works?

A reading of 2:6-11 could imply that one is saved by works. If there is one thing clearly taught in Romans and Paul's other epistles, it is that salvation is apart from works. Thus, this passage is either blatantly contradictory to what Paul says elsewhere (indeed in the next two chapters), or there is another explanation of what Paul is intending in this text. Two common solutions to the passage include the perseverance and hypothetical views. The former assumes the doctrine of the perseverance of the saints and concludes that true believers will, necessarily, live lives of consistent obedience. The latter holds that hypothetically one could be saved by works if the entire Law were kept. There is, however, a third possibility which I would simply call the "principle" view. Notice that verses 6 and 11 teach the same thing thus forming an inclusio. *The principle of the section is that God judges according to works, thus impartially. To say that we will be judged by works is not the same as saying that we are saved by works. The wicked will be judged by his works and will receive commensurate punishment in hell. The righteous will be judged by his works and will receive commensurate privilege and reward in the kingdom. Once more, Paul is presenting a principle of God's judgment, not telling people how to be saved. Based on the sinfulness of the Jew laid out in the preceding section (1-5) and the following section (12-29), this principle of judgment will result in full condemnation.*

c. Paul states that God's judgment is based on man's obedience to His revelation—2:12-16
   1) Paul states the principle that those who sin without the Law will perish without the Law and vice a versa—2:12
   2) Paul states that the Jew is justified for obeying the Law and not just hearing it—2:13
   3) Paul states that the Gentile has an innate sense of right and wrong and that the conscience functions as an accuser or excuser of their state. If this is true for the Gentile, how much more for the Jew who has the Law in written form—2:14-16

C. Paul continues to discuss the condemnation of the Jew in order to show that their privileges as Jews do not mean that they are guiltless in the sight of God but that they have more responsibility, thus God is just in condemning them—2:17-3:8

1. Paul states that the Jews' possession of the Law was not sufficient and was a basis of condemnation—2:17-24
   a. Paul notes the religious position of the Jew as being in covenant with God and possessing the Law to proclaim to the nations—2:17-20
   b. Paul notes that the Jew revealed hypocrisy in his actions and as a result dishonored God and the Law—2:21-24
2. Paul states that the Jews' possession of circumcision was not sufficient and was a basis of condemnation—2:25-29
   a. Circumcision without obedience to the Law makes the symbol meaningless—2:25
   b. If a Gentile observes the Law, his lack of circumcision does not matter—2:26
   c. The uncircumcised could be on a higher spiritual plane than the circumcised if the former obeys the law—2:27
   d. A true Jew is one who is one inwardly—2:28-29
3. Paul deals with Jewish objections based on their condemnation—3:1-8

Note #113: What is the advantage of the Jew?

Romans 3:1-8 is one of the strongest New Testaments texts to affirm the distinction of and national future for Israel. These verses belong to a larger section beginning in 2:1 where the Jews are taken to task for violation of the Law, hypocrisy, and trust in religious rites. Paul's condemnation reaches its pinnacle when he writes that the uncircumcised Gentile would be acceptable before God before the circumcised Jew. This castigation is so strong that it leads the apostle to imagine his readers asking a question: "What advantage then has the Jew, or what is the profit of circumcision?" The force of the question in 3:1 can only be appreciated when connected with chapter 2. Circumcision was the sign of the Abrahamic promises and therefore the question essentially has the sense of whether those promises are still in force? If the sign has no value, then that to which the sign points has no value. Paul continues in the passage to affirm that God will be faithful to his promises even if Israel is faithless. This is basically what dispensationalists mean by the "unconditional nature" of the Abrahamic Covenant. God has taken it on himself to see that the promises are ultimately fulfilled. This will occur in the future when the New Covenant is enacted for Israel as they are given a new heart and experience all of the features of that covenant.

   a. The first objection asks whether the Jews have any advantage and Paul says that they do because they have the oracles of God—3:1-2
   b. The second objection asks whether Jewish unbelief nullifies God's faithfulness and Paul affirms that God is faithful—3:3-4
   c. The third objection asks that if Jewish sin displays God's glory, why should God condemn them to which Paul answers that this would prevent God from judging anyone—3:5-8

D. Paul discusses the condemnation of the whole world in order to show that God is just in His dealings with the world and that all are therefore accountable to Him—3:9-20
   1. Paul states the charge that both Jew and Gentile are under sin—3:9

Note #114: Total Depravity

Paul asserts what is known as the doctrine of "total depravity" with his indictment in 3:9 of the entire human race, "all under sin." This phrase indicates that each person is under the domination and bondage of the sin principle. The issue is not that all commit acts of sin (though all do), but that all are bound by the power of sin as a force. Thomas Schreiner states well: "...'sin' is probably also a power [he is arguing that ἁμαρτίαν should not be limited to sinful acts]. For instance, sin is described as reigning (5:21), enslaving (6:6), ruling (6:12), and exercising lordship (6:14). People are described as slaves to (6:16, 17, 20) or freed from (6:18, 22)...Paul had a darker view of human ability than some Jews in that the latter believed that human beings had the capability to observe the law...Judaism acknowledged that all people without exception were sinners. But Paul thought that sin had wrapped its tentacles so tightly around human beings that they could not keep the law" (Thomas Schreiner, Romans Baker Exegetical Commentary on the New Testament [Grand Rapids: Baker, 2003], 164-65).

Total depravity does not mean that a person sins as much as he possible could or that he is unable to act in a dignified manner. Rather, all aspects of humanity have been affected by sin rendering the individual in a state of utter helplessness. Paul elucidates this doctrine in the following section. Notice the logic: no one has any righteousness—no one understands they have no righteousness (most people are hoping their good works will outweigh their bad works)—therefore, no one seeks after God since they see no need for his righteousness. Paul then develops these points by giving specific examples of how sin has affected each person.

2. Paul quotes Old Testament scripture in order to validate his claim that all are under sin—3:10-18
   a. The extent of sin is universal—3:10-12
   b. The nature of sin is depravity as seen in sins of the tongue and sins of action—3:13-17
   c. The source of sin springs from the fact that there is no fear of God—3:18
3. Paul applies these Old Testament quotes by observing that the Law confirms man's sinfulness and that man can never be righteous in God's sight thus showing that God is righteous in His judgment— 3:19-20

III. PAUL EXPOUNDS THE DOCTRINE OF JUSTIFICATION THROUGH FAITH IN ORDER TO SHOW HOW GOD CAN BE RIGHTEOUS IN HIS SAVING OF SINFUL MAN AND HIS KEEPING OF SINFUL MAN UNTO FULL AND COMPLETE SALVATION—3:21-8:39

A. Paul explains the doctrine of justification in order to show how God can be righteous in declaring sinners justified—3:21-31

Note #115: Justification

The doctrine of justification has been called "The chief article of Christian doctrine." Without it "we dwell in densest darkness." That which "cannot be sufficiently extolled" (Martin Luther, What Luther Says *[St. Louis: Concordia, 1986], 2:705). Dutch theologian G. C. Berkouwer remarked that "the confession of divine justification touches a man's life at its heart, at the point of its relationship with God; it defines the preaching of the Church, the existence and progress of the life of faith, the root of human security, and man's perspective of the future" (G. C. Berkouwer,* Studies in Dogmatics: Faith and Justification *[Grand Rapids: Eerdmans, 1954], 17). J. I. Packer, noting the systemic nature of the doctrine, observes that "like Atlas [it] bears a world on its shoulders" ("Introductory Essay," in* The Doctrine of Justification: An Outline of its History in the Church and of its Exposition from Scripture *[Edinburgh: The Banner of Truth Trust, 1984], viii). Romans 3:21-31 is the central New Testament text on the subject. Of this article [justification] nothing can be yielded or surrendered...even though heaven and earth, and whatever will not abide, should sink to ruin...And upon this article all things depend which we teach and practice in opposition to the Pope, the devil, and the [whole] world. Therefore, we must be sure concerning this doctrine, and not doubt; for otherwise all is lost, and the Pope and devil and all things gain the victory and suit over us ("Smalcald Articles," http://bookofconcord.org/smalcald.php#gospel, accessed 2/13/2014. The Second Part, Part II, Article I). The Smalcald Articles were written by Martin Luther for the Smalcald League which was a group of Lutheran princes who had formed to protect their religious interests in the Roman Empire (Carl Meyer, "Smalcald Articles," "Smalcald League," in* The New International Dictionary of the Christian Church, *J. D. Douglas editor [Grand Rapids: Zondervan, 1981], 908-09).*

Briefly defined, justification means to "declare righteous." It is a legal, forensic pronouncement by God. Importantly, it does not mean to "make righteous" as taught by the Roman Catholic Church. Observe below the contrasts between the Biblical and Roman views.

BIBLE	**ROME**[580]
Instantaneous	Gradual
Declared	Made
Imputed[581]	Infused
Faith Alone	Faith +

[580] See The Canons of Trent and Catechism of the Catholic Church for representative statements of the Roman position in Note 139.

[581] Hodge explains "imputation" as the "laying anything to one's charge, and treating him accordingly. It produces no change in the individual to whom the imputation is made; it simply alters his relation to the law" (Charles Hodge, *Commentary on Romans* [Grand Rapids: Eerdmans, 1977], 106).

The Biblical view of the doctrine can be elucidated through a debt/asset analogy.

Pre-Justification	
Debts	**Assets**
Original sin - sinful condition from Adam acquired at conception renders each person positionally guilty before God. Personal sins - each thought, act, or motive which violates God's standard; each thought, act, or motive which does not fulfill the expectation of God's standard. Personal sins accumulate as long as a person lives and are like deposits into God's bank of wrath to be withdrawn at the day of judgment (Romans 2:5)	

Post-Justification	
Debts	**Assets**
The merits of Christ's death (passive obedience) are imputed and all debits are erased. We are legally viewed as if we never inherited original sin and never committed any personal sin.	The merits of Christ's life (active obedience) are imputed and the assets column is full. We are legally viewed as if we lived the very life of Jesus Christ in thought, act, and motive.

Seven Summary Statements Regarding Justification[582]
Justification is:
an act, not a process
grace when condemnation is deserved
not subjective change like regeneration
not merely an executive act, but a legal one
the ground is the active/passive obedience of Christ
the obedience of Christ is imputed to our account
faith is the condition

[582] Adapted from Charles Hodge, *Systematic Theology* (Grand Rapids: Eerdmans, 1968), III:117-18.

1. Paul explains the manifestation of righteousness—3:21-23
   a. This is a righteousness apart from the Law—3:21a
   b. This righteousness was attested in the Old Testament—3:21b
   c. God is the source of this righteousness—3:22a

Note #116: Faith as a channel

*We are said to be justified by faith (simple dative Rom. 3:28; 5:2); by faith (ἐκ with the genitive Rom. 1:17; 3:30; 4:16 twice; 5:1; 9:30; 10:6; Gal. 2:16; 3:8, 11, 24; Heb. 10:38); through faith (δία with the genitive Rom. 3:22, 25, 30; Gal. 2:16; Phil. 3:9); upon faith (ἐπι with the genitive Phil. 3:9), and according to faith (κάτα with the accusative Heb. 11:7); but never are we said to be justified because of or account of faith (δία with the accusative). B. B. Warfield stated "The saving power of faith resides not in itself, but in the Almighty Savior on whom it rests...It is not, strictly speaking, even faith in Christ that saves, but Christ that saves through faith" (*Works of Benjamin B. Warfield *[Grand Rapids: Baker, 1978], II:504).*

   d. The channel for receiving righteousness is faith—3:22b

Note #117: Saving Faith

Saving faith includes the intellect, assent, and will. These aspects are often denoted with the Latin terms notitia, assensus, *and* fiducia *respectively. Probably starting with Luther and further developed by his friend Philip Melanchthon, the reformers were eager to distinguish true faith from false faith. This distinction is still needed today as skeptics of Christianity characterize faith as a blind leap which is just as valid as having faith in Zeus or Thor. Many Christians themselves mistake faith for a subjective experience ("you ask me how I know he lives, he lives within my heart"). Luther and Melanchthon explained that faith has three separate, but interconnected components.* Notitia *deals with the content of faith. One cannot have faith in nothing, and God never calls on a person to do so. Warfield wrote that "we cannot be said to believe or to trust in a thing or person of which we have no knowledge; implicit faith in this sense is an absurdity. Of course we cannot be said to believe or to trust the thing or person to whose worthiness of our belief or trust assent has not been obtained. And equally we cannot be said to believe that which we distrust too much to commit ourselves to it" (B. B. Warfield, "On Faith in its Psychological Aspects," The Princeton Theological Review 9:4 [October 1911], 566).* Assensus *deals with the confidence that the content is true. Thus, we move from knowing truth to being persuaded of it.* Fiducia *represents an act of the will in which one comes to rest in the truth of which he is persuaded.*

   e. The extent of this righteousness is to all who believe—3:22c
   f. There is no difference in this appropriation because all sinned—3:23

Note #118: Romans 3:23

This familiar verse demands four interpretive observations: 1) the significance of "for." Paul is expanding on verse 22 by stating the reason there is no difference in the way individuals are justified, 2) the meaning of "all have sinned." The construction in

3:23 is the same as the construction in 5:12 where it is translated "all sinned." It should be translated the same in 3:23 thus reflecting that Paul has in mind original sin when each member of the human race sinned in Adam, 3) the meaning of "fall short, come short." This translation could imply that sinners have some righteousness but just not enough, when in fact Paul is clear in Romans that sinners have no righteousness before God. Therefore, the issue in justification is not God giving the sinner enough righteousness to supplement what he already has, but giving him a divine righteousness which he completely lacks. The verb Paul uses here is ὑστερέω which is used 16 times in the New Testament (Matt. 19:20; Mark 10:21; Luke 15:14; 22:35; John 2:3; Rom. 3:23; 1 Cor. 1:7; 8:8; 12:24; 2 Cor. 11:5, 9; 12:11; Phil. 4:12; Heb. 4:1; 11:37; 12:15). The term can have the sense of "to lack" which would be appropriate in this context, and 4) the meaning of the "glory of God." There are several good possibilities of what Paul could mean here (the sinner lacks approval or honor from God; the sinner fails to glorify God; the sinner does not reflect the glory of God; the sinner has turned the glory from God to himself). However, a case can be made that in this passage, the glory of God, which fallen man is said to lack is the glory with which man was first created, that original glory, lost by the fall to be restored in the future. It is the glory given by God. When man was created, he was to act as God's regent and representative on earth. Man, acting for God, would rule and subdue the earth realm. In the book of Hebrews chapter 2, the writer refers to the creation of man and his kingly responsibilities in terms of his being "crowned with glory and honor." It becomes clear in Hebrews 2:5-8 that the glory and honor with which man was crowned is indeed a reference to man's creation and appointment over the earth.

However according to Genesis 3 and Hebrews 2, this glorious position was not retained very long. Hebrews 2 shows that sin resulted in the loss of the glory and honor of man in his role over God's creation. The word "glory" is used numerous times in the New Testament and it is used 16 times in the book of Romans alone. Sometimes the word will be used of the majesty of God for which mankind should render praise. However, it is interesting that 6 times in the book of Romans, Paul uses the word "glory" to refer to the future glory which will restore the original glory lost in the Garden of Eden through Adam's sin. For example, 5:2 says that we "rejoice in hope of the glory of God." Here Paul is referring to Christian's fixation on the glory which will be given to him in the future. Notice also that Paul uses the entire phrase "glory of God" just as in Romans 3:23 to refer to that future. In 8:18, again referring to the future, Paul writes "I reckon that the sufferings of the present time are not worthy to be compared with the glory which shall be revealed in us" which he then describes in the rest of that passage. In 8:21 he speaks of the "glorious liberty of the children of God." And in 8:30 he speaks of our glorification. There are two indications in 3:23 that Paul is thinking of this same glory. First, if "all sinned" refers to the fall of the race in Adam as it does in 5:12, this immediately makes reference to the Garden of Eden and the loss of the glory of man. The second is the linking word "and" in verse 23. "All sinned and lack or are destitute of the glory of God." The "and" implies that Paul is making two parallel statements. "All sinned—that is, all sinned in Adam," "and" building on that, "fall short of the glory of God—that is, they have lost the original glory with which man was created in his body and spirit and function in the world."

2. Paul explains the provision of righteousness—3:24-26

a. Paul notes how this provision of righteousness works to justify sinners—

3:24-25c

1) He says that the basis is grace—3:24a

2) He says that the method is redemption through the atoning work of Christ—3:24b-25b

Note #119: Redemption

"There is no one of the titles of Christ which is more precious to Christian hearts than 'Redeemer.' There are others, it is true, which are more often on the lips of Christians. The acknowledgment of our submission to Christ as our Lord, the recognition of what we owe to Him as our Saviour, - these things, naturally, are most frequently expressed in the names we call Him by. "Redeemer," however, is a title of more intimate revelation than either 'Lord' or 'Saviour.' It gives expression not merely to our sense that we have received salvation from Him, but also to our appreciation of what it cost Him to procure this salvation for us. It is the name specifically of the Christ of the cross. Whenever we pronounce it, the cross is placarded before our eyes and our hearts are filled with loving remembrance not only that Christ has given us salvation, but that He paid a mighty price for it" (B. B. Warfield, Opening Address, delivered in Miller Chapel, Princeton Theological Seminary, September 17, 1915).

"There are a variety of words for "redemption" in the New Testament. The word used in Romans 3:24 is avpolu,trwsij. It has the sense of 'buying back a slave or captive, making him free by payment of a ransom'" (William Arndt, F. Wilbur Gingrich and Frederick Danker, *A Greek-English Lexicon of the New Testament and Other Early Christian Literature* [Chicago: The University of Chicago Press, 1979], 96).

3) He says that the means of appropriation is faith—3:25c

b. Paul notes that the purpose of this provision is the vindication of God's righteousness in His dealings with men—3:25d-26

1) He says that in the past He demonstrated His justice by forbearing with sin because He anticipated Christ's work—3:25d

Note #120: The remission of sins

The term translated "remission" (KJV), "passed over" (ESV, NKJV, NASB), "left unpunished" (NIV) is the word πάρεσις which is found only here in the New Testament. In Koine Greek, this term referring to remission of punishment or debt, should be distinguished from ἄφεσις which refers to the remission of sin (Moulton and Milligan, The Vocabulary of the Greek New Testament [Grand Rapids: Eerdmans, 1974], 493). The phrase "remission for sins that are past" occurs in this section in which Paul is showing how God remains righteous in justification. The question which arises has to do with how God can be righteous for not prosecuting sins before the cross. Paul is saying that regarding the sins that are past, the full and final payment for them was postponed. With the prepositional phrase "through the forbearance of God" Paul is communicating the idea of self-restraint or tolerance. Because God was anticipating what would be done someday on Calvary, He tolerated and left unpunished those sins which were committed. It is as if they sinned on credit; the full bill being due when Jesus died.

2) He says that in the present God demonstrates His justice by justifying those who have faith in Jesus—3:26

3. Paul explains the inferences which result from justification—3:27-31
   a. There is no room for boasting because justification is through faith—3:27-28
   b. There is no distinction between Jew and Gentile—3:29-30
   c. The Law is established by faith because the Law has taken its proper place—3:31

B. Paul illustrates the doctrine of justification with the examples of Abraham and David in order to show that both before and after the Law men were justified through faith—4:1-25

1. Paul states the fact of Abraham's justification by faith in order to illustrate that before the giving of the Law men were justified by faith—4:1-3
2. Paul explains the nature of Abraham's justification—4:4-25
   a. Paul states how Paul was not justified—4:4-16
      1) Abraham was not justified by works—4:4-8
         a) He shows logically that if he were justified by works then the wages he received are an obligation and not a gift; therefore, righteousness is received through faith and not by works—4:4-6

Note #121: Faith is not a work

Paul asserts emphatically in 4:5 that faith is not a work. As stated earlier, faith is the channel through which we receive justification, it is not the basis on which we are justified. There is nothing magical about believing something—we do it all the time. John Murray lists nine arguments that faith is not a work, the ground of justification, or accepted by God in lieu of righteousness (The Epistle to the Romans The New International Commentary on the New Testament *[Grand Rapids: Eerdmans, 1980], 354-59). They are as follows. 1) in the context of Romans 4 with the Genesis 15:6 quote, more is involved in the imputation of righteousness than the imputation of faith, 2) Romans 10:10 has the expression "it is believed unto righteousness," 3) it cannot be questioned that the righteousness in justification is the righteousness "of God," 4) Christ himself is said to be made unto us righteousness, 5) the righteousness of justification is a gift, 6) we are pointed to the obedience of Christ as that through which we are justified in Romans 5:19, 7) "through faith" is not to be confused with "on account" of faith, 8) the righteousness of justification through Scripture does not allow faith to be substituted for righteousness, and 9) the prepositions used with justification indicate instrumentality.*

         b) He shows scripturally by the words of David that God credits righteousness apart from works—4:6-8
      2) Abraham was not justified by circumcision—4:9-12
         a) Abraham was justified before his circumcision—4:9-10
         b) Circumcision was intended as only a sign of righteousness—4:11a
         c) Abraham, by virtue of his faith, is the father of both the circumcised and the uncircumcised—4:11b-12
      3) Abraham was not justified by the Mosaic Law because the promises were by faith and grace so that the promises can be guaranteed to all of Abraham's descendants—4:13-16

b. Paul states how Abraham was justified—4:17-22

1) Paul states that the object of Abraham's faith was God—4:17

Note #122: Father of many nations

The fact that Abraham is called the father of many nations implies two things, 1) he fathered a number of races and 2) a father is an example to his children who ideally emulate what he does. In this case, Abraham's faith is something that is "copied" by his children.

2) Paul states the obstacles which Abraham's faith had to overcome—4:18-21

a) Negatively, he believed despite human weakness—4:18-19

b) Positively, he believed in the power of God—4:20-21

3) Paul states that the outcome of Abraham's faith was a declaration of righteousness—4:22

c. Paul applies the illustration of Abraham's faith to all men by showing that to anyone who believes their faith results in justification—4:23-25

C. Paul demonstrates the assurance that the one who believes can have in order to show the fullness and finality of justification and to show that as God deals righteously with people He can be trusted—5:1-8:39

Note #123: Structure

The writer is suggesting in this section that the unit consisting of 5:1-8:39 is dealing with the matter of assurance of salvation. Paul has been stating that a right standing before God comes without doing any works. The natural question would be one of hope, and the safety of this method. This is due to the fact that faith is a sort of intangible that cannot be seen whereas works are something that can be seen and measured. Therefore, Paul is showing in this section the great assurances God gives of complete and final salvation. Thus, this again shows how God deals righteously in His relationships with people.

It is also being suggested that this train of thought runs from 5:1-21 and is then interrupted in chapters 6:1-8:1 to answer two objections that arise from chapter 5—the believer's relationship to grace (chapter 6), the believer's relationship to the Law (chapter 7). After these objections are dealt with, Paul resumes the subject of assurance in 8:2-39 (8:1 is a verse linking providing a link back to chapter 5). The specifics of these points will become evident as the argument is unfolded.

1. Paul deals with the hope or expectation the justified person has regarding the future (proof #1)—5:1-11

a. Paul states that justification gives present peace and future hope of sharing in God's glory to show the assurance that comes from justification—5:1-2 (based on the flow of thought, I am assuming the indicative reading of "have" in 5:1 [ἔχομεν] rather than the subjunctive reading [ἔχωμεν]. Thus, the reading should be "we have peace with God, rather than "let us have peace with God."

b. Paul states that afflictions strengthen this hope in order to show that even tribulations cannot shake this assurance—5:3-5

c. Paul discusses God's love and the work of Christ on behalf of the believer in order to show certainty of assurance—5:6-11

2. Paul deals with how the believer's change in position took place in order to show that our union with Christ is another grounds of assurance (proof #2)—5:12-21

Note #124: All sinned

There has been a long history of interpretation related to the phrase "all sinned" in Romans 5:12. Summarily, there have been four major approaches. The first is Pelagianism named after Pelagius. Pelagius was a British monk who was born in the 4th century AD best known for his fierce debate with St. Augustine on the issue of the human will. One of the things that Pelagius taught (which was necessary in order to come out where he did on free will) was that Adam's sin did not have an effect on the rest of the human race. He held that there was no connection between Adam's sin and our sin. When we are born, according to Pelagius, we are born neutral and sinless just as Adam was when he was made. And so Pelagius would argue, we have the choice whether we sin or not. If we choose to sin we are merely following Adam's example, but there is no connection between his sin and ours. And so when Paul says "all sinned" he means just that: all sinned. We imitate what Adam did. Pelagius was eventually condemned by two African councils in 416 and by the council of Ephesus in 431 which affirmed both inherited and imputed sin. All major orthodox traditions of Christianity reject Pelagianism

*A second view of the phrase is that of Arminianism named after Jacob Arminius. In his introductory discussion of Arminian theology, Arminian scholar Roger Olson affirms that people are born morally and spiritually depraved "helpless to do anything good or worthy in God's sight without a special infusion of God's grace to overcome the affects [*sic?*] of original sin" (Roger Olson,* Arminian Theology: Myths and Realities *[Downers Grove: InterVarsity Press, 2006], 33). Olson goes on to argue that Christ's death precludes imputation of guilt to infants (Ibid.). "Thus, in Arminian theology all children who die before reaching the age of awakening...and falling into actual sin (as opposed to inbred sin) are considered innocent by God and are taken into paradise. Among those who commit actual sins only those who repent and believe have Christ as Savior" (Ibid.). Olson appears to be arguing that when an individual has the power of choice and then chooses to sin, he is rendered guilty.*

A third major position is known as Augustinianism, Realism, or Seminalism. The issue with this view is that the only way that God could fairly allow the consequences of Adam's sin to come upon the human race is if the race was somehow actually involved in Adam's sin—if it really was in a sense there sinning with Adam. It is then posited that we were there in that we were biologically in Adam, because he is the father of the human race; in him resided all of humanity, thus we were there sinning with him, we were participating with him—his sin is our sin.

A fourth view goes by the name of Federalism or the Representative view. This position states that Adam was the federal head of mankind. God appointed Adam as the representative for the human race. When Adam was put on probation, he was not only on probation for himself but for the entire human race as well. The reason this position is called "federalism" is taken from the way an ambassador might act on behalf of his country. There are strong contextual reasons that is what Paul means by "all sinned" in this passage. When one reads through the passage one thing that stands out clearly is that Paul is contrasting the one act of Adam and the one act of Christ. The point of the passage is that just as Adam's act of disobedience had consequences on the race, so Christ's act of obedience had consequences on the race.

This is seen in verse 12: "by one man sin entered into the world;" verse 15: "by the offense of one many are dead;" verse 16: "the judgment was by one to condemnation;" verse 17 "by one man's offense death reigned by one;" verse 18: "by the offense of one judgment came upon all men to condemnation;" and verse 19: "by one man's disobedience many were made sinners." So the drift of the passage is that Adam was acting on our behalf, which is why Paul says six times that things are as they are because of the negative act of one man. By contrast, if one holds that we were in Adam sinning because we were seminally in him, then in order to be consistent with the analogy Paul is making, we would also have to say that we were in Christ performing His act of obedience. That would turn salvation into a work.

What Paul means to say in regard to Christ is that His act of obedience—His life and His death—was performed by Him for us. He stood as our representative and we reaped the positive consequences. If that is true, then the opposite is true as well; Adam stood as our representative and we reaped the negative consequences of his act. What we have then is Adam's sin imputed to us just as Christ's righteousness is imputed to us. The first Adam standing as our representative failed and we were condemned; the second Adam standing as our representative succeeded and we were declared righteous.

This model results in three "imputations" in salvation history.

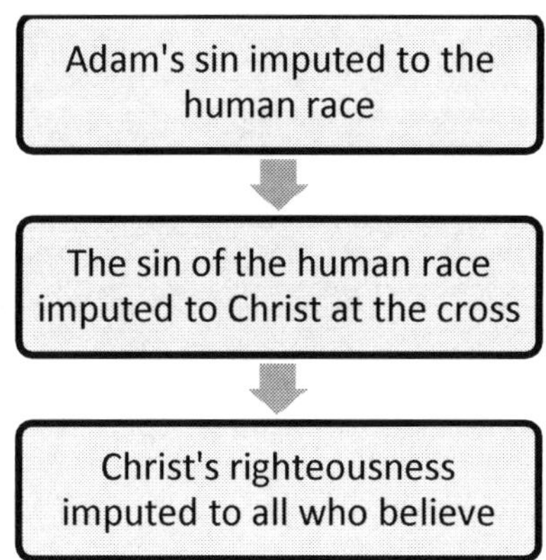

Romans 5:12-21 becomes one of the most important statements in the New Testament for understanding what a "Christian" is. In the Romans 5 description, a Christian is one who was spiritually in the realm of Adam, but who now is in the realm of Christ. He is "in Christ" in the sense that he is now in a sphere where he is associated with the benefits of the work of Christ.

SPIRITUAL REALM CONTRASTS ROMANS 5

TWO MEN:	**Adam**	**Christ**
TWO ACTS:	Trespass in the garden	Obedience on the cross
TWO RESULTS:	Sin/death	Righteousness/life
TWO DIFFERENCES:	Sin/death abound	Grace super-abounds

Schreiner states well, "Nor does the word mystical provide the best inroad for understanding Paul's 'in Christ' theology. Since mystical is a vague term with a diversity of connotations, it is too imprecise to prove useful in defining Paul's theology...Those who are in Adam experience all the liabilities of being descended from him. Similarly, those in Christ experience all the blessings that accrue to those who belong to God" (Thomas Schreiner, Paul Apostle of God's Glory in Christ: A Pauline Theology *[Downers Grove: InterVarsity Press, 2001], 157, 159). The troubling factor in this entire discussion is what is known as the* peccatum alienum *or "alien guilt." How can God treat the human race as guilty for a sin they did not commit? The oft quoted words of Pascal express the difficulty: "Without doubt, nothing is more shocking to our reason than to say that the sin of the first man has implicated in its guilt men so far from the original sin that they seem incapable of sharing it. This flow of guilt does not seem merely impossible to us, but indeed most unjust. What could be more contrary to the rules of our miserable justice than the eternal damnation of a child, incapable of will, for an act in which he seems to have so little part that it was actually committed 6, 000 years before he existed? Certainly nothing jolts us more rudely than this doctrine" (Blaise Pascal, Πενσέεσ [Harmondsworth: Penguin Books, 1966], 65. Four thoughts should be considered. First, we must beware of imposing our conception of fairness on God. The folly of this is addressed by Paul in Romans 9. Second, the concept of representation was common in the Old Testament. Third, in many world governments the same principle is followed in that elected officials make decisions for the country. Fourth, if the idea of representations is removed as unfair, then we have removed the basis for our salvation since we were represented by another.*

a. Paul states the first part of his proposition: sin entered the world through Adam and as the result death came for all men—5:12

b. Paul states how the effects of Adam's act were surpassed by the effects of Christ's act—5:13-17

  1) The effect of Adam's act was that death reigned even before the time of the law—5:13-14

  2) The effect of Christ's act was that grace and the gift of righteousness are available to all—5:15-17

c. Paul states the second part of his proposition: the representative act of one brings consequences on all—5:18-19

d. Paul states two questions at this point concerning the purpose of law and the purpose of grace—5:20-21

  1) The law was intended to reveal the sin of man—5:20

  2) Grace was intended to reveal the sufficiency of God's provision for that sin—5:21

BEGIN PARENTHESIS

Note #125: The Meaning of the Parenthesis

The fact that this is called a parenthetical section does not mean to imply that it is an afterthought or any less important than the rest of the letter. Nor does it mean to imply that it is unrelated to what precedes or follows it. Rather, as noted above, the section from 5:1-8:39 deals with assurance. Furthermore, it was suggested that that there is a break in this progression from 6:1-8:1 in which Paul is dealing with two objections that could arise from his discussion in 5:12-19. It was seen in 5:20 that he brings up the question of the law, and in 5:21 he brings up the question of grace dealing with the sin aroused by the law. It is thus necessary for Paul to say something about the believer's relationship to the law, for justification seems to have wiped it away, and the believer's relationship to grace, for grace seems to make sin not such a bad thing. He deals with the latter first (chapter 6) and then the former (chapter 7).

3. Paul explains the believer's relationship to grace in order to show that justification should result in holy living rather than an abuse of God's grace—6:1-23

a. Paul deals with the believer's freedom from the realm of sin in order to show the basis of holy living and to show that if one lives in the bondage of sin he is denying his justified position—6:1-14

b. Paul asks the question: shall we continue in sin that grace may abound?—6:1

1) Paul answers the question: "May it never be," and gives a number of reasons for this—6:2-11

a) He states that the believer died to sin—6:2a

b) He states that the believer was baptized into Christ's death—6:3-10

Note #126: Baptized by the Spirit

The baptism referred to here is Spirit baptism rather than water baptism. There are a number of reasons for this: 1) Paul normally uses the word to denote union with Christ, 2) the context is explaining how the believer was made dead to sin, and certainly this is not accomplished by water baptism, 3) "baptized" is in the passive voice suggesting something that was done to the believer, and 4) baptism is parallel to "planting" in v. 5. Thus, the baptism into Christ signifies union with Him and the participation of all of the privileges which that entails.

(1) Paul states the historical fact of being baptized into Christ's death—6:3

(2) Paul states the spiritual consequences of this union—6:4-11

(a) The believer's union with the death of Christ signifies that he is finished with the realm and reign of sin and raised to a new kind of life—6:4

(b) The believer has been raised with Christ to a new kind of life—6:5

(c) The old man was crucified so that the body of sin might be destroyed—6:6-7

Note #127: Old man/body of sin

From the context, the old man is the person the believer used to be in Adam, the person he was spiritually before he trusted Christ. The aorist tense suggests that the old man was permanently put to death. Thus, the old man is done away once and for all. Paul goes on to state that the purpose of this crucifixion of the old man was so that the "body of sin might be destroyed." Contextually, the "body" means the physical body (6:12, 13, 19). So, the body of sin refers to the physical body of which sin has taken possession. Sin reigns in the realm of the body and tries to control it. "Destroyed" has the idea of rendered powerless or ineffective as far as legal rights are concerned.

(d) This new life is a permanent one because it is united to an ever living Christ—6:8-10

2) Paul applies the truth of the believer's identification to Christ so that it would become effective in their lives—6:11-14

a) Paul tells them to count these facts as true in their lives—6:11

b) Paul tells them to not let sin reign in their mortal bodies—6:12

c) Paul tells them to not let their body be an instrument for sin—6:13

d) Paul tells them the reason for this exhortation is that they are in the realm of grace where the facts he has presented operate—6:14

c. Paul deals with the believer's enslavement to God's righteousness in order to show them that in the realm of righteousness and justification they have a new master—6:15-23

1) Based on the preceding point, Paul asks the question if they should sin because they are under grace and not law—6:15a

2) Paul answers "may it never be" and explains why this is true—6:15b-23

a) He notes that one's obedience determines one's enslavement and because they have been freed from sin they should now be the slaves of righteousness—6:15b-20

b) He notes that one's enslavement determines what one receives—6:21-23

4. Paul explains the believer's relationship to the law in order to show the place of the law during the present administration in their justified position—7:1-25

a. Paul shows the believer's freedom from the law in order to show that they have moved to a new realm of life—7:1-6

1) Paul states the principle that the law has authority over a man as long as he is alive—7:1

2) Paul illustrates the principle by noting that in the marriage relationship the partners are bound to each other until one of them dies—7:2-3
3) Paul applies the illustration by noting that the believer died (the death of the old man at justification) to the realm of the law in order to produce fruit in the realm of the Spirit—7:4-6

b. Paul explains the relationship of the law to sin and death in order to show that the law is not being deprecated by him—7:7-25
1) Paul speaks about the relationship of the law to sin—7:7-12
   a) The problem: is the law sin?—7:7a
   b) The answer: the law is holy and reveals sin—7:7b-12
2) Paul speaks about the relationship of the law to death—7:13-25
   a) Paul states that it is sin, not the law, that causes death—7:13
   b) Paul states the reason this is true is because the law is spiritual but man is carnal—7:14-25a
      (1) He contrasts the law as being spiritual with himself as being a slave to sin—7:14
      (2) He proves this point by showing the condemnation which the law brings—7:15-25

Note #128: What is the spiritual state of "the man?"

There are many interpretive issues related to 7:14-25. In fact, Nygren asserts that these verses are the "most discussed and fought over part of the epistle" (A. Nygren, A Commentary on Romans *[Philadelphia: Fortress, 1949], 284), and Martyn Lloyd-Jones asserted that "anyone who approaches this section without 'fear and trembling,' and without humility, is not really fit to expound Scripture at all" (Martyn Lloyd-Jones,* Romans: An Exposition of Chapters 7.1-8.4: The Law, Its Functions and Limits *[Grand Rapids: Zondervan, 1978], 177). The most important aspect of the section has to do with the spiritual state of "the man" in the second half of the chapter. For a discussion of other issues in this text see the major commentaries on Romans such as Douglas Moo,* The Epistle to the Romans *(Grand Rapids: Eerdmans, 1996), 442-452 and Thomas Schreiner,* Romans *(Grand Rapids: Baker, 2003), 372-394.*

The two major approaches to the spiritual state of the man is that he is either unsaved (Moo, Fee, Theissen, Meyer, the early church generally) or saved (Nygren, Barrett, Murray, Packer, Cranfield, Dunn, Morris, Mounce, Calvin, the Puritans, Reformers, and Princeton theologians generally). Schreiner argues that "the arguments on both sides are remarkably strong....I would suggest that the arguments are so finely balanced because Paul does not intend to distinguish believers from unbelievers in this text" (Schreiner, Romans, *390). Some of the textual evidence for the first view includes descriptions of being "under sin," "fleshly," and "captive to the law of sin." The textual evidence for the second view is that the person is at least struggling with sin and is said to "delight" in the Law. If the unsaved view is correct, then this is a matter of a person who needs to be saved; if the second view is correct, then this is a matter of a Christian struggling with sin in his life.*

There is another possibility for understanding this text which may fit better into the argument of this chapter which I have called the "awakened sinner" view. This position has three major components.

1. <u>Two types of individuals</u>. In Romans 1:18-3:20 Paul gives one of the most stark descriptions of the human race bound in sin apart from the grace of God as found anywhere in the New Testament. Summarily, he is said to have rejected God's revelation of himself through nature, judicially abandoned to the ever-increasing downward spiral of sin, in bondage to sin, no awareness of a lack of divine righteousness, no desire to seek God, and an actual enemy of God. Beginning in 3:21 Paul describes the individual whom God has graciously and mercifully declared righteous. This individual is freed from sin, death, and the law. Moreover, he is dead to sin and has the capacity to serve righteousness. It is my opinion that neither of these individuals is in view in Romans 7:14-25.

2. <u>The first half of Romans 7 is the key</u>. In Romans 7 Paul is discussing the relationship of the believer to the Law. He reaches the conclusion in 7:1-6 that the believer is free from the condemnation of the Law. At this point, he has accomplished what he set out to do. However, he imagines someone asking the question in 7:7 "what shall we say then? Is the Law sin?" Paul argued previously that the Law exacerbates the desire to sin (5:20) and now he is saying that we are freed from the Law. The logical query, therefore, is whether the Law is sinful. This leads the apostle in 7:7-13 to show emphatically that the Law is good. Essentially he is going to show the goodness of the Law by showing what the Law does, namely reveals sin. This is good because it shows our need of the righteousness of God and drives us to God to obtain the righteousness of

Christ. One of the key parts in this section is the three-fold progress in 7:9: alive...sin revived...I died (a) "I was alive once without the Law," (b) "but when the commandment came, sin revived," (c) "and I died."

(a) I was alive apart from the Law once. Calvin has captured the sense of this statement perfectly. "The meaning then is this, 'When I sinned, having not the knowledge of the law, the sin, which I did not observe, was so laid to sleep, that it seemed to be dead; on the other hand, as I seemed not to myself to be a sinner, I was satisfied with myself, thinking that I had a life of mine own'" (John Calvin, The Epistle to the Romans [Grand Rapids: Baker, 1979], 255). The legitimate question is then asked, at what time could Paul be said to be ignorant of the Law? Calvin continues: "It is indeed certain, that he had been taught the doctrine of the law from his childhood; but it was the theology of the letter which does not humble its disciples....So also he himself, while he had his eyes veiled, being destitute of the Spirit of Christ, was satisfied with the outward mask of righteousness...Hence he represents the law as absent, though before his eyes, while it did not really impress him with the consciousness of God's judgment" (Ibid.).

(b) But when the commandment came, sin revived. According to Paul's earlier teaching in Romans, all men are sinners. The reviving of sin by virtue of the Law refers to the awareness and sense of conviction which comes when the Law does its work. There is produced a sense of sinfulness that was not present before.

(c) I died. Paul states this concept several times in this section. In verse 9 he says "I died." In verse 10 he says that he found the commandment to be unto death, and in verse 11 he indicates that "sin by the commandment...slew me." The death of which he is speaking is the spiritual work of the Law. Previously, though Paul had the Law, it was an external guide he lived up to which left him assuming he was right with God (Phil. 3:4-6). However, when the Law did its spiritual work on his heart he "died" and was knocked down as he became awakened to his helpless, hopeless

condition before God.

3. <u>Illustration</u>. Having stated the function of the Law as something that is good, Paul concludes the chapter by illustrating the Law in action. The man, whoever he may be, has been awakened to his sinful condition and is a state of spiritual torment until he finally cries out for deliverance. The description of the man in the illustration is not the same as the description of mankind in the earlier chapters of Romans since they are impervious to their spiritual state. Furthermore, Paul is not talking about a Christian's struggle with sin (though true in fact) in this section since the flow of the argument deals, not with sanctification, but the work of the Law. The experience described in this illustration has been experienced by every Christian to one degree or another.

Godet sums up the idea of the passage well: "The apostle is speaking here neither of the natural man in his state of voluntary ignorance and sin, nor of the child of God, born anew, set free by grace, and animated by the Spirit of Christ; but of the man whose conscience, awakened by the law, has entered sincerely, with fear and trembling, but still in his own strength, into the desperate struggle against evil" (F. L. Godet, Commentary on St. Paul's Epistle to the Romans [Edinburgh: T. & T. Clark, 1890], 1:56).

END PARENTHESIS

5. Paul states the proposition that there is no condemnation for the believer because he has been freed from the law of sin and death because the righteousness of the law has been fulfilled (proof #3)—8:1-4

Note #129: Resumption of argument

Romans 8:1 is actually a hinge verse which brings Paul back to his discussion of assurance. One of the points of discussion in this verse is the antecedent of the "therefore" with which the verse begins. For the following three reasons it is valid to see the "therefore" of 8:1 picking up the argument from 5:21, 1) since Paul was dealing with questions regarding law and grace in chapters 6-7, those chapters were digressing from his main argument in chapter 5 which he now resumes in chapter 8, 2) the word "condemnation" in 8:1 occurs only two other times in the New Testament, 5:16, 18 which shows he is picking up that theme again, and 3) the phrase "in Christ" in 8:1 picks up that theme which was developed in the Adam/Christ contrast in chapter 5.

Note #130: The purpose of chapter 8

Chapter 8 is often understood to have as its theme the role of the Holy Spirit in sanctification. There is no doubt that the Holy Spirit is prominent in this section, and that sanctification is seen in this section, but it is the writer's view that sanctification is not the major part of this section. The great theme of this chapter seems to be the security of the Christian (of which the Holy Spirit is certainly a significant part). This dominant theme is sounded in the proposition in 8:1 and reaches its zenith in 8:28-39. This security and assurance flow of thought will be developed in the following argument.

6. Paul contrasts the life in the flesh with the life in the Spirit in order to show that the one who has been freed from condemnation and the law of sin and death has God's Spirit working in him (proof #4)—8:5-11

7. Paul notes that it is the believer's responsibility to put to death the deeds of the body because they are the recipients of the presence of God's Spirit who provides an inner assurance that we are God's children (proof #5)—8:12-17

Note #131: "Abba" isn't "daddy"

The title for this note is borrowed from James Barr's 1988 article "Abba Isn't Daddy," Journal of Theological Studies *39:1: 28-47. Barr points out that "abba" was not a form of address used by small children to their father, rather a form of address by adult children. The term was neither a term of childhood nor a particularly intimate one. The danger of using "daddy" is not only that it is inaccurate, but that it leads at worst to an irreverent familiarity or at best to an infantile relationship with God. As Barr states, "It was not a childish expression comparable with 'Daddy': it was a more solemn, responsible, adult address to a Father" (46).*

8. Because believers are sons, they are destined for an inheritance in glory even in the face of tribulation (proof #6)— 8:18-25
9. God has not left the believer to himself but has given him the assistance of the Holy Spirit (proof #7)—8:26-27

Note #132: The intercession of the Holy Spirit

In 8:27 Paul writes that the Holy Spirit intercedes for the believer. Five points of interpretation will make the argument clear: 1) the word "help" in verse 26 refers to "coming alongside to bear a load," 2) the reason this help is needed is because of our "infirmity" which refers to the weakened human condition, 3) the way the Spirit helps is in the area of prayer, 4) the way he helps in the area of prayer is by praying for us. He does not teach us "how" to pray, but he actually prays for us in times when we don't know "what" to pray for, and 5) his prayers are effective because he knows the mind of God.

10. God is at work in the whole scheme of salvation, from past to future (proof #8)—8:28-30
11. God is the one who is for us (proof #9)—8:31-34
12. Nothing shall separate us from the love of Christ (proof #10)—8:35-39

IV. PAUL DISCUSSES ISRAEL'S REJECTION OF GOD'S RIGHTEOUSNESS IN ORDER TO VINDICATE GOD'S RIGHTEOUS CHARACTER AS IT IS SEEN IN HIS DEALINGS WITH THE NATION—9:1-11:36

Note #133: Who chose whom? Two important questions

Romans 9-11 presents one of the clearest statements in Scripture regarding the doctrine of unconditional election. It is not the purpose of this note to present a detailed defense of this doctrine, other than to draw attention to one of the major textual arguments in its favor, namely, two questions which Paul asks. After asserting that God chose Jacob instead of Esau apart from anything they had done, Paul poses the first question: Is there unrighteousness with God? After asserting that God will have mercy on whom he will have mercy, Paul poses the second question: Why does he yet find fault? If Paul were not teaching unconditional election, these questions never would have been asked. They are only asked (as objections) because it appears unjust of God to choose some and not others. To object to the doctrine of unconditional election as unfair is proof that the doctrine has been understood correctly. Paul simply responds to the objection by saying the creature has no right to question the creator.

A. Paul presents the facts of God's selection and rejection of individuals in order to show
that God has the right to do as He pleases and that these facts are not inconsistent with
His justice and thereby vindicating Him—9:1-29

1. Paul states that God's rejection of the nation caused him sorrow and grief especially in light of the fact that they had been given such great privileges—9:1-5

2. Paul illustrates God's sovereign choice in order to show why Jewish involvement in God's program was decreasing in spite of their privileges and why Gentile involvement was increasing—9:6-18

a. God chose Isaac over Ishmael to establish the spiritual line of promise in order to show that current rejection was an example of God's sovereign choice established in the Old Testament—9:6-9

Note #134: They are not all Israel who are of Israel

Some covenant theologians insist that Romans 9:6 teaches that we are now part of the people of God called Israel (e.g. Sam Waldron, MacArthur's Millennial Manifesto: A Friendly Response *[Owensboro, KY: RBAP, 2008], 46-47). Of course, both Jews and Gentiles are saved the same way and are a part of the people of God in that sense; however, "Israel" cannot be redefined to include believing Jews and Gentiles for the following reasons: a) the contextual definition has been established in 9:4, b) the division in 9:6 is a division within Israel, c) the two occurrences of the term "Israel" in 9:27 fall plainly within this sense, d) the occurrence of "Israel" in 9:31 refers to ethnic Israel, e) the two occurrences of "Israel" in Romans 10 refer to ethnic Israel (19, 21), and f) the four occurrences of "Israel" in Romans 11 refer to ethnic Israel (2, 7, 25, 26). Here are numerous uses of the word "Israel" all of which refer to ethnic Israel (including 9:6 because of 9:4). It is therefore exegetically unlikely that we would have a new definition of "Israel" as Jews and Gentiles.*

b. God chose Jacob over Esau in order to show that election is not based on works but on God's choice—9:10-13

c. Paul presents the illustration of Pharaoh in order to show that God is just in His dealings and is sovereign in His choice—9:14-18

1) Paul anticipates the objection that God is unjust—9:14a

2) Paul states that God is not unjust and can sovereignly confer mercy on whomever He chooses—9:14b-15

3) Paul infers from this that man's efforts do not count but rather God's mercy—9:16-18

- **d.** Paul establishes God's right to elect individuals and that He has the right to be wrathful to some and merciful to others in order to establish God's sovereignty in His treatment of people—9:19-29
  - **1)** Paul establishes God's right to elect individuals—9:19-21
    - **a)** He anticipates the objection that man is not responsible because no one can resist God's will—9:19
    - **b)** Paul rebukes man for this irreverence—9:20
    - **c)** Paul illustrates this by noting that the created thing submits to the creator—9:21
  - **2)** Paul establishes God's right to be wrathful to some and merciful to others—9:22-29
    - **a)** He notes that God has deigned to make some the objects of His wrath—9:22
    - **b)** He notes that God has deigned to make some the objects of His mercy including both Jew and Gentile—9:23-29

B. Paul presents the stumbling of Israel through unbelief in order to show that Israel is culpable and that God is righteous in the way He is dealing with them—9:30-10:21

- **1.** Paul states that Israel is culpable because they repudiated righteousness by faith and tried to establish their own righteousness—9:30-10:4
- **2.** Paul states that Israel is culpable because they ignored the Old Testament teaching on righteousness by faith—10:5-13

Note #135: Deuteronomy 30

In 10:6-8 Paul quotes freely from Deuteronomy 30 where Moses charges Israel as they are about to enter Canaan. Since they had God's message near them, it was not necessary to have someone come down from heaven, or someone to rise from the dead to give them that message. In the same way, this generation had a message of righteousness by faith near them, and thus they had all they needed to be saved.

Paul notes in 10:9 that confession is necessary for salvation. This refers to an acknowledgement of the deity of Christ by Israel. Cranfield has noted that kurios *is used more than 6,000 times in the LXX to represent the Tetragrammaton. This is especially relevant in light of the Old Testament concerning Israel—they had to acknowledge that He was God's Messiah (C. E. B. Cranfield,* Romans *[Edinburgh: T. & T. Clark, 1982], 2:529).*

- **3.** Paul states that Israel is culpable because they refused the opportunity of accepting the message of righteousness through faith—10:14-21

C. Paul presents the future restoration of Israel in order to show that their rejection is not final thereby showing that God is just and faithful to His covenants and thus in His dealings with the nation—11:1-36

- **1.** Paul shows that Israel's rejection is not complete for there has always been a remnant—11:1-10
- **2.** Paul shows that Israel's rejection is not final—11:11-24

Note #136: The grafting in of the Gentiles

Fruchtenbaum has correctly noted that the grafting of the Gentiles into the olive tree does not refer to the replacement of Israel by the Church. Rather, the olive tree does not refer to Israel or the Church but to a place of privilege and blessing (Arnold Fruchtenbaum, Israelology *[Tustin, CA: Ariel Ministries, 2001], 499-503).*

a. He states that one reason for their rejection was so that blessing could be brought to the Gentiles—11:11-15
b. He states that their rejection is not final because of the earnest given to the Patriarchs—11:16
c. He presents the illustration of the olive tree in order to show the relation between Jew and Gentile in this plan—11:17-24
   1) He admonishes the Gentiles against pride because they were grafted into the tree and could be cut off since God did not spare even the natural branches—11:17-22
   2) He states that Israel will be re-grafted because God is able to do this and natural branches are easy to re-graft—11:23-24

3. Paul shows that Israel's future restoration is certain—11:25-32
   a. Israel's blindness is partial and temporary—11:25
   b. Israel's restoration will be complete—11:26-27
   c. He reviews by stating that in order to bring salvation to the Gentiles He had to deal with Israel as enemies but in relation to election they are God's beloved and will again be shown mercy—11:28-32
4. Paul concludes this sections with a doxology of praise to God in order to show the wisdom He displays in His righteous dealings with Israel and the Gentiles—11:33-36

V. PAUL EXPANDS ON THE RIGHTEOUS LIFESTYLE WHICH SHOULD CHARACTERIZE THE JUSTIFIED BELIEVER IN ORDER TO SHOW THAT THE RIGHTEOUSNESS SEEN IN GOD'S DEALINGS SHOULD ALSO BE SEEN IN THOSE TO WHOM HE HAS IMPUTED RIGHTEOUSNESS—12:1-15:13

A. Paul presents the conduct the justified believer should display in the church—12:1-8
   1. The foundation of the conduct of the believer is to consecrate himself to God—12:1-2

Note #137: The will of God

Romans 12:1-2 is teaching that when we consecrate ourselves to God, we come to understand that the will of God is good. In other words, with a renewed mind, we approve of the things God approves. The will of God which we come to see as good is described throughout the rest of the section in how we relate to believers, unbelievers, the state, and the rich and the strong. The will of God in Scripture is not something mysterious which we try to find, but is plainly revealed in Scripture.

   2. The believer is to walk humbly before God because each one is a part of the body and should serve the body as opportunities arise—12:3-8

B. Paul presents a number of commands showing how the believer should conduct himself in relation to other believers—12:9-13

C. Paul presents a number of commands showing how the believer should conduct himself in relation to unbelievers—12:14-21

Note #138: Heaping coals of fire on someone's head

Paul states in 12:20 that when we are kind to others we "heap coals of fire on his head." This phrase occurs in a larger context which deals with doing good things for one's enemies and leaving their judgment to God. The imagery of "coals of fire" is to be related to the Old Testament symbolism of divine anger and judgment (John Day, "'Coals of Fire' in Romans 12:19-20," Bibliotheca Sacra *160 [October-December 2003], 418). The idea of the passage then is that Christians can show kindness to the unbeliever and take comfort in the fact that if this kindness is spurned, God will render future judgment.*

D. Paul presents the conduct the believer should have in relation to the state—13:1-7

- **1.** He should submit himself to the government because it is of divine origin and because of the divine purpose of government—13:1-4
- **2.** He infers from this proposition that subjection to government will avoid punishment—13:5
- **3.** He infers from this proposition that the individual should support the government by taxes and honor—13:6-7

E. Paul presents the conduct the believer should have toward their neighbors in light of the future—13:8-14

- **1.** They are not to leave any outstanding debts—13:8a
- **2.** They are rather to love one another which captures the essence of the law—3:8b-10
- **3.** Paul presents the motivation for this love as being the fact that the return of Christ is imminent and therefore they should act accordingly—13:11-14

F. Paul presents the conduct the believer should have toward the weak and the strong (differing levels of maturity) in order to achieve harmony between Jew and Gentile—14:1-15:13

- **1.** Paul exhorts the believers to mutual forbearance and states several reasons for this—14:1-12
  - **a.** Paul says that they should mutually forbear because both are accepted by God using the illustrations of differences over food and days—14:1-5
  - **b.** Paul says that they should mutually forbear because both belong to Christ and are responsible to Him—14:6-9
  - **c.** Paul says that they should mutually forbear because both will be judged by God—14:10-12
- **2.** Paul exhorts the strong not to offend the weak—14:13-23
  - **a.** Paul concedes to the strong that certain things are not unclean but exhorts them not to destroy the weak because the Kingdom of God consists of more than food—14:13-18
  - **b.** Paul concludes that the strong are to build and not to destroy so that there would be unity in the body—14:19-21
  - **c.** Paul puts the practice in the principle of acting in faith—14:22-23

3. Paul exhorts the strong to help the weak as an imitator of Christ—15:1-6
    a. Paul states that the strong should bear up the weak and not please themselves which he illustrates by the example of Christ's unselfishness—15:1-4
    b. Paul appeals for unity in these matters in order to glorify God—15:5-6
4. Paul exhorts the believers to have mutual acceptance of one another in order to demonstrate the plan of God in which He accepts both Jew and Gentile—15:7-13
    a. Paul exhorts to mutual acceptance—15:7a
    b. Paul illustrates mutual acceptance by the ministry of Christ in which He vindicated God's truthfulness by confirming the promises made to the Patriarchs and including Gentiles in His plan of mercy—15:7b-12
    c. Paul applies the illustration by entreating them to joy and peace—15:13

VI. PAUL CONCLUDES THIS LETTER BY STATING HIS MOTIVATION FOR WRITING, HIS INTENTION OF VISITING SPAIN, PERSONAL GREETINGS, AND ADMONITIONS IN ORDER TO SHOW HIS AFFECTION FOR THE ROMAN CHRISTIANS AND TO DEFEND THE CONTENT OF HIS LETTER—15:14-16:27

A. Paul states that his motivation for writing was the persuasion of the progress of the Romans and His desire to present the Gospel to the Gentiles in order to defend the content of the letter—15:14-21
1. Paul commends the Romans for their progress in the Gospel—15:14
2. Paul says that he wrote to remind them again of his ministry to the Gentiles—15:15-21
    a. He says that he was bold in this presentation—15:15a
    b. He says that he used this boldness because he was appointed as a minister of Christ to minister to the Gentiles—15:15b-21

B. Paul states his intention of his visit to them in order for them to see his genuine concern for them—15:22-33
1. Paul states that in the past and the present he has desired to visit them and that he plans on going to Spain—15:22-24
2. Paul states that he made a detour in Jerusalem to deliver an offering in order that they would understand his delay in visiting them—15:25-29
3. Paul states his desire for the prayers of the Romans that he would be delivered from the unbelieving Jews in Jerusalem and would be accepted by the believing Jews—15:30-33

C. Paul states his final greetings and admonition—16:1-27
1. He recommends Phoebe to the Christians in Rome and asks them to receive her—16:1-2
2. He salutes various saints in the churches—16:3-16
3. He cautions the saints to beware of false teachers who cause division and teach contrary to what they had been taught—16:17-20
4. He sends the greetings of his companions—16:21-24
5. He states his benediction in which he acknowledges God as the one who will establish them in the faith that has now been revealed—16:25-27

Note #139: The Canons of Trent and *Catechism of the Catholic Church*

*In Roman Catholicism the "*magisterium*" (from the Latin word magister) refers to the teaching authority of the Church.*[583] *When an ecumenical council is called (an "extraordinary magisterium") which is both approved and presided over by the pope, its decrees are considered to be infallible. That these decrees are infallible does not imply that they cannot be improved upon or stated in more accurate language. Rather, they can never be refuted or rejected. The Roman Church has called 21 such councils in her history; the nineteenth of which was the Council at Trent. This Council convened on December 13, 1545 and would meet off and on for over 18 years thus meeting during several sessions. "Its main object was the definitive determination of the doctrines of the Church in answer to the heresies of the Protestants."*[584]

In 1985 a council was called to provide a summary of Church belief for Catholics worldwide. This catechism was written under the direction of Cardinal Ratzinger (later to become Pope Benedict XVI) and was approved by John Paul II. The English translation was released in 1994 with the title Catechism of the Catholic Church. I have provided selected, representative statements below from each document which touch on the matters of justification.

Trent's Sixth Session

DECREE ON JUSTIFICATION—CHAPTER VIII: And whereas the Apostle saith, that man is justified by faith and freely, those words are to be understood in that sense which the perpetual consent of the Catholic Church hath held and expressed; to wit, that we are therefore said to be justified by faith, because faith is the beginning of human salvation, the foundation, and the root of all Justification; without which it is impossible to please God, and to come unto the fellowship of His sons: but we are therefore said to be justified freely, because that none of those things which precede justification-whether faith or works-merit the grace itself of justification. For, if it be a grace, it is not now by works, otherwise, as the same Apostle says, grace is no more grace.

DECREE ON JUSTIFICATION—CHAPTER X: Having, therefore, been thus justified, and made the friends and domestics of God, advancing from virtue to virtue, they are renewed, as the Apostle says, day by day; that is, by mortifying the members of their own flesh, and by presenting them as instruments of justice unto sanctification, they, through the observance of the commandments of God and of the Church, faith co-

[583] "The task of giving an authentic interpretation of the Word of God, whether in its written form or in the form of Tradition, has been entrusted to the living, teaching office of the Church alone. Its authority in this matter is exercised in the name of Jesus Christ." This means that the task of interpretation has been entrusted to the bishops in communion with the successor of Peter, the Bishop of Rome" (*CCC*, 85). "The Church's Magisterium exercises the authority it holds from Christ to the fullest extent when it defines dogmas, that is, when it proposes, in a form obliging the Christian people to an irrevocable adherence of faith, truths contained in divine Revelation or also when it proposes, in a definitive way, truths having a necessary connection with these" (*CCC*, 88). "The Roman Pontiff, head of the college of bishops, enjoys this infallibility in virtue of his office, when, as supreme pastor and teacher of all the faithful—who confirms his brethren in the faith—he proclaims by a definitive act a doctrine pertaining to faith or morals...The infallibility promised to the Church is also present in the body of bishops when, together with Peter's successor, they exercise the supreme Magisterium," above all in an Ecumenical Council. When the Church through its supreme Magisterium proposes a doctrine "for belief as being divinely revealed," and as the teaching of Christ, the definitions "must be adhered to with the obedience of faith. This infallibility extends as far as the deposit of divine Revelation itself" (*CCC*, 891).

[584] "Council of Trent," http://www.newadvent.org/cathen/15030c.html accessed 2/12/2014.

operating with good works, increase in that justice which they have received through the grace of Christ, and are still further justified, as it is written; He that is just, let him be justified still; and again, Be not afraid to be justified even to death; and also, Do you see that by works a man is justified, and not by faith only.

DECREE ON JUSTIFICATION—CHAPTER XVI: And, for this cause, life eternal is to be proposed to those working well unto the end, and hoping in God, both as a grace mercifully promised to the sons of God through Jesus Christ, and as a reward which is according to the promise of God Himself, to be faithfully rendered to their good works and merits. For this is that crown of justice which the Apostle declared was, after his fight and course, laid up for him, to be rendered to him by the just judge, and not only to him, but also to all that love his coming. For, whereas Jesus Christ Himself continually infuses his virtue into the said justified,-as the head into the members, and the vine into the branches,-and this virtue always precedes and accompanies and follows their good works, which without it could not in any wise be pleasing and meritorious before God,-we must believe that nothing further is wanting to the justified, to prevent their being accounted to have, by those very works which have been done in God, fully satisfied the divine law according to the state of this life, and to have truly merited eternal life, to be obtained also in its (due) time.

CANON 5: If any one saith, that, since Adam's sin, the free will of man is lost and extinguished; or, that it is a thing with only a name, yea a name without a reality, a figment, in fine, introduced into the Church by Satan; let him be anathema.

CANON 9: If any one saith, that by faith alone the impious is justified; in such wise as to mean, that nothing else is required to co-operate in order to the obtaining the grace of Justification, and that it is not in any way necessary, that he be prepared and disposed by the movement of his own will; let him be anathema.

CANON 11: If any one saith, that men are justified, either by the sole imputation of the justice of Christ, or by the sole remission of sins, to the exclusion of the grace and the charity which is poured forth in their hearts by the Holy Ghost, and is inherent in them; or even that the grace, whereby we are justified, is only the favour of God; let him be anathema.

CANON 12: If any one shall say that justifying faith is nothing else than confidence in the divine mercy pardoning sins for Christ's sake, or that it is that confidence alone by which we are justified...let him be accursed.

CANON 14: If any one saith, that man is truly absolved from his sins and justified, because that he assuredly believed himself absolved and justified; or, that no one is truly justified but he who believes himself justified; and that, by this faith alone, absolution and justification are effected; let him be anathema.

CANON 30: If any one saith, that, after the grace of Justification has been received, to every penitent sinner the guilt is remitted, and the debt of eternal punishment is blotted out in such wise, that there remains not any debt of temporal punishment to be discharged either in this world, or in the next in Purgatory, before the entrance to the kingdom of heaven can be opened (to him); let him be anathema.

CANON 33: If any one saith, that, by the Catholic doctrine touching Justification, by this holy Synod inset forth in this present decree, the glory of God, or the merits of our Lord Jesus Christ are in any way derogated from, and not rather that the truth of our faith, and the glory in fine of God and of Jesus Christ are rendered (more) illustrious; let him be anathema.

Catechism of the Catholic Church
997: Our Lord tied the forgiveness of sins to faith and Baptism.

1026: He makes partners in his heavenly glorification those who have believed in him and remained faithful to his will.

1030: All who die in God's grace and friendship, but still imperfectly purified, are indeed assured of their eternal salvation; but after death they undergo purification, so as to achieve the holiness necessary to enter the joy of heaven.

1129: The Church affirms that for believers the sacraments of the New Covenant are necessary for salvation.

1213: Through Baptism we are freed from sin and reborn as sons of God; we become members of Christ, are incorporated into the Church.

1266: The Most Holy Trinity gives the baptized sanctifying grace, the grace of justification.

1285: the reception of the sacrament of Confirmation is necessary for the completion of baptismal grace.

1477: In the treasury, too, are the prayers and good works of all the saints, all those who have followed in the footsteps of Christ the Lord and by his grace have made their lives holy and carried out the mission the Father entrusted to them. In this way they attained their own salvation and at the same time cooperated in saving their brothers in the unity of the Mystical Body.

1524: In addition to the Anointing of the Sick, the Church offers those who are about to leave this life the Eucharist as viaticum. Communion in the body and blood of Christ, received at this moment of "passing over" to the Father, has a particular significance and importance. It is the seed of eternal life and the power of resurrection.

1989: Justification is not only the remission of sins, but also the sanctification and renewal of the interior man.

1992: Justification is conferred in Baptism, the sacrament of faith. It conforms us to the righteousness of God, who makes us inwardly just by the power of his mercy.

1993: Justification establishes cooperation between God's grace and man's freedom.

1995: justification entails the sanctification of his whole being.

2008: The merit of man before God in the Christian life arises from the fact that God has freely chosen to associate man with the work of his grace.

1 CORINTHIANS

Authorship

Pauline authorship of 1 Corinthians is almost universally accepted. Pauline authorship has strong external evidence from the church fathers with the earliest known statement coming from Clement of Rome in his *To the Corinthians* (AD 95). Internal evidence also supports this conclusion in light of 1:1 and 16:21, as well as the harmonious language and character with Paul's other epistles.

The Corinthian Church[585]

Historical

The city of Corinth was ideally situated just southwest of the Corinthian Isthmus which connected Northern Greece and Southern Greece (the Peloponnesus). The Isthmus was a four-mile rock-cut track connecting the two ports, enabling cargo and even small ships to be hauled across the isthmus (a narrow strip of land connecting two larger areas) to the other gulf. Cargo would be unloaded to vehicles which would take them from one gulf to the other. If a ship were small enough, the entire vessel could be pulled across. This eliminated taking the long voyage around Southern Greece. Later, the Greeks cut out a canal linking the two gulfs. This project was actually began by Nero but wasn't finished until 1893.

Corinth had angered Rome because Corinth was the chief city of the Achaean league. (*3rd-century-bc confederation of the towns of Achaea in ancient Greece. The 12 Achaean cities of the northern Peloponnese had organized a league by the 4th century BC to protect themselves against piratical raids from across the Corinthian Gulf, but this league fell apart after the death of Alexander the Great. The 10 surviving cities renewed their alliance in 280 BC, and under the leadership of Aratus of Sicyon, the league gained strength by the inclusion of his city, and later other non-Achaean cities, on equal terms. The league's activity initially centered on the expulsion of the Macedonians and the restoration of Greek rule*). Corinth had revolted rather than submit to Rome's demands to dissolve the league. The Roman military led to the league's inevitable defeat and the demolition of its leading city in 146 BC. Lucius Mummius, the Roman general, sacked and burned the city. Reportedly, the male population was killed, the women and children were sold into slavery. The year 146 BC marked the end of Corinth as a normally functioning city.

The town remained desolated and largely uninhabited for 102 years after this defeat. In 44 BC, shortly before his assassination, Julius Caesar decided to establish a Roman colony on the site. Rome established colonies to solve overcrowding in the city and to promulgate Roman civilization across the world. This resettlement created a new Roman heritage for Corinth.

Julius Caesar colonized the city with persons predominately belonging to the "freedman class." Crinagoras acidly referred to the Corinthian settlers as "those often sold, unstable or disreputable slaves." The city, however, was soon transformed from

585 The material in this section is cited and/or adapted from David Garland's excellent volume *1 Corinthians,* Baker Exegetical Commentary on the New Testament (Grand Rapids: Baker Academic, 2003), 1-14.

ruin to riches. The denizens (a person permitted residence in a foreign country) of Corinth in Paul's day were known for their wealth and ostentation (excessive display). Without an entrenched aristocracy, the citizens of Corinth were not fated, but had a real opportunity for upward social mobility. The favorable economic climate attracted settlers from all over the empire.

In Paul's time, Corinth had a mixed ethnic population of Roman freedmen, indigenous Greeks, and immigrants from far and wide. A strong Jewish community was well integrated and on good terms with the wider community.

Social/Economic

This letter must be read against the background of Corinth as a city imbued with Roman cultural values. In sum:

- The original freedmen settlers were still under obligation to their former masters in Italy.
- The official language of Latin predominates.
- The religious focal point of the Corinthian forum was the temple dedicated to the imperial family.
- Throngs attended the Isthmian games.
- Many inhabitants were so affluent that "wealth and **ostentatious display** became the hallmark of Corinth." The Corinthians indulged new attitudes and ways of life fueled by the new wealth and unbridled by ancestral tradition. **These values fed the zeal to attain public status**.

It is particularly critical to expand on this fifth socio/economic point. Crucial for any success and status in this culture was attaining the patronage of powerful people and giving favors to others to establish an array of influential friends and clients, exerting political enmity to ostracize opponents, and employing skillful oratory to persuade others in any assembly. To use terms from American culture: massaging a superior's ego, rubbing shoulders with the powerful, pulling strings, scratching each other's back, and dragging rivals' names through the mud, brownnosing, sucking up, etc.—all describe what was required to attain success in this society.

Unfortunately, most of the believers in Corinth were affected by the dominant culture surrounding them, even if they assimilated its values only subliminally. What they were ignorant of was that these values were hostile to the message of the cross (particularly those .related to honor and status through power) and percolated into the church, destroying its fellowship and unity.

Secular wisdom, which reflected the code of conduct of the social elites, had its hold on members of the church. Its values played havoc on Paul's attempt to build a community based on love. Corinthian society was riddled by competitive individualism, and this ethos spilled over into the relationships in the church as wealthier members competed for followers. Socially pretentious and self-important individuals appear to have dominated the church. It is likely that they flaunted their symbols of status, wisdom, influence, and family pedigree and looked down on others of lesser status. They appear to have wanted to preserve the social barriers of class and status that permeated their social world but were nullified in the cross of Christ. For some, the Christian community had become simply another arena to compete for status according to the societal norms. Paul pictures the church as divided into "haves" and "have-nots" (11:22). Since one needed to affirm one's wealth and social status to confirm one's identity in this culture, the "haves" show no qualms about humiliating the "have-nots" at the Lord's Supper, widening the division in the camp.

Corinth was a religious melting pot. The gods and the cults celebrated by the Corinthians included Apollo, Aphrodite/Venus, Asclepius, Athena, Athena Chalinitus, Demeter and Kore, Dionysus, Ephesian Artemis, Hera Acraea, Hermes/Mercury, Jupiter Capitolinus, Poseidon/Neptune, Tyche, Fortuna, and Zeus." Egyptian mystery cults, such as the worship of Isis, also were practiced.

In Paul's day many of the pagan religions included prostitution as part of the worship of their god or goddess. Consequently fornication flourished in Corinth. "Old Corinth had gained such a reputation for sexual vice that Aristophanes (*ca.* 450-385 BC) coined the verb *korinthiazo* (= to act like a Corinthian, i.e., to commit fornication)." "The old city had been the most licentious city in Greece, and perhaps the most licentious city in the Empire."

The most notorious shrine was the temple of Aphrodite that stood on top of an approximately 1,900 foot high mountain just south of the city, the Acrocorinth. Hundreds of female slaves served the men who "worshipped" there. Other major deities honored in Corinth included Melicertes, the patron of seafarers, and Poseidon, the sea god.

Christians were labeled "misanthropes," haters of humankind, because they refused to join in the worship and sacrificial meals offered to local traditional gods and in their great festivals that quickened local pride or to help polish a city's image as loyal to the emperor by taking part in the imperial cult. Christians may also have been deemed strange because they themselves had no temples or national temple. They met in private homes (or rented assembly halls) at night, greeted each other with a holy kiss, and partook of the body and blood of one who was crucified by Roman authorities in a provincial backwater. Christians also had no particular national identity and consequently had no established political ties with the Romans. Any repudiation of the imperial cult would have made them particularly vulnerable and politically suspect.

The most important religious influence in Corinth at this time was the imperial cult, which worshiped political power as divine. It required an overt display of reverence for the imperial house and the performing of sacrifices and conducting of festivals and feasts. Householders sacrificed on altars outside their homes as the cult procession passed by.

Paul's proclamation that Jesus alone is Lord (8:5-6) directly challenged the imperial cult. "Lord Jesus" was a different kind of "emperor," "savior," and "son of God" than Caesar. The problem for some was that this Lord offered no actual political favors in this worldly realm.

The Corinthian Correspondence and Contacts[586]

The number and nature of contacts Paul had with the Corinthian church is a debated subject. The following is a suggested scheme:

1. Paul founded the church on his first missionary journey (Acts 18:1-17).
2. Paul leaves Corinth for Ephesus in the fall of AD 52 accompanied by Priscilla and Aquila (Acts 18:18-19).
3. Paul later returned to Ephesus on his third missionary journey in the fall of AD

[586] This material is adapted from David Lowry, "1 Corinthians," in *The Bible Knowledge Commentary* (Wheaton: Victor Books, 1983), 506.

53 for a period of about 2 1/2 years (Acts 19). It was probably during this time that Paul wrote the letter mentioned in 1 Corinthians 5:9-13 that was misunderstood by the Corinthians and now lost.

4. Paul learned of this misunderstanding and additional problems in the Corinthian church from the household of Chloe (1 Cor. 1:11). Later, an official delegation brought Paul specific questions which were dividing the church (1 Cor. 16:17).
5. Paul wrote 1 Corinthians around AD 54-55 to address these problems.
6. Paul heard (probably from Timothy—4:17; 16:10) that the problems still were not resolved and that Paul's authority was being questioned (2 Cor. 10:10; 11:23; 12:6-7). Paul then decided to visit the church again which he called "the painful visit" (2 Cor. 1:15; 2:1).
7. After this second visit, he returned to Ephesus and sent a letter carried by Titus called "the severe letter" (2 Cor. 2:3-9; 7:8-12). This letter grieved him deeply because of its severe nature (2 Cor. 7:8-9).
8. Paul later left Ephesus because of the silversmiths' riot and went to Troas to find Titus. When he could not find him, he went on to Macedonia (2 Cor. 2:12-13; 7:5) concerned for Titus' safety. Titus reported that the worst was over, but that there was still a group which was opposed to Paul.
9. Paul wrote 2 Corinthians from Macedonia.
10. Paul made his third visit to the city in the winter of AD 56-57 (Acts 19:21; 20:3; 2 Cor. 13:1).

Purpose

It is evident from the content of the letter that Paul addresses three general problem areas in the church which were reported to him by various messengers. The first was a problem of divisions (1-4) and disorders (5-6). The second revolved around various questions concerning Christian living (7-14). And the third was in the area of the resurrection (15). A purpose statement could be put thusly: Paul addresses divisions, disorders, and difficulties in the Corinthian church in order to preserve unity, purity, and understanding of Christian truth in the local church.

Summary of Argument

I. PAUL RECORDS THE INTRODUCTION TO THE LETTER IN ORDER TO SALUTE HIS READERS AND MENTION THE THANKSGIVING HE HAS FOR THE EFFECTS OF GOD'S GRACE IN THEIR LIVES—1:1-9

A. Paul presents himself as an apostle by the will of God in order to establish his authority—1:1

B. Paul addresses the recipients as being in Christ in order to show that the church belongs to Christ and not any human—1:2-3

C. Paul thanks God for the effects of His grace on their behalf in order to show that God is at work in their midst—1:4-9

1. He thanks God for giving them many spiritual gifts in order to balance out the correction he is going to give later concerning them—1:4-7

2. He thanks God for giving them sustaining strength to the day of Christ—1:8-9

II. PAUL ADDRESSES THE PROBLEM OF DIVISIONS IN THE CORINTHIAN CHURCH IN ORDER TO GIVE THEM A PROPER UNDERSTANDING OF THE APOSTOLIC MESSAGE AND MESSENGER SO THAT THEY WOULD HAVE UNITY AMONG THEMSELVES—1:10-4:21

A. Paul states the reality of divisions in the church in order to show that they were caused by following men which was contrary to Paul's ministry in Corinth—1:10-17

1. He appeals to the church to have unity among themselves which he heard was a problem from the house of Chloe—1:10-11

2. He explains his charge by stating that some were rallying around Apollos, Paul, Cephas, or Christ—1:12

3. He notes the absurdity of such a thing because Christ is not divided—1:13

4. He validates his point by noting that during his ministry among them he did not baptize anyone (with a few possible exceptions) but preached the message of the gospel—1:14-17

B. Paul states that the remedy for divisions in the church was an understanding that the apostolic message was Christ crucified and the messengers of that fact were only God's servants in order to bring them to a point of unity—1:18-4:5

1. Paul observes that the apostolic message as Christ crucified is the true wisdom of God in order to correct their misconception of the truth—1:18-3:4

a. He notes that the message of Christ crucified was in reality the wisdom and power of God in order to contrast it with human wisdom which was causing their division—1:18-2:5

1) Paul states that the message of the crucified Christ was foolishness to the unbeliever but was the power and wisdom of God to the believer—1:18-25

2) Paul states the experience of the message in the Corinthians' lives to show that for them it proved to be the wisdom and power of God—1:26-31

3) Paul states that the message of Christ crucified in his message showed that it was the wisdom and power of God in contrast to human wisdom—2:1-5

b. He expands on the message of Christ crucified in order to show how it reveals the true wisdom of God—2:6-3:4

1) Paul states that the true wisdom of God originates and culminates in God but is hidden from the world which was demonstrated by their crucifixion of Christ—2:6-9

2) Paul states that though the truth is hidden from some it is revealed by the Spirit to those who possess the Spirit—2:10-13

Note #140: 1 Corinthians 2:9-13

There are many points in 2:9-13 which deserve comment. First, 2:9 is not a reference to eternity, but to the understanding of the apostolic message which is revealed to some and concealed from others. This is confirmed by the context and the past tense of 2:10. Second, v. 11 is explaining the reason the Spirit is the agent of revelation. Paul illustrates by asking "who among men (in general) knows the things (inner life and thoughts) of a man (in particular)? This is an aminori ad majus *argument and expects a negative answer. If humans cannot know each other's thoughts, how necessary for the Spirit to reveal the mind of God. Third, is the "we" in v. 12 an apostolic "we" or a general Christian "we?" It is no doubt the former and a reference to special revelation because of the concepts of revelation (v. 10), inspiration (v. 13), and the speaking by the apostles (v. 13). Fourth, the phrase "expressing spiritual truths in spiritual words" (NIV) is also difficult. It is possible, however, to take* pneumatikois *as masculine rather than neuter. With this understanding, the sense would be "expressing spiritual truth to spiritual men." This would fit better with the context, for the point Paul is making is the receiver of revelation.*

3) He shows that the true wisdom of God can be fully grasped only by the spiritually mature—2:14-3:4

a) The natural man cannot grasp the things from the Spirit like the mature man can because those things are spiritually discerned—2:14-16

Note #141: Illumination

Obviously, a natural man can objectively understand the Bible. The point in this section is that the natural man cannot perceive the implications of the truth. He is blind to how the truth applies to him. Thus, he cannot receive the message, but rather rejects it. The spiritual man, on the other hand, is the one who possesses the Spirit and is able to evaluate and appreciate spiritual truth. Thus illumination is not intellectual but affectional. Broughton Knox states the point well: "An intellectual apprehension of what the scriptures are saying is not difficult and does not require an outside interpreter. However, the acceptance of the truth of what is being said, and apprehension of our own relationship to it, is another matter and comes about only when the Spirit of God writes his word on our heart, that is, touches the inmost point of our personality so that we align ourselves with what is being said. This in turns leads to a much deeper apprehension and understanding of what the Bible is about" (Broughton Knox, Broughton Knox: Selected Works, *[Matthias Media, 2003], 2:122). For an exegesis of the entire section see Robert Pyne, "The Role of the Holy Spirit in Conversion,"* Bibliotheca Sacra *150:598 (Apr 1993), 204-218.*

b) The immature baby Christian has a limited capacity for grasping the truth—3:1-2a

c) The immature carnal Christian has willfully prevented his capacity for what the mature can grasp by reason of his divisions—3:2a-4

2. Paul observes that the apostles were only servants of God accountable to Him to show that there should not be divisions over the following of men but rather God should be followed who was the true source of blessing—3:5-4:5

a. Paul states that the messengers of God are His servants with varying duties but that it is God who ultimately is responsible for the increase of fruit—3:5-9
b. Paul states that the messengers of God will answer to Him for how they minister—3:10-17
    1) The one who builds wisely using gold, silver, and precious stones would be rewarded by God—3:10-14
    2) The one who builds unwisely using wood, hay, and stubble will lose reward—3:15
    3) If one destroys the temple (here the local church), he would be judged by God—3:16-17
c. Paul states that the messengers of God should not be self-deluded or be the objects of human boasting—3:18-23
    1) He says that they should not be fooled by the wisdom of the world—3:18-20
    2) He says that they should not be the objects of human boasting 3:21-23
d. Paul states that the messengers of God are to conduct themselves as faithful servants who will be judged by God alone when He comes—4:1-5

C. Paul concludes that the divisions in the Corinthian church were caused by their pride and self-elevation and that they needed to follow his example of self-abasement—4:6-21

1. Paul discusses the pride of the Corinthians in order to show them the root cause for divisions among them—4:6-8
2. Paul presents the abasement of the apostles in order to provide the Corinthians with an example to follow—4:9-13
    a. He states the submission they had toward humiliation before the world—4:9
    b. He states several specific examples in order to illustrate the way in which they had been humiliated—4:10-13
3. Paul admonishes the Corinthians as their spiritual father to imitate his humility so that he would be able to come to them with joy—4:14-21
    a. The basis of his admonishment is the fact that he is their one and only spiritual father—4:14-15
    b. His admonishment is that they imitate his life which will be validated by the report of Timothy—4:16-17
    c. He will see how they are doing when he comes to them—4:18-21

III. PAUL ADDRESSESS THE PROBLEM OF VARIOUS DISORDERS IN THE CHURCH INCLUDING IMMORALITY AND LAWSUITS IN ORDER TO SHOW THE CORINTHIANS THAT THEY NEED TO MAKE WISE MORAL DECISIONS AND MAINTAIN PURITY IN THE CHURCH—5:1-6:20

A. Paul rebukes the church for failing to judge blatant immorality because of pride and urges them to deal with the problem so that the church would be pure—5:1-13

1. **1.** Paul states the fact that there was an incestuous relationship reported in the church—5:1
2. **2.** Paul states that they were indifferent out of arrogance and therefore did nothing when they should have put the man out of the church—5:2
3. **3.** Paul states that his judgment of the matter is that the man be turned over to the sphere of Satan outside the church so that his sinful orientation would be changed—5:3-5
4. **4.** Paul deals with their responsibilities in such matters to remind them of how they should be dealing with these cases—5:6-13
   - **a.** Paul chides them for their boasting and instructs them to expel immorality so that the church would be pure—5:6-8
   - **b.** Paul tells them that instead of disassociating themselves from the people of the world they should remove the immoral from the church—5:9-13

Note #142: The incestuous man

In the preceding section Paul expresses shock over the sexual immorality that was reported in the Corinthian church. The interpretation of this section can be seen through a number of propositions.

1. *The term translated "immorality" or "fornication" is the Greek term πορνεία. It is a broad term describing all types of sexual sin. The fact that the man has involvement with his "father's wife" (though probably not his biological mother) indicates that the word is being used narrowly in this context.*
2. *Even though the Roman Empire was rife with immorality, incest was regarded as a "serious infraction" in the Greco-Roman world (J. F. Gardner,* Women in Roman Law and Society *[Bloomington, IN: Indiana University Press, 1986], 125-127). This is the cause for Paul's statement that this is "not tolerated, even among the pagans." Cicero illustrates the point in his In Defense of Cluentius, "The mother-in-law marries the son-in-law, no one looking favourably on the deed, no one approving it, all foreboding a dismal end to it. Oh, the incredible wickedness of the woman, and, with the exception of this one single instance, unheard of since the world began" (14, 15; http://www.perseus.-tufts.edu/hopper/text?doc=Perseus, accessed 6/26/14).*
3. *Paul indicates in 5:2 that there is pride in the church over this matter. This is subject to two possible understandings. Either they were boasting because of this sin or in spite of this sin. The latter is the better understanding; that is, they were ignoring it. Garland explains the logic in this culture. "The reasons for ignoring this sin are more likely to be sociological than theological....Greco-Roman religiosity normally did not affect moral behavior, and new converts would not have been accustomed to think through the religious implications of their conduct. It is more likely, then, that the church ignored this man's sin because of his higher social status and wealth than because of some theological stance" (David Garland, 1 Corinthians, 162).*
4. *Paul instructs the church to immediately remove the individual from the congregation. The Apostle indicates in verse 3 that he has made the pronouncement regarding the matter and that pronouncement still stands (Paul uses the perfect tense of κρίνω when indicating he had reached a judgment on*

the matter)

5. *The expulsion from the church somehow involves Satan. Evidently, God would allow Satan to be an agent of divine discipline.*
6. *The "destruction of the flesh" could have a referent to the man's physical body meaning that the judgment would be some type of illness or even death. A better explanation is to take "flesh" as referring to the man's sinful orientation. The goal of the discipline, therefore, is that the shock of this pronouncement and vulnerability before Satan would lead the man to repentance.*
7. *In the meantime, the church is not to associate with him. Paul is not calling on the church to have nothing to do with the man, but that the individual is to have no affiliation with the church.*

B. Paul rebukes the church for taking fellow believers to pagan law courts in order to remind them that they were competent to handle such disputes and to avoid division—6:1-11

1. Paul states that the problem was that they were taking their cases before unbelievers when they should have taken them before the believers in the church—6:1

Note #143: Christian lawsuits

When Paul prohibits Christians from taking one another to court, this is a reference to civil matters not criminal matters. Moreover, in this culture, the goal of bringing a person to court was to assassinate their character and take advantage of them through the corruption of the court system. This was to have no place in the church.

2. Paul states several reasons why they should not be doing this in order to show how illogical it was—6:2-11

a. He states that in the eschaton they would be judging the world and angels and therefore were competent to handle petty disputes—6:2-6

b. He states that they should rather suffer wrong than greedily try to profit from fellow believers—6:7-8

c. He states that their action with lawsuits was inconsistent with their position in Christ for they were acting just like the pagan—6:9-11

C. Paul rebukes the church for their immorality with prostitutes in order to show them that fornication is incompatible with the relationship they have with God—6:12-20

1. Paul states the Corinthian slogan "everything is permissible for me" in order to show that it should not be used as a cloak for immorality by showing that the phrase should be qualified by saying that any action needed to be beneficial to others and not cause mastery over a person—6:12

2. Paul states the Corinthian slogan "food for the stomach and the stomach for food" in order to show that there is not a parallel between eating when hungry and committing immorality when desired—6:13-14

3. Paul states three arguments against immorality introduced by the phrase "do you not know"—6:15-20

a. He notes that the Christian is a member of Christ's body and should therefore not be joined to a prostitute—6:15

b. He notes that one who is joined to a prostitute forms a new union which should be avoided—6:16-18

c. He notes that the body is the sacred dwelling place of the Holy Spirit which was bought with a price—6:19-20

IV. PAUL ADDRESSES VARIOUS DIFFICULTIES RAISED IN THE CORINTHIAN CHURCH IN ORDER TO GIVE THE CORINTHIANS INSTRUCTION AND UNDERSTANDING IN CHRISTIAN TRUTH—7:1-16:12

A. Paul discusses difficulties concerning marriage in order to give instruction on sexuality so that the immorality just described would be counteracted—7:1-40

Note #144: Marriage and divorce

The biblical teaching on marriage and divorce is a complicated one with 1 Corinthians 7 being one of the key passages in the discussion. See Chapter VIII, Sections 12 and 13 for a full discussion.

1. Paul gives instruction to married couples and those who were formerly married—7:1-24

a. Paul instructs married believers who thought that it was best to abstain from sex—7:1-7

1) Paul quotes a Corinthian slogan which felt that those who were married should abstain from sex—7:1

Note #145: Not to touch a woman

In the slogan "it is good for a man not to touch a woman," "to touch a woman" is a euphemism for sexual intercourse. This could be a reaction of the Corinthians from Paul's teaching in chapter 6, or a reflection of the branch of Greek thought that treated the body in an ascetic fashion. Only in extreme, temporary situations, should married couples withhold sex from their partner.

2) Paul emphasizes that the husband and wife have a sexual obligation to each other which would serve as a guard against immorality—7:2-7

b. Paul instructs the unmarried and widowed that they may marry again if they cannot control their sexual passion—7:8-9

c. Paul instructs believing partners that they are not to seek a divorce, but if one should occur, they should remain single or be reconciled to their mate—7:10-11

d. Paul instructs believers who are married to unbelieving partners that they should live harmoniously in marriage and separation with the goal of bringing the unbeliever to faith—7:12-16

e. Paul states the principle that believers should remain in the same situation they were in when saved because as slaves of Christ they should render Him obedience—7:17-24

2. Paul gives instructions to the unmarried (engaged couples) counseling that they remain unmarried but this is not mandatory— 7:25-38

a. Paul counsels that they remain unmarried because of the distressing times—7:25-28

b. Paul counsels that they remain unmarried so that they can have undistracted devotion to the Lord—7:29-35

c. Paul counsels the bridegroom (or possibly father of the bride) that it is alright to marry but not mandatory—7:36-38

3. Paul gives instruction to the widows that they are free to remarry if they wish but this is not preferred—7:39-40

B. Paul discusses issues involving Christian liberty in order to combat the pride and self-centeredness of the Corinthians—8:1-11:1

Note #146: Meat offered to idols

Beginning in chapter 8 Paul discusses the problem of how to deal with meat offered to idols. The test cases will involve eating meat in an idol temple, eating meat of an unknown origin, and eating meat in the home of an unbeliever. These scenarios have often been interpreted as a clash between the strong (able to eat meat) and the weak (not able to eat meat) about which they were asking Paul to reach a decision on. Paul's conclusion is that the strong are technically correct, but out of deference for the weak they should abstain lest they cause offense. However, Garland makes a strong case that this reconstruction is incorrect (David Garland, 1 Corinthians, *347-362). Instead of the meat issue being a disagreement between the weak and strong in the church; it is a disagreement between the church and Paul. The church was not asking Paul "can we eat idol food," but "why can't we eat idol food?" This would be particularly important in Corinthian culture since it would affect one's sociopolitical standing. Paul stoutly forbids the eating of any food in a pagan temple or any food which was known to be used for that purpose.*

1. Paul addresses the issue of a Christian eating meat offered to an idol to show that this is something that is always inappropriate for the believer—8:1-13

2. Paul illustrates the principle he has just enunciated regarding the use of privileges by giving a positive and negative example with their varying results in order to persuade the Corinthians to follow the positive example—9:1-10:13

a. Paul uses himself as a positive illustration in the matter of rights in the area where he was being criticized, namely his apostleship—9:1-27

1) Paul notes that his position as an apostle gave him the right to receive financial support—9:1-14

a) Paul asserts his apostleship based on his vision of the resurrected Lord—9:1-2

b) Paul notes the rights (freedom—*exousia* as in 8:9 thus linking the two chapters) he and others have—9:3-6

c) Paul uses six illustrations to show his right of support—9:7-14

(1) The soldier, farmer, and shepherd are all supported by their work—9:7

(2) The Old Testament spoke of remuneration with the

proverbial expression about not muzzling an ox—9:8-10

(3) If one brought spiritual riches to someone, it is not too much to expect to be reciprocated with material remuneration—9:11

(4) The church supported other ministers—9:12

(5) The priesthood was recompensed for their service—9:13

(6) Jesus taught that those who preach the Gospel should live of the Gospel—9:14

2) Paul notes that he had given up these rights he had in order to gain more converts and receive reward from God—9:15-27

a) He says that he gave up these rights because he had an inner compulsion to preach that was more important than his rights—9:15-18

b) He says that he gave up these rights so that he would win more converts—9:19-23

c) He says that he gave up these rights in the same way an athlete disciplines himself to win the prize and so that he would not be disqualified—9:24-27

Note #147: Athletic imagery

Paul's reference to the athletic games was an allusion to the Isthmian games which were held in Corinth every two years. They were founded in 581 BC. Next to the Olympic Games, these were the most splendid of all and one of the best attended national festivals of Greece (see firsthand descriptions by Pausanias, Guidebook to Greece. *Loeb, 1.7; 2.2 and Dio Chrysostom of Prusa, Loeb,* Concerning Virtue, *6, 9, 14, 15). Furthermore, Paul was in Corinth when the games of AD 49 and 51were held. The toil and discipline which the athletes endured brought them to the point of death (Philo,* Every Good Man is Free *110.113; Epictetus, Discourses 3.22.52). Paul refers to this in 1 Corinthians 9:25 as "agony." Paul says in this passage that he did this for an incorruptible crown (9:25). Evidently, Paul was referring to the celery/pine crown which was given to the winner at the Isthmian games. This crown elevated the winner to a divine status when he was crowned in the Temple of Zeus at the end of the games. While this crown withered, Paul was giving up his rights for a crown that would never fade away. It is also important to note that Paul brought up the possibility of being disqualified. In 9:25 Paul refers to the training required by those in the games. If these training rules were broken, athletes were disqualified from the celery crown. Thus Paul is not speaking of losing salvation here, but of being disqualified from reward.*

b. Paul uses Israel as a negative example of misusing privileges to warn the Corinthians of being disapproved by God and show how they were guilty of the same things—10:1-13

1) Paul enumerates the privileges of Israel in order to establish what they had—10:1-4

a) They were guided and protected by the cloud—10:1a

b) They experienced deliverance by the Red Sea—10:1b

c) They were united and identified with their spiritual head Moses—10:2

d) They enjoyed the manna from heaven—10:3

e) They were given water in the wilderness whose supernatural source in reality was Christ—10:4

2) Paul enumerates the sins of Israel and the consequent judgment that God brought on them—10:5-10

a) God scattered them across the desert for their misuse of these privileges—10:5

b) They lusted after the pleasures of Egypt—10:6

c) They were idolaters—10:7

d) They committed sexual immorality—10:8

e) They questioned God's purpose in bringing them to Canaan—10:9

f) They rebelled against Moses and Aaron—10:10

3) Paul applies this example to the Corinthians by warning them to not succumb to temptation in light of the privileges they had—10:11-13

a) He notes that what happened to Israel was intended as a warning for the Corinthians—10:11

b) He warns them that if they think they could live in sin without penalty they were wrong—10:12

c) He tells them that the temptations they were experiencing could be overcome by endurance rather than giving in to temptation as they were doing—10:13

c. Paul concludes the section by applying the principles regarding eating food sacrificed to idols—10:14-11:1

1) He states that eating idol meat in a pagan temple is inconsistent with Christian liberty and should be avoided—10:14-22

2) He states that purchasing idol meat and eating it at home is consistent with Christian principles—10:23-26

3) He states that eating idol meat when one is a guest in another person's home is against Christian principles—10:27-30

4) Paul summarizes the teaching by noting that all should be done to the glory of God and for the good of others—10:31-11:1

C. Paul discusses difficulties in the area of Christian worship to show the Corinthians that in this area of church life they needed to not be self-indulgent but rather glorify God and build up fellow believers—11:2-14:40

1. Paul commends them for their general obedience to the things he had taught them—11:2

2. Paul rebukes the church for the lack of subordination of the women to the men in the church—11:3-16

a. Paul notes that the covering of the woman's head was designed to show the headship of the man and for women to disregard it was a disgrace—11:3-6

Note #148: Man as the head of the woman

There is more than ample evidence that the idea of "head" is authority rather than source or origin. This meaning does more justice to the parallels between man/woman and Christ/God, as well as to the lexical evidence. For more support of this see James Hurley, Man and Woman in Biblical Perspective, *163-168. For a critique of the methodology used by those who argue for "source" or "origin" see D. A. Carson, Exegetical Fallacies, 36-38.*

- **b.** Paul notes five reasons why this insubordination should not exist in the church—11:7-16
  - **1)** It should not exist because of creation—11:7-9

Note #149: The order of creation

One of the bases Paul uses for the subordination of the woman to the man is the order of creation. This order of creation implies man's headship in at least two ways: 1) it is supported by the Old Testament law of primogeniture in which the firstborn male was invested with the highest honor and authority (Exod. 4:22; Jer. 31:9; Ps. 89:27; see the article by Beitzel, "The Right of the Firstborn in the Old Testament," in A Tribute to Gleason Archer*), and 2) Paul uses this argument to speak of Christ's headship in Colossians 1.*

- **a)** The man should not cover his head because he was created in the image and glory of God—11:7a
- **b)** The woman should cover her head because she is the glory of the man—11:7b-9

Note #150: Head coverings

In v. 7 Paul had said that the man is created in the image and glory of God. However, Paul says that the woman is the glory of the man. Does this imply that she is not in the image of God? Obviously, this is not what Paul means for they are both in the image of God. Paul is making a partial statement not an exhaustive statement. He is commenting on the woman's relationship to the man not the woman's relationship to God. So Paul is referring to authority relations not ontological relations. The woman is the glory of the man in the sense that she is his ally in exercising dominion over the earth. However, if she abdicates her God-given role in the hierarchical structure ordained by God (in this case by uncovering her head in the church), she is rebelling against this complimentary role. In addition, she would be considered immoral in this culture. Gill explains that "This [head covering] became an emblem for modesty and chastity. Presumably women who felt able to uncover their heads were considered immodest, unchaste, and therefore by definition un-Roman" (David Gill, "1 Corinthians," in Zondervan Illustrated Bible Backgrounds Commentary *[Grand Rapids: Zondervan, 2002], 157). See also James Hurley,* Man and Woman in Biblical Perspective *(Grand Rapids: Zondervan, 1981), 269-272; Bruce Waltke, "1 Corinthians 11:2-16: An Interpretation,"* Bibliotheca Sacra *135:537 (Jan 1978), 49.*

Regarding the matter of head coverings as a whole, there are two major issues to be addressed. The first is whether Paul has in mind a real head covering, or is he viewing the hair as the covering. It is my view that a real head covering fits better with the passage. Two comments are in order; first, the veil in the passage shows the woman's submission while her hair shows her glory; and second, Paul is making an analogy when he refers to hair and a material head covering. God has given the woman a covering (hair) by nature, and she should follow that example by wearing a veil in the assembly. The second is how this passage applies today. The range of positions are 1) there is no applicability today since Paul was just talking about a first century custom, 2) real head coverings should be worn by women today, or 3) a suitable, cultural parallel should be found in the present which would express the theological truth of the passage. The third option is the best, for Paul was telling the Corinthian women to abide by a social convention which upheld male/female roles; whereas in contemporary Western culture head coverings would be abnormal, not normal.

Regarding the enigmatic phrase "because of the angels" (11:10), Wilson lists the five major views: 1) a head covering would lessen the temptation of the church minister to lust, 2) a head covering would lessen the temptation of evil angels to lust, 3) a head covering would lessen the temptation of good angels to lust, 4) angels would be offended by a change in God's in that they are the guardians of the created order, and 5) the angels would be offended if the structured hierarchy were changed (Kenneth Wilson, "Should Women Wear Headcoverings?" Bibliotheca Sacra *148:592 [Oct 1991], 454).*

(1) She is the glory of the man because the man did not come from the woman but the woman came from the man—11:7b-8

(2) She is the glory of the man because the man was not created for the woman but the woman for the man—11:9

2) It should not exist because of the angels—11:10

3) It should not exist because the man and the woman are interdependent—11:11-12

a) They are interdependent because the man is not without the woman and the woman is not without the man—11:11-12b

(1) The reason the woman is dependent on the man is because she is of the man—11:12a

(2) The reason the man is dependent on the woman is because he is borne by the woman—11:12b

b) They are interdependent because both are from God—11:12

4) It should not exist because of natural revelation—11:13-15

a) A woman should not pray unveiled because it is improper—11:13

b) A woman should not pray unveiled because natural revelation teaches that long hair is a glory to a woman—11:14-15a

c) A woman's hair is a glory to her because it was given to her for a covering—11:15b

5) It should not exist because of church practice—11:16

3. Paul rebukes the church for their divisive and gluttonous behavior at the Lord's supper—11:17-34

Note #151: What was the problem at the Lord's Supper?

In 11:27 Paul tells the church that they are partaking of the Supper in an "unworthy manner" (ἀναξίως). It is important to observe that this word is an adverb, not an adjective. Therefore the problem was not that they were unworthy (unconfessed sin) when

they ate and needed to confess secret sins before they partook, but they were eating, or celebrating this event in an unworthy way. As stated in the introduction to 1 Corinthians, there was competition for status in the culture which had spilled over into the church. This had led to a segregation of the poor from the rich when the Lord's Supper was being taken. The poor were literally huddled in the kitchen eating a meal of basic fare, while the rich reclined in the dining room enjoying a sumptuous meal. Hence Paul condemns them for their divisions and bids them remember how the Lord broke bread for all the disciples indiscriminately.

- **a.** Paul states that the divisiveness and gluttony the Corinthians display at the Lord's supper results in the ordinance losing all of its significance—11:17-22
- **b.** Paul reminds the Corinthians that the purpose of the Lord's supper was to remember and honor Christ's death who gave himself equally for all—11:23-26
- **c.** Paul warns the Corinthians that if they partake of this ordinance in an unworthy manner (recognizing social distinctions), they are in danger of divine judgment which can be avoided if they first judge themselves—11:27-32
- **d.** Paul concludes this section by telling them to exercise discipline at the meal and that he would give further instructions when he came—11:33-34

4. Paul discusses the problem concerning spiritual gifts in the local church in order to show the Corinthians that their gifts needed to be regulated and controlled for the purpose of edifying others rather than using them for self-gratification—12:1-14:40

- **a.** Paul notes that spiritual gifts are given by the Holy Spirit to show the Corinthians that there is no room for pride in their possession of gifts—12:1-11
  - **1)** Spiritual gifts are tested as to their origin by whether or not they exalt the person of Christ—12:1-3
  - **2)** Spiritual gifts are diverse but they all have their source in the same Spirit—12:4-11
- **b.** Paul notes that spiritual gifts are diverse but they are all part of the same body to show the Corinthians that each gift should contribute to the unity of the body rather than to its division—12:12-31a
  - **1)** The unity of the believers into one body came as the result of the baptism by the Spirit into the body of Christ—12:12-13
  - **2)** Paul uses the illustration of the human body to show that each part is important and dependent on the other parts—12:14-26
  - **3)** Paul shows that not every person possesses each gift in order to show that what is true of the human body is true of the church body—12:27-31a

5. Paul discusses the subject of love to show the Corinthians that love is of greater value than any spiritual gift and should be the realm in which the gifts operate—12:32b-13:13

Note #152: The "perfect"

The primary issue in this section is to determine what is referred to by the word to teleion (perfect). There are three major views. The first is the maturity of the church view. This states that the "perfect" is the time when the church passes from immaturity to maturity. Consequently at this time, tongues would cease. The second is the canon view. This view states that the completion of the canon is the perfect thing, and at that time, miraculous gifts came to an end. The third is the present with the Lord view. This holds that the knowledge gleaned from the content of prophecies at the time Paul wrote will one day be replaced and completed by full knowledge when the individual is present with the Lord. This view is sometimes criticized because it is said to imply that the sign gifts are still operative today. This is invalid, however, because the purpose of the chapter is not to show when tongues cease but the superiority of love. Thus, Paul's purpose was not to prove the date of the cessation of the gifts, but rather the fact of their cessation. After a thorough historical examination of these views, a helpful conclusion can be drawn on the data.

The vast majority of biblical commentators throughout the history of the church have understood the expression τὸ τέλειον to be related in some way to the eschaton. Both the canon view and the mature body view are relatively recent interpretations that have developed out of the controversy over contemporary manifestations of the miraculous gifts. Both can be traced only to the mid or early twentieth century, though there were apparently some antecedents to both in the nineteenth century. The recency of a view does not necessarily disprove its hermeneutical legitimacy, but it should serve as a caution to the interpreter to be sure that there is an adequate and valid exegetical basis for it. Too often views have been adopted because they provide the "right answer" to controversial issues. It may well be that controversy stimulates a greater attention to a passage than had previously been given. The result may be greater theological precision. That was certainly true of the Christological controversies of the early centuries—though no new interpretations of problem passages resulted from the deliberations of the councils. Although the purpose of this paper has not included an exegetical evaluation of 1 Corinthians 13:10 in its context, it may be helpful to make some general observations on each of the three views based only on the arguments summarized above. In that regard, it would appear that the canon view is the weakest of the three. Not only does it labor under the cloud of recency, but it also requires one of two strategies to make sense of the passage. Either the time referred to in verse ten must be differentiated from verse twelve, or it is necessary to provide creative reinterpretations of verse twelve to harmonize it with a past (or perhaps gnomic) event. Both of these alternatives appear to be strained exegesis. None of the commentators surveyed above who have defended the canon view have provided an exegetical basis for either of these options. That does not mean that it could not be done, but until it has been provided the canon view should be regarded as a hypothesis rather than as an established position. The mature body view, in any of its forms, ought probably to be rated as the next most viable option—between the canon view and the eschatological view. Although it is perhaps of even more recent provenance than the canon view, it has offered an exegetical basis that is significantly broader. The crux of the position, however, hinges on the validity of the close association of 1 Corinthians 13 and Ephesians 4. Numerous parallels have been cited, but it does not appear to be clear that these go beyond verbal similarities. The contexts of 1 Corinthians 13 and Ephesians 4 seem to be much different, requiring major assumptions to reconcile. Although the background of the two epistles does have a common setting in Paul's ministry, and thus provides a possible conceptual link, that potential does not seem to be fulfilled in the actual statements of 1 Corinthians 13. It might also be asked why the passage should be understood in a corporate sense (maturity of the church) rather than individually (we know, I became a man, I will know..., etc.). The popularity of both these views has probably been a desire to establish a straightforward, single-passage proof text for the cessation of tongues in response to the abuses and extremes of the contemporary charismatic movement. Unless a more adequate exegetical basis for these views is forthcoming, however, it would appear that advocates have been inclined to be selective in their use of the text—the very thing for which the charismatics are often faulted. Those views which associate τὸ τέλειον with an eschatological event or condition not only have historical preponderance, but have far fewer exegetical problems and require fewer theological twists to harmonize the context (Rodney Decker, A History of Interpretation of "That Which Is Perfect" *(1 Cor 13:10) With Special Attention to the Origin of the "Canon View." [paper presented at the Council of Dispensational Hermeneutics, Clarks Summit, PA: September 2013]).*

6. Paul shows the Corinthians that prophecy is to be preferred over tongues because it edifies the church and then gives rules for the regulation of gifts so that there would be order in the church—14:1-40

Note #153: The identity of tongues

The word glossa *refers to known languages in the New Testament. Thus the tongues referred to here are known languages. The idea that ecstatic utterance from Hellenistic religion had been imported into the Corinthians church, though popular, is lacking convincing evidence (for an erudite discussion see Christopher Forbes,* Prophecy and Inspired Speech in Early Christianity and its Hellenistic Environment *[Peabody, MA: Hendrickson, 1997]). The scholarly support for the erroneous view of ecstatic speech for γλῶσσα comes from the esteemed* Greek-English Lexicon of the New Testament and Other Early Christian Literature *(Bauer, Arndt, Gingrich, and Danker, Chicago: University of Chicago Press, 1979), 162 and the article by Johannes Behm on γλῶσσα in* Theological Dictionary of the New Testament *(Grand Rapids: Eerdmans, 1964-74), I:719-726. However, both articles acknowledge that "language" is the normal meaning of γλῶσσα and, in my opinion, have offered no substantial evidence to the contrary. For a full discussion of these two articles see Thomas Edgar,* Miraculous Gifts: Are they for today? *(Neptune, NJ: Loizeaux Brother, 1983), 110-170. Though lexicons are immensely helpful and authoritative, Burton's caution should always be kept in mind when using lexicons: "No earnest student can consent always and on all points to accept on authority even of the ablest lexicographers the opinions which he has to hold on matters as vital as those with which New Testament lexicography has to deal" (Ernest Burton, "The Study of New Testament Words,"* The Old and New Testament Student *[March 1891], 12:136).*

1) He states that prophecy is superior to tongues because it edifies the church while uninterpreted tongues do not because they are unintelligible—14:1-19

a) He notes that prophecy is to be preferred because it edifies the church and tongues do not—14:1-5

b) He notes that tongues do not edify because they are unintelligible to the listener when not interpreted—14:6-19

2) He states that prophecy is superior to tongues because it convicts unbelievers of their need of salvation whereas uninterpreted tongues only bring mockery—14:20-25

Note #154: Purpose of tongues

It is important to comment on the purpose of tongues noted by Paul. In this connection, he quotes Isaiah 28:11-12. Because Israel refused to listen to God's message, Isaiah prophesied that another message (of judgment) would be delivered in a foreign tongue. This would be a reference to the Assyrian invaders who would be used by God to judge Israel. Thus tongues were a sign of judgment on unbelieving Jews. This is worked out in Acts where tongues are seen to be a sign to the Jews to overcome unbelief of God's program. The judgment aspect could be seen in that the change in program was necessitated by the rejection of the Jews of the Messiah. Judgment is coming again on Israel through Gentile foreigners, this time from the Romans in AD 70. Two other views as to the purpose of tongues include evangelistic and devotional. However, both of these views have difficulties. Regarding the evangelistic view 1) two international trade languages (Greek and Aramaic) were used in the areas delineated in Acts 2:9-11 so other languages/dialects would not be necessary, 2) tongues occurs two other times in Acts (10 & 19) and in both instances they occur after salvation has occurred, 3) this view goes against the clearly stated purpose in 1 Corinthians 14:22, 4) the conversions at Pentecost were not due to tongues-speaking but to Peter's sermon which was delivered in his known language, and 5) if this was an efficient way to bring people to faith, then why hasn't the gift continued? And why has it never been operative in the great revivals and awakenings in church history, not to mention the Reformation? The "devotional" view faces even more insurmountable problems 1) Paul's instructions for tongues in 1 Corinthians presume they will be used in the assembly, 2) a devotional use of tongues is contrary to the nature of spiritual gifts which are never for private edification, 3) devotional tongues are never found in Acts, 4) this view goes against the biblical stated purpose for tongues, 5) even if tongues continued today, Paul indicates in 1 Corinthians 12:30 that not everybody would speak with tongues. Therefore, only some believers would have the opportunity to commune with God on a deeper level, and 6) if a private "prayer language" helped the believer grow closer to God, then a steady stream of the most prominent figures of church history missed out on this.

3) He states that the exercise of gifts in the local church should be used in an orderly way so that edification would be the result—14:26-36
   a) He states that the general rule should be that all should be done for edification—14:26
   b) He states that concerning tongues they should be exercised by two or three men in turn followed by interpretation—14:27-28
   c) He states concerning prophecy it should be exercised by two or three men with an evaluation following but that women should keep silent in this matter—14:29-36

Note #155: Prayer and prophecy by women in the church

There seems to be a contradiction between 11:5 where Paul permits women to pray and prophesy and 14:33-35 where he tells them not to speak. Besides the suggestions that the text is inauthentic and Paul contradicts himself, there remain two options. The first says that Paul did not give women permission to speak in 11 but let that go by because it was not his purpose to address it. In 14, he addressed it because that was his concern. It is questionable whether Paul would let an objectionable practice go by for sake of argument. Further, chapter 11 would have been the perfect time to address the problem since he was dealing with insubordination. The second suggests that Paul is addressing different situations. Under this view, some have suggested that chapter 11 has informal meetings in view while chapter 14 has formal meetings in view. This is, however, impossible to demonstrate. Others have said that the situation in 14 was loud women who were yelling things from their "women's section" and disrupting this service. This is impossible to prove also since Paul nowhere deals with the subject of unruly women in the church meeting. A better solution is to interpret the prohibition contextually and say that women were permitted to pray and prophesy (ch. 11), but that they were not to judge the prophets (ch. 14). It is seen from the structure in the above outline, that 14:33b-35 occurs in the section dealing with the judging of the prophets. Thus, the issue is once again that of subordination. In Paul's mind, this act was one involving ecclesiastical authority and this was inconsistent with their role in the church. This view also fits with Paul's reference to the Old Testament in 14:34. The Law nowhere states that women are to remain silent at all times (Exod. 15:20-21; 2 Sam. 6:15; Ps. 148:12). But it is not difficult to imagine that it would be against the general tenor of Old Testament teaching of the hierarchy between man and woman.

4) He summarizes his teaching on gifts by noting that gifts should be preferred for their value to the church—14:37-40

Note #156: Spiritual gifts

The traditional view that a "spiritual gift is a special ability given to the believer at salvation to serve the body of Christ" is not without its difficulties. A more satisfying approach to the whole area has been explained by Kenneth Berding, What Are Spiritual Gifts: Rethinking the Conventional View *(Grand Rapids: Kregel, 2006). The salient points from his work are outlined below:*

- *Spiritual gifts are not special abilities but ministries or areas of service.*
- *The issue is not me discovering the special ability God has given me, but looking at my situation and determining where I can best serve the Body of Christ. This ministry could occur in a minute, an hour, or a lifetime.*
- *The Greek word* charisma *does not mean special ability.*
- *Apart from one occurrence in 1 Peter,* charisma *is used only by Paul in the New Testament. Of the sixteen Pauline uses, six cannot mean special ability; four probably don't; and, in six the meaning can only be determined after studying 1 Corinthians.*

The practical implications of this understanding are as follows:

- *The tension of natural talent vs. spiritual gift is eliminated.*
- *The tension of trying to find your spiritual gift is eliminated.*
- *The tension of whether I have one gift or several is eliminated.*
- *We can serve in a wide variety of ministries which strengthen the body of Christ rather than feeling locked into our "special ability."*
- *This removes guilt. What if I don't want to teach in the local church and serve in some other capacity? I am free to do so with this approach.*
- *Ministries can be short-term or long term depending on how God directs our lives.*

D. Paul discusses difficulties concerning bodily resurrection in which he shows its certainty and necessity so that the Corinthians would be clear on this issue—15:1-58

  1. Paul shows that the bodily resurrection of the Christian is linked to the resurrection of Christ historically, logically, theologically, and experientially in order to show them why they should believe in the resurrection—15:1-34

    a. He shows that historically the bodily resurrection of Christ is essential to the Gospel message which the Corinthians had believed—15:1-11

      1) The Gospel Paul preached was embraced by the Corinthians—15:1-2

      2) The primary content of the Gospel was the death and resurrection which was verified by eyewitnesses—15:3-10

      3) This resurrection gospel was preached by all the apostles and was embraced by the Corinthians—15:11

    b. He shows that logically the doctrine of bodily resurrection cannot be denied without rendering the Gospel as worthless—15:12-19

      1) It was illogical for some Corinthians to separate the bodily resurrection of the dead from the resurrection of Christ—15:12

      2) If the bodily resurrection is denied this involves denial of Christ's resurrection which then makes Christianity groundless—15:13-19

    c. He shows that theologically the bodily resurrection of Christ guarantees the bodily resurrection of the believer as well as Christ's final triumph over all things—15:20-28

      1) This is true because believers are identified with Christ in His resurrection—15:20-22

      2) This is true because there is a order of resurrection followed by the subduing of all things by Christ—15:23-28

    d. He shows that experientially this belief in a bodily resurrection should affect the conduct of believers—15:29-34

      1) The practice of baptism for the dead implies a confidence in the resurrection—15:29

Note #157: Baptism for the dead

Estimates for the number of interpretations of this phrase have ranged from 40-200. Most notable is the interpretation by the Mormon Church that baptism is essential for salvation. Proxy baptism can be accepted by the deceased while residing in the spirit world. See Doctrine and Covenants, *Section 124:29, 32, 33, 35, 39; Section 128; Section 138: 30, 33 (https://www.lds.org/scriptures/dc-testamentdc?lang=eng, accessed 5/15/2014). In light of the variety of interpretations, Fee's comments are apropos: "One may consider it as axiomatic that when there is such a wide divergence of opinion, no one knows what in fact was going on. The best one can do in terms of particulars is point out what appear to be the more viable options, but finally admit to ignorance. What is certain is how the text functions in the argument. Whatever it was that some of them were doing, those actions are a contradiction to the position that there is no resurrection of the dead" (Fee,* 1 Corinthians, *New International Commentary on the New Testament, 763). Reaume concludes that of the some 200 interpretations of the phrase, three remain as viable options: 1) the preposition "for" (ὑπέρ) has the sense of new believers being baptized to take the place of dead Christians, 2) take "for" with the sense of "in order to be reunited with their loved ones at the resurrection," or 3) take "for" as "because of. This would yield the understanding that a new believer's baptism is due to the influence of a deceased Christian (John Reaume, "Another Look at 1 Corinthians 15:29, 'Baptized for the Dead,'"* Bibliotheca Sacra *152:608 [Oct 1995], 475).*

2) The endurance of suffering is motivated by a belief in a future bodily resurrection—15:30-32

3) The exhortation to righteous living is based on a confidence in a future bodily resurrection—15:33-34

2. Paul answers certain objections that are raised in response to the doctrine of the resurrection—15:35-58

a. Paul discusses the resurrection from the dead in order to show how the resurrection is achieved and the nature of the resurrection body—15:35-49

1) He notes that the resurrection of the body does not occur until after death—15:35-36

2) He notes that the resurrection body is similar and yet diverse from the earthly body—15:37-49

a) He states the principle of similarity and diversity in his illustration from creation—15:37-41

b) He applies this principle to the resurrection body—15:42-49

(1) The resurrection body is incorruptible not corruptible—15:42

(2) The resurrection body is glorious not dishonorable—15:43a

(3) The resurrection body is powerful not weak—15:43b

(4) The resurrection body is given to spiritual use and not natural use—15:44

(5) The resurrection body is heavenly not earthly—15:45-49

b. Paul discusses the resurrection body of those saints who are alive at the rapture to show that they would have glorified bodies as well as those who died previously—15:50-57

1) There must be a radical transformation in the body because flesh and blood cannot inherit the Kingdom—15:50

2) Those believers who are alive at the rapture would instantaneosly be transformed into a resurrection body—15:51-53

3) This body would provide men with their ultimate victory over their

greatest enemy of death since those who have received their resurrection bodies will never be subject to death—15:54-57

c. Paul states that these resurrection facts should lead the believer into a life of steadfastness and abundant service—15:58

E. Paul discusses the offering for the poor saints in Jerusalem in order to show how the collection should be made and to provide a practical demonstration of their faith in the resurrection-16:1-4

1. Paul says that the collection should be made according to the rules he had left with them—16:1-2

2. Paul says that the offering should be handled by faithful men who would deliver it to Jerusalem—16:3-4

F. Paul discusses his travel plans in the future to visit Corinth—16:5-12

1. He says that after some ministry in Ephesus and Macedonia he hoped to visit Corinth—16:5-9

2. He says that Timothy might come to Corinth for Paul and he is to be treated with cooperation—16:10-11

3. He says that Apollos did not desire to return—16:12

V. PAUL STATES THE CONCLUSION TO THE LETTER BY EXHORTING THEM TO APPROPRIATE CONDUCT AND GIVING FINAL GREETINGS—16:13-24

A. He exhorts them to change their conduct so as to correct their deficiencies—16:13-18

B. He salutes various saints, pronounces a curse on those who do not love the Lord, and closes with a benediction and love for all—16:19-24

2 CORINTHIANS

Introduction

Paul left Ephesus in the spring of AD 56 and went to Troas where he hoped to meet with Titus. When he could not find Titus there, he went on to Macedonia where he finally found him. Titus reported that in general the Corinthian church was doing well (2 Cor. 7:6-16). This improvement in their situation came as the result of "the lost letter," 1 Corinthians, and "the severe letter." However, Titus also related to Paul that there was a faction in the church that was opposed to Paul and was undermining his apostolic authority (2 Cor. 10:1-13:10). In response to this attack on Paul's apostleship and message, Paul wrote 2 Corinthians from Macedonia around the fall or winter of AD 56. The other occasion for the writing of this epistle concerned the collection the Corinthians were taking for their poorer brethren in Jerusalem (for more background on the Corinthian epistles see the introduction to 1 Corinthians).

Accordingly, the structure of the letter centers around three major sections. The first (1-7) discusses Paul's ministry and his relationship to the Corinthians. This, no doubt, was in response to his adversaries' charge that his interest in the Corinthians was suspect and fickle. The second section (8-9) deals with the collection for the saints in Jerusalem. This was probably necessary because Paul's enemies could have been suggesting that Paul was not to be trusted with the money, and therefore the giving could have been slacking off. The third section (10-13) includes a defense of Paul's apostleship and an attack on those who opposed him. Thus, a purpose statement for 2 Corinthians could be as follows: <u>Paul gives an exposition of his ministry, instruction concerning the collection, and a defense of his apostleship in order to answer accusations brought against him by his adversaries to show the superiority of his ministry over theirs, and spur the Corinthians to obedience and renewed commitment to the Lord and himself</u>.

Summary of Argument

I. PAUL INTRODUCES HIS LETTER WITH THE CUSTOMARY SALUTATION IN ORDER TO ASSERT HIS APOSTLESHIP AND THANKSGIVING FOR GOD'S COMFORT IN AFFLICTION IN ORDER TO SHOW THE EXPERIENCE OF GOD'S GRACE EVEN IN DIFFICULT CIRCUMSTANCES—1:1-11

- **A.** Paul salutes the Corinthians by introducing himself and identifying them as the recipients—1:1-2
  - **1.** Paul introduces himself and Timothy and emphasizes that he was an apostle by the will of God in order assert his apostolic authority—1:1a
  - **2.** Paul identifies the recipients as the church in Corinth and all the saints throughout Macedonia—1:1b
  - **3.** Paul bids them grace and peace from God—1:2
- **B.** Paul thanks God for His comfort in affliction in order to show the experience of God's grace in suffering—1:3-11
  - **1.** Paul praises God as the source of compassion and comfort who comforts those in affliction so that they in turn can comfort others—1:3-4
  - **2.** Paul states that his suffering was due to his relationship to Christ but that the

consolation he received would match the suffering—1:5

3. Paul states that his suffering for the Corinthians would lead to their salvation (sanctification aspect) and he was confident that they would remain steadfast—1:6-7
4. Paul states that the suffering he endured caused him to despair but also to trust God who delivered him—1:8-11

II. PAUL GIVES A DEFENSE OF HIS CHANGE OF PLANS AND AN EXPOSTION OF HIS MINISTRY IN ORDER TO ANSWER INSINUATIONS RAISED BY HIS OPPONENTS CONCERNING HIS SINCERITY AND COMMITTMENT TO THE MINISTRY AND THE CORINTHIANS SO THAT THEY WOULD HAVE RENEWED CONFIDENCE IN HIM—1:12-7:16

A. Paul clarifies the reason he changed his plans to visit the Corinthians in order to answer the insinuation raised by the false teachers that Paul was really not sincere in his concern for the Corinthians and that a true apostle would not vacillate in his plans—1:12-2:11

1. Paul clarifies the reason he changed his plans to visit the Corinthians to refute the accusations brought against him and to affirm his love for them—1:12-2:4
   - **a.** Paul explains the sincerity of his actions to the Corinthians—1:12-14
     - **1)** He states that his conduct was motivated by the grace of God and sincerity and not the self-serving ambition of the world—1:12
     - **2)** He appeals to the Corinthians' knowledge of his conduct that he was honest so that they would see he did not have any secret motives—1:13-14
   - **b.** Paul explains the consistency of his actions to the Corinthians—1:15-22
     - **1)** He answers the charge of fickleness by stating that he had originally planned in good faith to visit them but was unable and so arranged his travel plans so that he could later visit them twice—(he explains these plans more fully beginning at v. 23)—1:15-16
     - **2)** He states that he did not make his plans in a self-serving manner—1:17
     - **3)** He presents an argument from ethical congruity with the Father by noting that God is faithful and since he proclaims His message he is faithful also—1:18
     - **4)** He presents an argument from Christ in that Christ is truth because he affirms God's promises and this is the one Paul preached—1:19-20
     - **5)** He presents an argument from the work of God among them which produces stability in them—1:21-22
   - **c.** Paul explains the loving motive of his change in plans to visit the Corinthians so that they would realize his love for them—1:23-2:4
     - **1)** He affirms with God as his witness that he did not visit them to avoid more grief in case the problem could be solved in another way—1:23-2:2

Note #158: The painful visit?

Possibly this is a reference to the "painful visit" which was the first part of the unfinished plans mentioned in 1:15-16. Evidently, some grievous event occurred which caused Paul and the Corinthians' pain (2:5?). In order to spare further grief, he deferred this second part of his visit.

2) He states that instead of making that visit he wrote a letter in order to demonstrate his deep love for them—2:3-4

Note #159: The lost letter?

In the scheme of things being suggested in the introduction to 1 Corinthians, this letter would have been the lost letter written after 1 Corinthians. Whatever the contents of that letter (possibly clues are seen in 2:5-11 and 7:5-12), it is evident that the letter contained deep feelings for the Corinthians (2:3-4).

2. Paul gives advice concerning the situation that had caused the grief so that Satan would not use this situation to drive a wedge between the relation of Paul and the church—2:5-11

a. He refers to the person who caused the sorrow as one who caused grief for Paul and the whole church—2:5

Note #160: Who is the "man?"

This man has often been identified as the incestuous man referred to in 1 Corinthians 5. However, this is doubtful when comparing the severity of that situation with the situation here, and with the unlikelihood that the letter referred to here is 1 Corinthians. What this person did is uncertain, but it probably involved an attack on Paul's apostolic authority.

b. He commends them for disciplining the man but warns them against disciplining him too severely—2:6-8

c. He states that he wants them to stand committed with him in this matter so that they would be unified—2:9-11

B. Paul describes his view of the ministry as triumphant and as superior to the old economy in order to defend his ministry from his attackers— 2:12-7:16

1. Paul states that his ministry was superior because it is triumphant and glorious because it was dependent on God and not man and that it had the internal attestation of the Spirit—2:12-3:6

a. He states that his ministry was glorious and triumphant because it was dependent on God and not man—2:12-17

1) He recounts for them about his rendezvous with Titus in order to show them that he was concerned for their welfare—2:12-13

2) He praises God that his ministry is one of triumph in spite of setbacks because it depends on God and that in this ministry he was sincere—2:14-17

Note #161: Roman triumph

Paul compares the advance of the gospel to the spectacle march known as the Roman triumph. Hubbard describes the scene: "Awarded by the senate to honor a victorious general, the triumph was essentially an enormous parade through the heart of Rome. It was designed to display the glory of the Roman general and offer thanks to Jupiter, the chief deity of the Roman pantheon, for granting victory. The festivities could last several days, and not only did the entire populace of Rome turn out to view the spectacle, but Rome itself was copiously adorned to embrace her conquering hero....The climax of the procession involved a sacrifice to the Roman deities and the execution of any eminent captives in the Forum....The imagery of the conquest and the triumph was disseminated throughout the empire on coinage" (Moyer Hubbard, "2 Corinthians," in Zondervan Illustrated Bible Backgrounds Commentary *[Grand Rapids: Zondervan, 2002], 206).*

- **b.** He also notes that the apostles formed a sweet smelling savor to God irrespective of the response of men which has as its background the aroma of the sacrifice going up to God (2:15-16b).
- **c.** He states that his ministry is internally attested in order to answer the charge that his credentials were inadequate—3:1-6
  - **1)** His devout life and their changed lives were his letters of commendation in order to answer the charge which could come from the preceding section that he commended himself because no one else would—3:1-3
  - **2)** This confidence is based on divine resources which had made him a competent minister of the New Covenant—3:4-6

2. Paul states that his ministry was superior because it was based on the glory of the New Covenant which was better than the old in order to contrast his ministry with that of the false apostles—3:7-18

- **a.** Paul contrasts the old and new covenants—3:7-11
  - **1)** The new covenant is more glorious than the old because it is permanent—3:7-8
  - **2)** The new covenant is more glorious than the old because it provides righteousness whereas the old produced condemnation—3:9-10
  - **3)** The new covenant is more glorious than the old because it remains while the old has passed away—3:11

Note #162: The Law as a unit has passed away

This is an important section to show that the Law as a unit has passed away. There is really no justification to say that the Law was divided into three parts (ceremonial, civil, and moral), and that the ceremonial and civil have been done away while the moral remains. This is seen in the text where that which Moses ministered is called a ministration of death which was engraved in stone. The only part of the Law which was written in stone was the Ten Commandments, thus they are said to be a ministration of death and have passed away. Therefore, the whole code is done away not just part of it. It should be borne in mind that just because a dispensation has been done away, this does not necessarily mean that everything in that dispensation cannot be found in another one. While there are differences between dispensations there are also at times similarities.

For a fuller discussion of the passing away of the Law, see Note 168.

Note #163: The church and the new covenant

The relationship of the Church to the New Covenant is a major point of contention in Biblical Studies. Second Corinthians 3 is a key text in the debate since Paul says that he is a minister of the New Covenant. George Gunn summarizes the five views on the subject ("Second Corinthians 3:6 and the New Covenant," in An Introduction to the New Covenant *[Hurst, TX: Tyndale Seminary Press, 2013], 204-205): 1) Replacement — National Israel has been superseded by the Church and it is fulfilling the New Covenant; 2) Partial—The Church is fulfilling part of the NC but it will be completely fulfilled by national Israel in the millennium; 3) Participation—The Church participates in some blessings of the NC; 4) Two Covenants—The Church has a NC and Israel has a NC; 5) No relationship—the Church is not directly related to the NC but is related to the Mediator and blood of the NC. View #1 is held by Covenant theologians, while views #2-5 have been/are held by dispensationalists. Gunn's article makes a strong case for view 5 and offers this conclusion of the 2 Corinthians 3 passage: "...the parties to the New Covenant are God and the houses of Israel and Judah...the realization of its blessings awaits that time when God brings Israel and Judah into the covenant. Until that time, others (viz. the Church) may be benefitting from the same blood that ratified the New Covenant, but there seems to be no exegetical necessity for seeing he Church as having been brought in as a new party to the covenant" (234-235).*

b. Paul states that because of the superiority of the ministry in which he was engaged he could be bold and candid in his execution of it as it was implemented by the Spirit—3:12-18

1) Because of the hope brought by the new covenant he could have boldness—3:12

2) This was in contrast to Moses who wore a veil over his face because of the unworthiness of the nation due to their hardness (confirmed by v. 14)—3:13

3) This blindness on Israel persists today unless God graciously shines the light of the gospel on them—3:14-16

4) This blindness is removed by the Holy Spirit—3:17

5) Christians are transformed progressively into the glory of Christ by the Spirit—3:18

3. Paul states that his ministry was superior because in the midst of hardship it provided sustainment through the power of God—4:1-15

a. He notes that the ministry was a source of encouragement in spite of difficult circumstances because the results were dependent on God—4:2-6

1) Because God had given him this ministry he did not give up—4:1

2) They could be honest in their presentation of the message since its results were God's business—4:2

3) Those who did reject the message did so because they were blinded by Satan in order to show that if his message was rejected it was not his fault—4:3-4

4) He advanced the cause of Christ not his own cause as his accusers were suggesting—4:5-6

b. He notes the contrasts between the message and the messenger in his ministry in order to show the glorious nature of the message and the mere mortality of the messenger—4:7-15

1) He says that the message is the knowledge of God but it is deposited in common vessels so that the power would be seen to be supernatural—4:7

2) He illustrates this contrast by four examples from his life—4:8-9

a) He is hard-pressed but not crushed—4:8a

b) He is perplexed but not in despair—4:8b

c) He is persecuted but not abandoned—4:9a

d) He is struck down but not destroyed—4:9b

3) He states that this kind of life is similar to the Lord's and shows that the power of Christ is working in him—4:10-11

4) He states that his suffering gave the Corinthians evidence of God's working but that when his suffering was over he was confident that he and his readers would be resurrected—4:12-14

5) He states that his suffering was for their good and God's glory—4:15

4. Paul states that his ministry was superior because of its eternal perspective—4:16-5:10

a. He shows its eternal perspective by contrasting the outward deterioration of the body with the inward renewal which would culminate in eternal glory—4:16-18

1) His sufferings were causing him to be destroyed outwardly but he was being renewed spiritually—4:16

2) His sufferings were light in comparison to the weight of glory he would receive at the bema—4:17

3) He fixed his eyes on the invisible things for they are eternal—4:18

b. He shows its eternal perspective by contrasting his present and future dwellings in order to give substance to the eternal things about which he has just spoken—5:1-10

Note #164: Is there an intermediate body at death?

The "intermediate state" is the time period between a person's death and resurrection. The Bible is clear that upon death, the believer immediately goes into a blissful state in the presence of God while the unbeliever goes to a place of conscious torment in hades. This, however, deals with the immaterial part of man. The question at issue here is whether the believer has a temporary body received at death as the permanent resurrection body is awaited, or does the believer exist in a disembodied state until the time of resurrection. Second Corinthians 5:1-10 is a central passage in this discussion. It would seem that the body under discussion in this text is the resurrection body since it is called "eternal" and Paul appears to be envisioning a period of not being clothed with a body in 5:3-4. Since Paul is speaking of only two states in this passage—clothed and unclothed—it seems unwarranted to posit a third state. If it is asked how a person can function without a body, one only need look at the members of the Godhead and the angels. There are also possible indications that the spirit can take on a recognizable form (1 Sam 28:13-14; Luke 16:19-31; Rev 6:9-11). Summarily, the intermediate state, therefore, is one of being with the Lord but without a body. Paul would prefer to be alive at the return of Christ and be clothed with his resurrection body, but even the intermediate state without it is far better than being in this world because the relationship there will be "inexpressibly rhapsodic."

1) He states that when the earthly body is destroyed we will be granted a resurrection body (given at the resurrection) prepared by God—5:1
2) He expands the idea of the resurrection body by using the figure of a garment which will replace the mortal cloak at the resurrection—5:2-4
3) He states that the giving of the Holy Spirit by God is a down payment on our resurrection body in order to show this is not just wishful thinking—5:5
4) He states that this gave him the confidence in his daily life that while he was in the body he was absent from the Lord and to be away from the body would be to be present with the Lord —5:6-8
5) He states that in light of this fact he makes it his goal to please God because he would one day give an account of his life to the Lord—5:9-10

Note #165: The bema seat judgment

*The judgment being referred to here is the bema seat of Christ where the Christian will have his life evaluated or more accurately, according to this text, "laid bare" (φανερόω). Arndt, Danker, and Bauer have "to cause to become visible, reveal, expose publicly" (*A Greek-English Lexicon of the New Testament and Other Early Christian Literature*, 1048). Certainly, his sins will not enter the picture from a salvific point of view. However, it is incorrect to assume from this that the believer will not be accountable before God. It seems correct to say that at the very least Paul is saying here that it is possible for the believer to lose rewards at this judgment. However, others go beyond this and argue for actual discipline of the slothful Christian at the judgment seat (J. D. Faust,* The Rod, will God Spare it? An Exhaustive Study of Temporary Punishment for Unfaithful Christians at the Judgment Seat and During the Millennial Kingdom *[Hayesville, NC: Schoettle Publishing, 2003]). The text does say that the believer will receive for the good* <u>and</u> *the evil. Robertson suggests: "Paul does not say merely that he shall receive according to what he has done in the body, but that he shall receive the things done—the very selfsame things he did" (cited by Alfred Plummer,* A Critical and Exegetical Commentary on 2 Corinthians *[Edinburgh: T. & T. Clark, 1915], 157). Therefore, it seems that the believer who lives a slothful, careless life will suffer some kind of discipline which will involve more than the loss of rewards. What this will involve, the Bible does not say.*

The position of being a child of God is, indeed, not forfeitable, but not the total fullness of the heavenly birthright. In this sense, there is urgent need to give diligence... "for thus shall be richly supplied unto you the entrance into the eternal kingdom of our Lord and Savior Jesus Christ (2 Peter 1:10-11)" (Eric Sauer, In the Arena of Faith *[United Kingdom: Paternoster, 1994], 154).*

5. Paul states that his ministry is superior because the heart of its message is reconciliation to God—5:11-6:2

a. He notes the impetus and goal behind his dispensing of this message—5:11-15

1) Paul says that the motive in spreading the message of reconciliation was the thought of standing before the judgment seat of Christ—5:11a

2) Paul says that the goal in spreading the message of reconciliation was to persuade men—5:11b

3) Paul says that the ministry was done in sincerity and he was willing to be thought of as a fool to show his sincerity—5:11c-13

4) Paul says that he felt this way because of the love of Christ for him which was seen when He died for all men—5:14-15

b. He illustrates how God's love and Christ's death changed his viewpoint about Christ thus showing an example of reconciliation—5:16-17

1) He states that before his conversion he looked at externals and saw Christ as a mere man of lowly origins but that since his conversion he saw Him in a new light—5:16

2) He infers from the preceding point that this new viewpoint comes at conversion—5:17

c. He now explains how the message of reconciliation is effected—5:18-21

1) God is the subject of reconciliation and the world is the object accomplished through the work of Christ—5:18

2) This was done by God when he imputed the sin of the world onto Christ thus putting the world into a saveable condition—5:19

3) He is now one who proclaims this message on behalf of God--5:20

4) The reason God did this was so that he could put the righteousness of Christ to the account of men—5:21

d. He applies the message of reconciliation to the readers—6:1-2

1) He warns the readers against believing the message of the false teachers instead of his message for this would be to receive the grace of God in vain—6:1

2) He urges his readers to accept his message during the era of salvation for there would be a day when it would be too late —6:2

6. Paul states that his message is superior and his motives sincere because he had been willing to suffer hardships for it—6:3-10

a. He affirms that his motives were sincere—6:3

b. He describes the hardships to show his sincerity in the gospel by means of his endurance—6:4-5

c. He describes the graces in his life through these trials—6:6-7a

d. He describes the conditions under which he ministered—6:7b-10

7. Paul appeals to the Corinthians on the basis of his preceding defense to accept his ministry and message and to reject the influence of the false apostles who opposed him—6:11-7:16

a. He appeals to the Corinthians to be accepting of him and consistent in their Christian walk—6:11-7:4

1) Paul states the appeal by asking that they be open-hearted to him as he had been toward them—6:11-13

2) Paul balances his appeal by cautioning them against being open-hearted to false teachers—6:14-7:1

a) He commands that they form no ecclesiastical liaison with the false apostles—6:14a

b) He shows the inconsistency of forming a liaison with them by pointing out five contrasts—6:14b-18

(1) Righteousness and wickedness have nothing in common—6:14b

(2) Light and dark cannot have fellowship—6:14c

(3) Christ and Satan are not in harmony together—6:15a

(4) Believers and unbelievers do not have anything spiritual in common—6:15b

(5) There is no agreement between the temple of God and idols which is substantiated by three Old Testament quotes—6:16a-18

c) Paul applies these quotations by noting that the believer should avoid all contamination as they pressed on in holiness—7:1

3) Paul restates his appeal that the Corinthians be open-hearted toward him and assures them of his love for them and confidence that they would respond properly—7:2-4

b. Paul rejoices in the encouraging response the Corinthians had displayed thus far in order to encourage them to continue on in their acceptance of him and lay the groundwork for the subsequent exhortation about the collection—7:5-16

1) He states the joy and encouragement he had when he met with Titus and was told of their response to his exhortation even though he had second thoughts about sending the letter—7:5-13a

2) He states the joy and encouragement that Titus had because of their response—7:13b-16

III. PAUL INSTRUCTS THE CORINTHIANS CONCERNING THE COLLECTION FOR THE POOR IN JERUSALEM SO THAT THEY WOULD RESUME THEIR GIVING IN SPITE OF WHAT THE FALSE TEACHERS WERE SAYING ABOUT HIM—8:1-9:15

A. Paul provides the Corinthians with two examples of giving in order to motivate them to generosity—8:1-9

1. Paul illustrates generosity in giving by pointing to the Macedonian churches—8:1-7

a. He states the generosity of the Macedonian churches—8:1-2

b. He states the characteristics that marked their giving—8:3-5

1) They gave sacrificially beyond their ability—8:3a

2) They gave of their own initiative—8:3b

3) They gave of their own free will and not from the pressure of others—8: 3c-4

4) They gave out of their personal dedication to God and Paul—8:5

c. He urges the Corinthians to excel in this grace of giving as had the other Macedonian churches—8:6-7

2. Paul illustrates generosity in giving by pointing to Christ—8:8-9

a. He hoped that the sincerity of their love would be motivated by the example of others—8:8
b. He states that the incarnation should be the greatest motive in giving—8:9

B. Paul provides the Corinthians with the rationale for the collection and arrangements for its handling—8:10-9:5

1. Paul states the rationale for the collection—8:10-15
   - **a.** He urges them to complete their collection since they desired to do this and had already started before the Macedonian churches—8:10-12
   - **b.** He explains to them that the objective of the collection was to equally distribute what existed not to make one poor and another rich—8:13-15
2. Paul provides arrangements for the handling of the collection—8:16-9:5
   - **a.** He stated that he was sending Titus to pick up the gift and affirmed Titus' love for the Corinthians—8:16-17
   - **b.** He stated that a highly respected representative from the churches would take the gift to Jerusalem and notes that he scrupulously arranged things so as to bring honor to the Lord—8:18-21
   - **c.** He stated that another brother would join the collection party who was zealous and an honor to the lord—8:22-24
   - **d.** He stated that he planned to visit Corinth shortly after the delegation arrived in order to further motivate the Corinthians to giving—9:1-5

C. Paul provides the Corinthians with the rewards they would receive in their generous giving in order to help them follow through with their purpose—9:6-15

1. The first reward is that the giver is enriched—9:6-10
2. The second reward is that the receivers' needs are met—9:11-12
3. The third reward is that God is glorified—9:13-15

Note #166: New Testament giving

In light of the fact that the Mosaic Law has been abrogated and therefore the Christian today is not under the tithing aspect of it, 2 Corinthians 8-9 becomes an important epistolary text on giving during this era. An excellent series of articles on the overall subject has been written by Ray Stedman and can be found in Bibliotheca Sacra, *107:427 (Jul 1950), 107:428 (Oct 1950), 108:429 (Jan 1951), 108:430 (Apr 1951). Several principles for giving emerge when bringing together various New Testament passages: 1) each individual should participate in giving, 2) the amount given is in proportion to God's blessing, 3) the amount given is a matter between the individual and God, 4) the attitude behind giving should be cheerful obedience, 5) giving should help meet the needs of the congregation, 6) sacrificial giving is pleasing to God.*

IV. PAUL SUPPLIES A DEFENSE OF HIS APOSTLESHIP BY ANSWERING THE CHARGES MADE AGAINST HIM, CENSURES THE FALSE APOSTLES, AND MAKES CLAIMS WHICH SUPPORT HIS APOSTLESHIP IN ORDER TO WIN THE DEVOTION OF THE CORINTHIANS BACK TO CHRIST AND HIMSELF—10:1-13:10

A. Paul begins by gently asking his readers to respond to apostolic authority so that when he came it would not have to be in a severe manner—10:1-2

B. Paul supplies a defense of his apostleship by answering the charges made against him—10:3-18

1. He replies to the charge of cowardice by noting that though he was human he did not utilize human weapons but spiritual weapons which were effective in spiritual warfare—10:3-6
2. He replies to the charge of weakness by noting that he is able to deal with them forcefully in person as well as by letter—10:7-11

C. Paul supplies a defense of his apostleship by censuring the false apostles on several counts—10:12-11:1

Note #167: False prophets

Views on the identity of these false apostles include: Hellenistic Jews, Gnostic Jews, or Palestinian Jews who claimed to be apostles of Christ. Though it is difficult to say for sure, there are certain characteristics of them which can be gleaned from the book: 1) they were claiming apostolic authority (v. 11:5, 13), 2) they were phonies (11:13-15), 3) they were Jews (11:22), 4) they undermined Paul's authority (10-13), and 5) they were perhaps some type of Judaizers who tried to impose the Mosaic Covenant because of Paul's discussion earlier in the letter about the superiority of the New Covenant over the old one.

1. The false apostles compared themselves with human standards rather than divine standards—10:12
2. The false apostles were not divinely appointed to minister to the Gentiles as he was—10:13-14
3. The false apostles had over-exaggerated their claims and while he was boasting about his accomplishments his boasting was in the Lord—10:15-11:1
4. He provides a warning to the Corinthians of their spiritual peril by noting the false appeals the false prophets were making—11:2-15
   a. He states his desire that they would be presented in a pure state to Christ but warns them that they were close to being deceived as Eve was because they were tolerating a different message—11:2-4
   b. He notes that the false apostles were claiming to be linked with the original disciples—11:5
   c. He notes that the false apostles were playing on the Corinthians' desire for rhetorical excellence—11:6
   d. He notes that the false apostles were wrongly receiving support from the churches unlike the practice of Paul—11:7-12
   e. He blasts the false apostles as being shams and servants of Satan whose end would be according to their work—11:13-15

D. Paul supplies a defense of his apostleship by presenting his apostolic credentials in order to show his divine accreditation and to show that they should see greatness not from a worldly perspective of outward human greatness but human weakness—11:16-12:10

1. Paul apologizes for having to come down to the Corinthians' level and resort to boasting but does so to persuade them of his genuineness (compare Prov.

26:5)—11:16-21

2. Paul mentions his pedigree—11:22-23a
    a. He was a Jew who was descended from Abraham—11:22
    b. He was a servant of Christ—11:23a
3. Paul mentions his sufferings in which he calls God as his witness that they were true—11:23b-33
4. Paul mentions the special revelation that he had received from God— 12:1-10
    a. He relates that he was caught up into the very presence of God and received a personal message but which he had not revealed so that he would not be thought of more highly than would be proper—12:1-6
    b. He relates that he was given a thorn in the flesh so that he would not become overly proud of the revelation he had received—12:7-8
    c. He relates that he rejoiced in this affliction for by his weakness the power of God would be seen—12:9-10

E. Paul concludes his defense by referring to his apostolic miracles and paternal love for the Corinthians so that he can urge them to a recommended response involving repentance and an affirmation of loyalty to his fellow-workers—12:11-13:10
1. Paul refers to his miracles and paternal love among the Corinthians in order to set the stage for his appeal to them—12:11-18
    a. Paul states that his defense was over but that it should not have been necessary because when he was with the Corinthians he had performed the signs of an apostle (i.e., signs, wonders, and miracles)—12:11-13
    b. Paul states that he was not craftily obtaining money indirectly through his associates which was demonstrated by the fact that he was self-supporting when among the Corinthians—12:14-18
2. Paul shares his concerns about his upcoming visit and urges the Corinthians to repentance and an affirmation of loyalty to him—12:19-13:10
    a. Paul states his concerns—12:19-21
        1) He states that he was concerned that they would not see that his apostolic defense was for their strengthening—12:19
        2) He states that he was concerned that when he visited them there would be carnality in the congregation—12:20-21
    b. Paul states his warnings—13:1-10
        1) He warns them that he would deal with any unresolved problems because of his apostolic authority—13:1-4
        2) He warns them that they should examine themselves and make sure they were being obedient to the faith—13:5-6
        3) He warns them that though his desire was for their obedience and maturity, he would deal with them severely if this did not take place—13:7-10

V. PAUL CONCLUDES THE LETTER WITH AN EXHORTATION, SALUTATION, AND BENEDICTION IN ORDER TO MOVE HIS READERS TO UNITY WITH ONE ANOTHER AND HIMSELF—13:11-14

A. Paul exhorts them to be obedient and to live in peace—13:11-12
B. Paul sends salutations from the saints—13:13
C. Paul invokes the blessing of the Triune God on their behalf—13:14

Note #168: The Law as a unit has passed away expanded

Other than Theonomy (also known as Christian Reconstructionism or Dominion theology) which teaches that society should be reconstructed by being brought under the Old Testament Law including its capital penalties, there are two major views as to the role the Mosaic Law plays today.

The Triad View of the Law

The first major view, and probably the most common, could be called the "triad" view. The Triad view divides the Mosaic Law into three divisions. The first division is the ceremonial. The ceremonial aspect of the Law includes laws dealing with sacrifices together with different religious rites and ceremonies. The second division is the civil and judicial aspect. This part of the Law encompasses regulations related to Israel as a civil state. And the third division is the moral. The moral part of the Law reflects those laws which flow from God's nature. Since God's nature does not change, then those moral laws which proceed from God's nature do not change and therefore they are binding on all people at all times. The believer today is neither under the ceremonial Law nor the civil Law. Thus, the part of the Law which applies to us today would be those laws under the moral aspect of the code.

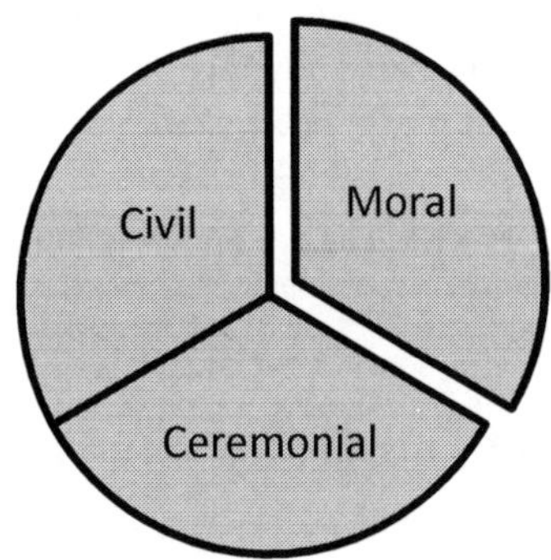

The Unified View of the Law

A second position could be called "the unified" view of the Law. This position states that the Law is not to be considered as made up of different parts, but that it is one unit. When Christ died, this rule of Law ended, and Christians today are not under any of the Mosaic Law. This view is preferable due to the following considerations.

1. *There is no evidence that the Jews ever viewed the Law as broken up into parts. This idea is a historical development not a Jewish distinction. The Jews viewed the Law as a unit, every part of which was equally binding on their lives. In fact, there was death sentences from different parts of the Law, thus one could be executed for breaking a non-religious law as much as for breaking a religious law.*

2. The division of the Law into parts is arbitrary. Moral, civil and ceremonial distinctions are imposed on the text and do not arise from it. For example, Leviticus 19:18 says to love your neighbor as yourself, the very next verse says, "Do not wear clothing woven of two kinds of material." The so-called moral, civil and ceremonial regulations occur together in the text with no indicators that there are such distinctions. Gordon Wenham makes the same observation in when he points out that "the arbitrariness of the distinction between moral and civil law is reinforced by the arrangement of the material in Leviticus. Love of neighbor immediately precedes a prohibition on mixed breeding; the holiness motto comes just before the law on executing unruly children" (Gordon Wenham, The Book of Leviticus *[Grand Rapids: Eerdmans, 1985], 34). This is why when the Law is read through, will be a constant flip-flopping between issues.*

3. It is sometimes difficult to determine into which of these three categories a law falls. The entire Law was theological in nature where even the most mundane laws like not planting a field with two kinds of seed, or not wearing a garment with two kinds of material were making the same theological point of the holiness and the separateness of God from what was profane. In fact, all of these kinds of legislations dealt with this overarching theological principle of God's holiness. How could it be said then that such parts of the law are not moral? For instance, rebellious children were to be executed. Is not rebellion a moral issue? If so, why should we not impose the penalty for this moral issue? When one reads through the entire Law as found in Exodus, Leviticus, Numbers, and Deuteronomy, it is a maze of confusion in trying to determine what is applicable and what is not. Thus, when we talk about the Law ending we must think of the Law as a unit ending as opposed to some parts ending and some parts not ending.

4. The historical context in which the Law was given must be remembered. The Mosaic Law was given to the nation of Israel—a nomadic, ancient Near Eastern people. It was never given to Gentiles as a rule of life. Specifically, it was given to the nation of Israel in relation to their enjoying the blessings of the Abrahamic Covenant. That is, if they were obedient to the Mosaic Law, they would possess the Promised Land, they would defeat their enemies, God would be visibly present, there would be material prosperity and health, etc.

5. There are several New Testament passages which show the Law as a unit ended. For example, the major pronouncement of the Jerusalem Council in Acts 15 was that the Gentiles were not obligated to keep the Law. They were only asked to curb their liberty for the sake of the Jews during this tenuous period in the early church. In Romans 7:1-6 and 10:4 Paul, viewing the Law as a unit, indicates that we are free from the Law and the Law has come to an end. In 2 Corinthians 3:7-11 Paul says that he is a minister of the New Covenant in contrast to that which was ministered by Moses which he calls a "ministration of death." Interestingly, he refers to the Mosaic Covenant as that which was written in stone. The only part of the Law written in stone was the Ten Commandments. He then writes in verse 11: For if what was being brought to an end came with glory, much more will what is permanent have glory. *Paul asserts the same point strongly in Galatians. The Judaizers were pressing the Law on the early Christians in terms of justification and sanctification. Paul warns them forcefully that they are not to turn again to the elements of the Law. He then makes the remarkable statement in 4:11:* I am afraid I may have labored over you in vain. *He is indicating that if they go back to the Law, then his work among them has been wasted.*

6. Though the Law as a unit has come to an end, there is such a thing as using the

Law lawfully (1 Tim. 1:8). Charles Ryrie wrote to the effect that we must distinguish between a code and transferable commandments among codes *(C. C. Ryrie, "The End of the Law,"* Bibliotheca Sacra *124:495 [Jul 19670], 240-247; see also Arnold Fruchtenbaum,* Israelology: The Missing Link in Systematic Theology *[Tustin, CA: Ariel Ministries, 2001], 373-380; 476-494; 588-601; 640-680). This means, regardless of one's theological persuasion, that God has operated in different ways in different times. God's demands before the Mosaic Law was given are different than after the Mosaic Law was given. God's demands in the present age, even if one adopts the triad view of the Law, are different than when God was working through the Mosaic Law. During the Kingdom age yet to come, God will be operating differently than he is now. And so what emerges is that there are various codes, not just the Mosaic code, but several codes, by which God has ruled things on earth. For example, murder in any age has always been prohibited by God. If a person refrains from murder today, this does not mean he is putting himself under the Mosaic Law; rather, murder is illustrative of the principle of* distinguishing between a code and transferable commandments among codes. *The same point can be seen when a person transfers their citizenship from one country to another. If one obeys a law which both countries happen to share in common, he is not putting himself under the law code of his old country. Instead, that law is kept because it is also a part of the laws of the country where he now resides. Thus, something may be retained from one code to the next and therefore become binding while the code itself has been entirely dismissed.*

7. How do we know what transfers from one dispensation to the next? There are four steps which help in answering this question.

- *First, begin with the premise that the Law as a unit has been done away and therefore is not binding.*
- *Second, when we examine an Old Testament text, we must look at that text by keeping in mind its historical, cultural, and theocratic contexts.*
- *Third, compare the Law to what is recorded in the New Testament and take note of what is said in the New Testament and what is not said. Are there passages in the New Testament which affirm something in the Law? Are there passages which repeal something said in the Law? Are there things in the Law not mentioned at all in the New Testament? This will begin to give us a feel for what has been transferred and what has not.*
- *Fourth, there are several New Testament passages which will help on this. The first is the Sermon on the Mount as recorded in Matthew 5-7. In the heart of Jesus' sermon we find an inclusio. In 5:17 Jesus refers to the Law and the Prophets and repeats this formula in 7:12. This is a way of bracketing an entire section of material. And as we look at that section, we observe that everything Jesus says is dealing with practical righteousness from the Law. Thus, we have a large teaching block speaking of that which is transferable from one time to another. Moreover, everything in that section is also reiterated in the Epistles. A second passage is the entire book of James. James is the earliest New Testament epistle, and is essentially an exposition of the Sermon on the Mount. And then a third passage is found in 1 Timothy 1. In verse 8 Paul writes that the Law is good if a man uses it lawfully? How do we use it lawfully? In the next two verses he tells us by giving a list of prohibitions which transfer from the Law to the present age, just as he does in other vice lists throughout the New Testament.*

The Law **as a unit** is abrogated

Determine the theocratic context of the passage

Compare the Law to the New Testament

Helpful New Testament passages

GALATIANS

Authorship

Paul clearly states that he is the author of this epistle (1:1; 5:2). He says that he departed from the normal practice of dictating his letters and wrote this one himself (6:11). The external evidence for Pauline authorship is provided by the church fathers. Even Marcion placed the epistle at the top of his list of genuine Pauline epistles (Harrison, *Introduction to the New Testament,* 255). Internal evidence also favors this view including Paul's mention of himself, his testimony, and his common themes.

Destination

Paul specifies the destination of the epistle to be the "churches of Galatia" (1:2). The question, however, is where these churches were. The traditional view is the North Galatian theory. This view states that the book was written to Gallic believers in the territory of Galatia whom Paul had won to Christ on his second missionary journey (advocates include Lightfoot, Betz, Kummel, and Harrison). There are three major supports for this view: 1) Luke used geographical names, 2) the Gallic lifestyle of fickleness, strife, anger, and impulsiveness, and 3) patristic support. In addition, it is important to point out that this view interprets Galatians 2:1-10 as the Jerusalem Council visit.

An alternative to the traditional view sees Galatians as written to Greek believers in the Roman province of Galatia (political Galatia) whom Paul won to Christ on his first missionary journey. This is known as the South Galatian theory (advocates include: Ramsey, Bruce, Hiebert, and Guthrie). There are several supports for this view: 1) Paul generally referred to groups of churches by the names of their Roman province, 2) "Galatia" was the best general term to describe the various ethnic groups in the southern area, 3) no mention is made of the Jerusalem Council verdict which would have occurred already assuming the Northern theory, 4) Barnabas is mentioned who accompanied Paul only in South Galatia, 5) since Paul visited the Galatian churches during the recovery from a bodily illness (4:13), it is unlikely that he made the difficult trip to the central plateau on which North Galatia was located. In the view of this theory, the visit to Jerusalem in 2:1-10 is a reference to the famine visit.

Though the southern view has chronological difficulties and the northern view has the problem of attributing the "again" in 2:1 to a third visit, the weight of evidence seems to be in favor of the Southern Galatian theory.

Date

In light of the acceptance of the Southern view, the date of the epistle would be around AD 48-49 from Antioch of Syria. Given the theme of the letter, this early date finds support from the fact that Paul did not make reference to the Jerusalem Council decree (ca. AD 49).

Interpreting Epistolary Literature

The word "epistle" comes from the Greek noun ἐπιστολη, which simply refers to a "letter." Letters were used widely in the ancient world and account for a large part of the New Testament. In fact, 21 of the 27 New Testament books are letters comprising about

35% of the entire New Testament. Thus, when speaking of the epistles reference is being made to the books of Romans through Jude. These represent letters written by an individual to another individual, a church, or to a locale where it was to be circulated among believers in that region. Typically, though not always, these letters would include an introduction, a body, and a conclusion. As one reads and interprets these letters, there are several principles to keep in mind.

Principle #1: The letters are meant to be read in one sitting, just as any letter we would receive in the present day.

Principle #2: The letters are authoritative substitutes. The letters of the New Testament would have been as authoritative to a local church as if an apostle were there personally.

Principle #3: The letters are occasional documents. Each New Testament letter was written in light of a particular situation or problem.

Principle #4: The letters are purposeful. Each letter was written to accomplish something--it had an end in view. This purpose will arise out of the occasion and will typically intend to give instruction in a special doctrinal area or to correct some type of misbehavior.

Principle #5: The letters have an argument or flow of thought. Every paragraph of the letter, every sentence in the letter, every verse of the letter will be a logically connected whole all of which will be the author's way of proving and developing his purpose. Each part of the letter is an indispensable link in the chain of the argument.

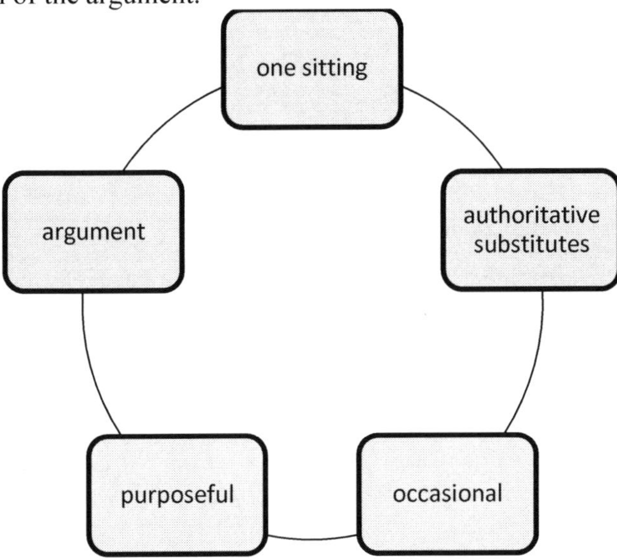

Who were the false teachers in Galatia?

Generally speaking, conservative scholars have assumed that Paul's foes were Judaizers, and they would then interpret the book in that light. However, over the past many decades in the history of interpretation, this identification of Paul's opponents has been challenged. One reason it has been challenged is because in chapters 5 and 6 the Apostle is dealing with the problem of antinomianism. Antinomianism is not a typical feature of Judaizers and therefore it has been felt that more is taking place in Galatians besides just Judaizers. By way of summary, there are three major views as to who these false teachers were (for more detailed discussion see John Barclay, "Mirror Reading a Polemic Letter: Galatians as a Test Case," *Journal for the Study of the New Testament* 31 [1988], 73-93; Walter B. Russell III, "Who Were Paul's Opponents in Galatia?" *Bibliotheca Sacra* 147:587 [Jul 1990], 330-350).

The first view is the traditional one that says the opponents of Paul were Judaizers. That is, these people were pressuring Gentiles to be saved and live as if they were Jews. This view has strong internal support based on Paul's discussion of circumcision, observing the Mosaic Law, and his interest in his readers being "sons of Abraham." A second view is that these opponents were actually two groups. There was a group of Judaizers and there was a group of antinomians. As mentioned earlier, this is primarily based on Paul's attacking of a Judaizing group in chapters 3-4 and a libertine group in chapters 5-6. A third view is what is known as the "gnostic/syncretistic Jewish Christian" view. This view argues that one group is in view in the epistle. This group belonged to a fringe within Judaism which had both legalistic and libertine traits.

It has been my opinion that the traditional view which identifies Paul's opponents as Judaizers is correct. Paul never seems to indicate that the problem with these people was their lack of desire for obedience to the Law. In fact, he says in 4:21 that the false teachers wanted the Galatians to be under the Law which Paul describes in 5:1 as a "yoke of slavery." Therefore, 5 & 6 are not disjointed from the rest of the letter, where Paul is suddenly talking to a second group of people. Instead, he is continuing to blast these Judaizers by showing his readers the failure of trying to live under the Law. Therefore, it is not that the Judaizers or these false teachers were promoting loose living in chapters 5 and 6, but rather the apostle is showing his readers where going back under the Law would lead them—namely, failed and frustrated living.

Barclay is correct when he writes, "taking the argument of the letter as a whole, there is sufficient evidence that the Galatians were informed of (and responded warmly to) the requirements of Torah-observance as the hallmark of the people of God" ("Mirror Reading a Polemic Letter: Galatians as a Test Case," 87).

Occasion

The Galatians had an enthusiastic beginning in the gospel (3:1-5). Evidently, this enthusiasm had waned (4:15) due to the opposition to Paul's authority and teaching by Judaizers who were spreading the idea that salvation came by Christ + Law and circumcision (1:6; 4:13-14). This adherence to the Law also seemed to include the sanctification process (5-6).

Purpose

In light of the above occasion and the contents of the epistle, it can be seen that Paul had at least three purposes in view: 1) to defend his apostleship (1-2), 2) to defend the doctrine of justification by faith (3-4), and 3) to show that holiness of life (and not license) should be the result of this doctrine (5-6). Thus, the message of Galatians could be put thusly: Paul writes concerning his apostleship and justification through faith in order to demonstrate his apostolic authority and show that the believer is free from the law in both justification and sanctification so that his readers would not return to the bondage of the Law.

Summary of Argument

I. PAUL INTRODUCES HIS LETTER BY SALUTING HIS READERS AND DENUNCIATING THEM FOR THEIR TURNING AWAY FROM THE GOSPEL MESSAGE IN ORDER TO SET THE TONE FOR THE REST OF THE LETTER BY POINTING OUT TO THEM THEIR PROBLEM—1:1-10

- **A.** Paul presents his salutation in which he introduces himself and his recipients—1:1-5
  - **1.** Paul introduces himself as an apostle in order to demonstrate his authority—1:1-2a
  - **2.** Paul states his recipients as the churches in Galatia who had been delivered from this present evil world in order to emphasize their freedom in Christ—1:2b-5
- **B.** Paul denunciates his readers for their quick turning away from the gospel in order to impress upon them the seriousness and folly of their action—1:6-10
  - **1.** He states his astonishment that they had so soon turned to another "gospel"—1:6-7
  - **2.** He states that if anyone preached another gospel other than what was first delivered to them they are worthy of eternal damnation—1:8-10

II. PAUL PRESENTS A DEFENSE OF HIS APOSTOLIC AUTHORITY IN ORDER TO DEMONSTRATE THAT THE GOSPEL HE WAS PROCLAIMING HAD DIVINE
APPROVAL—1: 11-2:21

- **A.** Paul discusses how he received the revelation of the Gospel from God independent of any other apostle in order to show the Galatians that his Gospel was true because its source was from God—1:11-24
  - **1.** He states his thesis that the Gospel he preached was neither made up nor something he received from other men but something he received by direct revelation from Jesus Christ—1:11-12
  - **2.** He states that before his conversion he was a zealous Jew but one who had been set apart by God from birth—1:13-15a
  - **3.** He states that during his conversion God revealed to him the truth about His Son and called him to minister to the Gentiles—1:15b-16a
  - **4.** He states that after his conversion he did not immediately confer with even the apostles and did not go to Jerusalem until three years after his conversion where he briefly met Peter and James—1:16b-24
- **B.** Paul discusses his interdependence with the other apostles and their approval in order to show that though he received the message directly from God it was the same message preached by the other apostles—2:1-10
  - **1.** He states that 14 years later he went to Jerusalem to present to the leaders there the gospel he preached to the Gentiles—2:1-2

Note #169: The famine visit

The problems in these verses revolve around the referent point from which Paul calculated the 14 years and which Jerusalem visit Paul had in mind. Paul visited Jerusalem at least five times after his conversion (after he left Damascus, the famine visit, the Council, the end of the second missionary journey, and his final visit). There are a number of reasons which favor taking this as the famine visit rather than the Jerusalem Council visit: 1) it takes "again" in its natural sense as a reference to his actual second visit following his conversion, 2) Galatians 2:1-10 records a private discussion not the public scenario of Acts 15, 3) the decrees from the council are missing in chapter 2, 4) Peter and Paul's dispute makes better sense pre-council, and 5) double revelation in 2:2 and Acts 11:28 confirm this (for further development see Stanley Toussaint, "The Chronological Problem of Galatians 2:1-10" Bibliotheca Sacra *120:480 [October-December], 334-340).*

Note #170: To run in vain

Paul's fear that "he should prove to have run in vain" should not be construed to mean he had doubts regarding the content of his gospel. Rather, his concern was that if he did not make contact with the Jerusalem apostles, his work might be undermined by some who would think they had not approved of his preaching to the Gentiles. Titus became a test case of a Gentile who was not required to become circumcised. Fung observes that "Paul's anxiety was...about a rupture of the one Church into two separate branches of Jewish and Gentile Christianity" (Ronald Fung, The Epistle to the Galatians, *New International Commentary on the New Testament [Grand Rapids: Eerdmans, 1988], 90).*

  2. He states that there were Judaizers present at this meeting but that they were unsuccessful in their attempts at imposing circumcision as a condition of salvation—2:3-5
  3. He states that James, Peter, and John agreed with Paul's message to the Gentiles and accepted him into the apostolic band—2:6-10

C. Paul discusses the incident in which he corrects Peter in order to further establish his apostolic authority and the truth of his message—2:11-21
  1. He states unequivocally that he opposed Peter in Antioch because Peter was in error—2:11
  2. He states that Peter was wrong because he withdrew from the uncircumcised Gentile believers when some Jewish visitors came from Jerusalem—2:12-13
  3. He states that he rebuked him openly because he was acting inconsistently and affecting many other believers—2:14

Note #171: The rebuke of Peter

Peter was eating with believers in Antioch who were both Jew and Gentile (cf. the sheet vision of Acts 10). Some Jews from Jerusalem came who thought Gentiles needed to be circumcised before becoming Christians. Evidently Peter was intimidated and withdrew from the Gentile Christians. This action was followed by other Jews. By doing this, they were denying by their actions the truth of the gospel that Jews and Gentiles are accepted equally by God. Paul told him that "you are a Jew, yet you live like a Gentile" referring to Peter's action that although he was a Jew, he was eating with the Gentiles thus showing his approval that both are accepted alike. But by withdrawing from them, he was reversing himself, and in essence saying the opposite and that they must be circumcised.

4. He develops the inconsistency displayed by Peter between his belief and actions—2:15-21
   a. Paul affirms that even Jews are saved through faith apart from the Law and because of this it is nonsensical to try and put the Gentiles under the Law—2:15-16
   b. Paul affirms that this method of justification does not lead to lawless behavior and if it did would imply that Christ promotes sin since He is the one in whom the believer trusted—2:17-18
   c. Paul affirms that in coming to Christ the believer is actually dead to the Law thus opening a way for him to live for God because he was identified to Christ in His death and resurrection—2:19-20
   d. Paul affirms that if what he is saying is false then Christ's death was meaningless—2:21

III. PAUL PRESENTS A DEFENSE OF THE DOCTRINE OF JUSTIFICATION THROUGH FAITH IN ORDER TO SHOW THAT THE WORK OF CHRIST DID NOT NEED TO BE SUPPLEMENTED BY HUMAN WORKS—3:1-4:31

A. Paul vindicates the doctrine of justification through faith by appealing to experience, scripture, and logic in order to dissuade his readers from returning to the Law—3:1-29

1. Paul vindicates the doctrine of justification by appealing to the experience of the Galatians—3:1-5
   a. They are acting as if they are under some kind of spell in light of the fact that Paul had clearly portrayed Christ crucified among them—3:1
   b. They had received the Spirit by faith—3:2
   c. They were being sanctified by faith—3:3
   d. Their sufferings for the doctrine would be meaningless—3:4
   e. They had seen miracles confirming the doctrine—3:5
2. Paul vindicates the doctrine of justification by appealing to Scripture in order to refute the legalists and to provide a basis for the previously mentioned experience—3:6-14
   a. Paul shows that it is incorrect to say that people became the sons of Abraham by conformity to the Law—3:6-9
      1) He cites Genesis 15:6 to show that Abraham was justified through faith—3:6
      2) He notes that men are sons of Abraham in that they are justified the same way in which Abraham was justified, through faith—3:7-9
   b. Paul shows that if one took his stand under the Law he would be cursed by the Law because no one could perfectly keep it—3:10-14

Note #172: Faith alone

Paul quotes five Old Testament passages to uphold the fact that one is justified through faith: Genesis 12:3—This passage shows the universal aspect of the Abrahamic Covenant to include Gentiles. This unconditional covenant was made before the Law was instituted; Deuteronomy 27:26—This is a cursing section in Deuteronomy and shows that the Law itself declared that if it was not kept in every detail it would lead to judgment; Habakkuk 2:4—This passage shows that the believer lives a lifestyle characterized by faith; Leviticus 18:5—Paul quotes this passage to show that Law and faith are mutually exclusive. The Law demanded perfect obedience or would result in physical death; Deuteronomy 21:23—this text shows that there is hope for those who have broken the Law. Christ was hung on a tree because he was cursed by God so that those who had broken the Law could be justified.

3. Paul vindicates the doctrine of justification by appealing to logic and showing the fallacy of relying on the Law—3:15-29
   a. Paul shows that the principle of faith continued after the giving of the Law in order to show that the Law did not terminate justification through faith—3:15-18

Note #173: Luther on 3:13

Luther famously wrote, "...Christ should become the greatest transgressor, murderer, adulterer, thief, rebel, and blasphemer, that ever was or could be in the world. For he being made a sacrifice for the sins of the whole world, is not now an innocent person and without sins, is not now the Son of God born of the Virgin Mary; but a sinner, which hath and carrieth the sin of Paul, who was a blasphemer, an oppressor, and a persecutor; of Peter, which denied Christ; of David, which was an adulterer, a murderer, and caused the Gentiles to blaspheme the name of the Lord; and briefly, which hath and beareth all the sins of all men in his body; not that he himself committed them, but for that he received them being committed or done by us, and laid them upon his own body, that he might make satisfaction for them with his own blood" (Martin Luther, A Commentary on Saint Paul's Epistle to the Galatians *[Grand Rapids: Baker, 1982], 272).*

Jonathan Edwards adds a similar sentiment. "God dealt with him as if he had been exceedingly angry with him, and as though he had been the object of his dreadful wrath. This made all the sufferings of Christ the more terrible to him, because they were from the hand of the Father, whom he infinitely loved, and whose infinite love he had had eternal experience of. Besides, it was an effect of God's wrath that he forsook Christ. This caused Christ to cry out...My God, my God, why hast thou forsaken me? This was infinitely terrible to Christ. Christ's knowledge of the glory of the Father, and his love to the Father, and the sense and experience he had had of the worth of his Father's love to him, made the withholding the pleasant ideas and manifestations of his father's love as terrible to him, as the sense and knowledge of his hatred is to the damned, that have no knowledge of God's excellency, no love to him, nor any experience of the infinite sweetness of his love" (Jonathan Edwards, "Of Satisfaction for Sin," in The Works of Jonathan Edwards *[Carlisle, PA: The Banner of Truth Trust, 1992], 2:575).*

Note #174: 430 years

It is probably best to see the 430 years as a reference to the period between the reiteration of the promises to Abraham in Beersheba as he left Canaan to settle in Egypt

(Gen. 46:2-4; ca. 1875 B.C.). So the 430 years went from the end of one era (promise) to the beginning of the other (Law). This would fit with Exodus 12:40.

b. Paul shows that the purpose of the Law was to provide protective custody until the coming of Christ in order to show that the Law did have value—3:19-25

Note #175: The Law as tutor

In developing the purpose of the Law, Paul uses the illustration of a tutor. During Paul's day, it was common for children from the age of six to puberty to be put under the care of a tutor who protected them from evil influences and gave them guidance. This is what the Law did for Israel. During their childhood as a nation, the Law was given to protect them by giving them parameters and providing guidance. The Law came along side the promise and led the Israelite up to the coming of Christ. Now that Christ has come and done His work, this period of custody is over.

c. Paul shows three results of not being under the supervision of the Law—3:26-29

1) They are now full grown adult sons with all of the privileges and rights which that entails by means of baptism into Christ —3:26-27

2) There is no distinction in spiritual status—3:28

3) There is heirship of the Abrahamic promise—3:29

B. Paul clarifies the doctrine of justification by faith by illustrations in order to show the condition of the believer as contrasted to the legalists thus helping them to abandon legalism—4:1-31

1. Paul uses a domestic (legal) illustration in order to show the change in status of the believer—4:1-7

a. He presents the illustration of an heir as a child and a son to show that he could not enjoy the privileges of sonship until the father appointed the time of maturity—4:1-2

b. He applies the illustration by noting that in their former state under the Law they were like slaves in bondage but now they had been made adult sons confirmed by the giving of the Spirit—4:3-7

Note #176: The fullness of times

The "fullness of times" would parallel the date set by the Roman father when he determined that his son was an adult. This fits with the logic of the illustration rather than positing the historical situation of the Roman Empire as the perfect time for God to send Christ. Fung elaborates on how this would apply to the coming of Christ. "It would seem that 'when the time had fully come' (RSV, NIV) does not mean that a certain divinely appointed period had elapsed (so NEB?), or that certain divinely ordained events had to transpire (cf. 2 Thess. 2:3ff.), or that God sent his Son into the world when all the conditions were ripe for his appearance. In view of the fact that the word 'came' denotes in the context (cf. 3:23, 25) the eschatological event of the coming of Christ and of the principle of justifying faith, the thought is rather that the appearance of the Son brought the 'fulness [sic] of the time,' marking the end of the present aeon (cf. 1:4) and ushering in the future aeon" (Fung, The Epistle to the Galatians, *184). "The basic elements of the world" could be the Law but this would not apply to the Gentiles. Rather, it probably has reference to the moral systems under which Jew and Gentile were bound. "Those under the Law" (v. 5) is a reference to the Jew, and "we" (v. 5) and "you" (v. 6) is a reference to all believers.*

2. Paul presents a personal appeal to his readers in order to persuade them not to return to the bondage of the Law—4:8-20
    a. He appeals to their past bondage and asks them how they could even think of going back to that—4:8-11
    b. He appeals to their past relationship with Paul in which they would have done anything for him—4:12-16
    c. He appeals to his present attitude toward them as one of love and concern—4:17-20
3. Paul presents a biblical illustration using Hagar and Sarah in order to show his readers that they were in danger of joining the wrong branch of Abraham's family—4:21-31
    a. He presents the biblical story where Abraham had two sons one by a slave woman Hagar who was born in the natural way and one by a free woman Sarah who was born in a supernatural way according to the promise—4:21-23
    b. He presents the interpretation of the allegory in which he notes that Hagar could be representative of the Mosaic Covenant and Judaism and Sarah could be representative of the Abrahamic Covenant and Christianity in order to emphasize the contrast between Law and grace—4:24-27
    c. He presents the application by noting three things—4:28-31
        1) The believer is like Isaac in that he experiences a supernatural birth and participates in the promise—4:28
        2) The believer is persecuted like Isaac by his so-called brethren—4:29
        3) The believer should exclude legalists from their midst as Abraham cast out Ishmael from his household—4:30
        4) He reminds them that they are children of the free woman and not the slave woman—4:31

Note #177: Allegory

It should be noted that Paul is not interpreting the Old Testament allegorically, but is explaining an allegory. Furthermore, the allegory is based on a literal story which does not lose its literal meaning. This is a far cry from allegorizing the Old Testament so that it loses its literal sense.

IV. PAUL PRESENTS HOW FREEDOM FROM THE LAW WORKS ITSELF OUT IN PRACTICAL LIVING IN ORDER TO SHOW THAT THE ABSENCE OF THE LAW DOES NOT LEAD TO ANTINOMIANISM—5:1-6:10

A. Paul instructs them on living without the Law by showing them the dangers of returning to the Law—5:1-12

1. He says that if they return to the Law they would be returning to slavery and this would make the work of Christ of no effect—5:1-2
2. He says that if they return to the Law they would be debtors to the whole Law—5:3
3. He says that if they return to the Law they would be fallen from the realm of grace—5:4-6

Note #178: Falling from grace

In this section Paul is showing the folly of these believers returning to the legal system. Thus, in verse 4 he is not telling them that they are in danger of losing their salvation, but rather they would be leaving the realm of grace to go to the realm of Law. Though commenting on 3:1, Chrysostom captures the pathos of Paul as he urges the Galatians not to go back to the Law, "These words convey both praise and blame; praise, for their implicit acceptance of the truth; blame, because Him whom they had seen, for their sakes, stripped naked, transfixed, nailed to the cross, spit upon, mocked, fed with vinegar, upbraided by thieves, pierced with a spear; (for all this is implied in the words, 'openly set forth, crucified,') Him had they left, and betaken themselves to the Law" (John Chrysostom. "Commentary of St. John Chrysostom, Archbishop of Constantinople, on the Epistle of St. Paul the Apostle to the Galatians." In Saint Chrysostom: Homilies on Galatians, Ephesians, Philippians, Colossians, Thessalonians, Timothy, Titus, and Philemon, *edited by Philip Schaff, translated by Gross Alexander with Anonymous. Vol. 13. A Select Library of the Nicene and Post-Nicene Fathers of the Christian Church, First Series. New York: Christian Literature Company, 1889). Logos 5.*

4. He says that if they return to the Law they would interfere with the spiritual progress of believers—5:7-10
5. He says that if they return to the Law they would remove the offense of the cross—5:11-12

B. Paul instructs them that their liberty from the Law should not lead to license to sin but to love in order to prevent them from going to the opposite extreme—5:13-15

1. Paul instructs them on living by the Holy Spirit to show how they could be successful over sin and live to the glory of God—5:16-26
2. He tells them that godliness is available for them if they choose to operate in the realm of the Spirit rather than in the realm of the flesh—5:16-18
3. He presents the works of the flesh which result when one operates outside of the realm of the Spirit—5:19-21
4. He presents the fruit of the Spirit which result when one lives obediently in the realm of the Spirit—5:22-23
5. He presents the basis for battling the flesh to be the believer's co-crucifixion with Christ—5:24-26

C. Paul instructs the believers on their responsibilities toward others in order to give some examples of how the fruit of the Spirit works itself out—6:1-10

1. The sinning Christian is to be gently and meekly restored—6:1
2. The burdened (contextually probably an excessive struggle with the flesh)

Christian should be given a helping hand—6:2-5
3. Teachers should be supported financially—6:6-9
4. They should do good toward all men—6:10

D. Paul concludes the letter by summarizing his important points and urging them to obedience—6:11-18
1. He states that he wrote this letter with his own hand in order to show the seriousness of the matter and his concern—6:11
2. He summarizes that the Judaizers were men-pleasers who were afraid of persecution and wanted to boast over the number of Galatians they had won—6:12-13
3. He states that his boast was in the cross of Christ—6:14-16
4. He states his benediction—6:17-18

Note #179: The Israel of God

There are a number of ways to take the "Israel of God" in 6:16: 1) the amillennialist takes the kai *(and the Israel of God) as apposition thus identifying the church with Israel. The sense would then be "those who walk by this rule (the Church) is even the Israel of God." But this is a rare usage of* kai *and there is no instance where Israel is used of the church, 2) others see this as a reference to the remnant of Israelites in the church thus balancing his attack on the Judaizers, 3) others see this to refer to the future redeemed nation of Israel. This is supported in part by the future tense of "walk." It is probably best to see this as a reference to the Christian Jews in the church (view 2) for a number of reasons: 1) a remnant is presented in such places as Romans 11, 2) the "Israel of God" would be a part of the whole Israel, 3) this is the usage of the term "Israel" throughout the Bible (ethnic Israel), 4) the two prepositions suggest two groups, 5) 67 other uses of "Israel" in the New Testament all refer to Jews, 6) this would fit the context where he is blasting the Judaizers, thus showing that he is not anti-Semitic by invoking a blessing on the Jewish remnant (for a full critique of the amillennial interpretation, see Jerry Hullinger, Review of "MacArthur's Millennial Manifesto,"* Journal of Dispensational Theology *[October 2009], 84-90).*

EPHESIANS

Author

There have been objections to Pauline authorship of Ephesians on linguistic, literary, and theological grounds. However, the book enjoys extensive external support in the early church. In addition, there are the following internal evidences for authorship by Paul: 1) direct claims, 2) structural affinities with his other epistles, 3) language and literary similarities, 4) theological affinities, and 5) pseudonymity was not practiced by the early Christians, and even if it were, it would be strange that another writer would be able to compose a book whose closest rival in excellence would be Paul's book of Romans.

Origin and Date

Paul was a prisoner when he wrote this letter (3:1; 4:1; 6:20). It seems most likely that this is a reference to the Roman imprisonment (Acts 28:30) in AD 60-62. Thus along with Ephesians, Philippians, Colossians, and Philemon were also written during this same period.

Destination

The traditional view is that the epistle was sent to the church in Ephesus as was held by the Church Fathers. However, an alternative has been to suggest that it was a circular letter sent to several churches in the province of Asia.

This is based on the facts that "in Ephesus" does not appear in three early Alexandrian manuscripts, and that Paul does not name anyone by name. Nevertheless, "in Ephesus" could certainly be genuine since there is a wide geographical distribution of manuscripts which do contain the phrase. Furthermore, the title "To the Ephesians" appears in all manuscripts of the epistle. Regarding the absence of names, it is difficult to determine what motivated Paul.

Purpose

Two key words stand out in determining the purpose of the book: love and unity. Concerning the first, it can be noted that more than 1/6 of Paul's references to love in his epistles occurs in Ephesians (see Harold Hoehner, *Ephesians: An Exegetical Commentary* [Grand Rapids: Baker, 2002], 102-105). Concerning the second word, the stress in 4:1-6 is the unity of the body, and that stress is said to be the outworking ("therefore" in 4:1) of the first three chapters. Thus, in chapter 1 Paul presents the unity of the believer with God because of His work in salvation. This becomes the basis for unity. Chapter 2 follows with how this unity worked out between Jew and Gentile. Paul continues this discussion in chapter 3 as he deals with the mystery of Jew and Gentile together in one body. Chapters 4-6 become the outworking in the church of the positional unity presented in the first part of the book. Lexical indicators of unity as a major theme of the book include: 1) the word translated "unity" (ἑνότης) in 4:3, 13 is used nowhere else in the New Testament, 2) the term "one" (ἓν) is used 14 times in the book, and 3) the preposition σύν (with) is combined with 14 words. A statement concerning message and purpose of the book could be stated as follows: <u>Paul presents the spiritual blessings which God bestowed on the believers and how this is executed in the believers' individual and</u>

corporate position in the body of Christ in order to spur the Ephesian Christians on to love and unity with one another.

Summary of Argument

I. PAUL INTRODUCES THE LETTER BY STRESSING THAT HIS APOSTLESHIP IS BY THE WILL OF GOD AND THAT THE EPHESIAN CHRISTIANS POSITIONALLY ARE IN CHRIST—1:1-2

II. PAUL PRESENTS THE INDIVIDUAL AND CORPORATE POSITION OF THE BELIEVER IN THE BODY OF CHRIST IN ORDER TO SHOW THE BASIS OF UNITY WITH GOD AND MAN—1:3-3:21

A. Paul praises the Triune God for the spiritual blessings which He bestowed on the believers so that they would know the basis of their unity with God and that He is the cause of it all—1:3-14

Note #180: The greatest sentence ever written

Verses 3-14 in the English translations represent but one sentence in the Greek text which is composed of 202 words. Interestingly, Paul presents God's work in salvation from the perspective of the economic trinity (the role each member of the Godhead performed in our salvation). God the Father a) chose us. The verb ἐκλέγομαι occurs 22 times in the New Testament and has the sense of "to pick" or "to choose." With one possible exception, the verb is always used in the middle voice which would indicate that God's selection is made for his own behalf or for his own interest. That "interest" is mentioned three times in the sentence as "to the praise of the glory of his grace." This sense is strengthened further when Paul adds that this election was made "before the foundation of the world." This is tantamount to saying that God's election was unconditional. i.e., there was nothing in the one chosen which moved God to act. The idea is similarly expressed in Romans 9:11 when God's choice of Isaac over Ishmael is said to be before the children were born "having done neither good or evil," b) predestined us. This aorist participle refers to the determining of one's destiny and relates to the ones chosen. This verbal is best understood in a causal sense. Hoehner explains: "In the counsels of God, the reason he chose the saints out of (ἐκ) the mass of humanity is because he predetermined their destiny" (Hoehner, Ephesians, *194). This destiny, according to Paul, is to become God's children. God the Son redeemed us. He paid the ransom price to deliver us from the bondage of sin. One of the benefits from this redemption is the forgiveness of sins. God the Spirit sealed us. The term can have a wide variety of uses including "authentication," "ownership," and "protection." The idea of ownership is probably dominant in this verse since Paul has been saying that the believer is God's possession. There have been those who have followed the theology of the "sealers" in which one has to earnestly seek the sealing of the Spirit. However, the two aorist participles "heard" and "believed" are best taken as simultaneous actions. Thus, when the Ephesians heard and believed, they were sealed.*

1. He presents the work of the Father in this process—1:3-6

a. He states that the Father blessed us with all spiritual blessings by virtue of our union with Christ—1:3

   b. He states that the Father selected some individuals (deals with the who) for Himself before the world began for salvation for the purpose of being holy—1:4
   c. He states that the Father predestined those individuals (deals with the what) to be adopted as full-fledged sons—1:5
   d. He states that the purpose of the Father's work was to the praise of His glorious grace—1:6
2. He presents the work of the Son in this process—1:7-12
   a. He states that the Son released us from slavery to sin with the price of His blood—1:7a
   b. He states that the Son provided the forgiveness of sin according to the wealth of God's grace—1:7b
   c. He states that this grace was lavished on the believer with wisdom (objective insight) and understanding (subjective apprehension) of the mystery whose end would be realized at the end of the Millennium when all things are put under Christ's feet—1:8-10
   d. He states that in Christ the Gentiles were also chosen and predestined to the praise of His glorious grace—1:11-12
3. He presents the work of the Spirit in this process—1:13-14
   a. He states that the Father sealed the believer with the Holy Spirit in order to show ownership of the believer by God—1:13
   b. He states that this giving of the Spirit becomes a down payment of more that is to come—1:14a
   c. He states that the purpose of this is to the praise of His glorious grace—1:14b

B. Paul prays that the believers might be filled with wisdom and revelation in the knowledge of God so that they might have a more intimate relationship with Him—1:15-23

1. He commends the Ephesians for their faith and love toward the saints—1:15-16
2. He addresses his prayer to the God of our Lord Jesus Christ the Father of glory—1:17a
3. The content of his prayer is that they would be given the spirit of insight into God Himself—1:17b
4. The object of this insight is that they would know God more intimately that which is possible because they had been enlightened (perfect tense)—1:17c-18a
5. The reasons that they might know God more intimately are given—1:18b-23
   a. The first is that they might know the past call of God which produces hope—1:18b
   b. The second is that they might know the future inheritance that God has in His saints—1:18c
   c. The third is that they might know the power that saved them—1:19-23
      1) This power is rooted in that which in the past was manifested in Christ's resurrection and ascension—1:19-21
      2) This power will be manifested in the future when Christ rules as the head of creation—1:22

3) This power is presently manifested by His headship over the church—1:23

C. Paul discusses how the blessings of God are executed individually and corporately on people in order to show that the work is entirely of God's grace thus presenting a basis of unity among believers—2:1-22

1. Paul presents how the blessings of God are executed individually in salvation in order to show the position of the individual in God's gracious plan—2:1-10

a. He discusses the old position of the individual as being dead in sins which he describes as following the ways of the world, following Satan, and following the desires of the flesh and mind thus being an object of wrath in order to show the hopeless condition before regeneration—2:1-3

b. He discusses the new position of the individual as being alive to God in order to show the grace of God which placed the believer into identification with Christ—2:4-10

1) God made them alive with Christ—2:4-5

2) God raised them up with Christ—2:6a

3) God seated them with Christ in heavenly places—2:6b

4) God did these things so that in the eternal state He may display the riches of His grace—2:7

5) He expands on the riches of His grace by noting that grace is the basis for this action and faith is the means which is seen by the fact that the believer is God's workmanship for whom He has prepared a path of good works—2:8-10

Note #181: To what does "that" refer?

There is debate which centers on the use of "that" (τουτο) in verse 2:8. Some have suggested that it refers back to grace and others to faith. However, it is probably best to take it as a reference to the entire concept of salvation which has grace as its basis and faith as its means. Thus the point is that salvation has its source in God. This is supported in that the demonstrative pronoun is neuter whereas "grace" and "faith" are feminine. Further, a reference back to either of these words would be redundant. Calvin concludes: "Here we must advert to a very common error in the interpretation of this passage. Many persons restrict the word gift to faith alone. But Paul is only restating the former sentiment. His meaning is, not that faith is the gift of God, but that salvation is given to us by God, or, that we obtain it by the gift of God" (John Calvin, Commentaries on the Epistles of Paul to the Galatians and Ephesians *[Grand Rapids: Baker, 1979], 228-229).*

2. Paul presents how the blessings of God are executed corporately in salvation in order to show the position of the entire body of Christ in God's gracious plan as being on equal footing—2:11-22

a. He provides a statement of the union of Jew and Gentile into one body in light of the alienation of the Gentile—2:11-13

1) In the past the Gentiles were without Christ, aliens, strangers, without hope, and without God—2:11-12

2) In the present the Gentiles have been brought near to God and the

Jew by the blood of Christ—2:13

b. He provides an explanation of this union between Jew and Gentile in order to clarify the peace that should exist between believers and God—2:14-18

1) He asserts that peace has been provided for Jew and Gentile by Christ's breaking down the spiritual enmity between them in order that they would be reconciled—2:14-16

Note #182: The stone wall in the temple

Paul could have in mind the stone wall which separated the Court of the Gentiles from the other Jewish Courts. Josephus wrote: "When you go through these cloisters, unto the second temple, there was a partition made of stone all round, whose height was three cubits: its construction was very elegant; upon it stood pillars, at equal distances from one another, declaring the law of purity, some in Greek, and some in Roman letters, that 'no foreigner should go within that sanctuary;' for that second [court of the] temple was called 'the Sanctuary;' and was ascended to by fourteen steps from the first court" ("The Wars of the Jews," in Works of Josephus, *Translated by William Whiston [Grand Rapids: Baker, 1980], 5.5.2).*

2) He asserts that this message of peace has been preached to both Jew and Gentile so that both parties would have an introduction to the Father by the same Spirit—2:17-18

c. He states that the consequence of this union is that Jew and Gentile are fellow citizens of the same house in which God lives by His Spirit—2:19-22

D. Paul presents a parenthetical expansion on the mystery about which he has just spoken in order to emphasize its reality to Jew and Gentile— 3:1-13

Note #183: The mystery

The word "mystery" in the Bible does not refer to something that is spooky, mysterious, or ethereal. Rather, the word "mystery" refers to something which to this point of time had not been revealed. First, it is important to point out what the mystery is not. It is not Gentile salvation for this was revealed in the Old Testament in the Abrahamic Covenant. Also, it is not the <u>*existence*</u> *of the Church (though this is not revealed in the OT). Rather, the mystery deals with the* <u>*nature*</u> *of the Church, namely, that the Jew and Gentile are on equal footing in this dispensation.*

That the nature of the church was a mystery does not *imply that the church was an afterthought in God's plan. Yet this continues to be a caricature of dispensationalists by some. For example, "How terribly wrong it is for those who call themselves Dispensationalists to say that the Christian Church was a mere afterthought in the mind of God, that He had never really intended it in eternity...The greatest thing in the universe, the greatest manifestation of God's own wisdom, an afterthought" (D. M. Lloyd-Jones,* The Unsearchable Riches of Christ: An Exposition of Ephesians 3 *[Grand Rapids: Baker, 1981], 86)!*

1. He is about to offer a prayer based on the preceding section but digresses to speak about the mystery—3:1

2. He describes the mystery in order to show that it involves the equal share of God's spiritual blessings—3:2-6
   a. He states that there was given to him an administration of God's grace—3:2
   b. He states that this administration was revealed to him but was not revealed previously—3:3-5

Note #184: Restrictive or descriptive?

There is a question related to the comparative adverb "as" (ὡς) in verse 5. Generally, amillennialists normally take it in a restrictive sense which would mean that the mystery was partially revealed in the Old Testament. Others take it to be descriptive which would mean that no revelation of the mystery was given in the Old Testament. There are several reasons which make the descriptive sense the better option: 1) both senses are found in the New Testament, 2) contextually, Paul states that this was not revealed formerly (v. 5), and 3) the parallel passage in Colossians 1:26 states that this was not revealed in the Old Testament.

   c. He defines the mystery as being the enjoyment of God's spiritual blessings by Jew and Gentile alike on the same plane—3:6
3. He discusses his ministry in spreading this mystery to the Gentiles—3:7-12
   a. He was graciously put into the ministry by God—3:7-8a
   b. He preached to the Gentiles the unsearchable riches of Christ and to make plain the administration of this ministry in order to show how his ministry functioned—3:8b-9
   c. He states that the purpose of this was that the wisdom of God in this mystery be displayed to the angelic hosts—3:10-12
4. He tells the Ephesians not to be discouraged at his sufferings because he was suffering due to the glory of this message—3:13

E. Paul prays that the Ephesians would experience Christ's love so that they would exhibit love toward another as they comprehended God's work in this new arrangement of the body—3:14-21

1. He approaches God the Father for this prayer—3:14-15
2. The content of the prayer is that the Ephesians would be strengthened in the inner man which would result in Christ being the dominating factor in their lives—3:16-17a
3. The purpose of the prayer is that the Ephesians would comprehend and know experientially the love of Christ and be filled with the fullness of God—3:17b-19
4. Paul concludes his prayer with an ascription of praise in order to show what God can accomplish between both Jew and Gentile—3:20-21

III. PAUL PRESENTS THE PRACTICE WHICH SHOULD RESULT FROM THE POSITION OF THE BELIEVER IN ORDER TO SHOW THE UNITY AND LOVE WHICH SHOULD BE PRESENT IN THE CHURCH BECAUSE OF THEIR INDIVIDUAL AND CORPORATE UNITY—4:1-6:20

A. Paul explains how the church is to walk in unity through the use of spiritual gifts so that they would grow up into a mature body—4:1-16

1. He exhorts the church to unity and shows its elements in order to provide the basis for their unity together—4:1-6
   a. He exhorts them to unity by asking them to walk worthy of their vocation (the call to unity) by loving one another and thereby maintaining their unified position—4:1-3
   b. He explains to them that the elements of unity are based on the three persons of the Trinity—4:4-6
2. He discusses the gifted believers which were given to the church in order to show the means of preserving unity in the body—4:7-16
   a. He notes the fact that various gifts were provided to different people—4:7-11

Note #185: The right to give gifts

Paul refers to Psalm 68 in order to confirm Christ's right to give gifts. The point in the psalm is that a military victor has the right to give gifts to those identified with him. Regarding Ephesians, Christ captured the enemies of the believer (the world, the devil, the flesh, cf. 2:1-3) and rescued sinful men by redeeming them and gave them as gifts to the church. There is some debate over the meaning of the phrase "he descended into the lower parts of the earth." Some have suggested that this is a genitive of comparison by which they posit that Christ descended into hades after his death and released Old Testament saints from one of the compartments and took them to paradise. This seems to read a lot into this passage, assumes that Old Testament saints did not go immediately into the presence of God, does not fit the context dealing with spiritual gifts, and fails to note that in Psalm 68 the ones taken captive are enemies not believers. Two options that would be better are to take "of the earth" as a genitive of apposition, "he descended into the lower parts that is the earth," i.e. the incarnation, or a genitive of possession, "he descended into the lower parts which belong to the earth," i.e., the grave. It should also be pointed out that there is a textual issue regarding the word "first" in the phrase "he also descended first into the lower parts of the earth" (KJV). As reflected in all the other translations, the word "first" should be omitted. If this is the case, then this would weaken the concept that Christ descended into hades (W. Hall Harris III, "The Ascent and Descent of Christ in Ephesians 4:9-10," Bibliotheca Sacra *151:602 [Apr 1994], 201-202; in this article, Harris argues that the "descent" is a reference to Pentecost).*

Note #186: Apostle, prophet, evangelist, pastor, teacher

Apostle. When the term "apostle" is used in its technical sense it carries the idea of "one who is sent bearing Christ's full authority." In the New Testament the apostle had at least six characteristics: a direct call from Christ; a direct witness of the ministry of Jesus; a direct witness of the resurrection of Jesus; a recipient of direct revelation; infallibility when speaking from the apostolic office; the ability to perform miracles. It is doubtful that any person today has any one of these characteristics, not to mention all six, therefore it is concluded that this office is not functioning today.

Prophet. A prophet is essentially a spokesperson for God. The ministry of a prophet usually consisted in giving a message from God to meet a local need, and on rarer occasions predicting the future. The common denominator in both of these functions was the reception of direct revelation. Since God is not directly speaking to people today, the office of prophet has ceased. Accordingly, as Paul states in Ephesians 2:20, the church is built on the foundation *of the apostles and prophets.*

Evangelist. The evangelist has been variously described as one who is unusually successful in presenting the gospel; as one who teaches people in the church how to evangelize; or, a type of revivalist. The term "evangelist" occurs only 3 times in the New Testament. The Ephesians 4 text just mentions the title but says nothing about function. Another use occurs in 2 Timothy 4:5 where Paul simply tells Timothy to do the work of an evangelist, but again with no explanation. The final use is in Acts 8 which relates to the ministry of Philip. This passage is unique because it is the only text where the evangelist's activities are seen. Philip travels to Samaria to preach and while he is there he performs several miracles including exorcism and healing. He is then told by an angel to leave the area. This ministry description leaves two alternatives: 1) the evangelist, Scripturally described, was a temporary office due to the miraculous nature of Philip's ministry. If this is correct, the responsibility of the Church to evangelize is still in place, but to be distinguished from the miraculous ministry evident in the book of Acts, or 2) the work of the evangelist is to take place outside of the church in bringing the gospel to those who have not heard—much like a modern missionary.

Pastor. The term for "pastor" (ποιμήν) is used 18 times in the New Testament with the sense of a "shepherd." In this instance, a pastor is one who gently cares for those to whom he ministers.

Teacher. The word "teacher" (διδάσκαλος) is used 59 times in the New Testament and refers to one who gives instructions based on what has been revealed in Scripture.

One of the major areas of discussion regarding pastors and teachers in this passage relates to the fact that in the Greek text one article governs the two nouns (τοὺς δὲ ποιμένας καὶ διδασκάλους // article-pastor-and-teacher). The question is whether these are two distinct offices to be translated "pastors and teachers," or one office to be translated "pastor-teacher." Wallace argues that the two offices are distinct but that there is some overlap between the two, and that to see this as one office is to misuse the Granville Sharp Rule (Wallace, Greek Grammar Beyond the Basics, *284). Thus, "these two gifts, pastoring and teaching, are distinct although it could be said that all pastors should be teachers but not all teachers are pastors" (Hoehner,* Ephesians: An Exegetical Commentary, *545).*

b. He notes that the purpose of these gifted men was to do the work of the ministry so that the body would be edified and unified—4:12-16

B. Paul discusses various injunctions to be worked out on a personal level in order to show how the unity of the body could be put into practice—4:17-32

1. He presents the nature and practice of the old man which shows what the believer was before his new position in the unified body in order to show how they should not act—4:17-19

2. He presents the nature and practice of the new man which shows what the believer is after his new position in the unified body in order to show how they should act—4:20-32

a. He shows the new position of the believer in Christ which shows them they should not live as they once did in order to show the basis for their behavior—4:20-24

b. He shows the new practice that should result in their lives from this new position—4:25-32

1) They are to be truthful with one another because they are members of Christ's body—4:25
2) They are to control their anger so that Satan would not gain a foothold in leading them into sin—4:26-27 (I am taking the NIV translation here, "in your anger do not sin," rather than an imperative to righteous anger as in the majority of other translations)
3) They are to work so that they would have something to share with others—4:28
4) They are to speak helpful words so as to edify each other —4:29
5) They are not to grieve the Spirit who has sealed them to the day of redemption—4:30
6) They are to be kind and compassionate because Christ in God is compassionate to the believer—4:31-32

C. Paul discusses that the believer should walk in love toward one another in order to give further demonstration of how unity is achieved in the body—5:1-6

1. He states that they should walk in love toward one another as an imitator of God—5:1-2
2. He states that they should abstain from evil practices because the ones who do such things do not inherit the kingdom of God—5:3-6

D. Paul discusses that the believer should walk in the light because of his new position—5:7-14

1. He instructs them not to become involved with evildoers because they have a changed position but rather to walk as children of light—5:7-10
2. He instructs them not to become involved with the works of evildoers but rather expose them because their works are shameful—5:11-14

E. Paul discusses that they should walk in wisdom by being filled with the Holy Spirit in order to show the enablement that is available to maintain unity and love—5:15-6:9

1. He admonishes them to skillful living in a manner that makes use of opportunities because the days are evil—5:15-16
2. He instructs them on the state of filling so that they would be able to walk in wisdom—5:17-21
   - **a.** He admonishes them not to be unwise but to understand what the will of God is so that they can carry it out—5:17
   - **b.** He notes that this wise conduct begins to works itself out when the believer is empowered by the Spirit—5:18-21

Note #187: Spirit filling

The concept of Spirit filling is significant enough to merit more extensive comment. The following observations (and some interpretation) can be noted.

1) *Spirit filling is not to be confused with the Spirit's work in baptism, indwelling, sealing, or witness.*
2) *There are three categories of Spirit filling to be seen as distinct in the New Testament. The first is an endowment of power for a lifelong ministry. This is rare but probably in view with John the Baptist (who was "filled" from his*

mother's womb), Saul's filling in Damascus after his conversion, and Jesus' endowment with the Spirit after his baptism. The second category is an occasion of power. This is given to individuals for an immediate task. This is an event of filling not a state of filling. The third category is found in the Ephesians 5 passage in which is envisioned an obedient, mature Christian walking in obedience in whose life the Spirit is producing His fruit.

3) *The word "*pimplemi*" (πίμπλημι) is used for the category 2 filling noted above. This is an event not a state. This has no conditions and is sovereignly bestowed by the Spirit.*
4) *The word "*pleres*" (πλήρης) is an abiding condition of Spirit fullness and is used for category 3 above. This is a state which need not be sought or prayed for. It is experienced when the believer walks in obedience to God's Word. Important in this regard is to notice Colossians 3:16. As the believer allows the word of Christ to dwell in him richly, the same results accrue as found in Ephesians 5:18-21.*
5) *The Spirit fullness of category 3 is demonstrable by character qualities as illustrated by Ephesians 5:19ff and Acts 6:3, for example.*
6) *Spirit fullness is not presented in the NT as a "struggling" concept. That is, it is characteristic of an obedient Christian.*
7) *Spirit filling is mentioned only one time in Paul's epistles. This leads to the conclusion that Spirit filling is simply one "metaphor" for looking at the responsibility the believer has in the Christian life—living in obedience to God's Word with the expectation that the Spirit will be at work in the life of the obedient Christian. In other words, "filling" as something distinct is not the "secret" to the Christian life.*
8) *Since all Christians possess the Spirit and all that is necessary for life and godliness, there is not a crisis moment or event which will bring the believer to a state of victory or new dimension of spirituality.*
9) *The idea of the "filling" as "control" should be eliminated as this implies passivity on the part of the believer. The analogy with drunkenness in 5:18 should not be understood as "control" but rather as source. Just as drunkenness is the source of debauchery, so obedience to the Spirit is the source of the experience of fullness.*
10) *Paul notes five results (all participles) in 19-21 of being filled with the Spirit as: speaking, singing, making music, giving thanks, and submitting. Notice that no spectacular manifestations of the Spirit are mentioned.*

Note #188: The function of verse 21 in the argument

The question arises as to whether verse 21 should be included with the preceding or following section. The answer to this question seems to be both. It is linked to the previous section by virtue of the fact that it is another participial clause appended to plerousthe *("be filled" 5:18). Syntactically, therefore, since the word is a participle rather than an imperative, it should be linked with the previous section. However, it is also to be noted that verse 22 does not include a verb of its own thus assuming that the verb is being carried over from verse 21.*

This raises the further question as to whether Paul is suggesting a mutual submission between husband and wife, for example. This is unlikely for three reasons: 1) the carryover of the verb of verse 21 is a heading for the entire section and not just the husband/wife section. Therefore, the three examples that follow (husband/wife; parent/child; slave/master) involve submission from different parties, not mutual submission within each arrangement, 2) the meaning of the word "submit" has the idea of a chain of command where one person subordinates themself to another, 3) it is possible to serve someone (the man the wife) without necessarily being subordinate to that person, and 4) the "to one another" phrase could be looking back at the preceding section of activity in the body of Christ.

3. He applies his exhortation to be filled with the Spirit in everyday relationships—5:22-6:9
  a. He applies his exhortation to the husband and wife relationship—5:22-33
    1) He tells wives to submit themselves to their husbands—5:22-24
    2) He tells husbands to love their wives as Christ loved the church—5:25-27
    3) He applies the preceding illustration by noting that as the church is an extension of Christ so the wife is an extension of the husband and one flesh—5:28-33
  b. He applies his exhortation to the child and parent relationship—6:1-4
    1) He tells children to obey and honor (take care of in their old age) their parents for this pleases the Lord, and will result in the likelihood that their children will care for them—6:1-3
    2) He tells fathers not to exasperate their children but rear and instruct them in the knowledge of the Lord—6:4
  c. He applies his exhortation to the slave and master relationship—6:5-9
    1) He tells slaves to obey their masters with respect, fear, sincerity, etc. so that, the Lord would reward them—6:5-8
    2) He tells masters to treat their slaves in the same way for they too are servants of an impartial master—6:9

F. Paul discusses the resources available to the believer to stand against evil forces so that they would understand that the demonic world is fighting against the love and unity of the body—6:10-20
  1. He admonished them to be strong in the Lord by putting on God's armor so that they would be able to stand against the schemes of Satan—6:10-13
  2. He instructs them on the various pieces of armor they are to employ—6:14-17
  3. He instructs them on the method they are to use as they take up the armor—6:18-20

IV. PAUL PRESENTS THE CONCLUSION TO THE LETTER BY TELLING THEM THAT TYCHICUS WOULD INFORM THEM ON HIS CONDITION, SALUTING THEM, AND INVOKING GOD'S GRACE ON ALL WHO LOVE THE LORD—6:21-24

PHILIPPIANS

Introduction

Paul first visited the city of Philippi on his second missionary journey. During his stay several people trusted Christ including Lydia, a demon-possessed girl, and the Philippian jailer (Acts 16). Soon after this, a church was established in the city.

Philippi was a fortified city of Macedonia, and as a Roman colony was granted the *Jus Italicum* (privileges of Italian citizens) which put it on the level of Roman colonies in Italy. The city became a military colony in 42 BC when Octavian won the battle of Philippi. Following the battle of Actium in 31 BC, in which Octavian defeated Anthony, its status was raised. Octavian forced some of the people in Italy to give up their homes there and live in Philippi. In exchange, they were given autonomous government, freedom from tribute, and all of the privileges of Roman citizenship (this provides the historical background for 3:20).

Author

Most scholars agree that Paul wrote the letter to the Philippians. This is supported internally by the claim in 1:1 and the reference to Timothy who was with Paul when he evangelized Philippi (Acts 16). The biographical section in 3:4-6 also harmonizes with this. Externally, Pauline authorship is attested by the church fathers.

Date and Origin

Philippians 1:7, 13, and 16 state that Paul was a prisoner when he wrote this letter. The problem is to identify whether this was the Caesarean, Ephesian, or Roman imprisonment. It is the view of the writer that the Roman imprisonment is in view which is given in Acts 28. This has several supports: 1) the reference to the "Praetorium" in 1:13 and "Caesar's household" in 4:22 indicate the imperial palace in Rome, 2) according to Philippians, Paul is anticipating judgment of either life or death which seems to fit only with the Roman imprisonment, and 3) the freedom to correspond and receive guests best fits with the Roman situation. Thus, the epistle originated from Rome and was written around AD 61 or 62.

Occasion

When the Philippians heard about Paul's imprisonment in Rome, they sent Epaphroditus to visit him and bring him a gift. While Epaphroditus was in Rome, he apparently became gravely ill (2:27). He did eventually recover, however, and was ready to return to Philippi. Paul took this occasion to pen the letter and send it back with him.

Purpose

From the historical occasion of the epistle, it can be seen that one of Paul's purposes in writing was to thank the Philippian church for their generous gift (see also 4:10-18). However, from an examination of the major portion of the contents of the book it can be seen that Paul had other concerns as well. It appears that one of the key verses in determining the major thrust of the epistle is 1:27-29. In this passage, Paul tells them to be united as they stand firmly in the Gospel regardless of what opposition they might face. Consequently, in 1:12-26 Paul speaks of the advance of the gospel amid his persecution; in 1:27-2:30 he speaks of their need to stand firmly in unity with one another; and in 3:1-27 he warns them about their enemies in the gospel. He then repeats his exhortation to unity in 4:1-3 as well as exhorting them to other Christian virtues. In light of this, a message and purpose statement could be as follows: Paul instructs the Philippians regarding the advance of the gospel amid persecution, the need for humility and unity, and opposition to false teachers in order to encourage them to a firm and united stand in their witness for the gospel.

Summary of Argument

I. PAUL INTRODUCES THE LETTER BY GREETING THE CHURCH IN PHILIPPI, PRAISING THEM FOR THEIR CONDUCT, AND PRAYING THAT THEIR LOVE WOULD ABOUND IN ORDER TO SHOW THEM HIS LOVE FOR THEM AND HIS CONCERN FOR THEIR CONTINUED ADVANCEMENT—1:1-11

A. Paul greets the church by identifying himself and the recipients of the letter—1:1-2

1. Paul sends greetings from himself and Timothy noting that they are servants of Christ in order to give an example of humility—1:1a

2. Paul identifies the recipients of the letter as the church in Philippi upon whom he invokes God's grace and peace—1:1b-2

B. Paul praises the church for their behavior in the gospel in order to show his appreciation and love for them—1:3-8

1. Paul praises them for their constant witness of the gospel—1:3-6

Note #189: He who has begun a good work

Though often used as a proof-text for eternal security and/or perseverance of the saints, there is good contextual reason to believe that Paul is not dealing with salvation/sanctification. Rather the phrase "good work" in verse 6 is referring back to the term "fellowship" (κοινωνία) in 1:5. The use of the term in Philippians would argue that this is a reference to the financial participation in Paul's efforts to preach the gospel (John Hart, "Does Philippians 1:6 Guarantee Progressive Sanctification?" A paper delivered at the annual meeting of the Evangelical Theological Society, November 1995).

2. Paul praises them for concern for the gospel as is seen in their aid of Paul—1:7

3. Paul affirms his love for the Philippians—1:8

C. Paul prays for the church that they would grow in love and in the fruit of righteousness in order to show his desire that they continue in their progress so that they would be blameless at Christ's coming—1:9-11

1. Paul prays that they would grow in their love so that they would be discerning and pure until the day of Christ—1:9-10

2. Paul prays that they would be filled with the fruit of righteousness so that God would be glorified—1:11

II. PAUL INFORMS THE PHILIPPIANS ABOUT HIS SITUATION IN ROME IN ORDER TO SHOW THEM THAT THE GOSPEL CAN ADVANCE DESPITE OPPOSITION AND IN LIGHT OF THIS THEY ALSO MUST STAND FIRM IN THE GOSPEL REGARDLESS OF THE OPPOSITION THEY FACE FROM FALSE TEACHERS—1:12-30

A. Paul tells the Philippians that the circumstances he faced in Rome were resulting in the furtherance of the gospel to show them that the cause of Christ continues despite opposition—1:12-18
 1. He informs them that his imprisonment has advanced the gospel because the palace knows that he was arrested for the cause of Christ which has resulted in additional boldness for other brethren—1:12-14
 2. He informs them that some preach Christ from good motives and others preach Christ from bad motives but either way the message was getting out and in this he rejoiced—1:15-18

B. Paul tells the Philippians that he is confident of his eventual release from prison and his return to minister to them again—1:19-26
 1. He states that because of their prayers for him he was confident that he would be delivered—1:19
 2. He states his hope that he would have courage whether he lived or died so that Christ would be exalted—1:20
 3. He states that he has this desire in life or death because if he lived it was for Christ, but if he died this would be to his gain—1:21
 4. He states the quandary whether he desired to live or die—1:22-24
 5. He repeats that he felt that he would probably remain alive so that he would be able to continue with them in the progress of the gospel—1:25-26

C. Paul applies his condition in Rome to the Philippian believers by exhorting them in their situation so that they would understand that for them suffering was a part of the gospel—1:27-30
 1. He tells them that whatever happens to him they needed to conduct themselves worthy of the gospel—1:27a
 2. This conduct consisted of standing firmly in a united spirit and contending for the faith of the gospel without being frightened—1:27b-28
 3. He explains to them that in their situation belief in the gospel was also accompanied by suffering—1:29-30

III. PAUL EXHORTS THE PHILIPPIANS TO HUMILITY AND LOVE SO THAT THE CHURCH WOULD BE UNIFIED AND AN EFFECTIVE WITNESS IN THE ADVANCE OF THE GOSPEL—2:1-30

A. Paul exhorts the Philippians to unity and humility toward those within the church—2:1-11
 1. He lists four certainties they had as believers in order to provide four grounds or incentives to unity—2:1
 2. He exhorts the believers to four demonstrations of unity that could be realized in their lives based on the four certainties preceding—2:2
  a. He exhorts them to be like-minded—2:2a
  b. He exhorts them to have love for each other—2:2b

c. He exhorts them to be one in spirit—2:2c
d. He exhorts them to be one in purpose—2:2d

3. He exhorts the believers to humility and a concern for the interests of others—2:3-4
4. He provides an example from Christ in order to show the supreme illustration of humility and concern for others—2:5-11
   a. He discusses the self-emptying which Christ endured during His incarnation—2:5-8
      1) Christ existed as the very essence of God but voluntarily set some of the privileges associated with this aside—2:6
      2) Christ emptied Himself of the privileges and position of deity—2:7a
      3) Christ took the nature of a servant by means of the incarnation—2:7b
      4) Christ humbled himself to the point of enduring death on the cross—2:8
   b. He discusses the result of His humiliation by noting that God highly exalted Him to be one day worshipped by the world—2:9-11

Note #190: The kenosis

There have been a variety of views as to the meaning of the kenosis (self-emptying). These include: Christ acted as if He did not have attributes; Christ surrendered all of His attributes; Christ surrendered some of His attributes; Christ disguised His attributes; Christ ceased to be God at His incarnation, etc. However, there seem to be two demonstrable points from the text which give content to this kenosis; 1) He laid aside the independent use of His attributes by becoming obedient to the Father during His earthly ministry (this is implied in the fact that he is the ultimate Servant of the Father; see also John 8 and Hebrews 10), and 2) He laid aside His manner of existence in the glory of heaven by becoming the form of a man (seen by the phrase "made himself of no reputation").

*There are also a number of other points to be made from this passage: 1) "being" (v. 6) is in the present tense emphasizing continued existence in the past and present, 2) "form" (*morphe *in v. 6) means form, shape, or appearance. It refers to the very essence of God or that which is intrinsic or essential to a thing. Thus He is what is intrinsic to God, 3) the phrase "did not regard equality with God a thing to be grasped" (v. 6) refers to the fact that Christ voluntarily set aside His exalted position in glory, 4) "emptied" refers to his laying aside of rights, privileges, and position, 5) "taking" implies addition not exchange, and 6) "likeness" and "fashion" emphasizes outward appearance. Essentially, therefore, he emptied himself of self—which is the place to which Paul wants to bring the Philippians.*

B. Paul exhorts the Philippians to work out their salvation by being unified with each other so that they could be effective in their ministry—2:12-18
   1. He exhorts them to work out their salvation knowing that God is at work in them to provide the means to do this—2:12-13
   2. He explains to them that this working out of their salvation means that they should do everything without complaining and arguing—2:14
   3. He notes that the goal of this is that they would be blameless in the world where they shine as lights and that Paul would not have labored in vain

among them—2:15-16
4. He repeats the fact that he had joy in his sufferings and rejoiced in their sacrificial faith—2:17-18

C. Paul speaks of the ministries of Timothy and Epaphroditus in order to provide the Philippians with two examples of servants who were concerned for the welfare of others—2:19-30
1. Paul mentions the ministry of Timothy in order to provide an example of one who was genuinely interested in the welfare of the Philippians and not in his own self-promotion—2:19-24
2. Paul mentions the ministry of Epaphroditus in order to provide an example of one who almost died for the Philippians and the cause of Christ—2:25-30

IV. PAUL WARNS THE PHILIPPIANS ABOUT THE WORK OF THE JUDAIZERS SO THAT THEY WOULD BE AWARE THAT THEY WERE ENEMIES OF THE CROSS AND THAT THEY SHOULD NOT PUT CONFIDENCE IN THE WORKS OF THE FLESH BUT HAVING BEEN JUSTIFIED BY FAITH WOULD PRESS ON IN THEIR CHRISTIAN WALK—3:1-21

A. Paul warns the Philippians about the work of the Judaizers so that they would not put confidence in the flesh but press on to maturity—3:1-14
1. He introduces his exhortation by entreating them to rejoice in the Lord and tells them it is for their safeguard for him to repeat this warning about the Judaizers—3:1
2. He warns them to beware of the Judaizers as men who do evil—3:2
3. He informs the Philippians that they are the true circumcision because they put no confidence in the flesh—3:3
4. He provides the proper example for them to follow regarding the problem of putting confidence in the flesh—3:4-14
   - **a.** He notes that if anyone had the right to trust in the flesh it was he—3:4-6
     1) He was circumcised the eighth day showing that as a boy he was circumcised according to the Law (Lev. 12:3)—3:4-5a
     2) He was of the stock of Israel showing that he was not a proselyte but one who could trace his lineage to Abraham—3:5b
     3) He was of the tribe of Benjamin showing that he was of the tribe that remained faithful during the division of the kingdom and from where Israel's first king came—3:5c
     4) He was a Hebrew of the Hebrews showing that he did not have mixed parents and knew Hebrew customs, language, etc.—3:5d
     5) He was a Pharisee showing that he was a member of the strictest and most orthodox sect touching the Law—3:5e
     6) He persecuted the church showing that no one could match his zeal in promoting Judaism—3:6a
     7) He was blameless in the Law showing that he meticulously adhered to all of its externals—3:6b
   - **b.** He notes that he considered all of these things worthless so that he could be found in Christ and thus gain a righteousness that is by faith apart from the Law—3:7-9

Note #191: The structure of 3:7-11

The structure of 3:7-11 is somewhat difficult. This outline understands them as follows: verses 7-9 are speaking of justification with verses 8-9 being parenthetical of verse 7; verses 10-11 are speaking of sanctification.

- **c.** He notes that having been justified he wanted to continue to know Christ in a deeper way, know the power and suffering that came from that, and to be a part of the resurrection from the dead—3:10-11

Note #192: The out-resurrection

Verse 11 seems to express doubt on Paul's part as to whether he would attain this resurrection or that he had to somehow earn it. The word translated "resurrection" literally means an "out-resurrection" i.e. out from other dead ones (ἐξανάστασις—used only here in the New Testament). This possibly is to be seen as reference to the rapture because of the partial nature suggested by the word. Therefore, the doubt which Paul expresses could be due to the fact that he did not know if he would be alive or dead at this event. In addition, the phrase translated "if by any means" could be translated as "and so somehow." This phrase (ἔι πως) occurs four times in the New Testament (Acts 27:12; Rom. 1:10; 11:14; Phil. 3:11) and each time reflects uncertainty about the matter stated, whether regarding its achievement or the manner in which it would be achieved. In summary, since Paul never expresses doubt in his epistles about the resurrection, he must be expressing uncertainty as to whether he would come to experience the time of resurrection to occur at the rapture.

- **d.** He notes that in light of this goal he vigorously presses on to his ultimate salvation in God's presence where he would be rewarded at the judgment seat of Christ—3:12-14

B. Paul instructs the Philippians on how to be wary of the Judaizers so as to protect them against their influence—3:15-21

1. He exhorts the Philippians to have a mature outlook of the things he has just spoken about and to live up to the light they had already received—3:15-16

2. He exhorts the Philippians to be watchful for their enemies and provides two reasons for this exhortation—3:17-21

- **a.** He tells them to be watchful for those who walk contrary to the pattern about which he had told them—3:17
- **b.** The first reason is that they are enemies of the cross, their end is destruction, and their present state is one of shame and carnality—3:18-19
- **c.** The second reason is that they are citizens of heaven from which will come the Savior and transform their bodies through the power which will enable him to put all things under His control— 3:20-21

V. PAUL PRESENTS A SERIES OF EXHORTATIONS IN ORDER TO PERSUADE THE PHILIPPIANS TO UNITY AND STEADFASTNESS AND THE DEVELOPMENT OF CHRISTIAN VIRTUES--4:l-9

A. He exhorts the Philippians to steadfastness and unity—4:1-3

1. He expresses his love for them and exhorts them to stand firmly—4:1
2. He singles out two women to iron out their differences and become united in the Lord—4:2-3

B. He exhorts the Philippians to develop various Christian virtues—4:4-9

1. He exhorts them to rejoice in the Lord—4:4
2. He exhorts them to gentleness because of the imminence of the Lord's return—4:5
3. He exhorts them to not be anxious but to trust in the Lord so that they would have God's peace which is beyond man's ability to understand—4:6-7
4. He exhorts them to think worthy thoughts—4:8
5. He exhorts them to be obedient to the things they ought to do and states the fact that the God of peace is with them—4:9

VI. PAUL PRAISES THE PHILIPPIANS FOR THEIR GIFT TO HIM AND TAKES THAT OPPORTUNITY TO EXPRESS TO THEM THAT GOD ENABLED HIM TO BE CONTENT REGARDLESS OF THE CIRCUMSTANCES AND THAT HE WAS CONFIDENT THAT GOD WOULD MEET THEIR NEEDS AS WELL—4:10-20

A. Paul praises them for their concern for him and notes that God has provided the strength for him to be content in every circumstance— 4:10-13

Note #193: I can do all things?

When Paul says in this verse that he can do "all things" through Christ who strengthens him. The "all things" of verse 13 are defined in verses 11-12. Verse 13, therefore, is a summary statement that he is able to be content in whatever circumstances God may bring. Thus contentment is achievable for the believer in any situation. This verse is not teaching that through Christ one can achieve any aspiration they may have.

B. Paul again praises them for their gift to him and expresses to them his conviction that God would meet their needs according to His glorious riches—4:14-19

Note #194: All needs met?

There obviously are times when all of the believers' needs are not met. With this in mind, there are three possible solutions: 1) Paul had a special insight from God that He would do this in the situation of the Philippians, 2) he was referring to a general wisdom principle, or 3) our needs will be met to accomplish whatever the will of God may be for us.

C. Paul praises God for His strength and provision—4:20

PAUL CONCLUDES THE LETTER WITH FINAL GREETINGS AND AN INVOCATION OF GOD'S GRACE ON ALL—4:21-23

COLOSSIANS

Occasion

The city of Colosse was situated in the Lycus Valley about 100 miles east of Ephesus. When Paul wrote the letter, the inhabitants were mainly Greek colonists although there were also Jews living there who had been relocated from Mesopotamia by Antiochus the Great (223-187 BC). The founding of the church appears to be linked with Epaphras (1:7; 4:12-13). He was a Colossian and had instructed the Christians who were there (1:7). He may have gone to Rome to acquaint Paul with the state of the gospel in the Lycus Valley and to secure Paul's help in battling the false doctrine there (1:7, 8; 4:12, 13).

There is debate over the precise identification of the Colossian heresy. Of the scores of suggestions (J. J. Gunther lists 34 views: "St. Paul's Opponents and Their Background. A Study of Apocalyptic and Jewish Sectarian Teachings," in *Novum Testamentum Supplements* [Leiden: Brill, 1973], 3-4), the basic ones include an Essene Judaism of a Gnostic variety (Lightfoot); a pagan mystery cult (Dibelius); or a syncretism of Jewish Gnosticism and pagan elements (Bornkamm). Given the fact that Paul does not give a formal expression of the heresy, only the marks of it can be deduced by examining key words he uses in the epistle. One thing that is certain is that this heresy was distorting the person and work of Christ hence the great declarations of 1:15-16 and 2:9. Furthermore, several other features can be noted: 1) it had some Jewish elements which stressed the need for observing Old Testament laws and ceremonies (2:8, 11, 16; 3:11), 2) it had some philosophical appeal perhaps emphasis on some higher knowledge (2:8), 3) it included the veneration of angels (2:18-19), 4) there was an ascetic emphasis (2:20-23), and 5) apparently an idea that only a certain elite group could experience spiritual maturity 1:20, 28; 3:11). It is probably correct to say that these emphases later developed into full-blown Greek Gnosticism, although in Colosse the Jewish element was much more prominent.

Author

External evidence for Pauline authorship is provided by the church fathers (e.g., Justin, Marcion, Irenaeus, Tertullian, Clement of Alexandria, etc.) and was not seriously questioned until the 19th century when German scholars questioned it on the basis of the letter's similarity to Ephesians, and their supposition that the heresy being combatted was 2nd century Gnosticism. The first objection does not prevent Paul from being the author, and the second assumes a full-blown Gnosticism being addressed in the letter. In addition, there are several indications of Pauline authorship: 1) first person references to Paul are found in 1:1; 2:23 and 4:18, 2) there are numerous references to Paul's associates (4:7, 9, 10, 12, 14, 17), 3) the conclusion of Ephesians confirms Tychicus as the carrier of Ephesians and Colossians (compare Eph. 6:21 and Col. 4:7), and 4) Colossians is closely linked with Philemon which enjoys strong Pauline authenticity (Col. 1:1 and Philemon 1; Col. 4:10-14 and Philemon 23-24; Col. 4:9 and Philemon 10).

Date and Origin

As has been argued for the other prison epistles, Colossians was written during Paul's Roman imprisonment. Accepting the Roman imprisonment, the book was probably written sometime between AD 60-62.

Purpose

From the occasion of the book, it becomes clear that Paul's primary purpose was to combat the false teaching that was present and to show that Christ's preeminence was sufficient for Christian living. A purpose statement could be given as follows: Paul explains the preeminence of the person and work Christ and how this is sufficient for life in order to warn the Colossians about the false teaching they were hearing and move them ahead on the proper road to maturity.

Summary of Argument:

I. PAUL INTRODUCES THE LETTER WITH A SALUTATION, THANKSGIVING, AND PRAYER FOR THE COLOSSIAN CHRISTIANS IN ORDER TO SHOW THEM HIS LOVE AND APPRECIATION—1:1-8

A. Paul begins the letter with a salutation in order to introduce himself and Timothy and to wish God's blessing on his readers—1:1-2

B. Paul expresses his thanksgiving for the Colossians so that they would know that he was aware of their progress in the gospel and rejoiced over it—1:3-8

1. When he and Timothy pray they thank God for the demonstration of their continuing trust in Christ—l:3-4a

2. They thank God for their love for other Christians—1:4b

3. They thank God for their hope in future blessings in heaven which comes from the dynamic gospel as they had heard from Epaphras—1:5-8

C. Paul prays for the Colossians that they would have full perception into God's will so that they would be able to distinguish the truth of the gospel from the falsehood of the heresy and thus glorify God in their conduct—1:9-14

1. The reason he prayed for them was the good report he had received from Epaphras—1:9a

2. The content of his prayer was that they might have full and exact knowledge of God's will for them—1:9b

3. The goal of this knowledge was that the Colossians might live in a manner which would glorify the Lord—1:10-14

a. He states the goal is to live in a way which is honoring to God—1:10a

b. He describes the content of a life which brings honor to God—1:10b-14

1) It includes bearing fruit in every good work—1:10b

2) It includes growing in the knowledge of God—1:10c

3) It includes patience which comes from the strengthening of God's power—1:11

4) It includes giving thanks to the Father—1:12-14

a) This thanks was for the fact that He qualified them to share in the inheritance of the Kingdom—1:12

b) The way He made this possible was by rescuing the believer from Satan's kingdom to God's kingdom via redemption and forgiveness—1:13-14

II. PAUL EXPLAINS THE PREEMINENT PERSON AND WORK OF CHRIST IN ORDER TO GIVE HIS READERS A FULLER INSIGHT INTO GOD'S WILL REGARDING CHRIST AND THEREBY SHOWING THEM THEY NEED TO

REJECT THE FALSE TEACHING THAT DEMEANED CHRIST —1:15-29

A. Paul expounds on the preeminent person of Christ by showing His relationship to the Father, creation, and the church—1:15-20

1. He shows His relationship to the Father by stating that He is the image of God—1:15a

Note #195: Image

"Image" (εἰκών) denotes here that Christ absolutely corresponds to the Father. He is the illumination of the inner core and essence of the Father. In other words, He is the visible representation and manifestation of God the Father. This is why Jesus said on numerous occasions, "If you have seen me, you have seen the Father" (John 1:18; 14:8-9). "What is this but to say that the very nature and being of God have been perfectly revealed in Him—that in Him the invisible has become visible" (F. F. Bruce, Commentary on the Epistle to the Colossians *[Grand Rapids: Eerdmans, 1980], 193).*

2. He shows His relationship to all creation—1:15b-17

a. He is the firstborn over all creation—1:15b

Note #196: Firstborn

The fact that Christ is the "firstborn of creation" does not mean that He was created. Rather, the word (πρωτότοκος) has the Old Testament background of primogeniture. The word implies that Christ has been appointed by the Father to have certain rights and privileges, namely, sovereignty over creation.

b. He is the origin, agent, and goal of creation in order to show why He was appointed the firstborn over all creation—1:16

c. He is pre-existent to and the sustainer of the universe—1:17-18

3. He shows His relationship to the church—1:18-20

a. Christ is the head (source of life and sovereign) over the universal church by virtue of his resurrection from the dead—1:18

b. He is supreme in the church because the totality of deity resides in Him—1:19

c. He is supreme in the church because of His work of reconciliation—1:20

Note #197: Reconciling all things

It is necessary to comment on the meaning of "reconciling all things to Himself." This verse cannot be teaching universalism because the Bible clearly states that many will be eternally damned, and the "all things" would include the angelic world which was not an object of redemption. Furthermore, it does not appear to go far enough to say that Christ's work merely put the world in a saveable state because the "all things" includes more than just mankind. It should be noted that peace can either be freely accepted or forcefully imposed. Bruce has commented well: "The principalities and powers whose conquest by Christ is described in 2:15 are certainly not depicted there as gladly surrendering to his grace, but as submitting against their wills to a power which they cannot resist. Everything in the universe has been subjected to Christ...By His reconciling work, the hosts of the high ones on high and sinful men on earth have been decisively subdued to the will of God" (Bruce, Commentary on the Epistle to the Colossians, *210).*

B. Paul expounds on the preeminent work of Christ in reconciliation as was seen in the experience of the Colossians and as was ministered by himself in order to give further assurance of the truth of the gospel— 1:21-29

1. Paul reminds the Colossians of their experience of reconciliation—1:21-23

a. They were once enemies of God—1:21

b. They were reconciled by the death of Christ so that they could be presented to God as blameless—1:22

c. This would be the case if they continued in the faith which was proclaimed to the whole world—1:23

Note #198: Perseverance, loss of salvation, or reward?

The discussion about 1:23 centers around how the phrase "if you continue in the faith" relates to 1:21-22. The "calvinistic" view asserts that continuing in the faith is a necessary mark of salvation, even a means of salvation. Therefore, if one does not persevere, then the individual was never truly saved. The "arminian" view asserts that one can be a true believer, but if perseverance in the faith does not occur, then salvation is lost. A third option is to be preferred and can be laid out through a number of propositions: 1) the book is written to believers. Colossians 1:1-14 could not make this clearer, 2) these believers are being warned of being led astray by false teaching, 3) the conditional statement in 1:23 goes back to the presentation before God in 1:22. This concept frequently refers to the believer's evaluation at the judgment seat (e.g. Rom 14:10), and 4) this fits with Paul's statement later in the chapter that he hopes to present his readers as mature at the judgment seat (1:28).

2. Paul reminds the Colossians of the message of reconciliation he ministered to the Gentiles in order for them to understand more fully this message and thereby press on to maturity—1:24-29

a. Paul tells the Colossians that suffering was a part of God's plan in order to qualify what he had just said about the success of the gospel—1:24

Note #199: Filling up the sufferings of Christ

Paul says that his sufferings somehow filled up what was lacking in the sufferings of Christ. This is, perhaps, the most difficult verse in the letter. Johnson has noted that τηλιπσεον *(translated here as "suffering") is never used in the New Testament of the atoning suffering of Christ (S. Lewis Johnson, "Studies in the Epistle to the Colossians Part V: The Minister of the Mystery," Bibliotheca Sacra 119:475 [Jul 1962], 229). Johnson lists four options suggested for this verse (230-231). 1) Christ's afflictions refer to the quota of suffering the church is destined to undergo, but this is foreign to the context which speaks of the contribution of Paul's sufferings to the welfare of the Colossians, 2) Paul was saying his sufferings were similar to Christ's, 3) the sufferings are sacrificial works which Christ left for believers to perform, but this would be a strange way to refer to Christ's afflictions, and 4) the afflictions of Christ are Christ's actual suffering now through Paul whom He indwelt. When the believer suffers, Christ suffers (Acts 9:4). The best option is probably #4.*

- **b.** Paul tells the Colossians that his message proclaimed to the Gentiles was the mystery that they could be on an equal spiritual plane with the Jew in this dispensation by virtue of Christ's indwelling of them which was a pledge that they would share in His future glory—1:25-27
- **c.** Paul tells the Colossians that the purpose in this message was to have people become mature in Christ—1:28
- **d.** Paul tells the Colossians that the enabling he had to do this came from the indwelling Christ who energized him—1:29

III. PAUL WARNS THE COLOSSIANS ABOUT THE PHILOSOPHIES OF MEN SO THAT THEY WOULD SHUN ERRONEOUS TEACHING AND PERSERVERE IN THE TRUTH—2:1-23

A. Paul exhorts the Colossians to persevere in the truth so that they would not drift into heresy—2:1-7

1. He states that he is concerned for them—2:1
2. He states that his goal is that they would have complete understanding so that they would understand the truth about Christ—2:2-3
3. He notes that thus far they were standing firmly but that he was concerned that this state would continue—2:4-5
4. He states the exhortation in which he urges them that just as they had accepted Christ as Lord and Master so they would continue in conduct that conformed to that doctrine—2:6
5. He describes the walk in which they were to continue with four participles—2:7
   - **a.** They had been permanently rooted (perfect tense)—2:7a
   - **b.** They were to continue being built up like a building—2:7b
   - **c.** They were to continue to be strengthened in the faith—2:7c
   - **d.** They were to continue to abound in thanksgiving—2:7d

B. Paul explains the true doctrine of Christ to the Colossians in order to provide reasons to abandon the false teaching and encourage them to remain faithful to this revelation they had received—2:8-15

1. He instructs them to not be fooled by philosophies of men which are empty and based on human tradition rather than on Christ—2:8

Note #200: Is philosophy bad?

"Philosophy" does not mean here the study of the basic questions of life and is therefore not a prohibition of Christians being involved in that field. Rather the term refers to the false ideas and speculations of false teachers.

2. He instructs them that Christ is sufficient for all their needs for in Him is deity and they are partakers of His fullness—2:9-10
3. He shows the sufficiency of Christ as it is seen in three things he has done for the believer—2:11-15
   a. The domination of the sinful nature was done away (spiritual circumcision) by means of the Spirit baptism into Christ—2:11-12
   b. He has provided the forgiveness of sin—2:13-14

Note #201: The debt has been canceled

Paul states that the unregenerate had a bill of debt to God because they had violated His law. The "handwriting" was the charge of indebtedness from breaking the law. This certificate was violent against us in the sense that it justly condemned us. The "ordinances" were the regulations which had been broken. The idea is that these charges were erased by placing them on Christ at the cross. Bruce writes, "Those sins represented, so to speak, a mountain of bankruptcy which you were bound to acknowledge, but could never have any hope of discharging. You had violated the ordinances of the law, and nothing that you might do could afford redress...He took that signed confession of indebtedness which stood as a perpetual witness against you, and cancelled it in His death; you might actually say that He took the document, ordinances and all, and nailed it to His cross as an act of triumphant defiance in the face of those blackmailing powers who were holding it over you as a threat" (Bruce, Commentary on the Epistle to the Colossians, *238).*

   c. He rendered inoperative the claims of the demonic on the believer—2:15

C. Paul explains the false doctrines of men in order to contrast them with the truth he has just presented so that his readers could more easily identify them—2:16-23
   1. He warns them about Jewish errors including dietary and festal observances which legitimately foreshadowed Christ but had now been done away—2:16-17
   2. He warns them about mystic errors involving self-abasement and the appeal to angels for this causes pride and a disconnection from the growth that is available in Christ—2:18-19

Note #202: Were the Colossians worshipping angels?

*All of the major translations of 2:18 say something about the "worship" of angels. The word translated "worship" is θρησκεία (*threskeia*) which is used four times in the New Testament (Acts 26:5; Colossians 2:18; James 1:26, 27). Most commentaries suggest various scenarios for what was occurring but there appears to be a consensus that there was some type of angelic veneration taking place. The question to be asked is, why was this occurring? At the end of his discussion, James Dunn interestingly writes: "these angels could be seen within the 'philosophy' as either benevolent, and therefore to be worshiped to attain their blessing, or malevolent, and therefore to be appeased" (James Dunn, The Epistles to the Colossians and to Philemon,* New International Greek Testament Commentary *[Grand Rapids: Eerdmans, 1996], 179). It is quite possible that the "worship" of angels involved calling on them for protection. Arnold has observed* *that "there are many inscriptions from Asia Minor mentioning angels. Most of these are invocations to angels for protection, deliverance, or assistance" (Clinton Arnold, "Colossians," in* Zondervan Illustrated Bible Backgrounds Commentary *[Grand Rapids: Zondervan, 2002], 390). Within Judaism, there was also a penchant for calling on an angel to thwart the working of a demon who was believed to be behind a particular ailment (391).*

3. He warns them about ascetic errors of buffeting the body and abstaining from things to gain God's favor—2:20-23

IV. PAUL EXHORTS THE COLOSSIANS IN AREAS OF PRACTICAL CHRISTIAN LIVING IN ORDER TO SHOW THEM THAT THE TRUE DOCTRINE OF CHRIST LEADS TO HOLINESS—3:1-4:6

A. He states the doctrinal basis for Christian living and general exhortations based on that doctrine so that they would see that their practice should grow out of their position—3:1-4

1. He states the premise that the believer has been united to Christ—3:1a

2. He urges them to set their hearts and seek earnestly the things above where Christ is seated at the right hand of God—3:1b

3. He urges them to set their minds on things above where their lives are safely deposited—3:2-4

B. He states the proper method for the above exhortation to show them how to work out this position in their lives—3:5-17

1. He urges them to violently put to death the sinful practices which stem from their earthly nature because these things bring the wrath of God—3:5-7

2. He urges them to put off sins of speech since these belong to their old self rather than to their new self which is in a process of development for both Jew and Greek—3:8-11

3. He urges them to put on positive virtues in order to replace the things they had taken off—3:12-17

a. Paul provides a list of virtues to be developed in interpersonal relationships because they are God's chosen people—3:12-14

b. Paul provides a list of four imperatives they should follow—3:15-17

1) They were to let the peace of God rule in their hearts—3:15a

2) They were to be thankful—3:15b

3) They were to let the word of Christ dwell in them richly—3:16

4) They were to do everything in harmony with the name of Christ—3:17

C. He instructs them in the area of personal relationships in order to show them how a proper understanding of Christ should work out in these areas—3:18-4:1

1. He instructs wives to submit to their husbands and for husbands to love their wives and not be harsh with them—3:18-19

2. He instructs children to obey their parents and for fathers not to provoke their children to anger—3:20-21

3. He instructs slaves to obey their masters and to remember that their work is done primarily for the Lord; and for masters to remember that they have a Master too—3:22-4:1

D. He instructs them on three essential practices they should develop in order to impress their importance on his readers—4:2-6

1. They were to devote themselves to prayer—4:2-4

2. They were to be wise in the way they behave toward those outside the church—4:5

3. They were to speak wisely so as to mirror the character of God and make sure that their speech was appropriate for the occasion so as to provide an attractiveness to their message—4:6

V. PAUL CONCLUDES THE LETTER WITH PERSONAL INFORMATION AND INSTRUCTION AS WELL AS GREETINGS IN ORDER TO IMPRESS ON THEM THE NEED FOR UNITY IN THE MIDST OF FALSE TEACHERS—4:7-18

A. Paul notes the men that are being sent from him so that they would know that these were trustworthy and faithful men—4:7-9

B. Paul presents greetings from several of his companions in order to stress the unity they had in sound doctrine with believers—4:10-17

C. Paul concludes the letter by noting that he signed it himself so as to authenticate his authorship, request prayer for himself, and wish that God's grace would rest on them—4:18

1 THESSALONIANS

Background and Occasion

The City of Thessalonica

The city was founded in 315 BC by the Macedonian general Cassander who named the city after his wife who was the stepsister of Alexander the Great. In 146 BC Rome organized Macedonia into a province and Thessalonica was made the capital of that province.

The Inhabitants of the City

Thessalonica soon grew into the second largest city of Macedonia, the largest being Philippi, with a population of about 200,000 by the time of the New Testament. The majority of the inhabitants were native Greeks but there were also Romans, Orientals, and a sizeable number of Jews who maintained a synagogue and wielded a proselyting influence on a number of the Gentiles. Like any large city there were the poor and the rich and the low moral standards of Thessalonica would have been similar to other cities.

The Status of the City

Another point of interest about the city is that it was made a "free city" in 42 BC by Anthony and Octavian. This meant that the city was autonomous in that it controlled its internal affairs through a board of magistrates who were known as "politarchs" (a city ruler). In the New Testament, the word "politarch" is only found two places (Acts 17:6, 8) relative to Thessalonica; and, does not occur in any extant Greek literature. However, the term is found in many ancient inscriptions. For the inscriptions themselves, see Ernest Burton, "The Politarchs," *The American Journal of Theology* Volume II (July 1898), 598-632. It is true that the Roman proconsul would have resided in the city, but he did not control its internal affairs and there would have been no Roman troops stationed there.

The Geography of the City

Geographically speaking, the city had an excellent location which contributed to its success. It was located on the banks of a harbor in the Thermaic Gulf which was near the northwest corner of the Aegean Sea. In Paul's day this was the chief seaport of Macedonia. Because of this, it was one of the busiest ports in the ancient world and of course made the city conducive to commerce.

A second item of geography which was significant was that the city was located on the famous "Egnatian Way." The Egnatian Way was the main Roman road from Rome to the East and this road passed through Thessalonica. That meant that this put the city in contact with the rest of the world and became one of the major arteries between Rome and the Eastern provinces not only by sea but by land.

Paul first visited Thessalonica on his second missionary journey accompanied by Silas and Timothy after being released from prison in Philippi. For at least three Sabbath days Paul ministered in the synagogue resulting in the salvation of many (Acts 17:2). Those who believed included Jews, proselytes, women, and pagans. When unbelieving Jews heard of the conversion of the proselytes, they stirred up a gang of bullies who attacked the home where Paul was staying. Because of the danger, Paul and Silas went by night to Berea (Acts 17:10). These same ruffians came down to Berea where Paul was ministering, causing him to go away to Athens while Silas and Timothy remained in Berea (Acts 17:14). Subsequent to this, Silas and Timothy rejoined Paul in Athens where Paul sent Silas back to Philippi and Timothy back to Thessalonica (Acts 17:15; 1 Thess. 4:11). Later, both men returned to Paul in Corinth with reports of their trips (Acts 18:3, 5).

It was Timothy's report of conditions within the Thessalonica church that moved Paul to write 1 Thessalonians. There were several problems which Paul wanted to address: l) the believers were being persecuted, 2) there was hostility to Paul, 3) there seems to have been some confusion over spiritual gifts, 4) there were incidents of sexual immorality, 5) some had abused the doctrine of the Lord's imminent return by quitting their jobs, and 6) some were worried that their loved ones who had died would somehow miss out on some of the blessings when the Lord returned.

Date

Given the background of the epistle, it becomes clear that Paul wrote the epistle in Corinth around AD 51. Thus, this would have been Paul's second inspired letter (Galatians being the first).

Purpose

There seem to be at least three purposes for the writing of 1 Thessalonians. The first was an encouragement to persevere in the faith despite persecution. The second was a defense by Paul of the charges brought against him. And the third was to correct some errors and give instruction in problem areas that had cropped up in the church. A purpose and message statement could be put into these words: **Paul** thanks God for the Thessalonians, reviews his ministry among them, and seeks to instruct them in certain areas in order to renew their confidence in him and enable them to persevere in the midst of persecution through a better understanding of practice and doctrine in light of the Lord's imminent return.

Summary of Argument

I. PAUL INTRODUCES THE LETTER BY IDENTIFYING HIMSELF AND HIS COMPANIONS, HIS ADDRESSEES, AND BY CONVEYING A GREETING TO THEM FROM GOD AND CHRIST— 1:1

II. PAUL PRESENTS HIS THANKSGIVING FOR THE THESSALONIANS, REVIEWS THE TYPE OF MINISTRY HE HAD WHILE HE WAS AMONG THEM, AND DISCUSSES HIS RELATIONS WITH THEM DURING HIS ABSENCE SO THAT THEY WOULD BE ENCOURAGED TO STAND FAST IN PERSECUTION AND WOULD REALIZE HIS LOVE FOR THEM SO THAT THEIR CONFIDENCE WOULD BE RENEWED—1:2-3:13

A. Paul gives thanks for several aspects of the Thessalonians' salvation in order to encourage them to stand fast in the faith despite the persecution they were facing—1:2-10

1. He states they always gave thanks for the Thessalonians in their prayers—

1:2

2. He states the reasons he gave thanks for the Thessalonians included their virtues, election, and testimony—1:3-10
   a. He thanks God for their virtues including work which was produced by faith, their labor which was prompted by love, and their patience which was inspired by hope (I am taking the three genitives as subjective)—1:3
   b. He thanks God for the assurance he had of their election—1:4-7
      1) He states that he has assurance of their election—1:4
      2) He states the first reason he had assurance of their election was the way the gospel was brought to them, namely, in power (with which the apostles were filled), in the Holy Spirit (who produced conviction), and with assurance (the certainty the apostles had of the message)—1:5
      3) He states the second reason he had assurance of their election was the effect the ministry had on the Thessalonians in that they were transformed, they welcomed the message with joy, and they became models to other believers—1:6-7
   c. He thanks God for the reports there were concerning them from other people—1:8-10
      1) Others reported that they had heard the gospel from them—1:8-9a
      2) Others reported that they had turned to God from idols to serve Him—1:9b
      3) Others reported that they were eagerly awaiting His Son from heaven—1:10

Note #203: The wrath to come

"The wrath to come" is probably a reference to the eschatological wrath that is coming in connection with the Day of the Lord during the Tribulation period. This is supported by the frequent references in the Thessalonian epistles to this period, in particular 1 Thessalonians 5 and 2 Thessalonians 2. In light of the other passages which teach that the believer will not experience any of God's wrath during this period, it is best to understand the preposition ek as "out of" rather than "away from." This also fits better with the idea of Christ the Deliverer rescuing the elect from this period in v. 10.

B. Paul reviews the type of ministry he had among the Thessalonians in order to renew their confidence in him and prepare the way for him to instruct them on some problem areas in the church—2:1-16
   1. He rehearses his ministry in Thessalonica in order to remind them how the gospel had been delivered to them—2:1-12
      a. He notes that the ministry there had been of value and continued despite persecution in order to show that he was not in the ministry for selfish reasons—2:1-2
      b. He notes that the ministry there was out of pure motives and was approved by God in order to show that he was not deceptive and was interested in pleasing God—2:3-4
      c. He notes the conduct of the messengers of the message in order to show

their reliability—2:5-12

1) Their conduct was not characterized by flattery, greed, or desire for recognition—2:5-6
2) Their conduct was characterized by gentleness, love, and generosity—2:7-8
3) Their work among them was characterized by hard work and dealings reminiscent of a father by encouraging, comforting, and exhorting—2:9-12

2. He rehearses how the ministry was received among them in order to further vindicate himself and remind them of their past belief in the message so that they would continue to herald it—2:13-16

a. He thanks God that they had received the word as from God rather than as from men—2:13

b. He notes that because they accepted the word in this way they became imitators of God and endured persecution because of it from their enemies who would eventually be judged—2:14-16

Note #204: The opposers

The source of opposition referred to in these verses seems to have been Gentiles because they are contrasted with the Jews in verse 14. However, it is also possible to see the term "countrymen" in a local rather than a racial sense and thus this would not exclude all reference to the Jews but would include those who were citizens of Thessalonica. This would be supported by the following invective against the Jews by Paul. This also finds support by the fact that most of the early persecution came from the hands of the Jews.

C. Paul expresses his concern for the Thessalonians since he was separated from them so that they would appreciate what they meant to him so that they would reject any notion that his interest in them was selfish—2:17-3:13

1. He tells them he had deeply desired to visit them but was hindered (the road had been made impassable) by Satan but nonetheless rejoiced in their ultimate victory—2:17-20

2. He tells them he could not stay away from them any longer so he sent Timothy to strengthen and encourage them in their persecution so that Satan would not take advantage of them in their suffering—3:1-5

3. He tells them Timothy had reported to him that they were withstanding persecution which led Paul to thank God for this and continue to pray that God would mature them in their faith—3:6-10

4. He prays for them in view of this report that God would clear the way (make the road passable) so that he could visit them and that their love would increase so that they would be strengthened spiritually and be blameless when Christ returned—3:11-13

III. PAUL PROVIDES PRACTICAL INSTRUCTIONS AND EXHORTATIONS IN ORDER TO PROMOTE THEIR MATURITY IN THE FAITH SO THAT THEY WOULD BE ABLE TO STAND PLEASING TO GOD IN THEIR PERSECUTION AS THEY WAITED FOR THE COMING OF THE LORD—4:1-5:24

A. Paul gives the Thessalonians some practical exhortations concerning Christian living—4:1-12

1. He exhorts them to continue to excel in the way they had been instructed so as to please God—4:1-2

2. He exhorts them to a life of sanctification—4:3-8

a. The basis for this exhortation is that it is the will of God—4:3a

b. This sanctification is worked out by abstaining from fornication and possessing one's own vessel in honor—4:3b-6a

Note #205: Master your passions vs. acquire a wife

*One of the most discussed passages in 1 Thessalonians is the central phrase in 4:3. There are two ways this is translated in the various versions: "control your body" (ESV, NIV, NLT, NRS); or, "possess your vessel" (KJV, NASB, NKJV,). The term κτάομαι can be translated either "control" or "possess." The term σκεῦος can be translated either "body" or "vessel." If the former, Paul is urging the Thessalonians to master their passions; if the latter, Paul is urging them to get married as a means of dealing with immorality. It is my opinion that the first view is correct for the following reasons: 1) Moulton and Milligan have shown that in the papyri the word κτάομαι had the sense of "to gradually obtain the complete mastery of the body" (*The Vocabulary of the Greek New Testament, *361-362) and is the preferred interpretation in this passage, 2) since all people struggle with their passions, then Paul would have to be instructing all of the Thessalonians to be married if they were not, 3) those who were already married still will struggle with sinful passions; therefore, there would be no instruction for them in the passage, 4) there is no place in Paul's writings where σκεῦος refers to a wife, 5) the pronoun translated "each one" would support this view, for mastery of the passions is something in which every individual is engaged, and 6) later in the passage where Paul is giving reasons for this injunction, he refers to the immorality of unsaved Gentiles.*

c. He tells them to pursue this sanctification for three reasons: its violation will bring God's vengeance, it is in harmony with the divine will, and its rejection is a rejection of God— 4:6b-8

3. He exhorts them to brotherly love and industry—4:9-12

a. He commends them for the brotherly love they were displaying—4:9-10a

b. He exhorts them to continue to abound in this love—4:10b

c. He exhorts them to a restful, nonmeddlesome, and industrious life so that they would meet their own needs and gain the approval of nonbelievers—4:11-12

B. Paul gives the Thessalonians some instruction regarding the dead in Christ in order to show them that those who had died in the Lord (Church age saints) would not miss out on any of the blessing of those who were alive at the rapture—4:13-18

1. He states the reason he gave this instruction was that he did not want them to be ignorant concerning the future or to grieve as those without hope—4:13

2. He presents the content of the instruction—4:14-17

a. He states the ground of assurance by noting that as assuredly as Christ died and rose from the dead so also he would bring the dead in Christ back with Him—4:14

b. He states the accurate form of teaching by noting that the Lord said that the living would have no advantage over the dead at His appearing—4:15

Note #206: The word of the Lord

This reference to the word of the Lord cannot be referring to the Olivet Discourse since this dealt only with the Second Advent and the future of Israel. Rather, this must be revelation which was given to Paul by revelation, or instruction from Jesus which was included in the Gospels (e.g. John 14:1-6).

c. He states that the Lord Himself would descend from heaven with a loud shout—4:16a

d. He states that the dead in Christ would rise first followed by living believers who would be caught up with them to meet the Lord in the air to ever be with Him—4:16b-17

e. He states that these instructions should be used to encourage one another in their suffering—4:18

Note #207: The rapture of the church

1 Thessalonians 4:13-18 is one of the central New Testament texts on the rapture of the Church. It should be noted, however, that this passage is not dealing with the timing of the event. Rather, Paul is explaining to the Thessalonians that their departed loved ones would not miss out on the blessings of this event. The actual word "rapture" is neither used in this passage nor in any New Testament passage. The term "rapture" comes from the Latin Vulgate rendering of the verse 17: deinde nos qui vivimus qui relinquimur simul **rapiemur** cum illis in nubibus obviam Domino in aera et sic semper cum Domino erimus. "Rapiemur" *(from* rapio *meaning "to seize, snatch, tear away" [*Cassell's New Latin Dictionary, *New York: Funk & Wagnalls, 1968], 500) is translating the Greek term ἁρπάζω (the text uses the future, passive form of the verb) in 4:17 which has the idea of "to seize," "to carry off," or "to snatch away." The verb is used 14 times in the New Testament (Matt 12:29; 13:19; John 6:15; 10:12, 28, 29; Acts 8:39; 23:10; 2 Cor 12:2, 1 Thess 4:17; Jude 23; Rev 12:5).*

C. Paul exhorts the Thessalonians to watchfulness so that they would be ready to meet the Lord in light of the imminent event which he has just described—5:1-11

1. He notes that the Day of the Lord's time is uncertain—5:1-2

2. He notes that those who are not ready for it would be caught in sudden destruction—5:3

3. He exhorts them to be alert and sober concerning things to come because they were not ignorant of these events for they had been revealed by Paul and they were children of light—5:4-7

4. He exhorts them to arm themselves with faith, love, and hope because they had not been appointed to wrath because of the death of Christ which had appointed them to deliverance (salvation)—5:8-10

Note #208: The Day of the Lord

1 Thessalonians 5:9 is one of the strongest verses in the New Testament to support a pretribulational rapture. This is based on several factors: 1) the context is the Day of the Lord, 2) it is solidly demonstrable that the Day of the Lord begins at the start of the Tribulation period, and 3) Paul says that they would be "saved" (delivered) from this period. The only way to rebut this logic is to prove that the Day of the Lord begins at the end of the Tribulation period. In the writer's opinion, this has not been successfully done. For a full discussion of the crucial theme of the Day of the Lord, see Note 210.

5. He exhorts them to continue to edify each other based on these truths—5:11

D. Paul exhorts the Thessalonians to obligations in church life in order to balance his exhortations of the future with their behavior in the present—5:12-15

1. He exhorts them to esteem their leaders—5:12-13
2. He exhorts them to warn the idle, encourage the timid, help the weak, and be patient with all men—5:14-15

E. Paul exhorts the Thessalonians in the area of individual responsibility so that they would know their duties—5:16-24

1. He instructs them in the area of personal actions and attitudes—5:16-18
   - **a.** They were to rejoice—5:16
   - **b.** They were to pray without ceasing (like a hacking cough)—5:17
   - **c.** They were to give thanks in all situations for this is God's will—5:18
2. He instructs them in the area of corporate actions and attitudes—5:19-22
   - **a.** They were not to quench the Spirit by hindering His work—5:19
   - **b.** They were not to despise prophecy on the one hand, but on the other hand they should have a critical spirit toward it to make sure it was in line with other revelation—5:20-21
   - **c.** They were to abstain from every prophecy which was proved false—5:22

Note #209: Abstain from all appearance of evil

Not a few Christians have been taught from this verse that they should refrain from any practice which might be construed as evil by another person. This idea is not even remotely hinted at in the passage. Observe the flow of thought in the context: v. 19 don't quench (stifle, put out the fire, and hinder the working) the Holy Spirit. What would be one example of how this is done? ⇨ v. 20 do not despise prophesying. In the first century, the Holy Spirit would give direct revelation to the prophets which revelation was then to be communicated to the church. It would be quenching the Holy Spirit's work if this revelation was despised. Does this mean that the church should abandon all discernment, and take anything someone had to say as a message from God? ⇨ v. 21 No! Prove all things. That is, when prophecies are given, they should be evaluated as to whether they are in concert with God's previous revelation (1 Cor. 14:29). If the prophecy is proved to be of God, what should we do? ⇨ v. 21 hold fast that which is good (the good being a reference to the approved prophecy). What if the prophecy is determined to be false and not from God at all after evaluation? ⇨ v. 22 abstain, having nothing to do with false revelation. Paul will continue this train of thought in his next letter to the Thessalonians. In 2 Thessalonians 2 he will observe that they are being troubled by false teaching which had come from false prophets.

3. Paul prays that they would be entirely sanctified knowing that God was the One who was working in them to provide enablement—5:23-24

IV. PAUL CONCLUDES THE LETTER IN ORDER TO ENCOURAGE SOME FINAL ACTIONS ON THE PART OF THE THESSALONIANS—5:25-28

A. He asks for their prayers—5:25
B. He asks them to greet the brethren—5:26
C. He asks them to read the letter to the whole church—5:27
D. He expresses his desire that God's grace would be with his readers—5:28

Note #210: The Day of the Lord expanded

The Importance of This Concept

The biblical phrase "Day of Yahweh" occupies a peerless place of importance in both the Old and New Testaments. L. Cerny has suggested that "The doctrine of the Day of Yahweh is not only the most interesting but perhaps also the most important of all the teachings of the Hebrew prophets. This is rather an understatement than an exaggeration."[587] *Consequently, there are a number of reasons which demonstrate the merit for studying this key phrase. First, it is a major strand of prophecy running throughout the Old Testament. The Hebrew phrases translated "Day of Yahweh," appear nineteen times in the Old Testament.*[588] *Furthermore, other phrases such as "that day," "the day," and the great day," are scattered throughout the prophets, as well as hundreds of passages referring to events within that time period.*

A second reason which shows the importance of this concept is the fact that the phrase "Day of the Lord" is found in four New Testament passages.[589] *Since the Old Testament provides the basis for understanding the use of this phrase in the New Testament, it is thus paramount that the phrase be understood in the interpretation of both Testaments. Beecher noted the importance of this when he writes:*

> *All doctrines in regard to the millennium, the second coming of Christ, and the final judgment depend greatly on the passages in the New Testament that use the formulas, "the day of the Lord"...The meaning of these passages is, in turn, greatly dependent on the relations that exist, both in ideas and in phraseology, between them and the texts of the Old Testament that speak of the "day of the Lord," that is, "the day of Jehovah." Necessarily, the study of these places in the Old Testament will be profitable, both in itself and for the light it throws on New Testament eschatology.*[590]

A final reason of importance for studying this concept can be seen from the difficulties with which it is beset. Some of these are as follows: (1) the origin of the phrase, (2) the definition and content of the events included in the phrase, (3) whether the

[587] L. Cerny, *The Day of Yahweh and Some Relevant Problems* (no publication data), i.

[588] These passages are as follows: Isaiah 2:12; 13:6, 9; Ezekiel 13:5; 30:3; Joel 1:15; 2:1,11,31; 3:14; Amos 5:18 (twice), 20; Obadiah 15; Zephaniah 1:7, 14 (twice); Zechariah 14:1; Malachi 4:5.

[589] These passages are as follows: Acts 2:20; 1 Thessalonians 5:2; 2 Thessalonians 2:2; 2 Peter 3:10.

[590] W. J. Beecher, "The Day of Jehovah in Joel," *The Homiletical Review* 18 (1889), 355.

day is fulfilled historically or eschatologically, (4) whether it is a time of judgment or blessing or both, and (5) when the day actually begins.

The Major Textual Data in the New Testament

In light of the incredible number of passages which deal with this subject, it is not possible to examine every text which speaks of the Day of the Lord. Therefore, only those central passages will receive specialized treatment. The purpose here is to observe the context and make a number of brief observations concerning those passages where the phrase "Day of the Lord" appears as a point of reference for later discussion.

Isaiah—739-681 BC[591]

Isaiah 2:12. *This verse is the first mention of the Day of the Lord in the prophecy of Isaiah. In 2:1-5, Isaiah has affirmed the future restoration of Judah and Jerusalem as he describes some of the characteristics of the Millennial Kingdom. These include the establishment of God's house (2:2a), the attraction of the nations to Jerusalem (2:2b-3a), the proclamation of the Law from Jerusalem, and the peace that will reign among the nations (2:4). Then in 2:6-11, he notes that Judah had taken on the values of the pagans around them, and in 2:11-22, the consequent judgment which these values would bring. It is in this judgment context where the Day of the Lord is described by Isaiah. From this passage the following characteristics are seen about the Day of the Lord:*

1. *It will be a time when the proud will be humbled–2:11, 12, 17.*
2. *It will be a time when the Lord will be exalted –2:10, 11, 17, 19, 21.*
3. *It will be a time of fear and hiding–2:10, 19, 21.*
4. *It will be a time when the Lord will shake the earth–2:19, 21.*
5. *It will be a time of judgment against Israel–2:6.*

It appears that the judgment referred to here is eschatological[592] *instead of historical judgment at the hands of Assyria and Babylon. This is so because of the eschatological emphasis of 2:1-5 and the cosmic disturbances as noted above.*[593]

Isaiah 13:6-16. *The next reference to the Day of the Lord in Isaiah is in the thirteenth chapter. In this section Isaiah is delivering an oracle of judgment against Babylon, and in it additional information is gleaned concerning the Day of the Lord. These are:*

1. *It is from God Himself–13:6, 11, 12, 13.*
2. *It is a time of destruction, wrath, and anger–13:6, 9, 11, 13, 15,16.*
3. *It is directed against sinners–13:9, 11.*
4. *The sun, moon, and stars will be darkened–13:10.*

---

[591] The dates given are approximations and follow the chronology suggested by Gleason Archer, *A Survey of Old Testament Introduction* (Chicago: Moody Press, 1974) . The purpose of the dates is to identify more easily the judgments in view in these prophecies.

[592] E. J. Young, *The Book of Isaiah* (Grand Rapids: Eerdmans, 1983), 1:123; G. A. Gay, "Day," in *Evangelical Dictionary of Theology* (Grand Rapids: Baker, 1984), 294; Henry Dosker, "Day of the Lord," in *International Standard Bible Encyclopedia* (Grand Rapids: Eerdmans, 1980), 2:799; A. J. Everson, "Days of Yahweh," *Journal of Biblical Literature* 93 (1974), 330.

[593]For an example of one who sees 2:1-4 as eschatological and 2:5ff. as present, see Herbert Wolf, *Interpreting Isaiah* (Grand Rapids: Zondervan, 1985), 76-78.

5. *God will shake the earth–13:13.*
6. *Men will be filled with fear-13:7, 8, 14.*
7. *A specific Gentile nation is involved–13:1, 19.*

Unlike the previous Isaiah passage, there seems to be both a near eschatological event in view as well as a far eschatological event. It seems clear that 13:1-8 refers to the relatively near event fulfilled by Babylon from 605-586 B.C.[594] *However, the description in 13:9-16 speaks of an event in the far future.*[595] *his seems clear again from the cosmic disturbances as well as the universality of judgment mentioned (13:11). This interplay between near and far eschatology is explained by Ladd where he writes that*

> *These two visitations, the near and the far, or, as we may for convenience call them, the historical and the eschatological, are not differentiated in time. In fact, sometimes the two blend together as though they were one day...This historical Day of the Lord is painted against the backdrop of the eschatological Day of the Lord.*[596]

It should be further noted that this near and far interplay in the prophets is not an unusual phenomenon, and is commonly referred to as "prophetic telescoping." Henry Virkler explains this prophetic device thusly: "Biblical prophecy may leap from one prominent peak in predictive topography to another, without notice of the valley between."[597] *Examples of this can be seen most notably when the prophets spoke of the first and second comings of Christ (e.g. Isa. 9:6; 61:1-2; Zech. 9: 9-10). As McClain observed, "the Oriental was interested in the next important event, not in the time which might intervene."*[598] *Amillennialists also recognize this principle. For example, Lenski in commenting on Acts 3:17 states that, "It must be well understood that the prophets always viewed the two comings of Christ together without having the interval between the two revealed to them."*[599] *So in principle, the same thing is happening in these day of the Lord prophecies.*

Jeremiah—626-582 BC

Jeremiah 46:10. *In Jeremiah 46:1–12, the prophet is delivering a message of judgment against Egypt. He prophesied that Egypt would be ravaged by the Babylonians. This defeat is called by Jeremiah "the day of the Lord God of hosts" (46:10). The following observations are made:*

1. *It is a time of judgment against a specific Gentile nation–46:1-2.*
2. *It is a time of God's vengeance–46:10.*
3. *It is a time of slaughter of God's enemies–46:10.*

[594] J. S. Wright, "Day of the Lord," *New Bible Dictionary* (Downers Grove: InterVarsity, 1996), 269; Young, *The Book of Isaiah,* 419.

[595] Richard Mayhue, "The Prophet's Watchword: Day of the Lord," *Grace Theological Journal* 6 (1985), 239; H. C. Leupold, *Exposition of Isaiah* (Grand Rapids: Baker, 1968), 1:234.

[596] G. E. Ladd, *The Presence of the Future* (Grand Rapids: Eerdmans, 1970), 66.

[597] Henry Virkler, *Hermeneutics: Biblical Principles and Processes of Biblical Interpretation* (Grand Rapids: Baker, 1981), 201.

[598] Alva McClain, *Daniel's Prophecy of the 70 Weeks* (Grand Rapids: Zondervan, 1981), 38.

[599] R. C. H. Lenski, *An Interpretation of the Acts of the Apostles* (Minneapolis: Augsburg, 1964), 77.

Because this prophecy is made against a specific nation, and because there are no judgments necessitating the end of the age, it is concluded that this was a day of the Lord fulfilled in 605BC when Nebuchadnezzar registered a major victory against the Egyptians.[600]

Ezekiel—592-570 BC

Ezekiel 13:5. *Ezekiel wrote in chapters 12-19 concerning the certainty of judgment to come upon Israel. The third message delivered by Ezekiel regarding this judgment is found in chapter thirteen where he denounces the false prophets and prophetesses who were contributing to Israel's sense of false security. Here it is observed that:*

1. *The judgment is from the Lord–13:8, 9.*
2. *The judgment is against the false prophets of Israel–13:3.*
3. *The judgment would involve the elements of nature–13:11, 13.*

In this first Ezekiel passage it seems best to understand the Day of the Lord as a reference to the beginning of Judah's deportation in 605 BC and to Jerusalem's destruction in 586 BC.[601]

Ezekiel 30:3

The next reference in Ezekiel about the Day of the Lord is found in 30:3. In this section the prophet is writing concerning the demise of Egypt and her allies at the hands of Babylon and refers to it as a "day of the Lord." Ezekiel refers to this day as:

1. *A time of woe, howling, and distress–30:2*
2. *A cloudy day–30:3*
3. *A time of death, pain, and desolation–30: 4, 5, 7*

As with the first Ezekiel passage, this one seems to refer to a near eschatological event, namely the destruction of Egypt (30:4, 6, 8, 10).

Joel–835 BC

The Day of the Lord is mentioned five times in the book of Joel and thus becomes a locus classicus *for a study of the subject. The difficulty as to whether to take the locust plague as literal or figurative in these chapters is well known.*[602] *It is not within the scope here to deal with this question; however it should be stated that the writer holds to what H. Hosch describes as a historical/near, eschatological/far view.*[603] *This view states that the locusts of chapter one are real. A near future invasion under the locust figure referring to either the Assyrians or Babylonians is in view in 2:1-17. Finally, 2:18-27 serves as a transition to far eschatology in 2:28-3:21. Thus the locust plague that*

---

[600]C. C. Ryrie, *What You Should Know About the Rapture* (Chicago: Moody Press, 1981), 93; Keil and Delitzsch, *Jeremiah, Lamentations* (Grand Rapids: Eerdmans, 1980), 178; R. K. Harrison, *Jeremiah and Lamentations* (Downers Grove: InterVarsity, 1973), 170.

[601] Charles Dyer, "Ezekiel," in *The Bible Knowledge Commentary* (Wheaton: Victor Books, 1985), 1251; G. A. Cooke, *The Book of Ezekiel* International Critical Commentary (Edinburgh: T & T Clark, 1936), 139.

[602]See H. Hosch, "The Concept of Prophetic Time in the Book of Joel," *Journal of the Evangelical Theological Society* 15 (1972), 32-38.

[603]Ibid., 32-33

destroyed the Judean countryside is used by Joel to picture near and far judgment to be brought by God. A number of observations can be made from Joel's treatment of the Day of the Lord.

Joel 1–the locust invasion

1. *It is destruction from the Almighty–1:15.*
2. *It will bring famine and drought which will affect men and animal –1:10-12; 16-20.*
3. *It will involve an invasion of Israel by a powerful army–2:6.*

Joel 2:1-17–near eschatology–the Assyrian and/or Babylonian invasion

1. *It will be from the Almighty – 2:1-4.*
2. *It will involve the land of Israel – 2:1.*
3. *It is great, terrible, dark, and gloomy – 2:2- 11.*
4. *It will involve an invasion of Israel by a powerful army – 2: 2-9.*
5. *The earth will quake, and the heavenly bodies will be affected – 2:10.*

Joel 2:28-3:21 – far eschatology

1. *The Spirit will be poured out – 2:28- 29.*
2. *The earth will quake, and the heavenly bodies will be affected – 2:30, 31.*
3. *The nations will be judged in the Valley of Jehoshaphat –3:2, 14.*
4. *The godless will be destroyed –3:13.*
5. *The Messiah will reign and the land will be blessed – 3:18.*

Amos—720-755 BC

Amos 5:18. *Amos wrote his prophecy to the Northern Kingdom when it was at a tremendous height in power and prosperity (cf. 3:15, 5:11, 6:1-6; 8:5). Unfortunately, this success brought with it social injustice (2:6-7; 5:7; 6:12; 8:4-6), immorality (2:7), and abominable worship (5:21-23). Evidently, the people mistakenly believed that the Lord was with them (5:14) and thus longed for the Day of the Lord (5:18a). Amos, however, decried their sins and warned them that the Day of the Lord held judgment for the nation (5:18b).*[604] *Amos' description of this time includes the following:*

1. *It will fall on Israel – 5:1*
2. *It will destroy the sinful of the nation – 9:1-10.*
3. *It is a time of judgment from the Lord – 5:17.*
4. *It is a day of darkness with no light –5:28, 20.*
5. *It is a time of woe – 5:16.*
6. *It will be a time of restoration and blessing – 9:11-15.*

While the passage concerning restoration is far eschatological (9:11-15), it is probably best to take the passage in 5:18-20 as a reference to the fall of Samaria in 7:22 BC (cf. 2 Kings 17).[605]

[604] See William Harper, *Amos and Hosea* International Critical Commentary (Edinburgh: T & T Clark, 1966), 131-132; G. A. Cooke, *A Critical and Exegetical Commentary on the Book of Ezekiel*, 139.

[605] J. S. Wright, "Day of the Lord,", 269;_ Colin Brown, "Day of the Lord," in *The Zondervan Pictorial Encyclopedia of the Bible* (Grand Rapids: Zondervan, 1975), 2:46; G. E. Ladd, *A Theology of the New Testament* (Grand Rapids: Eerdmans, 1983), 554; James Orr, "Eschatology," in *International Standard Bible*

Obadiah—848-841 BC

Obadiah's message is primarily one of doom and judgment against Israel's enemy Edom. The question of interest in Obadiah is whether the day of the Lord passage in vv. 15-21 relates to the near or far future. Some, such as Henderson, say that this was fulfilled in the Babylonian conquest of Idumea.[606] *Kaiser suggests a fulfillment in the Maccabean period.*[607] *On the other hand, Allen suggests that the scope of the reference simply goes beyond 587 BC. He writes that "He is still much concerned with Edom...but behind the fate of the nations...stands the fall of Jerusalem in 587."*[608] *Others like Gaebelein relate the fall of Edom to the time just before the establishment of the Millennium.*[609]

It is probably contextually best to regard vv. 1-14 as a near future reference to the destruction of Edom by Nebuchadnezzar. Yet, the language used in the rest of the book seems to point to the far future time of the Kingdom Age. Mayhue suggests five supports for this view:[610] *(1) vv. 1-14 deal with Edom followed by an abrupt shift in vv. 15-16 dealing with all nations, (2) Edom becomes a pattern for future nations (v.16) , (3) the destruction of the nations is an eschatological event, (4) Israel's full restoration (vv. 17-21) will occur in the millennium, and (5) it is stated that the kingdom will be the Lord's (v. 21). Having done with this, it can briefly be observed how Obadiah described the Day of the Lord.*

1. *It will come upon Edom – 1-14.*
2. *It will come upon all nations – 15.*
3. *Nations will be judged by their treatment of Israel – 15-16.*
4. *Israel will be delivered, returned to the land, and see the establishment of the Kingdom – 17-21.*

Zephaniah 1:7, 14—630 BC

The theme of Zephaniah's prophecy is the judgment to come upon Judah for her disobedience. Be this as it may, it is still revealed that a remnant would be preserved in keeping with God's faithfulness to the Covenant. The question which surfaces is how to relate the universality of judgment in 1:1-3 with the specific judgment on Judah by Babylon. Further, how does this relate to the future judgment of all nations pictured in 3:8 and the future restoration of Israel in 3:9-20? Again, it needs to be remembered as in the other prophecies, that the prophets often weave together a near eschatological strand with a far eschatological strand into one whole. Hannah explains that "Zephaniah saw Judah's destruction and universal judgment as two parts of one grand event, the day of the Lord."[611] *Likewise, Kaiser corroborates by noting that "they combined in one picture what history split into different times and events...Hence the day of the Lord ran*

Encyclopedia (Grand Rapids: Eerdmans, 1980), 2:977.

[606] E. Henderson, *The Books of the Twelve Minor Prophets* (London: Hamilton, Adams, and Co., 1845), 195.

[607] W. C. Kaiser, *Toward an Old Testament Theology* (Grand Rapids: Zondervan, 1978), 188.

[608] Leslie Allen, *The Books of Joel, Obadiah, Jonah and Amos* (Grand Rapids: Eerdmans, 1983), 160-61.

[609] Frank Gaebelein, *Four Minor Prophets* (Chicago: Moody Press, 1976), 33-35.

[610] Mayhue, "The Prophet's Watchword," 234-35.

[611] John Hannah, "Zephaniah," in *Bible Knowledge Commentary* (Wheaton: Victor Books, 1985), 1525.

throughout the history of the kingdom of God so that it occurred in each particular judgment as evidence its complete fulfillment."[612]

The following facts are observed about Zephaniah's contribution about the Day of the Lord:

1. *It is judgment from the Lord – 1: 1-4*
2. *It is judgment on Judah – 1:4*
3. *It is judgment on all nations – 3:8*
4. *It is judgment on the rich, leaders, mighty, hardened, and indifferent – 1:6-12*
5. *The ungodly will perish –1:17-18*
6. *Idolatry will cease –1:4-5*
7. *It is characterized by wrath, trouble, distress, desolation, darkness, gloominess, and clouds –1:15-17*
8. *It will involve blessing and restoration for Israel –3:9-18*

Zechariah 14:1—520 BC

Since Zechariah was a post-exilic prophet writing after the Assyrian and Babylonian judgments, his prophecy concerning the Day of the Lord has a far eschatological reference. Some, such as Leupold,[613] *have suggested that the prophecy of chapter fourteen is figurative describing New Testament times. However, if a literal hermeneutic is applied to this chapter, the prophecy has not come close to being fulfilled. From Zechariah's use of the Day of the Lord, the following observations can be made.*

1. *Israel will be plundered by Gentile nations –14:1*
2. *The Lord will fight against these armies –14:2*
3. *The Messiah will return to the Mt. of Olives –14:4a*
4. *There will be an earthquake –14:4b*
5. *It will be an eternal day – 14:7*
6. *There will be a sufficient water supply –14:8*
7. *The Lord will be king over a peaceful Jerusalem – 14:9-11*
8. *Israel's enemies will be destroyed – 14:12-15*
9. *The Kingdom will be one of worship and holiness –14:16-21*

Malachi 4:5—435 BC

The final use of the phrase "Day of the Lord" is found in Malachi 4:5. As many of the other prophets, Malachi is writing to Israel to enjoin them to faithfulness to the Covenant in order to enjoy its blessings. The phrase occurs at the very end of the book in which Malachi speaks of the coming of Elijah before the day of the Lord. Malachi pictures the Day of the Lord in 4:1-5 as a time of judgment, desolation, and pain.

Contents and Definition of the Day of the Lord

Having made a survey of the key texts in the preceding section, it is interesting to note the various views on what exactly the Day of the Lord is. These views have been grouped into headings designated by the writer.[614]

---

[612] Kaiser, *Toward an Old Testament Theology*, 188; Ladd, *The Presence in the Future*, 67.

[613] H. C. Leupold, *Exposition of Zechariah* (Grand Rapids: Baker, 1971), 259.

[614] Some writers are easier than others to put into categories. The difficult ones are those who do not treat

Future Judgment at Second Advent View

This view sees the Day of the Lord as a purely eschatological event consisting of judgment only to take place at the Second Advent of Christ. In many cases, proponents of this view substitute the Day of the Lord for the coming of Christ. For example, B. B. Warfield speaks of the Advent freely as the Day of the Lord, a term which from Joel's time on has stood for a synonym of the final judgment.[615] *Likewise, Berkhof states that "the terms parousia and Day of the Lord are used interchangeably."*[616] *Another advocate of this position is L. Cerny who writes: "We may say that the Day of Yahweh is the decreed, dark, dreadful, destructive and dangerous day...this term is always in our literary documents applied to the final and universal judgment, and not to any less decisive intervention of God in the course of human history."*[617] *From this view should be noted three things: (1) the term is applied to eschatological events, not historical, (2) the event takes place at the Second Advent, and (3) the event includes judgment but not blessing.*

Though it is difficult to determine what is included in their entire scheme of the Day of the Lord, Fausset,[618] *Alford,*[619] *and Milligan*[620] *appear to associate it strongly with the parousia as well. Whether these authors would admit to any historical aspects of the Day of the Lord is not known to the writer.*[621]

Historical and Future Judgment at Second Advent View

Those who espouse this view hold essentially the same position as those mentioned in the previous one. The difference is that these see the judgments in history as aspects of Day of the Lord as well as the great judgment still in the future. Thus "days of the Lord" occurred in historical circumstances and the "day of the Lord" will take place at the close of[622] *the Tribulation period at the Second Advent, and another Day of the Lord at the close of the Millennium. Of this view, Mayhue writes:*

> *The Day of the Lord is a biblical phrase used by God's prophets to describe either the immediate future or the ultimate eschatological consummation...I would also suggest that the Day of the Lord will occur only at the end of the tribulation period, not throughout its duration, and that the Day of the Lord will occur only at the end of the millennium, not throughout its duration.*[623]

---

the Day of the Lord as a major issue (i.e. most post- and amillennialists). In such cases, what has been written is considered.

[615] B. B. Warfield, *Biblical Doctrines* (NY: Oxford University Press, 1929), 603.

[616] L. Berkhof, *Systematic Theology* (Grand Rapids: Eerdmans, 1979), 696.

[617] L. Cerny, *The Day of Yahweh and Some Relevant Problems*, vii, 26.

[618] A. R,. Fausset, *A Commentary: Critical, Experimental, and Practical* (Grand Rapids: Eerdmans, 1978), 3:467.

[619] Henry Alford, *Alford's Greek Testament* (Grand Rapids: Baker, 1980), 3:267.

[620] George Milligan, *St. Paul's Epistle to the Thessalonians* (Grand Rapids: Eerdmans, 1952), 64, 98.

[621] See also, James Frame, *The Epistles of St. Paul to the Thessalonians*, International Critical Commentary (Edinburgh: T. & T. Clark, 1979), 178; William Hendriksen, *Exposition of I and II Thessalonians* (Grand Rapids: Baker, 1974), 122.

[622] The issue of timing in regard to the Day of the Lord is one of the most important features of this theme. See the subsequent discussion.

[623] Richard Mayhue, "The Prophet's Watchword: Day of the Lord," 245, 246.

Keil also seems to fall into this camp when, speaking of the Day of the Lord and the judgment of God, he avers that history is "a continuous judgment, which will conclude at the end of this course of the world with a great and universal act of judgment."[624] In a similar strain, Calvin observes concerning this event, "he calls it the day of Jehovah, because in that day God would stretch forth his hand to execute judgment...God calls it His own day, when he will openly shine forth and appear as the judge of the world."[625] In summarizing this view, four points should be noted: (1) it includes historical judgments, (2) it includes eschatological judgments, (3) it excludes eschatological blessing, and (4) it excludes the Tribulation period.

Historical Judgment and Future Judgment/ Blessing at Second Advent View

This view is identical to the preceding except for the fact that in the future aspect, it says that the Day of the Lord includes the judgments at the Second Advent plus *the blessings of the Millennium. Gaebelein, for instance, states that the "day of Jehovah is that lengthened period of time beginning with the return of the Lord in glory, and ending with the purgation of the heavens and earth by fire preparatory to the new heavens and new earth."[626] Likewise Chafer writes that this is the "lengthened period of a thousand years that begins, generally speaking with the second advent of Christ and the judgments connected therewith, and ends with the passing of the present heaven and the present earth...The Day of the Lord is characterized by the reign of Christ over Israel"[627]*

A final statement of this view is made by John Freeman who says that the Day of the Lord "begins at the second coming and will include the final judgment...It will include the millennial judgment and culminate in the new heavens and the new earth."[628] This is also the position of G. N. H. Peters,[629] H. C. Thiessen,[630] and The Scofield Reference Bible.[631]

In summarizing this position, several points are noteworthy: (1) the future aspect is emphasized almost to the exclusion of the historical, (2) the period begins with the premillennial advent, and (3) the period includes both judgment and blessing.

Historical Judgment and Future Judgment/ Blessing at Tribulation View

There are two basic differences between this view and the preceding. First, this view gives more of an emphasis to the historical aspects of the Day of the Lord. And second, this position sees the future aspect beginning with the Tribulation rather than with the Second Advent. It is the position of the writer that this view best squares with the textual data as found in the previous section.

By way of introduction a brief description needs to be given concerning the word "day." Most often the word "day" is used to specify a unit of time such as the hours of

---

[624]C. F. Keil, *The Minor Prophets* (Grand Rapids: Eerdmans, 1980), 186-187.

[625]John Calvin, *Joel-Nahum* (Grand Rapids: Baker, 1979), 36.

[626]A. C. Gaebelein, *Four Minor Prophets*, 33.

[627]L. S. Chafer, *Systematic Theology* (Dallas: Dallas Seminary Press, 1947-48), 4:398.

[628]John Freeman, "Day of the Lord," in *Zondervan Pictorial Bible Dictionary* (Grand Rapids: Zondervan, 1976), 204.

[629]G. N. H. Peters, *The Theocratic Kingdom* (Grand Rapids: Kregel, 1972), 2:410.

[630]H. C. Thiessen, *Introductory Lectures in Systematic Theology* (Grand Rapids: Eerdmans, 1952), 507.

[631]*Scofield Reference Bible*, p. 1349; Interestingly, Cooke states, "By Ezekiel and other post-exilic prophets the word was used with an added significance; the Day was to consummate the overthrown of heathenism and usher in the age of blessedness" (*A Critical and Exegetical Commentary on the Book of Ezekiel*, 78).

daylight (Gen. 1:5, 16; Josh. 6:15; Isa. 27:3), or a legal or civil day (Lev. 23:32).[632] *The word is also used however to speak of an unspecified period of time (Isa. 49:8; 2 Cor. 6:2). Such is the case with the Day of the Lord. Each time the phrase appears, it must be examined in its context to determine its duration. Cerny offers this helpful comment:*

> *Time is not only actually closely associated with all of the contents by which it is filled, but that it is identical with them, that they are its very "substance" because for the Hebrew mind time does not exist as an empty "form or frame"...When mention is made of the day of Jerusalem, Jezreel or Midian, then it applies to events of decisive importance in their lives, just as the Day of Yahweh is the violent actions, in which Yahweh more particularly manifests himself.*[633]

In a similar statement, G. A. Gay remarks that "In Semitic thought it was customary to designate events of importance with the term day."[634] *With this in mind, one could say that "day" with reference to Yahweh was a concept used to interpret momentous events in which Yahweh was present in the world through His ongoing activities.*[635] *As Wolff suggests, "day does not mean a definite extent of time, but rather a definite event in time whose nature is determined by the associated personal name."*[636] *Or more simply, the Day of Yahweh is a time which belongs to Him in which He intervenes into human history. Thus, as Allen notes, "In...the prophetic teaching handed down...the Day of Yahweh had a double, even a triple function."*[637] *With this as a background, it can now be examined how this is accomplished.*

Historical Judgment

It should be clear from the survey of texts noted previously that there were "days of the Lord" fulfilled in history. It was suggested that these included:

Judgment on God's enemies. Babylon was judged at the hands of the Assyrians (Isa. 13:6, 9); Egypt was judged at the hands of the Babylonians (Jer. 46:10; Ezek. 30: 2-4); Edom was judged at the hands of Nebuchadnezzar (Isa. 34: 8-9; Obad. 1-14).

Judgment on God's people. Not only did the Day of the Lord signify a judgment on God's enemies, but at times on His people as well. Judah is invaded by Assyria (Joel 1:15; 2:1, 11); Israel is deported by Assyria (Amos 5:18, 20); Judah is judged by the Babylonians (Ezek. 13:5; Zeph. 1:4-13).

Future Judgment

It was also seen in the preceding discussion that a great amount of the revelation concerning the Day of the Lord had a reference to far eschatological judgment. This is so

---

[632]For other uses see Francis Brown, S. R. Driver, and Charles Briggs, *A Hebrew and English Lexicon of the Old Testament* (Oxford: Clarendon Press, n.d.), 398-401.

[633]Cerny, *The Day of Yahweh,* 5.

[634]G. A. Gay, "Day of Christ, God, the Lord," in *Evangelical Dictionary of Theology* (Grand Rapids: Baker, 1984), 295.

[635]A. J. Everson, "Days of Yahweh," *Journal of Biblical Literature* 93 (1974), 335, 337.

[636]Hans Wolff, *Joel and Amos* (Philadelphia: The Fortress Press, 1977), 33.

[637]Allen, *The Books of Joel, Obadiah, Jonah, and Micah,* 100.

because if one follows literal interpretation the fulfillment of the judgment has not taken place.[638]

> *Judgment on the nations. It is revealed that there is a coming day of the Lord in which the nations will be judged (Obad. 15-16; Isa. 13:9, 11; Zeph. 3:8; Zech. 14. 2-3).*
> *Judgment on Israel. It is also seen that the nation of Israel will receive judgment (Zech. 14:2; Amos 9:9, 10).*
> *Judgment and nature. It should also be remembered that this future judgment will be one of terror and agony. In addition, at this time cosmic changes and earthquakes will temporarily occur (Joel 2:30-31; Isa. 2:19, 21).*

Conclusion

It is concluded that the prophets wove together aspects of near and far judgment. It is further seen that the prophets did not regard the Day of the Lord as a once and for all event. R. G. Gruenler puts it in these words:

> *The Lord will act in a might way to judge evil and redeem his people . . . which we may designate F1 (Future 1) and F2 (Future 2) respectively. In prophetic poetry the two themes are repeated and interwoven as highly charged eschatological warnings and promises that often refer to historical events just past or soon to come, as well as to the long-range messianic age.*[639]

Also relating the historical day of the Lord to the future day of the Lord, Kaiser explains: "that final time would be climactic and the sum of all the rest. Though the events of their own times fitted the pattern of God's future judgment, that final day was nevertheless immeasurably larger and more permanent in its salvific and judgmental effects."[640]

So, these "days of the Lord" in history are foretastes or trailers of the time in the future of climactic, decisive judgment.

Future Blessing

Not only does this view admit to historical and future judgment, but it also insists on future blessing unlike the first two views. Working from the analogy of a solar day which extended from sunset to sunset (Lev. 23:32), McClain suggests that similarly the Day of the Lord will be a period composed of both darkness and light.[641] *Feinberg concurs when he writes that this will be a time "of the rule of the Messiah of Israel over them in Jerusalem on the throne of David."*[642] *Walvoord agrees when he states: "The significant truth revealed here is that the day of the Lord which first inflicts terrible judgments ends with an extended period of blessing on Israel, which will be fulfilled in the millennial kingdom...a time of special divine blessing."*[643]

---

[638]For one who says these have been fulfilled in the present age, see Oswald Allis, *Prophecy and the Church* (Philadelphia: The Presbyterian and Reformed Publishing Co., 1945), 135.

[639]R. G. Gruenler, "Last Day, Days," in *Evangelical Dictionary of Theology* (Grand Rapids: Baker, 1984), 619.

[640]W. C. Kaiser, *Towards and Old Testament Theology*, 191.

[641]Alva McClain, *The Greatness of the Kingdom* (Winona Lake: BMH Books, 1983), 178.

[642]Charles Feinberg, *The Minor Prophets* (Chicago: Moody Press, 1976), 15.

[643]J. F. Walvoord, "Posttribulationism Today," *Bibliotheca Sacra* 134 (1977), 8.

When the day of the Lord passages are studied, this view seems to hold up. This is seen in a number of passages (e. g. Isa. 2:1-4; Joel 2:32; Amos 9: 11-15; Obad. 17-21; Zeph. 3:9-20; Zech. 14: 9-21). When these passages are examined, it is discovered that they occur in the same context as the judgment aspect of the Day of the Lord, and include restoration of Israel, the establishment of the Kingdom, the blessing of the land, etc. Based on these observations, Erich Sauer notes, "it is clear that he [Joel] connects the term day of the Lord not with the gloomy time of judgment only, but also, and as concerns the length of the period, even chiefly with the glorious time of the visible kingdom of God."[644] In the same manner, Colin Brown observes from the Amos passage that "Amos' vision of the day oscillates between battles, natural disasters and supernatural calamities, but he ends on a note of hope."[645] And finally, Allen remarks, "the Day of Yahweh thus reaches a climax in the fulfillment of covenant blessing of the penitent people in the land."[646] Thus, this period belonging to Yahweh not only displays His wrath, but His mercy and grace as well.

Beginning at the Tribulation

Among those who believe in a literal Tribulation yet to come, this is one of the key areas of debate when it comes to the subject of the Day of the Lord. The difficulty lies in the fact the Bible does not explicitly state when the future Day begins. However, when all of the references in both Testaments which speak of the Tribulation are examined, it seems safe to say that the Day of the Lord will include that seven year period. The purpose of the following survey is to see how passages throughout the Bible concerning the Tribulation compare to those already surveyed which use the phrase "day of the Lord."

Event(s)	***Old Testament "Day of the Lord"***	***Revelation 6 – 19***
earthquakes/cosmic	*Isa. 2:19, 21; Joel 2:30*	*Rev. 6: 12-14*
men hiding	*Isa. 2: 10, 19*	*Rev. 6:15*
wrath	*Zeph. 1:15; Isa. 13:6, 9, 11*	*Rev. 6:17*
trees and grass burned	*Zeph. 1:15*	*Rev. 8:7*
woe	*Joel 2:1-2; Ez. 30:2*	*Rev. 8: 13*
hail	*Ezek. 13: 11, 13*	*Rev. 8: 7*
Israel persecuted	*Isa. 2:6; Zech. 14: 2*	*Rev. 12:6, 16, 17; 13:7*
proud humbled	*Isa. 2:11, 12*	*Rev. 6:15*

---

[644]Erich Sauer, *From Eternity to Eternity* (Grand Rapids: Eerdmans, 1975), 77.

[645]Colin Brown, "Day of the Lord," 1:46; Clarence Mason, "The Day of the Lord," *Bibliotheca Sacra* 125 (1968), 354-355.

[646]Leslie Allen, *The Books of Joel, Obadiah, Jonah, and Micah*, 38.

darkness and pain	*Joel 2:31; Amos 5: 18, 20*	*Rev. 16: 2; 8-10*
wrath on nations	*Zeph. 1:15; Isa. 13:9, 11; Ob. 15, 16*	*Rev. 6: 15-17; 11:18*

It can be seen from this brief comparison that there is a great deal of similarity between the judgments of the Day of the Lord and those of the Tribulation period in Revelation 6-19. It is doubtful that these refer to two separate events or that these could all be restricted to the end of the Tribulation.

Other Old Testament references

There are hundreds of Old Testament passages which have an eye to the future Tribulation period. By examining a handful of them, the general teaching can be seen. It is said to be a time of devouring, desolation, and burning (Isa. 24:1, 3, 6); a time of earthquakes and punishment (Isa. 24: 19-21); a time of indignation (Isa. 26:20, 21); a time of vengeance and recompense (Isa. 34:8); a time of Jacob's trouble (Jer. 30:7); a time of desolations (Dan. 9:26); a time of seven years (Dan. 9:27); a time of unparalleled tribulation (Dan. 12: 1); and a time of fierce judgment on the wicked (Mal. 4:1). These too, appear to refer to the period of the Day of the Lord.

The Olivet Discourse

There are also a number of descriptions in the Olivet Discourse concerning the Tribulation which parallel with those of the Day of the Lord. These include a time of unprecedented tribulation (Matt. 24:21); a time of unprecedented turmoil (Matt. 24:6, 7); a lack of peace (Matt. 24: 1-7); a time of famine (Matt. 24:7); a time of death (Matt. 24: 7-8); and a time of persecution for Israel (Matt. 24:9).

Key New Testament Texts

Up to this point, the texts provided show the <u>reasonableness</u> of holding that the Day of the Lord includes the Tribulation period; however, it must be admitted that they do not prove it. There are though some key passages in the New Testament which further strengthen this position.

Matthew 24: 6, 7, 21 (cf., Dan. 12:1). These verses state that the Tribulation is a period of unique and unparalleled wrath. This being the case, it is difficult to imagine that the Old Testament foreshadowings of the future Day of the Lord would not include this period. This is further confirmed by the fact that Christ said that in the future the trouble of the Tribulation would never have been equaled. This would include the judgment to be poured out at the Second Advent. Therefore, it is probably best to view the whole period of unprecedented judgment included in the concept of the Day of the Lord.

Matthew 24:15—2 Thessalonians 2:3—Daniel 9:27. It is seen from Daniel 9:27, that the seventieth week (seven years) of Daniel begins with the signing of a covenant between the Antichrist and Israel. In the midst of the week (3 ½ years), he breaks this covenant (cf., 2 Thess. 2:4)[647] *In Matthew 24: 4 – 31, Christ lays out for the disciples the program*

[647] For a discussion and validation of this chronology, see Alva McClain, *Daniel's Prophecy of the Seventy*

of Daniel's seventieth week (the Tribulation). In this discourse, Christ cites Daniel's prophecy regarding the breaking of the covenant as the middle of the Tribulation period (Matt. 24:15), and that this event would mark a time of unprecedented trouble (Matt. 24:21). Thus, the Tribulation begins with the signing of the covenant, and the middle is marked by the breaking of that covenant. Finally, in 2 Thessalonians 2:2, Paul confirms that the Day of the Lord comes when the son of perdition is revealed (the beginning of the Tribulation), to be followed by the abomination of desolation at the middle of the period (2 Thess. 2:3).

In summary, it can be seen that Daniel and Jesus mark the beginning of the Tribulation as the signing of a covenant between Israel and the Antichrist. Likewise, they both mark the middle of the Tribulation by the breaking of that same covenant. Paul, then, equates the beginning of the Day of the Lord with the revelation of the Antichrist.

1 Thessalonians 5: 2-3. There are two points to be observed from this passage. The first is the fact that Paul says the Day of the Lord will come as a thief in the night. Since the Second Coming is preceded by signs (Matt. 24: 29 – 30), if the Day of the Lord came at this time, it would not be unexpected as a thief. Thus, the time which best describes this beginning of the Day of the Lord would be the beginning of the Tribulation rather than the end. The second point is that Paul says the Day of the Lord comes at a time when there is peace and safety. The end of the Tribulation could hardly be said to be a time of peace and safety, for at the end of the Tribulation all nations will surround Palestine (Zech. 12:3; 14:2; Rev. 16:14). Therefore, again the feeling of peace and safety would fit better with the beginning of the Tribulation (cf., Ezek. 38:11) especially due to the fact that the seventieth week begins with a covenant of peace.

Conclusion

In conclusion it can be said that the "historical judgment and future judgment/blessing view" best fits the biblical data. So it is seen that the Day of the Lord is a time of divine intervention into the affairs of men. This has taken place historically, which is but a picture of that future intervention of judgment and blessing beginning at the Tribulation and extending through the Millennium. Therefore, when Paul says in 1 Thessalonians 1:10 and 5:9 that the believer will be delivered from wrath, this is a strong indication that the Christian will not go through any of the Tribulation.

Weeks, 49-67; J. D. Pentecost, *Things to Come* (Grand Rapids: Zondervan, 1979), 239-250; Robert Anderson, *The Coming Prince* (Grand Rapids: Kregel, 1984), 121-123; Harold Hoehner, *Chronological Aspects in the Life of Christ* (Grand Rapids: Zondervan, 1977), 115-139. However, for a recent discussion of the issue which reaches a different conclusion, see Christopher Hughes, "The *Terminus ad Quem* of Daniel's 69th Week," *Journal of Dispensational Theology* (Summer/Fall, 2013).

2 THESSALONIANS

Introduction

The external attestation to the Pauline authorship of 2 Thessalonians is provided by the fact that no church father questioned the authenticity of the claims of the letter. Internally, Pauline authorship is stated in the letter (1:1; 3:17), and the premature ending is more suitable to Paul than to one who was trying to imitate him.

Occasion

The epistle suggests that Paul had heard about some current conditions within the Thessalonian church. This information could have come from the person who carried the first letter and returned to Paul, or some of the news had been given to Paul, Silas, and Timothy by others. Some of the news was good in that the believers were continuing to grow and remain faithful despite persecution. However, some news was bad in that there was false information concerning the Day of the Lord which was resulting in some misbehavior.

Origin and Date

The facts that Paul, Silas, and Timothy were together in Corinth (Acts 18:5), that 1 Thessalonians was written from Corinth, and since the topics alluded to in both epistles are similar, it is logical to assume that the second epistle was also written from Corinth. This being the case, the second letter was probably written shortly after 1 Thessalonians some time in the early 50s (perhaps AD 51).

Purpose

It was observed in the section dealing with the occasion of the epistle that some false teaching regarding the Day of the Lord had crept into the church. This was leading to confusion and causing some, for example, to panic and quit their jobs in expectation of the Lord's return. A message/purpose statement could be put in these words: Paul writes to correct the error in the church concerning the Day of the Lord in order to return some of them to proper conduct in light of this doctrine.

Summary of Argument

I. PAUL INTRODUCES THE LETTER BY NAMING HIMSELF, SILAS, AND TIMOTHY TO THE THESSALONIAN CHURCH AND INVOKING GOD'S GRACE ON THEM SO THAT THEY WOULD KNOW THAT THEY WERE STILL IMPORTANT TO THEM—1:1-2

II. PAUL THANKS GOD FOR THE STEADFASTNESS OF THE THESSALONIANS, ENCOURAGES THEM TO CONTINUE TO PERSEVERE, AND PRAYS FOR THEM SO THAT THEY WOULD BE MOTIVATED TO ENDURE HARDSHIP AND WOULD REALIZE THAT SUFFERING IS NOT INCOMPATIBLE WITH BEING KEPT FROM THE DAY OF THE LORD—1:3-12

A. Paul tells the Thessalonians that he thanked God for their growing faith and love amid persecution in order to commend them for what they were doing—1:3-4

B. Paul encourages the Thessalonians to continue to persevere by noting that their enemies would be destroyed and God would be glorified in them so that they would be able to continue to bear up under their trials—1:5-10

1. He tells them that God's judgment will be seen to be right toward them by the fact that

they will be granted to participate in His Kingdom by virtue of their faithful endurance—1:5

2. He tells them that God's judgment will be seen to be right toward their adversaries by

the fact that they will be destroyed—1:6-8

a. The outcome of this judgment will be that the enemies will be paid back and they will receive relief—1:6-7a

b. The Judge will be revealed when He comes from heaven in blazing fire with His angels—1:7b

c. The subjects of judgment will be those who do not know God and do not obey the Gospel—1:8

3. He tells them of the consequences of this judgment—1:9-10

a. The lost will be punished eternally and shut out from the loving presence of God—1:9

b. The saved will glorify God and be amazed over what God has wrought in them—1:10

Note #211: Does this section teach the church will go through the tribulation?

Verses 6-10 are sometimes used by posttribulationists to prove their view that the rapture will occur at the end of the Tribulation. They suggest that the release of believers from persecution is at the return of Christ to judge unbelievers. There is a sense in which that is true in that people who believe the Gospel during the Tribulation and survive that period, will be delivered when Christ returns. This is the sense of what Jesus said in Matthew 24:13 "he who endures to the end shall be saved." However, there are certain facts which militate against this text saying that the Church will go through the Tribulation: 1) Paul had previously told the Thessalonians in 1 Thessalonians 5 that they would be delivered from the wrath of the Day of the Lord, 2) if Paul had taught them posttribulationism, there would not have been the panic that gave rise to this letter, and 3) the context is not dealing with the rapture but vindicating God's future and righteous judgment.

C. Paul prays for the Thessalonians that they would have success in their suffering for the

Gospel—1:11-12

1. He prays that they would be approved by God and be filled with power to bring to expression the good purpose of God—1:11

2. He prays this for the purpose that God would be glorified—1:12

III. PAUL DISCUSSES THE DOCTRINE OF THE DAY OF THE LORD IN ORDER TO CORRECT THE FALSE UNDERSTANDING THEY HAD OF THIS

MATTER AND TO STABLIZE THE CHURCH— 2:1-12

A. Paul explains to the Thessalonians the events that had to occur at the beginning of the Day of the Lord so that they would realize that they were not in it—2:1-4

1. He urges them not to be alarmed by any reports that said they were now in the Day of the Lord—2:1-2

2. He notes that the Day would not come until the apostasy takes place—2:3a

3. He notes that the Day would not come until the man of sin was revealed whose character it will be to have himself worshiped—2:3b-4

Note #212: 2 Thessalonians 2:1-3

The centerpiece of 2 Thessalonians is 2:1-12. A number of the key issues are found in the first three verses and will be summarized here.

1) *The preposition "by" in 2:1 has the sense of "on behalf of" or even "in the interest of" (Leon Morris,* The First and Second Epistles to the Thessalonians *[Grand Rapids: Eerdmans, 1979], 214, footnote 1).*
2) *The term translated "coming" in 2:1 is παρουσία. The word is used 24 times in the New Testament emphasizing the presence of someone. It is used in a variety of contexts and is not a technical term for the Second Advent.*
3) *Paul further modifies the term "coming" with the phrase "and our gathering together with him." The construction of the entire concept is not an example of the Granville Sharp rule; and therefore, while the ideas are closely related, they are not identical. Powell correctly states that "The 'coming' and the 'gathering' seem to refer to related but distinct events. The phrase is in an article-substantive-καί-substantive construction, also known as a Granville Sharp construction. However, since the nouns are impersonal, they do not meet the criteria of Sharp's first rule"(Charles Powell, "The Identity of the 'Restrainer' in 2 Thessalonians 2:6-7,"* Bibliotheca Sacra *154:615 [Jul 1997], 323). Thus "the gathering" is defining what aspect of the "coming" is in view—the rapture of the church as described in 1 Thessalonians 4:13-18. So, Paul is writing to defend the "gathering together."*
4) *The reason this defense is necessary is because the Thessalonians had been rashly disturbed into thinking that they were in the Day of the Lord, the event from which Paul wrote in his first letter to them they would be spared.*
5) *Paul indicates they were not in the Day of the Lord because two events had to take place before its beginning. The first is called the "falling away" or the "apostasia." Though many take this to be a reference to a religious apostasy, there is strong evidence that this is a reference to the rapture of the Church; particularly in light of the fact that Paul is writing to defend the "gathering together." The second event is the revelation of the man of sin, or antichrist. According to Daniel's prophecy (9:27), his appearance and treaty with Israel will inaugurate the future Day of the Lord.*

B. Paul explains to the Thessalonians that this mystery of lawlessness was being presently restrained in order to further show them that they had not entered into the Day of the Lord—2:5-12

1. He reminds them that he had told them about these things in the past—2:5
2. He explains to them the restraint that is on the mystery of lawlessness—2:6-7
    a. He notes that the purpose of the restraint was so that the man of sin would be revealed at the proper time—2:6
    b. He notes that this restraint would continue until the restrainer stepped aside—2:7

Note #213: Who is the restrainer?

There have been a number of suggestions as to the identity of the restrainer: 1) the Roman Empire, but this has vanished, 2) government, but this does not restrain evil and will be present during the Tribulation, 3) Satan, or 4) the church. The best explanation is that the restrainer is the Holy Spirit. However it should also be pointed out that Paul is not dealing with the relation between the Spirit and the believer, or his relation to the world (i.e. removal) but the relation between the Spirit and the man of sin. Thus, Paul is not answering questions relating to the rapture here. He is simply saying that the man of sin will be made manifest when the Spirit allows him to be, or "steps aside."

3. He explains to them the career of the man of sin—2:8-12
    a. He will be revealed when the Restrainer allows him to be—2:8a
    b. He will be destroyed by Christ at His coming—2:8b
    c. He will operate by the power of Satan by performing signs and wonders which will deceive the unregenerate who refuse the truth —2:9-10
    d. These will be deceived because God would send them strong delusion—2:11-12

Note #214: The abomination of desolation

The passage says earlier (v. 4) that the man of sin will oppose God, proclaim himself as God, and will set up an image of him to be worshiped. This, no doubt, is a reference to the Abomination that makes Desolate. Summarily, he will proclaim that he is to be worshiped around the middle of the Tribulation period by setting up a worship system in the Temple. This will cause the faithful to desolate this sacred area.

Note #215: Do people get a second chance to be saved after the rapture?

Some have suggested that v. 11 teaches that one who has rejected the gospel before the rapture cannot be saved after it. This is not true for several reasons: 1) virtually no one accepts the gospel the first time they hear it, 2) of the 144,000 witnesses during the Tribulation and the myriads who are saved during this time, it is reasonable to assume that some of them had heard the gospel before, 3) the connective "for" in v. 11 gives the reason, based on v. 10, they are sent strong delusion--they "refused to love the truth and be saved." This is deliberate and decisive rejection, and 4) the time period in view in the context is speaking of people who reject the Gospel during the Tribulation, not the

Church age.

IV. PAUL THANKS GOD FOR THE THESSALONIANS AND PRAYS FOR THEIR STEADFASTNESS IN ORDER TO REMIND THEM OF THEIR CALLING SO THAT THEY WOULD HOLD FAST TO THEIR PROFESSION AND APOSTOLIC TEACHING—2:13-17

A. Paul thanks God because of His election of the Thessalonians to be saved and share in the blessings of the gospel—2:13-14
B. Paul exhorts the elect to hold on to the sound teaching they had received—2:15
C. Paul prays for the elect that God would encourage and strengthen them so that they would do and say what would be pleasing to Him—2:16-17

V. PAUL EXHORTS THE THESSALONIANS CONCERNING PRACTICAL MATTERS SO THAT THEY WOULD RETURN TO NORMAL CHRISTIAN LIVING IN LIGHT OF THE CORRECTED TEACHING HE HAD GIVEN THEM ON THE DAY OF THE LORD—3:1-15

A. Paul requests their prayers that the Word would spread rapidly and be honored and that they would be delivered from evil men—3:1-2
B. Paul expresses God's faithfulness to them and his confidence in them and prays that their love and patience would increase—3:3-5
C. Paul instructs them on the discipline of the disorderly to bring back orderliness to the church—3:6-15
   1. He commands the faithful to withdraw from the offenders—3:6

Note #216: How to deal with the idle in the church

Paul had already warned those who were idle in 1 Thess. 4:11 and 5:14 but evidently some had not responded. This idleness led to being a busybody, or perhaps spreading the false doctrine of the Day of the Lord, thus expecting support from the church. It is possible that these people either quit their jobs because of imminency or had lost their jobs due to persecution and were presuming and loafing off the church. This seems to be what Paul is trying to correct and is supported by 7-10.

2. He supports this command by apostolic example in which they provided for their own needs.and did not presume on the church—3:7-10
3. He gives specific instructions concerning the idle—3:11-13
   a. The idle were urged to settle down and support themselves—3:11-12.
   b. The faithful were urged to continue to do what was right—3:13
4. He gives further instructions if the idle did not repent—3:14-15
   a. The person is to be ostracized so that he would feel ashamed of his actions—3:14
   b. The person is not to be treated in a reactionary way but it is to be remembered that he is still a brother—3:15

VI. PAUL CONCLUDES THE LETTER WITH A PRAYER, SALUTATION, AND BENEDICTION—3:16-18

A. He prays that they would have peace in the midst of their persecutions—3:16
B. He greets the church noting that this was an authentic letter—3:17
C. He pronounces the benediction that God's grace would be with the whole church—3:18

1 TIMOTHY

Author

Of all Paul's letters, the authenticity of the Pastorals is the most disputed. This doubt over Pauline authorship revolves around four main areas. The first is the chronological setting. This objection states that it is impossible to fit the writing of the Pastorals in the chronological framework provided by Acts. This objection assumes that the ending of Acts marks the closing days of Paul's life. However, it is really not necessary to fit the Pastorals into the book of Acts, for they probably describe a period after Acts. Surely if Paul had been executed at the end of his imprisonment, Luke would have mentioned it. It is just as likely that he was released (ca. AD 62) and engaged in another period of ministry. Between AD 62 and 67 he traveled widely and was eventually arrested again and executed in Rome in AD 67. During this period of travel, he would have written 1 Timothy and Titus, and during his final imprisonment 2 Timothy.

A second objection to Pauline authorship is the ecclesiastical complexity described in the books. It is said that this is too advanced for the first century. However, the assignments of bishops/elders were a part of Paul's ministry in Acts (14:23; 15:2-6; 20:17-28) and of Peter's admonitions (1 Peter 5:1-4). Furthermore, proper order of worship was developed before the Pastorals (1 Cor. 11-14).

A third objection is the doctrinal viewpoint. This criticism suggests that the heresy fought by Paul is full-blown second century Gnosticism. Yet, the heresy in the Pastorals had a strong Jewish flavor (1 Tim. 1:3-10). This would correspond more to incipient Gnosticism as was refuted in Colossians, for example.

A fourth problem with Pauline authorship revolves around linguistic peculiarities. This objection notes that there are 175 *hapax legomena* in the Pastorals. But an author should be given the freedom to change vocabulary when writing concerning different subject matter and writing during a different period in his life. Or, this could reflect the use of an amanuensis.

Accordingly, critics of Pauline authorship suggest that the three letters are the work of a pseudonymous writer who had access to fragments of some of Paul's genuine letters. On the other hand, it can be noted that during the apostolic age and into the second century, the view of Pauline authorship was as strong as any of Paul's epistles except Romans and 1 Corinthians (Guthrie, *New Testament Introduction,* 585). Internally, the epistles claim to be Pauline and the characterization presented is distinctly Pauline.

Date and Origin

If Paul was released from prison in Rome in the early AD 60s, he probably wrote 1 Timothy and Titus during his travels between AD 62-67. Paul refers to Macedonia in 1:3 and this suggests that he may have been in Macedonia when he wrote it, but this is open to question.

Paul's Relationship with Timothy

Timothy apparently became a Christian during Paul's missionary work in Lystra (Acts 14:6-23). He later joined Paul on his second missionary journey when Paul passed through where Timothy lived (Acts 16:1-3). On this second journey, Timothy helped Paul in Troas, Philippi, Berea, Thessalonica, Athens, and Corinth. During the third missionary journey, Timothy was with Paul who then sent him to Macedonia (Acts 19:22). Later he was with Paul in Macedonia and traveled with him to Corinth (Rom. 16:21). On the way back to Ephesus Timothy accompanied Paul as far as Troas (Acts 20:3-6). Subsequent to this, Timothy was with Paul in Rome (Col. 1:1; Philemon 1; Phil. 1:1) and from there probably made a trip to Philippi (Phil. 2:19-23).

Occasion

After Paul's release from his first Roman imprisonment, he eventually arrived in Ephesus. When Paul departed from Ephesus he left Timothy in charge as his representative to continue the work there (1 Tim. 1:3). Sometime later, Timothy must have written to Paul asking if he could leave Ephesus. Paul evidently responded with 1Timothy to instruct him to remain in Ephesus where he was needed.

Purpose

With the occasion and contents of the book in view, a purpose statement of the book could be put in these words: Paul instructs Timothy regarding life in the local church and his responsibilities in it so that the church would remain orderly in practice and pure in doctrine as it proclaimed the Word of God to the world.

Summary of Argument

I. PAUL BEGINS THIS LETTER TO TIMOTHY WITH HIS IDENTIFICATION AS AN APOSTLE AND A WARM GREETING TO TIMOTHY IN ORDER TO SET THE TONE FOR THE REST OF THE LETTER—1:1-2

II. PAUL INSTRUCTS TIMOTHY CONCERNING SOUND DOCTRINE IN ORDER TO REMIND HIM OF THE DANGER OF FALSE TEACHING AND HIS RESPONSIBILITY TO CORRECT IT—1:3-20

- **A.** Paul warns Timothy of the danger of sound doctrine in Ephesus so that he would be aware of the task that he faced and what his responsibility was—1:3-11
  - **1.** Paul discusses the teachers who were teaching erroneous doctrine and what Timothy was to do—1:3-7

Note #217: False teachers in Ephesus

Paul gives in these verses several characteristics of the false teachers in Ephesus: 1) they taught another doctrine. This implies an objective standard from which they were deviating, 2) they taught legends and fables which had grown out of the allegorical interpretation of the genealogies of the Old Testament, 3) their speaking was vain and empty, and 4) they were attempting to teach the Law but had missed the point of it.

- **a.** He reminds Timothy that he was to stay in Ephesus and to command these men not to teach—1:3a
- **b.** He describes for Timothy the characteristics of their teaching—1:3b-4
  - **1)** They teach different doctrine—1:3b
  - **2)** They devote themselves to myths—1:4a
  - **3)** They devote themselves to endless genealogies—1:4b

    4) Their teaching promoted controversy—1:4c
  c. He tells Timothy that the goal of his instruction for him was to cultivate love in his hearers that rests on a pure heart, a conscience devoid of guilt, and a trust in God—1:5
  d. He tells Timothy that the false teachers had departed from these and they did not know what they were saying for they had missed the point of the Law—1:6-7

2. Paul discusses the fact that the Law is profitable in order to show that the false teachers were abusing the Law and to show that he was in no way disparaging the Law—1:8-11
  a. He states that the Law itself is good if it is used properly—1:8
  b. He states that the Law was needed because men are sinners thus the Law curbed unrighteousness and revealed God's holiness—1:9-11

Note #218: The Law

Paul did not include 1:8-9 to say that we are under the Law but to emphasize that in his attack on the Judaizers he was not undermining the Law. It should be remembered that the Law had many purposes and here he simply alludes to one of them. Namely, he emphasizes that the Law was given because men were sinners and the Law served to point out their sin and put a fence around them. Though the Law as a unit has been done away (2 Cor 3; Rom. 7), there are aspects of it which transcend dispensations. Some of those aspects are listed in this passage. In the present age, these aspect can be stressed and thus the Law be used lawfully. The false teachers, however, were evidently imposing the whole Law on the people.

B. Paul thanks God for the change which His grace had brought in his life in order to show the transformation God brings to those condemned by the Law and the grace He gives for His work in order to encourage Timothy—1:12-17
  1. He states that he was appointed to the ministry in part because God foresaw he would be faithful even though in the past he was a sinner—1:12-14

Note #219: Sinning ignorantly

When Paul said that he committed these sins in ignorance, he meant that motivation in his sin was to please God by persecuting a movement he thought dishonored God. From a human perspective, he did not have a full revelation as to who Christ was.

  2. He states that his conversion was planned as a pattern for other saints and sinners—1:15-17

Note #220: The chief of sinners?

There is discussion as to what Paul means at the end of the verse 15 when he writes "of whom I am chief." The difficulty is that Paul was not the worst sinner of all time because there have been other people who have lived longer and sinned more grievously. Furthermore, according to Paul's statements in Philippians 3, he belonged to the strict sect of the Pharisees and vigorously kept the Law. And so how can Paul claim to be the "chief" or "foremost" or worst" sinner? Remarkably, Hendriksen states the importance of this question when he claims that this clause "has caused a wider variety of interpretation than almost any other in Paul's writings" (William Hendriksen, Thessalonians, Timothy, and Titus *[Grand Rapids: Baker, 1986], 79. For a discussion of seven views on the phrase, see footnote 39, on pages 79-80). Probably the best explanation is the one given by Ernest Brown in his commentary on the Pastoral Epistles (The Pastoral Epistles [London: Methuen, 1917], 10) in which Paul would be expressing a sense of sinfulness which had been produced by the Law. This would fit with what called previously the "lawful use of the law." Brown writes, "The fact is that it is always the characteristic of a true saint to feel himself a real sinner. The air in a room seems to be clear, but when it is penetrated by the sunlight it is seen to be full of dust and other impurities; and so as men draw nearer to God, and are penetrated by the light of God, they see more clearly their own infirmities, and begin to feel for sin something of the hatred which God feels for it." The same thing is happening in Romans 7 (see note there) when after being slain by the Law he exclaims "O wretched man that I am." John Stott has also captured this well when he writes: "The truth is...that when we are convicted of sin by the Holy Spirit, an immediate result is that we give up all...such comparisons. Paul is so vividly aware of his own sins that he could not conceive that anybody could be worse. It is the language of every sinner whose conscience has been awakened and disturbed by the Holy Spirit. We may begin like the Pharisee in Jesus' parable 'God I thank you that I am not like other men,' but we end like the tax collector who beat his breast and said literally 'God be merciful to me, the sinner.' The Pharisee indulged in odious comparisons; as far as the tax collector was concerned, however, there were no other sinners with whom to compare himself " (John Stott,* The Message of 1 Timothy and Titus *[Downers Grove: InterVarsity, 2001], 53).*

C. Paul exhorts Timothy concerning his responsibility to sound doctrine in order to motivate him to action—1:18-20

Note #221: Renewed charge

The mention of the "charge" in 1:18 is a reference back to the command in 1:3 and 5 where Timothy is to promote sound doctrine and refute false teachers.

3. Paul exhorts him to fight the good fight of faith as he continued to trust God and maintain a good conscience—1:18-19a

4. Paul warns him about rejecting these and gives two examples of men who had done so with disastrous results—1:19b-20

III. PAUL INSTRUCTS TIMOTHY CONCERNING PUBLIC WORSHIP IN ORDER TO EMPHASIZE THE IMPORTANCE OF PRAYER AND THE PROPER PLACE OF MEN AND WOMEN—2:1-15

A. Paul instructs Timothy regarding the importance of prayer in church life in order to emphasize its importance and to show him how it is to be practiced—2:1-7

1. He states the types of prayers which should be made in order to emphasize its importance—2:1a

2. He states these prayers should be made on behalf of all men including those in authority—2:1b-2a

3. He states the reason for these prayers is so that the church could be at peace with pagan rulers so as to have a venue to present the gospel. This prayer pleases God because He delights in saving men—2:2b-4

Note #222: God's will

It should be pointed out that in 2:4 the aspect of God's will being spoken of is His desired will rather than His decreed will. God's desired will often falls short because He has not chosen in this age to enforce it (unlike in the Millennium). For example, God desires for men not to murder, but he has given them the freedom to obey or disobey this wish. In a similar way, God generally desires all men to be saved, that is, He does not delight in their damnation. However, God has a higher, decreed will which is inflexible. In this decree, He has not chosen all to be saved. Somehow, it will bring God more glory for some to perish rather than for all to be saved. If this were not the case then God would have created a world in which none would perish.

4. He states that there is one God, one way to God, and a ransom that has been provided in order to confirm what he has just said about God delighting in saving men—2:5-6
5. He states that he had been appointed to proclaim this to the Gentiles in order to further buttress his command to pray for all men—2:7

B. Paul instructs Timothy concerning the responsibility of men in the church meeting—2:8

1. Men are to lead in public prayer—2:8a
2. Men are to do so while maintaining a holy life, without harboring resentment toward others, and with the absence of arguments—2:8b

C. Paul instructs Timothy concerning the responsibility of women in the church meeting—2:9-15

1. Women are to dress modestly and decently and to perform the good works which are to be expected from one who is worshiping God—2:9-10
2. Women are to submit to the authority and leader ship of the men in the public meeting—2:11-15
   - **a.** Positively they are to learn in quietness and submission—2:11
   - **b.** Negatively they are not to teach or have authority over a man—2:12
   - **c.** The first reason is the creational priority of the man—2:13
   - **d.** The second reason is the fact that Eve was deceived—2:14

Note #223: The role of women in the church meeting

The role of women in the church meeting is clearly one of the most emotionally charged debates in the current day. The purpose of this note is simply to state in brief form the conclusions to which I have come on the issues mentioned by Paul in this Timothy text.

1) It is necessary at the beginning to eliminate the expected disclaimers. No one is asserting that women are ontologically inferior, should be abused, demeaned, taken advantage of, stifled, not be used in God's service, etc. The introduction of these kinds of terms, ideas, or anecdotes from history is to purposefully cloud the issue and turn it into an emotional climate. The goal is to determine what the text meant to the original audience.

2) *This is a relatively recent debate in that the consensus of church history from the ancient church to the 20th century has been that the authoritative teaching ministry in the church is to be done by men. See Daniel Doriani's historical survey "A History of the Interpretation of 1 Timothy 2," in Women in the Church: A Fresh Analysis of 1 Timothy 2:9-15 (Grand Rapids: Baker, 1995), 213-267. Either evangelical feminists (egalitarians) have discovered an exegesis of this passage which eluded the Christian Church for 20 centuries, or they are being influenced by the thinking of the culture.*
3) *The feminist literature is filled with the faulty assumption that subordination equals inferiority. Roles assigned by God have nothing to do with inferiority/superiority.*
4) *The term "learn" refers to learning through instruction.*
5) *The term "silence" refers to the mode of learning. That is, it is a demeanor of peace and rest which accepts what God has ordained.*
6) *The term "subjection" refers to an ordering under or arrangement under an authority.*
7) *The translation of the KJV of verse 12 "to usurp" authority is most unfortunate. This reading followed Erasmus' Latin translation and implies that what Paul is prohibiting is not women holding authoritative pastoral office, but a forcible seizing of it. The more modern translations have corrected this translational error with something to the effect of "have" authority or "exercise" authority.*
8) *The two infinitives in verse 12 "to teach" and "to have authority" are not grammatically to be taken as a hendiadys, but rather as two prohibitions. Thus what is prohibited is not women teaching authoritatively (it is okay for women to teach men as long as it is not done in this manner), but women neither teaching nor having authority over the man in the church.*
9) *"Teaching" in the Pastoral Epistles refers to the teaching of apostolic doctrine.*
10) *One reason women are not to have this teaching function over men is because of creational priority. For Paul, this indicates a role difference.*
11) *A second reason is that Eve was deceived. Since Paul refers to Eve's deception in this context would indicate that a role reversal occurred in the Garden, and should not be repeated in the church.*

e. He complements this prohibition by stating that they would find a life of fulfillment apart from the leadership of the church—2:15

Note #224: Saved through childbearing

The phrase "she shall be saved through child-bearing" has a number of interpretations: 1) some suggest that godly women are promised physical safety in childbirth, however this is empirically false, 2) others say that if a woman dies in childbirth she will be spiritually saved, however it is impossible to make this link, 3) others see spiritual salvation in view through the incarnation (This has a number of supports. First, Paul's mind is in Genesis 3:15. Second, this would provide a remedy to the Fall just mentioned. And third, there is an article before childbirth), and 4) the word for saved would have the idea of "delivered" with "childbirth" acting as a synecdoche. With this understanding, the idea is that as she accepts her role in the home (symbolized by childbirth) she would be persevered from the temptation of seizing men's roles thus being saved from the evils that could come to her as came to Eve. This view seems to balance Paul's argument the best by showing how women can find a life of fulfillment not as teachers and leaders but as mothers in the home. This seems to stay more on the line of Paul's thinking rather than jumping to salvation, etc. As for women who are single or who do not have children, Paul is probably looking at the typical situation.

IV. PAUL INSTRUCTS TIMOTHY CONCERNING CHURCH OFFICERS IN ORDER TO GIVE TIMOTHY GUIDANCE IN SELECTING INDIVIDUALS WHO WOULD DO THE MOST FOR THE CHURCH— 3:1-16

A. Paul describes for Timothy the qualifications for bishops—3:1-7

1. He reminds Timothy that for one to desire the office of bishop is proper for it is a noble office—3:1

Note #225: Bishop

The terms "bishop," "pastor," and "elder" all refer to the same office. For example, in Acts 20:17 a group of men is called "elders" and in Acts 20:28 the same group is called "bishops;" in Titus 1:5 instruction is given to ordain elders and in verse 7 they are called bishops. The different terms stress different aspects of the office. The term "bishop" stresses the responsibility of oversight and is being retained in the outline because of the Greek term Paul uses (ἐπισκοπη, episkope*). "Overseer" would also be a good translation of this. For an excellent discussion of the office of elder, see Alexander Strauch, Biblical Eldership: An Urgent Call to Restore Biblical Church Leadership (Littleton, CO: Lewis and Roth Publishers, 1995).*

2. Paul lists for Timothy the qualifications of the bishop—3:2-7

a. He is to be one against whom no obvious charge could be brought against to reproach the name of Christ (blameless)—3:2a

b. He is to be the husband of one wife—3:2b

Note #226: One woman man

This is the most debated of all the qualifications. The views include: 1) the exclusion of married men view which is held by some Roman Catholic scholars to support celibacy for the priesthood. The "one wife" is the church. This view is refuted in the context where Paul speaks of the elder having children, 2) the exclusion of unmarried men view. This is the opposite of the preceding and has a number of criticisms: it does not give proper force to the adjective "one." "One" wife is different from "a" wife; neither Paul nor Christ saw anything wrong with the single state, in fact Paul himself was an elder (compare 1 Tim. 4:14 with 2 Tim. 1:6) and he was unmarried (l Cor. 7:8); consistency of interpretation would demand that if the elder must be married, he must also have children (3:4), 3) the exclusion of polygamists, however, polygamy was forbidden in the Roman Empire; if 3:2 means polygamy than 5:9 means polyandry. It is doubtful that this was a problem in the early church, 4) the exclusion of remarried widowers view is very popular and holds that one can only have been married once. This has a number of problems; the dubious support from 5:9; the presupposition that marriage is a necessary evil; the appeal to church history comes from an ascetic milieu; was this such a problem in the early church that it was the only sexual problem singled out?; Paul did not oppose remarriage after the death of a spouse (1 Tim. 5:14; 1 Cor. 7:9), 5) the exclusion of one involved in marital sin view. This view states that if a man has committed adultery or been divorced, etc., he is disqualified from the ministry for life. This view has the support of the immorality that was prevalent in society and the emphasis on quality or character seen by the lack of the article before the two nouns. However, this view has some weaknesses which will be shown in the final view. The final view (favored by the writer) is in essential agreement with view #5. Yet, this sixth view differs in that it sees the prohibition concerning those presently involved in sexual sin. Thus, what is at issue is not the past but the present state of the individual. There are several supports for this: 1) it enjoys the support of the preceding view 2) all of the qualifications are of importance. No human being has lived up to all of the qualities his whole life. Thus, it is inconsistent to demand that some of the others can be broken and the man still be in line for leadership while at the same time saying that if the "husband of one wife" is broken then the man is disqualified for life, 3) the issue is what the person is like at the present. With this in mind, there are two disclaimers to be made. First, this is not to say that a past sin will not have present ramifications thus prohibiting a man from holding office. It certainly may. Second, if a man has had a past problem, sufficient time should have elapsed for this or any other problem to be resolved (3:2 and 3:10). Thus, the bottom line for this quality, as well as the others, is whether or not the man presently shows maturity in all of these areas.

c. He is to be sober, clear-headed, and well balanced (temperate)—3:2c
d. He is to be self-controlled and sensible (prudent)—3:2d
e. He is to be orderly, proper, dignified, of good behavior (respectable)—3:2e
f. He is to be one who is hospitable—3:2f
g. He is to be on who is qualified and competent to explain and defend God's truth (apt to teach)—3:2g
h. He is not to be one who is addicted to wine (lit. "one who sits long at the wine." The Bible nowhere condemns the use of alcoholic beverages. In fact, Scripture views them as a blessing of God. Total abstinence is essentially an American invention from the early 20th century. There is a difference between the use and abuse of God's creation. See also Paul's discussion on asceticism in 4:1-5)—3:3a
i. He is not to be a quick-tempered bully (not a striker)—3:3b
j. He is to be gentle and patient—3:3c
k. He is not to be quarrelsome or contentious—3:3d
l. He is to be free from the love of money—3:3e
m. He is to have the administrative ability to manage his household well so that it is under control—3:4-5
n. He is not to be a novice so that he is not tempted by the devil to pride—3:6
o. He is to have a good reputation among those outside the church—3:7

B. Paul lists for Timothy the qualifications of deacons—3:8-10

Note #227: What is a deacon?

The various words in the "deacon" word group occur around 100 times in the New Testament and emphasize various types of service. The noun occasionally designates the church office of deacon as it does in this passage. The office of deacon is not a teaching or ruling office. Rather, it involves serving, aiding, and assisting the bishop/elder/pastor in whatever practical ways would be of help.

1. He is to be a man of dignity and worthy of respect—3:8a
2. He is to be sincere not hypocritical—3:8b
3. He is not to be addicted to wine—3:8c
4. He is not to be a lover of money or greedy—3:8d
5. He is to be a man of conviction who behaves in harmony with his conscience concerning those beliefs—3:9
6. He should be beyond reproach in the past and present—3:10

Note #228: Potential deacons

The idea here is not that a man should be given a trial appointment as a deacon but rather that the church should constantly be examining men in the church so that when the need arises for a deacon they will know which are qualified.

C. Paul lists for Timothy the qualifications of women who assist the deacons—3:11
1. She is to be dignified and worthy of respect—3:11a
2. She is not to be a gossiper or slanderer—3:11b
3. She is to be temperate and well balanced—3:11c
4. She is to be completely trustworthy in all things—3:11d

Note #229: Who are the "women?"

After discussing the qualifications of bishops and deacons, Paul inserts one verse on the qualifications for some women and then proceeds to give more qualifications for the deacon in the next verse. The question centers on the identity of the "women." The Greek word γυνη, can be translated either "wife" or "woman." This has led to two major interpretations of the verse. The first view is that the women are the wives of deacons and the second view is that this is referring to an office of deaconess. In favor of the first view is that these are wives of deacons are the following: 1) if these were deaconesses, Paul could have indicated that by calling them such rather than using the word for "women," 2) in the next verse Paul continues to talk about the qualifications of deacons which would seem odd if he had introduced a third order of church officer here, and 3) one of the major objections to this view is that if these are wives of the deacons then why would he not have mentioned the wives of elders? The answer is: only the wives of deacons could assist their husbands in their work while the wives of elders could not because that was a function of authority.

In favor of the second view that this is an office of deaconess is the following: 1) the previous "wife" view is virtually arguing for this view, because if the wife had to have certain qualifications to serve with her husband, then practically speaking she is a deaconess, 2) the context of chapter 3 is dealing with church officers, 3) the conjunction translated "likewise." In verse 8 the word "likewise" marks a transition from the office of bishop to the office of deacon, and then in verse 11 the "even so" is the same conjunction indicating that now he is moving to a third office, 4) there is nothing in the office of deacon which would be wrong for a woman to do, 5) in 16:1 Phoebe is called a "deaconess" which granted could simply mean servant but it could also refer to an office, and 6) there are major early church documents which indicate an office of deaconess.

A third view, however, has been suggested by Robert Lewis ("The Women of 1 Timothy 3:11," Bibliotheca Sacra *136:542 [Apr 1979], 167-175) in which he posits that the "women" of this passage are unmarried women who assist the deacons. One of the strongest arguments for this view is a weakness which has not been adequately addressed by the other positions. The grammar of the passage argues that a distinct group is under consideration which supports the second view, but one of the flaws of this is that if this is a distinct office, then why would Paul resume talking about the office of deacon in the very next verse. This view is able to keep the distinction in mind, and yet show some relationship between the two, then allowing Paul to talk about deacons in the next verse.*

The reason these would be unmarried women is: 1) no qualifications are given for them which relate to the home, 2) the main ministry of women according to the letter is to be centered in the home (1 Tim. 2:15; 5:8, 14, 16; 2 Tim. 3:14-15; Titus 2:3-5) [this does not mean that she shouldn't be involved in the church but that the church be worked around her home responsibilities.], 3) historically speaking, at the close of the first century churches limited the office of deaconess almost exclusively to virgins and, 4) unmarried women are one of the most neglected individuals as far as untapped ministry potential.

D. Paul lists more qualities of deacons—3:12-13
- **1.** He is to be the husband of one wife—3:12a
- **2.** He must manage his household well—3:12b
- **3.** He states that the deacons' rewards are a good reputation and increased confidence with God that comes from a clear conscience—3:13

E. Paul explains to Timothy the importance of the charges he had just given him by noting the nature of the local church—3:14-16
- **1.** He said that these instructions were important because people needed to know how to conduct themselves in the local church since it was a household (a family of believers) and a pedestal (in that it holds up the testimony of each individual before the world)—3:14-15
- **2.** He said that these instructions were important because of the glorious message that is the possession of the church—3:16
  - **a.** Christ was revealed in the flesh at his incarnation—3:16a
  - **b.** Christ was proved righteous and vindicated by the Spirit at His resurrection—3:16b
  - **c.** Christ was worshipped by angels at His exaltation in heaven—3:16c
  - **d.** Christ was preached among the nations—3:16d
  - **e.** Christ was believed on by those who accepted the message—3:l6e
  - **f.** Christ was taken up to glory at the ascension—3:16f

V. PAUL INSTRUCTS TIMOTHY CONCERNING THE FALSE TEACHERS IN ORDER TO HELP HIM TO IDENTIFY THE HERESY AND TO INSTRUCT HIM

ON HIS RESPONSIBILITY IN DEALING WITH IT—4:1-16

A. Paul instructs Timothy about the false teachers including the time of their appearing and a description of their teaching so that he would be equipped to identify them and a refutation of their doctrine—4:1-5
  1. He gives the time of their appearing as being in the latter times—4:1a
  2. He gives a description of their teaching—4:1b-3a
    a. It causes an abandoning of the faith—4:1b
    b. It finds its source in demonic activity—4:1c
    c. It is promoted by hypocritical liars whose consciences have been cauterized by their refusal of the truth—4:2
    d. It promotes an asceticism which forbids to marry and enjoy certain foods—4:3a
  3. He gives a refutation of their teaching—4:3b-5
    a. He says that the things God created are to be enjoyed by the believer—4:3b
    b. He says these things are good and are sanctified by the Word and prayer—4:4-5

B. Paul instructs Timothy concerning his duties and responsibilities so that he would know his role in overcoming the influences of these ascetic apostates—4:6-16
  1. He was to point out the truth he had just been given to the church—4:6
  2. He was not to become embroiled in refuting these fables but rather should train himself in godliness which includes the fact of our hope in the living God who is the Savior of all men—4:7-10
  3. He was to teach sound doctrine—4:11
  4. He was to maintain the respect of the people by setting an example in word, conduct, love, faith, and purity—4:12
  5. He was to carry out a balanced public ministry including the public reading of the Scripture, preaching, and teaching—4:13
  6. He was to nurture the gift he possessed—4:14
  7. He was to be diligent in his personal life and public ministry—4:15-16

Note #230: Christians need to be saved too

In 4:4-16 Paul gives Timothy a series of instructions as to what he is to do in the local church. These include things such as teaching, setting an example, publicly reading Scripture, etc. Paul indicates in 4:16 that if Timothy does these things he will "save himself and those who hear him." In the Bible, "salvation" is multi-dimensional. Quite often the word refers to a full and meaningful spiritual life. Clearly Paul is not talking about initial salvation at this point since Timothy is already saved. Therefore, the salvation in view in this text is a deliverance from doctrinal error which would be accomplished by Timothy faithfully carrying out his ministry. By doing this, he would save himself and those in the congregation. Thus, Christians need to be saved too.

VI. PAUL INSTRUCTS TIMOTHY CONCERNING VARIOUS GROUPS IN THE CHURCH IN ORDER TO AID HIM IN INTERPERSONAL RELATIONSHIPS AND EDUCATE HIM ON HOW VARIOUS PEOPLE ARE TO BE TREATED—

5:1-6:10

A. He instructs Timothy on how to deal with various age groups—5:1-2
  1. He is to treat older men with respect and gentleness as fathers—5:1a
  2. He is to treat younger men as brothers—5:1b
  3. He is to treat older women as mothers—5:2a
  4. He is to treat younger women with the purity of a sister—5:2b
B. He instructs Timothy on how to deal with widows in order to show God's special care for them—5:3-16

Note #231: Instruction concerning widows

Going back to the Old Testament, widows have always been of special concern to God because of their vulnerability (Deut. 10:18; 24:17; Ps. 68:5; Isa. 1:17). Apparently, in the Ephesian churches instruction was needed due to problems in this area. Paul distinguished between two types of widows: those who had family to support them and those who did not. The latter group, known as "widows indeed," should receive financial support from the church if they met three qualifications: at least 60 years of age (the age at which in this culture she could not provide for her own needs and was unlikely to remarry), faithful in her marriage, and a pattern of good works. By contrast, younger widows were not to be supported by the church lest they become idle. Moreover, it would have been expected that a younger widow would remarry.

  1. Widows who are truly destitute without family should be cared for by the church—5:3
  2. Widows who have family members should be cared for by them—5:4
  3. The first type of widow is marked by her faith in God and should be supported but the widow of the first type who pursues pleasure rather than God does not qualify for support—5:5-6
  4. Timothy was to teach these things to the church including the fact that the family is responsible to provide for their own—5:7-8
  5. Three qualifications of "widows indeed" (mentioned in v. 3) to know who qualified for support—5:9-10
    a. She had to be at least 60 years of age thus incapable of providing for herself—5:9a
    b. She had to have been faithful to her spouse—5:9b
    c. She had to have established a pattern of good works including well raised children, hospitality, humble service, sensitive to the needy, and devoted to good works in general—5:10
  6. Younger widows should not be placed on the list of those to be supported—5:11-15
    a. This is because their sexual desires might give them the desire to remarry and this would cause reproach for it would break their pledge of joining the widows' list of not remarrying—5:11-12
    b. This is because younger widows would have a harder time resisting the temptations connected with idleness—5:13-15
  7. He states that financially capable women should maintain widows in their families in order not to be misunderstood concerning his charge in v. 8—

5:16

C. Paul instructs Timothy concerning elders in order to help deal properly with this group in the church—5:17-25
   1. Elders of the church were to direct the church and teach and were worthy of double remuneration which is supported by Deut. 25:4 and Lev. 19:13—5:17-18
   2. Accusations against elders are not to be heeded unless brought by 2-3 witnesses—5:19
   3. Those that are culpable were to be rebuked publicly so that others would fear—5:20
   4. These things were to be carried out in an objective manner—5:21
   5. He warns Timothy to be careful in his selection of elders in order to avoid problems in the first place—5:22
   6. He suggests, as a parenthesis in the argument, that Timothy use wine to relieve the stress of this process—5:23
   7. He continues the thought of verse 22 by noting that the better a potential elder can be known before ordination, the better, so that there are no surprises afterward—5:24-25

Note #232: The discipline of sinning elders

Beginning in 5:19, Paul enjoins Timothy to the difficult task of how to carry out discipline on elders in the church who sin. Paul's instructions will be laid out in a number of interpretive observations.

1) *Formal complaints against elders. The word translated "accusation" (κατηγορία) is used only 3 times in the New Testament (John 18:29; 1 Timothy 5:19; Titus 1:6). In broader Greek literature the term is "nearly always" of a legal nature (Bauer, Arndt, Gingrich, Danker, 423). Thus, what is being envisioned in this text is the lodging of a formal complaint.*
2) *Complaints must be factual. Paul indicates that a formal complaint must be accompanied by two or three witnesses. This would serve to protect the elder from an accusation, which even if shown to be false, could damage his credibility. Conversely, it would prevent frivolous accusations.*
3) *Discipline is required for single acts of sin. The question here has to do with the present participle "sin" in 5:20. Does the present tense indicate that discipline should only be pursued if the sin is continual? The answer is probably "no." The present tense most likely refers to the state of guilt of the elder.*
4) *What is the sin? Certainly no one holding church office is perfect and will commit acts of sin. What is in view is something that would cause the individual to stop being above reproach (1 Tim. 3:2) and would cause his ministry to lose credibility. Specific examples are found in the balance of Paul's list in chapter 3. This fact helps support the conclusion in #3.*
5) *The elder should be rebuked in public. If the elder is found guilty, should he be rebuked in private or before the entire congregation? I would argue for the latter. Since the accusation has been verified by several witnesses, the problem is already a public matter and therefore would demand dealing with it before the congregation. Not to do so would open the other leaders to complicity.*
6) *What is the goal of this process? It goes without saying that the culpable*

individual should be forgiven and received back into the assembly; however, the goal Paul gives in this text is that "the rest also may fear." While the "rest" could refer to the entire congregation, perhaps specifically, the other elders are in view. This would make the ultimate goal of the process to be the maintenance of respectability for the office.

7) *The process is to be carried out in an objective manner (5:21).*
8) *The "laying on of hands." Paul instructs Timothy in 5:22 not to rashly lay hands on elders. The interpretive question is: is Paul talking about the restoration of elders who have sinned? Or, is he talking about the initial laying on of hands at ordination? While either view is possible, I tend to the latter position. If correct, the purpose of this instruction is a safeguard which would prevent going through the discipline process. If care is taken in the initial ordination of an individual, then there is less likelihood that discipline will need to occur. This appears to be validated by the balance of the verse. If ordination occurred too hastily, then part of the blame would rest on those who ordained the man. This would also explain why the following verses talk about this process.*
9) *The importance of knowing potential elders. The section ends with the words in verses 24-25 "Some men's sins are clearly evident, preceding* them *to judgment, but those of some men follow later. Likewise, the good works of* some *are clearly evident, and those that are otherwise cannot be hidden" (NKJV). The "judgment" in view refers to the human evaluation of potential elders. The sins of some are evident even before this evaluation occurs; while the sins of others are detected after this evaluation. These directions explain why the laying on of hands should not occur until a time of deliberation.*

D. Paul instructs Timothy regarding slaves and masters—6:1-2
   1. Slaves are to respect their masters so that God's name is not slandered—6:1
   2. Slaves are to serve their masters even if they are unbelieving—6:2

E. Paul instructs Timothy regarding false teachers and the greedy—6:3-10
   1. Paul gives Timothy a description of the false teachers—6:3-5
      a. He describes the actions of false teachers as advocating false doctrine and rejection of true doctrine and godliness—6:3
      b. He describes their attitudes as being conceited and ignorant—6:4a
      c. He describes their fruits as being controversy and friction—6:4b-5a
      d. He describes their motivation as being greed—6:5b
   2. Paul gives Timothy instruction concerning money for those who desired to be rich—6:6-10
      a. True gain comes in the acquisition of godliness which includes an attitude of contentment—6:6
      b. There is no relation between godliness and material possessions because they are transitory—6:7
      c. The necessities of life should bring contentment—6:8
      d. The results of desiring to be rich—6:9-10
         1) Falling into temptation—6:9a
         2) Falling into a snare—6:9b
         3) Falling into senseless and harmful lusts—6:9c
         4) Potential eternal ruin—6:10a
         5) Wandering from the faith—6:10b

6) It causes many inward and outward griefs—6:10c

VII. PAUL PRESENTS HIS FINAL CHARGE TO TIMOTHY IN WHICH HE EXHORTS HIM TO GODLINESS AND INSTRUCTS HIM ON HOW TO DEAL WITH THE RICH—6:11-21

A. He exhorts Timothy to a life of godliness—6:11-16

1. He exhorts Timothy to flee from the snares of money and pursue righteousness—6:11

2. He exhorts Timothy to fight the good fight of faith—6:12-13a

3. He exhorts Timothy to keep the commandment of God as seen in the instructions he had been given until the appearing of Jesus Christ—6:13b-16

B. He instructs Timothy on how to instruct those who are rich in the church—6:17-19

1. He is to instruct them not to be proud—6:17a

2. He is to instruct them not to put their hope in wealth but in God—6:17b

3. He is to instruct them to be rich in good works, one of which is sharing with others, so that they would lay up treasure in heaven and really experience the fullness of eternal life—6:18-19

C. He concludes by charging Timothy to guard what had been entrusted to him, turn away from false teaching, and by wishing God's grace upon him—6:20-21

2 TIMOTHY

Occasion

As was suggested in the introduction to 1 Timothy, Paul ended up as a prisoner in Rome again (2:9). He had already gone through his initial hearing and was awaiting trial (4:16) during which he expected to be found guilty (4:6). Since Paul was executed shortly before the death of Nero in June of AD 68, and since he penned 2 Timothy (the last of his epistles) before his death, this book was probably written around AD 67.

Timothy was apparently still in Ephesus after receiving Paul's first letter (1:16-18; 4:14, 19). After the fire in Rome (AD 64) and the blame for this placed on Christians by Nero, it had become dangerous to be associated with Christianity. Quite possibly Timothy was tempted to assume a lower profile in his ministry due to these circumstances.

Purpose

In light of Paul's imminent execution and the danger associated with maintaining an aggressive ministry, Paul wrote this epistle to Timothy to encourage him to remain faithful and unashamed in his ministry. A purpose statement is as follows: Paul charges Timothy with various duties and responsibilities in his ministry in order to urge him to remain faithful in his calling as a minister of the Gospel in the face of hardship so that he would receive a full reward at the judgment seat.

Summary of Argument

I. PAUL INTRODUCES THE LETTER BY NOTING HIS APOSTLESHIP ACCORDING TO THE PROMISE OF LIFE IN THE GOSPEL AND BY GREETING TIMOTHY AS HIS BELOVED SON—1:1-2

A. Paul notes that his apostleship is by the will of God and according to the promise of eternal life in the Gospel in order to give Timothy strength and hope in hardship—1:1

B. Paul greets Timothy as his dear son and pronounces God's blessing on him in order to emphasize the affection he felt for him—1:2

II. PAUL THANKS GOD FOR TIMOTHY'S PAST FAITHFULNESS, CHARGES HIM TO CONTINUE TO REMAIN LOYAL, AND GIVES EXAMPLES OF FAITHFULNESS AND UNFAITHFULNESS IN ORDER TO STRENGTHEN HIS RESOLVE TO BE UNASHAMED OF THE GOSPEL—1:3-18

A. Paul thanks God for Timothy's past faithfulness in order to encourage him to continue being faithful—1:3-7

1. He tells Timothy that he thanks God continually for him and that he longed to see him—1:3-4

2. He tells Timothy that he rejoiced in the genuine faith that resided in him—1:5

3. He tells Timothy that, in view of his faith, he was to fan into a flame the gift of the ministry he was given—1:6
4. He tells Timothy that this was to be done because God wanted him to be characterized by power, love, and self-discipline—1:7

Note #233: Was Timothy really timid?

"God has ***not*** *given us a spirit of fear;* ***but*** *of power, and of love, and of a sound mind" (2 Tim. 1:7, NKJV). This verse has led many to the perception that Timothy was of a fearful, timid personality. For example, Kelly writes that Paul is "obliquely chiding Timothy for his timidity" (J. N. D. Kelly, A Commentary on the Pastoral Epistles [Grand Rapids: Baker, 1983], 160) while Knight says that Paul is reminding "Timothy of this both because of his own temperament and also because of the difficult situation in which he and Paul found themselves" (George Knight III, The Pastoral Epistles [Grand Rapids: Eerdmans, 2000], 371). It appears that this view of Timothy's personality rests largely on this text since there is really no other evidence in the New Testament description of Timothy that would suggest he was of a timid nature. Rather, as one of Paul's most trusted comrades, the opposite would be assumed. Based on this text, was Timothy really timid? There are two indicators which lead to a negative answer to this question.*

First, in his discussion of this verse, Fee zeroes in on the οὐ/ἀλλα, (not/but) contrast in Paul's writings. He observes that in the vast majority of instances where the formula is used, the negative part of the statement could essentially be eliminated since it is not the point being made. Rather, Paul is encouraging Timothy (just as he would encourage anyone) by the Spirit's activity in the life of the believer. Fee writes, "...the negative is not the point, although it is crucial to the point....But to get there [the positive, "but" part of the statement] Paul begins by setting up a contrast vital to the present argument, but expressed in such a way as to make his meaning almost impossible to render in English without some jockeying with the words and their word order" (Gordon Fee, God's Empowering Presence: The Holy Spirit in the Letters of Paul *[Peabody, MA: Hendrickson Publishers, 1994], 788-789). Mounce concurs, "...it is highly doubtful that Paul is implying that Timothy was a coward...Cowardice is merely a foil that serves to emphasize and define what Paul means by power" (William Mounce,* Pastoral Epistles *[Dallas: Word, 2000], 478).*

A second indicator is the word translated "fear" (δειλία). This word is used only here in the New Testament, but is used 9 times in the LXX. What is of interest in these other uses is that the term denotes something more intense than mere timidity. Therefore, if Paul were commenting on Timothy's temperament, he would be saying that he was a coward which does not fit with how the New Testament pictures him.

B. Paul charges Timothy to be courageous and unashamed in order to further encourage him to remain faithful and able to guard the deposit of the gospel—1:8-14

1. He charges Timothy to be courageous so that he would not be ashamed in his ministry—1:8-12
   a. He instructs him not to be ashamed of the gospel or of Paul by the grace and power of the Gospel which would see Christ destroy death and bring immortality—1:8-11

b. He tells Timothy that the gospel was the reason he was suffering so that Timothy's courage would be bolstered in light of the fact that even if his life ended, God would be faithful in preserving the message he had entrusted to him—1:12

Note #234: The deposit

The "deposit" could refer either to that which Paul had committed to God, namely his soul for salvation etc., or what God had committed to Paul, namely the Gospel message. If the first view is taken, the deposit is Paul's given to God, if the latter, then the deposit is God's entrusted to Paul. It appears best to take the latter view that the deposit is God's of the gospel message entrusted with Paul. This would be consistent with the other two uses where this is meant (1 Tim. 6:20; 2 Tim. 1:14), and with the theme in this letter to remain faithful.

2. He charges Timothy to guard the deposit they had been given—1:13-14

a. He instructs him to continue to preach the same message he had heard from Paul in order to protect him from the temptation of modifying the message—1:13

b. He instructs him to guard the good deposit by the aid of the Holy Spirit—1:14

C. Paul provides Timothy with examples of faithful and unfaithful service in order to impress upon him the need to remain faithful—1:15-18

1. He provides examples of unfaithfulness by noting that all (hyperbole) in Asia abandoned him (not the gospel) in his hour of need among whom were Phygelus and Hermogenes (perhaps he lists them because they were unexpected to do this)—1:15

2. He provides examples of faithfulness by noting that the household of Onesiphorus was not ashamed of his chains and that God would take this as an opportunity of showing mercy to him at the judgment seat of Christ to reward him more greatly than the unfaithful brethren (i.e., Phygelus and Hermogenes)—1:16-18

III. PAUL CHARGES TIMOTHY TO REMAIN STRONG IN HIS SERVICE OF CHRIST IN ORDER TO ENCOURAGE HIM TO PERSEVERE AND REMAIN SERVING FAITHFULLY IN HIS DUTIES AS A MINISTER—2:1-26

A. Paul charges Timothy to remain strong in his service for Christ and explains to him the specific responsibilities of that in order to encourage him to persevere and remain strong—2:1-13

1. He gives Timothy the general charge to remain strong in the grace that is in Christ Jesus—2:1

2. He gives Timothy specific responsibilities he was to carry out in his endurance—2:2-7

a. He tells Timothy to pass the message given him by Paul to other faithful men so that they would pass it to others—2:2

b. He tells Timothy to endure hardship and gives him three illustrations to impress this point on him—2:3-6

1) He is to be like the soldier who endures hardship, does not become entangled with lesser goals, and gives unquestioned obedience to his commander—2:3-4
2) He is to be like the athlete who trains according to the rules of the games and only then receives reward—2:5
3) He is to be like the farmer who toils diligently and then receives the fruit of his labor—2:6

c. He asks Timothy to mediate on what he had just said so that the Lord would help him to see the truth of these words—2:7

3. He gives Timothy the example of Christ in order to give him the ultimate example of enduring hardship—2:8-10

a. He urges Timothy to remember the work of Christ who was vindicated after His sufferings and that this gospel is why he was suffering—2:8-9

b. He states that because of the power of the gospel he endured all things so that the elect would come to faith—2:10

4. He presents a popular saying consisting of four couplets in order to remind Timothy to endure hardship and remain faithful—2:11-13

a. The first couplet notes that since the believer died with Christ he has been raised with him in newness of life in order to provide the comfort of this new position—2:11

b. The second couplet notes that if the believer endures the temptation to turn away he will one day reign with Christ—2:12a

Note #235: Faithfulness leads to reigning

The issue in these verses (as well as the whole book) is not salvation but the necessity of the believer remaining faithful in his service to Christ. Therefore, the believer who remains faithful in this life will receive greater rewards in the Kingdom as far as reigning, etc.

c. The third couplet notes that if the believer disowns Christ by not faithfully enduring he would be disowned at the judgment seat—2:12b

d. The fourth couplet notes that even if the believer is unfaithful to God, He would remain faithful in saving him—2:13

B. Paul charges Timothy to remain faithful in his service for Christ in order to motivate him to persevere—2:14-26

1. Paul urges Timothy to faithfulness in his public ministry—2:14-21

a. He is to warn the people of what he had told him and to not be embroiled in meaningless controversies—2:14

b. He is to be diligent in his work for God so that he would not be ashamed at the judgment which would occur if he handled the Word accurately—2:15

Note #236: "Study?" or "be zealous?"

The word "study" in 2:15 is oftentimes used as picturing a student. However, the word ἐργάτης is used of one who labors. Thus the idea is to be diligent or zealous. "Rightly dividing" is used only here and in the LXX at Proverbs 3:6 and means literally "to cut straight." Paul does not say which workman he has in mind (whether a tentmaker, a farmer, a builder, etc.). Be that as it may, it is clear that disapproval remains for the minister who misuses and is not precise in his handling of the text.

- **c.** He is to turn away from meaningless discussions because they provide an atmosphere of poison that hurts the body of Christ—2:16-17a
- **d.** He provides the examples of Hymenaeus and Philetus who taught that the resurrection had already occurred and had caused many to have the faith destroyed—2:17b-18
- **e.** He notes that even though the church was being upset it would continue to stand because God knows which servants are faithful and which are not (Num. 16:5—Aaron, Nadab and Abihu)—2:19
- **f.** He furthers his point by illustrating with vessels in the house: some are for noble and others for ignoble purposes in order to show that there were both kinds in the church and impress on Timothy the need to remain pure so that he would be a fit vessel for God's use—2:20-21

2. Paul urges Timothy to faithfulness in his conduct—2:22-26

- **a.** He urges Timothy to run away from evil desires and to pursue righteousness—2:22
- **b.** He urges Timothy to refuse to get caught up in immature debates which cause division—2:23
- **c.** He urges Timothy to promote peace and to gently teach the brethren in the hope that they would repent—2:24-26

IV. PAUL CHARGES TIMOTHY CONCERNING THE LAST DAYS SO THAT HE WOULD KNOW THE CHARACTERISTICS OF THAT PERIOD AND HIS DUTIES IN IT IN ORDER TO HELP HIM TO FAITHFULLY ENDURE—3:1-4:8

A. Paul describes for Timothy characteristics of the last days so that he would know that what was happening was to be expected and how to combat it intelligently—3:1-9

Note #237: The last days

The "last days" is a period (in the NT) extending from the first advent to the rapture of the Church. The writers of the New Testament regarded themselves as living in the last days (1 John 2:18; Acts 2:16-17; Heb. 1:1), because the end of the period was unknown. The "last days" in the Old Testament refers to the future time when God fulfills Israel's covenants.

1. Paul gives the description of the character of the last days—3:1-9

2. Paul provides a negative illustration of Jannes and Jambres (according to Jewish tradition these were the magicians who opposed Moses) in order to show Timothy that those who opposed him, like those who opposed Moses would be proved to be false—3:8-9

B. Paul presents a personal example, his childhood training, and the inspired Scriptures in order to provide Timothy with safeguards to inspire him to withstand apostasy—3:10-17

1. He reviews for Timothy his faithfulness in the midst of persecution to inspire and remind him that persecution will come—3:10-13
2. He reminds Timothy of his godly heritage and the part the Scriptures played in his past so that he would continue in that way—3:14-15
3. He reminds Timothy of the inspired (God-breathed) Scripture and its profitableness so that he would see the part it played in his present and future ministry—3:16-17

Note #238: All Scripture inspired

When the Greek word "all" or "every" (πᾶς) is used with a technical noun as "Scripture," it is better to render it as "all" rather than "every" (Wayne House, "Biblical Inspiration in 2 Timothy 3:16," Bibliotheca Sacra, *137:545 [Jan, 1980], 55). It is also to be noted that verse 16 has no verb but it has to be inserted. Some insert the copula so that the verse reads "every Scripture inspired by God is profitable..." Others insert it before God so that it reads "all Scripture is inspired by God..." This seems to be the better reading as is argued by Walter Lock, The Pastoral Epistles,* The International Critical Commentary *(Edinburgh: T. & T. Clark, 1978), 110 and others. Thus, "all Scripture is inspired by God and is profitable."*

C. Paul charges Timothy to proclaim the truth so that he would know what his primary role would be in the last days—4:1-5
   1. He presents the nature of the charge to be under the watchful eye of God and Christ in order to impress upon him the solemn nature of it—4:1
   2. He presents the content of the charge as the proclaiming of God's Word at all times—4:2
   3. He presents the method of proclaiming the Word as including correction, rebuke, and encouragement done with patience and with careful instruction—4:2b
   4. He presents the reason for the charge to be that many would turn away from the truth to things they wanted to hear—4:3-4
   5. He continues the charge by reminding him to stay alert, be willing to endure hardship, evangelize, and thus carry out the ministry entrusted to him—4:5
D. Paul tells Timothy that his role in these last days was his imminent death in order to further impress on him the need for remaining faithful and to provide an example for him to follow—4:6-8
   1. He states that he was already moving closer to his death (drink offering) and was getting ready for his soon departure—4:6
   2. He states that his life on earth consisted in fighting the good fight, finishing the race (according to the rules), and keeping the faith—4:7
   3. He states that because of his victorious life on earth just described he would be rewarded just as those would who long for the appearing of the Lord—4:8

V. PAUL CONCLUDES THE LETTER WITH PERSONAL INSTRUCTIONS AND INFORMATION FOR TIMOTHY SO THAT HE WOULD BE ABLE TO CARRY OUT THE APOSTLE'S LAST WISHES —4:9-22

A. Paul informs Timothy concerning his enemies and friends—4:9-15
   1. He urges Timothy to come and visit him quickly—4:9

2. He notes that Demas had forsaken him because of the allurement of the world—4:10a
3. He states that Crescens and Titus had gone presumably in the Lord's work—4:10b
4. He states that only Luke was with him and requests that Mark and Timothy would come to Rome and bring with them his cloak, books, and parchments—4:11-13
5. He states that Alexander had caused him problems but that the Lord would repay him for that and warns Timothy to watch out for him—4:14-15

B. Paul informs Timothy concerning his hearing in court—4:16-18

1. He states that at his preliminary hearing before his trial no one came to his defense—4:16
2. He states that the Lord was the only one who stood with him and strengthened him and allowed him up to that point to proclaim the Gospel to the Gentiles—4:17
3. He states that despite his impending death the Lord would provide the ultimate deliverance of bringing him into His presence—4:18

C. Paul provides additional greetings, instructions, and benediction—4:19-22

TITUS

Background and Occasion

Titus was a Gentile convert (Gal. 2:3) who had been won to Christ by the apostle Paul (Titus 1:4). Titus accompanied Paul and Barnabas on their mission to the Jerusalem church (Gal. 2:1-3). Titus was also a special representative to the church at Corinth during Paul's third missionary journey. In addition, he carried the "severe letter" from Ephesus (2 Cor. 12:18) and on his way back to Ephesus met with Paul in Macedonia (2 Cor. 7:6-16). Furthermore, he was the leader of a group sent to the churches in Macedonia by Paul to pick up the collection for the poor saints at Jerusalem (2 Cor. 8:6, 16).

During the time between his two Roman imprisonments, Paul and Titus traveled to Crete. After a brief visit, Paul left Titus in Crete to set the church in order there (Titus 1:5). He planned to send Artemas or Tychicus to relieve Titus so that Titus could join Paul in Nicopolis (probably the one in Illyricum) for the winter (Titus 3:12). Though uncertain, it is likely that Paul wrote the letter to Titus from Nicopolis. A traditional date between AD 62-66 seems safe for the composition of the letter.

Purpose

From the background to the letter and its content, the purpose was to instruct Titus on how he was to set in order the Cretan churches. This evidently included both organization and teaching. With this in mind, a purpose statement could be: <u>Paul instructs Titus on the appointment of elders, the correction of false teachers, and the godly behavior that should characterize the church so that the church would be set in order and the believers would love in a Christian manner</u>.

Summary of Argument

I. PAUL PRESENTS THE SALUTATION OF THE LETTER IN TYPICAL FASHION EXCEPT EXPANDS ON HIS OFFICE IN ORDER FOR THE CHURCH TO KNOW THAT TITUS IS AN APOSTOLIC REPRESENTATIVE—1:1-4

A. Paul designates himself as a servant and an apostle of Jesus Christ—1:1a
B. Paul notes that the ministry of his office was to bring God's elect to faith in Christ designed to produce godly living—1:1b
C. Paul notes that this ministry rests on the hope of eternal life which was promised by God and delegated to himself by divine command—1:2-3
D. Paul addresses the letter to Titus and invokes God's blessing on him—1:4

II. PAUL INSTRUCTS TITUS ON THE APPOINTMENT OF ELDERS SO THAT THE CHURCH WOULD BE SET IN PROPER ADMINISTRATIVE ORDER WITH QUALIFIED LEADERS—1:5-9

A. Paul tells Titus that the reason he left him in Crete was so that he might finish the business of appointing elders—1:5

B. Paul gives Titus the qualifications these elders should have in order to emphasize that the leadership of the church was very important (see notes on 1 Timothy 3 for discussion on the meaning of each trait)—1:6-9

1. He notes the general qualification that he should be blameless—1:6a

2. He notes several domestic qualifications including being the husband of one wife and having children who believe (i.e. are faithful while under his authority)—1:6b

3. He notes several personal qualifications including not self-willed, not quick tempered, not addicted to wine, not violent, not fond of money gained dishonestly, but hospitable, a lover of what is good, sensible, just, devout, and self-controlled—1:7-8

4. He notes several doctrinal qualifications including commitment to God's truth, able to exhort with the Scriptures, and able to point out false teaching and why it is wrong—1:9

III. PAUL INSTRUCTS TITUS CONCERNING THE CORRECTION OF FALSE TEACHERS IN ORDER TO EMPHASIZE TO HIM THE IMPORTANCE OF GUARDING THE CHURCH AGAINST HERESY —1:10-16

A. These false teachers were rebellious, empty talkers, and deceivers (especially those among the Jews) in order to inform Titus of their nature and characteristics—1:10

B. Their deeds included causing upheaval in the church, being greedy, and lying in order to show why they needed to be stopped

Note #239: Epimenedes

The poet to whom Paul refers was Epimenedes who was widely believed to be a religious prophet. The quotation may have generally referred to the lie that said Zeus was buried in Crete (which would have been offensive to those who believed in him), but by Paul's day, the saying became a proverb to emphasize the low esteem in which Cretans were held.

C. Paul charges Titus to rebuke these false teachers sharply—1:13b-16

1. They were to be sharply rebuked so that they could be restored to sound doctrine—1:13b

2. They were to be warned not to follow Jewish myths and commandments that came from men (perhaps abstaining from food as 1 Tim. 4)—1:14-15a

3. They were to be rebuked because their false teaching showed that they had polluted minds and consciences—1:15b

4. They were to be rebuked because they had a false profession which was belied by their works, and further they could not do anything which was approved by God—1:16

IV. PAUL INSTRUCTS TITUS ON THE CONDUCT OF THE SAINTS SO THAT THE CHURCH WOULD BE IN ORDER AND NOT SUSCEPTIBLE TO FALSE TEACHING—2:1-3:11

A. Paul instructs Titus on the conduct of various age groups in the church—2:1-15

1. He gives the introductory charge to Titus that he must teach that which is in harmony with sound doctrine—2:1

2. He is to teach the older men to be temperate, dignified, sensible, godly, sound in faith, in love, and in perseverance—2:2

3. He is to teach the older women to be reverent in the way they live, not slanderous or addicted to wine, and teachers of what is good—2:3

4. The older women are to teach the younger women to be lovers of their husbands, lovers of their children, sensible, pure, workers at home, kind, subject to their husbands so that God's word would not be maligned—2:4-5

5. He is to teach the young men to be sensible, examples of good works in order to show integrity in their teaching, dignified, and having speech that cannot be criticized so that the enemies of the church would have no basis for criticism—2:6-8

6. He is to teach slaves to be submissive to their masters, to please their masters, to refrain from talking back, to not steal, and to be trustworthy so that the gospel would be adorned—2:9-10

7. He gives the rationale for the behavior just described as being rooted in God's past grace and in His coming again—2:11-14

a. The reason for the aforementioned conduct is the grace of God that was manifested in Christ by providing salvation He states that this grace should lead the Christian to deny ungodliness and to live righteously—2:12

b. This behavior is done in light of the expectation of the return of Christ—2:13

c. The intent of Christ saving us was to redeem from wickedness so that we could be pure and do what is right—2:14

8. He gives Titus a concluding charge to teach all of these things with full authority without letting anyone intimidating him—2:15

B. Paul instructs Titus on the conduct of all believers in the church in order to clarify and enlarge on the responsibilities of all Christians —3:1-11

1. He gives Titus instructions on what to teach all of the people— 3:1-7

a. He was to remind them to be subject to the government by being obedient to it, to do good, to not speak slanderously, and to be peaceable, gentle, and considerate—3:1-2

b. He rehearses what their condition used to be in the world and what it was now in order to motivate his readers to obedience by emphasizing the grace of God—3:3-7

1) He notes that their former condition was one of enslavement to the bondage of sin—3:3

2) He notes that their present condition is changed because of the kindness and love of God who saved us because of His mercy which consisted in the cleansing from sin and the giving of the Holy Spirit so that they would became heirs of eternal life—3:4-7

2. He gives Titus instructions on his responsibility—3:8-11

a. He is to stress the trustworthy saying that those who have trusted Christ should practice good works—3:8

b. He is to shun foolish questions and debates promoted by the false teachers—3:9

c. He is to warn a false teacher twice and if he does not respond he is to have nothing to do with him—3:10-11

V. PAUL CONCLUDES THE LETTER TO TITUS BY GIVING HIM FURTHER INSTRUCTIONS SO THAT HE WOULD BE ABLE TO COMPLETE THE JOB OF SETTING THE CHURCH IN ORDER—3:12-15

A. He tells him that he would send someone to relieve him so that he could join him during the winter—3:12

B. He tells him to help Zenas and Apollos in whatever they need—3:13

C. He gives a final encouragement for the Cretans to provide for their own needs and live productive lives—3:14

D. He sends his love and greetings—3:15

PHILEMON

Historical Background

Philemon was apparently a wealthy slave owner who had been converted under Paul's influence (v. 19). One of Philemon's slaves named Onesimus escaped and made his way to Rome where he came in contact with Paul and was converted (v. 10). Following his conversion, Onesimus (helpful) became a helper to Paul (v. 11), yet Paul felt it was his responsibility to return him to his master and make things right between them (vv. 13-14).

When Paul sent Tychicus to Asia with the epistles of Ephesians and Colossians, Onesimus probably went with him. This letter was also sent along with the personal entreaty of Tychicus. Since this letter was sent with the letter to the Colossians, they were both probably written in Rome around AD 60-62.

Purpose

From the background to the letter, Paul's purpose was to pacify Philemon and affect reconciliation between him and Onesimus. Thus, a purpose statement could be: <u>Paul gives thanks to God for Philemon and pleads with him to receive Onesimus back with forgiveness in order to show the way faith in Christ affects the treatment of people</u>.

Summary of Argument

I. PAUL PRESENTS THE FORMAL GREETING TO THE LETTER IN ORDER TO SET THE FRIENDLY TONE FOR THE LETTER—1-3

- **A.** Paul introduces himself as a prisoner —1a
- **B.** Paul greets Philemon as a dear friend and fellow worker and other members of the church that met in his home—1b-2
- **C.** Paul wishes God's grace and peace on them—3

II. PAUL GIVES THANKS AND PRAYS FOR PHILEMON IN ORDER TO MOTIVATE HIM TO RESPOND TO THE REQUEST TO FOLLOW IN KEEPING WITH HIS CHRISTIAN VIRTUES— 4-7

- **A.** Paul thanks God for Philemon's faith in Christ and his love for all of the saints—4-5
- **B.** Paul prays that Philemon's sharing with others, which was an outgrowth of his faith, would increasingly abound—6
- **C.** Paul testifies that Philemon's love for the saints had a been a source of joy and comfort to him—7

III. PAUL APPEALS TO PHILEMON TO RECEIVE ONESIMUS BACK IN FORGIVENESS SO THAT ONESIMUS WOULD BE ABLE TO FULFILL HIS OBLIGATIONS AND THAT PHILEMON WOULD PROFIT FROM HIS CONVERSION—8-21

A. Paul presents his appeal—8-11

   1. He states that he has the authority to command Philemon but rather appeals to him on the basis of love—8-9
   2. He states the appeal for Onesimus because he had been saved and was now useful to both of them—10-11

B. Paul presents his motives—12-16

   1. He states that he loved Onesimus and would liked to have kept him but felt it was his responsibility to send him back—12-14
   2. He states that perhaps things transpired as they did so that Philemon would not only gain back a slave but a brother in Christ—15-16

C. Paul repeats his appeal that Onesimus be welcomed as if he were Paul—17

D. Paul presents his offer to Philemon in order to remove any obstacle that Philemon might have—18-20

   1. He offers to pay for any debts (or pilfering that was common among slaves) incurred by Onesimus—18
   2. He repeats that he would pay and reminds Philemon of the debt he owed to Paul—19
   3. He states that his receiving of Onesimus would be repayment and encouragement to him—20

E. Paul expresses his confidence in Philemon to do even more than he was requesting—21

IV. PAUL PRESENTS A CONCLUSION AND GREETINGS—22-25

A. Paul asks them to prepare a room for him as he hoped to come and visit—22

B. Paul sends greetings from Epaphras, Mark and others—23-24

C. Paul invokes God's grace on the whole church in Philemon's house—25

HEBREWS

Author

Candidates for authorship include Paul, Barnabas, Luke, Clement, Silvanus, Apollos, Philip, and Priscilla. Pauline authorship is virtually inconceivable based on anonymity, style of Greek, and the author's distancing of himself from the apostles (2:3-4). After a lengthy discussion, B. F. Westcott tersely remarks: "The Epistle cannot be the work of St. Paul" (*The Epistle to the Hebrews: The Greek Text with Notes and Essays* [Grand Rapids: Eerdmans, 1984], lxxviii). Though initially placed with Paul's letters in the Eastern church, the ancient church ultimately rejected Pauline authorship. Virtually no scholar today argues that Paul wrote the book. Therefore, its canonicity must be based on other grounds. De Silva summarizes the point in these words: "While the identity of the author cannot be known, Paul, at least, can be ruled out. The evidence of the early church fathers actually favors non-Pauline authorship. The internal evidence, however, is even more certain" (David de Silva, *An Introduction to the New Testament: Contexts, Methods & Ministry Formation* [Downers Grove: IVP Academic, 2004], 787). These internal features include, but are not limited to, Paul's distancing himself from the apostles (2:3-4) and the rhetorical and stylistic elegance of the book.

Date

An upper boundary for the date of the book can be set at around AD 95 since Hebrews is quoted in 1 Clement (for an example, compare 1 Clement 36:2-5 with Hebrews 1:3-5, 7, 13). Furthermore, because the author does not mention the destruction of Jerusalem in AD 70, and because he speaks of the Levitical priesthood in the present tense, it is safe to also assume a date of before AD 70. Other evidence for early dating has been provided by Guthrie who finds support from the facts of the mention of Timothy, the primitive ecclesiastical situation, and the fact that many of the readers appear to be the first converts in the community (Donald Guthrie, *New Testament Introduction,* 717). In addition, the note of urgency sounded by the author suggests that he foresaw the soon judgment on Jerusalem as predicted by Christ (Luke 21:5ff; Mark 13:14ff.). Because of these facts, a date of sometime in the late 60s is accepted.

Destination

There have been as many suggestions for destination as there have been for authorship. For example, the list includes: Colossae, Ephesus, Galatia, Syrian Antioch, Corinth, Cyprus, Berea, and Alexandria (Guthrie, *New Testament Introduction*, 711-715). However, the two main suggestions remain either Rome and Jerusalem or Palestine. The importance of this question lies in its impact on whether or not the warnings relate to the destruction of Jerusalem. There are several supports for a Roman destination: 1) the citation by clement of Rome in AD 95, 2) the salutation in 13:24, 3) the generosity of the Roman church fits the description of the readers, and 4) the persecution they had suffered could refer to Claudius' edict in AD 49. However, it can be pointed out that Hebrews 2:3 could be a problem if the readers were taught by eyewitnesses, and the Jerusalem believers also unselfishly shared their material possessions (Acts 2:44-45; 4:32-37). A strong case can be made for the Palestinian view: a) the emphasis on the Jewish sacrificial system would be more appropriate for a Palestinian locale, b) the "former days of suffering" mentioned in 10:32-34 could be a reference to Jewish persecution mentioned in Acts 8:1, c) the wording in the fourth warning in chapter 10 regarding "the day," "drawing near," "as you see," implies something of which the readers are aware and fits best with the crisis pending for Jerusalem, d) indications of the continuing operation of the temple, and e) Hellenistic Jews were a prominent feature of the Jerusalem church thus explaining heavy reliance on the LXX. For more pro-Palestine arguments see commentaries by Buchanan, Delitzsch, Hughes, Westcott and Carl Mosser, "No Lasting City: Rome, Jerusalem and the Place of Hebrews in the History of Earliest Christianity," PhD Dissertation, University of St. Andrews (Scotland, 2005), 275-321.

Recipients and Occasion

Without a doubt, the identification of the recipients of the letter is the most crucial for the interpretation of the book. There are a number of points to be made. First, the readers were *Jewish*. This is evident from the prominent place given to the Levitical system; the Old Testament quotations; the references to Moses, Aaron, Melchizedek, and Abraham; and the fact that Gentiles who were contemplating defection would not be greatly moved by the argumentation that perfection did not come through the Levitical priesthood. Second, it is evident that the recipients were Jewish *believers*. For example, in 3:1 they are called "holy brethren" and "partakers of a heavenly calling" (see also 3:12; 10:19), they have a great high priest (4:14), they are encouraged to draw near to the throne of grace (4:16), they are encouraged to press on to maturity (6:1), they had been enlightened (10:32), they had received a kingdom (12:28), etc. In addition, it should be noted that in the warning passages there is no differentiation between audiences, for each is introduced as an inference on preceding material with the author identifying himself with the group (2:1; 4:1; 6:1; 10:26; 12:25).

Third, these Jewish believers were undergoing *persecution* (10:32-36; 12:4; 13:3-5).

Fourth, these converts had retrogressed spiritually into a state of *stagnation* (5:11-14; 10:25) with a besetting sin of unbelief (3:12; 12:1). Because of the persecution causing this problem, they were being tempted to defect back into Judaism in order to avoid conflict (2:1; 3:12-14; 4:1; 6:8-9; 10:22-25; 12:25). Therefore, these believers were in need of encouragement to move on in their faith to maturity and to patiently endure the persecution they were facing (5:12-14; 10:24; 12:1-2; 13:5-7).

Purpose

It will be seen in the argument of the Epistle that the author is concerned to develop the theme of the superiority of Christ over the Levitical system. Growing out of these points, the author issues five warnings to his readers. This is all necessary, for as noted above, the readers were in need of moving on to maturity despite persecution. The warning passages serve to motivate them to do this, for if they did not, they would suffer chastening at the hand of God which would find its culmination in the destruction of Jerusalem in AD 70. With these points in mind, a purpose statement could be put thusly: The author demonstrates the superiority of Christ over the Levitical system in order to urge his readers to move on to maturity and not defect into the old order despite persecution so that they would avoid the chastening hand of God and receive a full reward in the eschaton.

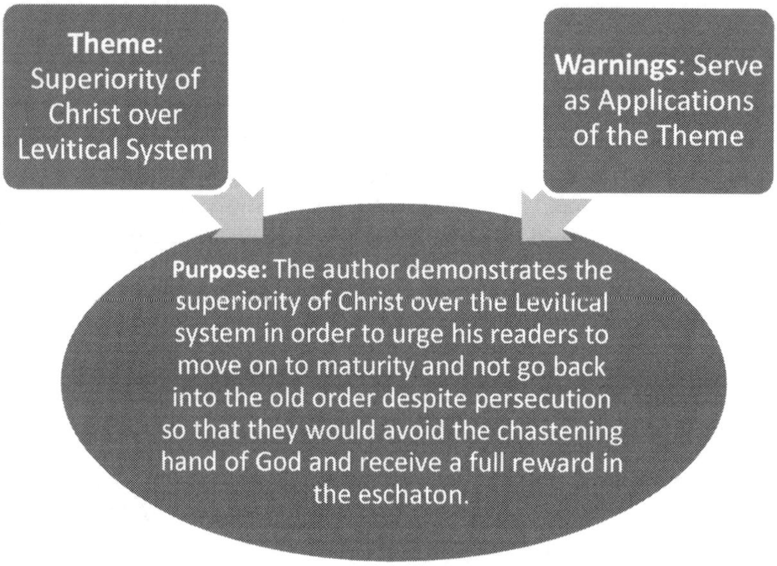

Theme: Superiority of Christ over Levitical System

Warnings: Serve as Applications of the Theme

Purpose: The author demonstrates the superiority of Christ over the Levitical system in order to urge his readers to move on to maturity and not go back into the old order despite persecution so that they would avoid the chastening hand of God and receive a full reward in the eschaton.

Summary of Argument

I. THE AUTHOR DEMONSTRATES THE SUPERIORITY OF THE SON IN HIS PERSON AND WORK OVER THE OLD SYSTEM IN ORDER TO PROVIDE A DOCTRINAL BASIS FOR URGING HIS READERS TO MATURITY SO THAT THEY WOULD AVERT THE CHASTENING HAND OF GOD—1:1-10:18

A. The author presents the theme of the epistle in which he contrasts the old and new revelations in order to show that Christ is the supreme and culmination of all revelation and therefore it would be folly to revert to an inferior system—1:1-3

1. The author contrasts the revelatory systems by noting that the old was partial, through the prophets, and anticipatory, while the new is complete, through the Son, and final—1:1-2a (the lack of the article before "Son" stresses his intrinsic character.)

Note #240: The last days

There are two important points to be made here. First, the Jews saw two ages—the present age and the one to come. So, by the phrase "these last days" the author is referring to the age preceding the Kingdom Age. Second, the aspect of Christ as Revealer was one of the most important reasons for His coming to earth, i.e., to reveal the Father. This chapter should be compared to John 1.

2. The author presents seven statements about Christ in order to show Christ's qualifications to reveal the Father—1:2b-3

a. Christ is appointed heir of all things (He has received from the Father the lawful possession and authority over all creation—cf. Ps. 2:8; Col. 1:15)—1:2b

b. Christ was the agent through which God made the worlds (possibly dispensations)—1:2c (his protological existence)
c. Christ is the shining out of the Father's glory—1:3a
d. Christ is the exact representation of the Father's nature—1:3b
e. Christ bears along all things to their appointed end—1:3c
f. Christ made purification of sins—1:3d
g. Christ sat down at the right hand of the Father thus showing the completeness of His work and that it was accepted by the Father—1:3e

Note #241: Summary of the seven statements about Christ

Statement	Meaning
Heir of all things	This refers to the inheritance of the earth Christ will receive during his millennial reign. Prominent passages include Daniel 7:13-14; Phil 2:9-11; Heb 2:5; Rev 5:7; 19:6.
Agent of creation	The term used here is not κόσμος but αἰῶνας. The latter term refers to the "ages of time" and the various dispensations through which time passes.
Radiance of God's glory	"Radiance" (ἀπαύγασμα) speaks of that which shines from a source. This refers to the inner glory which was veiled during the time of the incarnation.
Express image of God	"Express image" translates the Greek word χαρακτὴρ (used only here in the New Testament) indicating that Christ is the exact representation of the essence of God.
Bears all things	The verb used here is φέρω meaning "to carry," or "to lead." The Son is actively carrying all things to their appointed goal, primarily their consummation in the kingdom and beyond.
Purification for sins	In the priestly material of Hebrews, "purification" (καθαρισμός) will be a major theme and relates to the cleansing of the conscience
Sat down	His work is complete.

B. The author demonstrates the superiority of Christ over the angels by using arguments from the Old Testament, His sovereignty, and His humanity in order to show that He is a greater channel of revelation than the angels and thus the readers should be warned against going back to an inferior system—1:4-2:18

1. The author demonstrates the superiority of Christ over the angels with proof from the Old Testament—1:4-14
    a. He states that the Son is superior to the angels by virtue of the fact that he inherited a better name then they—1:4

Note #242: Angels in Hebrews

The term "angel" occurs 13 times in Hebrews and is thus a favorite word of the writer. The writer must demonstrate Christ's superiority to angels since they were the mediators of the Mosaic Law (Deut 33:2; Gal 3:19).

Note #243: The title "Son"

There are two general points to be made about 1:4-2:18. First, it should be observed that there are two types of sonship in Hebrews. In 1:1-3 the writer says that Christ is <u>Son by nature</u>; that is, he has the same essence as his father. Beginning in verse 4 he is said to be <u>Son by acquisition</u>. This is seen by the aorist participle γενόμενος translated "being made" (KJV) or better "having become" (ESV, NASB, NKJV, and NRS). This implies that something has been attained. The first sonship is known as his eternal, divine, or essential sonship. The latter is known as his mediatorial, functional, acquired, or eschatological sonship. The latter title has been acquired since he has been appointed by the Father to have this role during the Kingdom age.

    b. He quotes Psalm 2:7 in order to show His positional dignity as appointed by the Father in which He is called "Son" whereas angels are only collectively called "sons"—1:5a
    c. He quotes 2 Samuel 7:14 in order to relate Christ as the head of the covenant program thus anticipating His rule in the Millennium—1:5b
    d. He quotes Deuteronomy 32:43 in order to show that Christ will one day return in judgment at which time He will be worshiped by angels—1:6
    e. He quotes Psalm 104:4 in order to contrast the eternal character of Christ with the transitory nature of the ministry of angels—1:7
    f. He quotes Psalm 45:6-7 in order to show the deity and eternity of Christ—1:8-9
    g. He quotes Psalm 102:25-27 in order to show the immutability of Christ—1:10-12
    h. He quotes Psalm 110:1 in order to show Christ is seated in the presence of the Father while the angels are still being sent by God to minister to those who shall receive final and complete deliverance—1:13-14

2. The author presents his first warning to his readers, based on the truth he has just presented, to show them that this greater revelation had obligations and to ignore it would result in discipline—2:1-4

Note #244: The warning passages

Some view the warning passages in Hebrews as directed to professing believers within the believing community (e.g. Stanley Toussaint, "The Eschatology of the Warning Passages in the Book of Hebrews," Grace Theological Journal *3:1 [Spring, 1982], 67-80). There is no solid reason to suggest that the warnings are addressed to mere professors, rather the close connection of the warnings with the preceding material and the use of the pronouns "us" and "we" show true believers to be in view. Further, this is in keeping with the purpose of the book which is to spur believers on to maturity in order to avoid discipline. This is the premise which will underlie the interpretation of the other warning passages. Therefore, the warning here is addressed to true believers who were ignoring and neglecting the revelation as seen in Christ and were thus in danger of present discipline and loss of reward in the Kingdom. Their response to avoid this was to pay more attention in their application of the truth (2:1).*

- **a.** He warns them to pay close attention to what they had heard so that they do not drift away—2:1
- **b.** He notes that the message under the old system required obedience and lack of obedience resulted in discipline—2:2
- **c.** He notes that if the message under the old system required obedience how much more was this true of the new system—2:3
- **d.** He notes that this message was authenticated by signs and wonders—2:4

Note #245: Summary of the first warning

EXEGETICAL SUMMARY OF WARNING 1 (2:1-4)
Verse 1 "Therefore" (Διὰ τοῦτο) links the warning with the argument of Hebrews 1 showing that the warning is intended for the same audience being addressed previously.
"We must" (δεῖ περισσοτέρως) literally has the idea of "it is necessary more abundantly, or to a greater degree." It stresses the urgency of the warning. This kind of argument was known by Jewish interpreters as *qal wahomer*. This means that what applied in a lesser case will definitely apply more in a greater case. He is about to tell his readers that if something was true in the Mosaic era, it will apply to a greater degree in the Christian era. This serves to strengthen the thesis that the warnings build on previous material for the same audience.
"Give the more earnest heed" (KJV) προσέκειν has the idea of "pay attention."
"The things we have heard" (ἡμᾶς τοῖς ἀκουσθεῖσιν) refers to the truth presented in the first chapter; specifically, the seven dramatic statements about Christ and the superiority of Christ to angels as proved from the Old Testament.
"To slip" (KJV) or "drift away" (ESV, NASB, NIV, NKJV) (παραρυῶμεν) is used only here in the New Testament but has a colorful background. It was used of a ring that slipped off a finger; food that slipped down the throat; a thought that slipped out of the mind; or, a coarse joke that was slipped into a conversation—even of hair that slipped off the head. Thus the truth should not be allowed to slip from their awareness. It also could be used in a nautical sense to speak of a ship that drifted past the harbor because of

carelessness and neglect. This must not be the attitude of the Christian toward truth. Evidently there were readers who had grown complacent, lax, and careless in their Christian lives. Notice that they were neither rejecting the truth nor fighting against it; they were simply neglecting it and treating it lightly. As the captain sleeps, the ship drifts into peril.
Verse 2 "Steadfast" (βεβαιός) is an adjective which means "legally binding" and occurs four times in Hebrews (2:2; 3:14; 6:19; 9:17). The point is: if the Mosaic Law was legally binding in terms of its stipulations and punishments; how much more would the new revelation brought by Christ be legally binding.
Verse 3 "Escape" (ἐκφευχξμεθα). The escape in view here is not referring to escaping hell or eternal punishment. Remember, the warning is speaking to Christians who are neglecting the truth they have accepted. Therefore, the escape in view is a reference to the chastisement of God. If they did not right the ship, discipline would be inevitable.
"Salvation" (σωτηρίας) refers to that which the readers have already received and has been elaborated on in the previous chapter. It is the neglect of what they possess that would lead to discipline and even eventual loss in the kingdom. The latter sense of loss in the kingdom is prominent because all seven of the Old Testament quotations in chapter 1 refer to the future kingdom age. This is confirmed by 2:5 where the writer speaks of the "world to come *of which we are speaking*." Therefore, the readers of Hebrews face a dual consequence: temporal discipline and loss in the eschaton.

3. The author presents the superiority of Christ over the angels with proof from His sovereignty—2:5-9

Note #246: The sovereignty of Christ

The proof from His sovereignty goes back to Genesis 1-3 where man was appointed by God to rule over the earth. This outworking was partially marred by the Fall. Christ, as the ideal Man, will do what man failed to do when He rules in the Millennium. The Psalm 8 quote does not mean that Christ is the "son of man" in that psalm, rather he identifies with man so as to do what man failed to do.

   a. He states that the angels were not assigned with the future authority over the Kingdom—2:5
   b. He states the true destiny of man to rule the earth will be perfectly realized by the Son—2:6-9

4. The author presents the superiority of Christ over the angels with proof from His humanity and salvation in order to show why Christ became a man—2:10-18
   a. The first reason he became a man was to show God's grace in bringing many sons to glory—2:10-13

Note #247: "Perfect"

While "perfect" can have the idea of ethical perfection, it can also mean to bring to a desired end or complete as it does here. In verses 12-13, the writer uses three quotes to substantiate Christ's association with man: 1) Psalm 22:22 has Christ speaking after His resurrection in the midst of the congregation, 2) Isaiah 8:17 shows His relationship to the Father in His trust in Him just as a human must do, and 3) Isaiah 8:18 shows Isaiah and believers trusting God despite opposition and Jesus identified with that family. To say that he "learned obedience" does not mean that he learned to obey, but rather he experienced what obedience entails.

- **b.** The second reason he became a man was to overcome the prince of death—2:14
- **c.** The third reason he became a man was to establish man's freedom from the fear of death—2:15
- **d.** The fourth reason he became a man was to provide men with a merciful and faithful high priest who could help them in the conflicts they were facing—2:16-18

C. The author demonstrates the superiority of Christ over Moses in order to further emphasize to these believers the danger of defecting from the faith and their need to enter the rest which God has provided— 3:1-4:13

Note #248: Why Moses?

There are several reasons why Moses is presented in the argument: 1) the defection of the Old Testament was under Moses, 2) the whole Mosaic system is under discussion, 3) Moses was considered the epitome of faithfulness, 4) He was regarded by the Jews as the greatest man, 5) Moses was sent by God (apostle) and interceded for the people (priest). In spite of these facts which show the greatness of Moses, the author shows that Christ is even greater, and in addition, to bring up the possibility of there being another defection as there was under Moses in the Old Testament.

1. Christ is superior to Moses in His person and work—3:1-4
   - **a.** He points out that both Christ and Moses were apostles, high priests, and faithful to God—3:1-2
   - **b.** He points out that Christ is due greater honor than Moses because He built the house (the worship system) while Moses was a part of the house—3:3-4
2. Christ is superior to Moses in His position for while Moses is a servant in the house Christ is the ruler and heir—3:5-6
3. The author presents the second warning to his readers so that they would not miss the rest of God as their predecessors did under Moses—3:7-4:13

Note #249: What is "rest?"

The major challenge in this section is to determine what is implied by the term "rest." The views on rest include salvation rest, millennial rest, eternal rest, and daily faith rest. To start with, it is important to point out that the concept of rest has three aspects in Hebrews—God's rest in creation (4:4), Canaan rest (3:7-19) and faith rest

(4:1, 3a, 8, 9). It is also crucial to understand the Old Testament background presented in these verses in order to properly interpret the "rest" into which these believers are urged to enter. The first reference is to Psalm 95 (3:7-11) which describes Israel's faltering at Massah and Meribah for fear of dying from thirst. The second reference is to Numbers 13-14 and the Kadesh-Barnea incident where, despite God's assurance of victory in the Promised Land, the people failed to take the land because of unbelief in God's promise that they would conquer their enemies. Because of their rebellion they did not enter the land and thus forfeited the blessings of rest promised in the covenant. This led to their discipline as the disobedient generation died in the wilderness. However, they were still a covenant people, but had simply missed the blessings of the covenant (Deut. 28-30). Thus, the author is drawing a parallel between his present audience and the generation in the Old Testament. Both groups were redeemed and both were promised rest which involved the enjoyment of the blessings of their salvation. While the past generation had missed God's rest, the present generation is in danger of doing the same thing, and therefore they are urged by the author to not miss the peace and rest that can come to their daily lives as they respond in faith to the revelation God had provided them. It should also be noted that "rest" did not refer to the absence of conflict (as both groups faced this), but to the enjoyment and victory in the midst of conflict. This warning was apropos for the Hebrews because they were in danger of rejecting this victory in deference to returning to Judaism. Thus they are being warned to enter God's rest before it is too late. It is sometimes objected to this view that Psalm 95 is an enthronement psalm. Therefore, the rest is eschatological. While this is true, the writer is not emphasizing the enthronement motif in the psalm, but to the historical situation to which the psalm refers. This becomes evident from the context involving Numbers 13-14. This is especially true in light of the fact that Joshua and David were not promised the Millennium but victory through conflict and the enjoyment of temporal blessings.

Note #250: Views of warning 2 at a glance

1. Salvation Rest	2. Eternal Rest	3. Millennial Rest	4. Daily Rest
The rest and peace experienced by the unbeliever at the moment of salvation.	Also known as "heaven rest," the toil and weariness brought about by the Fall will be eliminated as the child of God enters the presence of God.	This view argues that the rest has reference to the millennial kingdom and participating in the reign of Christ.	This position says that the rest can be a present reality of the believer consisting of peace and blessing entered into by faith and obedience.

Note #251: Exegetical summary of the second warning

EXEGETICAL SUMMARY OF WARNING 2 (3:1-4:13)

3:1 "Partakers" (μέτοχοι). This term refers to a "partner" or "companion." In his excellent discussion of the term, Dillow clarifies the concept by noting that being Christ's partner is different than being his son—"only sons are partners, but not all sons are partners—only those who hold firmly to the end the confidence they had at first (Joseph Dillow, *The Reign of the Servant Kings: A Study of Eternal Security and the Final Significance of Man* [Hayesville, NC: Schoettle Publishing, 1992], 103). This passage then stresses the manward side of maintaining this partnership by obedience.

3:5-6 "House" (οἶκος). This term is most likely a reference to Numbers 12:7 and the place of worship, namely the Tabernacle. This observation helps solve the problem of interpreting "we are his house if we hold fast" in a way which is in concert with the letter. For the Hebrews, they would be a part of God's house (the worshiping community) if they remained faithful.

3:12 "Departing" (ἀποστῆναι φρομ ἀφίστημι). This is the term from which the concept of apostasy is taken. The question is: can a true Christian apostatize? The classic Reformed position would say "no." Therefore, if one were to defect, this would be an indication that they were never truly saved but merely professing to be so. While this certainly could be true; it does not hit at the heart of the debate. The question is not: can an unbeliever reveal his true colors by leaving the Christian community he falsely professed to be a part of. The question is: can one be a true believer and yet still apostatize. My position is "yes" which means I deny the doctrine known as the perseverance of the saints (not to be confused with the preservation of the saints). The term itself does not solve the problem because it can be used of both believers (this passage, Acts 15:38; 2 Timothy 2:12; 4:4 and unbelievers (Luke 13:27; 2 Thess 2:11). There are other passages which reveal that true believers can renounce the faith (Matt 10:33; Mark 8:32; 2 Tim 1:15; Rev 3:8). Therefore, each context must determine how the word is being used. Since this passage has as its background Kadesh-Barnea, it would most likely refer to the rebellion and apostasy which occurred at that event. The readers are in danger of turning away just as their forefathers did. If this is not the case, then one would have to prove that out of the millions of Jews who left Egypt, only Joshua and Caleb were saved. This goes against statements like Exodus 14:31 which appears to indicate the opposite. Those who apostatized did not lose their salvation, but they forfeited the blessings which could have been theirs had they entered the land in faith. Thus, true Christians can turn from God in deliberate rebellion.

"Evil heart of unbelief." The term "evil" is used twice in Numbers 14 (27, 35) to describe Israel. "Unbelief" hearkens back to Numbers 14:11 "how long will they not believe in me?" The context makes it clear that "evil" and "unbelief" are not to be thought of in the justification sense. It is not an unbelief in the gospel of Christ but the ability of God to deliver their enemies into their hands when they go into the land. In fact, the same two terms are used to describe Moses and Aaron in Numbers 20:12 and 24.

The redeemed state of the Exodus generation. Exodus 4:30-31 indicates that the people believed God, bowed low, and worshipped him. Randall Gleason lists nine reasons why this reaction is significant. 1) the Hiphil form of אמן (*aman*, 31) translated "believed" became a technical noun to express genuine faith in the OT (see *Theological*

Wordbook of the Old Testament, eds. Harris, Archer, and Waltke [Chicago: Moody Press, 1980], 1:51), 2) the six occurrences of "believe" in Exodus 4 mark the people's faith as a central theme of the chapter, 3) the genuineness of their faith is marked not only by their initial worship but also by their obedience regarding the Passover, 4) the Lord promised them "salvation" from the Egyptians (14:13), 5) their response to their deliverance is again that they "believed," but here it is added that they believed "in" the Lord (14:30-31) which indicates an entrance into a relationship of trust with the Lord, 6) the Song of Moses which follows the Red Sea incident refers to their "salvation," "redemption," and "purchase," 7) when their deliverance is referred to elsewhere in the OT, it is said that though they did sin, God redeemed, saved, and forgave them (Pss. 78:42; 106:10; Isaiah 63:9; Ps. 106:8, 10; Neh. 9:17; Pss. 78:38; 99:8), 8) the establishment of the Sinai covenant shows their redeemed status; 9) their redeemed status is affirmed in Hebrews 11:29, 39 (Randall Gleason, "A Moderate Reformed View," in *Four Views on the Warning Passages in Hebrews* [Grand Rapids: Kregel, 2007], 345-46).

4:1 "Let us fear" (Φοβηθῶμεν). That which is to be feared in this context is missing rest. This would occur if the Old Testament example were followed.

4:11 "Let us labor" (Σπουδάσωμεν). This aorist subjunctive has been variously translated (labor, strive, make every effort, etc.). Three points emerge: 1) the good news (called "gospel" in this passage) is that rest was still available for the very people who prompt the warning, 2) to enter rest would require effort. Moving ahead in the Christian life is not always an easy thing to do; nor is it automatic (read "let go and let God," "give it to the Lord," "commit it to the Lord"), and 3) not to labor to enter rest would constitute rebellion (apostasy).

- **a.** The author presents the example of failure in the wilderness and warning of unbelief in order to present an example of the danger his readers were facing—3:7-19
  - **1)** He presents the Old Testament example of the disobedience produced by unbelief of Israel by using Psalm 95 which looks to the beginning (Exodus 17) and ending (Numbers 14) of the wilderness wanderings in order to show that their lack of faith caused them to miss God's rest—3:7-11
  - **2)** He applies the lesson from the Old Testament by exhorting his readers to examine their hearts to see if they were in the same spiritual condition as their forefathers—3:12-15
  - **3)** He interprets the lesson by noting that a redeemed people disobeyed God through unbelief and forfeited the blessings of rest—3:16-19
- **b.** The author presents the availability of rest for the Hebrews and urges them to labor (believe) for this so that they would not be disciplined as were their ancestors—4:1-13
  - **1)** He warns his readers about the failure to enter the available rest—4:1-3a
  - **2)** He presents God's rest from creation (enjoyment of accomplishment not resting from weariness) in order to show that God is a God of rest—4:3b-4

3) He shows that rest had been prepared for Israel and they did not appropriate it for neither David nor Joshua brought permanent rest to the nation—4:5-8

4) He shows that though Israel rejected this rest it is still available for the believer today—4:9-10

5) He exhorts the believers to enter the available rest and not to miss it through disobedience—4:11

a) He presents the penetrating power of the Word of God in order to emphasize to his readers that God knows what they were thinking of doing because His truth penetrates to the inner depths where doubt arises—4:12-13

C. The author demonstrates the superiority of Christ over Aaron in order to provide his culminating argument and thus persuade his readers to obedience rather than defection—4:14-10:18

1. He states that Christ is superior to Aaron because He holds a better position in order to give his readers a basis on which they can hold firmly to the faith through a high priest to whom they can come for strength—4:14-16

a. He urges them to hold firmly to their confession of faith in light of the fact that they had a high priest who was permanently in the presence of God—4:14

b. He states that the reason they are to hold fast to their profession is because they have a high priest who can suffer along with their weaknesses in light of the fact that He was tempted as they were—4:15

Note #252: Tempted in all points

This verse does not imply that Jesus faced every conceivable temptation. For example, he did not have a sin nature, did not know the pressures of marriage, etc. Rather it has the idea that he faced the full force or measure of testing, a rating that no human could bear, and yet He faced it without sinning.

c. He states that the inference is to draw near to Him with confidence in order to receive divine help in the time of suffering—4:16

2. He states that Christ is superior to Aaron in his role as a priest—5:1-7:28

a. He notes the prerequisites for priesthood in order to show that Christ is qualified for this office—5:1-4

1) He must be human so that he can sympathize with human feelings—5:1-3

2) He must be divinely appointed to his office—5:4

b. He notes that Christ has fulfilled these qualifications—5:5-10

1) He states that Christ was divinely appointed to the priesthood by quoting Psalm 2:7 and 110:1 to show that He was appointed to a position of authority and as a priest forever respectively—5:5-6

2) He states that Christ was genuinely human as seen by His incarnation and suffering—5:7-10

Note #253: The garden prayer

The reference in 5:7 points back to the experience in Gethsemane, and helps us understand the content of what He prayed there. The author of Hebrews points out that Christ's prayer in the garden was "heard" which implies not only awareness but the granting of what was prayed for. With this in mind, it is also to be noted that there are three aspects to death: physical (separation of the body and soul), spiritual (separation of the soul from God), and eternal (permanent spiritual death). Since Christ experienced the first two types of death, he was praying that He would not be cast in a state of permanent spiritual death, though He was willing to be. His prayer, however, was answered for He was resurrected and returned to the presence of the Father. The "cup passed from him" in the sense that the Father fully accepted his sacrifice for sin.

c. The author presents his third warning in which he exhorts his readers to press on to maturity so that they would not be permanently confirmed in a state of stagnation—5:11-6:20

1) The author notes the fact of his readers' stagnation in order to show his concern for their lack of progress—5:11-14

Note #254: The spiritual state of the readers

These believers had retrogressed into a state of spiritual dullness when by this time they should have been quite advanced in their faith. Because of this they needed the milk rather than the meat of the word. "Solid food" does not mean an area of doctrine (e.g. prophecy) but the depth in an area. Also, it is interesting to note two evidences of maturity which these people lacked: the ability to put into practice what they knew, and the ability of spiritual discernment.

2) The author notes the danger of apostasy in order to show the readers the need for progression and to warn them of the finality of departing from the truth—6:1-8

a) He admonishes them to move on to maturity by listing six particulars they were to move beyond—6:1-3

Note #255: Leaving the first principles

When the author says to leave these things he does not mean to repudiate them, but to go beyond them in their experience. These probably refer to Old Testament practices because of the background of the book and the plural form of "baptisms." These particulars are: repentance from dead works—the works of the Levitical system which could not bring lasting privileges; faith toward God—belief in God's promises especially as in chapters 3-4; instructions about washings—ceremonial cleansings of the Old Testament; laying on of hands—OT appointment, identification, blessing, etc.; resurrection of the dead—Dan. 12:2; Isa. 26:18; Job 19:25; eternal judgment.

b) He warns them about the danger of not progressing to maturity—6:4-8

Note #256: The third warning

Views of the Third Warning at a Glance			
Arminian	**Reformed**	**Hypothetical**	**Immaturity**
The warning is written to saved people in danger of losing their salvation.	The warning is written to those professing to be saved. When they fall away, this proves their profession was false.	The warning refers to a sin that is impossible to commit. It is speaking to believers who are wavering and in a state of confusion. "Just think if you could do this, how frightening it would be."	The warning is written to immature Christians. If they do not move on to maturity, they will experience God's discipline.

This warning has been interpreted many ways: 1) the doom of the unsaved who may profess to be Christian (Calvin, Plummer, Westcott, Kelly, Morris), 2) the falling of the unsaved from Christ to damnation. This view differs from the preceding in that it sees the participles in a Christian light as what appears to be (Hoyt, Bruce, Hughes), 3) the loss of salvation by the saved (Lenski, Moffatt), 4) a hypothetical situation in which the readers are not expected to fall (Kent, Barnes, Griffith Thomas, Hewitt, Ryrie), and 5) a falling into sin by the saved (continuation in immaturity) so that they are in danger of divine chastisement (Gromacki, Hodges, Pentecost, Lang, Barker). This view is favored by the writer for several reasons: 1) the purpose of the book is to move the readers on to maturity; 2) the immediate context is dealing with their stagnation and need to move on, 3) the four participles describe true believers. "Enlightened" is used in 10:32 to refer to their past decision for Christ; "tasted of the heavenly gift" is used in 2:9 in reference to Christ's real and full experience; "partakers of the Holy Spirit" is used in 1:9; 3:1, 14; 12:8 to refer to full participants because of change of character which makes them "sons" and "holy brethren"; and "tasted of the good word of God..." indicates possession and enjoyment, and 4) in reference to their moving on into maturity, 6:3 states that this they would do if God permit. The implication is that God may not permit this and confirm them in a state of immaturity if they did not take heed to this warning.

The background, then, seems to be the Kadesh-Barnea experience referred to in chapters 3-4. Because of that generation's unbelieving disobedience they were confirmed in this state as they were confined to the wilderness wanderings—they missed out on blessing which could have been theirs. It is interesting to note that at a later time they tried to repent of this, but were refused admission to the land by God, thus being confirmed in this state. Thus, the writer of Hebrews is telling his readers that they are at their spiritual Kadesh. They had two choices: either move on in maturity or face the possibility of being confirmed in their stagnated state.

- **(1)** He states that the believer could be confirmed in this state (impossible to renew to repentance) because by defecting he was identifying with a generation which crucified and blasphemed Christ—6:4-6
- **(2)** He illustrates the warning with two different tracts of land which produce different crops though they receive the same blessings showing that believers can produce different fruits—6:7-8

3) The author records his persuasion of better things for his readers in order to comfort and encourage them that he was confident they would move on to maturity—6:9-12

- **a)** The author records the certainty of God's promises in order to show that God can be trusted so that they could imitate the men of faith who had gone before—6:13-20
  - **(1)** He uses the illustration of Abraham to show faith and endurance in light of a future event and that certainty is guaranteed by the oath of God—6:13-18
  - **(2)** He notes the entrance of Christ into heaven as our forerunner who would be followed by us in order to give the second base of assurance—6:19-20

Note #257: Summary of the third warning

EXEGETICAL SUMMARY OF WARNING 3 (5:11-6:20)
5:11 **"Sluggish" "Dull" (νωθροὶ).** Part of the key here is the verb "become" used with this adjective. This shows that this state had not always been true of them. This is a major support for the "immature" view. Supporting this contention that believers are in view is that the only other occurrence of the term in the New Testament is in 6:12 where the readers are told to imitate those who are patient.
6:1-2 **"Repentance from dead works"**=a change of mind regarding those things which lead to death.
"Faith toward God"=saving faith.
"Doctrine of baptisms"=a reference to various Old Testament washings or the variety of baptisms practiced in the New Testament and early Church.
"Laying on of hands"=a widespread practice used in ordinations and commissioning for service.
"Resurrection of the dead"=reception of a newly formed body.
"Eternal judgment"=the punishment for sin which awaits the wicked at resurrection.
Each of the six doctrines mentioned in these verses are absolutely vital to Christianity but

they are foundational to it. Thus the writer is not disparaging them but telling his readers that they need to move beyond them.

6:3 "if God permit." In the Greek text, this is a 3rd class condition (ἐάν + the subjunctive mood). Regarding the significance of the subjunctive in this condition, Boyer comments: "it seems to me that the use of the subjunctive points essentially to the condition expressed by the protasis as being doubtful, uncertain, undetermined (because it has not yet been determined). The term potential is accurate. It is 'not yet.' It may be, if…Perhaps the term contingent would be even clearer. In any case, the common denominator is futurity. Perhaps the best name for this type of condition is simply the Future Condition" (James L. Boyer, "Third (and Fourth) Class Conditions," *Grace Theological Journal* 3:2 [1982], 166). Very importantly, Boyer examines all third class conditions in the Greek New Testament in order to ascertain the degree of probability expressed.

His conclusions are as follows (168-169):

Fulfillment certain 19
Fulfillment probable 63
Fulfillment doubtful 20
Fulfillment improbable 16
Fulfillment possible 4
Fulfillment conceivable 30
Certain not to be fulfilled 7
No indication of probability 120

Based on this data, it appears that potentiality is not inherent in this construction and must be determined from the context. Boyer concludes that "What term can be used to express the essential meaning of the third class condition? Such terms as 'probable,' 'likely,' 'expectancy,' 'anticipatory' are all misleading and not suitable. 'Potential' or 'contingent' are neutral terms which express well the meaning if properly understood" (172). "Potential" and "contingent" fit well with the context of Hebrews. Moving on to maturity is potential if the readers heed the exhortation to move on.

6:4-6. These three verses contain five adjectival, substantival participles. A substantival participle is one which functions as a noun. The article τοὺς in 6:4 governs all five participles which serve as the object of "renew (ἀνακαινίζειν) to repentance." Thus the five participles (functioning adjectivally) describe the one who cannot be restored. The essential difference between the "reformed" and "immature" views is whether this description is of believers or professing believers. The evidence seems to indicate that these are true believers.

Participle 1 "enlightened" (φωτιςθέντας). This term is used one other time in Hebrews (10:32) and refers to genuine experience.

Participle 2 "tasted" (γευσαμένους). Outside of this passage the term is used one other time in Hebrews (2:9) and refers to genuine, full experience as Christ "tasted" death.

Participle 3 "become partakers" (μετόχους γενηθέντας). The term μετόχους means "to share" or "to participate" and is here linked with the participle "become." Again, this refers to genuine experience as the readers have already been told that they are "partakers of the heavenly calling" (3:1) and "partakers of Christ" (3:14).
Participle 4 "tasted" (γευσαμένους). See participle 2.
Participle 5 "fall away" (παραπεσόντας). Since this participle is parallel to the preceding four, it should not be translated with an "if" as is done by the ESV, KJV, NIV and NKJV, but is better rendered as it appears in the NASB as a fifth description of the one who cannot be renewed to repentance. It is erroneous to assume that this action can only be viewed soteriologically (reformed and Arminian views). The word is used nine times in the LXX five of which are in the canonical books. In fact, all five uses in the Old Testament are in Ezekiel (14:13; 15:8; 18:24; 20:27; 22:4) with the sense of "acting unfaithfully" or "acting treacherously." The word is used once in the Apostolic Fathers (1 Clement 51.1) and refers to a Christian committing a sin (For all our transgressions which we have committed through any of the wiles of the adversary, let us entreat that we may obtain forgiveness). It can also have the sense of "to make a mistake" or "to go astray." Importantly, the word is used only here in the New Testament. Therefore, the term's meaning in this passage must be governed by this context. The only sin mentioned in this passage is stagnation in the Christian life and a deliberate refusal to move forward. Thus the act of disobedience envisioned is a refusal to press on to maturity; it is a falling away from that path.
6:4 "Impossible" (Αδύνατον). This adjective is used three other times in Hebrews. In 6:18—it is impossible for God to lie; in 10:4—it is impossible for the blood of bulls and goats to take away sin; 11:6—without faith it is impossible to please him. Based on usage outside of this passage, it must be concluded that those described in this passage may be denied a renewal to a place of blessing (impossible not difficult). This is consistent with the refusal of God to allow the Kadesh generation to enter the Promised Land.

d. He notes that Jesus belongs to the Melchizedekian priesthood which is greater than the Aaronic in order to show that Jesus is a greater priest than Aaron—7:1-28

1) He states that the Melchizedekian priesthood is greater than the Aaronic due to its preeminence—7:1-10

Note #258: Who was Melchizedek?

Melchizedek is of crucial importance to the writer of Hebrews; however, outside of the book of Hebrews, he is only mentioned two other times in the Bible: Psalm 110 and Genesis 14. Despite his seeming insignificance, he will be of critical importance in the argument of Hebrews. At the beginning of Hebrews 7, the writer gives a brief historical summary of the account of Melchizedek from Genesis 14. Views on his identity have included, the son of Shem, an incarnation of the Holy Spirit, a sinless man, or a

Christophany. It is probably best to see him as a real, historical figure who typified Christ. There are at least four parallels to see in this typology. First, Melchizedek was a king over ancient Jerusalem. When Christ returns at his second advent, the capitol city of his reign will be Jerusalem. Second, the nature of their reigns is parallel. The name Melchizedek means "king of righteousness." When Christ reigns in his millennial kingdom, his kingdom will be "established in justice and righteousness from henceforth even forever" (Isaiah 9:7). Third, Melchizedek was both a king and a priest. This was true of no other individual in the Old Testament. The only other person in the Bible to exercise these two offices is Jesus Christ—he is a king priest. And fourth, Melchizedek was without father, without mother, without genealogy, having neither beginning of days nor end of life." To the Levitical priests genealogy was all important because that is what gave them the right to serve as priests—they had to have the proper lineage. A priest had to be able to show that he was a descendant of Levi and of the priestly family of Aaron. When the writer says that Melchizedek did not have father or mother; he is not indicating those things did not exist but simply that his priesthood did not rest on external circumstances, but rather on the direct call of God. How is this relevant for the Hebrews? For the Jew, there was no other priesthood than the Aaronic priesthood—that was the only way to approach God. If the writer is going to show that Christ is superior to Aaron, then he has to show that the Melchizedekian priesthood is superior to the Aaronic priesthood. Furthermore, Christ was not qualified to be a priest after the order of Aaron—he did not come from the right family line. Therefore, if he is going to be a priest, then he has to come from a different order, and that order has to be shown to be superior to the Aaronic. If the writer can prove that, then it would be sheer folly for the Hebrews to go back to an inferior priesthood. In the rest of the argument of chapter 7 the writer gives a number of reasons as to why the Melchizedekian priesthood is superior to the Aaronic priesthood.

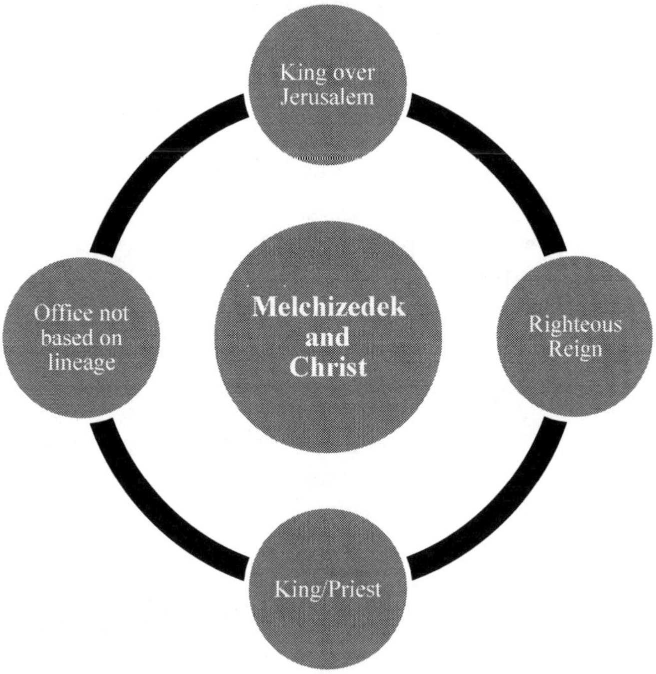

- **a)** He describes Melchizedek as a king/priest to whom Abraham paid tithes and who was without genealogy in order to show that he is a perfect type of Christ—7:1-3
- **b)** He states that Melchizedek is superior to Aaron in that Abraham paid tithes to Melchizedek which the lesser does to the greater—7:4-6a
- **c)** He states that Melchizedek is superior to Aaron in that Melchizedek blessed Abraham—7: 6b-7
- **d)** He states that Melchizedek is superior to Aaron in that there is no record of his death thus symbolizing that the Levitical order was ministered by dying men whereas the other was ministered by the living—7:8-10

2) He states that the Melchizedekian priesthood is greater than the Aaronic
due to its eternality—7:11-25

- **a)** The Aaronic priesthood was transitory and consequently could not perfect the worshiper—7:11-14
- **b)** The Aaronic priesthood was temporal—7:15-1
- **c)** The new order is immutable because it is based on the oath of Psalm 110—7:20-22
- **d)** The new order is uninterrupted—7:23-25

Note #259: The nature of Christ's intercession

Hebrews 7:23-25 is one of the most profound passages in the New Testament regarding the working out of the believer's salvation. The writer makes the point that the priesthood of Aaron was made up of many priests—and this was because of the most practical of reasons—they all died. In fact, there were 83 high priests from Aaron to the fall of the second temple in AD 70. It is said of Christ, however in 7:24, that he has an endless priesthood because he will never die. Theoretically, what would happen if Christ did die? This apparently is in the mind of the author because he has been talking about death in Aaronic order and never ending life in the Melchizedekian order. With this thought in mind, the author is going to explain what the consequences are in light of the fact that Christ's priesthood is perpetual.

The author is going to show that our security rests in with what Christ is doing now. The first word of verse 25 is "wherefore," "therefore," "consequently," depending on the translation. "Wherefore," that is, because his priesthood is based on an endless life, "he is able to save to the uttermost those that come unto God by him, seeing he ever lives to make intercession for them." The term translated "to make intercession" is a present active verb meaning "to petition," "to appeal," "to entreat."

To grasp the profundity of what is going on here, the following four propositions will bring out the meaning. First, intercession is to be distinguished from propitiation. There is no sense in which Christ is pleading with God so that he looks favorably on us. Second, this intercession is real. On one occasion on earth, Jesus interceded for Peter and said "I have prayed for you that your faith fail not." That intercession was in light of the truth "Satan has desired to have you." In John 17 Jesus prayed for all of the apostles and all of those who would ever believe—that they would be safely kept until they arrived in the presence of God. Third, this intercession baffles the understanding. Just because we cannot understand the complete mystery of this, does not mean that we abandon the doctrine. Fourth, the intercession involves our final salvation. Salvation is a package. It begins in eternity past with God's unconditional election before the foundation of the world, followed by the death of Christ, calling, regeneration, faith, sanctification, and glorification. Salvation cannot be limited to one piece of the process. In this text the writer refers to the final phase of salvation because he speaks of it in terms of being saved "to the uttermost." This means that there will be nothing left undone in our salvation, it will not fall short, and there will be no deficit to it. In the divine purpose of bringing many sons to glory, this is linked to the intercession of Christ and his unending priesthood. One commentator who has stated this well is the Puritan John Owen.: "wherefore we are to look unto this priesthood of Christ, as that which divine wisdom hath appointed as the only way and means whereby we may be saved...So great and glorious is the work of saving believers unto the utmost that it is necessary that the Lord Christ should lead a mediatory life in heaven, for the perfecting and accomplishing of it...It is generally acknowledged that sinners could not be saved without the death of Christ; but that believers could not be saved without the life of Christ following it, is not so much considered" (John Owen, An Exposition of the Epistle to the Hebrews *[Grand Rapids: Baker, 1980], 5:528, 542).*

            3) He concludes this section by giving a contrast of the superiority of Christ over Aaron in His character in that Christ perfectly meets human needs and is sinless and therefore does not need sacrifices for Himself—7:26-28

3. He states that Christ is superior to Aaron because He mediates a better covenant in order to show the things upon which His order rests are superior—8:1-13
   - **a.** The crowning feature of Christ's superiority is that He ministers at the right hand of the Father—8:1-5
   - **b.** From this place Christ mediates a better covenant than did Aaron because it is based on better promises—8:6-13
      - **1)** He makes the summary statement that Jesus' ministry is better because it mediates a better covenant which is based on better promises—8:6
      - **2)** He states the essence of this superiority—8:7-12
         - **a)** The old covenant was transitory and temporary—8:7
         - **b)** He quotes Jeremiah 31:31-34 in order to show that the prophets anticipated the doing away of the old covenant and to show some of the better promises of the new covenant including inner change, the knowledge of God, and the forgiveness of sin—8:8-12
      - **3)** He states that the covenant of Jeremiah was a new kind which implies that the old was temporary and has been displaced—8:13

Note #260: The new covenant

It is important to note why, in the flow of the argument of the passage, the author refers to the New Covenant. The purpose of the Jeremiah 31 quotation is not to deal with the current debate between dispensationalism and supersessionism; rather, it is simply to show the readers that the Scriptures anticipated a change in administration. If a New Covenant is prophesied, then clearly the Old Covenant is not meant to be permanent.

Note #261: The day of atonement

In chapters 9-10, the writer contrasts the Day of Atonement (the highest holy day in the Levitical system) with the work of Christ.[648] *If the writer can demonstrate the superiority of Christ's work over the Day of Atonement, this will be the capstone of his argument. The following chart summarizes these contrasts.*

Leviticus 16	Hebrews 9-10	Functional Difference
The high priest entered the holy of holies alone	Christ entered the immediate presence of God as a pioneer for his people	Christ entered the "real" presence of God which guarantees present access for the believer into a better sanctuary. In addition, his blood secures eschatological access when the believer sees God face to face
The high priest entered once a year	Christ remains in the presence of God	Because Christ remains in the presence of the Father, the believer has unlimited access now and in the future
The high priest sacrificed what was outside himself	Christ sacrificed himself	This shows the superiority of Christ's sacrifice and priesthood
The high priest offered for himself	Christ was without sin and needed no sacrifice	This also shows the superiority of his sacrifice
The high priest offered many sacrifices for the sin of the people	Christ offered one sacrifice for the sin of the people	Christ's sacrifice was potent enough to do its work in one offering
Levitical sacrifices effected outward cleansing	Christ's sacrifice effected inward cleansing	The Levitical system was instituted to remove ceremonial defilement because of the holiness of God's presence and therefore it was only efficacious in this sphere. Christ's sacrifice was able to cleanse the inward conscience and perfect the worshiper
The high priest ministered in an earthly tabernacle	Christ ministers in a greater, heavenly tabernacle	From the human perspective, the animal sacrifices were intended for an earthly, horizontal sphere, while Christ's sacrifice was intended for a heavenly, vertical sphere (though

[648] See Note 274 for an expanded discussion of the Day of Atonement.

		of course with horizontal ramifications)
The high priest entered the holy of holies with the blood of an animal	Christ entered the presence of God by virtue of his own blood	This again points to the fact that Christ's blood was needed to enter the real sanctuary and therefore operates in a different sphere
The high priest offered temporary sacrifice	Christ offered an abiding sacrifice	Christ's work is superior because it accomplished its objective with one offering
The high priest offered the sacrifice of an involuntary animal	Christ voluntarily offered himself	This points to Christ's superior sacrifice
Animal sacrifices operated in the sphere of the Mosaic Covenant	Christ's sacrifice operates in the sphere of the New Covenant	Animal sacrifices operated as a part of the Mosaic economy which was never intended to bring salvation. In contrast, Christ's sacrifice ratified the New Covenant which brings soteriological blessings
Animal blood cleansed the earthly sanctuary	Christ's blood cleansed the heavenly sanctuary	The sphere of the differing sacrifices is again contrasted as earthly/horizontal and heavenly/vertical
Aaron had to leave the presence of God	Christ remains in the presence of God	The heavenly/vertical sphere is always open because of the presence of Christ at the Father's right hand
Aaron reappeared from the Holy of Holies	Christ will one day reappear for his people	Christ will reappear from the presence of God and bring his people there with him
The Levitical priests stood before the Lord continually offering sacrifices	Christ sat down at the right hand of God because his work is finished	Christ's objectives in the spiritual sphere are complete

4. He states that Christ is superior to Aaron because He ministers in a better sanctuary than Aaron—9:1-10

a. He discusses the furniture of the Tabernacle in order to show that though the earthly Tabernacle was useful it was only temporary because it was of the earth—9:1-5

Note #262: "Censer" or "altar?"

Some suggest that the word θυμίατηριον in 9:4 should be translated as "censer" rather than "altar." However, since the censer was not an article of furniture, and since the high priest is said to have brought this into the Holy of Holies, it is better to render the word as the "altar of incense." Support for the censer translation is that this is the meaning in the LXX in 2 Chron. 26:19 and Ezekiel 8:11. This altar of incense was in the Holy Place because of Exodus 30:6-10 and 40:17-28; the priest was to burn incense on it daily (Exod. 30:7-8).

- **b.** He discusses the service in the Tabernacle in order to show the limitations of the old and thus the superiority of the new—9:6-10
  - **1)** The Holy of Holies was entered only by the high priest—9:6-7a
  - **2)** The Holy of Holies was entered only once a year—9:7b
  - **3)** He could enter only with blood—9:7c
  - **4)** It was only efficacious for sins of ignorance—9:7d
  - **5)** Direct access to God was impossible under the old system—9:8
  - **6)** The old could not permanently deal with the perfection of the worshiper—9:9-10
- **5.** He states that Christ is superior to Aaron because he provided a better sacrifice—9:11-10:18
  - **a.** He explains why Christ sacrifice is superior—9:11-14
    - **1)** It is superior because of its locale—9:11

Note #263: The identity of the tabernacle

There are at least four views as to what this "tabernacle" is. Some see it as the human nature of Christ (Owen); others take it as the church (Westcott); others take it as the hearts and souls of men (Bruce); and others see it as heaven itself (Hughes, Brown). For support of the "heaven" view see Philip Hughes, "The Blood of Jesus and His Heavenly Priesthood in Hebrews Part III: The Meaning of the "True Tent' and 'The Greater and More Perfect Tent,'" Bibliotheca Sacra *130:520 (Oct 1973), 305-314. In addition, it does not seem necessary to insist on an edifice in heaven which corresponds to each item in the Tabernacle. Kent states well that "heaven itself is the biblical phrase of the divine presence, answers to all the truth conveyed by the symbolism of the earthly holy of holies. It is in actual and not just the representational presence of God in heaven" (Homer Kent,* The Epistle to the Hebrews *[Grand Rapids: Baker, 1981], 147, 179-180). Thus, the divine arrangement in heaven was communicated in physical form on earth.*

- **2)** It is superior because the nature of it was not the blood of animals but His own blood—9:12a

Note #264: Did Christ carry his blood into heaven?

A much discussed phrase is "by his own blood he entered into the holy place." It has been suggested by many that Christ carried His literal blood into the presence of God (Bengel, Calvin, and Walter Brooks). There are a number of reasons which militate against this position: 1) the aorist participle euramenos *has the idea that he entered into heaven after He had secured redemption (see also the aorist participle in 10:12), 2) the preposition* dia *is best translated as "through" rather than "with." So the idea is that He entered heaven by means of His blood, or by virtue of His blood, 3) it is doubtful that Christ's resurrection body was bloodless, 4) Jesus cried on the cross "it is finished," and 5) there is dubious support for a secret ascension after His resurrection. Smeaton's words are classic, "It may we think be convincingly proved that the entrance of our High Priest to sprinkle the mercy seat took place at the moment of His death; that no moment of time intervened; and that the rending of the veil indicated His entry...While His lifeless body was hanging on the cross, the mercy seat was sprinkled" (George Smeaton,* The Apostles' Doctrine of the Atonement *[Grand Rapids: Zondervan, 1957], 339-340).*

3) It is superior because it has abiding and inward efficacy—9:12b-13
4) It is superior because it was voluntary—9:14a
5) It is superior because it was rational—9:14b
6) It is superior because it was offered through His eternal spirit—9:14c

b. He explains that Christ's sacrifice ratified the New Covenant in order to show the need for His death—9:15-22

1) He points out that this death was needed to bring the promises of the covenant to the Old Testament saints by dealing with their sins—9:15
2) He notes that a covenant has to be ratified by blood—9:16-17

Note #265: The "covenant"

There is debate as to whether diatheke *should be translated as "will" or "covenant." It seems best to hold to the latter for the context is discussing covenants not wills, and verse 18 explains how the first covenant was made.*

3) He illustrates this fact by noting that even the old covenant was ratified by blood but was done away, but the New would never be done away because of its unconditionality—9:18-22

c. He explains the ministry of Christ's sacrifice in the new tabernacle—9:23-28

1) He notes that the cleansing of the heavenly tabernacle was needed just as the earthly was—9:23

Note #266: Sacrifices

He probably uses the plural "sacrifices" to speak of Christ's death to show that all the Old Testament sacrifices were fulfilled in Him.

Rather than saying that the writer is just speaking figuratively, or that the dedication of the tabernacle is in view here, it is better to understand an actual cleansing as being necessary. Support for this would be that it would maintain the correspondences the author is making in the passage, and the heavens are defiled due to Satan's presence and the fact that creation is bound up in the effects of sin.

2) He notes that Christ entered into heaven once for all with a completed work—9:24-26
3) He notes that our Priest will reappear from the Holy of Holies for His people just as the High Priest did on the Day of Atonement—9:27-28

Note #267: Judgment after death

Verse 9:27 is stating the general principle that men die once and then are judged. This strengthens the fact that Christ died only once for he is associated with the human pattern. Because judgment follows death there is no repetition of death, and thus no need for further offering.

d. He presents the climax of his argument by noting the efficacy of Christ's sacrifice—10:1-18

1) He demonstrates the insufficiency of the Old Testament sacrifices in order to show the need for Christ's work—10:1-4

a) They were only a shadow and not the true reality—10:1a

b) They were repetitive—10:1b-2

c) They maintained a consciousness of sin because they could not permanently take sin away—10:3-4

2) He demonstrates the sufficiency of the sacrifice of Christ by showing that it came from perfect obedience which made it acceptable in order to show what can deal with sin if the Levitical sacrifices could not—10:5-10

Note #268: The submission of the Son

The author demonstrates Christ's willingness to die by quoting Psalm 40:6-8. In this psalm David prayed for God's deliverance and realized that God not only desired sacrifice but willing obedience. This was ultimately fulfilled in Christ. The LXX states "a body you have prepared for me" whereas the MT states "my ears thou has opened." This is probably a case of synecdoche where the part stands for the whole. When God created the ear, it was equivalent to creating the whole body. The ear would be associated with the hearing of God's will.

a) He states that Christ came in perfect obedience—10:5-7

b) He states that the Old Testament sacrifices are contrasted with obedience and thus Christ brought perfection by His sacrifice—10:8-10

3) He demonstrates the sufficiency of the sacrifice of Christ by contrasting His present position with the Levitical repetition —10:11-14

a) The Levitical priest was always standing because his work was never done while Christ sat down—10:11-13

b) The reason He sat down is because His work is done—10:14

4) He demonstrates the sufficiency of the sacrifice of Christ by showing it fulfilled the New Covenant in order to show that there is no more room for Levitical sacrifices—10:15-18

a) Christ's work enacted an inward change—10:15-16

b) Christ's work makes no room for the remembrance of sin—10:17

c) Christ's work is the final offering to be made—10:18

II. THE AUTHOR PRESENTS THE PRACTICAL APPLICATION OF CHRIST'S SUPERIORITY TO THE LIVES OF HIS READERS IN ORDER TO EXHORT

THEM TO OBEDIENCE AND FAITH IN THEIR SITUATION SO THAT THEY WOULD NOT EXPERIENCE THE CHASTENING HAND OF GOD—10:19-13:25

A. The author presents exhortations, a warning, and encouragement in order to persuade his readers to respond to the truth he has presented—10:19-39

1. He presents a series of exhortations to his readers in order to move them to improve on their areas of weakness—10:19-25

a. He states that they can have confidence to enter the Most Holy Place by the blood of Christ in order to show them the basis for access into God's presence—10:19-21

b. He exhorts them to draw near (devoted worship) in full assurance (as opposed to the trepidation on the Day of Atonement) which is based on the cleansing of the conscience and the washing of the body by pure water—10:22

c. He exhorts them to hold fast the profession of their faith they made at their baptism which they can do because God is faithful—10:23

d. He exhorts them to stimulate each other to love and good deeds which is done by not neglecting the local assembly (because of persecution) and by encouraging one another as the day is approaching—10:24-25

2. He presents his fourth warning to his readers to show them the consequences and dangers if they did not improve in these areas—10:26-31

Note #269: The fourth warning

This warning is often taken to refer to the unsaved because of the strong language which the writer uses (esp. v. 29) and the quotation of Isaiah 26:11 in 10:27 which contrasts the righteous with the wicked. While the language is admittedly strong, it should be noted that James uses an even stronger word in 4:4 to describe the believer who has an allegiance to the world, and the apparent quote from Isaiah may not actually be a quote but could be a borrowing of the language to emphasize the nearness of judgment.

In the preceding context the author has been addressing the saved (5:9; 7:25) and in 10 he addresses those who are "sanctified" (10:14) and notes that they have access to God's presence by the blood of Christ (10:22-25). Furthermore, the quotation in 10:30, "The Lord shall judge His people" shows that believers are in view. With this in mind, several points are to be made: 1) the description in 10:29 seems to be an apt one for the treatment which Christ received by the nation of Israel. The Hebrews were in danger of returning to Judaism and thus identifying with this nation which was under judgment, 2) the "willful sinning" of verse 26 then is the continued ignoring of the teachings concerning the superiority of Christ which the author has been expounding and a return to the Judaic system, 3) if they made this defection, they would be associating with a nation which had "trampled under foot the Son of God, treated as an unholy thing the blood of the covenant, and insulted the Spirit of grace," 4) by doing such a thing they would end up at a dead-end street for they would be in a system whose sacrifices had no efficacy for sin, 5) verse 28 shows physical death to be in view not spiritual, 6) "the day" of verse 25, is not the eschatological return of Christ (though it is prefigured) but the approaching judgment on the nation in AD 70 which Christ had predicted in Luke 21 and Peter in Acts 2. This is seen by the fact that it is said to be "drawing near" (v. 25), and it *is a day which is coming in a little while (v. 37). Furthermore, the quote from Habakkuk 2:3-4 refers not to the coming of the Messiah, but to the coming of the Babylonians in judgment. Thus, the believer who re-identified with this nation under judgment, and who perhaps returned to the city and the Temple would possibly be involved in the destruction of the city (*apoleia *in v. 39 refers to temporal ruin not eternal destruction—BAGD, 103). In this scenario, "forsaking the assembly" is not missing a church service, but defecting from the believing community entirely.*

Josephus, *The Wars of the Jews*, Translated by William Whitson (Grand Rapids: Baker, 1980).	*Neither did any other city ever suffer such miseries (5.10.5).*
	Their multitude was so great [Jews being slaughtered], *that room was wanting for the crosses, and crosses wanting for the bodies* (5.11.1).
	Now the number of those that were carried captive during this whole war was collected to be ninety-seven thousand, as was the number of those that perished during the whole siege eleven hundred thousand [1,100,000], *the greater part of whom were indeed of the same nation [with the citizens of Jerusalem], but not belonging to the city itself; for they were come up from all the country to the feast of unleavened bread, and were on a sudden shut up by an army, which, at the very first, occasioned so great a straitness among them that there came a pestilential destruction upon them, and soon afterward such a famine, as destroyed them more suddenly* (6.9.3).

a. He explains the danger of what they were contemplating and the results of it—10:26-28

b. He explains what is involved in this apostasy—10:29

c. He explains the reason that judgment would result, namely the character of God—10:30-31

3. He presents a word of encouragement to his readers in order to show them his confidence in them and to persuade them to patiently endure —10:32-39

a. He reminds them of their past courageous faith—10:32-34

b. He exhorts them to continued patient endurance by noting that their persecution would come to an end so that they would be rewarded by God—10:35-39

B. The author presents examples of patient endurance in order to show his readers that there may be an interval between what is promised and the fulfillment so that they would be encouraged to identify with those who endured by faith rather than with an apostate nation and thus be approved by God (note the inclusio of 2 and 39)—11:1-40

1. He gives to his readers an explanation of faith—11:1-3
   a. He notes that faith produces the certainty of what is unseen—11:1
   b. He notes that the ancients were approved by God for this—11:2
   c. He uses creation as an example of believing something which cannot be seen—11:3
2. He gives to his readers examples of faithful endurance—11:4-38
   a. He notes the faith of the antediluvian saints—11:4-7
      1) Abel—he displayed faith as he acted in spiritually motivated worship
      2) Enoch—he displayed faith through fellowship as he showed his endurance by faithfully pleasing God
      3) Noah—he displayed faithful endurance by his obedience of work for some 120 years
   b. He notes the faith of the patriarchs—11:8-22
      1) Abraham—he displayed faith in the promise of the possession of the land and his belief in God's ability to raise the dead
      2) Sarah—her ability to conceive was by faith even though she was impotent
      3) Isaac, Jacob, and Joseph—these all anticipated the literal fulfillment of the promises
   c. He notes the faith in the wilderness—11:23-31
      1) Moses—his decision was prompted by faith in identifying with God rather than Egypt
      2) Those he led—they demonstrated faith in the efficacy of the blood
      3) Rahab—since Jericho was the first victory of Israel, she could only believe that God gave the land to Israel, thus her faith was not based on a past conquest
   d. He notes the faith in trials of various saints in order to show that faithful endurance does not always have a happy ending but that it always triumphs even over death—11:32-38
3. He shows to his readers the victory of faith in order to demonstrate that all of these people anticipated the fulfillment of the promises so that they would see that they needed to have patience until they receive the fulfillment—11:39-40

C. The author presents an exhortation to patient endurance in which he gives the greatest example, some instruction on suffering, and a final warning in order to persuade them to patiently endure—12:1-29
   1. He gives the readers examples of patients endurance—12:1-3
      a. The first example is the saints in chapter 11 which is to lead the readers to remove all hindrances and run the race with patience—12:1

Note #270: Who are the witnesses?

There are basically two views as to who these "witnesses" are. The first sees them as actual spectators watching from heaven. The second interprets the word "witness" as one who testifies, that is, the saints of chapter 11 are testifying to present-day believers about the life of faith. Thus it is not so much they who look at us, but we who look at them for encouragement. This is latter view would better explain why the author went to so much detail in describing these people.

   b. The second example is the steadfastness of Christ amidst suffering on which the believer should focus his attention—12:2-3

Note #271: For the joy set before him

*The preposition in Hebrews 12:2 translated "for" in our English versions is the Greek word ἀντί. The translation "instead of" is to be preferred to "for." The preposition occurs only 22 times in the New Testament and there is strong evidence for the conclusion of the translation of this term as "instead of" in this verse. Murray Harris lists five arguments for this view (*Prepositions and Theology in the Greek New Testament: An Essential Reference Resource for Exegesis *[Grand Rapids: Zondervan, 2012], 56) which I paraphrase as follows: 1) the prevailing substitutionary sense of ἀντί, 2) the use of πρόκειμαι (was set before him) in Heb 6:18 and 12:1 to denote a present reality, not a future acquisition, 3) the translation of "instead of" in BDAG and TDNT, and 4) the common NT theme of voluntarily giving up personal rights for others. The idea, therefore, would be similar to Philippians 2 where Christ gave up the joys and worship of heaven to become humiliated in the incarnation. Likewise, the Hebrews are to give up the easy route of dealing with their problems which they perceive to be going back to Judaism.*

2. He instructs the readers on the purpose of sufferings in order to show them its positive results so the they would endure in light of these—12:4-11
   a. They had not yet suffered loss of life as some of the saints in chapter 11—12:4
   b. He quotes Proverbs 3:11-12 in order to remind them that discipline comes from a loving Father which is didactic—12:5-6
   c. The efficacy of discipline depends on the spirit in which it is received—12:7
   d. Divine discipline is a proof of sonship and should be endured in voluntary submission—12:8-9
   e. The reason they were to do this is because it produces peaceable fruit, even righteousness—12:10-11

3. He instructs the readers on the behavior they are to display as they endure these sufferings—12:12-14
   a. Their first obligation was to encourage one another and not cause each other to stumble—12:12-13
   b. Their second obligation was to live at peace with each other and pursue holiness—12:14

4. He presents the fifth warning passage in order to show the dangers which are present to the believer in suffering and the severity of losing God's blessing through a decision of selfishness—12:15-17

Note #272: Suffering

The concern of the author in this warning is how they would handle their suffering. He instructs them to appropriate God's grace (15a) so that they would not grow bitter and rebellious thereby damaging others. He also warns them against being immoral in only being concerned about gratifying the desires of the flesh. Esau is used of an example of one who forfeited, through one decision, his eligibility to enjoy covenant blessings even though afterward he repented. Likewise, the readers would be gratifying the flesh by trying to escape persecution, and in so doing would run the risk of losing the blessings of God through the temporal consequences of sin. It should be remembered the enjoyment of blessing, and not salvation is in view here.

5. He applies the lesson of Esau to his readers by picturing their privileges negatively, positively, and then the peril of neglecting them—12:18-29
- **a.** He presents a terrifying picture of Mt. Sinai in order to show his readers that if they defected to the old system they would be reverting to a system of fear which required obedience to the Law to be blessed—12:18-21
- **b.** He presents a glorious picture of Mt. Zion (representing the eternal destiny of the believers) in order to provide a contrast of all they would be turning their back on if they defected—12:22-24
- **c.** He presents his "sixth warning" in order to show his readers the danger of turning away from the revelation of this epistle—12:25-29

Note #273: Listen to God

He tells his readers that if they reject the voice of God from heaven, they are guilty of a greater sin than their forefathers and would not escape temporal (not salvific) judgment. The warning is based on Haggai 2:6 which looks forward to the millennial reign of Christ. The writer's purpose is to show the transitory nature of all things. Therefore, the readers can persevere because their afflictions are temporary, their kingdom is eternal which they will enter, and God is holy. Thus, they are not to go back to a system which will be the subject of eschatological judgment but to realize that they belong to a kingdom which will not be judged but will be established forever.

- **1)** They are warned not to refuse God's word for they would not escape judgment—12:25
- **2)** He notes that God would once more shake the earth in order to show its transitoriness—12:26-27
- **3)** He urges them to serve God because they are in the process of receiving an immoveable kingdom—12:28-29

D. The author presents the readers with a series of exhortations involving social, religious, and personal obligations in order to provide personal applications of the truth of the letter and show them how to live during persecution—13:1-25

1. He speaks of the social obligations they were to observe in order to show that difficult times do not change God's laws which include love, hospitality, compassion, sexual purity, and contentment—13:1-6

2. He speaks of the religious obligations they were to observe—13:7-17
- **a.** He reminds them of the faith of their past leaders which they were to imitate. They could do this because Christ is the same for them as he was for their leaders—13:7-8
- **b.** He urges them to complete devotion to Christ by showing them that Christ did as much and more than the old system did which should result

in their service and devotion—13:9-16

   c. He urges them to obey their present leaders—13:17

3. He speaks of the personal obligations they were to observe—13:18-25

   a. He asks for their prayer—13:18-19

   b. He pronounces a benediction on his readers in which he affirms many key doctrines of the book to remind them that God can meet their needs in present suffering—13:20-21

   c. He urges them to take heed to what he has written—13:22

   d. He instructs them that Timothy was released from prison and he may accompany him on a visit—13:23

   e. He sends greetings—13:24-25

Note #274: The Day of Atonement expanded[649]

The pinnacle of the Mosaic sacrificial system was the Day of Atonement. It has been correctly termed the "Good Friday" of the Old Testament, and the rabbis simply called it "the day."[650] *Herr agrees that this was the "most important day of the liturgical year."*[651] *However, this facet of God's revelation is not complete until it is correlated with Hebrews 9-10, for these two chapters are the New Testament commentary on the Old Testament Day. The Day of Atonement was instituted in light of the deaths of Nadab and Abihu (Lev. 10). This institution was to protect the high priest from experiencing a similar fate. Moreover, in light of the context in Leviticus 11-15, the wide-ranging nature of the uncleanness rules threatened to pollute the presence of God in the sanctuary.*

1. The Purpose of the Day of Atonement. *There are two demonstrable purposes for the Day. First and foremost, this was the day when the sanctuary was cleansed from the various pollutions that had infiltrated it due to the sin and uncleanness of the congregation and priests (Lev. 16:16, 19).*[652] *This would then permit the holy presence of God to continue dwelling among the people.*

Second, the Day of Atonement was the culminating day of sacrifice in the Mosaic system. Gayford has commented that the offerings of this day were "the highest in importance of all the atoning sacrifices; they summed up all the atoning power of the others."[653] *Likewise Kurtz states that "it was the highest, most perfect, and most comprehensive of all the acts of expiation."*[654] *And finally Ringgren writes, "This comprises a large number of expiatory practices to atone for sins of the high priest and the people during the preceding year."*[655] *The sacrifice on this occasion was the most*

---

[649] This excerpt is taken from Jerry Hullinger, "Two Atonement Realms: Reconciling Sacrifice in Leviticus and Hebrews," *Journal of Dispensational Theology* 32 (2007). Cited by permission.

[650] C. F. Keil and F. Delitzsch, *The Pentateuch* (repr., Commentary on the Old Testament; Grand Rapids: Eerdmans, 1980), 395-96.

[651] Moshe David Herr, "Day of Atonement," *Encyclopedia Judaica*, 5:1376.

[652] G. J. Wenham, *The Book of Leviticus* (NICOT; Grand Rapids: Eerdmans, 1985), 228. Margolis agrees that "by these rites the most holy place was rendered free from all impurities attaching to it through the intentional and unintentional entrance of the unclean persons into the sanctuary" (Max Margolis, "Atonement, Day of," *The Jewish Encyclopedia*), 2:284.

[653] S. C. Gayford, *Sacrifice and Priesthood: Jewish and Christian* (London: Methuen & Co., 1953), 85.

[654] J. H. Kurtz, *Sacrificial Worship of the Old Testament* (repr., Minneapolis: Klock & Klock, 1980), 386.

[655] H. Ringgren, *Sacrifice in the Bible* (NY: Association Press, 1962), 38. See also Allen Ross, *Holiness to the Lord: A Guide to the Exposition of the Book of Leviticus* (Grand Rapids: Baker, 2002), 313-14; Alfred Edersheim, *The Temple: Its Ministry and Services* (repr., Grand Rapids: Eerdmans, 1972), 303; Barclay, *The*

potent blood manipulation possible.[656]

2. The Ritual of the Day of Atonement. *The central passage for examining the Day of Atonement is Leviticus 16.*[657] *Leviticus 16:1-10 provides a general description of the ritual. The description is introduced with a warning: Aaron was not to come into the Holy of Holies whenever he chose.*[658] *This was due to God's presence above the mercy seat which would result in Aaron's death if he entered without proper preparation. Therefore, the rest of the chapter explains how he was to make his entrance.*

A detailing of the ritual is found in Leviticus 16:11-28. The first part of the ritual was the offering of the bullock (16:11-14) by Aaron to make atonement for his own sins. He took the blood of the bull along with a censer full of hot coals into the Holy of Holies. While Keil suggests that the incense was to prevent God from seeing the sinner, it seems better with Hertz and Hoffmann to understand this act as an attempt to protect the high priest from gazing on the divine presence and thereby averting his death.[659] *This appears to be the idea of verse 13 which says that the smoke covers the mercy seat rather than the high priest.*[660] *Consequently, the result was that "the high priest was unable to see the Lord, and this fact saved his life."*[661] *When he had entered the inner sanctuary, the high priest sprinkled some of the blood of the bull on the mercy seat and some in front of the mercy seat.*

The second part of the ritual dealt with the offering of the first goat (16:15-19) on behalf of the nation. Interestingly, no mention is made of the ceremony of the casting of lots regarding the two goats (cf., Lev. 16:8-9). Perhaps this casting of lots was done during the preparation phase of the ceremony. The lots were drawn and one was placed on the head of each goat.[662]

At this point, the high priest killed the goat which was designated for the Lord in order to offer it for the people. He then took its blood into the Holy of Holies and sprinkled it in the same manner as he had the blood of the bull (16:15). In addition, the sanctuary of the Holy Place needed to be cleansed (16:16). The text states that the holy place was defiled by the sin of the people. Morris explains: "The point of this is that the circumstances of everyday life made it easy for people to contract forms of ceremonial defilement...All this meant that they had defiled the place where they came to worship and this part of the day's ceremonies was directed to removing uncleanness."[663]

The third part of the Day of Atonement ritual was the sending away of the second,

---

Letter to the Hebrews, (Philadelphia: Westminster, 1958), 98.

656 N. Kiuchi, *The Purification Offering in the Priestly Literature: Its Meaning and Function* (Sheffield: Sheffield Academic Press, 1987), 159.

657 Other Old Testament references to the Day of Atonement include Exodus 30:10; Leviticus 23:26-32; Leviticus 25:9; Numbers 18; and Numbers 29:7-11.

658 "That he is not to come" is not an apodictic prohibition but merely a warning (J. Bright, "The Apodictic Prohibition: Some Observations," *Journal of Biblical Literature* 92 [1973]: 195-204). It is interesting that nothing is said about a fixed time for Aaron to enter the adytum. Milgrom suggests that the purgation rite was initially an emergency measure, and therefore Aaron could enter the adytum whenever he chose, but his successors could do so only on the annual Day of Atonement (Jacob Milgrom, *Leviticus 1—16* [AB, NY: Doubleday, 1991], 1012-13).

659 Keil & Delitzsch, *The Pentateuch*, 399; J. H. Hertz, *Leviticus* (London: Oxford, 1932), 156; D. Hoffmann, *Das Buch Leviticus I-II*, (Berlin: Poppelauer, 1905-06), 1:447.

660 Wenham, *The Book of Leviticus*, 231; Leon Morris, *The Atonement: Its Meaning and Significance* (Downers Grove: InterVarsity, 1983), 70.

661 R. K. Harrison, *Leviticus: An Introduction and Commentary* (Downers Grove: InterVarsity, 1980), 172.

662 For the details on this phase from Mishnaic sources, see Milgrom, *Leviticus 1-16*, 1019-20.

663 Leon Morris, *The Apostolic Preaching of the Cross* (Grand Rapids: Eerdmans, 1965), 71.

live goat into the wilderness (16:20-22). This part of the ceremony had two phases. In the first, the high priest laid both of his hands on the goat's head while confessing the sins of the people (16:21a). This symbolized the transference of the guilt of the people to the goat (16:21b; cf. Isa. 53:4).[664] *The second aspect of this part of the ritual involved the actual sending of the goat into the wilderness by a man appointed specifically for this job (16:21c-22).*[665] *While there has been considerable debate regarding the term "Azazel" (scapegoat) and the sending of the goat into the desert, what is being portrayed is clear.*[666] *The dismissal of this goat signified to the people that the consequences of their sins were removed from the presence of the Lord (cf., Ps. 103:12). W. Moeller summarizes the meaning of the dismissal of this goat.*

> *In order to make this transfer all the more impressive, both the hands are here brought into action, while in Leviticus 1:4 only one hand is used. The fact that*

---

[664] Kiuchi has also noted: "the guilt that Aaron has borne in purifying the defiled sancta is devolved upon the Azazel goat. Thus the relationship of the two rites is a continuous one" (Kiuchi, *The Purification Offering in the Priestly Literature*, 156).

[665] Geikie observes that in New Testament times, in order to prevent the goat returning to Jerusalem, it was led to a high mountain where it was pushed off and certainly killed (Cunningham Geikie, *The Holy Land and the Bible* [NY: James Pott & Co., 1888], 1:224-25).

[666] The etymology of the word "Azazel" is uncertain. Some derive "to drive away, something driven away" (Keil, *The Pentateuch*, 398; Hertz, *Leviticus*, 154; Brown, Driver, Briggs, 736b). Others follow the Septuagint and Vulgate and translate it as "scapegoat" (N. H. Snaith, *Leviticus and Numbers* [London: Thomas Nelson, 1967], 113; R. de Vaux, *Ancient Israel* [NY: McGraw-Hill, 1961], 508ff.), while others suggest an Arabic etymology meaning "rough ground" or "precipice" (G. R. Driver, "Three Technical Terms in the Pentateuch," *Journal of Semitic Studies* 2 [1956]: 98). Besides this, there have been four options proposed for understanding the phrase "for Azazel" (for a further discussion of all these options see Kurtz, *Sacrificial Worship of the Old Testament*, 396; Wenham, *The Book of Leviticus*, 234-35; Harrison, *Leviticus*, 170-71; Charles Feinberg, "The Scapegoat of Leviticus Sixteen " *Bibliotheca Sacra* 115 [1958]: 320-33): 1) the description of a place, 2) the description of the goat, 3) an evil demon to whom the goat is sent (possibly Satan) , and 4) an abstract noun signifying complete removal. The majority of commentators opt for the third view (e.g., Keil and Delitzsch, *The Pentateuch*, 1:404; George Bush, *Leviticus* [repr., Minneapolis: James Family Christian Publishers, 1979], 149; Morris, *The Apostolic Preaching of the Cross*, 98). This view is supported by the parallelism of "for the Lord" and "for Azazel," later Jewish literature which cites Azazel as the name of a demon (Enoch 8:1; 9:6), and the biblical citations looking at the wilderness as the haunt of demons (Lev. 17:17; Isa. 13:21; 34:14; Matt. 12:43; Mark 1:13). But as Hertz points out, "The offering of sacrifices to satyrs is spoken of as a heinous crime in the very next chapter (17:7); homage to a demon of the wilderness cannot, therefore be associated with the holiest of the Temple rites into the chapter immediately preceding" (Hertz, *Leviticus*, 156). This view is further weakened by the fact that both goats are said to constitute one sin offering to the Lord. In the writer's opinion, the best view is the fourth. First, this option fits the dual aspect of the one sacrifice. Second, this is a legitimate etymology of the word (Brown, Driver, Briggs, 736). Third it avoids the pitfall of offering an appeasement to a demon. Fourth, it is supported by the translation of the Septuagint (Wilhelm Moeller, "Azazel," *International Standard Bible Encyclopedia*, 1:344. Fifth, the function of the live goat is expressly said to bear the sins away into the wilderness (Lev. 16:21c-22). Thus the word visually symbolizes the removal of sin from the people (Feinberg, "The Scapegoat of Leviticus 16," 333; Harrison, *Leviticus*, 171; Hoffmann, *Das Buch Leviticus I-II*, 1:444; Hertz, *Leviticus*, 154).

Whichever view is adopted, however, Hoffmann's words are apropos. "Whether Azazel means, the mountain where the goat is destroyed, the sin which is given to destruction, or the evil angel who is given a bribe so that he does not become an accuser, it all comes back to the same basic idea: that sin is exterminated from Israel" (Hoffmann, 1:444; so, Ross, *Holiness to the Lord*, 319). The New Testament does not mention the scapegoat as typical of Christ directly, but since the Epistle of Barnabas (written c.a. AD 200), Christians have seen it as a type of Christ. As it was led out to die in the wilderness bearing the sins of the people, Christ was crucified outside the city of Jerusalem for the sins of the people (N. Micklem, "The Book of Leviticus," *Interpreters Bible*, 2:79ff.).

the goat is accompanied by somebody and that it is to be taken to an uninhabited place is to indicate the absolute impossibility of its return, i.e., the guilt has been absolutely forgiven and erased, a deep thought made objectively evident in a transparent manner and independently of the explanation of Azazel.[667]

It is probably best to see the two goats of this part of the ceremony as forming one offering. It is clearly stated in 16:5 that the two goats constituted a sin offering.[668] *Crawford suggests consequently that the two goats embodied two aspects of one sacrifice; the first exhibited the means, and the other the results of the atonement.*[669] *Erdman corroborates this thought. "The first goat signified the means of reconciliation to God, namely, by the death and sprinkled blood of a vicarious offering, so the dismissal of the second goat typified the effect of the expiation in the removal of the sin from the presence of a holy God."*[670]

Following the ritual of the two goats, the next stage of the procedure was the washing of the participants (16:23-28) so that new contamination to areas just cleansed would be prevented. Therefore, all who were involved in the activities were required to wash their clothes and flesh. The high priest at this point removed his white garments and put on his normal priestly garb (16:23-24). The fat of the sin offering was then burned on the altar while the bull and first goat were burned outside the camp.

The final part of the ritual involved duties which were incumbent on the people. First, they were to observe this day once each year on the given date. Second, they were to "afflict themselves." This probably carried the idea of self-examination, prayer, and fasting.[671] *Third, they were to do no work on this day.*

---

[667] Moeller, "Azazel," 1:344.

[668] Thus the living goat was the "alter ego" of the first as hircus redivivus (Kurtz, *Sacrificial Worship of the Old Testament,* 396; Edersheim, *The Temple: Its Ministry and Services,* 312). The first died as a sin offering, while the second visibly and strikingly conveyed the idea of the complete dismissal of sin.

[669] T. J. Crawford, *Doctrine of Holy Scripture Respecting Atonement* (NY: William Blackwood, 1888), 225.

[670] Charles Erdman, *The Book of Leviticus* (NY: Fleming Revell, 1951), 75. See also George Smeaton, *The Apostles' Doctrine of the Atonement* (repr., Grand Rapids: Zondervan, 1957), 25; Edersheim, *The Temple: Its Ministry and Services,* 319.

[671] Wenham, *The Book of Leviticus,* 236.

JAMES

Author

There are at least four men who bear the name of "James" in the New Testament. These include James, whose son Judas was one of the twelve apostles (Luke 6:16; Acts 1:13); James, the son of Alphaeus who was one of the twelve apostles (Luke 6:15; Acts 1:13); James, the brother of John, and son of Zebedee who was also one of the twelve apostles; and James, the half-brother of the Lord. The two most serious candidates for authorship are the apostle who was the son of Zebedee and the brother of John, or the half-brother of Jesus. The former is unlikely since he was martyred in AD 44 (Acts 12:2). The latter has several factors which support it: 1) there is a similarity of vocabulary between this letter and the letter sent from the Jerusalem Council (see Gromacki, *New Testament Survey,* 336), 2) the authority James displayed at the Council can be seen in this epistle, and 3) this was the external testimony of church fathers such as Origen, Eusebius, and Jerome.

Date

There is strong evidence to suggest that this was the earliest letter of the New Testament written around AD 45 and possibly even earlier than that. This is so for several reasons: l) the Jewish flavor of the letter fits with the early period of the church (see below), 2) there is no mention of the Jewish/Gentile controversies which is usually pinpointed around AD 45, 3) there is a close affinity to the Old Testament and the teachings of Christ, 4) the use of "synagogue" to describe the meeting place points to the early period when Christianity was largely confined to Jewish circles, and 5) the type of persecution seems to be religious from the Jews rather than political from the Romans.

Recipients

There are a number of important points to be noticed about the recipients of the letter. First, they were Jewish. This is seen in that they are addressed as the twelve tribes of the diaspora, the use of "synagogue," the use of such terms as "the Lord of Hosts" and "gehenna," the reverence for the Law, the use of Old Testament characters as illustrations, and the many allusions to Wisdom Literature. Second, they were believers. This is seen by the fact that they are called "brothers" (2:1) and they are told how to live as Christians. Third, they had been scattered throughout the Roman Empire. James would have personally known many who were driven out of Jerusalem in the persecution prompted by Stephen's martyrdom (Acts 8:1-4; 11:19). Fourth, it is also possible that James wrote to the Christian Jews who were scattered in the East. This would be supported by the facts that Peter wrote to the Christian Jews who were scattered in Pontus, Galatia, Cappadocia, Asia, and Bithynia and that James was accepted late by the Western churches.

Occasion

Given the early composition of the letter, several things can be noted concerning its occasion. For example, this would be a period in the history of the church when young believing Jews who were steeped in the Old Testament Law had to make the difficult transition experientially into the age of grace. Furthermore, both James and Peter were involved in this transition by their leadership of the Jews into this new era. This is seen by James as dependence on the Law and the teaching of Christ, as well as the emphasis on fruit and action which is what the Law sought to produce. Thus James, as the leader of the Jerusalem Church, would feel an added responsibility for these former members who had been scattered through persecution. This persecution involved ostracism from the synagogue which was the religious, social, and economic center for the Jew (see Joseph Mayor, *The Epistle of St. James* [Grand Rapids: Baker, 1978], cxxv).

Purpose

These believers knew factually that the era of Law had come to an end through the death of Christ, and that the age of grace had begun. The obvious need then is to know what kind of behavior or righteousness God expected at present. Or put another way, what is the ethical relationship of believers to the Law? Thus, a purpose statement could be: James presents various exhortations and instructions on righteous living in order to show the Jewish Christians of the diaspora how faith operates to produce the righteousness of the Law during this new age.

Summary of Argument

I. JAMES INTRODUCES HIMSELF AS A SERVANT OF GOD AND ADDRESSES THE TWELVE TRIBES WHICH ARE SCATTERED ABROAD—1:1

II. JAMES INSTRUCTS THE BELIEVERS IN THE REALM OF TESTING AND TEMPTATION IN ORDER TO SHOW THEM THAT OBEDIENT FAITH PROFITS FROM TESTING AND RESISTS TEMPTATION—1:2-18

Note #275: Testing

James uses the Greek noun πειρασμός and its verbal cognate πειράζω with different nuances in this section. Sometimes there will be a positive sense of testing to confirm one's character, while at other times there will be a negative sense of enticing to sin.

A. He instructs them regarding testing so that they would know how to handle testing and profit from it—1:2-12

1. Their attitude toward testing should be one of joy because testing produces endurance which leads to maturity—1:2-4

2. They should ask for wisdom in their testing so that they would see the good in it and know how to deal with it—1:5-8

3. The correct estimate of testing should be rejoicing because of the eternal benefits—1:9-11

4. The reward of enduring testing is the crown of life given to those who evince a love for God by their endurance—1:12

B. He instructs them regarding temptation so that they would have help in resisting it—1:13-18

1. The source of temptation is not God but sinful man—1:13-14

2. The consequences of yielding to temptation is a cycle which leads to physical frustration/death—1:15

3. He warns them about being deceived into thinking that temptation is from God by noting that He is the giver of good things which is preeminently illustrated by the gift of regeneration—1:16-18

III. JAMES INSTRUCTS THE BELIEVERS IN THE REALM OF THE RECEPTION OF THE WORD IN ORDER TO SHOW THEM THAT FAITH PRODUCES OBEDIENCE—1:19-27

A. He exhorts them on their attitudes and actions in order to show the preconditions for receiving the Word—1:19-21

1. They are to be quick to listen, slow to speak, and slow to become angry for this does not bring the righteous life which God desires—1:19-20

Note #276: The righteousness of God

"The righteousness of God" can be used in several ways in the Bible. It was seen in the notes on Romans that the phrase describes the fact that God is righteous in the way He deals with people. It is also used by Paul of the judicial and objective righteousness which He imputes to people. James, however, uses it in the sense of the righteous life which God desires as a standard of life. As James develops this idea in the epistle, he is heavily dependent on the righteousness portrayed in the Old Testament and the Sermon on the Mount (for twenty-five parallels between James and Matthew's version of the Sermon on the Mount, see Peter Davids, The Epistle of James: A Commentary on the Greek Text *[Grand Rapids: Eerdmans, 1982], 47-48).*

2. They are to rid themselves of moral filth and humbly receive the Word—1:21

B. He exhorts them to be obedient to the Word—1:22-27

1. He states the requirement of being obedient to the Word—1:22
2. He illustrates this requirement by one who looks in a mirror and does nothing in response and by one who looks into the mirror of the Word and does respond—1:23-25

Note #277: The law of liberty

By the "perfect law of liberty" James has reference to the righteousness depicted in the whole Old Testament and the Sermon on the Mount. The phrase "of liberty" has the idea of "that which liberates." Thus, it is righteousness that is distinct from enslaving, Pharisaic legalism with which they would have been familiar.

3. He applies the requirement by showing that a hearer and a doer will perform acts of mercy and lead a holy life—1:26-27

IV. JAMES INSTRUCTS THEM IN THE REALM OF PARTIALITY IN ORDER TO SHOW THEM THAT OBEDIENT FAITH TREATS ALL PEOPLE ON THE SAME LEVEL—2:1-13

A. He prohibits them to show favoritism and gives an illustration of how this could happen in their assembly and explains that by doing this they would be assuming the position of judge over people—2:1-4

B. He shows the results of partiality—2:5-11

  1. He contrasts the methods of judgment in order to show them that they ended up rejecting whom God had accepted—2:5-7

    a. He notes that God has chosen the poor to inherit the blessings of the Kingdom—2:5

    b. He notes that they have insulted the ones chosen by God in favor of the ones who were persecuting them—2:6-7

  2. He explains that partiality violates God's law—2:8-11

    a. He states that if one truly loves another he is keeping the royal law, but if he is not, he is breaking it—2:8-9

Note #278: The Sermon on the Mount

The law is called "royal" because it was given by Christ the King in the Sermon on the Mount. The law is the whole law of God and love toward one's neighbor is the crucial element governing human relationships.

    b. He states that if they break one part of the Law they were guilty of breaking all of it to show the seriousness of this one issue—2:10-11

  3. He exhorts them not to show partiality because they would one day be judged by the law of liberty—2:12-13

Note #279: The Judgment Seat

The reference here is to the judgment seat of Christ. The mercy here is not salvific mercy but that mercy which will come to the Christian at the day of judgment. Our mercy toward others now will provide God with a further occasion to show mercy to the individual on the Day of Judgment. An unmerciful attitude, on the other hand, restricts God's flow of mercy.

V. JAMES INSTRUCTS THEM IN THE REALM OF FAITH AND WORKS IN ORDER TO SHOW THEM THAT OBEDIENT FAITH PRODUCES GOOD WORKS—2:14-26

Note #280: Faith without works is dead

This section in James has been the occasion for much debate. The position of the writer will be set out in a number of propositions: 1) the book is addressing Christians (called "brethren" 15 times) regarding testing, suffering, the purpose of trials, and living out the faith by touching on matters such as obedience, the tongue, handling wealth, treating all people with love, worldliness, patience, submitting to God, sickness, and similar themes, 2) In the first half of chapter 2 the issue under discussion is the problem of favoritism. James tells his readers that when people come into the assembly they are to be treated equally regardless of social standing. The section beginning in verse 14 expands on this call to impartiality, 3) the term "saved" must be seen in its rich, varied biblical use. Dillow explains. "It would be difficult to find a concept which is richer and more varied in meaning than the biblical concept of salvation. The breadth of salvation is so sweeping and its intended aim so magnificent that in many contexts the words used defy precise definition. Yet these difficulties have not thwarted numerous interpreters from assuming, often without any contextual justification, that the words used invariably mean 'deliverance from hell' or 'go to heaven when you die.' It may come as a surprise to many that this usage of 'salvation'...would have been the least likely meaning to come to the mind of a reader of the Bible in the first century [particularly this early in the first century since James was the first epistle written]. Indeed, in 812 usages of the various Hebrew words translated 'to save' or 'salvation' in the Old Testament, only 58 (7.1 percent) refer to eternal salvation" (Joseph Dillow, The Reign of the Servant Kings, *112), 4) in the Wisdom Literature, which is rich in James, salvation is often used to refer the fullness of physical life and being delivered from the consequences of sin. In this context, specific emphasis is being delivered from the sin of partiality, 5) the preceding point is further supported by the fact that within this very text, James continues to speak of helping the poor, 6) while Paul speaks eloquently of justification before God through faith alone, James in his epistle is using the term differently to speak of justification or validation before men as to the reality of our faith. Thus it is said of Abraham (2:22) that his faith came to "completion" when he offered Isaac, 7) Abraham was justified with God* before *he offered Isaac; moreover, he was justified* before *Genesis 15:6. When the text says "and he believed the Lord," the* waw *(w) plus the perfect tense verb "believed" (הֶאֱמִן) would have a disjunctive idea "now he had believed" indicating that this was Abraham's pattern. Ross observes that "The verse may be a summary statement of Abraham's faith, or a transitional note between sections. It could be translated parenthetically as disjunctive clauses often are...The verb could be explained as having a characteristic nuance in the sense that he was a believer. In other words, the text does not necessarily mean that Abram came to faith here" (Allen Ross,* Creation & Blessing: A Guide to the Study and Exposition of Genesis *[Grand Rapids: Baker, 1988], 310), 8) a "dead" faith does not refer to a faith that is not present, but to a faith that is not active, therefore 9) "The faith which is mentioned in this section can be presupposed in every Christian...[James] intention is not dogmatically oriented, but practically oriented:* he wishes to admonish the Christian to practice their faith, i.e. their Christianity, by works" *(Martin Dibelius,* James *[Philadelphia: Fortress, 1976], 178). Summarily, it is possible for a Christian to have a "dead" faith, in the sense that his faith is not operative.*

- **A.** He presents his first thesis that faith without works is dead—2:14-17
    - **1.** He states that if faith is not living and productive then it is dead—2:14
    - **2.** He illustrates this by an example of one who says something without any action to accompany it—2:15-16
    - **3.** He concludes by stating that faith which does not produce action is dead—2:17
- **B.** He presents his second thesis that faith without works is demoniacal—2:18-20
    - **1.** He states that faith without works is incapable of demonstration—2:18
    - **2.** He states that faith without works is like that of demons—2:19-20
- **C.** He gives two illustrations in order to show faith and works go together—2:21-25
    - **1.** He gives the example of Abraham to show that his faith was confirmed to be alive by his obedient offering of Isaac—2:21-24

2. He gives the example of Rahab to show that her faith was confirmed to be alive by the aid which she gave to the spies—2:25

D. He concludes by showing that as the body is dead without the spirit so faith is dead (inoperative/nonproductive) without works—2:26

VI. JAMES INSTRUCTS THEM IN THE REALM OF THE TONGUE IN ORDER TO SHOW THEM THAT OBEDIENT FAITH IS ABLE TO CONTROL THE TONGUE—3:1-18

A. He instructs his readers on the importance of the tongue—3:1-5
   1. He warns that not many should be teachers because they would be judged for their teaching—3:1
   2. He states that the one who can control his tongue is mature and able to control the rest of his person—3:2
   3. He gives three illustrations in order to show the importance and power of the tongue—3:3-6

B. He instructs his readers on the insubordination of the tongue by noting that while men have the ability to tame animals they do not have the ability to tame the tongue—3:7-8

C. He instructs his readers on the incongruity of the tongue—3:9-12
   1. The tongue blesses God on the one hand, and curses man who is in the image of God on the other hand—3:9-10
   2. He condemns this inconsistency by noting the perversion of this in nature—3:11-12

D. He instructs his readers on the two kinds of wisdom in order to show wisdom's role in controlling the tongue—3:13-18
   1. He notes the demand for wisdom in that it needs to be shown in the life—3:13
   2. He notes that the control of false wisdom leads to selfishness and evil—3:14-16
   3. He notes that the control of true wisdom is pure, etc., and leads to righteousness—3:17-18

VII. JAMES INSTRUCTS THEM IN THE REALM OF WORLDLINESS IN ORDER TO SHOW THEM THAT OBEDIENT FAITH PRODUCES LOYALTY TO GOD—4:1-12

A. He describes worldliness in their situation and rebukes them for allowing it in their lives—4:1-6
   1. He gives a description of the condition so that they would be able to recognize it—4:1-3
   2. He rebukes the worldliness by noting that the one who is the friend of the world is an enemy of God—4:4-6

B. He exhorts those who are worldly in order to show the cure for worldliness—4:7-12
   1. He calls them to proper action to God—4:7-10
      a. He exhorts them to surrender to God's will—4:7a
      b. He exhorts them to resist the devil—4:7b

- **c.** He exhorts them to restore their fellowship to God—4:8a
- **d.** He exhorts them to moral cleansing—4:8b
- **e.** He exhorts them to inner purification—4:8c
- **f.** He exhorts them to sorrow over their sin—4:9a
- **g.** He exhorts them to mourn—4:9:b
- **h.** He exhorts them to joy over their repentance—4:9c
- **i.** He exhorts them to humility—4:10

2. He calls them to proper action toward man—4:11-12

- **a.** They are not to slander each other—4:11a
- **b.** They are not to slander because it sets themselves above the law and usurps the position that is God's alone—4:11b-12

VIII. JAMES INSTRUCTS THEM CONCERNING PRESUMP-TUOUS PLANNING IN ORDER TO SHOW THEM THAT OBEDIENT FAITH SHOWS DEPENDENCE ON GOD—4:13-17

A. He calls to attention those who do not feel their dependency on God as they make their plans—4:13

B. He says that this is wrong because of lack of knowledge and the brevity of life—4:14

C. He says that the correct attitude is one that recognizes God's authority and dependence on Him—4:15-16

D. He concludes that to know what should be done (the preceding) and not doing it is to sin—4:17

IX. JAMES INSTRUCTS THEM CONCERNING THE RICH, JESUS' COMING, AND PRAYER IN ORDER TO SHOW THEM HOW OBEDIENT FAITH ACTS IN THESE SITUATIONS—5:1-20

A. James instructs them on the fate of the rich and how they are to live in light of this—5:1-12

1. He notes that judgment is coming on the unsaved rich because they oppress the poor, are self-indulgent, and are violent against the righteous—5:1-6

2. He instructs them on how they are to live as they wait for judgment to come upon the rich—5:7-12

- **a.** He tells them to be patient as the farmer who waits for his crop—5:7-8a
- **b.** He tells them to stand firmly—5:8b
- **c.** He tells them to not grumble against each other—5:9
- **d.** He gives the example Job of patient endurance—5:10-11
- **e.** He tells them to be honest in all things thus not necessitating the taking of an oath—5:12

B. James instructs them in the area of prayer so that they would be helped in their present affliction—5:13-20

1. He says that those who are suffering hardship should pray, and those who are happy should sing songs of praise—5:13

2. He gives instruction for those who are sick—5:14-18

Note #281: The prayer of faith will save the sick

1. In James 5:14 the writer asks a question of his readers, which is similarly translated in almost all versions "is anyone among you sick?" The word "translated "sick" is ἀσθενέω which is used 33 times in the New Testament and simply means "weakness" (Bauer, Arndt, Gingrich, Danker, A Greek-English Lexicon of the New Testament and Other Early Christian Literature, *115), and can refer either to physical weakness (illness) or spiritual weakness. Statistically, the word more often refers to physical weakness rather than spiritual weakness; however, as long as the semantic range is established, context must be the determining factor.*

2. Also in 5:14 the sick person is to call for the elders to pray who will then "anoint" the individual with oil. The word translated "anoint" is ἀλείφω which occurs 9 times in the New Testament. Daniel Hayden suggests the following trend of the term: "James is not suggesting a ceremonial or ritual anointing as a means of divine healing; instead, he is referring to the common practice of using oil as a means of bestowing honor, refreshment, and grooming. It was in this sense that the sinful woman anointed...*Jesus' feet with ointment (Luke 7:38) and that a host would* anoint...*the head of a guest with oil (Luke 7:46). Jesus also suggested that a person who was fasting should not appear sad and ungroomed, but should* anoint...*his head and wash his face (Matt 6:17)" (Daniel Hayden, "Calling the Elders to Pray,"* Bibliotheca Sacra *138:551 [Jul 1981], 264-265).*

3. In James 5:15 occurs the second occurrence of the word "sick" which again is similarly translated in the versions as "the sick," "the sick person," "the one who is sick." However, in this second occurrence James uses a different Greek term than he used in verse 14. This time the term is κάμνω. This word is used only twice in the New Testament (James 5:15; Hebrews 12:3) and means to be "wearied" or "fatigued" (Bauer, Arndt, Gingrich, Danker, 402). While the term can refer to physical illness outside of the New Testament, the use in Hebrews clearly refers to spiritual weariness.

4. James states firmly in 5:15 that the prayer and anointing by the elders "will save the sick." As noted in the discussion on James 2, "salvation" frequently has a use quite apart from justification with this being another case in point. The absoluteness of this statement is not problematic if the weakness in view is spiritual in nature. Through the person's initiative in calling the elders, the anointing, and the prayers (and possibly the confession of sin), he will be delivered from spiritual discouragement. Contrariwise, if the weakness is physical in nature, the explanation of this clause is much more difficult and certainly inconsistent.

5. James says in 5:16 that if sin is involved in the weakness of the individual that confession will bring forgiveness and "healing" (ἰάομαι). Used 26 times in the New Testament, the most frequent use is found in the Gospels and Acts refers to physical healing. The term is used of spiritual, salvific healing in Acts 28:27 and 1 Peter 2:24. The word is then used in Hebrews 12:13 of the healing of the spiritually discouraged saint.

6. The inclusion of Elijah as an illustration could legitimately be argued to be merely a model of fervent, effective prayer. That granted, it is hard not to take into account that Elijah was a prominent example of a believer who became spiritually depressed.

7. There is a thematic inclusio to be noted in the structure of James. The book begins by addressing believers of the diaspora who are plagued by trials and the book concludes in 5:13 by addressing those who are suffering. Some will respond with prayer and others with rejoicing. However, others will become spiritually defeated.

8. It is also significant to see how the book ends in 5:19-20: Brethren, if anyone among you wanders from the truth, and someone turns him back, let him know that he who turns a sinner from the error of his way will save a soul from death and cover a multitude of sins *(NKJV).*

Conclusion. There is clear lexical evidence to support the view that James has physical illness in mind in this passage; a view held by many commentators (for example see Craig Blomberg, Mariam Kamell, James, *Zondervan Exegetical Commentary on the New Testament [Grand Rapids: Zondervan, 2008], 241-253). However, given the semantic range of the terms involved, the similar condition of the readers in Hebrews (where the terms clearly refer to spiritual weariness) and James, the use of the term "sick" in 5:15 to elucidate the use of the term "sick" in 5:14, and other considerations which have been mentioned; it is the conclusion reached here that some of the readers of this letter had grown into spiritual depression or weakness.*

- **a.** The sick person is to call for the elders of the church—5:14a
- **b.** The elders are to pray anointing him with oil—5:14b
- **c.** The prayer of faith will restore the individual—5:15-16a
- **d.** He illustrates from Elijah the fact that the prayer of a righteous man is powerful and effective—5:16b-18

X. JAMES CONCLUDES HIS INSTRUCTIONS BY SHOWING HOW AN OBEDIENT FAITH ACTS TOWARD THOSE WHO DO NOT HEED THE ADMONITIONS OF THE LETTER—5:19-20

- **A.** He presents the scenario of a brother wandering from this truth and being restored by another brother—5:19
- **B.** He notes that this act has saved this brother from physical death—5:20

1 PETER

Author

This epistle claims Petrine authorship and the traditional view supports this assertion. Externally, writers such as Irenaeus, Tertullian, and Eusebius have supported this. Internally, it is supported by the salutation (1:1), the claim to be a witness of the sufferings of Christ (5:1), and a number of analogies with the discourses of Peter in Acts.

Date

Those who reject the Petrine authorship of the book posit a date of around AD 80-100 during the reign of Domitian. However, the conservative view dates the book shortly before the outbreak of the Neronian persecution in AD 64. This is buttressed by the following evidence: 1) there is no hint of the readers being second generation Christians, 2) Peter advocates a loyal attitude toward government which suggests that official persecution has not taken place yet, and 3) the trend made it clear that trouble lay ahead (4:17-18).

Origin

Peter states at the end of chapter 5 that he was writing from Babylon. This identification is subject to at least four possibilities. First, it could be Antioch since this was the last place where Peter was, and since this is where the Diaspora settled. To a Jew, Babylon represented bondage, thus Antioch became their Babylon. Second, it could be the small town in Egypt with that name, but this was too insignificant a town to merit a visit by Peter. Third, it could be a cryptic reference to the city of Rome. This is supported by the tradition that Peter was in Rome at the end of his life, and the cryptic reference was to avoid persecution. A fourth view is to take it as the literal city on the Euphrates. This is supported because of the natural meaning of the term, it was the chief center of Jews in the Eastern dispersion, and it fits the order of the provinces if coming from the East. Whichever view is taken, it, does not affect the interpretation of the book.

Recipients

The most important introductory matter concerns the recipients because this can bear on the interpretation of 2:9, 10. Some see the readership as primarily Gentile with some Jewish element, and others see the readership as primarily Jewish with some Gentile element. The first view is the most commonly held for the following reasons: 1) the "abominable idolatries" would be most applicable to a Gentile audience (4:3), 2) the lack of the article before "scattered" (1:1), and 3) Peter's use of his Greek name rather than his Hebrew or Aramaic one.

In favor of a primarily Jewish readership the following evidence is to be noted: 1) the description of the unregenerate past would be applicable to both Jew and Gentile, 2) the regions named in the introduction had representatives in Jerusalem on Pentecost suggesting that these churches were started by those converts. This would allow the term Diaspora to have its normal, Jewish sense, 3) though Peter also had a ministry to Gentiles, he was primarily a leader to Jews. Though each view has its support, the writer favors the latter view primarily for the normal sense of Diaspora and the Old Testament ideas (Hosea 11) which are applied to the readers who, if they were Gentiles, would not have as much significance.

Occasion

There seem to be at least two primary factors which contributed to the writing of this epistle. The first is persecution. This appears to be primarily personal persecution rather than governmental persecution (2:12; 3:16-17; 4:3-4, 14) which was spotty, local, and intermittent. If this had been the persecution under Nero, it is doubtful that this would have been so vague. The second factor is that these believers had been scattered in the midst of a pagan society that did not know God, and therefore they needed exhortation and encouragement.

Purpose

The key vocabulary in the book helps illuminate the purpose Peter had in writing. For example, the word *anastrophe* (conduct) is used six times; the word *pascho* (suffer) is used twelve times; *hypotasso* (subject) is used six times, and *agathopoieo* (do good) is used four times. Furthermore, the structural ideas help determine the purpose. In 1:1-2:10 he writes concerning the greatness of salvation, in 2:11-3:7 he speaks of the various areas of subjection and duty, and in 3:8-5:14 he speaks about suffering and responsibilities in that suffering. From these facts, the following purpose statement could be suggested: Peter writes to persecuted Christians about their salvation, subjection, and suffering in order to encourage them in the light of their future glory and to exhort them to righteous living in a sinful world.

Summary of Argument

I. PETER INTRODUCES THE LETTER WITH A REFERENCE TO HIMSELF, TO HIS READERS, AND A GREETING—1:1-2

- **A.** He introduces himself as Peter an apostle of Christ—1:1a
- **B.** He gives a description of his readers in order to encourage them in light of their spiritual position—1:1b-2a
  - **1.** He notes their true nature as being elect—1:1b
  - **2.** He notes their geographical location—1:1c
  - **3.** He notes their spiritual pedigree—1:2a

Note #282: Foreknowledge

Peter asserts that his readers were elect/chosen according to the "foreknowledge" of God. The theological debate generated by this passage deals with the relationship of God's sovereignty, God's knowledge, and man's will. Of course the issues involved are much larger than this one text, but the purpose of this note is to summarily focus the options on this passage. There are at least five approaches: 1) open theism/neotheism/free-will theism (e.g. Clark Pinnock, John Sanders, Gregory Boyd, William Hasker, Richard Rice). This view separates itself from the "calvinistic" view that God determines the future and the "arminian" view that God simply knows the future. For, if God knows the future, then this leads to determinism which implies that human freedom is an illusion. Thus the future is *unknown to God because it has not happened yet since it is created by free, human choice. God, therefore, does not possess foreknowledge even in the passive, Arminian sense of God simply knowing beforehand what will occur. Hence, foreknowledge is virtually denied. The following statements from Pinnock are representative (Clark Pinnock, The Most Moved Mover [Grand Rapids: Baker, 2001]: "Though God knows all there is to know about the world, there are aspects about the future that even God does not know" (32); Scripture makes a distinction with respect to the future; God is certain about some aspects of it and uncertain about other aspects (47); "But no being, not even God, can know in advance precisely what free agents will do, even though he may predict it with great accuracy" (100), 2) the second view (I am at a loss to know how to label it) argues that there is neither a logical nor temporal connection between foreknowledge and election. Geisler states on 1 Peter 1:2 that "there is no chronological or logical priority of election and foreknowledge. As a simple Being, all of God's attributes are one with his indivisible essence. Hence, both foreknowledge and predetermination are one in God. Thus whatever God knows, he determines. And what he determines, he knows" (Norm Geisler, "God Knows All Things," in Predestination & Free Will [Downers Grove: InterVarsity Press, 1986], 70), 3) middle knowledge. The concept of "middle knowledge" is usually associated with the 16th century Jesuit theologian Luis de Molina (hence also known as "molinism") and is championed by current theologians such as William Lane Craig. This view divides God's knowledge into three categories. The <u>first category</u> is that God knows all things that are possible in all possible worlds with all possible contingencies. Thus God knows what each of his creatures could choose to do in any possible set of circumstances. This is referred to as God's "natural knowledge." In the <u>second category</u>, God knows what his creatures will do in a given set of circumstances. These circumstances are not forcing one to make a decision but simply noting how one would freely choose. Thus if God chooses to actuate a certain scenario, then certain results will follow. This second category is called "middle knowledge" because it occurs after the first category but before the third. In the <u>third category</u> of God's knowledge, God brings about one of the worlds from his middle knowledge through deliberation of every possibility. The application of this theory to the Peter text is explained by Craig, "Middle knowledge also serves to reconcile predestination and human freedom. On Molina's view predestination is merely that aspect of providence pertaining to eternal salvation; it is the order and means by which God ensures that some free creature attains eternal life. Prior to the divine decree, God knows via His middle knowledge how any possible free creature would respond in any possible circumstances, which include the offer of certain gifts of prevenient grace which God might provide. In choosing a certain possible world, God commits Himself, out of His goodness, to offering various gifts of grace to every person which are sufficient for his salvation. Such grace is not intrinsically efficacious in that it of itself produces its effect; rather it is extrinsically efficacious in accomplishing its end in those who freely cooperate with it. God knows that many will freely reject His sufficient grace and be lost; but He knows that many others will assent to it, thereby rendering it efficacious in effecting their salvation. Given God's immutable decree to actualize a certain world, those whom God knew would respond to His* *grace are predestined to do so in the sense that it is absolutely certain that they will respond to and persevere in God's grace. There is no risk of their being lost; indeed, in sensu composito it is impossible for them to fall away. But in sensu diviso they are entirely free to reject God's grace; but were they to do so, God would have had different middle knowledge and they would not have been predestined. Similarly those who are not predestined have no one to blame but themselves. It is up to God whether we find ourselves in a world in which we are predestined, but it is up to us whether we are predestined in the world in which we find ourselves" (http://www.leaderu.com/offices/billcraig/docs/middle2, accessed 8/11/2014), 4) foresight. This fourth view argues that "foreknowledge" simply refers to the fact that God knows the future without determining the future. Therefore, God knows in advance who will choose to accept the gospel. Edgar concludes, in his spirited article on the term, that "The exegetical evidence for proginōskō agrees with the objective lexical evidence for the meaning of this word. It means to know beforehand and has no deterministic meaning or inference such as electing, choosing, or intimate or loving relationship" (Thomas Edgar, "The Meaning Of ΠΡΟΓΙΝΩΣΚΩ ('To Foreknow')," Chafer Theological Seminary Journal 09:1 [Spring 2003], 73), and 5) foreknowledge as determination. A final view of the term is that it not only includes God's prescience, but his sovereign determination as well. Thus the election of Peter's readers by God is based upon his decision to save them.*

Of the five views, only the fourth and fifth deal seriously with textual considerations and remain the two most viable options. The overall solution to the larger theological debate as to who does what in salvation must correlate all of the Scriptural data, every branch of systematic theology, historical theology, and even missiological trends beginning in the Old Testament. The focus in this note, however, is merely the word "foreknowledge." The term used by Peter translated as "foreknowledge" is πρόγνωσιν.

"Foreknowledge" Usage

FORM	NEW TESTAMENT (SUBJECT)	LEXICONS
πρόγνωσις "foreknowledge" (noun) **2 Uses** Acts 2:23 1 Peter 1:2	**Acts 2:23 (God to Christ)** ESV **Acts 2:23** this Jesus, delivered up according to the definite plan and foreknowledge of God KJV **Acts 2:23** Him, being delivered by the determinate counsel and foreknowledge of God NAU **Acts 2:23** this *Man*, delivered over by the predetermined plan and foreknowledge of God NIV **Acts 2:23** This man was handed over to	*BAGD* "Of God's omniscient wisdom and intention...*κατὰ πρόγνωσιν θεου/ according to the predestination of God the Father* 1 Pt 1:2" (703-04). *Thayer's Greek Lexicon,*

	you by God's set purpose and foreknowledge **<u>1 Peter 1:2 (God to Man)</u>** ESV **1 Peter 1:2** according to the foreknowledge of God the Father KJV **1 Peter 1:2** Elect according to the foreknowledge of God the Father NAU **1 Peter 1:2** according to the foreknowledge of God the Father NIV **1 Peter 1:2** who have been chosen according to the foreknowledge of God the Father	<u>BibleWorks 6</u> "Foreknowledge" Judith 9:6; 11:19 [these are the only two references in the LXX which use the noun form]. "Forethought, prearrangement" 1 Peter 1:2
προγινώσκω "foreknow" (verb) **<u>5 Uses</u>** Acts 26:5 Romans 8:29 Romans 11:2 1 Peter 1:20 2 Peter 3:17	**<u>Acts 26:5 (Man to Man)</u>** ESV **Acts 26:5** They have known for a long time KJV **Acts 26:5** Which knew me from the beginning NAU **Acts 26:5** since they have known about me for a long time NIV **Acts 26:5** They have known me for a long time **<u>Romans 8:29 (God to Man)</u>** ESV **Romans 8:29** For those whom he foreknew he also predestined KJV **Romans 8:29** For whom he did foreknow, he also did predestinate NAU **Romans 8:29** For those whom He foreknew, He also predestined NIV **Romans 8:29** For those God foreknew he also predestined	<u>*The New International Dictionary of New Testament Theology*</u> "In the NT the vb. *προγινοσκο*, foreknow, know beforehand or in advance, choose beforehand, is found 5 times...In Paul the vb. *proginosko*, foreknow, choose beforehand, demonstrates the character of God's activity among men. It assumes the aspect of a personal relationship with a group of people which originates with God himself" (1:693).

	Romans 11:2 (God to Israel) ESV **Romans 11:2** God has not rejected his people whom he foreknew KJV **Romans 11:2** God hath not cast away his people which he foreknew NAU **Romans 11:2** God has not rejected His people whom He foreknew NIV **Romans 11:2** God did not reject his people, whom he foreknew **1 Peter 1:20 (God to Christ)** ESV **1 Peter 1:20** He was foreknown before the foundation of the world KJV **1 Peter 1:20** Who verily was foreordained before the foundation of the world NAU **1 Peter 1:20** For He was foreknown before the foundation of the world NIV **1 Peter 1:20** He was chosen before the creation of the world **2 Peter 3:17 (Man to Events)** ESV **2 Peter 3:17** You therefore, beloved, knowing this beforehand KJV **2 Peter 3:17** Ye therefore, beloved, seeing ye know *these things* before NAU **2 Peter 3:17** You therefore, beloved, knowing this beforehand NIV **2 Peter 3:17** Therefore, dear friends, since you already know this	

The seven texts listed above are the only New Testament examples of the noun "foreknowledge" and the verb "to foreknow." Two of the seven uses deal with what man knows including some facts about Paul (Acts 26:5) and that false teachers will twist

Paul's writings (2 Peter 3:17). These two uses simply refer to the natural knowledge possessed by man. Five of the seven uses have God as the subject. In these instances more is being indicated than awareness of what is going to take place. Acts 2:23 links God's foreknowledge with his "determinate counsel." It would be odd of Peter to say that God knew Christ would be crucified apart from any aspect of determination. 1 Peter 1:2 associates God's foreknowledge with his election. There is nothing in this passage that speaks of God foreseeing the action of faith in his creatures. To say that God knew in advance that some would choose Him and then elect them makes the concept of election meaningless. To speak of God choosing someone because they choose him is nonsensical. Moreover, the 1 Peter 1:20 use of "foreknow" speaks of Christ being "foreknown" before the foundation of the world. Surely more is meant than God knew in advance about Christ; especially in light of the fact that Peter had preached in Acts 2:23 that Christ was delivered up by the determinate counsel of God. This is why the KJV translates the term as "foreordained" and the NIV as "chosen." Thus Christ died to fulfill God's preordained plan. If the 1:20 text is clear, then this should inform Peter's meaning in 1:2. As Hiebert states, "divine foreknowledge involves God's favorable regard for people as part of his deliberate plans and purposes" (D. Edmond Hiebert, First Peter: An Expositional Commentary [Chicago: Moody Press, 1984], 38). Romans 8:29 says that God foreknew certain individuals. It should be noted that the object of the foreknowing act is not an action but a person. <u>People</u> are foreknown, not their action of faith. This point is confirmed by Paul's only other use of the term in Romans 11:2 where he writes that God foreknew Israel. It is inconceivable that this simply means that God knew about Israel in advance. Rather, God chose Israel rather than choosing Egypt, Assyria, Babylon, France, Japan, America, etc. Thus the prophet's words to the nation: "you only have I known of all the families of the earth" (Amos 3:2). Because of this Paul says, God will not cast his people away. It would have been impossible for God to have foreseen anything positive in Israel since their past has been one of running from God not to him; and, their future will be one of God catching them and giving them a new heart and blessing.

Schreiner brings together the Pauline and Petrine uses of the term: "The term 'foreknow' at a minimum means that God knew from the beginning those who would belong to Jesus Christ...It is likely, however, that the term means even more than this when attributed to God. God's knowledge of his people in the OT refers to his covenantal love by which he set his affection on his people...It seems, then, that the word 'foreknow' virtually takes on the meaning 'choose beforehand.' Such a conclusion is supported by Rom. 11:2, where Paul discusses whether God has abandoned Israel as his people. He asserts, 'God has not rejected his people whom he foreknew.' The words 'rejected' and 'foreknew' function as antonyms in the verse...The definition proposed fits as well with 1 Peter 1:20 where Christ was foreknown before the world began. This does not mean merely that God foresaw Christ would arrive; it indicates also that God planned in his love to choose Jesus of Nazareth to be the Christ" (Thomas Schreiner, New Testament Theology: Magnifying God in Christ [Grand Rapids: Baker Academic, 2008], 339-340).

C. He greets his readers with the hope that abundant grace and peace would be theirs—1:2b

II. PETER EXTOLS THE GREATNESS OF THE READERS' SALVATION IN ORDER TO ENCOURAGE THEM CONCERNING THEIR FUTURE DESTINY WHICH WILL HELP THEM IN THEIR PRESENT PERSECUTION AND RESPONSIBILITIES—1:3-2:10

A. Peter praises God for salvation in order to encourage his readers in light of their future destiny—1:3-12

1. Peter gives a description of salvation in order to assure his readers that it is based on God's work and because of this they can have hope—1:3-5

a. The author of salvation is God Himself—1:3a-b

b. The hope of salvation is grounded in Christ's resurrection and an imperishable inheritance—1:3c-4a

c. The inheritance and the heir are guarded by the power of God—1:4b-5

Note #283: Salvation as deliverance

It should be kept in mind that the word "salvation" means "deliverance" and can be used in a wide variety of ways. The "salvation" in 1:5 and 9 appears to be eschatological deliverance from persecution rather than to soteriological deliverance.

2. Peter gives a description of the present experiences related to salvation so that they would have joy—1:6-9

a. On the one hand they rejoice in their salvation—1:6a

b. On the other hand they are experiencing suffering—1:6b

c. The purpose of this suffering is to demonstrate the genuine nature of their faith so that God would be praised—1:7

d. They are sustained by a love and faith in Christ which gives them joy because they are participating in their faith which will be consummated in their future deliverance—1:8-9

3. Peter extols the greatness of their salvation so that they would see its magnificence—1:10-12

a. The problem of suffering and glory was the subject of intense prophetic search—l:10-12a

b. It has been proclaimed through Christian preaching—1:12b

c. It is the subject of angelic inquiry—1:12c

B. Peter exhorts his readers to righteous behavior based on their salvation so that they would know what is expected of them both personally in relation to God and corporately in relation to each other—1:13-2:10

1. They are to live in hope which is done by clear thinking and self-control (the main verb is "hope" and the other verbs are imperatival participles)—1:13

2. They are to live in holiness because God is holy—1:14-16

3. They are to live in godly fear because God is judge and salvation was costly—1:17-21

4. They are to live in love toward one another because of their experience of regeneration through the instrumentality of the Word—1:22-25

5. They are to live in spiritual growth—2:1-3
   a. The preparation for spiritual growth is the removal of hindering vices—2:1
   b. The duty to promote growth is the craving of the pure word of God—2:2a
   c. The goal of growth is maturity in salvation—2:2b
   d. The motive for growth is the experience of the goodness of the Lord—2:3
6. They are to offer spiritual sacrifices to God as a holy priesthood—2:4-8
7. They are to be a testimony to the world as they proclaim to them the praises of God—2:9-10

Note #284: The Hosea quote and the use of the Old Testament in the New

First Peter 2:10 has been the occasion for discussion since Peter applies a passage from Hosea to the Church which was originally applied to Israel. This is one of several instances in the New Testament where a New Testament author uses an Old Testament text in a way that it was not originally intended. This would seem to weaken the dispensational distinction between Israel and the Church. When Hosea 1-3 is examined it will be seen that Hosea married an immoral woman who would continue in immorality while married to the prophet. His children's names symbolized the scattering and rejection of Israel by God. However, their names were later changed by God to picture the return of Israel to the land and blessing to occur in the eschaton. If a Gentile readership is accepted for 1 Peter, Peter could simply be using the Hosea passage as an illustration. According to many amillennialists, however, this would be an indication that the Hosea promise was fulfilled in full or in part in the Church. If Jewish readership is held, then it can be said that Peter was indicating that the believing Jews enjoyed a restored relationship to God which is similar to the one to be experienced in the future by the entire nation.

The larger questions at issue are 1) how the New Testament uses the Old Testament, and 2) the matter of sensus plenior. *Regarding #1, dispensationalists have presented numerous, legitimate ways the New Testament uses the Old which demonstrates that the New Testament writers are not teaching any kind of supersessionism. Arnold Fruchtenbaum lists the following: a) literal prophecy plus literal fulfillment, b) literal plus typical, c) literal plus application, and d) summation (Arnold Fruchtenbaum,* Israelology *[Tustin, CA: Ariel Ministries], 843-845). In addition to biblical examples of each category, Fruchtenbaum draws on the research of Emil Shuer and David Cooper to show that since the New Testament was written by Jews, it would be logical that they would use the methods consistent with their way of utilizing literature. The Rabbinic categories which would mirror letters a-d above are:* pshat *meaning "simple, plain;"* remez *meaning "hint," "clue," or "suggestion;"* drash *meaning "exposition" or "investi-gation;" and* sod *meaning "mystery" or "secret." This final term was so called because it did not deal with a single passage but summarized what was said on a topic ("Rabbinic Quotations of the Old Testament and how it Relates to Joel 2 and Acts 2." http://www.pre-trib.org/data/pdf/Fruchtenbaum-RabbinicQuotationsoftheOl.pdf. Accessed 4/25/2014). Roy Zuck suggests 10 ways the New Testament uses the Old: 1) to point up the accomplishment or realization of an OT prediction, 2) to confirm that a NT* *incident agrees with an OT principle, 3) to explain a point in the OT, 4) to support a point being made in the NT, 5) to illustrate a NT truth, 6) to apply the OT to NT incident or truth, 7) to summarize an OT concept, 8) to use OT terminology, 9) draw a parallel with an OT incident, and 10) to relate an OT incident to Christ (*Basic Bible Interpretation *[Wheaton: Victor Books, 1991], 260-270). For an excellent discussion of the general issue see Michael Vlach, "Part 3: Supersessionism and Hermeneutics," in* Has the Church Replaced Israel: A Theological *Evaluation (Nashville: B&H Publishing Group, 2010), 79-120. Regarding #2, though the issues are large, this comes down to the question of whether the modern interpreter should imitate how the writers of the New Testament used the Old Testament. This question must be answered in the negative. There is a vast difference between an author of Scripture, writing under the supervision of the Spirit, using an inspired document and a modern exegete taking creative liberty with the text. For an excellent discussion arguing for this viewpoint, see Robert Thomas, "The New Testament Use of the Old Testament," in* Dispensationalism Tomorrow & Beyond *(Fort Worth, TX: Tyndale Seminary Press, 2003), 165-188. For a discussion of the related issue of the usage of the "fulfillment" terminology in the New Testament, see Charles Dyer, "Biblical Meaning of 'Fulfillment,'" in* Issues in Dispensationalism *(Chicago: Moody Press, 1994), 51-72.*

III. PETER EXHORTS HIS READERS TO SUBJECTION IN VARIOUS AREAS OF LIFE SO THAT THEY WOULD BE A PROPER TESTIMONY IN THEIR ROLE OF WITNESSING TO THE WORLD—2:11-3:12

- **A.** Peter appeals to his readers for appropriate personal conduct consisting of self-discipline and good behavior toward those outside of the church so that they would glorify God—2:11-12
- **B.** Peter tells them to be subject to the state—2:13-17
  - **1.** He tells them to submit to all forms of authority because it is their function to reward the good and punish the bad—2:13-14
  - **2.** He tells them that the reason for this submission is to impact foolish men—2:15
  - **3.** He tells them that as they submit they should utilize their freedom, live as servants of God, respect everyone, love one another, fear God, and honor the king—2:16-17
- **C.** Peter tells them to be subject in the household—2:18-25
  - **1.** He tells the servants to be subject to their masters whether good or bad including patiently enduring unjust suffering—2:18-20
  - **2.** He gives the example of the suffering of Christ in order to illustrate one who suffered unjustly—2:21-25
- **D.** Peter tells them to be subject in the family—3:1-7
  - **1.** He tells the wife to be subject to her husband so that if he is an unbeliever, he may be won to the faith by her godly behavior which is to be mainly concerned with the inward character—3:1-6
  - **2.** He tells the husband to be considerate of the wife and to live with her as the weaker vessel so that their prayers would not be hindered—3:7

Note #285: The weaker vessel

There are two valid suggestions for interpreting the phrase "weaker vessel." The first stresses the fact that the wife is more fragile and easily damaged and therefore should be treated with the utmost sensitivity and respect. Another suggestion (perhaps better) relates to the position which the wife has assumed due to her submission. This submissive position could possibly put the wife in a vulnerable position. Therefore, Peter is telling the husband not to exploit her, take advantage of her, or abuse his authority.

E. He tells them to be in subjection to each other in daily ethics—3:8-12

1. They are to live in loving and humble harmony with each other—3:8

2. They are to not seek revenge on those who abuse them—3:9

3. He confirms his appeal by quoting the Old Testament which notes that in order to have a good and positive life it is necessary to do good and seek peace in light of the fact that God is pleased with such conduct—3:10-12

IV. PETER ADDRESSES THE PROBLEM OF SUFFERING WHICH THESE READERS WERE FACING IN ORDER TO SHOW THEM THE PROFIT OF SUFFERING FOR RIGHTEOUSNESS' SAKE, TO EQUIP THEM FOR SUFFERING, AND TO ENCOURAGE THEM TO STEADFASTNESS IN SUFFERING—3:13-5:11

A. Peter addresses the experience of suffering for righteousness' sake in order to show his readers the profit in their suffering—3:13-17

1. He tells them that even though it is unnatural to suffer for what is right they are blessed—3:13a

2. He gives them certain directives in order to show them how to profit in their sufferings—3:13b-16

a. He tells them to not be afraid—3:13b

b. He tells them to be ready to give a defense of their Christian hope—3:14-16

3. He assures them that it is better to suffer for good than for evil—3:17

B. Peter presents the experience of Christ suffering for righteousness' sake in order to give them a pattern for unjust suffering including the profit and deliverance that came from it—3:18-22

1. He states that Christ was just but died for the unjust so that He might bring the unrighteous to God—3:18a

2. He states that Christ preached through Noah to the people in his day and though Noah was persecuted he was delivered from the destruction that came on his persecutors in order to provide the type for what they would experience—3:18b-21

Note #286: Preaching to the spirits in prison

"The preaching to the spirits in prison" has been subject to a number of interpretations which I have summarized below:

VIEW	VARIANTS/EXPLANATION
Preaching in the underworld to people during the *triduum mortis* (a period of three days after death for those holding the Christ variant)	1. Enoch preached 2. the spirits of the dead apostles preached 3. Christ preached a. announces to the righteous of their release from the underworld b. announces to the unrighteous condemnation c. announces to the unrighteous a second chance for salvation
Preaching in the underworld to fallen angels during the *triduum mortis*	1. an announcement of victory 2. an announcement of condemnation
Preaching done after the ascension	1. different options for where this is done 2. probably not in the underworld 3. Christ announces victory over evil powers
Christ preaching in the days of Noah	1. Christ preaches during his preexistent state 2. the preaching is done through Noah to unbelievers who are now in prison (hades)

Though admittedly a difficult passage, the view preferred here is the final view that Christ preached by the Holy Spirit through Noah to unbelievers on earth during Noah's day who were in hades when Peter wrote his epistle. With this interpretation, the following would be the salient points of interpretation:

1. *The "spirits" could refer to human or angelic spirits but with this interpretation would refer to human spirits.*

2. *The imprisonment would be occurring at the time Peter wrote the letter, not when the spirits were preached to.*

3. *The spirits were preached to when Noah was building the ark, thus "because they formerly did not obey, when God's patience waited in the days of Noah, while the ark was being prepared" (ESV).*

4. *God was patiently waiting for unbelievers to come to repentance from Noah's preaching. Thus again, the audience is unbelieving humans.*

5. *The content of the preaching was the opportunity to repent in light of coming judgment.*

6. *Christ being "put to death" (crucifixion) and "made alive" (resurrection) illustrates for his readers that the trials they are facing are temporary and will result in ultimate victory.*

7. Earlier in his letter, Peter indicates that Christ was preaching through the prophets regarding his passion and glory (1:11). Similarly, Christ preached through the message of Noah during the time when the ark was being built.

The final task which remains for the interpretation of this passage is to note how it fits into Peter's argument in this passage. Given the purpose of 1 Peter as stated previously in the introduction section (Peter writes to persecuted Christians about their salvation, subjection, and suffering in order to encourage them in the light of their future glory and to exhort them to righteous living in a sinful world), the logic of Peter's thought becomes is as follows: Christ suffered and was raised by the Spirit ⇨Christians who suffer will be vindicated ⇨ another example of the same truth is Noah. As Noah preached during his day, he was ridiculed; however, the story ended with Noah being vindicated and his enemies being physically destroyed and now residing in hades ⇨ just as water saved Noah, so baptism saves the Christian—in that it is a type picturing the cleansing of the believer which leads to their salvation from their persecutors. Or, 3:21 stated in a more expanded way: in Noah's day, the event of the ark carried away by the flood delivered Noah from the judgment which came on his persecutors. In the same way, the readers' baptism (which corresponds to the whole event of the ark/flood) is a copy (or representation/correspondence) to what happened to Noah in that it shows them to be separated from their persecutors who would be judged. Because their baptism pictures their cleansed conscience, it "saves" them in the sense of delivering them from the judgment to come on their persecutors.

For further discussion of the view presented here see John Feinberg, "1 Peter 3:18-20, Ancient Mythology, and the Intermediate State," Westminster Theological Journal *48:2 (Fall 1986), 304-336; Wayne Grudem "Christ Preaching Through Noah: 1 Peter 3:19-20 In The Light of Dominant Themes in Jewish Literature,"* Trinity Journal *7:2 (Fall 1986), 3-31.*

   3. He states that Christ is now glorified in the presence of the Father just as they would be—3:22

C. Peter instructs his readers on the equipment they are to employ as they face suffering so that they would know the attitudes they should have when suffering—4:1-19

   1. He calls on them to be armed with the same patient attitude that Christ displayed which should be motivated by their sinful past, and the future judgment on their enemies—4:1-6

Note #287: Done with sin 4:1

The phrase "he who has suffered in his body has ceased with sin" has been interpreted in several ways including: sinless perfection, physical death, cessation of sin's dominion, and the link with Romans 6 and the believer's identification with the death of Christ. It seems best to take it as the latter so that Peter is saying that Christ's death conquered sin's dominion, and by virtue of the believer's union with that, he is freed from its dominion. Thus he is giving a reason why the believer can arm himself with the attitude which Christ had. This view is also supported by the perfect tense of the verb which looks to the past.

Note #288: Preaching to the dead

Another difficult verse is verse 4:6. William Dalton, in his Christ's Proclamation to the Spirits *(Rome: Editrice Pontificio Istituto Biblico, 1989), 51-59; has outlined the four main solutions of this verse to include: Christ preached salvation to the pre-Christian dead after his death, Christ preached salvation to the just of Old Testament times, the apostles preached to those spiritually dead during their ministries, and the dead are Christians who had the gospel preached to them and who then died. In the judgment of God, the opinions of men will be reversed and they will live in the new resurrection realm. The death of fellow members in the church would have been a cause for perplexity in the church. So this offers comfort by stating that though they were wrongly judged by men in the flesh they were judged rightly by God. The "for" probably looks back to the whole paragraph (1-5) and states that the Gospel brings two results: the blame of men and the approval of God.*

2. He calls on them to obedience to various injunctions in the realm of mutual love and service so that God would be glorified—4:7-11
3. He calls on them to joy and steadfastness in their suffering for it shows their identification with Christ and that the worst suffering was yet to come for the unbeliever—4:12-18
4. He presents his summary exhortation to the sufferers in which they should commit themselves to God and continue to do good—4:19

D. Peter provides concluding exhortations to the elders and the church as a whole in order to give further instructions on their roles—5:1-11

1. He gives instructions to the elders so that they would faithfully shepherd the flock of God—5:1-4
    - **a.** He exhorts them to shepherd the flock in a willing manner not with the motive of greed or lording over the flock but rather as examples—5:1-3
    - **b.** He states that the reward for such service would be a crown of glory given by the Chief Shepherd—5:4
2. He gives instructions to the members of the church—5:5-11
    - **a.** He tells the young men to be submissive to the older—5:5a
    - **b.** He tells all to be humble one toward another—5:5b-7
    - **c.** He tells all to be watchful because Satan is seeking an opportunity to destroy them and therefore they must resist him in the faith—5:8-9
    - **d.** He encourages them by stating that after they had experienced this short experience of suffering they could be assured that God would restore them—5:10-11

V. PETER CLOSES HIS LETTER IN TYPICAL EPISTOLARY STYLE—5:12-14

A. He states that with the help of Silvanus he had written this letter to encourage them in order that they would stand fast—5:12

B. He greets his readers and gives a benediction of peace—5:13-14

2 PETER

Authorship and Canonicity

Of all the books in the New Testament, none has been disputed more regarding authorship and canonicity than 2 Peter. These two things go hand in hand because if there is a doubt as to its apostolic authorship, then there is also some doubt as to its canonicity. The following are objections to the Petrine authorship of the book: 1) no long line of tradition supported Petrine authorship traced to Eusebius' and Jerome's day, 2) the style is different than that of 1 Peter, 3) Peter's name was used in connection with Gnostic literature, 4) knowledge of 2 Peter was geographically limited, 5) the book is dependent on Jude, 6) the Hellenistic language and imagery cannot be ascribed to a Galilean fisherman, 7) the problem of the delay of the Parousia (Christ's coming) is a second century problem, 8) 2 Peter is not mentioned by Christian writers in the second century, 9) the collection of the Pauline corpus referred to in 2 Peter 3:15-16 was made in the second century, and 10) if Peter wrote it, why was there so much doubt about it.

Though seemingly formidable, these objections are answerable: 1) normal circulation patterns could have been hindered by persecution or if the destination of the letter was not on one of the mainly traveled routes, 2) the style is different from 1 Peter, but it should be noted that 1 Peter also has 62 *hapax legomena* (words used only one time) (Charles Bigg, *A Critical and Exegetical Commentary on the Epistles of St. Peter and St. Jude* [Edinburgh: T. & T. Clark, 1901], 224-225), there are many similarities (Kenneth Gangel, "2 Peter," in *The Bible Knowledge Commentary* [Wheaton: Victor Books, 1983], 860), he could have used a different amanuensis, and the mood and purpose of the letters are different, 3) while there is pseudonymous literature associated with Peter, the fact that the early church finally accepted 2 Peter showed its superiority over them, 4) its geographical limitation is answered the same as the first objection, 5) even if Peter used Jude, this does not preclude 2 Peter from being authentic. Furthermore, this dependence has not been conclusively proven, 6) the extent of Hellenistic influence on Peter is not known, and even if it were, an amanuensis could explain this problem, 7) the delay of the Parousia was also a first century problem (John 20:21-23; Acts 1:6-11; 2 Thess. 2:1-4), 8) the reference to the Pauline corpus could represent the letters known at the present time, 9) there is evidence of references to 2 Peter in the second century (Bigg, *A Critical and Exegetical Commentary on the Epistles of St. Peter and St. Jude,* 199-210), and 10) its late acceptance could be accounted for, as already noted, because of its destination, persecution, and suspicion the early church had of forgeries. For more discussion related to the objections of lack of external attestation, stylistic/literary arguments, and historical/doctrinal inconsistencies, see Michael Kruger, "The Authenticity of 2 Peter," *Journal of the Evangelical Theological Society* 42:4 (December 1999), 645-671.

In addition, there are other positive points that can be made for Petrine authorship: 1) the book claims to have been written by Peter and refers to events witnessed by him, 2) what was the motive of a forger? 3) this epistle was separated from spurious works containing Peter's name, 4) the letter does not give reason to posit second century problems, 5) the sovereignty of God must not be overlooked, and 6) it was accepted by Origen, Athanasius, Jerome, Augustine, and the Third Council of Carthage in AD 397.

If Petrine authorship is held, the date is usually viewed as between AD 64-68. The date is bracketed by the beginning of the Neronian persecution in AD 64 and the death of

Nero in AD 68 (Hiebert, *An Introduction to the New Testament,* 3:152). Furthermore, the collection of Paul's letters suggests that many of them were in circulation which would make the earliest date to be around AD 60. Thus the book was probably written shortly before Peter's death (1:12-15).

Origin and Destination

Rome is usually suggested for origin because Peter was known to have been there, and the destination could have been the same as 1 Peter—somewhere in Asia Minor.

Occasion

The occasion can be inferred from the contents of the book. The immediate occasion seems to have been that Peter knew that his time on earth was short and that his readers were facing the danger of false teachers. From the book's statements concerning them, it can be seen that they denied the soon return of Christ, lived immoral lives, denied blood redemption, were greedy of money, and were antinomian.

Purpose

The major purpose of Peter seems to have been the desire to fortify his readers against the false teachers who were infiltrating the church. Thus, in chapter 1 he shows the nature of the Christian life with challenges to growth in order to establish them on a sure foundation to fight false teachers. In chapter 2 he presents a description of the false teachers, and in chapter 3 he refutes the primary heresy of the apostates. It should also be pointed out that Peter seems to view "knowledge" as one of the greatest safeguards against apostasy. Consequently, he uses various cognates of the verb "to know" throughout the letter (1:2, 3, 5, 6, 8, 12, 14, 16, 20; 2:9, 20. 21; 3:3, 17, 18). A purpose statement could be put in these words: <u>Peter presents his readers with a reminder of the safeguards they have against apostasy as well as a denunciation of the apostates in order to fortify them against these false teachers so that the readers would continue to grow in their faith</u>.

Summary of Argument

I. PETER PRESENTS THE INTRODUCTION TO THE LETTER IN ORDER TO INTRODUCE HIMSELF AND NOTE THE SPIRITUAL TREASURE POSSESSED BY HIS READERS—1:1-2

A. He introduces himself as Peter an apostle and servant of Christ—1:1a
B. He speaks of his readers as those who have received an equal-valued faith through the righteousness of God—1:1b
C. He prays for God's grace and peace to be on them and notes that it comes through the knowledge of God and Christ—1:2

II. PETER REMINDS HIS READERS OF THE NATURE OF THE CHRISTIAN LIFE WITH ITS CHALLENGE TO GROWTH, ITS FOUNDATION ON THE TESTIMONY OF THE APOSTLES, AND THE ORIGIN OF SCRIPTURE IN ORDER TO SHOW THEM THE SAFEGUARDS THEY HAD AGAINST APOSTASY—1:3-21

A. Peter reminds his readers of the bestowal of new life and stresses the cultivation of that new life so that they would be safeguarded against falling into error—1:3-11

1. The believer has been given a new life through which they had been made partakers of the divine nature and given the ability to escape the corruption in the world—1:3-4

2. The necessity of spiritual growth should logically come out of this new life—1:5-11

a. Diligence is required for effective growth—1:5a

b. Several qualities need to be nurtured—1:5b-7

1) Moral excellence translated into vigorous action—1:5b

2) Knowledge—1:5c

3) Self-Control—1:6a

4) Perseverance—1:6b

5) Godliness—1:6c

6) Brotherly Kindness—1:7a

7) Love—1:7b

c. Two motives to spiritual growth—1:8-9

1) The one who is abounding in these traits will be fruitful in their relationship with God—1:8

2) The one who is not abounding in these things is blind and has spiritual amnesia—1:9

d. He exhorts his readers to spiritual growth so that they would confirm their election—1:10a

e. He notes the results that will accrue from their spiritual growth —1:10b-11

1) In the present they would be in less danger of falling prey to false teachers—1:10b

2) In the future they would receive an abundant entrance into the Kingdom—1:11

B. Peter reminds his readers while he still has life that what he is telling them does not have its basis in mere stories but in eyewitness accounts and in the authority of Scripture so that they would know their faith rests on a sure foundation—1:12-21

1. He tells them that what he is writing them rests on eyewitness accounts of the life of Christ—1:12-18

a. He tells them that he will remind them of these things as long as he is living knowing that he will soon leave the tent of his body —1:12-15

b. He tells them that the truth he had told them about the Second Coming was not a fairy tale but based on an eyewitness account of the Kingdom glory revealed on the Mount of Transfiguration—1:16-18

2. He tells them that what he is writing rests on the authoritative Scriptures which originated with God—1:19-21

a. He notes that the character of the prophetic word is certain— 1:19a

Note #289: The certainty of the prophetic word

The statement in 1:19a is affirming that the prophetic word has the quality of being "more firm, sure, or reliable." The NASB has rendered this to suggest that what was seen at the Transfiguration made the prophetic word more sure. In view of the coordinating kai, *however, it seems that Peter is giving a second grounds for assurance that is even more reliable than the testimony of the apostles, namely, the prophetic word. The expression "the prophetic Word" is comprehensive enough to include numerous prophecies which were fulfilled in Christ's life and death.*

b. The present function of the prophetic word is to is to shine in a dark world—1:19b

Note #290: The function of the prophetic word

Having pointed out the certainty of the prophetic word, he proceeds to describe its function. He first tells them to pay attention to it. He then compares it to a lamp which sheds light in a dark world on the future. He then notes that this prophetic lamp would one day be replaced. It is possible to place a comma after "dawns" referring to the day when Christ returns; and the morning star arising in the heart" refers to the subjective attitude of assurance that should be in the person.

c. The origin of the prophetic word resides in God as he superintended the recording of it by men—1:20-21

Note #291: Private interpretation

There have been various views as to the meaning of "no private interpretation" in verse 20. Some say that the individual layman does not have the ability to interpret prophecy; others say that prophecy must be interpreted in its context; others feel that it is the Holy Spirit who must interpret prophecy. The most likely view is that the concern is the origin of prophecy as it relates to the prophet himself (see D. Edmond Hiebert, "The Prophetic Foundation for the Christian Life," Bibliotheca Sacra *141:562 [1984], 158-168). The meaning then is that no prophecy arose out of the prophet's own solution to the scenes he confronted when he received revelation. This view is supported by the flow of the argument, the natural meaning of the verb "came about," and is in accord with the following verse.*

III. PETER GIVES A DESCRIPTION OF THE FALSE TEACHERS SO THAT HIS READERS WOULD BE KNOWLEDGEABLE CONCERNING THEM AND ENCOURAGED BY THEIR FUTURE DESTRUCTION—2:1-22

A. Peter gives a concise picture of the methods of these false teachers—2:l-3a

1. By historical analogy there have always been false teachers and there will continue to be—2:1a
2. They secretly introduce destructive heresies even to the point of denying aspects of the work of Christ—2:1b
3. These false teachers will gain many followers—2:2
4. They will be governed by greed as they make up lies to exploit people—2:3a

B. Peter gives a picture of the judgment to come on these false teachers—2:3b-9

1. He states the principle that judgment is hanging over them—2:3b

2. He gives three examples of judgment in order to show a precedent for God's judgment—2:4-9

a. He gives the example of fallen angels—2:4

Note #292: The angels who sinned

Second Peter 2:4 is one of the most interesting but challenging verses in the epistle. Most importantly the main point of the verse is clear. Peter is asserting the sure judgment to come on false teachers, and the purpose of this verse is to give an example of judgment in the past in order to show that God will judge in the future. In fact, in verses 4-9, Peter will give a total of three examples of judgment to show a precedent. However, there are some curious points about this first example to be noted.

1. *The grammatical structure of 2:4-9. The section begins with a first class conditional sentence which is composed of a three-part protasis (an "if" clause—that which expresses the condition) in 2:4-8 and an apodosis (a "then" clause—that which expresses the consequence) in 2:9. The protasis in the first class conditional sentence is assuming reality though at times it may not necessarily correspond to reality. The logic of the six verses can be laid out as follows:*

2 Peter 2:4-8

If...

The angels who sinned	*God did not spare them*
The flood	*God did not spare the ancient world* *God preserved Noah*
Sodom and Gomorrah	*God turned them to ashes* *God rescued Lot*

2 Peter 2:9

Then...

The present situation	*God will deliver the godly from trials* *God will punish the ungodly in the eschaton*

By giving these three examples, Peter is laying out the certainty of both the deliverance of the righteous and the condemnation of the unrighteous. In the angelic example, the certainty of judgment is perhaps heightened in that the noun "angels" is anarthrous in the Greek text (i.e., lacks an article) yielding the sense "so more emphatic, even angels" (A. T. Robertson, Word Pictures in the New Testament *[Grand Rapids: Baker, 1933], VI:162). Therefore, if God judged angels, how much more will he judge these false teachers?*

2. *What angelic sin does Peter have in mind? This is by far the most difficult question in the passage. The suggestions have included 1) the prehistoric*

rebellion of angels, 2) the tradition that the "sons of men" in Genesis 6 were angels who had sexual intercourse with the daughters of men, or 3) Peter is referring to an event not recorded in Scripture. Each of these views has difficulties and it ultimately must be acknowledged that neither Peter nor Jude identified what the event was. Despite the linking of the 2 Peter and Jude passages with Genesis 6, I remain unconvinced that that text is referring to angels or that even a sexual sin was occurring. The bottom line for Peter is that a precedent for judgment has been set.

3. *The identity of ταρταρόω (*tartaroo*). This term is an aorist active nominative masculine singular participle. The English versions are rather unanimous in their translations as "cast/deliver into hell" (ESV, KJV, NKJV, NAU, NIV, NLT, NRS). The curious point, however, is that Peter does not use the term "hades" or "gehenna." Rather he opts for a word that is used 17 times in Classic literature and only here in the New Testament. The term "hades" is used is used 108 times in the LXX and 10 times in the New Testament while "gehenna" is used 12 times in the New Testament. Why would Peter choose such an obscure term rather than ones which were more common and which he would have familiarity? It seems rather odd that Peter would use ταρταρόω as a synonym for hades or gehenna. Rather than a synonym, it seems more likely that Peter was using a classical term from Greek literature to refer to a place invested with the meaning of a distinct place where these angels had been confined. This may or may not argue that Peter was familiar with classical literature, but that the idea was common enough to be understood by his readers. Bauckham writes that "the verbs ταρταροῦν and (rather more common) καταταρταροῦν mean 'to cast into Tartarus,' and were almost always used with reference to the early Greek theogonic myths, in which the ancient giants, the Cyclopes and Titans, were imprisoned in Tartarus, the lowest part of the underworld" (Richard Bauckham,* 2 Peter, Jude *[Dallas: Word, 1988], 249). For example, "tartarus" is used three times in Homer's* Iliad. *In 8.13-14 we read "I shall take him [sc. the disobedient god] and dash him down to the murk of Tartaros, far below, where the uttermost depth of the pit lies under earth." In 8:478-81, "not if you stray apart to the undermost limits of earth and sea, where Iapetos and Kronos seated have no shining of the sun god Hyperion to delight them nor winds' delight, but Tartaros stands deeply about them." And finally in 14.278-80, Thus he [* sc *Sleep] spoke, and the goddess, white-armed Hera, failed not to obey, but swore as he asked, and invoked by name all the gods below Tartarus, that are called Titans" (Daniel Kolligan, "Τάρταροζ" in* Poetic Language and Religion in Greece and Rome *[Cambridge: Cambridge Scholars Publishing, 2013], 118-119). This would not indicate that Peter is endorsing the entire concept in Greek literature, but as stated above, this would be "invested with the meaning of a distinct place where these angels had been confined." This view is buttressed by the fact that Peter says these angels are still awaiting a future judgment; therefore, this could not be a reference to hell.*

4. *"Chains" or "pits" of darkness? There is a textual variant in the Greek manuscripts as to whether the word should be "chains" (σειραῖς) or "pits" (σιροῖς). Though this is a difficult call, the translation "chains" would be preferred (ESV, KJV, NRSV, David Jones, "The Apostate Angels of 2 Pet. 2:4 and Jude 6,"* Faith and Mission *23:2 [Spring 2006], 22; Gene Green,* Jude and 2

Peter *[Grand Rapids: Baker, 2008], 251). For "pits" see NAU, NLT, Thomas Schreiner,* 1, 2 Peter, Jude *(Nashville: Broadman & Holman, 2003), 337. Thus, the angels that sinned are completely restrained until the time of future judgment.*

   b. He gives the example of the flood—2:5
   c. He gives the example of Sodom and Gomorrah—2:6-9

C. Peter gives a picture of the character of these false teachers—2:10-22
   1. He notes that they despise authority—2:10a
   2. He notes that they are proud and boastful—2:10b-12a

Note #293: Slander

The reference to "slandering celestial beings" probably refers to the irreverent speech of the false teachers about unseen powers by which they would be pridefully thinking they were stronger. This is confirmed by the following reference to the respect for evil angels given by good angels.

   3. They are animalistic—2:12b
   4. They are deceitful—2:13
   5. They are chronic sinners—2:14
   6. They are mercenary—2:15-16

Note #294: The way of Balaam

The "way of Balaam" goes back to Numbers 22-24 when Balaam urged the Moabites to trick the Israelites into illicit relationships with Moabite women thereby introducing immorality into the camp. Thus the "way of Balaam" is that love of money and immorality which leads people astray.

   7. They have the appearance of providing refreshment and blessing but are empty and hypocritical—2:17
   8. They entice people with boastful words and lustful desires—2:18
   9. They promise freedom but they themselves are enslaved—2:19
   10. Even if they had known the truth and turned from it they are worse off and have shown their true colors—2:20-22

Note #295: Those who turn from the truth

There is debate as to who is being described in verses 20-22. Suggestions include: the false teachers, the unsaved listeners, believers who lose their salvation, or new believers who are warned against carnality. The third view does not carry any weight, and therefore it is probably a combination of the first and second or the fourth. The fourth is weak in that the context and analogy with Balaam seem to support the first. Further v. 21a would not follow if a saved person is in view, and v. 22 is referring to the true nature of a person.

IV. PETER GIVES A REFUTATION OF THE APOSTATES' ERROR IN DENYING THE RETURN OF THE LORD IN ORDER TO PROVIDE STABILITY FOR HIS

READERS AND THEIR ETHICS DURING THE INTERIM—3:1-18

A. Peter presents the denial of Christ's return—3:1-4
   1. He exhorts them to remember the words spoken by the Apostles and Christ—3:1-2
   2. He reminds them that scoffers will come who will follow their own evil desires—3:3
   3. He reminds them that they will deny Christ's promised coming on the basis that things have always been the same—3:4
B. Peter presents a refutation of this denial—3:5-10
   1. This is not true for after creation there was the flood which is a token of the future judgment that would come on the apostate—3:5-7
   2. They had overlooked God's time perspective in that what may seem like a long time to the scoffer is a short time with God—3:8
   3. God's delay is due to His gracious character—3:9

Note #296: God is not willing

*Peter says that God is not "willing" that any should perish. The proper interpretation of this phrase is yielded when one reads with close attention the pronouns in the passage. In verse 8, Peter is speaking to the saved since he calls them "beloved." He then uses the pronoun "us" in verse 9 to refer back to the beloved. So the object of God's desire that none perish is the people of God. Put within the framework of biblical theology, God is holding off judgment until all of his elect are brought to faith. He is longsuffering toward "us", not willing that any of [us] should perish but that all [of us] should come to repentance. Another viable option is to take "willing" in its sense of "desire." This interpretation would be drawing on the different aspects of God's will found in Scripture. "Three aspects of the will of God may be observed in Scripture: (1) the sovereign will of God (Isa. 46:9-11; Dan. 4:17, 35; Heb. 2:4; Rev. 17:17); (2) the moral will of God, i.e. His moral law (Mk. 3:35; Eph. 6:6; Heb. 13:21); and (3) the desires of God coming from His heart of love (Ezek. 33:11; Mt. 23:37; 2 Pet. 3:9). The sovereign will of God is certain of complete fulfillment, but the moral law is disobeyed by men, and the desires of God are fulfilled only to the extent that they are included in His sovereign will. God does not desire that any should perish, but it is clear that many will not be saved (Rev. 21:8)" (*New Scofield Reference Bible, *[Oxford: 1967], 1340-1341).*

   4. The Day of the Lord will come suddenly bringing destruction—3:10
C. Peter presents the ethical standards they should employ before the Day of the Lord transpires—3:11-18
   1. They are to live holy and godly lives in view of the fact that the world is to be destroyed some day—3:11-13
   2. They are to make every effort to be morally pure—3:14
   3. They are to remember that the Lord's patience means salvation—3:15-16
   4. They are to be on guard—3:17
   5. They are to grow in the grace and knowledge of Christ—3:18

1 JOHN

Author

The traditional view is that the author of this epistle is the same as that of the Gospel of John, namely, the beloved Apostle. Externally, this is perhaps the best attested general epistle. Internally, it is seen that the writer speaks as an eyewitness of Jesus' life and speaks with the authority of an apostle.

Date

The traditional dating of the epistle is anytime between AD 80-97. Those who date the book late note that there is no reference to state persecution which could then date the book after the death of Domitian in AD 96. Or, there is the suggestion that the book was written before the persecution under Domitian, which according to Eusebius (*Ecclesiastical History* 3.18), began in the latter part of his reign. Thus, a date between AD 80-85 is possible.

Origin and Destination

Most would agree that the book originated in Ephesus which is in direct agreement with the statement of Ireneaus (*Against Heresies* 3.1.1) and the fact that the earliest known references to the letter are by the church leaders from Asia (Glenn Barker, *1, 2, 3 John,* Expositor's Bible Commentary: Volume 12 [Grand Rapids: Zondervan, 1981], 294). John probably ministered to the surrounding churches in Asia Minor while he was in Ephesus. Most likely then, the epistle was a circular letter to the believers in the environs of Ephesus.

Occasion: The "Problem" of Christ's Humanity

Jesus was born into a world which had come to believe that matter was morally evil. Much of this could be traced back to Greek philosophy and its greatest proponents like Plato. One of his ideas came to be known as Platonic Dualism. Plato taught that things in the material world were fleeting and temporary because they were simply manifestations of an ideal counterpart in the spiritual world. In addition, it was believed that the human soul existed in this perfect, spiritual world before it came to reside in a physical body. The goal for a person was to attain the knowledge necessary to escape the prison of the body so as to return at death to the eternal world.

When the second member of the Trinity came to earth, Plato's ideas were being expounded in a variety of ways and applied to and mixed with Christian thought. In the second century AD the great church father and apologist Tertullian was born. One of his most famous statements was "what indeed has Athens to do with Jerusalem" (Tertullian. "The Prescription Against Heretics." In *The Ante-Nicene Fathers: Latin Christianity: Its Founder, Tertullian*, edited by Alexander Roberts, James Donaldson, and A. Cleveland Coxe, translated by Peter Holmes. Vol. 3. Buffalo, NY: Christian Literature Company, 1885. Chapter VII)? Tertullian was trying to get his readers to steer clear of heresy which he believed was rooted in Greek philosophy—particularly in those like Platonism which produced a dialectic Christianity. Indeed what does Athens have to do with Jerusalem? The answer is, very little.

One tack this mixture took was the notion that the material was evil. The thought was that it was impossible for God to become man because that would mean that God had become imperfect. This led to two early Christological heresies both of which denied the humanity of Christ. These two heresies were not necessarily in their full-blown form when John wrote his letter, but the seeds were present.

The first was known as "Cerinthianism" sometimes called "adoptionism." Cerinthus taught that Jesus was born naturally as Mary had relations with Joseph or some other man. For some reason, God chose Jesus to put the Christ-spirit upon which occurred at Jesus' baptism. This spirit enabled him to teach for God and to do miracles, but the Christ-spirit left him at some point before his crucifixion. So, the man Jesus was not God in flesh but simply a vehicle for divine revelation.

There is an interesting story told by the church historian Eusebius, who was born in the third century, from Irenaeus' work *Against Heresies,* about a time when the Apostle John and Cerinthus were in a bathhouse in Ephesus at the same time.

> The Apostle John one day went into a bathhouse to take a bath, but when he found Cerinthus inside he leaped out of the place and ran for the door, since he could not endure to be under the same roof. He urged his companions to do the same, crying 'Let's get out of here lest the place fall in: Cerinthus, the enemy of the truth, is inside!'(Eusebius, *The Church History*, trans. Paul Maier, [Grand Rapids: Kregel, 2007], 103).

> Irenaeus himself wrote regarding Cerinthus, "Cerinthus, again, a man who was educated in the wisdom of the Egyptians, taught that the world was not made by the primary God, but by a certain Power far separated from him, and at a distance from that Principality who is supreme over the universe, and ignorant of him who is above all. He represented Jesus as having not been born of a virgin, but as being the son of Joseph and Mary according to the ordinary course of human generation, while he nevertheless was more righteous, prudent, and wise than other men. Moreover, after his baptism, Christ descended upon him in the form of a dove from the Supreme Ruler, and that then he proclaimed the unknown Father, and performed miracles. But at last Christ departed from Jesus, and that then Jesus suffered and rose again, while Christ remained impassible, inasmuch as he was a spiritual being" (Irenaeus of Lyons. "Irenæus Against Heresies." In *The Apostolic Fathers with Justin Martyr and Irenaeus*, edited by Alexander Roberts, James Donaldson, and A. Cleveland Coxe. Vol. 1. The Ante-Nicene Fathers. Buffalo, NY: Christian Literature Company, 1885), 26.1. Logos 5.

The second Christological heresy which denied the humanity of Christ was known as "Docetism." The word "docetism" comes from the Greek word doke,w which can have the idea of "to appear" or "to seem." Thus the docetics said that Christ was a pure spirit who just appeared to be in human form but he was not truly human.

In his first epistle, John will deal with these matters and the collateral damage they are inflicting on his readers.

Purpose

Perhaps the most crucial issue regarding 1 John is to discern why it was written and to determine what John was trying to accomplish. One of the most common views is known as the "tests of life" view whereby John presents criteria so that his readers might see whether they are saved or not. This position goes back at least as far as the work done by Robert Law (1860-1919). (See Robert Law, *The Tests of Life: A Study of the First Epistle of St. John: Being the Kerr Lectures for 1909* [Edinburgh: T. & T. Clark, 1909]). Law wrote: "One peculiarity of the Epistle among the writings of the New Testament is that the practical purpose for which it is avowedly written is a purpose of testing. To exhibit those characteristic of the Christian life, each of which is an indispensable criterion, and all of which conjointly form the incontestable evidence of its genuineness, is the aim that determines the whole plan of the Epistle, and dictates almost every sentence: 'These things I write unto you, that ye may know that ye have Eternal Life' (5:13)" (Robert Law, *Tests of Life*, 208). The "evidence of genuineness" centers around three tests—belief, righteousness, and love. That is, do we believe Christ came in the flesh; are we practicing righteousness; and, are we loving the brethren? Thus, John is writing so that his readers may acquire assurance if they are saved. This line of thinking has been followed by many commentaries.

However, there are a number of objections to be made to this understanding. 1) John never says he is writing to give tests to his readers to see *if* they are saved, but rather writes to them *because* they are saved. For instance he writes in 2:12-14 "I write to you, little children, Because your sins are forgiven you for His name's sake. I write to you, fathers, Because you have known Him *who is* from the beginning. I write to you, young men, Because you have overcome the wicked one. I write to you, little children, Because you have known the Father. I have written to you, fathers, Because you have known Him *who is* from the beginning. I have written to you, young men, Because you are strong, and the word of God abides in you, And you have overcome the wicked one." To this can be added the number of times he refers to them as "brothers" and "little children," 2) this view rests heavily on 5:13. Yet, the formula "these things I have written" occurs throughout the letter (e.g. 1:4; 2:1; 2:26). "These things" always refers to the content of what was just discussed. To pour the letter's entire purpose on one of these instances is to ignore the balance of the letter, 3) even if 5:13 is the purpose statement of the letter, it is assumed by this view that "eternal life" is used in the justification sense rather than observing that John often uses the concept in the qualitative sense of a full, growing, and vibrant relationship with God in the present, 4) this view often puts to much weight on the present tense verbs in the letter (see note #9 below), 5) a good case can be made that 1 John is an exposition of the Upper Room Discourse. If this is true, then John is expanding on the truth of abiding in fellowship through obedience, which according to the Discourse, a Christian may or may not do, and 6) admittedly, this view is seen by many through the debatable lens of perseverance (not preservation) of the saints.

An alternative to the "tests of life" view to the letter is the "tests of fellowship" view. There are two ingredients which would formulate this understanding of the epistle. The first ingredient is "fellowship." John's foremost purpose in writing is to lead his readers into a joyful fellowship with God. This is stated at the beginning of the epistle. "That which we have seen and heard we declare to you, that you also may have fellowship with us; and truly our fellowship *is* with the Father and with His Son Jesus Christ. And these things we write to you that your joy may be full." The second ingredient is polemic. John will warn his readers in this letter of false teaching circulating in Asia Minor. This erroneous teaching would lead John's readers away from this intimate fellowship with God which he desired for them. Thus, John is not writing to provide tests for the assurance of salvation, but he is writing that they might know God better and experience a full and joyful eternal life despite the heresy they were hearing. A purpose statement could read as follows: John warns his readers about false doctrine and the importance of true doctrine in order to lead them into a joyful fellowship with God.

Summary of Argument

I. JOHN PRESENTS THE PROLOGUE TO HIS EPISTLE IN ORDER TO AFFIRM THE REALITY OF THE INCARNATION SO THAT HIS READERS WOULD HAVE A BASIS FOR PRODUCING THE PROPER KIND OF LIVING WHICH WOULD LEAD TO FELLOWSHIP WITH GOD AND ONE ANOTHER—1:1-4

- **A.** John presents the historical encounter with the Word of Life in order to show that his message was based on eyewitness testimony—1:1-2
- **B.** John states that he was writing these things so that they would have fellowship and joy—1:3-4

Note #297: The "beginning" and foundation of the letter

The reader is referred to the notes on John 1 to see the difference between the "beginning" presented in each document. Here, it seems to be a reference to the start of the earthly ministry of Christ. This fits with the heresy John is dealing with in this letter, thus he begins with the apostles' experience of the bodily, incarnate Christ.

It should also be noted that 1:3-4 provides a basis for understanding the purpose of the epistle. John states that the goal of what he is writing is fellowship and joy. Fellowship and joy come as the result of proper doctrine and living. Thus Roman numeral I has provided the doctrinal basis on which this can be achieved. The rest of the letter shows the practical righteousness which should be pursued by the believer which will maintain fellowship and joy with God and the brethren. Thus, fellowship is not synonymous with conversion, but rather it is the continual walk and participation in the life of God.

II. JOHN PRESENTS THE PROPER WALK OF THE BELIEVER IN ORDER TO SHOW HOW
RIGHTEOUS LIVING SHOULD WORK OUT IN THEIR LIVES SO THAT THEY COULD ENJOY FELLOWSHIP WITH GOD AND MAN—1:5-5:21

- **A.** John instructs his readers on walking in the light—1:5-2:28
  1. He states the proposition that God is light in order to show that the basis for fellowship is God's character of holiness—1:5
  2. He presents a series of negative and positive statements in order to show that walking in the light involves holiness—1:6-10

Note #298: A Christian must choose

One of the most discussed questions regarding this epistle is to determine whether or not John is speaking of believers or unbelievers (see the discussion under "purpose" above). It is the writer's opinion that he is speaking of believers as to what their lives should be like. This is because he is writing about fellowship which involves only believers. Further, if a believer walks in darkness (morally)—1:6a; he is not "living by the truth"—1:6b. This implies that he knows the truth, but that he is simply not living in accord with it. The same is true of 1:8. If a believer denies personal sin, the truth is not acting as a controlling influence. Another example can be seen in 2:9 where John says that the one who hates his brother is in the dark. The very fact that one has a brother to hate shows that he is a believer. This finds a parallel, for example, in Galatians 5:4b where Paul tells his believing readers that they could fall from grace. The point was that if they defected to Judaism, they were still believers, but would be operating in the realm of law rather than grace. The same could also be seen in Hebrews where the believing readers were considering defection to a nation and system which was under the judgment of God. Thus, the readers of 1 John are exhorted to live righteous lives so that they might have fellowship with God rather than be led astray by the false ethics of the heretics.

- **a.** If one walks in darkness he cannot have fellowship with God—1:6
- **b.** If one walks in the light he can have fellowship with God—1:7
- **c.** If one denies personal sin he is deceived—1:8

Note #299: Denial of sin

For one to say he had no sin probably referred to a denial of personal guilt rather than a denial of a sin nature for several reasons: 1) John's use of "to have sin" (John 9:41; 15:22, 24; 19:11), 2) this is what a gnostic would say in blaming his body, and 3) the context is speaking of cleansing of personal sin and not the sin nature.

- **d.** Confession of sin brings forgiveness—1:9
- **e.** Denial of sin is to ignore the truth—1:10

3. He records two reactions to his discussion on sin and forgiveness in order to show how fellowship and walking in the light is maintained—2:1-2
- **a.** The fact of forgiveness should not lead to careless living—2:1a
- **b.** The fact of forgiveness should not lead to despair because when sin occurs we have a defense attorney—2:1b-2

4. He notes that walking in the light involves obedience which shows the maturity of true love—2:3-6

Note #300: "Know"

As suggested previously, the purpose of the author is the desire for obedience that leads to fellowship. Therefore, "know" should be understood in the sense of fellowship rather than salvation.

5. He notes that walking in the light involves love—2:7-11
- **a.** He says that the command to love is old in that it finds its roots in the Old Testament and in the teaching of Christ but that it is also

new in quality and degree (there are always new ways to express love)—2:7-8

b. He applies this lesson to show that brothers should have love for one another and that the one who loves is walking in the light—2:9-11

6. He addresses the various groups in the church in order to show the bases of his appeals and to commend them for the spiritual assets they possessed—2:12-14

Note #301: Spiritual stages

*Some have suggested that John is dividing his readers according to chronological age and others hold that he is dividing them according to spiritual maturity. The term "little children" (τεκνιον) is used for all of the readers (2:1, 12, 28; 3:7, 18; 4:4; 5:21) as is the expression "children" (*paidion*; 2:13, 18; 3:7). Therefore, each term of address is referring to all the readers in each case, and each experience ascribed to them fits the category named.*

7. He presents to his readers the hindrances to walking in the light—2:15-28
   a. The first hindrance to walking in the light is worldliness—2:15-17
      1) He states the prohibition that they are not to love the world or the things that are in the world—2:15a
      2) He states the reason for this prohibition is that the love of the world and love of God are antagonistic to each other—2:15b
      3) He presents verification of this fact—2:16-17
   b. The second hindrance to walking in the light is apostates—2:18-27
      1) He presents the reality of the crisis by noting that many antichrists were present and had seceded from the church— 2:18-19
      2) He notes that the believer has the anointing of the Holy Spirit in order to show their safeguard against false teachers—2:20-23

Note #302: The anointing

The "anointing" is a reference to the Holy Spirit since the anointing is said to teach (v. 27). Because of this anointing, they had adequate instruction on knowing the truth about Christ (the definition of "all things" in v. 27).

      3) He presents several bases for confidence which they had in the light of false teachers—2:24-28
         a) They were to persevere in what they had heard—2:24-26
         b) They are reminded of the anointing of the Holy Spirit—2:27
         c) They are to abide or continue to walk in the light—2:28

B. John instructs his readers on walking in righteousness and love in order to show his readers how they should live and help them to recognize a true child of God in contrast to the antichrists about which he has just spoken—2:29-5:21

1. He states the proposition that since God is righteous the one who does righteousness is born of God—2:29

Note #303: Doing righteousness

The converse of this statement in 2:29 does not follow, namely, everyone who is born of God does righteousness (see 1:6, 8; 2:1). Christians can walk in darkness and thereby conceal their new birth. John is simply saying that one can see the new birth through actions. This is what was expected in the Old Testament and Sermon on the Mount, for example. Thus, John is showing his readers that righteousness should flow from their faith and provide them with some objective base on which they could discern false teachers.

2. He states that the motive for righteousness is the love displayed by God in the new birth and its culmination at the coming of Christ—3:1-3

Note #304: To be like him—consequence or pre-requisite for seeing Christ?

An interesting question turns on the preposition "for" in the phrase "we shall be like him for we shall see him as he is" (3:2). The preposition could be expressing the necessary consequence of seeing Christ, or it could be expressing the requirement for seeing Christ. We will be like him because we will see him (consequence); or, we will be like him so that we can see him (pre-requisite). Virtually all commentators take the first view (Boice, Barker, Lloyd-Jones, Stott, Bruce, Robertson, Plummer, Marshall, Smalley, Dodd, and Hiebert), while others do not discuss the issue.

When individuals have visions of deity in Scripture, it becomes clear that God cannot be viewed in his pure, full effulgence. God said to Moses that no one could see his face and live (Exod. 33:20), therefore, we are to assume that when God reveals himself to men in their fallen states, they are only seeing a shadow of the divine essence. Based on this consideration, it seems reasonable that our transformation at resurrection is not a consequence of seeing Christ, but the pre-requisite necessary to see him. Calvin has caught this sense: "...except our nature were spiritual, and endued with a heavenly and blessed immortality, it could never come so nigh to God...He intimates a new and an ineffable manner of seeing him, which we enjoy not now; for as long as we walk by faith, we are absent from him. And when he appeared to the fathers, it was not in his own essence...hence the majesty of God, now hid, will then only be in itself seen, when the veil of this mortal and corruptible nature shall be removed" (John Calvin, The First Epistle of John *[Grand Rapids: Baker, 1979], 206).*

3. He states the hindrances to righteousness and love—3:4-4:6

a. Sin is a hindrance to righteousness and love and hate is something that is displayed by the children of the devil and not the children of God—3:5-10a

Note #305: Christians cannot continually sin (?)

First John 3:9 is one of the most discussed verses in the book. The first challenge is to determine what is meant by the term "seed." It could mean the Word of God (2:24), the Holy Spirit (2:27), or the divine nature given to each believer (John 1:13; 2 Peter 1:4; and the many references to "child" in the letter which would lend itself to the idea of the child partaking of the nature of the parent). It is most likely the latter.

A more difficult problem is what is meant by "not sinning," or "does not commit sin"

with views ranging widely and including, 1) a reference to mortal sins as opposed to venial, 2) God views sin in Christians differently than he does in his children, 3) John is speaking of an ideal which has not been experienced yet by his readers, or 4) this is a description of willful sin. By far, the most common interpretation is that the believer does not "make a practice of sinning." The idea being that though all Christians sin and sometimes heinously so, true Christians will never persist in that kind of lifestyle. If they do, then this is proof they were never truly saved. The exegetical basis for this view from the passage is the use of the present tense of the verb "sin." However, appeal to the present tense and the basis for this view are dubious for a number of reasons. First, there are different uses of the present tense in the New Testament. Just because a verb appears in the present tense does not necessarily mean that the action in view is continuously taking place. Louw explains (emphasis is in the original): "An item like ἁμαρτάνει 'he sins' does not explicitly denote duration, it is merely unmarked as for completion. This means that in some contexts ἁμαρτάνει may ***refer*** *to a process as a duration but this decision on its reference is not one on its meaning. In other words: since ἁμαρτάνει is unmarked as to completion, it may in certain contexts be used for duration* ***if the context positively suggestions duration;*** *but we cannot reverse the statement by assuming that because ἁμαρτάνει is unmarked with respect to completion it must of necessity denote duration! In fact, many presents in Greek need not be pressed for durative aspect. In 1 Jh. 2:1 Τεκνία μου ταῦτα γράφω ὑμῖν ἵνα μὴ ἁμάρτητε 'my children, I write you this so that you will not sin' is a mere statement of fact" ((J.P. Louw, "Verbal Aspect in the First Letter of John" Neotestamentica 9 [1975], 100).*

Second, there are Greek words which mean "continually" which could have been added by John if he wanted to stress a continual and habitual action. For example, the word "pantos" is found in Luke 24:53 translated: "and were continually in the temple praising God." (cf. Mark 5:5; Acts 10:2; 24:16; Rom. 11:10; Heb. 9:6). Third, if this way of interpreting the present tense were used consistently in 1 John, it would lead to contradictions within this very book. For example, in 5:16 the text says: "if any man see his brother sin a sin which is not unto death." Sin is in the present tense: "if any see his brother continually and habitually sinning a sin which is not unto death." This would contradict 3:9. If the present tense demands a durative sense, then 5:16 teaches that a brother <u>*can*</u> *habitually sin. This shows that continual action is not inherent in the tense. Therefore, to make the theological point that true Christians cannot sin continually, while permitted by the use of the present, cannot be proved by it. This removes from this passage at least an exegetical basis for perseverance of the saints. Fourth, do not all Christians continue to sin until the day of their death? Furthermore, do not all Christians sin daily? Is not daily sin a continuation in doing it? It would seem that no Christian could claim not to sin continually.*

What John is saying here (and going back to 3:6) is this: when we as Christians are abiding in Him, that is a sinless experience. This does not mean that Christians are free from sin; but notice the connection of verses 5 and 6. Verse 5 ends by saying that "in him is no sin." Then verse 6: if we are abiding in him, that is, if we are living in fellowship and obedience with the sinless one, then we are at that moment of abiding, not sinning. This follows the flow of thought John is making; it also recognizes the absolute contrast John is making in this passage. If we are walking in righteousness; if we are abiding in fellowship with the sinless one, then we are not sinning.

b. Hatred is a hindrance to righteousness and love in order to show how righteousness expresses itself in Christian love—3:10b-24

1) He provides a negative example of hatred and murder in order to show what love is not—3:10b-15
2) He provides a positive example of love and expressions of love in order to show what love is—3:16-18
3) He provides the assurances that will arise in the believer from the demonstration of love—3:19-24
    a) It will provide assurance that he is participating experientially in the truth—3:19-20
    b) It will provide assurance that his prayers will be answered—3:21-22
    c) It will provide assurance that he is in fellowship with God and that this is the manifestation of that—3:23-24

c. False doctrine is a hindrance to righteousness and love—4:1-6

1) He tells them to test the spirits in light of the fact that there are many false prophets in the world—4:1
2) He tells them that the criteria for testing the spirits is whether they admit that Jesus has come in the flesh—4:2-3
3) He tells them that the criteria for testing those through whom the spirits speak is to identify their origin—4:4-6

4. He describes the evidences of walking in love—4:7-5:3a

- **a.** He discusses brotherly love and its source by noting that love stems from a new nature and fellowship with God—4:7-16
- **b.** He states that love produces confidence to stand before God's presence on the day of judgment—4:17-18
- **c.** He states that walking in love produces an affection for the brethren—4:19-21
- **d.** He states that love is evinced for God by the keeping of His commands—5:1-3a

5. He describes the empowerment available to walk in love—5:3a-15

- **a.** He states that God's commands can be carried out by means of his overcoming faith—5:3a-5
- **b.** He refers to the coming of Christ in order to show the one in whom this faith rests—5:6-8

Note #306: The Johannine comma

One of the most famous textual issues in the New Testament is the so-called Comma Johanneum *(Latin for "Johannine Sentence"). The reference is to the additional words in the* Textus Receptus *"in heaven, the Father, the Word, and the Holy Spirit, and these three are one; and there are three that testify on earth." The Comma reading is found in only eight late manuscripts, four of which include it as a marginal reading. There is no sure evidence for this reading in any Greek manuscript until the 16th century (W. Hall Harris,* 1, 2, 2 John *[Biblical Studies Press and the Author, 2003], 214). The reading probably had its roots in a fourth century Latin homily "in which the text was allegorized to refer to members of the Trinity. From there, it made its way into copies of the Latin Vulgate, the text used by the Roman Catholic Church" (Dan Wallace, bible.org/article/textual-problem-1-*

john-57-8, accessed 5/2/2014). In fact, when Erasmus produced his first Greek New Testament in 1516 he did not include the additional words because he could find it in no Greek manuscript available to him. He inserted the Comma in his third edition when presented with an Irish manuscript Codex Montfortianus (James White, The King James Only Controversy: Can You Trust the Modern Translations? *[Minneapolis, MN: Bethany House, 1995], 60-61).*

- **c.** He notes that God has witnessed concerning His Son and that we can be sure of the one in whom our faith rests—5:9-12
- **d.** He says that he has written these things (previous context) so that his readers would be assured of their eternal life despite what the false teachers were saying—5:13
- **e.** He states that whatever is prayed for according to God's will is assured of being answered especially the empowerment to walk in love—5:14-15

6. He describes the practice of love—5:16-21

- **a.** It should intercede on behalf of a brother in sin who is not sinning unto death—5:16-17
- **b.** It should be assured of the knowledge that the child of God should live a holy life, that he is a child of God though the world is in the hands of Satan, and that Christ has come and given understanding—5:18-20
- **c.** It should remain loyal to God—5:21

2 JOHN

Introduction

Regarding questions of authorship, date, destination, and origin see notes on 1 John. The specific question of destination involves the understanding of the designation "elect lady." John is either writing to a literal lady or is personifying the church. This latter view is favored by the writer for: 1) the church is personified elsewhere (Eph. 5), 2) no personal names are mentioned as in 3 John, 3) John switches from singular pronouns (1-9) to plural ones (10-12), and then back to the singular, and 4) the Greek term for "lady" (κυρία) was also used as a sociopolitical subdivision of the term translated "church" in the New Testament (Robert Yarbrough, "2 John," in *Zondervan Illustrated Bible Background Commentary* [Grand Rapids: Zondervan, 2002], 214).

Another introductory question concerns the occasion. Evidently, the problem in this church also revolved around antichrists who were itinerant preachers in this area. They seem to have had docetic tendencies in denying the incarnation (7, 9).

The purpose of this letter seems to be to commend this church for its love and loyalty to the truth, and to exhort them to not extend hospitality to these heretics.

Summary of Argument

I. JOHN PRESENTS THE CUSTOMARY INTRODUCTION TO THE LETTER—1-3

A. He identifies himself as the elder—1a
B. He identifies the recipients as the elect lady and her children—1b
C. He states that he loves them in the truth because of its enduring character—1c-2
D. He invokes God's grace, mercy, and peace on the church—3

II. JOHN PRESENTS THE BODY TO THE EPISTLE IN ORDER TO EXHORT THEM TO CONTINUE IN THEIR OBEDIENCE AND PROTECT THE TRUTH—4-11

A. He exhorts them to continue practicing the truth—4-6
 1. He commends them and tells them of his joy because of their general walking in the truth—4
 2. He asks them to continue in love which consists in obedience—5-6

B. He exhorts them to protect the truth—7-11
 1. He warns them of many deceivers in the world who deny that Jesus is come in the flesh—7
 2. He warns them to be watchful so that they do not lose a full reward—8-9
 3. He exhorts them not to provide support for false teachers—10-11

Note #307: Hospitality

This is not a prohibition against having cult members, for example, in one's home.

Rather, the situation these readers were facing was the itinerant ministry of false teachers. He is telling his readers not to provide room and board for these heretics thereby supporting them in the area while they promoted their false teaching.

III. JOHN PRESENTS THE CONCLUSION TO THE LETTER—12-13

A. He states his future plans to visit them so that they would be joyful—12
B. He sends greetings—13

3 JOHN

Introduction

For general introductory matters see the notes on 1 John. The recipient of this letter is a man named Gaius. Three men named Gaius appear in the New Testament in connection with Paul (Acts 19:29; 20:24; Rom. 16:23). It is generally agreed though that the Gaius of 3 John is not to be identified with one of these three (D. Edmond Hiebert, "Studies in 3 John Part 1: An Exposition of 3 John 1-4," *Bibliotheca Sacra* 144:573 [Jan 1987], 58). Gaius was a common name in the Graeco-Roman world, and nothing is known for certain about him other than what is revealed in the letter. Bruce adds that "Gaius was a common name in the Roman world; it was one of the eighteen names from which Roman parents could choose a *praenomen* [first or personal name of a Roman citizen] for one of their sons" (*The Gospels and Epistles of John* [Grand Rapids: Eerdmans, 1994], 147).

Occasion

The occasion of 3 John is almost the opposite of 2 John. While 2 John speaks of the people from whom hospitality is to be withheld, 3 John speaks about those to whom hospitality is to be extended. The situation in 3 John is that a man by the name of Diotrephes (nourished by Zeus) was not practicing hospitality to itinerate preachers of the truth. The purpose of the letter then is to commend Gaius for his hospitality and to condemn Diotrephes for his lack of it.

Purpose

John commends Gaius for his hospitality and condemns Diotrephes for his lack of hospitality in order to encourage support for preachers of the truth.

Summary of Argument

I. JOHN INTRODUCES THE LETTER BY IDENTIFYING HIMSELF AS THE ELDER AND HIS RECIPIENT AS GAIUS WHOM HE LOVES IN THE TRUTH—1

II. JOHN GREETS GAIUS AND CONFIRMS HIM IN HIS ACTIVITY IN ORDER FOR HIM TO KNOW THAT HE WAS DOING WHAT WAS RIGHT—2-8

- **A.** He prays that Gaius would enjoy prosperity in all areas—2
- **B.** He expresses joy over the reports that Gaius was walking in the truth—3-4
- **C.** He commends Gaius for his hospitable treatment of preachers of the truth and states that this was the proper behavior—5-8

III. JOHN CONDEMNS DIOTREPHES SO THAT HE WOULD KNOW THAT HIS LACK OF HOSPITALITY WAS WRONG—9-11

- **A.** He notes his character as one who loves to have preeminence which was shown by his rejection of the gospel messengers—9

B. He says that if he comes he will deal with the situation and repeats the charge that Diotrephes is not accepting the brethren and is putting them out of the church—10

C. He exhorts Gaius not to imitate the evil that Diotrephes is doing—11

IV. JOHN COMMENDS DEMETRIUS FOR THE GOOD REPORTS THAT WERE GIVEN OF HIM—12

V. JOHN CONCLUDES THE LETTER BY EXPRESSING HIS DESIRE TO SEE GAIUS SOON AND SENDS GREETINGS FROM HIS FRIENDS—13-14

JUDE

Authorship

There are seven men in the New Testament named Jude. The four major possibilities of authorship include a pseudonymous author from the second century, Judas the apostle (Acts 1:13), Judas a leader in the early Jerusalem church (Acts 15:22), or Judas the half-brother of Christ. It is probably the latter for several reasons: 1) verse 17 seems to indicate that he did not consider himself an apostle, 2) he calls himself the brother of James who would have been the best known one, and 3) this Jude was an itinerant preacher (1 Cor. 9:5).

Date

It is difficult to date Jude because he does not directly identify the recipients of the letter. The traditional view is to date it anywhere from AD 40-90, however a date of somewhere between AD 67-80 is commonly held.

Origin

The place of writing is uncertain, but two possibilities are Egypt and Palestine.

Recipients

The fixing of the destination is also speculative. Since Jude did not mention a specific place, it is probable that this was a circular letter to places where he had itinerated. Given the references to Old Testament incidents and extra-biblical literature, it is plausible that he was writing to Christian Jews in Palestine.

Occasion

Jude had initially intended to write a treatise on soteriology (v. 3). This changed, however, when he heard of the infiltration of false teachers. These appear to be similar apostates as were addressed by 2 Peter, namely, those with gnostic tendencies. They were arrogant, immoral, and hypocritical.

Purpose

Jude's purpose in light of the occasion was to give a scathing denunciation of these heretics. In addition, he wanted to show his readers their responsibility in light of heresy so that they could withstand this danger and be presented as perfect in the presence of God.

Jude's Relationship to 2 Peter

Even a cursory reading of Jude 4-18 and 2 Peter 2 reveals an obvious similarity. In light of this, there has been much discussion over dependence. There are three basic positions: both drew from a common source; Jude used 2 Peter; or, Peter used Jude. It is quite possible that both drew from a common source but this is impossible to prove. The following is given as support that Jude used 2 Peter and was thus written later: 1) Jude 18 is almost an exact quote of 2 Peter 3:3, 2) 2 Peter uses the future tense in speaking about false teachers while Jude uses the present tense, 3) the lesser would borrow from the greater, 4) the fact that Jude quoted from other sources makes it more likely that he borrowed from Peter. Others argue that Jude was written first and Peter used him. The following is offered for support: 1) the shorter is written first, 2) Jude is more vivid, 3) Peter left out Jude's apocryphal references. Whichever view is taken does not have to affect the Petrine authorship of 2 Peter or the authority of either letter (see Guthrie, *New Testament Introduction,* 926). Since the evidence is inconclusive, either position may be held without undermining the text. Jude gives a thorough description and scathing denunciation of false teachers so that his readers would recognize them and see the necessity of contending for the truth so that they would be presented perfect before the presence of God.

Jude's Use of Sources

Another perceived problem in the book of Jude is the fact that he quotes extra-biblical sources. He refers to the *Assumption of Moses* in v. 9, and the *Book of Enoch* in vv. 14-15. This raises the question as to whether Jude is canonical and whether the apocryphal sources are inspired. It is the writer's opinion that this does not affect the authority of Jude or the nature of non-biblical sources: 1) Jude does not call these allusions Scripture, 2) inspiration does not mean to exclude human documents as sources of divine truth. Truth is truth no matter where it is found, 3) the Bible elsewhere uses non-biblical sources (Josh. 10:13; Acts 17:28; 1 Cor. 10:4; 15:33; Titus 1:12), 4) the prophecy is not presenting any new fact, therefore Jude is simply affirming that particular truth, and 5) God has promised to guard the writers in the presentation of the truth (John 16:13; 2 Peter 1:21).

Summary of Argument

I. JUDE INTRODUCES THE LETTER BY IDENTIFYING HIMSELF AS A SERVANT OF CHRIST AND THE BROTHER OF JAMES, NAMING HIS RECIPIENTS AS THOSE WHO ARE CALLED AND KEPT, AND WISHING MERCY, PEACE, AND LOVE ON THEM—1-2

II. JUDE DISCUSSES THE PROBLEM OF APOSTASY SO THAT HIS READERS WOULD KNOW THE DANGER THEY FACED AND HAVE THE ABILITY TO RECOGNIZE THE APOSTATES SO THAT THEY COULD CONTEND FOR THE FAITH—3-16

A. He states the reason for the letter—3-4
  1. He initially was going to write about their common salvation—3a
  2. He felt he had to change and write to them to contend for the objective body of truth entrusted to the church—3b
  3. He had to do this because of the number of heretics that had slipped in the church and were perverting the grace of God and the person of Christ—4

B. He provides three examples of judgment in order to show the fate of these apostates—5-7
  1. The judgment on the Jewish nation after their deliverance from Egypt—5
  2. The judgment on the angels who rebelled—6
  3. The judgment on Sodom and Gomorrah who were presently suffering eternal damnation—7

C. He describes the apostates so that his readers would recognize them and see the foolishness of following them—8-13

  1. They pollute their bodies—8a
  2. They reject authority and slander celestial beings which even Michael did not do—8b-10a
  3. They are ignorant and unreasoning animals—10b
  4. They had gone in the way of Cain in terms of false religion—11a
  5. They had gone in the error of Balaam in deceiving many for profit—11b
  6. They had rebelled as Korah over religious authority with their doom being certain—11c
  7. They are selfish, hypocritical, and shameful—12-13

D. He denounces the apostates—14-16

  1. He notes their denunciation by Enoch who prophesied that they would be judged by the Lord and His saints—14-15
  2. He denounces them by describing their character as evil, proud, and greedy—16

III. JUDE PRESENTS THE DUTY OF THE BELIEVER IN ORDER TO SHOW THEM HOW TO BE PROTECTED FROM THESE MEN AND CONTEND FOR THE FAITH—17-23

A. They are to remember that it had been foretold that there would be these types of men who would scoff and follow their evil desires—17-19

B. They are to remain in the love of God by building themselves up and praying—20-21

C. They are to be merciful to those who are doubting, attempt to save those who are caught in the snare of apostasy from eternal death, and minister to those caught in immorality in a way that would not cause them to be defiled by sin—22-23

IV. JUDE PRAISES GOD FOR HIS ABILITY TO KEEP THESE BELIEVERS FROM STUMBLING AND FOR THE FACT THAT GOD WILL ONE DAY PRESENT THEM FAULTLESS IN HIS PRESENCE—24-25

REVELATION

Author

The author calls himself John without further qualification. The traditional view has understood this designation to be a reference to the Apostle John, the brother of James. The external evidence for this identification is strong and early as is attested by Justin Martyr and Irenaeus. In addition, Irenaeus knew Polycarp who was a personal disciple of John (*Against Heresies* 3.3.4). For additional external evidence see the discussions by D. E. Hiebert, *Introduction to the New Testament: The Non-Pauline Epistles and Revelation* (Chicago: Moody, 1977), 240-241; Guthrie, *New Testament Introduction,* 934-935; and Everett Harrison, *Introduction to the New Testament* (Grand Rapids: Eerdmans, 1971), 428-431. Internally, 1) the author is known by the Asiatic churches and speaks to them with apostolic authority; 2) he prophesies in his own name being conscious of receiving direct revelation (1:1, 11, 19; 10:10; 12:6-9); 3) there are similarities in the description of John in the Synoptics and in Revelation (Guthrie, *New Testament Introduction,* 938); and 4) similarities between Revelation, the Gospel of John and the Epistles of John (Guthrie, *New Testament Introduction,* 938-940).

Origin and Date

John had been exiled to the isle of Patmos (1:9; an island in the Aegean Sea about 70 miles southwest of Ephesus) by Domitian during the latter part of his reign (ca. AD 90-95). John was possibly freed from his banishment when Domitian was succeeded by Nerva in AD 96. Eusebius writes: "After Domitian had ruled fifteen years, Nerva succeeded. By decree of the Roman senate, the honors of Domitian were annulled and those banished unjustly returned and had their property restored. At that time also, early Christian tradition relates, the apostle John, after his island exile, resumed residence at Ephesus" (*Eusebius: The Church History*, 96).

The traditional date of writing is some time in the mid 90s AD and is to be preferred. Those who take the preterist view of Revelation argue for a date of pre-70 AD thus making it a prophecy of the destruction of Jerusalem in AD 70. For the preterist date see Kenneth Gentry, *Before Jerusalem Fell: Dating the Book of Revelation* (San Francisco: Christian Universities Press, 1997). For a rebuttal to the early date see Mark Hitchcock, "A Defense of The Domitianic Date of the Book of Revelation" (Ph.D. dissertation, Dallas Theological Seminary), 2005. Hitchcock's dissertation is available for free download: www.pre-trib.org.

Destination

The destination of the book is the seven churches in the Roman province of Asia (1:4, 11). However, the representative character of the churches and the wide scope of the prophetic events presented indicate that it is also applicable to the Christian church as a whole.

Occasion

The immediate occasion for the book is the direct command of the Lord who appeared to John (1:10-11, 19). Beyond this it can be said that the church was experiencing persecution from Rome (cf. the date) and compromise from within (2-3).

Purpose

The first verse of the book states that what is to be revealed was a disclosure of Jesus Christ. The genitive (revelation *of Jesus Christ*) could be either subjective (the revelation came from Him) objective (the revelation was about Him), or plenary (both ideas are present). The book also presents ethical demands of Christ as found in the letters to the churches. Following this, it reveals the events to transpire immediately before, during, and after the Second Advent of Christ. In light of the historical setting, this information would serve to encourage the believer to persevere in light of persecution and present the ethical demands of Christ before He returned. Additionally, it could be stated that it is fitting that this is the last book of the Bible. Genesis begins with God's irruption into human history to conquer the evil one and establish God's rule on earth. The rest of the Bible presents the unfolding of this plan which culminates in this book. Furthermore, the followers of Christ had seen Him crucified and removed from the scene, so this book fittingly shows that He will one day return in triumph over all enemies and establish His Kingdom. In light of these facts, a purpose statement could be put thusly: <u>John presents a revelation of Jesus Christ as it is seen in His ethical demands and events surrounding His Second Coming in order to encourage his readers to perseverance and obedience in light of the ultimate victory that would transpire when Christ returns</u>.

Interpretive Approaches to Revelation

There are four major methods of approaching the interpretation of Revelation: 1) the preterist approach—this view sees the content of Revelation as a picture of the conflicts of the early church period which have been mostly fulfilled by AD 70, 2) the historicist approach—this view sees the Revelation as a picture of the conflict during the entire church age, 3) the idealist approach—this view sees the book as a symbolic struggle between good and evil and utilizes heavily the allegorical approach of spiritualizing the text, and 4) the futurist approach—this view sees the churches of 2-3 as descriptive of the apostolic period (though some see them as also representative of the stages of church history) and 4-22 as yet future encompassing the Tribulation, Millennium and eternal state. The view one adopts depends largely on his hermeneutical presuppositions. The futurist approach will be followed in this discussion for the writer feels that it deals most normally with the text of Revelation and the some 278-400 allusions to the Old Testament.

Preterist	**Historic**	**Idealist**	**Futuristic**
Fulfilled in AD 70	Fulfilled throughout Church history	Symbolic struggle of Good and evil	Most fulfilled in the future during the Tribulation, Millennium, and Eternal State

Millennial Views

In addition to the various interpretive philosophies of the book, there are four millennial approaches associated with the book which are illustrated as follows.

Postmillennialism

Postmillennial Order of Events			
1. Preach	2. Kingdom	3. Return	4. New Heaven/Earth

Amillennialism

Tenets of Amillennial View	
Church Age is the Millennium	Christ reigns from Heaven
	Satan is bound
New Heaven and New Earth	Second Coming
	Resurrection and Judgment

Historic/Covenant Premillennialism

Tenets of Premillennial View
There is no distinction between Israel and the Church
The second coming occurs, followed by the Millennium

Dispensational Premillennialism

Dispensational Premillennial Order of Events		
1. Church Age	2. Tribulation	3. Millennium

The Literary Structure of Revelation

There are at least three points that deserve comment in this regard. The first concerns the organizational key to the book found in 1:19. When this command is taken in its normal grammatical sense, it yields a tripartite division of the message given to John: "the things which you have seen" (1:12-18); "the things which are" (2:1-3:22); "the things which shall take place after these things" (4:1-22:5).

The second point relates to the relationship of the seals, trumpets, and bowls. The question is should these three groups of seven be taken in a concurrent, successive, or telescopic arrangement? The concurrent view would see the three groups as taking place simultaneously with the repetition serving to show the intensification and emphatic nature of the judgments. The second sees the three groups in a consecutive arrangement, thus envisioning twenty-one judgments. The latter sees a consecutive arrangement but with the seventh seal introducing the trumpet series, and the seventh trumpet introducing the bowl series. Therefore, the seven trumpets are an explanation of the seventh seal, and the seven bowls are an explanation of the seventh trumpet. Furthermore, these series of judgments form a linear sequence leading toward the goal of Christ's coming. The writer prefers the last understanding for several reasons: 1) succession is seen within each series by the use of ordinal numbers, the description of them sounding sequentially rather than simultaneously, and the pronouncement of three more woes implies succession, 2) succession is suggested by the fact that the seventh seal and the seventh trumpet are proleptic of the six trumpets and six bowls respectively, 3) the three series of judgments are not merely recapitulations, but are successive sets of judgments which increase in severity, 4) succession is also seen by the fact that the first seal introduces the Antichrist while the bowls destroy his kingdom which flourishes during the Tribulation period, and 5) the book is replete with time markers, the most significant ones being "after this" (4:1; 7:1; 18:1; 19:1) showing progress in movement.

A third question relates to the relationship of the intercalations to the chronological arrangement of the judgments (7:1-17; 10:1-11:13; 12:1-14:20; 17:1-19:10). These will be fully discussed in regard to function during the course of the argument. However here it can be stated that these sections serve to join the major sections by elucidating previous events and introducing various player oftentimes to show the grace and encouragement of God.

Interpreting Symbols/Symbolic Language

One of the intimidating factors in the interpretation of Revelation is the presence of symbolic language. The word "symbol" simply refers to an object or action which depicts the qualities of something else. There are a number of hermeneutical principles which can serve as an aid as one studies this book.

1. A symbol will have its basis in reality. A symbol is based on a literal object like a basket of fruit, a lion, a lamb, a pot, a goat, incense, a serpent, etc. When a symbol is identified in the text, the literal item to which the symbol is corresponding needs to be discovered. However, there will be instances when the symbol will be fanciful in nature like a beast with seven heads and ten horns in Revelation 17 or a leopard with wings in Daniel 7. Even in these rarer cases, the items deal with things that individually have a basis in reality such as heads, horns, a leopard, and wings.
2. Identify the symbol and the referent of the symbol. In Amos 8:1-2 there is a symbol consisting of a basket of fruit and the referent which is Israel. In Revelation Jesus is called both a lion and lamb. The lion and lamb are the symbols while Jesus is the referent. Quite often the text will indicate what the referent of the symbol is. I have listed below 44 symbols in Revelation which are explained in the book.

44 Examples of Figures Interpreted by the Text of Revelation[672]		
PASSAGE	**FIGURE**	**INTERPRETATION**
1:13//20	Seven stars	Seven angels
1:16//20	Seven candlesticks	Seven churches
2:28//22:16	Morning star	Jesus
3:12//21:2	City of my God	New Jerusalem
4:5	Seven lamps of fire	Seven spirits of God
5:6	Seven eyes	Seven spirits of God
5:8	Smoke	Prayers of the saints
9:1//11	The fallen star	The angel of the pit
11:8	The great city	Jerusalem
11:8	Sodom	Jerusalem
11:8	Egypt	Jerusalem
12:4//9	Stars of heaven	Fallen angels
12:5//19:15	Male child	Christ
12:9	Dragon	Satan
12:9	Serpent	Satan
12:14//6	Time, times, half a time	1260 days
13:11//19:20	Beast of the earth	False prophet
17:18	Woman	The great city
17:18	Woman	Babylon
17:1//15	Waters	Multitudes of people
17:9	Seven heads	Seven mountains (kingdoms)
17:10	Seven heads	Seven kings (kings and mountains are used interchangeably in prophetic literature)
17:11	Beast	Eighth king
17:12	Horns	Kings
17:14	Lamb	Lord of lords
17:14	Lamb	King of kings
18:10	Great city	Babylon
19:7//21:9, 11	Lamb's wife	Holy Jerusalem
19:8	Fine linen	Righteousnesses of the saints
19:11	Rider of white horse	Faithful
19:11	Rider of white horse	True
19:13	Rider of white horse	Word of God
19:16	Rider of white horse	King of kings
19:16	Rider of white horse	Lord of lords
19:16//17:14	Rider of white horse	Lamb
20:4, 5	On thrones/beheaded/ didn't worship beast	Those raised in the first resurrection
20:14	Lake of fire	Second death
21:9	Bride	Lamb's wife
21:9, 10	Bride	The great city

[672]This chart is substantively taken from J. B. Smith, *A Revelation of Jesus Christ* (Scottsdale, PA: Herald Press, 1961), 18-19. However, Smith actually lists 46 examples. I have removed his sixteenth example (the devil is Satan from 12:9) since I would not consider this to be a valid example. I have also omitted his twentieth example (the woman sits on seven hills which is Rome from 17:18) since the text does not say the seven hills refer to Rome (which I do not think they do). In addition, I have removed the two references to the woman as pointing to Rome; since in my opinion, this is an unwarranted interpretation of the text. Therefore, in the above table, I simply refer to the woman as "the great city" and "Babylon."

21:9	Bride	Holy Jerusalem
21:22	Lord God/Lamb	Temple of the city
21:23	Lamb	Light of the city
22:16	Root of David	Jesus
22:16	Offspring of David	Jesus

3. If the text does not interpret the symbol, then other passages can be checked where the symbol is used. To put this in perspective, Revelation contains 404 verses, and 278 of the 404 make allusion to the Old Testament. The majority of allusions are from Daniel followed by Isaiah, Ezekiel and then the Psalms. If the text being studied does not interpret the symbol, then other passages should be checked where the symbol is used.
4. If the passage does not indicate the interpretation then it is necessary to determine what the characteristics of the symbol are which are held in common with the referent. Based on the context of the passage, a determination is made as to which char-acteristic would be most apropos.
5. It should not be assumed that just because a passage contains a symbol that everything in the passage is symbolic. For example, in Zechariah 12, Zechariah is describing events associated with Messiah's second coming and he writes in verse 4 that God will make Jerusalem a "burdensome stone for all peoples." Clearly, as the text indicates, the symbol of a burdensome stone is referring to Jerusalem. Before the second coming of Christ the nations will try to completely destroy Jerusalem, and Zechariah says she will be like a burdensome stone that cannot be lifted and carried away. Likewise, God will preserve Israel so that her attackers will not ultimately be able to prevail. Though the stone is a symbol, this does not mean that Jerusalem is a symbol or foreign armies attacking Jerusalem are symbols, or the conversion of Israel is a symbol. In Revelation 19 where John describes the second coming of Christ, there are several symbols in the passage but they all relate to the literal coming of Christ to this earth.
6. One should not turn something into a symbol if there is a plausible explanation for it not being a symbol. In Revelation 17 & 18 there is a discussion of Babylon. Many have argued that Babylon is symbolic of the Roman Catholic Church or some other religious entity; however, there is no reason textually that Babylon has to be a symbol of anything other than being a literal city. This is particularly true when it is observed that in 18:10 Babylon is called a city, and back in 14:8 she is called a city. In chapter 8 of the same book we are told that the sun, moon, and stars will be darkened. This is entirely plausible even more so since God did the same thing literally back in ancient Egypt. In chapter 7 John refers to 144,000 Jews who will be sealed and protected during the Tribulation. Is there any good reason from the text that number has to be a symbol? It makes perfect sense to take it at face value. This is supported by the fact that in the passage John goes on to refer to the literal tribes of Israel.

Summary of Argument

I. JOHN RECORDS THE INTRODUCTION TO THE BOOK IN ORDER TO EXPLAIN ITS PURPOSE AND TO PREPARE HIS READERS FOR THE

REVELATION TO FOLLOW BY GLORIFYING THE TRINITY—1:1-8

A. John records the preface to the book in order to show that what he is about to write is a revelation from God—1:1-3
  1. The content of the book involves a revelation of Jesus Christ which God gave to show what would happen in the future—1:1
  2. The method by which God gave this information was through His angel to John and that it is the very Word of God—1:2
  3. There is a promised blessing to those who comprehend and keep the things in this prophecy—1:3

Note #308: Things that must soon take place/the time is near

John writes in 1:1 that the things shown John will "soon take place (τάχος)," and in 1:3 that the time is "near" (εγγύς). Many have used these two phrases as a proof that the futurist interpretation of Revelation cannot be correct since most of the events in this view have not transpired. Regarding 1:1, while the term can refer to something which happens after a short time, it can also refer to the manner in which something will take place. Walvoord writes: "That which Daniel declared would occur 'in the latter days' is here described as 'shortly,'...that is, quickly or suddenly coming to pass,' indicating rapidity of execution after the beginning takes place. The idea is not that the event may occur soon, but that when it does, it will be sudden (cf. Luke 18:8; Acts 12:7; 22:18; 25:4; Rom. 16:20). A similar word, tachys, *is translated 'quickly' seven times in Revelation (2:5, 16; 3:11; 11:14; 22:7, 12, 20)" (John Walvoord,* The Revelation of Jesus Christ *[Chicago: Moody Press, 1981], 35). Regarding 1:3, this simply refers to something that could occur at any moment (Alan Johnson, "Revelation," in* The Expositor's Bible Commentary *[Grand Rapids: Zondervan, 1981], 12:416-418; Robert Mounce,* The Book of Revelation *[Grand Rapids: Eerdmans, 1980], 65).*

B. John records the salutation to the book in order to heighten his readers' appreciation and expectation of what they are about to read—1:4-8
  1. He introduces himself as John and identifies his readers as the seven churches in the province of Asia—1:4a
  2. He pronounces a benediction of grace and peace on his readers—1:4b
  3. He describes the sources of grace and peace in order to glorify the Trinity with a special emphasis on the glory of the Son—1:4c-6
    a. He describes the Father as Jehovah I AM—1:4c
    b. He describes the Spirit in His fullness (Isa. 11:2-3)—1:4d
    c. He describes the Son—1:5-6
      1) He is the faithful witness because He faithfully revealed the Father (John 1:18)—1:5a
      2) He is the firstborn from the dead because He was resurrected and appointed to a position of authority—1:5b
      3) He is the ruler of the kings of the earth by virtue of His appointment (Psalm 110)—1:5c
      4) He is the One who loves the saints and loosed them from their bondage to sin by His death—1:5d
      5) He is the One who made the saints to be a kingdom and priests—1:6

4. He affirms the promise of Christ's coming with special reference to Israel—1:7
5. He affirms the sovereignty of the Father to show that He has the right to judge—1:8

II. JOHN PRESENTS THE "THINGS WHICH HE HAS SEEN" INVOLVING A VISION OF THE GLORIFIED CHRIST IN ORDER TO SET FORTH THE PLAN OF THE BOOK AND TO ESTABLISH THE PERSON OF CHRIST IN LIGHT OF THE EVENTS WHICH ARE TO TRANSPIRE—1:9-20

A. John presents the background of the vision—1:9-11

1. He was suffering as they were which was showed by his banishment on the isle of Patmos because of the testimony of Christ—1:9
2. On the Lord's Day he was instructed by an authoritative voice (like a trumpet) to write down and send what he was told to the seven churches of Asia—1:10-11

Note #309: The Lord's day

The phrase "the Lord's Day" has three possible meanings: 1) a day of the week possibly Sunday, but Sunday is never called the Lord's Day in the Bible, 2) the eschatological Day of the Lord, but this would be referring to the Tribulation/Millennium, or 3) "Lord" is an adjective describing the day as characterized by Lordship. The third view is probably the best.

B. John presents the vision of the glorified Christ in order to show His character and thereby prepare John and his readers for what was to follow—1:12-16

1. He sees seven golden candlesticks which represent the churches in their intended function of giving light—1:12
2. He sees the Son of Man in the midst of these candles—1:13-16

Note #310: Amidst the lamps

Christ can be said to be standing in the middle of these lamps because when the seven cities are located on the map they form a semi-circle. The title "Son of Man" is meant to conjure up the Messianic image of Daniel 7. The Messiah is evaluating his Church with his watchful eye.

a. He is clothed with a long robe and golden sash in order to picture Him in His priestly function in relation to the church—1:13
b. His head and hair were white like wool in order to show His purity and wisdom—1:14a
c. His eyes were like a blazing fire in order to emphasize His piercing judgment and understanding—1:14b
d. His feet were like bronze in order to show judgment (Isa. 60-61)—1:15a
e. His voice was like the sound of rushing waters in order to emphasize his authoritative power—1:15b
f. He held in his right hand seven stars, had a sword coming out of His

mouth, and His face shone like the sun in order to show His authority over the churches, the weapon of His judgment, and the righteousness of His character respectively—1:16

C. John presents the consequences of this vision—1:17-20

1. He was overwhelmed by this vision of glory and fell lifeless before Him—1:17a
2. Christ laid His comforting hand of power on Him and identified Himself as eternal and the resurrected One who had the authority over hell and death—1:17b-18
3. Christ instructed him to write what he had seen (see introduction on 1:19) and explains that the seven stars were the seven messengers of the churches and the seven candlesticks were the seven churches themselves—1:19-20

III. JOHN PRESENTS THE "THINGS WHICH ARE" IN ORDER TO SHOW THE CHURCHES THE ETHICAL DEMANDS THAT WERE REQUIRED BY THE GLORIFIED CHRIST AS THEY WAITED FOR HIS RETURN—2:1-3:22

Note #311: Interpretive approaches to the seven letters

There are three views which should be noted for the interpretation of these letters. The first is the prophetical view. This view says that the churches addressed were not in existence during the first century but will come into being during the Day of the Lord (Bullinger, Welch). The second view (historical view) states that the seven churches were in actual existence in the first century and their traits may characterize other local churches at various times in church history. The third view (historico-prophetical) sees the churches in existence in the first century, but also suggests that they prophetically reveal in the history of the church seven successive periods until the Rapture. These are:

REFERENCE	CHURCH	PERIOD OF CHURCH HISTORY
2:1-7	Ephesus	Apostolic era 33-64
2:8-11	Smyrna	Period of persecution 64-313
2:12-17	Pergamum	Official patronage 313-606
2:18-29	Thyatira	Middle ages 606-1520
3:1-6	Sardis	Protestant reformation 1520-1750
3:7-13	Philadelphia	Missionary era 1750-1900
3:14-22	Laodicea	Modern period 1900-?

The writer favors the historical view because this is the way the other New Testament epistles are interpreted together with the following weaknesses of the historico-prophetical view: 1) the correspondences are arbitrarily contrived, 2) Rev. 1:19 means that the prophetic part of the book does not begin in these chapters, 3) the rapture could not be imminent if 2-3 are taken in this sense, 4) this way of reading church history is selective, and 5) these correspondences are true only for Western Christianity.

A. John writes to the church at Ephesus in order to commend them for their labors and perseverance and to exhort them to rekindle their former love—2:1-7

1. The letter is addressed to the church at Ephesus from Christ—2:1

Note #312: Angels of the churches

The term "angel" could be a reference to a human messenger since that is a use of the term ἄγγελος. However, the possibility that this is a reference to a spirit being should not be dismissed. If correct, this would mean that the letter is given to the angel by Christ who then gives it to John. This would be consistent with the chain already presented in 1:1 "The Revelation of Jesus Christ, which God gave Him to show His servants—things which must shortly take place. And He sent and signified it by His angel to His servant John" (NKJV).

2. Christ commends the church for their hard work, discipline of false teachers, and perseverance in the midst of persecution—2:2-3
3. Christ rebukes the church for a loss of love for Him (or doctrine?)—2:4
4. Christ exhorts the church to remember how they used to feel and to repent back to their former works lest he comes with temporal judgment resulting in their loss of testimony-2:5-6

Note #313: Nicolaitans

*The Nicolaitans appear to be a group which exaggerated the doctrine of Christian liberty by overindulging in the pleasures of the flesh. Irenaeus wrote: "The Nicolaitanes are the followers of that Nicolas who was one of the seven first ordained to the diaconate by the apostles. They lead lives of unrestrained indulgence. The character of these men is very plainly pointed out in the Apocalypse of John, [when they are represented] as teaching that it is a matter of indifference to practise adultery, and to eat things sacrificed to idols" (*Against Heresies, *1.26.3).*

5. Christ promises to the one who overcomes the right to eat of the tree of life—2:7

Note #314: Who are the overcomers?

There is debate as to the identity of the "overcomers." Some feel that this is a reference to all Christians. This is based on passages like 1 John 5:4 and the reference to the "second death" in Revelation 2:11. Others feel that the "overcomers" refer to those Christians who are faithful to the instructions of these letters. Though this is a difficult question, the writer feels that the latter is in view for several reasons: 1) 1 John 5:4 can be explained as what is true of every believer in a positional sense, however, not every believer puts this into practice, and this is what is being called for in Rev. 2-3. Though a different author, the idea is similar to when Paul says that God killed the "old man" (Rom. 6:6), but then tells the believer to put off the old man (Eph. 4:22), 2) the passage in 2:11 can be explained by litotes (see notes there), 3) the precise reason for these letters is the very fact that many were not overcoming as is shown, by the rebuke sections, 4) the letters seem to express aspiration not certainty, 5) not all believers demonstrate the overcoming traits, and 6) the concept of rewards in the ancient world was that only those who faithfully endured and followed the rules of the games would be rewarded (see notes on 1 Cor. 9). Fuller states well: "Some have argued, however, that the term 'overcomer' applies to all Christians. While that is a more debatable interpretation in I John, it is not exegetically sound in Revelation, and it virtually eliminates each of the letters' respective motivations to remain faithful as well as the very need to urge faithfulness. A command that everyone keeps is superfluous, and a reward that everyone receives for a virtue that not everyone has is nonsense. Surely the burden of proof is on the shoulders of those who would argue that the warnings are not genuinely addressed to true believers as they seem to be and that the promises are genuinely addressed to all believers (as they do not seem to be). Hence the 'overcomer' is the individual Christian who enjoys special benefits in eternity for refusing to give up his faith in spite of persecution during life on earth" (J. William Fuller, "I Will Not Erase His Name From the Book Of Life," Journal of the Evangelical Theological Society *26:3 [Sep 1983], 299).*

The "tree of life" hearkens back to Gen. 2:9 and 3:22 where the tree's fruit was apparently a means of preserving life in a blissful state (Allen Ross, Creation and Blessing, *[Grand Rapids: Baker, 1988],124). The term is also used metaphorically in Proverbs four times where its nuance is more temporal rather than eternal. The tree of life then seems to depict a source of life and blessing while eating often depicts fellowship (see also Rev 3:20). The overcomer is promised intimate fellowship with Christ during the Kingdom age. The "paradise" of God terminology apparently arose from the influence of the LXX of Gen. 2:9. Paradise was originally a Persian word which signified an enclosed garden or park (Colin Hemer,* The Letters to the Seven Churches of Asia in Their Local Setting, *[Sheffield, England: University of Sheffield, 1986], 50).*

B. John writes to the church at Smyrna (myrrh—the embalming fluid associated with death) in order to commend them for their endurance of persecution and to exhort them to remain faithful even to the point of death—2:8-11

1. He addresses the letter to the church at Smyrna and notes that it is from the resurrected One in order to encourage them in the fact of death—2:8
2. Christ commends them for their endurance of affliction and poverty—2:9
3. Christ exhorts them not to fear their adversaries—2:10a
4. Christ promises that the one who faithfully endures and overcomes would be given the crown of life and would not be hurt of the second death—2:10b-11

Note #315: The second death

All are agreed that the second death is a reference to eternal damnation and separation from the presence of God. This is often said to be a glaring weakness of the view adopted above of the overcomers, since the implication appears to be that the Christian who does not overcome will be hurt by the second death. One possible interpretation has been suggested by Hodges: "By litotes [a figure of speech in which an affirmative idea is expressed by the negation of its opposite—in this case doubly negated] this intimates a superlative triumph over the second death. But since the second death is actual banishment from the presence and life of God, the litotes also intimates a splendid experience of the divine life and presence" (Zane Hodges, Grace in Eclipse *[Dallas: Redencion Viva, 1985], 107-111).*

C. John writes to the church at Pergamum in order to commend them for their faithfulness to Christ and to encourage them to reject the false teaching in their midst—2:12-17

1. He addresses the letter to the church from the one with the sharp two-edged sword—2:12

Note #316: Two-edged sword

The reference to the two-edged sword may refer to the fact that Roman governors were divided into two groups: those that had the right to execute and those who did not. Pergamum was given the power of life and death. Similarly, Christ had the power of life and death. Johnson explains: "It is interesting that Pergamum was a city to which Rome had given the rare power of capital punishment...which was symbolized by the sword. The Christians in Pergamum were thus reminded that though they lived under the rule of an almost unlimited imperium, *they were citizens of another kingdom—that of him who needs no other sword than that of his mouth" (Alan Johnson, "Revelation," in* The Expositor's Bible Commentary *[Grand Rapids: Zondervan, 1981], 440).*

2. Christ commends the church for their faithfulness in not renouncing Him during the time when Antipas was martyred—2:13

Note #317: Antipas

Concerning Antipas, Tatford has suggested: "Antipas is said to have been a dentist and a physician, but the aesculapiades *suspected that he was propagating Christianity secretly and they accused him of disloyalty to Caesar. He was condemned to death and was shut up in a brazen bull, which was then heated until it was red-hot." (Frederick Tatford,* The Patmos Letters *[Grand Rapids: Kregel, 1969], 75). "Where Satan lives" is probably a reference to the many cults and temples that resided in the city. The most notable was Asceplios—the god of healing who was emblemized by a serpent.*

3. Christ rebukes the church for allowing the doctrines of Balaam and the Nicolaitans—2:14-15

Note #318: Doctrine of Balaam

The doctrine of the Nicolaitans has already been commented on above. The doctrine of Balaam refers back to Numbers 25 where Balaam told Balak that he could defeat Israel if he involved them in Moabite religious feasts and intermarriage. This would render them unfaithful to God and consequently subject to discipline. Evidently, these believers were being tempted to idolatry and fornication in pagan feasts and in principle were being drawn away from God as was Israel.

4. Christ exhorts the church to repent lest they face judgment—2:16
5. Christ promises the church that the ones who overcome would receive hidden manna and a white stone with a new name—2:17

Note #319: Hidden manna and the white stone

The idea of manna goes back to the wilderness wanderings where the nation was sustained by the gracious provision of God. The Christians of Pergamum could find their spiritual nourishment in Christ apart from pagan festivals. The fact that it is "hidden" could be a reference to the location of the manna in the Holy of Holies, or possibly that Christ is hidden from the unbeliever. The full experience of this nourishment would be enjoyed by the overcomer during the Kingdom age.

The "white stone" could be a reference to the ancient practice of voting where the jurors cast black or white pebbles into an urn. This would then denote the vindication of the believer or his participation in the judging activities during the Millennium. It could also denote a token of acceptance into the precincts of the temple. The stone bore the secret name of the deity represented by the idol (Tatford, The Patmos Letters, *82). With this understanding, the white stone would have to do with activity in the marriage supper of the Lamb, and the name would be "overcomer" or the like. For five other possibilities see Hemer,* Letters, *96.*

D. John writes to the church in Thyatira (continued sacrifice) in order to commend them for their service and to warn them to reject idolatry and sinful practices—2:18-29

1. He addresses the church from the One with eyes of blazing fire and feet like bronze—2:18
2. Christ commends them for their good deeds, patient endurance, and increasing zeal—2:19
3. Christ rebukes the church tolerating the influence of Jezebel—2:20-23

Note #320: Trade guilds

Trade guilds are well attested in ancient Thyatira. Those in the same trade were often organized into "guilds" (somewhat similar to modern trade unions) which helped set standards for their profession as well protecting their economic interests. The guilds could pose potential problems for converts to Christianity because they were linked to the patron Roman deity of that guild. For those in Thyatira the participation in a feast associated with the deity of a guild created a problem. "The clubs bound their members closely together in virtue of the common sacrificial meal, a scene of enjoyment following on a religious ceremony. They represented in its strongest form the pagan spirit in society...To hold aloof from the clubs was to set oneself down as a mean-spirited, grudging, ill-conditioned person, hostile to existing society, devoid of generous impulse and kindly neighbourly feeling an enemy of mankind.Such revels were not merely condoned by pagan opinion, but were regarded as a duty, in which graver natures ought occasionally to relax their seriousness, and yield to the impulses of nature, in order to return again with fresh zest to the real work of life.Thus, this controversy was of the utmost importance in the early Church. It affected and determined more than any other, the relation of the new religion to the existing forms and character of Graeco-Roman city society" (William Ramsay, The Letters to the Seven Churches *[Grand Rapids: Baker, 1985], 348-350).*

Jezebel was historically the one who attempted to set up Baal worship in Israel (1 Kings 16:31-33; 21:25-26). Evidently, there was a woman in Thyatira, who like the Old Testament Jezebel, was promoting idolatrous syncretism and immorality with the local trade guilds. The immorality could legitimately be either physical or spiritual.

4. Christ exhorts the church who had not accepted her teachings to continue in their good conduct—2:24-25
5. Christ promises to those who remain faithful the privilege of reigning with Him and the morning star—2:26-29

Note #321: To reign with Christ

Those who are faithful to Christ are promised the privilege of reigning with Christ. This is a common idea in the New Testament (Matt. 25:14-30; 1 Tim. 2:12; Rev. 20:4-6), and clearly admits to degrees as is seen by Matthew's parable. A further reward is the morning star. This is a reference to Christ Himself (Rev. 22:16). This could be a reference to an emblem of His sovereignty (Num. 24:17 and Matt. 2:2) in which the believer would share as he reigns with Christ.

E. John writes to the church at Sardis (those escaping) to commend the few faithful and to exhort the others to remembrance and obedience—3:1-6
   1. He addresses the church from the One who holds the seven stars—3:1a
   2. Christ commends them for their reputation but rebukes them for their deadness—3:1b
   3. Christ exhorts them to wake up, repent, and obey lest He come in judgment—3:2-3
   4. Christ promises that the faithful overcomers would be dressed in white and would not have his name blotted out from the book of life but confessed before the Father—3:4-6

Note #322: Clothed in white

The white clothing seems to gain its significance from the Roman triumph procession. This was originally a procession of a victorious Roman general to the temple of Jupiter (Ramsay, The Letters, 386-388). On that day, all work ceased and the true Roman citizen donned a white toga. A specially privileged few (friends or relatives of the general, for example) actually had a part in the procession. These Sardian believers were exhorted to remain faithful so that they would participate in the day of Christ's triumph and thereby "walk with Him in white."

There is also the issue of what is meant by "I will not blot his name from the book of life." The "book of life" is a list of the names of the elect inscribed before the foundation of the world. With the writer's understanding of the overcomers, this does not have to imply that the non-overcomer would have his name blotted out. Again, this could be another example of litotes. Thus, the overcomer's name would be especially glorious. Tatford notes that "If, on the other hand, a citizen had performed some outstanding exploit deserving special distinction, honor was bestowed on him, either by the recording of the deed in the city roll or by his name being encircled in gold (or overlaid with gold) in the roll" (Tatford, The Patmos Letters, *116-117). This would probably involve what was meant by the words "I will acknowledge his name before my Father." In a similar vein, Fuller suggests that "name" can carry the idea of "reputation." Indeed, the idea of a "good name" is common in Scripture (Job 30:8; Prov. 22:1; Isa. 56:4-5). The believer who overcomes will have a good reputation through eternity. "When the context of Rev 3:5 is honored, it is best understood not in soteriological terms but in the sense of promising the preservation of more than the faithful Christian's eternal existence: It promises a unique and honorable eternal identity. The unfaithful Christian, conversely, will find that even as he on earth was ashamed of Christ's* onoma, *Christ will in heaven be ashamed of his (Matt 10:33; 2 Tim 2:12). It is this promise and threat that makes endurance through the kinds of trials and temptations catalogued in Revelation 2–3 conceivable" (J. William Fuller, "I Will Not Erase His Name From the Book Of Life," 306).*

F. John writes to the church at Philadelphia (brotherly love) in order to praise them for their faithfulness and encourage them to persevere— 3:7-13
   1. He addresses the letter church from the One who is holy and true and holds the keys of authority—3:7
   2. Christ commends the church for their deeds and the fact that they had not denied His name—3:8

Note #323: Open door

The "open door" seems to be the opportunity which was afforded to this church by God by virtue of their geographical setting. Ramsay explains that "Philadelphia lay at the upper extremity of a long valley, which opens back from the sea. After passing Philadelphia the road along this valley ascends to the Phrygian land...the main mass of Asia Minor...The road was the one which led...to the East in general...The Imperial Post Road from Rome to the provinces farther east and southeast coincided for some considerable distance with this trade-route" (The Letters, 404-405).

   3. Christ presents several promises to the church—3:9-13
      a. Their Jewish antagonists would bow before their presence and acknowledge their error—3:9

Note #324: Synagogue of Satan

The "synagogue of Satan" corroborates the fact that the major opposition to Christianity came from the Jews, and the city of Philadelphia was no exception. Tait has noted that "the most inveterate enemy of the church of Christ was the Jews. We read of them in Thessalonica, in Smyrna, and here in Philadelphia...In Palestine they were the sole persecutors of the church; and elsewhere, if they did not directly oppose the Gospel, they instigated others to do so" (Andrew Tait, The Messages to the Seven Churches of Asia Minor: An Exposition of the First Three Chapters of Revelation *[London: Hodder & Stoughton; Reprint, 1884], 352).*

      b. They would be kept from the hour of testing—3:10

Note #325: Pre-trib rapture

This is a key text to support the pretribulational rapture. It lends support because of the following: 1) τερεο εκ has the idea of "to keep out of." If posttribulationism were correct, the construction would have been τερεο εν, εισ or δια, 2) the article emphasizes the hour, 3) the purpose of the hour is "to try the whole earth," 4) v. 11 closely links the Second Coming with this hour, 5) the "people on the earth" is a moral classification (6:10; 11:10; 13:8), and 6) if this refers to a "keeping through," then Christ fails miserably in light of the martyrdom in the Tribulation (these are believers who come to faith during this period). For further support see Jeff Townsend, "The Rapture in Revelation 3:10," Bibliotheca Sacra *166:663 (July-September 2009), 350-365.*

There are two other grammatical issues which are often over-looked in this text. These have been discussed by John Niemela, "For You Have Kept My Word: The Grammar of Revelation 3:10," Chafer Theological Seminary Journal *6:1 (January-March 2000), 14-38. The first is the first word of the verse ὅτι ("because"). The implication is that only the faithful will be delivered from the hour of testing. Niemela demonstrates, however, that the conjunction is subordinate to 3:9 and not 3:10b. The second issue is the punctuation with which 3:10a should end. In this case it should be a period rather than a comma.*

Another interpretive issue, also addressed by Niemela ("For You Have Kept My Word: The Theology of Revelation 3:10," Chafer Theological Seminary Journal 6*:4 (October 2000), 52-67), is how the promise of deliverance in this verse would relate to the first century reader since the rapture did not occur then. The conclusion reached is that Revelation 3:10 is not a rapture passage per se, but does address the issue of the rapture. That is, the New Testament promised earlier that believers are not destined to the Tribulation, but this is not a promise specifically to the Philadelphia church as to how that will be accomplished. Universally, no church age believer will go through the Tribulation but there are different means by which this will be accomplished. i.e. death or rapture.*

c. The overcomer would be made a pillar in the temple with a new name written on him—3:11-13

Note #326: A pillar in the temple

One of the major drawbacks of living in Philadelphia was that it was the subject of earthquakes. In AD 17 a devastating earthquake leveled twelve cities of Asia overnight, and was especially hard on Philadelphia (Robert Mounce, The Book of Revelation *[Grand Rapids: Eerdmans, 1980], 115). Ramsay notes that "the effects lasted for years after. The trembling of the earth continued for a long time, so that the inhabitants were afraid to repair the injured houses, or did so with careful provision against collapse. Two or three years later, when Strabo wrote, shocks of earthquakes were an everyday occurrence. The walls of houses were constantly gaping in cracks; and now one part of the city, now another part, was suffering" (The Letters, 407). A pillar suggests strength, stability, and constancy. The overcomers, therefore, are promised this in contrast to the lack thereof in their present setting. The fact that they "will no more go in and out" is reminiscent of the fact that after AD 17 many of the residents moved out of the city, and others fled when there was the slightest tremor (Henry Swete,* Commentary on Revelation *[Grand Rapids: Kregel, 1977], 53; Alan Johnson, "Revelation," 451). Barclay suggests on the idea of a new name that a faithful servant or distinguished priest was sometimes honored by having a special pillar added to one of the temples with his named inscribed (William Barclay,* The Revelation of John *[Philadelphia: The Westminster Press, 1976], 89).*

G. John writes to the church at Laodicea (judgment of the people) in order to shake them out of their complacency—3:14-22

1. He addresses the letter to the church from the one who is faithful and true and ruler of God's creation—3:14

2. Christ rebukes the church for their lukewarmness and their false sense of security and independence—3:15-17

Note #327: Lukewarm

Drinks, to be useful, are served either cold or hot. The Laodiceans knew how the Lord felt, for their city drinking water was piped from a spring six miles to the south via an aqueduct and arrived disgustingly lukewarm (George Beasley-Murray, The Book of Revelation *[Grand Rapids: Eerdmans, 1999], 105). Their spirituality was just as useless. The Lord's vomiting them out does not imply the loss of salvation, but rather His disgust at their state. The city was wealthy from the production of wool cloth, banking, and health care which evidently led to their self-sufficient attitude.*

3. Christ exhorts the church to be earnest and repent and to enjoy fellowship with Him—3:18-20

Note #328: Knocking at the door—but why?

Many Christians have been moved by the Warner Sallman painting "Christ at Heart's Door" based on Revelation 3:20. The question is: why is Christ knocking? A common view is that this is a picture of Christ knocking at the heart's door which, if the individual chooses to open, will bring salvation. A less common view has been proposed by Thomas in which he argues that the door is an eschatological one through which Christ will enter when he returns. It is therefore urgent that people seek a right relationship with God (Robert Thomas, Revelation 1-7 *[Chicago: Moody Press, 1992], 321). A more probable explanation is that Christ is seeking renewed fellowship with the Laodicean Church. Wallace lists a series of considerations which would argue against the "salvation" view (Dan Wallace,* Greek Grammar Beyond the Basics: An Exegetical Syntax of the New Testament *[Grand Rapids: Zondervan, 1996], 380-381). 1) there is every indication that the individuals being addressed are saved. This is confirmed by the preceding verse "as many as I love, I rebuke and chasten. Therefore be zealous and repent." Moreover, the "therefore" connects the ones Christ loves with those who are called on to repent, 2) the term "love" (φιλέω) is never used of God's love for an unbeliever in the New Testament, 3) the preposition πρὸς does not mean "into" but "toward." The phrase "come toward" (εἰσέρχομαι πρὸς) in its eight uses in the New Testament never means penetration.*

4. Christ promises the overcomer that he would sit with Christ on His throne—3:21-22

IV. JOHN PRESENTS THE "THINGS WHICH SHALL BE HEREAFTER" IN ORDER TO SHOW THE FUTURE EVENTS SURROUNDING THE COMING OF CHRIST IN ORDER TO PROVIDE COMFORT AND ENCOURAGEMENT OF THE

ULTIMATE VICTORY OF CHRIST AND HIS SAINTS AND TO UNDERSCORE GOD'S SOVEREIGNTY IN HIS ACTIONS TOWARD THE WORLD—4:1-22:5

A. John presents a glorious picture surrounding the throne of God in order to provide an introduction to the judgments of the Tribulation by revealing the character of the Judge and giving the heavenly perspective of what is to take place—4:1-5:14

1. John gives a description of the scene in the throne-room of heaven—4:1-11

a. John was invited into heaven after the revelation he had received so that he could be shown what would take place after the Church Age—4:1

Note #329: Is 4:1 a rapture passage?

The invitation for John to "come up" (ἀναβαίνω) through the open door is not a reference to the rapture of the Church, but the place from which he will receive further revelation.

b. He describes the scene that he witnesses—4:2-11

1) He describes the glory of God the Father as He is seated on His throne (cf. v. 8)—4:2-3

2) Twenty-four elders were seated on 24 thrones which surrounded the throne of God—4:4

3) From the throne of God proceeded lightning (symbol of judgment) before which was the Spirit of God and a sea of glass—4:5-6a

4) In the center of the circle were four living creatures who incessantly worship God the Father—4:6b-8

5) The 24 elders likewise worship—4:9-11

2. John gives a description of the scroll and the Lamb in order to provide a heavenly perspective of the One who is worthy to judge—5:1-14

a. John describes the scroll as having writing on both sides and is sealed with seven seals—5:1

Note #330: The twenty-four elders

The identity of these individuals is not easy to determine. They could refer to human beings. If correct, it would need to be determined whether they are representatives of Israel, the Church, or both. Another option is to say they are angels.

Note #331: The little scroll

Suggestions as to what this scroll is includes: the Lamb's book of life, the Old Testament, and God's eternal plan. It seems that the scroll contains the judgments to follow and the title deed to the land of the earth. In Jeremiah 32, the prophet is told by God to buy a piece of property in Palestine which was the family inheritance. However, the property would be worthless because of approaching captivity, but in obedience to God Jeremiah bought it anyway and was given a scroll which was the title deed to the land. Similarly, in Revelation 5, the scroll has to do with the title deed to the earth—that is, Christ's right to rule over it. In Zechariah 5 a scroll is opened containing a record of judgments. So, the two ideas in the scroll are judgment and reigning. Christ will reign after a period of judgment.

The seals were composed of wax or clay so that the contents contained on the scroll would remain secret. There is a difference of opinion as to where the seals are on the scroll. Some argue that a seal would be broken and then the scroll unrolled until it came to the next seal, and so forth. Others view all of the seals on the outside of the scroll.

b. John describes the Lamb as the opener of the scroll—5:2-7
- **1)** He laments the fact that no one on earth, in heaven, or under the earth was worthy to open the scroll—5:2-4
- **2)** He describes the Lamb in order to show His worthiness to judge and reign—5:5-7
  - **a)** He is called the Lion of the Tribe of Judah which is a Messianic title from Gen. 49:8-10— 5:5a
  - **b)** He is called the root of David which is a Messianic title emphasizing His humanity from Isaiah 11:1—5:5b
  - **c)** He notes that the Lamb appeared as though He had passed through the slaughter (perpetual reminder of his crucifixion throughout eternity)—5:6a
  - **d)** He had seven horns symbolizing power (Deut. 33; Ps. 18), and seven eyes symbolizing omniscience—5:6b
  - **e)** He notes that the Lamb took the scroll from the hand of Father—5:7

c. John describes the response in heaven to the action of the Lamb—5:8-14
- **1)** The 24 elders and 4 creatures worshiped the Lamb with a special emphasis on His sacrifice—5:8-10
- **2)** An innumerable host of angels join in with these—5:11-12
- **3)** Every living creature joins in with these—5:13-14

B. John presents the seal judgments and one intercalation in order to show the first wave of judgment that would come during the Tribulation period—6:1-8:1

Note #332: Three waves of tribulation judgment at a glance

Name	Judgments	Time
Seals	Antichrist War Famine/Inflation Death Vengeance Earthquake	#1 inaugurates the 7-year Tribulation #s 2-6 occur toward the middle of the first half of the period
Trumpets	Vegetation Seas Drinking water Light Demonic assault A great army	Occur sequentially through the second half of the period
Bowls	Ulcers Sea	Occur in rapid succession at the end of the Tribulation associated with the

	Fresh water Heat Darkness Euphrates dried Earthquake	Second Coming

Note #333: Seal judgments

The seal judgments are the first wave of judgment which inaugurate the Tribulation. This is because the first seal speaks of the coming of the Antichrist. According to Daniel 9:27 the 70th Week of Daniel begins with the covenant of peace between Israel and the Antichrist. Seals 2-6 appear to take place in rapid succession toward the middle of the Tribulation.

1. The first seal is the Antichrist who is pictured as a military leader—6:1-2

Note #334: Rider on the white horse

Though some have attempted to identify this rider as Christ (Zane Hodges, "The First Horseman of the Apocalypse," Bibliotheca Sacra *119:476 [October 1962], 324-334), this would present a chronological problem since Christ does not return until after the Tribulation, the fact that the descriptions between 6:1-2 and 19:11 are much different, and the first horseman is seen in relation to the other three.*

2. The second seal is war—6:3-4
3. The third seal is famine and inflation brought about by war—6:5-6
4. The fourth seal is death that comes about from seals 2 and 3—6:7-8
5. The fifth seal pictures martyred saints as the result of the seal judgments who ask for the avenging of their blood—6:9-11

Note #335: Seal five

This seal is different in that it mentions saints in heaven. This seal is a result of judgment and not judgment itself. It shows that there is a remnant in the Tribulation and it is giving the basis of further judgment since these saints are pleading for this to occur.

6. The sixth seal consists of a great earthquake and disruption of the course of nature which causes terror on the earth—6:12-17

(Break in Chronology)

7. John presents the first intercalation (or parenthesis) looking back over the first wave of judgment in order to show how God will be merciful and gracious during this period of judgment and what would happen to those who belonged to God during this time—7:1-17
   a. He shows the sealing of 144,000 Israelites during the Tribulation in order to show that they would be protected and preserved as they are separated to a special ministry—7:1-8

Note #336: Tribe of Dan

The tribe of Dan is not mentioned in this list possibly because of their idolatry (Judges 18:30). However, they will receive a portion of land during the Millennium (Ezek. 48:1-2). Other proposals for the tribe's absence include a textual corruption that replaced Dan with Manasseh; the Antichrist will arise from Dan; Dan had become extinct (Robert Thomas, Revelation 1-7 *[Chicago: Moody, 1992], 480-481. For other peculiarities of the list see the discussion in Thomas.*

The special ministry of the 144,000 consists of the proclamation of the Gospel of the Kingdom. This is the same message that was preached by John and Jesus and entailed two parts: repent for the kingdom is at hand and behold the Lamb of God who takes away the sin of the world. Acceptance of this message would secure one's position in the coming Messianic reign.

- **b.** He shows that a great multitude from the earth will be saved in order to show the fruit of the ministry of the 144,000—7:9-17

(Chronology Resumes)

8. The seventh seal consists of the seven trumpets which are preceded by a period of silence in order to emphasize what God is doing and to provide an opportunity to repent—8:1

C. John presents the trumpet judgments and two intercalations in order to describe the second wave of judgment to come during the Tribulation period—8:2-14:20

Note #337: Trumpet judgments

It has already been noted that the seal judgments begin at the first part of the Tribulation and are concentrated during the mid-point. The trumpet judgments seem to cover the second half of the period and characterize it as the time of great Tribulation. The question of the literalness of these judgments might be answered in comparing them to the plagues on Egypt in Exodus.

1. John records the introduction to the trumpet judgments in order to show that God is sending judgment in answer to the prayers of His people (Exod. 3:7-10; Rev. 6:10-11; 8:3-4)—8:2-6

- **a.** Seven angels are handed the seven trumpets—8:2
- **b.** An angel offers the prayers of the saints at the altar and then throws coals to earth symbolizing judgment—8:3-6

2. The first trumpet consists of a judgment on the vegetation of earth—8:7

3. The second trumpet consists of judgment on the sea which would affect food and commerce—8:8-9

4. The third trumpet consists of judgment on the drinking water—8:10-11

5. The fourth trumpet affects the heavenly light bodies in that there will be four less hours of daylight and four hours of night in which there will be no luminaries as stars or moon—8:12

6. John sees an eagle fly through the sky warning of the woes of the last three trumpets yet to come—8:13

7. The fifth trumpet consists of an attack of demons who are loosed from the abyss who occupy specially prepared locust bodies (cf. the literal locust in Joel and Egypt and the swine in the Gospels) to inflict pain on all who do not have the seal of God—9:1-11

Note #338: The star

The "star" who opens the shaft of the abyss is possibly Christ, Satan, or another fallen angel. Most likely this refers to an angel from heaven who is carrying out God's bidding. These locust-like creatures are led by Satan (Abaddon in Hebrew and Apollyon in Greek both of which mean destroyer). Crown=victory; man=intelligence; teeth= destructiveness.

8. The sixth trumpet consists of a great army that is turned loose to bring judgment on the earth—9:12-21

(Break in Chronology)

9. John provides his second intercalation giving information between the sixth and seventh trumpets in order to confirm John's call to prophesy and the ministry of the two witnesses—10:1-11:14
   a. John presents supplementary material about his preparation to prophesy again—10:1-11
      1) He describes the appearance of a mighty angel (Christ) who has a little scroll (of judgment) and plants his feet on the land and sea in order to
      show the ownership of the land by Christ; he says something of judgment which John is not allowed to record—10:1-4
      2) The angel announces that there would be no more delay in the consummation of the covenanted program—10:5-7
      3) The angel instructed him to eat the scroll (it would be bitter because of its judgment but sweet because of what is being accomplished) and that he must prophesy again—10:8-11
   b. John presents supplementary material about the temple in Jerusalem and the ministry of the two witnesses in order to show that God is still in control and that there will be a ministry of grace during the Tribulation—11:1-14
      1) John is told to measure the temple and informed that the Gentiles will trample the city for 42 months—11:1-2

Note #339: Measuring the temple

The act of measuring indicates that the area belongs to God. The first verse is reminiscent of Zechariah's third night vision which anticipates the rebuilding of the temple (2:1-5) after Gentile domination. This verse then seems to be looking forward to the millennial temple. Revelation 11:2 however, seems to be dealing with the temple that will be rebuilt by the Jews before or during the first half of the Tribulation (For support that this is a literal, tribulation temple, see Randall Price, The Temple and Bible

Prophecy: A Definitive Look at Its Past, Present, and Future *[Eugene, OR: Harvest House, 2005], 317-319). The period of Gentile domination refers to the last half of the Tribulation for several reasons: 1) Daniel 9:27 says that during the first half Israel will be at peace through the covenant with the Antichrist, and 2) the abomination occurs at the middle of the Tribulation which will mark persecution of Israel for 3 1/2 years. A new temple will be built during the Millennium.*

2) John presents the events surrounding the two witnesses—11:3-13

a) He notes the ministry of the two witnesses to include proclamation which is authenticated by miracles—11:3-6

Note #340: Two witnesses

It is stated that these witnesses will be active for 3 1/2 years probably during the second half of the Tribulation. These are most likely two men who will be living at that time rather than a reincarnate Elijah, Enoch, or Moses.

b) The two witnesses will be put to death by the beast and rejoiced over—11:7-10

c) The two witnesses will be resurrected by God and taken to heaven—11:11-13

d) This will be followed by an earthquake that will kill a large number—11:13-14

(Chronology Resumes)

10. John records the seventh trumpet in order to present the Second Coming of Christ as the climax in the judgment program of God and the fulfillment of the covenanted program (Dan. 2; Ps. 2; Zech. 14)—11:15-19

Note #341: Trumpet seven

It appears that the seventh trumpet judgment is looking forward to the Second Advent at which Christ establishes His Millennial reign. At this point in the book, John does not describe the judgments to accompany this seventh trumpet. That judgment is contained in the seven bowls in chapter 16. Therefore, chapters 12-14 are another intercalation about this period of the Great Tribulation giving more information. Revelation 11:18 refers to the various judgments to occur at the Second Advent.

(Break in Chronology)

11. John provides his third intercalation in order to provide some information on the actors during the Tribulation period—12:1-14:20

a. He records the activity of Satan in order to show his plans and to show that he is the empowering force during this period—12:1-13:1

1) He describes a woman who was pregnant and cried out because she was about to give birth—12:1-2

Note #342: The players in chapter 12

The players include Israel (the woman), Christ (the child), Satan (the dragon), Antichrist (beast from sea), and the False Prophet (beast from the earth). Revelation 12:1-5 seems to speak of history and 6-17 of the future. Thomas remarks "The method of narration beginning at this point differs from anything previous, because it focuses on the secret maneuvers that lie behind the visible conflict to be portrayed under the seven bowls...That future struggle is merely the outworking of a conflict between God and Satan" (Robert Thomas, Revelation 8-22 *[Chicago: Moody, 1995], 117).*

2) He describes a dragon who was waiting to devour the child that was born of the woman—12:3-4
3) The male child was born and caught up into heaven so the dragon turns to persecute Israel for the last half of the Tribulation—12:5-6
4) There was a war in heaven between Michael and the dragon and his angels and that the dragon was hurled out of heaven to earth—12:7-9
5) There was rejoicing in heaven over this expulsion but woe to the earth because of the great wrath he would have for earth dwellers—12:10-12

Note #343: Satan's expulsion

Satan has access to heaven now (Job 1:6; Rev. 12:10), but at the mid-point of the Tribulation he will be expelled.

6) Satan takes out his vengeance on the woman and her seed for 3 1/2 years—12:13-17

Note #344: Persecution of the woman

The primary object of Satan during the last half of the Tribulation is Israel. The "wings" in v. 14 suggest divine enablement provided by God for the nation to flee (Deut. 32:11-12). The wilderness to which she flees could possibly be a reference to the Gentiles which would fit with Matthew 25:35-46 where Gentiles alive during this period are judged on how they helped Israel.

b. He records the activity of the two beasts in order to show the two primary personages through whom Satan will work—13:2-18
   1) He describes the character and activity of the beast out of the sea—13:1-10

Note #345: The beast

John indicates in his first epistle that there were in his time many antichrists in the world. The picture which emerges when comparing New Testament passages is that those who are anti- Christ foreshadow the one who will be the consummate Antichrist (see John's distinction between the two in 1 John 2:18). All one can know from Scripture is that this individual is coming with some description of what he will do. It is futile and dangerous to speculate as to his identity (for a history of the sad attempt in identifying him, see Stephen Nichols, "Prophecy Makes Strange Bedfellows: On the History of Identifying the Antichrist," Journal of Evangelical Theology *44:1 [Mar 2001], 76-85).*

Some argue that the second beast, rather than the first, is the Antichrist, but it appears that the first is the Antichrist for several reasons: 1) the meaning of anti as "instead of" fits better with the ministry of the first beast more than the second in that the first is prominent, 2) the fact that the second beast is called a lamb (the Jews are awaiting a kinglike Messiah rather than a lamblike one), 3) the second beast is the servant and executive of the first, and 4) there are several parallelisms between the first beast and the man of sin, little horn, and willful king (2 Thess. 2; Dan. 7; 11).

The Greek word for "beast" signifies a wild beast who is interested in brute force. Most see this beast as somehow connected with the Roman Empire, however just what this connection is remains a point of dispute. The preterist view sees it as the Roman empire during John's day; the historic view sees it as the Roman church; the idealist view sees it as the Roman empire and the idea of the beast throughout the church age as a movement; the futurist view sees it as a future revived form of the Roman Empire (4th kingdom of Daniel), or better, the final form of Gentile power (this view would not see the beast as "revived Rome"). John presents the beast as both a king and a kingdom.

The sea represents the unsettled state of humanity. This beast is probably a Gentile: 1) John defines the "sea" as a reference to Gentile nations (17:15), 2) the little horn arises out of the final Gentile empire, 3) Antiochus is a type of the Antichrist and was a Gentile (Dan. 11), and 4) one does not need to be a Jew to sign a covenant with Israel especially because he would be energized by Satan.

While some see the 7 heads as Roman emperors, it seems better to see them as 7 successive imperial governments (Egypt, Assyria, Babylon, Persia, Greece, Roman, the 7th is the ten-nation federation in the first half of the Tribulation and the eighth is the world empire headed by Antichrist during the last half (for further comments see the discussion on the seven hills in Rev. 17:9).

The ten horns represent ten kings during the final form of this Gentile empire and the ten horns the despotic power that these kings will enjoy.

The mongrel nature of the beast (leopard, bear, lion—Babylon, Media-Persia, Greece) suggests that the beast will embody all of these traits as the consummate world power.

The deadly wound has been explained by the following views: Nero Redivivus; judgment at the cross; national revival; personal revival. The writer favors the latter for 1) the wound is also mentioned in 13:12, 14; 17:8, 11 and seems to refer to an individual, 2) the healing leads people to wonder and worship at that which would they would see, 3) the word for "wound" is used in 5:6 to speak of the wounds inflicted on Christ, 4) this "death and resurrection" could be a parody on the death of Christ, 5) 13:14 says it is caused by the sword, 6) this seems to cause a change in the Antichrist (13:5-7), and 7) this "resurrection" could be a deceptive ploy by the second beast (see 11-15).

The text says that the beast would rule intensely for 3 ½ years which refers to the last half of the Tribulation because of the nature of his behavior.

a) It comes out of the sea—13:1a
b) It has seven heads, ten horns, and ten crowns—13:1b
c) It is a mongrel—13:2a
d) It has derived power from the dragon—13:2b
e) It receives a fatal wound and is healed which leads to worship

and intimidation by the beast—13:3-4

f) It is blasphemous and exercises its horrendous power and persecution for 42 months—13:5-7

g) It is to be worshiped by all—13:8-10

2) He describes the character and activity of the beast from the land—13:11-18

a) He notes the person of the second beast as being from the earth in order to show his humanity; as being like a lamb in order to show his peaceful appearance; as having two horns in order to show his civil and religious power as one who seeks to have all worship the first beast—13:11-12

b) He notes the work of the false prophet as calling fire form heaven, and giving life to an image of the beast in order to show that he would authenticate his work by miracles—13:13-15

c) He notes that the false prophet will impose a literal (use of the word) mark on earth dwellers for them to enjoy a relatively normal life in order to show the culmination of human effort—13:16-18

c. He records the triumph of the 144,000 and the judgment to come during the Tribulation in order to show the certainty of judgment to come on the beast and his followers—14:1-20

1) He records the triumph of the 144,000 on Mt. Zion in order to show the victory of God's sealed servants over the rule of the beast—14:1-5

Note #346: Mt. Zion

Mt. Zion is to be understood as the earthly Jerusalem (possibly the Mt. of Olives) rather than the heavenly city because of the Scriptural use of the term (2 Sam. 5:7; Isa. 2:3; Ps. 50, 51, 53, 69, 74, 84, 99 et al.), and because this group makes it safely through the Tribulation and moves into the millennial earth without going into God's presence.

2) He records the judgment to come on the beast and his kingdom—14:6-20

Note #347: The winepress

This judgment is the same as 11:15 ff. and 19:17-21 to take place at the Second Advent. Judgment has been committed to the Son (John 5) and he uses the sickle (a threshing instrument). A picture is also given of taking grapes and putting them into a winepress where they are trodden down. The word for "ripe" signifies something that is ripe or possibly past its peak (14:15; the word for "ripe" in 14:18 seems to signify that while in one sense the judgment is overdo, on the other hand it is right on divine schedule). Grapes were put in a winepress outside the city wall which had holes in the sides of the vat near the bottom to allow the juice to flow out. This describes the judgment that will take place in the bowl-like valley of Jezreel in Northern Israel (i.e., Armageddon). The "eternal gospel" is the good news that God is going to judge this evil system.

- **a)** An angel announces the coming judgment—14:6-7
- **b)** An angel announces the fall of Babylon—14:8
- **c)** An angel announces the fate of the beast worshippers—14:9-12
- **d)** The announcement of the triumph of the righteous dead—14:13
- **e)** Christ is seen on a cloud of Shekinah as he comes to reap God's harvest—14:14-16
- **f)** The angles are seen as involved in this reaping as well—14:17-20

(Chronology Resumes)

D. John presents the bowl judgments and two intercalations in order to show the third wave of judgment during the Tribulation, namely the form of the judgments to fall on the world at the Second Advent—15:1-19:21

- **1.** John gives the introduction to the bowl judgments in order to show the preparation for the final wave of judgment—15:1-8
  - **a.** He announces the last judgments as the completion of God's wrath (This verse serves as a heading for the balance of Tribulation judgment)—15:1
  - **b.** He notes the praise of the holiness and righteousness of God by the Tribulation martyrs—15:2-4
  - **c.** He notes the preparation of the angels to pour out the judgment—15:5-8
- **2.** John presents the bowl judgments in order to show the climactic judgments at the end of the Tribulation—16:1-21

Note #348: The bowl judgments

The bowl judgments are the third major wave of judgment to occur during the Tribulation. These are best seen as concentrated toward the end of the 7-year period. If correct, these judgments could occur during what Joel called "the great and terrible" day of the Lord.

It should be noted that the bowl judgments are similar to the plagues on Egypt. In Exodus the plagues were a polemic against the gods of Egypt (see Jerry Hullinger, "The Egyptian Religious Background of Pharaoh's Hard Heart," Journal of Dispensational Theology *16:47 [April 2012], 24-39). The same thing seems to be happening here, for this is the ultimate conflict between God and the false system of the Satan and the beast.*

- **a.** John hears the directive given to the angels to commence pouring out their bowls on the earth—16:1
- **b.** The first bowl consists of sores or boils on the beast worshipers—16:2
- **c.** The second bowl is the destruction of all sea life—16:3
- **d.** The third bowl is the contaminating of all fresh water by blood—16:4-7
- **e.** The fourth bowl is climatic changes involving a higher degree of heat intensity from the sun—16:8-9
- **f.** The fifth bowl is darkness—16:10-11
- **g.** The sixth bowl is the drying up of the Euphrates River which prepares the way for the Kings of the East—16:12

Note #349: The Euphrates

The drying up of the Euphrates should not be viewed as something that enables the armies to cross, for they would be capable of crossing a river. Rather, the literal drying up of the river seems to suggest the removal of restraint by God to lead to this final phase. Thus it is not the drying up of the river that is the judgment but that to which this leads. See other passages where the drying of water is associated with God's mighty actions (Exod. 14; Josh. 3; Isa. 11:15; Zech. 10:11).

h. He presents a parenthesis in order to describe the gathering of the nations—16:13-16

1) Three demons are loosed which influence the kings of the earth to go to war against the beast (?) while Satan's purpose is to gather them to do war against God—16:13-14

2) There is a warning to unbelievers that His coming will be sudden and for believers to live properly—16:15

3) The demons gather all of the armies at Armageddon—16:16

Note #350: Armageddon

Revelation 16:16 is the only place in the Bible where the word ~Αρμαγέδων is used. John says that in the Hebrew tongue this is "Har-Magedon" (there is an "h" in Hebrew but not an "h" in Greek). The transliteration is for the sake of John's Greek readers in Asia Minor. While some take Har to refer to a hill on which Megiddo stood, or a reference to Mt. Carmel, the term can have the sense of a mountain region or hill country (Brown, Driver, Briggs, Hebrew and English Lexicon of the Old Testament *[Oxford: Clarendon Press, n.d.), 251). Hence, this is most likely a reference to the hill country surrounding the Jezreel Valley (14 x 20 miles) including the hill on which the town of Megiddo was situated. Of course this valley cannot hold all of the armies of the world and so this could be a place of troop deployment (Thomas,* Revelation 8-22, *270-271).*

i. The seventh bowl is poured out causing a destructive earthquake accompanied with large hail stones—16:17-21

Note #351: Earthquakes

As one reads through Revelation, many earthquakes as are seen. They are all precursors and types of this final, climactic one.

(Chronology Resumes)

3. John presents an intercalation concerning Babylon in order to summarize one of the great movements during the Tribulation period— 17:1-19:10

Note #352: Babylon

There are several points to be noted about chapters 17-18, 1) it appears that they are describing one Babylon rather than two (see Dyer's discussion in "The Identity of Babylon in Revelation 17-18: Part 1" Bibliotheca Sacra *144:575 [Jul 1987]), 2) the description of Babylon as a "mystery" in 17:5 is not to be understood as part of her name, but rather what is written on her forehead is a mystery (something previously unrevealed), 3) 17:18 identifies the woman as a city not as a religious system, 4) the focus in these chapters seems to be on her prostitution of all that is noble for economic gain as a means to power and luxury, 5) while the seven hills are often understood as a reference to the city of Rome, there is another explanation: the word translated "hill" in Revelation 17 is used seven other places in the book and is always translated as "mountain." The word "mountain" is often a symbol of a kingdom or national power (Isa. 2:2; 41:15; Jer. 51:25; Dan. 2:35, 44; Zech. 4:7). Thus, it is likely that the seven hills refer to successive imperial governments (Egypt, Assyria, Babylon, Persia, Greece, and Rome). The seventh head represents a Gentile power in the first half of the Tribulation including the ten nation federation, and the eighth represents the final Gentile government during the second half of the Tribulation. This would explain why the seventh head is only in power a short time. Therefore, Babylon is a literal city that will dominate the world. It is characterized as a harlot who prostitutes her moral values for luxury. She will obtain control over Antichrist and the entire earth, but will eventually be destroyed during the Tribulation.*

It is also to be observed that there is a linkage between John's description in 17-18 and Jeremiah's description of Babylon in 50-51 (see Charles Dyer, "The Identity of Babylon in Revelation 17-18: Part 2" Bibliotheca Sacra *144:576 [Oct 1987]. It seems that Jeremiah 50-51 requires the literal city of Babylon to be rebuilt during this period for several reasons: 1) Babylon is to be destroyed suddenly (51:8), 2) it is to be destroyed completely (50:3, 13), 3) the building materials will never be reused (51:26), 4) believers will flee the city (50:8; 51:6), and 5) Israel and Judah will be reunited (50:4-5). Since these things have never happened, it is strong support that the literal city will be rebuilt, only to be razed to the ground by the beast. The other option is to view Old Testament passages as a genre which is not to be taken literally.*

- **a.** John is invited by an angel to see the punishment of the prostitute who polluted the world with her adulteries—17:1-2
- **b.** John sees a vision of the system—17:3-6
  - **1)** The woman is seen sitting on a scarlet beast who had seven heads and ten horns to show her control over it—17:3
  - **2)** The woman is dressed brilliantly holding a cup which is filled with abomination—17:4
  - **3)** The woman has a mysterious name "Babylon the great, the mother of prostitutes and of the abominations of the earth"—17:5
  - **4)** The woman is drunk with the blood of the saints—17:6
- **c.** John is given the beast part of the interpretation by the angel—17:7-14
  - **1)** He states that the beast (same as ch. 13) will cause astonishment and that one of his heads had existed and then passed out of existence—17:7-8
  - **2)** He states that the seven heads are seven hills and seven kings—17:9
  - **3)** He states that five of these have fallen (Egypt, Assyria, Babylon, Persia, Greece), one is (Rome), one is to come (the form under the beast—the ten nation federation for the first half of the trib.) and that for a little while —17:10
  - **4)** He states that there will be an eighth kingdom (the world-wide

government under the beast during the last half of the tribulation) which is related to the seven and will be destroyed—17:11

5) He states that the ten horns are ten kings who will be allies of the beast—17:12

6) He states that the ten horns will give power and authority to the beast—17:13

7) He states that they will make war with the Lamb and be defeated—17:14

d. John is given the harlot part of the interpretation by the angel—17:15-18

1) The waters on which the prostitute sat were the nations signifying her control and influence over them—17:15

2) The beast and the ten horns will hate and destroy the harlot—17:16-17

3) The woman is the great city that rules over the kings of the earth—17:18

e. John sees the destruction of the city of Babylon explaining the "how" of 17:16—18:1-24

1) The announcement of judgment is made—18:1-3

2) The description of judgment is given—18:4-8

3) The reactions to the judgment are given—18:9-20

4) The execution of the judgment is given—18:21-24

f. John sees the rejoicing in heaven over the destruction of Babylon and the preparation for the marriage supper of the Lamb—19:1-10

(Chronology Resumes)

4. John presents the Second Coming of Christ—19:11-21

a. He describes the return of the majestic Christ and His saints to judge and defeat the nations—19:11-16

b. He describes the scene of carnage on the earth as the armies of the beast fight against Christ and are destroyed—19:17-21

E. John presents the millennial reign of Christ in order to inform his readers as to the events to transpire when Christ returns to earth— 20:1-15

Note #353: 1,000 years

One of the most important debates regarding Revelation in particular and eschatology in general, is the interpretation of Revelation 20:1-6. John Walvoord states the importance of this passage: "Few verses in the Bible are more crucial to the interpretation of the Bible as a whole than the opening verses of Revelation 20. They are determinative in their support of the three major millennial views: postmillennialism, amillennialism, and premillennialism. They are of vital importance to the doctrine of the righteousness of God and His ultimate triumph over evil. They relate pointedly to the question of the resurrection of both the righteous and the wicked. Further, they are essential to the doctrine of satanology, that is, the present power and program of Satan as well as his destiny" (John Walvoord, "The Theological Significance of Revelation 20:1-6," in Essays in Honor of J. Dwight Pentecost *[Chicago: Moody, 1986], 227). The issues within the passage have to do with 1) the time and nature of Satan's binding, 2) the nature and timing of the first resurrection, 3) whether the 1,000 years is symbolic or literal, 4) the nature of the "millennium," and 5) the relationship between Revelation 19 and 20. The following chart summarizes the views taken on these areas (this is a general overview of the various approaches to this text which recognizes that there is room for variation within the major positions). The writer feels that the premillennial view is the correct one.*

Issue	**Amillennial**	**Postmillennial**	**Premillennial**
Binding of Satan	Satan is currently bound so that his activities are limited. This binding occurred during the ministry of Christ	Satan is bound progressively as the world is more and more Christianized	Satan's activities will be completely eliminated during the future, earthly reign of Christ
First Resurrection	A spiritual resurrection at regeneration or the translation of the soul to heaven upon death	A spiritual resurrection (variously interpreted in postmillennial literature in agreement with the amillennial description or even things like a revival)	A future, physical resurrection to occur at the beginning of the Millennium
1,000 Years: Symbolic or Literal?	Symbolic—variously described as a long period of time; complete period of time; indefinite period of time, etc.	Symbolic (generally)	A future, literal period of time giving the duration of Christ's earthly reign which is promised throughout the Scripture
Nature of the Millennium	A spiritual reign currently taking place in heaven, in the Church, or in the life of the individual	Christ reigns from heaven exercising dominion through the saints on earth	A future, earthly reign of Christ
Relationship Between Revelation 19 and 20	The events of Revelation 20:1-6 take place before the events of Revelation 19:11-21 (recapitulation)	Recapitulation (generally)	The events of Revelation 20:1-6 take place after the events of Revelation 19:11-21 (sequential)

1. Satan is bound in the abyss for 1,000 years—20:1-3
2. John sees those who are rewarded and given thrones of authority during this period—20:4a
3. John sees those who were martyred during the Tribulation and are

resurrected constituting the participants in the first resurrection—20:4-6b

Note #354: The first resurrection

The other participants in the first resurrection are Christ, the church age saints at the rapture, and the OT saints. The "rest of the dead" in v. 5 refers to the wicked dead who will be raised at the end of the Millennium. The "first resurrection" refers to a resurrection of "kind" namely eternal life. The "second resurrection" also refers to one of kind namely damnation.

4. Satan is loosed, goes out to deceive the nations and gathers them to the battle of Gog and Magog where they are defeated, and Satan is cast into the lake of fire with the beast and false prophet—20:7-10

Note #355: Mixed population in the millennium

These verses show that there will be children born with sin natures to non-resurrected, saved individuals who enter the Kingdom. These children will have the opportunity to be saved during this period. At the end of the millennium, Satan will deceive those who have rejected the gospel into thinking that they would be better off submitting to his authority rather than to that of Christ. He gathers them to Jerusalem to do battle with Christ and the saints at which time they will be decisively crushed.

*The idea of a mixed population in the millennium often meets with objections. Amillennialist Kim Riddlebarger says, "According to premillenarians, the millennium is a period in which people who have been raised from the dead and who now live on earth in resurrected bodies coexist with people who have not been raised from the dead and who remain in the flesh. How can this be? Where does Scripture teach about such a mixture of resurrected and nonresurrected individuals" (*A Case for Amillennialism: Understanding the End Times *[Grand Rapids: Baker, 2013], 232)? See similar statements by Sam Storms ("Problems with Premillennialism," eschatologystuff.wordpress.com, accessed 5/1/2014) and Vern Poythress, "2 Thessalonians 1 Supports Amillennialism," http://www.frame-poythress.org/2-thessalonians-1-supports-amillennialism, accessed 5/1/2014. Obviously, this debate deals with larger issues than simply how can glorified and non-glorified people exist side by side. However, consider the following facts to show the concept to at least be reasonable, 1) there are numerous passages in the Old Testament and New Testament describing the kingdom age as a time where Christ rules on earth with a rod of iron. Moreover, victorious Christians are promised that they will join Christ in this reign. These texts indicate a mixed multitude during the period, 2) an allegorical interpretation of Revelation 20 presents more exegetical difficulties than a literal one which yields a mixed multitude during the millennium (for a common sense, concise, and straightforward presentation of these, see Matthew Waymeyer,* Revelation 20 and the Millennial Debate *[The Woodlands, TX: Kress Christian Publications, 2004]), 3) the resurrected Christ mingled with two disciples on the road to Emmaus, the apostles, and had numerous appearances to hundreds of other individuals, culminating in the ascension as the apostles gazed in amazement, 4) whether resurrected, or raised to die again, one must deal with the odd account in Matthew 27:51-53 of people rising from the dead and then appearing to people in Jerusalem, and 5) in Zechariah 14:3 the Messiah* *returns in judgment and it is indicated that those who remain on the earth go to Jerusalem yearly to worship (14:16ff).*

5. The judgment of the wicked—20:11-15
   a. The wicked dead are presented before the Great White Throne of God at a place located between heaven and earth (cf. 2 Peter 3)—20:11-12a
   b. The books are opened—20:12b

Note #356: The books

The books represent the deeds of the unbeliever. These deeds will determine the degree of punishment in the lake of fire they experience. The book of life is the record of all the elect from the foundation of the world. The absence of those at this judgment from this book will demonstrate the justice of their fate.

   c. The dead are resurrected and judged according to their deeds—20:13
   d. Death and hades (the present temporary place of judgment where the unsaved dead await this judgment) are cast into the lake of fire—20:14
   e. All individuals whose names are not in the book of life are cast into the lake of fire—20:15

Note #357: Eternal punishment

The doctrine of eternal punishment is admittedly difficult to ponder; however, it is clearly taught in Scripture. See Note 361 for a larger overview of the matter. Besides the larger issue, one question which Christian people have, and yet find it difficult to acknowledge they have, is how the lostness of a friend or relative will affect them in the eternal state. This is something that touches every Christian and there is no pat answer to be given. Yet two considerations are appropriate: 1) we must acknowledge that our current perspective is extremely limited and what seems impossible to grasp now may be seen in a different light in the future, and 2) God loves the lost more than any person is able. Yet God exists and will continue to exist in a perfect state of felicity. If this is possible for a being whose love is greater than ours, is it not reasonable to conclude that we will be capable of the same?

F. John presents the conditions of the eternal state in order to show the readers their final home—21:1-22:5

Note #358: The eternal state

It seems that this is a description of the eternal state rather than the Millennium for three reasons: 1) the chronological development, 2) the fact that the first heaven and first earth are passed away, and 3) there is no temple in it.

6. He describes the conditions to exist in the eternal state—22:1-8
7. He describes the New Jerusalem—21:9-22:5

Note #359 <u>Some</u> fast facts on the New Jerusalem

1. *It will be the capital of the new creation.*
2. *Its inhabitants will include many people groups. Revelation 21:3 indicates God will dwell with men ("peoples"). Israel is usually designated with the singular "people." This would relate to the original promise to Abraham that through Israel God will bless many nations.*
3. *There will be no tears. These are tears which were caused by things in the old creation.*
4. *There will be no sin. Why? Because there will be no unbelievers and all believers will have their resurrection bodies.*
5. *The city will have a radiant glow.*
6. *The city will have 12 gate-towers. The city will be square and on each wall there will be three of these towers which will be points of access into the city.*
7. *There will be angelic guards to the city; not because there are any threats but to enhance the point that there is perfect security.*
8. *Directions and time will exist.*
9. *The base of the city is square with each side measuring approximately 1,500 miles. That is about the distance from Philadelphia to Dallas; or Dallas to Los Angeles; keeping in mind that is just one side of the base. In addition, the city is said to be 1,500 miles high.*
10. *Each gate tower will be carved from one pearl.*
11. *The city will contain no temple. This is because the city is a virtual temple in which the presence of God resides. A temple proper will not be necessary because there will be no uncleanness to contaminate God's presence.*
12. *There will be no sun, moon, or stars. God's glory will illuminate the entire city and beyond.*
13. *National identities will be retained in the city.*
14. *The gates of the city will remain open because there will be no enemies of the city.*
15. *The means of entrance into the city will be having one's name in the book of life.*
16. *Pure, unpolluted water will issue from God's throne.*
17. *God's throne will be positioned at the head of the main street of the city.*
18. *The river from God's throne will divide into two branches around the tree of life.*
19. *The tree will perpetually bear fruit with a new crop each month.*
20. *The saints will serve the Lamb.*
21. *The saints will see God's face.*
22. *Faithful believers will have more authority in this city than those who have been less faithful. This goes back to the overcomer passages in Revelation 2-3.*
23. *The city walls will be about 72 yards thick.*

V. JOHN RECORDS THE EPILOGUE TO THE BOOK IN ORDER TO COMFORT AND WARN HIS READERS—22:6-21

A. He states the things he has written are true and that it is certain that Christ will return—22:6-7

B. He states that he responded to these things by wrongly worshiping the angel—22:8-9

C. He notes that he was told to proclaim this revelation and that if people reject it there is nothing left for them and that Christ is returning with His rewards—

22:10-15

D. He repeats that the author of the work is Christ given to the churches—22:16

E. He invites the spiritually thirsty to find eternal life—22:17

F. He warns against adding or deleting from the book of Revelation lest right to the tree of life be forfeited—22:18-19

Note #360: Book of life or tree of life?

The translation "book of life" found in the KJV is traceable back to Erasmus' use of the Latin Vulgate when creating his Greek text. Apart from the Vulgate there is no manuscript evidence to support the reading "book of life." Hence the Majority Text, the UBS text, and the 27th Nestle-Aland text all have "tree of life" which is the preferred rendering.

G. He repeats Christ's promise to come quickly (swiftly) and affirms his desire for this—22:20-21

Note #361: Eternal punishment through history

The discussion of the Great White Throne judgment and eternal punishment is not an easy one. It has been my position that the truth of eternal, conscious torment is one of the easiest doctrines to prove but one of the most difficult to grasp. While I hold the doctrine with confidence because it is clearly taught in Scripture (certainly by Jesus himself), I do not feel that it is rational from the limited, human perspective any more than the doctrine of the Trinity or hypostatic union. I am well aware of the argument that sin is against an infinite Being and therefore deserves infinite punishment; and the argument that hell is eternal because sin is perpetually being committed in hell, etc. I find both of these explanations to be unsatisfactory which just beg the question and never get at the heart of the matter as to why God would knowingly create a being he would end up infinitely punishing. I share the sentiment of Jonathan Edwards who remarked "'tis an awful doctrine, but 'tis of God." I hold the doctrine because as Edwards said it 'tis of God; I do not hold it because I can prove it intellectually (apart from Scripture) or rationally. The criterion for truth, however, must never be human reason, but the revelation of Scripture. This neither means that Scripture is unreasonable; nor, does it mean that human reason is not used in interpreting the Bible. Rather, it seeks to follow the Reformers' distinction of the magisterial (bad) and ministerial (good) use of reason. The magisterial use of reason will always lead to philosophical rationalism and ultimately to theological liberalism. This in no way shows a weakness or compromise on this truth; simply an admission that we should come to grips with the fact that we cannot grasp this now since God has not been pleased to allow us to. For the sake of academic interest and the challenge faced to defend this doctrine, I have included below the views held on the subject and some statements reflecting these views (though not presented in any particular order).

Views of Hell[673]

Traditional

Some people (perhaps even a majority of the human race) will not be saved. • Each person is judged once and for all at death and given either eternal life or eternal condemnation. • Hell is a place of endless, conscious punishment for sin. This punishment is sometimes interpreted literally (physical torment) and sometimes metaphorically (a state of being, spiritual suffering, separation from God). • Once a person is in hell, there is no exit. • Some versions of this view argue that there are variations in punishment depending upon the severity of a person's sins. • Some (Calvinist) versions emphasize God's sovereignty in punishing those whom he chooses to punish, while other versions emphasize the freedom of human choice. • The Roman Catholic view distinguishes between hell and purgatory, a place of temporary purification for those who are destined for heaven.

Conditional Immortality or Annihilationism

Some people will not be saved. • The human soul is not naturally immortal. Eternal existence is a gift of God to the redeemed. • The unrepentant will be punished, but this period of conscious punishment will be temporary. • At the final resurrection, the unrepentant will be destroyed and cease to exist. The biblical "fire" of hell is a consuming, rather than tormenting, fire. • Some conditionalists believe that after death a person will receive a second chance to accept or reject God.

Restorationism or Universalism

All people will eventually be saved, and God will restore the creation to perfect harmony. • Eternal punishment contradicts the love of God, since God wills the salvation of all and has the power to overcome sin and evil. God's love is stronger than human resistance. • If there is a hell, it is not eternal. Punishment is temporary and remedial, leading the sinner towards repentance and union with God. • Even the devil can ultimately repent and be saved. • Some theologians throughout history have maintained a more cautious "hopeful universalist" stance: We cannot say dogmatically that all will be saved, but neither can we deny the possibility.

Miscellaneous Comments

"Let me say at the outset that I consider the concept of hell as endless torment in body and mind an outrageous doctrine, a theological and moral enormity, a bad doctrine of the tradition which needs to be changed. How can Christians possibly project a deity of such cruelty and vindictiveness whose ways include inflicting everlasting torture upon his creatures, however sinful they may have been? Surely a God who would do such a thing is more nearly like Satan than like God, at least by any ordinary moral standards, and by the gospel itself...Surely the God and Father of our Lord Jesus Christ is no fiend; torturing people without end is not what our God does"[674]

– Clark Pinnock

[673] This helpful summary of the three major positions is taken from *The History of Hell: Christian History Guide #1,* Christian History Magazine (2011), 3.

[674] Clark Pinnock, "The Destruction of the Finally Impenitent," *Criswell Theological Review* 4/2 (1990), 246-247.

"Is it not folly to assume that eternal punishment signifies a fire lasting a long time, while believing that eternal life is life without end? For Christ, in the very same passage, included both punishment and life in one and the same sentence when he said, "So those people will go into eternal punishment, while the righteous will go into eternal life" (Matt 25:46). If both are "eternal," it follows necessarily that either both are to be taken as long-lasting but finite, or both as endless and perpetual. The phrases "eternal punishment" and "eternal life" are parallel and it would be absurd to use them in one and the same sentence to mean: "Eternal life will be infinite, while eternal punishment will have an end." Hence, because the eternal life of the saints will be endless, the eternal punishment also, for those condemned to it, will assuredly have no end"[675]

– Augustine

"The fire itself is termed "eternal" and "unquenchable," but it would be very odd if what is thrown into it proves indestructible. Our expectation would be the opposite: it would be consumed forever, not tormented forever. Hence it is the smoke (evidence that the fire has done its work) which "rises for ever and ever?"[676]

–John Stott

"[O]ur expectation would be that the smoke would die out after the fire had finished its work. How could the smoke from the fire rise forever if its fuel had been consumed?"[677]

–Robert Peterson

"It is therefore one and the same God the Father who has prepared good things with Himself for those who desire His fellowship, and who remain in subjection to Him; and who has prepared the eternal fire for the ringleader of the apostasy, the devil, and those who revolted with him, into which [fire] the Lord has declared those men shall be sent who have been set apart by themselves on His left hand. And this is what has been spoken by the prophet, "I am a jealous God, making peace, and creating evil things; thus making peace and friendship with those who repent and turn to Him, and bringing [them to] unity, but preparing for the impenitent, those who shun the light, eternal fire and outer darkness, which are evils indeed to those persons who fall into them.[678]

– Irenaeus of Lyons

"John's use of the symbol [of the lake of fire] shows that he views it as the alternative to the city of God, the new Jerusalem...Its significance for humanity thus begins with the new creation. That it does not have the meaning of annihilation is indicated by 20:10. The lake of fire signifies not extinction in opposition to existence, but torturous existence in the society of evil in opposition to life in the society of God."[679]

–G.R. Beasley-Murray

---

675 Augustine, "City of God," in *Basic Writings of St. Augustine* (Grand Rapids: Baker, 1992), 21, 23-24.

676 John Stott, *Evangelical Essentials* (Downers Grove, IL: InterVarsity, 1988), 316.

677 Robert A. Peterson, "A Traditionalist Response To John Stott's Arguments For Annihilationism," *Journal of the Evangelical Theological Society* 37:4 (December, 1994), 560.

678 Irenaeus of Lyons. (1885). *Irenæus against Heresies*. In A. Roberts, J. Donaldson, & A. C. Coxe (Eds.), *The Ante-Nicene Fathers: The Apostolic Fathers with Justin Martyr and Irenaeus* (Vol. 1, p. 523). Buffalo, NY: Christian Literature Company.

679 G. R. Beasley-Murray, *The Book of Revelation*, (Grand Rapids: Eerdmans, 1978), 304.

"Further, the magnitude of the punishment matches the magnitude of the sin...Now a sin that is against God is infinite; the higher the person against whom it is committed, the graver the sin—it is more criminal to strike a head of state than a private citizen—and God is of infinite greatness. Therefore an infinite punishment is deserved for a sin committed against him."[680]

–*Thomas Aquinas*

"Objection: An eternal hell seems to mean that God is not totally or finally victorious over evil. Heaven and hell seem coeternal forever. But this is Manichaean dualism, where good and evil exist as equal and opposite warring ultimates. In that case God is not omnipotent. This contradicts both Scripture and reason. It contradicts Scripture because Scripture says God will, in the end, be totally victorious over evil, and will be "all in all" (1 Cor 15:12–28, 54–57). It contradicts reason because it is inherent in the nature of evil to be self-destructive, not to last forever.

Reply: This objection...wrongly assumes that hell implies an eternal coexistence of good (heaven) and evil (hell). But coexistence implies a common field of some kind of time and/or place in which to coexist. But neither heaven nor hell are in time, in history. They are at the end of history. A parallel: another person's death can occur in my life's time, but my own death cannot. My own death ends my life's time. Whatever eternity is, it is not time, not even endless time.

Scripture is quite clear both that hell is eternal and that there is no eternal Manichaean dualism, no stalemate between good and evil, only God's final triumph. How both these doctrines can be true may not be clear from Scripture, but that they are both true is clear. This is given as our data, just as both divine predestination and human free will and responsibility are both given as data, but not how the two are to be reconciled. In both cases, our limited understanding of time and eternity prevents us from seeing the answer clearly."[681]

–*Peter Kreeft*

"Assuredly he may fear to die, who, not being regenerated of water and the Spirit, is delivered over to the fires of Gehenna; he may fear to die who is not enrolled in the cross and passion of Christ; he may fear to die, who from this death shall pass over to a second death; he may fear to die, whom on his departure from this world eternal flame shall torment with never-ending punishments."[682]

–*Cyprian of Carthage*

[680] Thomas Aquinas, *Summa Theologiae* (New York: McGraw-Hill, 1974), 1a2ae.87,4.

[681] Peter Kreeft, *Handbook on Christian Apologetics*, (Downers Grove: InterVarsity, 1994), 306-307.

[682] Cyprian of Carthage. (1886). On the Mortality. In A. Roberts, J. Donaldson, & A. C. Coxe (Eds.), R. E. Wallis (Trans.), *The Ante-Nicene Fathers: Fathers of the Third Century: Hippolytus, Cyprian, Novatian, Appendix* (Vol. 5, p. 472). Buffalo, NY: Christian Literature Company.

"All souls are immortal, even those of the wicked, for whom it were better that they were not deathless. For, punished with the endless vengeance of quenchless fire, and not dying, it is impossible for them to have a, period put to their misery."[683]

–Clement of Alexandria

"With regard to a complementary doctrine, the unconditional immortality of mankind has generally been universally accepted both in and outside of the church...We have found that so far back as we can penetrate there is evidence of the fact that it has been natural to man to believe in some sort of existence after death. From the fifth century A.D. until the latter half of the nineteenth century, no orthodox leader seriously challenged the doctrine of hell."[684]

–Richard Mayhue

"It is doubtful that there is a doctrine in the Bible easier to prove than that of eternal punishment."[685]

–S. Lewis Johnson

"We now come to the final phase of the tragic episode of sin—the ultimate and utter destruction of the unrepentant sinner if he willfully clings to his sin... The writers of the Old Testament seem to have exhausted the resources of the language at their command—the Hebrew tongue—to affirm the complete destruction of the intractable sinner. The major Hebrew verb roots (such as destroy, perish, consume, cut off, burn up) are literal, and are used to signify the total extinction, or excision, of such animate beings."[686]

–Le Roy Froom

"The history of the doctrine of universal salvation (or apokatastasis) is a remarkable one. Until the nineteenth century almost all Christian theologians taught the reality of eternal torment in hell. Here and there, outside the theological mainstream, were some who believed that the wicked would be finally annihilated (in its commonest form this is the doctrine of 'conditional immortality'). Even fewer were the advocates of universal salvation, though these few included some major theologians of the early church. Eternal punishment was firmly asserted in official creeds and confessions of the churches. It must have seemed as indispensable a part of universal Christian belief as the doctrines of the Trinity and the incarnation. Since 1800 this situation has entirely changed, and no traditional Christian doctrine has been so widely abandoned as that of eternal punishment. Its advocates among theologians today must be fewer than ever before. The alternative interpretation of hell as annihilation seems to have prevailed even among many of the more conservative theologians. Among the less conservative, universal salvation, either as hope or as dogma, is now so widely accepted that many

---

683 Clement of Alexandria. (1885). Fragments of Clemens Alexandrinus. In A. Roberts, J. Donaldson, & A. C. Coxe (Eds.), W. Wilson (Trans.), *The Ante-Nicene Fathers: Fathers of the Second Century: Hermas, Tatian, Athenagoras, Theophilus, and Clement of Alexandria (Entire)* (Vol. 2, p. 580). Buffalo, NY: Christian Literature Company.

684 Richard L. Mayhue, "Hell: Never, Forever, or Just a Little While?" *Master's Seminary Journal* 9:2 (Fall 98), 133.

685 S. Lewis Johnson, "God Gave Them Up," *Bibliotheca Sacra* 129 (April-June 1972), 131.

686 Le Roy Froom, *The Conditionalist Faith of our Fathers* [Washington, D.C.: Review and Herald, 1966], 1:105.

theologians assume it virtually without argument."[687]

–Richard Bauckham

We, however, so understand the soul's immortality as to believe it "lost," not in the sense of destruction, but of punishment, that is, in hell.[688]

–Tertullian

"The apostolic teaching is that the soul, having a substance and life of its own, shall, after its departure from the world, be rewarded according to its deserts, being destined to obtain either an inheritance of eternal life and blessedness, if its actions shall have procured this for it, or to be delivered up to eternal fire and punishments, if the guilt of its crimes shall have brought it down to this."[689]

–Origen

Some Miscellaneous Statements from Jonathan Edwards[690]

This doctrine is indeed awful and dreadful yet 'tis of God.

'Tis the infinite almighty God that shall become the fire of the furnace.

It will be a dreadful sight to them when they come to their bodies again, those bodies which were formerly approved by them as the organs and instruments of sin and wickedness...and they shall very unwillingly enter into them.

The symbols are very probably literal. The body is literal and there is no reason why it shouldn't be taken this way. After all, it takes real fire to burn heaven and earth.

'Tis probable that this earth after the conflagration shall be the place of the damned. It is fit that man should suffer in body and soul because he was created such and sinned in both. In hell man is deprived of all pleasure derived through the sense; in fact, he is tormented through each sense. Still the torments of the soul will be greater.

The all-important feature of heaven and of hell is God himself. He is the one who makes heaven, heaven. He is the one who makes hell, hell. Indeed, according to Edwards, he is hell and he is heaven. Eternity for sinner and saint will be spent in the immediate presence and sight of God. God will be the hell of one and the heaven of the other.

After we have said our utmost and thought our utmost, all that we have said or thought is but a faint shadow of what really is.

---

[687] Richard Bauckham, "Universalism: A Historical Survey," *Themelios* (January 1979), 48.

[688] Tertullian. (1885). On the Resurrection of the Flesh. In A. Roberts, J. Donaldson, & A. C. Coxe (Eds.), P. Holmes (Trans.), *The Ante-Nicene Fathers: Latin Christianity: Its Founder, Tertullian* (Vol. 3, p. 569). Buffalo, NY: Christian Literature Company.

[689] Origen. (1885). De Principiis. In A. Roberts, J. Donaldson, & A. C. Coxe (Eds.), F. Crombie (Trans.), *The Ante-Nicene Fathers: Fathers of the Third Century: Tertullian, Part Fourth; Minucius Felix; Commodian; Origen, Parts First and Second* (Vol. 4, p. 240). Buffalo, NY: Christian Literature Company.

[690] I have gleaned the statements from Edwards from John Gerstner's discussion of Edwards' theology in *The Rational Biblical Theology of Jonathan Edwards* (Powhatan, VA: Berea Publications, 1991), III:501-540. I am enamored with Edwards' way of putting things.

Their pain is a mixture of sorrow and rage.

The damned in hell would give the world to have the number of their sins one less. The sinner spends all his time here gathering fuel for his own fire there. The longer sinners live the more wrath they accumulate. It would be far better for the unawakened to have spent the time in hell, than on earth. It would be better for you if your breath was taken from your nostrils, this day, and that you were nailed up in your coffin and that your would should be amongst the damned this night.

All men partake equally of original sin, but men do not partake equally of actual sins. After they have endured misery a thousand years they may have a more dreadful sense of an eternity of misery than they had at first.

Let what has been said on this subject lead sinners to consider what they are ripening for. There are two kinds of persons that are here in this world in a preparatory state, elect and reprobates.

Both are continued here in a state of preparation for an eternal state. Elect are here to be prepared for heaven. Reprobates are preparing for hell. They are ripening. And there are none who stand still, neither saints nor sinners.

As sinners go on sinning, they become more and more adapted to their new home.

Wicked men in hell will remember how things were with them here in this world.

How will you bear to hear them singing for joy of heart, when your work day and night will be nothing but to cry for sorrow of heart and howl.

Eternity is the sting of the doctrine. [He lists some of eternity's properties: 1) it cannot be divided into parts, 2) there is no half of eternity, 3) it cannot be distinguished by periods such as youth and old age, 4) a thousand ages is as much less as a minute, 5) the eternality of hell cannot be made more or less by addition or subtraction, 6) it will forever only be beginning].

One reason hell is eternal is that their nature is unchanged therefore they continue sinning. While they are suffering they continue sinning and so contract new debt, and again while they are paying that they contract another and so in infinitum.

God won't be any more inclined to pity them after they have lain there millions of ages than he was at the first moment.

New Testament Book Purpose Statements

BOOK	PURPOSE STATEMENT
Matthew	Matthew records selected events in the life of Christ in order to demonstrate that He is the covenanted Messiah and to shed light on the Kingdom program in light of the rejection of the King so that persecuted Jewish Christians would be encouraged and receive instruction on how they should live in the present age.
Mark	Mark presents the deity of Christ in the role of a servant of God in order to give the suffering Roman church a pattern of discipleship in the midst of adversity so that they would be encouraged to stand as strong disciples during difficult times.
Luke	Luke records selected events from the life of Christ in order to confirm Theophilus in the faith and to present Christ as the Son of Man to the Gentile world so that they would know that they are included in the Kingdom program and offered salvation.
John	John records selected signs and discourses from the ministry of Jesus in order to demonstrate that He is the Son of God Who reveals the Father so that his readers would put their faith in Him and gain a dynamic and growing eternal life.
Acts	Luke records the events surrounding the sovereign progression of the Gospel message From Jews in Jerusalem to Gentiles in Rome in order to show that the kingdom will be populated with believers from every race.
Romans	Paul presents a comprehensive statement of justification by faith which is available to both Jew and Gentile in order to show that God is just in His dealings with both groups in order to unify them thereby gaining support for his Spanish mission.
First Corinthians	Paul addresses divisions, disorders, and difficulties in the Corinthian church in order to preserve unity, purity, and understanding of Christian truth in the local church.
Second Corinthians	Paul gives an exposition of his ministry, instruction concerning the collection, and a defense of his apostleship in order to answer accusations brought against him by his adversaries to show the superiority of his ministry over theirs, and spur the Corinthians to obedience and renewed commitment to the Lord and himself.

Galatians	Paul writes concerning his apostleship and justification through faith in order to demonstrate his apostolic authority and show that the believer is free from the law in both justification and sanctification so that his readers would not return to the bondage of the Law.
Ephesians	Paul presents the spiritual blessings which God bestowed on the believers and how this is executed in the believers' individual and corporate position in the body of Christ in order to spur the Ephesian Christians on to love and unity with one another.
Philippians	Paul instructs the Philippians regarding the advance of the gospel amid persecution, the need for humility and unity, and opposition to false teachers in order to encourage them to a firm and united stand in their witness for the gospel.
Colossians	Paul explains the preeminence of the person and work Christ and how this is sufficient for life in order to warn the Colossians about the false teaching they were hearing and move them ahead on the proper road to maturity.
First Thessalonians	Paul thanks God for the Thessalonians, reviews his ministry among them, and seeks to instruct them in certain areas in order to renew their confidence in him and enable them to persevere in the midst of persecution through a better understanding of practice and doctrine in light of the Lord's imminent return.
Second Thessalonians	Paul writes to correct the error in the church concerning the Day of the Lord in order to return some of them to proper conduct in light of this doctrine.
First Timothy	Paul instructs Timothy regarding life in the local church and his responsibilities in it so that the church would remain orderly in practice and pure in doctrine as it proclaimed the Word of God to the world.
Second Timothy	Paul charges Timothy with various duties and responsibilities in his ministry in order to urge him to remain faithful in his duty and calling as a minister of the Gospel in the face of hardship so that he would receive a full reward at the judgment seat.
Titus	Paul instructs Titus on the appointment of elders, the correction of false teachers, and the godly behavior that should characterize the church so that the church would be set in order and the believers would love in a Christian manner.
Philemon	Paul gives thanks to God for Philemon and pleads with him to receive Onesimus back with forgiveness in order to show the way faith in Christ affects the treatment of people.

Hebrews	The author demonstrates the superiority of Christ over the Levitical system in order to urge his readers to move on in maturity and not go back into the old order despite persecution so that they would avoid the chastening hand of God and receive a full reward in the eschaton.
James	James presents various exhortations and instructions on righteous living in order to show the Jewish Christians of the diaspora how faith operates to produce the righteousness of the Law during this new age.
First Peter	Peter writes to persecuted Christians about their salvation, subjection, and suffering in order to encourage them in the light of their future glory and to exhort them to righteous living in a sinful world.
Second Peter	Peter presents his readers with a reminder of the safeguards they have against apostasy as well as a denunciation of the apostates in order to fortify them against these false teachers so that they would continue to grow in their faith.
First John	John warns his readers about false doctrine and the importance of true doctrine in order to lead them into a joyful fellowship with God.
Second John	The purpose of this letter is to commend this church for its love and loyalty to the truth, and to exhort them to not extend hospitality to heretics.
Third John	John commends Gains for his hospitality and condemns Diotrephes his lack of hospitality in order to encourage support for preachers of the truth.
Jude	Jude gives a thorough description and scathing denunciation of false teachers so that his readers would recognize them and see the necessity of contending for the truth so that they would be presented perfect before the presence of God.
Revelation	John presents a revelation of Jesus Christ as it is seen in His ethical demands and events surrounding His Second Coming in order to encourage his readers to perseverance and obedience in light of the ultimate victory that would transpire when Christ returns.

New Testament Book Backgroud Summary

BOOK	AUTHOR	DATE	ORIGIN	DESTINATION	OCCASION
Matthew	Matthew	ca AD 50[691]	?? Palestine, Antioch, Syria	Jewish converts	Kingdom not established with the coming of the Messiah
Mark	Mark	AD 64-68	Rome	Gentile Christians	Persecution under Nero
Luke	Luke	AD 58-60	??	Theophilus	Theophilus' need for instruction
John	Apostle John, son of Zebedee	ca AD 85-95	Ephesus	Ephesian Gentiles	Confusion over Christ's person and life he came to offer
Acts	Luke	AD 60-62	Rome	Theophilus	Continuation of instruction to Theophilus on a new scroll
Romans	Paul	AD 57	Corinth	Jews/Gentiles (mostly) in Rome	The projected trip of Phoebe to Rome
First Corinthians	Paul	AD 54-55	Ephesus	Christians in Corinth	Paul hears of problems in the church
Second Corinthians	Paul	AD 55	Macedonia	Christians in Corinth	Though conditions had improved in Corinth, there was still a faction opposed to Paul
Galatians	Paul	AD 48-49	Antioch of Syria	Greek believers in the Roman province of Galatia (Southern Galatian theory)	The Galatians' post-conversion enthusiasm had waned due to the teaching of the Judaizers
Ephesians	Paul	AD 60-62	Rome	Christians in Ephesus	A need for unity
Philippians	Paul	AD 60-62	Rome	Christians in Philippi	The visit of Epaphroditus
Colossians	Paul	AD 60-62	Rome	Christians in Colosse	The Colossian Heresy
First Thessalonians	Paul	AD 51	Corinth	Christians in Thessalonica	Doctrinal/ behavioral problems and distrust of Paul
Second Thessalonians	Paul	AD 51	Corinth	Christians in Thessalonica	Misinformation on the Day of the Lord

691 Matthean priority.

First Timothy	Paul	AD 62-67	Macedonia	Timothy	Timothy's desire to leave Ephesus and disorder in the church
Second Timothy	Paul	AD 67	Rome	Timothy	Danger of being a Christian with temptation to defect
Titus	Paul	AD 62-67	Nicopolis	Titus	Titus' mission of setting the churches in order in Crete
Philemon	Paul	AD 60-62	Rome	Philemon	The conversion of an escaped slave named Onesimus
Hebrews	?	AD 68-69	?	Jewish Christians in Palestine/ Jerusalem (Rome is also a common view)	Spiritual retrogression due to difficulties
James	James, the half-brother of Jesus	ca AD 45	Jerusalem (?)	Jewish Christians of the Diaspora	Period of Jewish transition out from under the Law
First Peter	Peter	ca AD 64	"Babylon"	Jewish readership primarily in Asia Minor	Christians scattered throughout the Empire during a time of persecution
Second Peter	Peter	AD 64-68	Rome (?)	Jewish readership primarily in Asia Minor	Peter knew his time was short and was aware of the danger of false teachers
First John	Apostle John, son of Zebedee	AD 80-85	Ephesus	Circular letter to believers around Ephesus	False doctrinal system in Asia Minor
Second John	Apostle John, son of Zebedee	AD 80-85	Ephesus	Circular letter to believers around Ephesus	False, itinerant preachers
Third John	Apostle John, son of Zebedee	AD 80-85	Ephesus	Gaius	Lack of proper hospitality
Jude	Judas, half-brother of Christ	AD 67-80	Egypt or Palestine	Christian Jews in Palestine (?)	Infiltration of false teachers
Revelation	Apostle John, son of Zebedee	AD 90-95	Island of Patmos	Churches in Asia Minor	The direct command of the Lord in light of persecution and compromise in the churches

BIBLIOGRAPHY

1 Clement. Accessed January 2014. http://www.ntslibrary.com/PDF%20Books/First%20Epistle%20of%20Clement%20to%20the%20Corinthians.pdf.

Achtemeier, Paul J. "Provinces." In *Harper's Bible Dictionary*. San Francisco: Harper & Row, 1985.

Adams, Sean. "Paul the Roman Citizen: Roman Citizenship in the Ancient World and Its Importance for Understanding Acts 22:22-29." Accessed June 16, 2014. https://www.academia.edu/3793625/Paul_the_Roman_Citizen_Roman_Citizenship_in_the_Ancient_World_and_its_Importance_for_Understanding_Acts_22_22-29.

"Against Heresies (Book III, Chapter 1)." CHURCH FATHERS: Against Heresies, III.1 (St. Irenaeus). Accessed August 22, 2014. http://www.newadvent.org/fathers/0103301.htm.

Aland, Kurt, and Barbara Aland. *The Text of the New Testament*. Grand Rapids: Eerdmans, 1987.

Alexander, Ralph. *Ezekiel*. Chicago: Moody Press, 1976.

Alford, Henry. *Alford's Greek Testament*. Vol. 3. Baker: Grand Rapids, 1980.

Allen, Leslie. *The Books of Joel, Obadiah, Jonah, and Amos*. Grand Rapids: Eerdmans, 1983.

_____, Leslie C. *Ezekiel*. Waco, TX: Word Books, 1994.

Allis, Oswald T. *Prophecy and the Church: An Examination of the Claim of Dispensationalists That the Christian Church Is a Mystery Parenthesis Which Interrupts the Fulfilment to Israel of the Kingdom Prophecies of the Old Testament*. Philadelphia: Presbyterian and Reformed Pub., 1945.

Anderson, Megory, and Philip Culbertson. "The Inadequacy of the Christian Doctrine of Atonement." *Anglican Theological Review* 7 (1977).

Anderson, Robert. *The Coming Prince*. Grand Rapids: Kregel, 1984.

"Antonia Fortress - First Century Jerusalem." Antonia Fortress. Accessed June 21, 2014. http://www.bible-history.com/jerusalem/firstcenturyjerusalem_antonia_fortress.html.

The Apocrypha: Revised Standard Version of the Old Testament: Translated from the Greek and Latin Tongues, Being the Version Set Forth A.D. 1611, Revised A.D. 1894, Compared with the Most Ancient Authorities and Revised A.D. 1957. New York: T. Nelson, 1957.

Appianus. *The Histories of Appian: The Civil Wars*. Edited by E. H. Warmington. Loeb Classical Library. Cambridge, MA: Harvard Univ. Press, 1912.

Apuleius. *The Golden Ass*. Vol. 3. The Loeb Classical Library.

Aquinas, Thomas. *Summa Theologiae*. New York: McGraw-Hill, 1974.

Archer, Gleason. *A Survey of Old Testament Introduction*. Chicago: Moody Press, 1974.

Aristotle. *Politics - Aristotle*. S.l.: Nuvision Publications, 2009.

Arndt, William, F. Wilbur Gingrich, Frederick W. Danker, and Walter Bauer. *A Greek-English Lexicon of the New Testament and Other Early Christian Literature: A Translation and Adaptation of the Fourth Revised and Augmented Edition of Walter Bauer's Griechisch-deutsches Wörterbuch Zu Den Schriften Des Neuen Testaments Und Der Übrigen Urchristlichen Literatur*. Chicago: University of Chicago Press, 1979.

Arnold, Clinton. "Acts." In *Zondervan Illustrated Bible Backgrounds Commentary*. Grand Rapids: Zondervan, 2002.

_____. "Colossians." In *Zondervan Illustrated Bible Backgrounds Commentary*. Grand Rapids: Zondervan, 2002.

_____. "Revelation." In *Zondervan Illustrated Bible Backgrounds Commentary*, 317. Grand Rapids, MI: Zondervan, 2002.

Augustine. "City of God." In *Basic Writings of St. Augustine*. Grand Rapids: Baker, 1992.

_____. "On Christian Doctrine." In *A Select Library of the Nicene and Post-Nicene Fathers of the Christian Church, First Series, Volume II: St. Augustin's City of God and Christian Doctrine*, translated by J. F. Shaw. Buffalo: Christian Literature Company, 1887.

_____. "Reply to Faustus the Manichæan." Translated by R. Stothert. In *A Select Library of the Nicene and Post-Nicene Fathers of the Christian Church, First Series, Volume IV: St. Augustine: The Writings against the Manichaeans and against the Donatists*, edited by P. Schaff. Buffalo: Christian Literature Company, 1900.

Bailey, Kenneth. "The Manger and the Inn: The Cultural Background of Luke 2:7." *Bible and Spade* 20, no. 4 (Fall 2007).

Balsdon, J. P. V. D. *Romans and Aliens*. London: Duckworth, 1979.

Baltensweiler, Heinrich. *Die Verklärung Jesu: Abhandlungen Zur Theologie Des Alten Und Neuen Testaments*. Zurich: Zwingli-Verlag, 1959.

Barclay, John. "Mirror Reading a Polemic Letter: Galatians as a Test Case." *Journal for the Study of the New Testament* 31 (1988).

Barclay, William. *The Acts of the Apostles*. Philadelphia: Westminster Press, 1976.

_____. *The Letter to the Hebrews*. Philadelphia: Westminster Press, 1976.

_____. *The Letters to the Corinthians*. Philadelphia: Westminster Press, 1975.

_____. *The Letters to Timothy, Titus, and Philemon*. Philadelphia: Westminster Press, 1975.

_____. *The Revelation of John*. Philadelphia: Westminster Press, 1976.

Barker, Glenn. "1, 2, 3 John." In *Expositor's Bible Commentary*. Vol. 12. G: Zondervan, 1981.

Barnes, Albert. *Notes on the Old Testament: Isaiah*. Grand Rapids: Baker, 1950.

Barnett, Paul. *Jesus & the Rise of Early Christianity: A History of New Testament times*. Downers Grove, IL: InterVarsity Press, 1999.

Barr, James. "Abba Isn't Daddy." *Journal of Theological Studies* 39, no. 1 (1988).

Barrett, C. K. *A Commentary on the First Epistle to the Corinthians*. New York: Harper & Row, 1968.

Barth, Karl, and Edwyn Clement Hoskyns. *The Epistle to the Romans*. London: Oxford University Press, H. Milford, 1933.

Bauckham, Richard. *2 Peter, Jude*. Word Biblical Commentary. Dallas: Word, 1988.

_____. "Universalism: A Historical Survey." *Themelios*, January 1979.

Bauer, Walter, William Arndt, Felix Wilbur. Gingrich, and Frederick W. Danker. *A Greek-english Lexicon of the New Testament and Other Early Christian Literature*. 2nd ed. Chicago: University of Chicago Press, 1979.

Beale, G. K. "The Millennium in Revelation 20:1-10: An Amillennial Perspective." *Criswell Theological Review* 11, no. 1 (Fall 2013): 29.

Beasley-Murray, G. R. "Ezekiel." In *New Bible Commentary*. Wheaton, IL: Tyndale Press, 1953.

_____. *The Book of Revelation*. Grand Rapids: Eerdmans, 1999.

Beecher, W.J. "The Day of Jehovah in Joel." *The Homiletical Review* 18 (1889).

Behm, Johannes. "Glw/ssa." In *Theological Dictionary of the New Testament*. Vol. I. Grand Rapids: Eerdmans, 1964-74.

Beitzel, B. "The Right of the Firstborn in the Old Testament." In *A Tribute to Gleason Archer*. Chicago: Moody Press, 1986.

Berding, Kenneth. *What Are Spiritual Gifts? Rethinking the Conventional View*. Grand Rapids: Kregel, 2006.

Berenbaum, Michael, and Fred Skolnik, eds. *Encyclopaedia Judaica*. Vol. 2. Detroit: Thomson/Gale, 2007.

Berkhof, L. *Systematic Theology*. Grand Rapids: Eerdmans, 1979.

Berkouwer, G. C. *Studies in Dogmatics: Faith and Justification*. Grand Rapids: Eerdmans, 1954.

Bernardin, Joseph. "The Transfiguration." *Journal of Biblical Literature* 52 (1933).

Bigg, Charles. *A Critical and Exegetical Commentary on St. Peter and St. Jude*. International Critical Commentary. Edinburgh: T. & T. Clark, 1901.

Bing, Charles. "Why Lordship Faith Misses the Mark for Discipleship." *Journal of the Grace Evangelical Society* 12, no. 2 (1999).

_____. "Why Lordship Faith Misses the Mark for Salvation." *Journal of the Grace Evangelical Society* 12, no. 1 (1999).

Bird, Michael. "The Crucifixion of Jesus as the Fulfillment of Mark 9:1." *Trinity Journal* 24 (2003).

Blaiklock, E. M. *The World of the New Testament*. London: Ark, 1981.

Blinzler, Josef. *The Trial of Jesus; the Jewish and Roman Proceedings against Jesus Christ Described and Assessed from the Oldest Accounts*. Westminster, MD: Newman Press, 1959.

Blomberg, Craig. *Interpreting the Parables*. Downers Grove, IL: InterVarsity Press, 1990.

_____. *James*. Zondervan Exegetical Commentary on the New Testament. Grand Rapids: Zondervan, 2008.

_____. *Matthew*. Nashville: Broadman Press, 1992.

Bock, Darrell L. *Acts*. Grand Rapids, MI: Baker Academic, 2007.

_____. *Jesus According to Scripture: Restoring the Portrait from the Gospels*. Grand Rapids, MI: Baker Academic, 2002.

_____. *Luke: Volume 1: 1:1-9:50. Baker Exegetical Commentary on the New Testament*. Grand Rapids, MI: Baker Books, 1999.

_____. *Luke: Volume 2: 9:51-24:53. Baker Exegetical Commentary on the New Testament*. Grand Rapids, MI: Baker, 1998.

Bock, Darrell L., and Gregory J. Herrick. *Jesus in Context: Background Readings for Gospel Study*. Grand Rapids: Baker, 2005.

Boobyer, G. H. *St. Mark and the Transfiguration Story*. Edinburgh: T. & T. Clark, 1942.

Boston, Thomas. *Human Nature in Its Fourfold State: Of Primitive Integrity, Entire Depravity, Begun Recovery, and Consummate Happiness or Misery*. Carlisle, PA: Banner of Truth Trust, 1989.

Botterweck, G. Johannes., Helmer Ringgren, John T. Willis, Heinz-Josef Fabry, David E. Green, and Douglas W. Stott. *Theological Dictionary of the Old Testament*. Grand Rapids, MI: Eerdmans, 1974.

Bouquet, A. C. *Everyday Life in New Testament times*. New York: Charles Scribner, 1955.

Boyer, James. "Third (and Fourth) Class Conditions." *Grace Theological Journal* 3, no. 2 (1982).

Brettler, Marc A., and Michael Poliakoff. "Rabbi Simeon Ben Lakish at the Gladiator's Banquet: Rabbinic Observations on the Roman Arena." *The Harvard Theological Review* 83, no. 1

(1990): 94-97.

Bright, J. "The Apodictic Prohibition: Some Observations." *Journal of Biblical Literature* 92 (1973).

Brisco, T. V. "The Hellenistic Period." In *Holman Bible Atlas*. Nashville, TN: Broadman & Holman, 1998.

Bromiley, Geoffrey William. *The International Standard Bible Encyclopedia*. Grand Rapids, MI: Eerdmans, 1980.

Broneer, Oscar. "The Apostle Paul and the Isthmian Games." *The Biblical Archaeologist* 25 (1962).

_____. "Corinth: Center of Paul's Missionary Work in Greece." *The Biblical Archaeologist* 14 (1951).

_____. "The Isthmian Victory Crown." *American Journal of Archaeology* 66 (1962).

_____. "Paul and the Pagan Cults at Isthmia." *Harvard Theological Review* 64 (1971).

Brooks, James A. *Mark, New American Commentary*. Nashville: Broadman & Holman, 1991.

Brower, Kent. "Mark 9:1: Seeing the Kingdom in Power." *Journal for the Study of the New Testament* 2 (1979).

Brown, Colin. "Day of the Lord." In *The Zondervan Pictorial Encyclopedia of the Bible*. Grand Rapids: Zondervan, 1975.

_____. *Philosophy & the Christian Faith: A Historical Sketch from the Middle Ages to the Present Day*. Downers Grove, IL: InterVarsity Press, 1968.

Brown, Ernest. *The Pastoral Epistles*. London: Methuen, 1917.

Brown, Francis, S. R. Driver, and Charles Briggs. *A Hebrew and English Lexicon of the Old Testament*. Oxford: Clarendon Press, 1951.

Brown, Francis, S. R. Driver, Charles A. Briggs, Edward Robinson, and Wilhelm Gesenius. *A Hebrew and English Lexicon of the Old Testament, with an Appendix Containing the Biblical Aramaic*. Oxford: Clarendon Press, 1952.

Brown, Raymond. *The Birth of the Messiah: A Commentary on the Infancy Narratives in Matthew and Luke*. Garden City: Image Books, 1979.

_____. *The Gospel According to John I-XII The Anchor Bible*. Garden City, NY: Doubleday, 1966.

Bruce, Alexander Balmain. *The Training of the Twelve*. Grand Rapids: Kregel Publications, 1971.

Bruce, F. F. *The Book of the Acts*. New International Commentary on the New Testament. Grand Rapids, MI: Eerdmans, 1980.

_____. *Commentary on the Epistle to the Colossians*. Grand Rapids: Eerdmans, 1980.

_____. *The Gospels and Epistles of John*. Grand Rapids: Eerdmans, 1994.

_____. *New Testament History*. Garden City, NY: Doubleday, 1980.

Brunner, Emil. *The Theology of Crisis*. New York: C. Scribner's Sons, 1929.

Bullinger, E. W. "Matthew." In *The Companion Bible*. London: Oxford University Press, N.d.

Burge, Gary M., Gene L. Green, and Lynn H. Cohick. *The New Testament in Antiquity*. Grand Rapids, MI: Zondervan, 2009.

_____. *Jesus and the Jewish Festivals*. Grand Rapids, MI: Zondervan, 2012.

Burke, G. T. "Sermon on the Mount." In *Evangelical Dictionary of Theology*. Grand Rapids: Baker, 1984.

Burton, Ernest. "The Politarchs." *The American Journal of Theology* II (July 1898).

_____. "The Study of New Testament Words." *The Old and New Testament Student*, March 1891.

Bush, George. *Leviticus*. Reprint ed. Minneapolis: James Family Christian Publishers, 1979.

Buttrick, George Arthur., ed. *Interpreter's Bible*. Vol. 9. New York: Abingdon, 1954.

Caird, G. B. "The Transfiguration." *The Expository times* 67 (1956).

Calvin, Jean, and William Pringle. *Commentary on a Harmony of the Evangelists, Matthew, Mark, and Luke*. Grand Rapids: W.B. Eerdmans Pub., 1949.

Calvin, John. *Commentaries on the Epistles of Paul to the Galatians and Ephesians*. Calvin's Commentaries. Baker: Grand Rapids, 1979.

_____. "The Epistle Dedicatory to Simon Grynaeus: A Man Worthy of All Honour." In *Commentaries on the Epistle of Paul the Apostle to the Romans*, edited by Henry Beveridge. Grand Rapids, MI: Baker Academic, 1979.

_____. *Epistle to the Romans*. Calvin's Commentaries. Grand Rapids: Baker, 1979.

_____. *The First Epistle of John*. Calvin's Commentaries. Grand Rapids: Baker, 1979.

_____. *Joel-Nahum*. Calvin's Commentaries. Grand Rapids: Baker, 1979.

Campbell, Donald. "Interpretation and Exposition of the Sermon on the Mount." PhD diss., Dallas Theological Seminary, 1953.

Campbell, Ken. "What Was Jesus' Occupation?" *Journal of the Evangelical Theological Society* 48, no. 3 (September 2005): 502-19.

Carcopino, Jérôme, Henry T. Rowell, and E. O. Lorimer. *Daily Life in Ancient Rome*. NY: Bantam, 1971.

Carson, D. A. *Exegetical Fallacies*. Grand Rapids: Baker, 1984.

_____. *From Sabbath to Lord's Day: A Biblical, Historical, and Theological Investigation*. Grand Rapids, MI: Zondervan, 1982.

_____. *The Gospel According to John*. Grand Rapids: Eerdmans, 1991.

_____. "Matthew." In *The Expositor's Bible Commentary*. Vol. 8. Grand Rapids: Zondervan, 1984.

_____. *The Sermon on the Mount: An Evangelical Exposition*. Grand Rapids: Baker, 1984.

Cassell's New Latin Dictionary. NY: Funk & Wagnalls, 1968.

Catechism of the Catholic Church. Accessed October 2013. Logos 5.

Cerny, L. *The Day of Yahweh and Some Relevant Problems*. Nd.

Chafer, Lewis S. "Christology." In *Systematic Theology*. Vol. 5. Dallas: Dallas Seminary Press, 1947-48.

_____. *Systematic Theology*. Dallas, TX: Dallas Seminary Press, 1978.

Chancey, Mark, and Eric Meyers. "How Jewish Was Sepphoris in Jesus' Time?" In *Israel: An Archeological Journey*, edited by Sarah Yeomans. Washington D.C.: Biblical Archeological Society, 2009. Accessed July 21, 2014. http://www.bib-arch.org/e-books/pdf/israel.pdf.

Chary, T. "Le Temple D'Ezechiel." *Le Monde De La Bible* 40 (1985).

Chilton, B. D. "The Transfiguration: Dominical Assurance and Apostolic Vision." *New Testament Studies* 27 (1980).

Chisholm, Robert. "A Theology of Isaiah." In *A Biblical Theology of the Old Testament*. Chicago: Moody Press, 1991.

"Christ Preaching through Noah: 1 Peter 3:19-20 in the Light of Dominant Themes in Jewish Literature." *Trinity Journal* 7, no. 2 (Fall 1986).

Chrysostom, Dio. *Concerning Virtue*. Heinemann: William, 1961.

_____. *Concerning Virtue*. London: William Heinemann, 1961.

_____. *The First Discourse on Kingship*. Vol. 1. Accessed June 16, 2014. http://penelope.uchicago.edu /Thayer/E/Roman/Texts/Dio_Chrysostom/Discourses/1.

_____. *The Twenty-First Discourse: To the People of Rhodes*. London: William Heinemann, 1961.

Chrysostom, John. "Commentary of St. John Chrysostom, Archbishop of Constantinople on the Epistle of St. Paul the Apostle to the Galatians." In *A Select Library of the Nicene and Post-Nicene Fathers of the Christian Church*, edited by Philip Schaff. Logos 5.

Cicero. *Against Verres*.

_____. "In Defense of Cluentius." Accessed June 2014. http://www.perseus.tufts.edu/hopper/.

_____. *The Letters of Cicero*. Translated by Evelyn S. Shuckburgh. Vol. 1. London: George Bell & Sons, 1899.

_____. *Speech before Roman Citizens on Behalf of Gaius Rabirius, Defendant against the Charge of Treason*.

Clement of Alexandria. "Fragments of Clemens Alexandrinus." *Logos 5*.

Clifford, Richard J. *The Cosmic Mountain in Canaan and the Old Testament*. Cambridge, MA: Harvard University Press, 1972.

Coleridge, Samuel. *Table Talk*. Oxford: Oxford University Press, N.d.

Conybeare, William John, and J. S. Howson. *The Life and Epistles of St. Paul*. Grand Rapids: W.B. Eerdmans Pub., 1966.

Coogan, Michael. *Studies from Ancient Canaan*. Philadelphia: Westminster Press, 1978.

Cooke, G. A. *The Book of Ezekiel*. International Critical Commentary. Edinburgh: T. & T. Clark, 1936.

Cooper, Lamar, Sr. *Ezekiel*. The New American Commentary. Nashville, TN: Broadman & Holman, 1994.

Cothenet, E. "Influence D'Ezechiel Sur La Spiritualite De Qumran." *Revue De Qumran* 13 (1988).

"Council of Trent." Accessed February 12, 2014. http://www.newadvent.org/cathen/15030.

Countess, Robert. "The Translation of QEOS in the New World Translation." *Bulletin of the Evangelical Theological Society* 10, no. 3 (1967): 160.

Craig, William L. "Middle Knowledge." Accessed August 2014. http://www.leaderu.com/offices/billcraig/docs/middle.

Craigie, Peter C. *Ezekiel*. Philadelphia: Westminster Press, 1983.

Cranfield, C. E. B. *The Gospel According to Saint Mark, an Introduction and Commentary*. Cambridge: University Press, 1959.

_____. *Romans: Volume I I-VIII*. International Critical Commentary. Edinburgh: T. & T. Clark, 1985.

_____. *Romans Volume II IX-XVI*. International Critical Commentary. Edinburgh: T. & T. Clark, 1979.

Crawford, Thomas J. *The Doctrine of Holy Scripture Respecting the Doctrine of the Atonement*. New York: Blackwood, 1888.

Cyprian of Carthage. "On the Mortality." *Logos 5.*

Dalton, William. *Christ's Proclamation to the Spirits*. Rome: Editrice Pontificio Istituto Biblico, 1989.

Danby, Herbert. *The Mishnah.* Oxford: Clarendon Press, 1933.

Davids, Peter. *The Epistle of James: A Commentary on the Greek Text*. Grand Rapids: Eerdmans, 1982.

Davidson, A. B. "The Epistle to the Hebrews." In *Handbooks for Bible Classes and Private Students*. Edinburgh: T. & T. Clark, 1882.

_____. *Ezekiel.* Cambridge: University Press, 1924.

_____. *The Theology of the Old Testament*. Edinburgh: T. & T. Clark, 1904.

Davies, Douglas. "An Interpretation of Sacrifice in Leviticus." *Zeitschrift Fur Die Alttestamentliche Wissenschaft* 89 (1977).

Day, John. "Coals of Fire in Romans 12:19-20." *Bibliotheca Sacra* 160 (October 2003).

Decker, Rodney. Address, Council of Dispensational Hermeneutics, Baptist Bible Seminary, Clarks Summit, September 2013.

_____. ""The Use of Euvqu, J ('immediately') in Mark"" *Journal of Ministry and Theology* 1, no. 1 (1997): 90-121.

Deines, Roland. "The Pharisees—Good Guys with Bad Press." *Biblical Archaeology Review*, July/August 2013.

Deissmann, Adolf, and Lionel R. M. Strachan. *St. Paul; a Study in Social and Religious History*. London: Hodder and Stoughton, 1912.

_____. "Appendix II: On the Altar of an Unknown God." In *St. Paul; a Study in Social and Religious History*. London: Hodder and Stoughton, 1912.

_____. *Light from the Ancient East; the New Testament Illustrated by Recently Discovered Texts of the Graeco-Roman World.* Grand Rapids: Baker Books, 1978.

Derickson, Gary W., and Earl D. Radmacher. *The Disciplemaker: What Matters Most to Jesus*. Salem, OR: Charis Press, 2001.

DeSilva, David Arthur. *An Introduction to the New Testament: Contexts, Methods & Ministry Formation*. Downers Grove, IL: InterVarsity Press, 2004.

_____. *An Introduction to the New Testament: Contexts, Methods & Ministry Formation.* Downers Grove, IL: InterVarsity Press, 2004.

Dewar, Lindsay. "The Biblical Use of the Term Blood." *Journal of Theological Studies* 4 (1953).

Dibelius, Martin. *James*. Philadelphia: Fortress Press, 1976.

Dillow, Joseph. *The Reign of the Servant Kings*. Hayesville: Schoettle Publishing, 1992.

Doctrine and Covenants. Accessed May 2014. https://www.lds.org/scriptures/dc-testament.

Dodd, C. H. *The Parables of the Kingdom*. London: Nisbet, 1936.

Doriani, Daniel. "A History of the Interpretation of 1 Timothy 2." In *Women in the Church: A Fresh Analysis of 1 Timothy 2:9-15*. Grand Rapids: Baker, 1995.

Dosker, Henry. "Day of the Lord." In *International Standard Bible Encyclopedia*. Grand Rapids: Eerdmans, 1980.

Douglas, J. D. *The New International Dictionary of the Christian Church*. Grand Rapids: Zondervan Pub., 1981.

Drees, Ludwig. *Olympia; Gods, Artists, and Athletes*. New York: Praeger, 1968.

Driver, G. R. "Three Technical Terms in the Pentateuch." *Journal of Semitic Studies* 2 (1956).

Dunn, James. *The Epistles to the Colossians and to Philemon*. New International Greek Testament Commentary. Grand Rapids: Eerdmans, 1996.

Durant, Will, and Ariel Durant. *The Lessons of History*. New York: Simon and Schuster, 1968.

Durant, Will. *The Story of Philosophy*. New York: Simon and Schuster, 1961.

Duty, Guy. *Divorce and Remarriage*. Minneapolis, MN: Bethany House Publ., 1983.

Dyer, Charles. "Biblical Meaning of 'Fulfillment'" In *Issues in Dispensationalism*. Chicago: Moody Press, 1994.

_____. "Ezekiel." In *The Bible Knowledge Commentary*. Wheaton: Victor Books, 1985.

_____. "The Identity of Babylon in Revelation 17-18: Part 1." *Bibliotheca Sacra* 144, no. 575 (July 1987): 305-16.

_____. "The Identity of Babylon in Revelation 17-18: Part 2." *Bibliotheca Sacra* 144, no. 576 (October 1987): 433-49.

_____. "Do the Synoptics Depend on Each Other?" *Bibliotheca Sacra* 138, no. 551 (July 1981): 230-44.

Edersheim, Alfred. *The Life and times of Jesus the Messiah*. Vol. 1. Grand Rapids, MI: Eerdman, 1980.

_____. *The Temple: Its Ministry and Services, as They Were at the Time of Jesus Christ*. Grand Rapids, MI: W.B. Eerdmans Pub., 1972.

Edgar, Thomas. "The Meaning Of ΠΡΟΓΙΝΩΣΚΩ ('To Foreknow')." *Chafer Theological Seminary Journal* 09, no. 1 (Spring 2003).

_____. *Miraculous Gifts: Are They for Today?* Neptune: Loizeaux Brothers, 1983.

Edwards, David L., and John R. W. Stott. *Evangelical Essentials: A Liberal-evangelical Dialogue*. Downers Grove, IL: InterVarsity Press, 1989.

Edwards, Jonathan. "The Great Christian Doctrine of Original Sin Defended." In *The Works of Jonathan Edwards*, 224. Carlisle: Banner of Truth Trust, 1992.

_____. "Of Satisfaction for Sin." In *The Works of Jonathan Edwards*. Vol. 2. Carlisle: Banner of Truth Trust, 1992.

_____. *The Works of Jonathan Edwards*. Carlisle, PA: Banner of Truth Trust, 1974.

Edwards, William, Wesley Gabel, and Floyd Hosmer. "Crucifixion (and Related Incidents) on the Physical Death of Jesus Christ." *Journal of the American Medical Association* 255, no. 11 (1986).

Eichrodt, Walther. *Ezekiel; a Commentary*. Philadelphia: Westminster Press, 1970.

_____. *Theology of the Old Testament*. Philadelphia: Westminster Press, 1961.

Elliott, Ralph. "Atonement in the Old Testament." *Review and Expositor* 59 (1962).

Encyclopedia Britannica. http://www.britannica.com.

Encyclopedia Judaica. Jerusalem: Encyclopedia Judaica, 1971.

Enns, Paul P. *Ezekiel*. Grand Rapids, MI: Zondervan, 1986.

_____. *The Moody Handbook of Theology*. Chicago, IL: Moody Press, 1989.

Enslin, Morton Scott, and John Henry Paul Reumann, eds. *Understanding the Sacred Text: Essays in Honor of Morton S. Enslin on the Hebrew Bible and Christian Beginnings*. Valley Forge: Judson Press, 1972.

Epictetus. *Discourses*. London: William Heinemann, 1969.

_____. *Encheiridion*. London: William Heinemann, 1969.

"The Epistle of Barnabas." CHURCH FATHERS: Epistle of Barnabas. Accessed August 22, 2014. http://www.newadvent.org/fathers/0124.htm.

Epstein, Isidore. *The Babylonian Talmud*.. London: Soncino Press, 1961.

Erdman, Charles Rosenbury. *The Book of Leviticus, an Exposition*. New York: Revell, 1951.

Erickson, Millard J. *Christian Theology*. Grand Rapids: Baker Book House, 1985.

Eusebius. *Eusebius--the Church History*. Translated by Paul L. Maier. Grand Rapids, MI: Kregel Publications, 2007.

Evans, W. Glyn. "Will Babylon Be Restored?" *Bibliotheca Sacra* 107, no. 427 (July 1950): 335-42.

Everson, A. J. "Days of Yahweh." *Journal of Biblical Literature* 93 (1974).

_____. "Days of Yahweh." *Journal of Biblical Literature* 93 (1974).

Fairbairn, Patrick. *An Exposition of Ezekiel.* Reprint Ed. Grand Rapids: Zondervan Pub. House, 1960.

Fausset, A.R. *A Commentary: Critical, Experimental, and Practical.* Grand Rapids: Eerdmans, 1978.

Faust, J. D. *The Rod, Will God Spare It? An Exhaustive Study of Temporary Punishment for Unfaithful Christians at the Judgment Seat and during the Millennial Kingdom.* Hayesville: Schoettle Publishing, 2003.

Fee, Gordon D., and Douglas K. Stuart. *How to Read the Bible for All Its Worth: A Guide to Understanding the Bible.* Grand Rapids, MI: Zondervan, 2003.

_____. *The First Epistle to the Corinthians.* Grand Rapids, MI: W.B. Eerdmans Pub., 1987.

_____. *God's Empowering Presence: The Holy Spirit in the Letters of Paul.* Peabody: Hendickson, 1994.

Feinberg, Charles Lee. *The Prophecy of Ezekiel; the Glory of the Lord.* Chicago: Moody Press, 1969.

_____. "The Rebuilding of the Temple." In *Prophecy in the Making: Messages Prepared for Jerusalem Conference on Biblical Prophecy*, edited by W. A. Criswell and Carl F. H. Henry. Carol Stream, IL: Creation House, 1971.

_____. "The Scapegoat of Leviticus Sixteen." *Bibliotheca Sacra* 115 (1958).

Feinberg, John. "1 Peter 3:18-20, Ancient Mythology, and the Intermediate State." *Westminster Theological Journal* 48, no. 2 (Fall 1986).

Feldman, Emanuel. *Biblical and Post-Biblical Defilement and Mourning: Law as Theology.* New York: KTAV Pub. House, 1977.

Ferguson, Everett. *Backgrounds of Early Christianity.* Grand Rapids, MI: W.B. Eerdmans, 1993.

Finegan, Jack, Jerry Vardaman, and Edwin M. Yamauchi, eds. *Chronos, Kairos, Christos: Nativity and Chronological Studies Presented to Jack Finegan.* Winona Lake: Eisenbrauns, 1989.

Finkel, Irving. "Cyrus Cylinder - Translation." British Museum. Accessed July 8, 2012. http://www.britishmuseum.org/explore/highlights/articles/c/cyrus_cylinder_-_translation.aspx.

Forbes, Christopher. *Prophecy and Inspired Speech in Early Christianity and Its Hellenistic Environment.* Peabody: Hendrickson, 1997.

Frame, James. *The Epistles of St. Paul to the Thessalonians.* International Critical Commentary. Edinburgh: T. & T. Clark, 1979.

France, R. T. *The Evidence for Jesus*. Downers Grove, IL: InterVarsity Press, 1986.

Freeman, Hobart E. *An Introduction to the Old Testament Prophets*. Chicago: Moody Press, 1968.

Freeman, James M., and Harold J. Chadwick. *Manners & Customs of the Bible*. North Brunswick, NJ: Bridge-Logos Publishers, 1998. Logos 5.

Freeman, John. "Day of the Lord." In *Zondervan Pictorial Bible Dictionary*. Grand Rapids: Zondervan, 1976.

Friedlander, Gerald. *The Jewish Sources of the Sermon on the Mount*. New York: KTAV Publishing House, 1969.

Froom, Le Roy. *The Conditionalist Faith of Our Fathers*. Washington, D.C.: Review and Herald, 1966.

Fruchtenbaum, Arnold G. *The Footsteps of the Messiah: A Study of the Sequence of Prophetic Events*. Tustin CA: Ariel Ministries, 2002.

_____. *Israelology: The Missing Link in Systematic Theology*. Tustin, CA: Ariel Ministries, 2001.

_____. *The Sabbath*. San Antonio, Tx.: Ariel Ministries, 2012.

_____. "Rabbinic Quotations of the Old Testament and How It Relates to Joel 2 and Acts 2." April 2014. http://www.pre-trib.org/data/pdf/Fruchtenbaum-RabbinicQuotationsofthe Ol.pdf.

Fuller, J. William. "I Will Not Erase His Name from the Book of Life." *Journal of the Evangelical Theological Society* 26, no. 3 (September 1983).

Fung, Ronald. *The Epistle to the Galatians*. New International Commentary on the New Testament. Grand Rapids: Eerdmans, 1988.

"Funus." In *A Dictionary of Greek and Roman Antiquities by Various Authors*, edited by William Smith, 558-62. London: John Murray, 1875.

Gaebelein, A. C. *The Gospel of Matthew*. Neptune, NJ: Loizeaux Bros., 1961.

Gaebelein, Frank. *Four Minor Prophets*. Chicago: Moody, 1976.

Gammie, John G. *Holiness in Israel*. Minneapolis: Fortress Press, 1989.

Gangel, Kenneth. "2 Peter." In *The Bible Knowledge Commentary*. Wheaton: Victor Books, 1983.

Gardiner, E. Norman. *Athletics of the Ancient World*. Chicago: Ares, 1930.

_____. *Greek Athletic Sports and Festivals*. London: Macmillan and, 1910.

Gardner, J. F. *Women in Roman Law and Society*. Bloomington: Indiana University Press, 1986.

Garland, David. *1 Corinthians*. Baker Exegetical Commentary on the New Testament. Grand Rapids: Baker Academic, 2003.

Gay, G. A. "Day." In *Evangelical Dictionary of Theology*. Grand Rapids: Baker, 1984.

Gayford, S. C. *Sacrifice and Priesthood: Jewish and Christian*. London: Methuen, 1953.

Geikie, Cunningham. *The Holy Land and the Bible: A Book of Scripture Illustrations Gathered in Palestine*. New York: Pott, 1888.

_____. *The Life and Words of Christ*. New York: D. Appleton and Company, 1893.

Geisler, Norman. "God Knows All Things." In *Predestination and Free Will*. Downers Grove: InterVarsity, 1986.

_____. "Gnosticism." In *Baker Encyclopedia of Christian Apologetics*. Grand Rapids: Baker Books, 1999.

_____. *Systematic Theology*. Minneapolis, MN: Bethany House, 2002.

Geisler, Norman, and Joshua Betancourt. *Is Rome the True Church? A Consideration of the Roman Catholic Claim*. Wheaton: Crossway Books, 2008.

Geisler, Norman L., and R. C. Sproul. *Miracles and Modern Thought*. Grand Rapids, MI: Zondervan Pub. House, 1982.

Geisler, Norman L., and William E. Nix. *A General Introduction to the Bible*. Chicago: Moody Press, 1977.

Geldenhuys, Norval. *Commentary on the Gospel of Luke*. Grand Rapids: Eerdmans, 1951.

Gentry, Kenneth. *Before Jerusalem Fell: Dating the Book of Revelation*. San Francisco: Christian Universities Press, 1997.

Gerstner, John. *The Rational Biblical Theology of Jonathan Edwards*. Vol. III. Powhatan: Berea Publications, 1991.

Gill, David. "1 Corinthians." In *Zondervan Illustrated Bible Backgrounds Commentary*. Grand Rapids: Zondervan, 2002.

Glaser, Mitch, and Zhava Glaser. *The Fall Feasts of Israel*. Chicago: Moody Press, 1987.

Gleason, Randall. "A Moderate Reformed View." In *Four Views on the Warning Passages in Hebrews*. Grand Rapids: Kregel, 2007.

Godet, F. L. *Commentary on St. Paul's Epistle to the Romans*. Edinburgh: T. & T. Clark, 1890.

Godet, Frédéric Louis. *Commentary on the Gospel of Luke*. Grand Rapids, MI: Zondervan, 1955.

Govett, Robert. *The Sermon on the Mount*. Miami Springs: Conley & Schoettle, 1984.

Gray, George Buchanan. *Sacrifice in the Old Testament: Its Theory and Practice*. New York: Ktav Pub. House, 1971.

Greek and Roman Authors on LacusCurtius.

http://penelope.uchicago.edu/Thayer/E/Roman/Texts/home.html.

Green, Gene. *Jude and 2 Peter*. Grand Rapids: Baker, 2008.

Green, Michael. *The Second Epistle General of Peter, and the General Epistle of Jude: An Introduction and Commentary*. Grand Rapids, MI: Eerdmans, 1973.

Gregg, D. L. "Alexander." In *Eerdmans Dictionary of the Bible*, edited by David Noel Freedman, Allen C. Myers, and Astrid B. Beck. Grand Rapids, MI: W.B. Eerdmans, 2000. Logos 5.

Grigsby, Bruce. "Gematria and John 21:11--Another Look at Ezekiel 47:10." *Expository Times* 95 (1984).

Gruenler, R. G. "Last Days, Days." In *Evangelical Dictonary of Theology*. Grand Rapids: Baker, 1984.

Guelich, Robert. *The Sermon on the Mount: A Foundation for Understanding*. Waco: Word Books, 1982.

Gundry, Robert, and Russell Howell. "The Sense and Syntax of John 3:14-17 with Special Reference to the Use of]OUTWS...]WSTE in John 3:16." *Novum Testamentum* 41 (January 1999).

Gundry, Robert Horton. *A Survey of the New Testament*. 4th ed. Grand Rapids: Zondervan, 2003.

_____. *Matthew*. Grand Rapids: Eerdmans, 1994.

Gunn, George. "Second Corinthians 3:6 and the New Covenant." In *An Introduction to the New Covenant*. Hurst: Tyndale Seminary Press, 2013.

Gunther, J. J. "St. Paul's Opponents and Their Background. A Study of Apocalyptic and Jewish Sectarian Teaching." In *Novum Testamentum Supplements*. Leiden: Brill, 1973.

Guthrie, Donald. *New Testament Introduction*. Downers Grove, IL: Inter-Varsity Press, 1990.

Hamilton, Floyd Eugene. *The Basis of Millennial Faith*. Grand Rapids, MI: Wm. B. Eerdmans Pub., 1942.

Hannah, John. "Zephaniah." In *Bible Knowledge Commentary*. Wheaton: Victor Books, 1985.

"Harmony - J B Phillips New Testament." Harmony - J B Phillips New Testament. Accessed May 3, 2014. http://www.ccel.org/bible/phillips/JBPhillips.htm.

Harper, William. *Amos and Hosea*. International Critical Commentary. Edinburgh: T. & T. Clark, 1966.

Harris, Harold Arthur. *Sport in Greece and Rome*. Ithaca, NY: Cornell University Press, 1972.

Harris, Murray. *Prepositions and Theology in the Greek New Testament: An Essential Reference Resource for Exegesis*. Grand Rapids: Zondervan, 2012.

Harris, R., Gleason Archer, and Bruce Waltke, eds. *Theological Workbook of the Old Testament:*

'Aleph-Mem. Vol. 1. Chicago: Moody Press, 1980.

Harris, R. Laird, Gleason L. Archer, and Bruce K. Waltke. *Theological Wordbook of the Old Testament: Volume II Nun-Taw*. Chicago: Moody Press, 1980.

Harris, W. H. "The Ascent and Descent of Christ in Ephesians 4:9-10." *Bibliotheca Sacra* 151, no. 602 (April 1994).

_____. *1, 2, 3 John*. Biblical Studies Press, 2003.

Harrison, E. F. "The Transfiguration." *Bibliotheca Sacra* 93 (1936).

_____. *Introduction to the New Testament. Second Printing*. London: Pickering & Inglis, 1966.

_____. *Introduction to the New Testament*. Grand Rapids: Eerdmans, 1971.

Harrison, R. K. *Jeremiah and Lamentations*. Downers Grove: InterVarsity, 1973.

_____. *Leviticus, an Introduction and Commentary*. Downers Grove, IL: Inter-Varsity Press, 1980.

Hart, John. "Does Philippians 1:6 Guarantee Progressive Sanctification?" Proceedings of Evangelical Theological Society. 1995.

Hartley, John E. *Leviticus*. Dallas, TX: Word Books, 1992.

Hayden, Daniel. "Calling the Elders to Pray." *Bibliotheca Sacra* 138, no. 551 (July 1981).

Heater, Homer. "Do the Prophets Teach That Babylon Will Be Rebuilt In The Eschaton?" *Journal of the Evangelical Theological Society* 41, no. 1 (March 1998): 23-43.

Hegre, T. A. *The Cross and Sanctification*. Minneapolis: Bethany, 1960.

Heller, John. "Burial Customs of the Romans." *The Classical Weekly* XXV, no. 24 (1932): 193-97.

Hemer, Colin. *The Letters to the Seven Churches of Asia in Their Local Setting*. Sheffield: University of Sheffield, 1986.

Henderson, E. *The Books of the Twelve Minor Prophets*. London: Hamilton, Adams, and, 1845.

Hendrikesen, William. *Thessalonians, Timothy, and Titus*. Grand Rapids: Baker, 1986.

_____. *Exposition of I and II Thessalonians*. Grand Rapids: Baker, 1974.

Hengel, Martin. *Crucifixion in the Ancient World and the Folly of the Message of the Cross*. Philadelphia: Fortress Press, 1982.

Henry, Carl. *Christian Personal Ethics*. Grand Rapids: Eerdmans, 1957.

Herodotus. *Book VIII*.

Herr, David. "Day of Atonement." In *Encyclopedia Judaica*. Vol. 5.

Hertz, J. H. *Leviticus*. London: Oxford University Press, 1932.

Heth, William A., and Gordon J. Wenham. *Jesus and Divorce: Towards an Evangelical Understanding of New Testament Teaching*. London: Hodder and Stoughton, 1984.

Hiebert, D. Edmond. *First Peter: An Expositional Commentary*. Chicago: Moody Press, 1984.

_____. *An Introduction to the New Testament*. Chicago: Moody Press, 1981.

_____. *Introduction to the New Testament: The Non-Pauline Epistles and Revelation*. Chicago: Moody, 1977.

_____. *Mark: A Portrait of the Servant*. Chicago: Moody Press, 1974.

_____. "The Prophetic Foundation of the Christian Life." *Bibliotheca Sacra* 141, no. 562 (1984).

_____. "Studies in 3 John Part 1: An Exposition of 3 John 1-4." *Bibliotheca Sacra* 144, no. 573 (January 1987).

Hillyer, Norman. "1 Peter and the Feast of Tabernacles." *Tyndale Bulletin* 21 (1970).

The History of Hell: Christian History Guide #1. Christian History Magazine, 2011.

Hitchcock, Mark. "A Defense of the Domitianic Date of the Book of Revelation." PhD diss., Dallas Theological Seminary, 2005.

Hock, Ronald F. *The Social Context of Paul's Ministry: Tentmaking and Apostleship*. Philadelphia: Fortress Press, 1980.

Hodge, Charles. *Commentary on Romans*. Grand Rapids: Eerdmans, 1977.

_____. *Systematic Theology*. Grand Rapids: Eerdmans, 1968.

Hodges, Zane. "The First Horseman of the Apocalypse." *Bibliotheca Sacra* 119, no. 476 (1962).

_____. *Grace in Eclipse*. Dallas: Redencion Viva, 1985.

_____. "Problem Passages in the Gospel of John Part 3: Water and Spirit—John 3:5." *Bibliotheca Sacra* 135, no. 539 (July 1978).

_____. "Problem Passages in the Gospel of John Part 8: The Woman Taken in Adultery (John 7:53-8:11): The Text." *Bibliotheca Sacra* 136, no. 544 (October 1979).

Hoehner, Harold. *Ephesians: An Exegetical Commentary*. Grand Rapids: Baker, 2002.

_____. *Chronological Aspects of the Life of Christ*. Grand Rapids: Zondervan Pub. House, 1977.

_____. *Herod Antipas*. Cambridge: University Press, 1972.

Hoekema, Anthony A. *The Bible and the Future*. Grand Rapids, MI: Eerdmans, 1979.

Hoffmann, D. *Das Buch Leviticus*. Berlin: Poppelauer, 1905-06.

Hogg, C. F., and W. E. Vine. *The Epistles of Paul the Apostle to the Thessalonians*. Shreveport, LA: Lambert Book House, 1977.

Holwerda, David E. *Jesus and Israel: One Covenant or Two?* Grand Rapids, MI: W.B. Eerdmans, 1995.

Horton, Michael Scott. *Putting Amazing Back into Grace*. Grand Rapids, MI: Baker Books, 1995.

_____. *Where in the World Is the Church?: A Christian View of Culture and Your Role in It*. Chicago: Moody Press, 1995.

Hosch, H. "The Concept of Prophetic Time in the Book of Joel." *Journal of the Evangelical Theological Society* 15 (1972).

House, H. Wayne., ed. *Divorce and Remarriage: Four Christian Views*. Downers Grove, IL: InterVarsity Press, 1990.

_____. "The Understanding of the Church Fathers regarding the Olivet Discourse and the Fall of Jerusalem." Address, Pre-Trib Conference, 2009.

_____. "Biblical Inspiration in 2 Timothy 3:16." *Bibliotheca Sacra* 137, no. 545 (January 1980).

Hubbard, Moyer. "2 Corinthians." In *Zondervan Illustrated Bible Backgrounds Commentary*. Grand Rapids: Zondervan, 2002.

Hudson, Henry. *Papal Power*. Unicoi: Trinity Foundation, 2008.

Hughes, Christopher. "The Terminus Ad Quem of Daniel's 69th Week." *Journal of Dispensational Theology*, Summer 2013.

Hughes, Philip. "The Blood of Jesus and His Heavenly Priesthood in Hebrews Part III: The Meaning of the 'true Tent' and 'the Greater and More Perfect Tabernacle'" *Bibliotheca Sacra* 130, no. 520 (October 1973).

Hui, Timothy. "The Purpose of Israel's Annual Feasts." *Bibliotheca Sacra* 147, no. 586 (April 1990).

Hullinger, Jerry. "The Egyptian Religious Background of Pharaoh's Hard Heart." *Journal of Dispensational Theology* 16, no. 47 (April 2012).

_____. "The Function of the Sacrifices in Ezekiel's Temple, Part 1." *Bibliotheca Sacra* 167, no. 665 (2010): 40-57.

_____. "The Function of the Sacrifices in Ezekiel's Temple, Part 2." *Bibliotheca Sacra* 167, no. 666 (2010).

_____. "The Historical Background of Paul's Athletic Allusions." *Bibliotheca Sacra* 161, no. 643 (2004): 343-59.

_____. "The Realization of Ezekiel's Temple." In *Dispensationalism Tomorrow & Beyond: A Theological Collection in Honor of Charles C. Ryrie*, edited by Christopher Cone, 375-96. Fort Worth, TX: Tyndale Seminary Press, 2008.

_____. "Review of MacArthur's Millennial Manifesto." Review of *MacArthur's Millennial Manifesto*. *Journal of Dispensational Theology*, October 2009.

_____. "Two Atonement Realms: Reconciling Sacrifice in Leviticus and Hebrews." *Journal of Dispensational Theology* 32 (2007).

Hurley, James. *Man and Woman in Biblical Perspective*. Grand Rapids: Zondervan, 1981.

Ice, Thomas, and Kenneth Gentry. *The Great Tribulation past or Future? Two Evangelicals Debate the Question*. Grand Rapids: Kregel, 1999.

Ice, Thomas. "Dispensational Hermeneutics." In *Issues in Dispensationalism*, edited by Wesley R. Willis, John R. Master, and Charles Caldwell Ryrie. Chicago, IL: Moody Press, 1994.

Instone-Brewer, David. *Divorce and Remarriage in the Bible: The Social and Literary Context*. Grand Rapids, MI: W.B. Eerdmans, 2002.

The International Standard Bible Encyclopedia. Edited by James Orr. Grand Rapids, MI: W.B. Eerdmans, 1980.

Irenaeus. *Against Heresies*. Logos 5.

Jacobs, P., and H. Krienke. "Foreknowledge, Providence, Predestination." In *New International Dictionary of New Testament Theology*. Vol. 1. Grand Rapids: Zondervan, 1981.

Jaeggli, J. Randolph. "The Interpretation of Old Testament Prophecy." *Detroit Baptist Seminary Journal* 2 (1997): 3-17.

"James, 1-2 Peter, 1-3 John, Jude." In *Ancient Christian Commentary on Scripture*, edited by Gerald Bray. Downers Grove: InterVarsity, 2000.

Jeffers, James S. *The Greco-Roman World of the New Testament Era: Exploring the Background of Early Christianity*. Downers Grove, IL: InterVarsity Press, 1999.

Jeremias, Joachim. *Jerusalem in the Time of Jesus: An Investigation into Economic and Social Conditions during the New Testament Period*. Philadelphia: Fortress Press, 1989.

"JewishEncyclopedia.com." AGRIPPA I. Accessed August 23, 2013. http://www.jewishencyclopedia.com/articles/912-agrippa-i.

Johnson, Alan. "Revelation." In *The Expositor's Bible Commentary*. Grand Rapids: Zondervan, 1981.

Johnson, Elliott. "Premillennialism Introduced: Hermeutics." In *The Coming Millennial Kingdom: A Case for Premillennial Interpretation*, edited by Donald K. Campbell and Jeffrey L. Townsend. Grand Rapids, MI: Kregel Publications, 1997.

_____. "A Traditional Dispensational Hermeneutic." In *Three Central Issues in Contemporary Dispensationalism: A Comparison of Traditional and Progressive Views*, edited by Herbert W. Bateman. Grand Rapids, MI: Kregel Publications, 1999.

_____. "What I Mean by Historical-grammatical Interpretation and How That Differs from

Spiritual Interpretation." *Grace Theological Journal* 11 (1990).

Johnson, S. L. "God Gave Them up." *Bibliotheca Sacra* 129 (April 1972).

______"Studies in the Epistle to the Colossians Part V: The Minister of the Mystery." *Bibliotheca Sacra* 119, no. 475 (July 1962).

______. "The Gospel That Paul Preached." *Bibliotheca Sacra* 128, no. 512 (October 1971).

______. "The Transfiguration of Christ." *Bibliotheca Sacra* 124 (1967).

Jones, A. H. M. *The Greek City from Alexander to Justinian*. Oxford: Clarendon Press, 1940.

Jones, David. "The Apostate Angels of 2 Pet. 2:4 and Jude 6." *Faith and Mission* 23, no. 2 (Spring 2006).

Josephus, Flavius. *The Antiquities of the Jews*. Translated by William Whiston. Grand Rapids, MI: Baker Academic, 1980.

______. *The Wars of the Jews*. Translated by William Whiston. Grand Rapids, MI: Baker Academic, 1979.

______. "The Life of Flavius Josephus." Translated by William Whiston. In *Works of Josephus*. Vol. II. Grand Rapids: Baker, 1980.

Kaiser, Walt. "The Promised Land: A Biblical-Historical View." *Bibliotheca Sacra* 138, no. 552 (1981).

______. *Toward an Old Testament Theology*. Grand Rapids: Zondervan, 1978.

______. "The Promise of the Arrival of Elijah in Malachi and the Gospels." *Grace Theological Journal* 3 (1982).

______. "The Promised Land: A Biblical-Historical View." *Bibliotheca Sacra* 138 (1981).

Kaploun, Uri. *The Synagogue*. Philadelphia: Jewish Publication Society of America, 1973.

Keener, Craig S. *And Marries Another: Divorce and Remarriage in the Teaching of the New Testament*. Peabody, MA: Hendrickson, 1991.

______. *The IVP Bible Background Commentary: New Testament*. Downers Grove, IL: InterVarsity Press, 1993.

Keil, Carl Friedrich, and Franz Delitzsch. *Jeremiah, Lamentations*. Grand Rapids: Eerdmans, 1980.

______. *The Pentateuch*. Reprint Ed., Commentary on the Old Testament. Grand Rapids, MI: Eerdmans, 1980.

Keil, Carl Friedrich. *Ezekiel, Daniel*. Vol. IX. Commentary on the Old Testament in Ten Volumes. Grand Rapids, MI: Eerdmans, 1982.

_____. *The Minor Prophets*. Grand Rapids: Eerdmans, 1980.

Kelly, J. N. D. *A Commentary on the Pastoral Epistles: Timothy I & II, Titus*. Grand Rapids, MI: Baker Academic, 1983.

_____. *A Commentary on the Epistles of Peter and Jude*. Grand Rapids, MI: Baker Academic, 1987.

_____. *An Commentary on the Pastoral Epistles*. Grand Rapids: Baker, 1983.

Kent, Homer. *The Epistle to the Hebrews*. Grand Rapids: Baker, 1981.

Kidner, Derek. "Sacrifice—Metaphors and Meaning." *Tyndale Bulletin* 33 (1982).

Kittle, Gerhard, ed. *Theological Dictionary of the New Testament*. Vol. 1. Grand Rapids: Eerdmans, 1971.

Kiuchi, N. *The Purification Offering in the Priestly Literature: Its Meaning and Function*. Sheffield: Sheffield Academic Press, 1987.

Klein, Ralph W. *Ezekiel: The Prophet and His Message*. Columbia, SC: University of South Carolina Press, 1988.

Klein, William W., Craig Blomberg, and Robert L. Hubbard. *Introduction to Biblical Interpretation*. Nashville, TN: Thomas Nelson, 2004.

Knight, George. *The Pastoral Epistles*. The New International Greek Testament Commentary. Grand Rapids: Eerdmans, 2000.

Knox, Broughton. *Broughton Knox: Selected Works*. Vol. 2. Matthias Media, 2003.

Kolligan, Daniel. "Ta,rtaroj." In *Poetic Language and Religion in Greece and Rome*. Cambridge: Cambridge Scholars Publishing, 2013.

Komoszewski, J. Ed., M. James. Sawyer, and Daniel B. Wallace. *Reinventing Jesus: How Contemporary Skeptics Miss the Real Jesus and Mislead Popular Culture*. Grand Rapids, MI: Kregel Publications, 2006.

Konig, Eduard. *Geschichte Der Alttestamentlichen Relgion*. Gutersloh: C. Bertelsmann, 1924.

Kostenberger, Andreas, and Justin Taylor. "Why We Believe We Can Know the Exact Date Jesus Died." First Things. Accessed April 22, 2014. http://www.firstthings.com/web-exclusives/2014/04/april-3-ad-33.

Kostenberger, Andreas. *John*. Grand Rapids: Baker, 2004.

Kraus, C. Norman. *Dispensationalism in America*. Richmond: John Knox Press, 1958.

Kreeft, Peter. *Handbook on Christian Apologetics*. Downers Grove: InterVarsity, 1994.

Kruger, Michael. "The Authenticity of 2 Peter." *Journal of the Evangelical Theological Society* 42, no. 4 (December 1999).

Kurtz, J. H. *Sacrificial Worship of the Old Testament*. Edinburgh: T. & T. Clark, 1863.

Ladd, G.E. *The Presence of the Future*. Grand Rapids: Eerdmans, 1970.

_____. *Crucial Questions about the Kingdom of God*. Grand Rapids: Eerdmans, 1952.

_____. *A Theology of the New Testament*. Grand Rapids: Eerdmans, 1983.

Lane, William. *The Gospel of Mark*. Grand Rapids: Eerdmans, 1979.

_____. *The Gospel According to Mark: The English Text with Introduction, Exposition, and Notes*. Grand Rapids: Eerdmans, 1979.

Laney, J. Carl. *The Divorce Myth*. Minneapolis, MN: Bethany House Pub., 1981.

Lange, Johann Peter. *The Gospel According to Matthew: Together with a General Theological, and Homiletical Introduction to the New Testament*. New York: C. Scribner, 1865.

Law, Robert. *The Tests of Life: A Study of the First Epistle of St. John: Being the Kerr Lectures for 1909*. Edinburgh: T. & T. Clark, 1909.

Lee, Hugh. "Athletic Arete in Pindar." *The Ancient World* 7 (1983).

Lenski, R. C. H. *The Interpretation of St. Matthew's Gospel*. Minneapolis, MN: Augsburg, 1961.

_____. *An Interpretation of the Acts of the Apostles*. Minneapolis: Augsburg, 1964.

Lescelius, Robert. *Lordship Salvation: Some Crucial Questions and Answers*. Asheville: Revival Literature, 1992.

Leupold, H. C. *Exposition of Isaiah*. Grand Rapids: Baker, 1968.

Levine, Baruch A. *Leviticus: The Traditional Hebrew Text with the New JPS Translation*. Philadelphia: Jewish Publication Society, 1989.

Lewis, Robert. "The Women of 1 Timothy 3:11." *Bibliotheca Sacra* 136, no. 542 (April 1979).

Licht, Jacob. "An Ideal Town Plan from Qumran—The Description of the New Jerusalem." *Israel Exploration Journal* 29 (29).

Liefeld, Walter L. *Luke: The Expositor's Bible Commentary*. Grand Rapids: Zondervan, 1984.

Linnemann, Eta. *Jesus of the Parables; Introduction and Exposition*. New York: Harper & Row, 1966.

Livius, Titus. *The History of Rome*. 45th ed. Vol. 6. Series 12. London: London: J.M. Dent & Sons, 1905.

Livy. *Book XXIII: From the Founding to the City*. Cambridge, MA: Harvard, 1966.

_____. *The History of Rome, by Titus Livius. Books Nine to Twenty-Six*. Edited by D. Spillan. Medford MA: Henry G. Bohn, 1896.

Lloyd-Jones, David M. *The Unsearchable Riches of Christ: An Exposition of Ephesians 3*. Grand Rapids: Baker, 1981.

_____. *The Church and the Last Things*. Wheaton, IL: Crossway Books, 1998.

_____. *Studies in the Sermon on the Mount*. Grand Rapids: Baker, 1986.

_____. *Romans: An Exposition of Chapters 7.1-8.4*. Grand Rapids: Zondervan, 1978.

Lock, Walter. *The Pastoral Epistles*. International Critical Commentary. Edinburgh: T. & T. Clark, 1978.

Lohmeyer, Ernst. "Die Verklarung Jesus Nach Dem Markus-Evangelium,"" *Zeitschrift Fur Die Neutestamentliche Wissenschaft* 21 (1922).

Longenecker, Richard. "Acts." In *Expositor's Bible Commentary*. Vol. 9. Grand Rapids: Zondervan, 1981.

_____. *The Acts of the Apostles*. Grand Rapids: Zondervan, 1981.

_____. "The Acts of the Apostles." In *The Expositor's Bible Commentary*. Grand Rapids, MI: Zondervan Pub. House, 1981.

Longenecker, Richard N., and Merrill C. Tenney. *New Dimensions in New Testament Study*. Grand Rapids: Zondervan Pub. House, 1974.

Louw, J. P. "Verbal Aspect in the First Letter of John." *Neotestamentica*, 1975.

Lucillius. *Greek Anthology*. London: William Heinemann, 1918.

Luther, Martin. *The Bondage of the Will*. Translated by Henry Cole. Grand Rapids: Baker Academic, 1983.

_____. *Commentary on Romans*. Grand Rapids: Kregel, 1977.

_____. *A Commentary on St. Paul's Epistle to the Galatians*. Grand Rapids: Baker, 1982.

_____. *Luther's Works*. Edited by Theodore Bachmann. Philadelphia: Muhlenberg Press, 1960.

_____. "The Smalcald Articles." Book of Concord. Accessed February 2014. http://bookofconcord.org/smalcald.

_____. *Works of Luther, Volume 14: Selected Psalms III*. St. Louis: Concordia Publishing House, 1955.

Maalouf, Tony. "Were the Magi from Persia or Arabia?" *Bibliotheca Sacra* 156, no. 624 (October 1999).

MacArthur, John F. *The Gospel According to Jesus*. Grand Rapids: Zondervan, 1988.

MacKay, Cameron. "Why Study Ezekiel 40-48." *Evangelical Quarterly* 37 (1965).

Maier, Paul, trans. *Eusebius: The Church History*. Grand Rapids: Kregel, 2007.

Malamat, A. "Doctrines of Causality in Historiography." *Vetus Testamentum* 5 (1955).

Man, Ronald. "The Value of Chiasm for New Testament Interpretation." *Bibliotheca Sacra* 141, no. 562 (1984): 146-57.

Manek, Jindrich. "The New Exodus in the Books of Luke." *Novum Testamentum* 2 (1957).

Mantey, Julius. "Evidence That the Perfect Tense in John 20:23 and Matthew 16:19 Is Mistranslated"." *Journal of the Evangelical Theological Society* 163, no. 3 (Summer 1973).

Margolis, Max. "Atonement, Day of." In *The Jewish Encyclopedia*. Vol. 2.

Marshall, I. Howard. *The Gospel of Luke: A Commentary on the Greek Text*. Grand Rapids: Eerdmans, 1978.

Mason, Clarence. "The Day of the Lord." *Bibliotheca Sacra* 125 (1968).

Maspero, G., and A. H. Sayce. *The Dawn of Civilization*. London: Society for Promoting Christian Knowledge, 1910.

Mayhue, Richard. "For What Did Christ Atone in Isa 53:4-5?" *Master's Seminary Journal* 6, no. 2 (Fall 1995).

_____. "Hell: Never, Forever, or Just a Little White?" *Master's Seminary Journal* 9, no. 2 (Fall 1998).

_____. "The Prophet's Watchword: Day of the Lord." *Grace Theological Journal* 6 (1985).

Mayor, Joseph. *The Epistle of St. James*. Grand Rapids: Baker, 1978.

McArthur, Harvey. *Understanding the Sermon on the Mount*. New York: Harper, 1960.

McCarthy, Dennis. "Further Notes on the Symbolism of Blood and Sacrifice." *Journal of Biblical Literature* 92 (1973).

McClain, Alva. *Daniel's Prophecy of the Seventy Weeks*. Grand Rapids: Zondervan, 1969.

_____. *The Greatness of the Kingdom: An Inductive Study of the Kingdom of God as Set Forth in the Scriptures*. Winona Lake: BMH Books, 1983.

McClean, John A. "Did Jesus Correct the Disciples' View of the Kingdom." *Bibliotheca Sacra* 139 (1982).

McCoy, Brad. "Chiasmus: An Important Structural Device Commonly Found in Biblical Literature." *Chafer Theological Seminary Journal* 9, no. 2 (2003): 18.

McCurley, Foster. "And After Six Days: A Semitic Literary Device." *Journal of Biblical Literature* 93 (1974).

McCurley, Foster, and Charles Carlston. "Transfiguration and Resurrection." *Journal of Biblical Literature* 80 (1961).

McNeile, Alan. *The Gospel According to St. Matthew*. Grand Rapids: Baker, 1980.

Merrill, Eugene H. *Everlasting Dominion: A Theology of the Old Testament*. Nashville, TN: Broadman & Holman, 2006.

_____. "Paul's Use of 'about 450 Years' in Acts 13:20." *Bibliotheca Sacra* 138, no. 551 (July 1981).

_____. "The Sign of Jonah." *Journal of the Evangelical Theological Society* 23, no. 1 (March 1980).

Metzger, Bruce A. *A Textual Commentary on the Greek New Testament*. New York: United Bible Societies, 1971.

Meyer, Carl. "Smalcald Articles, Smalcald League." In *New International Dictionary of the Christian Church*. Grand Rapids: Zondervan, 1981.

Meyer, Heinrich. *Critical and Exegetical Handbook to the Gospel of Matthew*. Edinburgh: T. & T. Clark, 1879.

Meyers, Allen. "Writing." In *Eerdmans Bible Dictionary*. Grand Rapids: Eerdmans, 1987.

Micklem, N. *The Book of Leviticus*. Edited by George Buttrick. Vol. 2. Interpreter's Bible. New York: Abingdon, 1953.

Milgrom, Jacob. *Cult and Conscience: The Asham and the Priestly Doctrine of Repentance*. Leiden: Brill, 1976.

_____. "Israel's Sanctuary: The Priestly Picture of Dorian Gray." *Revue Biblique* 83 (1976).

_____. *Leviticus 1-16: A New Translation with Introduction and Commentary*. New York: Doubleday, 1991.

_____. *Numbers*. New York: Jewish Publication Society, 1990.

_____. "Sin Offering or Purgation Offering." *Vetus Testamentum* 21 (1971).

_____. "Two Kinds of Hatta't"." *Vetus Testamentum* 26 (1976).

Miller, Stephen. "Excavations at Nemea." *Hesperia* 48 (1979).

Milligan, George. *St. Paul's Epistle to the Thessalonians*. Grand Rapids: Eerdmans, 1952.

Mishnah. *Sukkah*.

Moller, Wilhelm. "Azazel." In *The International Standard Bible Encyclopedia*. Vol. 1. Grand Rapids: Eerdmans, 1980.

Moo, Douglas. *The Epistle to the Romans*. Grand Rapids: Eerdmans, 1996.

Morris, Leon. *The Apostolic Preaching of the Cross*. Grand Rapids: Eerdmans, 1965.

_____. "'Asham'" *Evangelical Quarterly* 30 (1958).

_____. *The Atonement, Its Meaning and Significance*. Downers Grove, IL: Inter-Varsity Press, 1983.

_____. "The Biblical Use of the Term Blood." *Journal of Theological Studies* 3 (1952).

_____. *The First and Second Epistles to the Thessalonians*. New International Commentary on the New Testament. Grand Rapids: Eerdmans, 1979.

_____. *The Gospel According to John*. Grand Rapids: Eerdmans, 1979.

Mosser, Carl. "No Lasting City: Rome, Jerusalem and the Place of Hebrews in the History of Earliest Christianity." PhD diss., University of St. Andrews, 2005.

Moulton, James Hope, and George Milligan. *The Vocabulary of the Greek New Testament*. Grand Rapids: Eerdmans, 1974.

_____. *The Vocabulary of the Greek Testament*. Peobody, MA: Hendrickson Publishers, 1997.

Mounce, Robert. *The Book of Revelation*. Grand Rapids: Eerdmans, 1980.

Mounce, William. *Pastoral Epistles*. Word Biblical Commentary. Dallas: Word, 2000.

Muir, Steven. "Vivid Imagery in Galatians 3:1-Roman Rhetoric, Street Announcing, Graffiti, and Cricifixions." *Biblical Theology Bulletin* 44, no. 2 (2014).

Murphy-O'Connor, J. *St. Paul's Corinth: Texts and Archaeology*. Wilmington, DE: Michael Glazier, 1983.

Murray, John. *Divorce*. Philadelphia, Penn.: Presbyterian and Reformed Pub., 1961.

_____. *The Epistle to the Romans*. The New International Commentary on the New Testament. Grand Rapids: Eerdmans, 1980.

Negev, Avraham. *The Archaeological Encyclopedia of the Holy Land*. New York: Prentice Hall Press, 1990. Logos 5.

Neil, William. *The Acts of the Apostles*. Grand Rapids: Eermans, 1981.

Neimela, John. "For You Have Kept My Word: The Grammar of Revelation 3:10." *Chafer Theological Seminary Journal* 6, no. 1 (January 2000).

_____. "For You Have Kept My Word: The Theology of Revelation 3:10." *Chafer Theological Seminary Journal* 6, no. 4 (2000).

Nelson, Neil. "This Generation' in Matthew 24:34: A Literary Critical Perspective." *Journal of the Evangelical Theological Society* 38, no. 3 (September 1996).

Neusner, J. *The Rabbinic Traditions about the Pharisees before 70*. Vol. 3. Leiden: Brill, 1974.

New English Translation. Biblical Studies Press, 2001.

New English Translation: First Beta Edition. Biblical Studies Press, 2001.

New Scofield Reference Bible. Oxford, 1967.

New World Translation of the Holy Scriptures. S.l.: Watchtower Bible and Tract Society of New York, 1984.

Neyrey, Jerome. "The Apologetic Use of the Transfiguration." *The Catholic Biblical Quarterly* 42 (1980).

Nichols, Stephen. "Prophecy Makes Strange Bedfellows: On the History of Identifying the Antichrist." *Journal of the Evangelical Theological Society* 44, no. 1 (March 2001).

Nock, Arthur. "Cremation and Burial in the Roman Empire." *The Harvard Theological Review* 25, no. 4 (1932): 322.

Noordtzij, A. *Leviticus*. Grand Rapids, MI: Zondervan Pub. House, 1982.

Noth, Martin. *Leviticus: A Commentary*. Philadelphia: Westminster Press, 1977.

Nygren, A. *A Commentary on Romans*. Philadelphia: Fortress Press, 1949.

Obbink, H. "The Horns of the Altar in the Semitic World, Especially in Yahwism." *Journal of Biblical Literature* 56 (1937).

Oesterley, W. O. E. *Sacrifices in Ancient Israel, Their Origin, Purposes and Development*. London: Hodder and Stoughton, 1937.

Olson, Roger. *Arminian Theology: Myths and Realities*. Downers Grove: InterVarsity, 2006.

Open Theism. Accessed July 2014. theism/neotheism/free-will theism.

Oppian. *Cynegetica*. London: William Heinemann, 1933.

Origen. *Contra Celsum*. Logos 5.

_____. "De Principiis." *Logos 5*.

_____. "De Principiis." Translated by F. Crombie. In *The Ante-Nicene Fathers, Volume IV: Fathers of the Third Century: Tertullian, Part Fourth; Minucius Felix; Commodian; Origen, Parts First and Second*, edited by A. Roberts, J. Donaldson, and A. C. Coxe. Buffalo: Christian Literature Company, 1885.

Orr, James, ed. *The International Standard Bible Encyclopedia*. Grand Rapids: Eerdmans, 1980.

_____. "Eschatology." In *International Standard Bible Encyclopedia*. Grand Rapids: Eerdmans, 1980.

Osborne, Grant R. *Revelation: Baker Exegetical Commentary on the New Testament*. Grand Rapids, MI: Baker Academic, 2002.

Otto, Randall. "The Fear Motivation in Peter's Offer to Build Treij Skhnaj." *Westminster Theological Journal* 59 (1997).

Ovid. "Metamorphoses." Accessed January 2014. http://classics.mit.edu/Ovid/metam.8.

Owen, John. *An Exposition of the Epistle to the Hebrews*. Vol. 5. Grand Rapids: Baker.

Packer, J. I. *Evangelism & the Sovereignty of God*. Downers Grove, IL: Intervarsity Press, 1961.

_____. "Introductory Essay." In *The Doctrine of Justification: An Outline of Its History in the Church and of Its Exposition from Scripture*. Edinburgh: Banner of Truth Trust, 1984.

_____. "Poor Health May Be the Best Remedy." *Christianity Today*, 1982.

_____. "Carpenter, Builder, Workman, Craftsman, Trade." In *The New International Dictionary of New Testament Theology*, edited by Colin Brown. Grand Rapids, MI: Zondervan Pub. House, 1981.

Papachatzis, Nicos D. *Ancient Corinth: The Museums of Corinth, Isthmia and Sicyon*. Athens: Edotike Athenon, 1991.

Papalas, A. "The Development of Greek Boxing." *The Ancient World* 9 (1984).

Pascal, Blaise. *Pensees*. Harmondsworth: Penguin Books, 1966.

Pausanias. *Description of Greece*. Cambridge, MA: Harvard, 1978.

_____. *Guidebook to Greece*. Loeb Classical Library. Cambridge: Harvard, 1978.

Penner, James A. "Revelation and Discipleship in Matthew's Transfiguration Account." *Bibliotheca Sacra* 152 (1995).

Pentecost, Dwight J. "The Purpose of the Law." *Bibliotheca Sacra* 128, no. 511 (July 1971): 227-33.

_____. *Things to Come*. Grand Rapids: Zondervan, 1979.

_____. *The Parables of Jesus*. Grand Rapids, MI: Zondervan, 1982.

_____. *The Sermon on the Mount: Contemporary Insights for a Christian Lifestyle*. Portland: Multnomah Press, 1980.

_____. *Thy Kingdom Come: Tracing God's Program and Covenant Promises throughout History*. Wheaton, IL: Victor Books, 1990.

Pentecost, J. Dwight, and John Danilson. *The Words and Works of Jesus Christ: A Study of the Life of Christ*. Grand Rapids, MI: Zondervan Pub. House, 1981.

Peters, George Nathaniel Henry. *The Theocratic Kingdom of Our Lord Jesus, the Christ, as Covenanted in the Old Testament and Presented in the New Testament*. Grand Rapids, MI: Kregel Publications, 1972.

Peterson, Robert. "A Traditionalist Response to John Stott's Arguments for Annihilationism." *Journal of the Evangelical Theological Society* 37, no. 4 (December 1994).

Petry, Ray C., and Clyde L. Manschreck. *A History of Christianity: Readings in the History of the Church, Volume 1 The Early and Medieval Church*. Grand Rapids, MI: Baker Book House, 1981.

Pfitzner, V. C. *Paul and the Agon Motif. Traditional Athletic Imagery in the Pauline Literature*. Leiden: E.J. Brill, 1967.

Phillips, Anthony. "The Undetectable Offender and the Priestly Legislators." *Journal of Theological Studies* 36 (1985).

Philo. *Every Good Man Is Free*. Cambridge, MA: Harvard, 1929.

_____. *Every Good Man Is Free*. Loeb Classical Library. Cambridge: Harvard, 1929.

Philostratus. *The Life of Apollonius of Tyana*. Book V. London: William Heinemann, 1926.

Pindar. *The Olympian Odes*. Cambridge, MA: Harvard, 1961.

Pinnock, Clark. "The Destruction of the Finally Impenitent." *Criswell Theological Review*, 1990th ser., 4, no. 2.

_____. *The Most Moved Mover*. Grand Rapids: Baker, 2001.

Plass, Ewald M. *What Luther Says*. St. Louis: Concordia, 1986.

Plummer, Alfred. *A Critical and Exegetical Commentary on 2 Corinthians*. International Critical Commentary. Edinburgh: T. & T. Clark, 1915.

_____. *A Critical and Exegetical Commentary on the First Epistle of St. Paul to the Corinthians*. Edinburgh: T. & T. Clark, 1983.

_____. *A Critical and Exegetical Commentary on the Gospel According to S. Luke*. Edinburgh: T. & T. Clark, 1922.

_____. *An Exegetical Commentary on the Gospel According to S. Matthew*. Grand Rapids, MI: Baker Academic, 1982.

Plutarch. "On Those Who Are Punished by the Deity Late." Accessed June 2014. http://www.readbookonline.net/readOnLine/49202.

_____. *Plutarch's Lives: Marcellus*. London: William Heinemann, 1917.

Polhill, John B. *Acts*. Nashville, TN: Broadman Press, 1992.

_____. *The New American Commentary - Acts*. Nashville, TN.: Broadman Press, 1992.

Poliakoff, Michael. *Combat Sports in the Ancient World: Competition, Violence, and Culture*. New Haven: Yale University Press, 1987.

Powell, Charles. "The Identity of the 'Restrainer' in 2 Thessalonians 2:6-7." *Bibliotheca Sacra* 154, no. 615 (July 1997).

Poythress, Vern. "2 Thessalonians 1 Supports Amillennialsm." Accessed May 2014. http://www.frame-poythress.org/2-thessalonians-1-supports-amillennialism.

Price, Randall. "Prophetic Postponement." In *The Popular Encyclopedia of Bible Prophecy*. Eugene: Harvest House, 2004.

_____. *The Temple and Bible Prophecy: A Definitive Look at Is Past, Present, and Future*. Eugene: Harvest House, 2005.

Pritchard, James B. *Ancient near Eastern Texts*. Princeton, NJ: Princeton University Press, 1969.

Pyne, Robert. "The Role of the Holy Spirit in Conversion." *Bibliotheca Sacra* 150, no. 598 (April 1993).

"Rabbinics Resources Online." Rabbinics Resources Online. http://www.rabbinics.org/.

Rackham, Richard. *The Acts of the Apostles*. Grand Rapids: Baker, 1978.

Rainey, A. F. "The Order of Sacrifices in Old Testament Ritual Texts." *Biblica* 51 (1970).

Ramm, Bernard L. *Protestant Biblical Interpretation: A Textbook of Hermeneutics*. Boston: W.A. Wilde, 1950.

_____. *Them He Glorified: A Systematic Study of the Doctrine of Glorifcation*. Grand Rapids: Eerdmans, 1963.

Ramsay, William. *The Letters to the Seven Churches*. Grand Rapids: Baker, 1985.

Ramsay, William Mitchell. *The Letters to the Seven Churches*. Grand Rapids, MI: Baker Academic, 1985.

Ramsey, Arthur Michael. *The Glory of God and the Transfiguration of Christ*. London: Longmans, Green, 1949.

Raubitschek, Antony. "The Agonistic Spirit in Greek Culture." *The Ancient World* 7 (1983).

Reaume, John. "Another Look at 1 Corinthians 15:29, Baptized for the Dead." *Bibliotheca Sacra* 152, no. 608 (October 1995).

"Religion: Babylonian Talmud." Babylonian Talmud. http://www.jewishvirtuallibrary.org/jsource/Talmud/talmudtoc.html.

Reymond, Robert. *The Reformation's Conflict with Rome: Why It Must Continue*. Great Britain: Christian Focus Publications, 2001.

Richards, E. Randolph. "An Honor/Shame Argument for Two Temple Clearings." *Trinity Journal* 29, no. 1, 20-43.

_____. "An Honor/Shame Argument for Two Temple Clearings." *Trinity Journal* 29, no. 1 (Spring

2008): 30-31.

Richardson, Alan. *An Introduction to the Theology of the New Testament*. London: SCM Press, 1958.

Ridderbos, H. N. *Matthew*. Grand Rapids: Eerdmans, 1987.

Riddlebarger, Kim. *A Case for Amillennialism: Understanding the End times*. Grand Rapids: Baker, 2013.

Ridge, Donna R., and E. R. Clendenen. "Emperor Worship." In *Holman Illustrated Bible Dictionary*. Nashville, TN: Holman Bible Publishers, 2003.

Rieske, Susan. "What Is the Meaning of 'This Generation' in Matthew 23:36," (24:36) [sic]." *Bibliotheca Sacra* 165, no. 658 (April 2008).

Ringgren, Helmer. *Sacrifice in the Bible*. New York: Association Press, 1963.

Roberts, Alexander, James Donaldson, and A. Cleveland Coxe, eds. *Fathers of the Third and Fourth Centuries: Lactantius, Venantius, Asterius, Victorinus, Dionysius, Apostolic Teaching and Constitutions, Homily, and Liturgies*. Vol. 7. The Ante-Nicene Fathers. Buffalo: Christian Literature Company, 1886. Logos 5.

Robertson, A. T. *Word Pictures in the New Testament*. Vol. 6. Grand Apids: Baker, 1933.

Robertson, O. Palmer. *The Christ of the Prophets*. Phillipsburg, NJ: P & R Pub., 2004.

Rodriguez, Angel M. *Substitution in the Hebrew Cultus*. Berrien Springs, MI: Andrews University Press, 1979.

Roehers, Walter. "God Tabernacles Among Men." *Concordia Theological Monthly* 35 (1964).

Romano, David. "The Ancient Stadium: Athletes and Arete." *The Ancient World* 7 (1983).

Rooker, Mark F. *Leviticus*. Nashville, TN: Broadman & Holman, 2000.

Ross, Allen. *Creation and Blessing*. Grand Rapids: Baker, 1988.

_____. *Holiness to the Lord: A Guide to the Exposition of the Book of Leviticus*. Grand Rapids, MI: Baker Academic, 2002.

_____. *Recalling the Hope of Glory: Biblical Worship from the Garden to the New Creation*. Grand Rapids, MI: Kregel Publications, 2006.

Rowley, H. H. *Worship in Ancient Israel; Its Forms and Meaning*. Philadelphia: Fortress Press, 1967.

Russell, Walter, III. "Who Were Paul's Opponents in Galatia?" *Bibliotheca Sacra* 147, no. 587 (July 1990).

Ryrie, Charles Caldwell. *The Basis of the Premillennial Faith*. New York: Loizeaux Bros., 1953.

_____. *Dispensationalism Today*. Chicago: Moody Press, 2007.

_____. "The End of the Law." *Bibliotheca Sacra* 124, no. 495 (July 1967).

_____. *What You Should Know About the Rapture*. Chicago: Moody, 1981.

Samarin, William. "The Linguisticality of Glossolalia." Accessed January 21, 2014. http://philosophy-religion.info/handouts/pdfs/samarin-pages 48-75.

_____. *Tongues of Men and Angels*. New York: Macmillan, 1972.

Sanford, La Sor William, David Allan. Hubbard, and Frederic William. Bush. *Old Testament Survey: The Message, Form, and Background of the Old Testament*. Grand Rapids, MI: Eerdmans, 1982.

Sauer, Eric. *In the Arena of Faith*. United Kingdom: Paternoster, 1994.

_____. *From Eternity to Eternity*. Grand Rapids: Eerdmans, 1975.

_____. *The Triumph of the Crucified; a Survey of Historical Revelation in the New Testament*. Grand Rapids: Eerdmans, 1952.

Savelle, Charles. "A Reexamination of the Prohibitions in Acts 15." *Bibliotheca Sacra* 161, no. 644 (October 2004).

Schaff, Philip, ed. *Lange's Commentary on the Holy Scriptures*. Vol. 12. Reprint Ed. Grand Rapids: Zondervan, 1980.

_____. *History of the Christian Church*. Grand Rapids: Eerdmans, 1981.

Schiffman, Lawrence, and Mark Powell. "Annas." In *The HarperCollins Bible Dictionary*. New York: HarperCollins, 2011. Logos 5.

Schnabel, Eckhard J. *Acts: Zondervan Exegetical Commentary on the New Testament*. Grand Rapids, MI: Zondervan, 2012.

Schreiner, Thomas. *1, 2 Peter, Jude*. Nashville: Broadman & Holman, 2003.

_____. *New Testament Theology: Magnifying God in Christ*. Grand Rapids: Baker Academic, 2008.

_____. *Paul, Apostle of God's Glory in Christ: A Pauline Theology*. Downers Grove: InterVarsity, 2001.

_____. *Romans*. Baker Exegetical Commentary on the New Testament. Grand Rapids: Baker, 2003.

Schreiner, Thomas R., and Bruce A. Ware. *The Grace of God, the Bondage of the Will*. Grand Rapids, MI: Baker Books, 1995.

Schürer, Emil. *The History of the Jewish People in the Age of Jesus Christ*. London: Bloomsbury T & T Clark, 2014.

_____. *A History of the Jewish People in the Time of Jesus*. New York: Schocken Books, 1967.

Scott, J. Julius. *Jewish Backgrounds of the New Testament*. Grand Rapids, MI: Baker Books, 2000.

Sefaria.org : A Living Library of Jewish Texts Online. http://www.sefaria.org/.

Shepard, J. W. *The Christ of the Gospels, an Exegetical Study*. 3rd ed. Grand Rapids: Wm. B. Eerdmans Pub., 1946.

Showers, Renald E. *There Really Is a Difference!: A Comparison of Covenant and Dispensational Theology*. Bellmawr, NJ: Friends of Israel Gospel Ministry, 1990.

_____. *What on Earth Is God Doing? Satan's Conflict with God*. Neptune: Loizeaux Brothers, 1974.

Singer, Isidore, ed. *The Jewish Encyclopedia*. Funk & Wagnalls, 1906.

Smalley, Stephen. "The Delay of the Parousia." *Journal of Biblical Literature* 83 (1964).

Smeaton, George. *The Apostles' Doctrine of the Atonement*. Grand Rapids: Zondervan, 1957.

_____. *The Apostles' Doctrine of the Atonement: With Historical Appendix*. Grand Rapids: Zondervan Pub. House, 1957.

Smith, Gary V. *Isaiah 1-39*. Nashville, TN: Broadman & Holman, 2007.

Smith, J. B. *A Revelation of Jesus Christ*. Scottsdale: Herald Press.

Smith, Josiah R. *Xenophon: Memorabilia*. Medford, MA: Ginn and Company, 1903.

Smith, Michael. "The Role of the Pedagogue in Galatians." *Bibliotheca Sacra* 650, no. 163 (2006): 207.

Snaith, Norman H. *Leviticus and Numbers*. London: Nelson, 1967.

_____. "The Sin-Offering and the Guilt-Offering." *Vetus Testamentum* 15 (1965).

Snowden, James H. *The Coming of the Lord: Will It by Premillennial?* New York: Macmillan, 1919.

Sola, D. A., and M. J. Raphall. "Eighteen Treatises from the Mishna." Index. http://www.sacred-texts.com/jud/etm/index.htm.

Stalker, D. M. G. *Ezekiel. Introduction and Commentary. (Second Impression.)*. London: SCM Press, 1971.

Stallard, Mike. *The Gathering Storm*. Springfield, MO: Century Press, 2005.

_____. "Literal Interpretation: The Key to Understanding the Bible." *The Journal of Ministry and Theology* 4 (2000).

Stedman, Ray. "Giving under Grace Part 1." *Bibliotheca Sacra* 107, no. 427 (July 1950).

Stedman, Ray. "Giving under Grace Part 2." *Bibliotheca Sacra* 107, no. 428 (October 1950).

_____. "Giving under Grace Part 3." *Bibliotheca Sacra* 108, no. 429 (January 1951).

_____. "Giving under Grace Part 4." *Bibliotheca Sacra* 108, no. 430 (April 1951).

Stern, E. "The Archeology of Persian Palestine." In *The Cambridge History of Judaism*, edited by W. D. Davies and L. Finkelstein. Vol. 1. Cambridge University Press, 1984.

Stern, Frank. *A Rabbi Looks at Jesus' Parables*. Lanham, MD: Rowman & Littlefield Publishers, 2006.

Stigers, H.G. "House." In *The Zondervan Pictorial Encyclopedia of the Bible*, edited by Merrill C. Tenney. Grand Rapids: Zondervan Pub. House, 1976.

Storms, Sam. "Problems with Premillennialism." Accessed May 2014. eschatologystuff.wordpress.com.

Stott, John. *The Message of 1 Timothy and Titus*. Downers Grove: InterVarsity, 2001.

_____. *The Message of Romans*. Leicester: InterVarsity, 1994.

Strack, Hermann, and Paul Billerbeck. *Kommentar Zum Neuen Testament: Das Evangelium Nach Matthaus Erlautert Aus Talmud Und Midrash*. Vol. 1. Munich: C.H. Beck'sche Verlagsbuchhandlung, 1961.

Strauch, Alexander. *Biblical Eldership: An Urgent Call to Restore Biblical Church Leadership*. Littleton: Lewis and Roth Publishers, 1995.

Strauss, Mark L. *Four Portraits, One Jesus: An Introduction to Jesus and the Gospels*. Grand Rapids, MI: Zondervan, 2007.

Sweet, Waldo E. *Sport and Recreation in Ancient Greece: A Sourcebook with Translations*. New York: Oxford University Press, 1987.

Swete, Henry Barclay. *Commentary on Mark*. Grand Rapids, MI: Kregel Publications, 1977.

_____. *Commentary on Revelation*. Grand Rapids: Kregel, 1977.

"Synagogue." In *International Standard Bible Encyclopedia*, edited by Geoffrey W. Bromiley. Grand Rapids: W. B. Eerdmans, 1988. Logos 5.

Synge, F. C. "The Transfiguration Story." *The Expository times* 83 (1970).

Tacitus. *Annals*. http://classics.mit.edu/Tacitus/annals.

Tait, Andrew. *The Messages to the Seven Churches of Asia Minor: An Exposition of the First Three Chapters of Revelation*. London: Hodder & Stoughton, 1884.

Tatford, Frederick. *The Patmos Letters*. Grand Rapids: Kregel, 1969.

Taylor, John B. *Ezekiel; an Introduction and Commentary*. Downers Grove, IL: Inter-Varsity

Press, 1969.

Tenney, Merrill C. *John: The Gospel of Belief*. Grand Rapids: Eerdmans, 1979.

_____. *The Zondervan Pictorial Bible Dictionary*. Grand Rapids: Zondervan Pub. House, 1976.

Terry, Milton Spenser. *Biblical Hermeneutics: A Treatise on the Interpretation of the Old and New Testaments*. Grand Rapids, MI: Zondervan Pub. House, 1974.

Tertullian. "On the Resurrection of the Flesh." *Logos 5*.

_____. "The Prescription against Heretics." *Logos 5*.

Thayer's Greek Lexicon. Accessed August 2014. BibleWorks 6.

Thelwall, S., trans. "De Spectaculis." In *Latin Christianity: Its Founder, Tertullian*, compiled by A. C. Coxe. Vol. 3. Buffalo: Christian Literature Company, 1885.

Theocritus. "The Herdsman." In *Idyll IV*. Accessed July 2014. http://allpoetry.com/Idyll-IV.--The-Herdsmen.

Thiessen, H. C. *Introductory Lectures in Systematic Theology*. Grand Rapids: Eerdmans, 1952.

Thomas, Robert. "The New Testament Use of the Old Testatment." In *Dispensationalism Tomorrow and Beyond*. Fort Worth: Tyndale Seminary Press, 2003.

_____. *Revelation 1-7*. Chicago: Moody Press, 1992.

_____. *Revelation 8-22*. Chicago: Moody Press, 1995.

Thorne, C. G. "Persecution." In *The New International Dictionary of the Christian Church*. Grand Rapids: Zondervan, 1981.

Thrall, Margaret. "Elijah and Moses in Mark's Account of the Transfiguration." *New Testament Studies* 16, no. 4 (1970).

"Toga," A Dictionary of Greek and Roman Antiquities. http://penelope.uchicago.edu/Thayer/E/Roman/Texts/home.html.

Toussaint, Stanley. *Behold the King: A Study of Matthew*. Portland: Multnomah Press, 1981.

_____. "The Chronological Problem of Galatians 2:1-10." *Bibliotheca Sacra* 120, no. 480 (October 1963).

_____. "A Critique of the Preterist View of the Olivet Discourse." *Bibliotheca Sacra* 161, no. 644 (October 2004).

_____. "The Eschatology of the Warning Passages in the Book of Hebrews." *Grace Theological Journal* 3, no. 1 (Spring 1982).

_____. "Israel and the Church of a Traditional Dispensationalist." In *Three Central Issues in Contemporary Dispensationalism: A Comparison of Traditional and Progressive Views*.

Grand Rapids: Kregel, 1999.

Toussaint, Stanley D., and Charles H. Dyer, eds. *Essays in Honor of J. Dwight Pentecost.* Chicago: Moody Press, 1986.

Toussaint, Stanley, and Jay Quine. "No, Not Yet: The Contingency of God's Promised Kingdom." *Bibliotheca Sacra* 164, no. 654 (April 2007).

Townsend, Jeff. "The Rapture in Revelation 3:10." *Bibliotheca Sacra* 166, no. 663 (July 2009).

_____. "Fulfillment of the Land Promise in the Old Testament." *Bibliotheca Sacra* 142 (1985).

Trench, Richard Chenevix. *Studies in the Gospels.* New York: Charles Scribner, 1867.

_____. *Synonyms of the New Testament.* Grand Rapids: Eerdmans, 1985.

Turner, David. "The Continuity of Scripture and Eschatology: Key Hermeneutical Issues." *Grace Theological Journal* 6 (1985).

_____. *Matthew.* Grand Rapids: Baker Academic, 2008.

Tyndale, William. "Tyndale's Preface to the Romans." Accessed February 2014. http://www.luminarium.org/renlit/tyndalebib.

Tzaferis, Vassilios. "Crucifixion: The Archeological Evidence." *Biblical Archeology Review* 11, no. 1 (1985).

VanGemeren, Willem. *New International Dictionary of Old Testament Theology & Exegesis.* Grand Rapids, MI: Zondervan Pub. House, 1997.

Vaux, Roland De. *Ancient Israel: Its Life and Institutions.* New York: McGraw-Hill, 1961.

_____. *Studies in Old Testament Sacrifice.* Cardiff: University of Wales Press, 1964.

Verbrugge, Verlyn D. *A Not-so-silent Night: The Unheard Story of Christmas and Why It Matters.* Grand Rapids, MI: Kregel Publications, 2009.

"Verse." Bible.org. Accessed August 22, 2014. https://bible.org/byverse/matthew24%3A36%2C%20accessed%2010/12/2013.

Virkler, Henry A., and Karelynne Gerber Ayayo. *Hermeneutics: Principles and Processes of Biblical Interpretation.* Grand Rapids, MI: Baker Academic, 2007.

_____. *Hermeneutics: Principles and Processes of Biblical Interpretation.* Grand Rapids: Baker Academic, 2007.

Vlach, Michael. *Has the Church Replaced Israel: A Theological Evaluation.* Nashville: B & H Publishing Group, 2010.

Vos, Geerhardus. *Biblical Theology.* Grand Rapids: Eerdmans, 1977.

Waldron, Sam. *MacArthur's Millennial Manifesto: A Friendly Response.* Owensboro: RBAP,

2008.

Walker, P. W. L. *In the Steps of Paul: An Illustrated Guide to the Apostle's Life and Journeys*. Grand Rapids, MI: Zondervan, 2008.

Wallace, Daniel. "1 John 5:7-8." Accessed May 2014. bible.org/article/textual-problem-1-john-57-8.

_____. *Greek Grammar beyond the Basics: An Exegetical Syntax of the New Testament*. Grand Rapids: Zondervan, 1996.

Waltke, Bruce. "1 Corinthians 11:2-16." *Bibliotheca Sacra* 135, no. 537 (1978).

Walton, John. "Inspired Subjectivity and Hermeneutical Objectivity." *The Master's Seminary Journal* 13 (2002).

Walvoord, John F., and Roy B. Zuck, eds. *The Bible Knowledge Commentary: New Testament*. Wheaton, IL: Victor Books, 1983.

_____, eds. *The Bible Knowledge Commentary: Old Testament*. Wheaton, IL: Victor Books, 1985.

Walvoord, John F. *Matthew: Thy Kingdom Come*. Chicago: Moody Press, 1974.

_____. "Interpreting Prophecy: Part 4—The Kingdom of God in the New Testament." *Bibliotheca Sacra* 139 (1982).

_____. "Part 1: Does the Church Fulfill Israel's Program?" *Bibliotheca Sacra* 137, no. 545 (January 1980): 25-30.

_____. "Posttribulationism Today." *Bibliotheca Sacra* 134 (1977).

_____. *The Revelation of Jesus Christ*. Chicago: Moody, 1981.

_____. "Spiritual Life in the Millennium." *Bibliotheca Sacra* 115 (1958).

Warfield, B. B. Address, Opening Address, Miller Chapel, Princeton Theological Seminary, September 17, 1915.

_____. "On Faith in Its Psychological Aspects." *The Princeton Theological Review* 9, no. 4 (October 1911).

_____. *Works of Benjamin B. Warfield*. Vol. II. Grand Rapids: Baker, 1978.

_____. *Biblical Doctrines*. NY: Oxford University Press, 1929.

Waymeyer, Matthew. *Revelation 20 and the Millennial Debate*. The Woodlands: Kress Christian Publications, 2004.

Wells, Bruce. "Exodus." In *Zondervan Illustrated Bible Backgrounds Commentary: Volume 1 Genesis, Exodus, Leviticus, Numbers, Deuteronomy*, by John Walton. Grand Rapids: Zondervan, 2009.

Wenham, Gordon. *The Book of Leviticus*. New International Commentary on the Old Testament. Grand Rapids: Eerdmans, 1985.

_____. *The Book of Leviticus*. Grand Rapids, MI: W.B. Eerdmans, 1979.

Wessell, Walter. "Mark." In *The Expositor's Bible Commentary*. Vol. 8. Grand Rapids: Zondervan, 1984.

Westcott, B. F. *The Epistle to the Hebrews: The Greek Text with Notes and Essays*. Grand Rapids: Eerdmans, 1984.

When the Trumpet Sounds. Edited by Thomas Ice and Timothy J. Demy. Eugene, Or.: Harvest House Publishers, 1995.

White, James R. *The King James Only Controversy: Can You Trust the Modern Translations?* Minneapolis, MN: Bethany House, 1995.

Wilken, Robert Louis. *The Christians as the Romans Saw Them*. New Haven, CT: Yale University Press, 1984.

Williams, David John. *Paul's Metaphors: Their Context and Character*. Peabody, MA: Hendrickson Publishers, 2004.

Wilson, Kenneth. "Should Women Wear Headcoverings?" *Bibliotheca Sacra* 148, no. 592 (October 1991).

Witherington, Ben. *The Acts of the Apostles: A Socio-rhetorical Commentary*. Grand Rapids, MI: W.B. Eerdmans Pub., 1998.

_____. *New Testament History: A Narrative Account*. Grand Rapids, MI: Baker Academic, 2001.

Wolf, Herbert. *Interpreting Isaiah*. Grand Rapids: Zondervan, 1985.

_____. "A Solution to the Immanuel Prophecy in Isaiah 7:14-8:22." *Journal of Biblical Literature* 91 (December 1972).

Wolff, Hans. *Joel and Amos*. Philadelphia: Fortress Press, 1977.

Wood, D. R. W., and I. Howard. Marshall. *New Bible Dictionary*. Leicester, England: InterVarsity Press, 1996. Logos 5 Bible Software.

Wright, David. "Tertullian." In *The New International Dictionary of the Christian Church*, edited by J. D. Douglas. Grand Rapids, MI: Zondervan, 1981.

Wright, Frederick. "Olympic Games." In *The Oxford Classical Dictionary*, edited by M. Cary. Oxford: Clarendon Press, 1949.

Wright, J.S. "Day of the Lord." In *New Bible Dictionary*. Downers Grove: InterVarsity, 1996.

Xenophon, Henry Graham. Dakyns, and Florence Melian. Stawell. *Cyropaedia: The Education of Cyrus*. United Kingdom: Dodo Press., 2008.

Yamauchi, Edwin. "Cultural Aspects of Marriage in the Ancient World." *Bibliotheca Sacra* 135 (1978): 247.

_____. "The Episode of the Magi." In *Chronos, Kairos, Christos: Nativity and Chronological Studies Presented to Jack Finegan*. Eisenbrauns, 1989.

Yarbrough, Robert. "2 John." In *Zondervan Illustrated Bible Backgrounds Commentary*. Grand Rapids: Zondervan, 2002.

Young, David. "Professionalism in Archaic and Classical Greek Athletics." *The Ancient World* 7 (1983).

Young, E. J. *The Book of Isaiah*. Grand Rapids: Eerdmans, 1983.

Zias, Joseph, and Eliezer Sekeles. "The Crucified Man from Giv'at Ha-Mivtar: A Reappraisal." *Israel Exploration Journal* 35, no. 1 (1985): 22-27.

Zimmerli, Walther, Douglas W. Stott, and Walter Brueggemann. *I Am Yahweh*. Atlanta: John Knox Press, 1982.

Zimmerli, Walther, Frank Moore. Cross, and Klaus Baltzer. *Ezekiel: A Commentary on the Book of the Prophet Ezekiel*. Philadelphia: Fortress Press, 1979.

Zimmerman, J. E. *Dictionary of Classical Mythology*. New York: Bantam Books, 1971.

Zohar, Noam. "Repentance and Purification: The Significance and Semantics of TaJx in the Pentateuch." *Journal of Biblical Literature* 107 (1988).

Zuck, Roy B., and Darrell L. Bock, eds. *A Biblical Theology of the New Testament*. Chicago: Moody Press, 1994.

Zuck, Roy. *Basic Bible Interpretation*. Wheaton: Victor Books, 1991.

Made in the USA
San Bernardino, CA
25 August 2016